The Editor

STEPHEN H. A. SHEPHERD is Associate Professor of English at Loyola Marymount University. His honors include fellowships to the Huntington Library and the Bibliographical Society of America. He is the editor of the Early English Text Society edition of the Middle English *Pseudo-Turpin Chronicle* and of the Norton Critical Edition of *Middle English Romances*.

A NORTON CRITICAL EDITION

Sir Thomas Malory

LE MORTE DARTHUR

or

The Hoole Book of Kyng Arthur
and of His Noble Knyghtes of The Rounde Table

AUTHORITATIVE TEXT

SOURCES AND BACKGROUNDS

CRITICISM

Edited by

STEPHEN H. A. SHEPHERD

SOUTHERN METHODIST UNIVERSITY

W • W • NORTON & COMPANY • *New York* • *London*

W. W. Norton & Company has been independent since its founding in 1923, when William Warder Norton and Mary D. Herter Norton first published lectures delivered at the People's Institute, the adult education division of New York City's Cooper Union. The Nortons soon expanded their program beyond the Institute, publishing books by celebrated academics from America and abroad. By mid-century, the two major pillars of Norton's publishing program—trade books and college texts—were firmly established. In the 1950s, the Norton family transferred control of the company to its employees, and today—with a staff of four hundred and a comparable number of trade, college, and professional titles published each year—W. W. Norton & Company stands as the largest and oldest publishing house owned wholly by its employees.

First Edition

The text of this book is composed in Fairfield Medium and Cloister Black
with the display set in Bernhard Modern.
Composition by Binghamton Valley Composition.
Manufacturing by the LSC Communications.
Book design by Antonina Krass.
Production manager: Benjamin Reynolds.

Library of Congress Cataloging-in-Publication Data
Malory, Thomas, Sir, 15th cent.
[Morte d'Arthur]
Le morte Darthur, or, The hoole book of Kyng Arthur and of his noble knyghtes of the
Rounde Table: authoritative text, sources and backgrounds, criticism / Sir Thomas
Malory ; edited by Stephen H. A. Shepherd.
p.   cm. — (A Norton critical edition)
Includes bibliographical references.

ISBN 0-393-97464-2 (pbk.)

1. Arthurian romances. 2. Malory, Thomas, Sir, 15th cent. Morte d'Arthur.
3. Arthurian romances—History and criticism. 4. Knights and knighthood in literature.
5. Kings and rulers in literature. I. Title: Hoole book of Kyng Arthur and of his noble
knyghtes of the Rounde Table. II. Shepherd, S. H. A. III. Title.
PR2041 .M37 2002
823'.2—dc21   2002026534

W. W. Norton & Company, Inc., 500 Fifth Avenue, New York, N.Y. 10110
www.wwnorton.com

W. W. Norton & Company Ltd., 15 Carlisle Street, London W1D 3BS

4 5 6 7 8 9 0

Contents

for Shelli

Preface

Malory's 'hoole book,' it is clear, has undergone major revisions at the hands of successive generations of editors. And, given the lack of an authoritative copy of the work, it is necessary to conclude that the exemplar which lay behind the sole surviving manuscript may be as much the product of editorial intervention as Caxton's or Vinaver's versions. But to acknowledge the differences in the interpretations which these various texts generate, and the extent to which the process of editing itself determines critical judgements, is to alert us to the open-ended nature of the act of reading, and to its shaping by historical and ideological circumstance. And as readers of Malory today, we should recognize that we actively participate in the creation of meaning.[1]

Even if we did have an authoritative copy—presumably a holograph, a manuscript in Malory's own hand—the shaping of its reading by historical and ideological circumstance would still be unavoidable, and there would remain some doubt about the degree to which what Malory wrote represents what he intended; and any plan to share the text in a more "accessible" form (even, say, at the level of deciding upon a typeface) would necessitate an interventionist editorial presence. Any more ambitious editorial attempt to recover the "original" Malory must admit to being part of a project continually, if learnedly, deferred. The present edition, though precluded in its received format from being a "scholarly edition," does stake a claim to being part of such a project insofar as it recovers certain powerful visual and organizational features of the surviving manuscript omitted from previous editions and offers an unabridged original-language text with a number of new and—I believe (in the absence of certainty)—more authentic readings, many of them recommended by the recent published work of several scholars.[2]

1. Carol M. Meale, " 'The Hoole Book': Editing and the Creation of Meaning in Malory's Text," in *A Companion to Malory*, ed. Elizabeth Archibald and A.S.G. Edwards (Cambridge, Brewer, 1996), 17. "Caxton": the first printed editions of Malory by William Caxton, 1485. "Vinaver": the standard scholarly edition of Malory, about which see the next note. Vinaver's edition is based mainly upon the text of the only known surviving manuscript, the Winchester Manuscript, discovered in 1934, sometimes also referred to as the "Malory Manuscript," about which see, p. xxvii, xxxiv, xliv.
2. I am especially indebted to the following: P. J. C. Field, *Malory: Texts and Sources* (Cambridge: Brewer, 1996); Tsuyoshi Mukai, "De Worde's 1498 *Morte Darthur* and Caxton's Copy-Text," *Review of English Studies* 51 (2000): 24–40; Takako Kato, *Caxton's "Morte Darthur": The Printing Process and the Authenticity of the Text* (a Medium Ævum Monograph, forthcoming); Shunichi Noguchi, "Reading Malory's Text Aloud" and "The Winchester Malory," both in *The Malory Debate: Essays on the Texts of "Le Morte Darthur,"* ed. Bonnie Wheeler, Robert L. Kindrick, and Michael Salda, Arthurian Studies 47 (Cambridge: Brewer, 2000), 117–125, 301–314; and Sir Thomas Malory, *Le Morte Darthur: The Winchester Manuscript*, ed. Helen Cooper (Oxford: Oxford University Press, 1998). The collective implication of much of this work supports Field's assessment that "a reader who wants a version of Malory's book as near as possible to that which Malory intended, should prefer the Winchester text to Caxton's, and should prefer a well-edited modern edition based on the Winchester manuscript to either" (*Malory*, 24). I have accordingly based this edition on Winchester, with emendations from Caxton (for further details, see "Editorial Procedure/Reading the Edition," p. xliii). In addition to the scholarship just mentioned, I am also very much indebted to *The Works of Sir Thomas Malory*, 3rd ed., 3 vols. (Oxford: Clarendon Press, 1990), the standard scholarly edition by Eugène Vinaver and P. J. C. Field, the erudition and logic of whose emendations in the overwhelming majority of cases is unquestionable.

One of the more obvious visual features of the manuscript represented in this edition is rubrication.[3] Helen Cooper finds that its effect in the manuscript "is overwhelmingly to call attention to the *names,* the identities announced to the world of the people they represent—a visual equivalent to Malory's presentation of a . . . knightliness that consists in 'worship,' honor, the glory that accrues to the name."[4] Cooper also finds that "the consistency with which [the rubrication] is done . . . suggests that it may have been a feature of the exemplar." Whether that exemplar so represented Malory's intention we cannot say—perhaps not, as one wonders, for example, whether the rubrication (with capitalization) of *genytrottys* ("genitals," fol. 77ᵛ) is the result of a scribe's misconstrual of the word as a proper name (though the identity of the giant upon whom these reddened parts are sliced apart is violently sexual). Whatever the case, as Carol Meale observes, "this form of highlighting enables a reader to find her or his way around the text more readily" and so "constitutes a form of signposting within the text which is formalized by the introduction of chapter breaks in Caxton's edition."[5] As a practical aid to readers of an edition based on a manuscript that has relatively few major division markers, representation of the rubrication is an obvious advantage; but it is clear also that it reveals levels of contemporaneous interpretive information that have yet to be fully explored.

The same may be said of two other features of the manuscript I have imported into the edition: large capitals and the paraph (¶, tagged for insertion in the manuscript by a double virgule [//] and corresponding in large part to the modern paragraph break). In such features Helen Cooper again sees potential access to greater authenticity, noting the remarkably close correspondence in the Winchester Manuscript of large capitals and double virgules with many of Caxton's frequent chapter breaks: the possibility is that the features as they appear in Winchester "appeared in similar form in Caxton's copy-text" and may "derive from a common exemplar underlying both: and that puts the system of capitalization and the weightier punctuation within reach of Malory himself."[6]

The simple counterargument to this is that Caxton used the Winchester Manuscript itself as his guide for textual division; we know that it was in his printing shop around the time that he was producing his edition of Malory, even though he must have had a second, probably messier, exemplar upon which he depended for Malory's words.[7] A further objection to the claim of authenticity is that the two scribes of the Winchester Manuscript appear to have had different habits of capitalization and paragraphing: Scribe A seems less inclined than Scribe B to use initials over two lines in height, and "seems to have disliked the

---

3. For a detailed account of the disposition of this and other features in the edition, see "Editorial Procedure/Reading the Edition," p. xliii.
4. "Opening Up the Malory Manuscript," in *The Malory Debate,* 273.
5. "The Hoole Book," 10.
6. "Opening Up the Malory Manuscript," 265.
7. For the revelation that Winchester was in Caxton's shop, see Lotte Hellinga, "The Malory Manuscript and Caxton," in *Aspects of Malory,* ed. Toshiyuki Takamiya and Derek Brewer (Cambridge: Brewer, 1981), 127–141 (revised from *The British Library Journal* 3 [1977–78]: 91–101). For evidence that Caxton's main copy-text was in a condition that hindered the purposes of establishing text divisions, see Kato, *Caxton's "Morte Darthur,"* chap. III.2 ("Caxton's Irregular Setting-Copy").

breaks caused by the diagonal strokes."[8] Be that as it may, I would urge further meditation on Cooper's hypothesis. There is one surviving manuscript of a Middle English romance that we know to be a holograph; extraordinarily, the manuscript preserves in its binding, in the same hand as the manuscript proper, a portion of the author/translator's draft.[9] The draft, though cramped, employs a pattern of paragraphing and hierarchical capitalization that is transferred with some consistency to the fair copy: it serves as perhaps the most apposite reminder available that Middle English authors, and not just scribes, used organizational signs with deliberation in their own copy. If Malory used such features himself, they must have stood a chance of persisting in some form in subsequent manuscript copies, transmitted perhaps through the same kind of care manifested by Caxton.

Leaving aside the question of their authenticity, such signs at the very least remain important descriptors of the earliest known reception of the *Morte Darthur*. And what emerges are frequent reconfigurations of meaning: if one observes the distinctions of Winchester's paragraphing against the usual practices of modern editions, there are, for instance, realignments of dialogues into narrative units rather than speaker-exclusive paragraphs, realignments of episodic boundaries, emphatic isolations of short statements (sometimes within single speeches), emphatic or suspenseful separations of clauses,[1] delineations of parentheses, clarifications of syntax, the visual privileging of certain characters' speeches, the highlighting of rapid-fire exchanges of dialogue, and the signaling of colophonic direction. The relative line height and decorative elaboration of large capitals suggest additional representations of hierarchies, affinities, and distinctions, not the least of which concern some narrative divisions notoriously overridden by Vinaver.[2] Interestingly, such "restored" functions (and no doubt others) are common in the deployments of both scribes, despite their different habits, and with further study (necessarily incorporating a check for correlations in Caxton's increasingly reappreciated witness) may bring us back to the question of authorial nuance.

The items I have chosen for the Chronologies (p. xvii) and the Sources and Backgrounds and Criticism sections are designed to contribute to what I would describe as the contextualizing model of the volume. They represent my concern that readers develop a studious caution about inclinations they may have to mystify or reify Malory at the expense of

---

8. N. R. Ker, *The Winchester Malory: A Facsimile*, Early English Text Society, Supplementary Series 4 (Oxford: Oxford University Press, 1976), xviii.
9. This is *Sir Ferumbras*, written around 1380 and preserved in Oxford, Bodleian Library, MS Ashmole 33. The standard edition (with a parallel edition of the draft) is by Sidney J. Herrtage, Early English Text Society, Extra Series 34 (Oxford: Oxford University Press, 1879). For a survey of some of the translator/author/binder's methods, see Stephen H. A. Shepherd, "The Ashmole *Sir Ferumbras*: Translation in Holograph," in *The Medieval Translator,* ed. Roger Ellis (Cambridge: Brewer, 1989), 103–121.
1. For further consideration of the Malorian clause, see D. Thomas Hanks and Jennifer Fish, "Beside the Point: Medieval Meanings vs. Modern Impositions in Editing Malory's *Morte Darthur*," *Neuphilologische Mitteilungen* 98, 3rd ser. (1997): 273–289, esp. 277–278.
2. See Murray J. Evans, "The Explicits and Narrative Division in the Winchester MS: A Critique of Vinaver's Malory," *Philological Quarterly* 58 (1979): 263–281 and "Ordination and Narrative Links: The Impact of Malory's Tales as a 'hoole book,'" in *Studies in Malory,* ed. James W. Spisak (Kalamazoo, Mich.: University of Western Michigan, 1985), 29–52; see also "Opening Up the Malory Manuscript," 258–264.

not seeing his work as mediated, in its creation and its representation, by a variety of histories, discourses, technologies, speculations, and subjectivities (including those of editors). I am uncomfortable about characterizing my choices further. I do make some attempt to qualify their illustrative potential in brief dedicated headnotes and footnotes, but at the same time I do not wish to create the impression that I view those choices—or indeed my comments anywhere else in this volume—as somehow essential to anyone's experience of Malory.[3]

---

3. In an effort to resist the fixities imposed by its bibliographic form, this volume has a dedicated Web site with additional support materials similar to those that I offer for *Middle English Romances*; it can be reached by following links from the publisher's Norton Critical Edition Web site (www.wwnorton.com/college/english/nce_home.htm).

Acknowledgments

I am grateful to several libraries for permission to transcribe from their manuscripts and early printed books; the specific contributions of each library are acknowledged under "The Text," p. xliv, and in the source notes to each selection that appears in Sources and Backgrounds. Michael Boggan, Superintendent of the Manuscripts Reading Room of the British Library, was extremely helpful in negotiating to have the Winchester Manuscript removed from its exhibition case long enough for me to complete a record of the manuscript's rubrication and other uses of color. Professor P. J. C. Field has very patiently answered my questions about potential revised readings, helped make available research in advance of publication, and provided several much needed "reality checks." Professor Field's revised edition of Vinaver's Malory, a compendium of decades of work, has been an indispensable control and reference standard at every stage of the present edition's preparation. Takako Kato most generously made available a copy of her forthcoming *Medium Ævum* monograph, a work I believe is of considerable consequence for editors of Malory. To Carol Bemis, my editor at W. W. Norton & Company, go continuing thanks for having entertained my initial proposal for this edition, for her liberal attitude toward my requests for elaborate typesetting measures, and then for her great patience and understanding in seeing the project to its completion. Above all, I thank my dear wife, Shelli Carnes Shepherd, for her devoted assistance and tireless encouragement.

Any errors in this volume are, of course, mine alone to regret.

Chronologies

Arthur Before Malory†

409 C.E.	Rome loses control of Britain.
c. 468	Riothamus, King of the Britons, possibly to be identified with the historical Arthur, leads an army against the Visigoths in Gaul.
Late 5th to early 6th century	Various historical records imply that an unnamed British warlord—potentially the historical Arthur—experiences some successes against invading forces of Angles and Saxons.
Late 6th century	Poems by the (Welsh) bard Taliesin and others speak of an Arthur as a famous warrior, sometimes with supernatural associations.
c. 610	The *Gododdin* of Aneirin, a collection of northern elegies preserved in Welsh, evaluates a certain warrior as "no Arthur," thus suggesting the already legendary status of the name.
c. 800	The *Historia Brittonum,* a chronicle attributed to the Welsh monk Nennius, lists twelve victories over the Saxons won by Arthur, *dux bellorum* (leader of battles); Nennius embellishes by noting that Arthur slew 960 opponents singlehandedly in one battle.
c. 960–80	The *Annales Cambriae* (Annals of Wales) place the death of Arthur, and one Medraut (i.e., Mordred), at the battle of Camlann.
c. 1000–1100	Development of a body of Welsh Arthurian tales with much marvellous content, the most important of which is *Culhwch and Olwen,* later to be included among the *Mabinogion* tales, and possibly an indicator of the Celtic origin of aspects of the Grail quest.
c. 1136	The *Historia Regum Brittaniae* (History of the kings of Britain), written by the cleric Geoffrey of Monmouth, produces a combination of features of Arthur's story that will form the basis of much

† This chronology is selective, concentrating on texts and events that have some demonstrable legacy in Malory. The full range of Arthurian representation in the Middle Ages is vast; for introductions to further study, see "Arthurian Origins" in the Bibliography, p. 947.

	subsequent Arthurian literature: Merlin and his prophecies, the Roman campaign, Arthur's battle with Mordred, and his final repair to the Isle of Avalon.
1155	Wace finishes his Anglo-Norman *Brut*, a poem based mainly on Geoffrey, but introducing the Round Table and "modernizing" Arthur's court into a chivalric institution.
c. 1160–80	Marie de France writes her *Lais*, including two Arthurian poems, *Lanval* and *Chevrefeuil*.
c. 1160–91	Chrétien de Troyes produces arguably the first, the finest, and the most influential of all medieval Arthurian romances, *Eric et Enide*, *Cligés*, *Le Chevalier de la Charette*, *Le Chevalier au Lion* (*Yvain*), and *Le Conte du Graal* (*Perceval*); introduction of Camelot, Lancelot, Gawain, and Perceval.
c. 1170	Beroul writes his Anglo-Norman *Roman de Tristan*, an early "noncourtly" rendering of the legend of Tristan and Iseult.
c. 1190	Layamon completes his *Brut*, a translation of Wace, and the first Arthurian retelling in English.
1190	"Discovery" of the grave of Arthur and Guinevere at Glastonbury Abbey (an event advantageous to the impecunious abbey and to Henry II, who was faced with claims by rebellious Celtic peoples that Arthur would return to fight against him).
c. 1191–1210	Robert de Boron produces *Joseph d'Arimathie*, *Merlin*, and probably the *Didot Perceval*; he christianizes the Grail of Chrétien's *Perceval* and makes it the object of knightly quests.
c. 1210–30	*Perlesvaus* (*Le Haut Livre de Graal*) composed, with some knowledge of de Boron's *Joseph* and Chrétien's *Perceval*.
	Composition of the French prose Vulgate Cycle, an attempt to represent a full range of Arthurian legend, with a didactic cast: *Estoire del Saint Graal*, *Estoire de Merlin*, *Roman de Lancelot*, *Queste del Saint Graal*, *Mort Artu*.
c. 1240	French prose *Tristan* renders the story of Tristan and Iseult in a more thoroughly Arthurian context than its predecessors (e.g., Tristan becomes a knight of the Round Table).
c. 1250–1300	Production of *Arthour and Merlin*, the earliest known Arthurian metrical romance in English.
1278	Edward I reinters the (alleged) bones of Arthur at Glastonbury—a gesture in part to demoralize the Welsh (cf. the entry for 1190).

c. 1300–1350	Construction of the Winchester "Round Table" (see n. 5, p. 61)
1348	Edward III founds the Order of the Garter in imitation of the institution of the Round Table.
c. 1350	Composition of the alliterative *Morte Arthure*.
c. 1387–1400	Chaucer writes the *Canterbury Tales*; the "Wife of Bath's Tale" and the "Squire's Tale" feature Arthurian elements.
	Thomas Chestre writes *Sir Launfal*, and possibly *Libeaus Desconus*.
	Composition of the stanzaic *Morte Arthur*.
c. 1400–30	Composition of the *Awntyrs off Arthure at the Terne Wathelyne*.
c. 1450	Production of the earliest English prose romance, *Merlin*.
	Henry Lovelich produces his *History of the Holy Grail*, the first English translation of the *Estoire del Saint Graal*.
1465	Completion of John Hardyng's *Chronicle*.
c. 1469	Malory begins *Le Morte Darthur*.

The Wars of the Roses†

Feb. 1399	Richard II seizes the lands of his exiled cousin Henry Bolingbroke, Duke of Lancaster (of the House of Lancaster).
July 1399– Feb. 1400	Bolingbroke (soon to be Henry IV) returns to England and usurps the throne from Richard II. Richard is imprisoned first in the Tower of London and then at Pontefract Castle, where he is secretly murdered (before his death, Richard had unofficially identified Roger Mortimer, Earl of March, as his heir).
1400–09	Henry IV suppresses rebellions of Owen Glendower in Wales and, in England, Henry Percy (Hotspur), the Earls of Northumberland and Worcester, and Richard Scrope, Archbishop of York; King James I of Scotland captured.
Mar. 20, 1413	Death of Henry IV, who is succeeded by his son, Henry V.

† This chronology begins by listing events that led up to the Wars of the Roses proper and generally emphasizes events that may have some resonance with the *Morte Darthur*. The chronology also lists events that continue past Malory's death, but are included to provide some sense of historical contiguity up to and beyond the time of the first printed publication of Malory's work in 1485. For guides to further reading see the Selected Bibliography.

1415	Richard, Earl of Cambridge, plots to overthrow Henry V to place Edmund Mortimer, son of Roger, on the throne; Edmund betrays the plot to Henry; Richard is executed.
Oct. 25, 1415	Battle of Agincourt; Henry V defeats a French army three times the size of his with severe losses among French knights and nobility; Edward, Duke of York is killed, whose title passes to Richard, son of the Earl of Cambridge, thus founding the House of York.
By May 1420	Henry V conquers much of northern France and is recognized as heir to the French throne; he marries Catherine, daughter of Charles VI of France, June 2, 1420.
Aug. 31, 1422	Henry V dies in France, something of a legend in his own time; his son and heir, Henry, is only nine months old.
1428–37	Nation governed by a royal council until the end of Henry's minority; Henry emerges as a sovereign little concerned with secular matters and with a distaste for war; English hold on territories in France wavers. Henry is easily led by a small group of ambitious advisers, especially William de la Pole, Earl of Suffolk.
Dec. 2, 1431	Henry crowned King of France in Paris.
1441	Humphrey, Duke of Gloucester, a principal opponent of Henry's ambitious advisers, is discredited when his wife is accused of sorcery (cf. n. 4, p. 17) and forced to endure public penance; Gloucester dies in 1447, imprisoned by his enemies, probably murdered.
1444	Henry marries Margaret of Anjou, niece of Charles VII.
1447	The Earl of Suffolk instigates an attack on the Duke of Brittany, ally of Charles VII; Charles retaliates, and by 1453 all English possessions in France, with the exception of Calais, are lost. Lawlessness and corruption become common traits of local governance throughout England (cf. pp. 759–68).
1450	The Earl of Suffolk executed on his way into exile. Jack Cade's Rebellion arises in Kent in protest at abuses brought about under Suffolk's influence and culminates in murderous riots in London. Richard, Duke of York, heir apparent as well as heir to the Mortimer claim on the throne, returns from virtual banishment in Ireland to challenge the authority of Henry VI's new favorite, and a rival claimant to the throne as grandson of Edward III, Edmund Beaufort, Duke of Somerset.

Aug. 1453	Henry VI suffers the first of several periods of vegetative insanity; his son Edward (now the new heir apparent) is born two months later: the Lancastrian claim to the throne is revitalized, but many believe that the child is Somerset's (see the entry for Mar. 1454).
Mar. 1454	Richard, Duke of York, appointed Protector of the Realm; the Duke of Somerset is arrested—in the Queen's apartments—and imprisoned in the Tower of London.
Dec. 1454	Henry recovers from insanity; Somerset released; Henry expresses surprise at the birth of his son, claiming he must have been conceived by the Holy Spirit.
Feb. 1455	York dismissed as Protector.
May 22, 1455	First battle of St. Albans, the first major battle of the Wars of the Roses: Yorkists encounter Somerset and Henry VI; Somerset is killed; York, evidently satisfied with the result, renews his oath of alliegance to the King. From this time until 1459 the Queen, Margaret of Anjou, attempts to consolidate Lancastrian control of court and government, to the increasing consternation of the Yorkists.
Oct. 1459	York's forces defeated at Ludford Bridge by an army raised by the Queen; York flees to Ireland, and other Yorkists flee to Calais, including the Earl of Warwick and York's son Edward, Earl of March (soon to be King Edward IV).
June 1460	A Yorkist army from Calais lands at Sandwich; men of the surrounding southeastern counties join with these forces (cf. n. 3, p. 683).
July 2, 1460	Yorkists enter London and besiege the Tower of London with cannon (cf. n. 8, p. 679).
July 10, 1460	Battle of Northampton: partly due to defections from the Lancastrian army, the Yorkists prevail, led by Warwick and the Earl of March.
Sept.–Oct. 1460	Richard, Duke of York, returns from Ireland and advances his claim to the throne (see p. 768); the lords of the realm reject the claim, but reinstate Richard as Protector and recognize him as heir to the throne, thus disinheriting Henry VI's son Edward; Henry is detained in London; the Queen flees north.
Dec. 30, 1460	Battle of Wakefield: forces assembled by the Queen rout forces led by Richard, Duke of York; Richard is killed, and his head, wearing a paper crown, is spiked on the gates of York.

Feb. 2, 1461   Battle of Mortimer's Cross: Edward, son of Richard and now Duke of York (aged eighteen) defeats a large Lancastrian force. Before the battle Edward's army sees in the sky what appear to be three suns that merge into one; Edward takes the vision as a sign of the Trinity's favor of his cause.

Feb. 17, 1461   Second battle of St. Albans: forces of Queen Margaret, pillaging their way toward London, defeat Yorkists led by Richard Neville, Earl of Warwick (the Kingmaker). Margaret arranges for her seven-year-old son, Prince Edward, to order the executions of several captured Yorkist leaders. Henry VI is recovered from his captors; nevertheless, in the following two weeks Margaret and her forces fail to gain entry into London and turn northward to Yorkshire.

Mar. 1, 1461   Edward, Duke of York, is acclaimed King of England (as Edward IV) and is so proclaimed at Westminster Abbey on March 4 (he is crowned later, June 28).

Mar. 29, 1461   Battle of Towton (Palm Sunday Field, the bloodiest battle ever fought on English soil, with more than twenty thousand dead—for a contemporary account, see p. 772): the Lancastrians are decisively routed; Henry, Margaret, and Prince Edward escape to Scotland; Edward IV's claim to the throne is effectively secured.

By 1464   Edward IV acts swiftly to eliminate Lancastrian resistance (cf. his Act of Attainder, p. 774); Margaret of Anjou returns to France with Prince Edward; Henry remains a fugitive in the north. Lancastrian strongholds in Northumberland, such as Bamburgh, Dunstanborough, and Alnwick, are repeatedly won and lost (Malory was at the 1462 sieges with the Yorkists; see p. xxvi).

May 1464   Edward IV marries Elizabeth Woodville, widow of a Lancastrian knight, much to the consternation of the ambitious Kingmaker Richard, Earl of Warwick, who was in the process of arranging the King's marriage to a French princess.

July 1465   The fugitive Henry is captured in Lancashire and imprisoned in the Tower of London, where he remains for the next five years.

1468   Having been embarrassed and rejected by Edward IV in frustrating his various diplomatic efforts in France, Richard, Earl of Warwick, reinvents his role as Kingmaker and rebels in favor of George, Duke of Clarence, the King's brother.

1469   Warwick the Kingmaker orchestrates uprisings in the north and lands with an army from Calais;

	Edward IV is captured, but subsequent local unrest forces Warwick to reconcile with and restore Edward.
Spring 1470	Warwick orchestrates new rebellions in Lincolnshire and Wales, which Edward successfully suppresses; Warwick and Clarence flee to France and by July form an alliance with Margaret of Anjou to support the Lancastrian cause.
Sept. 1470	Warwick arranges a diversionary rebellion in York and lands in the south, gathering much local support; Edward IV, unable to return to London, flees to the Netherlands.
Oct. 3, 1470	Henry VI restored to the throne (the Readeption); Warwick swears alliegance, but is now the practical ruler of the nation.
Apr. 11, 1471	Edward IV, having landed in Yorkshire with an army of mercenaries, and now having the support of Clarence, evades opposing forces and enters London.
Apr. 14, 1471	Battle of Barnet Heath: Lancastrian forces are routed; Warwick is killed. Margaret of Anjou returns from France with Prince Edward and begins a march toward Lancastrian strongholds in Wales; Edward IV marches to intercept.
May 4, 1471	Battle of Tewkesbury: Edward IV decisively defeats Margaret's forces; Prince Edward is slain and Margaret captured and thence imprisoned in the Tower of London (she is ransomed five years later by her father).
May 21, 1471	Edward IV returns to London; Henry VI (now held in the Tower of London, separately from Margaret) is murdered.
Feb. 18, 1478	The Duke of Clarence, having continued in treasonous nuisances, is executed, reputedly by drowning in a butt (cask) of wine.
To 1483	Edward secures peace and order for the realm and relieves the Crown from the debtor habits it had assumed under Lancastrian rule. He becomes friend and patron to William Caxton, first printer in England. Edward also gains notoriety for indulging his tastes for wine, women, and song.
Apr. 9, 1483	Edward IV dies, having appointed his brother Richard, Duke of Gloucester, as Regent during the minority of his eldest son, Edward V, then twelve years old.
June 22, 1483	Richard has Edward IV's marriage declared invalid and his sons illegitimate (Edward V and his younger

	brother, Richard, who have been held in the Tower of London, are soon murdered there).
July 6, 1483	Richard crowned as Richard III.
Autumn 1483	Henry Stafford, Duke of Buckingham, Richard's principal co-conspirator in his move to claim the throne, rebels after allying with the exiled Henry Tudor, earl of Richmond, surviving head of the House of Lancaster; Richard suppresses the rebellion and Stafford is executed.
Aug. 22, 1485	Battle of Bosworth Field: Henry Tudor invades with an army of French mercenaries, and his forces meet Richard in open battle; Richard is unhorsed and killed (the last English monarch to die in battle); Tudor is proclaimed Henry VII.
Jan. 18, 1486	Henry VII marries Princess Elizabeth of York, daughter of Edward IV, thus uniting the two houses; all subsequent sovereigns of England can be identified as descended by blood from this union.
Sept. 20, 1486	Henry's eldest son, Arthur, Prince of Wales, is born; Henry arranges for him to be born in the legendary Arthurian capital of Winchester (cf. n. 5, p. 61) and chooses his name to commemorate the unification of England that the child embodies; Arthur dies fifteen years later, eight years before the death of his father.

Malory: Life Events†

c. 1415–1417	Thomas is born into a Warwickshire gentry family, the son of Philippa Chetwynd and John Malory (who died 1433/4 and was at various times sheriff, Member of Parliament [M.P.], and justice of the peace for Warwickshire).
Oct. 8, 1441	First record describing Thomas as a knight.
Oct. 10, 1443	Malory accused of having insulted, wounded, and imprisoned Thomas Smythe of Spratton, Northamp-

---

† The chronology is that of Sir Thomas Malory of Newbold Revel, Warwickshire; several other men of the same name have been put forward as candidates for the author of *Le Morte Darthur,* but current scholarly consensus is that the Newbold Revel candidate is the most feasible. That said, given the fragmentary, often contradictory, and sometimes fraudulent nature of 15th-century records, there is no guarantee that all of the events listed here actually pertain to the same man; no claim to an authoritative "biography" can be made. Details of this chronology are abstracted mainly from two works by P. J. C. Field: *The Life and Times of Sir Thomas Malory* (Cambridge: Brewer, 1993) and "The Malory Life-Records," in *A Companion to Malory,* ed. Elizabeth Archibald and A. S. G. Edwards (Cambridge: Brewer, 1996), 115–130. Further information about Malory's time in Newgate is taken from Anne F. Sutton, "Malory in Newgate: A New Document," *The Library* 7th ser., 1 (2000): 243–262.

tonshire, and stealing £40's worth of his goods (the matter apparently did not go to trial).

By Feb. 5, 1448   Married to Elizabeth Walsh of Wanlip, Leicestershire.

Jan. 1445–
Apr. 1446   M.P. for Warwickshire.

c. 1447–48   Birth of son Robert.

Aug. 23, 1451   Malory is charged at Nuneaton, Warwickshire, in the presence of Humphrey Stafford, Duke of Buckingham, with the following crimes:

- Attempted murder of the Duke of Buckingham, by ambush with twenty-six other men, in the Abbot's woods at Combe, Warwickshire, Jan. 4, 1450.
- "Rape" (*raptus*) of Joan Smith, at Coventry, May 23, 1450.[1]
- Extortion of money from two monks of Monks Kirby, Warwickshire, May 31, 1450.
- Second "rape" of Joan Smith, and theft of £40's worth of goods from her husband, Aug. 6, 1450.
- Extortion of money from another monk of Monks Kirby, Aug. 31, 1450.
- Theft of seven cows, two calves, 335 sheep, and a cart worth £22 at Cosford, Warwickshire, June 4, 1451.
- Theft of six does and infliction of £500's worth of damage in the duke of Buckingham's deer park at Cauldon, Warwickshire, July 20, 1451.
- Escaping imprisonment at the house of Sheriff Sir William Montford at Coleshill, Warwickshire (Malory swims the moat at night), July 27, 1451.
- Robbery, with ten accomplices, of £46 in money and £40's worth of ornaments from Combe Abbey, July 28, 1451.
- Further robbery at Combe Abbey, with one hundred accomplices, of £40 in money and five rings, a small psalter, two silver bells, three rosaries, and two bows, and three sheaves of arrows.

By Jan. 27,
1452, and until
July 1460   Held at various prisons in London (Ludgate, King's Bench, the Tower of London, and Newgate) awaiting a trial that never happened. During this period Malory is released on bail several times; during two of these periods of temporary freedom he is implicated in further crimes:

- Theft of four oxen from Lady Katherine Peyto at Sibbertoft, Northamptonshire.
- Harboring another alleged criminal, his servant

---

1. For a consideration of this crime, see the essay by Catherine Batt, p. 797 herein.

	John, and attempting with him to steal horses in the environs of Great Easton, Essex.
	For the latter, he is jailed at Colchester, Essex, from whence he escapes, Oct. 30, 1454. He is recaptured and returned to prison in London. Not long after the seizure of London by Yorkist forces in July 1460, Malory is probably freed from prison.
Oct. 24, 1462	Issued a general pardon (i.e., amnesty) by the new king, Edward IV.
Autumn 1462	Probable marriage of son Robert to Elizabeth Pulteney of Misterton, Leicestershire.
Oct. 1462–Jan. 1463	Malory participates in the military expedition of Edward IV and Richard, Earl of Warwick against Lancastrian strongholds in the Northumbrian castles of Alnwick, Bamburgh, and Dunstanborough.
Between Aug. 2, 1466 and July 26, 1467	Birth of grandson Nicholas.
July 14, 1468	Malory is explicitly excluded from a general pardon of Edward IV for any crimes committed; the exclusion generally names Lancastrian sympathizers. Presumably Malory is back in prison at this time, even though no charges against him are recorded, and there is no record of his having been brought to trial (see next two entries).
Apr. 20, 1469	Twenty-one men, including Malory, are recorded as witnesses to a deathbed declaration of Thomas Mynton, inmate of Newgate Prison; presumably Malory is also an inmate there—a prison less likely to hold political prisoners than the Tower of London (cf. the entry for Mar. 14, 1471).
Between Mar. 4, 1469 and Mar. 3, 1470	*Le Morte Darthur* completed (see n. 4, p. 698); to judge from Malory's references throughout to being in prison, he may well have written most, if not all, of the work while incarcerated (see pp. 112, 227, 327, and 698).
Feb. 22, 1470	Malory is explicitly excluded from another general pardon of Edward IV.
Mar. 14, 1471	Malory dies, possibly still a prisoner, as he is buried at Greyfriars Church in the immediate vicinity of Newgate. If he was still a prisoner, then his imprisonment on political grounds seems less likely, as the throne had reverted to Henry VI in the previous year (see the chronology, p. xxiii). According to a sixteenth-century transcription, his epitaph read as follows (the actual tombstone is lost, probably sold in 1545, with many others from the churchyard, to raise money for Henry VIII):

> *Dominus Thomas Malleré valens miles obiit 14 Mar 1470*[2] *de parochia Mokenkyrby in comitatu Warwici* (Sir Thomas Malory, a valiant knight of the parish of Monks Kirby in Warwickshire, died 14 March 1471).

Receptions of *Le Morte Darthur* to 1934[†]

c. 1471–83   Production of the "Winchester Manuscript" of *Le Morte Darthur* for an unknown patron; the manuscript was present in the printing shop of William Caxton at least between 1480 and 1489, but was not used as his primary copy-text for his own edition of Malory. The manuscript later ends up at Winchester College, where it remains effectively unknown until 1934.

July 31, 1485   William Caxton finishes the first printed edition of Malory, introducing his own chapter divisions, changing spellings, and making thousands of other small changes to the readings of his copy-text; Caxton is also probably responsible for the extreme abridgment of his edition of the Roman war episode. Many readings in Caxton's edition, however, appear to be closer to Malory's known sources than comparable readings in Winchester. For Caxton's own comments about his edition, see p. 814. Caxton's edition becomes the only known copy-text for postmedieval editors until 1934.

1498   Wynkyn de Worde, Caxton's apprentice and successor, reprints the edition, with minor corrections—possibly from Caxton's copy-text—and adds twenty dedicated woodcut illustrations. In book XX, chapter 12, he adds a moralizing interpolation, warning readers to consider

> how and in what manner ought ye to be so desirous of . . . mundane honour so dangerous.

2. In England at this time the calendar year was calculated as beginning on March 25 (Lady Day, about which see n. 6, p. 212); thus the year of the epitaph translates to a modern dating of 1471.
† Malory's influence is vast and since the 19th century has grown exponentially; with the exception of listing all editions before 1868, the present chronology can tabulate only critical and artistic highlights. Critical quotations taken from the works cited are by no means intended to be definitive but are intended to stimulate further reading with an awareness that current ideas and debates about Malory often have genealogies of considerable antiquity. For guides to critical studies of Malory mainly after 1934 (the date of the discovery of the Winchester Manuscript), see the Bibliography; see also the essays reprinted in this volume, beginning p. 795. For direction to treatments of Malory's creative heritage, especially after 1934—including literature, music, drama, film, and other visual arts—see the Bibliography. The present chronology is particularly indebted to the following studies: Marylyn Jackson Parins, *Malory: The Critical Heritage* (New York: Routledge, 1988); A. S. G. Edwards, "The Reception of Malory's *Morte Darthur*," in *A Companion to Malory*, ed. Elizabeth Archibald and A. S. G. Edwards (Cambridge: Brewer, 1996), 241–252; and Beverly Taylor and Elizabeth Brewer, *The Return of King Arthur* (Cambridge: Brewer, 1983).

Therefore me thinketh this present book call La Morte Darthur is right necessary often to be read, for in it shall ye find the gracious, knightly, and virtuous war of most noble knights of the world, whereby they gat praising continual. Also me seemeth by the oft reading thereof ye shall greatly desire to accustom yourself in following of those gracious knightly deeds, that is to say, to dread God, and to love rightwiseness, faithfully and courageosly to serve your sovereign prince.

c. 1450(?)–1500   Composition of *The Weddyng of Syr Gawen and Dame Ragnell,* a Middle English metrical romance burlesquing Arthurian values; a "loathly lady" romance as well as the "Wife of Bath's Tale," and possibly the *Awntyrs off Arthure,* are sources, but the poem also claims to be written by someone in jail and employs character names in combinations otherwise unique to Malory.[1]

1529   de Worde produces another edition, with "modernized" syntax and normalized vocabulary; he also adds some new illustrations.

1557   Edition of William Copeland, based on de Worde 1529.
John Bale (bishop of Ossory), *Scriptorium Illustrium Maioris Britanniae:* "In my view, [Malory's] work abounds in old wives' tales which need to be expurgated lest the historical veracity of the work be compromised. In our times, Malory enjoys an illustrious reputation" (trans. Parins).

1570   Roger Ascham (Renaissance scholar and tutor to Elizabeth I), *The Scholemaster:*

In our forefathers tyme, whan Papistrie, as a standyng poole, covered and overflowed all England, fewe bookes were read in our tong, savyng certaine bookes of Chevalrie, as they sayd, for pastime and pleasure, which, as some say, were made in Monasteries, by idle Monkes, or wanton Chanons: as one for example, *Morte Arthure:* the whole pleasure of which booke standeth in two speciall poyntes, in open mans slaughter, and bold bawdrye: In which booke those be counted the noblest Knightes, that do

---

1. P. J. C. Field has suggested that the poem was in fact written by Malory: "Malory and *The Wedding of Sir Gawain and Dame Ragnell,*" in P. J. C. Field, *Malory: Texts and Sources* (Cambridge: Brewer, 1998), 284–294 (reprinted from a 1982 article in *Archiv*). I am more inclined to see the poem as a parodic reception of the *Morte Darthur* along with other Arthurian texts: see Stephen H. A. Shepherd, "No poet has his travesty alone: *The Weddynge of Syr Gawen and Dame Ragnell*" in *Romance Reading on the Book,* ed. J. Fellows et al. (Cardiff: University of Wales Press, 1996), 112–128.

kill most men without any quarell, and commit fowlest adulteries by sutlest shiftes. . . . What toyes, the dayly readyng of such a booke, may worke in the will of a yong jentleman, or a yong mayde, that liveth welthelie and idleie, wise men can judge, and honest men do pitie.

1575   Robert Laneham (mercer of London) in a letter describes festivities during Queen Elizabeth's visit to Kenilworth Castle and showing considerable familiarity with Malory's work, identifies a minstrel's song as derived from I.26 of (de Worde's) Morte Darthur.

c. 1577   Thomas East's edition, based on de Worde 1529 and Copeland.

1577   Nathaniel Baxter (Puritan author, tutor in Greek to Sir Philip Sydney), Dedicatory Epistle to his translation of Calvin's sermons on the prophet Jonas: "vile and blasphemous, or at least . . . prophane and frivolous bookes, such as are that infamous legend of King Arthur . . . with the horrible actes of those whoremasters, Launcelot du Lake, Tristram de Liones, Gareth of Orkney, Merlin, the Lady of the Lake, with the vile and stinking story of the Sangreall, of King Peleus, etc."

1578–83   Sir Philip Sydney reveals a likely acquaintance with Malory in his Defense of Poesie (c. 1579) and Arcadia (1578–83).

1590–96   Edmund Spenser makes a strong allusion to Malory (corresponding to Caxton XVIII.8–20) in his View of the Present State of Ireland (1596). His most famous work, the Faerie Queene (1590–1596), also suggests the likelihood of Malorian influence.

1597–98   Shakespeare's 2 Henry IV casually refers to Sir Dagonet (III.iii.272, corresponding to Caxton X.11–12), suggesting the playwright's greater familiarity with Malory.

1611   Robert Chester's Birth, Life and Death of Honourable Arthur King of Brittaine borrows heavily, often verbatim, from Malory.

1634   Edition of William Stansby (based on that of East): the Preface (possibly written by one Jacob Blome), taking an antiquarian stance, notes of Malory's writing that "the reader may see the best forme and manner of writing and speech that was in use at those times." The editor also claims—falsely, as it turns out—to have expurgated "prophane [and] superstitious speeches." The Preface later claims that the

	text as edited "may passe for a famous piece of antiquity, revived almost from the gulf of oblivion." Another new edition of Malory will not appear until 1816.
1638–67	John Milton early considers writing an epic poem on the subject of King Arthur, but ultimately rejects is for the religious matter of his great work *Paradise Lost* (1667); slight details in the poem do, however, reveal Milton's familiarity with Malory.
1662	In *Hudibras*, Samuel Butler, influenced by the frontispiece of Stansby's edition, mocks the Arthurian milieu, claiming that the Round Table was a hooped petticoat with which Arthur would store food for his knights.
1672	*Chaucer's Ghoast: or, a piece of Antiquity . . . with the History of Prince Corniger* (author unknown); an eclectic parody of the *Morte Darthur*, the work of someone who has closely read a pre-Stansby edition.
1696	William Nicholson speaks of Malory as a historian in the *English Historical Library*: "Thomas Malory . . . wrote King Arthur's story in English; a book that is, in our days, often sold by the ballad-singers."
1748	William Oldys writes an entry on Malory in the *Biographia Britannica*, claiming that his work "seems to have been kept in print, for the entertainment of the lighter and more insolid readers."
1762, 1777	In *Observations on the Faerie Queene* (1762) and *History of English Poetry* (1777), Thomas Warton provides what can be called the first scholarly studies of the *Morte Darthur*, researching Malory's influence on subsequent writers, offering estimations of his sources, and raising the issue of the questionable "unity" of his work.
1765	In his edition of Shakespeare, Samuel Johnson observes that "Nations, like individuals, have their infancy. . . . The study of those [in England] who then aspired to plebeian learning was laid out upon adventures, giants, dragons, and enchantments. *The Death of Arthur* was the favourite volume."
1792–1824	The great Romantic novelist and early medievalist Sir Walter Scott studies the *Morte Darthur*, with increasingly positive evaluations, culminating in his 1824 "Essay on Romance" for the *Encyclopaedia Britannica*: "Sir Thomas Malory, indeed, compiled, from various French authorities, his celebrated *Morte d'Arthur*, indisputably the best Prose Romance the language can boast."

1816   The first two new editions of Malory since 1634 are published. Both are based on the Stansby edition but with modernized spelling: of these two, the Walker's British Classics edition is known to have been owned by Keats and Wordsworth, and both that and the Wilkes edition are owned by Tennyson.

1817   Edition of Robert Southey, the first to make an earnest (if often erroneous) attempt at identifying Malory's sources; an attempt is also made to retain Caxton's original spellings. Southey observes, "the fashion for such works has passed away; and now for the full enjoyment of them a certain aptitude is required, as it is for poetry and music: where that aptitude exists, perhaps no works of imagination produce so much delight."

1822   Kenelm Digby publishes *The Broad Stone of Honour, or Rules for the Gentlemen of England*, with extensive exemplary quotation from Malory.

1828   Wordsworth writes "The Egyptian Maid," acknowledging some influence from Malory.

1842–85   Publication by 1842 of Alfred, Lord Tennyson's *Morte d'Arthur, Sir Lancelot and Queen Guenevere, The Lady of Shalott* and *Sir Galahad*, followed between 1859 and 1885 by incremental publication of perhaps the single most important Malory-influenced work of literature yet published, the *Idylls of the King*.

1853   Characters in Charlotte Yonge's *The Heir of Redclyffe* intelligently debate the artistic maturity of Malory's work.

1858   Edition of Thomas Wright, based on Stansby, but with annotations about original Caxton readings, and the first critical study of all prior editions.
Publication of William Morris's *The Defence of Guenevere and other Poems*, showing (as can be argued for his well-known visual art) some influence from Malory.

1859   David Masson, *British Novelists and their Styles*: "[The *Morte Darthur*] is the kind of book into which a poet may go for hints and fancies already made to his hands, in dealing with which by way of elaboration and expansion he may follow his own free will without sense of constraint, evolving meanings where they seem concealed, or fitting his own meanings to visual imaginations which start out of their apparent arbitrariness into pre-established connexion with them." (The observation could be said to

	prefigure the directions that postmodern criticism of Malory will begin to take nearly 150 years later.)
1868[2]	Edition of Richard Strachey, which, though occasionally modernized, contains an introduction of unprecedented critical scope, considering the editorial history of "our English epic," its modification of sources, unique characterizations, its "unity," its depiction of geography, and "the morality of the book."
1880	*The Boy's King Arthur,* the first American edition of Malory, produced by the poet Sidney Lanier: "No book ever needed less pointing-out of its intrinsic faults and beauties than this frank work of a soul so transparent that one is made to think of the Wakulla Spring in Florida where one can see a penny on the bottom at a hundred feet depth."
1888–89	Frederick Ryland, essay in *English Illustrated Magazine*: "The *Morte Darthur* is in fact a very typical product of the art of the Middle Ages, which always tends to subordinate form to matter, rejoicing in rich multiplicity of detail, in beautiful luxuriance of colour, and in unspeakable wealth of ornament."
1889	Mark Twain's *A Connecticut Yankee in King Arthur's Court* employs Malory as a central influence and interpolates extensively from Strachey's edition.
1889–91	Edition of H. Oskar Sommer: text (the first since Caxton to leave Caxton's text unaltered) plus two volumes of commentary, with a comprehensive and detailed revelation of the intricacies of Malory's handling of sources; Sommer says of Malory, "truth demands that we should not rate him too highly. To put it mildly, his work is very unequal—sometimes he excels, but often he falls beneath, oftener still, he servilely reproduces his originals. Nor can his selection of material be unreservedly praised."
1893	W. P. Ker, introduction to *English Prose Selections*, defends Malory's style: "Malory's prose, and not Chaucer's, is the prose analogue of Chaucer's poetry; summing up as it does some of the great attainments of the earlier Middle Ages, and presenting them in colours more brilliant, with a more conscious style, than they had possessed in their first rendering."
1893–94	Edition of F. J. Simmons, with illustrations by the then-controversial modern artist Aubrey Beardsley;

2. Beyond this date editions of Malory begin to proliferate in many forms; mention of editions hereafter in this chronology is selective.

	in 1906 this is reissued as the popular Dent/Everyman edition.
1891–1907	American poet Richard Hovey publishes *Launcelot and Guenevere: A Poem in Dramas,* much influenced by Malory.
1894–97	Harvard professor George Lyman Kittredge puts forward detailed evidence for Sir Thomas Malory of Newbold Revel, Warwickshire, as the most likely candidate for the author of the *Morte Darthur,* this remains the most accepted identification (see the chronology on p. xxiv).
1896	Swinburne's poem "The Tale of Balen," a close adaptation of Malory's story of Balin le Saveage.
1898	George Saintsbury, *A Short History of English Literature:* "Criticisms have been made on Malory's manner of selecting and arranging his materials—criticisms which, like all unsuccessful exercises of the most difficult of arts, come from putting the wrong questions to the jury—from asking, 'Has this man done what *I* wanted him to do?' or 'Has he done it as *I* should have done it?' instead of 'Has he done what *he* meant to do?' and 'Has he done this well?' "
1912	W. H. Schofield, *Chivalry in English Literature: Chaucer, Malory, Spenser, and Shakespeare.*
1917	Vida D. Scudder, *Le Morte Darthur of Sir Thomas Malory: A Study of the Book and its Sources;* the first book-length study of Malory; praises his "original genius."
1917–27	Pulitzer Prize–winning American poet Edwin Arlington Robinson publishes *Merlin* (1917), *Launcelot* (1920), and *Tristram* (1927), long poems with a framework based on Malory.
1922	E. K. Chambers, *Malory,* a pamphlet making the important proposition that Malory's purposes sometimes differed from those of his sources.
1923	Laurence Binyon, *Arthur: A Tragedy,* a drama based on the closing books of the *Morte Darthur.*
1926–32	American novelist John Erskine publishes *Galahad: Enough of His Life to Explain His Reputation* and *Tristan and Isolde: Restoring Palamede,* both based on Malory.
1929	Eugène Vinaver, *Malory,* an insightful, if not altogether complementary, study of Malory's handling of French sources; Vinaver's views will become more favorable over the next forty years with his work on the now-standard scholarly edition of Malory, based on the Winchester Manuscript.

1934   Discovery by librarian Walter Oakeshott, in a safe in
            the Warden's lodgings of Winchester College, of a
            fifteenth-century manuscript copy of Malory's work
            (the "Winchester Manuscript"); the manuscript pro-
            vides extra autobiographical information, divides
            and decorates the text differently from Caxton, and
            has thousands of readings at variance with Caxton.
            Stemming from these differences, a new era of
            Malory studies is born.

Reading Malory's English[†]

Malory's English is sufficiently late—some may prefer to call it "Early Modern" rather than "Middle" English—that it usually presents few persistent difficulties for new readers. The main challenges in reading come from negotiating unfamiliar syntax, discerning "false friends," acquiring new (i.e., old) vocabulary, and establishing a sense of suitable pronunciation when reading aloud. The footnotes and Glossary (p. 907) are designed to address the first three of these challenges in most instances, but part I of this guide offers a more systematic understanding, which should reduce the frequency with which a new reader may have to turn away from the main text.

Malory's work, like the Middle English verse romances that are sometimes his sources, has a strong oral/declamatory ethos—most evident in a heavy reliance on direct discourse—and can make for a shamelessly Falstaffian indulgence when read aloud. Perhaps a more immediate incentive for attending to the orality of the text, however, emerges from a consideration of the records of Malory's life (p. xxiv): if they can be trusted as pertaining to the right man, one feature of his character that stands out is that he was able—it seems dangerously able, as far as those who wanted him in jail were concerned—to press rather large groups of people into following him; there can be little doubt that he was as compelling a speaker as he was a writer. To silence the sonic components of his surviving words against their inscribed signification, or to succumb to the ease with which one can modernize the sounds as one reads, risks being counterauthorial and countercontextual. In theory, at least, this principle must hold some conviction; it may not be wholly practicable, however, because, in the absence of a holograph of Malory's writing, we cannot be as confident as possible of how he pronounced his words. A comprehensive analysis, moreover, of authorial dialectal features that may be preserved by or beneath the scribal forms of the Winchester Manuscript has yet to be published. Nevertheless, if we assume Malory's origin in Warwickshire, the remarks in part II (p. xxxviii), based on a model of Midland English, should provide a serviceable approximation of Malory's pronunciation.

---

† Portions of this section are reprinted, with extensive adaptation, from M. H. Abrams et al., eds., *The Norton Anthology of English Literature,* 7th ed. 2 vols. (New York, 1993), I: 15–18, with permission of W. W. Norton & Company, New York. Examples are taken from the text of the Winchester Manuscript only.

I. Parts of Speech and Grammar

1. Nouns

The plural and possessive of nouns most often end in *es, ys,* or *is,* formed by adding *es, ys,* or *is* to the singular: *knight, knightes; roote, rootes; syege, syegis; salve, salves, salvys* (sometimes *s* alone is added); a final consonant is sometimes doubled before *es, ys,* or *is: God, Goddis.* A common irregular plural is *even* (spelled variously, including *eyn, yen, eghne, eyghen*— "eyes").

2. Pronouns

Where they appear, the chief differences from Modern English are as follows:

Modern English	Middle English
I	*I,* but occasionally *Y*
you (singular)*	*thou* (subjective); *the(e)* (objective)
she	*she,* but very occasionally *he* (from Old English *heo*)
her	*hir, hyr, her*
it	*hit(te), it*
its	*his*
you (plural)*	*ye* (subjective); *you* (objective)
their	*hir, hyr(e), her*
them	*hem, them*
those	*tho(o)*

* Note: In formal speech, the second person plural is often used for the singular as a gesture of respect and deference, and conversely the second person singular is sometimes used disrespectfully or overfamiliarly where the more formal choice is appropriate: the observance of these distinctions is often a significant element in Malory's characterizations: cf. n. 3, p. 649. The possessive adjectives *my, thy* take *n(e)* before a word beginning with a vowel or *h: thyne hede, myne adventure.*

3. Adjectives

Adjectives are compared by adding *er(e)* for the comparative, *est(e)* or *ist(e)* or *yst(e)* for the superlative. Sometimes the stem vowel is shortened or altered in the process: *sweete, swettere, swettest; long, lenger, lengest.*

4. Adverbs

Adverbs are formed from adjectives by adding *ly,* though sometimes are uninflected, as is the case for some instances of *fair* (courteously) and *lyke* (equally).

5. Verbs

Middle English verbs, like Modern English verbs, are either "weak" or "strong." Weak verbs form their preterites and past participles with a *t* or *d* suffix and preserve the same stem vowel throughout their systems, although it is sometimes shortened in the preterite and past participle:

love, loved; bend, bent; hear, heard; meet, met. Strong verbs do not use the *t* or *d* suffix, but vary their stem vowel in the preterite and past participle: *take, took, taken; begin, began, begun; find, found, found.*

The inflectional endings are the same for strong verbs and weak verbs, except in the preterite singular and the imperative singular. In the following standardized paradigms (where not every example appears in Malory's text and additional spellings are attested), the weak verbs *loven* (to love) and *hyren* (to hear), and the strong verbs *taken* (to take) and *slayen* (to slay) serve as models.

	PRESENT INDICATIVE	PRETERITE INDICATIVE
I	love, hyre	loved, herde
	take, sle(e)	toke, slew
thou	lovyst; heryst	loved, lovedyst; herde, herdyst
	takyst; sleyst	toke, tokyst; slew, slewyste
he, she, it	lovyth, hyryth	loved, herde
	takyth, sleyth	toke, slew
we, ye, they	love(th), hyre(th)[1]	loved, herde
	take(th), sle(e)(th)	toke, slew
	PRESENT SUBJUNCTIVE	PRETERITE SUBJUNCTIVE
Singular	love, hyre	oved, herde
	take, sle(e)	toke, slew
Plural	love, hyre	loved, herde
	take, sle(e)	toke, slew

The infinitive of most verbs is *e* or *en*: *love(n), hyre(n), take(n), bynde(n).*

The past participle of weak verbs is the same as the preterite without inflectional ending: *loved, herde.* In strong verbs the ending is either *e* or *en*: *take(n), bounde(n).* The prefix *y-* or *i-* often appears on past participles: *i-horsed, y-fared, i-taught.*

6. Prepositions

Malory often employs familiar prepositions with more senses than their modern counterparts:

> *of* can have the sense of "from," "in," or "on" (e.g., respectively, p. 27, line 19; p. 355, line 35; p. 289, line 2).
> *at* can mean "of" (e.g., p. 14, line 13).
> *for* can mean "about" (e.g., p. 372, line 37).
> *in* can mean "on" (e.g., p. 68, line 38).
> *with* can mean "by" (e.g., p. 190, line 31).

The prepositional senses of "to" and "unto" can apply to *tyll(e)* (e.g., p. 675, line 33; p. 470, line 5).

7. Conjunctions

Malory's conjunctions conform predominantly with modern usage, but the following common variations are worthy of note:

1. In Caxton's text *-en* is often used for the present plural indicative.

And very often carries the sense of "if" (e.g., p. 65, line 41).

The phrase *but if* typically carries the sense of "unless" (e.g., p. 22, line 33; p. 647, line 37)

Without can carry the sense of "unless" (e.g., p. 261, line 20)

8. *Syntax*

Often as a result of the exigencies of translation or adaptation of sources, sometimes perhaps as a result of scribal miscopying, Malory's sentences can seem "experimental" to the point of chaos; in such cases the foot-notes will provide guidance. A few normative features of Malory's writing that might, however, seem persistently irregular to the modern reader are listed here:

Double- and sometimes triple-negatives are the usual form of negation (e.g., p. 184, lines 31–32; p. 594, line 16).

Indirect and direct discourse can be combined without notice (e.g., p. 179, lines 14–15; p. 115, line 1; p. 509, line 16).

Grammatical discontinuity can arise between adjacent clauses (i.e., anacoluthon: e.g., p. 55, lines 14–15; p. 228, lines 2–3; p. 690, lines 20–22).

Essential sense components—subjects, objects, nouns, pronouns, verbs—are often left implicit (i.e., ellipsis: e.g., p. 101, line 15; p. 104, line 1; p. 495, line 12; p. 614, line 4; p. 636, line 2).

II.A. The Sounds of Middle English: General Rules

The following general analysis of the sounds of Middle English will enable the reader who does not have time for detailed study to read Malory's text aloud so as to preserve some of its most essential characteristics, without, however, giving heed to many important details. Section II.B, "Detailed Analysis," is designed for the reader who wishes to go more deeply into the pronunciation of Middle English. Malory's English differs from Modern English in two principal respects: (1) the pronunciation of the long vowels *a, e, i* (or *y*), *o,* and *u* (spelled *ou, ow*); and (2) the fact that all Middle English consonants are sounded.

1. *Long Vowels*

Middle English vowels are long when they are doubled (*aa, ee, oo*) or when they are terminal (*he, to, holy*); *a, e,* and *o* are long when followed by a single consonant plus a vowel (*name, mete, note*). Middle English vowels are short when they are followed by two consonants.

Long *a* is sounded like the *a* in Modern English *father: maker, pass* (pace).

Long *e* may be sounded like the *a* in Modern English *name* (ignoring the distinction between the close and open vowel): *be, pees* (peace).

Long *y* (or *i*) is sounded like the *i* in Modern English *machine: lynage, wist, myght, holy.*

Long *o* may be sounded like the *o* in Modern English *note* (again ignoring the distinction between the close and open vowel): *do, sone* (soon).

Long *u* (spelled *ou, ow*) is sounded like the *oo* in Modern English *goose: aboute* (about), *rou(gh)te, prowese.*

Note that in general Middle English long vowels are pronounced like long vowels in modern languages other than English. Short vowels and diphthongs, however, may be pronounced as in Modern English.

2. *Final e*

Final *e* is commonly suppressed except when it is the only vowel (e.g., *sle* for "sley"). In other cases where it is likely to have been pronounced, the edition indicates this with -*é*.

3. *Consonants*

Middle English consonants are pronounced separately in all combinations—*gnasted: g-nasted; knave: k-nave; write: w-rite; folkys: fol-kys.* In a simplified system of pronunciation the combination *gh* as in *night* or *thought* may be treated as if it were silent.

II.B. The Sounds of Middle English: Detailed Analysis

1. *Simple Vowels*

Sound	Pronunciation	Example
long *a* (spelled *a, aa*)	*a* in *father*	*maker, pass*
short *a*	*o* in *hot*	*wan*
long *e* close (spelled *e, ee*)	*a* in *name*	*be, peerys*
long *e* open (spelled *e, ee*)	*e* in *there*	*mete, peeres*
short *e*	*e* in *set*	*hem*
long *i* (spelled *i, y*)	*i* in *machine*	*I, ryde*
short *i*	*i* in *in*	*in*
long *o* close (spelled *o, oo*)	*o* in *note*	*sone, good*
long *o* open (spelled *o, oo*)	*oa* in *broad*	*go, foo*
short *o*	*o* in *oft*	*of*
long *u* when spelled *ou, ow*	*oo* in *goose*	*aboute, prowesse*
long *u* when spelled *u*	*u* in *pure*	*vertu*
short *u* (spelled *u, o*)	*u* in *full*	*ful, love*

Doubled vowels and terminal vowels are always long, whereas single vowels before two consonants other than *the* and *ch* are always short. The vowels *a, e,* and *o* are long before a single consonant followed by a vowel: *nāme, sēke* (sick), *hōly.* In general, words that have descended into Modern English reflect their original Middle English quantity: *livith* (he/she lives), but *lȳf* (life).

The close and open sounds of long *e* and long *o* may often be identified by the Modern English spellings of the words in which they appear. Original long close *e* is generally represented in Modern English by *ee*: *sweet, knee, teeth,* and *see* have close *e* in Middle English, but so does *be*; original long open *e* is generally represented in Modern English by *ea*; *meat, heath, sea, great,* and *breath* have open *e* in Middle English. Similarly, original long close *o* is now generally represented by *oo*: *soon, food, good,* but also *do,* and *to*; original long open *o* is represented either by *oa* or by *o*: *coat, boat, moan,* but also *go, bone, foe,* and *home.* Notice that original close *o* is now almost always pronounced like the *oo* in *goose,* but that original open *o* is almost never so pronounced; thus it is often possible to identify the Middle English vowels through Modern English sounds.

The nonphonetic Middle English spelling of *o* for short *u* has been preserved in a number of Modern English words (*love, son, come*), but in others *u* has been restored: *nunnery* (*nonnery*), *sunbeam* (*sonnebeame*).

For the treatment of final *e,* see "General Rules," "Final *e*" (p. xxxix).

During the fifteenth century, primarily in the environs of London, the long vowels began to be "raised" with an elevation of the tongue and more closing of the mouth such that many of them began to approach their pronunciation in modern (British) English. David Crystal provides a useful illustration of the effect:

The post-vowel-shift sentence

so it is time to see the shoes on the same feet now

would have sounded more like this in pre-vowel-shift Middle English:

saw it is team to say the shows on the sarm fate noo.[2]

It is difficult to assess the extent to which Malory would have been affected by the "Great Vowel Shift," but, seeing as he was of provincial birth, from the earlier part of the century, and was probably in his late fifties when he wrote the *Morte Darthur,* his speech is likely to have been conservative.

2. *Diphthongs*

Sound	Pronunciation	Example
ai, ay, ei, ey	between *ai* in *aisle* and *ay* in *day*	*vitailled, day, counceile seyde*
au, aw	*ou* in *out*	*daunger, lawys*
eu, ew	*ew* in *few*	*deuke, nevew*
oy	*oy* in *joy*	*joye*
ou, ow	*ou* in *thought*	*thought, trow(e)*

2. David Crystal, *The English Language* (London: Penguin, 1988), 184. The development of the umlauts *ai* in modern *time* and *au* in modern *now* may not, however, have occurred until Shakespeare's time.

Note that in words with *ou, ow* that in Modern English are sounded with the *ou* of *about,* the combination indicates not the diphthong but the simple vowel long *u* (see "Simple Vowels").

3. *Consonants*

In general, all consonants except *h* were always sounded in Middle English, including consonants that have become silent in Modern English such as the *g* in *gnaw;* the *k* in *knight,* the *l* in *folk,* and the *w* in *write.* In noninitial *gn,* however, the *g* was silent as in Modern English *sign.* Initial *h* was silent in short common English words and in words borrowed from French and may have been almost silent in all words. The combination *gh* as in *night* or *thought* was sounded like the *ch* of German *ich* or *nach.* Note that Middle English *gg* represents both the hard sound of *dagger* and the soft sound of *bridge.*

Editorial Procedure/
Reading the Edition

Footnotes and Glossary

The footnotes serve the following functions, sometimes in combination: (1) glossing of the relatively frequent instances of "false friends" in Malory's prose, where a word appears to have a modern form but conceals a medieval sense (e.g., where *defended* means "forbidden" or *defamed* means "famed"); (2) explanation of difficult phrases, sentences, or longer passages; (3) contextualizing of details or events described in the text; (4) cross-references; and (5) explanation of selected variant readings or other editorial decisions. The glossary addresses the premodern vocabulary and usage of the *Morte Darthur* and, along with "Reading Malory's English" above, is intended to be the primary resource in this edition for readers still familiarizing themselves with Malory's writing.

Marginal Annotations

Each Winchester Manuscript folio number appears beside the line in the edition corresponding to the first line of the folio. Numbers in square brackets represent Caxton's corresponding chapter numbers and are placed beside the lines in the text where Caxton's chapters begin. Caxton book numbers appear in square brackets in the running titles. Numbers in angle brackets in the Roman war episode represent corresponding line numbers in the alliterative *Morte Arthure* (see n. †, p. 113 for further details).

Annotations written by the scribes of the Winchester Manuscript are included because it is possible that some, if not all, are authorial.[3] A marginal illustration is also included on the same grounds (see n. 3, p. 510). These items are placed in approximately the same position in the margins as they occupy in the manuscript. The text does not reproduce either scribe's line breaks.

---

3. See P. J. C. Field, "Malory's Own Marginalia," *Medium Ævum* 70 (2001), 226–239.

The Text

The base text is that of the "Winchester Manuscript," London, British Library, Additional Manuscript 59,678, printed with the permission of the British Library. Emendations are supplied from the Pierpont Morgan copy of Caxton's 1485 edition, printed with permission of the Pierpont Morgan Library, New York. For the purposes of transcription the texts were consulted in facsimiles: N. R. Ker, *The Winchester Malory: A Facsimile*, Early English Text Society, Supplementary Series 4 (Oxford: Oxford University Press, 1976), and Paul Needham, *"Le Morte D'Arthur," Printed by William Caxton 1485: Facsimile* (London: Scolar Press, 1976). For the purpose of confirming all instances of its rubrication, the Winchester Manuscript was consulted at firsthand.

The use of *u* and *v*, *i*, and *j* has been modernized; þ and 3 have been replaced by modern equivalents (the former to *th* and the latter to *gh, y,* or *z*, depending on the letter's position in a word). Roman numerals and abbreviations have been expanded silently in accordance with unabbreviated spellings as found in the manuscript; ſ has been expanded to *-es* (in accordance with the practice of O³). A special measure has been adopted in the representation of abbreviations of Merlin's name: see n. 4, p. 17.[4] Word division, punctuation, and capitalization are editorial, except in the case of large capitals and paragraphs (see below). Otherwise, and excepting the correction of obvious scribal errors, the orthography of the texts has not been regularized.

Emendation

All text appearing inside square brackets is from Caxton's edition, unless otherwise noted (as in the case of titles; see the following section). Angle brackets are used in the tale of the Roman war for readings imported from the alliterative *Morte Arthure;* for further details of the special editorial procedures employed for that tale, see n. †, p. 113. In an effort to reduce an intimidating clutter of brackets unsuitable for this kind of edition, I have not signaled corrections of brief and obvious mechanical copying errors (e.g., p. 15, line 40: *after* for manuscript *aftr*; p. 15, line 41: *the desire* for manuscript *thy desire,* etc.). Emendations are usually marked for one or more of the following reasons: (1) if, even when responding to clearly mechanical errors, they extend to more than three or four words, thus increasing the odds that not all of the words taken from Caxton's model are authentic; (2) if readings are supplied because the manuscript is damaged; (3) if the error corrected is assumed to have resulted from some form of eye skip;[5] (4) if Caxton's

---

4. The measure has been adopted on the basis of Helen Cooper's observations in "M. for Merlin: The Case of the Winchester Manuscript," in *Medieval Heritage: Essays in Honour of Tadahiro Ikegami,* ed. Masahiko Kanno et. al. (Tokyo: Yushodo Press, 1997), 93–107.
5. E.g., p. 29, lines 30–32, "they [put in the cyté . . . also they] had of othir," where the Winchester scribe (or a prior copyist) has skipped over a lengthy portion of text by looking at the wrong *they*

text is demonstrably closer to Malory's likely source (the demonstration usually having been recorded in O^3, the most comprehensive study of such lections available);[6] and (5) if the emendation is a conjectural construction not attested in any surviving witness (in which case an explanatory note always attends such readings).

An argument could be made that even these five kinds of emendations should go unmarked in an edition of this type, where a consistently detailed accounting for them in a discursive apparatus is not feasible or even desireable. I believe their identification has instructive potential, however, reminding readers that what they have before them is a representation of Malory rather than an invariably authentic replication; I also hope that this awareness will point interested readers toward a fuller exploration of the scholarly record and its debates, starting with O^3. Indeed, the provision in this edition of corresponding Winchester folio numbers and Caxton book and chapter numbers is intended to encourage comparative study.

Large Capitals, Major Divisions in the Text, and Titles

Lombardic capitals in the manuscript are represented with lombardic capitals in this edition and at the same relative line height as they have in the manuscript: i.e., a capital that is three handwritten lines high in the manuscript is three typeset lines high in this edition (where Caxton's is the only witness available, these and the following comments also apply). Capitals that appear in the margin of the manuscript are placed in the margin of this edition. The three large floriated capitals that survive in the manuscript, and one more that is postulated for the now-missing first page, are represented with floriated counterparts in this edition. As they are printed from existing typesetters' fonts, however, all of these capitals are to be understood as representations, not facsimiles, of the actual letters in the manuscript.

Major divisions in the manuscript are signaled by lombardic capitals, often in combination with preceeding blank space or placement at the top of a page, and sometimes with a colophon or statement of closure in the previous section. This edition attempts to reproduce all such markers of division as placed (with the exception of noting, but not printing, blank pages) and does not create divisions that are not sanctioned by the manuscript. The first footnote to each major section makes an attempt to confirm the nature of the division as it appears in the manuscript.

There are no section titles in Caxton or Winchester, but I provide titles at the beginnings of the major sections for the convenience of readers and instructors; in each case, however, the title is extracted from

---

of his exemplar: Caxton supplies the missing text. This kind of error is quite common and often demonstrates how Caxton is not a direct copy of Winchester.

6. For published sources of recommendations for other emendations, many of which are adopted in this edition and which represent the "recovery" of Winchester readings, see n. 2, p. xi. Significant emendations that are otherwise original to this edition are identified and justified in dedicated footnotes.

the appropriate Malorian colophons or introductory sentences and is attended by a footnote to explain its editorial origin.

Paragraphing

A paragraph break accompanied by the symbol ¶ signifies a paragraph break as sanctioned by the Winchester Manuscript; I have attempted to reproduce every marked occurrence, though in some fainter instances the existence of a mark is open to interpretation (e.g. fols. 53ᵛ, line 23; 149ʳ, line 17; 359ᵛ, line 21). Usually the scribes signal the insertion of a paragraph mark with a double virgule (//: these were possibly intended later to have been covered over with alternating red and blue paraph marks, but the job was never started). The style of the symbol chosen for this edition reflects that chosen by the scribes on the rare occasions when they actually write out a paraph symbol (at fols. 182ʳ, line 22 and 191ʳ, margin); I have waived use of the virgule form itself in order to take advantage of readers' preexisting familiarity with some of the functions of the paraph symbol (initial double slashes also have a decidedly "unfinished" look in a typeset space). ℂ is the symbol chosen to represent paragraph marks in those sections of the text that have to be incorporated from Caxton, as that symbol more closely corresponds to the style of Caxton's mark and serves as a reminder that, where comparison with Winchester is possible, Caxton's choices are fewer and sometimes different from those of the manuscript.

In one sense, preceding these symbols with an indented line-break as with modern paragraphing, is a redundancy; in another more important sense doing so also removes the emphatic framing effect of paraph symbols appearing on either side of a particular passage. Nevertheless, not to follow the modern practice will result in a solid block of text, which can prove fatiguing to readers used to postmedieval typesetting conventions, in a text whose late-medieval prosody may already present something of a challenge.

A paragraph that begins without a symbol is editorial; editorial paragraphs are kept to a minimum, but again are introduced to relieve long stretches of unbroken text. I have introduced such breaks using one or more of the following criteria: (1) where the scribe appears to have broken with his usual local practice when dealing with repeating narrative structures, such as colophons or lists; (2) where a sentence begins at the left-hand margin and is marked by a capital letter; (3) where there are forms of punctuation, such as a mid-line dot (*punctus*) or single virgule or one of each, indicating the end of a sentence; (4) where a larger-than-usual space precedes a capital letter within the body of script (i.e., where a space may have been reserved for the insertion of a paraph, but the usual virgules were forgotten); and (5) where the scribes employ an unusually large capital letter in their standard script. In the case of text incorporated from Caxton, editorial paragraphs are introduced at my own discretion, but usually correspond to words favored in Winchester for double virgule tags, and match with one of

Caxton's many single virgules, used by him in the main to separate clauses and sentences.

Rubrication and Other Changes of Script

For additional comment on my rationale for representing the rubrication of the manuscript, see the Preface (p. xii). I have endeavored to represent the location of rubrication exactly, including where it has been rendered erroneously by the scribes (e.g., where they have forgotten to change back to their black pens or have forgotten or decided not to rubricate where they normally would). I have not emended, first as a reminder that the rubrication is not necessarily the product of attention to an authorial plan, and second because there exists no other record of this information with the exception of the Winchester Manuscript itself (the distinction of red ink often fails to transfer to the black-and-white photographs of the Ker facsimile, and the British Library has no color reproduction of the whole manuscript).[7] The only place where representation of rubrication is conjectural is in text imported from Caxton's edition. There I have followed the usual practices of the Winchester scribes: rubrication of proper names and the enlarged scripts of opening lines.

The two scribes use different calligraphic styles when rubricating: Scribe A shifts from his usual anglicana script to a more formal textura script, whereas Scribe B (probably A's apprentice)[8] uses only a secretary script, which is sometimes enlarged in red. Scribe A's practice has been applied throughout; a black-letter font has been chosen as a style that will be familiar to most readers and yet that also offers a reasonable approximation to Scribe A's original. Readers wishing to know which scribe writes which portions of the manuscript are directed to the Ker facsimile.

In the case of some opening lines, where large textura script is used both in black and red, the text in red is represented by extra boldface. Shifts to the larger script are represented with corresponding changes of font and size.

Inscriptions and Epistolary Material

If simply for the aesthetics of having some additional notional landmarks within the great expanse of this text, I have followed and elaborated upon Vinaver's practice of rendering quoted inscriptions in capitals; I have also set them off on a separate line; this has the additional, if spurious, advantage of reflecting the usual medieval

7. My diplomatic rendering of the rubrication extends to the manuscript's atypical use of abbreviation for Merlin's name, remarked upon by Helen Cooper; see n. 4, p. 17.
8. See N. R. Ker, *The Winchester Malory: A Facsimile,* Early English Text Society, Supplementary Series 4 (Oxford: Oxford University Press, 1976), xiv.

practice for public inscriptions, such as those that appear on monuments, stained-glass windows, and other objects (especially those with heraldic displays) which typically allude to their own provenance or present some expression of piety, or both. Small capitals have been adopted so as to retain proper-noun distinctions that may otherwise be ambiguous to new readers. As another way of providing landmarks, I have set off the texts of quoted epistolary matter (i.e., letters addressed by one character to another) in indented paragraphs. I emphasize that I adopt both of these practices without sanction from the manuscript.

Abbreviations

The following are the principal abbreviations used in the footnotes and headnotes.

aMA   *alliterative Morte Arthure*

c.   *circa*

cf.   *compare*

ed.   *edition*

EETS   *Early English Text Society*

ES   *Extra Series*

esp.   *especially*

ff.   *and following*

fol.   *folio*

fols.   *folios*

l.   *line*

ll.   *lines*

ME   *Middle English*

MER   *Middle English Romances,* A Norton Critical Edition, selected and edited by Stephen H. A. Shepherd (New York, 1995)

MS   *manuscript*

MSS   *manuscripts*

n.   *(foot)note*

no.   *number*

nos.   *numbers*

O³   *The Works of Sir Thomas Malory,* 3rd ed., 3 vols., ed. Eugène Vinaver, rev. P. J. C. Field (Oxford, Clarendon Press, 1990)

OS   *Original Series*

p.   *page*

pp.   *pages*

r   *recto (front)*

sMA   *stanzaic Morte Arthur*

SS   *Supplementary Series*

v	*verso (back)*
vol.	*volume*
vols.	*volumes*

Page Numbers in This Edition Corresponding to Vinaver (O³) Section Titles†

† Although most of Vinaver's titles and breaks have little sanction in either the Winchester Manuscript or in Caxton's edition, they are listed here because they have become something of a standard means of locating and referring to portions of Malory's narrative.

LE MORTE DARTHUR[†]

or

The Hoole Book of Kyng Arthur and of His Noble Knyghtes of the Rounde Table

❧

FRO THE MARYAGE OF KYNGE UTHER UNTO KYNG ARTHURE THAT REGNED AFTIR HYM AND DED MANY BATAYLES‡

How Uther Pendragon Gate the Noble Conqueror Kyng Arthur[1]

It[2] befel in the dayes of Uther Pendragon, when he was Kynge of all Englond and so regned, that there was a myghty duke in Cornewaill that helde warre ageynst hym long tyme, and the duke was called the Duke of **Tyntagil.** And so by meanes Kynge **Uther** send for this 5 duk, chargyng hym to brynge his wyf with hym, for she was called a fair lady and a passynge wyse—and her name was called **Igrayne.**

So whan the duke and his wyf were comyn unto the Kynge, by the meanes of grete lordes they were accorded bothe. The Kynge lyked and loved this lady wel, and he made them grete chere oute 10 of mesure[3]—and desyred to have lyen by her. But she was a passyng good woman and wold not assente unto the Kynge.

And thenne she told the duke her husband, and said, "I suppose that we were sente for that I shold be dishonoured; wherfor, husband, I counceille yow that we departe from hens sodenly, that we 15 maye ryde all nyghte unto oure owne castell." And in lyke wyse as she said, so they departed, that neyther the Kynge nor none of his counceill were ware of their departyng. Also soone as Kyng **Uther** knewe of theire departyng soo sodenly, he was wonderly wrothe. Thenne he called to hym his pryvy counceille and told them of the 20 sodeyne departyng of the duke and his wyf.

¶Thenne they avysed the Kynge to send for the duke and his wyf by a grete charge: "And yf he wille not come at your somons, thenne may ye do your best; thenne have ye cause to make myghty werre upon hym." Soo that was done, and the messagers hadde 25 their ansuers—and that was thys, shortly: that neyther he nor his wyf wold not come at hym. Thenne was the Kyng wonderly wroth;

---

‡ The title is taken editorially from the conclusion to this section (p. 112, lines 18–19). It is important to remember that neither Caxton nor the Winchester MS sanction the placement of titles at the beginning of new sections. Malory's principal source for this section is the French prose *Suite de Merlin,* for illustrative selections from which, see p. 709. The first gathering of the Winchester MS is missing, probably comprising some sixteen folio sides. Text corresponding to that which is missing is supplied from Caxton's edition. Caxton's chapter-number headings have been removed. The floriation and size of the first capital and the enlarged rubricated font of the opening line are conjectured on the basis of similar features at other major beginnings in the MS, at pp. 113, 496, and 588. Caxton's opening capital is also floriated and five lines high. *Fro:* from. *Unto:* i.e., until. *Regned:* reigned. *Ded:* did, fought.

1. The subtitle is editorially taken from Caxton's prologue to his edition; for the full text of that prologue, see p. 814. *Gate:* begot.
2. I.e., it.
3. *Out of mesure:* immeasurably.

and thenne the Kyng sente hym⁴ playne word ageyne and badde hym be redy and stuffe hym and garnysshe hym,⁵ for within fourty dayes he wold fetche hym oute of the byggest castell that he hath.

ℭWhanne the duke hadde thys warnynge, anone he wente and furnysshed and garnysshed two stronge castels of his, of the whiche the one hyght **Tyntagil** and the other castel hyght **Terrabyl**. So his wyf Dame **Igrayne** he putte in the castell of **Tyntagil**, and hymself he putte in the castel of **Terrabyl**, the whiche had many yssues and posternes oute.⁶ Thenne in all haste came **Uther** with a grete hoost and leyd a syege aboute the castel of **Terrabil**, and ther he pyght many pavelyons; and there was grete warre made on bothe partyes, and moche peple slayne.

Thenne for pure angre and for grete love of fayr **Igrayne**, the Kyng **Uther** felle seke. So came to the Kynge **Uther** Syre **Ulfius**, a noble knyght, and asked the Kynge why he was seke. "I shall telle the,"⁷ said the Kynge, "I am seke for angre and for love of fayre **Igrayne**, that I may not be hool." "Wel, my lord," said Syre **Ulfius**, "I shal seke **Merlyn**⁸ and he shalle do yow remedy, that youre herte shal be pleasyd."

So **Ulfius** departed; and by adventure he mette **Merlyn**, in a beggars aray. And ther **Merlyn** asked **Ulfius** whome he soughte; and he said he had lytyl ado to telle hym. "Well," saide **Merlyn**, "I knowe whome thou sekest, for thou sekest **Merlyn**; therfore seke no ferther, for I am he. And yf Kynge **Uther** wille wel rewarde me and be sworne unto me to fulfille my desyre, that shall be his honour and profite more than myn, for I shalle cause hym to have all his desyre." "Alle this wyll I undertake," said **Ulfius**, "that ther shalle be nothyng resonable but thow shalt have thy desyre."⁹ "Well," said **Merlyn**, "he shall have his entente and desyre; and therfore," saide **Merlyn**, "ryde on your wey, for I wille not be long behynde."

ℭhenne **Ulfius** was glad and rode on more than a paas¹ tyll that he came to Kynge **Uther Pendragon**, and told hym he had met with **Merlyn**. "Where is he?" said the Kyng. "Sir," said **Ulfius**, "he wille not dwelle long." Therwithal **Ulfius** was ware where **Merlyn** stood at the porche of the pavelions dore, and thenne **Merlyn** was bounde to come to the Kynge. Whan Kyng **Uther** sawe hym, he said he was welcome. "Syr," said **Merlyn**, "I knowe al your hert, every dele. So ye wil be sworn unto me, as ye be a true kynge enoynted, to fulfille my desyre, ye shal have your desyre." Thenne the Kyng was sworne upon the four Evangelistes.²

[2]

---

4. I.e., the Duke of Tintagel.
5. *Stuffe hym and garnysshe hym*: furnish himself with men, provisions, and equipment for defense.
6. *Yssues and posternes oute*: passageways and (hidden) exits.
7. Thee.
8. Merlin's first appearance in Malory is made without the explanation or the extensive foregrounding of what would have been his likely source, if he had chosen to use it, the French Vulgate Prose *Merlin*. Evidently Malory expected his readership already to know of Merlin's legendary status as magician, creator of the Round Table, and prophet and facilitator of Arthur's reign; for such accounts of Arthur's background, as related in the Prose *Merlin*, see p. 705.
9. That, within reason, you shall have what you desire.
1. At great speed.
2. I.e., the king swore (an oath of loyalty) upon a MS containing the four Gospels.

"Syre," said Merlyn, "this is my desyre: the first nyght that ye shal lye by Igrayne ye shal gete a child on her; and whan that is borne, that it shall be delyverd to me for to nourisshe there as I wille have it—for it shal be your worship and the childis availle, as mykel as the child is worth."[3] "I wylle wel," said the Kynge, "as thow wilt have it."

"Now make you redy,"said Merlyn. "This nyght ye shalle lye with Igrayne in the castel of Tyntigayll; and ye shalle be lyke the duke her husband, Ulfyus shal be lyke Syre Brastias, a knyghte of the dukes, and I will be lyke a knyghte that hyghte Syr Jordanus, a knyghte of the dukes. But wayte ye make not many questions with her nor her men, but saye ye are diseased; and soo hye yow to bedde and ryse not on the morne tyll I come to yow, for the castel of Tyntygaill is but ten myle hens." Soo this was done as they devysed.

But the Duke of Tyntigail aspyed hou the Kyng rode fro the syege of Tarabil, and therfor that nyghte he yssued oute of the castel at a posterne for to have distressid the Kynges hooste, and so thorowe his owne yssue the duke hymself was slayne or ever the Kynge cam at the castel of Tyntigall. So after the deth of the duke, Kyng Uther lay with Igrayne more than thre houres after his deth, and begat on her that nyght Arthur; and, or day cam, Merlyn cam to the Kyng and bad hym make hym redy. And so he kist the lady Igrayne and departed in all hast. But whan the lady herd telle of the duke her husband, and by all record he was dede or ever Kynge Uther[4] came to her, thenne she mervelled who that myghte be that laye with her in lykenes of her lord. So she mourned pryvely and held hir pees.

Thenne alle the barons by one assent prayd the Kynge of accord betwixe the Lady Igrayne and hym. The Kynge gaf hem leve, for fayne wold he have ben accorded with her; soo the Kyng put alle the trust in Ulfyus to entrete bitwene them. So by the entreté, at the last the Kyng and she met togyder.

"Now wille we doo wel," said Ulfyus. "Our Kyng is a lusty knyghte and wyveles,[5] and my Lady Igrayne is a passynge fair lady; it were grete joye unto us all and[6] hit myghte please the Kynge to make her his quene." Unto that they all well accorded and meved it to the Kynge. And anone, lyke a lusty knyghte, he assentid therto with good wille, and so in alle haste they were maryed in a mornynge with grete myrthe and joye.

And Kynge Lott of Lowthean and of Orkenay thenne wedded Margawse that was Gawepns[7] moder, and Kynge Nentres of the land of Garlot wedded Elapne. Al this was done at the request of Kynge Uther. And the thyrd syster, Morgan le Fey, was put to scole in a

---

3. It shall be delivered to me so that I may raise it according to my plans—for it shall be to your honor and the child's advantage, as noble as the child is.
4. I.e., King Uther disguised as the Duke.
5. Wife-less, unmarried.
6. I.e., if.
7. Margeuse is sister to Igrayne. Her future son, Gawayne, is to be one of the knights of the Round Table, renowned for his courtesy. He also will tragically become one of the principal agents in the dissolution of Arthur's achievements: see p. 657 ff.

nonnery, and ther she lerned so moche that she was a grete clerke
of nygromancye—and after she was wedded to Kynge Uryens of the
lond of Gore that was Syre Ewayns le Blaunche Maynys fader.

Thenne Quene Igrayne waxid dayly gretter and gretter. So it
befel after within half a yere, as Kyng Uther lay by his quene,
he asked hir, by the feith she ought to hym whos was the child
within her body. Thenne was she sore abasshed to yeve ansuer.
"Desmaye you not," said the Kyng, "but telle me the trouthe, and
I shall love you the better, by the feythe of my body. "Syre," saide
she, "I shalle telle you the trouthe. The same nyghte that my lord
was dede—the houre of his deth, as his knyghtes record—ther
came into my castel of Tyntigaill a man lyke my lord in speche and
in countenaunce, and two knyghtes with hym in lykenes of his two
knyghtes Barcias and Jordans. And soo I went unto bed with hym
as I ought to do with my lord; and the same nyght, as I shal ansuer
unto God, this child was begoten upon me." "That is trouthe,"
saide the Kynge, "as ye say, for it was I myself that cam in the
lykenesse—and therfor desmay you not, for I am fader to the
child." And ther he told her alle the cause, how it was by Merlyns
counceil.

Thenne the Quene made grete joye whan she knewe who was
the fader of her child. Sone come Merlyn unto the Kyng and said,
"Syr, ye must purvey yow[8] for the nourisshyng of your child." "As
thou wolt," said the Kyng, "be[9] it." "Wel," said Merlyn, "I knowe a
lord of yours in this land that is a passyng true man and a feithful,
and he shal have the nourysshyng of your child; and his name is
Sir Ector, and he is a lord of fair lyvelode in many partyes in
Englond and Walys. And this lord Sir Ector, lete hym be sent for,
for to come and speke with you, and desyre hym yourself,[1] as he
loveth you, that he will put his owne child to nourisshynge to
another woman, and that his wyf nourisshe yours. And whan the
child is borne, lete it be delyverd to me at yonder pryvy posterne,
uncrystned." So like as Merlyn devysed it was done.

And whan Syre Ector was come he made fyaunce to the Kyng for
to nourisshe the child lyke as the Kynge desyred; and there the
Kyng graunted Syr Ector grete rewardys. Thenne when the lady was
delyverd[2] the Kynge commaunded two knyghtes and two ladyes to
take the child, bound in a cloth of gold, "and that ye delyver hym
to what poure man ye mete at the posterne yate of the castel." So
the child was delyverd unto Merlyn, and so he bare it forth unto
Syre Ector and made an holy man to crysten hym, and named hym
Arthur. And so Sir Ectors wyf nourysshed hym with her owne pappe.

Thenne, within two yeres, Kyng Uther felle seke of a grete
maladye. And in the meanewhyle hys enemyes usurpped upon hym
and dyd a grete bataylle upon his men and slewe many of his peple.

8. *Purvey yow*: arrange.
9. I.e., so be.
1. *Desyre hym yourself*: express your desire.
2. Had given birth.

"Sir," said Merlyn, "ye may not lye so as ye doo, for ye must to[3] the feld, though ye ryde on an hors-lyttar; for ye shall never have the better of your enemyes but yf your persone be there, and thenne shall ye have the vyctory."

So it was done as Merlyn had devysed, and they caryed the Kynge forth in an hors-lyttar with a grete hooste towarde his enemyes; and at Saynt Albons ther mette with[4] the Kynge a grete hoost of the North. And that day Syre Ulfyus and Sir Bracias dyd grete dedes of armes, and Kyng Uthers men overcome the Northeryn batayle and slewe many peple and putt the remenaunt to flight.

And thenne the Kyng retorned unto London and made grete joye of his vyctory. And thenne he fyll passynge sore seke, so that thre dayes and thre nyghtes he was specheles; wherfor alle the barons made grete sorow and asked Merlyn what counceill were best. "There nys none other remedye," said Merlyn, "but God wil have His wille. But loke ye al barons be bifore Kynge Uther tomorne, and God and I shalle make hym to speke."

So on the morne alle the barons with Merlyn came tofore the Kyng. Thenne Merlyn said aloud unto Kyng Uther, "Syre, shall your sone Arthur be kyng, after your dayes, of this realme with all the appertenaunce?" Thenne Uther Pendragon torned hym,[5] and said in herynge of them alle, "I gyve hym Gods blissyng and myne, and byd hym pray for my soule, and righteuously and worshipfully that he clayme the croune, upon forfeture of my blessyng"[6]—and therwith he yelde up the ghost. And thenne was he enterid as longed to[7] a kyng, wherfor the Quene, fayre Igrayne, made grete sorowe, and alle the barons.

Thenne stood the reame in grete jeopardy long whyle, for every lord that was myghty of men maade hym stronge, and many wende to have ben kyng.[8] Thenne Merlyn wente to the Archebisshop of Caunterbury[9] and counceilled hym for to sende for all the lordes of the reame and alle the gentilmen of armes,[1] that they shold to London come by Cristmas, upon payne of cursynge,[2] and for this cause: that Jesu, that was borne on that nyghte, that He wold of His grete mercy shewe some myracle, as He was come to be Kynge of Mankynde, for to shewe somme myracle who shold be rightwys kynge of this reame.

So the Archebisshop, by the advys of Merlyn, send for alle the lordes and gentilmen of armes that they shold come by Crystmasse

3. I.e., go to.
4. I.e., against.
5. Turned himself.
6. *Upon forfeture of my blessyng*: i.e., upon my death.
7. Befitted.
8. *Thenne stood the reame . . . wende to have ben kyng*: The observation is not matched in Malory's source, but strikes a familiar ring as a sanguine reflection of the motivations behind the dynastic conflicts—the so-called Wars of the Roses—of Malory's own time. For a summary of the major events of the wars, see p. xix. Cf. Malory's direct comments on his own times at p. 680, lines 25–40.
9. The supreme head of the Church in England and the most appropriate choice to preside over the coronation of the king.
1. Men with family coats of arms, armigerous gentry.
2. I.e., excommunication.

even unto London; and many of hem made hem clene of her lyf,[3]
that her prayer myghte be the more acceptable unto God. Soo in
the grettest chirch of London (whether it were Powlis[4] or not, the
Frensshe booke maketh no mencyon) alle the estates[5] were longe
or day in the chirche for to praye. And whan matyns and the first   5
Masse was done, there was sene in the chircheyard ayenst the hyhe
aulter a grete stone four square, lyke unto a marbel stone; and in
myddes therof was lyke an anvylde of stele a foot on hyghe, and
theryn stack a fayre swerd naked by the poynt[6]—and letters there
were wryten in gold about the swerd that saiden thus: 10

> WHOSO PULLETH OUTE THIS SWERD OF THIS STONE AND
> ANVYLD IS RIGHTWYS KYNGE BORNE OF ALL ENGLOND.

Thenne the peple merveilled and told it to the Archebisshop. "I   15
commande, said th'Archebisshop, "that ye kepe yow within your
chirche and pray unto God still, that[7] no man touche the swerd
tyll the Hyhe Masse be all done." So whan all Masses were done,
all the lordes wente to beholde the stone and the swerd. And whan
they sawe the scripture, som assayed, suche as wold have ben   20
Kyng, but none myght stere the swerd nor meve hit. "He is not
here," said the Archebisshop, "that shall encheve the swerd—but
doubte not God will make hym knowen. But this is my counceill,"
said the Archebisshop, "that we lete purvey[8] ten knyghtes, men of
good fame, and they to kepe this swerd." So it was ordeyned, and   25
thenne ther was made a crye that every man shold assay that wold
for to wynne the swerd.

And upon Newe Yeers Day the barons lete maake a justes and
a tournement, that alle knyghtes that wold juste or tourneye there
myght playe. And all this was ordeyned for to kepe the lordes togy-   30
ders, and the comyns, for the Archebisshop trusted that God wold
make hym knowe that[9] shold wynne the swerd. So upon New Yeres
Day, whan the servyce was done, the barons rode unto the feld,
some to juste and som to torney. And so it happed that Syre Ector,
that had grete lyvelode aboute London, rode unto the justes, and   35
with hym rode Syr Kaynus,[1] his sone, and yong Arthur that was hys
nourisshed broder (and Syr Kay was made knyght at Al Halowmas[2]
afore).

So as they rode to the justes-ward,[3] Sir Kay had lost his suerd,
for he had lefte it at his faders lodgyng, and so he prayd yong Arthur   40

3. *Made hem clene of her lyf*: i.e., were absolved of their sins (by a priest).
4. I.e., St. Paul's Cathedral (the principal church of London).
5. *The Frensshe booke*: Malory, as do other writers of the period, often alludes to a source
with the intention of reminding his readership of his concern for rendering an authoritative
version of the story. In this case the allusion is accurate, but sometimes Malory's source
is not as he describes it, and the information he provides is likely to be of his own invention.
Alle the estates: all (higher) ranks of society.
6. I.e., unsheathed.
7. I.e., such that.
8. *Lete purvey*: assign.
9. I.e., who.
1. I.e., Sir Kay.
2. All Saints' Day, November 1.
3. Toward the jousts.

for to ryde for his swerd. "I wyll wel," said Arthur, and rode fast after the swerd. And whan he cam home, the lady and al were out to see the joustyng. Thenne was Arthur wroth, and saide to hymself, "I will ryde to the chircheyard and take the swerd with me that stycketh in the stone, for my broder Sir Kay shal not be without a swerd this day." So whan he cam to the chircheyard Sir Arthur alight and tayed his hors to the style, and so he wente to the tent and found no knyghtes there, for they were atte justyng. And so he handled the swerd by the handels, and lightly and fiersly pulled it out of the stone, and took his hors and rode his way untyll he came to his broder Sir Kay, and delyverd hym the swerd.

And as sone as Sir Kay saw the swerd, he wist wel it was the swerd of the stone; and so he rode to his fader Syr Ector and said, "Sire, loo! here is the swerd of the stone—wherfor I must be kyng of thys land!" When Syre Ector beheld the swerd, he retorned ageyne and cam to the chirche, and there they alighte, al thre, and wente into the chirche; and anon he made Sir Kay to swere upon a book[4] how he came to that swerd. "Syr," said Sir Kay, "by my broder Arthur, for he brought it to me."

"How gate ye this swerd?" said Sir Ector to Arthur. "Sir, I will telle you. When I cam home for my broders swerd, I fond nobody at home to delyver me his swerd, and so I thought my broder Syr Kay shold not be swerdles; and so I cam hyder egerly and pulled it out of the stone withoute ony payn." "Found ye ony knyghtes about this swerd?" seid Sir Ector. "Nay," said Arthur.

"Now," said Sir Ector to Arthur, "I understande ye must be kynge of this land." "Wherfore I?" sayd Arthur, "and for what cause?" "Sire," saide Ector, "for God wille have hit soo, for ther shold never man have drawen oute this swerde but he that shal be rightwys kyng of this land. Now lete me see whether ye can putte the swerd ther as it was and pulle hit oute ageyne." "That is no maystry,"[5] said Arthur; and soo he put it in the stone. Therwithalle Sir Ector assayed to pulle oute the swerd, and faylled.

"Now assay," said Syre Ector unto Syre Kay; and anon he pulled at the swerd with alle his myghte, but it wold not be. "Now shal ye assay," said Syre Ector to Arthur. "I wyll wel," said Arthur— and pulled it out easily. And therwithalle Syre Ector knelyd doune to the erthe, and Syre Kay. "Allas!" said Arthur, "myne own dere fader and broder, why knele ye to me?" "Nay, nay, my lord Arthur, it is not so; I was never your fader nor of your blood, but I wote wel ye are of an hygher blood than I wende ye were." And thenne Syre Ector told hym all how he was bitaken hym for to nourisshe hym, and by whoos commandement, and by Merlyns delyveraunce.

Thenne Arthur made grete doole when he understood that Syre Ector was not his fader. "Sir," said Ector unto Arthur, "woll ye be my good and gracious lord[6] when ye are Kyng?" "Els were I to blame,"

[5]
[6]
[10]
[15]
[20]
[25]
[30]
[35]
[40]
[45]

4. I.e., a religious book (such as a copy of the Gospels, a psalter, or the Bible).
5. Requires no skill.
6. I.e., will you engage me in a mutually binding compact as my (feudal) lord? (The essence of feudalism—a pervasive institution in western Europe from about the 9th to the 15th centuries—concerns the management of large estates, provinces, even nations. According to the system, chief land-owning lords ("liege" lords, including the king) granted a portion

said Arthur, "for ye are the man in the world that I am most beholdyng to—and my good lady and moder your wyf, that, as wel as
her owne, hath fostred me and kepte. And yf ever hit be Goddes
will that I be Kynge, as ye say, ye shall desyre of me what I may
doo, and I shalle not faille yow—God forbede I shold faille yow."

"Sir," said Sire Ector, "I will aske no more of yow but that ye wille
make my sone, your foster broder Syre Kay, senceall of alle your
landes." "That shalle be done," said Arthur, "and more, by the feith
of my body: that never man shalle have that office but he, whyle
he and I lyve." Therewithall they wente unto the Archebisshop and
told hym how the swerd was encheved and by whome. And on
Twelfth Day[7] alle the barons cam thyder, and to assay to take the
swerd, who that wold assay.

But there, afore hem alle, ther myghte none take it out but
Arthur—wherfor ther were many lordes wroth, and saide it was
grete shame unto them all and the reame to be over-governyd with
a boye of no hyghe blood borne.[8] And so they fell oute at that tyme,
that it was put of tyll Candelmas,[9] and thenne all the barons shold
mete there ageyne; but alwey the ten knyghtes were ordeyned to
watche the swerd day and nyght, and so they sette a pavelione over
the stone and the swerd, and fyve always watched.

Soo at Candelmasse many moo grete lordes came thyder for to
have wonne the swerde, but there myghte none prevaille; and right
as Arthur dyd at Cristmasse, he dyd at Candelmasse, and pulled
oute the swerde easely—wherof the barons were sore agreved and
put it of in delay till the hyghe feste of Eester. And as Arthur sped
afore, so dyd he at Eester. Yet there were some of the grete lordes
had indignacion that Arthur shold be kynge, and put it of in a delay
tyll the feest of Pentecoste.[1]

of their land (known variously as a "feoff," "fief," "feud," or land held "in fee") to a tenant
("vassal") in return for "fealty"—sworn loyal service, including the payment of various
taxes and rents and the provision of military service on demand. The swearing of an oath
of fealty was part of a most important feudal ritual. Performed annually, the ritual involved
first the act of homage, in which the vassal would, kneeling, place his hands between those
of the lord; he would then swear the oath of fealty and agree to become the lord's "man."
As well as rights of enfeoffment, the vassal also obtained in this relationship the right to
request assistance from his lord in protecting his own interests and in enforcing laws (as
does Gawayne, in his conflict with Launcelot near the end of Malory's work, p. 659, lines
17–21). By Malory's day, the loyalties required by such arrangements had been complicated by the introduction of contracts secured by annuities rather than loyalty-based grants
of estates; this brought about the destabilizing presence of what were in practice private
standing armies that gave rebellious barons enough power against the throne to take the
law into their own hands—whence the so-called Wars of the Roses. For additional consideration of these times, see the chronology on p. xix, as well as p. 759 and Malory's own
comments at pp. 595, 624–25, and 680.)

7. January 6, the twelfth day after Christmas, and traditionally the last day of Christmas
celebrations. It is also known as the festival of Epiphany, commemorating the manifestation of Christ's divine nature, as represented by the Magi, to the Gentiles.

8. By a boy of low birth.

9. February 2, the feast of the purification of the Blessed Virgin and the presentation of
Christ in the Temple (see Luke 2.22–39; called Candelmas because a procession with
lighted candles is held during the Mass on that day).

1. Pentecost is usually the day of the grandest feast at Arthur's court. Also known as Whitsunday, it is the fiftieth day after Easter, the day on which Christ's Apostles "were all filled
with the Holy Ghost" (Acts 2:4) and on which the numbers of those following in Christ's
teachings was seen to increase: "all that believed were together, and had all things common; and sold their possesions and goods, and parted them to all men, as every man had
need" (Acts 2:44–45). Thus the day symbolically commemorates the founding of the
Christian Church.

Thenne the Archebisshop of Caunterbury, by 𝔐𝔢𝔯𝔩𝔶𝔫𝔰 provyd-ence, lete purveye thenne of the best knyghtes that they myghte gete, and suche knyghtes as 𝔘𝔱𝔥𝔢𝔯 𝔓𝔢𝔫𝔡𝔯𝔞𝔤𝔬𝔫 loved best and moost trusted in his dayes. And suche knyghtes were put aboute 𝔄𝔯𝔱𝔥𝔲𝔯 as Syr 𝔅𝔞𝔴𝔡𝔢𝔴𝔶𝔫 of 𝔅𝔯𝔢𝔱𝔞𝔶𝔫, Syre 𝔎𝔞𝔶𝔫𝔢𝔰, Syre 𝔘𝔩𝔣𝔶𝔲𝔰, Syre 𝔅𝔞𝔯𝔰𝔦𝔞𝔰— [5] all these, with many other, were alweyes about 𝔄𝔯𝔱𝔥𝔲𝔯, day and nyghte, till the feste of 𝔓𝔢𝔫𝔱𝔢𝔠𝔬𝔰𝔱.

𝔄nd at the feste of 𝔓𝔢𝔫𝔱𝔢𝔠𝔬𝔰𝔱 alle maner of men assayed to pulle [7] at the swerde that wold assay; but none myghte prevaille but 𝔄𝔯𝔱𝔥𝔲𝔯, and pulled it oute afore all the lordes and comyns that were [10] there—wherfor alle the comyns cryed at ones, "We wille have 𝔄𝔯𝔱𝔥𝔲𝔯 unto our kyng. We wille put hym no more in delay, for we all see that it is Goddes wille that he shalle be our kynge—and who that holdeth ageynst it, we wille slee hym." And therwithall they knelyd at ones, both ryche and poure, and cryed[2] 𝔄𝔯𝔱𝔥𝔲𝔯 mercy [15] bycause they had delayed hym so longe. And 𝔄𝔯𝔱𝔥𝔲𝔯 foryaf hem, and took the swerd bitwene both his handes and offred it upon the aulter where the Archebisshop was; and so was he made knyghte of the best man that was there.

And so anon was the coronacyon made. And ther was he sworne [20] unto his lordes and the comyns for to be a true kyng, to stand with true justyce fro thensforth the dayes of this lyf. Also thenne he made alle lordes that helde of the croune[3] to come in and to do servyce as they oughte to doo. And many complayntes were made unto Sir 𝔄𝔯𝔱𝔥𝔲𝔯 of grete wronges that were done syn the dethe of [25] Kyng 𝔘𝔱𝔥𝔢𝔯, of many londes that were bereved lordes, knyghtes, ladyes, and gentilmen; wherfor Kynge 𝔄𝔯𝔱𝔥𝔲𝔯 maade the londes to be yeven ageyne unto them that oughte hem.

❡Whanne this was done, that the Kyng had stablisshed alle the countryes aboute London, thenne he lete make Syr 𝔎𝔞𝔶 Sencial of [30] Englond, and Sir 𝔅𝔞𝔲𝔡𝔢𝔴𝔶𝔫 𝔬𝔣 𝔅𝔯𝔢𝔱𝔞𝔶𝔫𝔢 was made Constable, and Sir 𝔘𝔩𝔣𝔶𝔲𝔰 was made Chamberlayn, and sire 𝔅𝔯𝔞𝔰𝔱𝔦𝔞𝔰 was maade Wardeyn to wayte upon the Northe, fro Trent forwardes, for it was that tyme the most party[4] the Kynges enemyes; but within fewe yeres after, 𝔄𝔯𝔱𝔥𝔲𝔯 wan alle the North, Scotland, and alle that were [35] under their obeissaunce; also Walys, a parte of it, helde ayenst 𝔄𝔯𝔱𝔥𝔲𝔯, but he overcam hem al—as he dyd the remenaunt, thurgh the noble prowesse of hymself and his knyghtes of the Round Table.[5]

𝔗henne the Kyng remeved into Walys and lete crye a grete feste, [8] [40] that it shold be holdyn at 𝔓𝔢𝔫𝔱𝔢𝔠𝔬𝔰𝔱 after the incoronacion of hym at the cyté of 𝔆𝔞𝔯𝔩𝔶𝔬𝔫. Unto the fest come Kyng 𝔏𝔬𝔱𝔱 of Low-thean and of Orkeney, with fyve hondred knyghtes with hym; also

---

2. I.e., asked of.
3. *Helde of the croune:* held their lands and titles as given to them by the king.
4. The river Trent is here used to mark the border with the north. *The most party:* for the most part.
5. Malory is here referring to Arthur's future conquests. As with his first mention of Merlin (see n. 8, p. 4), Malory evidently assumes his readers' prior familiarity with the legendary status of the Round Table. For an account of its origin through the agency of Merlin, see p. 707.

ther come to the feste Kynge **Uryens** of Gore, with four hondred
knyghtes with hym.

℣. Also ther come to that feeste Kyng **Nayntres** of Garloth, with
seven hundred knyghtes with hym; also ther came to the feest the
Kynge of Scotland, with sixe honderd knyghtes with hym (and he
was but a yong man); also ther came to the feste a kyng that was
called the Kyng with the Honderd Knyghtes, but he and his men
were passyng wel bisene at al poyntes;[6] also ther cam Kyng **Carados**
with fyve honderd knyghtes. And Kyng **Arthur** was glad of their
comynge, for he wende that al the kynges and knyghtes had come
for grete love and to have done hym worship at his feste; wherfor
the Kyng made grete joye and sente the kynges and knyghtes grete
presentes.

But the kynges wold none receyve, but rebuked the messagers
shamefully and said they had no joye to receyve no yeftes of a
berdles[7] boye that was come of lowe blood, and sente hym word
they wold[8] none of his yeftes, but that they were come to gyve hym
yeftes—"with hard swerdys betwixt the neck and the sholders!"
And therfore they came thyder—so they told to the messagers
playnly—for it was grete shame to all them to see suche a boye to
have a rule of soo noble a reaume as this land was.

With this ansuer the messagers departed and told to Kyng **Arthur**
this ansuer; wherfor, by the advys of his barons, he took hym to a
strong towre[9] with fyve hondred good men with hym. And all the
kynges aforesaid in a maner leyd a syege tofore hym. But Kyng
Arthur was well vytailled, and within fyftene dayes ther came **Merlyn**
amonge hem into the cyté of Carlyon. Thenne all the kynges were
passyng gladde of **Merlyn**, and asked hym, "For what cause is that
boye **Arthur** made your kynge?" "Syres," said **Merlyn**, "I shalle telle
yow the cause: for he is Kynge **Uther Pendragons** sone, borne in
wedlok, goten on **Igrayne**, the Dukes wyf of **Tyntigail**." "Thenne is
he a bastard," they said al.

"Nay!" said **Merlyn**, "After the deth of the duke, more than thre
houres, was **Arthur** begoten; and thirtene dayes after, Kyng **Uther**
wedded **Igrayne**;[1] and therfor I preve hym he is no bastard. And,
who[2] saith nay, he shal be Kyng and overcome alle his enemyes;
and, or he deye,[3] he shalle be long Kynge of all Englond and have
under his obeyssaunce Walys, Yrland, and Scotland, and moo rea-
mes than I will now reherce."

Some of the Kynges had merveyl of **Merlyns** wordes and demed
well that it shold be as he said; and som of hem lough hym to

---

6. *Passyng wel bisene at al poyntes:* surpassingly good-looking in every respect.
7. Beardless; i.e., young.
8. I.e., would have.
9. I.e., fortified tower.
1. The conditions of Arthur's conception and birth satisfy the technicalities of medieval
   canon (religious) law: he is Uther's legitimate heir because he was conceived after the
   death of the Duke of Tintagel and born after Uther's marriage to Igraine, the Duke's
   widow.
2. I.e., regardless of who.
3. Before he dies.

scorne,[4] as Kyng Lot—and mo other called hym a wytche.[5] But
thenne were they accorded with Merlyn that Kynge Arthur shold
come oute and speke with the kynges; and to come sauf and to goo
sauf, suche suraunce ther was made. So Merlyn went unto Kynge
Arthur and told hym how he had done and badde hym fere not,
"but come oute boldly and speke with hem, and spare hem not,
but ansuere them as their kynge and chyvetayn, for ye shal overcome hem all, whether they wille or nylle."[6]

Thenne Kynge Arthur came oute of his tour and had under his
gowne a jesseraunte of double maylle, and ther wente with
hym the Archebisshop of Caunterbury, and Syr Baudewyn of Bretayne, and Syr Kay, and Syre Brastias: these were the men of moost
worship that were with hym. And whan they were mette there was
no mekenes but stoute wordes on bothe sydes; but alweyes Kynge
Arthur ansuerd them and said he wold make them to bowe[7] and he
lyved—wherfore they departed with wrath (and Kynge Arthur badde
kepe hem wel, and they bad the Kynge kepe hym wel).[8] Soo the
Kynge retornyd hym to the toure ageyne, and armed hym and alle
his knyghtes.

"What will ye do?" said Merlyn to the kynges. "Ye were better for
to stynte, for ye shalle not here prevaille, though ye were ten so
many." "Be we wel avysed to be aferd of a dreme-reder?"[9] said Kyng
Lot. With that Merlyn vanysshed aweye and came to Kynge Arthur
and bad hym set on hem fiersly; and in the menewhyle there were
thre honderd good men of the best that were with the kynges, that
wente streyghte unto Kynge Arthur—and that comforted hym gretely. "Syr," said Merlyn to Arthur, "fyghte not with the swerde that
ye had by myracle til that ye see ye go unto the wers; thenne drawe
it out and do your best."

So forthwithalle Kynge Arthur sette upon hem, in their lodgyng;
and Syre Bawdewyn, Syre Kay, and Syr Brastias slewe on the right
hand and on the lyfte hand, that[1] it was merveylle—and alweyes
Kynge Arthur on horsback leyd on with a swerd and dyd merveillous
dedes of armes, that many of the kynges had grete joye of his dedes[2]
and hardynesse. Thenne Kynge Lot brake out on the bak syde, and
the Kyng with the Honderd Knyghtes, and Kyng Carados, and sette
on Arthur fiersly behynde hym. With that Syre Arthur torned with
his knyghtes and smote behynd and before—and ever Sir Arthur
was in the formest prees[3] tyl his hors was slayne undernethe hym;
and therwith Kynge Lot smote doune Kyng Arthur.

4. *Lough hym to scorne:* derided him.
5. In the Middle Ages the term *witch* could apply to a man or a woman.
6. I.e., will not follow you.
7. I.e., bow in submission.
8. The observation that the opponents parted with literal farewells may indeed be ironic, but
   it also draws attention to their status as men of a certain dignity and honor.
9. I.e., Merlin.
1. I.e., such that.
2. I.e., deeds of arms.
3. *Formest prees:* forefront of the press of battle.

With that his[4] four knyghtes receyved hym and set hym on horsback. Thenne he drewe his swerd Excalibur;[5] but it was so bryght
in his enemyes eyen that it gaf light lyke thirty torchys, and therwith he put hem on bak,[6] and slewe moche peple. And thenne the
comyns of Carlyon aroos with clubbis and stavys and slewe many   5
knyghtes; but alle the kynges helde them togyders with her knyghtes that were lefte on lyve,[7] and so fled and departed. And Merlyn
come unto Arthur and counceilled hym to folowe hem no further.

So after the feste and journeye, Kynge Arthur drewe hym unto   [10]
London; and soo by the counceil of Merlyn the Kyng lete calle   10
his barons to counceil, for Merlyn had told the Kynge that the sixe
kynges that made warre upon hym wold in al haste be awroke on
hym and on his landys—wherfor the Kyng asked counceil at[8] hem
al. They coude no counceil gyve, but said they were bygge[9] ynough.
"Ye saye well," said Arthur. "I thanke you for your good courage,   15
but wil ye al that loveth me speke with Merlyn? Ye knowe wel that
he hath done moche for me, and he knoweth many thynges; and
whan he is afore you I wold that ye prayd hym hertely of his best
avyse." Alle the barons sayd they wold pray hym and desyre hym;
soo Merlyn was sente for and fair desyred of al the barons to gyve   20
them best counceil.

"I shall say you," said Merlyn, "I warne yow al, your enemyes are
passyng strong for yow, and they are good men of armes as ben on
lyve—and by thys tyme they have goten to them four kynges mo
and a myghty duke—and onlesse that our Kyng have more chy-   25
valry[1] with hym than he may make within the boundys of his own
reame, and he fyghte with hem in batail, he shal be overcome and
slayn." "What were best to doo in this cause?" said al the barons.

"I shal telle you," said Merlyn, "myne advys: ther ar two bretheren
beyond the see, and they be kynges bothe and merveillous good   30
men of her handes;[2] and that one hyghte Kynge Ban of Benwic, and
that other hyght Kyng Bors of Gaule (that is, Fraunce). And on
these two kynges warrith a myghty man of men, the Kynge Claudas,
and stryveth with hem for a castel; and grete werre is betwixt them.
But this Claudas is so myghty of goodes[3] wherof he geteth good   35
knyghtes, that he putteth these two kynges moost parte to the
werse. Wherfor this is my councell: that our Kyng and soveraynlord
sende unto the kynges Ban and Bors by two trusty knyghtes with
letters wel devysed, that, and they wil come and see][4] Kynge Arthur   fol.9r
and his courte and to helpe hym in hys warrys, that he wolde be   40
sworne unto them to helpe hem in theire warrys agaynst Kynge
Claudas. Now, what sey ye unto thys counceyle?" seyde Merlyon.

---

4. I.e., Arthur's.
5. The name of the famous sword is here (perhaps overenthusiastically) misapplied; Arthur
   does not actually receive Excalibur until later (see p. 43).
6. Back, in retreat.
7. Alive.
8. I.e., of.
9. I.e., strong.
1. I.e., knights.
2. *Good men of her handes:* valorous men in battle.
3. Powerful through wealth.
4. The surviving text of the Wichester MS begins after this point.

"Thys ys well councelde," seyde the Kynge. And in all haste two
barownes ryght so were ordayned to go on thys message unto thes
two kyngis, and lettirs were made in the moste plesauntist wyse,
accordynge unto Kynge Arthurs desyre. And Ulphuns and Brascias
were made the messyngers, and so rode forth well horsed and well   5
i-armed (and as the gyse was that tyme), and so passed the see and
rode towarde the cité of Benwyk. And there besydes were eyght
knyghtes that aspyed hem, and at a strayte passage they mette with
Ulphuns and Brascias and wolde a takyn them presoners. So they
preyde them that they myght passe, for they were messyngers unto   10
Kyng Ban and Bors i-sente frome Kynge Arthure.

"Therefore," seyde the knyghtes, "ye shall dey othir be presoners,
for we be knyghtes of Kynge Claudas." And therewith two of them
dressed their sperys unto Ulphuns and Brascias—and they dressed
their speris—and ran togydir with grete random. And Claudas his[5]   15
knyghtes brake theire spearis; and Ulphuns and Brascias bare the
two knyghtes oute of theire sadils to the erth, and so leffte them
lyynge and rode their wayes. And the other six knyghtes rode before
to a passage to mete with them ayen; and so Ulphuns and Brascias
othir two[6] smote downe, and so paste on hir wayes. [And at the   20
thirde passage there mette two for two, and bothe were leyde unto
the erthe.][7] And at the fourthe passage there mette two for two,
and bothe were leyde unto the erthe—so there was none of the
eyght knyghtes but he was hurte sore othir brused.

And whan they com to Benwyke, hit fortuned both the kynges be   25
there, Ban and Bors. Than was hit tolde[8] the two kyngis how there
were com two messyngers. And anone there was sente unto them
two knyghtes of worship, that one hyght Lyonses, lorde of the contrey of Bayarne, and Sir Pharyaunce, a worshipfull knyght; and anone
asked them frome whens they com; and they seyde, "frome Kyng   30
Arthure, Kynge of Ingelonde." And so they toke them in theire armys
and made grete joy eche of othir.[9]

But anone, as they wyste they were messyngers of Arthurs, there
was made no taryynge, but forthwith they spake with the kyngis.
And they welcommed them in the moste faythfullyst wyse and   35
seyde they were moste welcom unto them before all the kynges
men lyvynge. And therewith they kyssed the lettirs[1] and delyvird
them; and whan Kynge Ban and Bors undirstoode them and the
lettirs, than were they more welcom than they were tofore. And,
after the haste[2] of the lettirs, they gaff hem thys answere: that they   40
wolde fulfille the desire of Kyng Arthurs wrytynge, and bade Sir
Ulphuns and Sir Brascias tarry there as longe as they wolde, for they

fol.9v

5. *Claudas his*: i.e, Claudas's.
6. I.e., two others.
7. In order to render the correct total of eight knights, this sentence is supplied editorially,
   on the model of the next sentence.
8. I.e., told to.
9. I.e., of each other.
1. The kissing of the letters signifies the knights' reverence for their contents and their
   ultimate author, King Arthur.
2. I.e., in response to the urgency.

shulde have such chere as myght be made for them in thys marchis.

Than **Ulphuns and Brascias** tolde the kynges of theire adventure at the passagis for the eyght knyghtes. "A-ha!" seyde **Ban and Bors**, "they were oure good frendis. I wolde I had wyste of them, and they sholde nat so a ascaped."[3] So thes two knyghtes had good chere and grete gyfftis, as much as they myght bere away, and had theire answere, by mowth and by wrytynge, that the two kynges wolde com unto **Arthure** in all the haste that they myght. So thes two knyghtes rode on afore and passed the see and com to their lorde, and tolde hym how they had spedde; wherefore Kyng **Arthure** was passyng glad, and seyde, "How suppose you—at what tyme woll thes two kynges be here?"

¶"Sir," they seyde, "before All Halowmasse."[4]

¶Than the Kynge lette purvey for a grete feste, and also he lette cry both turnementis and justis thorowoute all his realme, and the day appoynted and sette at All Halowmasse. And so the tyme drove on, and all thynges redy i-purveyed. Thes two noble kynges were entirde[5] the londe, and comyn ovir the see with three hondred knyghtes full well arayed both for the pees and also for the werre. And so royally they were resceyved and brought towarde the cité of London.

¶And so **Arthure** mette them ten myle oute of London, and there was grete joy made as couthe be thought. And on All Halowmasse day, at the grete feste, sate in the halle the three kynges; and Sir **Kay** the Seneschall served in the halle, and Sir **Lucas** the Butler that was Duke **Corneus** son, and Sir **Gryfflet** that was the son of God of **Cardal**: thes three knyghtes had the rule of all the servyse that served the kyngis. And anone, as they were redy and wayshen, all the knyghtes that wolde juste made hem redy. And be than[6] they were redy on horsebak there was seven hondred knyghtes. And Kynge **Arthure, Ban, and Bors**, with the Archebysshop **of Caunterbyry**, and Sir **Ector, Kays** fadir, they were in a place covirde with clothys of golde, lyke unto an halle, with ladyes and jantillwomen for to beholde who dud beste and thereon to gyff a jugemente.

And Kyng **Arthure** with the two kyngis lette departe the seven hondred knyghtes in two partyes; and there were three hondred knyghtes of the realme of **Bentwyke and Gaule** that turned on the othir syde.[7] And they dressed their shyldis and began to couche[8] hir sperys, many good knyghtes. So Sir **Gryfflet** was the firste that sette oute, and to hym com a knyght—hys name was Sir **Ladynas**—and they com so egirly togydir that all men had wondir; and they so sore fought that hir shyldis felle on pecis, and both horse and man felle to the erthe. And both the Frensh knyght and the Englysh knyght lay so longe that all men wente they had bene dede.

3. I.e., escaped our rebuke.
4. See n. 2, p. 8.
5. I.e., entered into.
6. I.e., by the time.
7. I.e., the side representing Ban and Bors.
8. I.e., secure in saddle rests.

Whan **Lucas** the Butler saw Sir **Gryfflet** ly so longe, he horsed hym[9]
agayne anone, and they too ded many mervelous dedis of armys
with many bachelers. Also Sir **Kay** com oute of a bushemente with
fyve knyghtes with hym, and they six smote othir six downe. But
Sir **Kay** dud that day many mervaylous dedis of armys, that there   5
was none that dud so welle as he that day.

Than there com **Ladynas and Grastian**, two knyghtes of Fraunse,
and dud passynge well, that all men praysed them. Than com in
Sir **Placidas**, a good knyght, that mette with Sir **Kay** and smote hym
downe, horse and man—wherefore Sir **Gryfflet** was wroth and   10
mette with Sir Placidas so harde that horse and man felle to the
erthe.

❡But whan the fyve knyghtes wyst that Sir Kay had a falle, they
were wroth oute of mesure and therewithall ech of them fyve bare
downe a knyght.   15

Whan Kynge **Arthur** and the two kynges saw hem begynne wexe
wroth on bothe partyes, they leped on smale hakeneyes[1] and lette
cry that all men sholde departe unto theire lodgynge. And so they
wente home and unarmed them, and so[2] to evynsonge and souper.
And aftir souper the three kynges wente into a gardyne and gaff   20
the pryces unto Sir **Kay** and unto Sir **Lucas** the Butler and unto Sir
Gryfflet. And than they wente unto counceyle, and with hem **Gwenbaus**, brothir unto Kynge **Ban and Bors**, a wyse clerke; and thidir
wente **Ulphuns, Brascias and Merlion**. And aftir they had ben in her
counceyle they wente unto bedde. And on the morne they harde   25
Masse, and to dyner and so to theire counceyle, and made many
argumentes what[3] were beste to do.

So at the laste they were concluded that **Merlion** sholde go with
a tokyn of Kynge **Ban**,[4] that was a rynge, unto hys men, and Kynge
Bors, Gracian, and Placidas sholde go agayne and kepe their castels   30
and theire contreyes, for Kynge **Ban of Bentwyke** and Kynge **Bors of
Gaule** had ordayned them all thynge. And so passed they the see
and com to **Bentwyke**. And whan the people sawe Kynge **Bannys**
rynge, and **Gracian and Placidas**, they were glad and asked how theire
kynge fared and made grete joy of their welfare. And accordyng   fol.10v   35

---

9. Set him on his horse.
1. I.e., ordinary riding horses (as opposed to war horses).
2. I.e., so went.
3. I.e., about what.
4. I.e., Merlin should go with evidence of his allegiance to King Ban. This is the first instance
in the surviving portion of the Winchester MS where Merlin's name is represented only
with a red "**M.**"; all such instances are recorded in this edition with an expansion in italics.
No other name is so severely abbreviated in the MS, and Helen Cooper has suggested
that, beyond its being a possible reflection of similar abbreviation in Malory's source, this
singular procedure may have been employed for one or more specific reasons (though its
use cannot be said to be absolutely consistent in any of these circumstances, and there is
no guarantee of authorial, as opposed to scribal, intention): (1) superstition about naming
a power that may bring bad luck, (2) an indication that Merlin has appeared unannounced,
(3) an indication that he is in disguise, or (4) that he is to be understood as otherwise
unfamiliar to those who meet him (for reference to Cooper's article, see n. 4, p. xlvi).
Often those occasions in which Merlin's name is written out in full coincide with points
at which he first appears in a scene or when he has not been mentioned for some time.
Caxton always prints Merlin's name in full, and so one can only conjecture how the
Winchester MS would have represented the name in those portions now missing. Whatever the degree of authority, deliberation, and consistency behind this abbreviation, the
impression is of a variable occultness consistent with that of Merlin's activities in general.

unto theire soveraigne lordis desire, the men of warre made hem
redy in all haste possible, so that they were fyftene thousand on
horsebacke and foote—and they had grete plenté of vitayle by **Merlions** provisions. But **Gracian and Placidas** were leffte at home to fur-
nysh and garnysh the castels for drede of Kyng **Claudas**.   5

Ryght so **Merlion** passed the see well vitayled bothe by watir and
by londe.[5] And whan he com to the see he sente home the footemen agayne, and toke no mo with hym but ten thousand men on
horsebake—the moste party of men of armys—and so shipped and
passed the see into Inglonde and londed at **Dovir**. And thorow the   10
wytte of **Merlion**, he ledde the oste northwarde the pryveyst wey
that coude be thought, unto the foreste of **Bedgrayne**, and there in
a valey lodged hem secretely. Than rode **Merlion to Arthure** and to
the two kynges, and tolde hem how he had spedde, whereof they
had grete mervayle that ony man on erthe myght spede so sone to   15
go and com.

So **Merlion** tolde them how ten thousande were in the forest of
Bedgrayne, well armed at all poyntis.[6] Than was there no more to
sey, but to horsebak wente all the oste, as **Arthure** had before provyded. So with twenty thousand he passed by nyght and day. But   20
there was made such an ordinaunce afore by **Merlyon** that there
sholde no man of warre ryde nothir go in no contrey on this syde
Trente watir[7] but if he had a tokyn frome Kynge **Arthure**,
wherethorow the Kynges enemyes durst nat ryde as they dud tofore
to aspye.   25

And so wythin a litill whyle the three kyngis com to the forest   [12]
of Bedgrayne and founde there a passynge fayre felyship and
well besene, whereof they had grete joy—and vitayle they wanted
none. Thys was the causis of the northir hoste: that they were rered
for the despite and rebuke that the six kyngis had at Carlyon. And   30
tho six kyngis by hir meanys gate unto them fyve othir kyngis, and
thus they began to gadir hir people.

And now they swore, nother for welle nothyr wo,[8] they sholde
nat lyve[9] tyll they had destroyed **Arthure**—and than they made an
othe; and the first that began the othe was the Deuke of **Candebenet**,   35
that he wolde brynge with hym fyve thousand men of armys, the
which were redy on horsebakke. Than swore Kynge **Brandegoris of
Strangore** that he wolde brynge with hym fyve thousand men of
armys on horsebacke. Than swore Kynge **Claribaus of Northumbirlonde** that he wolde brynge three thousand men of armys with hym.   40
Than swore the Kynge with the Hondred Knyghtes, that was a
passynge good man and a yonge, that he wold brynge foure thousand good men of armys on horsebacke.   fol.11r

Than there swore Kynge **Lott**—a passyng good knyght, and fadir
unto Sir **Gawayne**—that he wolde brynge fyve thousand good men   45

---

5. *Well vitayled bothe by watir and by londe:* i.e., well provisioned with food from land and
   sea.
6. In every respect.
7. I.e., south of the river Trent.
8. I.e., no matter what
9. I.e., carry on normal lives.

of armys on horsebak. Also there swore Kynge **Uryens**, that was Sir **Uwaynes** fadir, of the londe of **Goore**; and he wolde brynge six thousand men of armys on horsebak. Also there swore Kynge **Idres of Cornuweale** that he wolde brynge fyve thousand men of armys on horsebake.

⁋Also there swore Kynge **Cradilmans** to brynge fyve thousand men on horsebacke. Also there swore Kyng **Angwysshauns** of Irelonde to brynge fyve thousand men of armys on horsebak.

⁋Also there swore Kynge **Nentres** to brynge fyve thousand men on horsebak. Also there swore Kynge **Carados** to brynge fyve thousand men of armys on horsebak.

⁋So hir hole oste was of clene[1] men of armys: on horsebacke was fully fyffty thousand, and on foote ten thousand of good mennes bodyes. Than they were sone redy and mounted uppon horsebacke, and sente forthe before[2] the foreryders. For thes a eleven[3] kynges in hir wayes leyde a sege unto the castell of **Bedgrayne**. And so they departed and drew towarde **Arthure**, and leffte a fewe to byde at the sege, for the castell of **Bedgrayne** was an holde of Kynge **Arthurs** and the men that were within were Kynge **Arthurs** men all.

So by **Merlyons** advice there were sente foreryders to skymme the contrey; and they mette with the foreryders of the Northe and made hem to telle which way the oste com.

⁋And than they tolde Kynge **Arthure**, and, by Kynge **Ban and Bors** his counceile,[4] they lette brenne and destroy all the contrey before them there[5] they sholde ryde. The Kynge of the Hondred Knyghtis that tyme mette a wondir dreme two nyghtes before the batayle: that there blew a grete wynde and blew downe hir castels and hir townys, and aftir that com a watir and bare hit all away. And all that herde of that swevyn seyde hit was a tokyn of grete batayle.

⁋Than, by counceile of **Merlion**, whan they wyst which wey the an eleven[7] kynges wolde ryde and lodge that nyght, at mydnyght they sette uppon them as they were in their pavilions. But the scowte-wacche by hir oste cryed, "Lordis, to harneys![8] for here be oure enemyes at youre honde."[9]

Than Kynge **Arthur** and Kynge **Ban and Bors** with hir good and trusty knyghtes sette uppon them so fersely that he made them overthrowe hir pavilons on hir hedis. But the eleven kynges, by manly prouesse of armys, toke a fayre champion[1]—but there was slayne that morow tyde ten thousand good mennes bodyes. And so

[5]

[10]

[15]

[20]

[13]

[25]

Sompnus[6]

[30]

[35]

[14]

fol.11v

[40]

---

1. I.e., excellent.
2. I.e., ahead
3. This group of eleven.
4. *by Kynge Ban and Bors his counceile:* by the counsel of Kings Ban and Bors.
5. I.e., there where.
6. *Sompnus:* a dream. This is the first surviving example—and the only one in Latin—of a series of marginal annotations produced by the two main scribes of the Winchester MS (rendered in red throughout). There is a possibility that some or all of them are authorial; see n. 3, p. xliii.
7. I.e., the group of eleven.
8. Arm yourselves.
9. I.e., at hand, near.
1. *Toke a fayre champion:* secured strategically advantageous ground.

they had before hem a stronge passage; yet were there fyffty thousand of hardy men. Than hit drew toward day.

⁋"Now shall ye do by myne advice," seyde Merlyon unto the three
kyngis—and seyde, "I wolde Kynge Ban and Bors with hir felyship
of ten thousand men were put in a woode here besyde, in an inbusshemente, and kept them prevy, and that they be leyde or[2] the
lyght of the day com, and that they stire nat tyll that ye and youre
knyghtes a fought with hem[3] longe. And whan hit ys daylyght,
dresse youre batayle evyn before them and the passage, that they
may se all youre oste—for than woll they be the more hardy whan
they se you but aboute twenty thousande—and cause hem to be
the gladder to suffir you and youre oste to com over the passage."
All the three kynges and the hole[4] barownes seyde how Merlion
devised passynge well; and so hit was done.

So on the morn, whan aythir oste saw othir, they of the Northe
were well comforted. Than Ulphuns and Brascias were delyvirde[5]
three thousand men of armys, and they sette on them fersely in
the passage, and slew on the ryght honde and on the lyffte honde,
that hit was wondir to telle.

⁋But whan the eleven kynges saw that there was so few a felyship that dud such dedis of armys, they were ashamed and sette
on hem agayne fersely. And there was Sir Ulphuns horse slayne;
but he dud merveylously on foote.

⁋But the Duke Eskanse of Candebenet and Kynge Clarivaunce of
Northehumbirlonde were allwey grevously set on Ulphuns. Than Sir
Brascias saw his felow y-fared so withall,[6] he smote the duke with
a spere, that horse and man felle downe. That saw Kyng Clarybauns,
and returned unto Sir Brascias; and eythir smote othir so that horse
and man wente to the erthe. And so they lay longe astoned, and
theire horse[7] knees braste to the harde bone. Than com Sir Kay
the Senesciall with six felowis with hym and dud passynge well.

⁋So with that com the eleven kyngis: and there was Gryfflette
put to the erth, horse and man—and Lucas the Butler, horse and
man, Kynge Brandegoris, and Kynge Idres and Kynge Angwyshaunce.
Than wexed the medlee passyng harde on bothe parties. Whan Sir
Kay saw Sir Gryfflet on foote, he rode unto Kynge Nentres and smote
hym downe, and ledde his horse unto Sir Gryfflette and horsed hym
agayne.

⁋Also, Sir Kay with the same spere smote downe Kynge Lotte
and hurte hym passynge sore. That saw the Kynge with the Hondred Knyghtes and ran unto Sir Kay and smote hym downe, and
toke hys horse and gaff hym[8] Kynge Lotte—whereof he seyde "Gramercy!"

⁋Whan Sir Gryfflet saw Sir Kay and Sir Lucas de Butler on foote,

2. Lie in place until.
3. I.e., the eleven kings' forces.
4. I.e., whole number of.
5. I.e., sent by the eleven kings.
6. I.e., when *y-fared so withall*: treated in such a way.
7. I.e., horses'.
8. I.e., gave him to.

he with a sherpe spere grete and square⁹ rode to Pynnel, a good
man of armys, and smote horse and man downe; and than he toke
hys horse and gaff hym unto Sir Kay. Than Kyng Lotte saw Kynge
Nentres on foote, he ran unto Meliot de la Roche and smote hym
downe horse and man, and gaff unto Kynge Nentres the horse and
horsed hym agayne. Also the Kynge with the Hondred Knyghtes
saw Kynge Idres on foote; he ran unto Gwyniarte de Bloy and smote
hym downe, horse and man, and gaff Kynge Idres the horse and
horsed hym agayne. Than Kynge Lotte smote downe Clarinaus de la
Foreyste Saveage and gaff the horse unto Duke Escans.

And so whan they had horsed the kyngis agayne, they drew hem
all eleven kynges togydir, and seyde they wolde be revenged of the
damage that they had takyn that day. The meanewhyle, com in
Kyng Arthure with an egir countenans, and founde Ulphuns and
Brascias on foote, in grete perell of dethe, that were fowle defoyled
undir the horse feete. Than Arthure as a lyon ran unto Kynge Cra-
dilment of North Walis and smote hym thorow the lyffte syde, that
horse and man felle downe. Than he toke the horse by the reygne
and led hym unto Ulphuns and seyde, "Have this horse, myne olde
frende, for grete nede hast thou of an horse."

⁋"Gramercy," seyde Ulphuns. Than Kynge Arthure dud so mer-
vaylesly in armys that all men had wondir. Whan the Kyng with
the Hondred Knyghtes saw Kynge Cradilmente on foote, he ran unto
Sir Ector, Sir Kayes fadir, that was well i-horsed and smote horse
and man downe, and gaff the horse unto the kynge and horsed
hym agayne. And whan Kynge Arthure saw that kynge ryde on Sir
Ectors horse he was wrothe, and with hys swerde he smote the
kynge on the helme, that a quarter of the helme and shelde clave
downe; and so the swerde carve downe unto the horse necke, and
so man and horse felle downe to the grounde. Than Sir Kay com
unto Kynge Morganoure, senesciall with the Kynge of the Hondred
Knyghtes, and smote hym downe, horse and man, and ledde the
horse unto hys fadir, Sir Ector. Than Sir Ector ran unto a knyght
that hyght Lardans and smote horse and man downe, and lad the
horse unto Sir Brascias, that grete nede had of an horse and was
gretly defoyled.

⁋Whan Brascias behelde Lucas the Butler that lay lyke a dede
man undir the horse feete—and ever Sir Gryflet dud mercyfully for
to reskow hym, and there were allwayes fourtene knyghtes upon
Sir Lucas—and than Sir Brascias smote one of them on the helme,
that hit wente unto his tethe; and he rode unto another and smote
hym, that hys arme flowe into the felde. Than he wente to the
thirde and smote hym on the shulder, that sholdir and arme flow
unto the felde.

And whan Gryfflet saw rescowis¹ he smote a knyght on the tem-
plis, that hede and helme wente of to the erthe; and Gryfflet toke
that horse and lad hym unto Sir Lucas, and bade hym mownte

fol.12v

9. I.e., of square cross section.
1. I.e., the opportunity for rescue.

uppon that horse and revenge his hurtis—for² Sir **Brastias** had slayne a knyght tofore—and horsed Sir **Lucas**. Than Sir **Lucas** saw Kynge **Angwysschaunce** that nyghe³ had slayne **Maris de la Roche**; and **Lucas** ran to hym with a sherpe spere that was grete, and he gaff hym suche a falle that the horse felle downe to the erthe.

[15]
The dethe of Marys
del Roche
5

Also, **Lucas** founde there on foote **Bloyas de la Flaundres** and Sir **Gwynas**, two hardy knyghtes, and, in that woodnes that **Lucas** was in, he slew two bachelers and horsed them agayne. Than wexed the batayle passynge harde one bothe partyes. But Kynge **Arthure** was glad that hys knyghtes were horsed agayne. And than they fought togiders, that the noyse and the sowne range by the watir and woode.

¶Wherefore Kynge **Ban and Bors** made hem redy and dressed theire shyldis and harneysse, and were so currageous that their enemyes shooke and byverd for egirnesse. All thys whyle Sir **Lucas**, **Gwynas**, **Bryaunte, and Bellias of Flaundres** helde strong medlé agaynste six kynges, which were **Kynge Lott**, Kynge **Nentres**, Kynge **Brandegoris**, Kynge **Idres**, Kyng **Uriens**, and Kynge **Angwysshauns**. So, with the helpe of Sir **Kay** and of Sir **Gryfflet**, they helde thes six kyngis harde, that unneth they had ony power to deffende them.⁴

But whan Kynge **Arthure** saw the batayle wolde nat be ended by no maner, he fared woode as a lyon and stirred his horse here and there, on the ryght honde and on the lyffte honde, that he stynted nat tylle he had slayne twenty knyghtes. Also he wounded Kynge **Lotte** sore on the shulder and made hym to leve that grownde, for Sir **Kay with Sir Gryfflet** dud with Kynge **Arthure** grete dedis of armys there. Than Sir **Ulphuns, Brastias, and Sir Ector** encountirde agaynste the Duke **Escans**, and Kynge **Cradilmante**, and Kynge **Claribauns** of Northhumbirlonde, and Kynge **Carados**, and the Kynge with the Hondred Knyghtes. So thes kynges encountird with thes knyghtes, that they made them to avoyde the grounde.

¶Than Kynge **Lotte** made grete dole for his damagis and his felowis, and seyde unto the kyngis, "But if we woll do as I have devised, we all shall be slayne and destroyed:

¶"Lette me have the Kynge with the Hondred Knyghtes, and Kynge **Angwysshaunce**, and Kynge **Idres**, and the Duke of **Candebenet**; and we fyve kyngis woll have ten thousand men of armys with us, and we woll go on one party, whyle the six kynges holde the medlé with twelve thousand. And whan we se that ye have foughtyn with hem longe, than woll we com on freysshly—and ellis shall we never macche them," seyde Kynge Lotte, "but by thys means."

So they departed as they here devised, and thes six kyngis made theire party stronge agaynste Kyng **Arthure** and made grete warre longe in the meanewhyle. Than brake the bushemente of Kynge

fol.13r

---

2. I.e., and, because.
3. Nearly. The MS here reads *nyght*, but Maris resurfaces, alive, below (p. 26, line 13); the emendation follows that of Vinaver, O³, p. 30., line 7. The marginal annotation proclaiming Maris's death seems unlikely to be authorial, but cf. the reference in the Preface, n. 3, p. xliii.
4. I.e., themselves.

𝕭anne and 𝕭ors; and 𝕷ionse and 𝕻hariaunce had that advaunte-garde,[5]
and they two knyghtes mette with Kynge 𝕴dres, that was nere dis-
comfited. That saw Kynge 𝕬ngwysshaunce, and put 𝕷yonses and
𝕻hariaunce in poynte of dethe, for the Duke of 𝕮andebenet com on
with a grete felyship. So thes two knyghtes were in grete daungere   5
of their lyves, that they were fayne to returne; but allweyes they
rescowed hemselff and hir felyship merveylously.

¶Whan Kynge 𝕭ors saw tho knyghtes put on bak[6] hit greved
hym sore. Than he com on so faste that his felyship semed as blak
as inde.[7]   10

¶Whan Kynge 𝕷otte had aspyed Kynge 𝕭ors, he knew hym well,
and seyde, "Jesu defende us frome dethe and horryble maymes, for
I se well we be in grete perell of dethe; for I se yondir a kynge, one
of the moste worshipfullyst men, and the best knyghtes of the
worlde be inclyned unto his felyship."   15

¶"What[8] ys he?" seyde the Kynge with the Hundirde Knyghtes.
"Hit ys," he seyde, "Kynge 𝕭ors of 𝕲aule." "I mervayle," seyde he,
"how they com unto this contrey withoute wetynge of us all."

¶"Hit was by 𝕸erlions advice," seyde a knyght.

¶"As for me," seyde Kynge 𝕮arados, "I woll encountir with Kynge   20
𝕭ors, and ye woll rescow me whan myster ys."[9] "Go on," seyde they,
"for we wol[1] all that we may." Than Kynge 𝕮arados and hys oste
rode on a soffte pace[2] tyll they com as nyghe Kynge 𝕭ors as a bowe-
draught. Than eythir lette theire horsys renne as faste as they   fol.13v
myght (and 𝕭leobris, that was godson unto Kynge 𝕭ors; he bare his   25
chyeff standard[3] that was a passyng good knyght).

"Now shall we se," seyde Kynge 𝕭ors, "how thes northirne Bret-
ons can bere theire armys!" So Kynge 𝕭ors encountird with a
knyght and smote hym thorowoute with a spere, that he felle dede
unto the erthe; and aftirwarde drew hys swerde and dud mervay-   30
lous dedis of armys, that all partyes had grete wondir thereof. And
his knyghtes fayled nat, but dud hir parte. And Kynge 𝕮arados was
smytten to the erthe.

¶With that com the Kynge with the Hondred Knyghtes and rescowed Kynge Carados myghtyly by force of armys, for he was a   35
passynge good knyght, and but a yonge man. Be than[4] com into   [16]
the felde Kynge 𝕭an, as ferse as a lyon, with bondis of grene and
thereuppon golde.[5] "A-ha!" seyde Kynge 𝕷ott, "we muste be discomfite, for yondir I se the most valiante knyght of the worlde, and

---

5. Held the advance guard (that would be ambushed first).
6. *Put on bak:* set back, repulsed.
7. I.e., so quickly that his army seemed to be a mass as dark as indigo (dye).
8. I.e., who.
9. *Whan myster ys:* when necessary.
1. I.e., will do.
2. At a steady pace.
3. Carried the King's main heraldic flag. The standard-bearer holds a position of great honor,
   representing the army's will to fight. (This Bleobris, incidentally, is not to be confused
   with Bleoberys de Ganys.)
4. By that time.
5. *With bondis of grene and thereuppon golde:* with heraldic stripes of green (on his coat of
   arms) with a gold background.

the man of moste renowne, for such[6] two brethirne as ys Kynge
Ban and Kynge Bors ar nat lyvynge. Wherefore we muste nedis
voyde or dye, and but if[7] we avoyde manly and wysely there ys but
dethe." So whan thes two kyngis, Ban and Bors, com into the
batayle, they com in so fersely that the strokis rebounded agayne   5
fro the woode and the watir.

¶Wherefore Kynge Lotte wepte for pité and dole that he saw so
many good knyghtes take their ende.

¶But thorow the grete force of Kynge Ban they made bothe the
northirne batayles that were parted hurteled togidirs for grete   10
drede. And the three kynges and their knyghtes slew on ever, that
hit was pité to se and to beholde the multitude of peple that fledde.

¶But kyng Lott, and the Kynge with the Hundred Knyghtes, and
Kynge Morganoure, gadred the peple togydir passynge knyghtly,[8]
and dud grete proues of armys, and helde the batayle all the day   15
lyke harde.

¶Whan the Kynge with the Hundred Knyghtes behelde the grete
damage that Kynge Ban [dyd] he threste unto hym with his horse
and smote hym an hyghe on the helme a grete stroke and stoned
hym sore. Than Kynge Ban was wood wrothe with hym and folowed   20
on hym fersely. The othir saw that and caste up hys shelde and
spored hys horse forewarde, but the stroke of Kynge Ban downe
felle and carve a cantell of the shelde, and the swerde sloode downe
by the hawbirke byhynde hys backe and kut thorow the trappoure
of stele, and the horse, evyn in two pecis, that the swerde felle to   fol.14r   25
the erth. Than the Kynge of the Hundred Knyghtes voyded the
horse lyghtly, and with hys swerde he broched the horse of Kynge
Ban thorow and thorow.

¶With that Kynge Ban voyded lyghtly frome the dede horse and
smote at that othir so egirly on the helme that he felle to the erthe.   30
Also in that ire he felde Kynge Morganoure, and there was grete
slawghtir of good knyghtes and muche peple. Be that tyme com
into the prees Kynge Arthure and founde Kynge Ban stondynge
amonge the dede men and dede horse, fyghtynge on foote as a
wood lyon, that there com none nyghe hym as farre as he myght   35
reche with hys swerde but he caught a grevous buffette.

¶Whereof Kynge Arthure had grete pité. And Kynge Arthure was
so blody that by hys shylde[9] there myght no man know hym, for
all was blode and brayne that stake on his swerde and on hys
shylde. And as Kynge Arthure loked besyde hym he sawe a knyght
that was passyngely well horsed. And therewith Kynge Arthure ran   40
to hym and smote hym on the helme, that hys swerde wente unto
his teeth, and the knyght sanke downe to the erthe, dede. And
anone Kynge Arthure toke hys horse by the rayne and ladde hym
unto Kynge Ban and seyde, "Fayre brothir, have ye thys horse, for   45

---

6. I.e., another such.
7. Unless.
8. *Passynge knyghtly:* in a surpassingly knightly fashion.
9. By the coat of arms on his shield.

ye have grete myster thereof, and me repentys sore of youre grete damage."

¶"Hit shall be sone revenged," seyde Kynge Ban, "for I truste in God myne hurte ys none suche but som of them[1] may sore repente thys." "I woll welle," seyde Kynge Arthure, "for I se youre dedys full actuall![2] Nevertheles, I myght nat com to you at that tyme." But whan Kynge Ban was mounted on horsebak, than there began a new batayle whych was sore and harde, and passynge grete slaughtir. And so thorow grete force Kyng Arthure, Kynge Ban, and Kynge Bors made hir knyghtes alyght to wythdraw hem to a lytyll wood, and so over a litill ryvir; and there they rested hem, for on the nyght before they had no grete reste in the felde. And than the eleven kyngis put hem on an hepe[3] all togydirs, as men adrad and oute of all comforte. But there was no man that myght passe them; they helde hem so harde togydirs, bothe behynde and before, that Kynge Arthure had mervayle of theire dedis of armys and was passynge wrothe.

"A, Sir Arthure," seyde Kynge Ban and Kynge Bors, "blame hem nat, for they do as good men ought to do." "For be my fayth," seyde Kynge Ban, "they ar the beste fyghtynge men and knyghtes of moste prouesse that ever Y saw other herde off speke. And tho eleven kyngis ar men of grete worship; and if they were longyng to you, there were no kynge undir hevyn that had suche eleven kyngis, nother off suche worship." "I may nat love hem," seyde Kynge Arthure, "for they wolde destroy me."

"That know we well," seyde Kyng Ban and Kynge Bors, "for they ar your mortall enemyes, and that hathe bene preved beforehonde. And thys day they have done theire parte, and that ys grete[4] pité of their wylfulnes." Than all the eleven kynges drew hem togydir, and than seyde Lott, "Lordis, ye muste do othirwyse than ye do, othir ellis the grete losses ys behynde:[5] for ye may se what peple we have loste and what good men we lese because we wayte allweyes on thes footemen, and ever in savyng of one of thes footemen we lese ten horsemen for hym. Therefore thys ys myne advise: lette us putte oure footemen frome us, for hit ys nere nyght. For thys noble Kynge Arthure woll nat tarry on the footemen, for they may save hemselff—the woode ys nerehonde. And whan we horsemen be togydirs, looke every of you kyngis lat make such ordinaunce that none breke, uppon payne of deth—and who that seeth any man dresse hym to fle, lyghtly that he be slayne: for hit ys bettir we sle a cowarde than thorow a coward all we be slayne:

¶"How sey ye?" seyde Kynge Lotte, "Answere me, all ye kynges." "Ye say well," seyde Kynge Nentres. So seyde the Kynge with the Hondred Knyghtes; the same seyde Kynge Carados and Kynge Uryens; so seyde Kynge Idres and Kynge Brandegoris; so dud Kyng

fol.14v

---

1. I.e., those who have injured me.
2. I see real evidence of your deeds.
3. *Put hem on an hepe:* gathered themselves into a band.
4. I.e., the great.
5. Otherwise the great defeat will have happened.

Cradilmasse and the Duke of Candebenet; the same seyde Kynge Clar-
paunce, and so dud Kynge Angwyssbaunce—and swore they wolde
never fayle other for lyff nothir for dethe, and whoso that fledde,
all they sholde be slayne. Than they amended their harneyse and
ryghted their sheldis, and toke newe speris and sette hem on theire   5
thyghes, and stoode stylle as[6] hit had be a plumpe of woode.

¶Whan Kynge Arthure and Kynge Ban and Bors behelde them   [17]
and all hir knyghtes, they preysed them much for their noble chere
of chevalry, for[7] the hardyeste fyghters that ever they herde other
sawe. So furthwith there dressed a fourty[8] knyghtes, and seyde   10
unto the three Kynges they wolde breke their batayle. And thes
were their namys: Lyonses, Phariaunce, Ulphuns, Brascias, Ector,   fol.15r
Kayus, Lucas de Butler, Gryfflet la Fyse de Deu, Marrys de la Roche,
Gwynas de Bloy, Bryaunte de la Foreyste Saveage;

¶Bellaus, Morians of the Castel Maydyns, Flaundreus of the Castel of   15
Ladyes, Annecians (that was Kynge Bors godson, a noble knyght), and
Ladinas de la Rouse, Emerause, Caulas, Graciens le Castilion, Bloyse de
la Case, and Sir Colgrevaunce de Goore. All thes knyghtes rode on
before with sperys on theire thyghes and spurred their horses
myghtyly.   20

And the eleven kyngis with parte of hir knyghtes rushed furthe
as faste as they myght with hir sperys, and there they dud, on bothe
partyes, merveylous dedes of armys. So there com into the thycke
of the prees Arthure, Ban, and Bors, and slew downeryght on bothe
hondis, that hir horses wente in blood up to the fittlockys. But ever   25
the eleven Kyngis and the oste was ever in the visage of Arthure—
wherefore Kynge Ban and Bors had grete mervayle, consyderyng
the grete slaughter that there was; but at the laste they were dryven
abacke over a litill ryver.

¶With that com Merlion on a grete blacke horse and seyde unto   30
Kynge Arthure, "Thou hast never done![9] Hast thou nat done inow?
Of three score thousande thys day hast thou leffte on lyve[1] but
fyftene thousand. Therefore hit ys tyme to sey 'Who!' for God ys
wroth with the,[2] for thou wolt never have done. For yondir a eleven
Kynges at thys tyme woll nat be overthrowyn; but, and[3] thou tary   35
on them ony lenger, thy fortune woll turne and they shall encres:

¶"And therefore withdraw you unto youre lodgynge and reste
you as sone as ye may, and rewarde youre good knyghtes with golde
and with sylver, for they have well deserved hit. There may no
ryches be to dere[4] for them, for of so fewe men as ye have, there   40
was never men dud more worshipfully in proues than ye have done
today—for ye have macched thys day with the beste fyghters of
the worlde." "That ys trouthe," seyde Kynge Ban and Bors. Than

6. I.e., as if.
7. I.e., as.
8. A group of forty. The subsequent list names only twenty-one, and so the roman numerals
   of the actual MS reading may represent a misreading in the copy text of *xxi* for *xl*.
9. I.e., you are never finished.
1. *On lyve:* alive.
2. thee
3. I.e., if.
4. I.e., costly to you.

Merlyon bade hem, "Withdraw where ye lyste, for thys three yere[5] I
dare undirtake they shall nat dere you; and by that tyme ye shall
hyre newe tydyngis."

¶Than Merlion seyde unto Arthure, "Thes eleven Kyngis have
more on hande than they ar ware off, for the Sarezynes[6] ar londed
in their contreies, mo than fourty thousande, and brenne and sle
and have leyde syege to the Castell Wandesborow, and make grete
destruccion. Therefore drede you nat thys [thre] yere;

¶"Also, sir, all the goodis that be gotyn at this batayle, lette hit[7]   fol.15v
be serched, and whan ye have hit in your hondis lette hit be geffyn
frendly unto thes two kyngis, Ban and Bors, that they may rewarde
their knyghtes wythall—and that shall cause straungers to be of
bettir wyll to do you servyse at nede. Also ye be able to rewarde
youre owne knyghtes at what tyme somever hit lykith you."

¶"Ye sey well," seyde Arthure, "and as thou haste devised, so
shall hit be done."

¶Whan hit was delyverde to thes kynges, Ban and Bors, they gaff
the godis as frely to theire knyghtes as hit was gevyn to them. Than
Merlion toke hys leve of Kynge Arthure and of the two kyngis, for to
go se hys mayster Bloyse that dwelled in Northhumbirlonde. And
so he departed and com to hys mayster, that was passynge glad of
hys commynge. And there he tolde how Arthure and the two kynges
had spedde at the grete batayle, and how hyt was endyd, and tolde
the namys of every kynge and knyght of worship that was there.
And so Bloyse wrote[8] the batayle worde by worde as Merlion tolde
hym, how hit began and by whom, and in lyke wyse how hit was
ended and who had the worst.

¶And all the batayles that were done in Arthurs dayes, Merlion
dud[9] hys mayster Bloyse wryte them. Also he dud wryte all the
batayles that every worthy knyght ded of Arthurs courte.

¶So aftir this Merlion departed frome his mayster and com to
Kynge Arthure that was in the castell of Bedgrayne, that was one of
the castels that stondith in the Foreyste of Sherewood.

¶And Merlion[1] was so disgysed that Kynge Arthure knew hym
nat, for he was all befurred in blacke shepis skynnes, and a grete
payre of bootis, and a boowe and arowis, in a russet gowne, and
brought wylde gyese in hys honde. And hit was on the morne aftir
Candilmasse[2] Day. But Kynge Arthure knew hym nat.

¶"Sir," seyde Merlion unto the Kynge, "woll ye geff me a gyffte?"

¶"Wherefore," seyde Kynge Arthure, "sholde I gyff the a gyffte,
chorle?"

---

5. For the next three years.
6. *On hande:* i.e., to concern them. *Sarezynes:* Saracens; typically Muslim Arabs, but sometimes in Malory the name is simply used to designate those who are unchristened. The
word probably derives, by way of Greek, Latin, and then French, from an Arabic word for
easterner.
7. I.e., them.
8. I.e., wrote an account of. The purpose of this reference is twofold: firstly, to relate the
validation of the events of Arthur's reign as worthy enough to be written down, and secondly, to demonstrate the proximity of the current text to an authoritative source.
9. I.e., had.
1. On the abbreviation of Merlin's name in the Winchester MS, see n. 4, p. 17.
2. See n. 9, p. 10.

¶"Sir," seyd *Merlion*, "ye were bettir to gyff me a gyffte that ys nat in youre honde than to lose grete rychesse:

¶"For here in the same place there the grete batayle was, ys grete tresoure hydde in the erthe."

¶"Who tolde the so, chorle?"

¶"Sir, Merlyon tolde me so," seyde he.

¶Than Ulphuns and Brascias knew hym well inowghe and smyled.

¶"Sir," seyde thes two knyghtes, "hit ys Merlion that so spekith unto you!"

¶Than Kynge Arthure was gretly abaysshed and had mervayle of Merlion, and so had Kynge Ban and Bors. So they had grete disporte at hym. Than in the meanewhyle there com a damesell that was an erlis doughter; hys name was Sanam and hir name was Lyonors, a passyng fayre damesell. And so she cam thidir for to do omage[3] as other lordis ded aftir that grete batayle. And Kynge Arthure sette hys love gretly on hir, and so ded she uppon hym, and so the Kynge had ado with hir and gate on hir a chylde. And hys name was Borre, that was aftir a good knyght, and of the Table Rounde.

Than there com worde that Kynge Ryens of North Walis made grete warre on Kynge Lodegreaunce of Camylarde, for the whiche Kynge Arthure was wrothe, for he loved hym welle and hated Kyng Royns, for allwayes he was ayenst hym.

¶So, by ordinauns of the three Kynges, ther were sente home unto Benwyke all that wolde departe, for drede of Kynge Claudas.[4] Thes knyghtes, Pharyaunce, Anthemes, Graciens, and Lyonses of Payarne, were the leders of them that sholde kepe the two kynges londis.

And than Kynge Arthure, Kynge Ban, and Kynge Bors departed with hir felyship—a twenty thousande—and cam within seven dayes into the contrey of Camylarde, and there rescowed Kynge Lodegraunce, and slew there muche people of Kynge Ryons, unto the numbir of ten thousand, and putte hem to flyght. And than had thes thre kynges grete chere of Kynge Lodegraunce, and he thanked them of[5] theire grete goodnes that they wolde revenge hym of his enemyes. And there had Arthure the firste syght of queene Gwenybere, the Kyngis doughter of the londe of Camplarde, and ever afftir he loved hir. And aftir, they were wedded, as hit tellith in the booke.[6]

¶So, breffly to make an ende, they toke there leve to go into hir owne contreyes, for Kynge Claudas dud grete destruction on their londis. Than seyde Arthure, "I woll go with you." "Nay," seyde the kyngis, "ye shall nat at thys tyme, for ye have much to do yet in thys londe. Therefore we woll departe. With the grete goodis that we have gotyn in this londe by youre gyfftis we shall wage good knyghtes and withstonde the Kynge Claudas hys malice,[7] for, by the

fol.16r

[18]

---

3. Cf. n. 6, p. 9.
4. I.e., fearing an attack by Claudas on the lands of Ban and Bors while Ban, Bors, and Arthur are off fighting Ryons, reinforcements are sent back.
5. I.e, for.
6. Cf. n. 5, p. 8.
7. The malice of King Claudas.

grace of God, and[8] we have nede, we woll sende to you for succour; and ye have nede, sende for us, and we woll nat tarry, by the feythe of oure bodyes."

¶ "Hit shall nat nede,"[9] seyde **Merlion**, "thes two Kynges to com agayne in the wey of warre. But I know well Kynge **Arthure** may nat be longe frome you—for within a yere or two ye shall have grete nede; than shall he revenge you of youre enemyes, as ye have done on his. For thes eleven Kyngis shall dye all in one day by the grete myght and prouesse of armys of two valyaunte knyghtes." (As hit tellith aftir, hir namys were **Balyne le Saveage and Balan**, hys brothir, that were merveylous knyghtes as ony was tho lyvynge.)

¶ Now turne we unto the eleven Kynges that returned unto a cité that hyght **Surhaute**, which cité was within Kynge **Uriens** londe. And there they refreysshed them as well as they myght, and made lechys serche their woundis, and sorowed gretly for the deth of hir people.

So with that there com a messyngere and tolde how there was comyn into theyre londis "people that were lawles, as well as Sarezynes a fourty thousande, and have brente and slayne all the people that they may com by withoute mercy, and have leyde sege unto the Castell **Wandesborow**." "Alas," seyde the eleven Kyngis, "here ys sorow uppon sorow; and if we had nat warred agmaynste **Arthure** as we have done, he wolde sone a revenged us. And as for Kynge **Lodegreaunce**, he lovithe **Arthure** bettir than us; and as for Kynge Royens, **he hath ynow** ado with Kynge **Lodegreauns**, for he hath leyde sege unto hym." So they condescended[1] togydir to kepe all the marchis of Cornuwayle, of Walis, and of the Northe.

So firste they put Kynge **Idres** in the cité of Nauntis in Bretayne, with foure thousand men of armys to wacche bothe watir and the londe; also they [put in the cyté of **Wyndesan** Kynge **Nauntres** of Garlott with four thousand knyghtes to watche both on water and on lond; also they] had of othir men of warre mo than eyght thousand for to fortefye all the fortresse in the marchys of Cornuwayle; also they put mo kyngis in all the marchis off Walis and Scotlonde with many good men of armys. And so they kept hem togydirs the space of three yere and ever alyed hem with myghty kynges and dukis.

And unto them felle[2] Kynge **Royns** of Northe Walis, which was a myghty Kynge of men, and **Nero** that was a myghty man of men. And all thys whyle they furnysshed and garnysshed hem of good men of armys and vitayle and of all maner of ablemente that pretendith to warre, to avenge hem for the batayle of **Bedgrayne**, as hit tellith in the booke of aventures.

Than aftir the departynige of Kynge **Bans and Bors**, Kynge **Arthure** rode unto the cité of **Carlyon**. And thydir com unto hym Kynge **Lottis** wyff of Orkeney in maner of a message, but she was sente

8. I.e., if.
9. I.e., be necessary for.
1. I.e., agreed.
2. I.e., joined.

thydir to aspye the courte of Kynge Arthure, and she com rychely
beseyne with hir foure sonnes, Gawayne, Gaheris, Aggravayne, and
Gareth, with many other knyghtes and ladyes, for she was a passynge fayre lady. Wherefore the Kynge caste grete love unto hir
and desired to ly by her. And so they were agreed, and he begate 5
uppon hir Sir Mordred. And she was syster on the modirs syde,
Igrayne, unto Arthure.[3] So there she rested hir a monthe, and at the
laste she departed. Than the Kynge dremed a mervaylous dreme
whereof he was sore adrad. But all thys tyme Kynge Arthure knew
nat that Kynge Lottis wyff was his sister. 10

¶But thus was the dreme of Arthure: hym thought there was com
into hys londe gryffens and serpentes, and hym thought they
brente and slowghe all the people in the londe; and than he
thought he fought with them and they dud hym grete harme and
wounded hym full sore, but at the laste he slew hem. 15

¶Whan the Kynge waked, he was passynge hevy of hys dreme.
And so to putte hit oute of thought, he made hym redy with many
knyghtes to ryde on huntynge. And as sone as he was in the foreste,
the Kynge saw a grete harte before hym. "Thys harte woll I chace,"
seyde Kynge Arthure, and so he spurred hys horse and rode aftir 20
longe. And so be fyne force[4] oftyn he was lyke to have smytten the
herte. Wherefore as the Kynge had chased the herte so longe that
hys horse lost his brethe and felle downe dede, than a yoman fette
the Kynge another horse. So the Kynge saw the herte imboced and
hys horse dede, he sette hym downe by a fowntayne, and there he 25
felle downe[5] in grete thought.

¶And as he sate so hym thought he herde a noyse of howundis
to the som of thirty, and with that the Kynge saw com towarde
hym the strongeste beste that ever he saw or herde of. So thys
beste wente to the welle and dranke, and the noyse was in the 30
bestes bealy [lyke unto the questyng of thirty coupyl houndes, but
alle the whyle the beest dranke there was no noyse in the bestes
bely]. And therewith the beeste departed with a grete noyse,
whereof the Kynge had grete mervayle; and so he was in a grete
thought, and therewith he felle on slepe. 35

¶Ryght so there com a knyght on foote unto Arthure, and seyde,
"Knyght full of thought and slepy, telle me if thou saw any stronge
beeste passe thys way." "Such one saw I," seyde Kynge Arthure,
"that ys paste nye two myle.[6] What wolde ye with that beeste?"
seyde Arthure. "Sir, I have folowed that beste longe and kylde[7] myne 40
horse, so wolde God I had another to folow my queste."

Ryght so com one with the Kyngis horse; and whan the knyght
saw the horse he prayde the Kynge to gyff hym the horse, "for I
have folowed this queste thys twelvemonthe, and othir I shall

fol.17r

A dreme of Arthur

fol.17v

---

3. I.e., she was Arthur's half sister on the side of their mother, Igrayne. Mordred, the child
of this incestuous union between Arthur and King Lott's wife, Morgawse, will be instrumental in Arthur's ultimate downfall; see p. 679.
4. *be fyne force*: through superior strength.
5. Became absorbed.
6. Nearly two miles back.
7. I.e., it killed.

encheve hym othir blede of the beste bloode in my body." (Whos name was Kynge 𝕻𝖊𝖑𝖑𝖞𝖓𝖔𝖗 that[8] tyme folowed the Questynge Beste[9]—and afftir hys dethe Sir 𝕻𝖆𝖑𝖔𝖒𝖞𝖉𝖊𝖘 folowed hit.) "Sir knyght," seyd the Kynge, "leve that queste and suffir me to have hit, and I woll folowe hit anothir twelvemonthe." [20]

¶"A, foole!" seyde the kynge unto 𝕬𝖗𝖙𝖍𝖚𝖗𝖊, "hit ys in vayne thy desire, for hit shall never be encheved but by me other by my nexte[1] kynne." And therewithe he sterte unto the Kyngis horse and mownted into the sadyl, and seyde, "Gramercy—for this horse ys myne owne!"

¶"Well," seyde the Kynge, "thou mayste take myne horse by force, but, and I myght preve hit, I wolde weete whether thou were bettir[2] worthy to have hym or I."

¶Whan the kynge[3] herde hym sey so, he seyde, "Seke me here whan thou wolte, and here, nye thys welle, thou shalte fynde me," [and soo passyd on his weye. Thenne the Kyng sat in a study,] and bade hys men fecche another horse as faste as they myght.

¶Ryght so com by hym 𝕸𝖊𝖗𝖑𝖞𝖔𝖓, lyke[4] a chylde of fourtene yere of ayge, and salewed the Kynge and asked hym whye he was so pensyff. "I may well be pensiff," seyde the Kynge, "for I have sene the mervaylist syght that ever I saw."

¶"That know I well," seyde 𝕸𝖊𝖗𝖑𝖞𝖔𝖓, "as welle as thyselff, and of all thy thoughtes. But thou arte a foole to take thought for hit that woll nat amende the.[5]

¶"Also I know what thou arte, and who was thy fadir, and of whom thou were begotyn: for Kynge Uther was thy fadir and begate the on 𝕴𝖌𝖗𝖆𝖞𝖓𝖊." "That ys false!" seyde Kynge 𝕬𝖗𝖙𝖍𝖚𝖗𝖊. "How sholdist thou know hit? For thou arte nat so olde of yerys to know my fadir." "Yes, seyde 𝕸𝖊𝖗𝖑𝖞𝖔𝖓, "I know hit bettir than ye or ony man lyvynge." "I woll nat beleve the," seyde 𝕬𝖗𝖙𝖍𝖚𝖗𝖊, and was wrothe with the chylde.

¶So departed 𝕸𝖊𝖗𝖑𝖞𝖔𝖓, and com ayen in the lyknesse of an olde man of foure score yere of ayge—whereof the Kynge was passynge glad, for he semed to be ryght wyse.

¶Than seyde the olde man, "Why ar ye so sad?" "I may well be sad," seyde 𝕬𝖗𝖙𝖍𝖚𝖗𝖊, "for many thynges. For ryght now there was a

---

8. I.e., who that.
9. Malory's choice of name for this creature is ingeniously multivalent and enhances its enigmatic staus; the name invokes not only the sound of hounds' baying made by the beast but also the beast's involvement in a knight's quest, a quest of rather vague origin and motivation and one that we are told Pellynor will not achieve (likewise, Palomydes's later taking up of the quest is seemingly arbitrary and remains unresolved; see p. 293). There is also the suggestion that the beast is on its own quest, whatever that may be. Perhaps in both circumstances we are to be reminded that subjectively the quest and questor cannot really be dissociated and that the relationship can exist without a terminal purpose. In the French, by contrast, the name *Beste Glatissant* refers only to the sound made by the creature, and the knight who pursues it has a determinant mission: a legend claims that the best knight of his bloodline will kill the beast, and he seeks to know if he is that knight.
1. I.e., next of.
2. I.e., more.
3. I.e., Pellynor.
4. I.e., disguised as.
5. To concern yourself with that which cannot help you.

chylde here, and tolde me many thynges that me[6] semythe he sholde nat knowe, for he was nat of ayge to know my fadir."

¶"Yes," seyde the olde man, "the chylde tolde you trouthe, and more he wolde a tolde you and[7] ye wolde a suffirde hym:

¶"But ye have done a thynge late that God ys displesed with you, for ye have lyene by youre syster and on hir ye have gotyn a childe that shall destroy you and all the knyghtes of youre realme."

¶"What ar ye," seyde Arthure, "that telle me thys tydyngis?" "Sir, I am Merlion, and I was he in the chyldis lycknes." "A," seyde the Kynge, "ye ar a mervaylous man. But I mervayle muche of thy wordis, that I mon dye in batayle." "Mervayle nat," seyde Merlion, "for hit ys Goddis wylle that youre body sholde be punysshed for your fowle dedis. But I ought ever to be hevy," seyde Merlion, "for I shall dye a shamefull dethe, to be putte in the erthe quycke; and ye shall dey a worshipfull dethe."

And as they talked thus, com one with the Kyngis horse; and so the Kynge mownted on hys horse, and Merlion on anothir, and so rode unto Carlyon. And anone the Kynge askyd Ector and Ulphuns how he was begotyn, and they tolde hym how Kynge Uther was hys fadir, and Quene Igrayne hys modir—"So Merlion tolde me. I woll that my modir be sente for, that I myght speke with hir; and if she sey so hirselff, than woll I beleve hit."

So in all haste the quene was sente for, and she brought with hir Morgan le Fay, hir doughter, that was a fayre lady as ony myght be; and the Kynge welcommed Igrayne in the beste maner. Ryght so com in Ulphuns, and seyde opynly that the Kynge and all myght hyre that were fested[8] that day, "Ye ar the falsyst lady of the worlde, and the moste traytoures unto the Kynges person."

¶"Beware," seyde Kynge Arthure, "what thou seyste; thou spekiste a grete worde." "Sir, I am well ware," seyde Ulphuns, "what I speke, and here ys my gloove[9] to preve hit uppon ony man that woll sey the contrary, that thys Quene Igrayne ys the causer of youre grete damage and of youre grete warre; for and she wolde have uttirde hit in the lyff of Uther, of the birth of you, and how ye were begotyn, than had ye never had the mortall warrys that ye have had. For the moste party of your barownes of youre realme knewe never whos sonne ye were, ne of whom ye were begotyn. And she that bare you of hir body sholde have made hit knowyn opynly, in excusynge of hir worship and youres, and in lyke wyse to all the realme. Wherefore I preve hir false to God and to you and to all youre realme. And who woll sey the contrary, I woll preve hit on hys body."[1]

¶Than spake Igrayne and seyde, "I am a woman and I may nat fyght; but rather than I sholde be dishonoured, there wolde som

---

6. I.e., to me.
7. I.e., if.
8. *Opynly that*: openly so that. *Were fested*: i.e., sitting at the feast.
9. A glove, or gauntlet, was traditionally thrown down as a sign of a grave challenge (cf n. 7, p. 390).
1. *I woll preve hit on hys body*: i.e., I will prove it through trial by combat.

good man take my quarell.[2] But," thus she seyde, "Merlion knowith   fol.18v
well—and ye, Sir Ulphuns—how Kynge Uther com to me into the
castell of Tyntagyl in the lyknes of my lorde, that was dede three
owres tofore, and there begate a chylde that nyght uppon me; and
aftir the thirtenth day Kynge Uther wedded me. And by his com-   5
maundemente—

℔"Whan the chylde was borne hit was delyvirde unto Merlion
and fostred by hym. And so I saw the childe never aftir, nothir
wote nat what ys hys name—for I knew hym never yette." Than
Ulphuns seyde unto Merlion, "Ye ar, than, more to blame than the   10
queene."

℔"Sir, well I wote I bare a chylde be my lorde Kynge Uther, but
I wote never where he ys becom."[3]

℔Than the Kynge toke Merlion by the honde, seyng thys wordis:
"Ys this my modir?" "Forsothe, sir, yee." And therewith com in Sir   15
Ector, and bare wytnes how he fostred hym by Kynge Uthers com-
maundemente. And therewith Kyng Arthure toke his modir Quene
Igrayne in hys armys and kyssed her, and eythir wepte uppon other.
Than the Kynge lete make a feste that lasted eyght dayes.

So on a day there com into the courte a squyre on horsebacke   20
ledynge a knyght tofore hym, wounded to the deth, and tolde how
there was a knyght in the foreste that had rered up a pavylon by a
welle, "that hath slayne my mayster, a good knyght—hys name was
Myles—wherefore I besech you that my maystir may be buryed,
and that som knyght may revenge my maystirs dethe." Than the   25
noyse[4] was grete of that knyghtes dethe in the courte, and every
man seyde hys advyce.

℔Than com Gryfflet that was but a squyre, and he was but yonge
of ayge. So he besought the Kynge for all hys servyse that he had
done hym to gyff hym the order of knyghthoode. "Thou arte but   [22]   30
yonge and tendir of ayge," seyd Kynge Arthure, "for to take so hyghe
an order uppon you." "Sir," seyde Gryfflet, "I beseche you to make
me knyght."

℔"Sir," seyde Merlion, "hit were pité to lose Gryfflet, for he woll
be a passynge good man whan he ys of ayge, and he shall abyde   35
with you the terme of hys lyff. And if he aventure his body with
yondir knyght at the fountayne, hit ys in grete perell[5] if ever he
com agayne, for he ys one of the beste knyghtes of the worlde and
the strengyst man of armys."

℔"Well, seyde Arthure, "at thyne owne desire thou shalt be made   40
knyght."

℔"Now, seyde Arthure unto Gryfflet, "sith I have made the[6]
knyght, thou muste gyff me a gyffte."

℔"What ye woll," seyde Gryfflet. "Thou[7] shalt promyse me by thy   fol.19r
feyth of thy body, whan thou haste justed with that knyght at the   45

2. Some good man would take up my cause.
3. Igrayne is speaking. *Where he ys becom:* what has become of him.
4. I.e., scandal.
5. *Hit ys in grete perell:* it is very doubtful.
6. thee.
7. Arthur is speaking.

fountayne, whether hit falle ye be on horsebak othir on foote, that ryght so ye shall com agayne unto me withoute makynge ony more debate."

¶"I woll promyse you," seyde Gryfflet, "as youre desire ys." Than toke Gryfflet hys horse in grete haste and dressed hys shelde and toke a spere in hys honde, and so he rode a grete walop tylle he com to the fountayne. And thereby he saw a ryche pavilion, and thereby undir a cloth stood an horse well sadeled and brydyled, and on a tre hynge a shelde of dyvers coloures, and a grete spere thereby. Than Gryfflet smote on the shylde with the butte of hys spere, that the shylde felle downe.

¶With that the knyght com oute of the pavilion and seyde, "Fayre knyght, why smote ye downe my shylde?" "Sir, for I wolde juste with you," seyde Gryfflet. "Sir, hit ys bettir ye do nat," seyde the kynge, "for ye ar but yonge and late made knyght, and youre myght ys nat to⁸ myne."

¶"As for that," seyde Gryfflet, "I woll jouste with you." "That ys me loth," seyde the knyght, "but sitthyn I muste nedis, I woll dresse me thereto:

¶"Of whens be ye?" seyde the knyght. "Sir, I am of Kynge Arthurs courte." So the two knyghtes ran togydir, that Gryffletis spere all to-shevirde. And therewithall he smote Gryfflet thorow the shelde and the lyffte syde, and brake the spere, that the truncheon stake in hys body, and horse and man felle downe to the erthe.

¶Whan the knyght saw hym ly so on the grounde, he alyght, and was passyng hevy, for he wente he had slayne hym. And than he unlaced hys helme and gate hym wynde;⁹ and so, with the truncheon, he sette hym on his horse and gate hym wynde, and so betoke hym to God and seyde he had a myghty herte, and seyde if he myght lyve, he wolde preve a passyng good knyght. And so rode forthe Sir Gryfflet unto the courte, whereof passyng grete dole was made for hym. But thorow good lechis he was heled and saved.

Ryght¹ so com into the courte twelve knyghtes that were aged men, whiche com frome the Emperoure of Rome. And they asked of Arthure trwage for hys realme, othir ellis the Emperour wolde destroy hym and all hys londe. "Well," seyde Kynge Arthure, "ye ar messyngers, therefore ye may sey what ye woll—othir ellis ye sholde dye therefore—

¶"But thys ys myne answere: I owghe the Emperour no trewage, nother none woll I yelde hym, but on a fayre fylde I shall yelde hym my 'trwage'—that shall be with a sherpe spere othir ellis with a sherpe swerde—and that shall nat be longe, be my fadirs soule

[23]

fol.19v

---

8. *Nat to:* not equal to.

9. Let him (Gryfflet) have some air.

1. From here to *an evyll tyme com they* (in the following paragraph), Malory is following his source, with a brief account of events that begin Arthur's Roman war, a story that Malory later relates at length in his *Noble Tale Betwyxt Kynge Arthure and Lucius the Emperour of Rome*. There Malory starts over again with the visit of the emperor's messengers, but the details have changed materially (see pp. 113 ff.). An obvious implication of this difference is that Malory's plans for his work changed as he continued to write and that he forgot or did not have time to correct traces of earlier intentions (cf. n. 9, p. 39).

Uther!"[2] And therewith the messyngers departed passyngly wrothe, and Kynge Arthure as[3] wrothe; for in an evyll tyme com they. But the Kynge was passyngly wrothe for the hurte of Sir Gryfflet, and so he commaunded a prevy man of hys chambir that, or hit were day, his beste horse and armoure, "and all that longith to my person, be withoute[4] the cité or tomorow day." 5

⁋Ryght so he mette with his man and his horse, and so mownted up, and dressed his shelde and toke hys spere, and bade hys chambirlayne tary there tylle he com agayne. And so Arthure rode a soffte pace tyll hit was day. And than was he ware of thre chorlys chasyng Merlion, and wolde have slayne hym. 10

⁋Than the Kynge rode unto them, and bade hem, "Fle, chorlis!" Than they fered sore whan they sawe a knyght com, and fledde. "A, Merlion," seyde Arthure, "here haddist thou be slayne for[5] all thy crafftis, had nat I bene." "Nay," seyde Merlyon, "nat so: for I cowde a saved myselffe and I had wolde.[6] But thou arte more nere thy deth than I am, for thou goste to thy dethe-warde[7]—and God be nat thy frende." So as they wente thus talkynge, they com to the fountayne and the ryche pavilion there by hit. Than Kynge Arthure was ware where sate a knyght armed in a chayre. 15

20

⁋"Sir knyght," seyde Arthure, "for what cause abydist thou here, that there may no knyght ryde thys way but yf he juste with the? I rede the to leve that custom."

⁋"Thys custom," seyde the knyght, "have I used and woll use magré who seyth nay. And who that ys agreved with my custum lette hym amende hit." "That shall I amende," seyde Arthure. "And I shall defende the," seyde the knyght. 25

⁋And anone he toke hys horse, and dressed hys shelde and toke a grete spere in hys honde, and they com togydir so harde that eythir smote other in mydde the shyldis, that all to-shevird theire speris. 30

⁋Therewith anone Arthure pulled oute his swerde. "Nay, nat so," seyde the knyght, "hit ys bettir that we twayne renne more togydirs with sherpe sperys." "I woll well," seyde Arthure, "and I had ony mo sperys here." "I have inow," seyde the knyght. So there com a squyre and brought forthe two sperys, and Arthure chose one and he another. So they spurred theire horsis and com togydir with all theire myghtes, that eyther brake their sperys to[8] their hondis. Than Arthure sette honde on his swerde. 35

fol.20r

"Nay," seyde the knyght, "ye shall do bettir. Ye ar a passyng good juster as ever Y mette withall, and onys for the hyghe order of knyghthode lette us jouste agayne." "I assente me," seyde Arthure. And anone there was brought forth two grete sperys, and anone 40

2. *Be my fadirs soule Uther:* (I swear) by the soul of my father, Uther.
3. I.e., was as.
4. I.e., waiting outside.
5. I.e., despite.
6. *And I had wolde:* if I had wished it.
7. Toward your death.
8. I.e., up to.

every[9] knyght gate a spere; and therewith they ran togiders, that Arthures spere all to-shevirde. But this other knyght smote hym so harde in myddis the shelde that horse and man felle to the erthe. And therewith Arthure was egir, and pulde oute hys swerde, and seyde, "I woll assay the,[1] sir knyght, on foote—for I have loste the honoure on horsebacke," seyde the Kynge.

¶"Sir, I woll be on horsebacke stylle to assay the."[2] Than was Arthure wrothe, and dressed his shelde towarde hym with his swerde drawyn.

¶Whan the knyght saw that, he alyght, for hym thought no worship to have a knyght at such avayle, he to be on horsebacke and hys adversary on foote; and so he alyght and dressed his shelde unto Arthure. And there began a stronge batayle with many grete strokis, and so they hew with hir swerdis that the cantels flowe unto the feldys, and muche bloode they bledde bothe, that all the place there as they fought was ovirbledde with bloode. And thus they fought longe and rested them. And than they wente to the batayle agayne, and so hurteled togydirs lyke too rammes, that aythir felle to the erthe. So at the laste they smote togyders, that bothe hir swerdis mette evyn togyders. But Kynge Arthurs swerde brake in two pecis, wherefore he was hevy.

¶Than seyde the knyght unto Arthure, "Thou arte in my daungere, whethir me lyste[3] to save the or sle the; and but thou yelde the to me as overcom and recreaunte, thou shalt dey."

¶"As for that," seyde Kynge Arthure, "dethe ys wellcom to me whan hit commyth. But to yelde me unto the, I woll nat." And therewithall the Kynge lepte unto Kynge Pellynore, and toke hym by the myddyll, and overthrew hym, and raced of hys helme. So whan the knyght felte that, he was adradde, for he was a passynge bygge man of myght; and so forthewith he wrothe Arthure undir hym and raced of hys helme, and wolde have smytten off hys hede.

¶And therewithall com Merlion and seyde, "Knyght, holde thy honde, for and thou sle that knyght thou puttyst thys realme in the gretteste damage that evir was realme, for thys knyght ys a man of more worshyp than thou wotist off."

¶"Why, what ys he?" seyde the knyght. "For hit ys Kynge Arthure," seyde Merlyon. Than wolde he have slayne hym for drede of hys wratthe, and so he lyffte up hys swerde. And therewith Merlion caste an inchauntemente on the knyght, that he felle to the erthe in a grete slepe.

¶Than Merlion toke up Kynge Arthure and rode forthe on the knyghtes horse.

¶"Alas," seyde Arthure, "what hast thou do, Merlion? Hast thou slayne thys good knyght by thy craufftis? For there lyvith nat so worshipfull a knyght as he was—for I had levir than the stynte of

[24]   fol.20v

9. I.e., each.
1. Thee.
2. Thee.
3. *Me lyste*: it pleases me.

my londe a yere that he were on lyve."[4] "Care ye nat," seyde Merlion, "for he ys holer than ye; he ys but on slepe and woll awake
within thys owre. I tolde you," seyde Merlyon, "what a knyght he
was. Now here had ye be slayne had I nat bene:

¶"Also there lyvith nat a bygger knyght than he ys one; and afftir 5
this he shall do you goode servyse. And hys name ys Kynge Pellinore, and he shall have two sonnes that shall be passyng good men
as ony lyvynge. Save one,[5] in thys worlde they shall have no felowis[6]
of prouesse and of good lyvynge, and hir namys shall be Percyvall
and Sir Lamorake of Walis. And he shall telle you the name of 10
youre owne son, begotyn of youre syster, that shall be the destruccion of all thys realme."

¶Ryght so the Kynge and he departed and wente unto an ermy- [25]
tage, and there was a good man and a grete leche. So the ermyte
serched the Kynges woundis and gaff hym good salves. And so the 15
Kyng was there three dayes; and than wer his woundis well
amended, that he myght ryde and goo, and so departed. And as
they rode, Kynge Arthur seyde, "I have no swerde." "No force,"[7]
seyde Merlyon, "hereby ys a swerde that shall be youre, and I may."[8]

So they rode tyll they com to a laake the which was a fayre watir 20
and brode. And in the myddis Arthure was ware of an arme clothed
in whyght samyte, that helde a fayre swerde in that honde. "Lo!"
seyde Merlion, "yondir ys the swerde that I spoke off." So with that
they saw a damesell goynge uppon the laake. ["What damoysel is
that?" said Arthur. "That is the Lady of the Lake,"] seyde Merlion. 25
"There ys a grete roche, and therein ys as fayre a paleyce as ony
on erthe, and rychely besayne. And thys damesel woll com to you
anone, and than speke ye fayre to hir, that she may gyff you that   fol.21r
swerde."

So anone com this damesel to Arthure and salewed hym, and he 30
hir agayne. "Damesell," seyde Arthure, "what swerde ys that yondir
that the arme holdith aboven the watir? I wolde hit were myne, for
I have no swerde." "Sir Arthure," seyde the damesel, "that swerde
ys myne, and if ye woll gyff me a gyffte whan I aske hit you, ye   Here ys a mencion
shall have hit." "Be my feyth," seyde Arthure, "I woll gyff you what   of the Lady of the
gyffte that ye woll aske."   Laake, whan
        sheasked Balyne le
¶"Well," seyde the damesell, "go ye into yondir barge, and rowe   Saveage his hede
youreselffe to the swerde, and take hit and the scawberde with
you. And I woll aske my gyffte whan I se my tyme." So Kyng Arthure
and Merlion alyght and tyed their horsis unto two treys, and so they 40
wente into the barge; and whan they com to the swerde that the
honde hylde, than Kyng Arthure toke hit up by the hondils and bare
hit with hym, and the arme and the honde wente undir the watir.

---

4. *I had levir than the stynte of my londe a yere that he were on lyve*: I would sooner he were
   alive than have a year's worth of revenue from my lands.
5. A couched prediction of the advent of Galahad, who will be chief among the three knights
   in the achievement of the Grail Quest (see pp 582 ff.).
6. I.e., peers
7. That does not matter.
8. *And I may*: if I can cause it to happen.

And so he com unto the londe and rode forthe. And Kyng **Arthure** saw a ryche pavilion. "What signifieth yondir pavilion?"

"Sir, that ys the knyghtes pavilys that ye fought with laste, Sir **Pellynore**; but he ys oute. He ys nat at home, for he hath had ado with a knyght of youres that hyght **Egglame**, and they had foughtyn togyddyr. But at the laste **Egglame** fledde—and ellis he had bene dede—and he hath chaced hym evyn to **Carlion**. And we shall mete with hym anone in the hygheway." "That ys well seyde," seyde **Arthure**. "Now have I a swerde, I woll wage batayle with hym and be avenged on hym."

"Sir," seyde **Merlion**, "nat so; for the knyght ys wery of fyghtynge and chasynge, that ye shall have no worship to have ado with hym. Also, he woll nat lyghtly be macched of[9] one knyght lyvynge; and therefore hit ys my counceile, latte hym passe, for he shall do you good servyse in shorte tyme—and hys sonnes afftir hys dayes. Also, ye shall se that day in shorte space that ye shall be ryght glad to gyff hym youre syster to wedde for hys good servyse. Therefore have nat ado with hym whan ye se hym." "I woll do as ye avise me." Than Kyng **Arthure** loked on the swerde and lyked hit passynge well.

Than seyde **Merlion**, "Whethir lyke ye bettir the swerde othir the scawberde? "I lyke bettir the swerde," seyde **Arthure**. "Ye ar the more unwyse, for the scawberde ys worth ten of the swerde; for whyles ye have the scawberde uppon you, ye shall lose no blood, be ye never so sore wounded.[1] Therefore kepe well the scawberde all-weyes with you."

¶So they rode unto **Carlion**, and by the wey they mette with Kyng **Pellinore**; but **Merlion** had done suche a crauffte unto[2] Kyng Pelli-nore [that **Pellinore**] saw nat Kyng **Arthure**, and so passed by with-oute ony wordis. "I mervayle," seyde **Arthure**, "that the knyght wold nat speke." "Sir, he saw you nat; for had he seyne you, ye had nat lyghtly parted." So they com unto **Carlion**, whereof hys knyghtes were passynge glad.

¶And whan they herde of hys adventures, they mervayled that he wolde joupardé his person so alone. But all men of worship seyde hit was myrry to be under such a chyfftayne that wolde putte hys person in adventure as other poure knyghtis ded.

¶So thys meanewhyle com a messyngere frome Kyng **Royns** of Northe Walls (and kyng he was of all Irelonde and of Iles). And this was hys message, gretynge well Kyng **Arthure** on thys maner of wyse, sayng that Kyng **Royns** had discomfite and overcom eleven kyngis, and every[3] of them dud hym omage. And that was thus to sey: they gaff theire beardes clene flayne off, as much as was bearde[4]—wherefore the messyngere com for Kyng **Arthures** berde.

¶For Kyng **Royns** had purfilde a mantel with Kyngs berdis, and there lacked one place of the mantel; wherefore he sente for hys

9. I.e., by.
1. No matter how sorely wounded you are.
2. *Done suche a crauffte unto:* enchanted.
3. I.e., each.
4. *As much as was bearde:* for as much skin as had beard.

bearde—othir ellis he wolde entir into his londis and brenne and sle, and nevir leve tylle he hathe the hede and the bearde, bothe.

¶"Well," seyde Arthure, "thou haste seyde thy message, the whych ys the moste orgulus and lewdiste message that evir man had i-sente unto a kyng. Also, thou mayste se my bearde ys full yonge yet to make off a purphile!— 5

¶"But telle thou thy kyng thus: that I owghe hym none homage, ne none of myne elders; but, or hit be longe to,[5] he shall do me omage on bothe his knees—other ellis he shall lese hys hede, by the fayth of my body. For thys ys the moste shamefullyste message 10 that ever Y herde speke off. I have aspyed thy kyng never yette mette with worshipfull man. But telle hym I woll have hys hede withoute[6] he do me omage." Than thys messyngere departed.

"Now, ys there ony here that knowyth Kyng Royns?" Than answerde a knyght that hyght Naram: "Sir, I know the kyng well; he 15 ys a passynge good man of hys body as fewe bene lyvynge, and a passynge proude man. And, sir, doute ye nat he woll make on you a myghty puyssaunce."[7]

¶"Well," seyde Arthure, "I shall ordayne for hym[8] in shorte tyme." fol.22r

¶Than[9] Kyng Arthure lette sende for all the children that were [27] 20 borne in May Day, begotyn of lordis and borne of ladyes; for Merlyon tolde Kyng Arthure that he that sholde[1] destroy hym and all the londe sholde be borne on May Day. Wherefore he sente for hem all, in[2] payne of dethe, and so there were founde many lordis sonnys and many knyghtes sonnes, and all were sente unto the Kyng— 25 and so was Mordred sente by Kyng Lottis wyff. And all were putte in a shyppe to the se; and som were foure wekis olde and som lesse.[3] And so by fortune the shyppe drove unto a castelle, and was all to-ryven and destroyed the moste party, save that Mordred was cast up; and a good man founde hym and fostird hym tylle he 30 was fourtene yere of age, and than brought hym to the courte—as hit rehersith aftirward and towarde the ende of the *Morte Arthure*.[4]

---

5. *Or hit be longe to:* before long.
6. *Mette with:* in the company of. *Withoute:* i.e., unless.
7. Bring a great power to bear against you.
8. Make commandments concerning him.
9. From here to the end of the paragraph, Malory's account of the whole episode differs substantially from that in his known source for most of the rest of this section—the *Suite de Merlin*. There Arthur has the children rounded up with the intention of killing them but spares them on the advice of a monitory dream. Nor is mention made of Mordred's subsequently being raised at Arthur's court. On the basis of the latter detail, the unfulfilled promise to relate an episode from *Morte Arthure*, and some compelling traces of alliteration, P. J. C. Field has suggested that Malory was influenced by an epiosde from a now-lost version of the English alliterative *Morte Arthure*, a known source for other parts of his work. In that text, Arthur is on the whole rendered as more potentially tyrannical than he usually is in Malory. An implication of this possible influence is that, as with the unfulfilled promise, Malory may have had intentions for the direction his work was to take which he either forgot or abandoned. For evidence of other such intentions later overridden, see n. 1, p. 34 and n. 2, p. 56.
1. I.e., would.
2. I.e., on.
3. Clearly not all the boys were born on the same day; Malory overlooks a detail in his source that says that Arthur seized those born throughout the month of May.
4. Malory does not in fact go on to relate this story anywhere else; the reference to *Morte Arthure* may therefore be to one of his sources, the alliterative *Morte Arthure,* which does mention Mordred's youth at Arthur's court (about the alliterative *Morte,* see n. †, p. 714).

So, many lordys and barownes of thys realme were displeased for[5] hir children were so loste; and many putte the wyght on **Merlion** more than on Arthure. So, what for drede and for love, they helde their pece.

But whan the messynger com to the Kyng **Royns**, than was he woode oute of mesure, and purveyde hym for a grete oste,[6] as hit rehersith aftir in the booke **of Balyne le Saveage** that folowith nexte aftir: that was the adventure how **Balyne** gate the swerde.

The Tale of Balyn and Balan[1]

Afftir the deth of **Uther** regned **Arthure**, hys son, which had grete warre in hys dayes for to gete all Inglonde into hys honde— for there were many kyngis within the realme of Inglonde and of Scotlonde, Walys, and Cornuwayle. So hit befelle on a tyme whan Kynge **Arthure** was at London, there com a knyght and tolde the Kynge tydyngis how the Kynge **Royns** of Northe Walis had rered a grete numbir of peple and were entred in the londe and brente and slew the Kyngis trew lyege people. "Iff thys be trew," seyde **Arthure**, "hit were grete shame unto myne astate but[2] that he were myghtyly withstonde."

¶ "Hit ys trouthe," seyde the knyght, "for I saw the oste myselff." "Well," seyde the Kynge, "I shall ordayne to wythstonde hys malice." Than the Kynge lette make a cry[3] that all the lordis, knyghtes, and jantilmen of armys sholde draw unto the castell called **Camelot** in tho dayes, and there the Kynge wolde lette make a councelle-generall and a grete justis. So whan the Kynge was com thidir with all his baronage and logged as they semed beste, also there was com [a damoisel] the which was sente frome the grete Lady **Lyle of Avilion.** And whan she com before Kynge **Arthure**, she tolde fro whens she com and how she was sente on message unto hym for thys causis. Than she lette hir mantell falle that was rychely furred; and than was she gurde with a noble swerde, whereof the Kynge had mervayle and seyde, "Damesel, for what cause ar ye gurte with that swerde? Hit besemyth you nought."[4]

"Now shall I telle you," seyde the damesell. "Thys swerde that I am gurte withall doth me grete sorow and comberaunce, for I may nat be delyverde of thys swerde but by a knyght, and he muste be a passynge good man of hys hondys and of hys dedis, and withoute velony other[5] trechory, and withoute treson. And if I may fynde

[II.1]

15

20

25

fol.22v

30

35

40

---

5. I.e., that.
6. Provided himself with a great army.
1. The title is taken editorially from the last sentence of this subsection (see p. 61). In the Winchester MS, only the two-line-high initial "A," without any blank line-space separation, marks the beginning of the tale. Malory's pricipal source for this section is the French *Suite de Merlin;* for illustrative selections, see p. 709.
2. I.e., unless.
3. I.e., proclamation.
4. *Besemyth you nought:* does not befit you.
5. *Delyverde:* i.e., relieved. *Other:* i.e., or.

such a knyght that hath all thes vertues, he may draw oute thys swerde oute of the sheethe. For I have bene at Kynge Royns, for hit was tolde me there were passyng good knyghtes; and he and all his knyghtes hath assayde and none can spede."

¶"Thys ys a grete mervayle," seyde Arthure. "If thys be sothe, I woll assay myselffe to draw oute the swerde, nat presumynge myselff that I am the beste knyght; but I woll begynne to draw youre swerde in gyvyng an insample to all the barownes, that they shall assay everych one aftir othir whan I have assayde." Than Arthure toke the swerde by the sheethe and gurdil and pulled at hit egirly, but the swerde wolde nat oute.[6]

¶"Sir," seyd the damesell, "ye nede nat for to pulle halffe so sore, for he that shall pulle hit oute shall do hit with litill myght." "Ye sey well," seyde Arthure. "Now assay ye, all my barownes." "But beware ye be nat defoyled with shame, trechory, nother gyle, for than hit woll nat avayle," seyde the damesel, "for he muste be a clene knyght withoute vylony and of jantill strene of fadir syde and of modir syde." The moste parte of all the barownes of the Rounde Table that were there at that tyme assayde all be rew,[7] but there mýght none spede.

¶Wherefore the damesel made grete sorow oute of mesure, and seyd, "Alas! I wente in this courte had bene the beste knyghtes of the worlde withoute trechory other treson." "Be[8] my faythe," seyde Arthure, "here ar good knyghtes as I deme as ony be in the worlde, but their grace ys nat to helpe you, wherefore I am sore displeased."

Than hit befelle so that tyme there was a poore knyght with Kynge Arthure that had bene presonere with hym half a yere for sleyng of a knyght which was cosyne unto Kynge Arthure. And the name of thys knyght was called Balyne, and by good meanys of the barownes he was delyverde oute of preson, for he was a good man named of his body,[9] and he was borne in Northehumbirlonde. And so he wente pryvaly into the courte, and saw thys adventure, whereoff hit reysed his herte, and wolde assayde as othir knyghtes ded—but for[1] he was poore and poorly arayde, he put hymselff nat far in prees.[2] But in hys herte he was fully assured to do as well, if hys grace happed hym, as ony knyght that there was.

And as the damesell toke her leve of Arthure and of all the bar-ownes, so departynge, thys knyght Balyn called unto her and seyde, "Damesell, I pray you of youre curteysy suffir me as well to assay as thes other lordis. Thoughe that I be pourely arayed yet in my herte me[3] semyth I am fully assured as som of thes other, and me semyth in myne herte to spede ryght welle."

¶Thys damesell than behelde thys poure knyght, and saw he was a lyckly man; but for hys poure araymente she thought he

fol.23r

[2]

---

6. I.e., come out.
7. *All be rew:* in turn, in succession.
8. I.e., by.
9. *A good man named of his body:* a man reputed for his physical prowess.
1. *Wolde:* i.e., he would have. *But for:* i.e., because.
2. *Put hymselff nat far in prees:* did not push himself forward.
3. I.e., to me.

sholde nat be of no worship[4] withoute vylony or trechory. And than
she seyde unto that knyght, "Sir, hit nedith nat you[5] to put me to
no more payne, for hit semyth nat you to spede there as all thes
othir knyghtes have fayled."

¶"A, fayre damesell!" seyde Balyn, "worthynes and good tacchis   5
and also good dedis is nat only in araymente, but manhode and
worship [ys hyd] within a mannes person, and many a worshipfull
knyght ys nat knowyn unto all peple—and therefore worship and
hardynesse ys nat in araymente."

¶"Be God," seyde the damesell, "ye sey soth. Therefore ye shall   10
assay to do what ye may."

¶Than Balyn toke the swerde by the gurdyll and shethe, and
drew hit oute easyly; and whan he loked on the swerde hit pleased
hym muche. Than had the Kynge and all the barownes grete mervayle that Balyne had done that aventure. Many knyghtes had grete   15
despite at hym.

"Sertes," seyde the damesell, "thys ys a passynge good knyght
and the beste that ever Y founde, and moste of worship, withoute
treson, trechory, or felony—and many mervayles shall he do:

¶"Now, jantyll and curtayse knyght, geff me the swerde agayne."   fol.23v   20
"Nay!" seyde Balyne, "for thys swerde woll I kepe, but[6] hit be takyn
fro me with force."

¶"Well," seyde the damesell, "ye ar nat wyse to kepe the swerde
fro me, for ye shall sle with that swerde the beste frende that ye
have, and the man that ye moste love in the worlde—and that   25
swerde shall be youre destruccion." "I shall take the aventure,"
seyde Balyn, "that God woll ordayne for me:

¶"But the swerde ye shall nat have at thys tyme, by the feythe
of my body." "Ye shall repente hit within shorte tyme," seyde the
damesell, "for I wolde have the swerde more for youre avauntage   30
than for myne; for I am passynge hevy for youre sake, for and ye
woll nat leve that swerde, hit shall be youre destruccion—and that
ys grete pité." So with that departed the damesell, and grete sorow
she made.

¶And anone afftir, Balyn sente for hys horse and armoure, and   35
so wolde departe frome the courte, and toke his leve of Kynge
Arthure. "Nay," seyde the Kynge, "I suppose ye woll nat departe
so lyghtly from thys felyship. I suppose that ye ar displesyd that I
have shewed you unkyndnesse. But blame me the lesse, for I was
mysseinfourmed ayenste you; but I wente ye had nat bene such a   40
knyght as ye ar of worship and prouesse. And if ye woll abyde in
thys courte amonge my felyship, I shall so avaunce you as ye shall
be pleased." "God thanke youre hyghnesse," seyde Balyne. "Youre
bounté may no man prayse halff unto the valew,[7] butt at thys tyme
I muste nedis[8] departe, besechynge you allway of youre good   45
grace."

4. He would not be of any standing.
5. *Hit nedith nat you:* you need not.
6. I.e., unless.
7. *Youre bounté may no man prayse halff unto the valew:* no man can estimate even half of
the value of your generosity.
8. Must.

❡"Truly," seyde the Kynge, "I am ryght wroth of youre departynge. But I pray you, fayre knyght, that ye tarry nat longe frome
me, and ye shall be ryght wellcom unto me and to my barownes—
and I shall amende all mysse that I have done agaynste you." "God
thanke youre good grace," seyde **Balyn**, and therewith made hym   5
redy to departe. Than the moste party of the knyghtes of the
Rounde Table seyde that **Balyne** dud nat this adventure only by
myght, but by wycchecrauffte.

❡So the meanewhyle that thys knyght was makynge hym redy   [3]
to departe, there com into the courte the Lady of the Laake, and   10
she com on horsebacke rychely beseyne, and salewed Kynge **Arthure**
and there asked hym⁹ a gyffte that he promysed her whan she gaff
hym the swerde. "That ys sothe," seyde **Arthure**, "a gyffte I promysed   fol.24r
you, but I have forgotyn the name of my swerde that ye gaff me."
"The name of hit," seyde the lady, "ys **Excalibur**—that ys as muche   15
to sey as 'Kutte Stele.' "¹

❡"Ye sey well," seyde the Kynge. "Aske what ye woll and ye shall
have hit, and² hit lye in my power to gyff hit."

❡"Well," seyde thys lady, "than I aske the hede of thys knyght
that hath wonne the swerde, othir ellis the damesels hede that   20
brought hit. I take no force though³ I have both theire hedis, for
he slew my brothir, a good knyght and a trew; and that jantillwoman was causer of my fadirs deth." "Truly," seyde Kynge **Arthure**,
"I may nat graunte you nother of theire hedys with my worship;
therefore aske what ye woll els,⁴ and I shall fulfille youre desire."   25
"I woll aske none other thynge," seyde the lady.

❡So whan **Balyn** was redy to departe, he saw the Lady of the
Lake, which by hir meanys had slayne hys modir; and he had
sought hir three yere before. And whan hit was tolde⁵ hym how
she had asked hys hede of Kynge **Arthure**, he wente to hir streyght   *The dethe of the* 30
and seyde, "Evyll be ye founde; ye wolde have myne hede, and   *Lady of the Lake*
therefore ye shall loose youres." And with hys swerde lyghtly he
smote of hyr hede before Kynge **Arthure**.

"Alas, for shame!" seyde the Kynge. "Why have ye do so? Ye have
shamed me and all my courte, for thys lady was a lady that I was   35
much beholdynge to, and hyder she com undir my sauffconduyghte. Therefore I shall never forgyff you that trespasse."

❡"Sir," seyde **Balyne**, "me forthynkith of⁶ youre displeasure, for
this same lady was the untrwyste lady lyvynge, and by inchauntement and by sorcery she hath bene the destroyer of many good   40
knyghtes—and she was causer that my modir was brente, thorow
hir falsehode and trechory."

❡"For what cause soever ye had," seyde **Arthure**, "ye sholde have
forborne in my presence. Therefore, thynke nat the contrary; ye
shall repente hit, for such anothir despite had I nevir in my courte.   45

---

9. I.e., of him.
1. I.e., a sword that can cut through steel.
2. I.e., if.
3. *I take no force though*: I do not mind if.
4. What else you would have.
5. I.e., told to.
6. *Me forthynkith of*: I grieve over.

Therefore, withdraw you oute of my courte in all the haste that ye may." Than Balyn toke up the hede of the lady and bare hit with hym to hys ostry, and there mette with hys squyre, that was sory he had displeased Kynge Arthure; and so they rode forthe oute of towne.

¶"Now," seyde Balyne, "we muste departe; therefore, take thou thys hede and bere hit to my frendis, and telle hem how I have spedde—and telle hem in Northhumbirlonde how my moste foo ys dede. Also telle hem how I am oute of preson, and what adventure befelle me at the getynge of this swerde." "Alas," seyde the squyre, "ye ar gretly to blame for to displease Kynge Arthure." "As for that," seyde Balyne, "I woll hyghe me in all the haste that I may to mete with Kyng Royns and destroy hym, othir ellis to dye therefore. And iff hit may happe me to wynne hym, than woll Kynge Arthure be my good frende." "Sir, where shall I mete with you?" seyde his squyre. "In Kynge Arthurs courte," seyde Balyne. So his squyre and he departed at that tyme. Than Kynge Arthure and all the courte made grete dole and had grete shame of the Lady of the Lake. Than the Kynge buryed hir rychely.

¶So at that tyme there was a knyght, the which was the Kynges son of Irelonde,[7] and hys name was Launceor, the which was an orgulus knyght and accompted hymselff one of the beste of the courte. And he had grete despite at Balyne for the enchevynge of the swerde, that ony sholde be accompted more hardy or more of prouesse; and he asked[8] Kynge Arthure licence to ryde afftir Balyne and to revenge the despite that he had done. "Do youre beste," seyde Arthur. "I am ryght wrothe with Balyne. I wolde he were quytte of the despite that he hath done unto me and my courte." Than thys Launceor wente to his ostré to make hym redy. So in the meanewhyle com Merlyon unto the courte of Kynge Arthure, and anone was tolde hym[9] the adventure of the swerde and the deth of the Lady of the Lake.

¶"Now shall I sey you," seyde Merlion, "thys same damesell that here stondith,[1] that brought the swerde unto youre courte, I shall telle you the cause of hir commynge. She ys the falsist damesell that lyveth—she shall nat sey nay![2] For she hath a brothir, a passyng good knyght of proues, and a full trew man; and thys damesell loved anothir knyght that hylde her as paramoure. And thys good knyght, her brothir, mette with the knyght that helde hir to paramoure, and slew hym by force of hys hondis. And whan thys false damesell undirstoode this, she wente to the Lady Lyle of Avylion and besought hir of helpe[3] to be revenged on hir owne brothir: "And so thys Lady Lyle of Avylion toke hir[4] this swerde that she brought with hir, and tolde there sholde no man pulle hit oute

7. The son of the King of Ireland.
8. I.e., asked of.
9. I.e., to him.
1. The damsel has evidently come back to Arthur's court.
2. I.e., she will not disagree (with me).
3. Asked her help.
4. *Toke hir:* took to her (the damsel).

fol.24v

[4]

[5]   fol. 25r

of the sheethe but yf he be one of the beste knyghtes of thys realme, and he sholde be hardy and full of prouesse—and with that swerde he sholde sle hys brothir. Thys was the cause, dame- sell, that ye com into thys courte—I know hit as well as ye! God wolde ye had nat com here, but ye com never in felyship of wor- shipfful folke for to do good, but allwayes grete harme. And that knyght that hath encheved the swerde shall be destroyed thorow the swerde, for the which woll be grete damage, for there lyvith nat a knyght of more prouesse than he ys. And he shall do unto you, my Lorde **Arthure**, grete honoure and kyndnesse; and hit ys grete pité he shall nat endure but a whyle, for of his strengthe and hardinesse I know hym nat lyvynge hys macche."[5]

So thys knyght of **Irelonde** armed hym at all poyntes and dressed his shylde on hys sholdir and mownted uppon horsebacke and toke hys glayve in hys honde, and rode aftir a[6] grete pace as muche as hys horse myght dryve.[7] And within a litill space on a mowntayne he had a syght of **Balyne**, and with a lowde voice he cryde, "Abyde, knyght! for ells ye shall abyde, whethir ye woll other no.[8] And the shelde that ys tofore you shall nat helpe you," seyde thys Iryshe knyght, "therefore com I affter you!"

❡"Peradventure," seyde **Balyne**, "ye had bene bettir to have holde you at home. For many a man wenyth to put hys enemy to a rebuke, and ofte hit fallith on hymselff. Oute of what courte be ye com fro?" seyde **Balyn**. "I am com frome the courte of Kynge **Arthure**," seyde the knyght of Irelonde, "that am com hydir to revenge the despite ye dud thys day unto Kynge **Arthure** and to his courte."

"Well, seyde **Balyne**, "I se well I muste have ado with you, that[9] me forthynkith that I have greved Kynge **Arthure** or ony of hys courte. And youre quarell ys full symple," seyde **Balyne**, "unto me,[1] for the lady that ys dede dud to me grete damage—and ellis I wolde have bene lothe as ony knyght that lyvith for to sle a lady." "Make you redy," seyde the knyght **Launceor**, "and dresse you unto me, for[2] that one shall abyde in the fylde."

Than they fewtred their spearis in their restis and com togidirs as muche as their horsis myght dryve. And the Irysh knyght smote **Balyn** on the shylde that all wente to shyvers of hys spere.[3] And **Balyne** smote hym agayne[4] thorow the shylde—and the hawbirk perysshed—and so bore hym thorow the body and over the horse crowpen; and anone turned his horse fersely and drew oute hys swerde, and wyst nat that he had slayne hym.

Than[5] he saw hym lye as a dede corse, he loked aboute hym and was ware of a damesel that com rydynge full faste as the horse

fol.25v

How Balyn slew Launceor

[6]

---

5. *I know hym nat lyvynge hys macche:* I know no one living who is his match.
6. I.e., at a.
7. I.e., hasten.
8. *Other no:* or not.
9. I.e., such that.
1. Your argument is insubstantial to me.
2. *Dresse you:* ready yourself. *For:* i.e., so.
3. *All wente to shyvers of hys spere:* his spear completely shattered into splinters.
4. I.e., in return.
5. I.e., Then when.

myght dryve, on a fayre palferey. And whan she aspyed that Launceor was slayne, she made sorow oute of mesure, and seyde, "A,
Balyne! two bodyes thou haste slayne in one herte, and two hertes
in one body, and two soules thou hast loste." And therewith she
toke the swerde frome hir love that lay dede, and felle to the   5
grounde in a swowghe.

And whan she arose, she made grete dole oute of mesure, which
sorow greved Balyn passyngly sore. And he wente unto hir for to
have tane the swerde oute of hir honde; but she helde hit so faste
he myght nat take hit oute of hir honde but yf⁶ he sholde have hurt   10
hir—and suddeynly she sette the pomell to the grounde, and rove
hirselff thorowoute the body.

⁋Whan Balyne aspyed hir dedis he was passynge hevy in his
herte and ashamed that so fayre a damesell had destroyed hirselff
for the love of⁷ hys dethe. "Alas!" seyde Balyn, "me repentis sore   15
the dethe of thys knyght for the love of thys damesel, for there was
muche trew love betwyxte hem." And so for sorow he myght no
lenger beholde them, but turned hys horse and loked towarde a
fayre foreste. And than was he ware by hys armys⁸ that there com
rydyng hys brothir Balan. And whan they were mette they put of   20
hyr helmys and kyssed togydirs and wepte for joy and pité.

⁋Than Balan seyde, "Brothir, I litill wende to have mette with
you at thys suddayne adventure, but I am ryght glad of youre delyveraunce of⁹ youre dolerous presonment—for a man tolde me in
the Castell of Foure Stonys that ye were delyverde, and that man   25
had seyne you in the courte of Kynge Arthure; and therefore I com
hydir into thys contrey, for here I supposed to fynde you." And
anone Balyne tolde hys brothir of hys adventure of the swerde and
the deth of the Lady of the Laake, and how Kynge Arthure was
displeased with hym. "Wherefore he sente thys knyght afftir me   fol.26r   30
that lyethe here dede—and the dethe of thys damesell grevith me
sore." "So doth hit me," seyde Balan, "but ye must take the adventure that God woll ordayne you."

"Truly," seyde Balyne, "I am ryght hevy that my lorde Arthure ys
displeased with me, for he ys the moste worshypfullist kynge that   35
regnith now in¹ erthe; and hys love I woll gete—othir ellis I woll
putte my lyff in adventure.² For Kynge Ryons lyeth at the sege of
the Castell Terrable, and thydir woll we draw in all goodly haste
to preve oure worship and prouesse uppon hym." "I woll well,"
seyde Balan, "that ye so do, and I woll ryde with you and put my   40
body in adventure with you, as a brothir ought to do."

⁋"Now go we hense," seyde Balyne, "and well we beth mette."   [7]
The meanewhyle, as they talked, there com a dwarff frome the cité
of Camelot on horsebacke as much³ as he myght, and founde the
dede bodyes, wherefore he made grete dole, and pulled hys heyre   45

6. *But yf*: unless.
7. *For the love of*: on account of.
8. I.e., coat of arms.
9. I.e., from.
1. I.e., on.
2. *In adventure*: at risk.
3. I.e., fast.

for sorowe, and seyde, "Which of two knyghtes have done this dede?" "Whereby askist thou?" seyde Balan. "For I wolde wete!" seyde the dwarff. "Hit was I," seyde Balyn, "that slew this knyght, in my defendaunte; for hyder he com to chase me, and othir I muste sle hym, other[4] he me. And this damesell slew hirself for his love, which repentith me.[5] And for hir sake I shall owghe all women the bettir wylle and servyse all the dayes of my lyff."

"Alas," seyde the dwarff, "thou hast done grete damage unto thyselff. For thys knyght that ys here dede was one of the moste valyauntis men that lyved—and truste well, **Balyne**, the kynne of thys knyght woll chase you thorow the worlde tylle they have slayne you."

"As for that," seyde **Balyne**, "them I fere nat gretely, but I am ryght hevy that I sholde displease my lorde, Kynge **Arthure**, for the deth of thys knyght." So as they talked togydirs there com a Kynge of **Cornuwayle** rydyng, which hyght Kyng **Marke**. And whan he saw thes two bodyes dede, and undirstood howe they were dede, by the two knyghtes abovenseyde, thenne made the kynge grete sorow for the trew love that was betwyxte them, and seyde, "I woll nat departe tyll I have on thys erth made a towmbe." And there he pyght his pavylyons and sought all the contrey to fynde a towmbe, and in a chirch they founde one was[6] fayre and ryche. And than the kyng lette putte hem[7] bothe in the erthe, and leyde the tombe uppon them, and wrote the namys of hem bothe on the tombe— how

HERE LYETH **Launceor**, THE KYNGIS SON OF IRELONDE,
THAT AT HYS OWNE REKEYSTE
WAS SLAYNE BY THE HONDIS OF **Balyne**

—and how

THIS LADY **Columbe**, AND PARAMOUR TO HYM,
SLEW HIRSELFE WITH HYS SWERDE, FOR DOLE AND SOROW.

The meanewhyle as thys was adoynge, in com **Merlion**[8] to Kynge **Marke** and saw all thys doynge.

¶"Here shall be," seyde **Merlion**, "in this same place, the grettist bateyle betwyxte two men that ever was or ever shall be, and the trewyst lovers—and yette none[9] of hem shall slee other." And there Merlion wrote hir namys uppon the tombe with lettirs of golde, that shall feyght in that place, which namys was **Launcelot du Lake and Trystrams**.[1] "Thou art a merveylous man," seyde Kynge **Marke** unto **Merlion**, "that spekist of such mervayles. Thou arte a

fol.26v

How the Lady Columbe slew hirselfe for the deth of Launceor

[8]

4. *Othir . . . other*: either . . . or.
5. *Which repentith me*: about which I am sorry.
6. I.e., that was.
7. Allowed them to be put.
8. On the abbreviation of Merlin's name in the Winchester MS, see n. 4, p. 17.
9. I.e., neither.
1. Merlin here prophecies the combat that occurs at p. 343; the prophecy is not matched in Malory's source.

boysteous man and an unlyckly, to telle of suche dedis. What ys
thy name?" seyde Kynge Marke. "At thys tyme," seyde Merlion, "I
woll nat telle you. But at that tyme Sir Trystrams ys takyn with his
soveraigne lady,[2] than shall ye here and know my name—and at
that tyme ye shall here othir tydynges that shall nat please you.   5

A, Balyne," seyde Merlion, "thou haste done thyselff grete hurte
that[3] thou saved nat thys lady that slew herselff; for thou myghtyst
have saved hir and thou haddist wold."[4]

¶"By the fayth of my body," seyde Balyne, "I myght nat save hir,
for she slewe hirselff suddeynly."   10

"Me repentis hit," seyde Merlion. "Because of the dethe of that
lady, thou shalt stryke a stroke moste dolerous[5] that ever man
stroke—excepte the stroke of Oure Lorde Jesu Cryste[6]—for thou
shalt hurte the trewyst knyght and the man of moste worship that
now lyvith. And thorow that stroke three kyngdomys shall be   15
brought into grete poverté, miseri, and wrecchednesse, twelve[7]
yere—and the knyght shall nat be hole of that wounde many[8]
yerys." Than Merlion toke hys leve.

"Nay!" seyde Balyn, "nat so! For and[9] I wyste thou seyde soth, I
wolde do so perleous a dede that I wolde sle myself to make the[1]   20
a lyer!" Therewith Merlion vanysshed away suddeynly, and than
Balyn and his brother toke their leve of Kynge Marke. "But first,"
seyde the kynge, "telle me youre name." "Sir," seyde Balan, "ye may
se he beryth two swerdis, and thereby ye may calle hym 'the Knyght
with the Two Swerdis.'"   25

And so departed Kynge Marke unto Camelot to Kynge Arthure. And   fol.27r
Balyne toke the way to Kynge Royns; and as they[2] rode togydir, they
mette with Merlion disgysed so that they knew hym nought. "But
whotherward ryde ye?" seyde Merlion. "We had litill ado to telle
you," seyde thes two knyghtes. "But what ys thy name?" seyde   30
Balyn. "At thys tyme," seyde Merlion, "I woll nat telle." "Hit ys an
evyll sygne," seyde the knyghtes, "that thou[3] arte a trew man, that
thou wolt nat telle thy name." "As for that," seyde Merlion, "be[4] as
hit be may. But I can telle you wherefore ye ryde thys way: for to
mete with Kynge Royns. But hit woll nat avayle you withoute[5] ye   35
have my counceyle." "A!" seyde Balyn, "ye ar Merlion. We woll be
ruled by youre counceyle." "Com on," seyde Merlion, "and ye shall
have grete worship—and loke that ye do knyghtly, for ye shall have

2. A prophecy of the time when Trystram will be caught with his secret lover, and Mark's
   wife, Isode (pp. 268 ff.) Again, the prophecy is not matched in Malory's source.
3. I.e., in that, because.
4. *And thou haddist wold*: if you had wished.
5. *A stroke moste dolerous*: a prophecy of the Dolorous Stroke, through which Balyn stabs
   King Pellam and lays waste to three countries (see p. 56).
6. I.e. the piercing of Christ's side at the Crucifixion.
7. I.e., for twelve.
8. I.e., for many.
9. I.e., if.
1. Thee.
2. I.e., Balyn and Balan.
3. I.e., as thou.
4. I.e., be it.
5. I.e., unless.

nede." "As for that, seyde **Balyne**, "dred you nat, for we woll do what we may."

Than there lodged **Merlion** and thes two knyghtes in a woode amonge the levis, besydes the hyghway, and toke of the brydyls of their horsis and putte hem to grasse, and leyde hem downe to reste tyll hit was nyghe mydnyght. Than Merlion bade hem ryse and make hem redy—"for here commyth the kynge nyghehonde, that was stoolyn away frome his oste with a three score[6] horsis of hys beste knyghtes." And twenty of them rode tofore the lorde to warne the Lady de Vaunce that the kynge was commynge—for that nyght Kynge **Royns** sholde have lyen with hir.

"Which[7] ys the kynge?" seyde **Balyn**. "Abyde," seyde **Merlion**, "for here in a strete ye shall mete with hym." And therewith he shewed **Balyn** and hys brothir the kynge. And anone they mette with hym and smote hym downe, and wounded hym freyshly and layde hym to the growunde. And there they slewe on the ryght honde and on the lyffte honde mo than fourty of hys men; and the remanaunte fledde.

¶Than wente they agayne unto Kynge **Royns** and wolde have slayne hym, had he nat yelded hym unto hir grace. Than seyde he thus: "Knyghtes full of prouesse, sle me nat, for be[8] my lyff ye may wynne, and by my dethe litill."[9] "Ye say sothe," seyde the knyghtes, and so leyde hym on an horse littur. So with that **Merlion** vanysshed, and com to Kynge **Arthure** aforehonde and tolde hym how hys moste enemy was takyn and discomfite. "By whom?" seyde Kynge **Arthure**. "By two knyghtes," seyde **Merlion**, "that wolde fayne have youre lordship—and tomorow ye shall know what knyghtis they ar."

So anone aftir com the Knyght with the Two Swerdis and hys brothir, and brought with them Kynge **Royns** of Northe Waalis, and there delyverde hym to the porters, and charged[1] hem with hym; and so they two returned ayen in the dawnyng of the day. Than Kynge **Arthure** com to Kynge **Royns** and seyde, "Sir Kynge, ye ar wellcom. By what adventure com ye hydir?" "Sir," seyde Kynge **Royns**, "I com hyder by an harde adventure."

¶"Who wanne you?" seyde Kynge **Arthure**. "Sir," seyde he, "the Knyght with the Two Swerdis and hys brothir, which ar two mervayles knyghtes of prouesse." "I know hem nat," seyde **Arthure**, "but much am I beholdynge unto them." "A, sir!" seyde **Merlion**, "I shall telle you. Hit ys **Balyn** that encheved the swerde, and his brothir **Balan**, a good knyght—there lyvith nat a bettir[2] of proues, nother of worthynesse. And hit shall be the grettist dole of hym that ever Y knew of knyght,[3] for he shall nat longe endure."

fol.27v

---

6. *A three score:* a group of sixty.
7. I.e., Which one.
8. I.e., by.
9. I.e., you will profit little.
1. I.e., entrusted.
2. I.e., better man.
3. *The grettist dole of hym that ever Y knew of knyght:* the most sorrowful experience I ever knew a knight to have.

¶"Alas," seyde Kynge Arthure, "that ys grete pité, for I am muche beholdynge unto hym, and I have evill deserved hit agayne[4] for hys kyndnesse."

¶"Nay, nay," sede Merlion, "he shall do much more for you— and that shall ye know in haste—but, sir, ar ye purveyde?" seyde Merlion, "for tomorne the oste of Kynge Nero, Kynge Royns brothir, woll sette on you, or none,[5] with a grete oste. And therefore make you redy, for I woll departe frome you."

Than Kynge Arthure made hys oste redy in ten batayles; and Nero was redy in the fylde afore the Castell Terrable with a grete oste—and he had ten batayles with many mo peple than Kynge Arthure had. Than Nero had the vawarde with the moste party of the people. And Merlion com to Kynge Lotte of the Ile of Orkeney, and helde hym with a tale of the prophecy tylle Nero and his peple were destroyed. And there Sir Kay the Senesciall dud passyngely well, that dayes[6] of hys lyff the worship wente never frome hym; and Sir Hervis de Revel, that dud merveylous dedys of armys that day with Arthur; and Kynge Arthure slew that day twenty knyghtes, and maymed fourty.

So at that tyme com in the Knyght with the Two Swerdis and his brothir, but they dud so mervaylously that the Kynge and all the knyghtes mervayled of them; and all they that behelde them seyde they were sente frome hevyn as angels—other[7] devilles frome helle. And Kynge Arthure seyde hymself they were the dough-tyeste knyghtes that ever he sawe, for they gaff such strokes that all men had wondir of hem.

¶So in the meanewhyle com one to Kynge Lotte and tolde hym whyle he tarryed there how Nero was destroyed and slayne with all his oste. "Alas," seyde Kynge Lotte, "I am ashamed; for in[8] my defaute there ys [many a worshipful man slayne—for and[9] we had ben togyders, there hadde ben] none oste undir hevyn were able to have macched us—but thys faytoure with hys prophecy hath mocked me!"

¶All that dud Merlion, for he knew well that, and Kynge Lotte had bene with hys body at the first batayle, Kynge Arthure had be slayne and al hys peple distressed.[1] And well Merlion knew that one of the Kynges sholde be dede that day; and lothe was Merlion that ony[2] of them bothe sholde be slayne, but of the tweyne he had levir Kyng Lotte of Orkeney had be slayne than Arthure. "What ys beste to do?" seyde Kynge Lotte. "Whether ys me bettir[3] to trete with Kynge Arthur othir to fyght? For the gretter party of oure peo-ple ar slayne and distressed."

"Sir," seyde a knyght, "sette ye on Arthure, for they ar wery and

[10]

10

15

20

fol.28r

25

30

35

40

---

4. *Evill deserved hit agayne:* badly repaid.
5. *Or none:* before noon.
6. I.e., all the days.
7. I.e., or.
8. I.e., through.
9. I.e., if.
1. *With hys body:* i.e., in person. *Distressed:* i.e., defeated.
2. I.e., any one.
3. *Whether ys me bettir:* Is it better for me.

forfoughtyn, and we be freyssh." "As for me," seyde Kynge Lott, "I wolde that every knyght wolde do hys parte as I wolde do myne." Than they avaunced baners[4] and smote togydirs and brused hir sperys. And Arthurs knyghtes, with the helpe of the Knyght with Two Swerdys and hys brothir Balan, put Kynge Lotte and hys oste to the warre.[5]

¶But allwayes Kynge Lotte hylde hym ever in the forefronte and dud merveylous dedis of armys; for all his oste was borne up by hys hondys,[6] for he abode all knyghtes. (Alas, he myght nat endure, the whych was grete pité, so worthy a knyght as he was one—that he sholde be overmacched, that of late tyme before he had bene a knyght of Kynge Arthurs, and wedded the syster of hym. And for because that Kynge Arthure lay by hys wyff and gate on her Sir Mordred, therefore Kynge Lott helde ever agaynste Arthure.)[7]

So there was a knyght that was called the Knyght with the Strange Beste, and at that tyme hys ryght name was called Pellynore, which was a good man off prouesse as few[8] in tho dayes lyvynge. And he strake a myghty stroke at Kynge Lott as he fought with hys enemyes; and he fayled of hys stroke and smote the horse necke, that he foundred to the erthe with Kyng Lott. And therewith anone Kynge Pellinor smote hym a grete stroke thorow the helme and hede unto the browis.

Than all the oste of Orkeney fledde for the deth of Kynge Lotte— and there they were takyn and slayne, all the oste. But Kynge Pellynore bare the wyte of the dethe of Kynge Lott, wherefore Sir Gawayne revenged the deth of hys fadir the tenthe yere aftir he was made knyght, and slew Kynge Pellynor hys[9] owne hondis. Also there was slayne at that batayle twelve kynges on the syde of Kynge Lott with Nero, and were buryed in the chirch of Seynte Stevins in Camelot; and the remanent of knyghtes and other were buryed in a grete roche.

¶So at the enterement com Kyng Lottis wyff, Morgause, with hir foure sonnes, Gawayne, Aggravayne, Gaheris, and Gareth; also there com thydir Kyng Uryens, Sir Uwaynes fadir, and Morgan le Fay, his wyff, that was Kynge Arthurs syster—all thes com to the enterement. But of all the twelve kyngis, Kynge Arthure lette make the tombe of Kynge Lotte passynge rychely, and made hys tombe by hymselff.[1] And than Arthure lette make twelve images of laton and cooper and overgylte with golde, in the sygne of[2] the twelve kynges; and eche one of hem helde a tapir of wexe in hir honde that brente nyght and day. And Kynge Arthure was made in the sygne of a fygure stondynge aboven them with a swerde drawyn in hys honde; and all the twelve fygures had countenaunce lyke unto men that were

fol.28v

[11]

---

4. Raised their battle flags.
5. *Put . . . to the warre:* defeated.
6. *Borne up by hys hondys:* i.e., sustained by his deeds.
7. In Malory's source, Lot's enmity is said to stem from his resentment over Arthur's killing of the May Day children (see, p. 39), not his adultery.
8. *Off prouesse as few:* among few of such prowess.
9. I.e., with his. For confirmation of the death of Pellinore, see p. 369, line 12.
1. I.e., separate from that of the other kings.
2. *Images:* i.e., statues. *In the sygne of:* to represent.

overcom. All thys made Merlion by hys subtyle craufte—and there he tolde the Kynge how that whan he was dede, thes tapers sholde brenne no lenger, "aftir the adventures of the Sankgreall[3] that shall com amonge you and be encheved." Also he tolde Kynge Arthure how Balyn, the worshipfull knyght, "shall gyff the Dolerouse Stroke—whereof shall falle grete vengeaunce."[4]

¶"A![5] where ys Balyne, Balan, and Pellinore?" "As for Kynge Pellinore," seyde Merlion, "he woll mete with you soone. And as for Balyne, he woll nat be longe frome you. But the other brothir woll departe; ye shall se hym no more." "Be my fayth," seyde Arthur, "they ar two manly knyghtes, and namely that Balyne passith of[6] proues off ony knyght that ever Y founde—for much am I beholdynge unto hym. Wolde God he wolde abyde with me!" "Sir, seyde Merlion, "loke ye kepe well the scawberd of Excaleber, for ye shall lose no bloode whyle ye have the scawberde uppon you, thoughe ye have as many woundis uppon you as ye may have."

So aftir, for grete truste, Arthure betoke the scawberde unto Morgan le Fay, hys sister. And she loved another knyght bettir than hir husbande Kynge Uriens—othir Arthure. And she wolde have had Arthure hir brother slayne; and therefore she lete make anothir scawberd for Excaliber [lyke it, by enchauntement, and gaf the scauberd Excalibur[7] to her love—] and the knyghtes name was called Accolon, that aftir had nere slayne Kynge Arthure. But aftir thys Merlion tolde unto Kynge Arthure of the prophecy that there sholde be a grete batayle besydes Salysbiry,[8] and Mordred hys owne sonne sholde be agaynste hym. Also he tolde hym that Bagdemagus was his cosyne germayne, and unto[9] Kynge Uryens. So within a day or two Kynge Arthure was somwhat syke, and he lette pycch hys pavilion in a medow, and there he leyde hym downe on a paylet to slepe, but he myght have no reste.

¶Ryght so he herde a grete noyse of an horse, and therewith the Kynge loked oute at the porche dore of the pavilion and saw a knyght commynge evyn by hym makynge grete dole.

¶"Abyde, fayre sir," seyde Arthure, "and telle me wherefore thou makyst this sorow." "Ye may litill amende me," seyde the knyght, and so passed forth to the Castell of Meliot. And anone aftir that com Balyne, and whan he saw Kyng Arthur he alyght of hys horse and com to the Kynge one foote, and salewed hym. "Be my hede,"[1] seyde Arthure, "ye be wellcom:

¶"Sir, ryght now com rydynge thys way a knyght makynge grete mone, and for what cause I can nat telle. Wherefore I wolde desire of you, of your curtesy and of your jantilnesse, to fecche agayne that knyght, othir by force othir by his good wylle."

¶"I shall do more for youre lordeship than that," seyde Balyne,

---

3. The Holy Grail, for the "adventures" of which, see *The Noble Tale of the Sankgreal*, p. 496.
4. I.e., acts of vengeance.
5. Arthur is speaking here.
6. Surpasses.
7. I.e. the real scabbard of Excalibur.
8. Events leading up to this catastrophic battle begin at p. 683.
9. *Cosyne germayne:* first cousin. I.e., cousin unto.
1. By my head.

"othir ellis I woll greve hym." So **Balyn** rode more than a pace[2] and founde the knyght with a damesell undir a foreyste, and seyde, "Sir knyght, ye muste com with me unto Kynge **Arthure** for to telle hym of youre sorow." "That woll I nat," seyde the knyght, "for hit woll harme me gretely and do you none avayle." "Sir," seyde **Balyne**, "I pray you make you redy, for ye muste go with me, othir ellis I muste fyght with you and brynge you by force—and that were me lothe to do."

¶"Woll ye be my warraunte," seyde the knyght, "and[3] I go with you?"

¶"Yee," seyde **Balyne**, "othir ellis, by the fayth of my body, I woll dye therefore." And so he made hym redy to go with **Balyne**, and leffte the damesell stylle. And as they were evyn before Arthurs pavilion, there com one[4] invisible, and smote the knyght that wente with **Balyn** thorowoute the body with a spere.

¶"Alas!" seyde the knyght, "I am slayne undir youre conduyte with[5] a knyght called **Garlonde**. Therefore take my horse, that is bettir than youres, and ryde to the damesell and folow the queste that I was in as she woll lede you—and revenge my deth whan ye may." "That shall I do," seyde **Balyn**, "and that I make avow to God and knyghthode." And so he departed frome Kynge **Arthure** with grete sorow. So Kynge **Arthure** lette bury this knyght rychely, and made mencion on his tombe how

fol.29v

Here Garlonde that
went inbisyble slew
Harlews le Barbeus
under the conduyt of
Balyn

HERE WAS SLAYNE **Berbeus**

—and by whom the trechory was done—

OF THE KNYGHT **Garlonde**

But ever the damesell bare the truncheon of the spere with hir that Sir **Harleus le Berbeus** was slayne withall.

SO **Balyne** and the damesell rode into the foreyste, and there mette with a knyght that had bene an-hontynge. And that knyght asked **Balyn** for what cause he made so grete sorow.

¶"Me lyste nat to telle," seyde **Balyne**. "Now," seyde the knyght, "and I were armed as ye be, I wolde fyght with you but iff ye tolde me." "That sholde litell nede,"[6] seyde **Balyne**, "I am nat aferde to telle you," and so tolde hym all the case how hit was. "A!" seyde the knyght, "ys thys all? Here I ensure you by the feyth of my body never to departe frome you whyle my lyff lastith." And so they wente to their ostré and armed hem, and so rode forthe with **Balyne**. And as they com by an ermytage evyn by a chyrche-yerde, there com **Garlonde** invisible and smote this knyght, **Peryne** de Mounte Belyarde, thorowoute the body with a glayve. "Alas!"

[13]

Here Garlonde invis-
ible slew Peryne de
Mounte Beliard
under the conduyght
of Balyn

2. *More than a pace:* fast.
3. I.e., if.
4. I.e., someone.
5. I.e., by.
6. There is little need for that.

seyde the knyght, "I am slayne by thys traytoure knyght that rydith invisible."

"Alas," seyde **Balyne**, "thys ys nat the firste despite that he hath done me." And there the ermyte and **Balyne** buryed the knyght undir a ryche stone and a tombe royall. And on the morne they 5
founde letters of golde wretyn, how that

SIR **Gawayne** SHALL REVENGE HIS FADIRS DETHE ON KYNGE **Pellynore**.

10

And anone aftir this **Balyne** and the damesell rode forth tylle they com to a castell, and anone **Balyne** alyghte and wente in. And as sone as [**Balyn** came within the castels yate] the portecolys were lette downe at his backe, and there felle many men aboute the damesell and wolde have slayne hir. fol.30r 15

¶Whan **Balyne** saw that, he was sore greved, for he myght nat helpe her. But than he wente up into a towre, and lepte over the wallis into the dyche, and hurte nat hymselff; and anone he pulled oute his swerde and wolde have foughtyn with them. And they all seyde nay, they wolde nat fyght with hym, for they dud nothynge 20 but the olde custom of thys castell; and tolde hym that hir lady was syke and had leyne many yeres, and she myght nat be hole but yf she had bloode in a sylver dysshe full, of a clene[7] mayde and a kynges doughter—"and therefore the custom of thys castell ys that there shall no damesell passe thys way but she shall blede of hir 25 bloode a sylver dysshe full."

¶"Well," seyde **Balyne**, "she shall blede as much as she may blede, but I woll nat lose the lyff of hir whyle my lyff lastith."

¶And so **Balyn** made hir to bleede by hir good wylle; but hir bloode holpe nat the lady. And so she and he rested there all that 30 nyght and had good chere, and in the mornynge they passed on their wayes (and as hit tellith aftir in the **Sankgreall**,[8] that Sir **Percivall** his syster[9] holpe that lady with hir blood, whereof she was dede). Than they rode three or foure dayes and nevir mette with [14] adventure. And so by fortune they were lodged with a jantilman; 35 and as they sate at souper **Balyn** herde one complayne grevously by hym in a chambir.

¶"What ys thys noyse?" seyde **Balyn**. "Forsothe," seyde his oste, "I woll telle you. I was but late at a justynge, and there I justed with a knyght that ys brothir unto Kynge **Pellam**, and twyse I smote 40 hym downe; and than he promysed to quyte me on my beste frende. And so he wounded thus my son, that can nat be hole tylle I have of that knyghtes bloode—and he rydith all invisyble, but I know nat hys name." "A!" seyde **Balyne**, "I know that knyghtes name, which ys **Garlonde**, and he hath slayne two knyghtes of myne 45 in the same maner—therefore, I had levir mete with that knyght than all the golde in thys realme for the despyte he hath done me."

7. I.e., pure.
8. For the episode, see p. 572.
9. I.e., Percival's sister.

¶"Well," seyde hys oste, "I shall telle you how: Kynge **Pellam** off **Lystenoyse** hath made do cry[1] in all the contrey a grete feste that shall be within thes twenty dayes, and no knyght may com there but he brynge hys wyff with hym, othir hys paramoure—and that your enemy, and myne, ye shall se that day." "Than I promyse you," seyde **Balyn**, "parte of his bloode to hele youre sonne withall."

fol.30v 5

¶"Than we woll be forewarde tomorne," seyde he. So on the morne they rode all three towarde Kynge **Pellam**, and they had fyftene dayes journey or they com thydir. And that same day began the grete feste; and so they alyght and stabled their horsis and wente into the castell, but **Balynes** oste myght not be lette in because he had no lady.

¶But **Balyne** was well receyved and brought unto a chambir, and unarmed hym.[2] And there was brought hym robis to his plesure— and wolde[3] have had **Balyn** leve his swerde behynde hym. "Nay," seyde **Balyne**, "that woll I nat, for hit ys the custom of my contrey a knyght allweyes to kepe hys wepyn with hym. Other ells," seyde he, "I woll departe as I cam."

Than they gaff hym leve with his swerde, and so he wente into the castell and was amonge knyghtes of worship, and hys lady afore[4] hym. So aftir this **Balyne** asked a knyght and seyde, "Ys there nat a knyght in thys courte which his name ys **Garlonde**?" "Yes, sir, yondir he goth, the knyght with the blacke face—for he ys the mervaylyste knyght that ys now lyvynge; and he destroyeth many good knyghtes, for he goth invisible."

¶"Well," seyde **Balyn**, "ys that he?" Than **Balyn** avised hym[5] longe, and thought, "If I sle hym here, I shall nat ascape; and if I leve hym now, peraventure I shall never mete with hym agayne at such a stevyn, and muche harme he woll do and[6] he lyve."

¶And therewith thys **Garlonde** aspyed that **Balyn** vysaged hym, so he com and slapped hym on the face with the backe of hys honde, and seyde, "Knyght, why beholdist thou me so? For shame, ete thy mete and do that[7] thou com fore."

¶"Thou seyst soth," seyde **Balyne**, "thys ys nat the firste spite that thou haste done me—and therefore I woll do that I come fore"—and rose hym up fersely and clave his hede to the sholdirs.

How Balyn slew
Garlon the knyght
that wente invisible

¶"Now geff me youre troncheon," seyde **Balyn**, "that he slew youre knyght with." And anone she gaff hit hym, for allwey she bare the truncheoune with hir; and therewith **Balyn** smote hym thorow the body, and seyde opynly, "With that troncheon thou slewyste a good knyght, and now hit stykith in thy body." Than **Balyn** called unto hys oste and seyde, "Now may ye fecche blood inowghe to hele youre son withall."

fol.31r 40

¶So anone all the knyghtes rose frome the table for to sette on

[15]

---

1. Caused to be proclaimed.
2. I.e., himself.
3. I.e., his hosts would.
4. I.e., was ahead of.
5. *Avised hym:* considered to himself.
6. I.e., if.
7. I.e., that which.

Balyne. And Kynge **Pellam** hymself arose up fersely, and seyde, "Knyght, why hast thou slayne my brothir? Thou shalt dey therefore or thou departe."

¶"Well," seyde **Balyn**, "do hit youreselff!" "Yes!" seyde kyng **Pellam**, "there shall no man have ado with the but I myselff, for the love of my brothir." Than Kynge **Pellam** caught in his hand a grymme wepyn and smote egirly at **Balyn**; but he put hys swerde betwyxte hys hede and the stroke, and therewith hys swerde braste in sundir.[8] And whan **Balyne** was wepynles he ran into a chambir for to seke a wepyn—fro chambir to chambir—and no wepyn coude he fynde; and allwayes Kyng **Pellam** folowed afftir hym. And at the last he enterde into a chambir which was mervaylously dyght and ryche, and a bedde arayed with cloth of golde, the rychiste that myght be—and one[9] lyyng therein. And thereby stoode a table of clene golde; and uppon the table stoode a mervaylous spere strangely wrought.

¶So whan **Balyn** saw the spere, he gate hit in hys honde, and turned to Kynge **Pellam** and felde hym and smote hym passyngly sore with that spere, that Kynge **Pellam** felle downe in a sowghe. And therewith the castell brake, rooffe and wallis, and felle downe to the erthe. And **Balyn** felle downe and myght nat styrre hande nor foote; and for[1] the moste party of that castell was dede thorow the Dolorouse Stroke—

¶Ryght so lay Kynge **Pellam** and **Balyne** three dayes. Than **Merlion** com thydir, and toke up **Balyn** and gate hym a good horse, for hys was dede, and bade hym voyde oute of that contrey.

¶"Sir, I wolde have my damesell," seyde **Balyne**. "Loo," seyde **Merlion**, "where she lyeth, dede."

And Kynge **Pellam** lay so many yerys sore wounded, and myght never be hole tylle that **Galaad** the hawte prynce heled hym in the Queste of the **Sankgreall**.[2] For in that place was parte of the bloode of Oure Lorde Jesu Cryste, which **Joseph** off **Aramathy** brought into thys londe,[3] and there hymselff lay in that ryche bedde. And that was the spere whych **Longeus**[4] smote Oure Lorde with to the herte. And Kynge **Pellam** was nyghe of **Joseph** his kynne,[5] and that was the moste worshipfullist man on lyve in tho dayes—and grete pité hit was of hys hurte, for thorow that stroke hit turned to grete dole, tray, and tene.

Here is a pronosticacion of the Sankgreall

[16]

fol.31v

8. Asunder.
9. I.e., someone.
1. I.e., because.
2. For the episode, see p. 584. Malory's account of the maiming of Pellam here seems to be unique to his version of the story of Balyn and Balan and does not match at all with his later account of it given during the Grail Quest (p. 563); on such discrepancies, cf. n. 9, p. 39. For the corresponding passage from the French *Suite de Merlin*, see p. 709. The story of the Dolerous Stroke has mythic origins and is related to stories of the Fisher King and the Waste Land; see n. 6, p. 563.
3. On the legend of Joseph of Arimathea, see n. 7, p. 464 and *The Noble Tale of the Sankgreal*, esp. pp. 507–8.
4. Apochryphal legend held that the man who pierced Christ's side was a blind soldier named Longius (or Longinus), whose vision was restored by Christ's blood. Cf. n. 6, p. 48. Perhaps the most famous medieval English account of Longius is that given in Passus 18 of *Piers Plowman* (B text).
5. Was close to Joseph's blood line.

¶Than departed **Balyne** frome **Merlyon**, for he seyde, "Nevir in
thys worlde we parte nother meete no more." So he rode forthe
thorow the fayre contreyes and citeys and founde the peple dede
slayne on every syde, and all that evir were on lyve cryed and seyde,
"A, **Balyne**, thou hast done and caused grete vengeaunce in thys 5
contreyes! For the Dolerous Stroke thou gaff unto Kynge **Pellam**,
thes three contreyes ar destroyed—and doute nat but the vengeaunce woll falle on the[6] at the laste."

¶But whan **Balyn** was past tho contreyes he was passynge fayne;
and so he rode eyght dayes or he mette with any adventure. And 10
at the last he com into a fayre foreyst in a valey, and was ware of
a towure; and there besyde he mette with a grete horse tyed to a
tree, and besyde there sate a fayre knyght on the grounde, and
made grete mournynge (and he was a lyckly man and a well made).

¶**Balyne** seyde, "God you save. Why be ye so hevy? Telle me, and 15
I woll amende hit, and I may, to my power."[7] "Sir knyght," he seyde,
"thou doste me grete gryeff, for I was in my thoughtes and now
thou puttist me to more payne."

¶Than **Balyn** went a litill frome hym and loked on hys horse.

¶Than herde **Balyne** hym sey thus: "A, fayre lady! Why have ye 20
brokyn my promyse? For ye promysed me to mete me here by
noone—and I may curse you that ever ye gaff me that swerde, for
with thys swerde I woll sle myselff," and pulde hit oute.

¶And therewith com **Balyne**, and sterte unto hym and toke hym
by the honde. 25

¶"Lette go my hande," seyde the knyght, "or ellis I shall sle the!"
"That shall nat nede," seyde **Balyn**, "for I shall promyse you my
helpe to gete you youre lady and ye woll telle me where she ys."

¶"What ys your name?" seyde the knyght.

¶"Sir, my name ys **Balyne le Saveage**." "A, Sir, I know you well 30
inowghe: ye ar the Knyght with the Two Swerdis, and the man of
moste proues of youre hondis lyvynge."

¶"What ys youre name?" seyde **Balyne**. "My name ys **Garnysh** of
the Mownte, a poore mannes sonne, and be my proues and hardynes a deuke made me knyght and gave me londis. Hys name ys 35
Duke **Harmel**, and hys doughter ys [she[8] that I love, and she me,
as I demed." "Hou fer is she hens?" sayd **Balyn**. "But six myle," said
the knyghte.

"Now ryde we hens!" sayde these two knyghtes. So they rode
more than a paas tyll that they cam to a fayr castel wel wallyd and 40
dyched. "I wylle[9] into the castel," sayd **Balyn**, "and loke yf she be
ther." Soo he wente in and serched fro chamber to chambir and
fond her bedde, but she was not there. Thenne **Balyn** loked into a
fayr litil gardyn, and under a laurel tre he sawe her lye upon a quylt
of grene samyte, and a knyght in her armes, fast halsynge eyther 45

6. Thee.
7. *To my power:* to the best of my ability.
8. Two leaves are missing in the Winchester MS at this point; text is supplied from the
   corresponding passages in Caxton.
9. I.e., will go.

other, and under their hedes grasse and herbes. Whan 𝕭𝖆𝖑𝖞𝖓 sawe
her lye so—with the fowlest knyghte that ever he sawe, and she a
fair lady—thenne 𝕭𝖆𝖑𝖞𝖓 wente thurgh alle the chambers ageyne
and told the knyghte how he fond her as she had slepte fast, and
so brought hym in the place there she lay fast slepynge.   5

And whan 𝕲𝖆𝖗𝖓𝖞𝖘𝖘𝖍 beheld hir so lyeng, for pure sorou his mouth   [17]
and nose brast oute on bledynge—and with his swerd he smote of
bothe their hedes; and thenne he maade sorowe oute of mesure,
and sayd, "O, 𝕭𝖆𝖑𝖞𝖓, moche sorow hast thow brought unto me, for
haddest thow not shewed me that syght I shold have passed my   10
sorow." "Forsoth," said 𝕭𝖆𝖑𝖞𝖓, "I did it to this entent, that it sholde
better thy courage, and that ye myght see and knowe her falshede,
and to cause yow to leve love of suche a lady. God knoweth, I dyd
none other but as I wold ye dyd to me."

"Allas," said 𝕲𝖆𝖗𝖓𝖞𝖘𝖘𝖍𝖊, "now is my sorou doubel, that I may not   15
endure—now have I slayne that[1] I moost loved in al my lyf!" And
therwith, sodenly, he roofe hymself on his own swerd unto the
hyltys. When 𝕭𝖆𝖑𝖞𝖓 sawe that, he dressid hym thensward,[2] lest
folke wold say he had slayne them, and so he rode forth.

And within thre dayes he cam by a crosse; and theron were   20
letters of gold wryten that said,

IT IS NOT FOR NO KNYGHT ALONE TO RYDE TOWARD THIS CASTEL.

Thenne sawe he an old hore gentylman comyng toward hym, that   25
sayd, "𝕭𝖆𝖑𝖞𝖓 𝖑𝖊 𝕾𝖆𝖛𝖊𝖆𝖌𝖊, thow passyst thy bandes to come this waye;
therfor torne ageyne, and it will availle the," and he vanysshed
awey anone. And soo he herd an horne blowe, as it had ben the
dethe of a best.[3] "That blast," said 𝕭𝖆𝖑𝖞𝖓, "is blowen for me, for I
am the pryse—and yet am I not dede." Anone withal he sawe an   30
hondred ladyes and many knyghtes that welcommed hym with fayr
semblaunt and made hym passyng good chere unto his syght, and
ledde hym into the castel; and ther was daunsynge, and mynstral-
sye, and alle maner of joye.

Thenne the chyef lady of the castel said, "Knyghte with the Two   35
Suerdys, ye must have adoo and juste with a knyght hereby that
kepeth an iland, for ther may no man passe this way but he must
juste or[4] he passe." "That is an unhappy[5] customme," said 𝕭𝖆𝖑𝖞𝖓,
"that a knyght may not passe this wey but yf he juste." "Ye shalle
not have adoo but with one knyghte," sayd the lady.   40

"Wel" sayd 𝕭𝖆𝖑𝖞𝖓, "syn I shalle, therto I am redy. But traveillynge
men are ofte wery, and their horses to: but though my hors be
wery, my hert is not wery—I wold be fayne ther my deth shold
be."[6] "Syr," said a knyght to 𝕭𝖆𝖑𝖞𝖓, "me thynketh your sheld is not
good; I wille lene yow a byggar, therof I pray yow." And so he tooke   45

1. I.e., the one that.
2. *Dressid hym thensward:* led himself away from there.
3. I.e., as if it had signified the killing of some beast (in a hunt).
4. I.e., before.
5. I.e., dire, objectionable.
6. *Ther:* i.e., there where. *Shold be:* i.e., is destined to be.

the sheld that was unknowen and lefte his owne, and so rode unto
the iland, and put hym and his hors in a grete boote.

And whan he came on the other syde he met with a damoysel,
and she said, "O knyght Balyn, why have ye lefte your owne sheld?
Allas, ye have put yourself in grete daunger, for by your sheld[7] ye   5
shold have ben knowen. It is grete pyté of yow as ever was of
knyght, for of thy prowesse and hardynes thou hast no felawe
lyvynge." "Me repenteth," said Balyn, "that ever I cam within this
countrey; but I maye not torne now ageyne for shame, and what
aventure shalle falle to me, be it lyf or dethe, I wille take the adven-   10
ture that shalle come to me." And thenne he loked on his armour
and understood he was wel armed, and therwith blessid hym[8] and
mounted upon his hors.

Thenne afore hym he sawe come rydynge oute of a castel a   [18]
knyght, and his hors trapped all reed,[9] and hymself in the same   15
colour. Whan this knyghte in the reed beheld Balyn, hym thought
it shold be his broder Balyn bycause of his two swerdys, but
bycause he knewe not his sheld he demed it was not he. And so
they aventryd theyr speres and came merveillously fast togyders,
and they smote other in the sheldes, but theire speres and theire   20
cours were soo bygge that t bare doune hors and man, that they
lay bothe in a swoun. But Balyn was brysed sore with the falle of
his hors, for he was wery of travaille.

And Balan was the fyrst that rose on foote, and drewe his swerd
and wente toward Balyn; and he aroos and wente ageynst hym. But   25
Balan smote Balyn fyrste, and he put up his shelde and smote hym
thorow the shelde and tamyd his helme. Thenne Balyn smote hym
ageyne with that unhappy swerd, and wel-nyghe had fellyd his
broder Balan—and so they fought ther togyders tyl theyr brethes
faylled. Thenne Balyn loked up to the castel and sawe the towres   30
stand ful of ladyes. Soo they went unto bataille ageyne and
wounded everyche other dolefully, and thenne they brethed[1] oftymes, and so wente unto bataille that alle the place there as they
fought was blood reed. And att that tyme ther was none of them
bothe but they hadde eyther smyten other seven grete woundes,   35
so that the lest[2] of them myght have ben the dethe of the myghtyest
gyaunt in this world.

Thenne they wente to batail ageyn so merveillously that doubte[3]
it was to here of that bataille for the grete bloodshedynge—and
their hawberkes unnailled,[4] that naked they were on every syde.   40
Atte last Balan, the yonger broder, withdrewe hym a lytel and leid
hym doune. Thenne said Balyn le Saveage, "What knyghte arte
thow? For or now I found never no knyght that matched me." "My
name is," said he, "Balan, broder unto the good knyght Balyn."

---

7. I.e., by the coat of arms on your shield.
8. *Blessid hym:* i.e., crossed himself.
9. *Trapped all reed:* all in red trappings.
1. I.e., rested.
2. I.e., least injurious.
3. I.e., a fearsome thing.
4. I.e., broke apart.

℃."Allas!" sayd **Balyn**, "that ever I shold see this day," and therwith he felle backward in a swoune. Thenne **Balan** yede on al four feet and handes, and put of[5] the helme of his broder, and myght not knowe hym by the vysage, it was so ful hewen and bledde; but whan he awoke he sayd, "O, **Balan**, my broder, thow hast slayne me, and I the,[6] wherfore alle the wyde world shalle speke of us bothe." "Allas!" sayd **Balan**, "that ever I sawe this day, that thorow myshap I myght not knowe yow—for I aspyed wel your two swerdys, but bycause ye had another shild I demed ye had ben another knyght!"

"Allas" saide **Balyn**, "all that maade[7] an unhappy knyght in the castel, for he caused me to leve myn owne shelde to our bothes destruction—and, yf I myght lyve, I wold destroye that castel for ylle customes." "That were wel done," said **Balan**, "for I had never grace[8] to departe fro hem syn that I cam hyther, for here it happed me to slee a knyght that kept this iland, and syn myght I never departe—and no more shold ye, broder, and ye myght[9] have slayne me as ye have and escaped yourself with the lyf."

Ryght so cam the lady of the toure with four knyghtes and six ladyes and six yomen unto them, and there she herd how they made her[1] mone eyther to other, and sayd, "We came bothe oute of one wombe, that is to say one moders bely, and so shalle we lye bothe in one pytte." So **Balan** prayd the lady of her gentylnesse, for his true servyse, that she wold burye them bothe in that same place there the bataille was done, and she graunted hem, with wepynge, it shold be done rychely in the best maner. "Now wille ye sende for a preest, that we may receyve our sacrament and receyve the blessid body of Our Lord Jesu Cryst?" "Ye," said the lady, "it shalle be done." And so she sente for a preest and gaf hem her ryghtes.[2]

"Now," sayd **Balen**, "whan we are buryed in one tombe, and the mensyon made over us how two bretheren slewe eche other, there wille never good knyght nor good man see our tombe but they wille pray for our soules"—and so alle the ladyes and gentylwymen wepte for pyté. Thenne anone **Balan** dyed, but **Balyn** dyed not tyl the mydnyghte after. And so were they buryed bothe, and the lady lete make a mensyon of **Balan**, how he was ther slayne by his broders handes—but she knewe not **Balyns** name.

In the morne cam **Merlyn** and lete wryte **Balyns** name on the tombe with letters of gold—that   [19]

Here lyeth Balyn le Sabeage
that was the Knyght with the Two Swerdes
and he that smote the Dolorous Stroke

---

5. Took off.
6. Thee.
7. I.e., was caused by.
8. I.e., permission.
9. *And ye myght*: if you could.
1. I.e., their.
2. I.e., last rites.

Also 𝕸erlyn lete make there a bedde, that ther shold never man lye therin but he wente oute of his wytte—yet 𝕷auncelot de 𝕷ake fordyd[3] that bed thorow his noblesse. And anone after 𝕭alyn was dede, 𝕸erlyn toke his swerd and toke of the pomel and set on another pomel. So 𝕸erlyn] bade a knyght that stood before hym to handyll that swerde; and he assayde hit and myght nat handyll hit.

    ❡Than 𝕸erlion lowghe.

    ❡"Why lawghe ye?" seyde the knyght.

    ❡"Thys ys the cause," seyde 𝕸erlion: "there shall never man handyll thys swerde but the beste knyght of the worlde, and that shall be Sir 𝕷auncelot, othir ellis 𝕲alahad, hys sonne. And 𝕷auncelot with thys swerde shall sle the man in the worlde that he lovith beste—that shall be Sir 𝕲awayne."[4] And all thys he lette wryte in the pomell of the swerde.

    Than 𝕸erlion lette make a brygge of iron and of steele into that ilonde, and hit was but halff a foote brode—"and there shall never man passe that brygge nother have hardynesse to go over hit but yf he were a passynge good man withoute trechery or vylany." Also the scawberd off 𝕭alyns swerde, 𝕸erlion lefte hit on thys syde the ilonde, that 𝕲alaad sholde fynde hit. Also 𝕸erlion lette make by hys suttelyté that 𝕭alynes swerde was put into a marbil stone stondynge upryght, as grete as a mylstone, and hoved allwayes above the watir, and dud many yeres. (And so by adventure hit swamme downe by the streme unto the cité of 𝕮amelot, that ys in Englysh called 𝖂ynchester.[5] And that same day 𝕲alaad the haute prynce com with Kynge 𝕬rthure; and so 𝕲alaad brought with hym the scawberde and encheved the swerde that was in the marble stone hovynge uppon the watir. And on Whytsonday[6] he enchevyd the swerde, as hit ys rehersed in the booke of the Sankgreall.)[7]

    Sone aftir thys was done 𝕸erlion com to Kynge 𝕬rthur and tolde hym of the Dolerous Stroke that 𝕭alyn gaff Kynge 𝕻ellam, and how 𝕭alyn and 𝕭alan fought togydirs the merveylyste batayle that evir was herde off, and how they were buryed bothe in one tombe.

    ❡"Alas," seyde Kynge 𝕬rthure, "thys ys the grettist pité that ever I herde telle off of two knyghtes, for in thys worlde I knewe never such two knyghtes."

    ❡Thus endith the tale of 𝕭alyn and 𝕭alan, two brethirne that were borne in Northhumbirlonde, that were two passynge good knyghtes as ever were in tho dayes.

𝕰xplicit.[8]

---

3. I.e., sometime later destroyed.
4. For the sequence of events linked to this sword that eventually lead to his death, see pp. 497–502, 557–58, and 676–82.
5. Malory is the first known Arthurian writer to equate Winchester with Camelot, though he may have got the idea from the presence there in his own day of a great round table, said to have been the original. The top of the table still survives, mounted on the wall of the great hall of Winchester Castle; modern scientific studies date the table to no earlier than the reign of Edward I (1272–1307). Cf. Caxton's skeptical comments in the preface to his edition, Criticism, pp. 815–16.
6. On this date, see n. 1, p. 10.
7. See pp. 499 ff.
8. (Here) ends (the tale).

The Weddyng of Kyng Arthur[1]

IN the begynnyng of Arthure, aftir he was chosyn Kynge by adventure and by grace—for the moste party of the barowns knew nat he was Uther Pendragon son but[2] as Merlyon made hit opynly knowyn, but yet many kyngis and lordis hylde hym grete werre[3] for that cause—

¶But well Arthur overcom hem all. The moste party dayes of hys lyff he was ruled by the counceile of Merlyon; so hit felle on a tyme Kyng Arthur seyde unto Merlion, "My barownes woll let me have no reste but nedis I muste take a wyff—and I wolde none take but by thy counceile and advice."

¶"Hit ys well done," seyde Merlyon, "that ye take a wyff, for a man of youre bounté and nobles scholde not be withoute a wyff. Now is there ony," seyde Marlyon, "that ye love more than another?" "Ye," seyde Kyng Arthure, "I love Gwenypere, the Kynges doughtir of Lodegrean, of the londe of Camelerde, the whyche holdyth in his house the Table Rounde that ye tolde me he had hit of my fadir Uther. And this damesell is the moste valyaunte and fayryst that I know lyvyng, or yet that ever I coude fynde." "Sertis," seyde Marlyon, "as of her beauté and fayrenesse, she is one of the fayrest on lyve. But, and ye loved hir not so well as ye do, I scholde fynde you a damesell of beauté and of goodnesse that sholde lyke you and please you—and youre herte were nat sette: but there as[4] mannes herte is sette, he woll be loth to returne." "That is trouthe," seyde Kyng Arthur.

But Marlyon warned the Kyng covertly that Gwenyber was nat holsom[5] for hym to take to wyff, for he warned hym that Launcelot scholde love hir, and sche hym agayne. And so he turned his tale to the aventures of the Sankegreal. Than Merlion[6] desyred of the Kyng for to have men with hym that scholde enquere of Gwenyber, and so the Kyng graunted hym. And so Merlyon wente forthe unto Kyng Lodegrean of Camplerde, and tolde hym of the desire of the Kyng that he wolde have unto his wyff Gwenyber, his doughter.

"That is to me," seyde Kyng Lodegreauns, "the beste tydynges that ever I herde, that so worthy a kyng of prouesse and noblesse wol wedde my doughter. And as for my londis, I wolde geff hit hym yf I wyste hit myght please hym—but he hath londis inow, he nedith none. But I shall sende hym a gyffte that shall please hym muche more, for I shall gyff hym the Table Rounde—

[III.1]   fol.35

fol.35v

---

1. The title is taken editorially from the *explicit,* or closing notation, to this section (see p. 77). Malory's principal source for this section is the French *Suite de Merlin;* for illustrative selections, see p. 709. In the Winchester MS, this section appears to mark a major division, beginning on a new page, with the previous page having been left completely blank. The initial "I" is in red, and the first "n" "h" and "b" of the opening line are touched in yellow.
2. I.e., except.
3. *Hylde hym grete werre:* waged extensive war against him.
4. I.e., where.
5. I.e., beneficial, healthy.
6. On the abbreviation of Merlin's name in the Winchester MS, see n. 4, p. 17.

❡"Whych **Uther**, hys fadir, gaff me: and whan hit ys fullé complete,[7] there ys an hondred knyghtes and fyfty. And as for an hondred good knyghtes, I have myselff; but I wante fyfty, for so many
hathe be[8] slayne in my dayes." And so Kynge **Lodgreaunce** delyverd hys
doughtir **Gwenyver** unto **Merlion**, and the Table Rounde with the   5
hondred knyghtes; and so they rode freysshly with grete royalté,[9]
what by watir and by londe, tyll that they com nyghe unto London.

Whan Kynge **Arthure** herde of the commynge of Quene **Gwenyver**   [2]
and the hondred knyghtes with the Table Rounde, than Kynge
Arthure made grete joy for hir commyng and that ryche presente,   10
and seyde opynly, "Thys fayre lady ys passyngly wellcom to me, for
I have loved hir longe, and therefore there ys nothynge so leeff to
me; and thes knyghtes with the Table Rownde pleasith me more
than ryght grete rychesse." And in all haste the Kynge lete ordayne
for the maryage and the coronacion in the moste honorablyst wyse   15
that cowude be devised.

❡"Now, **Merlion**," seyde Kynge **Arthure**, "go thou and aspye me[1]
in all thys londe fyfty knyghtes which bene of moste prouesse and
worship." So within shorte tyme Merlion had founde such knyghtes that sholde fulfylle[2] twenty and eyght knyghtes, but no mo   20
wolde he fynde. Than the Bysshop of Caunturbiry[3] was fette, and
he blyssed the segis with grete royalté and devocion, and there
sette the eyght and twenty knyghtes in her segis. And whan thys
was done **Merlion** seyde, "Fayre sirres, ye muste all aryse and com
to Kynge **Arthure** for to do hym omage; he woll the better be in   25
wylle[4] to maynteyne you." And so they arose and dud their omage.
And whan they were gone **Merlion** founde in every sege lettirs of
golde that tolde the knyghtes namys that had sitten there, but two
segis were voyde.

❡And so anone com in yonge **Gawayne** and asked[5] the Kynge a   30
gyffte.

❡"Aske," seyde the Kynge, "and I shall graunte you."

❡"Sir, I aske that ye shall make me knyght that same day that
ye shall wedde Dame **Gwenyver**." "I woll do hit with a goode wylle,"
seyde Kynge **Arthure**, "and do unto you all the worship that I may,   35
for I muste be reson[6] ye ar my nevew, my sistirs son." Forthwithall   [3]
there com a poore man into the courte, and brought with hym a   fol.36r
fayre yonge man of eyghtene yere of ayge, rydynge upon a lene
mare. And the poore man asked all men that he mette, "Where
shall I fynde Kynge **Arthure**?" "Yondir he ys," seyde the knyghtes.   40
"Wolt thou onythynge[7] with hym?" "Ye," seyde the poore man,
"therefore I cam hydir." And as sone as he com before the Kynge,

---

7. *Whan hit ys fullé complete:* when a full complement of knights sits at it.
8. *Wante:* i.e., lack. *Be:* i.e., been.
9. I.e., regal splendor, magnificence.
1. Search out for me.
2. I.e., make up the number of.
3. On this ecclesiastical position, see n. 9, p. 7.
4. *The better be in wylle:* be the more willing. On feudal relationships, see n. 6, p. 9.
5. I.e., asked of.
6. I.e., for the reason that.
7. Do you have any business.

he salewed hym and seyde, "Kynge 𝕬𝖗𝖙𝖍𝖚𝖗𝖊, the floure of all kyngis, I beseche Jesu save the!

¶ "Sir, hit was tolde me that at thys tyme of youre maryaige ye wolde gyff ony man the gyffte that he wolde aske you, excepte hit were unresonable." 5

¶ "That ys trouthe," seyde the Kynge, "such cryes I lette make, and that woll I holde, so hit appayre nat my realme nor myne astate."

¶ "Ye sey well and graciously," seyde the pore man—

¶ "Sir, I aske nothynge elis but that ye woll make my sonne 10 knyght."

¶ "Hit ys a grete thynge thou askyst off me," seyde the Kynge.

¶ "What ys thy name?" seyde the Kynge to the poore man.

¶ "Sir, my name ys 𝕬𝖗𝖞𝖊𝖘 the cowherde." "Whethir commith thys of the,[8] other ells of thy sonne?" seyde the Kynge. "Nay, sir," seyd 15 𝕬𝖗𝖞𝖊𝖘, "thys desyre commyth of my son and nat off me. For I shall telle you, I have thirtene sonnes, and all they woll falle to what laboure I putte them and woll be ryght glad to do laboure; but thys chylde woll nat laboure for nothynge that my wyff and I may do, but allwey he woll be shotynge, or castynge dartes, and glad for to 20 se batayles and to beholde knyghtes:

¶ "And allwayes day and nyght he desyrith of me to be made knyght."

¶ "What ys thy name?" seyde the Kynge unto the yonge man. "Sir, my name ys 𝕿𝖔𝖗𝖗𝖊." Than the Kynge behelde hym faste and saw he 25 was passyngly well vysaged and well made of[9] hys yerys. "Well," seyde Kynge 𝕬𝖗𝖙𝖍𝖚𝖗𝖊 unto 𝕬𝖗𝖞𝖊𝖘 the cowherde, "go fecche all thy sonnes before me that I may se them." And so the pore man dud, and all were shapyn muche lyke the poore man; but 𝕿𝖔𝖗𝖗𝖊 was nat lyke hym, nother in shappe ne in countenaunce, for he was muche 30 more than ony of hem. "Now," seyde Kynge 𝕬𝖗𝖙𝖍𝖚𝖗 unto the cowherde, "where ys the swerde he shall be made knyght withall?" "Hyt ys here," seyde 𝕿𝖔𝖗𝖗𝖊. "Take hit oute of the shethe," sayde the Kynge, "and requyre me to make you knyght."

¶ Than 𝕿𝖔𝖗𝖗𝖊 alyght of hys mare and pulled oute hys swerde, 35 knelynge and requyrynge the Kynge to make hym knyght, and that   fol.36v he made hym knyght of the Table Rounde. "As for a knyght, I woll make you," and therewith smote hym in the necke with the swerde. "Be ye a good knyght—and so I pray to God ye may be—and if ye be of proues and worthynes ye shall be of the Table Rounde." 40

¶ "Now, 𝕸𝖊𝖗𝖑𝖎𝖔𝖓," seyde 𝕬𝖗𝖙𝖍𝖚𝖗𝖊, "whethir thys 𝕿𝖔𝖗𝖗𝖊 shall be a goode man?"

¶ "Yee, hardely, sir, he ought to be a good man, for he ys com of good kynrede as ony on lyve—and of kynges bloode."

¶ "How so, sir?" seyd the Kynge. "I shall telle you," seyde 𝕸𝖊𝖗- 45 lion. "Thys poore man 𝕬𝖗𝖞𝖊𝖘 the cowherde ys nat his fadir, for he ys no sybbe to hym; for Kynge 𝕻𝖊𝖑𝖑𝖞𝖓𝖔𝖗𝖊 ys hys fadir." "I suppose nat!" seyde the cowherde.

---

8. Does this request come from thee?
9. Well vysaged: handsome of face. Of: i.e., for.

¶ "Well, fecch thy wyff before me," seyde **Merlion**, "and she shall nat sey nay." Anone the wyff was fette forth, which was a fayre houswyff. And there she answerde **Merlion** full womanly, and there she tolde the Kynge and **Merlion** that whan she was a mayde and wente to mylke hir kyne, "there mette with me a sterne knyght, and half be[1] force he had my maydynhode; and at that tyme he begate my sonne **Torre**, and he toke awey fro me my grayhounde that I had that tyme with me, and seyde he wolde kepe the grayhounde for my love." "A," seyde the cowherde, "I wente hit had nat be thus, but I may beleve hit well, for he[2] had never no tacchys of[3] me."

Sir **Torre** seyde unto **Merlion**, "Dishonoure nat my modir." "Sir," seyde **Merlion**, "hit ys more for your worship than hurte, for youre fadir ys a good knyght and a kynge, and he may ryght well avaunce you and youre modir both, for ye were begotyn or evir she was wedded." "That ys trouthe," seyde the wyff. "Hit ys the lesse gryff unto me," seyde the cowherde. So on the morne Kynge **Pellynor** com to the courte of Kynge **Arthure**. And he had grete joy of hym and tolde hym of Sir **Torre**, how he was hys sonne, and how he had made hym knyght at the requeste of the cowherde.

¶ Whan Kynge **Pellynor** behelde Sir **Torre**, he plesed hym muche. So the Kynge made **Gawayne** knyght—but Sir **Torre** was the firste he made at that feste.

¶ "What ys the cause," seyde Kynge **Arthure**, "that there ys two placis voyde in the segis?" "Sir," seyd **Merlion**, "there shall no man sitte in tho placis but they that shall be moste of worship. But in the Sege Perelous[4] there shall nevir man sitte but one—and yf there be ony so hardy to do hit he shall be destroyed—and he that shall sitte therein shall have no felowe." And therewith **Merlyon** toke Kynge **Pellinor** by the honde, and in[5] that one hande nexte[6] the two segis, and the Sege Perelous, he seyde in opyn audiens, "Thys is your place, for beste ar ye worthy to sitte thereinne of ony that here ys." And thereat had Sir **Gawayne** grete envy, and tolde **Gaherys** hys brothir, "Yondir knyght ys putte to grete worship, whych grevith me sore, for he slewe oure fadir Kynge **Lott**. Therefore I woll sle hym," seyde **Gawayne**, "with a swerde that was sette me that ys passynge trencheaunte."

¶ "Ye shall nat so," seyde **Gaherys**, "at thys tyme, for as now I am but youre squyre, and whan I am made knyght I woll be avenged on hym. And therefore, brothir, hit ys beste to suffir tyll another tyme, that we may have hym oute of courte, for and[7] we dud so we shall trouble thys hyghe feste."

¶ "I woll well,"[8] seyde **Gawayne**. Than was thys feste made redy, and the Kynge was wedded at **Camelot** unto Dame **Gwenyvere** in the

---

1. I.e., by.
2. I.e., Torre.
3. I.e., like.
4. The seat is destined for Galahad; see p. 500. Percyvale will sit to its right (p. 368).
5. I.e., holding him by.
6. I.e., next to.
7. I.e., if.
8. *I woll well:* I agree.

chirche of Seynte Stephyns, with grete solempnité. Than as every man was sette as hys degré asked,[9] Merlion wente to all the knyghtes of the Rounde Table and bade hem sitte stylle—"that none of you remeve, for ye shall se a straunge and a mervailous adventure."

¶Ryght so as they sate, there com rennynge inne a whyght herte into the hall, and a whyght brachet nexte hym, and thirty couple of blacke rennynge houndis com afftir with a grete cry. And the herte wente aboute the Rounde Table, and as he wente by the syde bourdis the brachet ever boote hym by the buttocke and pulde outte a pece, wherethorow the herte lope a grete lepe and over-threw a knyght that sate at the syde bourde. And therewith the knyght arose and toke up the brachet, and so wente forthe oute of the halle, and toke hys horse and rode hys way with the brachett.

Ryght so com in a lady on a whyght palferey, and cryed alowde unto Kynge Arthure and seyd, "Sir, suffir me nat to have thys despite, for the brachet ys myne that the knyght hath ladde away." "I may nat do therewith,"[1] seyde the Kynge. So with thys there com a knyght rydyng all armed on a grete horse, and toke the lady away with forse wyth hym, and ever she cryed and made grete dole.

¶So whan she was gone the Kynge was gladde, for she made such a noyse.

¶"Nay!" seyde Merlion, "ye may nat leve hit so—thys adventure—so lyghtly, for thes adventures muste be brought to an ende, othir ellis hit woll be disworshyp to you and to youre feste."

¶"I woll," seyde the Kynge, "that all be done by your advice." Than he lette calle Sir Gawayne—"for he muste brynge agayne the whyght herte." "Also, sir,[2] ye muste lette call Sir Torre, for he muste brynge agayne the brachette and the knyght, othir ellis sle hym:

¶"Also lette calle Kynge Pellynor, for he muste brynge agayne the lady and the knyght, othir ellis sle hym. And thes three knyghtes shall do mervayles adventures or they com agayne." Than were they called, all three as hit ys rehersed afore, and every of them toke their charge and armed them surely. But Sir Gawayne had the firste requeste; and therefore we woll begynne at hym, and so forthe to thes other.[3]

Here begynnith the fyrst batayle that ever Sir Gawayne ded after he was made knyght

Syr Gawayne rode more than a pace, and Gaheris his brothir rode with hym in the stede of a squyre to do hym servyse. So as they rode they saw two knyghtes fyght on horsebacke passynge sore. So Sir Gawayne and hys brothir rode betwyxte them and asked them for what cause they fought so.

¶One of the knyghtes seyde, "We fyght but for a symple mater, for we two be two brethirne and be begotyn of oo man and of oo woman."

fol.37v

[6]

9. *As hys degré asked:* according to his rank.
1. *I may nat do therewith:* I cannot do anything about that.
2. Merlin is speaking.
3. I.e., other two knights.

¶"Alas!" seyde Sir **Gawayne**. "Sir," seyde the elther brother, "there com a whyght herte thys way thys same day and many houndis chaced hym, and a whyght brachett was allwey nexte hym. And we undirstood hit was an adventure made for the hyghe feste of **Arthure**. And therefore I wolde have gone afftir to have wonne me worship; and here my yonger brothir seyde he wolde go aftir the harte, for he was bygger knyght than I—and for thys cause we felle at debate, and so we thought to preff which of us was the bygger knyght."

¶"Forsoth thys ys a symple cause," seyde **Gawayne**, "for uncouth men ye sholde debate withall, and no brothir with brothir. Therefore do be my counceyle: othir I woll have ado⁴ with you bothe, other yelde you to me and that ye go unto Kynge **Arthure** and yelde you unto hys grace."

¶"Sir knyght," seyde the two brethirne, "we ar forfoughten and much bloode have we loste thorow oure wylfulnes, and therefore we wolde be loth to have ado with you."

¶"Than do as I woll have you do," seyde Sir **Gawayne**. "We agré to fulfylle youre wylle—but by whom shall we sey that we be thydir sente?"

¶"Ye may sey, 'by the knyght that folowith the queste of the herte.'

¶"Now what ys youre name?" seyde **Gawayne**.

¶"Sir, my name ys **Sorluse** of the Foreyste," seyde the elder. "And my name ys," seyde the yonger, "**Bryan** of the Foreyste." And so they departed and wente to the Kyngis courte. And Sir **Gawayne** folowed hys queste; and as he folowed the herte by the cry of the howndis, evyn before hym there was a grete ryver, and the herte swam over. And as Sir **Gawayn** wolde a folowed afftir, there stood a knyght on the othir syde, and seyde, "Sir knyght, com nat over aftir thys harte but if thou wolt juste with me." "I woll nat fayle, as for that," seyde Sir **Gawayne**, "to folow the queste that I am inne"—and so made hys horse swymme over the watir. And anone they gate their glayves, and ran togydirs fulle harde, but **Gawayne** smote hym of hys horse, and [torned his hors and] than he bade hym yelde hym. "Nay," seyde the knyght, "nat so! for thoughe ye have the better of me on horsebak, I pray the, valyaunte knyght, alyght on foote and macche we togidir with oure swerdis."

¶"What ys youre name?" seyde Sir **Gawayne**. "Sir, my name ys **Alardyne** of the Oute Iles." Than aythir dressed their shyldes and smote togydir, but Sir **Gawayne** smote hym so harde thorow the helme that hit wente to the brayne and the knyght felle downe dede. "A," seyde **Gaherys**, "that was a myghty stroke of a yonge knyght!"

Than Sir **Gawayne** and **Gaherys** [rode more than a paas after the whyte herte, and let slyppe at⁵ the herte thre couple of grey-houndes; and so they chace the herte into a castel, and in the chyef

Marginal notes:

fol.38r

Now Sir Gawayne
slew Alerdyne,
knyght of the Iles

[7]

Line numbers: 5, 10, 15, 20, 25, 30, 35, 40, 45

---

4. *Be*: i.e., by. *Have ado*: fight.
5. *More than a paas*: quickly. *Lete slyppe at*: released against.

place of the castel they slewe the hert. Sir Gauayne and Gaheryse]
folowed afftir. Ryght so there com a knyght oute of a chambir with
a swerde drawyn in hys honde and slew two of the grayhoundes
evyn in the syght of Sir Gawayne, and the remanente he chaced
with hys swerde oute of the castell. And whan he com agayne he   5
seyde, "A, my whyght herte! me repentis that thou arte dede, for
my soveraigne lady gaff the to me, and evyll have I kepte the—and
thy dethe shall be evyl bought and I lyve.[6] And anone he wente
into hys chambir and armyd hym, and com oute fersely. And there
he mette with Sir Gawayne—and he seyde, "Why have ye slayne my   10
howndys? I wolde that ye had wrokyn youre angir uppon me rather
than uppon a dome beste." "Thou seyst trouth," seyde the knyght.
"I have avenged me on thy howndys—and so I woll on the or thou
go."

¶Than Sir Gawayne alyght on foote and dressed hys shylde, and[7]   15
stroke togydirs myghtyly, and clave their shyldis and stooned their
helmys and brake their hawbirkes that their blode thirled downe
to their feete. So at the last Sir Gawayne smote so harde that the
knyght felle to the erthe, and than he cryed mercy and yelded hym,
and besought hym as he was a jantyll knyght to save hys lyff. "Thou 20
shalt dey," seyd Sir Gawayne, "for sleynge of my howndis!" "I woll
make amendys," seyde the knyght, "to[8] my power." But Sir Gawayne
wolde no mercy have, but unlaced hys helme to have strekyn of
hys hede. Ryght so com hys lady oute of a chambir and felle over
hym—and so he smote of hir hede by myssefortune. "Alas," seyde   25
Gaherys, "that ys fowle and shamefully done! For that shame shall
never frome[9] you:

¶"Also ye sholde gyff mercy unto them that aske mercy, for a
knyght withoute mercy ys withoute worship."

¶So Sir Gawayne was sore astoned of the deth of this fayre lady,   30
that he wyst nat what he dud, and seyde unto the knyght, "Aryse,
I woll gyff the[1] mercy."

¶"Nay, nay!" seyd the knyght, "I take no forse of[2] thy mercy
now, for thou haste slayne with vilony my love and my lady that I
loved beste of all erthly thynge." "Me sore repentith hit," seyde Sir 35
Gawayne, "for I mente the stroke unto the. But now thou shalt go
unto Kynge Arthure and telle hym of thyne adventure, and how thou
arte overcom by the knyght that wente in the queste of the whyght
harte."

¶"I take no force," seyde the knyght, "whether I lyve othir dey."   40
But at the last, for feare of dethe, he swore to go unto Kynge
Arthure—and he made hym to bere the one grehownde before hym
on hys horse and the other behynde hym. "What ys youre name,"
seyde Sir Gawayne, "or we departe?" "My name ys," seyde the
knyght, "Blamoure of the Maryse." And so he departed towarde [8] 45

6. *Evyl bought and I lyve:* disastrously paid for if I live.
7. I.e., and they.
8. I.e., to the extent of.
9. I.e., go from, leave.
1. Thee.
2. Am not concerned for.

fol. 39r

Camelot; and Sir Gawayne wente unto the castell and made hym redy to lye there all nyght, and wolde have unarmed hym.

❡"What woll ye do?" seyde Gaherys. "Woll ye unarme you in thys contrey? Ye may thynke ye have many fooes in thys contrey."

❡He had no sunner seyde the worde but there com in foure knyghtes well armed and assayled Sir Gawayne harde, and seyde unto hym, "Thou new-made knyght, thou haste shamed thy knyght-hode, for a knyght withoute mercy ys dishonoured. Also thou haste slayne a fayre lady, to thy grete shame unto the worldys ende—and doute the nat thou shalt have grete nede of mercy or thou departe frome us." And therewith one of hem smote Sir Gawayne a grete stroke, that nygh he felle to the erthe. And Gaherys smote hym agayne sore; and so they were assayled on the one syde and on the othir, that Sir Gawayne and Gaherys were in jouparté of their lyves. And one with a bowe, an archer, smote Sir Gawayne thorow the arme that hit greved hym wondirly sore.

And as they sholde have bene slayne, there com foure fayre lad-yes and besought the knyghtes of grace for Sir Gawayne; and goodly at the requeste of thes ladyes, they gaff Sir Gawayne and Gaherys their lyves and made them to yelde them as presoners. Than Sir Gawayne and Gaherys made grete dole. "Alas!" seyde Sir Gawayne, "myn arme grevith me sore, that I am lyke to be maymed," and so made hys complaynte pyteuously. So erly on the morne there com to Sir Gawayne one of the foure ladyes that had herd hys com-playnte, and seyd, "Sir knyght, what chere?"[3] "Nat good."

"Why so? Hit ys youre owne defaute," seyde the lady, "for ye have done passynge foule for the sleynge of thys lady, the whych woll be[4] grete vylony unto you. But be ye nat of Kynge Arthurs?" seyde the lady.

❡"Yes, truly," seyde Syr Gawayne.

❡"What ys youre name?" seyde the lady, "for ye muste telle or ye passe." "Fayre lady, my name ys Sir Gawayne, the Kynges son Lotte of Orkeney, and my modir ys Kynge Arthurs sister." "Than ar ye nevew unto the Kynge," seyde the lady. "Well," seyde the lady, "I shall so speke for you that ye shall have leve to go unto Kynge Arthure for hys love." And so she departed and tolde the foure knyghtes how the presonere was Kynge Arthurs nevew—"and hys name ys Sir Gawayne, Kynge Lottis son of Orkeney." So they gaff hym leve and toke hym the hartes hede, because hit was in the queste; and than they delyverde hym undir thys promyse, that he sholde bere the dede lady with hym on thys maner: the hede of her was hanged aboute hys necke, and the hole body of hir before hym on hys horse mane.

fol. 39v

❡Ryght so he rode forthe unto Camelot. And anone as he was com Merlion dud make Kynge Arthure[5] that Sir Gawayne was sworne to telle of hys adventure, and how he slew the lady, and how he wolde gyff no mercy unto the knyght, wherethorow the lady was

3. How are you?
4. I.e., confer, attribute.
5. *Make Kynge Arthure:* make King Arthur ensure.

slayne. Than the Kynge and the Quene were gretely displeased
with Sir Gawayne for the sleynge of the lady; and there by ordynaunce of the Queene there was sette a queste of ladyes uppon
Sir Gawayne, and they juged hym for ever whyle he lyved to be with
all ladyes and to fyght for hir quarels, and ever that he sholde be 5
curteyse, and never to refuse mercy to hym that askith mercy. Thus
was Sir Gawayne sworne uppon the foure Evaungelystis that he
sholde never be ayenste lady ne jantillwoman, but if he fyght for a
lady and hys adversary fyghtith for another. And thus endith the
adventure of Sir Gawayne that he dud at the mariage of Arthure. 10

Whan Sir Torre was redy, he mounted uppon horsebacke [9]
and rode afftir the knyght with the brachett. And so as
he rode he mette with a dwarff, suddeynly, that smote hys horse
on the hede with a staff, that he reled bakwarde hys spere lengthe.[6] 15
¶"Why dost thou so?" seyde Sir Torre. "For thou shalt nat passe
thys way but if thou juste with yondir knyghtes of the pavilions."
Than was Sir Torre ware where were two pavilions, and grete sperys
stood oute, and two shildes hangynge on treys by the pavilions. "I
may nat tarry," seyd Sir Torre, "for I am in a queste that I muste 20
nedys folow." "Thou shalt nat passe thys wey!" seyde the dwarff, fol. 40r
and therewithall he blew hys horne.
¶Than there com one armed on horsebacke and dressed hys
shylde and com fast towarde Sir Torre—and than he dressed hym
ayenste hem and so ran togydirs, and Sir Torre bare hym frome hys 25
horse; and anone the knyght yelded hym to hys mercy—"but, sir,
I have a felow in yondir pavilyon that woll have ado with you
anone." "He shall be wellcom," seyde Sir Torre. Than was he ware
of another knyght commynge with grete rawndom, and eche of
hem dressed to other, that mervayle hit was to se. 30
¶But the knyght smote Sir Torre a grete stroke in myddys the
shylde, that his spere all to-shyverde. And Sir Torre smote hym
thorow the shylde benethe, that hit wente thorow the coste of the
knyght—but the stroke slew hym nat. And therewith Sir Torre
alyght and smote hym on the helme a grete stroke, and therewith 35
the knyght yelded hym and besought hym of mercy. "I woll well,"
seyde Sir Torre, "but ye and youre felow muste go unto Kynge
Arthure and yelde you presoners[7] unto hym."
¶"By whom shall we sey we ar thydir sente?"
¶"Ye shall sey, 'by the knyght that wente in the queste of the 40
knyght with the brachette.'
¶"Now, what be your two namys?" seyde Sir Torre. "My name
ys," seyde that one, "Sir Phelot of Langeduke." "And my name ys,"
seyde the othir, "Sir Petipace of Wynchilsee." "Now go ye forthe,"
seyde Sir Torre, "and God spede you and me." Than cam the dwarff, 45
and seyde unto Sir Torre, "I pray you gyff me my bone."[8] "I woll
well," seyde Sir Torre, "aske and ye shall have." "I aske no more,"

6. The length of his spear.
7. I.e., as prisoners.
8. I.e., boon, request.

seyde the dwarff, "but that ye woll suffir me to do you servyse, for
I woll serve no more recreaunte knyghtes." "Well, take an horse,"
seyde Sir Torre, "and ryde one⁹ with me." "For I wote,"¹ seyde the
dwarff, "ye ryde afftir the knyght with the whight brachette, and I
shall brynge you where he ys," seyde the dwarff. And so they rode
thorowoute a foreste, and at the laste they were ware of two pavilions evyn by a pryory, with two sheldes, and that one shylde was
enewed with whyght and that othir shylde was rede.

Therewith Sir Torre alyght, and toke the dwarff² hys glayve, and
so he com to the whyght pavilion. He saw three damesels lye in
hyt on a paylette, slepynge; and so he wente unto the tother pavylyon and founde a lady lyynge in hit slepynge—but therein was
the whyght brachett that bayed at hym faste. And than Sir Torre
toke up the brachette and wente hys way and toke hit to the
dwarffe. And with the noyse the lady com oute of the pavilion, and
all hir damesels, and seyde, "Woll ye take my brachette frome me?"

❡"Ye," seyde Sir Torre, "this brachett have I sought, frome Kynge
Arthures courte hydir." "Well," seyde the lady, "sir knyght, ye shall
nat go farre with hir but that ye woll be mette with and greved."
"I³ shall abyde what adventure that commyth, by the grace of
God"—and so mownted uppon hys horse and passed on hys way
towarde Camelot. But hit was so nere nyght he myght nat passe but
litill farther. "Know ye any lodgyng here nye?" seyde Sir Torre.

"I know none," seyde the dwarff, "but here besydys ys an ermytaige, and there ye muste take lodgynge⁴ as ye fynde." And within
a whyle they com to the hermytage and toke such lodgynge as was
there, and as⁵ grasse and otis and brede for their horsis. Sone hit
was spedde, and full harde was their souper. But there they rested
them all nyght tylle on the morne, and herde a Masse devoutely,
and so toke their leve of the ermyte. And so Sir Torre prayde the
ermyte to pray for hym—and he seyde he wolde—and betoke hym
to God, and so mownted uppon horsebacke and rode towardis Camelot a longe whyle.

❡So with that they herde a knyght calle lowde that com afftir
them, and seyde, "Knyght, abyde and yelde my brachette that thou
toke frome my lady!"

❡Sir Torre returned agayne and behelde hym how he was a
semely knyght and well horsed and armed at all poyntes.⁶ Than Sir
Torre dressed hys shylde and toke hys glayve in hys hondys; and so
they com fersely on as freysshe men, and droff both horse and man
to the erthe. Anone they arose lyghtly and drew hir swerdis as egirly
as lyons, and put their shyldis before them, and smote thorow their
shyldys, that the cantels felle on bothe partyes. Also they tamed
their helmys, that the hote bloode ran oute; and the thycke mayles

9. I.e., on.
1. *For I wote:* Since I know.
2. I.e., the dwarf took.
3. Torre is speaking.
4. I.e., such lodging.
5. I.e., such as was there.
6. *At all poyntes:* in every respect.

of their hawbirkes they carff and rooffe in sundir,[7] that the hote
bloode ran to the erthe. And bothe they had many woundys and
were passynge wery. But Sir Torre aspyed that the tothir knyght
faynted, and than he sewed faste uppon hym and doubled hys
strokis and stroke hym to the erthe on the one syde. Than Sir Torre
bade hym yelde hym.

¶ "That woll I nat," seyde Abelleus, "whyle lastith the lyff and the
soule in my body—onles that thou wolte geff me the brachette."
"That woll I nat," seyde Sir Torre, "for hit was my queste to brynge
agayne the brachette, thee, other bothe."

¶ With that cam a damesell rydynge on a palferey as faste as she
myght dryve, and cryed with lowde voice unto Sir Torre. "What
woll ye with me?" seyde Sir Torre. "I beseche the," seyde the damesell, "for Kynge Arthurs love, gyff me a gyffte. I requyre the, jantill
knyght, as thou arte a jantillman."

¶ "Now," seyde Sir Torre, "aske a gyffte and I woll gyff hit you."

¶ "Grauntemercy," seyde the damesell. "Now I aske the hede of
thys false knyght, Abelleus, for he ys the moste outerageous knyght
that lyvith—and the grettist murtherer."

¶ "I am lothe," seyde Sir Torre, "of that gyffte I have gyvyn you;
but[8] lette hym make amendys in that he hathe trespasced agayne
you."

¶ "Now," seyde the damesell, "I may nat, for he slew myne owne
brothir before myne yghen—that was a bettir knyght than he, and
he had had grace.[9] And I kneled halfe an owre before hym, in the
myre, for to sauff my brothirs lyff that had done hym no damage,
but fought with hym by adventure of armys—and so, for all that
I coude do, he strake of hys hede. Wherefore I requyre the, as
thou arte a trew knyght, to gyff me my gyffte, othir ellis I shall
shame the in all the courte of Kynge Arthure; for he ys the falsyste
knyght lyvynge, and a grete destroyer of men, and namely of good
knyghtes."

¶ So whan Abellyus herde thys he was more aferde and yelded
hym and asked mercy.

¶ "I may nat now," seyde Sir Torre, "but I sholde be founde false
of my promyse, for erewhyle, whan I wolde have tane you to mercy,
ye wolde none aske but iff ye had the brachett agayne that was my
queste." And therewith he toke off hys helme, and therewith he
arose and fledde, and Sir Torre afftir[1] hym—and smote of hys hede
quyte. "Now, sir," seyde the damesell, "hyt ys nere nyght. I pray
you com and lodge with me hereby at my place." "I woll well,"
seyde Sir Torre "for my horse and I have fared evyll syn we
departed frome Camelot." And so he rode with her, and had passynge good chere with hir. And she had a passyng fayre olde knyght
unto hir husbande that made hym good chere and well easyd both
hys horse and hym. And on the morne he herde hys Masse and

fol.41r

[11]

fol.41v

7. Asunder, apart.
8. I.e., instead.
9. *And he had had grace*: if he had received mercy.
1. I.e., fled after.

brake hys faste, and toke hys leve of the knyght and of the lady, that besought hym to telle hys name.

"Truly," he seyde, "my name ys Sir Torre, that was late made knyght—and thys was the firste queste of armys that ever Y ded, to brynge agayne that[2] thys knyght Abelleus toke away frome Kynge Arthurs courte." 5

"Now, fayre knyght," seyde the lorde and the lady, "and ye come here in oure marchys, se here youre poore[3] lodgynge, and hit shall be allwayes at youre commaundemente." So Sir Torre departed and com to Camelot on the third day by noone. And the Kynge and the 10 Quene and all the courte was passynge fayne of hys commynge, and made grete joy that he was com agayne—for he wente frome the courte with litill succour but as Kynge Pellynor, hys fadir, gaff hym an olde courser, and Kynge Arthur gaff hym armour and swerde; other ellis had he none other succour, but rode so forthe 15 hymself alone. And than the Kynge and the Quene, by Merlions advice, made hym swere to telle of hys adventures; and so he tolde and made prevys of hys dedys, as hit ys before reherced—wherefore the Kynge and the Quene made grete joy.

¶"Nay, nay!" seyde Merlion, "thys ys but japis that he hath do, 20 for he shall preve a noble knyght of proues as few lyvynge, and jantyl and curteyse and of good tacchys, and passyng trew of hys promyse, and never shall he outerage." Wherethorow Merlions wordis Kynge Arthure gaff an erledom of londis that felle unto[4] hym. And here endith the queste of Sir Torre, Kynge Pellynors sonne. 25

THan Kynge Pellynore armed hym and mownted uppon hys horse, and rode more than a pace after the lady that the knyght lad away.[5] And as he rode in a foreyste he saw in a valey a damesell sitte by a well, and a wounded knyght in her armys. And Kynge Pellynor salewed hir, and whan she was ware of hym, she 30 cryed on lowde and seyde, "Helpe me, knyght, for Jesuys sake!" [12]   fol. 42r

¶But Kynge Pellynore wolde nat tarry, he was so egir in hys queste—and ever she cryed an hondred tymes aftir helpe.

¶Whan she saw he wolde nat abyde, she prayde unto God to 35 sende hym[6] as much nede of helpe as she had, and that he myght feele hit or he deyed. So, as the booke tellith, the knyght there dyed that was wounded—wherefore for pure sorow the lady slew hirselff with hys swerde. As Kynge Pellynore rode in that valey he mette with a poore man, a laborer, and seyde, "Sawyst thou ony 40 knyght rydynge thys way ledyng a lady?"

¶"Ye, sir," seyde the man. "I saw that knyght and the lady, that made grete dole. And yondir beneth in a valey there shall ye se two pavilions; and one of the knyghtes of the pavilions chalenged[7] that lady of that knyght, and seyde she was hys cosyne nere, wherefore 45

2. I.e., that which.
3. I.e., humble.
4. *Felle unto*: were befitting to.
5. See p. 66.
6. I.e., her knight.
7. I.e., challenged possession of.

he sholde lede hir no farther. And so they waged batayle in that quarell; that one seyde he wolde have hir by force, and that other seyde he wold have the rule of her, for he was hir kynnesman and wolde lede hir to hir kynne." So for thys quarell he leffte hem fyghtynge—"and if ye woll ryde a pace ye shall fynde them fyghtynge, and the lady was leffte with two squyers in the pavelons."

"God thanke the," seyde Kynge Pellynor. Than he rode a walop tylle he had a syght of the two pavilons and the two knyghtys fyghtynge. And anone he rode unto the pavilons and saw the lady how she was there—for she was hys queste—and seyde, "Fayre lady, ye muste go with me unto the courte of Kynge Arthure." "Sir knyght," seyde the two squyres, "yondir ar two knyghtes that fyght for thys lady:

❡"Go ye thyder and departe[8] them, and be ye agreed with them, and than may ye have hir at youre plesure."

❡"Ye sey well," seyde Kynge Pellynor. And anone he rode betwixte hem and departed them, and asked them their causis why they fought.   fol.42v

❡"Sir knyght," seyde that one, "I shall telle you. Thys lady ys my kynneswoman nye, my awntis doughtir, and whan I herde hir complayne that she was with hym magré hir hede,[9] I waged batayle to fyght with hym." "Sir knyght," seyde thys other, whos name was Outelake of Wentelonde, "and thys lady I gate be my prouesse of hondis and armys thys day at Arthurs courte." "That ys nat trew," seyde Kynge Pellynor, "for ye com in suddeynly there as we were at the hyghe feste and toke awey thys lady or ony man myght make hym redy—and therefore hit was my queste to brynge her agayne and you bothe, othir ellis that one of us to leve[1] in the fylde. Therefore thys lady shall go with me, othir I shall dye therefore, for so have I promysed Kynge Arthur. And therefore fyght ye no more, for none of you shall have parte of hir at thys tyme—and if ye lyst for to fyght for hir with me, I woll defende hir."

❡"Well, seyde the knyghtes, "make you redy, and we shall assayle you with all oure power." And as Kynge Pellynor wolde have put hys horse frome hym, Sir Outelake roff hys horse thorow with a swerde, and seyde, "Now art thou afoote as well as we ar."

❡Whan Kynge Pellynore aspyed that hys horse was slayne, lyghtly he lepe frome hys horse and pulled oute hys swerde and put hys shylde afore hym, and seyde, "Knyght, kepe the[2] well, for thou shalt have a buffette for the sleynge of my horse." So Kynge Pellynor gaff hym such a stroke uppon the helme that he clave the hede downe to the chyne, and felle downe to the erthe dede. Than he turned [13] hym to the other knyght, that was sore wounded—but whan he saw that buffette he wolde nat fyght, but kneled downe and seyde, "Take my cosyn, thys lady, with you, as ys youre queste, and I

8. I.e., separate.
9. *Magré hir hede*: despite her wishes.
1. *To leve*: i.e., be left dead.
2. Thee.

require you, as ye be a trew knyght, put hir to no shame nother vylony."

¶"What?" seyde Kynge **Pellynore**, "woll ye nat fyght for hir?"

¶"No," seyde the knyght, "I woll nat fyght with such a knyght of proues as ye be." 5

¶"Well," seyde Kynge **Pellynore**, "I promyse you she shall have no vyllany by me, as I am trew knyght." "But now me wantis an horse," seyde Kynge **Pellynor**, "but I woll have **Outelakis** horse." "Sir, ye shall nat nede," seyde the knyght, "for I shall gyff you such an horse as shall please you, so that ye woll lodge with me, for hit ys 10 nere nyght." "I woll well," seyde Kynge **Pellynore**, "abyde with you all nyght." And there he had with hym ryght good chere and fared fol.43r of the beste with passyng good wyne, and had myry reste that nyght; and on the morne he harde Masse and dyned. And so was brought hym a fayre bay courser, and Kynge **Pellynors** sadyll sette 15 uppon hym. "Now, what shall I calle you," seyde the knyght, "inasmuch as ye have my cousyn at youre desyre of youre queste?"

"Sir, I shall telle you. My name ys Kynge **Pellynor**, Kynge of the Ilis, and knyght of the Table Rounde."

¶"Now am I glad," seyde the knyght, "that such a noble man 20 sholde have the rule of my cousyn." "Now, what ys youre name?" seyde Kynge **Pellynor**. "I pray you telle me."

¶"Sir, my name ys Sir **Meliot de Logurs**, and thys lady, my cosyn, hir name ys called **Nenyve**. And thys knyght that was in the other pavilion was my sworne brother, a passynge good knyght, and hys 25 name ys **Bryan** of the Ilis—and he ys full lothe to do ony wronge or to fyght with ony man but if he be sore sought on."[3] "Hit ys mervayle," seyde Kynge Pellynor, "he wolde nat have ado with me."

¶"Sir, he woll nat have ado with no man but if hit be at hys requeste." 30

¶"I pray you brynge hym to the courte one of thes dayes," seyde Kynge **Pellynor**. "Sir, we woll com togydirs." "Ye shall be wellcom," seyde Kynge **Pellynore**, "to the courte of Kynge **Arthure**, and ye shall be gretely alowed for youre commynge." And so he departed with the lady and brought her to **Camelot**. But so as they rode in a valey, 35 hit was full of stonys, and there the ladyes horse stumbled and threw her downe, and hir arme was sore bruised, that nerehonde she swooned for payne. "Alas!" seyde the lady, "myn arme ys oute of lythe,[4] wherethorow I muste nedys reste me."

¶"Ye shall well," seyde Kynge **Pellynor**. And so he alyght undir a 40 tre where was fayre grasse, and he put hys horse thereto, and so rested hem undir the tre and slepte tylle hit was ny nyght. And whan he awooke he wolde have rydden forthe, but the lady seyde, "Ye may as well ryde backwarde as forewarde, hit ys so durke." So they abode stylle and made there theire lodgyng. Than Kynge **Pel-** 45 **lynor** put of[5] hys armoure. Than so, a litill tofore mydnyght, they herde the trottynge of an horse.

---

3. *Sore sought on:* greatly provoked.
4. *Oute of lythe:* dislocated.
5. *Put of:* took off.

❡"Be ye stylle," seyde Kynge Pellynor, "for we shall hyre of som   [14]
adventure." And therewith he armed hym.   fol.43v

❡So ryght evyn before hym there mette two knyghtes, that one
com frowarde Camelot, and that othir com from the Northe, and
eyther salewed other and asked.[6] "What tydynges at Camelot?" seyde   5
that one knyght.

❡"Be[7] my hede, there have I bene and aspied the courte of Kynge
Arthure, and there ys such a felyship that they may never be brokyn—and well-nyghe all the world holdith with Arthure, for there
ys the floure of chevalry. And now for thys cause am I rydyng into   10
the Northe, to telle oure chyfftaynes of the felyship that ys withholdyn with Kynge Arthure." "As for that," seyde the othir knyght,
"I have brought a remedy with me that ys the grettist poysen that
ever ye herde speke off. And to Camelot woll I with hit, for we have
a frende ryght nyghe the Kynge, well cheryshed, that shall poysen   15
Kynge Arthur—for so hath he promysed oure chyfftaynes, and
receyved grete gyfftis for to do hit."

"Beware," seyde the othir knyght, "of Merlion, for he knowith all
thynges by[8] the devylles craffte." "As for that, woll I nat lett," seyde
the knyght; and so they departed in sondir. And anone aftir that   20
Kynge Pellynor made hym redy, and hys lady, and rode towarde
Camelot. And as they com by the welle there as the wounded knyght
was and the lady, there he founde the knyght and the lady etyn
with[9] lyons other with wylde bestis—all save the hede.

❡Wherefore he made grete sorow, and wepte passynge sore, and   25
seyde, "Alas! hir lyff myght I have saved, but I was so ferse in my
queste that I wolde nat abyde."

❡"Wherefore make ye such doole?" seyde the lady. "I wote nat,"
seyde Kynge Pellinore, "but my herte rwyth sore of the deth of hir
that lyeth yondir, for she was a passyng fayre lady, and a yonge."   30

❡"Now,[1] woll ye do by myne advise? Take this knyght and lette
hym be buryed in an ermytage, and than take this ladyes hede and
bere hit with you unto Kynge Arthure." So Kynge Pellynor toke thys
dede knyght on hys shyld and brought hym to the ermytage, and
charged the heremyte with the coorse, that servyse sholde be done   35
for the soule—"and take ye hys harneyse for youre payne."

❡"Hit shall be done," seyde the hermyte, "as I woll answere to
God." And therewith they departed and com there as the lady lay,   [15]   fol.44r
with a fayre yalow here. That greved Kynge Pellynore passynge sore
whan he loked on hit, for much hys herte caste unto that vysage.   40
And so by noone they com unto Camelot, and the Kynge and the
Quene was passyng fayne of hys commyng to the courte. And there
he was made to swere uppon the foure Evangelistes to telle the
trouthe of hys queste, frome the one ende to that other.

❡"A, Kynge Pellynor," seyde Quene Gwenyver, "ye were gretly to   45
blame that ye saved nat thys ladyes lyff."

---

6. I.e., inquired of each other.
7. I.e., by.
8. I.e., through.
9. I.e., by.
1. The lady is speaking.

❡"Madam," seyde Kynge Pellynore, "ye were gretely to blame and² ye wolde nat save youre owne lyff and ye myght:

❡"But, saff youre displesure,³ I was so furyous in my queste that I wolde nat abyde—and that repentis me,⁴ and shall do dayes⁵ of my lyff."

❡"Truly ye ought sore to repente hit," seyde Merlion, "for that lady was youre owne doughtir, begotyn of the Lady of the Rule. And that knyght that was dede was hir love and sholde have wedded hir, and he was a ryght good knyght of a yonge man, and wolde a preved a good man. And to this courte was he commynge, and hys name was Sir Myles of the Laundis; and a knyght com behynde hym and slew hym with a spere, and hys name was Lorayne le Saveage, a false knyght and a cowherde. And she for grete sorow and dole slew hirselff with his swerde, and hyr name was Alyne—and because ye wolde nat abyde and helpe hir, ye shall se youre beste frende fayle you whan ye be in the grettist distresse that ever ye were othir shall be. And that penaunce God hath ordaynd you for that dede, that he that ye sholde truste moste on of ony man on lyve, he shall leve you there ye shall be slayne."

❡"Me forthynkith hit," seyde Kynge Pellynor, "that thus shall me betyde—but God may well fordo desteny."

❡Thus whan the queste was done of the whyght herte, the whych folowed Sir Gawayne, and the queste of the brachet, whych folowed Sir Torre, Kynge Pellynors son, and the queste of the lady that the knyghte toke away, whych at that tyme folowed Kynge Pellynor, than the Kynge stablysshed all the knyghtes and gaff them rychesse and londys—and charged them never to do outerage nothir mourthir, and allwayes to fle treson, and to gyff mercy unto hym that askith mercy, uppon payne of forfiture of their worship and lordship of Kynge Arthure for evirmore; and allwayes to do ladyes, damesels, and jantilwomen and wydowes [socour], strengthe hem in hir ryghtes, and never to enforce them, uppon payne of dethe. Also, that no man take no batayles in a wrongefull quarell, for no love ne for no worldis goodis. So unto thys were all knyghtes sworne of the Table Rounde, both olde and yonge; and every yere so were they sworne at the hyghe feste of Pentecoste.⁶

fol.44v

Explicit the Weddyng of Kyng Arthur.

2. I.e., if.
3. *Saff youre displesure:* may it not displease you.
4. *Repentis me:* I repent.
5. I.e., all the days.
6. See n. 1, p. 10. Vinaver calls the oath Arthur has his knights swear, which is not found in Malory's known Arthurian sources, "perhaps the most complete and authentic record of Malory's conception of chivalry" (O³, p. 1335). Although the oath does not have a match in the known sources, it does reflect the oaths of actual chivalric orders in Malory's day; for instance, the ceremonial for making Knights of the Order of the Bath, which, as Richard Barber has observed, is very close to Malory's oath (see p. 780).

Aftir Thes Questis[1]

$$S$$O aftir thes questis of Syr Gawayne, Syr Tor and Kynge Pellynore, than hit befelle that Merlyon felle in dotage on the
damesell that Kynge Pellynore brought to courte, and she
was one of the damesels of the Lady of the Laake, that hyght
Nenyve. But Merlion wolde nat lette her have no reste, but allwayes
he wolde be wyth her. And ever she made Merlion[2] good chere
tylle sche had lerned of hym all maner of thynge that sche desyred;
and he was assoted uppon hir, that he myght nat be from hir.

¶So on a tyme he tolde to Kynge Arthure that he scholde[3] nat
endure longe, but for all his craftes he scholde be putte into the
erthe quyk. And so he tolde the Kyng many thyngis that scholde
befalle—but allwayes he warned the Kyng to kepe well his swerde
and the scawberde, [for he told hym how the swerd and the scau-
bard] scholde be stolyn by a woman frome hym, that he moste
trusted.

¶Also he tolde Kyng Arthure that he scholde mysse hym—"and
yett had ye levir than all youre londis have me agayne."

¶"A," sayde the Kyng, "syn ye knowe of youre evil adventure,
purvey for hit, and putt hit away by youre crauftes, that mysseadventure." Nay," seyde Merlion, "hit woll not be." He departed
frome the Kyng, and within a whyle the damesell of the Lake
departed, and Merlyon went with her evermore wheresomever she
yeode. And oftyntymes Merlion wolde have had hir prevayly away[4]
by his subtyle crauftes. Than she made hym to swere that he sholde
never do none inchauntemente uppon hir if he wolde have his wil;
and so he swore.

Than she and Merlyon wente over the see unto the londe of Benwyke there as Kyng Ban was kyng, that had grete warre ayenste
Kyng Claudas. And there Merlion spake with Kyng Bayans wyff, a
fayre lady and a good—hir name was Elayne. And there he sawe
yonge Launcelot. And there the queene made grete sorowe for the
mortal werre that Kyng Claudas made on hir lordis.

¶"Take none hevynesse," seyde Merlyon, "for this same chylde,
yonge Launcelot, shall within this twenty yere revenge you on Kyng
Claudas,[5] that all Crystendom shall speke of hit—and this same
chylde shall be the moste man of worship of the worlde. And his

[IV.1] fol.45r

5

10

15

20

25

30

35

fol.45v

---

1. The title is taken editorially from the opening sentence. In the Winchester MS, this section
   appears to mark a major division, beginning on a new page with the bottom two-thirds of
   the previous page left blank after the *explicit* to the previous section. The initial "S" is in red
   and the letters "o" and initial letters "s" of the first eight words are filled in yellow. The
   MS provides no real indication of a name for this subsection, which presents a wide variety
   of adventures. There is a colophon, but it refers only generally to this and the previous
   sections, from the beginning (p. 112). In his Prologue, Caxton lists the section as *how
   Merlyn was assotted* [i.e., besotted], *and of warre maad to Kyng Arthur;* this describes,
   however, only the opening episodes of the section. Malory's principal source for this subsection is the French prose *Suite de Merlin;* for illustrative selections, see p. 709.
2. On the abbreviation of Merlin's name in the Winchester MS, see n. 4, p. 17.
3. I.e., would.
4. *Prevayly away:* secretly taken away.
5. The revenge is later confirmed implicitly, p. 671, lines 44–45.

fyrst name ys Galahad—that know I well," seyde Merlyon—"and syn[6] ye have confermed[7] hym Launcelot." "That is trouth," seyde the quene, "his name was fyrst Galahad. A, Merlyon," seyde the quene, "shall I lyve to se my son suche a man of prouesse?" "Yee, hardely, lady, on my perelle[8] ye shall se hit—and lyve many wyntirs aftir."

¶Than sone aftir the lady and Merlyon departed. And by weyes[9] he shewed hir many wondyrs, and so come into Cornuayle. And allwayes he lay aboute to have hir maydynhode, and she was ever passynge wery of hym and wolde have bene delyverde of hym, for she was aferde of hym for cause he was a devyls son,[1] and she cowde not be skyfte of hym by no meane.

¶And so one[2] a tyme Merlyon ded shew hir in a roche whereas was a grete wondir, and wrought by enchauntement, that went undir a grete stone. So by hir subtyle worchyng she made Merlyon to go undir that stone to latte hir wete of the mervayles there; but she wrought so there for hym that he come never oute for all the craufte he coude do—and so she departed and leffte Merlyon. And as Kyng Arthure rode to Camelot—and helde there a grete feste with myrth and joy—

¶And sone aftir he returned unto Cardolle. And there come unto Arthure newe tydynges that the Kyng of Denmarke and the Kyng of Irelonde, that was his brothir, and the Kyng of the Vale and the Kynge of Sorleyse and the Kyng of the Ile of Longtaynse, all these fyve kynges with a grete oste was entirde into the londis of Kyng Arthure, and brent and slewe and distroyed clene byfore hem bothe the citeis and castels, that hit was pité to here.

¶"Alas!" seyde Arthure, "yet had I never reste one monethe syne I was Kyng crowned of this londe. Now shall I never reste tylle I mete with tho kyngis in a fayre felde—that I make myne avow, for my trwe lyege peple shall nat be destroyed in my defaughte.[3] Therefore go with me who so woll, and abyde who that wyll."

¶Than Kyng Arthure lette wryte unto Kyng Pellynor and prayde hym in all haste to make hym redy "with suche peple as we myght lyghtlyeste arere"—and to hyghe hym aftir in haste. Than all the barownes were wrothe prevaily that the Kynge wolde departe so suddaynly; but the Kynge by no meane wolde abyde, but made wrytyng[4] unto them that were nat ther and bade hyghe them aftir hym suche as were nat at that tyme at that courte.

¶Than the Kynge come to Quene Gwenyver and seyde unto her, "Madame, make you redy, for ye shall go with me—for I may nat longe mysse you. Ye shall cause me to be the more hardy, what adventure so befalle me—yette woll I nat wyghte my lady to be in no joupardye." "Sir, she seyde, "I am at youre commaundemente,

---

6. I.e., since that naming.
7. I.e., named through the sacrament of Confirmation.
8. *On my perelle:* (I swear) on peril of my salvation.
9. *By weyes:* on the way.
1. *For cause:* because. For an account of Merlin's origins that Malory was likely to have known, see p. 705.
2. I.e., on.
3. *In my defaughte:* through my fault.
4. *Made wrytyng:* had letters sent.

and shall be redy at all tymes." So on the morne the Kyng and the Quene departed with suche felyship as they had and come into the North, into a forerste besyde Humbir, and there lodged hem.

¶So whan this worde come unto the fyve kynges abovynseyde that Arthure was besyde Humbir in a foreste, so there was a knyght, brothir unto one of the fyve kynges, that gaff hem suche[5] counseyle: "Ye knowe well that Sir Arthur hath the floure of chevalry of the worlde with hym—and hit[6] preved by the grete batayle he did with the eleven kynges—and therefore hyghe ye unto hym nyght and day tyll that we be nyghe hym, for the lenger he taryeth the bygger he is, and we ever the weyker. And he is so corageous of hymself that he is com to the felde with lytyll peple, and therefore lette us sette uppon hym or day and we shall sle downe of his knyghtes that none shall helpe other of them."

¶Soo unto this counseyle these fyve kynges assented; and so they passed forth with hir oste thorow North Walys and come uppon Arthure be nyght, and sette uppon his oste as the Kynge and his knyghtes were in theire pavylyons. So Kynge Arthure was unarmed and leyde hym to reste with his Quene Gwenyvere. "Sir," seyde Sir Kayyus, "hit is nat beste we be unarmed." "We shall have no nede," seyde Sir Gawayne and Sir Gryflet, that lay in a lytyll pavylyon by the Kynge.

¶So with that they harde a grete noyse and many cryed "Treson!"

¶"Alas," seyde Arthure, "we be betrayed—unto armys, felowys!" than he cryed. So they were armed anone at all poyntes.

¶Than come there a wounded knyght unto the Kynge, and seyde, "Sir, save youreself and my lady the Quene, for oure oste is destroyed, and slayne is much of oure peple." So anone the Kynge and the Quene and the three knyghtes toke hir horses and rode toward Humbir to passe over hit. And the watir was so rowghe that they were aferde to passe over hit.

¶"Now may ye chose," seyde Kynge Arthure, "whethir ye woll abyde and take the adventure on this syde—for and[7] ye be takyn they wol sle you." "Yet were me lever[8] to dey in this watir than to falle in youre enemyes handis," seyde the Quene, "and there to be slayne."

¶And as they stode talkyng, Sir Kayus saw the fyve kynges commynge on horsebak by hemself alone, wyth hir sperys in hir hondis, evyn towarde hem.

¶"Lo!" seyde Sir Kayus, "yondir be tho fyve kynges—lette us go to them and macche hem." "That were foly," seyde Sir Gawayne, "for we ar but foure and they be fyve." "That is trouth," seyde Sir Gryfflette. "No force,"[9] seyd Sir Kayus. "I woll undirtake for two of the beste of hem, and than may ye three undirtake for all the othir three."

5. I.e., the following.
6. I.e., it being.
7. I.e., if.
8. Were me lever: I would prefer.
9. No force: that does not matter.

¶And therewithall Sir Kay lette his horse renne as faste as he myght to encountir with one of them, and strake one of the kynges thorow the shelde and also the body a fadom, that the kyng felle to the erthe starke dede.

¶That sawe Sir Gawayne and ran unto anothir kyng so harde that he smote hym downe and thorow the body with a spere, that he felle to the erthe dede.

¶Anone Sir Arthure ran to anothir and smote hym thorow the body with a spere, that he fell to the erthe dede.

¶Than Sir Gryfflet ran to the fourth Kynge and gaff hym suche a falle that his necke brake in sondir.

¶Than Sir Kay ran unto the fyfth kynge and smote hym so harde on the helme that the stroke clave the helme and hede to the erthe. "That was well stryken," seyde Kynge Arthure, "and worshipfully haste thou holde thy promyse—therefore I shall honoure the[1] whyle that I lyve." And therewithall they sate the Quene in a barge into Humbir—but allwayes Quene Gwenyvere praysed Sir Kay for his dedis, and seyde, "What[2] lady that ye love, and she love you nat agayne, she were gretly to blame. And amonge all ladyes," seyde the Quene, "I shall bere your noble fame, for ye spake a grete worde[3] and fulfylled hit worshipfully."

¶And therewith the Quene departed.

¶Than the Kynge and the three knyghtes rode into the forerste, for there they supposed to here of them that were ascapid,[4] and there founde the moste party of his peple, and tolde hem how the fyve kynges were dede—"and therefore lette us holde us togedyrs tyll hit be day:

¶"And whan hir oste have aspyed that their chyfteynes be slayne, they woll make such dole that they shall nat helpe hemself." And ryght as the Kynge seyde, so hit was, for whan they founde the fyve kynges dede they made such dole that they felle downe of there horsis.

¶And therewithall com in Kyng Arthure but with a fewe peple and slewe on the ryght honde and the lyffte honde,[5] that well-nye there ascaped no man, but all were slayne to the numbir of thirty thousand. And whan the batayle was all ended, the Kynge kneled downe and thanked God mekely. And than he sente for the Quene, and anone she was com and made grete joy of the overcommynge of that batayle.

¶Therewithall come one[6] to Kynge Arthure and tolde hym that Kynge Pellynore was within three myle with a grete oste, and seyde, "Go unto hym and let hym undirstonde how we have spedde." So within a whyle Kyng Pellynore com with a grete oste and salewed the peple and the Kynge, and there was grete joy on every syde.

---

1. Thee.
2. I.e., Whatever.
3. I.e., promise.
4. I.e., escaped from the previous battle.
5. I.e., on all sides.
6. I.e., someone.

❡Than the Kynge let serch how many peple he had slayne,[7] and there was founde but lytyll paste two hondred men slayne—and eyght knyghtes of the Table Rounde, in their pavylyons.

❡Than the Kynge lat rere and devyse,[8] in the same place there as the batayle was done and made, a fayre abbay, and endewed hit with grete lyvelode,[9] and let calle hit the Abbay of **La Beale Adventure.** But whan som of them come into there contrayes there as the fyve kynges were kynges, and tolde hem how they were slayne, there was made grete dole. And all the Kynge **Arthurs** enemyes— as the Kynge of North Walis and the kynges of the Northe—knewe of this batayle; they were passynge hevy. And so the Kynge retourned unto **Camelot** in haste, and whan he was com to **Camelot** he called Kyng **Pellynore** unto hym, and seyde, "Ye undirstonde well that we have loste eyght knyghtes of the beste of the Table Rounde; and by youre advyse we muste chose eyght knyghtes of the beste we may fynde in this courte." "Sir," seyde **Pellynore,** "I shall counsayle you aftir my conceyte the beste wyse:[1]

❡"There ar in youre courte full noble knyghtes bothe of olde and yonge; and be myne advyse ye shall chose half of the olde and half of the yonge." "Whych be the olde?" seyde Kynge **Arthure.** "Sir, mesemyth Kynge **Uryence,** that hath wedded youre sistir **Morgan le Fay;** and the Kynge of the Lake; and Sir **Herbyse de Revell,** a noble knyght; and Sir **Galagars,** the fourthe." "This is well devysed," seyde **Arthure,** "and ryght so shall hit be:

❡"Now, whyche ar the foure yonge knyghtes?" "Sir, the fyrste is Sir **Gawayne,** youre nevew, that is as good a knyght of his tyme as is ony in this londe; and the secunde as mesemyth beste is Sir **Gryfflette le Fyse de Du,** that is a good knyght and full desyrous[2] in armys—and who may se hym lyve, he shall preve a good knyght; and the thirde as mesemyth ys well worthy to be one of the Table Rounde, Sir **Kay the Seneschall,** for many tymes he hath done full worshipfully—and now at youre laste batayle he dud full honorably for to undirtake to sle two Kynges."

❡"Be my hede," seyde **Arthure,** "ye sey soth. He is beste worthy to be a knyght of the Rounde Table of ony that is rehersed yet, and[3] he had done no more prouesse his lyve dayes."

❡"Now," seyde Kynge **Pellynore,** "chose you of two knyghtes that I shall reherce whyche is moste worthy, of Sir **Bagdemagus and Sir Tor,** my son—but for because he is my son, I may nat praysa hym, but ellys, and he were nat my son, I durste say that of his age there is nat in this londe a better knyght than he is, nother of bettir condycions, and loth to do ony wronge and loth to take ony wronge."

❡"Be my hede," seyde **Arthure,** "he is a passyng good knight as ony ye spake of this day. That wote I well," seyde the Kynge, "for

---

7. *Let serch:* caused to be found out. *He had slayne:* i.e., of his that were slain.
8. *Lat rere and devyse:* caused to be planned and raised.
9. *Grete lyvelode:* a large source of income, an endowment.
1. *Aftir my conceyte the beste wyse:* according to my best judgment.
2. I.e., eager.
3. I.e., even if.

I have sene hym proved; but he seyth but lytil, but he doth much more—for I know none in all this courte, and he were as well borne on his modir syde as he is on youre syde, that is lyke hym of prouesse and of myght. And therefore I woll have hym at this tyme, and leve Sir Bagdemagus tyll anothir tyme."

¶So whan they were chosyn by the assent of the barouns, so were there founden in hir seges every knyghtes name that here ar reherced. And so were they sette in hir seges—whereof Sir Bagdemagus was wondirly wrothe that Sir Tor was avaunced afore hym. And therefore soddeynly he departed frome the courte and toke his squyre with hym, and rode longe in a foreste tyll they come to a crosse, and there he alyght and seyde his prayers devoutely. The meanewhyle, his squyre founde wretyn uppon the crosse that Bagdemagus sholde never retourne unto the courte agayne tyll he had wonne a knyght of the Table Rounde, body-for-body.[4]

¶"Loo!" seyde his squyer, "here I fynde wrytyng of[5] you; therefore I rede you, returne agayne to the courte." "That shall I never," seyde Bagdemagus, "tyll men speke of me ryght grete worship,[6] and that I be worthy to be a knyght of the Rounde Table."

And so he rode forth, and there by the way he founde a braunche of holy[7] herbe, that was the signe of the Sancgreall—and no knyght founde no suche tokyns but he were a good lyver and a man of prouesse.

¶So as Sir Bagdemagus rode to se many adventures, so hit happed hym to com to the roche there as the Lady of the Lake[8] had put Merlyon[9] undir the stone, and there he herde hym make a grete dole—wherefore Sir Bagdemagus wolde have holpyn hym, and wente unto the grete stone, and hit was so hevy that an hondred men myght nat lyffte hit up.

¶Whan Merlyon wyste that he was there, he bade hym leve his laboure, for all was in vayne—for he myght never be holpyn but by her that put hym there. And so Bagdemagus departed and dud many adventures, and preved aftir a full good knyght, and come ayen to the courte and was made knyght of the Rounde Table.

¶So on the morne there befelle new tydyngis and many othir adventures.

Than hit befelle that Arthure and many of his knyghtes rode on huntynge into a grete foreste. And hit happed Kynge Arthure and Kynge Uryence and Sir Accalon of Gawle folowed a grete harte; for they three were well horsed, and so they chaced so faste that within a whyle they three were more than ten myle from her felyshep. And at the laste they chaced so sore that they slewe hir horsis undirnethe them—and the horses were so fre that

4. One-on-one.
5. I.e., about
6. *Speke of me ryght grete worship*: say very honorable things about me.
7. As an evergreen plant, holly is a traditional symbol of eternal life; this, combined with its blood red berries and thorny leaves, has also made it a traditional symbol of Christ and the implications of His life and death.
8. I.e., Nenyve, "one of the damesels of the Lady of the Laake" (p. 78, line 7).
9. This is the last instance in the Winchester MS of the abbreviation of Merlin's name to M., about which see n. 4, p. 17.

they felle downe dede. Than were all three on foote, and ever they saw the harte before them, passynge wery and inboced.

"What shall we do?" seyde Kynge Arthure, "we ar harde bestadde."[1] "Lette us go on foote," seyde Kynge Uryence, "tyll we may mete with somme lodgyng."

¶Than were they ware of the harte that lay on a grete watir banke, and a brachette bytyng on his throte—and mo othir houndis come aftir.

¶Than Kynge Arthure blewe the pryce[2] and dyght the harte. Than the Kynge loked aboute the worlde and sawe before hym in a grete water a lytyll shippe, all apparayled with sylke downe to the watir. And the shippe cam ryght unto them and landed on the sandis. Than Arthure wente to the banke and loked in and saw none erthely creature therein.

¶"Sirs," seyde the Kynge, "com thens, and let us se what is in this shippe." So at the laste they wente into the shippe, all three, and founde hit rychely behanged with cloth of sylke. So by that tyme hit was durke nyght, there suddeynly was aboute them an hondred torchis sette uppon all the shyppebordis, and hit gaff grete lyght. And therewithall there come twelve fayre damesels and salued Kynge Arthure on hir kneis, and called hym be his name and seyde he was ryght wellcom, and suche chere as they had he sholde have of the beste.[3] Than the Kynge thanked hem fayre.

¶Therewythall they ledde the Kynge and his felawys into a fayre chambir, and there was a clothe leyde rychely beseyne[4] of all that longed to a table, and there were they served of all wynes and metys that they coude thynke of. But of that the Kynge had grete mervayle, for he never fared bettir in his lyff as for one souper.

¶And so whan they had souped at her leyser, Kyng Arthure was lad into a chambir—a rycher besene chambir sawe he never none—and so was Kynge Uryence served and lad into such anothir chambir, and Sir Accolon was lad into the thirde chambir, passyng rychely and well besayne. And so were they leyde in their beddis easyly, and anone they felle on slepe and slepte merveylously sore all the nyght.

And on the morne Kynge Uryence was in Camelot, abedde in his wyves armys, Morgan le Fay. And whan he woke he had grete mervayle how he com there, for on the evyn before he was two dayes jurney frome Camelot. And whan kyng Arthure awoke he founde hymself in a durke preson, heryng aboute hym many complayntes of wofull knyghtes. "What ar ye that so complayne?" seyde Kyng Arthure. "We bene here twenty knyghtes presoners, and som of us hath layne here eyght yere, and som more and somme lesse." "For what cause?" seyde Arthure. "We shall tell you," seyde the knyghtes:

¶"This lorde of this castell, his name is Sir Damas, and he is the

fol.49v 10

5

15

20

25

30

35

fol.50r

40

[7]

45

---

1. Hard pressed, in difficulty.
2. *Blewe the pryce:* blew a horn to signal the dogs' seizure of the prey.
3. *Suche chere as they had he sholde have of the beste:* he would receive the best welcome they could offer.
4. *Rychely beseyne:* magnificently presented.

falsyst knyght that lyvyth, and full of treson, and a very cowarde as lyvyth. And he hath a yonger brothir, a good knyght of prouesse, and his name is Sir **Oughtlake**. And this traytoure **Damas**, the elder brother, woll geff hym no parte of his londis, but as Sir **Outlake** kepyth thorow prouesse of his hondis[5]—and so he kepith frome hym a full fayre maner and a rych, and therein Sir **Outlake** dwellyth worshypfully and is well beloved with all peple. And this Sir **Damas** oure mayster is as evyll beloved,[6] for he is withoute mercy, and he is a cowarde—and grete warre hath bene betwyxte them. But **Outlake** hath ever the bettir,[7] and ever he proferyth Sir **Damas** to fyght for the lyvelode, body-for-body—but he woll nat of[8] hit—other ellys to fynde a knyght to fyght for hym:

❡ "Unto that Sir **Damas** hath grauntid to fynde a knyght, but he is so evyll beloved and hated that there is no knyght woll fyght for hym. And whan **Damas** saw this, that there was never a knyght wolde fyght for hym, he hath dayly layne a wayte[9] wyth many a knyght with hym, and takyn all the knyghtes in this contray to se and aspye[1] hir aventures—he hath takyn hem by force and brought hem to his preson. And so toke he us severally, as we rode on oure adventures; and many good knyghtes hath deyde in this preson for hunger—to the numbir of eyghtene knyghtes. And yf ony of us all that here is, or hath bene, wolde have foughtyn with his brother **Outlake**, he wolde have delyverde us.

❡ "But for because this **Damas** ys so false and so full of treson, we wolde never fyght for hym to dye for hit—and we be so megir for hungir that unnethe we may stonde on oure fete. God delyver you for His grete mercy!"

❡ Anone withall come a damesel unto **Arthure**, and asked hym, "What chere?" "I can nat sey," seyde **Arthure**. "Sir," seyde she, "and ye woll fyght for my lorde, ye shall be delyverde oute of preson—and ellys ye ascape never with the lyff." "Now," seyde **Arthure**, "that is harde. Yet had I lever fyght with a knyght than to dey in preson—

❡ "Wyth this,"[2] seyde **Arthure**, "I may be delyverde, and all thes presoners, I woll do the batayle." "Yes, seyde the damesell. "Than I am redy," seyde **Arthure**, "and I had horse and armoure." "Ye shall lak none," seyde the damesell. "Mesemethe, damesell, I shold have sene you in the courte of **Arthure**." "Nay," seyde the damesell, "I cam never there. I am the lordis doughter of this castell"—yet was she false, for she was one of the damesels of **Morgan le Fay**. Anone she wente unto Sir **Damas** and tolde hym how he wolde do batayle for hym. And so he sente for **Arthure**, and whan he com he was well coloured and well made of his lymmes, that all knyghtes that sawe hym seyde hit were pité that suche a knyght sholde dey in preson.

fol.50v

---

5. *Thorow prouesse of his hondis:* i.e., by force.
6. *As evyll beloved:* i.e., held in as low esteem as Outlake's is in high.
7. *Hath ever the bettir:* always prevails in combat.
8. *Nat of:* i.e., not agree to.
9. I.e., lie in wait.
1. *Takyn:* i.e., seized. *Se and aspye:* watch and look into.
2. *Wyth this:* Provided that.

¶So Sir Damas and he were agreed that he sholde fyght for hym uppon this covenaunte, that all the othir knyghtes sholde be dely-verde—and unto that was Sir Damas sworne unto Arthur, and also he to do[3] the batayle to the uttermoste. And with that all the twenty knyghtes were brought oute of the durke preson into the halle and delyverde, and so they all abode to se the batayle.

¶Now turne we unto Accalon of Gaule, that whan he awoke he founde hymself by a depe welles syde, within half a foote, in grete perell of deth. And there com oute of that fountayne a pype of sylver, and oute of that pype ran water all on hyghe in a stone of marbil. Whan Sir Accolon sawe this, he blyssed hym and seyde, "Jesu, save my lorde Kynge Arthure and Kynge Urpence, for thes damysels in this shippe hath betrayed us—they were fendis and no women, and if I may ascape this mysadventure I shall distroye them all that I may fynde of thes false damysels that faryth thus with theire inchauntementes."

¶And ryght with that there com a dwarf with a grete mowthe and a flatte nose, and salewed Sir Accalon, and tolde hym how he cam fromme Quene Morgan le Fay—"and she gretys yow well and byddyth you be of stronge herte, for ye shall fyght tomorne wyth a knyght at the houre of pryme.[4] And therefore she hath sent the[5] Excalebir, Arthurs swerde, and the scawberde, and she byddyth you as ye love her that ye do that batayle to the uttirmoste with-oute ony mercy—lyke as ye promysed hir whan ye spoke laste togedir in prevyté—and what damesell that bryngyth her the knyghtes hede whyche ye shall fyght withall, she woll make hir a quene."

¶"Now I undirstonde you," seyde Accalon. "I shall holde that[6] I have promysed her, now I have the swerde. Sir, whan sawe ye my lady Morgan le Fay?" "Ryght late," seyde the dwarff. Than Accalon toke hym in his armys, and sayde, "Recommaunde me unto my lady the quene and telle hir all shall be done that I promysed hir, and ellis I woll dye for hit:

¶"Now I suppose," seyde Accalon, "she hath made all this crauftis and enchauntemente for this batayle." "Sir, ye may well beleve hit!" seyde the dwarff.

¶Ryght so there come a knyght and a lady wyth six squyers, and salewed Accalon and prayde hym to aryse and com and reste hym at his maner.

¶And so Accalon mounted uppon a voyde horse and wente with the knyght unto a fayre maner by a pryory, and there he had pas-syng good chere.

¶Than Sir Damas sente unto his brothir Outelake and bade make hym redy be tomorne at the houre of pryme, and to be in the felde

fol.51r

[8]

---

3. I.e., fight.
4. Prime was the first of the eight canonical Hours making up the Divine Office, the sequence of prayer said every day and night by priests and other religious individuals. Typically, Prime would begin at about six o'clock in the morning and end at nine; Malory here uses the term less precisely to signify sometime in the later morning.
5. Thee.
6. *Holde that*: keep that which.

to fyght with a good knyght—for he had founden a knyght that was redy to do batayle at all poyntis.[7]

¶Whan this worde come to Sir Outlake he was passyng hevy, for he was woundid a lytyll tofore thorow bothe his thyghes with a glayve, and he made grete dole; but[8] as he was wounded, he wolde a takyn the batayle an[9] honde.

¶So hit happed at that tyme—by the meanys of Morgan le Fay—Accalon was with Sir Oughtlake lodged. And whan he harde of that batayle, and how Oughtlake was wounded, he seyde that he wolde fyght for hym because that Morgan le Fay had sent hym Excaliber and the shethe for to fyght with the knyght on the morne.

¶This was the cause Sir Accalon toke the batayle uppon hym.

¶Than Sir Outelake was passyng glad, and thanked Sir Accolon with all his herte that he wolde do so muche for hym. And therewithall Sir Outlake sente unto his brother Sir Damas that he hadde a knyght redy that sholde fyght with hym in the felde be the houre of pryme.

¶So on the morne Sir Arthure was armed and well horsed, and asked Sir Damas, "Whan shall we to the felde?" "Sir, seyde Sir Damas, "ye shall hyre Masse." And so Arthure herde a Masse.

¶And whan Masse was done, there com a squyre and asked Sir Damas if his knyght were redy—"for oure knyght is redy in the felde."

¶Than Sir Arthure mounted uppon horsebak. And there were all the knyghtes and comons of that contray; and so by all their advyces there was chosyn twelve good men of the contrey for to wayte uppon the two knyghtes. And ryght as Arthure was on horsebak, there com a damesel fromme Morgan le Fay and brought unto Sir Arthure a swerde lyke unto Excaliber, and the scawberde, and seyde unto Arthure, "She sendis here youre swerde for grete love." And he thanked hir and wente hit had bene so; but she was falce, for the swerde and the scawberde was counterfete, and brutyll, and false.

Than they dressed hem on two partyes of the felde and lette their horses ren so faste that aythir smote other in the myddis of the shelde; and their sperys helde, that bothe horse and man wente to the erthe—and than they stert up bothe and pulde oute their swerdis.

¶The meanewhyle that they were thus at the batayle com the Damesel of the Lake into the felde, that put Merlyon undir the stone. And she com thidir for the love of Kynge Arthur, for she knew how Morgan le Fay had ordayned for Arthur shold have bene slayne that day, and therefore she com to save his lyff. And so they went egerly to the batayle and gaff many grete strokes. But allwayes Arthurs swerde bote nat lyke Accalons swerde, and for the moste party every stroke that Accalon gaff he wounded Sir Arthure sore, that hit was mervayle he stood—and allwayes his blood felle frome

---

7. At all poyntis: in every respect.
8. I.e., except.
9. I.e., in.

hym faste. Whan Arthure behelde the grounde so sore be-bledde, he was dismayde; and than he demed treson, that his swerde was chonged, for his swerde bote nat steele as hit was wonte to do.[1] Therefore he dred hym sore to be dede, for ever hym semyd[2] that the swerde in Accalons honde was Excaliber, for at every stroke that Accalon stroke, he drewe bloode on Arthure.

¶"Now, knyght," seyde Accolon unto Arthure, "kepe the[3] well frome me!" But Arthure answerde not agayne, but gaff hym suche a buffette on the helme that he made hym to stowpe, nyghe fallyng to the erthe.

¶Than Sir Accalon wythdrewe hym a lytyll, and com on wyth Excaliber on heyght,[4] and smote Sir Arthure suche a buffette that he fylle ny to the erthe. Than were they bothe wrothe oute of mesure and gaff many sore strokis. But allwayes Sir Arthure loste so muche bloode that hit was mervayle he stoode on his feete—but he was so full of knyghthode that he endured the payne. And Sir Accolon loste nat a dele of blood; therefore he waxte passynge lyght—and Sir Arthure was passynge fyeble, and wente veryly to have dyed; but for all that he made countenaunce as he myght welle endure, and helde Accolon as shorte[5] as he myght.

¶But Accolon was so bolde because of Excalyber that he wexed passyng hardy. But all men that behelde hem seyde they sawe nevir knyght fyght so well as Arthur ded, conciderynge the bloode that he had bled—but all that peple were sory that thes two brethirne wolde nat accorde. So allwayes they fought togedir as fers knyghtes, and at the laste Kynge Arthure withdrew hym a lytyll for to reste hym; and Sir Accolon callyd hym to batayle, and seyde, "Hit is no tyme for me to suffir the to reste." And therewith he come fersly uppon Arthure, but Arthur therewith was wroth for the bloode that he had loste, and smote Accolon on hyghe uppon the helme so myghtyly that he made hym nyghe falle to the erthe. And therewith Arthurs swerde braste at the crosse and felle on the grasse amonge the bloode—and the pomell and the sure handyls[6] he helde in his honde.

¶Whan Kynge Arthure saw that, he was in grete feare to dye, but allwayes he helde up his shelde and loste no grounde nother batyd no chere.[7] Than Sir Accolon began with wordis of treson, and seyde, "Knyght, thou art overcom and mayste nat endure, and also thou art wepynles, and loste thou haste much of thy bloode—and I am full loth to sle the; therefore yelde the to me recreaunte."

¶"Nay," seyde Sir Arthur, "I may nat so, for I promysed by the feythe of my body to do this batayle to the uttermuste whyle my lyff lastith. And therefore I had levir to dye with honour than to

fol.52v
fol.53r
[10]

1. *His swerde bote nat steele as hit was wonte to do*: see p. 43 on the meaning of the sword's name. Arthur is about to prove his heroic ability to master the supernatural advantage of his own sword.
2. *Hym semyd*: it seemed to him.
3. Thee.
4. On high, raised up.
5. *Helde Accolon as shorte*: i.e., pressed Accolon as hard.
6. *Sure handyls*: hilt guards.
7. *Nother batyd no chere*: nor abated his defiant look.

lyve with shame; and if hit were possible for me to dye an hondred tymes, I had levir to dye so oufte than yelde me to the. For though I lak wepon, yett shall I lak no worshippe—and if thou sle me wepynles, that shall be thy shame."

¶"Welle," seyde Accolon, "as for that shame, I woll nat spare— now kepe the fro me, for thou art but a dede man!" And therewith Accolon gaff hym such a stroke that he felle nyghe to the erthe, and wolde have had Arthure to have cryed[8] hym mercy. But Sir Arthure preced unto Accolon with his shelde and gaff hym, wyth the pomell in his honde, suche a buffette that he reled three strydes abake.

¶Whan the Damesell of the Lake behelde Arthure—how full of prouesse his body was, and the false treson that was wrought for hym to have had hym slayne—she had grete peté that so good a knyght and such a man of worship sholde so be destroyed.

¶And at the nexte stroke Sir Accolon stroke at hym suche a stroke that, by the damesels inchauntemente, the swerde Excaliber fell oute of Accalons honde to the erthe; and therewithall Sir Arthure lyghtly lepe to hit and gate hit in his honde—and forthwithall he knew hit, that hit was his swerde Excalyber. "A" seyde Arthure, "thou haste bene frome me all to longe and muche damage hast thou done me!"And therewith he aspyed the scawberde by his syde, and suddaynly he sterte to hym and pulled the scawberte frome hym, and threw hit frome hym as fer as he myght throw hit.

¶"A, sir knyght," seyde Kynge Arthur, "this day haste thou done me grete damage wyth this swerde. Now ar ye com unto youre deth, for I shall nat warraunte you but ye shall be as well rewarded with this swerde, or ever we departe, as ye have rewarded me—for muche payne have ye made me to endure, and much bloode have Y loste."

And therewith Sir Arthure raced on hym with all his myght and pulde hym to the erthe, and than raced of his helme and gaff hym suche a buffette on his hede that the bloode com oute at his erys, nose, and mowthe.

¶"Now woll I sle the, " seyde Arthure. "Sle me ye may well," seyde Sir Accolon, "and[9] hit please you, for ye ar the beste knyght that ever I founde—and I se well that God is with you:

¶"But for I promysed," seyde Accolon, "to do this batayle to the uttirmyst and never to be recreaunte while I leved, therefore shall I never yelde me with my mowthe—but God do with my body what He woll."

¶Than Sir Arthure remembirde hym[1] and thought he scholde have sene this knyght.

¶"Now telle me," seyde Arthure, "or I woll sle the, of what contrey ye be and of what courte."

¶"Sir knyght," seyde Sir Accolon, "I am of the ryall courte of Kyng Arthure, and my name is Accolon of Gaule." Than was Arthure more dismayde than he was toforehonde, for than he remembirde hym

8. I.e., begged.
9. I.e., if.
1. Recollected to himself.

of his sistir Morgan le Fay, and of the enchauntement of the shippe. "A, sir knyght, I pray you, who gaff you this swerde, and by whom ye had hit?"

¶Than Sir Accolon bethought hym[2] and seyde, "Wo worthe[3] this swerde, for by hit I have gotyn my deth!" [11]

¶"Hit may well be," seyde the Kynge.

¶"Now, Sir," seyde Accolon, "I woll tell you. This swerde hath bene in my kepynge the moste party of this twelvemonthe, and Morgan le Fay, Kyng Uryence wyff, sente hit me yestirday by a dwarfe to the entente to sle Kynge Arthure, hir brothir—for ye shall undirstonde that Kynge Arthur ys the man in the worlde that she hatyth moste, because he is moste of worship and of prouesse of ony of hir bloode. Also she lovyth me oute of mesure as paramour—and I hir agayne—and if she myght bryng hit aboute to sle Arthure by hir crauftis, she wolde sle hir husbonde Kynge Uryence lyghtly. And than had she devysed to have me kynge in this londe, and so to reigne, and she to be my quene. But that is now done," seyde Accolon, "for I am sure of my deth."

¶"Well," seyde kyng Arthure, "I fele by you ye wolde have bene kynge of this londe, yett hit had be[4] grete damage to have destroyed your lorde," seyde Arthure. "Hit is trouthe," seyde Accolon, "but now I have tolde you the trouthe, wherefore I pray you tell me of whens ye ar and of what courte."

¶"A, Accolon," seyde Kynge Arthure, "now Y let the wete that I am Kynge Arthure that thou haste done grete damage to."

¶Whan Accolon herd that, he cryed on lowde,[5] "Fayre swete lorde, have mercy on me—for I knew you nat!" "A, Sir Accolon," seyde Kynge Arthur, "mercy thou shalt have, because I fele be thy wordis at this tyme thou knewest me nat: fol.54v

¶"But I fele by thy wordis that thou haste agreed to the deth of my persone: and therefore thou art a traytoure—but I wyte the[6] the lesse, for my sistir Morgan le Fay by hir false crauftis made the to agré to hir fals lustes. But I shall be sore avenged uppon hir, that all Crystendom shall speke of hit. God knowyth I have honoured hir and worshipped hir more than all my kyn, and more have I trusted hir than my wyff and all my kyn aftir."

¶Than Kynge Arthure called the kepers of the felde, and seyde, "Sirres, commyth hyder, for here ar we two knyghtes that have foughtyn unto grete damage unto us bothe, and lykly eche of us to have slayne other—and had ony of us knowyn othir,[7] here had bene no batayle nothir no stroke stryken."

¶Than all alowde cryed Accolon unto all the knyghtes and men that were there, and seyde, "A, lordis, this knyght that I have foughten withall is the moste man of prouesse and of worship in the

---

2. *Bethought hym*: thought to himself.
3. *Wo worthe*: may woe befall.
4. I.e., been.
5. Aloud.
6. Thee.
7. I.e., each other.

worlde—for hit is hymself Kynge **Arthure**, oure [alther][8] lyege lorde—and with myssehappe and mysseadventure have I done this batayle with the lorde and kynge that I am witholdyn withall."[9]

¶Than all the peple felle downe on her knees and cryed Kynge **Arthure** mercy. "Mercy shall ye have," seyde **Arthure**. "Here may ye se what soddeyn adventures befallys ouftyn of arraunte knyghtes, how that I have foughtyn with a knyght of myne owne, unto my grete damage and his bothe—

¶"But, syrs, because I am sore hurte and he bothe, and I had grete nede of a lytyll reste, ye shall undirstonde this shall be the opynyon betwyxte you two brethirne: as to the, Sir **Damas**, for whom I have bene champyon and wonne the felde of this knyght, yett woll I juge—because ye, Sir **Damas**, ar called an orgulus knyght and full of vylony, and nat worth of prouesse of youre dedis:

¶"Therefore woll I that ye geff unto youre brother all the hole maner with the apportenaunce, undir this fourme: that Sir **Outelake** holde the maner of[1] you and yerely to gyff you a palfrey to ryde uppon—for that woll become you bettir to ryde on than uppon a courser!—

¶"Also I charge the, Sir **Damas**, uppon payne of deth, that thou never distresse no knyghtes araunte that ryde on their adventure—

¶"And also that thou restore thyse twenty knyghtes that thou haste kepte longe presoners of[2] all theire harmys that[3] they be contente; or and ony of them com to my courte and complayne on the, be my hede thou shalt dye therefore:

¶"Also, Sir **Oughtlake**, as to you, because ye ar named a good knyght and full of prouesse, and trew and jantyll in all youre dedis, this shall be youre charge I woll gyff you: that in all goodly hast ye com unto me and my courte, and ye shall be a knyght of myne; and if youre dedis be thereaftir,[4] I shall so proferre you by the grace of God that ye shall in shorte tyme be in case as for to lyve as worshipfully as youre brother **Damas**." "God thonke youre large-nesse of youre grete goodnesse and of youre bounté. I shall be frome hensforewarde in all tymes at your commaundement—for," said Sir **Oughtlake**, "as God wolde, I was hurte but late[5] with an adventures knyght thorow bothe the thyghes, and ellys had I done[6] this batayle with you."

"God wolde," seyde Sir **Arthure**, "hit had bene so, for than had nat I bene hurte as I am. I shall tell you the cause why: for I had nat bene hurte as I am, had nat bene myne owne swerde that was stolyn frome me by treson—and this batayle was ordeyned afore-honde to have slayne me, and so hit was broughte to the purpose by false treson and by enchauntment."

8. *Oure alther:* of us all.
9. *Witholdyn withall:* retained by (in loyal feudal service).
1. I.e., from.
2. I.e., for.
3. I.e., such that.
4. *Be thereaftir:* turn out to accord with this.
5. I.e., recently.
6. I.e, fought.

[12]

5

10

fol.55r

15

20

25

30

35

40

fol.55v

❡"Alas," seyde Sir **Outlake**, "that is grete pyté that ever so noble a man as ye ar of your dedis and prouesse, that ony man or woman myght fynde in their hertis to worche ony treson ayenst you." "I shall rewarde them," seyde **Arthure**. "Now telle me," seyde **Arthure**, "how far am I frome **Camelot**?" "Sir, ye ar two dayes jurney." "I wolde be at som place of worship," seyde Sir **Arthure**, "that I myght reste me." "Sir," seyde **Outlake**, "hereby is a ryche abbey of youre elders foundacion, of nunnys, but three myle hens."

❡So the Kynge toke his leve of all the peple and mounted uppon horsebak, and Sir **Accolon** with hym. And whan they were com to the abbey, he lete fecch lechis[7] and serchid his woundis and Sir **Accolons** bothe. But Sir **Accolon** deyed within foure dayes, for he had bled so much blood that he myght nat lyve.

❡But Kynge **Arthure** was well recoverde. So whan **Accolon** was dede he lette sende hym in an horse-bere with six knyghtes unto **Camelot**, and bade, "Bere hym unto my systir, **Morgan le Fay**, and sey that I sende her hym to[8] a present. And telle hir I have my swerde **Excalyber**—and the scawberde." So they departed with the body.

❡The meanewhyle, **Morgan le Fay** had wente Kynge **Arthure** had bene dede. So on a day she aspyed Kynge **Uryence** lay on slepe on his bedde; than she callyd unto hir a mayden of her counseyle and sayde, "Go fecche me my lordes swerde, for I sawe never bettir tyme to sle hym than now." "A, madame," seyde the damesell, "and ye sle my lorde ye can never ascape." "Care the[9] not," sayde **Morgan**, "for now I se my tyme is beste to do hit—and therefore hyghe the faste and fecche me the swerde."

❡Than this damesell departed, and founde Sir **Uwayne** slepyng uppon a bedde in anothir chambir. So she wente unto Sir **Uwayne** and awaked hym, and bade hy aryse "—and awayte on my lady youre modir, for she woll sle the Kynge youre fadir slepynge on his bedde, for I go to fecch his swerde." "Well," seyde Sir **Uwayne**, "go on your way and lette me dele." Anone the damesell brought the quene the swerde, with quakyng hondis. And lyghtly she toke the swerde and pullyd hit oute, and wente boldely unto the beddis syde and awayted how and where she myght sle hym beste; and, as she hevyd up the swerde to smyte, Sir **Uwayne** lepte unto his modir and caught hir by the honde, and seyde, "A, fende! what wolt thou do? And thou were nat my modir, with this swerde I sholde smyte of thyne hede. A," seyde Sir **Uwayne**, "men seyde that **Merlyon** was begotyn of a fende, but I may sey an erthely fende bare me!"

"A, fayre son **Uwayne**, have mercy uppon me! I was tempted with[1] a fende, wherefore I cry the mercy. I woll nevermore do so—and save[2] my worship and discover me nat." "On this covenaunte," seyde Sir **Uwayne**, "I wol forgyff you, so ye woll never be aboute[3] to do such dedis."

"Nay, son—and that I make you assuraunce."

[13]

fol.56r

---

7. *Lete fecch lechis:* had physicians fetched.
8. I.e., as.
9. Thee.
1. I.e., by.
2. I.e., preserve.
3. I.e., scheming.

Than come tydynges unto **Morgan le Fay** that **Accolon** was [14]
dede, and his body brought unto the chirche, and how Kyng
Arthure had his swerde ayen.

¶But whan Quene **Morgan** wyste that **Accolon** was dede, she was
so sorowfull that nye hir herte to-braste—but bycause she wolde   fol.56v   5
nat hit were knowyn oute, she kepte hir countenaunce and made
no sembelaunte of dole. But welle sche wyste, and[4] she abode tylle
hir brother **Arthure** come thydir, there sholde no golde go for hir
lyff.[5]

¶Than she wente unto the Quene **Gwenyvere** and askid hir leve   10
to ryde into hir contrey.

¶"Ye may abyde," seyde the Quene, "tyll youre brother the
Kynge com home."

¶"I may nat, madame," seyde **Morgan le Fay**, "for I have such
hasty tydynges."   15

¶"Well," seyde the Quene, "ye may departe whan ye woll."

¶So erely on the morne, or hit was day, she toke hir horse and
rode all that day and moste party of the nyght; and on the morne
by none she com to the same abbey of nonnys whereas lay Kynge
Arthure—and she wyste that he was there; and anone she asked   20
where he was, and they answerde and seyde how he was leyde
hym on his bedde to slepe—"for he had but lytyll reste this three
nyghtes."

¶"Well," seyde she, "I charge that none of you awake hym tyll I
do." And than she alyght of hir horse and thought for to stele away   25
Excaliber, his swerde. And she wente streyte unto his chambir—
and no man durste disobey hir commaundement—and there she
found **Arthur** aslepe on his bedde, and **Excalyber** in his ryght honde,
naked.

¶Whan she sawe that, she was passyng hevy that she myght nat   30
com by the swerde withoute[6] she had awaked hym, and than she
wyste welle she had bene dede.[7] So she toke the scawberde and
went hir way to horsebak.

¶Whan the Kynge awoke and myssid his scawberde, he was
wroth, and so he asked who had bene there; and they seyde his   fol.57r   35
sister Quene **Morgan le Fay** had bene there and had put the scawberde undir hir mantell "—and is gone." "Alas," seyde **Arthure**,
"falsly have ye wacched me!" "Sir," seyde they all, "we durst nat
disobey your sistyrs commaundemente."

¶"A," seyde the Kynge, "lette fecch me the beste horse that may   40
be founde, and bydde Sir **Outlake** arme hym in all hast and take
anothir good horse and ryde with me." So anone the Kynge
and Sir **Outlake** were well armyd, and rode aftir this lady. And so
they com be a crosse and founde a cowherde, and they asked the
pore man if there cam ony lady late rydynge that way. "Sir," seyde   45
this pore man, "ryght late com a lady rydynge this way with a

---

4. I.e., if.
5. No amount of gold could purchase her safety.
6. I.e., unless.
7. I.e., she would have ended up dead.

fourty[8] horses, and to yonder forest she rode." And so they folowed
faste. And within a whyle **Arthur** had a syght of **Morgan le Fay**; than
he chaced as faste as he myght. Whan she aspyed hym folowynge
her, she rode a grete pace thorow the foreste tyll she com to a
playn. And when she sawe she myght nat ascape she rode unto a   5
lake thereby, and seyde, "Whatsoever com of me, my brothir shall
nat have this scawberde." And than she lete throwe the scawberde
in the deppyst of the watir. So hit sanke, for hit was hevy of golde
and precious stonys.

⁋Than she rode into a valey where many grete stonys were, and   10
whan she sawe she muste be overtake, she shope hirself, horse,
and man, by enchauntemente unto grete marbyll stonys. And
anone withall come Kynge **Arthure** and Sir **Outlake** whereas the
Kynge myght know[9] his sistir and her men and one knyght frome
another.   15

⁋"A," seyde the Kynge, "here may ye se the vengeaunce of God!
And now am I sory this mysaventure is befalle." And than he loked
for the scawberde, but hit wold nat be founde; so he turned to the
abbey there she come fro.

⁋So whan **Arthure** was gone, they turned[1] all there lyknesse as   fol.57v   20
she and they were before, and seyde, "Sirs, now may we go where
we wyll."

⁋Than seyde **Morgan le Fay**, "Saw ye of **Arthure**, my brother?"   [15]
"Yee," seyde hir men, "and that ye sholde have founde, and we
myght a stered of one stede, for by his amyvestyall[2] countenaunce   25
he wolde have caused us to have fledde." "I beleve you," seyde the
quene.

⁋So anone after as she rode she mette a knyght ledynge another
knyght on horsebake before hym, bounde hande and foote, blyndefelde, to have drowned hym in a fowntayne. Whan she sawe this   30
knyght so bounde she asked, "What woll ye do with that knyght?"

⁋"Lady," seyde he, "I woll drowne hym."

⁋"For what cause?" she asked. "For I founde hym with my
wyff—and she shall have the same deth anone."

⁋"That were pyté," seyde **Morgan le Fay**. "Now, what sey ye,   35
knyght? Is hit trouthe that he seyth of you?" "Nay, truly, madame,
he seyth nat ryght on me." "Of whens be ye," seyde the quene,
"and of what contrey?" "I am of the courte of Kynge **Arthure**, and
my name is **Manessen**, cosyn unto **Accolon of Gaule**." "Ye sey well,
and for the love of hym ye shall be delyverde—and ye shal have   40
youre adversary in the same case[3] that ye were in." So this **Manessen**
was loused, and the other knyght bounde.

⁋And anone **Manessen** unarmed hym and armede hymself in his

---

8. A group of forty.
9. The Winchester MS here reads *myght nat knowe*, but, as Vinaver notes (O³, p. 1351), the
elimination of *nat* is consistent with both Caxton and Malory's French source, where
Arthur recognizes the forms of his sister and her knights in the stone.
1. I.e., returned.
2. *And we myght a stered of one stede*: if we could have caused but one horse to move.
Amyvestyall appears to be a word of Malory's own devising; in context, the sense would
seem to be that of "menacing" or "threatening."
3. I.e., situation.

harneyse, and so mounted on horsebak, and the knyght afore
hym—and so threw hym in the fountayne and so drowned hym.
And than he rode unto **Morgan** ayen and asked if she wolde onythyng unto[4] **Arthure**. "Telle hym," seyde she, "that I rescewed the
nat for the love of hym, but for the love of **Accolon**; and tell hym I
feare hym nat whyle I can make me and myne[5] in lyknesse of
stonys—and lette hym wete I can do much more whan I se my
tyme." And so she departed into the contrey of **Gore**, and there was
she rychely receyved, and made hir castels and townys stronge, for
allwey she drad muche Kyng **Arthure**.

   Whan the Kynge had well rested hym at the abbey, he rode unto
Camelot and founde his quene and his barownes ryght glad of his
commyng. And whan they herde of his stronge adventures, as hit
is before rehersed, they all had mervayle of the falshede of **Morgan**
le Fay. Many knyghtes wysshed hir brente.

   ¶Than come **Manessen** to courte and tolde the Kynge of his
adventure.

   ¶"Well," seyde the Kyng, "she is a kynde sister![6] I shall so be
avengid on hir, and I lyve, that all Crystendom shall speke of hit."

   ¶So on the morne there cam a damesell on message frome **Mor-**
gan le Fay to the Kynge, and she brought with hir the rycheste
mantell that ever was sene in the courte, for hit was sette all full
of precious stonys as one myght stonde by another,[7] and therein
were the rycheste stonys that ever the Kynge saw. And the damesell
seyde, "Your sister sendyth you this mantell and desyryth that ye
sholde take this gyfte of hir—and what thynge[8] she hath offended,
she wol amende hit at your owne plesure."

   ¶Whan the Kyng behelde this mantell hit pleased hym much;
he seyde but lytyll.

   ¶With that come the Damesell of the Lake unto the Kynge, and
seyde, "Sir, I muste speke with you in prevyté." "Sey on," seyde the
Kynge, "what ye woll."

   ¶"Sir," seyde this damesell, "putt nat uppon you this mantell
tylle ye have sene more—and in no wyse lat hit nat com on you,
nother on no knyght of youres, tyll ye commaunde the brynger
thereof to putt hit uppon hir."

   ¶"Well," seyde the Kynge, "hit shall be as you counseyle me."

   ¶And than he seyde unto the damesell that com frome his sister,
"Damesell, this mantell that ye have brought me, I woll se hit
uppon you." "Sir," she seyde, "hit woll nat beseme[9] me to were a
kynges garmente."

   ¶"Be my hede," seyde **Arthure**, "ye shall were hit or hit com on
my bak, other on ony mannys bak that here is."

   ¶And so the Kynge made to putt hit uppon hir. And forthwithall

fol.58r

10

15

20

25

[16] 30

35

fol.58v

40

4. *Wolde onythyng unto*: would send any message to.
5. I.e., my followers.
6. The additional Middle English sense of *kynde* as "natural" enhances the irony of Arthur's
comment.
7. *As one myght stonde by another*: set together as closely as possible.
8. *What thynge*: in whatever matter.
9. I.e., be seemly for, be appropriate for.

she fell downe deede, and never spoke worde after, and brente to colys.

¶Than was the Kynge wondirly wroth—more than he was toforehande—and seyde unto Kynge **Uryence**, "My sistir, your wyff, is allway aboute to betray me, and welle I wote other ye or my nevewe, your son, is accounseyle with hir to have me distroyed. But as for you," seyde the Kynge unto Kynge **Uryence**, "I deme nat gretly that ye be of counseyle, for **Accolon** confessed to me his[1] owne mowthe that she wolde have distroyed you as well as me; therefore Y holde you excused. But as for your son Sir **Uwayne**, I holde hym suspecte; therefore I charge you, putt hym oute of my courte." So Sir **Uwayne** was discharged. And whan Sir **Gawayne** wyste that, he made hym redy to go with hym, "—for whoso banyshyth my cosyn jarmayne shall banyshe me." So they too departed and rode into a grete foreste, and so they com unto an abbey of monkys, and there were well logged.

¶Butt whan the Kynge wyste that Sir **Gawayne** was departed frome the courte, there was made grete sorowe amonge all the astatis.

¶"Now," seyde **Gaherys**, **Gawaynes** brother, "we have loste two good knyghtes for the love of one." So on the morne they herde their Masses in the abbey and so rode forth tyll they com to the grete foreste.

¶Than was Sir **Gawayne** ware, in a valey by a turrette, twelve fayre damesels and two knyghtes armed on grete horses, and the damesels wente to and fro by a tre. And than was Sir **Gawayne** ware how there hynge a whyght shelde on that tre, and ever as the damesels com by hit they spette uppon hit, and som threwe myre uppon the shelde.

¶Than Sir **Gawayne** and Sir **Uwayne** wente and salewed them, and asked why they dud that dispyte to the shelde. "Sir, seyde the damesels, "we shall telle you:

¶"There is a knyght in this contrey that owyth this whyght shelde, and he is a passyng good man of his hondis—but he hatyth all ladyes and jantylwomen, and therefore we do all this dyspyte to that shelde."

¶"I shall sey you," seyde Sir **Gawayne**, "hit besemyth evyll[2] a good knyght to dispyse all ladyes and jantyllwomen; and peraventure, thoughe he hate you, he hath som cause, and peraventure he lovyth in som other placis ladyes and jantyllwomen, and ys belovyd agayne—

¶"And[3] he be suche a man of prouesse as ye speke of. Now, what is his name?" "Sir," they seyde, "his name is Sir **Marhaus**, the Kynges son of **Irelonde**." "I knowe hym well," seyde Sir **Uwayne**. "He is a passynge good knyght as ony on lyve, for I sawe hym onys preved at a justys where many knyghtes were gadird, and that tyme there myght no man withstonde hym."

1. I.e., with his.
2. *Besemyth evyll*: ill suits.
3. I.e., if.

⁋"A," sayde Sir Gawayne, "damesels, methynke ye ar to blame, for hit is to suppose⁴ he that hyng that shelde there, he woll nat be longe therefro; and than may tho knyghtes macche hym on horsebak—and that is more youre worshyp than thus to do,⁵ for I woll abyde no lenger to se a knyghtes shelde so dishonoured." And therewith Sir Gawayne and Sir Uwayne departed a lytyll fro them. And than ware they ware where Sir Marhaus com rydynge on a grete horse streyte toward hem. And whan the twelve damesels sawe Sir Marhaus they fledde to the turret as they were wylde, that som of hem felle by the way. Than that one of the knyghtes of the towre dressed his shylde, and seyde on hyghe, "Sir Marhaus, defende the!" And so they ran togedyrs that the knyght brake his spere on Sir Marhaus—but Marhaus smote hym so harde that he brake his necke and his horse⁶ bak.

⁋That sawe the other knyght of the turret and dressed hym to Marhaus, that so egerly they mette that this knyght of the turret was smyte doune, horse and man, dede.

And than Sir Marhaus rode unto his shylde and sawe how hit was defoyled, and sayde, "Of this dispyte of⁷ parte I am avenged—but yet, for hir love that gaff me this whyght shelde, I shall were the and hange myne where thou was." And so he honged hit aboute his necke.

⁋Than he rode streyte unto Sir Gawayne and to Sir Uwayne and asked them what they dud there. They answerde hym and seyde they come frome Kynge Arthurs courte for to se aventures.

⁋"Welle," seyde Sir Marhaus, "here am I redy, an adventures knyght that woll fulfylle any adventure that ye woll desyre"—

⁋And so departyd frome hem to fecche his raunge.⁸ "Late hym go," seyde Sir Uwayne unto Sir Gawayne, "for he is a passynge good knyght os ony lyvynge. I wolde not be⁹ my wylle that ony of us were macched with hym." "Nay," seyde Sir Gawayne, "nat so! Hit were shame to us and he were nat assayed, were he never so good a knyght."

⁋"Welle," seyde Sir Uwayne, "I wolle assay hym before you, for I am weyker than ye; and yff he smyte me downe than may ye revenge me."

⁋So thes two knyghtes come togedir with grete raundom, that Sir Uwayne smote Sir Marhaus that his spere braste in pecis on the shelde. And Sir Marhaus smote hym so sore that horse and man he bare to the erthe, and hurte Sir Uwayne on the lefte syde. Than Sir Marhaus turned his horse and rode thidir as he com fro, and made hym redy with his spere.

When Sir Gawayne saw that, he dressed his shelde—and than they feautirde their sperys, and they com togedyrs with all the

[fol.59v]

[18,19]

[fol.60r]

---

4. *Hit is to suppose*: it is likely.
5. *That is more youre worshyp than thus to do*: that is more to your honor than what you are doing.
6. I.e., horse's.
7. I.e., in.
8. *Fecche his raunge*: begin his run.
9. I.e., by.

myght of their horses, that eyther knyght smote other so harde in
myddis the sheldis—but Sir Gawaynes spere brake—but Sir Marhaus
speare helde—and therewith Sir Gawayne and his horse russhed
downe to the erthe. And lyghtly Sir Gawayne wan on[1] his feete and
pulde oute his swerde and dressed hym toward Sir Marhaus on   5
foote. And Sir Marhaus saw that; he pylde oute his swerde, and
began to com to Sir Gawayne on horsebak.

¶"Sir knyght," sayde Sir Gawayne, "alyght on foote, or elles I woll
sle thyne horse."

¶"Gramercy," sayde Sir Marhaus, "of your jentylnesse! Ye teche   10
me curtesy, for hit is nat commendable one knyght to be on
horsebak and the other on foote."

¶And therewith Sir Marhaus sette his spere agayne a tre, and
alyght and tyed his horse to a tre, and dressed his shelde—and
eyther com unto other egirly and smote togedyrs with hir swerdys,   15
that hir sheldis flew in cantellys, and they bresed their helmys and
hawbirkes and woundid eyther other.

¶But Sir Gawayne, fro[2] hit was nyne of the clok, wexed ever strenger and strenger, for by than[3] hit cam to the howre of noone he
had three tymes his myght encresed.   20

¶And all this aspyed Sir Marhaus and had grete wondir how his
myght encreced. And so they wounded eyther other passyng sore.
So whan hit was [past noone, and whan it drewe] toward evynsonge, Sir Gawayns strength fyebled and woxe passyng faynte, that
unnethe he myght dure no lenger.   25

¶And Sir Marhaus was than bygger and bygger. "Sir knyght,"
seyde Sir Marhaus, "I have welle felt that ye ar a passynge goode   fol.60v
knyght and a mervaylous man of myght as ever I felte ony, whyle
hit lastyth; and oure quarellys ar nat grete, and therefore hit were
pyté to do you hurte, for I fele ye ar passynge fyeble."   30

¶"A," seyde Sir Gawayne, "jantyll knyght, ye say the worde that I
sholde sey!" And therewith they toke of her helmys, and eyther
kyssed other, and there they swore togedyrs eythir to love other as
brethirne. And Sir Marhaus prayde Sir Gawayne to lodge with hym
that nyght, and so they toke their horsis and rode towarde Sir   35
Marhaus maner. And as they rode by the way, "Sir knyght," seyde
Sir Gawayne, "I have mervayle of you, so valyaunte a man as ye be
of prouesse, that ye love no ladyes and damesels." "Sir," seyde Sir
Marhaus, "they name me wrongfully, for hit be the damesels of the
turret that so name me, and other suche[4] as they be: 40

¶"Now shal I telle you for what cause I hate them, for they be
sorsserers and inchaunters many of them, and be a knyght never
so good of his body and as full of prouesse as a man may be, they
woll make hym a starke cowerde, to have the bettir of hym—and
this is the pryncipall cause that I hate them. And all good ladyes   45
and jantyllwomen, I owghe them my servyse, as a knyght ought to
do. (For as the booke rehersyth in Freynsch, there was this many

---

1. *Wan on:* gained.
2. I.e., from the time that.
3. I.e., by the time that.
4. *Name:* i.e., repute. *Other suche:* i.e., such others.

knyghtes that overmacched Sir Gawayne, for all[5] his thryse-double myghte that he had: Sir Launcelot de Lake, Sir Trystrams, Sir Bors de Ganys, Sir Percivale, Sir Pelleas, Sir Marhaus—thes six knyghtes had the bettir of Sir Gawayne.)[6]

¶Than within a lytyll whyle they come to Sir Marhaus place, which was in a lytyll pryory, and there they alyght, and ladyes and damesels unarmed them and hastely loked to their hurtes,[7] for they were all three hurte. And so they had good lodgyng with Sir Marhaus—and good chere, for whan he wyste that they were Kynge Arthurs syster-sonnes[8] he made them all the chere that lay in his power. And so they sojourned there a sevennyght[9] and were well eased of their woundis, and at the laste departed.

¶"Nay," sayde Sir Marhaus, "we woll nat departe so lyghtly, for I woll brynge you thorow the foreste." So they rode forth all three—and Sir Marhaus toke with hym his grettyste spere. And so they rode thorow the foreste, and rode day be day well-nye a seven dayes[1] or they founde ony aventure. So at the laste they com into a grete foreste that was named the contrey and foreste of Arroy—and the contrey is of strong adventures.

"In this contrey," seyde Marhaus, "cam nevir knyght syn hit was crystynde[2] but he founde strange adventures." And so they rode and cam into a depe valey full of stonys, and thereby they sawe a fayre streme of watir. Aboven thereby was the hede of the streme, a fayre founteyne—and three damesels syttynge thereby. And than they rode to them and ayther salewed othir. And the eldyst had a garlonde of golde aboute her hede, and she was three score wyntir of age or more, and hir heyre was whyght undir the garlonde.

¶The secunde damesell was of thirty wyntir of age, wyth a cerclet of golde aboute her hede.

¶The thirde damesel was but fiftene yere of age, and a garlonde of floures aboute hir hede.

¶Whan thes knyghtes had so beholde them, they asked hem the cause why they sate at the fountayne.

¶"We be here," seyde the damesels, "for this cause: if we may se ony of arraunte knyghtes, to teche hem unto stronge aventures; and ye be three knyghtes adventures, and we be three damesels—and therefore eche one of you muste chose one of us. And whan ye have done so, we woll lede you unto three hyghewayes, and there eche of you shall chose a way, and his damesell with hym. And this day twelve moneth[3] ye muste mete here agayne—and God sende you the lyves[4]—and thereto ye muste plyght your trouth." "This is well seyde," seyde Sir Marhaus.

¶"Now shall everyche of us chose a damesell." "I shall tell you,"

fol.61r

fol.61v

[20]

5. *For all:* i.e., despite.
6. The most notable of such encounters is that with Launcelot, in which Gawain receives a wound that later proves mortal; see pp. 676 ff.
7. I.e., wounds.
8. I.e., nephews.
9. I.e., for a week.
1. Very nearly a week.
2. *Syn hit was crystynde:* since it was converted to Christianity.
3. Twelve months from today.
4. *God sende you the lyves:* God keep you.

seyde Sir Uwayne, "I am yongyst and waykest of you bothe;
therefore lette me have the eldyst damesell, for she hath sene
much and can beste helpe me whan I have nede—for I have moste
nede of helpe of you bothe."

¶"Now," seyde Sir Marhaus, "I woll have the damesell of thirty   5
wyntir age, for she fallyth beste[5] to me."

¶"Well," seyde Sir Gawayne, "I thanke you! for ye have leffte me
the yongyst and the fayryste, and hir is me[6] moste levyste."

¶Than every damesell toke hir knyght by the reygne of his brydyll and brought hem to the three wayes; and there was made   10
promesse to mete at the fountayne that day twelve monthe—and[7]
they were lyvynge. And so they kyssed and departed, and every
knyght sette his lady behynde hym.

¶And Sir Uwayne toke the way that lay weste; and Sir Marhaus
toke the way that lay sowthe.   15

¶And Sir Gawayne toke the way that lay northe:

¶Now woll we begyn at Sir Gawayne, that helde that way tyll that
he com to a fayre maner where dwelled an olde knyght and a good
householder. And there Sir Gawayne asked the knyght if he knewe
of any aventures.   20

¶"I shall shewe you tomorne," seyde the knyght, "mervelos
adventures."

¶So on the morne they rode all in same[8] to the foreste of aventures tyll they com to a launde, and thereby they founde a crosse.
And as they stood and hoved, there cam by them the fayreste   25
knyght and the semelyest man that ever they sawe—but he made
the grettyst dole that ever man made; and than he was ware of Sir
Gawayne and salewed hym, and prayde to God to sende hym muche
worshyp. "As for that," sayde Sir Gawayne, "gramercy; also I pray to   fol.62r
God sende you honoure and worshyp." "A," sayde the knyght, "I   30
may lay that on syde,[9] for sorow and shame commyth unto me
after worshyppe."

And therewyth he passed unto that one syde of the lawnde;   [21]
and on that other syde saw Sir Gawayne ten knyghtes that
hoved and made hem redy with hir sheldis and with hir   35
sperys agaynste that one knyght that cam by Sir Gawayne.

¶Than this one knyght feautred a grete spere, and one of the
ten knyghtes encountird with hym. But this wofull knyght smote
hym so harde that he felle over his horse tayle.

¶So this dolorous knyght served them all, that at the leste way[1]   40
he smote downe horse and man—and all he ded with one spere.
And so whan they were all ten on foote, they wente to the one
knyght—and he stoode stone-stylle and suffyrde hem to pulle hym
downe of his horse—and bounde hym honde and foote, and tyed
hym undir the horse bely; and so led hym with hem. "A, Jesu!"   45

5. *Fallyth beste:* is most suitable.
6. I.e., to me.
7. I.e., if.
8. *In same:* together.
9. *Lay that on syde:* set that aside, dispense with that.
1. Leastways.

seyde Sir Gawayne, "this is a dolefull syght, to se the yondir knyght
so to be entreted—and hit semyth by the knyght that he sufferyth
hem to bynde hym so, for he makyth no resistence."

¶"No," seyde his hoste, "that is trouth, for and he wolde, they
all were to[2] weyke for hym." "Sir," seyde the damesell unto Sir
Gawayne, "mesemyth hit were your worshyp[3] to helpe that dolerouse knyght, for methynkes he is one of the beste knyghtes that
ever I sawe." "I wolde do[4] for hym," seyde Sir Gawayne, "but hit
semyth he wolde have no helpe." "No," seyde the damesell, "methynkes ye have no lyste to helpe hym!"

¶Thus as they talked they sawe a knyght on the other syde of
the launde all armed, save the hede.

¶And on the other syde there com a dwarff on horsebak—all
armed, save the hede—with a grete mowthe and a shorte nose.

¶And whan the dwarff com nyghe, he seyde, "Where is this lady[5]
sholde mete us here?" And therewithall she com forth oute of the
woode. And than they began to stryve for the lady, for the knyght
seyde he wolde have hir, [and the dwerf said he wold have her].

¶"Woll we do welle?"[6] seyde the dwarff. "Yondir is a knyght at
the crosse. Lette hit be putt uppon hym,[7] and as he demeth hit,
so shall hit be." "I woll well," seyde the knyght. And so they wente
all three unto Sir Gawayne and tolde hym wherefore they strooff.
"Well, sirres, woll ye putt the mater in myne honde?" "Ye, sir," they
seyde bothe.

¶"Now, damesell," seyde Sir Gawayne, "ye shall stonde betwyxte
them bothe, and whethir[8] ye lyste bettir to go to, he shall have
you."

¶And whan she was sette betwene hem bothe, she lefte the
knyght and went to the dwarff.

¶And than the dwarff toke hir up and wente his way, syngyng;
and the knyght wente his way, with grete mournyng.

¶Than com there two knyghtes all armed, and one cryed on
hyght, "Sir Gawayne, knyght of the courte of Kynge Arthure, make
the[9] redy in haste and juste with me!" So they ran togedirs, that
eyther felle downe; and than on foote they drew there swerdis and
dud full actually.

¶The meanewhyle the other knyght went to the damesell and
asked hir why she abode with that knyght, and seyde, "If ye wolde
abyde with me, I wolde be your faythefull knyght." "And with you
woll I be," seyde the damesell, "for I may nat fynde in my herte to
be with hym; for ryght now here was one knyght that scomfyted
ten knyghtes, and at the laste he was cowardly ledde away—and
therefore let us two go whyle they fyght."

---

2. I.e., too.
3. *Your worshyp:* to your honor.
4. I.e., fight.
5. I.e., lady who.
6. *Do welle:* i.e., conduct ourselves properly.
7. *Lette hit be putt uppon hym:* I.e., Let the matter be entrusted to him.
8. I.e., which of the two.
9. Thee.

¶And Sir Gawayne fought with that othir knyght longe, but at
the laste they accorded bothe. And than the knyght prayde Sir
Gawayne to lodge with hym that nyght. So as Sir Gawayne wente
with this knyght, he seyde, "What knyght is he in this contrey that
smote downe the ten knyghtes? For whan he had done so manfully,   5
he suffirde hem to bynde hym hande and foote, and so led hym
away."

"A" sayde the knyght, "that is the beste knyght I trow in the
worlde, and the moste man of prouesse—and hit is the grettyst
pyté of hym as of ony knyght lyvynge, for he hath be served[1] so as   10
he was this tyme more than ten tymes. And his name hyght Sir
Pelleas—and he lovyth a grete lady in this contrey, and hir name
is Ettarde. And so whan he loved hir there was cryed in this contray
a grete justis three dayes,[2] and all this knyghtes of this contrey
were there, and jantyllwomen. And who that preved hym the beste   15
knyght sholde have a passyng good swerde and a cerclet of golde;
and that cerclet the knyght sholde geff hit to the fayryste lady that
was at that justis.

"And this knyght Sir Pelleas was far the beste of ony that was
there—and there were fyve hondred knyghtes—but there was   20
nevir man that ever Sir Pelleas met but he stroke hym downe, other
ellys frome his horse, and every day of three dayes he strake downe
twenty knyghtes. And therefore they gaff hym the pryce; and furthewithall he wente there as the lady Ettarde was, and gaff her the
cerclet, and seyde opynly she was the fayreste lady that there was,   25
and that wolde he preve uppon ony knyght that wolde sey nay:

¶"And so he chose hir for his soveraygne lady, and never to love   [22]
other but her. But she was so prowde that she had scorne of hym,   fol.63v
and seyde she wolde never love hym, thoughe he wolde dye for
hir—wherefore all ladyes and jantyllwomen had scorne of hir that   30
she was so prowde, for there were fayrer than she; and there was
none that was there but, and Sir Pelleas wolde have profyrde hem
love, they wolde have shewed hym the same for his noble prouesse.
And so this knyght promysed Ettarde to folow hir into this contray,
and nevir to leve her tyll she lovid hym; and thus he is here the   35
moste party nyghe[3] her and logged by a pryory. And every weke she
sendis knyghtes to fyght with hym, and whan he hath putt hem to
the worse, than woll he suffir hem wylfully to take hym presonere,
because he wolde have a syght of this lady. And allwayes she doth
hym grete dispyte, for somtyme she makyth hir knyghtes to tye   40
hym to his horse tayle, and somtyme bynde hym undir the horse
bealy.

"Thus in the moste shamfullyste wyse that she can thynke he is
brought to hir—and all she doth hit for to cawse hym to leve this
contrey and to leve his lovynge. But all this can nat make hym to   45
leve, for and he wolde a fought on foote, he myght have had the
bettir of the ten knyghtes as well on foote as on horsebak."

1. I.e., treated.
2. *A grete justis three dayes:* a great three-day joust.
3. *The moste party nyghe:* for the most part close by to.

❡"Alas," sayde Sir Gawayne, "hit is grete pyté of hym, and aftir this nyght I woll seke hym tomorow in this foreste to do hym all the helpe I can."

❡So on the morow Sir Gawayne toke his leve of his oste Sir Caradoß and rode into the foreste; and at the laste he mette with Sir Pelleas, makynge grete mone oute of mesure—so eche of hem salewed other—and asked hym why he made suche sorow; and as hit above rehersyth, Sir Pelleas tolde Sir Gawayne. "But allwayes I suffir her knyghtes to fare so with me as ye sawe yestirday, in truste[4] at the laste to wynne hir love—for she knoweth well all hir knyghtes sholde nat lyghtly wynne me and[5] me lyste to fyght with them to the uttirmoste:

❡"Wherefore, and I loved hir nat so sore, I had lever dye an hondred tymes, and I myght dye so ofte, rathir than I wolde suffir that dispyte; but I truste she woll have pyté uppon me at the laste. For love causyth many a good knyght to suffir to have his entente—but, alas, I am infortunate."

❡And therewith he made so grete dole that unnethe he myght holde hym on his horse bak.

❡"Now, sayde Sir Gawayne, "leve your mournynge, and I shall promyse you by the feyth of my body to do all that lyeth in my powere to gete you the love of your lady—and thereto I woll plyghte you my trouthe."

❡"A," seyd Sir Pelleas, "of what courte ar ye?" "Sir, I am of the courte of Kynge Arthure, and his sistir son, and Kynge Lotte of Orkeney was my fadir, and my name is Sir Gawayne." "And my name is Sir Pelleas, born in the Iles, and of many iles I am lorde—and never loved I lady nother damesel tyll nowe. And, sir knyght, syn ye ar so nye cosyn unto Kyng Arthure and ar a kynges son, therefore betray me nat, but help me, for I may nevir com by hir but by[6] som good knyght. For she is in a stronge castell here faste by, within this foure myle—and over all this contrey she is lady off:[7]

❡"And so I may never com to hir presence but as I suffir hir knyghtes to take me, and but if I ded so that I myght have a syght of hir, I had bene dede longe ar this tyme. And yet fayre worde had I never none of hir; but whan I am brought tofore hir, she rebukyth me in the fowlyst maner; and than they take me, my horse, and harneyse, and puttyth me oute of the yatis, and she woll nat suffir me to ete nother drynke. And allwayes I offir me to be her presoner—

❡"But that woll she nat suffir me—for I wolde desire no more, what[8] paynes that ever I had, so that I myght have a syght of hir dayly." "Well," seyde Sir Gawayne, "all this shall I amende, and ye woll do as I shall devyse. I woll have your armoure, and so woll I ryde unto hir castell and tell hir that I have slayne you, and so shall

fol.64r

fol.64v

---

4. I.e., hope.
5. I.e., if.
6. I.e., with the aid of.
7. She is the chief lady of all this country.
8. I.e., no matter what.

I com within hir[9] to cause hir to cheryshe me. And than shall I do my trew parte, that ye shall nat fayle to have the love of hir."

And there, whan Sir Gawayne plyght his trouthe unto Sir Pelleas to be trew and feythfull unto hym, so eche one plyght their trouthe to other, and so they chonged horse and harneyse. And Sir Gawayne departed and com to the castel where stood hir pavylyons withoute the yate. [23]

¶And as sone as Ettarde had aspyed Sir Gawayne, she fledde in toward the castell. But Sir Gawayne spake on hyght and bade hir abyde, for he was "nat Sir Pelleas—I am another knyght that have slayne Sir Pelleas." "Than do of[1] your helme," seyde the Lady Ettarde, "that I may se your vysage." So whan she saw that hit was nat Sir Pelleas, she made hym alyght and lad hym into hir castell, and asked hym feythfully whethir he had slayne Sir Pelleas, and he seyde yee.

¶Than he tolde hir his name was Sir Gawayne, of the courte of Kynge Arthure, and his sistyrs son—

¶And how he had slayne Sir Pelleas. "Truly," seyde she, "that is grete pyté, for he was a passynge good knyght of his body. But of all men on lyve I hated hym moste, for I coude never be quytte of hym—and for ye have slayne hym, I shall be your woman and to do onythynge that may please you."

¶So she made Sir Gawayne good chere. Than Sir Gawayne sayde that he loved a lady, and by no meane she wolde love hym. "Sche is to blame," seyde Ettarde, "and she woll nat love you, for ye that be so well borne a man and suche a man of prouesse, there is no lady in this worlde to good for you."

¶"Woll ye," seyde Sir Gawayne, "promyse me to do what that ye may do, be the fayth of your body, to gete me the love of my lady?" "Yee, sir, and that I promyse you be my fayth."

¶"Now," seyde Sir Gawayne, "hit is yourself that I love so well—therefore holde your promyse." "I may nat chese," seyde the Lady Ettarde, "but if I sholde be forsworne." And so she graunted hym to fulfylle all his desyre.

¶So hit was in the monthe of May[2] that she and Sir Gawayne wente oute of the castell and sowped in a pavylyon—and there was made a bedde, and there Sir Gawayne and Ettarde wente to bedde togedyrs. And in another pavylyon she leyde hir damesels; and in the thirde pavylyon she leyde parte of hir knyghtes, for than she had no drede of Sir Pelleas. And there Sir Gawayne lay with hir in the pavylyon two dayes and two nyghtes. And on the thirde day, on the morne erly, Sir Pelleas armed hym, for he hadde never slepte syn Sir Gawayne promysed hym by the feythe of his body to com to hym unto his pavylyon by the pryory within the space of a day and a nyght.

¶Than Sir Pelleas mounted uppon horsebak and com to the

fol.65r

---

9. *Within hir:* i.e., within her house.
1. *Do of:* take off.
2. May was seen as a traditional time for the initiation of courtships; cf. Malory's famous comments near the end of his work, pp. 624–25.

pavylyons that stood withoute the castell, and founde in the fyrste pavylyon three knyghtes in three beddis, and three squyres lyggynge at their feete.

¶Than wente he to the secunde pavylyon and founde foure jantyllwomen lyggyng in foure beddis.

¶And than he yode to the thirde pavylyon and founde Sir Gawayne lyggyng in the bed with his Lady Ettarde, and aythir clyppynge other in armys;

¶And whan he sawe that, his hert well-nyghe braste for sorow, and sayde, "Alas, that ever a knyght sholde be founde so false!" And than he toke his horse and myght nat abyde no lenger for pure sorow.

¶And whan he had ryden nyghe half a myle, he turned agayne and thought for to sle hem bothe.

¶And whan he saw hem lye so bothe slepynge faste, than unnethe he myght holde hym on horsebak for sorow, and seyde thus to hymself: "Though this knyght be never so false, I woll never sle hym slepynge—for I woll never dystroy the hyghe ordir of knyghthode," and therewith he departed agayne.

¶And or he had rydden half a myle, he returned agayne, and thought than to sle hem bothe, makynge the grettyst sorow that ever man made. And whan he come to the pavylyons, he tyed his horse to a tre and pulled oute his swerde naked in his honde, and wente to them there as they lay—and yet he thought shame to sle hem, and leyde the naked swerde overthwarte bothe their throtis— and so toke his horse and rode his way. And whan Sir Pelleas com to his pavylyons, he tolde his knyghtes and his squyers how he had spedde, and seyde thus unto them: "For youre good and trew servyse ye have done me I shall gyff you all my goodes, for I woll go unto my bedde and never aryse tyll I be dede;

¶"And whan that I am dede, I charge you that ye take the herte oute of my body and bere hit her[3] betwyxte two sylver dysshes, and telle her how I sawe hir lye wyth that false knyght, Sir Gawayne." Ryght so Sir Pelleas unarmed hymself and wente unto his bedde, makyng merveylous dole and sorow.

¶Than Sir Gawayne and Ettarde awoke of her slepe and founde the naked swerde overthwarte their throtis.

¶Than she knew hit was the swerde of Sir Pelleas. "Alas," she seyde, "Sir Gawayne, ye have betrayde Sir Pelleas and me! But had he bene so uncurteyse unto you as ye have bene to hym, ye had bene a dede knyght. But ye have dissayved me, that all ladyes and damesels may beware be you and me." And therewith Sir Gawayne made hym redy and wente into the foreste.

¶So hit happed the Damesell of the Lake, Nynyve, mette with a knyght of Sir Pelleas that wente on his foote in this foreste, makynge grete doole, and she askede hym the cause. And so the wofull knyght tolde her all how his mayster and lorde was betrayed thorow a knyght and a lady, and how "he woll never aryse oute of his bedde

fol.65v

fol.66r

5

10

15

20

25

30

35

40

45

3. I.e., to her.

tyll he be dede." "Brynge me to hym," seyde she anone, "and Y woll
waraunte his lyfe. He shall nat dye for love—and she that hath
caused hym so to love, she shall be in as evylle plyte as he is or hit
be longe, to:[4]

¶"For hit is no joy of suche a proude lady that woll nat have no
mercy of suche a valyaunte knyght." Anone that knyght broute hir
unto hym, and whan she sye hym lye on his bedde, she thought
she sawe never so lykly a knyght.

¶And therewith she threw an enchauntemente uppon hym, and
he fell on slepe. And than she rode unto the lady Ettarde, and
charged that no man scholde awake hym tyll she come agayne. So
within two owres she brought the lady Ettarde thidir, and bothe the
ladyes founde hym on slepe.

¶"Loo," seyde the Damesell of the Lake, "ye oughte to be
ashamed for to murther suche a knyght." And therewith she threw
such an inchauntemente uppon hir that she loved hym so sore that
well-nyghe she was nere oute of hir mynde.

¶"A, Lorde Jesu," seyde this lady Ettarde, "how is hit befallyn
unto me that I love now that[5] I have hatyd moste of ony man on
lyve?" "That is the ryghteuouse jugemente of God," seyde the
damesell.

¶And than anone Sir Pelleas awaked and loked uppon Ettarde,
and whan he saw hir, he knew her—and than he hated hir more
than ony woman on lyve, and seyde, "Away, traytoures! and com
never in my syght." And whan she herde hym sey so, she wepte
and made grete sorow oute of mynde.

¶"Sir knyght Pelleas," seyde the Damesel of the Lake, "take your
horse and com forthwith oute of this contrey, and ye shall love a
lady that woll love you."

¶"I woll well," seyde Sir Pelleas, "for this lady Ettarde hath done
me grete dispyte and shame." And there he tolde hir the begynnyng
and endyng, and how he had never purposed to have rysen agayne
tyll he had bene dede—"and now suche grace God hath sente me
that I hate hir as much as I have loved hir."

¶"Thanke me therefore," seyde the Lady of the Lake.

¶Anone Sir Pelleas armed hym and toke his horse, and commaunded his men to brynge aftir his pavylyons and his stuffe where
the Lady of the Lake wolde assyngne them.

¶So this lady Ettarde dyed for sorow; and the Damesel of the
Lake rejoysed Sir Pelleas, and loved togedyrs duryng their lyfe.

Now turne we unto Sir Marhaute, that rode with the damesel of
thirty wynter of ayge southwarde. And so they come into a
depe foreste, and by fortune they were nyghted and rode longe in
a depe way, and at the laste they com unto a courtlage, and there
they asked herborow. But the man of the courtlage wolde nat logge
them for no tretyse that they coude trete—

¶But this much the good man seyde: "And[6] ye woll take the

---

4. *Or hit be longe, to:* before long, too.
5. I.e., that which.
6. I.e., If.

adventure[7] of youre herbourage, I shall bryng you there ye may be herbourde." "What aventure is that that I shall have for my herborow?" seyde Sir Marhaute. "Ye shall wete whan ye com there," seyde the good man. "Sir, what adventure so hit be, I pray the to brynge me thidir, for I am wery, my damesel and my horse both." 5

¶So the good man wente uppon his gate before hym in a lane, and within an houre he brought hym untyll a fayre castel. And than the pore man called the porter, and anone he was lette into the castell. And so he tolde the lorde how he had brought hym a knyght arraunte, and a damesell wolde be lodged with hym. 10

¶"Lette hym in," seyde the lorde, "for hit may happen he shall repente that they toke theire herborow here." So Sir Marhaute was let in with a torche lyght—and there was a grete syght of goodly men that welcomed hym.

¶And than his horse was lad into a stable, and he and the damesel were brought into the halle—and there stoode a myghty duke, and many goodly men aboute hym. 15

¶Than this duke asked hym what he hyght, and fro whens he com and with whom he dwelte.

¶"Sir, he seyde," I am a knyght of Kynge Arthurs and knyght of 20 the Table Rounde, and my name is Sir Marhaute, and borne I was in Irelonde." "That me repentes,"[8] seyde the duke, "for I love nat thy lorde, nother none of thy felowys of the Table Rounde—and therefore ease thyself this nyght as well as thou mayste, for as tomorne I and my six sonnes shall macch with you." 25

¶"Is there no remedy," seyde Sir Marhaute, "but that I muste have ado with you and your six sunnes at onys?"

¶"No," seyde the duke, "for this cause I made myne avowe: for Sir Gawayne slew my sevynth sonne in a recountre; therefore I made myne avow that there sholde never knyght of Kynge Arthurs courte 30 lodge with me or com there as I myght have ado with hym but I wolde revenge me of my sonnes deth." "What is your name?" sayde Sir Marhaute, "I requyre you telle me, and hit please you."

¶"Wete thou well, I am the Duke of Southe Marchis."

¶"A!" seyde Sir Marhaute, "I have herde seyde that ye have bene 35 longe tyme a grete foo unto my lorde Arthure and unto his knyghtes." "That shall ye fele tomorne," seyde the duke, "and ye leve so longe."

¶"Shall I have ado with you?" seyde Sir Marhaute. "Ye," seyde the duke, "thereof shalt thou not chose. And therefore let take hym 40 to his chambir and lette hym have all that tyll hym longis."[9]

¶So Sir Marhaute departed and was led unto his chambir, and his damesel was led in tyll hir chambir. And on the morne the duke sente unto Sir Marhaute and bade hym make hym redy.

¶And so Sir Marhaute arose and armed hym. And than there was 45 a Masse songe afore hym, and brake his faste,[1] and so mounted

fol.67r

fol.67v

---

7. I.e., risk.
8. I regret that.
9. *That tyll hym longis:* that is fitting to him.
1. *Brake his faste:* had breakfast.

on horsebak in the courte of the castell there they sholde do batayle. So there was the deuke all ready on horsebak and clene armed, and his six sonnys by hym, and everyche had a spere in his honde. And so they encountirde, whereas the deuke and his [two] sonnys brake her sperys uppon hym.

¶But Sir Marhaute hylde up his spere and touched none of hem.

¶Than come the foure sonnes by couple, and two of them brake their sperys—and so dud the other two—and all this whyle Sir Marhaute towched hem nat.

¶Than Sir Marhaute ran to the deuke and smote hym downe with his speare, that horse and man felle to the erthe—and so he served his sonnes.

Than Sir Marhaute alyght downe and bade the deuke yelde hym, other he wolde sle hym.

¶Than som of his sonnes recovirde and wolde have sette uppon Sir Marhaute. Than Sir Marhaute seyde, "Sir deuke, cese thy sonnys! and ellys I woll do the uttirmust to you all."

¶Than[2] the deuke sye he myght nat ascape the deth, he cryed to his sonnes and charged them to yelde them to Sir Marhaute; and than they kneled alle adowne and putt the pomels of their swerdis to the knyght, and so he receyvid them. And than they hove up their fadir on his feete—

¶And so by their comunal assent promysed to Sir Marhaute never to be fooys unto Kynge Arthure, and thereuppon at Whytsonday[3] next aftir to com, he and his sonnes, and there to putt them in the Kynges grace.

¶Than Sir Marhaute departed. And within two dayes Sir Marhautes damesel brought hym whereas was a grete turnemente that the Lady Vawse had cryed; and who that dud beste sholde have a ryche cerclet of golde worth a thousand besauntis.[4] And there Sir Marhaute dud so nobely that he was renomed, and had smeten doune fourty knyghtes—and so the cerclet of golde was rewarded hym.

¶Than he departed thens with grete honoure. And so within sevennyght his damesel brought hym to an erlys place; his name was the Erle Fergus, that aftir was Sir Trystrams knyght. And this erle was but a yonge man and late com to[5] his londis; and there was a gyaunte faste by hym that hyght Taulurd, and he had another brother in Cornuayle that hyght Taulas,[6] that Sir Trystram slewe whan he was oute of his mynde.

¶So this erle made his complaynte unto Sir Marhaute that there was a gyaunte by hym that destroyed all his londis, and how he durste nowhere ryde nother go for[7] hym. "Sir," seyde he, "whether usyth he to fyght on horsebak othir on foote?"

2. I.e., When.
3. Whitsunday, also known as Pentecost; about the day, see n. 1, p. 10.
4. A bezant was a gold coin (identified with its first use in Byzantium), approximately equal to one pound (£1); in Malory's day the annual income required for knighthood was on the order of £20 to £40.
5. I.e., had recently inherited.
6. For the episode, see p. 303.
7. I.e., because of.

¶"Nay," seyde the erle, "there may no horse bere hym."

¶"Well," seyde Sir Marhaute, "than woll I fyght with hym on foote."

¶So on the morne Sir Marhaute prayde the erle that one of his men myght brynge hym where the gyaunte was, and so one brought hym where he syghe hym sytte undir a tre of hooly—and many clubbis of ironne and gysernes aboute hym. So this knyght dressed hym to the gyaunte and put his shylde before hym, and the gyaunte toke an ironne club in his honde, and at the fyrste stroke he clave Syr Marhautis shelde. And there he was in grete perell, for the gyaunte was a sly fyghter—but at the laste Sir Marhaute smote of his ryght arme aboven the elbow.

¶Than the gyaunte fledde, and the knyght affter hym; and so he drove hym into a watir—but the gyaunte was so hyghe that he myght nat wade aftir hym. And than Sir Marhaute made the Erle Fergus, man[8] to fecche hym stonys.

¶And with that[9] stonys the knyght gave the gyaunte many sore strokis tylle at the laste he made hym falle downe in the watir—and so was he there dede.

¶Than Sir Marhalte wente into the gyauntes castell, and there he delyverde[1] foure and twenty knyghtes oute of the gyauntes preson, and twelve ladyes—and there he had grete rychesse oute of numbir, that dayes of his lyff he was nevir poore man.

¶Than he returned to the Erle Fergus, the whyche thanked hym gretly and wolde have yevyn hym half his londys—but he wolde none take.

¶So Sir Marhaute dwellid with the erle nye half a yere—for he was sore brused with the gyaunte.

¶So at the laste he toke his leve; and as he rode by the way with his damysel, he mette with Sir Gawayne and wyth Sir Uwayne. So by adventure he mette with foure knyghtes of Arthurs courte: the fyrst was Sir Sagramour le Desyrus, Sir Ozanna le Cure Hardy, Sir Dodynas le Saveage, and Sir Felotte of Lystynoyse. And there Sir Marhaute, with one spere, smote downe these foure knyghtes, and hurte them sore—and so departed to mete at his day.[2]

Now turne we unto Sir Uwayne that rode westwarde with his damesell of three score wyntir of age. And there was a turnemente nyghe the marche of Walys, and at that turnemente Sir Uwayne smote doune thirty knyghtes. Therefore was gyffyn hym the pryce, and that was a jarfaucon and a whyght stede trapped with cloth of golde.

¶So than Sir Uwayne ded many strange adventures by the meanys of the olde damesel—and so she brought hym to a lady that was called the Lady of the Roch, the whyche was curtayse.

¶So there was in that contrey two knyghtes that were brethirne, and they were called two perelous knyghtes—that one hyght Sir

---

8. Earl Fergus's man.
9. I.e., those.
1. I.e., freed.
2. *Mete at his day*: rendezvous at his appointed day.

Edwarde of the Rede Castell, and that other Sir Hew of the Rede
Castell—and these two brethirne had disheryted the Lady of the
Roche of a baronnery of londis by their extorsion.

And as this knyghte was lodged with this lady, she made hir
complaynte to hym of thes two knyghtes. "Madam," seyde Sir 5
Uwayne, "they ar to blame, for they do ayenste the hyghe order of
knyghthode and the oth[3] that they made. And if hit lyke you I woll
speke with hem, because I am a knyght of Kyng Arthurs, and to
entrete them with fayrenesse—and if they woll nat, I shall do
batayle with hem for Goddis sake, and in the defence of your 10
ryght."

¶"Gramercy," seyde the lady, "and there as I may nat acquyte
you, God shall."

¶So on the morne the two knyghtes were sente fore, that they
sholde speke with the Lady of the Roche—and wete you well, they 15
fayled nat, for they com with an hondred horses. But whan this
lady sawe them in suche maner so bygge,[4] she wolde nat suffir Sir
Uwayne to go oute to them, upon no sureté ne of fayre langage,[5]
but she made hym to speke with them over[6] a toure.

¶But fynally thes two brethirne wolde nat be entreted, and 20
answerde that they wolde kepe that they had.

¶"Well, seyde Syr Uwayne, "than woll I fyght with one of you,
and preve that ye do this lady wronge."

¶"That woll we nat," seyde they, "for and we do batayle, we two
woll fyght bothe at onys with one knyght; and therefore, yf ye lyste 25
to fyght so, we woll be redy at what oure ye woll assygne:

¶"And yf ye wynne us in batayle, she to[7] have hir londis agayne." fol.69v

¶"Ye say well," seyde Sir Uwayne. "Therefore make you redy, and
that[8] ye be here tomorne in the defence of this ladyes ryght."

¶So was there sykernesse made on bothe partyes that no treson [28] 30
sholde be wrought. And so thes knyghtes departed and made them
redy. And that nyght Sir Uwayne had grete chere, and on the morne
he arose erly and harde Masse and brake his faste, and so rode
into the playne withoute the gatis, where hoved the two brethirne
abydyng hym. 35

¶So they ran togedyrs passynge sore, that Sir Edwarde and Sir
Hew brake their sperys uppon Sir Uwayne—and Sir Uwayne smote
Sir Edwarde, that he felle over his horse, and yette his spere braste
nat.

¶And than he spurred his horse and com uppon Sir Hew and 40
overthrew hym. But they sone recoverde and dressed their shyldes,
and drew oute their swerdes andbade Sir Uwayne alyght and do his
batayle to the utteraunce. Than Sir Uwayne devoyded his horse
delyverly and put his shylde before hym and drew his swerde; and

3. I.e., oath of knighthood; cf. p. 77.
4. I.e., strong.
5. Uppon no sureté ne of fayre langage: i.e., regardless of an assurance of safety or courteous
discussion.
6. I.e., from atop.
7. I.e., is to.
8. I.e., see that.

so they threste togedyrs, and eythir gave other grete strokis. And
there thes two brethirne wounded Sir Uwayne passyng grevously,
that the Lady of the Roche wente he sholde have deyed.

¶And thus they fought togedyrs fyve oures, as men outraged of
reson,[9] and at the laste Sir Uwayne smote Sir Edwarde upon the
helme suche a stroke that his swerde kerved unto his canellbone.
And than Sir Hew abated his corrage; but Sir Uwayne presed faste
to have slayne hym.

¶That saw Sir Hew, and kneled adowne and yelded hym to Sir
Uwayne; and he of his jantylnesse resceyved his swerde and toke
hym by the honde, and wente into the castell togedirs.

¶Than this Lady of the Roche was passyng glad—and Sir Hew
made grete sorow for his brothirs deth. But this lady was restored
ayen of all hir londis, and Sir Hew was commaunded to be at the
courte of Kynge Arthure at the next feste of Pentecoste.[1]

¶So Sir Uwayne dwelled with this lady nyghe halfe a yere—for
hit was longe or he myght be hole of his grete hurtis. And so whan
hit drew nyghe the terme day that Sir Gawayne, Sir Marhaute, and
Sir Uwayne made to mete at the crosseway, than every knyght drew
hym thydir to holde his promyse that they made. And Sir Marhalte
and Sir Uwayne brought their damesels with hem—but Sir Gawayne
had loste his damesel.

Ryght so at the twelve monthis ende they mette all three knyghtes at the fountayne, and theire damesels—but the damesell
that Sir Gawayne had coude sey but lytyll worshyp of hym.

¶So they departed frome the damesels and rode thorowe a grete
foreste; and there they mette with a messyngere that com from
Kynge Arthurs courte that had sought hem well-nyghe a twelvemonthe thorowoute all Ingelonde, Walis, and Scotlonde, and
charged yf ever he myght fynde Sir Gawayne and Sir Uwayne to haste
hem unto the courte agayne—and than were they all glad.

¶And so they prayde Sir Marhaute to ryde with hem to the Kynges
courte.

¶And so within twelve dayes they come to Camelot, and the
Kynge was passyng glad of their commyng, and so was all the
courte.

¶Than the Kynge made hem to swere upon a booke[2] to telle
hym all their adventures that had befalle them that twelvemonthe
before, and so they ded. And there was Sir Marhaute well knowyn,
for there were knyghtes that he had macched aforetyme, and he
was named one of the beste knyghtes lyvyng.

¶So agayne the feste of Pentecoste cam the Damesell of the
Laake, and brought with hir Sir Pelleas.

¶And at that hyghe feste there was grete Joustys. Of all knyghtes
that were at that justis Sir Pelleas had the pryce, and Syr Marhaute
was named next—but Sir Pelleas was so stronge that there myght
but fewe knyghtes stonde hym a buffette with a spere.

9. Bereft of reason through rage.
1. See n. 1, p. 10.
2. See n. 4, p. 9.

¶And at the next feste Sir 𝔓elleas and Sir 𝔐arhalt were made knyghtes of the Rounde Table—for there were two segis voyde, for two knyghtes were slayne that twelvemonthe. And grete joy had Kynge 𝔄rthure of Sir 𝔓elleas and of Sir 𝔐arhalte. But 𝔓elleas loved never aftir Sir 𝔊awayne but[3] as he spared hym for the love of the Kynge—but oftyntymes at justis and at turnementes Sir 𝔓elleas quytte Sir 𝔊awayne, for so hit rehersyth in the booke of Frensh. So Sir 𝔗rystrams many dayes aftir fought with Sir 𝔐arhaute in an ilande; and there they dud a grete batayle, but at the laste Sir 𝔗rystrams slew hym.[4] So Sir 𝔗rystrams was so wounded that unnethe he myght recover, and lay at a nunrye half a yere.

¶And Sir 𝔓elleas was a worshypfull knyght, and was one of the foure that encheved the 𝔖anfgreal.[5] And the Damesel of the Laake made by her meanes that never he had ado with Sir 𝔏auncelot 𝔡e 𝔏aake, for where Sir 𝔏auncelot was at ony justis or at ony turnemente, she wolde not suffir hym to be there that day but yf hit were on the syde of Sir 𝔏auncelot. Here endyth this tale, as the Freynshe booke seyth, fro the maryage of Kynge 𝔘ther, unto Kyng 𝔄rthure that regned aftir hym and ded many batayles.

¶And this booke endyth whereas Sir 𝔏auncelot and Sir 𝔗rystrams com to courte. Who that woll make ony more, lette hym seke other bookis[6] of Kynge 𝔄rthure or of Sir 𝔏auncelot or Sir 𝔗rystrams; for this was drawyn by a knyght presoner, Sir 𝔗homas 𝔐alleorré,[7] that God sende hym good recover. "Amen &c!"[8]

𝔈xplicit.

---

3. I.e., except.
4. For the episode of Trystram's slaying of Marhaut and his recovery thereafter, see p. 235.
5. Although Sir Pelleas does enter into the Grail Quest, he does not in fact achieve the Grail; perhaps Malory was thinking of King Pelles, who is able to recognize those who have achieved the Grail (see p. 581).
6. Malory's injunction to readers and prospective authors to turn to other books for further sources has engendered considerable scholarly debate about his intentions for creating a "unified" Arthuriad. On the one hand, Malory seems to suggest that he intended at this point to write nothing more; on the other, his predictions in the previous paragraph show a clear anticipation of, and interest in, further adventures—about which he does end up writing. It is possible that all Malory is saying here is that, as a prisoner, his access to sources is limited, and readers seeking greater literary authority would do well to look elsewhere.
7. On the possible circumstances of Malory's imprisonment, see the chronology on p. 26.
8. The "&c," an abbreviation for *et cetera* (Latin for "and the rest") is usually ignored by editors, but implies the continuation of a conventional (and thus easily abbreviated) line of prayer that responds to the previous clause. The prayer was probably meant to take the following form: *Amen per Dominum—benedicamus Domino!* (Be it so really, according to the Lord—let us bless the Lord!).

The Noble Tale Betwyxt Kynge Arthure and Lucius the Emperour of Rome†

Hyt befelle whan **Kyng Arthur** had wedded Quene **Gwenybere** and fulfylled the Rounde Table, and so aftir his mervelous knyghtis and he had venquyshed the moste party of his enemyes—

⁋Than sone aftir com Sir **Launcelot de Lake** unto the courte, and Sir **Trystrams** come that tyme also—

⁋And [helde¹ a ryal feeste and Table Rounde with his alyes of kynges, prynces, and noble knyghtes, all of the Rounde Table—there cam in to his halle, he syttynge in his throne ryall, twelve auncyen men berynge eche of them a braunche of olyve in token that they cam as embassatours and messagers fro the Emperour **Lucyus** (whiche was called at that tyme Dictatour or Procurour of the Publyke Wele of Rome). Whiche sayde messagers, after their entryng and comyng into the presence of Kynge **Arthur**, dyd to hym theyr obeyssaunce in makyng to hym reverence, and said to hym in this wyse:

"The hyghe and myghty Emperour **Lucyus** sendeth to the Kyng of Bretayne gretyng, commaundyng the² to knouleche hym for thy lord and to sende hym the truage due of this royamme unto th'Empyre,³ whiche thy fader and other tofore, thy precessours,

fol.71r
<26>

5

[V.1]

<80>

10

15

20

---

† *Betwyxt:* i.e., of the war between. The title is taken editorially from the *explicit*, or closing notation, to this section (see p. 151). The floriated initial "*H*" (in red with sprays in regular black ink) indicates a major division in the Winchester MS, that status reinforced by the section's beginning on a new page. Malory's principal source for this section is the Middle English *aMA*, written in the north of England c. 1400—a provenance that accounts for the unusually high degree of alliteration and northern and specialized alliterative vocabulary found in Malory's prose throughout the section. For illustrative selections from the *aMA*, and another less pervasively influential source, see p. 714.

The editing of this section is complicated by the fact that the texts of the Winchester MS and Caxton differ at this point much more substanitally than they usually do. On the face of it, Winchester, at twice the length of Caxton for this section, would seem more authoritative; but Caxton's text, especially at the beginning, where Winchester shows signs of having been severely abridged, appears to preserve some readings that better represent the source—and presumably, therefore, Malory's rendering of the source. The abridgment in Caxton after that point, to judge from the linguistic and textual studies of scholars such as P. J. C. Field, Lotte Hellinga, Yuji Nakao, Shunichi Noguchi, Arthur O. Sandved, Jan Simko, and Jeremy Smith seems very likely to have been done by Caxton himself, who was probably interested in streamlining the narrative while also reducing (but not eliminating) those alliterative and dialectal features of the text that he may have thought his principal market—London and the South—would have found difficult or unfashionable. The reductions at the beginning of the Winchester text may represent similar motives brought to Malory's text by another, unknown, redactor; whatever the case, Caxton's readings in the opening pages often appear to be more authentic and have been adopted in the present edition according to a reconstruction articulated by Field (*Malory: Texts and Sources,* pp. 144–161). Paragraphing within extended Caxton readings is introduced in correspondence with that of the Winchester MS wherever possible. Further readings wanting in Winchester, but found to be substantially common to Caxton and the *aMA*, have also been introduced into this edition; in rarer cases where Winchester shows substantial signs of scribal corruption of readings descended from the *aMA* but which are omitted altogether in Caxton, the *aMA* reading is adopted. All quotations from *aMA* are taken from the edition of Mary Hamel, with modernization of some letter forms; readings taken from *aMA* are set within angle brackets. Numbers in angle brackets in the margins correspond to line numbers of Hamel's edition. As usual, readings from Caxton are set within square brackets.

1. I.e., Arthur held.
2. thee.
3. I.e., the Empire.

have paid—as is of record—and thou, as rebelle, not knowynge hym as thy soverayne, withholdest and reteynest,[4] contrary to the statutes and decrees maade by the noble and worthy **Julius Cezar**, conqueror of this royame and fyrst Emperour of Rome."]

¶Whan Kynge **Arthure** wyste what they mente, he loked up with his gray yghen, and angred[5] at the messyngers passyng sore.   5

¶Than were this messyngers aferde, and knelyd stylle and durste nat aryse, they were so aferde of his grymme countenaunce.

¶Than one of the knyghtes messyngers spake alowde and seyde, "Crowned kynge, myssedo no messyngers, for we be com at his   <126>   10
commaundemente, as servytures sholde."

¶Than spake the Conquerrour,[6] "Thou recrayed and coward knyghte, why feryst thou my countenaunce? There be[7] in this halle, and they were sore aggreved, thou durste nat for a deukedom of londis loke in their facis."   15

¶"Sir," seyde one of the senatoures, "so Cryste me helpe, I was   <136>
so aferde whan I loked in thy face that myne herte wolde nat serve for to sey my message. But sytthen hit is my wylle for to sey myne erande:

¶"The[8] gretis welle **Lucius**, the Emperour of Roome, and com-   20
maundis the uppon payne that woll falle[9] to sende hym the trewage of this realme that thy fadir **Uther Pendragon** payde; [and yf thou refuse his demaunde and commaundement, knowe thou for cer- tayne that he shal make stronge werre ageynst the, thy royames, and londes, and shall] bereve the all thy realmys that thou weldyst,   25
[and] [chastyse the and thy subgettys, that it shal be ensample perpetuel unto alle kynges and prynces for to denye their truage unto that noble Empyre whiche domyneth upon the unyversal world."]

¶"Thow seyste well," seyde **Arthure**, "but for all thy brym wordys   30
I woll nat be to overhasty—and therfore thou and thy felowys shall abyde here seven dayes—and shall calle unto me my counceyle of   fol.71v
my moste trusty knyghtes and deukes, and regeaunte kynges, and erlys and barowns, and of my moste wyse doctours:

¶"And whan we have takyn oure avysement, ye shall have your   35
answere playnly, suche as I shall abyde by." [Thenne somme of the yonge knyghtes, heryng this their message, wold have ronne on them to have slayne them, sayenge that it was a rebuke to alle the knyghtes there beyng present to suffre them to saye so to the Kynge; and anone the Kynge commaunded that none of them,   40
upon payne of dethe, to myssaye them ne doo them ony harme.]

¶Than the noble Kynge commaunded Sir **Clegis** to loke that   <156>
thes men be seteled and served with the beste, that there be no deyntés spared uppon them, that nother chylde[1] nor horse faught

---

4. I.e., retain, keep back.
5. I.e., was angered.
6. I.e., King Arthur.
7. *There be:* i.e., There are some men.
8. thee.
9. I.e., befall you.
1. I.e., page, boy servant.

nothynge—"for they ar full royall peple; and thoughe they have greved me and my courte, yet we muste remembir on oure wor-shyp." So they were led into chambyrs and served as rychely of deyntés that myght be gotyn.

¶So the Romaynes had therof grete mervayle.

¶Than the Kynge unto counsayle called his noble [lordes and] knyghtes, and within a towre there they assembled, the moste party of the knyghtes of the Rounde Table. Than the Kynge com-maunded hem of theire beste counceyle.

¶"Sir," seyde Sir **Cador of Cornuayle**, "as for me, I am nat hevy of this message, for we have be many dayes rested now. The lettyrs[2] of **Lucius** the Emperoure lykis me well, for now shall we have warre and worshyp." "Be Cryste, I leve welle," seyde the Kyng, "Sir **Cador**, this message lykis the! But yet they may nat be so answerde, for their spyteuous speche grevyth so my herte that truage to Roome woll I never pay. Therefore counceyle me, my knyghtes, for Crystes love of hevyn—

¶"For this muche have I founde in the cronycles of this londe: that Sir **Belyne** and Sir **Bryne**,[3] of my bloode elders, that borne were in Bretayne, and they hath ocupyed the empyreship eyght score wyntyrs;

¶And aftir, **Constantyne** oure kynnesman conquerd hit—and dame **Elyneys son, of Ingelonde**, was Emperoure of Roome—and he recoverde the crosse that Cryste dyed uppon:[4]

¶"And thus was the Empyre kepte be my kynde elders, and thus have we evydence inowghe to the empyre of[5] hole Rome."

¶Than answerde Kynge **Angwysshaunce** unto **Arthure**, "Sir, thou oughte to be aboven all othir Crysten kynges, for of knyghthode and of noble counceyle, that is allway in the—[6]

¶"And **Scotlonde** had never scathe syne ye were crowned Kynge—

¶"And whan the Romaynes raynede uppon us they raunsomed oure elders and raffte us of oure lyves:

¶"Therefore I make myne avow unto mylde **Mary** and unto **Jesu Cryste** that I shall be avenged uppon the **Romayns**—and to farther thy fyght I shall brynge the[7] ferse men of armys, fully twenty thou-sand of tyred men. I shall yeff hem my wages for to go and warre on the Romaynes and to dystroy hem, and all shall be within two ayges[8] to go where the lykes."

<282>
fol.72r

2. I.e., dispatches.
3. According to the very influential (and often highly inventive) *Historia Regum Brittaniæ* (History of the Kings of Britain), written by Geoffrey of Monmouth, c. 1137, the Britons Belinus and Brennius conquered Rome long before Julius Caesar invaded Britain.
4. Legend held that the mother of the Roman Emperor Constantine, Helena (c. 225–c. 330) had discovered the True Cross while on a visit to the Holy Land. The real Helena and Constantine were people of the Mediterranean; their recasting as Britons is an invention of medieval chroniclers such as Geoffrey of Monmouth, perhaps derving from confusion over another Helena, wife of a 5th-century emperor over Gaul, Spain, and Britian, who had a son named Constantine; or over the genuine fact that Constantine was declared Emperor in 306 in York while serving in Britain as a Roman soldier.
5. *Evydence inowghe to the empyre of:* ample evidence of our claim to imperial power over.
6. Thee.
7. Thee.
8. *Within two ayges:* within the extremes of youth and age.

¶Than the Kyng of Lytyll **Brytayne** sayde unto Kynge **Arthure**,   <304>
"Sir, answere thes alyauntes and gyff them their answere, and I
shall somen my peple—and thirty thousand men shall ye have at
my costis and wages." "Ye sey well," seyde the Kynge, **Arthure**.

¶Than spake a myghty deuke that was lorde of Weste Walys: 5
"Sir, I make myne avowe to God to be revenged on the Romaynes,
and to have the vawarde, and there to vynquyshe with vyctory the
Vyscounte of Roome:

¶"For onys, as I paste on pylgrymage all by the Poynte **Tremble**,
than the Vyscounte was in **Tuskayne**, and toke up my knyghtys and   10
raunsomed them unresonablé.

¶"And than I complayned me to the Potestate, the Pope hymself—but I had[9] nothynge ellys but plesaunte wordys. Other reson[1]
at Roome myght I none have, and so I yode my way sore rebuked.   fol.72v
And therefore to be avenged I woll arere of my wyghteste Walshe-   15
men—and of myne owne fre wagis brynge you thirty thousand."

¶Than Sir **Ewayne** and his son **Ider** that were nere cosyns unto   <337>
the Conquerrour, yet[2] were they cosyns bothe twayne, and they
helde **Irelonde and Argayle** and all the Oute Iles. "Sir," seyde they
unto Kynge **Arthure**, "here we make oure avowes untoo Cryste   20
manly[3] to ryde into **Lumbardy** and so unto **Melayne** wallys, and so
over the Poynte **Tremble** into the vale of **Vyterbe**, and there to vytayle
my knyghtes—and for to be avenged on the Romayns, we shall
bryng the thirty thousand of good mennys bodyes."

¶Than leepe in yong Sir **Launcelot de Laake** with a lyght herte,   25
and seyde unto Kynge **Arthure**, "Thoughe my londis marche[4] nyghe
myne enemyes, yet shall I make myne avow aftir[5] my power that
of good men of armys, aftir my bloode, thus[6] many I shall brynge
with me: twenty thousand helmys in haubirkes attyred, that shall
never fayle you whyles oure lyves lastyth."   30

¶Than lowghe Sir **Bawdwyn of Bretayne** and carpys to the Kynge: <382>
"I make myne avow unto the Vernacle[7] noble for to brynge with
me ten thousand good mennys bodyes that shall never fayle whyle
there lyvis lastyth."

¶"Now I thanke you," seyde the Kynge, "with all my trew herte.   35
I suppose by[8] the ende be done and dalte the Romaynes had bene
bettir to have leffte their proude message!"

¶So whan the sevennyghte was atte an ende, the senatours
besought the Kynge to have an answere. "Hit is well," seyde the
Kynge—   40

¶"Now sey ye to youre Emperour that I shall in all haste me

---

9. I.e, received.
1. I.e., reasonable judgement.
2. I.e., indeed.
3. I.e., valiantly.
4. The assumption is that Launcelot is speaking of his lands in France.
5. I.e., according to.
6. *Aftir my bloode:* in addition to my kin. *Thus:* i.e., this.
7. The Vernicle is a holy relic, a handkerchief believed to have been offered by Saint Veronica
   to Jesus on His way to Calvary and upon which a representation of His face was miraculously impressed.
8. I.e., by the time that.

redy make with my keene knyghtes, and by the rever of Rome holde
my Rounde Table. And I woll brynge with me the beste peple of
fyftene realmys, and with hem ryde on the mountaynes in the maynelondis, and myne doune the wallys of **Myllayne** the proude, and
syth ryde unto Roome with my royallyst knyghtes: 5

¶"Now ye have youre answere; hygh you that ye were hense,
and[9] frome this place to the porte there ye shall passe over. And I
shall gyff you seven dayes to passe unto **Sandwyche**:

"**N**Ow spede you, I counceyle you, and spare nat youre horsis,   <449>
and loke ye go by Watlynge Strete[1] and no way ellys; and   10
where nyght fallys on you, loke ye there abyde—be hit felle other
towne, I take no kepe,[2] for hit longyth nat to none alyauntis for to
ryde on nyghtes. And[3] may ony be founde a spere-lengthe oute of
the way, and that ye be in the watir[4] by the sevennyghtes ende,
there shall no golde undir God pay for youre raunsom."   15

¶"Sir," seyde this **senatoures**, "this is an harde conduyte. We beseche you that we may passe saufly." "Care ye nat," seyde the Kynge,
"youre conduyte is able."

¶Thus they passed fro **Carleyle** unto **Sandwyche**-warde, that hadde
but seven dayes for to passe thorow the londe. And so Sir **Cador**   20
brought hem on her wayes; but the **senatours** spared for no horse,
but hyred hem hakeneyes frome towne to towne, and by the sonne
was sette at the seven dayes ende they com unto **Sandwyche**—so
blythe were they never! And so the same nyght they toke the watir
and passed into Flaundres, [Almayn,] and aftir that over the grete   25
mountayne that hyght **Godarde**, and so aftir thorow **Lumbardy** and
thorow **Tuskayne**. And sone aftir they come to the Emperour **Lucius**,
and there they shewed hym the lettyrs of Kynge **Arthure**, and how   fol.73v
he was the gastfullyst man that ever they on loked.

¶Whan the Emperour **Lucius** hadde redde the lettyrs and undir-   30
stoode them welle of theire credence, he fared as a man were rased
of his wytte.[5] "I wente that **Arthure** wold have obeyed you and served
you [hymself] unto your honde,[6] for so he besemed—other ony
kynge crystynde—for to obey ony senatour that is sente fro my
persone."   35

¶"Sir," sayde the senatours, "lette be suche wordis. For that we
have ascaped on lyve, we may thonke God ever; for we wolde nat
passe ayen to do that message, for all your brode londis. And therfore, sirres, truste to our sawys, ye shall fynde hym your uttir ene-
mye. And seke ye hym and ye lyste, for into this londis woll he   40
com—and that shall ye fynde within this half-yere, for he thynkys
to be emperour hymself:

¶"For he seyth ye have ocupyed the empyre with grete wronge,

---

9. *Hygh you that ye were hense:* hasten to be gone from here. *And:* i.e., and hasten.
1. Watling Street is a long Roman road (now modernized, but still largely in use) running
   from Dover through London and north to a point near Shrewsbury.
2. I do not care.
3. I.e., if.
4. *And that ye be in the watir:* i.e., unless you are at sea.
5. *Were rased of his wytte:* who was out of his wits.
6. *Served you hymself unto your honde:* i.e., waited on you hand and foot.

for all his trew auncettryes sauff his fadir Uther were emperoures
of Rome. And of all the soveraynes that we sawe ever, he is the
royallyst Kynge that lyvyth on erthe:

¶"For we sawe on Newerys Day at his Rounde Table nyne kyngis,
and the fayryst felyship of knyghtes ar with hym that durys on
lyve—and thereto of wysedome and of fayre speche and all royalté
and rychesse they fayle of[7] none:

¶"Therefore, sir, be my counsayle, rere up your lyege peple and
sende kynges and dewkes to loke unto your marchis, and that the
mountaynes of Almayne be myghtyly kepte."

¶"Be Estir," seyde the Emperour, "I caste me[8] for to passe
Almayne and so furth into Fraunce and there bereve hym his londis.
I shall brynge with me many gyauntys of Geene, that one of them
shall be worth an hondred of knyghtes, and perleous passage shall
be surely kepte with my good knyghtes."

¶Than the Emperoure sente furth his messyngers of wyse olde
knyghtes unto a contrey callyd Ambage, and Arrage, and unto Aly-
sundir, to Ynde, to Ermony that the rever of Eufrate rennys by, and to
Assy, Aufryke, and Europe the large, and to Ertayne, and Elampe, to
the Oute Yles, to Arrabé, to Egypte, to Damaske, and to Dampake, and
to noble deukis and erlys—also the Kynge of Capydos, and the Kyng
of Tars, and of Turké, and of Pounce, and of Pampoyle, and oute of
Preter Johanes londe,"[9] also the Sowdon of Surré. And frome Nero[1]
unto Nazareth, and frome Garese to Galely, there come Sarysyns[2]
and becom sudgettis unto Rome. So they come glydyng in galyes.
Also there come the Kynge of Cypres, and the Grekis were gadirde
and goodly arayed with[3] the Kynge of Macidony, and of Calabe and
of Catelonde bothe kynges and deukes, and the Kynge of Portyngale
with many thousande Spaynardis.

¶Thus all thes kynges and dukys and admyrallys noblys assembled with syxtene Kynges at onys—and so they com unto Rome
with grete multytude of peple.

¶Whan the Emperoure undirstood their comynge, he made redy
all his noble Romaynes and all men of warre betwyxte hym and
Flaundyrs.

¶Also he had gotyn with hym fyffty gyauntys that were engendirde with fendis,"[4] and all tho he lete ordeyne for to awayte on
his persone and for to breke the batayle of the frunte[5] of Arthurs
knyghtes—

¶But they were so muche of their bodyes that horsys myght nat
bere them. And thus the Emperour, with all hys horryble peple,
drew to passe Almayne to dystroy Arthures londys that he wan thorow
warre of his noble knyghtes.

---

7. *Fayle of:* i.e., are second to.
8. I intend.
9. Prester John was a legendary Christian king, thought to have ruled in some part of the
   Orient.
1. I.e., the Nile.
2. On Saracens, see n. 6, p. 27.
3. I.e., by.
4. *Engendirde with fendis:* born of devils.
5. Break the front line of battle.

¶And so **Lucius** com unto **Cullayne**, and thereby a **castelle** besegys, and wanne hit within a whyle, and feffed hit with Saresyns. And thus **Lucius** within a whyle destryed many fayre contrayes that **Arthure** had wonne before of[6] the myghty Kynge **Claudas**. So this **Lucius** dispercled abrode his oste, syxty myle large, and commaunde hem to mete with hym in **Normandy**, in the contray of **Constantyne**— "and at **Barflete** there ye me abyde; for the Douchery of **Bretayne**, I shall thorowly dystroy hit."

NOw leve we Sir **Lucius** and speke we of Kyng **Arthure**, that commaunded all that were undir his obeysaunce, aftir the utas of **Seynte Hyllary**[7] that all shulde be assembled for to holde a parlement at Yorke, within the wallys. And there they concluded shortly to areste all the shyppes of this londe, and within fyftene dayes to be redy at **Sandwych**. "Now, sirrys," seyde **Arthure**, "I purpose me to passe many perelles wayes and to ocupye the Empyre that myne elders afore have claymed. Therefore I pray you, counseyle me that may be beste[8] and moste worshyp."

¶The Kynges and knyghtes gadirde hem unto counsayle and were condecended for to make two chyfftaynes—that was Sir **Baudwen of Bretayne**, an auncient and an honorable knyght, for to counceyle and comforte Sir **Cadore** son of **Cornuayle**, that was at that tyme called Sir **Constantyne**, that aftir was kynge aftir **Arthurs** dayes.[9]

¶And there in the presence of all the lordis, the Kynge resyned all the rule unto thes two lordis and Quene **Gwenyvere** (and Sir **Trystrams** at that tyme he left with Kynge **Marke** of Cornuayle, for the love of La Beale **Isode**—wherefore Sir **Launcelot** was passyng wrothe).[1]

¶Than Quene **Gwenyver** made grete sorow that the Kynge and all the lordys sholde so be departed, and there she fell doune on a swone, and hir ladyes bare hir to her chambir.

¶Than the Kynge commaunded hem to God and belefte the Quene in Sir **Constantynes** and Sir **Baudewens** hondis, and all Inglonde holy to rule as themselfe demed beste.

¶And whan the Kynge was an horsebak he seyde in herynge of all the lordis, "If that I dye in this jurney, here I make the, Sir **Constantyne**, my trew ayre, for thou arte nexte of my kyn, save Sir **Cadore** thy fadir; and therefore, if that I dey, I woll that ye be crowned kynge."

¶Ryght so he sought, and his knyghtes, towarde **Sandewyche** where he founde before hym many galyard knyghtes—for there

fol.74v

5

[3]
<625>   10

15

20

25

30

fol.75r

35

<720>

40

---

6. I.e., from.
7. *The utas of Seynte Hyllary*: the eighth day after the Feast of Saint Hilary (thus January 21).
8. I.e., best to do.
9. In the *aMA* and generally in the tradition established by Geoffrey of Monmouth, Arthur entrusts the care of the nation to Mordred, who then goes on to wage war against Arthur's realm in the king's absence. Malory's substitution here is consistent with his changes to the end of this section, which in the sources would mark the end of Arthur's reign (for a selection from the end of the *aMA*, see p. 717). Malory relocates Mordred's disastrous treachery to near the end of his whole work (p. 679) and so does not allow his immediate account of the imperial achievements of Arthur's Roman war to be rounded off with ignominy.
1. For the (briefly told) episode, see p. 272.

were the moste party of all the Rounde Table redy on tho bankes[2]
for to sayle whan the Kynge lyked.

⁊Than in all haste that myght be, they shypped their horsis and
harneyse and all maner of ordynaunce that fallyth for the werre—
and tentys and pavylyons many were trussed—and so they shotte   5
frome the bankes many grete caryckes and many shyppes of forestage,[3] with coggis and galeyes—and spynnesse full noble with[4] galeyes—and galyottys rowyng with many ores. And thus they strekyn
forth into the stremys, many sadde[5] hunderthes.
                                                                        10

Here folowyth the dreme of Kynge Arthure.[6]

As the Kynge was in his cog and lay in his caban, he felle in a   [4]   <756>
slumberyng and dremed how a dredfull **dragon** dud drenche
muche of his peple, and com fleyng one wynge oute of the weste   15
partyes. And his hede, hym semed,[7] was enamyled with **asure**, and
his shuldyrs shone as the golde, and his wombe[8] was lyke mayles
of a merveylous hew; and his tayle was fulle of tatyrs, and his feete
were florysshed as hit were fyne sable, and his clawys were lyke
clene golde—and an hydeouse flame of fyre there flowe oute of   20
his mowth, lyke as[9] the londe and the watir had flawmed all on
fyre.

⁊Than hym semed there com oute of the oryent a grymly **beare**   fol.75v
all blak, in a clowde, and his pawys were as byg as a poste. He was
all to-rongeled with lugerande lokys—and he was the fowlyst beste   25
that ever ony man sye; he romed and rored so rudely that merveyle
hit were to telle.

⁊Than the dredfull dragon dressyd hym ayenste hym and come   <786>
in the wynde lyke a **faucon**, and freyshely strykis the **beare**. And
agayne[1] the gresly **beare** kuttis with his grysly tuskes, that his breste   30
and his brayle was bloodé—and hit rayled [reed][2] all over the
see.

⁊Than the worme[3] wyndis away and fleis uppon hyght and com
downe with such a sowghe, and towched the beare on the rydge
that fro the toppe to the tayle was ten foote large; and so he rentyth   35
the beare, and brennys hym up clene that all felle on pouder, bothe
the fleysh and the bonys—and so hit flotered abrode on the see.

⁊Anone the Kynge waked [and was sore abasshed] of his dreme,

---

2. I.e., shores.
3. *Of forestage:* with forecastles.
4. I.e., escorting.
5. I.e., valiant.
6. Malory's source for this episode is one of the more striking poetic passages in the alliterative *aMA*; it is reprinted on p. 714.
7. It seemed to him.
8. I.e., belly.
9. *Lyke as:* as if.
1. I.e., in return.
2. Red. The reading is here supplied on the basis of a reference to *red* in both Caxton and
   the *aMA*. As the phrasing of this passage differs substantially in all three texts, however,
   the relative point of insertion into the Winchester text must be conjectural; the present
   emendation assumes the possibility that the word was omitted by the the scribe through
   an eye-skip error on the final "ed" of *rayled*.
3. I.e., the dragon.

and in all haste he sente for a 𝕻𝖍𝖎𝖑𝖔𝖟𝖔𝖕𝖍𝖊𝖗 and charged hym to telle what sygnyfyed his dreme.

❡ "Sir," seyde the 𝕻𝖍𝖞𝖑𝖔𝖟𝖔𝖕𝖍𝖊𝖗, "the 𝖉𝖗𝖆𝖌𝖔𝖓 thou dremyste of beto-kyns thyne owne persone that thus here sayles with thy syker knyghtes; and the coloure of his wyngys is thy kyngdomes that thou haste with thy knyghtes wonne; and his tayle that was all to-tatered sygnyfyed your noble knyghtes of the Rounde Table. And the 𝖇𝖊𝖆𝖗𝖊 that the dragon slowe above in the clowdis betokyns som tyraunte that turmentis thy peple—other[4] thou art lyke to fyght with som 𝖌𝖞𝖆𝖚𝖓𝖙𝖊 boldely in batayle be thyself alone: <814>

❡ "Therefore of this dredfull dreme drede the but a lytyll, and care nat now, Sir Conquerroure, but comforte thyself."

❡ Than within a whyle they had a syght of the bankys of Nor-mandy, and at the same tyde the Kynge aryved at 𝕭𝖆𝖗𝖋𝖋𝖑𝖊𝖙𝖊 and founde there redy many of his grete lordis, as he had commaunded at 𝕮𝖗𝖞𝖘𝖙𝖊𝖒𝖆𝖘𝖘𝖊 before hymselfe. fol.76r

𝕿han come there an husbandeman oute of the contrey and talk-yth unto the Kyng wondurfull wordys, and sayde, "Sir, here is a [grete][5] 𝖌𝖞𝖆𝖚𝖓𝖙𝖊 𝖔𝖋 𝕲𝖊𝖓𝖊 that turmentyth thy peple—mo than fyve hundred, and many mo of oure chyldren, that hath bene his sus-tynaunce all this seven wynters. Yet is the sotte never cesid, but in the contrey of 𝕮𝖔𝖓𝖘𝖙𝖆𝖓𝖙𝖞𝖓𝖊 he hath kylled [and destroyed] all oure knave chyldren. And this nyght he hath cleyghte the Duches of 𝕭𝖗𝖊𝖙𝖆𝖞𝖓𝖊 as she rode by a ryver with her ryche knyghtes—and ledde hir unto yondir mounte to ly by hir whyle hir lyff lastyth: [5]

❡ "Many folkys folowed hym—mo than fyve hundird barounes and bachelers and knyghtes full noble—but ever she shryked won-dirly lowde, that the sorow of that lady cover shall we never: <856>

❡ "She was thy cousyns wyff, Sir 𝕳𝖔𝖜𝖊𝖑𝖑 the hende, a man that we calle nyghe of thy bloode:

❡ "Now, as thou arte oure ryghtwos Kynge, rewe on this lady and on thy lyege peple, and revenge us as a noble conquerroure sholde." "Alas," seyde Kynge 𝕬𝖗𝖙𝖍𝖚𝖗𝖊, "this is a grete myscheffe. I had levir than all the realmys I welde unto my crowne that I had bene before that freyke a furlonge way[6] for to have rescowed that lady, and I wolde have done my payne.[7]

❡ "Now, felow," seyde 𝕬𝖗𝖙𝖍𝖚𝖗𝖊, "woldist thou ken me where that carle dwellys? I trowe I shall trete with hym or I far passe."

❡ "Sir Conquerrour," seyde the good man, "beholde yondir two fyrys, for there shalte thou fynde that carle beyonde the colde strendus. And tresoure oute of numbir there mayste thou sykerly fynde—more tresoure, as I suppose, than is in all Fraunce aftir."[8]

❡ The Kynge seyde, "Good man, pees, I and carpe to me no more. Thy soth sawys have greved sore my herte." fol.76v

❡ Than he turnys towarde his tentys and carpys but lytyl.

4. I.e., or.
5. The Winchester MS reads *foule,* but Caxton and *aMA* both agree with "great" as the modifier.
6. *Before that freyke a furlonge way:* within an eighth of a mile of that man.
7. *Done my payne:* i.e., been at all pains to do it.
8. I.e., in the rest of France.

¶Than the Kynge [called][9] unto Sir Kay in counceyle,[1] and to Sir Bedwere the bolde thus seyde he: "Loke that ye two aftir evyn-songe be surely armed, and your beste horsis, for I woll ryde on pylgrymage prevaly, and none but we three. And whan my lordis is servyd, we woll ryde to Seynte Mychaels Mounte where mervayles ar shewed."

¶Anone Sir Arthure wente to his wardrop and caste on his armoure, bothe his Gesseraunte and his Basnet with his brode shylde. And so he buskys hym tyll his stede that on the bente hoved. Than he stertes uppon loffte[2] and hentys the brydyll, and stirres hym stoutly. And sone he fyndis his knyghtes two, full clenly arayed; and than they trotted on stylly togedir over a blythe contray full of many myrry byrdis. And whan they com to the forlonde, Arthure and they alyght on hir foote, [and the Kynge commaunded them to tarye there.]

¶"Now fastenys," seyde Arthure, "oure horsis that none nyghe other, for I woll seche this seynte[3] be myself alone—and speke wyth this maystir-man that kepys this mountayne."

¶Than the Kynge yode up to the creste of the cragge, and than he comforted hymself with the colde wynde. And than he yode forth by two welle-stremys—and there he fyndys two fyres flamand full hyghe; and at that one fyre he founde a carefull wydow wryn-gande hir handys, syttande on a grave that was new marked.

¶Than Arthure salued hir, and she hym agayne, and asked hir why she sate sorowyng.

¶"Alas," she seyde, "carefull knyght, thou carpys over[4] lowde! Yon is a werlow woll destroy us bothe. I holde the unhappy![5] What doste thou on this mountayne?

¶"Thoughe here were suche fyffty,[6] ye were to feyble for to macche hym all at onys. Whereto berys thou armoure? Hit may be lytyll avayle, for he nedys none other wepyn but his bare fyste:

¶"Here is a douches dede, the fayryst that lyved. He hath murth-ered that mylde withoute ony mercy—he forced hir by fylth of hymself,[7] and so aftir slytte hir unto the navyll."

¶"Dame," seyde the Kynge, "I com fro the conquerrour Sir Arthure, for to trete with that tirraunte for[8] his lyege peple."

¶"Fy on suche tretyse!" she seyde than, "for he settys nought by the Kynge, nother by no man ellys—

¶"But, and thou have brought Arthurs wyff, Dame Gwenybere, he woll be more blyther of hir than thou haddyste gefyn hym halfen-dele Fraunce! And but yf thou have brought hir, prese hym nat to

9. The Winchester MS reads *seyde,* but Caxton and *aMA* both agree with forms of "call."
1. I.e., private.
2. *Uppon loffte:* aloft.
3. *I woll seche this seynte:* i.e., I will seek out the patron saint of this place. Arthur's reference to a saint here is decidedly ironic; cf. n. 2, p. 124.
4. I.e., too.
5. *The:* thee. *Unhappy:* i.e., unlucky.
6. *Suche fyffty:* fifty such as you.
7. *He forced hir by fylth of hymself:* out of lust he raped her.
8. I.e., for the sake of.

nyghe.[9] Loke what he hath done unto fyftene kynges: he hath made hym a coote full of precious stonys, and the bordoures thereof is the berdis of fyftene kynges—and they were of the grettyst blood that dured on erthe. Othir farme had he none of fyftene realmys:

¶"This presente was sente hym to this laste Crystemasse—they sente hym in faythe for savyng of their peple. And for Arthurs wyff he lodgys hym here, for he hath more tresoure than ever had Arthure or ony of his elders.

¶"And now thou shalt fynde hym at souper with[1] syx knave chyldirne—and there he hath made pykyll and powder[2] with many precious wynes—and three fayre maydens that turnys the broche that bydis to go to his bed, for they three shall be dede within foure oures or the fylth is fulfylled that his fleyshe askys."[3]

¶"Well," seyde Arthure, "I woll fulfylle my message, for alle your grym wordis."

¶"Than fare thou to yondir fyre that flamys so hyghe, and there thou shalt fynde hym sykerly, forsothe."

¶Than he paste forth to the creste of the hylle and syghe where he sate at his soupere alone, gnawyng on a lymme of a large man; and there he beekys his brode lendys by the bryght fyre—and brekelys hym semys. And three damesels turned three brochis, and thereon was twelve chyldir but late borne—and they were broched in maner lyke birdis.

¶Whan the Kyng behylde that syght his herte was nyghe bledyng for sorow.

¶Than be haylesed hym with angirfull wordys: "Now He that all weldys geff the sorow, theeff, there thou syttes! For thou art the fowlyste freyke that ever was fourmed, and fendly thou fedyst the[4]—the devill have thy soule!

¶"And by what cause, thou carle, hast thou kylled thes Crysten chyldern? Thou haste made many martyrs by mourtheryng of[5] this londis:

¶"Therefore thou shalt have thy mede thorow Mychael that owyth this mounte. And also, why haste thou slayne this fayre douches?

¶"Therefore dresse the, doggys son, for thou shalt dye this day thorow the dynte of my hondis."

¶Than the gloton gloored and grevid full foule. He had teeth lyke a grayhounde—he was the foulyst wyghte that ever man sye— and there was never suche one fourmed on erthe, for there was never devil in helle more horryblyer made—for he was fro the hede to the foote fyve fadom[6] longe and large. And therewith sturdely he sterte uppon his leggis and caughte a clubbe in his honde all of clene iron. Than he swappis at the Kynge with that kyd wepyn.

<1037>

fol.77v   20

<1074>

5   I.e., hard.
1.   I.e., eating.
2.   I.e., seasoning.
3.   Or the fylth is fulfylled that his fleyshe askys: before the lust of his flesh is satisfied.
4.   Thee, thyself.
5.   I.e., of the people of.
6.   Five fadom: thirty feet.

He cruysshed downe with the club the coronal doune to the colde
erthe. The Kyng coverde hym with his shylde and rechis a boxe
evyn infourmede[7] in the myddis of his forehede that the slypped
blade unto the brayne rechis.

⁋Yet he shappis at Sir Arthure, but the Kyng shuntys a lytyll and
rechis hym a dynte hyghe uppon the haunche—and there he swappis his genytrottys in sondir.[8]

⁋Than he rored and brayed and yet angurly he strykes, and fayled of[9] Sir Arthure and the erthe hittis, that he kutte into the swarffe
a large swerde-length and more.

⁋Than the Kynge sterte up unto hym and raught hym a buffette
and kut his baly in sundir, that oute wente the gore, that the grasse
and the grounde all foule was begone.

⁋Than he kaste away the clubbe and caughte the Kynge in his
armys and handeled the Kynge so harde that he crusshed his ryb-
bes.

⁋Than the balefull maydyns wronge hir hondis and kneled on
the grounde and to Cryste called [for helpe and comforte of Arthur.]
With that the warlow wrath Arthure undir, and so they waltyrde and
tumbylde over the craggis and busshys, and eythir cleyght other
full faste in their armys—and other whyles Arthure was aboven and
other whyle undir—and so [weltryng and walowynge they rolled
doune the hylle.] They never leffte tyll they fylle there as the floode
marked.[1] But ever in the walterynge Arthure <smyttez and> hittis
hym with a shorte dagger up to the hyltys—and in his fallynge
there braste of the gyauntes rybbys three evyn at onys. And by
fortune they felle there as the two knyghtes aboode with theire
horsis.

⁋Whan Sir Kay saw the Kynge and the gyaunte so i-cleyght togyder, "Alas," sayd Sir Kay, "we ar forfete for ever! Yondir is oure
lorde overfallen with a fende." "Hit is nat so," seyde the Kynge,
"but helpe me, Sir Kay, for this corseynte have I clegged oute of
the yondir clowys!"[2]

⁋"In fayth," seyde Sir Bedwere, "this is a foule carle"—and
caughte the "corseynte" oute of the Kynges armys; and there he
seyde, "I have mykyll wondir, and[3] Mychael be of suche a makyng,
that ever God wolde suffir hym to abyde in Hevyn—and if seyntis
be suche that servys Jesu, I woll never seke for none, be the fayth
of my body!" The Kynge than lough at Bedwers wordis, and seyde,
"This seynte have I sought nyghe unto my grete daungere. But
stryke of his hede and sette hit on a trouncheoune of a speare, and
geff hit to thy servaunte that is swyffte-horsed, and bere hit unto
Sir Howell that is in harde bondis; and bydde hym be mery, for his

7. *Evyn infourmede:* well-directed.
8. *In sondir:* asunder.
9. Missed.
1. *There as the floode marked:* i.e., to the edge of the water.
2. *This corseynte have I clegged oute of the yondir clowys:* I have clutched this holy body from
   those steep valleys. *Corseynte* typically refers to the body of a saint preserved as a relic;
   again, Arthur makes ironic reference to the giant as a surrogate to Michael, the true patron
   saint of the mount; cf. n. 3, p. 122.
3. I.e., if.

<1124>
fol.78r

<1152>

enemy is destroyed. And aftir, in **Barflete**, lette brace hit on a **bar-** fol.78v
bycan, that all the comyns of this contrey may hit beholde.

¶"And than ye two go up [to the montayn] and fecche me my
shelde, my swerde, and the boystouse clubbe of iron—and yf ye 5
lyste ony tresoure, take what ye lyst, for there may ye fynde tresoure oute of numbir. So[4] I have the curtyll [and the clubbe,]
I kepe no more. For this was a freysh gyaunte and mykyll of
strength, for I mette nat with suche one this fyftene wyntir—sauff
onys in the mounte of Arrabé I mette with suche another; but 10
this was fersar—that had I nere founden, had nat my fortune be
good."

¶Than the knyghtes fecched the clubbe and the coote and all <1194>
the remenaunte, and toke with hem what tresoure that hem lyked.
Than the Kynge and they sterte uppon their horsys, and so they 15
rode fro thens there as they come fro.

And anone the clamoure was howge aboute all the contrey, and
than they wente with one voyse tofore the Kynge and thanked God
and hym that their enemy was destroyed.

¶"All thanke ye God," seyde **Arthure**, "and no man ellys. Looke[5] 20
that the gooddys be skyffted, that none playne of his parte."

¶Than he commaunded his cosyn, Sir **Howell**, to make a kyrke
on that same cragge in the worshyppe of Seynte **Mychael**. On the
morne, frome **Barflete** remevyth the Kynge with all his grete batayle
proudly arayed.

¶And so they shooke over the stremys into a fayre champayne, 25
and thereby doune in a valey they pyght up hir tentys. And evyn at
the metewhyle come two messyngers, that one was the **Marchall** of
Fraunce, that seyde to the Kynge how the Emperoure was [entryd]
into Fraunce—"and hath destroyed much of oure marchis, and is
com into **Burgayne**, and many borowys hath destroyed, and hath 30
made grete slaughtir of your noble people. And where that he
rydyth all he destroyes—and now he is comyn into dowse Fraunce, fol.79r
and there he brennys all clene:

¶"Now all the **Dowseperys**,[6] bothe deukys and other, and the <1254>
peerys of **Parys** towne, ar fledde downe into the Lowe Contrey 35
towarde **Roone**—and but yf thou helpe them the sunner, they
muste yelde hem all at onys, bothe the bodyes and townys. They
can[7] none othir succour, but nedys they muste yelde them in
haste."

Than the Kyng byddis Sir **Borce**, "Now bowske the[8] blythe, and [6] 40
Sir **Lionel** and Sir **Bedwere**—loke that ye fare with Sir **Gawayne**,
my nevew—with you, and take as many good knyghtes. And loke
that ye ryde streyte unto Sir **Lucius** and sey I bydde hym in haste
to remeve[9] oute of my londys. And yf he woll nat, so bydde hym

4. I.e., So long as.
5. See, make sure.
6. The chief noblemen of France—from Old French *douze pers* (twelve peers), originally the
   twelve bravest knights of the Emperor Charlemagne.
7. I.e., know.
8. thee.
9. I.e., remove his forces.

dresse his batayle and lette us redresse oure ryghtes with oure handis—and that is more worshyppe than thus to overryde maysterlesse men."

¶Than anone in all haste they dressed hem to horsebak, thes noble knyghtes.

¶And whan they com to the grene wood they sawe before hem
many prowde pavylyons of sylke, of dyverse coloures, that were sette in a medow besyde a ryvere; and the Emperoures pavylyon was in the myddys, with an egle displayed on loffte.[1]

¶Than thorow the wood oure knyghtes roode tylle that they com unto the Emperoures tente.

¶But behynde them they leffte stuff[2] of men of armys in a boyshemente. And there they leffte in the boyshemente Sir Lyonel and Sir Bedwere; Sir Gawayne and Sir Borce wente with the message.

¶So they rode worthyly into the Emperoures tente and spoke bothe at onys with hawté wordys:

¶"Now geff[3] the sorow, Sir Emperour, and all thy sowdyars the aboute!

¶"For why ocupyest thou with wronge the empyreship of Roome? That is Kynge Arthures herytage be kynde[4] of his noble elders—there[5] lakked none but Uther, his fadir. Therefore the Kyng commaundyth the to ryde oute of his londys, other ellys to fyght for all and knyghtly hit wynne."

¶"Ye sey well," seyde the Emperour, "as youre lorde hath you commaunded:

¶"But [saye] your lorde I sende hym gretynge, but I have no joy of youre renckys thus to rebuke me and my lordys:

¶"But sey youre lorde I woll ryde downe by Sayne and wynne all[6] that thereto longes, and aftir ryde unto Roone and wynne hit up clene." "Hit besemys the[7] ylle," seyde Sir Gawayne, "that ony such an elffe[8] sholde bragge suche wordys, for I had levir than all Fraunce to fyght ayenste the." "Other[9] I," seyde Sir Borce, "than to welde all Bretayne other Burgayne the noble."

¶Than a knyght that hyght Sir Gayus, that was cosyn unto the Emperour, he seyde thes wordys: "[Loo how] thes Englyshe Bretouns be braggars of kynde,[1] for ye may see how they boste and bragge as[2] they durste bete all the worlde!

¶Than grevid Sir Gawayne at his grete wordys, and with his bowerly bronde that bryght semed he stroke of the hede of Sir Gayus the knyght. And so they turned their horsis and rode over watyrs

<1281>

5

10

fol.79v

15

20

25

30

<1346>

35

The deth of Sir Gayus

40

---

1. Aloft.
2. I.e., forces.
3. I.e., may God give.
4. *Be kynde:* by right of birth.
5. I.e., of that.
6. I.e., all the territory.
7. thee.
8. *Ony such an elffe:* that any such a diminutive creature as you.
9. I.e., or.
1. *braggars of kynde:* natural braggarts.
2. I.e., as if.

and woodys into[3] they com ny the busshemente there Sir **Lyonell**
and Sir **Bedwere** were hovyng stylle.

¶Than the Romaynes folowed faste on horsebak and on foote
over a fayre champeyne unto a fayre wood.

¶Than turnys hym Sir **Borce** wyth a freyshe wylle and sawe a   5
gay[4] knyght [come fast on], all floryshed in golde, that bare downe
of **Arthures** knyghtes wondirfull many.

¶Than Sir **Borce** aspyed hym, he kaste in feautir[5] a spere and
gyrdis hym thorowoute the body, that his guttys fylle oute, and the
knyght [fylle] to the grounde that gresly gronyd.   10

¶Than preced in a bolde barowne all in purpull[6] arayed. He   <1374>
threste into the prece of Kyng **Arthures** knyghtes and fruysshed
downe many good knyghtes—and he was called **Calleborne**, the
strengyste of Pavynes londis. And Sir **Borce** turned hym to and bare   fol.80r
hym thorow the brode shylde and the brode of his breste, that he   15
felle to the erthe as dede as a stone.

¶Than Sir **Feldenake** the myghty that was a praysed man of armys,
he gurde to Sir **Gawayne** for greff of Sir **Gayus** and his other
felowys—and Sir **Gawayne** was ware and drew **Galantyne**, his swerde,
and hyt hym such a buffette that he cleved hym to the breste; and   The deth of Sir   20
than he caughte his courser and wente to his ferys.   Feldenak

¶Than a rych man of Rome, one of the senatours, called to his   <1391>
felowys and bade hem returne—"for yondir ar shrewed messengers
and bolde boosters. If we folow them ony farther, the harme shall
be owrys." And so the Romaynes returned lyghtly to theire tentys   25
and tolde the Emperour how they had spedde—and how the marchall of Rome was slayne, and mo than fyve thousand in the felde
dede. But yet ore they wente and departe, oure bushemente brake
on bothe sydys of the Romaynes, and there the bolde **Bedwer** and
Sir **Lyonel** bare downe the Romaynes on every syde.   30

¶There oure noble knyghtes of mery Ingelonde bere hem thorow
the helmys and bryght sheldis and slew hem downe, and there the
hole roughte returned unto the Emperour and tolde hym at one
worde his men were destroyed, ten thousand, by batayle of tyred
knyghtes—"for they ar the brymmyst men that evir we saw in   35
felde!" But allwayes Sir **Borce** and Sir **Gawayne** freyshly folowed on
the Romaynes, evyn unto the Emperoures tentes.

¶Than oute ran the Romaynes on every syde, bothe on horse
and on foote—to many oute of numbir.[7] But Sir **Borce** and Sir **Berel**
were formeste in the frunte and freyshly faught as ever dud ony   40
knyghtes. But Sir **Gawayne** was on the ryght honde and dud what
he myght, but there were so many hym agaynste he myght nat

3. I.e., until.
4. I.e., exuberant, splendid.
5. *Kaste in feautir:* fixed in its rest (on the knight's armor).
6. Purple has been used for millenia to distinguish people of high rank, such as emperors,
   senators, kings, bishops, and cardinals; the word itself derives from the Greek name given
   to the Mediterranean shellfish that originally provided the valuable purple dye. The actual
   color could range from true purple to a deep red or crimson.
7. *To many oute of numbir:* too many to count.

helpe there his ferys, but was fayne to turne on his horse, othir his lyffe muste he lese.

¶Sir **Borce** and Sir **Berell**, the good barounnes, fought as two boorys[8] that myght no farther passe.[9]

¶But at the laste, thoughe they loth were, they were yolden and takyn, and saved their lyves—yet the stale stoode a lytyll on fere with[1] Sir **Gawayne**, that made sorow oute of mesure for thes two lordys. But than cam in a freysh knyght clenly arayed, Sir **Idres**, Sir **Uwaynes** son, a noble man of armys. He brought fyve hondred good men in haubirkes attyred, and whan he wyste Sir **Borce** and Sir **Berel** were cesed of werre: "Alas," he sayde, "this is to muche shame and overmuche losse!

¶"For with Kynge **Arthure**, and[2] he know that thes two knyghtes bene thus loste, he woll never mery be tyll this be revenged." "A, fayre knyght," sayde Sir **Gawayne**, "thou moste nedis[3] be a good man, for so is thy fadir—I knowe full well thy modir; in Ingelonde was thou borne. Alas, thes Romaynes this day have chaced us as wylde harys, and they have oure noble chyfften takyn in the felde. There was never a bettir knyght that strode uppon a steede—

¶"Loo, where they lede oure lordys over yondir brode launde! I make myne avowe," seyde Sir **Gawayne**, "I shall never se my lorde **Arthure** but yf I reskew hem that so lyghtly ar ledde us fro."

¶"That is knyghtly spokyn," seyde Sir **Idres**—and pulde[4] up her brydyls and halowed over that champayne. There was russhynge of sperys and swappyng of swerdis—and Sir **Gawayne** with Galantyne, his swerde, dud many wondyrs.

¶Than he threste thorow the prece unto hym that lad Sir **Bors**, and bare hym thorow up to the hyltys, and lade away **Sir Bors** strayte unto his ferys. Than Sir **Idrus** the yonge, Sir **Uwaynes** son, he threste unto a knyght that had Sir **Berell**, that the brayne and the blode clevid on his swerde.

¶There was a proude senatoure preced[5] aftir Sir **Gawayne**, and gaff hym a grete buffet. That sawe Sir **Idres**, and aftir rydyth and had slayne the senatour, but that he yelded hym in haste. Yet he was loth to be yoldyn but that he nedys muste.

¶And with that Sir **Idrus** ledde hym oute of the prees unto Sir **Lyonel** and unto Sir **Lovel**, **Idrus** brothir, and commaunded hem to kepe hym on payne of theire hedis.[6] Than there began a passyng harde stoure, for the Romaynes ever wexed ever bygger.

¶Whan Sir **Gawayne** that aspyed, he sente forth a knyght unto Kyng **Arthure**—"And telle hym what sorow we endure, and how we have takyn the chefe chaunceler of Rome—and Petur is presonere, a senatoure full noble—and odir proude pryncis, we knowe nat

fol.80v

<1433>

5

10

15

20

25

30

fol.81r

35

40

<1543>

---

8. Wild boars can be quite ferocious and were considered in the Middle Ages to be a worthy test of a hunter's prowess.
9. *That myght no farther passe:* i.e., that had been cornered.
1. *On fere with:* at a distance from.
2. I.e., if.
3. *Moste nedis:* must.
4. I.e., they pulled.
5. I.e., who pressed.
6. *On payne of theire hedis:* on pain of losing their heads.

theire namys. And pray hym, as he is oure lorde, to rescowe us betyme, for oure presoners may pay rychesse[7] oute of numbir—and telle hym that I am wounded wondirly sore."

¶Whan the messyngers com to the Kyng and tolde hym thes wordys, the Kynge thanked Cryste, clappyng his hondys—"And for thy trew sawys, and I may lyve many wyntyrs, there was never no knyght better rewardid—but there is no golde undir God that shall save[8] their lyvys, I make myne avow to God, and[9] Sir Gawayne be in ony perell of deth, for I had levir that the Emperour and all his chyff lordis were sunkyn into helle than ony lorde of the Rounde Table were byttyrly wounded!"

¶So forth the presoners were brought before Arthure, and he commaunded hem into kepyng of the conestablys warde, surely to be kepte as noble presoners.

¶So within a whyle com in the foreryders, that is for to say Sir Bors, Sir Bedwere, Sir Lyonell, and Sir Gawayne that was sore wounded, with all hir noble felyshyp—they loste no man of worshyppe.

¶So anone the Kyng lete rensake Sir Gawayne anone in his syght, and sayde, "Fayre cosyn, me ruys of thyne hurtys. And yf I wyste hit myght glad thy hert othir fare the[1] bettir with hit, I sholde presente the with hir hedys thorow whom thou art thus rebuked!" "That were[2] lytyll avayle," sayde Sir Gawayne, "for theire hedys had they lorne, and I had wolde myself—and hit were shame to sle knyghtes whan they be yolden."

¶Than was there joy and game amonge the knyghtes of Rounde Table, and spoke[3] of the grete prouesse that the messyngers ded that day thorow dedys of armys.

¶ So on the morne, whan hit was day, the Kyng callyd unto hym Sir Cador of Cornuaple, and Sir Clarrus of Cleremounte, a clene man of armys, and Sir Cloudres, Sir Clegis, two olde noble knyghtes, and Sir Bors, Sir Berell, noble good men of armys, and also Sir Bryan de les Ylyes, and Sir Bedwere the bolde; and also he called Sir Launcelot in heryng of all peple, and seyde, "I pray the, Sir, as thou lovys me, take hede to[4] thes other knyghtes and boldely lede thes presoners unto Paryse towne, there for to be kepte surely[5] as thou my love woll have—and yf ony rescowe[6] befalle, moste I affye me in the, as Jesu me helpe."

¶Than Sir Launcelot and Sir Cador with thes other knyghtes attyred oute of their felyshyp ten thousand be tale[7] of bolde men arayed of the beste of their company, and than they unfolde baners and let hem be displayed.

fol.81v

<1601>

---

7. I.e., riches in ransom.
8. I.e., purchase.
9. I.e., if.
1. Thee.
2. I.e., would be.
3. I.e., the knights spoke.
4. *Hede to*: care of.
5. I.e., securely.
6. I.e., attempt at rescue.
7. *Be tale*: by count.

Ow turne we to the Emperour of Rome that wyste by a spye
whethir this presoners sholde wende. He callyd unto hym Sir
Edolf and Sir Edwarde, two myghty kynges, and Sir Sextore of Lybye,
and senatours many, and the Kyng of Surré, and the senatoure of
Rome Sawtre. All thes turned towarde Troyes with many proved
knyghtes to betrappe the Kynges sondismen that were charged
with the presoners.

¶Thus ar oure knyghtes passed towarde Paryse. A busshemente
lay before them of sixty thousand men of armys.

¶"Now, lordis," seyde Sir Launcelot, "I pray you, herkyns me a
whyle. I drede that in this woodys be leyde afore us many of oure
enemyes. Therefore, be[8] myne advyse, sende[9] we three good knyghtes." "I assente me," seyde Sir Cador—and all they seyde the same,
and were aggreed that Sir Clegis, Sir Claryon, and Sir Clement the
noble, that they sholde dyscover[1] the woodys, bothe the dalys and
the downys. So forth rode thes three knyghtes and aspyed in the
woodis men of armys rydyng on sterne horsys.

¶Than Sir Clegys cryed on lowde, "Is there ony knyght, kyng,
other cayser, that dare for his lordis love that he servyth[2] recountir
with a knyght of the Rounde Table? Be he kyng other knyght, here
is his recounter redy!"

¶An erle hym answeryd angirly agayne,[3] and seyde, "Thy lorde
wenys with his knyghtes to wynne all the worlde; I trow your currage shal be aswaged in shorte tyme."

¶"Fye on the, cowarde!" seyde Sir Clegis, "as a cowarde thou
spekyste—for, by Jesu, myne armys ar knowyn thorowoute all
Inglonde and Bretayne, and I am com of olde barounes of auncetry
noble—and Sir Clegis is my name, a knyght of the Table Rounde—
and frome Troy, Brute brought myne elders."[4]

¶"Thou besemeste well," seyde the kyng,[5] "to be one of the good,
be thy bryght browys,[6] but for all that thou canst conjeoure other
sey, there shall none that is here medyll with the this tyme."

¶Than Sir Clegis returned fro the ryche kyng and rode streyghte
to Sir Launcelot and unto Sir Cadore and tolde hem what he had
seyne in the woodis, of the fayryste syght of men of armys to the
numbir of sixty thousand—"and therefore, lordynges, fyght you
behovys,[7] other ellys shunte for shame; chose whether[8] ye lykys."

¶"Nay, be my fayth," sayde Sir Launcelot, "to turne is[9] no tyme,
for here is all olde knyghtes of grete worshyp that were never

[7]

5

10

15

fol.82r

<1649>

20

25

30

<1706>

35

---

8. I.e., according to.
9. I.e., send out as scouts.
1. I.e., search out.
2. For love of the lord he serves.
3. I.e., in reply.
4. According to legend dating back at least to the *Historia Brittonum* (History of the Britons,
   written around 800 and usually attributed to the Welsh monk Nennius), one Brutus, great-
   grandson of Æneas of Troy (the hero of Virgil's *Æneid* and predecessor of the Roman
   emperors), colonized the island whose people then became named after him—Britons.
   Clegis thus claims an ancient and prestigious lineage.
5. I.e., the King of Surré.
6. *Be thy bryght browys:* to judge from your handsome looks.
7. *Fyght you behovys:* it behooves you to fight.
8. I.e., which of the two.
9. I.e., there is.

shamed—and as for me and my cousyns of my bloode, we ar but late made knyghtes, yett wolde we be loth to lese the worshyp that oure eldyrs have deservyd." "Ye sey well," seyde Sir **Cador** and all these knyghtes, "of[1] youre knyghtly wordis comfortis us all, and I suppose here is none woll be glad to returne[2]—and as for me," seyde Sir **Cador**, "I had lever dye this day than onys to turne my bak."

❡"Ye sey well," seyde Sir **Borce**, "lette us set on hem freyshly, and the worshyp shall be oures and cause oure Kyng to honoure us for ever and to gyff us lordshyppis and landys for oure noble dedys—and he that faynes hym to fyght, the devyl have his bonys! And who save ony knyghtes for lycoure of goodys tylle all be done and know who shal have the bettir,[3] he doth nat knyghtly, so Jesu me helpe."

❡Than anone Sir **Launcelot** and Sir **Cador**, tho two myghty dukis, dubbed knyghtys worshyp to wynne.[4] **Joneke** was the fyrste, a juster full noble; Sir **Hectimer** and Sir **Alyduke**, bothe of Inglonde borne; and Sir **Hamerel** and Sir **Hardolf**, full hardy men of armys; also Sir **Harry** and Sir **Harygall** that good men were bothe.

❡"Now, felowys," seyde Sir **Launcelot** and Sir **Cador** the kene, "com hydir. Sir **Bedwere** and Sir **Berel**, take with you Sir **Raynolde** and Sir **Edwarde** that ar Sir **Roulondis** chyldir, and loke that ye take kepe to[5] thes noble presoners. What chaunce so us betyde,[6] save them and yourself. This commaundement we geff you as ye woll answere to oure soverayne lorde; and for ony stowre that ever ye se us bestadde, stondys in your stale[7] and sterte ye no ferther. And yf hit befalle that ye se oure charge is to muche, than recover yourself unto som kydde castell, and than ryde you faste unto oure Kynge and pray hym of soccour,[8] as he is oure kynde lorde."

❡And than they fruyshed forth all at onys, of the bourelyest knyghtes that ever brake brede, with mo than fyve hondred at the formyst frunte, and caste their spears in feawter all at onys—and save trumpettes, there was no noyse ellys.

❡Than the Romaynes oste remeved a lytyll, and the lorde that was Kynge of **Lybye**, that lad all the formyste route, he keste his spere in feautyr and bare his course evyn to Sir **Berel**, and strake hym thorow the gorge, that he and his horse felle to the grounde— and so he was brought oute of his lyff.

❡"Alas," sayde Sir **Cadore**, "now carefull[9] is myne herte that now lyeth dede my cosyn that I beste loved." He alyght off his horse, and toke hym in hys armys, and there commaunded knyghtes to kepe well the corse.

fol.82v

<1738>

The deth of Sir Berel

fol.83r

---

1. I.e., all of.
2. *Woll:* i.e., who will. *Returne:* i.e., turn away.
3. *Who save ony . . . shal have the bettir:* he who greedily spares any knights until the end of the battle in order to size them up for material gain (through ransom).
4. Dubbed new knights worthy of winning honor.
5. Take care of.
6. *What chaunce so us betyde:* whatever happens to us.
7. *Stondys in your stale:* hold your position.
8. *Pray hym of soccour:* ask him for help.
9. I.e., sorrowful.

¶Than the kynge craked grete wordys on lowde, and seyde, "One of yon prowde knyghtes is leyde full lowe!"

¶"Yondir kyng," seyde Sir Cador, "carpis grete wordis—but, and I may lyve or this dayes ende, I shall countir with yondir kynge, so Cryste me helpe!"

¶"Sir," seyde Sir Launcelot, "meve you nat to sore,[1] but take your spear in your honde and we shall you not fayle."

¶Than Sir Cador, Sir Launcelot, and Sir Bors, the good men of armys, thes three feawtyrd their sperys amd threste into the myddys and ran thorowoute the grete oste twyse other three tymes— and whan their sperys were brokyn, they swange oute their swerdis and slowe of noble men of armys mo than an hondred—and than they rode ayen to theire ferys.

¶Than alowde the Kynge of Lybye cryed unto Sir Cador, "Well have ye revenged the deth of your knyght, for I have loste for one knyght an hondred by seven score."[2] And therewith the batayle began to joyne, and grete slaughter there was on the Sarysens party—but thorow the noble prouesse[3] of Kyng Arthurs knyghtes, ten were takyn and lad forth as presoners. That greved sore Sir Launcelot, Sir Cador, amd Sir Bors the brym. The Kynge of Lybye behelde their dedis and sterte on a sterne horse and umbelyclosed oure kmyghtes and drove downe to the grounde many a good man—for there was Sir Aladuke slayne, and also Sir Ascamour sore wounded, and Sir Herawde and Sir Heryngale hewyn to pecis, and Sir Lovell was takyn, and Sir Lyonell als—and ne had Sir Clegis and Sir Cleremonde nat bene with the knyghthode of Sir Launcelot, tho newe-made knyghtes had be slayne everych one.

The deth of three knyghtes: Sir Aladuke, Sir Herawde, and Sir Heryngale

¶Than Sir Cador rode unto the Kyng of Lybye with a swerde well stelyd and smote hym an hyghe uppon the hede, that the brayne folowed.

The deth of the Kyng of Lybye

¶"Now haste thow," seyde Sir Cador, "corne-boote agaynewarde[4]—and the devyll have thy bonys that ever thou were borne!"

¶ Than the Sowdan of Surré was wood wrothe, for the deth of that kynge grevid hym at his herte, and recomforted his peple and sette sore on oure knyghtes.

<1843>
fol.83v

¶Than Sir Launcelot and Sir Bors encountyrs with hym sone, and within a whyle, as tellyth the romaynes,[5] they had slayne of the Sarazens mo than fyve thousand. And Sir Kay the kene had takyn a captayne, and Edwarde had takyn two erlys, and the Sawdon of Surré yeldid hym up unto Sir Launcelot, and the senatur of Sautre yeldid hym unto Sir Cador.

¶Whan the Romaynes and the Sarezens aspyed how the game yode, they fledde with all hir myght to hyde there hedis.

---

1. *Meve you nat to sore:* do not get overly emotional.
2. *An hondred by seven score:* past a hundred and closer to a hundred and forty.
3. I.e., prowess that kept them alive.
4. *Corne-boote agaynewarde:* proper payment in return.
5. As it happens the only surviving copy of the *aMA* says at the corresponding point that "fyfty thousande of folke was fellide" (line 1851); another copy could easily have had Malory's reading, since the alliteration, despite the number, remains unchanged.

¶Than oure knyghtes folowed with a freysshe fare and slew downe of the Sarezens [on every syde].

¶And Sir **Launcelot** ded so grete dedys of armys that day that Sir **Cador** and all the Romaynes had mervayle of his myght, for there was nother kynge, cayser, nother knyght that day myght stonde 5 hym ony buffette. Therefore was he honoured dayes of his lyff— for never ere or[6] that day was he proved so well, for he, and Sir **Bors**, and Sir **Lyonel** was but late afore at an hyghe feste made all three knyghtes.[7]

¶And thus were the Romaynes and the Sarezens slayne adowne 10 clene—save a fewe were recovirde thereby into a lytyll castell. And than the noble renckys of the Rounde Table, there as the felde was, toke up hir good bodyes of the noble knyghtes and garte sende them[8] unto Kyng **Arthure**, into the erthe to be caste. So they all rode unto **Paryse** and beleffte the presoners there with the pure 15 proveste,[9] and than they were delyverde into sure sauffgarde. Than every knyght toke a spere and dranke of the colde wyne, and than fersely in a brayde returned unto the Kynge.

¶Whan the Kynge his knyghtes sawe, he was than mervelously rejoyced and cleyght knyght be knyght in his armys, and sayde, "All 20 the worshyp in the worlde ye welde, be my fayth!

¶"There was never kyng sauff myselff that welded evir such knyghtes." "Sir," seyde Sir **Cador**, "there was none of us that fayled othir, but of the knyghthode of Sir **Launcelot** hit were mervayle to telle. And of[1] his bolde cosyns ar proved full noble knyghtes—but 25 of wyse wytte and of grete strengthe of[2] his ayge, Sir **Launcelot** hath no felowe."

¶Whan the Kyng herde Sir **Cador** sey such wordys, he seyde, "Hym besemys for to do such dedis."

¶And Sir **Cadore** tolde **Arthure** whyche of the good knyghtis were 30 slayne: "the Kynge of **Lybye**—and he slew the fyrste knyght on oure syde, that was Sir **Berell**; and Sir **Aladuke** was another, a noble man of armys, and Sir **Maurel** and Sir **Mores** that were two brethyrn, with Sir **Manaduke** and Sir **Mandyff**, two good knyghtes."

¶Than the Kynge [wepte and] with a keverchoff wyped his iyen, <1920> 35 and sayde, "Youre corrage and youre hardynesse nerehande had you destroyed, for and ye had turned agayne, ye had loste no wor- shyp—for I calle hit but foly to abyde whan knyghtes bene over- macched."

"Not so," sayde Sir **Launcelot**, "the shame sholde ever have bene 40 oures." "That is trouthe," seyde Sir **Clegis** and Sir **Bors**, "for knygh- tes ons shamed recoverys hit never."

¶Now leve Sir **Arthure** and his noble knyghtes and speke we of [8] a senatoure that ascaped fro the batayle. Whan he com to **Lucius** the Emperour of Rome, he seyde, "Sir, withdraw the! What doste 45

fol.84r

6. *ere or:* before.
7. *Late:* i.e., lately. *Made all three knyghtes:* all three dubbed knights.
8. *Garte sende them:* caused them to be sent.
9. *The pure proveste:* the provost (the chief magistrate) himself.
1. I.e., the contingent of.
2. I.e., for.

thou here in this marchis and to overren poore peple? Thou shalt wynne nothyng ellys, and if thou dele with Kynge **Arthure** and his doughty knyghtes thou wynnys naught ellys but grete strokys oute of mesure—for this day one of **Arthurs** knyghtes was worth in batayle an hondred of oures." 5

¶"Fye on the," seyde **Lucyus**, "for cowardly thou spekyste! Yf my harmys me greve, thy wordys greveth me muche more."

¶Than he called to hym his counceyle, men of noble bloode.

¶So by all theire advyse he sent forth a knyght that hyght Sir **Leompe**. He dressed[3] his peple, and hyghe hym[4] he bade, and take fol.84v 10 hym of the beste men of armys many sad hundrethis—"and go before, and we woll folow aftir."

¶But the Kynge of their commynge was prevely warned, and than into **Sessoyne** he dressid his peple and forstalled the Romaynes from the kyd castels and the walled townes. And there Sir **Vyllers** 15 the valyaunte made his avow evyn byfore the Kynge to take other to sle the Vycounte of Rome, or ellys to dye therefore.

Than the Kyng commaunded Sir **Cadore** to take hede to[5] the <2002> rerewarde—"and take renkys of the Rounde Table that the[6] beste lykes, sauff Sir **Launcelot** and Sir **Bors**, with many mo othir— 20 Sir **Kay**, Sir **Clegis** shall be there als, and Sir **Marroke**, Sir **Marhaulte** shall be with me in fere—and all thes with mo other shall awayte uppon my persone."

¶Thus Kynge **Arthure** dispercled all his oste in dyverse partyes that they[7] sholde nat ascape, but to fyght them behovys. Whan the 25 Emperoure was entyrd into the vale of **Sessoyne** he myght se where Kyng **Arthure** hoved in batayle with baners displayed. On every syde was he besette, that he myght nat ascape; but other to fyght other to yelde hym, there was none other boote.

¶"Now I se well," seyde Sir **Lucyus**, "yondir traytoure hath 30 betrayed me!"Than he redressis his knyghtes on dyverse partyes, and sette up a dragon with eglys many one enewed with sabyl.[8]

¶And than he lete blow up with trumpettes and with tabours, that all the vale dyndled. And than he lete crye on lowde, that all men myght here: 35

¶"Syrs, ye know well that the honoure and worshyp hath ever folowyd the Romaynes. And this day let hit nevir be loste for the defaughte of herte—for I se well by yondyr ordynaunce this day shall dye much peple. And therefore do doughtly this day, and the fol.85r felde is ourys." Than anone the Welshe Kyng was so nyghe that he 40 herde Sir **Lucyus**. Than he dressed hym to the Vycounte, his avow for to holde. His[9] armys were full clene—and therein was a dole-full[1] dragon—and into the vawarde he pykys hym with styff spere in honde. And there he mette wyth the valyaunte Vyllers, hymself

3. I.e., made ready.
4. I.e., Sir Leomye.
5. Take command of.
6. Thee.
7. I.e., the Romans.
8. Set up a heraldic battle standard with many eagles colored in black (cf. n. 3, p. 23).
9. I.e., The Viscount's.
1. I.e., as his coat of arms was a dreadful.

that was Vycounte of Rome;[2] and there he[3] smote hym thorow the shorte rybbys with a speare, that the bloode braste oute on every syde, and so fylle to the erthe and never spake mo wordys aftir.

¶Than the noble Sir Uwayne boldely approched and gyrde thorowoute the Emperoures batayle where was the thyckest prece, and slew a grete lorde by the Emperours standard—and than flow to the baner and strake hit thorowoute with his bryght swerde, and so takyth hit fro hem and rydyth with hit away unto his felyshyp.

¶Than Sir Launcelot lepe forth with his stede evyn streyght unto Sir Lucyus, and in his wey he smote thorow a kynge that stoode althirnexte hym, and his name was Jacounde, a Sarezen full noble. And than he russhed forth unto Sir Lucyus and smote hym on the helme with his swerde, that he felle to the erthe; and syth he rode thryse over hym on a rowe, and so toke the baner of Rome and rode with hit away unto Arthure hymself—and all seyde that hit sawe there was never knyght dud more worshyp in his dayes.

¶Than dressed hym Sir Bors unto a sterne knyght and smote hym on the umbrell, that his necke braste. Than he joyned his horse untyl a sterne gyaunte, and smote hym thorow bothe sydys— and yet he slewe in his way, turnyng two other knyghtes. Be than the bowemen of Inglonde and of Bretayne began to shote, and these othir, Romaynes and Sarezens, shotte with dartis and with crossebowys. There began a stronge batayle on every syde, and muche slaughter on the Romaynes party—and the Douchemen with quarels dud muche harme, for they were with the Romaynes with hir bowys of horne.

¶And the grete gyauntes of Gene kylled downe many knyghtes, with clubbys of steele crusshed oute hir braynes—also they sqwatte oute the braynes of many coursers.

¶Whan Arthure had aspyed the gyauntes workes, he cryed on lowde that knyghtes myght here, and seyde, "Fayre lordys, loke youre name be nat loste! Lese nat oure worshyp for yondir bare-legged knavys—and ye shal se what I shall do as for my trew parte!" He toke there oute Excalyber and gurdys towarde Galapas, that grevid hym moste. He kut hym of by the kneis clenly there in sondir.

¶"Now art thou of a syse," seyde the Kyng, "lyke unto oure ferys!"—and than he strake of his hede swyftely.

¶Than come in Sir Cadore and Sir Kay, Sir Gawayne and good Sir Launcelot, Sir Bors, Sir Lyonel, and Sir Ector de Marys, and Sir Ascamore, the good knyght that never fayled his lorde, Sir Pelleas and Sir Marhault, that were proved men of armys. All thes grymly knyghtes sette uppon the gyauntys, and by[4] the dyntys were dalte and the dome yoldyn[5] they had felled hem starke dede of fyffty[6] all to the bare erthe.

¶So forth they wente wyth the Kynge, tho knyghtes of the

<2073>

<2025>

fol.85v

2. *And there he mette . . . that was Vycounte of Rome:* and there he that was Viscount of Rome met with the valiant Vyllers (the Welsh king).
3. I.e., Vyllers, the Welsh King.
4. I.e., by the time that.
5. *The dome yoldyn:* the decsion of victory given.
6. *Hem starke dede of fyffty:* fifty of them utterly dead.

Rounde Table. Was never kyng nother knyghtes dud[7] bettir syn God made the worlde: they leyde on with longe swerdys and swapped thorow braynes; shyldys nother no shene armys myght hem nat withstonde tyll they leyde on the erthe ten thousand at onys. 5

¶Than the Romaynes reled a lytyl, for they were somwhat rebuked. <2153>

¶But Kyng **Arthure** with his pryce knyghtes preced sore aftir. fol.86r

¶Than Sir **Kay**, Sir **Clegis**, and Sir **Bedwere** the ryche encountyrs with them by a clyffsyde, and there they three by good meanys 10 slowe in that chace mo than fyve hondred. And also Sir **Kay** roode unto a Kyng of **Ethyope** and bare hym thorow, and as he turned hym agayne towarde his ferys a tyrraunte strake hym betwyxte the breste and the bowellys.

¶And as he was hurte, yet he turned hym agayne and smote the 15 todir on the hede, that to the breste hit raughte, and seyde, "Thoughe I dey of thy dente, thy praysyng shall be lytyll!"

¶Whan Sir **Clegys** and Sir **Bedwere** saw that Sir **Kay** was hurt, they fared with the Romaynes as grayhoundis doth with harys. And than they returned ayen unto noble Kynge **Arthure** and tolde hym 20 how they had spedde. "Sir Kyng," sayde Sir **Kay**, "I have served the[8] longe. Now bryng me unto som beryellys for my fadyrs sake, and commaunde me to Dame **Gwenyvere**, thy goodly quene—and grete wel my worshypfull wyff that wratthed me never, and byd hir for my love to worche for my soule."[9] 25

¶Than wepte Kynge **Arthure** for routhe at his herte, and seyde, "Thou shalt lyve for ever, my herte thynkes." And therewith the Kynge hymself pulled oute the truncheoune of the speare and made lechis to seche hym sykerly, and founde nother lyvir nor lungys nother bowelles that were attamed. 30

¶And than the Kyng putte hym in hys owne tente with syker knyghtes, and sayde, "I shall revenge thy hurte and I may aryght rede."[1]

¶Than the Kynge in this malyncoly metys with a kynge, and with **Excalyber** he smote his bak in sundir. Than in that haste he metys <2204> 35 with anothir, and gurde hym in the waste thorow bothe sydes. Thus he russhed here and there thorow the thyckyst prees more than thirty tymes.

¶Than Sir **Launcelot**, Sir **Gawayne**, and Sir **Lovel**, ys son, gerde oute one[2] that one[3] hande where **Lucyus** the Emperoure hymself in 40 a launde stoode. Anone, as Sir **Lucyus** sawe Sir **Gawayne**, he sayde fol.86v all on hyght, "Thou art welcom iwys, for thou sekyst aftir sorow! Here thou shalt be sone overmacched."

¶Sir **Launcelot** was wroth at hys grymme wordys and gurde to

---

7. I.e., who did.
8. Thee.
9. *Worche for my soule*: i.e., pray for my salvation.
1. *And I may aryght rede*: i.e., if I can manage it rightly.
2. I.e., on.
3. I.e., one.

hym with his swerde aboven uppon hys bryght helme, that the raylyng bloode felle doune to his feete.

¶And Sir Gawayne wyth his longe swerde leyde on faste, that three amerallys deyde thorow the dynte of his hondis.

How Sir Gawayne slew three amprallys in bataple

¶And so Lovel fayled nat in the pres: he slew a kynge and a deuke, that knyghtes were noble.

¶Than the Romaynes releved: whan they sye hir lorde so hampred they chaced and choppedde doune many of oure knyghtes good—and in that rebukyng they bare the bolde Bedwere to the colde erthe, and wyth a ranke swerde he was merveylously wounded.

¶Yet Sir Launcelot and Sir Lovel rescowed hym blyve. With that come in Kynge Arthure with the knyghtes of the Table Rounde and rescowed the ryche men, that never were lyke to ascape at that tyme (for oftetymes thorow envy grete hardynesse is shewed, that hath bene the deth of many kyd knyghtes—for thoughe they speke fayre many one unto other, yet whan they be in batayle eyther wolde beste be praysed).[4]

None as Kynge Arthure had a syght of the Emperoure Lucyus, for kynge nother for captayne he taryed no lenger. And eythir with her swerdys swapped at othir; so Sir Lucyus with his swerde hit Arthure overthwarte the nose and gaff hym a wounde nyghe unto the tunge; Sir Arthure was wroth and gaff hym another with all the myght that in his arme was leved, that frome the creste of his helme unto the bare pappys hit wente adoune—and so ended the Emperour.

How Kyng Arthure slew the Emperour of Rome Sir Lucius

¶Than the Kyng mette with Sir Cadore, his kene cousyn, and prayde hym, "Kylle doune clene for love of Sir Kay, my foster brother, and for the love of Sir Bedwer that longe hath me served. Therefore save none for golde nothir for sylver—for they that woll accompany them with Sarezens, the man that wolde save them were lytyll to prayse[5]—and therefore sle doune and save nother hethyn nothir Crystyn." Than Sir Cadore, Sir Clegis, they caughte to her swerdys; and Sir Launcelot, Sir Bors, Sir Lyonel, Sir Ector de Marys, they whyrled thorow many men of armys. And Sir Gawayne, Sir Gaherys, Sir Lovell and Sir Florens, his brothir (that was gotyn of Sir Braundyles systir uppon a mountayne),[6] all thes knyghtes russhed forth in a frunte with many mo knyghtes of the Rounde Table that here be not rehersid.

<2261>
fol.87r

¶They hurled over hyllys, valeyes, and clowys, and slow downe on every honde wondirfull many, that thousandis in an hepe lay thrumbelyng togedir. But for all that the Romaynes and the

---

4. This parenthetical statement appears to represent one of relatively few places where Malory departs from his matter and his sources to address his reader directly with a monitory (and personally revealing) observation; cf. other such comments—some of them among the most well-known of all passages from Malory's work—at pp. 595, 625, and 680.

5. *They that woll accompany . . . were lytyll to prayse:* that man deserves little praise who would save those (for ransom) who allied themselves with the Saracens.

6. According to its likely source in the Second Continuation of Chrétien's *Perceval,* this story is in actuality about Lovel's other brother, Guinglain; perhaps Malory had access to a different version or just remembered incorrectly.

Sarezens cowde do other speke[7] to yelde themself, there was none
saved, but all yode to the swerde. For evir Kynge **Arthure** rode in
the thyckeste of the pres and raumped downe lyke a lyon many
senatours noble.

⸿He wolde nat abyde uppon no poure man for no maner of   5
thyng—and ever he slow slyly[8] and slypped to another, tylle all
were slayne to the numbir of a hondred thousand (and yet many
a thousande ascaped thorow prevy frendys).

⸿And than relevys the Kynge with his noble knyghtes and ren-   <2278>
saked over all the feldis for his bolde barouns. And tho that were   10
dede were burryed as their bloode asked;[9] and they that myght be
saved, there was no salve spared, nother no deyntés to dere[1] that
myght be gotyn for golde other sylver. And thus he let save many
knyghtes that wente never to recover—but for Sir **Kayes** recovir
and of Sir **Bedwers** the ryche was never man undir God so glad as   15
hymself was.

⸿Than the Kynge rode streyte there as the Emperoure lay, and   fol.87v
garte lyffte hym up lordely with barounes full bolde. And the Sawdon of **Surré** and of **Ethyope** the Kyng, and of **Egypte** and of **Inde** two
knyghtes full noble, wyth seventene other Kynges were takyn up   20
als, and also syxty senatours of **Roome** that were honoured full
noble men, and all the elders.

⸿The Kynge let bawme all thes with many good gummys and
setthen lette lappe hem in syxtyfolde of sendell large,[2] and than
lete lappe hem in lede that for chauffynge other chongyng they   25
sholde never savoure—and sytthen lete close them in chestys full
clenly arayed, and their baners abovyn on their bodyes, and their
shyldys turned upwarde, that eviry man myght knowe of what contray they were.

⸿So on the morne they founde in the heth three senatours of   <2306>   30
Rome. Whan they were brought to the Kynge, he seyde thes wordis:

⸿"Now to save your lyvys I take no force grete, with that[3] ye woll
meve on my message unto grete Rome and presente thes corses
unto the proude **Potestate** and aftir [shew] hym my lettyrs and my   35
hole entente. And telle hem in haste they shall se me—and I trow
they woll beware how they bourde with me and my knyghtes."

⸿Than the Emperour hymself was dressed in a charyot, and
every[4] two knyghtys in a charyot cewed aftir other, and the senatours com aftir by cowplys in acorde.   40

⸿"Now sey ye to the **Potestate** and all the lordys aftir, that I sende
hem the trybet that I owe to Rome—for this is the trew trybet that
I and myne elders have loste this ten score wyntyrs:

⸿"And sey hem as mesemes I have sent hem the hole somme;

---

7. I.e., say.
8. I.e., skilfully.
9. *As their bloode asked:* according to their estate.
1. *No deyntés to dere:* no fine remedies too expensive.
2. *In syxtyfolde of sendell large:* sixty times in wide swathes of silk.
3. *Take no force grete, with that:* have no great concern, unless.
4. I.e., each.

and yf they thynke hit nat inowe, I shall amende hit whan that I com. [And ferthermore, I charge yow to saye to them that I commaunde them upon payne of theyre hedes never to demaunde trybute ne taxe of me ne of my londes], for suche tresoure muste they take as happyns us[5] here." 5

¶So on the morne thes senatours rayked unto **Rome**, and within eyghtene dayes they come to the **Potestate** and tolde hym how they hadde brought the taxe and the trewage of ten score wynters, bothe of Ingelonde, Irelonde, and of all the est londys—"for Kyng **Arthure** commaundys you nother trybet nother taxe ye never none aske, 10 uppon payne off youre hedys, but yf youre tytil be the trewer than ever ought ony of your elders:

¶"And for these causys we have foughtyn in **Fraunce**, and there us is foule happed,[6] for all is chopped to the deth, bothe the bettir and the worse. Therefore I rede you store you wyth stuff, for war 15 is at honde. For in the moneth of **May** this myscheff befelle in the contrey of **Constantyne**, by the clere stremys, and there he heryed us with his knyghtes, and heled them that were hurte that same day and to bery them that were slayne."

NOw turne we to **Arthure** with his noble knyghtes that entryth 20 streyghte into **Lushburne** and so thorowe **Flaundirs** and thàn to **Lorayne**. He laughte up all the lordshyppys, and sytthen he drew hym into **Almayne** and unto **Lumbardy** the ryche—and sette lawys in that londe that dured longe aftir—and so into **Tuskayne**, and there the tirrauntys destroyed. And there were captaynes full kene 25 that kepte[7] **Arthurs** comyng and at streyte passages slew muche of his peple, and there they vytayled and garnysshed many good townys.

¶But there was a cité kepte[8] sure defence agaynste **Arthure** and his knyghtes—and therewith angred **Arthure**, and seyde all on 30 hyght, "I woll wynne this towne, other ellys many a doughty shall dye."

¶And than the Kynge approched to the wallis withoute shelde, sauff his bare harneys.

¶"Sir," seyde Sir **Florence**, "foly thou workeste for to nyghe so 35 naked[9] this perleouse cité." "And thow be aferde," seyde Kyng **Arthure**, "I rede the[1] faste fle, for they wynne no worshyp of[2] me but to waste their toolys, for there shall never harlot[3] have happe, by the helpe of Oure Lord, to kylle a crowned Kynge that with **Creyme**[4] is anoynted." 40

¶Than the noble knyghtes of the Rounde Table approched unto the cité and their horsis levys. They hurled on a frunte streyght unto the barbycans, and there they slewe downe all that before

fol.88r

<2358>

[9]

fol.88v

---

5. As has befallen us here (i.e., the bodies of Roman worthies).
6. *Us is foule happed:* evil has befallen us.
7. I.e., hindered.
8. I.e., that kept.
9. *To nyghe so naked:* to come so close so poorly dressed.
1. Thee.
2. I.e., from.
3. *Toolys:* i.e., weapons. *Harlot:* i.e., rascal.
4. A reference to one of the rites of coronation.

them stondys; and in that bray the brydge they wanne—and had nat the garnyson bene, they had wonne within the yatys, and the cité wonne thorow wyghtnesse of hondys.

¶And than oure noble knyghtes withdrew them a lytyll and wente unto the Kynge and prayde hym to take his herborgage. And than he pyght his pavylyons of palle, and plantys all aboute the sege,[5] and there he lette sett up suddeynly many engynes.

¶Than the Kynge called unto hym Sir **Florens**, and seyde these wordys: "My folk ys wexen feble for wantynge of vytayle, and hereby be forestes full fayre—and there as oure foomen many, and I am sure they have grete store of bestes. And thyder shall thou go to forrey that forestes, and with the shall go Sir **Gawayne**, and Sir **Wysharde** with Sir **Walchere**, two worshypfull knyghtes, with all the wyseste men of the weste marchis—

¶"Also Sir **Cleremount** and Sir **Clegis** that were comly in armys, and the Captayne of **Cardyff**, that is a knyght full good:

¶"Now go ye and warne all this felyshep that hit be done as I commaunde."

¶So with that forth yode Sir **Florens**, and his felyshyp was sone redy; and so they rode thorow holtys and hethis, thorow foreste and over hyllys. And than they com into a lowe medow that was full of swete floures, and there thes noble knyghtes bayted her [horses].

¶And in the grekynge of the day Sir **Gawayne** hente his hors wondyrs for to seke.

¶Than was he ware of a man armed walkynge a paase[6] by a woodis ease, by a revers syde, and his shelde braced on his sholdir, and he on a stronge horse rydys withoute man wyth hym save a boy alone that bare a grymme speare.

¶The knyght bare in his shelde of golde glystrand three gryffons in sabyll and charbuckkle, the cheff of sylver.[7] Whan Sir **Gawayne** was ware of that gay knyght, than he gryped a grete spere and rode streyght towarde hym on a stronge horse, for to mete with that sterne knyght where that he hoved.

¶Whan Sir **Gawayne** com hym nyghe, in Englyshe he asked hym what he was. And that other knyght answerde in his langage of **Tuskayne**, and sayde, "Whother pryckyst thou, pylloure, that profers the so large?[8] Thou getest no pray, prove whan the[9] lykys, for my presoner thou shalt be, for all thy proude lokys."

¶"Thou spekyste proudly," seyde Sir **Gawayne**, "but I counseyle the, for all thy grymme wordis, that thou grype to the thy gere or more grame falle."

Than hir launcis they handylde by crauffte of armys, and com on spedyly with full syker dyntes, and there they shotte thorow

<2483>

5

10

15

20

<2510>

25

fol.89r

30

35

<2533>

40

[10]

---

5. *Plantys all aboute the sege*: establishes a state of siege around the town.
6. *A paase*: at some speed.
7. Bore on his shield as his coat of arms three gold griffins on a black background with carbuncles and a silver band across the top. A griffin is a legendary beast with the head and wings of an eagle and the body of a lion. A carbuncle is a rubious gemstone believed to have the power to shine in the dark.
8. *Profers the so large*: presents yourself so boastfully.
9. *Prove*: i.e., put it to the test. *The*: thee.

shyldys and mayles, and thorow there shene shuldyrs they were thorow-borne the brede of an hande.

¶Than were they so wroth that away[1] wolde they never, but rathly russhed oute their swerdys and hyttys on their helmys with hatefull dyntys and stabbis at hir stomakys with swerdys well ste-led—so freysshly tho fre men fyghtes on the grounde, whyle the flamynge fyre flowe oute of hir helmys."

¶Than Sir Gawayne was grevid wondirly sore, and swynges his [good] swerde Galantyne, and grymly he strykys, and clevys the knyghtes shylde in sundir, and thorowoute the thycke haubirke made of sure mayles, and the rubyes that were ryche, he russhed hem in sundir that men myght beholde the lyvir and longes. Than groned the knyght for his grymme woundis, and gyrdis to Sir Gawayne and awkewarde[2] hym strykes, and brastyth the rere-brace and the vawm-brace bothe, and kut thorow a vayne—that Gawayne sore greved, for so worched his wounde that his wytte chonged, and therewithall his armure was all blody berenne.

¶Than that knyght talked to Sir Gawayne and bade hym bynde up his wounde—"or thy ble chonge, for thou all be-bledis this horse and thy bryght wedys—for all the barbers[3] of Bretayne shall nat thy blood staunche—

¶"For who that is hurte with this blaade, bleed shal he ever."

¶"Be God," sayde Sir Gawayne, "hit grevys me but lytyll; yet shalt thou nat feare[4] me for all thy grete wordis. Thow trowyste with thy talkynge to tame my herte, but yet thou betydys tene or thou parte hense[5] but thou telle me in haste who may stanche my bledynge!" "That may I do, and I woll, so thou wolt succour me that I myght be fayre[6] crystynde and becom meke for my mysdedis:

¶"Now mercy I Jesu[7] beseche, and I shall becom Crysten and in God stedfastly beleve—and thou mayste for thy manhode have mede to[8] thy soule." "I graunte," seyde Sir Gawayne, "so God me helpe, to fullfyll all thy desyre—thou haste gretly hit deservyd—so[9] thou say me the soth, what thou sought here thus sengly thyself alone, and what lorde or legeaunce thou art undir."

"Sir," he seyde, "I hyght Priamus, and a prynce is my fadir, and he hath bene rebell unto Rome and overredyn muche of hir londis. And my fadir is com of Alysaundirs bloode that was overleder of kynges, and of Ector also was he com by the ryght lyne; and many mo were of my kynrede, bothe Judas Macabeus and deuke Josué—and ayre I am althernexte of Alysaundir and of Aufryke and of all the oute iles. Yet woll I beleve on thy Lorde that thou belevyst on, and

---

1. I.e., turn away.
2. I.e., with a backward stroke.
3. In the Middle Ages barbers were also practioners of surgery and dentistry.
4. I.e., frighten.
5. *Yet thou betydys tene or thou parte hense:* and yet you will experience sorrow before you leave from here.
6. I.e., graciously.
7. I.e., of Jesus.
8. *Mede to:* a reward for.
9. I.e., provided that.

take[1] the for thy labour tresour inow. For I was so hauté in my herte I helde no man my pere—so was I sent into this werre by the assente of my fadir, with seven score knyghtes—and now I have encountred with one[2] hath geevyn [me of] fyghtyng my fylle. Therefore, sir knyght, for thy kynges sake telle me thy name." fol.90r   5

❡"Sir," seyde Sir Gawayne, "I am no knyght, but I have be brought <2620>
up in the wardrope[3] with the noble Kyng Arthure wyntyrs and dayes[4] for to take hede to his armoure and all his other wedis, and to poynte[5] all the paltokkys that longe to hymself, and to dresse doub-lettis for deukys and erlys. And at Yole he made me yoman and 10
gaff me good gyfftys—more than an hondred pounde, and horse and harneyse rych—

❡"And yf I have happe <to> my hele[6] to serve my lyege lorde I shall be well holpyn in haste."

❡"A," sayde Sir Priamus, "and his knavys be so kene, his knyghtes <2632>   15
ar passynge good:

❡"Now for thy Kynges love of Hevyn and for thy kyngys love, whether thou be knave other knyght, telle thou me thy name." "Be God," seyde Sir Gawayne, "now woll I telle the soth: [my name is Syre Gawayn]; I am knowyn in his courte and kyd in his chambir 20
and rolled[7] with the rychest of the Rounde Table, and I am a deuke dubbed wyth his owne hondis. Therefore grucche nat, good sir, if me[8] this grace is behappened—hit is the goodnesse of God that lente me this strength."[9]

❡"Now am I bettir pleased," sayde Sir Pryamus, "than thou had- 25
dest gyff me the Provynce [and] Perysie the ryche, for I had levir have be toryn with foure wylde horse than ony yoman had suche a loose[1] wonne of me, other els ony page other prycker sholde wynne of me the pryce, in this felde gotyn. But now I warne the, Sir knyght of the Rounde Table, here is by[2] the Deuke of Lorayne 30
with his knyghtes, and the doughtyeste of Dolphyne landys, with many Hyghe Duchemen, and many lordis of Lumbardy, and the garneson of Godarde, and men of Westwalle, worshypfull kynges, and of Syssoyne and of Southlonde Sarezyns many numbirde—and there named ar in rollys sixti thousand of syker men of armys. 35
Therefore, but thou hyghe the fro this heth, hit woll harme us both, fol.90v
and sore be we hurte, never lyke to recover. But take thou hede [to[3] my] haynxman that he no horne blow, for and he do, than loke that he be hewyn on pecis, for here hovys at thy honde[4] a hondred of good knyghtes that ar of my retynew and to awayte uppon my 40

1. I.e., give.
2. I.e., one who.
3. I.e., king's private quarters.
4. *Wyntyrs and dayes:* i.e., for many years and days.
5. I.e., care for.
6. *Happe to my hele:* good fortune with my health.
7. I.e., enrolled, included.
8. I.e., to me.
9. I.e., power, status.
1. I.e., fame.
2. I.e., nearby.
3. *Take thou hede to:* notice.
4. *At thy honde:* near you.

persone. For and thou be raught with that rought,[5] raunsom nother
rede golde woll they none aske."

¶Than Sir Gawayne rode over a water for to gyde hymself,[6] and
that worshypfull knyght hym folowed, sore wounded. And so they
rode tylle they com to their ferys that were baytand hir horsys in a
low medow where lay many lordys lenyng on there shyldys with
lawghyng and japyng and many lowde wordys.

¶Anone as Sir Wycharde was ware of Sir Gawayne and aspyed that
he was hurte, he wente towarde hym wepyng and wryngyng his
hondys.

¶Than Sir Gawayne tolde hym how he had macched with that
myghty man of strengthe. "Therefore greve yow nat, good sir, for
thoughe my shylde be now thirled and my sholdir shorne,[7] yett
thys knyght Sir Pryamus hath many perelouse woundys. But he
hath salvys, he seyth, that woll hele us bothe—but here is new
note in honde nere than ye wene,[8] fore by an houre aftir none I
trow hit woll noy us all."

¶Than Sir Pryamus and Sir Gawayne alyght bothe and lette hir
horsys bayte in the fayre medow. Than they lette brayde of hir
basnettys and hir brode shyldys. Than eythir bled so muche that
every man had wondir that they myght sitte in their sadyls or
stonde uppon erthe.

¶"Now fecche me," seyde Sir Pryamus, "my vyall that hangys by
the gurdyll of my haynxman, for hit is full of the floure[9] of the
foure good watyrs that passis from Paradyse,[1] <that> mykyll
fruyte in fallys that at one day fede shall us all:

¶"Putt that watir in oure fleysh where the syde is tamed,[2] and
we shall be hole within foure houres." Than they lette clense their
woundys with colde whyght wyne, and than they lete anoynte them
with bawme over and over, and holer men than they were within
an houres space was never lyvyng syn God the worlde made. So
whan they were clensed and hole they broched barellys and
brought them the wyne wyth brede and brawne and many ryche
byrdys.

¶And whan they had etyn, Sir Gawayne seyde, "Lordynges, go to
armys!" And whan they were armed and assembled togedyrs, with
a clere claryon callys them togedir to counceyle, and Sir Gawayne
of the case hem tellys.

¶"Now tell us, Sir Pryamus, all the hole purpose of yondir pryce
knyghtes."

¶"Sirs," seyde Sir Pryamus, "for to rescow me they have made a
vowe, other ellys manfully on this molde to be marred all at onys.

<2668>

5

10

15

<2704>

25

fol.91r

30

35

40

---

5. *Raught with that rought*: caught by that band of warriors.
6. *Gyde hymself*: find his way.
7. I.e., cut through.
8. Here is more new business at hand than you expect.
9. I.e., flower, choicest thin.
1. Four rivers, the sources of the Ganges, the Tigris, the Nile, and the Euphrates, were
   believed to flow from Paradise (the Garden of Eden), thought to be located somewhere
   in the Far East. Their waters were held to have physically and spiritually restorative powers.
2. I.e., injured.

This was the pure purpose, whan I passed thens at hir perellys,[3] to preff me[4] uppon payne of their lyvys."

❧"Now, good men," seyde Sir **Gawayne**, "grype[5] up your hertes, and yf we *gettles* go thus away, hit woll greffe oure Kynge. And Sir **Florens** in this fyght shall here abyde for to kepe the stale[6] as a knyght noble, for he was chosyn and charged in chambir with the Kynge chyfften of this chekke and cheyff of us all; and whethir he woll fyght other fle, we shall folow aftir—for as for me, for all yondir folkys faare, forsake[7] hem shall I never." <2725>

❧"A, fadir," seyde **Florens**, "full fayre now ye speke," for I am but a fauntekyn to fraysted men of armys, and yf I ony foly do, the faughte muste be youres—therefore lese nat youre worshyp. My wytt is but symple, and ye ar oure allther[8] governoure—therefore worke as ye lykys."

❧"Now, fayre lordys," seyde Sir **Pryamus**, "cese youre wordys, I warne you betyme, for ye shall fynde in yondir woodys many perellus knyghtes. They woll putte furth beystys to bayte you oute of numbir, and ye ar fraykis in this fryth nat paste seven hondred— and that is, feythfully, to fewe to fyght with so many, for harlottys and haynxmen wol helpe us but a lytyll, for they woll hyde them in haste for all their hyghe wordys." fol.91v 20

❧"Ye sey well," seyde Sir **Gawayne**, "so God me helpe."

❧"Now, fayre sonne," sayde Sir **Gawayne** unto **Florens**, "woll ye take youre felyshyp of the beste provyd men to the numbir of a hondred knyghtes and prestly prove yourself and yondir pray wynne?" "I assent me with good hert," seyde **Florence**. 25

Than Sir **Florens** called unto hym Sir **Florydas** with fyve score knyghtes, and forth they flynged a faste trotte, and the folke of[9] the bestes dryvys. Than folowed aftir Sir **Florens** with noble men of armys fully seven hondred. And one Sir **Feraunte** of Spayne before on a fayre stede, that was fostred in Farmagos—the Fende was his fadir—he flyttys towarde Sir **Florens**, and sayde, "Whother flyest thou, false knyght?" Than "Sir **Florens** was fayne, and in feautyr castis his spere, and rydys towarde the rought and restys no lenger—and full-but in the forehede he hyttys Sir **Feraunte** and brake his necke-bone. [11] <2755>

How Sir Florens slew Sir Feraunte

❧Than **Feraunte** his cosyn[1] had grete care and cryed full lowde, "Thou haste slayne a knyght and kynge anoynted that or this tyme founde never frayke that myght abyde hym a buffette; therefore ye shall dey—there shall none of you ascape!" 40

❧"Fye on the," seyde Florydas, "thou eregned wrecche!" And therewith to hym he flyngis with a swerde that all the fleysshe of his flanke he flappys in sundir, that all the fylth[2] of the freyke and many of his guttys fylle to the erthe.

---

3. *At hir perellys*: in danger of them.
4. *Preff me*: to demonstrate my commitment.
5. I.e., lift.
6. *Kepe the stale*: stand firm.
7. I.e., refuse contact with.
8. *Oure allther*: of all of us.
9. I.e., with.
1. *Feraunte his cosyn*: Fraunte's cousin.
2. I.e., foul internal matter.

Than lyghtly rydis a raynke for to rescowe that barowne, that
was borne in the Rodis, and rebell unto Cryste. He preced in
proudly and aftir his pray wyndys. But the raynke **Rycharde** of the
Rounde Table on a rede stede rode hym agaynste and threste hym
thorow the shylde evyn to the herte. Than he rored full rudely—
but rose he nevermore.

¶Than alle his feerys, mo than fyve hondred, felle uppon Sir
Florence and on his fyve score knyghtes. Than Sir **Florens** and Sir
Florydas in feautir bothe castys their spearys, and they felled fyve
at the frunte at the fyrste entré. And sore they assayled oure folke
and brake browys and brestys and felde many adowne.

¶Whan Sir **Pryamus** the pryse knyght perceyved their gamys, he
yode to Sir **Gawyne** and thes wordys seyde: "Thy pryse men ar sore
begone[3] and put undir, for they ar oversette with Sarezens mo than
fyve hondred. Now wolde thou suffir me, for the love of thy God,
with a small parte of thy men to succoure hem betyme?"

¶"Sir, grucch ye nat," seyde Sir **Gawayne**, "the gré is there owne,
for they mowe have gyfftys full grete i-graunted of my lorde.
Therefore lette them fyght whylys hem lystes, the freysh knyghtes,
for som of hem fought nat their fylle of all this[4] fyve wyntyr.
Therefore I woll nat styrre wyth my stale half my steede length,
but yf they be stadde wyth more stuff[5] than I se hem agaynste."

¶So by that tyme was Sir **Gawayne** ware by the woodys syde men
commynge woodly with all maner of wepon, for there rode the Erle
of **Ethelwolde**, havyng on eyther half many hole thousandys; and the
Deuke of Douchemen dressys[6] hym aftir and passis with **Pryamus**
knyghtes.[7] Than **Gawayne** the good knyght, he chered his knyghtes,
and sayde, "Greve you nat, good men, for yondir grete syght, and
be nat abaysshed of yondir boyes in hir bryghte weedis, for and we
feyght in fayth, the felde is ourys."

¶Than they haled up their brydyls and began walop, and by that
they com nygh by a londys length[8] they jowked downe with her
hedys many jantyll knyghtes—a more jolyar joustynge was never
sene on erthe. Than the ryche men of the Rounde Table ran thorow the thykkeste[9] with hir stronge sperys, that many a raynke for
that prouesse ran into the grevys—and durste no knavys but knyghtes kene of herte fyght more in this felde, but fledde.

¶"Be God," seyde Sir **Gawayne**, "this gladys my herte, that yondir
gadlynges be gone, for they made a grete numbir:

¶"Now ar they fewer in the felde than they were fyrst num-
byrd—by twenty thousand, in feyth, for all their grete boste."

¶Than **Jubeaunce of Geane**, a myghty gyaunte, he feautred his
speare to Sir **Garrarde**, a good knyght of Walys; he smote the Waylshe knyght evyn to the herte. Than our knyghtes myghtyly

---

3. *Sore begone:* sorely beset.
4. *Of all this:* i.e., for the duration of.
5. I.e., forces.
6. I.e., postitioned.
7. *Passis with Pryamus knyghtes:* i.e., the Duke of Douchemen now has command of Priamus's men.
8. By the time they had traveled the length of the field.
9. I.e., thickest part of the battle.

<2784>

fol.92r

<2811>

fol.92v

<2883>

<2889>

meddeled[1] wyth hir myddylwarde. But anone at all assemble[2] many Saresyns were destroyed, for[3] the soveraynes of Sessoyne were salved for ever.

⁊By that tyme Sir Pryamus, the good prynce, in the presence of lordys royall, to his penowne he rode and lyghtly hit hentys, and rode with the royall rought of the Rounde Table—and streyte all his retynew folowed hym aftyr oute of the woode. They folowed as shepe oute of a folde, and streyte they yode to the felde and stood by their kynde lorde. And sytthyn they sente to the deuke[4] thes same wordis: "Sir, we have bene thy sowdyars all this seven wynter—and now we forsake the for the love of oure lyege lorde Arthure, for we may with oure worshype wende where us lykys—for garneson nother golde have we none resceyved." "Fye on you[5]—the devyll have your bonys! For suche sowdyars I sette but a lytyll."

⁊Than the deuke dressys his Dowchmen streyte unto Sir Gawayne and to Sir Pryamus; so they two gryped their spearys, and at the gaynyste in he[6] gurdys wyth hir noble myghtes—and there Sir Pryamus metyth with the Marquesse of Moyses-londe and smytyth hym thorow.

⁊Than Chastelayne, a chylde[7] of Kyng Arthurs chambir (he was a warde of Sir Gawaynes of the weste marchis) he chasis to Sir Cheldrake that was a chyfteyne noble, and with his spere he smote thorow Cheldrake—and so that chek that chylde cheved by chaunce of armys.

⁊But than they chaced that chylde that he nowhere myght ascape, for one with a swerde the halse of the chylde he smote in too.

⁊Whan Sir Gawayne hit sawe, he wepte wyth all his herte and inwardly he brente for sorow.

⁊But anone Gotelake, a good man of armys, for Chastelayne the chylde he chongyd his mode that the wete watir wente doune his chykys.

⁊Than Sir Gawayne dressis hym and to a deuke rydys; and Sir Dolphyn the deuke droff harde agaynste hym, but Sir Gawayne hym dressyth with a grete spere, that the grounden hede droff to his herte; yette he gate hit oute and ran to another one, Sir Hardolf, an hardy man of armys, and slyly in he lette hit slyppe thorow; and sodeynly he fallyth to the erthe. Yet he slow in the slade of men of armys mo than syxty with his hondys.

⁊Than was Sir Gawayne ware of the man that slew Chastelayne his chylde, and swyfftly with his swerde he smyttyth hym thorow. "Now and thou haddyst ascaped withoutyn scathe, the scorne had bene oures!" And aftir Sir Gawayne dressis hym unto the route and russhyth on helmys, and rode streyte to the rerewarde and so his

[marginal notes:]
The deth of the Marquesse

The deth of Chastelayne fol.93r

The deth of Sir Dolphyn

<2979>

---

1. I.e., mixed in.
2. I.e., encounters.
3. I.e., and.
4. I.e., the Duke of Douchemen.
5. The Duke is speaking.
6. I.e., each man.
7. I.e., noble youth.

way holdyth—and Sir **Pryamus** hym allthernexte—gydynge[8] hym
his wayes. And there they hurtelyth and hewyth downe hethyn
knyghtes many—and Sir **Florence** on the other syde dud what he
myght. There the lordys of **Lorayne** and of **Lumbardy** both were takyn
and lad away with oure noble knyghtes. For suche a chek oure
lordys cheved by chaunce of that werre that they were so avaunced,
for hit avayled hem ever.

¶Whan Sir **Florence** and Sir **Gawayne** had the felde wonne, than
they sente before[9] fyve score of knyghtes, and her prayes[1] and hir
presoners passyth hem aftir. And Sir **Gawayne** in a streyte passage
he hovyth tyll all the prayes were paste that streyte patthe, that so
sore he dredith. So they rode tyll they the cité sawe—and sothly
the same day with asawte hit was gotyn.

¶Than Sir **Florence** and Sir **Gawayne** harborowed surely their
peple, and sytthen turnys to a tente and tellyth the Kynge all the
tale truly, that day how they travayled and how his ferse men fare
welle all. "And fele of thy foomen ar brought oute of lyff, and many
worshypfull presoners ar yolden into oure handys. But **Chastelayne**,
thy chylde, is chopped of the hede—yette slewe he a cheff knyghte
his owne hondys this day."

" **N**Ow thanked be God," sayde the noble Kynge, "but I mervayle
muche of that bourely knyght that stondyth by the, for hym
semys to be a straungere, for presonere is he none lyke." "Sir,"
seyde Sir **Gawayne**, "this is a good man of armys—he macched me
sore this day in the mournyng—and had nat his helpe bene, that
had I [never] founden.[2] And now is he yolden unto God and to me,
Sir Kyng, for to becom Crysten and on good beleve. And whan he
is crystynde and in the fayth belevys, there lyvyth nat a bettir
knyght nor a noblere of his hondis."

¶Than the Kynge in haste crystynde hym fayre and lette con-
ferme hym **Priamus**, as he was afore, and lyghtly lete dubbe hym a
deuke with his hondys and made hym knyght of the Table Rounde.
And anone the Kynge lette cry asawte unto the towne; and there
was rerynge of laddyrs and brekynge of wallys—the payne that the
peple had was pyté to se.

¶Than the duches hir dressed with damesels ryche, and the
Countes of **Clarysyn** with hir clere maydyns; they kneled in their
kyrtyls there the kynge hovyth and besought hym of socoure for
the sake of Oure Lorde—"And sey us som good worde and cetyl
thy peple or the cité suddeynly be with asawte wonne—for than
shall dye many a soule that grevid the never."

¶The Kynge [av]alys[3] his vyser with a knyghtly countenaunce,

<3001>

10

fol.93v

15

20

[12]

25

30

35

<3044>

40

---

8. I.e., with Gawayne guiding.
9. I.e., ahead.
1. I.e., prizes.
2. I.e., discovered. The MS reads *bene that had I founden.* Caxton's corresponding *we shold
never have rotorned* provides *never,* and the emendation follows the model of a similar
phrase found earlier in the Winchester text (line 10, p. 125).
3. I.e., lifts up. The Winchester MS here reads *of Walys lyffte up:* the first two words represent
a scribal miscopying of *avalys,* a reading supported by Caxton's *avalyd* and by the present-
tense form of its counterpart in *aMA, veres; lyffte up* represents a scribe's attempt to replace
the necessary action obliterated by the *of Walys* copying error.

and kneled to hir myldely with full meke wordes, and seyde, "Shall   fol.94r
none myssedo you, madam, that to me longis, for I graunte the
chartyrs,[4] and to thy cheff maydyns, unto thy chyldern, and to thy
chyff men in chambir that to the longis—

⁋"But[5] thy deuke is in daunger, my drede ys the lesse—   5

⁋"But ye shall have lyvelode to leve by as to thyne astate fallys."[6]

⁋Than **Arthure** sendyth on eche syde wyth sertayne lordis for to
cese of their sawte, for the cité was yolden; and therewith the
deukeis eldyst sonne com with the keyes and kneled downe unto
the Kynge and besought hym of his grace.   10

⁋And there he cesed the sawte by assente of his lordis, and the
deuke was dressed to Dover with the Kynges dere knyghtes, for to
dwelle in daunger and dole dayes of his lyff.

⁋Than the Kynge with his crowne on his hede recoverde the
cité and the castell; and the captaynes and connestablys knew[7]   15
hym for lorde, and there he delyverde and dalte byfore dyverse
lordis a dowré for the deuches and hir chyldryn.

⁋Than he made wardens to welde all that londis. And so in
Lorayne and Lumbardy he lodged as a lorde in his owne, and sette
lawys in the londis as hym beste lyked.   20

⁋And than at Lammas[8] he yode—unto **Lusarne** he sought[9]—and   <3078>
lay at his leyser with lykynges inowe.

⁋Than he mevys over the mountaynes and doth many mervayles,
and so goth in by **Godarte**—that **Gareth** sone wynnys.

⁋Than he lokys into **Lumbardy**, and on lowde spekyth: "In yondir   25
lykynge londis as lorde woll I dwelle." Sir **Florence** and Sir **Floridas**
that day passed with fyve hondred good men of armys unto the
cité of [**Urbyne**]. They sought at the gaynyste[1] and leyde there a
buysshement as hem beste lykys. So there [yssued] oute of that
cité many hundretthis and skyrmysshed wyth oure foreryders as   30
hem beste semed. Than broke oute oure buysshemente and the
brydge wynnys, and so rode unto their borowys with baners up
dysplayed. There fledde much folke oute of numbir for ferde of Sir   fol.94v
Florence and his fers knyghtes. Than they busked up a baner abovyn
the gatis—and of Sir **Florence** in fayth so fayne were they never.   35
The Kynge than hovyth on an hylle and lokyth to the wallys, and
sayde, "I se be yondir sygne the cité is wonne." Than he lete make
a cry thorow all the oste that uppon payne of lyff and lymme, and
also lesynge of his goodys, that no lyege man that longyth to his
oste sholde lye be[2] no maydens ne ladyes nother no burgessis wyff   40
that to the cité longis.

⁋So whan this conquerrour com into the cité he passed into the
castell, and there he lendis and comfortis the carefull men with

---

4. *The:* thee. *Chartyrs:* i.e., pardons.
5. I.e., Except that.
6. *As to thyne astate fallys:* as befits your rank in society.
7. I.e., accepted.
8. Lammas Day, August 1.
9. I.e., advanced.
1. *At the gaynyste:* by the shortest way.
2. *Lye be:* lie by, rape.

many knyghtly wordis; and made there a captayne[3] a knyght of his owne contrey—and the commons accorded theretyll.

¶Whan the soveraygnes of **Myllayne** herde that the cité was <3134> wonne, they sente unto Kynge **Arthure** grete sommys of sylver, syxty horsys well charged, and besought hym as soverayne to have ruthe of the peple, and seyde they wolde be sudgectes untyll hym for ever and yelde hym servyse and sewte surely for[4] hir londys—bothe for **Plesaunce** [and **Pavye**] and **Petresaynte** and for the Porte **Trembyll**, and so mekly to gyff [yerly] for **Myllayne** a myllyon of golde, and make homage[5] unto **Arthure** all hir lyff tymes. Than the Kynge by his counceyle a conduyte hem sendys so to com in and know[6] hym for lorde.

¶Than into **Tuskayne** he turned whan hym tyme semed,[7] and <3150> there he wynnys towrys and townys full hyghe—and all he wasted in his warrys there[8] he away ryddys.

¶Than he spedys towarde **Spolute** with his spedfull knyghtys; and so unto **Vyterbe** he vytayled his knyghtes, and to the vale of **Vysecounte**; he devysed there to lygge in that vertuouse vale amonge vynys full—and there he suggeournys, that soveraigne, with solace fol.95r at his harte, for to wete whether the **senatours** wolde hym of succour beseke.

¶But sone after, on a Saturday, sought unto Kynge **Arthure** all the senatoures that were on lyve, and of the cunnyngyst **Cardynallis** that dwelled in the courte, and prayde hym of pece[9] and profird hym full large;[1] and besought hym as a soverayne, moste governoure undir God, for to gyff them lycence for syx wekys large, that they myght be assembled all, and than in the cité of **Syon** (that is **Rome** callyd) to crowne hym there kyndly[2] with crysemed hondys,[3] with septure, forsothe, as an emperoure sholde.

¶"I assente me," seyde the Kynge, "as ye have devysed, and <3213> comly be Crystmas to be crowned—hereafter to reigne in my asstate[4] and to kepe my Rounde Table with the rentys of **Rome** to rule as me lykys—

¶"And than, as I am avysed, to gete me over the salte see with good men of armys to deme[5] for His deth that for us all on the Roode dyed."

---

3. I.e., a governor of the city.
4. I.e., in return for.
5. On the act of homage, see n. 6, p. 9.
6. I.e., acknowledge.
7. *Whan hym tyme semed*: i.e., when the time seemed right to him.
8. *Wasted*: i.e., laid waste to. *There*: i.e., where.
9. Requested peace from him.
1. *Profird hym full large*: made generous offers.
2. I.e., lawfully, appropriately.
3. *With crysemed hondys*: hands annointed with holy oil.
4. *In my asstate*: according to my rank.
5. I.e., act in judgment. Here Arthur considers a crusade, a popular thing for sovereigns to propose (if not act on) in the later Middle Ages. Strictly speaking, this would be anachronistic for a historical King Arthur, as the age of crusading against the Muslims in Palestine did not begin until the end of the 11th century and lasted through the 13th century; but for Malory's time, a non-Christian threat from the eastern Mediterranean remained in the form of the Turks, who by 1456 had reached as far north as Belgrade, having conquered Constantinople, the center of the Eastern Christian world, in 1453. Of all Middle English romances, the poem *Capystranus* represents the most direct response to

¶Whan the **senatours** had this answere, unto Rome they turned and made rydy for his corownemente in the moste noble wyse. And at the day assigned, as the romaynes[6] me tellys, he was crowned Emperoure by the **Poopys** hondis, with all the royalté[7] in the worlde to welde for ever.

¶There they suggeourned that seson tyll aftir the tyme and sta-belysshed all the londys frome **Rome** unto **Fraunce**, and gaff londis and rentys unto knyghtes that had hem well deserved. There was none that playned on his parte, ryche nothir poore. Than he com-maunded Sir **Launcelot** and Sir **Bors** to take kepe unto their fadyrs landys that Kynge **Ban** and Kynge **Bors** welded, and her fadyrs: "Loke that ye take seynge in all your brode londis, and cause youre lyege men to know you as for their kynde lorde—and suffir never your soveraynté to be alledged[8] with your subjectes, nother the soveraygne of your persone and londys:

¶"Also the myghty Kynge **Claudas** I gyff you for to parte betwyxte you evyn,[9] for to mayntene your kynrede that be noble knyghtes, so that ye and they to the Rounde Table make your repeyre."

¶Sir **Launcelot** and Sir **Bors de Gaynys** thanked the Kynge fayre, and sayde their hertes and servyse sholde ever be his owne.

¶"Where[1] art thou, **Priamus**? Thy fee is yet behynde.[2] Here I make the and gyff the deukedom of **Lorayne** for ever unto the and thyne ayres, and whan we com into Ingelonde, for to purvey[3] the of horse-mete a thousand pounde quarterly, for to mayntene thy servauntes. So thou leve not my felyship, this gyffte ys thyne owne."

¶The knyght thankys the Kynge with a kynde wylle, and sayde, "As longe as I lyve my servys[4] is youre owne."

¶Thus the Kynge gaff many londys. There was none that wolde aske that myghte playne of his parte, for of rychesse and welth they had all at her wylle.

¶Than the knyghtes and lordis that to the Kynge longis called a counsayle uppon a fayre morne, and sayde, "Sir Kynge, we beseche the for to here us all. We ar undir youre lordship well stuffid, blyssed[5] be God, of many thynges—and also we have wyffis wed-

fol.95v

---

the Turkish threat; that poem is edited in *MER,* with an introductory headnote on the crusading context.

6. To the contrary, at this point in Malory's main romance source for this tale, the *aMA* (and indeed according to Arthurian tradition generally, as established by Geoffrey of Mon-mouth), Arthur receives word of Mordred's rebellion at home; he then turns back to Britain without being crowned emperor, and meets with the destruction of his kingdom. The *Chronicle* of John Hardyng is the only other known text that has Arthur crowned emperor; this may be the source Malory is referring to here, for it seems likely that he knew the text and used it elsewhere in this tale (see p. 719), but it is equally likely that he is simply positing a "phantom" source to cover what is perhaps the most radical of all changes he makes to Arthurian tradition. Malory evidently wished Arthur's Roman war to establish the legendary promise of a great king rather than depict a territorial distraction that led to his downfall (cf. n. 9, p. 119).

7. I.e., sovereign power.

8. I.e., lessened.

9. *Kynge Claudas I gyff . . . betwyxte you evyn:* i.e. I grant you the ransom you receive for King Claudas to divide evenly between you.

1. Arthur is speaking.

2. *Fee:* i.e., reward. *Yet behynde:* i.e., still to come.

3. I.e., provide.

4. I.e., homage.

5. *Stuffid:* i.e., provided. *Blyssed:* i.e., blessed.

did; we woll beseche youre good grace to reles us to sporte[6] us with oure wyffis, for, worshyp be Cryste, this journey is well overcom." Ye say well," seyde the Kynge, "for inowghe is as good as a feste— for to attemte[7] God overmuche, I holde hit not wysedom:

¶"And therefore make you all redy and turne we into Inge-londe."   5

¶Than there was trussynge of harneyse with caryage[8] full noble. And the Kynge toke his leve of the holy fadir the **Pope** and **Patryar-kys** and cardynalys and senatoures full ryche, and leffte good gov-ernaunce in that noble cité and all the contrays of **Rome** for to   10 warde and to kepe, on payne of deth, that in no wyse his com-maundement be brokyn. Thus he passyth thorow the contreyes of all partyes.[9] And so Kyng **Arthure** passed over the see unto **Sandwyche** haven.   fol.96r

¶Whan Quene **Gwenyvere** herde of his commynge, she mette   15 with hym at **London**, and so dud all other quenys and noble ladyes. For there was never a solempner metyng in one cité togedyrs, for all maner of rychesse they brought with hem at the full.

¶Here endyth the tale of the noble Kynge **Arthure** that was Emperoure hymself thorow dygnyté of his hondys; and here folow-   20 yth afftir many noble talys of Sir **Launcelot de Lake**.

**Explycit the noble tale betwyxt Kynge
Arthure and Lucius the Emperour of Rome.**

A Noble Tale of Sir Launcelot Du Lake†

SOne aftir that Kynge **Arthure** was com from **Rome** into Inge-   [VI.1]
londe, than all the knyghtys of the Rounde Table resorted
unto the Kynge and made many joustys and turnementes. And som
there were, that were but knyghtes, encresed in armys and worshyp   35
that passed all other of her felowys in prouesse and noble dedys—
and that was well proved on many. But in especiall hit was prevyd
on Sir **Launcelot de Lake**, for in all turnementes, justys, and dedys of
armys, both for lyff and deth, he passed all other knyghtes—and   40
at no tyme was he ovircom but yf hit were by treson other inchaun-   fol.96v
tement.

---

6. I.e., sport, play.
7. I.e., tempt.
8. I.e., transport, baggage.
9. I.e., regions.
† The title is taken from the *explicit*, or closing notation, to this section (see p. 177). In the Winchester MS the beginning of this section does not appear as a major division, starting at the bottom third of the page, immediately after the previous explicit and with only a line space for separation. The impression, indeed, is that Malory may have seen this section as a dependent sequel to the Roman war. Malory's principal source for the section is the French Prose *Launcelot*; for illustrative selections, see p. 720.

¶So this Sir **Launcelot** encresed so mervaylously in worship and honoure: therefore he is the fyrste knyght that the Freynsh booke makyth mencion of aftir Kynge **Arthure** com frome **Rome.** Wherefore Quene **Gwenyvere** had hym in grete favoure aboven all other knyghtis, and so he loved the Quene agayne[1] aboven all other ladyes dayes[2] of his lyff, and for hir he dud many dedys of armys, and saved her frome the fyre thorow his noble chevalry.[3]

¶Thus Sir **Launcelot** rested hym longe with play and game; and than he thought hymself to preve in straunge adventures, and bade his nevew, Sir **Lyonell,** for to make hym redy—"for we muste go seke adventures." So they mounted on their horses, armed at all ryghtes,[4] and rode into a depe foreste and so into a playne. So the wedir was hote aboute noone, and Sir **Launcelot** had grete luste[5] to slepe.

Than Sir **Lyonell** aspyed a grete appyll tre that stoode by an hedge, and seyde, "Sir, yondir is a fayre shadow; there may we reste us and oure horsys." "Hit is trouthe," seyde Sir **Launcelot,** "for this seven yere I was not so slepy as I am nowe." So there they alyted and tyed there horsys unto sondry treis; and Sir **Launcelot** layde hym downe undir this appyll tre, and his helmet undir his hede. And Sir **Lyonell** waked whyles he slepte. So Sir **Launcelot** slepte passyng faste; and in the meanewhyle com there three knyghtes rydynge, as faste fleynge as they myght ryde, and there folowed hem three but one knyght.

¶And whan Sir **Lyonell** hym sawe, he thought he sawe never so grete a knyght nother so well-farynge a man and well appareyld unto all ryghtes. So within a whyle this stronge knyght had overtakyn one of the three knyghtes, and there he smote hym to the colde erth that he lay stylle. And than he rode unto the secunde knyght and smote hym so that man and horse felle downe—and so streyte unto the thirde knyght, and smote hym behynde his horse ars a spere-lengthe.

¶And than he alyght downe and rayned his horse on the brydyll and bounde all three knyghtes faste with the raynes of theire owne brydelys.

¶Whan Sir **Lyonell** had sene hym do thus, he thought to assay hym, and made hym redy, and pryvaly he toke his horse and thought nat for to awake Sir **Launcelot**—and so mounted uppon his hors and overtoke the strong knyght. He bade hym turne; and so he turned and smote Sir **Lyonell** so harde that hors and man he

fol.97r

---

1. I.e., in return.
2. I.e., all the days.
3. *he loved the Quene . . . thorow his noble chevalry.* For Launcelot's rescue of Gwenyvere, see p. 654 ff. Throughout this section, in passages not matched in Malory's sources, Launcelot is challenged with, and repeatedly denies, insinuations that he is engaged in an adulterous relationship with Gwenyvere. The impression, between Malory's narratorial comment here and Launcelot's comments hereafter, is of a love acknowledged but resistant to definition, platonic in the written presence Malory desires to give it, but carnal in implicit deed. Malory's comments on the nature of the love in later sections presents a similar tension; cf. n. 9, p. 625; n. 6, p. 633; and n. 6, p. 638. Malory omits any account of the first meeting between Launcelot and Gwenyvere; for the account as given in the prose *Launcelot,* see p. 720.
4. *All ryghtes:* every respect.
5. I.e., desire.

bare to the erth. And so he alyght downe and bounde hym faste
and threw hym overthwarte his owne horse as he had served the
other three, and so rode with hem tyll he com to his owne castell.

¶Than he unarmed them and bete them with thornys all naked,
and aftir put them in depe preson where were many mo knyghtes   5
that made grete dole.

¶So whan Sir Ector de Marys wyste that Sir Launcelot was paste   [2]
oute of the courte to seke adventures, he was wroth with hymself
and made hym redy to seke Sir Launcelot. And as he had redyn longe
in a grete foreste, he mette with a man was lyke a foster. "Fayre   10
felow," seyde Sir Ector, "doste thou know this contrey or ony adventures that bene here nyghe honde?"[6]

"Sir," seyde the foster, "this contrey know I well. And hereby
within this myle is a stronge maner, and well dyked; and by that
maner, on the lyffte honde, there is a fayre fourde for horse to   15
drynke off, and over that fourde there growys a fayre tre, and
thereon hongyth many fayre shyldys that welded somtyme good
knyghtes; and at the b[oole] of the tre hongys a basyn of couper
and latyne. And stryke uppon that basyn with the butte of thy spere
three tymes, and sone aftir thou shalt hyre new tydynges—and   20
ellys haste thou the fayreste grace[7] that ever had knyghte this many
yeres that passed thorow this foreste!"

¶"Gramercy," seyde Sir Ector, and departed and com unto this
tre, and sawe many fayre shyldys; and amonge them all he sawe   fol.97v
hys brothirs shylde, Sir Lyonell—and many mo that he knew that   25
were of his felowys of the Rounde Table, the whyche greved his
herte—and promysed to revenge his brother.

¶Than anone Sir Ector bete on the basyn as he were woode,[8]
and than he gaff his horse drynke at the fourde. And there com a
knyghte behynde hym and bade hym com oute of the water and   30
make hym redy. Sir Ector turned hym shortly, and in feawtir caste
his spere, and smote the other knyght a grete buffette that his
horse turned twyse abowte.

¶"That was well done," seyde the stronge knyght, "and knyghtly
thou haste strykyn me." And therewith he russhed his horse on Sir   35
Ector and caught hym undir his ryght arme and bare hym clene
oute of the sadyll—

¶And so rode with hym away into his castell, and threw hym
downe in myddyll of the floure. [The name of thys knyghte was
Syre Turquyne.]   40

Than this seyde[9] Tarquyn seyde unto Sir Ector, "For thou hast
done this day more unto me than ony knyght dud this twelve yere—

¶"Now woll I graunte the[1] thy lyff, so thou wolt be sworne to
be my trew presoner." "Nay," sayde Sir Ector, "that woll I never
promyse the, but that I woll do myne advauntage."[2] "That me   45

6. Near at hand.
7. *The fayreste grace*: i.e., the best luck.
8. I.e., mad.
9. I.e., foresaid.
1. thee.
2. *Do myne advauntage*: i.e., look after myself.

repentis," seyde Sir **Tarquyn**. Than he gan unarme hym and bete hym with thornys all naked, and sytthyn put hym downe into a depe dongeon—and there he knewe many of his felowys.

But whan Sir **Ector** saw Sir **Lyonell**, than made he grete sorow. "Alas, brother," seyde Sir **Ector**, "how may this be, and where is my brothir Sir **Launcelot**?" "Fayre brother, I leffte hym on slepe, whan that I frome hym yode, undir an appil tre, and what is becom of hym I can nat telle you."

¶"Alas," seyde the presoneres, "but yf[3] Sir **Launcelot** helpe us we shall never be delyverde—

¶"For we know now no knyght that is able to macch with oure maystir **Tarquyne**." fol.98r

Now leve we thes knyghtes presoners, and speke we of Sir **Launcelot de Lake** that lyeth undir the appil tre slepyng aboute the none. So there com by hym foure queenys of a grete astate; and, for the hete sholde nat nyghe hem, there rode foure knyghtes aboute hem and bare a cloth of grene sylke on foure sperys betwyxte hem and the sonne— [3]

¶And the quenys rode on foure whyghte mulys.

¶Thus as they rode they herde a grete horse besyde them grymly nyghe.

¶Than they loked and were ware of a slepynge knyght lay[4] all armed undir an appil tre. And anone as they loked on his face they knew well hit was Sir **Launcelot**, and began to stryve for[5] that knyght, and every of hem seyde they wolde have hym to hir love.

¶"We shall nat stryve," seyde **Morgan le Fay**, that was Kyng **Arthurs** sister. "I shall put an inchauntement uppon hym that he shall nat awake of all this seven owres, and than I woll lede hym away unto my castell:

¶"And whan he is surely within my holde, I shall take the inchauntement frome hym and than lette hym chose whych of us he woll have unto paramour." So this enchauntemente was caste uppon Sir **Launcelot**, and than they leyde hym uppon his shylde and bare hym so on horsebak betwyxte two knyghtes, and brought hym unto the Castell Charyot; and there they leyde hym in a chambir colde, and at nyght they sente unto hym a fayre dameselle with his souper redy i-dyght (be that[6] the enchauntement was paste).

¶And whan she com, she salewed hym and asked hym what chere.[7] "I can not sey, fayre damesel," seyde Sir **Launcelot**, "for I wote not how I com into this castell, but hit be by inchauntemente."

¶"Sir," seyde she, "ye muste make good chere—and yf ye be suche a knyght as is seyde ye be, I shall telle you more tomorn be pryme[8] of the day." "Gramercy, fayre damesel," seyde Sir **Launcelot**, fol.98v

---

3. *but yf*: i.e., unless.
4. I.e., who lay.
5. *stryve for*: i.e., fight over.
6. By that time.
7. *What chere*: how he was doing.
8. I.e., the beginning. Prime was the first of the eight canonical hours making up the Divine

"of your good wylle." And so she departed; and there he laye all that nyght withoute ony comforte.

⟨And on the morne erly com thes foure quenys passyngly well besene, and all they byddynge hym good morne, and he them agayne.

⟨"Sir knyght," the foure quenys seyde, "thou muste undirstonde thou art oure presonere, and we know the[9] well, that thou art Sir **Launcelot du Lake**, Kynge **Bani**s sonne. And because that we undirstonde youre worthynesse, that thou art the noblest knyght lyvyng, and also we know well there can no lady have thy love but one, and that is Quene **Gwenybere**[1]—and now thou shalt hir love lose for ever, and she thyne. For hit behovyth the now to chose one of us foure: for I am Quene **Morgan le Fay**, Quene of the londe of Gore; and here is the Quene of **North Galys**, and the Quene of **Estlonde**, and the Quene of the **Oute Iles**. Now chose one of us, whyche that thou wolte have to thy paramour, other ellys to dye in this preson."

⟨"This is an harde case," seyde Sir **Launcelot**, "that other I muste dye other to chose one of you:

⟨"Yet had I lever dye in this preson with worshyp than to have one of you to my paramoure, magré myne hede.[2] And therefore ye be answeryd: I woll none of you, for ye be false[3] enchaunters. And as for my lady, Dame **Gwenybere**, were I at my lyberté as I was, I wolde prove hit on youres[4] that she is the treweste lady unto hir lorde lyvynge."

⟨"Well," seyde the quenys, "ys this your answere, that ye woll refuse us?"

⟨"Ye, on my lyff," seyde Sir **Launcelot**, "refused ye bene of me."

⟨So they departed and leffte hym there alone that made grete sorow.

⟨ So aftir that noone com the damesel unto hym with his dyner and asked hym what chere.

⟨"Truly, damesel," seyde Sir **Launcelot**, "never so ylle."

⟨"Sir," she seyde, "that me repentis; but, and ye woll be ruled by me, I shall helpe you oute of this dystresse—and ye shall have no shame nor velony, so that ye woll holde my promyse."

⟨"Fayre damesel, I graunte you; but sore I am of thes quenys crauftis aferde, for they have destroyed many a good knyght."

⟨"Sir," seyde she, "that is soth, and for the renowne and bounté that they here of you, they woll have your love—

⟨"And, sir, they sey youre name is Sir **Launcelot du Lake**, the floure of knyghtes—and they be passyng wroth with you that ye have refused hem:

⟨"But, sir, and ye wolde promyse me to helpe my fadir on

fol.99r

[4]

Office, the sequence of prayer said every day and night by priests and other religious professionals. Typically, Prime would begin at about six o'clock in the morning and end at nine.

9. Thee.
1. On this charge, see n. 3, p. 152.
2. *magré myne hede*: against my will.
3. I.e., treacherous.
4. *Prove hit on youres*: i.e., prove it against your freedom.

Tewysday next commynge, that hath made[5] a turnemente betwyxt hym and the Kynge of North Galys—for the laste Tewysday past my fadir loste the felde thorow three knyghtes of Arthurs courte—and yf ye woll be there on Tewysday next commynge and helpe my fadir, and tomorne be pryme by the grace of God I shall delyver you clene."[6]

¶"Now, fayre damesell," seyde Sir Launcelot, "telle me your fadyrs name, and than shall I gyff you an answere."

¶"Sir knyght," she seyde, "my fadyrs name is Kynge Bagdemagus, that was foule rebuked at the laste turnemente."

¶"I knowe your fadir well," seyde Sir Launcelot, "for a noble kyng and a good knyght; and by the fayth of my body, your fadir shall have my servyse—and you bothe—at that day."

¶"Sir," she seyde, "gramercy, and tomorne loke ye be redy betymys, and I shall delyver you and take you your armoure, your horse, shelde, and spere. And hereby wythin this ten myle is an abbey of whyght monkys,[7] and there I pray you to abyde[8] me, and thydir shall I brynge my fadir unto you." "And all this shall be done," seyde Sir Launcelot, "as I am trew knyght." And so she departed and come on the morne erly and founde hym redy.

¶Than she brought hym oute of twelve lockys, and toke hym his armour and his owne horse; and lyghtly he sadyld hym[9] and toke his spere in his honde and so rode forth, and sayde, "Damesell, I shall nat fayle, by the grace of God."

¶And so he rode into a grete foreste all that day, and never coude fynde no hygheway, and so the nyght fell on hym; and than was he ware in a slade of a pavylyon of rede sendele.

¶"Be my feyth," seyde Sir Launcelot, "in that pavylyon woll I lodge all this nyght." And so he there alyght downe, and tyed his horse to the pavylyon, and there he unarmed hym; and there he founde a bed, and layde hym therein, and felle on slepe sadly.[1]

¶Than within an owre there com that knyght that ought the pavylyon. He wente that his lemman had layne in that bed, and so he leyde hym adowne by Sir Launcelot and toke hym in his armys and began to kysse hym. And whan Sir Launcelot felte a rough berde kyssyng hym, he sterte oute of the bedde lyghtly—and the othir knyght after hym. And eythir of hem gate their swerdys in their hondis, and oute at the pavylyon dore wente the knyght of the pavylyon—and Sir Launcelot folowed hym. And there by a lytyll slad Sir Launcelot wounded hym sore, nyghe unto the deth. And than he yelded hym to Sir Launcelot, and so he graunted hym so that he wolde telle hym why he com into the bed.

¶"Sir" sayde the knyghte, "the pavylyon is myne owne:

¶"And as this nyght I had assigned my lady to have slepte with hir, and now I am lykly to dye of this wounde."

---

5. I.e., arranged.
6. I.e., utterly.
7. *Whyght monkys:* white monks; i.e., Cistercian monks, who wear white habits.
8. I.e., wait for.
9. *Sadyld hym:* set himself in his saddle.
1. I.e., soundly.

¶"That me repentyth," seyde Sir Launcelot, "of youre hurte, but I was adrad of treson, for I was late[2] begyled. And therefore com on your way into youre pavylyon, and take youre reste—and as I suppose[3] I shall staunche your bloode." And so they wente bothe into the pavylyon, and anone Sir Launcelot staunched his bloode.

¶Therewithall com the knyghtes lady that was a passynge fayre lady. And whan she aspyed that her lorde Belleus was sore wounded, she cryed oute on Sir Launcelot, and made grete dole oute of mesure.

¶"Pease, my lady and my love," seyde Sir Belleus, "for this knyght is a good man and a knyght of aventures." And there he tolde hir all the case how he was wounded—"and whan that I yelded me unto hym he laffte[4] me goodly, and hath staunched my bloode."

¶"Sir," seyde the lady, "I require the, telle me what knyght thou art, and what is youre name."

¶"Fayre lady," he sayde, "my name is Sir Launcelot du Lake." "So me thought ever be youre speche,[5] seyde the lady, "for I have sene you oftyn or[6] this, and I know you bettir than ye wene. But now wolde ye promyse me of youre curtesye, for the harmys that ye have done to me and to my lorde, Sir Belleus, that whan ye com unto Kyng Arthurs courte for to cause hym to be made knyght of the Rounde Table? For he is a passyng good man of armys and a myghty lorde of londys of many oute iles."

¶"Fayre lady," sayde Sir Launcelot, "latte hym com unto the courte the next hyghe feste, and loke ye com with hym, and I shall do my power;[7] and he preve hym doughty of his hondis[8] he shal have his desyre."

¶So within a whyle the nyght passed and the day shone.

¶Than Sir Launcelot armed hym and toke his horse, and so he was taughte to the abbey. And as sone as he come thydir, the daughter of Kyng Bagdemagus herde a grete horse trotte on the pavymente; and she than arose and yode to a wyndowe, and there she sawe Sir Launcelot. And anone she made men faste to take his horse frome hym, and lette lede hym into a stable, and hymself unto a chambir, and unarmed hym.

¶And this lady sente hym a longe gowne, and com hirself and made hym good chere—and she seyde he was the knyght in the worlde that was moste welcom unto hir.

¶Than in all haste she sente for hir fadir Bagdemagus that was within twelve myle of that abbey, and afore evyn he come with a fayre felyshyp of knyghtes with hym. And whan the kynge was alyght of his horse, he yode streyte unto Sir Launcelotte his chambir, and there he founde his doughtir. And than the Kynge toke hym in his armys, and eythir made other good chere.

fol.100r

5

10

15

20

25

[6]   30

35

fol.100v

40

---

2. I.e., recently.
3. I.e., believe.
4. I.e., left off striking.
5. *So me thought ever be youre speche*: so I thought from the beginning, by the sound of your voice.
6. I.e., before.
7. I.e., all in my power.
8. *doughty of his hondis*: i.e., valiant in battle.

¶Than Sir **Launcelot** made his complaynte unto the kynge how he was betrayed, and how he was brother unto Sir **Lyonell**, whyche was departed frome hym, he wyste not where, and how his dough-ter had delyverde hym oute of preson.

¶"Therefore, whyle that I lyve, I shall do hir servyse, and all hir kynrede."

¶"Than am I sure of your helpe," seyde the kyng, "on Tewysday next commyng?"

¶"Yee, sir," seyde Sir **Launcelot**, "I shall nat fayle you, for so have I promysed my lady youre doughter.

¶"But, sir, what knyghtes be tho of my lorde Kyng **Arthurs** that were with the Kyng of **North Galys**?"

¶"Sir, hit was Sir **Madore de la Porte** and Sir **Mordred** and Sir Gahalantyne that all forfared my knyghtes, for agaynste hem three I nother none of myne myght bere no strengthe." "Sir," seyde Sir **Launcelot**, "as I here sey, that the turnement shall be here within this three myle of this abbay:

¶"But, sir, ye shal sende unto me three knyghtes of youres suche as ye truste—and loke that the three knyghtes have all-whyght sheldis and no picture on their shyldis, and ye shall sende me another[9] of the same sewte—and we foure wyll oute of a lytyll wood in myddys of bothe partyes com, and we shall falle on the frunte of oure enemys and greve hem that we may.[1] And thus shall I not be knowyn what maner a knyght I am."

¶So they toke their reste that nyght. And this was on the Sonday, and so the kynge departed and sente unto Sir **Launcelot** three knygh-tes with foure whyght shyldys. And on the Tewysday they lodged hem in a lytyll leved wood besyde there as the turnemente sholde be.

¶And there were scaffoldys and [holes], that[2] lordys and ladyes myght beholde and gyff the pryse.

¶Than com into the fylde the Kynge of **North Galys** with nyne score helmys;[3] and than the three knyghtis of Kyng **Arthurs** stood by themself.

¶Than com into the felde Kynge **Bagdemagus** with foure score helmys; and than they feautred their sperys and come togydyrs with a grete daysshe. And there was slayne of knyghtes at the fyrste recountir twelve knyghtes of Kynge **Bagdemagus** parté, and syx of the Kynge of **North Galys** syde and party; and Kynge **Bagdemagus** his party were ferre sette asyde and abak.

Wyth that com in Sir **Launcelot**, and he threste in with his spere in the thyckyst of the pres; and there he smote downe with one spere fyve knyghtes—and of foure of them he brake their backys. And in that thrange he smote downe the Kynge of **North Galys**, and brake his thygh in that falle.

¶All this doynge of Sir **Launcelot** saw the three knyghtes of

---

9. I.e., another shield.
1. *That we may*: in whatever way we can.
2. *Scaffoldys*: i.e., platforms, risers. *Holes*: i.e., windows. *That*: i.e., such that.
3. *Nyne score helmys*: i.e., one hundred and eighty armed men.

Arthurs. "Yondir is a shrewde geste," [sayd Syre Madore de la Port,] "therefore have here ons at hym!"[4]

¶So they encountred, and Sir Launcelot bare hym downe, horse and man, that his sholdir wente oute of joynte.

¶"Now hit befallyth me," seyde Sir Mordred, "to stirre me, for Sir Mador hath a sore falle."

¶And than Sir Launcelot was ware of hym, and gate a spere in his honde and mette with hym. And Sir Mordred brake his spere uppon hym;

¶And Sir Launcelot gaff hym suche a buffette that the arson of the sadil brake, and so he drove over the horse tayle that his helme smote into the erthe a foote and more, that nyghe his nek was broke—and there he lay longe in a swowe.

¶Than com in Sir Gahalantyne with a grete spere, and Sir Launcelot agaynste hym in all[5] that they myght dryve, that bothe hir sperys to-braste evyn[6] to their hondys; and than they flange oute with her swerdes and gaff many sore strokys.

fol.101v

¶Than was Sir Launcelot wroth oute of mesure, and than he smote Sir Gahalantyne on the helme, that his nose, erys and mowthe braste oute on bloode—and therewith his hede hynge low, and with that his horse ran away with hym, and he felle downe to the erthe.

¶Anone therewithall Sir Launcelot gate a speare in his honde, and or[7] ever that speare brake he bare downe to the erthe syxtene knyghtes—som horse and man, and som the man and nat the horse—and there was none that he hitte surely but that he bare none armys that day.

¶And than he gate a spere and smote downe twelve knyghtes— and the moste party of hem never throoff aftir. And than the knyghtes of the Kyng of North Galys party wolde jouste no more, and there the gré was gevyn to Kyng Bagdemagus. So eythir party departed unto his owne, and Sir Launcelot rode forth with Kynge Bagdemagus unto his castel. And there he had passynge good chere bothe with the kyng and with his doughter—and they profyrde hym grete yefftes.

¶And on the morne he toke his leve and tolde the kynge that he wolde seke his brothir Sir Lyonell that wente frome hym whan he slepte.

¶So he toke his horse and betaughte hem all to God; and there he seyde unto the Kynges doughter, "Yf that ye have nede ony tyme of my servyse, I pray you let me have knowlecche, and I shall nat fayle you, as I am trewe knyght."

¶And so Sir Launcelot departed, and by adventure he com into the same foreste there[8] he was takynge his slepe before; and in the myddys of an hygheway he mette a damesel rydynge on a whyght palfray, and there eythir salewed other.

---

4. *Have here ons at hym:* have at (i.e., attack) him at once.
5. *In all:* with all speed.
6. I.e., right.
7. I.e., before.
8. I.e., where.

¶"Fayre damesel," seyde Sir Launcelot, "know ye in this contrey ony adventures nere[9] hande?"

¶"Sir knyght," seyde the damesel, "here ar adventures nyghe, and thou durste preve hem."

¶"Why sholde I not preve?" seyde Sir Launcelot. "For for that cause com I hydir."

¶"Welle," seyde she, "thou semyst well to be a good knyght, and yf thou dare mete with a good knyght, I shall brynge the where is the beste knyght and the myghtyeste that ever thou founde—

¶"So[1] thou wolte telle me thy name and what knyght thou art." "Damesell, as for to telle you my name, I take no grete force.[2] Truly, my name is Sir Launcelotte du Lake." "Sir, thou besemys well. Here is adventures fast by that fallyth[3] for the:

¶"For hereby dwellyth a knyght that woll nat be overmacched for no man I know, but[4] ye do overmacche hym, and his name is Sir Tarquyn. And, as I undirstonde, he hath in his preson, of Arthurs courte, good knyghtes three score and foure that he hath wonne with his owne hondys—

¶"But whan ye have done that journey,[5] ye shall promyse me, as ye ar a trew knyght, for to go and helpe me and other damesels that ar dystressed dayly with[6] a false knyght."

¶"All youre entente, damesell, and desyre I woll fulfylle—so ye woll brynge me unto this knyght."

¶"Now, fayre knyght, com on youre way." And so she brought hym unto the fourde and the tre where hynge the basyn.

¶So Sir Launcelot lette his horse drynke, and sytthen he bete on the basyn with the butte of his spere tylle the bottum felle oute— and longe dud he so, but he sye no man.

¶Than he rode endlonge the gatys of that maner nyghe halfe an howre.

¶And than was he ware of a grete knyght that droffe an horse afore hym, and overthwarte the horse lay an armed knyght bounden. And ever as they com nere and nere, Sir Launcelot thought he sholde know hym.

¶Than was he ware that hit was Sir Gaherys, Gawaynes brothir, a knyght of the Table Rounde.

¶"Now, fayre damesell," seyde Sir Launcelot, "I se yondir a knyght faste i-bounden that is a felow of myne, and brother he is unto Sir Gawayne. And at the fyrste begynnynge, I promyse you, by the leve of God, for to rescowe that knyght. But yf his[7] maystir sytte the bettir in his sadyl, I shall delyver all the presoners that he hath oute of daungere, for I am sure he hath two bretherne of myne presoners with hym." But by that tyme that eythir had sene other, they gryped theyre sperys unto them.

9. I.e., near at.
1. I.e., if.
2. I.e., trouble.
3. I.e., are suitable.
4. I.e., unless.
5. I.e., day's work.
6. I.e., by.
7. *But yf:* unless. *His:* i.e., Gaherys's.

❡"Now, fayre knyght," seyde Sir **Launcelot**, "put that wounded knyghte of[8] that horse and lette hym reste a whyle, and lette us too[9] preve oure strengthis. For, as hit is enfourmed[1] me, thou doyste and haste done me grete despyte, and shame unto knyghtes of the Rounde Table—and therefore now defende the." "And thou be of the Rounde Table," seyde Terquyn, "I defye the and all thy felyshyp!" "That is overmuche[2] seyde," Sir **Launcelot** seyde, "of[3] the at thys tyme."

And than they put there sperys in their restys, and come toge- [8] dyrs with hir horsis as faste as they myght ren; and aythir smote other in myddys of their shyldis, that both their horsys backys braste undir them, and the knyghtes were bothe astoned. And as sone as they myght, they avoyded their horsys and toke their shyldys before them and drew oute their swerdys and com togydir egirly; and eyther gaff other many stronge strokys, for there myght nothir shyldis nother harneyse holde their strokes.

❡And so within a whyle they had bothe many grymme woundys, and bledde passyng grevously.

❡Thus they fared two owres and more, trasyng and rasyng eyther othir where they myght hitte ony bare place.

❡Than at the laste they were brethles bothe, and stode lenyng on her swerdys.

❡"Now, felow," seyde Sir **Terquyne**, "holde[4] thy honde a whyle, and telle me that I shall aske of the." "Sey on," seyde Sir **Launcelot**. Than Sir **Terquyn** seyde, "Thou art the byggyst man that ever I mette withall, and the beste-brethed,[5] and as lyke one knyght that I hate abovyn all other knyghtes; so be hit that thou be not he, I woll lyghtly acorde with the:

❡"And for thy love I woll delyver all the presoners that I have— that is three score and foure—so thou wolde telle me thy name. And thou and I woll be felowys togedyrs—and never to fayle the whyle that I lyve." "Ye sey well," seyde Sir **Launcelot**, "but sytthyn hit is so that I may have thy frendeshyppe—

❡"What knyght is that that thou hatyste abovyn all thynge?" "Feythfully," seyde Sir **Terquyn**, "his name is Sir **Launcelot de Lake**, for he slowe my brothir Sir **Carados** at the Dolerous Towre, that was one of the beste knyghtes on lyve—and therefore hym I excepte of alle knyghtes, for may I hym onys mete, the tone shall make an ende, I make myne avow:

❡"And for Sir **Launcelottis** sake I have slayne an hondred good knyghtes, and as many I have maymed all uttirly, that they myght never aftir helpe themself—and many have dyed in preson. And yette have I three score and foure, and all shall be delyverde, so thou wolte telle me thy name—so be hit that thou be nat Sir **Launcelot**."

8. I.e., off.
9. I.e., two.
1. I.e., told to.
2. I.e., too hastily.
3. I.e., by.
4. I.e., withhold.
5. I.e., least easily exhausted.

❡"Now se I well," seyde Sir Launcelot, "that suche a man I myght be, I myght have pease; and suche a man I myghte be that there sholde be mortall warre betwyxte us:

❡"And now, sir knyght, at thy requeste I woll that thou wete and know that I am Sir Launcelot du Lake, Kynge Bannys son of Benwyke, and verry knyght of the Table Rounde. And now I defyghe the— and do thy beste!"

❡"A!" seyde Sir Tarquyne, "thou arte to me moste welcom of ony knyght, for we shal never departe tylle the tone of us be dede."

❡Than they hurteled togedyrs as two wylde bullys, russhynge and laysshyng with hir shyldis and swerdys, that somtyme they felle bothe on their nosys. Thus they foughte stylle two owres and more and never wolde have reste, and Sir Tarquyne gaff Sir Launcelot many woundys, that all the grounde there as they faughte was all besparcled with bloode.

❡Than at the laste Sir Terquyne wexed faynte and gaff somwhatt abakke,[6] and bare his shylde low for werynesse.

❡That aspyed Sir Launcelot, and lepte uppon hym fersly and gate hym by the bavoure of hys helmette and plucked hym downe on his kneis; and anone he raced of his helme and smote his necke in sundir.

❡And whan Sir Launcelot had done this he yode unto the damesell, and seyde, "Damesell, I am redy to go with you where ye woll have me, but I have no horse."

❡"Fayre sir," seyde [she, "take this wounded knyghtes] hors, and [sende hym] into this maner and [commaunde hym to] delyver all thes presoners."

❡So he toke Sir Gaheris horse and prayde hym nat to be greved.

❡"Nay, fayre lorde, I woll that ye have hym[7] at your commaundemente, for ye have bothe saved me and my horse. And this day I sey ye ar the beste knyght in the worlde, for ye have slayne this day in my syght the myghtyeste man and the beste knyght excepte you that ever I sawe—

❡"But, fayre sir," seyde Sir Gaherys, "I pray you telle me your name." "Sir, my name is Sir Launcelot du Lake, that ought to helpe you of ryght for Kynge Arthurs sake—and in especiall for my lorde Sir Gawayne his sake, youre owne brother. And whan that ye com within yondir maner, I am sure ye shall fynde there many knyghtes of the Rounde Table; for I have sene many of their shyldys that I know hongys on yondir tre. There is Sir Kayes shylde, and Sir Galphuddys shylde, and Sir Bryan de Lystenoyse his shylde, and Sir Alyduhis shylde, with many mo that I am nat now avysed of, and Sir Marhaus, and also my too brethirne shyldis, Sir Ector de Marys and Sir Lyonell. Wherefore I pray you grete them all frome me, and sey that I bydde them to take suche stuff there as they fynde, that in ony wyse my too brethirne go unto the courte and abyde me there

fol.103v   15

[9]

The deth of Terquyn
by Sir Launcelot

6. Gave way somewhat.
7. I.e., the horse.

tylle that I com. For by the feste of 𝔓𝔢𝔫𝔱𝔢𝔠𝔬𝔰𝔱𝔢[8] I caste me to be there—for as at thys tyme I muste ryde with this damesel for to save my promyse." And so they departed frome 𝔊𝔞𝔥𝔢𝔯𝔶𝔰; and 𝔊𝔞𝔥𝔢𝔯𝔶𝔰 yode into the maner, and there he founde a yoman porter kepyng many keyes.   5

¶Than Sir 𝔊𝔞𝔥𝔢𝔯𝔶𝔰 threw the porter unto the grounde and toke the keyes frome hym, and hastely he opynde the preson dore, and there he lette all the presoners oute, and every man lowsed other[9] of their bondys.

¶And whan they sawe Sir 𝔊𝔞𝔥𝔢𝔯𝔶𝔰, all they thanked hym, for they   10
wente that he had slayne Sir 𝔗𝔢𝔯𝔮𝔲𝔶𝔫𝔢 because that he was wounded.

¶"Not so, syrs," seyde Sir 𝔊𝔞𝔥𝔢𝔯𝔶𝔰, "hit was Sir 𝔏𝔞𝔲𝔫𝔠𝔢𝔩𝔬𝔱 that slew hym worshypfully with his owne hondys. And he gretys you all well and prayeth you to haste you to the courte—and as unto you, Sir   15
𝔏𝔶𝔬𝔫𝔢𝔩𝔩 and Sir 𝔈𝔠𝔱𝔬𝔯 𝔡𝔢 𝔐𝔞𝔯𝔶𝔰, he prayeth you to abyde hym at the courte of Kynge 𝔄𝔯𝔱𝔥𝔲𝔯𝔢." "That shall we nat do," seyde his bretherne. "We woll fynde hym and[1] we may lyve." "So shall I," seyde Sir 𝔎𝔞𝔶, "fynde hym or I com to the courte, as I am trew knyght."

¶Than they sought the house there as the armour was, and than   20
they armed them; and every knyght founde hys owne horse and all that longed unto hym. So forthwith there com a foster with foure horsys lade[2] with fatte venyson.

¶And anone Sir 𝔎𝔞𝔶 seyde, "Here is good mete for us for one meale, for we had not many a day no good repaste." And so that   25
venyson was rosted, sodde, and bakyn. And so aftir souper som abode there all nyght; but Sir 𝔏𝔶𝔬𝔫𝔢𝔩𝔩 and Sir 𝔈𝔠𝔱𝔬𝔯 𝔡𝔢 𝔐𝔞𝔯𝔶𝔰 and Sir Kay rode aftir Sir 𝔏𝔞𝔲𝔫𝔠𝔢𝔩𝔬𝔱 to fynde hym yf they myght.

¶Now turne we to Sir 𝔏𝔞𝔲𝔫𝔠𝔢𝔩𝔬𝔱 that rode with the damesel in a   [10]
fayre hygheway. "Sir," seyde the damesell, "here by this way haun-   30
tys a knyght that dystressis all ladyes and jantylwomen, and at the leste he robbyth them other lyeth by hem."

¶"What?" seyde Sir 𝔏𝔞𝔲𝔫𝔠𝔢𝔩𝔬𝔱, "is he a theff and a knyght and a ravyssher of women? He doth shame unto the order of knyghthode, and contrary unto his oth.[3] Hit is pyté that he lyvyth: 35

¶"But, fayre damesel, ye shall ryde on before, youreself, and I   fol.104v
woll kepe myself in coverte; and yf that he trowble yow other dystresse you, I shall be your rescowe and lerne hym to be ruled[4] as a knyght." So thys mayde rode on by the way a souffte amblynge pace—   40

¶And within a whyle com oute a knyght on horsebak owte of

---

8. On Pentecost, see n. 1, p. 10.
9. I.e., each other.
1. I.e., if.
2. I.e., laden.
3. *Is he a theff . . . and contrary unto his oth:* Launcelot here could well speak in the voice of Malory's own accusers, if the charges outlined in the chronolgy (p. xxv) do in fact apply to the author of *Le Morte Darthur.* Launcelot's expression of outrage and a number of other details in the rest of this episode, including Launcelot's rejection of both marriage and adultery (line 33, p. 163), are not matched in Malory's known sources (see p. 723 for the corresponding passages in the French Prose *Lancelot*).
4. *Lerne:* i.e., teach. *Be ruled:* i.e., behave.

the woode, and his page with hym; and there he put the damesell frome hir horse—and than she cryed.

¶With that com Sir Launcelot as faste as he myght tyll he com to the knyght, sayng, "A, false knyght and traytoure unto knyghthode, who dud lerne the to distresse ladyes, damesels and jantyll-women?"

¶Whan the knyght sy Sir Launcelot thus rebukynge hym, he answerde nat but drew his swerde and rode unto Sir Launcelot. And Sir Launcelot threw his spere frome hym and drew his swerde, and strake hym suche a buffette on the helmette that he claffe his hede and necke unto the throte.

Here Sir Launcelot slew Perys de Forest Savvage 10

¶"Now haste thou thy paymente that longe thou haste deserved!" "That is trouth," seyde the damesell—

¶"For lyke as Terquyn wacched to dystresse good knyghtes, so dud this knyght attende to destroy and dystresse ladyes, damesels, and jantyllwomen—and his name was Sir Perys de Foreste Savage." "Now, damesell," seyde Sir Launcelot "woll ye ony more servyse of me?"

15

¶"Nay, sir," she seyde, "at thys tyme, but allmyghty Jesu preserve you wheresomever ye ryde or goo, for the curteyst knyght thou arte—and mekyste unto all ladyes and jantylwomen—that now lyvyth:

20

¶"But one thyng, sir knyght, methynkes ye lak—

¶"Ye that ar a knyght wyveles, that ye woll nat love som mayden other jantylwoman. For I cowde never here sey that ever ye loved ony of no maner of degré, and that is grete pyté:

25

¶"But hit is noysed that ye love Quene Gwenyvere,[5] and that she hath ordeyned by enchauntemente that ye shall never love none other but hir, nother none other damesell ne lady shall rejoyce[6] you—wherefore there be many in this londe, of hyghe astate and lowe, that make grete sorow."

fol.105r 30

¶"Fayre damesell," seyde Sir Launcelot, "I may nat warne[7] peple to speke of me what[8] hit pleasyth hem. But for to be a weddyd man, I thynke hit nat, for than I muste couche with hir and leve armys and turnamentis, batellys and adventures. And as for to sey to take my pleasaunce with paramours, that woll I refuse—in pren-cipall[9] for drede of God, for knyghtes that bene adventures sholde nat be advoutrers nothir lecherous, for than they be nat happy[1] nother fortunate unto the werrys;[2] for other they shall be over-com with a sympler[3] knyght than they be hemself, other ellys they shall sle by unhappe and hir cursednesse bittir men than they be hemself:

35

40

5. On this charge, see n. 3, p. 152.
6. I.e., enjoy, possess.
7. I.e., forbid.
8. I.e., whatever.
9. *In prencipall:* principally.
1. I.e., lucky.
2. *Unto the werrys:* in battle.
3. I.e., of lower rank.

❡"And so who that usyth paramours shall be unhappy, and all thynge unhappy that is aboute them."[4]

❡And so Sir Launcelot and she departed. And than he rode in a depe foreste two dayes and more, and hadde strayte lodgynge. So on the thirde day he rode on a longe brydge, and there sterte uppon hym suddeynly a passyng foule carle. And he smote his horse on the nose, that he turned aboute, and asked hym why he rode over that brydge withoute lycence. "Why sholde I nat ryde this way?" seyde Sir Launcelotte, "I may not ryde besyde." "Thou shalt not chose!"[5] seyde the carle, and laysshed at hym with a grete club shodde with iron.

Than Sir Launcelot drew his swerde and put the stroke abacke,[6] and clave his hede unto the pappys. And at the ende of the brydge was a fayre vyllage, and all peple, men and women, cryed on Sir Launcelot, and sayde, "Sir knyght, a worse dede duddyst thou never for thyself, for thou haste slayne the chyeff porter of oure castelle."

❡Sir Launcelot lete hem sey what they wolde, and streyte he rode into the castelle. And whan he come into the castell he alyght and tyed his horse to a rynge on the walle; and there he sawe a fayre grene courte,[7] and thydir he dressid hym, for there hym thought was a fayre place to feyght in. So he loked aboute hym and sye muche peple in dorys and in wyndowys, that sayde, "Fayre knyghte, thou arte unhappy to com here!"

None withall there com uppon hym two grete Gyauntis, well armed all save there hedys, with two horryble clubbys in their hondys.

❡Sir Launcelot put his shylde before hym and put[8] the stroke away of that one gyaunte, and with hys swerde he clave his hede in sundir.

❡Whan his felowe sawe that, he ran away as he were woode[9]— and Sir Launcelot aftir hym with all his myght, and smote hym on the shuldir, and clave hym to the navyll.

❡Than Sir Launcelot wente into the halle, and there com afore hym three score of ladyes and damesels, and all kneled unto hym and thanked God and hym of his delyveraunce. "For," they seyde, "the moste party of us have bene here this seven yere presoners, and we have worched all maner of sylke workys for oure mete, and we ar all grete jentylwomen borne. And blyssed be the tyme, knyght, that ever thou were borne, for thou haste done the moste worshyp that ever ded knyght in this worlde—that woll we beare recorde. And we all pray you to telle us your name, that we may telle oure frendis who delyverde us oute of preson." "Fayre damesellys," he seyde, "my name is Sir Launcelot du Laake."

fol.105v

[11]

Here Sir Launcelot slew two gyauntes in the castel of Tyntagil

---

4. *But for to be a weddyd man. . . . that is aboute them.* This extraordinary passage is not matched in Malory's known sources; see n. 3, p. 163.
5. I.e., choose for yourself.
6. *Put the stroke abacke:* returned the stroke.
7. I.e., courtyard.
8. I.e., deflected.
9. I.e., mad, insane.

"A, sir," seyde they all, "well mayste thou be he, for ellys save yourself—as we demed—there myght never knyght have the bettir of thes jyauntis; for many fayre knyghtes have assayed, and here have ended. And many tymes have we here wysshed aftir you— and thes two gyauntes dredde never knyght but you." 5

¶"Now may ye sey," seyde Sir Launcelot, "unto your frendys, and grete them all fro me; and yf that I com in ony of your marchys, shew me such chere as ye have cause. And what tresoure that there is in this castel, I yeff hit you for a rewarde for your grevaunces: fol.106r

¶"And the lorde that is ownere of this castel, I wolde he ressayved hit as is his ryght." 10

¶"Fayre sir," they seyde, "the name of this castell is called Tyntagyll, and a deuke ought hit somtyme that had wedded fayre Igrayne. And so aftir that she was wedded to Uther Pendragon, and he gate on hir Arthure." "Well," seyde Sir Launcelot, "I undirstonde to whom this castel longith." 15

And so he departed frome them and betaught hem unto God; and than he mounted uppon his horse and rode into many stronge contreyes and thorow many watyrs and valeyes—and evyll was he lodged. And at the laste by fortune hym happynd ayenste[1] nyght 20 to com to a fayre courtelage, and therein he founde an olde jantylwoman that lodged hym with goode wyll; and there he had good chere for hym and his horse.

¶And whan tyme was, his oste brought hym into a garret over the gate, to his bedde. 25

¶There Sir Launcelot unarmed hym and set his harneyse by hym and wente to bedde, and anone he felle on slepe.

¶So aftir, there com one on horsebak, and knokked at the gate in grete haste. Whan Sir Launcelot herde this, he arose up and loked oute at the wyndowe, and sygh by the moonelyght three knyghtes 30 com rydyng aftir that one man, and all three laysshynge on hym at onys with swerdys; and that one knyght turned on hem knyghtly agayne and defended hym. "Truly," seyde Sir Launcelot, "yondir one knyght shall I helpe, for hit were shame for me to se three knyghtes on one—and yf he be there slayne, I am partener of[2] his deth." 35 And therewith he toke his harneys and wente oute at a wyndowe by a shete downe to the foure knyghtes.

¶And than Sir Launcelot seyde on hyght, "Turne you, knyghtis, unto me, and leve this feyghtyng with that knyght!" And than they three leffte Sir Kay and turned unto Sir Launcelot, and assayled hym fol.106v 40 on every honde.

¶Than Sir Kay dressid hym to have holpen Sir Launcelot. "Nay, sir," sayde he, "I woll none of your helpe; therefore as ye woll have my helpe, lette me alone with hem." Sir Kay, for the plesure of that knyght, suffyrd hym for to do his wylle, and so stoode on syde. 45

¶Than anone, within seven strokys, Sir Launcelot had strykyn hem to the erthe; and than they all three cryed, "Sir knyght, we

---

1. I.e., near to.
2. *Partener of:* complicit in.

yelde us unto you as a man of myght makeles." "As to that, I woll
nat take youre yeldyng unto me, but so that ye woll yelde you unto
thys knyght; and on that covenaunte I woll save youre lyvys, and
ellys nat."

¶"Fayre knyght, that were us loth,[3] for as for that knyght, we   5
chaced hym hydir, and had[4] overcom hym, had nat ye been.
Therefore to yelde us unto hym it were no reson."

¶"Well, as to that, avyse you[5] well, for ye may chose whether ye
woll dye other lyve; for and ye be yolden, hit shall be unto Sir 𝕶𝖆𝖞."

¶"Now, fayre knyght," they seyde, "in savyng of oure lyvys, we   10
woll do as thou commaundys us."

¶"Than shall ye," seyde Sir 𝕷𝖆𝖚𝖓𝖈𝖊𝖑𝖔𝖙, "on Whytsonday[6] nexte
commynge go unto the courte of Kynge 𝕬𝖗𝖙𝖍𝖚𝖗𝖊, and there shall ye
yelde you unto Quene 𝕲𝖜𝖊𝖓𝖞𝖛𝖊𝖗𝖊 and putte you all three in hir grace
and mercy—and say that Sir 𝕶𝖆𝖞 sente you thydir to be her pre-   15
soners." "Sir," they seyde, "hit shall be done, by the feyth of oure
bodyes, and we be men lyvyng." And there they sware every knyght
uppon his swerde, and so Sir 𝕷𝖆𝖚𝖓𝖈𝖊𝖑𝖔𝖙 suffyrd hem to departe. And
than Sir 𝕷𝖆𝖚𝖓𝖈𝖊𝖑𝖔𝖙 cnocked at the gate with the pomell of his
swerde; and with that come his oste, and in they entyrd, he and   20
Sir 𝕶𝖆𝖞. "Sir," seyde his oste, "I wente ye had bene in your bed."

¶"So I was, but I arose and lepe oute at my wyndow for to helpe
an olde felowe of myne."

¶So whan they come nye the lyght, Sir 𝕶𝖆𝖞 knew well hit was
Sir 𝕷𝖆𝖚𝖓𝖈𝖊𝖑𝖔𝖙—and therewith he kneled downe and thanked hym of   25
all his kyndenesse, that he had holpyn hym twyse frome the deth.
"Sir," he seyde, "I have nothyng done but that me ought for to do—
and ye ar welcom; and here shall ye repose you and take your
reste."

¶Whan Sir 𝕶𝖆𝖞 was unarmed, he asked aftir mete. Anone there   30
was mete fette for hym, and he ete strongly. And whan he had
sowped, they wente to their beddys and were lodged togydyrs in
one bed.[7]

¶So on the morne Sir 𝕷𝖆𝖚𝖓𝖈𝖊𝖑𝖔𝖙 arose erly and leffte Sir 𝕶𝖆𝖞
slepyng. And Sir 𝕷𝖆𝖚𝖓𝖈𝖊𝖑𝖔𝖙 toke Sir 𝕶𝖆𝖞𝖊𝖘 armoure and his shylde   35
and armed hym; and so he wente to the stable and sadylde his
horse, and toke his leve of his oste and departed. Than sone aftir
arose Sir 𝕶𝖆𝖞 and myssid Sir 𝕷𝖆𝖚𝖓𝖈𝖊𝖑𝖔𝖙; and than he aspyed that he
had his armoure and his horse:

¶"Now, be my fayth, I know welle that he woll greve som of the   40
courte of Kyng 𝕬𝖗𝖙𝖍𝖚𝖗𝖊, for on[8] hym knyghtes woll be bolde and
deme that hit is I—and that woll begyle them. And bycause of his
armoure and shylde I am sure I shall ryde in pease." And than sone
Sir 𝕶𝖆𝖞 departed and thanked his oste.

Here Sir Launcelot
bete three knyghtes
and rescowed Sir
Kay

fol.107r

---

3. *Were us loth:* would be loathsome to us.
4. I.e., would have.
5. *Avyse you:* think, consider.
6. On Whitsunday, see n. 1, p. 10.
7. The (nonsexual) sharing of beds was common in medieval hostelries.
8. I.e., toward.

Ow turne we unto Sir Launcelot that had ryddyn longe in a [12]
grete foreste, and at the laste he com unto a low contrey full
of fayre ryvers and fayre meedys; and before hym he sawe a longe
brydge, and three pavylyons stood thereon, of sylke and sendell of
dyverse hew. And withoute[9] the pavylyons hynge three whyght 5
shyldys on trouncheouns of sperys, and grete longe sperys stood
upryght by the pavylyons—and at every pavylyon dore stoode three
freysh knyghtes. And so Sir Launcelot passed by hem and spake no
worde.

¶But whan he was paste, the three knyghtes knew hym and 10
seyde hit was the proude Sir Kay: "He wenyth[1] no knyght so good
as he—and the contrary is oftyn proved!"

¶"Be my fayth," seyde one of the knyghtes—his name was Sir
Gawtere—"I woll ryde aftir hym and assay hym for all his pryde;
and ye may beholde how that I spede." 15

¶So Sir Gawtere armed hym and hynge his shylde uppon his fol.107v
sholdir, and mounted uppon a grete horse, and gate his speare in
his honde, and wallopte aftir Sir Launcelot. And whan he come
nyghe hym he cryed, "Abyde, thou proude knyght, Sir Kay! For
thou shalt nat passe all quyte." So Sir Launcelot turned hym, and 20
eythir feautyrd their sperys and com togedyrs with all their myghtes. And Sir Gawters speare brake, but Sir Launcelot smote hym
downe, horse and man.

And whan he was at the erthe, his brethyrn seyde, "Yondir
knyght is nat Sir Kay, for he is far bygger than he. "I dare ley my 25
hede," seyde Sir Gylmere, "yondir knyght hath slayne Sir Kay and
hath takyn hys horse and harneyse." "Whether hit be so other no,"
seyde Sir Raynolde, "lette us mounte on oure horsys and rescow
oure brothir, Sir Gawtere. For payne of deth, we all shall have worke
inow to macche that knyght—for ever mesemyth by his persone 30
hit is Sir Launcelot, other Sir Trystrams, other Sir Pelleas, the good
knyght."

¶Than anone they toke their horsys and overtoke Sir Launcelot.
And Sir Gylmere put forth his speare and ran to Sir Launcelot; and
Sir Launcelot smote hym downe that he lay in a sowghe. 35

¶"Sir knyght," seyde Sir Raynolde, "thou arte a stronge man, and
as I suppose[2] thou haste slayne my two bretherne, for the whyche
rysyth my herte sore agaynste the. And yf I myght, wyth my worshyppe,[3] I wolde not have ado with the, but nedys I muste take
suche parte as they do—and therefore, knyght, kepe thyselfe!" 40

¶And so they hurtylde togydyrs with all their myghtes and all
to-shevird bothe there spearys, and than they drew hir swerdys and
laysshed togydir egirly.

¶Anone therewithall arose Sir Gawtere and come unto his
brother Sir Gyllymere, and bade hym aryse—"and helpe we oure 45
brothir, Sir Raynolde, that yondir mervelously macchyth yondir

<hr />

9. I.e., outside.
1. I.e., believes there to be.
2. I.e., believe.
3. *Wyth my worshyppe:* i.e, and retain my honor.

good knyght." Therewithall they hurteled unto Sir **Launcelot**; and whan he sawe them com, he smote a sore stroke unto Sir **Raynolde**, that he felle of his horse to the grounde—and than he caste to the othir two bretherne, and at two strokys he strake hem downe to the erthe.

⟨Wyth that Sir **Raynolde** gan up sterte with his hede all blody, and com streyte unto Sir **Launcelot**. "Now let be," seyde Sir **Launcelot**, "I was not far frome the whan thou were made knyght, Sir **Raynolde**, and also I know thou arte a good knyght, and lothe I were to sle the." "Gramercy," seyde Sir **Raynolde**, "of your goodnesse, and I dare say as for me and my bretherne, we woll nat be loth to yelde us unto you, with[4] that we know youre name—for welle we know ye ar not Sir **Kay**!"

"As for that, be as be may,[5] for ye shal yelde you unto Dame **Gwenyvere**; and loke that ye be there on Whytsonday and yelde you unto hir as presoners—and sey that Sir **Kay** sente you unto hir."

⟨Than they swore hit sholde be done—and so passed forth Sir **Launcelot**—and ecchone of the bretherne halpe other as well as they myght. So Sir **Launcelotte** rode into a depe foreste, and thereby in a slade he sey foure knyghtes hovynge undir an oke, and they were of **Arthurs** courte: one was Sir **Sagramour le Desyrus**, and Sir **Ector de Marys**, and Sir **Gawayne**, and Sir **Uwayne**. And anone as these foure knyghtes had aspyed Sir **Launcelot**, they wende by his armys that hit had bene Sir **Kay**.

⟨"Now, be my fayth," seyde Sir **Sagramoure**, "I woll preve Sir **Kayes** myght," and gate his spere in his honde and com towarde Sir Launcelot. Than Sir **Launcelot** was ware of his commyng and knew hym well, and feautred his speare agaynste hym and smote Sir **Sagramoure** so sore that horse and man wente bothe to the erthe.

⟨"Lo, my felowys," seyde Sir **Ector**, "yondir may ye se what a buffette he hath gyffen; methynkyth that knyght is muche bygger than ever was Sir **Kay**. Now shall ye se what I may do to hym."

⟨So Sir **Ector** gate his spere in his honde and walopte towarde Sir **Launcelot**; and Sir **Launcelot** smote hym evyn thorow the shylde and his sholdir, that man and horse wente to the erthe—and ever his spere helde.

⟨"Be my fayth," sayde Sir **Uwayne**, "yondir is a stronge knyght, and I am sure he hath slayne **Kay**. And I se be his grete strengthe hit woll be harde to macche hym." And therewithall Sir **Uwayne** gate his speare and rode towarde Sir **Launcelot**; and Sir **Launcelot** knew hym well, and lette his horse renne on the playne, and gaff hym suche a buffette that he was astooned, and longe he wyste nat where he was.

⟨"Now se I welle," seyde Sir **Gawayne**, "I muste encountir with that knyght," and dressed his shylde and gate a good speare in his honde, and lete renne at Sir **Launcelot** with all his myght; and eyther knyght smote other in myddys of the shylde. But Sir **Gawaynes** spere

fol.108r

5

Here Sir Launcelot overcom thre bretherne uppon a brydge   10

15

[13]

20

25

30

fol.108v

35

40

45

---

4. I.e., provided.
5. Be that as it may.

braste, and Sir Launcelot charged so sore uppon hym that his horse reversed up-so-downe—and muche sorow had Sir Gawayne to avoyde his horse. And so Sir Launcelot passed on a pace, and smyled and seyde, "God gyff hym joy that this spere made, for there cam never a bettir in my honde!"

¶Than the foure knyghtes wente echone to other and comforted eche other, and seyde, "What sey ye by this geste," seyde Sir Gawayne, "that with one spere hath felde us all foure?" "We commaunde[6] hym to the devyll," they seyde all, "for he is a man of grete myght." "Ye may say hit well," seyde Sir Gawayne, "that he is a man of myght, for I dare ley my hede hit is Sir Launcelot—I know hym well by his rydyng."[7] "Latte hym go," seyde Sir Uwayne, "for whan we com to the courte, we shall wete."

¶Than had they much sorow to gete their horsis agayne.

¶Now leve we there, and speke we of Sir Launcelot, that rode a grete whyle in a depe foreste. And as he rode he sawe a blak brachette sekyng in maner as[8] hit had bene in the feaute of an hurte dere. And therewith he rode aftir the brachette, and he saw lye on the grounde a large feaute of bloode.

¶And than Sir Launcelot rode faster—and ever the brachette loked behynde hir—and so she wente thorow a grete marys, and ever Sir Launcelot folowed. And than was he ware of an olde maner—and thydir ran the brachette, and so over a brydge.

¶So Sir Launcelot rode over that brydge, that was olde and feble; and whan he com in the myddys of a grete halle, there he seye lye dede a knyght that was a semely man, and that brachette lycked his woundis. And therewithall com oute a lady wepyng and wryngyng hir hondys, and sayde, "Knyght, to[9] muche sorow hast thou brought me."

¶"Why sey ye so?" seyde Sir Launcelot, "I dede never this knyght no harme, for hydir by the feaute of blood this brachet brought me—and therefore, fayre lady, be nat dyspleased with me, for I am full sore agreved for your grevaunce."

¶"Truly, sir," she seyde, "I trowe hit be nat ye that hath slayne my husbonde, for he that dud that dede is sore wounded and is never lykly to be hole—that shall I ensure hym."

¶"What was youre husbondes name?" seyde Sir Launcelot. "Sir, his name was called Sir Gylberd the Bastarde,[1] one of the beste knyghtys of the worlde—and he that hath slayne hym, I know nat his name."

¶"Now God sende you bettir comforte," seyde Sir Launcelot. And so he departed and wente into the foreste agayne, and there he mette with a damesell the whyche knew hym well. And she seyde on lowde, "Well be ye founde, my lorde! And now I requyre you of your knyghthode helpe[2] my brother that is sore wounded and never

Here Sir Launcelot with one spere smote downe Sir Sagramour, Sir Ector, Sir Uwayne, and Sir Gawayne

5

10

[14] 15

fol.109r

20

25

30

35

40

45

6. I.e., recommend.
7. I.e., horsemanship.
8. I.e., as if.
9. I.e., too.
1. I.e., son of unwed, but noble, parents.
2. I.e., to help.

styntyth bledyng; for this day he fought with Sir **Gylberte** the Bastarde and slew hym in playne batayle, and there was my brother
sore wounded. And there is a lady—a sorseres—that dwellyth in a
castel here bysyde, and this day she tolde me my brothers woundys
sholde never be hole tyll I coude fynde a knyght wolde[3] go into the
Chapel Perelus, and there he sholde fynde a swerde and a blody
cloth that the woundid knyght was lapped in; and a pece of that
cloth and that swerde sholde hele my brother, with[4] that his woundis were serched with the swerde and the cloth."

    ¶"This is a mervelouse thyng," seyde Sir **Launcelot**, "but what is
your brothirs name?" "Sir, she seyde, "Sir **Melyot de Logyrs**." "That
me repentys," seyde Sir **Launcelotte**, "for he is a felow of the Table
Rounde, and to his helpe I woll do my power."

    ¶Than she sayde, "Sir, folow ye evyn this hygheway, and hit woll
brynge you to the Chapel Perelus; and here I shall abyde tyll God
sende you agayne—and yf you spede[5] nat, I know no knyght
lyvynge that may encheve that adventure."

R yght so Sir **Launcelot** departed, and whan he com to the Chapell
  Perelus he alyght downe and tyed his horse unto a lytyll gate.
And as sone as he was within the chyrcheyerde, he sawe on the
frunte of the chapel many fayre ryche shyldis turned up-so-
downe[6]—and many of tho shyldis Sir **Launcelot** had sene knyghtes
bere byforehande. With that he sawe by hym there stonde a thirty
grete knyghtes—more[7] by a yerde than any man that ever he had
sene—and all they grenned and gnasted at Sir **Launcelot**. And whan
he sawe their countenaunce he dredde hym sore, and so put his
shylde before hym and toke his swerde in his honde redy unto
batayle; and they all were armed all in blak harneyse redy, with her
shyldis and her swerdis redy drawyn.

    ¶And as Sir **Launcelot** wolde have gone thorow them, they skaterd
on every syde of hym and gaff hym the way,[8] and therewith he
wexed bolde and entyrde into the chapel. And there he sawe no
lyght but a dymme lampe brennyng, and than was he ware of a
corpus hylled with a clothe of sylke.

    ¶Than Sir **Launcelot** stouped doune and kutte a pese away of that
cloth:

    ¶And than hit fared undir hym as the grounde had quaked a
lytyll; therewithall he feared. And than he sawe a fayre swerde lye
by the dede knyght, and that he gate in his honde and hyed hym
oute of the chapell.

    ¶Anone as ever[9] he was in the chapell-yerde all the knyghtes
spake to hym with grymly voyces, and seyde, "Knyght, Sir **Launcelot**,
lay that swerde frome the, or thou shalt dye." "Whether that I lyve

fol.109v   5

   10

   15

[15]

   20

   25

   30

   35

fol.110r

   40

3. I.e., who would.
4. I.e., provided.
5. I.e., succeed.
6. The hanging of the shields upside-down is a sign of disrespect.
7. A *thirty*: a group of thirty. *More*: i.e., taller.
8. I.e., gave way to him.
9. *As ever*: i.e., as soon as.

other dye," seyde Sir Launcelot, "with no wordys grete gete ye hit agayne—therefore fyght for hit and ye lyst."[1]

¶Than ryght so he passed thorowoute them. And byyonde the chapell-yarde there mette hym a fayre damesell, and seyde, "Sir Launcelot, leve that swerde behynde the, other thou wolt dye for hit." "I leve hit not," seyde Sir Launcelot, "for no thretyng." 5

¶"No," seyde she, "and thou dyddyste leve that swerde, Quene Gwenyvere sholde thou never se." "Than were I a foole and I wolde leve this swerde."

¶"Now, jantyll knyghte," seyde the damesel, "I requyre the to kysse me but onys." "Nay," seyde Sir Launcelot, "that God me for-bede."[2] Well, Sir," seyde she, "and thou haddyst kyssed me, thy lyff dayes had be done—and now, alas," she seyde, "I have loste all my laboure, for I ordeyned this chapell for thy sake and for Sir Gawayne. And onys I had hym within[3] me, and at that tyme he fought with this knyght that lyeth dede in yondir chapell, Sir Gylberte the Bastarde, and at that tyme he smote the lyffte honde of Sir Gylberte. And, Sir Launcelot, now I telle the, I have loved the this seven yere; but there may no woman have thy love but Quene Gwenyver[4]—and sytthen I myght nat rejoyse[5] the nother thy body on lyve, I had kepte no more joy in this worlde but to have thy body dede: 10 15 20

¶"Than wolde I have bawmed hit and sered hit, and so to have kepte hit my lyve dayes—and dayly I sholde have clypped the and kyssed the, dispyte of Quene Gwenyvere." "Ye sey well," seyde Sir Launcelot. "Jesu preserve me frome your subtyle crauftys." And therewithall he toke his horse and so departed frome hir. And as the booke seyth— 25

¶Whan Sir Launcelot was departed, she toke suche sorow that she deyde within a fourtenyte; and hir name was called Hallewes the Sorseres, Lady of the castell Nygurmous. And anone Sir Laun-celot mette with the damesel, Sir Melyottis systir; and whan she sawe hym she clapped hir hondys and wepte for joy. And than they rode into a castell thereby where lay Sir Melyot, and anone as Sir Laun-celot sye hym he knew hym, but he was passyng paale as the erthe for bledynge. fol.110v 30 35

¶Whan Sir Melyot saw Sir Launcelot, he kneled uppon his kneis and cryed on hyghte, "A, lorde, Sir Launcelot, helpe me anone!"

¶Than Sir Launcelot lepe unto hym and towched his woundys with Sir Gylbardys swerde, and than he wyped his woundys with a parte of the bloody cloth that Sir Gylbarde was wrapped in; and anone an holer man in his lyff was he never. And than there was grete joy betwene hem, and they made Sir Launcelot all the chere that they myghte.

Here Sir Launcelot heled Sir Melyot de Logrys with Sir Gylberde the Basterdis swerde

¶And so on the morne Sir Launcelot toke his leve and bade Sir

---

1. *and ye lyst:* if you would like.
2. *That God me forbede:* i.e., God forbid.
3. I.e., with.
4. On this charge, see n. 3, p. 152.
5. I.e., enjoy.

Melyot hyghe hym "to the courte of my lorde Arthure, for hit drawyth nyghe to the feste of Pentecoste—and there, by the grace of God, ye shall fynde me." And therewith they departed.

¶And so Sir Launcelot rode thorow many stronge[6] contrayes, over mores and valeis, tyll by fortune he com to a fayre castell; and as he paste beyonde the castell, hym thought he herde [two][7] bellys rynge, and than he was ware of a faucon com over his hede fleyng towarde an hyghe elme, and longe lunes aboute her feete. And she flowe unto the elme to take hir perche, the lunes overcast aboute a bowghe.

¶And whan she wolde have tane hir flyght, she hynge by the leggis faste; and Sir Launcelot syghe how he[8] hynge, and behelde the fayre faucon Perygot,[9] and he was sory for hir.

¶The meanewhyle cam a lady oute of a castell and cryed on hyghe, "A, Launcelot, Launcelot! as thow arte floure of all knyghtes, helpe me to gete me my hauke, for and my hauke be loste my lorde wolde destroy me—for I kepte the hauke, and she slypped fro me; and yf my lorde my husbande wete hit, he is so hasty that he wyll sle me."

¶"What is your lordis name?" seyde Sir Launcelot. "Sir," she seyde, "his name is Sir Phelot, a knyght that longyth unto the Kynge of North Galys."

¶"Welle, fayre lady, syn that ye know my name and requyre me of knyghthode to helpe, I woll do what I may to gete youre hauke— and yet God knowyth I am an evyll clymber, and the tre is passynge hyghe, and fewe bowys to helpe me withall!"

¶And therewith Sir Launcelot alyght and tyed his horse to the same tre, and prayde the lady to onarme hym.

¶And so whan he was unarmed he put of[1] all his clothis unto his shurte and his breche, and with myght and grete force he clambe up to the faucon, and tyed the lunes to a grete rotyn boysh, and threwe the hauke downe with the buysh; and anone the lady gate the hauke in hir honde.

¶And therewithall com oute Sir Phelot oute of the grevys sud- deynly, that was hir husbonde, all armed and with his naked swerde in his honde, and sayde, "A knyght, Sir Launcelot, now I have founde the as I wolde"—he stondyng at the boole of the tre to sle hym.

¶"A, lady!" seyde Sir Launcelot, "why have ye betrayed me?"

¶"She hath done," seyde Sir Phelot, "but as I commaunded hir, and therefore there is none othir boote but thyne oure is com that thou muste dye."

¶"That were shame unto the," seyde Sir Launcelot, "thou an

[16]

5

10

15

fol.11r

20

25

30

35

40

6. I.e., strange.
7. Caxton's reading is inserted here according to the recommendation of P.J.C. Field, who notes that a study of medieval hunting by John Cummins "shows that in the Middle Ages hawk bells were normally made in pairs, and according to one authority, the pairs were made to ring a semi-tone apart" (*Malory: Texts and Sources*, p. 112).
8. she.
9. I.e., from the region of Périgord in France.
1. I.e., off.

armed knyght to sle a nakyd man by treson." "Thou gettyste none other grace," seyde Sir Phelot, "and therefore helpe thyself and thou can."

¶"Truly," seyde Sir Launcelot, "that shall be thy shame. But syn thou wolt do none other, take myne harneys with the and hange my swerde there uppon a bowghe that I may gete hit—and than do thy beste to sle me and thou can."

¶"Nay," seyde Sir Phelot, "for I know the[2] bettir than thou wenyste! Therefore thou gettyst no wepyn and I may kepe the therefro."

¶"Alas," seyde Sir Launcelot, "that ever a knyght sholde dey wepynles!" And therewith he wayted above hym and undir hym, and over hym above his hede he sawe a rowgh spyke, a bygge bowghe leveles; and therewith he brake hit of by the body and than he com lowar, and awayted[3] how his owne horse stoode, and suddenyly he lepe on the farther syde of his horse froward the knyght.

¶And than Sir Phelot layshed at hym egerly to have slayne hym, but Sir Launcelot put away the stroke with the rowgh spyke, and therewith toke hym on the hede, that downe he felle in a sowghe to the grounde.

¶So than Sir Launcelot toke his swerde oute of his honde and strake his necke in two pecys.

¶"Alas!" than cryed that lady, "why haste thou slayne my husbonde?" "I am nat causer," seyde Sir Launcelot, "but with falshede ye wolde have had me slayne with treson—and now hit is fallyn on you bothe." And than she sowned as though she wolde dey. And therewith Sir Launcelot gate all his armoure as well as he myght and put hit uppon hym for drede of more resseite[4]—for he dredde hym that the knyghtes castell was so nyghe hym—and as sone as he myght he toke his horse and departed, and thanked God that he had escaped that harde adventure.

So Sir Launcelot rode many wylde wayes, thorowoute morys and mares; and as he rode in a valay, he sey a knyght chasyng a lady with a naked swerde to have slayne hir. And by fortune, as this knyght sholde have slayne thys lady, she cryed on Sir Launcelot and prayde hym to rescowe her.

¶Whan Sir Launcelot sye that myschyff, he toke his horse and rode betwene hem, sayynge, "Knyght, fye for shame! Why wolte thou sle this lady? Shame unto the and all knyghtes!"

¶"What haste thou to do betwyxte me and my wyff? I woll sle her magré thyne hede."[5]

¶"That shall ye nat," sayde Sir Launcelot, "for rather we woll have ado[6] togydyrs."

¶"Sir Launcelot," seyde the knyght, "thou doste nat thy parte, for thys lady hath betrayed me."

¶"Hit is not so," seyde the lady, "truly, he seyth wronge on me.

2. Thee.
3. I.e., watched.
4. *More resseite:* receiving further attacks.
5. *Magré thyne hede:* against your will, despite you.
6. *Have ado:* fight.

And for bycause I love and cherysshe my cousyn jarmayne,[7] he is jolowse betwyxte me and hym; and as I mutte answere to God, there was never sene betwyxte us none suche thynges—

fol.112r

¶"But, sir," seyde the lady, "as thou arte called the worshypfullyest knyght of the worlde, I requyre the of trewe knyghthode, kepe me and save me—for whatsomever he sey he woll sle me, for he is withoute mercy."

¶"Have ye no doute, hit shalle nat lye in his power."

¶"Sir," seyde the knyght, "in your syght I woll be ruled as ye woll have me." And so Sir Launcelot rode on the one syde and she on the other syde. And he had nat redyn but a whyle but the knyght bade Sir Launcelot turne hym and loke behynde hym, and seyde, "Sir, yondir com men of armys aftir us rydynge."

¶And so Sir Launcelot turned hym and thought[8] no treson; and therewith was the knyght and the lady on one syde—and suddeynly he swapped[9] of the ladyes hede.

¶And whan Sir Launcelot had aspyed hym what he had done, he seyde and so called hym: "Traytoure! Thou haste shamed me for evir!" And suddeynly Sir Launcelot alyght of his horse and pulde oute his swerde to sle hym; and therewithall he felle to the erthe and gryped Sir Launcelot by the thyghes and cryed mercy.

¶"Fye on the," seyde Sir Launcelot, "thou shamefull knyght! Thou mayste have no mercy—therefore aryse and fyghte with me."

¶"Nay," sayde the knyght, "I woll never aryse tylle ye graunte me mercy."

¶"Now woll I proffyr the fayre:[1] I woll unarme me unto[2] my shyrte, [and I wylle have nothyng upon me but my sherte] and my swerde in my honde; and yf thou can sle me, quyte be thou for ever." "Nay, sir, that woll I never."

¶"Well," seyde Sir Launcelot, "take this lady and the hede, and bere it uppon the; and here shalt thou swere uppon my swerde to bere hit allwayes uppon thy bak and never to reste tyll thou com to my lady, Quene Gwenyver." "Sir, that woll I do, by the feyth of my body."

Here Sir Launcelot made Sir Pedyvere bere the dede body of the lady to Quene Gwenyvere

¶"Now what is youre name?" "Sir, my name is Sir Pedyvere." "In a shamefull oure were thou borne," seyde Sir Launcelot. So Sir Pedyvere departed with the lady dede and the hede togydir, and founde the Quene with Kynge Arthure at Wynchestir; and there he tolde all the trouthe.

fol.112v

¶"Sir knyght," seyde the Quene, "this is an horryble dede and a shamefull, and a grete rebuke unto Sir Launcelot—but natwythstondyng[3] his worshyp is knowyn in many dyverse contreis:

¶"But this shall I gyff you in penaunce—make ye as good skyffte as ye can: ye shall bere this lady with you on horsebak unto the Pope of Rome, and of hym resseyve youre penaunce for your foule dedis.

---

7. *Cousin jarmayne:* first cousin.
8. I.e., suspected.
9. I.e., struck.
1. *Proffyr the fayre:* make you a fair offer.
2. I.e., down to.
3. Despite that.

And ye shall nevir reste one nyght there as ye do another;[4] and ye go to ony bedde, the dede body shall lye with you."

¶This oth he there made and so departed. And as hit tellyth in the Frenshe booke, whan he com unto Rome—

¶The Pope there bade hym go agayne unto Quene Gwenyver—and in Rome was his lady buryed, by the Popys commaundement. And after, thys knyght Sir Pedyvere fell to grete goodnesse and was an holy man and an hermyte.

¶Now turne we unto Sir Launcelot du Lake that com home two [18] dayes before the feste of Pentecoste—and the Kynge and all the courte were passyng fayne.

¶And whan Gawayne, Sir Uwayne, Sir Sagramoure, and Sir Ector de Mares sye Sir Launcelot in Kayes armour, than they wyste well that hit was he that smote hem downe all wyth one spere.

¶Than there was lawghyng and smylyng amonge them. And ever now and now com all the knyghtes home that were presoners with Sir Terquyn, and they all honoured Sir Launcelot.

¶Whan Sir Gaherys herde hem speke, he sayde, "I sawe all the batayle from the begynnynge to the endynge"—and there he tolde Kynge Arthure all how hit was and how Sir Terquyn was the strongest fol.113r knyght that ever he saw excepte Sir Launcelot—and there were many knyghtes bare hym recorde,[5] three score.

¶Than Sir Kay tolde the Kynge how Sir Launcelot rescowed hym whan he sholde have bene slayne, and how "he made the three knyghtes yelde hem to me and nat to hym" (and there they were, all three, and bare recorde). "And by Jesu," seyde Sir Kay, "Sir Launcelot toke my harneyse and leffte me his, and I rode in Goddys pece and no man wolde have ado with me."

¶Anone therewith com three knyghtes that fought with Sir Launcelot at the longe brydge; and there they yelded them unto Sir Kay, and Sir Kay forsoke them and seyde he fought never with hem. "But I shall ease your hertes," seyde Sir Kay, "yondir is Sir Launcelot that overcam you."

¶Whan they wyste that, they were glad.

¶And than Sir Melyot de Logrys com home and tolde the Kynge how Sir Launcelot had saved hym frome the deth—and all his dedys was knowyn:[6] how the quenys sorserers foure had hym in preson, and how he was delyverde by the Kynge Bagdemagus doughter. Also there was tolde all the grete armys that Sir Launcelot dud betwyxte the two kynges—that ys for to say the Kynge of North Galys and Kyng Bagdemagus; all the trouth Sir Gahalantyne dud telle, and Sir Mador de la Porte, and Sir Mordred, for they were at the same turnement.

¶Than com in the lady that knew Sir Launcelot whan that he wounded Sir Belleus at the pavylyon; and there at the requeste of Sir Launcelot, Sir Belleus was made knyght of the Rounde Table.

¶And so at that tyme Sir Launcelot had the grettyste name of ony

---

4. *Nevir reste . . . as ye do another:* i.e., never rest in the same place twice.
5. *Bare hym recorde:* who bore witness to his deeds.
6. I.e., made known.

knyght of the worlde, and moste he was honoured of hyghe and lowe.[7]

Explicit a noble tale of Sir Launcelot du Lake. Here
folowyth Sir Gareth is tale of Orkeney
that was callyd Bewmaynes by Sir Kay.

5

The Tale of Sir Gareth of Orkeney†

In Arthurs dayes, whan he helde the Rounde Table moste plenoure,[1] hit fortuned the Kynge commaunded that the hyghe feste of Pentecoste[2] sholde be holden at a cité and a castell, in tho dayes that was called Kynkekenadoune, uppon the sondys that marched[3] nyghe Walys.

[VII.1]   fol.113v

20

¶So evir the Kynge had a custom that at the feste of Pentecoste in especiall, afore other festys in the yere, he wolde nat go that day to mete unto[4] that he had herde other sawe of a grete mervayle.

¶And for[5] that custom, all maner of strange adventures com byfore Arthure, as at that feste before all other festes.

25

¶And so Sir Gawayne, a lytyll tofore the none of the day of Pentecoste, aspyed at a wyndowe three men uppon horsebak and a dwarfe uppon foote; and so the three men alyght, and the dwarff kepte their horsis, and one of the men was hyghar than the tothir tweyne by a foote and an half.

30

¶Than Sir Gawayne wente unto the Kyng, and sayde, "Sir, go to your mete, for here at hande commyth strange adventures."

¶So the Kynge wente unto his mete with many other kynges; and there were all the knyghtes of the Rounde Table, onles that ony were presoners other slayne at recountyrs:

35

---

7. *Of hyghe and lowe:* i.e., by all ranks of people.
† The title is taken editorially from the colophon to this section (see p. 227). In the Winchester MS the impression is of a relatively major division, as the section begins at the top of the page; however, the colophon of the previous section has had to be squeezed into the bottom of the previous page, apparently with no intention of leaving blank space on the next page, and the initial "I", though long and red, with a fine black border, and followed by a capital "N" filled in yellow, is not floriated and not accompanied by an extensive font change across the first line, such as that found in other beginnings (see, e.g., pp. 62, 78, and 113 above; a more comparable division might be that marked in the previous section, p. 151). No major direct source is known for this often highly amusing section, and it has been argued that the tale is Malory's own invention, as opposed to a translation; be that as it may, the text has close analogues—most notably the story of *La Cote Male Taillé*, which Malory translates in his *Book of Sir Trystram* (see p. 702); for an account of other possible sources and analogues, see p. 702.
1. *Moste plenoure:* with the fullest number of knights.
2. On Pentecost, see n. 1, p. 10.
3. I.e., bordered.
4. I.e., until.
5. I.e., because of.

¶Than at the hyghe feste evermore they sholde be fulfylled the hole numbir of an hondred and fyffty—for than was the Rounde Table fully complysshed.

¶Ryght so com into the halle two men well besayne and rychely, and uppon their sholdyrs there lened the goodlyest yonge man and the fayreste that ever they all sawe; and he was large and longe and brode in the shuldyrs, well-vysaged—and the largyste and the fayreste[6] handis that ever man sye.

¶But he fared as he myght nat go[7] nothir bere hymself but yf he lened uppon their shuldyrs.

¶Anone as the Kynge saw hym there was made peas and rome, and ryght so they yode with hym unto the hyghe deyse withoute seyynge of ony wordys.

¶Than this yonge muche man pullyd hym abak and easyly streyghte upryght, seynge, "The moste noble kynge, Kynge Arthure, God you blysse and all your fayre felyshyp, and in especiall the felyshyp of the Table Rounde:

¶"And for this cause I come hydir, to pray you and requyre you to gyff me three gyftys—and they shall nat be unresenablé asked, but that ye may worshypfully graunte hem me, and to you no grete hurte nother losse:

¶"And the fyrste done and gyffte I woll aske now, and the tothir two gyfftes I woll aske this day twelvemonthe,[8] wheresomever ye holde your hyghe feste."

¶"Now aske ye," seyde Kyng Arthure, "and ye shall have your askynge."

¶"Now, sir, this is my petycion at this feste, that ye woll geff me mete and drynke suffyciauntly for this twelvemonthe, and at that day I woll aske myne other two gyfftys."

¶"My fayre son," seyde Kyng Arthure, "aske bettyr, I counseyle the,[9] for this is but a symple askyng; for myne herte gyvyth me to the gretly, that thou arte com[1] of men of worshyp—and gretly my conceyte fayleth me but thou shalt preve a man of ryght grete worshyp."

¶"Sir," he seyde, "thereof be as be may,[2] for I have asked that I woll aske at this tyme."

¶"Well, seyde the Kynge, "ye shall have mete and drynke inowe—I nevir forbade hit my frynde nother my foo—

¶"But what is thy name, I wolde wete?"

¶"Sir, I can nat tell you."

¶"That is mervayle," seyde the Kynge, "that thou knowyste nat thy name, and thou arte one of the goodlyest yonge men that ever I saw."

¶Than the Kyng betoke hym to Sir Kay the Styewarde, and charged hym that he had of all maner of metys and drynkes of the

---

6. I.e., most uncalloused (a sign of nobility).
7. I.e., walk.
8. *this day twelvemonthe:* a year from today.
9. thee.
1. I.e., descended.
2. I.e., be that as it may.

fol.114r

beste, and also that he had all maner of fyndynge as though he were a lordys sonne.

¶"That shall lytyll nede," seyde Sir Kay, "to do suche coste[3] uppon hym, for I undirtake he is a vylayne borne, and never woll make man—for and he had be com of jantyllmen, he wolde have axed[4] horse and armour; but as he is, so he askyth— 5

¶"And sythen he hath no name, I shall gyff hym a name whyche shall be called Bewmaynes—that is to say 'Fayre Handys'—

¶"And into the kychyn I shall brynge hym, and there he shall have fatte browes every day, that he shall be as fatte at the twel- fol.114v 10 vemonthe ende as a porke hog!" Ryght so the two men departed and lefte hym with Sir Kay, that scorned and mocked hym.

¶Thereat was Sir Gawayne wroth. And in especiall Sir Launcelot [2] bade Sir Kay leve his mockyng—"for I dare ley my hede he shall preve a man of grete worshyp." "Lette be," seyde Sir Kay, "hit may 15 not be by reson, for as he is, so he hath asked."

¶"Yett beware," seyde Sir Launcelot, "so ye gaff the good knyght Brunor, Sir Dynadans brothir, a name, and ye called hym La Cote Male Taylé[5]—and that turned you to anger aftirwarde."

¶"As for that," seyde Sir Kay, "this shall never preve none suche, 20 for Sir Brunor desyred ever worshyp, and this[6] desyryth ever mete and drynke and brotthe. Uppon payne of my lyff, he was fosterde up[7] in som abbey—and, howsomever hit was, they fayled mete and drynke, and so hydir he is com for his sustynaunce."

¶And so Sir Kay bade gete hym a place and sytte downe to mete. 25 So Bewmaynes wente to the halle dore and sette hym downe amonge boyes and laddys, and there he ete sadly.[8]

¶And than Sir Launcelot aftir mete bade hym com to his chambir, and there he sholde have mete and drynke inowe, and so ded Sir Gawayne; but he refused them all, for he wolde do none other but 30 as Sir Kay commaunded hym, for no profyr.[9] But as towchyng Sir Gawayne, he had reson to proffer hym lodgyng, mete, and drynke, for that proffer com of his bloode, for he was nere kyn to hym than he wyste off; but that Sir Launcelot ded was of his grete jantylnesse and curtesy. 35

¶So thus he was putt into the kychyn and lay nyghtly as[1] the kychen boyes dede. And so he endured all that twelvemonthe and never dyspleased man nother chylde, but allwayes he was meke and mylde. But ever whan he saw ony justyng of knyghtes, that wolde he se and he myght.[2] And ever Sir Launcelot wolde gyff hym 40 golde to spende, and clothis, and so ded Sir Gawayne. And where there were ony mastryes doynge, thereat wolde he be; and there fol.115r myght none caste barre nother stone to[3] hym by two yardys.

---

3. *To do suche coste*: i.e., to expend so much. 45
4. I.e., asked for.
5. I.e., the one in the badly tailored tunic. For the events Launcelot alludes to, see p. 280 ff.
6. I.e., this one.
7. *Fosterde up*: i.e., raised as an orphan.
8. I.e., fully.
9. *For no profyr*: for no kind of offer.
1. I.e., where.
2. *And he myght*: if he could.
3. I.e., as far as.

¶Than wolde Sir **Kap** sey, "How lykyth you my boy of the
kychyn?" So this paste on tyll the feste of **Whytsontyde,**[4] and at that
tyme the Kynge hylde hit at **Carlyon,** in the moste royallyst wyse
that myght be, lyke as he dud yerely. But the Kyng wolde no mete
ete uppon **Whytsonday** untyll he harde of som adventures. Than   5
com there a squyre unto the Kynge, and seyde, "Sir, ye may go to
your mete, for here commyth a damesell with som strange adventures."

¶Than was the Kyng glad and sette hym doune. Ryght so there
cam a damesell unto the halle and salewed the Kyng, and prayde   10
hym of succoure. "For whom?" seyde the Kynge "What is the
adventure?"

¶"Sir" she seyde, "I have a lady of grete worshyp to[5] my sustir,
and she is beseged with a tirraunte, that she may nat[6] oute of hir
castell. And bycause here ar called the noblyst knyghtes of the   15
worlde, I com to you for succoure."

"What is youre lady called, and where dwellyth she? And who is
he and what is his name that hath beseged her?" "Sir Kynge," she
seyde, "as for my ladyes name, that shall nat ye know for[7] me as
at thys tyme, but I lette you wete she is a lady off grete worshyp   20
and of grete londys; and as for that tyrraunte that besegyth her and
destroyeth hir londys, he is kallyd the Rede Knyght of the Rede
Laundys." "I know hym nat," seyde the Kyng. "Sir," seyde Sir
Gawayne, "I know hym well, for he is one of the perelest knyghtes
of the worlde. Men sey that he hath seven mennys strengthe—and   25
from hym I ascapyd onys full harde[8] with my lyff."

¶"Fayre damesell," seyde the Kynge, "there bene knyghtes here
that wolde do hir power[9] for to rescowe your lady, but bycause ye
woll not telle hir name nother where she dwellyth, therfore none
of my knyghtes that here be nowe shall go with you be my wylle."   30
"Than muste I seke forther," seyde the damesell.

¶So with thes wordys com **Beawmaynes** before the Kyng whyle   [3]   fol.115v
the damesell was there, and thus he sayde: "Sir Kyng, God thanke
you, I have bene this twelvemonthe in your kychyn and have had
my full sustynaunce; and now I woll aske my other two gyfftys that   35
bene behynde."[1]

¶"Aske on now, uppon my perell,"[2] seyde the Kynge.

¶"Sir, this shall be my fyrst gyffte of the two gyfftis: that ye woll
graunte me to have this adventure of this damesell, for hit belon-
gyth unto me."   40

¶"Thou shalt have it," seyde the Kyng, "I graunte hit the."

¶"Than, Sir, this is that other gyffte that ye shall graunte me:
that Sir **Launcelot du Lake** shall make me knyght, for of hym I woll

---

4. About the date, see n. 1, p. 10.
5. I.e., as.
6. I.e., not come.
7. I.e., from.
8. *Full harde:* i.e., with the greatest difficulty.
9. I.e., do everything in their power.
1. I.e., still to come.
2. I.e., salvation.

be made knyght, and ellys of none. And whan I am paste,[3] I pray you lette hym ryde aftir me and make me knyght whan I requyre hym."

¶"All thys shall be done," seyde the Kynge.

¶"Fy on the!" seyde the damesell, "Shall I have none but one that is your kychyn knave?" Than she wexed angry, and anone she toke hir horse.

¶And with that there com one to Bewmaynes and tolde hym his horse and armour was com for hym—and a dwarff had brought hym all thyng that neded hym[4] in the rycheste wyse. Thereat the courte had muche mervayle from whens com all that gere. So whan he was armed there was none but fewe so goodly a man as he was; and ryght so he cam into the halle and toke his leve of Kyng Arthure and Sir Gawayne and of Sir Launcelot, and prayde hym to hyghe aftyr hym. And so he departed and rode afftyr the damesell.

But there wente many aftir to beholde how well he was horsed and trapped[5] in cloth of golde, but he had neyther speare nother shylde. Than Sir Kay seyde all opynly in the hall, "I woll ryde aftir my boy of the kychyn to wete whether he woll know me for his bettir."

¶"Yet," seyde Sir Launcelot and Sir Gawayne, "abyde at home."

¶So Sir Kay made hym redy and toke his horse and his speare, and rode aftir hym.

¶And ryght as Beawmaynes overtoke the damesell, ryght so com Sir Kay, and seyde, "Beawmaynes! What, sir, know ye nat me?"

¶Than he turned his horse and knew hit was Sir Kay that had done all the dyspyte to hym, as ye have herde before.

¶Than seyde Beawmaynes, "Yee, I know you well for an unjantyll knyght of the courte, and therefore beware of me."

¶Therewith Sir Kay put his spere in the reest and ran streyght uppon hym.

¶And Beawmaynes com as faste uppon hym with his swerde and with a foyne threste hym thorow the syde, that Sir Kay felle downe as he had bene dede.

¶Than Beawmaynes alyght downe and toke Sir Kayes shylde and his speare and sterte uppon his owne horse and rode his way.

¶All that saw Sir Launcelot, and so dud the damesell. And than he bade his dwarff sterte uppon Sir Kayes horse, and so he ded; by that Sir Launcelot was com.

¶And anone he profyrde Sir Launcelot to juste; and ayther made hem redy and com togydir so fersly that eyther bare other downe to the erthe, and sore were they brused.

¶Than Sir Launcelot arose and halpe hym frome his horse, and than Beawmaynes threw his shylde frome hym and profyrd to fyght wyth Sir Launcelot on foote. So they russhed togydyrs lyke two borys, trasyng and traversyng and foynyng the mountenaunce of an houre.

Marginal notes:
5
[4]
15
fol.116r
20
25
Here Beawmaynes had allmoste slayne Sir Kay
30
35
40
45

3. I.e., passed.
4. *That neded hym:* that he would need.
5. I.e., dressed.

¶And Sir Launcelot felte hym so bygge that he mervayled of his strengthe, for he fought more lyker a gyaunte than a knyght—and his fyghtyng was so passyng durable and passyng perelous.

¶For Sir Launcelot had so much ado with hym that he dred hymself to be shamed—

¶And seyde, "Beawmaynes, feyght nat so sore! Your quarell and myne is nat so grete but we may sone leve of." "Truly that is trouth," seyde Beawmaynes, "but hit doth me good to fele your myght. And yet, my lorde, I shewed nat the utteraunce."[6]

¶"In Goddys name," seyde Sir Launcelot, "for I promyse you be the fayth of my body, I had as muche to do as I myght have to save myself fro you unshamed—and therefore have ye no dought of none erthely knyght." "Hope ye so that I may ony whyle[7] stonde a proved knyght?"

¶"Do as ye have done to me," seyde Sir Launcelot, "and I shall be your warraunte."

¶"Than I pray you," seyde Beawmaynes, "geff me the order of knyghthod."

¶"Sir, than muste ye tell me your name of ryght, and of what kyn ye be borne."

¶"Sir, so that ye woll nat dyscover me,[8] I shall tell you my name."

¶"Nay, Sir," seyde Sir Launcelotte, "and that I promyse you by the feyth of my body, untyll hit be opynly knowyn."

¶Than he seyde, "My name is Garethe, and brothir unto Sir Gawayne of fadir syde and modir syde."

¶"A, Sir, I am more gladder of you than I was! For evir me thought ye sholde be of grete bloode, and that ye cam nat to the courte nother for mete nother drynke."

¶Than Sir Launcelot gaff hym the order of knyghthode; and than Sir Gareth prayde hym for to departe, and so he to folow the lady.

¶So Sir Launcelot departed frome hym and com to Sir Kay, and made hym to be borne home uppon his shylde—and so he was heled harde with the lyff. And all men scorned Sir Kay, and in especiall Sir Gawayne. And Sir Launcelot seyde that hit was nat his parte to rebuke no yonge man—"for full lytyll knowe ye of what byrth he is com of, and for what cause he com to the courte."

And so we leve of Sir Kay and turne we unto Beawmaynes. Whan that he had overtakyn the damesell, anone she seyde, "What doste thou here? Thou stynkyst all of the kychyn—thy clothis bene bawdy[9] of the grece and talow.

¶"What! Wenyste thou," seyde the lady, "that I woll alow the for yondir knyght that thou kylde? Nay, truly, for thou slewyst hym unhappyly[1] and cowardly. Therefore turne agayne, thou bawdy kychyn knave! I know the[2] well, for Sir Kay named the Beawmaynes.

6. *The utteraunce:* i.e., my utmost.
7. *Hope:* i.e., believe. *Ony whyle:* for any length of time.
8. *Dyscover me:* disclose me to others.
9. I.e., filthy.
1. I.e., by unlucky chance.
2. Thee.

What art thou but a luske and a turner of brochis and a ladyll-waysher?"

❡"Damesell," seyde Sir Beawmaynes, "sey to me what ye woll, yet woll nat I go fro you, whatsomever ye sey, for I have undirtake to Kynge Arthure for to encheve your adventure; and so shall I fynyssh hit to the ende—other ellys I shall dye therefore."

❡"Fye on the, kychyn knave! Wolt thou fynyssh myne adventure? Thou shalt anone be mette³ withall, that thou woldyst nat for all the broth that ever thou souped onys to loke hym in the face." "As for that, I shall assay," seyde Beawmaynes. So ryght thus as they rode in the wood, there com a man fleyng all that ever he myght.

❡"Whother wolt thou?" seyde Beawmaynes. "A, lorde," he seyde, "helpe me, for hereby in a slade is six theffis that have takyn my lorde and bounde hym sore, and I am aferde lest that they woll sle hym."

❡"Brynge me thydir," seyde Beawmaynes. And so they rode togydirs unto they com there as was the knyght bounden—and streyte he rode unto them and strake one to the deth, and than another, and at the thirde stroke he slew the thirde. And than the other three fledde, and he rode aftir them and overtoke them; and than they three turned agayne and assayled Sir Beawmaynes harde—but at the laste he slew them, and returned and unbounde the knyght. And the knyght thanked hym and prayde hym to ryde with hym to his castell there a lytyll besyde, and he sholde worshypfully rewarde hym for his good dedis.

❡"Sir," seyde Beawmaynes, "I woll no rewarde have. Sir, this day I was made knyght of noble Sir Launcelot, and therefore I woll no rewarde have but God rewarde me—and also I muste folowe thys damesell."

❡So whan he com nyghe to hir, she bade hym ryde uttir—"for thou smellyst all of the kychyn. What, wenyst thou that I have joy of the for all this dede? For that thou haste done is but myssehappe; but thou shalt se sone a syght that shall make the to turne agayne—and that lyghtly."

❡Than the same knyght rode aftir the damesell and prayde hir to lodge with hym all that nyght. And because hit was nere nyght, the damesell rode with hym to his castell, and there they had grete chere—and at souper the knyght sette Sir Beawmaynes afore the damesell.

❡"Fy, fy!" than seyde she. "Sir knyght, ye ar uncurtayse to sette a kychyn page afore me; hym semyth bettir to styke a swyne than to sytte afore a damesell of hyghe parage."

❡Than the knyght was ashamed at hir wordys, and toke hym up and sette hym at a syde bourde and sate hymself before hym. So all that nyght they had good chere and myrry reste.

❡And on the morne the damesell toke hir leve and thanked the knyght, and so departed and rode on hir way untyll they come to

5

10

15

20

25

30

fol.117v

35

40

45

[6]

3. I.e., met by an opponent.

a grete foreste; and there was a grete ryver and but one passage, and there were redy two knyghtes on the farther syde to lette the passage.

¶"What seyst thou?" seyde the damesell. "Woll ye macche yon- dir two knyghtis, other ellys turne agayne?" "Nay," seyde Sir Bew- maynes, "I woll nat turne ayen, and they were six mo." And therewithall he russhed unto the watir, and in myddys of the watir eythir brake her sperys upon other to[4] their hondys. And than they drewe their swerdis and smote egirly at othir—and at the laste Sir Beawmaynes smote the othir uppon the helme, that his hede stoned,[5] and therewithall he felle downe in the watir, and there was he drowned. And than he spored his horse upon the londe, and therewithall the tother knyght felle uppon hym and brake his speare; and so they drew hir swerdys and fought longe togydyrs.

¶But at the laste Sir Beawmaynes clevid his helme and his hede downe to the shuldyrs; and so he rode unto the damesell and bade hir ryde furth on hir way. "Alas," she seyde, "that ever suche a kychyn payge sholde have the fortune to destroy such two knygh- tes! Yet thou wenyste thou haste done doughtyly? That is nat so, for the fyrste knyght his horse stumbled, and there he was drowned in the watir, and never hit was be thy force nother be thy myghte; and the laste knyght, by myshappe thou camyste behynde hym, and by myssefortune thou slewyst hym."

¶"Damesell," seyde Beawmaynes, "ye may sey what ye woll, but whomsomever I have ado withall, I trust to God to serve hym or[6] I and he departe—and therefore I recke nat what ye sey, so that I may wynne your lady."

¶"Fy, fy, foule kychyn knave! Thou shalt se knyghtes that shall abate thy boste."

¶"Fayre damesell, gyff me goodly langgage,[7] and than my care is paste—for what knyghtes somever they be, I care nat, ne I doute hem nought."

¶"Also," seyde she, "I sey hit for thyne avayle, for yett mayste thou turne ayen with thy worshyp; for and thou folow [me], thou arte but slayne—for I se all that evir thou doste is by mysseadven- ture, and nat by proues of thy hondys."

¶"Well, damesell, ye may sey what ye woll, but wheresomever ye go, I woll folow you."

¶So this Beawmaynes rode with that lady tyll evynsonge,[8] and ever she chydde hym and wolde nat reste. So at the laste they com to a blak launde, and there was a blak hauthorne, and thereon hynge a baner, and on the other syde there hynge a blak shylde, and by hit stoode a blak speare grete and longe, and a grete blak horse covered wyth sylk, and a blak stone faste by.

¶Also there sate a knyght all armed in blak harneyse, and his

*Here Sir Beawmay-
nes slew two knygh-
tes at a passage
fol.118r*

5

10

20

25

30

35

[7]   40

45

4. I.e., down to.
5. I.e., was stunned.
6. I.e., before.
7. *Gyff me goodly langgage:* i.e., speak more courteously to me.
8. Evening prayer, early evening (cf. n. 8, p. 154).

name was called the Knyght of the Blak Laundis. This damesell, whan she sawe that knyght, she bade hym fle downe that valey, for his hors was nat sadeled.

¶"Gramercy," seyde Beawmaynes, "for allway ye wolde have me a cowarde." So whan the Blak Knyght saw hir, he seyde, "Damesell, have ye brought this knyght frome the courte of Kynge Arthure to be your champyon?"

¶"Nay, fayre knyght, this is but a kychyn knave that was fedde in Kyng Arthurs kychyn for almys."

¶Than sayde the knyght, "Why commyth he in such aray? For hit is shame that he beryth you company." "Sir, I can not be dely- verde of hym, for with me he rydyth magré my hede.[9] God wolde," seyde she, "that ye wolde putte hym from me—other to sle hym and ye may—for he is an unhappy[1] knave, and unhappyly he hath done this day thorow myssehappe; for I saw hym sle two knyghtes at the passage of the watir, and other dedis he ded beforne ryght mervaylouse, and thorow unhappynesse."[2]

¶"That mervayles me," seyde the Blak Knyght, "that ony man of worshyp woll have ado with hym." "Sir, they knewe hym nat," seyde the damesell, "and for bycause he rydyth with me, they wene that he be som man of worshyp borne."

¶"That may be," seyde the Blak Knyght. "Howbehit as ye say that he is no man of worshyp borne, he is a full lykly persone, and full lyke to be a stronge man. But this muche shall I graunte you," seyde the knyght, "I shall put hym downe on foote, and his horse and harneyse he shall leve with me, for hit were shame to me to do hym ony more harme."

¶Whan Sir Beawmaynes harde hym sey thus, he seyde, "Sir knyght, thou arte full large of[3] my horse and harneyse! I lat the wete hit coste the[4] nought, and whether thou lyke well othir evyll, this launde woll I passe magré thyne hede—and horse ne harneyse gettyst thou none of myne but yf thou wynne hem with thy hondys. Therefore lat se what thou canste do." "Seyste thou that?" seyde the Blak Knyght. "Now yelde thy lady fro the, for hit besemed never a kychyn knave to ryde with such a lady."

¶"Thow lyest," seyde Beawmaynes. "I am a jantyllman borne, and of more hyghe lynage than thou—and that woll I preve on thy body."

¶Than in grete wretth they departed[5] their horsis and com togy- dyrs as hit had bene thundir, and the Blak Knyghtes speare brake, and Beawmaynes threste hym thorow bothe sydis—and therewith his speare brake, and the truncheon was left stylle in his syde. But nevirtheles the Blak Knyght drew his swerde and smote many egir strokys of grete myght, and hurte Bewmaynes full sore. But at the

---

9. *Magré my hede*: against my will.
1. I.e., unfortunate, troublesome.
2. I.e., misfortune, mischance.
3. *full large of*: very generous with.
4. thee.
5. I.e., separated.

laste the Blak Knyght, within an owre and an half, he felle downe
of his horse in a sowne and there dyed.

¶And than[6] Sir Bewmaynes sy hym so well horsed and armed,
than he alyght downe and armed hym in his armour, and so toke
his horse and rode aftir the damesell.

¶Whan she sawe hym com, she seyde, "Away, kychyn knave,
oute of the wynde! For the smelle of thy bawdy clothis grevyth
me—

¶"Alas," she seyde, "that ever such a knave sholde by myssehappe sle so good a knyght as thou hast done—but all is thyne
unhappynesse:

¶"But hereby is one that shall pay the all thy paymente—and
therefore yett I rede the flee." "Hit may happyn me," seyde Bewmaynes, "to be betyn other slayne; but I warne you, fayre damesell,
I woll nat fle away nothir leve your company for all that ye can
sey—for ever ye sey that they woll sle me othir bete me, but howsomever hit happenyth, I ascape and they lye on the grounde:

¶"And therefore hit were as good for you to holde you stylle thus
all day rebukyng me, for away[7] wyll I nat tyll I se the uttermuste
of this journay, other ellys I woll be slayne othir thorowly betyn.
Therefore ryde on your way, for folow you I woll, whatsomever
happyn me."

Thus as they rode togydyrs, they sawe a knyght comme dryvande
by them, all in grene, bothe his horse and his harneyse. And
whan he com nye the damesell, he asked hir, "Is that my brothir
the Blak Knyght that ye have brought with you?"

"Nay, nay," she seyde, "this unhappy kychyn knave hath slayne
thy brothir thorow unhappynes."

¶"Alas!" seyde the Grene Knyght, "that is grete pyté that so
noble a knyght as he was sholde so unhappyly be slayne—and
namely of a knavis honde, as ye say that he is—

¶"A, traytoure!" seyde the Grene Knyght, "thou shalt dye for
sleyng of my brothir. He was a full noble knyght, and his name
was Sir Perarde." "I defye the!" seyde Sir Bewmaynes, "for I lette the
wete, I slew hym knyghtly and nat shamfully." Therewythall the
Grene Knyght rode unto an horne that was grene, and hit hynge
uppon a thorne.[8] And there he blew three dedly motis, and anone
there cam two damesels and armed hym lyghtly. And than he toke
a grete horse, and a grene shylde, and a grene spere; and than they
ran togydyrs with all their myghtes, and brake their sperys unto
their hondis. And than they drewe their swerdys and gaff many
sad[9] strokys, and eyther of them wounded other full ylle; and at
the laste at an ovirtwarte stroke Sir Bewmaynes with his horse strake
the Grene Knyghtes horse uppon the syde, that he felle to the
erthe—and than the Grene Knyght voyded his horse delyverly and
dressed hym on foote.

5

[8]

fol.119v

10

15

20

25

30

35

40

45

6. I.e., when.
7. I.e., go away.
8. I.e., hawthorne tree.
9. I.e., heavy.

❡That sawe **Bewmaynes**, and therewithall he alyght; and they russhed togydyrs lyke two myghty kempys a longe whyle—and sore
they bledde bothe.

❡Wyth that come the damesell, and seyde, "My lorde the Grene
Knyght, why for shame stonde ye so longe fyghtynge with that
kychyn knave? Alas, hit is shame that evir ye were made knyght to
se suche a lad to macche you as the wede growyth over the corne."[1]

❡Therewith the Grene Knyght was ashamed—and therewithall
he gaff a grete stroke of myght and clave his shylde thorow.

❡Whan **Beawmaynes** saw his shylde clovyn asundir, he was a lytyll
ashamed of that stroke—and of hir langage.

❡And than he gaff hym suche a buffette upon the helme that
he felle on his kneis, and so suddeynly **Bewmaynes** pulde hym on
the grounde grovelynge; and than the Grene Knyght cryed hym
mercy, and yelded hym unto **Bewmaynes** and prayde hym nat to sle
hym.

❡"All is in vayne," seyde **Bewmaynes**, "for thou shalt dye but yf
this damesell that cam with me pray me to save thy lyff"—and
therewithall he unlaced his helme lyke as he wolde sle hym.

❡"Fye uppon the, false kychyn payge! I woll never pray the to
save his lyff, for I woll nat be so muche in thy daunger."[2]

❡"Than shall he dye," seyde **Beawmaynes**. "Nat so hardy,[3] thou
bawdy knave!" seyde the damesell, "that thou sle hym."

❡"Alas," seyde the Grene Knyght, "suffir me nat to dye for a
fayre worde spekyng:[4]

❡"Fayre knyght," seyde the Grene Knyght, "save my lyfe and I
woll forgyff the[5] the deth of my brothir, and for ever to becom thy
man—

❡"And thirty knyghtes that hold of[6] me for ever shall do you
servyse."

❡"In the devyls name," seyde the damesell, "that suche a bawdy
kychyn knave sholde have thirty knyghtes servyse, and thyne!"

❡"Sir knyght," seyde **Bewmaynes**, "all this avaylyth the nought but
yf my damesell speke to me for thy lyff"—and therewithall he made
a semblaunte to sle hym.

❡"Lat be," seyde the damesell, "thou bawdy kychyn knave! Sle
hym nat, for and thou do thou shalt repente hit."

❡"Damesell," seyde **Bewmaynes**, "your charge is to me a plesure,
and at youre commaundemente his lyff shall be saved, and ellis
nat."

❡Than he sayde, "Sir knyght with the grene armys, I releyse the
quyte at this damesels requeste, for I woll nat make hir wroth, for
I woll fulfylle all that she chargyth me."

❡And than the Grene Knyght kneled downe and dud hym homage with his swerde.

fol.120r

Here Sir Bewmaynes overcome the Grene Knyght

1. I.e., wheat.
2. I.e., power.
3. *Nat so hardy:* Be not so bold.
4. *for a fayre worde spekyng:* i.e., on the condition of a gracious word.
5. thee.
6. *hold of:* owe alliegance to.

¶Than sayde the damesell, "Me repentis of this Grene Knyghtes damage—and of your brothirs deth, the Blak Knyght—for of your helpe I had grete mystir:

¶"For I drede me sore to passe this foreste."

¶"Nay, drede you nat," seyde the Grene Knyght, "for ye all shall lodge with me this nyght, and to-morne I shall helpe you thorow this forest."

¶So they toke their horsys and rode to his maner that was faste by. And ever this damesell rebuked Bewmaynes and wolde nat suffir hym to sitte at hir table, but as the Grene Knyght toke hym and sate with hym at a syde table. "Damesell, mervayle me thynkyth," seyde the Grene Knyght, "why ye rebuke this noble knyghte as ye do, for I warne you he is a full noble man, and I knowe no knyght that is able to macche hym. Therefore ye do grete wronge so to rebuke hym, for he shall do you ryght goode servyse. For whatsomever he makyth hymself, he shall preve at the ende that he is com of full noble blood and of Kynges lynage."

¶"Fy, fy!" seyde the damesell, "hit is shame for you to sey hym suche worshyp." "Truly," seyde the Grene Knyght, "hit were shame to me to sey hym ony dysworshyp, for he hath previd hymself a bettir knyght than I am—and many is the noble knyght that I have mette withall in my dayes—

¶"And never or this tyme founde I no knyght his macche." And so that nyght they yoode unto reste, and all nyght the Grene Knyght commaundede thirty knyghtes prevyly to wacche Bewmaynes for to kepe hym from all treson. [And soo on the morne] they all arose and herde their Masse and brake their faste. And than they toke their horsis and rode their way.

¶And the Grene Knyght conveyed hem thorow the foreste.

¶Than the Grene Knyght seyde, "My lorde, Sir Bewmaynes, my body and this thirty knyghtes shall be allway at your somouns, bothe erly and late at your callynge, and whothir that ever ye woll sende us." "Ye sey well," seyde Sir Bewmaynes. "Whan that I calle upon you, ye muste yelde you unto Kynge Arthure, and all your knyghtes, if that I so commaunde you."

¶"We shall be redy at all tymes," seyde the Grene Knyght.

¶"Fy, fy upon the, in the devyls name!" seyde the damesel, "that ever ony good knyght sholde be obedyent unto a kychyn knave."

¶So than departed the Grene Knyght and the damesell, and than she seyde unto Bewmaynes, "Why folowyste thou me, kychyn knave? Caste away thy shylde and thy spere and fle away. Yett I counseyle the betyme, or thou shalt sey ryght sone 'Alas!' For and thou were as wyght as Sir Launcelot, Sir Trystrams, or the good knyght Sir Lamerok, thou shalt not passe a pace[7] here that is called the Pace Perelus."

¶"Damesell," seyde Bewmaynes, "who is aferde, let hym fle, for hit were shame to turne agayne syth I have ryddyn so longe with

7. I.e., pass.

you." "Well," seyde she, "ye shall sone, whether ye woll or woll not."

¶So within a whyle they saw a whyght towre as ony snowe, well macchecolde all aboute and double-dyked, and over the towre gate there hynge a fyffty[8] shyldis of dyvers coloures. And undir that towre there was a fayre medow; and therein was many knyghtes and squyres to beholde, scaffoldis, and pavylons—for there uppon the morne sholde be a grete turnemente. And the lorde of the towre was within his castell, and loked oute at a wyndow and saw a damesell, a dwarff, and a knyght armed at all poyntis.

¶"So God me helpe," seyde the lorde, "with that knyght woll I juste, for I se that he is a knyght arraunte." And so he armed hym and horsed hym hastely. Whan he was on horsebak with his shylde and his spere, hit was all rede, bothe his horse and his harneyse and all that to hym belonged.

¶And whan that he com nyghe hym he wente hit had be his brother the Blak Knyght.

¶And than lowde he cryed, and seyde, "Brothir, what do ye here in this marchis?"

¶"Nay, nay," seyde the damesell, "hit is nat he, for this is but a kychyn knave that was brought up for almys in Kynge 𝕬𝖗𝖙𝖍𝖚𝖗𝖘 courte."

¶"Neverthelesse, seyde the Rede Knyght, "I woll speke with hym or he departe."

¶"A," seyde this damesell, "this knave hathe slayne your brother—and Sir 𝕶𝖆𝖞 named hym 𝕭𝖊𝖜𝖒𝖆𝖞𝖓𝖊𝖘—and this horse and this harneyse was thy brothirs, the Blak Knyght;

¶"Also I sawe thy brothir, the Grene Knyght, overcom of his hondys:

¶"But now may ye be revenged on hym—for I may nevir be quyte of hym!"

¶Wyth this every[9] knyght departed in sundir and cam togydir all that[1] they myght dryve; and aythir of their horsis felle to the erthe.

¶Than they avoyde theire horsis, and put their shyldis before hem and drew their swerdys; and eythir gaff other sad strokys— now here, now there, trasyng, traversyng, and foynyng, rasyng and hurlyng lyke two borys, the space of two owrys.

¶Than she cryde on hyght to the Rede Knyght, "Alas, thou noble Rede Knyght, thynke what worshyp hath evermore folowed the— lette never a kychyn knave endure the so longe as he doth!"

¶Than the Rede Knyght wexed wroth and doubled his strokes, and hurte 𝕭𝖊𝖜𝖒𝖆𝖞𝖓𝖊𝖘 wondirly sore, that the bloode ran downe to the grounde, that hit was wondir to see that stronge batayle.

¶Yet at the laste 𝕭𝖊𝖜𝖒𝖆𝖞𝖓𝖊𝖘 strake hym to the erthe.

¶And as he wolde have slayne the Rede Knyght, he cryed, "Mercy, noble knyght! Sle me nat, and I shall yelde me to the wyth fyffty knyghtes with me that be at my commaundemente, and

[10]

5

10

15

20

fol.121v

25

30

35

40

45

---

8. A *fyffty*: a quantity of fifty.
9. I.e., each.
1. *All that*: as fast as.

forgyff the all the dispyte that thou haste done to me, and the deth
of my brothir the Blak Knyght, and the wynnyng[2] of my brothir the
Grene Knyght."

¶"All this avaylyth nat," seyde Beawmaynes, "but if my damesell
pray me to save thy lyff"—and therewith he made semblaunte to
stryke of his hede.

¶"Let be, thou Bewmaynes, and sle hym nat, for he is a noble
knyght; and nat so hardy, uppon thyne hede,[3] but that thou save
hym."

¶Than Bewmaynes bade the Rede Knyght to stonde up—"and
thanke this damesell now of thy lyff."

¶Than the Rede Knyght prayde hym to se his castell and to
repose them all that nyght.

¶So the damesell graunte hym, and there they had good chere—
but allwayes this damesell seyde many foule wordys unto Bewmaynes, whereof the Rede Knyght had grete mervayle. And all that
nyght the Rede Knyght made three score knyghtes to wacche Bewmaynes, that he sholde have no shame nother vylony.

¶And uppon the morne they herde Masse and dyned, and the
Rede Knyght com before Bewmaynes with his three score knyghtes,
and there he profyrd hym his omage and feawté at all tymes, he
and his knyghtes to do hym servyse.

¶"I thanke you," seyde Bewmaynes, "but this ye shall graunte me:
whan I calle uppon you, to com before my lorde, Kynge Arthure,
and yelde you unto hym to be his knyghtes." "Sir," seyde the Rede
Knyght, "I woll be redy, and all my felyship, at youre somouns."

¶So Sir Bewmaynes departed and the damesell—and ever she
rode chydyng hym in the fowleste maner wyse that she cowde.
"Damesell," seyde Bewmaynes, "ye ar uncurteyse so to rebuke
me as ye do, for mesemyth I have done you good servyse—
and ever ye thretyn me I shall be betyn wyth[4] knyghtes that we
mete; but ever, for all your boste, they all lye in the duste or in the
myre. And therefore, Y pray you, rebuke me no more; and whan
ye se me betyn or yoldyn as recreaunte, than may you bydde me
go from you shamfully. But erste, I let you wete, I woll nat departe
from you—for than I were worse than a foole and[5] I wolde departe
from you all the whyle that I wynne worshyp."

¶"Well," seyde she, "ryght sone shall mete the a knyght that
shall pay the all thy wagys, for he is the moste man of worshyp of
the worlde excepte Kyng Arthure." "I woll well," seyde Bewmaynes,
"the more he is of worshyp the more shall be my worshyp to have
ado with hym."

¶Than anone they were ware where was afore them a cyté rych
and fayre, and betwyxte them and the cyté, a myle and more, there
was a fayre medow that semed new mowyn, and therein was many
pavylons fayre to beholde.

Here Sir Bewmay-
nes overcom the Rede
Knyght

fol.122r

[11]

fol.122v

---

2. I.e., defeat.
3. *Nat so hardy, uppon thyne hede:* be not so bold, as you value your head.
4. I.e., by.
5. I.e., if.

¶"Lo," seyde the damesell, "yondir is a lorde that owyth yondir cyté, and his custom is, whan the wedir is fayre, to lye in this medow, to juste and to turnay. And ever there is aboute hym fyve hondred knyghtes and jantyllmen of armys, and there is all maner of gamys that ony jantyllman can devyse."

¶"That goodly lorde," seyde **Bewmaynes**, "wolde I fayne se."

¶"Thou shalt se hym tyme inowe,"[6] seyde the damesell.

¶And so as she rode nere, she aspyed the pavelon where the lorde was.

¶"Lo," seyde she, "syeste thou yondir pavyvlyon that is all of the coloure of inde, and all maner of thyng that there is aboute?" (Men and women and horsis, trapped shyldis and sperys, was all of the coloure of inde.) "And his name is Sir **Parsaunte of Inde**, the moste lordlyest knyght that ever thou lokyd on."

¶"Hit may well be," seyde Sir **Bewmaynes**, "but be he never so stoute a knyght, in this felde I shall abyde tyll that I se hym undir his shylde."

¶"A, foole," seyde she, "thou were bettir to flee betymes."

¶"Why?" seyde **Bewmaynes**. "And he be suche a knyght as ye make hym, he woll nat sette uppon me with all his men—for and there com no more but one at onys, I shall hym nat fayle whylys my lyff may laste."

¶"Fy, fy!" seyde the damesell, "that evir suche a stynkyng kychyn knave sholde blowe suche a boste!"

¶"Damesell," he seyde, "ye ar to blame so to rebuke me, for I had lever do fyve batayles than so to be rebuked—

¶"Lat hym com, and than lat hym doo his worste!"

¶"Sir," she seyde, "I mervayle what thou art and of what kyn thou arte com, for boldely thou spekyst and boldely thou haste done—that have I sene. Therefore, I pray the, save thyself and thou may, for thyne horse and thou have had grete travayle, and I drede that we dwelle ovirlonge[7] frome the seege—for hit is hens but seven myle, and all perelous passages we ar paste, sauff all only[8] this passage, and here I drede me sore last[9] ye shall cacche som hurte. Therefore I wolde ye were hens, that ye were nat brused nothir hurte with this stronge knyght—but I lat you wete this Sir **Persaunte** of Inde is nothyng of myght nor strength unto[1] the knyght that lyeth at the seege aboute my lady."[2] "As for that," seyde **Bewmaynes**, "be as be may, for sytthen I am com so nye this knyght, I woll preve his myght or I departe frome hym—and ellis I shall be shamed and I now withdrawe fro hym:

¶"And therefore, damesell, have ye no doute, by the grace of

fol. 123r

---

6. *Tyme inowe:* soon enough.
7. *Dwelle ovirlonge:* stay away too long.
8. *All only:* alone.
9. I.e., lest.
1. I.e., in comparison with.
2. "*Sir,*" *she seyde, "I mervayle . . . at the seege aboute my lady*": here the lady begins to speak to Bewmaynes in a new way, first by implicitly valuing his skills in trying to preserve him for the fight at the nearby siege and also by employing the more respectful pronoun forms *ye* and *you* (instead of the more familiar, even insulting *thee* or *thou;* on this distinction see p. xxxvi).

God I shall so dele with this knyght that within two owrys after none I shall delyver hym—and than shall we com to the seege be daylyght."

¶"A, Jesu, mervayle have I," seyde the damesell, "what maner a man ye be, for hit may never be other but that ye be com of jantyll bloode; for so fowle and shamfully dud never woman revyle a knyght as I have done you, and ever curteysly ye have suffyrde me—and that com never but of jantyll bloode."

¶"Damesell," seyde Bewmaynes, "a knyght may lytyll do that may nat suffir a jantyllwoman, for whatsomever ye seyde unto me, I toke none hede to your wordys—for the more ye seyde the more ye angred me, and my wretthe I wrekid uppon them that I had ado withall. [And therefor alle] the mysseyyng that ye mysseyde me in my batayle furthered me much and caused me to thynke[3] to shew and preve myselffe at the ende what I was; for peraventure, thoughe hit lyst me to be fedde in Kynge Arthures courte, I myght have had mete in other placis, but I ded hit for to preve my frendys—and that shall be knowyn another day, whether that I be a jantyllman borne or none—

¶"For I latte yow wete, fayre damesell, I have done you jantyllmannys servyse, and peraventure bettir servyse yet woll I do or I departe frome you."

¶"Alas," she seyde, "fayre Bewmaynes, forgyff me all that I have mysseseyde or done ayenste you." "With all my wyll," seyde he, "I forgeff hit you, for ye dud nothyng but as ye sholde do, for all youre evyll wordys pleased me—

¶"Damesell," seyde Bewmaynes, "syn hit lykyth you to sey thus fayre unto me, wote ye well hit gladdyth myne herte gretly; and now mesemyth there is no knyght lyvyng but I am able inow for hym."

¶Wyth this Sir Persaunte of Inde had aspyed them as they hoved in the fylde, and knyghtly he sente unto them[4] whether he cam in warre or in pece.

¶"Sey to thy lorde I take no force, but whether[5] as hym lyste."

¶So the messyngere wente ayen unto Sir Persaunte and tolde hym all his answere. "Well, than I woll have ado with hym to the utteraunce!"[6] And so he purveyede hym and rode ayenste hym.

¶Whan Bewmaynes sawe hym, he made hym redy—and mette[7] with all theire myghtes togedir as faste as their horse myght ren, and braste their spearys eythir[8] in three pecis, and their horsis [rassed so togyders that bothe their horses] felle downe to the erthe. And delyverly they avayded their horsis and put their shyldis before them and drew their swerdys and gaff many grete strokys, that somtyme they hurled so togydir that they felle grovelyng on the grounde.

---

3. I.e., intend.
4. *Sente unto them*: i.e., sent someone to inquire of them.
5. *Take no force*: do not care. *Whether*: i.e., whichever.
6. I.e., death.
7. I.e., they met.
8. I.e., both.

❡Thus they fought two owres and more, that there shyldes and hawbirkes were all forhewyn, and in many placis [were they] wounded.

❡So at the laste Sir 𝕭𝖊𝖜𝖒𝖆𝖞𝖓𝖊𝖘 smote hym thorow the coste of the body, and than he retrayed hym here and there and knyghtly maynteyned his batayle longe tyme.

❡And at the laste, though hym loth were,[9] 𝕭𝖊𝖆𝖜𝖒𝖆𝖞𝖓𝖊𝖘 smote Sir 𝕻𝖊𝖗𝖘𝖆𝖚𝖓𝖙𝖊 abovyn uppon the helme, that he felle grovelynge to the erthe; and than he lepte uppon hym overthwarte and unlaced his helme to have slayne hym.

fol.124r

❡Than Sir 𝕻𝖊𝖗𝖘𝖆𝖚𝖓𝖙𝖊 yelded hym and asked hym mercy.

Here Sir 𝕭𝖊𝖜𝖒𝖆𝖞-
𝖓𝖊𝖘 overcom 𝕾𝖎𝖗
𝕻𝖊𝖗𝖘𝖆𝖚𝖓𝖙𝖊 of 𝕴𝖓𝖉𝖊

❡Wyth that com the damesell and prayde hym to save his lyff. "I woll well," he seyde, "for hit were pyté this noble knyght sholde dye." "Gramercy," seyde Sir 𝕻𝖊𝖗𝖘𝖆𝖚𝖓𝖙𝖊, "for now I wote well hit was ye that slew my brother, the Blak Knyght, at the Blak Thorne. He was a full noble knyght; his name was Sir 𝕻𝖊𝖗𝖆𝖗𝖉𝖊. Also, I am sure that ye ar he that wan myne other brother, the Grene Knyght; his name is Sir 𝕻𝖊𝖗𝖙𝖍𝖔𝖑𝖔𝖕𝖊. Also ye wan my brother the Rede Knyght, Sir 𝕻𝖊𝖗𝖞𝖒𝖔𝖓𝖊𝖘. And now, sir, ye have wonne me. This shall I do for to please you: ye shall have homage and feawté of me and of an hondred knghtes to be allwayes at your commaundemente, to go and ryde where ye woll commaunde us." And so they wente unto Sir 𝕻𝖊𝖗𝖘𝖆𝖚𝖓𝖙𝖊𝖘 pavylyon and dranke wyne and ete spycis. And afterwarde Sir 𝕻𝖊𝖗𝖘𝖆𝖚𝖓𝖙𝖊 made hym to reste uppon a bedde untyll supper tyme, and aftir souper to bedde ayen.

❡So whan Sir 𝕭𝖊𝖜𝖒𝖆𝖞𝖓𝖊𝖘 was abedde, Sir 𝕻𝖊𝖗𝖘𝖆𝖚𝖓𝖙𝖊 had a doughter, a fayre lady of eyghtene yere of ayge, and there he called hir unto hym and charged hir and commaunded hir uppon his blyssyng to go unto the knyghtis bed and lye downe by his syde—"and make hym no strange chere but good chere, and take hym in your armys and kysse hym; and loke that this be done, I charge you, as ye woll have my love and my good wylle."

❡So Sir 𝕻𝖊𝖗𝖘𝖆𝖚𝖓𝖙𝖎𝖘 doughter dud as hir fadir bade hir, and so she yode unto Sir 𝕭𝖊𝖜𝖒𝖆𝖞𝖓𝖊𝖘 bed and pryvyly she dispoyled hir and leyde hir downe by hym. And than he awooke and sawe her and asked her what she was.

❡"Sir," she seyde, "I am Sir 𝕻𝖊𝖗𝖘𝖆𝖚𝖓𝖙𝖎𝖘 doughter, that by the commaundemente of my fadir I am com hydir." "Be ye a pusell or a wyff?" "Sir," she seyde, "I am a clene maydyn."

❡"God deffende me," seyde he, "than that ever I sholde defoyle you to do Sir 𝕻𝖊𝖗𝖘𝖆𝖚𝖓𝖙𝖊 suche a shame. Therefore I pray you, fayre damesell, aryse oute of this bedde, other ellys I woll." "Sir," she seyde, "I com nat hydir by myne owne wyll, but as I was commaunded."

fol.124v

❡"Alas," seyde Sir 𝕭𝖊𝖜𝖒𝖆𝖞𝖓𝖊𝖘, "I were a shamefull knyght and[1] I wolde do youre fadir ony dysworshyp." But so he kyste her, and so she departed and com unto Sir 𝕻𝖊𝖗𝖘𝖆𝖚𝖓𝖙𝖊 hir fadir and tolde hym

9. *Hym loth were:* was loath to him.
1. I.e., if.

all how she had sped. "Truly," seyde Sir Persaunte, "whatsomever he be, he is com of full noble bloode." And so we leve hem there tyll on the morne.

¶And so on the morne the damesell and Sir Bewmaynes herde [13] Masse and brake there faste and so toke their leve. 5

¶"Fayre damesell," seyde Sir Persaunte, "whothirwarde ar ye away ledynge this knyght?" "Sir," she seyde, "this knyght is goynge to the Castell Daungerous there as my systir is beseged."

¶"A-ha," seyde Sir Persaunte, "that is the Knyght of the Rede Launde, whyche is the moste perelyste knyght that I know now 10 lyvynge, and a man that is wythouten mercy—and men sey that he hath seven mennes strength. God save you, Sir Bewmaynes, frome that knyght, for he doth grete wronge to that lady; and that is grete pyté, for she is one of the fayreste ladyes of the worlde—and mese-myth that your damesell is hir sister. Ys nat your name Lyonet?" 15 "Sir, so I hyght, and my lady my sister hyght Dame Lyones."

"Now shall I tell you," seyde Sir Persaunte, "this Rede Knyght of the Rede Laundys hath layne longe at that seege, well-nye this two yerys, and many tymes he myght have had hir and he had wolde,[2] but he prolongyth the tyme to this entente, for to have Sir Launcelot 20 du Lake to do batayle with hym—or with Sir Trystrams, othir Sir Lamerok de Galys, other Sir Gawayne—and this is his taryynge[3] so longe at the sege:

¶"Now, my lorde," seyde Sir Persaunt of Inde, "be ye stronge and of good herte, for ye shall have ado with a good knyght." "Let me 25 dele," seyde Sir Bewmaynes. "Sir," seyde this damesell Lyonet, "I requyre you that ye woll make this jantyllman knyght or evir he fol.125r fyght with the Rede Knyght." "I woll, with all myne herte," seyde Sir Persaunte, "and hit please hym to take the order of knyghthode of so symple a man as I am." 30

¶"Sir," seyde Bewmaynes, "I thanke you for [your good wil, for] I am bettir spedde, for sertaynly the noble knyghte Sir Launcelot made me knyght."

¶"A," seyde Sir Persaunte, "of a more renomed man myght ye nat be made knyghte of, for of all knyghtes he may be called cheff of 35 knyghthode, and so all the worlde seythe that betwyxte three knyghtes is departed clerely[4] knyghthode, that is Sir Launcelot du Lake, Sir Trystrams de Lyones and Sir Lamerok de Galys—thes bere now the renowne. Yet there be many other noble knyghtis, as Sir Palomydes the Saresyn and Sir Saphir, his brothir; also Sir Bleobrys 40 and Sir Blamour de Ganys, his brothir; also Sir Bors de Ganys, and Sir Ector de Marys, and Sir Percivale de Galys—thes and many mo bene noble knyghtes, but there be none that bere the name but thes three abovyn seyde. Therefore God spede you well," seyde Sir Persaunte, "for and ye may macche that Rede Knyght, ye shall be 45 called the fourth of the worlde."

---

2. *And he had wolde:* if he had wished.
3. I.e., his reason for tarrying.
4. *Departed clerely:* clearly shared.

¶"Sir," seyde Bewmaynes, "I wolde fayne be of good fame and of knyghthode:

¶"And I latte you wete, I am com of good men, for I dare say my fadir was a nobleman. And so that ye woll kepe hit in cloce,[5] and this damesell, I woll tell you of what kynne I am com of."

¶"We woll nat discover[6] you," seyde they bothe, "tylle ye commaunde us, by the fayth we owe to Jesu."

¶"Truly," than sayde he, "my name is Sir Gareth of Orkenay, and Kynge Lott was my fadir, and my modir is Kyng Arthurs sistir—hir name is Dame Morgawse; and Sir Gawayne ys my brothir, and Sir Aggravayne and Sir Gaherys; and I am yongeste of hem all—and yette wote nat Kynge Arthure nother Sir Gawayne what I am."

¶So the booke seyth that the lady that was beseged had worde of hir sisteris comyng by the dwarff, and a knyght with hir, and how he had passed all the perelus passages.

¶"What maner a man is he?" seyde the lady. "He is a noble knyght truly, madam," seyde the dwarff, "and but a yonge man, but he is as lykly a man as ever ye saw ony."

¶"What is he, and of what kynne," seyde the lady, "is he com, and of whom was he made knyght?" "Madam," seyde the dwarff, "he was kynges son of Orkeney, but his name I woll nat tell you as at this tyme—but wete you well, of Sir Launcelot was he made knyght, for of none other wolde he be made knyght. And Sir Kay named hym Bewmaynes." "How ascaped he," seyde the lady, "frome the brethyrn of Sir Persaunte?" "Madam," he seyde, "as a noble knyght sholde:

¶"First, he slew two bretherne at a passage of a watir." "A!" seyde she, "they were two good knyghtes, but they were murtherers: that one hyght Sir Gararde le Breuse and that other hyght Sir Arnolde le Bruse." "Than, madam, he recountird at[7] the Blak Knyght and slew hym in playne batayle; and so he toke his hors and his armoure and fought with the Grene Knyght and wanne hym in playne batayle; and in lyke wyse he served the Rede Knyght; and aftir, in the same wyse, he served the Blew Knyght and wanne hym in playne batayle."

"Than," sayde the lady, "he hath overcom Sir Persaunte of Inde that is one of the noblest knyghtes of the worlde." "Trewly, madam," seyde the dwarff, "he hath wonne all the foure bretherne and slayne the Blak Knyght—and yet he dud more tofore: he overthrew Sir Kay and leffte hym nye dede upon the grounde:

¶"Also he dud a grete batayle wyth Sir Launcelot, and there they departed on evyn hondis.[8] And than Sir Launcelot made hym knyght."

¶"Dwarff," seyde the lady, "I am gladde of thys tydynges. Therefore go thou unto an hermytage of myne hereby and bere with the of my wyne in too flagons of sylver—they ar of two galons

fol.125v

[14]

fol.126r

5. *In cloce:* secret.
6. I.e., identify.
7. *Recountird at:* encountered with.
8. *On evyn hondis:* i.e., evenly matched.

—and also two caste of brede, with the fatte venyson i-bake, and
deynté foules; and a cuppe of golde here I delyver the that is ryche
of precious stonys. And bere all this to myne hermytage and putt
hit in the hermytis hondis. And sytthyn go thou to my sistir and
grete her welle, and commaunde me unto that jantyll knyght and
pray hym to ete and drynke and make hym stronge:

⁋"And say hym I thanke hym of his curtesy and goodnesse that
he wolde take uppon hym suche labur for me that[9] never ded hym
bounté nother curtesy:

⁋"Also pray hym that he be of good herte and corrage hymself,
for he shall mete with a full noble knyght, but he is nother of
curtesy, bounté, nother jantylnesse, for he attendyth unto nothyng
but to murther—and that is the cause I can nat prayse hym nother
love hym."

⁋So this dwarff departed and com to Sir **Persaunt**, where he
founde the damesell **Lynet** and Sir **Bewmaynes**, and there he tolde
hem all as ye have herde. And than they toke their leve; but Sir
Persaunte toke an amblynge hakeney and conveyed them on their
wayes, and than betoke he them unto God. And so within a lytyll
whyle they com to the hermytage, and there they dranke the wyne
and ete the venyson and the foulys bakyn.

⁋And so whan they had repasted them well, the dwarff retourned ayen with his vessell unto the castell; and there mette wyth
hym the Rede Knyght of the Rede Laundys, and asked hym from
whens he com, and where he had ben.

⁋"Sir," seyde the dwarff, "I have bene with my ladyes sistir of
the castell, and she hath bene at Kynge **Arthurs** courte and brought
a knyght with her."

⁋"Than I acompte her travayle but lorne, for though she had
brought with hir Sir **Launcelot**, Sir **Trystrams**, Sir **Lameroke**, othir Sir
Gawayne, I wolde thynke myself good inowe for them all." "Hit may
well be," seyde the dwarff, "but this knyght hathe passed all the
perelouse passages, and slayne the Blak Knyghte and other two
mo, and wonne the Grene Knyght, the Rede Knyght, and the Blew
Knyght." "Than is he one of thes foure that I have before reher-
syd?"

⁋"He is none of thes," seyde the dwarff, "but he is a kynges
son."

⁋"What is his name?" seyde the Rede Knyght of the Rede Laundis. "That woll I nat tell you, but Sir **Kay** on scorne named hym
Bewmaynes." "I care nat," seyde the knyght, "whatsomevir he be,
for I shall sone delyver hym—and yf I overmacche hym he shall
have a shamfull deth, as many othir have had."

⁋"That were pyté," seyde the dwarff, "and hit is pyté that ye
make suche shamfull warre uppon noble knyghtes."

NOw leve we the knyght and the dwarff and speke we of **Bewmaynes**, that all nyght lay in the hermytage; and uppon the
morne he and the damesell **Lynet** harde their Masse and brake their

5

10

15

20

25

fol.126v

30

35

40

45

[15]

9. I.e., who.

faste, and than they toke their horsis and rode thorowoute a fayre
foreste. And than they com to a playne and saw where was many
pavylons and tentys, and a fayre castell, and there was muche
smoke and grete noyse.

¶And whan they com nere the sege, Sir **Bewmaynes** aspyed on
grete trees, as he rode, how there hynge full goodly armed knyghtes
by the necke, and their shyldis aboute their neckys with their swerdis and gylte sporys uppon their helys.

¶And so there hynge nyghe a fourty knyghtes shamfully with
full ryche armys. Than Sir **Bewmaynes** abated[1] his countenaunce,
and seyde, "What menyth this?"

¶"Fayre Sir," seyde the damesell, "abate nat youre chere for all
this syght, for ye muste corrage youreself, other ellys ye bene all
shente:

¶"For all these knyghtes com hydir to this sege to rescow my
sistir, Dame **Lyones**, and whan the Rede Knyght of the Rede
Launde had overcom hem he put them to this shamefull deth withoute mercy and pyté—and in the same wyse he woll serve you but
yf ye quyte you the bettir."

¶"Now Jesu defende me," seyde Sir **Bewmaynes**, "frome suche
vylans deth and shendeshyp of harmys, for rathir than I sholde so
be faryn withall[2] I woll rather be slayne in playne batayle."

¶"So were ye bettir,"[3] seyde the damesell, "for trust nat, in hym
is no curtesy, but all goth to the deth other shamfull mourthur—
and that is pyté," seyde the damesell, "for he is a full lykly man
and a noble knyght of proues, and a lorde of grete londis and of
grete possessions."

¶"Truly," seyde Sir **Bewmaynes**, "he may be well a good knyght,
but he usyth shamefull customys, and hit is mervayle that he
enduryth so longe, that none of the noble knyghtes of my lorde
Arthurs have nat dalte with hym."

¶And than they rode unto the dykes and sawe them double-
dyked wyth full warly wallys, [and there were lodged many grete
lordes nyghe the wallys,] and there was grete noyse of mynstralsy.
And the see bete uppon that one syde of the wallys, where were
many shyppis and marynars noyse with "hale and how!"[4]

¶And also there was faste by a sygamoure tre, and thereon hynge
an horne, the grettyst that ever they sye, of an olyvauntes bone[5]—
"and[6] this Knyght of the Rede Launde hath honged hit up there
to this entente, that yf there com ony arraunte knyghte, he muste
blowe that horne, and than woll he make hym redy and com to
hym to do batayle:

¶"But, sir, I pray you," seyde the damesell, "blow ye nat the
horne tyll hit be hygh none, for now hit is aboute pryme, and now

fol.127r   5

10

15

20

25

30

35

40

1. I.e., cast down.
2. *So be faryn withall:* be so treated.
3. I.e., better off.
4. *Hale and how!:* i.e. heave-ho!.
5. Elephant's tusk.
6. The damsel is speaking.

encresyth his myght, that as men say he hath seven mennys
strength."

¶"A, fy, for shame! Fayre damesell, sey ye nevir so more to me:

¶"For and he were as good a knyght as ever was ony, I shall
never fayle hym in his moste myght, for other I woll wynne worshyp 5
worshypfully, othir dye knyghtly in the felde." And therewith he
spored his horse streyte to the sygamoure tre, and so blew the horne
egirly that all the seege and the castell range thereoff.

¶And than there lepe oute many knyghtes oute of their tentys
and pavylyons; and they within the castell loked ovir the wallys and 10
oute at wyndowis.

¶Than the Rede Knyght of the Rede Laundis armed hym hastely, and too barouns sette on his sporys on his helys—and all was
blood-rede, his armour, spere, and shylde. And an erle buckled his
helme on his hede, and than they brought hym a rede spere and a 15
rede stede; and so he rode into a lytyll vale undir the castell, that
all that were in the castell and at the sege myght beholde the
batayle.

¶"Sir," seyde the damesell Lynet unto Sir Bewmaynes, "loke ye be
glad and lyght, for yondir is your dedly enemy—and at yondir wyn- 20
dow is my lady, my sistir Dame Lyones." "Where?" seyde Bewmaynes.
"Yondir," seyde the damesell, and poynted with her fyngir. "That
is trouth," seyde Bewmaynes, "she besemyth afarre the fayryst lady
that ever I lokyd uppon; and truly," he seyde, "I aske no better
quarell than now for to do batayle, for truly she shall be my lady 25
and for hir woll I fyght." And ever he loked up to the wyndow with
glad countenaunce.

¶And this lady Dame Lyones made curtesy[7] to hym downe to the
erth, holdynge up bothe her hondys.

¶Wyth that the Rede Knyghte called unto Bewmaynes and seyde, 30
"Sir knyght, leve thy beholdyng and loke on me, I counsayle the!
For I warne the well, she is my lady, and for hir I have done many
stronge batayles."

¶"Geff thou so have done," seyde Bewmaynes, "mesemyth hit was
but waste laboure, for she lovyth none of thy felyshyp; and thou 35
to love that[8] lovyth nat the is but grete foly. For and I undirstoode
that she were nat ryght glad of my commynge, I wolde be avysed[9]
or I dud batayle for hir; but I undirstonde by the segynge of this
castell she may forbere thy felyshyp. And therefore wete thou well,
thou Rede Knyght, I love hir and woll rescow hir, othir ellys to dye 40
therefore."

"Sayst thou that?" seyde the Rede Knyght. "Mesemyth thou
oughtyste of reson to beware by yondir knyghtes that thou sawyste
hange on yondir treis."

¶"Fy for shame!" seyde Bewmaynes, "that ever thou sholdyst sey 45
so or do so evyll, for in that thou shamest thyself and all knyghthode—and thou mayste be sure there woll no lady love the that

7. I.e., courteous acknowledgment.
8. I.e., that which.
9. *Be avysed:* i.e., reconsider.

knowyth the and thy wykked customs. And now thou wenyste that
the syght of tho honged knyghtes shulde feare me? Nay, truly, nat
so; that shamefull syght cawsyth me to have courrage and hardynesse ayenst the[1] muche more than I wolde have agaynste the
and thou were a well-ruled knyght."

¶"Make the redy," seyde the Rede Knyght, "and talke no more
with me."

¶Than they putt their sperys in the reste and com togedyrs with
all the myght that they had bothe, and aythir smote other in the
myddys of their shyldis, that the paytrels, sursynglys, and crowpers
braste, and felle to the erthe bothe, and the raynys of their brydyls
in there hondys.

¶And so they lay a grete whyle sore astoned, that all that were
in the castell and in the sege wente their neckys had bene broste.

¶Than many a straunger and othir seyde that the straunge
knyght was a bygge man and a noble jouster—"for or now we sawe
never no knyght macche the Rede Knyght of the Rede Laundys."
Thus they seyde bothe within and withoute.

¶Than lyghtly and delyverly they avoyded their horsis and putt
their shyldis afore them and drew theire swerdys, and ran togydyrs
lyke two fers lyons—and eythir gaff othir suche two buffettys
uppon their helmys that they reled bakwarde bothe two stredys.
And than they recoverde bothe and hew grete pecis of othyrs harneyse and their shyldys, that a grete parte felle in the fyldes.

And than thus they fought tyll hit was paste none, and never
wolde stynte, tyll at the laste they lacked wynde bothe—and
than they stoode waggyng, stagerynge, pantynge, blowynge, and
bledyng, that all that behelde them for the moste party wepte for
pyté.

¶So whan they had rested them a whyle they yode to batayle
agayne, trasyng, traversynge, foynynge, and rasynge as two borys—
and at som tyme they toke their bere[2] as hit had bene two rammys
and horled togydyrs, that somtyme they felle grovelynge to the
erthe; and at som tyme they were so amated that aythir toke others
swerde in the stede of his owne. And thus they endured tyll
evynsonge—

¶That there was none that behelde them myght know whethir[3]
was lyke to wynne the batayle. And theire armoure was so forhewyn
that men myght se their naked sydys, and in other placis they were
naked, but ever the nakyd placis they dud defende. And the Rede
Knyghte was a wyly knyght in fyghtyng, and that taught **Bewmaynes**
to be wyse—but he abought hit full sore or he did asspye his
fyghtynge.[4]

¶And thus by assente of them both they graunted aythir othir
to reste; and so they sette hem downe uppon two mollehyllys there
besydys the fyghtynge place, and eythir of them unlaced theire

1. Thee.
2. *Toke their bere:* built up momentum.
3. I.e., which of (the) two.
4. I.e., style of fighting.

helmys and toke the colde wynde (for aythir of their pagis was faste
by them to com whan they called them to unlace their harneyse,
and to sette hem on agayne at there commaundemente).

¶And than Sir **Bewmaynes**, whan his helme was off, he loked up
to the wyndowe, and there he sawe the fayre lady Dame **Lyones**,
and she made hym suche countenaunce that his herte waxed lyght
and joly; and therewith he bade the Rede Knyght of the Rede Laundis make hym redy—"and lette us do oure batayle to the utteraunce." "I woll well," seyde the knyght. And than they laced on
their helmys, and avoyded⁵ their pagys, and yede togydyrs and
fought freysshly. But the Rede Knyght of the Rede Laundys
awayted hym at an overthwarte⁶ and smote hym [within the hand,]
that his swerde felle oute of his honde—and yette he gaff hym
another buffette uppon the helme, that he felle grovelynge to the
erthe; and the Rede Knyghte felle over hym for to holde hym
downe.

¶Than cryed the maydyn **Lynet** on hyght and seyde, "A, Sir **Bewmaynes**, where is thy corrayge becom? Alas! my lady my sistir
beholdyth the, and she shrekis and wepys so that hit makyth myne
herte hevy."

¶Whan Sir **Bewmaynes** herde hir sey so, he abrayded up with a
grete myght, and gate hym uppon hys feete, and lyghtly he lepe to
his swerde and gryped hit in his honde and dowbled his pace unto
the Rede Knyght—and there they fought a new batayle togydir.

¶But Sir **Bewmaynes** than doubled his strokys and smote so thycke that his swerde felle oute of his honde—and than he smote
hym on the helme, that he felle to the erthe. And Sir **Bewmaynes**
felle uppon hym and unlaced his helme to have slayne hym; and
than he yelded hym and asked mercy, and seyde with a lowde
voyce, "A, noble knyght, I yelde me to thy mercy!"

¶Than Sir **Bewmaynes** bethought hym on⁷ his knyghtes that he
had made to be honged shamfully, and than he seyde, "I may nat
with my worship to save thy lyff, for the shamefull dethys that thou
haste caused many full good knyghtes to dye."

¶"Sir," seyde the Rede Knyght, "holde youre hande and ye shall
knowe the causis why I putte hem to so shamefull a deth."

¶"Sey on," seyde Sir **Bewmaynes**. "Sir, I loved onys a lady fayre,
and she had hir bretherne slayne, and she tolde me hit was Sir
Launcelot du Lake othir ellys Sir **Gawayne**; and she prayed me as I
loved hir hertely that I wolde make hir a promyse by the faythe of
my knyghthode for to laboure in armys dayly untyll that I had mette
with one of them; and all that I myght overcom, I sholde put them
to vylans deth:

¶"And so I ensured her to do all the vylany unto **Arthurs** knyghtes, and that I sholde take vengeaunce uppon all these knyghtes—
and, sir, now I woll telle the that every day my strengthe encresyth
tylle none, untyll I have seven mennys strength."

fol.129r

Here Sir Bewmay-
nes overcom the Rede
Knyght of the Rede
Laundys

fol.129v

---

5. I.e., dismissed.
6. Waited for an opportunity to strike him crosswise.
7. *Bethought hym on:* thought to himself about.

¶Than cam there many erlys and barowns and noble knyghtes [18]
and prayde that knyght to save his lyff—"and take hym to[8] your
presoner"—and all they felle uppon their kneis and prayde hym of
mercy that he wolde save his lyff. "And, sir," they all seyde, "hit
were fayrer of hym to take omage and feauté and lat hym holde 5
his londys of you than for to sle hym, for by his deth ye shall have
none advauntage—and his myssededys that be done may not be
undone. And therefore make ye amendys for all partyes, and we
all woll becom youre men and do you omage and feauté."

¶"Fayre lordys," seyde Bewmaynes, "wete you well I am full loth 10
to sle this knyght; neverthelesse he hath done passynge ylle and
shamefully—

¶"But insomuche all that he dud was at a ladyes requeste, I
blame hym the lesse; and so for your sake I woll relece hym, that
he shall have his lyff uppon this covenaunte: that he go into this 15
castell and yelde hym to the lady, and yf she woll forgyff and quyte
hym, I woll well; with this, he make hir amendys of all the trespasse
that he hath done ayenst hir and hir landys:

¶"And also, whan that is done, that he goo unto the courte of
Kyng Arthur, and that he aske Sir Launcelot mercy, and Sir Gawayne, fol.130r 20
for the evyll wylle he hath had ayenst them."

¶"Sir," seyde the Rede Knyght, "all this woll I do as ye commaunde me, and syker assuraunce and borowys ye shall have."

¶So whan the assurauns was made, he made his omage and
feauté, and all tho erlys and barouns with hym. And than the may- 25
den Lynet com to Sir Bewmaynes and unarmed hym and serched his
woundis and staunched the blood; and in lyke wyse she dud to the
Rede Knyght of the Rede Laundis. And there they suggeourned
ten dayes in there tentys.

¶And ever the Rede Knyght made all his lordis and servauntys 30
to do all the plesure unto Sir Bewmaynes that they myght do.

¶And so within a whyle the Rede Knyghte yode unto the castell
and putt hym in her grace; and so she resseyved hym uppon suffyc-
iaunte sureté so that all her hertys were well restored of all that she
coude complayne. 35

¶And than he departed unto the courte of Kynge Arthure, and
there opynly the Rede Knyght putt hymself in the mercy of Sir
Launcelot and of Sir Gawayne; and there he tolde opynly how he was
overcom and by whom, and also he tolde all the batayles, frome
the begynnyng to the endynge. 40

¶"Jesu mercy!" seyde Kynge Arthure and Sir Gawayne, "we mervayle muche of what bloode he is com, for he is a noble knyght."

¶"Have ye no mervayle," seyde Sir Launcelot, "for ye shall ryght
well know that he is com of full noble bloode—and as for hys
myght and hardynesse, there bene but full few now lyvynge that is 45
so myghty as he is, and of so noble prouesse."

¶"Hit semyth by you," seyde Kynge Arthure, "that ye know his
name and frome whens he com."

8. I.e., as.

¶"I suppose I do so," seyde Sir Launcelot, "or ellys I wolde not have yeffyn hym the hyghe order of knyghthode; but he gaff me suche charge at that tyme that I woll never discover hym untyll he requyre me, or ellis hit be knowyn opynly by som other."

¶Now turne we unto Sir Bewmaynes, that desyred of Dame Lynet that he myght se hir lady.

¶"Sir," she seyde, "I wolde ye saw hir fayne."

¶Than Sir Bewmaynes all armed toke his horse and his spere and rode streyte unto the castell; and whan he com to the gate, he founde there men armed, and[9] pulled up the drawbrygge and drew the portcolyse.

¶Than he mervayled why they wolde nat suffir hym to entir, and than he loked up to a wyndow and there he sawe fayre Dame Lyones, that seyde on hyght, "Go thy way, Sir Bewmaynes, for as yet thou shalt nat have holy[1] my love unto the tyme that thou be called one of the numbir of the worthy knyghtes—and therefore go and laboure in worshyp this twelvemonthe, and than ye shall hyre newe tydyngis."

¶"Alas, fayre lady!" seyde Sir Bewmaynes, "I have nat deserved that ye sholde shew me this straungenesse. And I hadde wente I sholde have had ryght good chere with you—and unto my power I have deserved thanke; and well I am sure I have bought your love with parte of the beste bloode within my body."

¶"Fayre curteyse knyght," seyde Dame Lyonesse, "be nat displeased, nother be nat overhasty, for wete you well youre grete travayle nother your good love shall nat be loste, for I consyder your grete laboure and your hardynesse, your bounté and your goodnesse, as me ought to do:

¶"And therefore go on youre way and loke that ye be of good comforte, for all shall be for your worshyp and for the best—and, pardé, a twelvemonthe woll sone be done. And trust me, fayre knyght, I shall be trewe to you and never betray you, but to my deth I shall love you and none other." And therewithall she turned frome the wyndowe, and Sir Bewmaynes rode awaywarde frome the castell makynge grete dole. And so he rode now here, now there, he wyste nat whother, tyll hit was durke nyght.

¶And than hit happened hym to com to a pore mannys house, and there he was herborowde all that nyght.

¶But Sir Bewmaynes had no reste, but walowed and wrythed for the love of the lady of that castell.

¶And so upon the morne he toke his horse and rode untyll undyrn, and than he com to a brode watir; and there he alyght to slepe and leyde his hede upon hys shylde and betoke his horse to the dwarff and commaunded the dwarff to wacche all nyght.

¶Now turne we to the lady of the same castell, that thought muche upon Bewmaynes. And than she called unto hir Sir Gryngamoure, hir brother, and prayde hym in all maner, as he loved hir

fol.130v
[19]

fol.131r

9. I.e., and who.
1. I.e., wholly.

hertely, that he wolde ryde afftir Sir Bewmaynes—"and ever have ye
wayte uppon hym tyll ye may fynde hym slepyng, for I am sure in
his hevynesse he woll alyght adowne in som place and lay hym
downe to slepe. And therefore have ye youre wayte uppon hym in
prevy maner, and take his dwarff and com your way wyth hym as   5
faste as ye may:

¶"For my sistir Lynet tellyth me that he can telle of what kynrede
he is com of; and in the meanewhyle I and my sistir woll ryde untyll
your castell to wayte whan ye brynge with you the dwarff, and than
woll I have hym in examynacion myself—for tyll that I know what   10
is his ryght name and of what kynrede he is commyn, shall I never
be myrry at my herte."

"Sistir," seyde Sir Gryngamour, "all this shall be done aftir your
entente." And so he rode all that other day and the nyght tyll he
had lodged hym; and whan he sawe Sir Bewmaynes faste on slepe   15
he com stylly stalkyng behynde the dwarff and plucked hym faste
undir his arme and so rode his way with hym untyll his owne castell.

¶And this Sir Gryngamoure was all in blak, his armour and his
horse and all that tyll hym longyth. But ever as he rode with the   fol.131v   20
dwarff towarde the castell, he cryed untyll his lorde and prayde
hym of helpe; and therewyth awoke Sir Beawmaynes, and up he
lepte lyghtly and sawe where the blak knyght rode his way wyth
the dwarff, and so he rode oute of his syght.

¶Than Sir Bewmaynes put on his helme and buckeled on his   [20]   25
shylde and toke his horse and rode afftir hym all that ever he
myght, thorow mores and fellys and grete sloughis, that many
tymes his horse and he plunged over their hedys in depe myres—
for he knewe nat the way, but toke the gayneste way in that woodenesse[2]—   30

¶That many tymes he was lyke to peryshe. And at the laste hym
happened to com to a fayre grene way, and there he mette with a
poore man of the contray and asked hym whether he mette nat
with a knyght uppon a blak horse and all blak harneyse, and a lytyll
dwarff syttynge behynde hym with hevy chere.   35

¶"Sir," seyde the poore man, "here by me com Sir Gryngamoure
the knyght with suche a dwarff—and therefore I rede you nat to
folow hym, for he is one of the perelyst knyghtes of the worlde,
and his castell is here nerehonde but two myle. Therefore, we avyse
you, ryde nat aftir Sir Gryngamour but yf ye owe hym good wylle."   40

¶So leve we Sir Bewmaynes rydyng toward the castell, and speke
we of Sir Gryngamoure and the dwarff. Anone as the dwarff was com
to the castell, Dame Lyonesse and Dame Lynet, hir systir, asked the
dwarff where was his mastir borne and of what lynage was he
com—"and but yf thou telle me," seyde Dame Lyonesse, "thou shalt   45
never ascape this castell, but ever here to be presonere." "As for
that," seyde the dwarff, "I feare nat gretly to telle his name and of
what kynne he is commyn of:

2. I.e., madness, anger.

❡"Wete you well, he is a kynges son and a quenys, and his fadir   fol.132r
hyght Kynge Lot of Orkeney, and his modir is sistir to Kyng Arthure,
and he is brother to Sir Gawayne, and his name is Sir Gareth of
Orkenay. And now I have tolde you his ryght name, I pray you, fayre
lady, lat me go to my lorde agayne, for he woll never oute[3] of this   5
contrey tyll he have me agayne—and yf he be angry he woll do
harme or that he be stynted, and worche you wrake[4] in this contrey." "As for that, be as be may."

❡"Nay," seyde Sir Gryngamoure, "as for that thretynge, we woll
go to dynere." And so they wayshed and wente to mete and made   10
hem mery and well at ease. Bycause the Lady Lyonesse of the Castell Perelus was there, they made the gretter joy.

❡"Truly, madam," seyde Lynet unto hir sistir, "well may he be a
kyngys son, for he hath many good tacchis; for he is curtyese and
mylde, and the most sufferynge[5] man that ever I mette withall. For   15
I dare sey there was never jantyllwoman[6] revyled man in so foule
a maner as I have rebuked hym—and at all tymes he gaff me goodly
and meke answers agayne."[7] And as they sate thus talkynge, there
cam Sir Gareth in at the gate with hys swerde drawyn in his honde,
and cryed alowde that all the castell myght hyre, "Thou traytour   20
knyght, Sir Gryngamoure! Delyver me my dwarff agayne, or by the
fayth that I owghe to God and to the hygh ordir of knyghthode, I
shall do the all the harme that may lye in my power."

❡Than Sir Gryngamour loked oute at a wyndow, and seyde, "Sir
Gareth of Orkenay, leve thy bostyng wordys, for thou gettyst nat thy   25
dwarff agayne."

❡"Than, cowarde knyght," seyde Gareth, "brynge hym with the,
and com and do batayle with me, and wynne hym and take hym."

❡"So woll I do," seyde Sir Gryngamoure, "and me lyste, but for all
thy grete wordys thou gettyst hym nat." A, fayre brother," seyde   fol.132v   30
Dame Lyonesse, "I wolde he hadde his dwarff agayne, for I wolde
he were nat wroth; for now he hath tolde me all my desyre, I kepe
no more of the dwarff—

❡"And also, brother, he hath done muche for me, and delyverde
me frome the Rede Knyght of the Rede Laundis: 35

❡"And therefore, brother, I owe hym my servyse afore all knyghtes lyvynge—and wete you well that I love hym byfore all othyr
knyghtes lyvynge, and full fayne I wolde speke with hym. But in
no wyse I wolde nat that he wyste what I were, but as I were anothir
strange lady."   40

❡"Well, sistir," seyde Sir Gryngamour, "sythen that I know now
your wyll, I woll obey me now unto hym." And so therewith he
wente downe, and seyde, "Sir Gareth, I cry you mercy, and all that
I have myssedone I woll amende hit at your wylle. And therefore
I pray you that ye wolde alyght and take suche chere as I can make   45
you in this castell."

3. I.e., go out.
4. *Worche you wrake:* bring ruin to you.
5. I.e., patient.
6. I.e., a gentlewoman who.
7. I.e., in reply.

¶"Shall I have my dwarff?"seyde Sir Gareth. "Yee, sir, and all the plesure that I can make you, for as sone as your dwarff tolde me what ye were and of what kynde ye ar com, and what noble dedys ye have done in this marchis, than I repented me of my dedys."

¶Than Sir Gareth alyght, and there com his dwarff and toke his horse.

¶"A, my felow," seyde Sir Gareth, "I have had muche adventures for thy sake!" And so Sir Gryngamoure toke hym by the honde and ledde hym into the halle where his owne wyff was.

¶And than com forth Dame Lyones arayde lyke a prynces, and [21] there she made hym passyng good chere, and he hir agayne, and they had goodly langage and lovely countenaunce. And Sir Gareth thought many tymes, "Jesu, wolde that the lady of this Castell Perelus were so fayre as she is." And there was all maner of gamys and playes, of daunsyng and syngynge, and evermore Sir Gareth behelde that lady; and the more he loked on her, the more he brenned in love, that he passed hymself farre in his reson.[8] And forth towardys nyght they yode unto souper.

¶And Sir Gareth myght nat ete, for his love was so hoote that he wyst nat where he was. All thes lokys aspyed Sir Gryngamour, and fol.133r than aftir souper he called his sistir Dame Lyonesse untyll a chambir, and sayde, "Fayre sistir, I have well aspyed your countenaunce betwyxte you and this knyght, and I woll, sistir, that ye wete he is a full noble knyght, and yf ye can make hym to abyde here, I woll do hym all the plesure that I can; for and ye were bettir[9] than ye ar, ye were well bewared[1] uppon hym."

¶"Fayre brother," seyde Dame Lyonesse, "I undirstonde well that the knyght is a good knyght, and com he is oute of a noble house. Natwithstondyng, I woll assay hym bettir, howbehit I am moste beholde to hym of ony erthely man, for he hath had grete labour for my love and passed many dangerous passagis."

¶Ryght so Sir Gryngamour wente unto Sir Gareth, and seyde, "Sir, make ye good chere, for ye shall have none other cause,[2] for this lady my sistir is youres at all tymes, hir worshyp saved, for wete you well she lovyth you as well as ye do hir—and bettir, yf bettir may be."

¶"And I wyste that," seyde Sir Gareth, "there lyved nat a gladder man than I wolde be."

¶"Uppon my worshyp," seyde Sir Gryngamoure, "truste unto my promyse. And as longe as hit lykyth you, ye shall suggeourne with me, and this lady shall be wyth us dayly and nyghtly to make you all the chere that she can."

¶"I woll well," seyde Sir Gareth, "for I have promysed to be nyghe this contray this twelvemonthe, and well I am sure Kynge Arthure and other noble knyghtes woll fynde me where that I am wythin this twelvemonthe, for I shall be sought and founden yf that I be on lyve."

---

8. *Passed hymself farre in his reson:* went out of his mind.
9. I.e., even more noble.
1. I.e., bestowed.
2. *none other cause:* no cause to do otherwise.

¶And than Sir Gareth wente unto the lady Dame Lyonesse and kyssed hir many tymes, and eythir made grete joy of other, and there she promysed hym hir love, sertaynly to love hym and none other dayes of hir lyff.

¶Than this lady Dame Lyonesse by the assent of hir brother tolde Sir Gareth all the trouthe what she was, and how she was the same lady that he dud batayle fore, and how she was lady of the Castell Perelus. And there she tolde hym how she causid hir brother to take away his dwarff:

¶"For this cause, to know the[3] sertayne, what was your name, and of what kyn ye were com." And than she lette fette[4] before hym hir systir Lynet, that had ryddyn with hym many a wylsom way.

¶Than was Syr Gareth more gladder than he was tofore. And than they trouthe-plyght other[5] to love and never to fayle whyle their lyff lastyth.

¶And so they brente bothe in hoote love that they were acorded to abate their lustys secretly.

¶And there Dame Lyonesse counceyled Sir Gareth to slepe in none other place but in the halle, and there she promysed hym to com to his bed a lytyll afore mydnyght.

¶This counceyle was nat so prevyly kepte but hit was undirstonde,[6] for they were but yonge bothe and tendir of ayge, and had nat used suche craufftis toforne.

¶Wherefore the damesell Lyonett was a lytyll dysplesed, and she thought hir sister Dame Lyonesse was a lytyll overhasty that she myght nat abyde hir tyme of maryage; and for savyng of hir worshyp she thought to abate their hoote lustis. And she lete ordeyne[7] by hir subtyle craufftes that they had nat theire intentys neythir with othir as in her delytes[8] untyll they were maryed. And so hit paste on; at[9] aftir souper was made a clene avoydaunce,[1] that every lorde and lady sholde go unto his reste.

¶But Sir Gareth seyde playnly he wolde go no farther than the halle—"for in suche placis," he seyde, "was convenyaunte for an arraunte knyght to take his reste in."

¶And so there was ordayned grete cowchis, and thereon fethir beddis, and there he leyde hym downe to slepe; and within a whyle came Dame Lyonesse wrapped in a mantell furred with ermyne,[2] and leyde hir downe by the sydys of Sir Gareth—and therewithall he began to clyppe hir and to kysse hir. And therewithall he loked before hym and sawe an armed knyght with many lyghtes aboute hym, and this knyght had a longe gysarne in his honde and made a grymme countenaunce to smyte hym.

fol.133v

[22]

---

3. thee.
4. *Lette fette:* had fetched.
5. I.e., each other.
6. *Nat so prevyly kepte but hit was undirstonde:* not so closely kept that it did not become known to others.
7. *Lete ordeyne:* arranged.
8. *As in her delytes:* according to their delights.
9. I.e., at the time.
1. I.e., clearing of the hall.
2. Conjoined pelts of the white fur of the ermine (a kind of weasel), evenly punctuated by the black tips of the creatures' tails, are a distinctive feature of royal robes.

¶Whan Sir Gareth sawe hym com in that wyse, he lepte oute of his bedde, and gate in his hande a swerde and lepte towarde that knyght.

¶And when the knyght sawe Sir Gareth com so fersly uppon hym, he smote hym with a foyne thorow the thycke of the thygh, that the wounde was a shafftemonde brode and had cutte a-too[3] many vaynes and synewys. And therewithall Sir Gareth smote hym uppon the helme suche a buffette that he felle grovelyng; and than he lepe over hym, and unlaced his helme, and smote off his hede fro the body. And than he bled so faste that he myght not stonde; but so he leyde hym downe uppon his bedde, and there he sowned and lay as he had bene dede.

¶Than Dame Lyonesse cryed alowde that Sir Gryngamoure harde hit and com downe; and whan he sawe Sir Gareth so shamfully wounded he was sore dyspleased, and seyde, "I am shamed that this noble knyght is thus dishonoured—

¶"Sistir," seyde Sir Gryngamour, "how may this be that this noble knyght is thus wounded?"

¶"Brothir," she seyde, "I can nat telle you, for hit was nat done by me nother be myne assente—for he is my lorde and I am his, and he muste be myne husbonde:

¶"Therefore, brothir, I woll that ye wete I shame[4] nat to be with hym nor to do hym all the plesure that I can."

¶"Sistir," seyde Gryngamour, "and I woll that ye wete hit, and Gareth bothe, that hit was never done by me, nother be myne assente this unhappy dede was never done." And there they staunched his bledyng as well as they myght, and grete sorow made Sir Gryngamour and Dame Lyonesse. And forthwithall com Dame Lyonett and toke up the hede in the syght of them all, and anoynted hit with an oyntemente there as hit was smyttyn off, and in the same wyse he[5] ded to the othir parte there as the hede stake.[6]

¶And than she sette hit togydirs, and hit stake as faste as ever hit ded—and the knyght arose lyghtly up, and the damesell Lyonett put hym in hir chambir. All this saw Sir Gryngamour and Dame Lyonesse, and so ded Sir Gareth—and well he aspyed that hit was Dame Lyonett that rode with hym thorow the perelouse passages.

¶"A, well, damesell," seyde Sir Gareth, "I wente ye wolde nat have done as ye have done."

¶"My lorde Sir Gareth," seyde Lyonett, "all that I have done I woll avowe hit—and all shall be for your worshyp and us all." And so within a whyle Sir Gareth was nyghe hole, and waxed lyght and jocounde, and sange and daunced—

¶That agayne Sir Gareth and Dame Lyonesse were so hoote in brennynge love that they made their covenauntes, at the tenthe nyght aftir, that she sholde com to his bedde. And because he was wounded afore, he leyde his armour and his swerde nygh his beddis syde.

3. I.e., in two.
4. I.e., am ashamed.
5. She.
6. I.e., stuck, joined.

¶And ryght as she promysed she com.   [23]

¶And she was nat so sone in his bedde but she aspyed an armed
knyght commynge towarde the bed, and anone she warned Sir
Gareth—and lyghtly, thorow the good helpe of Dame Lyonesse, he
was armed; and they hurled togydyrs with grete ire and malyce all   5
aboute the halle.

¶And there was grete lyght as hit had be the numbir of twenty
torchis bothe byfore and behynde.

¶So Sir Gareth strayned hym so that his olde wounde braste ayen
on bledynge; but he was hote and corragyous and toke no kepe,   10
but with his grete forse he strake downe the knyght, and voyded
hys helme, and strake of his hede.

¶Than he hew the hede uppon[7] an hondred pecis, and whan he
had done so he toke up all tho pecis and threw them oute at a
wyndow into the dychis of the castell. And by[8] this done, he was   15
so faynte that unnethis he myght stonde for bledynge, and by than
he was allmoste unarmed, he felle in a dedly sowne in the floure.[9]

¶Than Dame Lyonesse cryed, that Sir Gryngamoure herde her; and
whan he com and founde Sir Gareth in that plyght he made grete
sorow. And there he awaked Sir Gareth and gaff hym a drynke that   20
releved hym wondirly well.

¶But the sorow that Dame Lyonesse made there may no tunge   fol.135r
telle, for she so fared with hirself as she wolde have dyed.

¶Ryght so come this damesell Lyonett before hem all, and she
had fette all the gobbettis of the hede that Sir Gareth had throwe   25
oute at the wyndow; and there she anoynted hit as she dud tofore,
and put them to the body in the syght of hem all.

¶"Well, damesell Lyonett," seyde Sir Gareth, "I have nat deserved
all this dyspyte that ye do unto me." "Sir knyght," she seyde, "I
have nothynge done but I woll avow hit, and all that I have done   30
shall be to your worshyp and to us all."

¶Than was Sir Gareth staunched of his bledynge; but the lechis
seyde there was no man that bare the lyff[1] sholde heale hym thorowly of his wounde but yf they heled them that caused the stroke
by enchauntemente.[2]   35

¶So leve we Sir Gareth there wyth Sir Gryngamour and his sisters,
and turne we unto Kyng Arthure that at the nexte feste of Pentecoste
[helde his feest]. There cam the Grene Knyght and fyfty knyghtes
with hym, and yeldyd them all unto Kynge Arthure. Than there com
the Rede Knyghte, his brother, and yelded hym to Kynge Arthure   40
wyth three score knyghtes with hym.

¶Also there com the Blew Knyght, his brother, [with an honderd
knyghtes] and yelded hem to Kyng Arthure. And the Grene Knyghtes name was Sir Partholype, and the Rede Knyghtes name was Sir
Perymones, and the Blew Knyghtes name was Sir Persaunte of Inde.   45

---

7. I.e., into.
8. I.e., with.
9. I.e., floor.
1. *bare the lyff:* was alive.
2. *but yf they . . . stroke by enchauntemente:* unless those who caused the enchanted stroke
   healed his wounds.

Thes three bretherne tolde Kynge **Arthure** how they were overcom
by a knyght that a damesell had with hir, and she called hym Sir
Bewmaynes.

"Jesu!" seyde the Kynge, "I mervayle what knyght he is and of
what lynage he is com. Here he was with me a twelvemonthe, and
poorely and shamefully he was fostred—and Sir **Kay** in scorne
named hym **Bewmaynes**." So ryght as the Kynge stode so talkyng
with thes three bretherne, there com Sir **Launcelot du Lake** and tolde
the Kynge that there was com a goodly lorde with fyve hondred
knyghtys with hym.

⸿Than the Kynge was at **Carlyon**, for there was the feste holde,
and thidir com to hym this lorde and salewed the Kynge with
goodly maner.

⸿"What wolde ye?" seyde Kynge **Arthure**, "and what is your
erande?" "Sir," he seyde, "I am called the Rede Knyght of the Rede
Laundis, but my name Sir **Ironsyde**. And, sir, wete you well, hydir
I am sente unto you frome a knyght that is called Sir **Bewmaynes**,
for he wanne[3] me in playne batayle hande-for-hande[4]—and so ded
never knyght but he that ever had the bettir of me this twenty
wyntir—and I am commaunded to yelde me to you at your wyll."

⸿"Ye ar welcom," seyde the Kynge, "for ye have bene longe a
grete foo of owres, to me and to my courte; and now, I truste to
God, I shall so entrete you that ye shall be my frende." "Sir, bothe
I and thes fyve hondred knyghtes shall allwayes be at your sommons to do you suche servyse as may lye in oure powers."

⸿"Gramercy," seyde Kynge **Arthure**, "I am muche beholdyng unto
that knyght that hath so put his body in devoure[5] to worshyp me
and my courte—

⸿"And as to the, Sir **Ironsyde**, that is called the Rede Knyght of
the Rede Laundys, thou arte called a perelouse knyght; and yf thou
wolte holde of[6] me, I shall worshyp the and make the knyght of
the Table Rounde, but than thou muste be no man-murtherer."

⸿"Sir, as to that, I have made my promyse unto Sir **Bewmaynes**
never more to use such customs, for all the shamefull customs
that I used I ded hit at the requeste of a lady that I loved. And
therefore I muste goo unto Sir **Launcelot** and unto Sir **Gawayne** and
aske them forgyffnesse of the evyll wyll I had unto them; for all
tho that I put to deth was all only for the love of Sir **Launcelot** and
of Sir **Gawayne**." "They bene here," seyde the Kynge, "before the:
now may ye sey to them what ye woll."

⸿And than he kneled downe unto Sir **Launcelot** and to Sir
Gawayne, and prayde them of forgeffnesse of his enmyté that he
had ayenste them.

⸿Than goodly they seyde all at onys, "God forgyff you, and we
do. And we pray you that ye woll telle us where we may fynde Sir
Bewmaynes." "Fayre lorde," sayde Sir **Ironsyde**, "I can nat telle you,

---

3. I.e., defeated.
4. I.e., hand-to-hand.
5. *Put his body in devoure:* put himself at mortal risk.
6. *Holde of:* owe alliegance to.

for hit is full harde to fynde hym—for such yonge knyghtes as he is, whan they be in their adventures, bene never abydyng in no place." But to sey the worshyp that the Rede Knyght of the Rede Laundys and Sir Persaunte and his bretherne seyde by hym, hit was mervayle to hyre.   5

¶"Well, my fayre lordys," seyde Kynge Arthure, "wete you well I shall do you honour for the love of Sir Bewmaynes; and as sone as ever I may mete with hym I shal make you all uppon a day knyghtes of the Table Rounde. And as to the, Sir Persaunte of Inde, thou hast bene ever called a full noble knyght, and so hath evermore thy   10
three bretherne bene called. But I mervayle," seyde the Kynge, "that I here nat of the Blak Knyght, your brother. He was a full noble knyght."

¶Sir," seyde Pertolype the Grene Knyght—

¶"Sir Bewmaynes slew hym in a recountir with hys spere: his   15
name was Sir Perarde." "That was grete pyté," seyde the Kynge—and so seyde many knyghtes, for thes foure brethyrne were full well knowyn in Kynge Arthures courte for[7] noble knyghtes, for long tyme they had holdyn werre ayenste the knyghtes of the Rownde Table.   20

Than Partolype the Grene Knyght tolde the Kyng that at a passage of the watir of Mortayse there encountird Sir Bewmaynes with too bretherne that ever for the moste party kepte that passage, and they were two dedly knyghtes. And there he slew the eldyst brother in the watir, and smote hym uppon the hede suche a buffette that   *fol.136v*   25
he felle downe in the watir and there was he drowned: and his name was Sir Garrarde le Brewse. And aftir he slew the other brother uppon the londe: hys name was Sir Arnolde le Brewse. So than the   [25,26]
Kynge [and they] wente to mete and were served in the beste maner. And as they sate at the mete, there com in the Quene of   30
Orkenay with ladyes and knyghtes a grete numbir.

¶And than Sir Gawayne, Sir Aggravayne, and Sir Gaherys arose and wente to hir modir and salewed hir uppon their kneis and asked hir blyssynge—for of fifteen yere before they had not sene hir.

¶Than she spake uppon hyght to hir brother, Kynge Arthure,   35
"Where have ye done[8] my yonge son, Sir Gareth? For he was here amongyst you a twelvemonthe, and ye made a kychyn knave of hym—the whyche is shame to you all—

¶"Alas, where have ye done my nowne dere son that was my joy and blysse?"   40

¶"A, dere modir," seyde Sir Gawayne, "I knew hym nat." "Nothir I," seyde the Kynge. "That now me repentys, but, thanked be God, he is previd a worshypfull knyght as ony that is now lyvyng of his yerys—and I shall nevir be glad tyll that I may fynde hym."

¶"A, brothir!" seyde the quene, "ye dud yourself grete shame   45
whan ye amongyst you kepte my son in the kychyn and fedde hym lyke an hogge."

7. I.e., as.
8. I.e., put.

❡"Fayre sistir," seyde Kynge Arthure, "ye shall ryght well wete that I knew hym nat, nother no more dud Sir Gawayne nothir his bretherne. But sytthe hit is so," seyde the Kynge, "that he thus is gone frome us all, we muste shape a remedy to fynde hym—

❡"Also, sistir, mesemyth ye myght have done me to wete of his commynge; and than, if I had nat done well to hym, ye myght have blamed me; for whan he com to this courte, he cam lenynge uppon too mennys sholdyrs as though he myght nat have gone.[9] And than he asked me three gyfftys; and one he asked that same day, and that was that I wolde gyff hym mete inowghe that twelvemonthe. And the other two gyfftys he asked that day twelvemonthe, and that was that he myght have the adventure of the damesel Lyonett; and the thirde, that Sir Launcelot sholde make hym knyght whan he desyred hym. And so I graunted hym all his desyre. And many in this courte mervayled that he desyred his sustynaunce for a twelvemonthe—and thereby we demed, many of us, that he was nat com oute of a noble house."

❡"Sir," seyde the Quene of Orkenay unto Kynge Arthure her brother, "wete you well that I sente hym unto you ryght well armed and horsed and worshypfully besene of his body, and golde and sylver plenté to spende."

❡"Hit may be so," seyde the Kyng, "but thereof sawe we none, save that same day that he departed frome us, knyghtes tolde me that there com a dwarff hyder suddeynely, and brought hym armour and a good horse full well and rychely beseyne; and thereat all we had mervayle frome whens that rychesse com. Than we demed all that he was com of men of worshyp."

❡"Brother," seyde the quene, "all that ye sey we beleve hit, for ever sytthen he was growyn he was [merveillously wytted, and ever he was] feythfull and trew of his promyse:

❡"But I mervayle," seyde she, "that Sir Kay dud mok and scorne hym, and gaff hym to[1] name Bewmaynes; yet Sir Kay," seyde the quene, "named hym more ryghteuously[2] than he wende, for I dare sey he is as fayre an handid man[3] [and wel disposed]—and[4] he be on lyve—as ony lyvynge."

❡"Sistir," seyde Arthure, "lat this langage now be stylle, and by the grace of God he shall be founde and he be within this[5] seven realmys. And lette all this passe, and be myrry, for he is proved to be a man of worshyp, and that is my joy."

❡Than seyde Sir Gawayne and his bretherne unto Kynge Arthure, "Sir, and ye woll gyff us leve, we woll go seke oure brother."

❡"Nay," sayde Sir Bawdwyn, "that shall not nede." And so seyde Sir Bawdwyn of Brytaygne: "For as by oure advyse, the Kynge shall sende unto Dame Lyonesse a messyngere and pray hir that she wolle come to the courte in all haste that she may—and doute ye nat

9. I.e., been able to walk.
1. I.e., as a.
2. I.e., correctly.
3. As fair-handed (i.e., noble) a man.
4. I.e., if.
5. I.e., these.

she woll com—and than she may gyff you the beste counceyle where ye shall fynde Sir Gareth." "This is well seyde of you," seyde the Kynge.

¶So than goodly lettyrs were made, and the messyngere sente forth, that nyght and day wente tyll he com to the Castell Perelous. And than the lady Dame Lyonesse was sente fore there as she was with Sir Gryngamour hir brother and Sir Gareth; and whan she undirstoode this messyngere, she bade hym ryde on his way unto Kynge Arthure, and she wolde com aftir in all the moste goodly haste.

¶Than she com unto Sir Gryngamour and to Sir Gareth, and tolde hem all how Kyng Arthure hadde sente for hir. "That is because of me," seyde Sir Gareth. "Now avyse ye me," seyde Dame Lyonesse, "what I shall sey, and in what maner I shall rule me." "My lady and my love," seyde Sir Gareth, "I pray you in no wyse be ye aknowyn where I am. But well I wote my modir is there and all my bretherne, and they woll take uppon hem to seke me; I woll that they do:

¶"But this, madam, I woll ye sey and avyse the Kynge, whan he questyons with you of me—than may ye sey this is your avyse: that, and hit lyke his good grace, ye woll do make a cry ayenst the Assumpcion of Oure Lady,[6] that what[7] knyght that prevyth hym beste, he shal welde you and all your lande:

¶"And yf so be that he be a wedded man that wynnes the degré, he shall have a coronall of golde sette with stonys of vertu to the valew of a thousand pounde, and a whyght jarfawcon."

¶So Dame Lyonesse departed. And to com off,[8] and to breff this tale—

¶Whan she com to Kynge Arthure she was nobly resseyved, and there she was sore questyonde of[9] the Kynge, and of the quene of Orkeney. And she answerde: where Sir Gareth was, she coude not tell.

¶But this muche she seyde unto Kynge Arthure: "Sir, by your avyse I woll let cry a turnemente that shall be done before my castell at the Assumpcion of Oure Lady, and the cry shall be this, that you, my lorde Arthure, shall be there and your knyghtes, and I woll purvey that my knyghtes shall be ayenste youres; and than I am sure I shall hyre of Sir Gareth." "This is well avysed," seyde Kynge Arthure. And so she departed; and the Kynge and she made grete provysion to[1] the turnemente.

¶Whan Dame Lyonesse was com to the Ile of Avylyon—that was the same ile there as hir brother Sir Gryngamour dwelled—than she tolde hem all how she had done, and what promyse she had made to Kynge Arthure. "Alas!" seyde Sir Gareth, "I have bene so sore wounded with unhappynesse sitthyn I cam into this castell that I

---

6. *Do make a cry ayenst the Assumpcion of Oure Lady:* have it proclaimed just before the Feast of the Assumption. The feast is held on August 15 to celebrate the bodily taking up of the Virgin Mary into heaven after her death.
7. I.e., whichever.
8. *Com off:* proceed.
9. I.e., by.
1. *Provysion to:* preparation for.

shall nat be able to do at that turnemente lyke a knyght; for I was never thorowly hole syn I was hurte."

¶"Be ye of good chere," seyde the damesell **Lyonett**, "for I undirtake within this fyftene dayes to make you as hole and as lusty as ever ye were." 5

¶And than she leyde an oynemente and salve to hym as hit pleased hir, that he was never so freyshe nother so lusty as he was tho.

¶Than seyde the damesell **Lyonett**, "Sende you unto Sir **Persaunte of Inde**, and assumpne hym that he be redy there with hys hole 10 assomons of knyghtes, lyke as he made his promyse;

¶"Also that[2] ye sende unto **Ironsyde** that is Knyght of the Rede Laundys, and charge hym that he be there with you wyth his hole somme of knyghtes, and than shall ye be able to macche wyth Kynge **Arthure** and his knyghtes." 15

¶So this was done, and all knyghtes were sente fore unto the Castell Perelous.

¶Than the Rede Knyght answerde and sayde unto Dame **Lyonesse** and to Sir **Gareth**, "Ye shall undirstonde that I have bene at the courte of Kynge **Arthure**, and Sir **Persaunte of Inde** and his broth- 20 erne, and there we have done oure omage as ye comaunded us:

fol.138v

¶"Also," seyde Sir **Ironsyde**, "I have takyn uppon me with Sir **Persaunte of Inde** and his bretherne to holde party[3] agaynste my lorde Sir **Launcelot** and the knyghtes of that courte; and this have I done for the love of my lady Dame **Lyonesse**, and you, my lorde Sir 25 **Gareth**." "Ye have well done," seyde Sir **Gareth**, "butt wete ye well, we shall be full sore macched with the moste nobleste knyghtes of the worlde; therefore we muste purvey us of good knyghtes where we may gete hem."

¶"Ye sey well," seyde Sir **Persaunte**, "and worshypfully." And so 30 the cry was made in Ingelonde, Walys, Scotlonde, Irelonde, and Cornuayle, and in all the Oute Iles, and in Bretayne and many contrayes, that at Oure Lady Day the Assumpsion next folowynge, men sholde com to the Castell Perelus besyde the Ile of Avylon;

¶And there all knyghtes, whan they com there, sholde chose 35 whethir them lyste to be on the tone party with the knyghtes of the castell, other to be with Kyng **Arthur** on the tothir party. And two monthis was to the day that the turnamente sholde be.

¶And so many good knyghtys that were at hir large[4] helde hem for the moste party all this tyme ayenste Kynge **Arthure** and the 40 knyghtes of the Rounde Table; and so they cam in the syde of [them of the] castell.

¶And Sir **Epynogrys** was the fyrste, and he was the Kynges son of Northumbirlonde;

¶And Sir **Palamydes** the Saresyn was another, and Sir **Safere** and 45 Sir **Segwarydes**, hys bretherne (but they bothe were crystynde), and Sir **Malegryne**, and Sir **Bryan de les Iles**, a noble knyght, and Sir

---

2. I.e., see that.
3. *Holde party:* unite.
4. *At hir large:* at large, at liberty.

Grummor Grummorson, a noble knyghte of Scotlond, and Sir Carados of the Dolowres Towre, a noble knyght, and Sir Terquyne his brother, and Sir Arnolde and Sir Gauter, two bretherne, good knyghtes of Cornuayle.

¶Also there com Sir Trystrams de Lyones, and with hym Sir Dynas the Senesciall, and Sir Saduk (but this Sir Trystrams was nat at that tyme knyght of the Rounde Table—but he was at that tyme one of the beste knyghtes of the worlde). And so all thes noble knyghtes accompanyed hem with the lady of the Castell, and with the Rede Knyght of the Rede Laundys. But as for Sir Gareth, he wolde nat take uppon hym but as othir meane knyghtis.[5]

Than turne we to Kynge Arthure that brought wyth hym Sir Gawayne, Aggravayne, Gaherys, his brethern; and than his nevewys, as Sir Uwayne le Blaunche Maynes, and Sir Agglovale, Sir Tor, Sir Percivale de Galys, Sir Lamerok de Galys. Than com Sir Launcelot du Lake with his bretherne, nevewys, and cosyns, as Sir Lyonell, Sir Ector de Marys, Sir Bors de Gaynys, and Sir Bleobrys de Gaynes, Sir Blamour de Gaynys and Sir Galyhodyn, Sir Galyhud, and many mo of Sir Launcelottys kynne; and Sir Dynadan, Sir La Cote Male Taylé, his brother, a knyght good, and Sir Sagramoure le Desyrus, Sir Dodynas le Saveage; and all the moste party of the Rounde Table. Also there cam with Kynge Arthure thes kynges: the Kyng of Irelonde, Kynge Angwysauns, and the Kynge of Scotlonde, Kynge Carados, and Kynge Uryens of the londe of Gore, and Kynge Bagdemagus and his son Sir Mellyagauns, and Sir Galahalte, the noble prynce—all thes prynces and erlys, barowns and noble knyghtes, as Sir Braundyles, Sir Uwayne les Avoutres, and Sir Kay, Sir Bedyvere, Sir Melyot de Logres, Sir Petypace of Wynchilsé, Sir Gotlake—all thes com with Kynge Arthure and mo that be nat here rehersid.

¶Now leve we of thes knyghtes and kynges, and lette us speke of the grete aray that was made within the castell and aboute the castell; for this lady Dame Lyonesse ordayned grete aray uppon hir party for hir noble knyghtys, for all maner of lodgynge and vytayle that cam by londe and by watir, that there lacked nothynge for hir party, nother for the othir party; but there was plenté to be had for golde and sylver for Kynge Arthure and all his knyghtes. And than there cam the herbygeours frome Kynge Arthure for to herborow hym and his kyngys, deukis, erlys, barons, and knyghtes.

¶Than Sir Gareth prayde Dame Lyonesse and the Rede Knyght of the Rede Laundys, and Sir Persaunte and his bretherne, and Sir Gryngamour, that in no wyse there sholde none of them telle his name, and make no more of hym than of the leste knyght that there was—"for," he seyde, "I woll nat be knowyn of neythir more ne lesse,[6] nothir at the begynnynge nother at the endyng."

¶Than Dame Lyones seyde unto Sir Gareth, "Sir, I wolde leve with you a rynge of myne; but I wolde pray you, as ye love me hertely, lette me have hit agayne whan the turnemente is done, for

fol.139r 5

[28]

10

15

20

25

30

fol.139v

35

40

45

---

5. *He wolde nat . . . othir meane knyghtis:* he would not present himself beyond the status of other ordinary knights.
6. *Of neythir more ne lesse:* i.e., by nobody.

that rynge encresyth my beawté muche more than hit is of myself—and the vertu of my rynge is this: that that is grene woll turne to rede, and that that is rede woll turne in lyknesse to grene, and that that is blewe woll turne to whyghte, and that that is whyght woll turne in lyknesse to blew; and so hit woll do of all maner of coloures; also who that beryth this rynge shall lose no bloode. And for grete love I woll gyff you this rynge."

¶"Gramercy," seyde Sir Gareth, "myne owne lady. For this rynge is passynge mete for me; for hit woll turne[7] all maner of lyknesse that I am in, and that shall cause me that I shall nat be knowyn."

¶Than Sir Gryngamour gaff Sir Gareth a bay coursor that was a passynge good horse. Also he gaff hym good armour and sure, and a noble swerde that somtyme Sir Gryngamours fadir wan uppon[8] an hethyn tyrraunte. And so thus every knyght made hym redy to that turnemente.

¶And Kynge Arthure was commyn two dayes tofore the Assumpcion of Oure Lady. And there was all maner of royalté, of all maner of mynstralsy that myght be founde.

¶Also there cam Quene Gwenyvere and the Quene of Orkeney, Sir Garethis mother. And uppon the Assumpcion day, whan Masse and matyns was done, there was herodys with trumpettis commaunded to blow to[9] the felde; and so there com oute Sir Eppynogrys, the Kynges son of Northumbirlonde, frome the castell; and there encountyrde with hym Sir Sagramoure le Desyrous, and eythir of them brake there sperys to theire handis. And than com in Sir Palomydes oute of the castell; and there encountyrd with hym Sir Gawayne, and eythir of them smote other so harde that bothe good knyghtes and their horsis felle to the erthe. And than the knyghtes of eythir party rescowed other.

¶Than cam in Sir Safer and Sir Segwarydes, bretherne to Palamydes; and there encountyrd Sir Aggravayne with Sir Safer, and Sir Gaherys encountyrd with Sir Segwarydes. So Sir Safer smote downe Sir Aggravayne, [Syr Gawayns broder, and Sir Segwarydes, Syr Saferys broder, smote downe Sir Gaherys].[1] And Sir Malegryne, a knyght of the castell, encountyrd with Sir Uwayne le Blaunche Maynes; and [Sir Uwayne] smote downe Sir Malegryne that he had allmoste broke his necke.

¶Than Sir Bryan de les Iles and Grummor Grummorson, knyghtes of the castell, encountyrde with Sir Agglovale and Sir Tor; and [Sir Agglovale and Sir Tor][2] smote them of the castell downe.

¶Than com in Sir Carados of the Dolowres Towre, and Sir Terquyne, knyghtes of the castell; and there encountyrd with hem Sir Percivale de Galys, and Sir Lamerok, his brother; and there

fol.140r

[29]

7. I.e., change, transform.
8. I.e., from.
9. *Blow to:* i.e., summon competitors to.
1. The last four words are neither in Caxton nor the Winchester MS, but are here extrapolated editorially as inevitable in context and confirmed by Wynkyn de Worde's 1498 edition.
2. These five words are supplied editorially on the same grounds as those cited in the previous note.

[encountred Syr **Percyvale** with Syre **Caradus**, and eyther brake their speres unto their handes, and thenne Syr **Turquyn** with Syre **Lamerak**, and eyther] smote downe othir, hors and man, to the erthe. And eythir partyes rescowed other and horsed them agayne. And Sir **Arnolde** and Sir **Gawter**, knyghtes of the castell, encountird wyth Sir **Brandyles** and Sir **Kay**; and thes foure knyghtes encountyrde myghtely, and brake their sperys to theyre handis.

¶Than com in Sir **Trystrams**, Sir **Saduk**, and Sir **Dynas**, knyghtes of the castell; and there encountyrd with Sir **Trystrams** Sir **Bedyvere**; and Sir **Bedyvere** was smyttyn to the erthe, bothe horse and man. And Sir **Sadoke** encountyrde wyth Sir **Petypace**, and there Sir **Sadoke** was overthrowyn. And there Sir **Uwayne les Avoutres** smote downe Sir **Dynas the Seneschall**. Than com in Sir **Persaunte of Inde**, a knyght of the castell; and there encountyrde with hym Sir **Launcelot du Lake**, and there he smote Sir **Persaunte**, horse and man, to the erthe.

¶Than come in Sir **Pertolype** frome the castell; and there encountyrde with hym Sir **Lyonell**, and there Sir **Pertolype**, the Grene Knyght, smote downe Sir **Lyonell**, brothir to Sir **Launcelot**. And all this was marked wyth noble herrodis,[3] who bare hym beste, and their namys. And than com into the felde Sir **Perimones**, the Rede Knyght, Sir **Persauntis** brothir, that was a knyght of the castell, and he encountyrde wyth Sir **Ector de Marys**; and aythir of hem smote other so harde that hir sperys and horsys and they felle to the erthe.

¶And than com in the Rede Knyght of the Rede Laundis and Sir **Gareth**, frome the castell; and there encountyrde with hem Sir **Bors de Ganys** and Sir **Bleobrys**. And there the Rede Knyght and Sir **Bors** smote other so harde that hir sperys braste and their horsys felle grovelynge to the erthe. Than Sir **Blamour** brake another spere uppon Sir **Gareth**; but of that stroke Sir **Blamour** felle to the erthe. That sawe Sir **Galyhuddyn**, and bade Sir **Gareth** kepe hym; and Sir **Gareth** smote hym anone to the erthe.

¶Than Sir **Galyhud** gate a spere to avenge his brother; and in the same wyse Sir **Gareth** served hym; and in the same maner Sir **Gareth** served Sir **Dynadan** and his brother, Sir **La Kote Male Taylé**, and Sir **Sagramoure le Desyrus**, and Sir **Dodynas le Saveage**: all these knyghtes he bare hem downe with one speare. Whan Kynge **Anguyshauns** of Irelonde sawe Sir **Gareth** fare so, he mervayled what knyght he was, for at one tyme he semed grene, and another tyme at his gaynecommynge hym semed blewe. And thus at every course that he

fol.140v

fol.141r

---

3. *Marked wyth noble herrodis:* recorded by noble heralds. Malory here links the list of knights and encounters he has just provided with the matter of serious official business. At the tournament, the heralds' records are necessary to determine the final apportioning of prizes; and on the battlefield, where the heralds would be expected to establish the identities of the dead, their records would help determine the apportioning of the knights' properties either through inheritance or as spoils of war—both motives being a common preoccupation of the nobility in Malory's time, during the Wars of the Roses—(cf. Edward IV's Act of Attainder, p. 774, and John Keegan's comments on Agincourt, p. 791, and the *Oath of a Herald*, p. 783). Malory's love of such lists has been connected with the practices of chroniclers concerned to record the past; Malory can also be considered, however, a kind of herald of Arthurian endeavor, looking to the future of the Arthurian legacy and employing the proper textual manifestation of that heraldry. Cf. Malory's comments on his own times, n. 4, p. 595 and n. 6, p. 680.

rode too and fro he chonged whyght to rede and blak, that there myght neyther kynge nother knyght have no redy cognysshauns of hym.

¶Than Kynge Anguyshaunce, the Kynge of Irelonde, encountyrde with Sir Gareth, and there Sir Gareth smote hym frome his horse, sadyll and all. And than com in Kynge Carados of Scotlonde, and Sir Gareth smote hym downe horse and man; and in the same wyse he served Kynge Uryens of the londe of Gore. And than come in Sir Bagdemagus, and Sir Gareth smote hym downe horse and man to the erthe; and Kynge Bagdemagus son, Sir Mellyagauns, brake a spere uppon Sir Gareth myghtyly and knyghtly. And than Sir Galahalte the noble prynce cryed on hyght, "Knyght with the many coloures, well haste thou justed! Now make the redy, that I may juste with the!" Sir Gareth herde hym, and gate a grete spere, and so they encountyrde togydir, and there the prynce brake his spere—but Sir Gareth smote hym uppon the buff syde of the helme, that he reled here and there, and had falle downe had nat his men recoverde hym.

¶"So God me helpe," seyde Kynge Arthure, "that same knyght with the many coloures is a good knyght!" Wherefore the Kynge called unto hym Sir Launcelot and prayde hym to encountir with that knyght. "Sir," seyde Sir Launcelot, "I may well fynde in myne herte for to forbere hym as at this tyme, for he hath had travayle inowe this day—and whan a good knyght doth so well uppon som day, hit is no good knyghtes parte to lette hym of his worshyp, and namely whan he seyth a good knyghte hath done so grete labur. For peraventure," seyde Sir Launcelot, "his quarell is here this day, and peraventure he is beste beloved with this lady of all that bene here; for I se well he paynyth hym[4] and enforsyth hym to do grete dedys. And therefore," seyde Sir Launcelot, "as for me, this day he shall have the honour; thoughe hit lay in my power to put hym frome hit, yet wolde I nat."

¶Than whan this was done there was drawynge of swerdys, and than there began a sore turnemente. And there dud Sir Lameroke mervaylus dedys of armys; and bytwyxte Sir Lameroke and Sir Ironsyde, that was the Rede Knyght of the Rede Laundys, there was a stronge batayle. And Sir Palompydes and Sir Bleobrys, betwyxte them was full grete batayle. And Sir Gawayne and Sir Trystrams mett; and there Sir Gawayne had the worse, for he pulled Sir Gawayne frome his horse, and there he was longe uppon foote and defouled.

¶Than com in Sir Launcelot, and he smote Sir Terquyn, and he hym; and than cam therein Sir Carados, his brother, and bothe at onys they assayled hym, and he, as the moste noblyst knyght of the worlde, worshypfully fought with hem bothe and helde them hote,[5] that all men wondred of the nobles[6] of Sir Launcelot. And than com in Sir Gareth, and knew that hit was Sir Launcelot that fought with tho perelous knyghtes, and parted them in sundir; and no stroke wolde he smyte Sir Launcelot. That aspyed Sir Launcelot, and demed

4. *Paynyth hym:* pains himself.
5. *Helde them hote:* pressed them hard.
6. I.e., nobility.

hit sholde be the good knyght Sir Gareth. And than Sir Gareth rode
here and there and smote on the ryght honde and on the lyffte
honde—

¶That all folkys myght well aspye where that he rode. And by
fortune he mette with his brother, Sir Gawayne; and there he put
hym to the wors, for he put of his helme. And so he served fyve or
six knyghtes of the Rounde Table, that all men seyde he put hym
in moste payne and beste he dud his dever.

¶For whan Sir Trystrams behylde hym, how he fyrste justed and
aftir fought so welle with a swerde—

¶Than he rode unto Sir Ironsyde and to Sir Persaunte of Inde, and
asked hem be their fayth, "What maner a knyght yondir knyght is
that semyth in so many dyvers coloures?"

¶"Truly mesemyth," seyde Sir Trystrams, "that he puttyth hymself in grete payne, for he never sesyth." "Wote nat ye what he is?"
seyde Ironsyde. "No," seyde Sir Trystrams. "Than shall ye knowe
that this is he that lovyth the lady of the castell, and she hym
agayne; and this is he that wanne me whan I beseged the lady of
this castell; and this is he that wanne Sir Persaunte of Inde and his
three brethirne."

"What is his name?" seyde Sir Trystrams, "and of what bloode is
he com?" "Sir, he was called in the courte of Kynge Arthure Bewmaynes, but his ryght name is Sir Gareth of Orkeney, brother unto Sir
Gawayne." "By my hede," seyde Sir Trystrams, "he is a good knyght
and a bygge man of armys; and yf he be yonge, he shall preve a
full noble knyght."

¶"Sir, he is but a chylde," he seyde, "and of Sir Launcelot he was
made knyght."

¶"Therefore is he muche the bettir," seyde Sir Trystrams. And
than Sir Trystrams, Sir Ironsyde, and Sir Persaunte and his bretherne
rode togydyrs for to helpe Sir Gareth. And than there was many
sadde strokis, and than Sir Gareth rode oute on the tone syde to
amende his helme.

¶Than seyde his dwarff, "Take[7] me your rynge, that ye lose hit
nat whyle that ye drynke." And so whan he had drunkyn he gate
on hys helme, and egirly toke his horse and rode into the felde,
and leffte his rynge with his dwarff—for the dwarf was glad the
rynge was frome hym, for than he wyste well he sholde be knowyn.[8]
And whan Sir Gareth was in the felde, all folkys sawe hym well and
playnly that he was in yealow colowres. And there he raced of
helmys and pulled downe knyghtes, that Kynge Arthure had mervayle what knyght he was; for the Kynge sawe by his horse that hit
was the same knyght, "but byfore he was in so many coloures, and
now he is but in one coloure, and that is yolowe:

¶"Now goo," seyde Kynge Arthure unto dyvers herowdys, and
bede hem ryde aboute hym, "and aspye yf ye can se what maner
of knyght he is; for I have spered of many knyghtes this day that
is uppon his party, and all sey that they knowe hym nought."

7. I.e., Give.
8. I.e., exposed, identified.

¶But at the laste an herrowde rode nyghe Sir Gareth as he coude, and there he sawe wryten aboute his helme in golde, seyynge,

This helme is sir Garethis of Orkeney

Than the heroude cryed as he were woode—and many herowdys with hym: "This is Sir Gareth of Orkenay in the yealow armys!" Thereby all the kynges and knyghtes of Kynge Arthurs party behelde and awayted; and than they presed all knyghtes to beholde hym— and ever the herrowdys cryed and seyde, "This is Sir Gareth, Kynge Lottys son of Orkeney!" And whan Sir Gareth aspyed that he was discoverde, than he dowbled his strokys and smote downe there Sir Sagramoure, and his brother Sir Gawayne. "A, brother," seyde Sir Gawayne, "I wente ye wolde [not] have smyttyn me so." Whan he herde hym sey so, he thrange here and there, and so with grete payne he gate oute of the pres, and there he mette with his dwarff.

¶"A, boy!" seyde Sir Gareth, "thou haste begyled me fowle this day of my rynge:

¶"Geff hit me faste, that I may hyde my body withall." And so he toke⁹ hit hym, and than they all wyste [not] where he was becom.

¶And Sir Gawayne had in maner¹ aspyed where Sir Gareth rode, and than he rode aftir with all his myght.

¶That aspyed Sir Gareth and rode wyghtly into the foreste; for all that Sir Gawayne coude do, he wyste nat where he was becom. And whan Sir Gareth wyste that Sir Gawayne was paste, he asked the dwarff of beste counsayle.

¶"Sir," seyde the dwarff, "mesemyth hit were beste, now that ye ar ascaped frome spyynge, that ye sende my lady Dame Lyones of the castell hir rynge." "Hit is well avysed," seyde Sir Gareth:

¶"Now have hit here and bere hit her, and sey that I recommaunde me unto hir good grace; and sey hir I woll com when I may, and pray hir to be trewe and faythfull to me as I woll be to hir."

¶"Sir," seyde the dwarff, "hit shall be done as ye commaunde me." And so he rode his way and dud his erande unto the lady.

¶Than seyde she, "Where is my knyght, Sir Gareth?" "Madam, he bade me sey that he wolde nat be longe frome you."

¶And so lyghtly the dwarff com agayne unto Sir Gareth that wolde full fayne have had a lodgynge, for he had nede to be reposed. And than fell there a thundir and a rayne, as hevyn and erthe sholde go togydir.

¶And Sir Gareth was nat a lytyll wery, for of that day he had but lytyll reste—nother his horse nor he.

¶So thus Sir Gareth rode longe in that foreste untyll nyght cam; and ever hit lyghtned and thundirde as hit had bene wylde. At the laste by fortune he cam to a castell, and there he herde the waytis uppon the wallys.

fol.143r

9. I.e., gave.
1. In some way.

¶Than Sir Gareth rode unto the barbycan of the castell, and prayed the porter fayre to lette hym into the castell.

[32]

¶The porter answerde ungoodly agayne,[2] and sayde, "Thou get-tyste no lodgynge here." "Fayre sir, sey not so, for I am a knyght of Kynge Arthurs; and pray the lorde and the lady of this castell to gyff me herborow for the love of Kynge Arthour."

5

¶Than the porter wente unto the douches and tolde hir how there was a knyght of Kynge Arthures wolde have herborow. "Latte hym in," seyde the douches, "for I woll see that knyght—and for Kynge Arthurs love he shall nat be herborowles."

10

¶Than she yode up into a towre over a gate with tourchis i-lyght.

¶Whan Sir Gareth saw that lyght, he cryed on hyghe, "Whethir thou be lorde or lady, gyaunte other champyon, I take no forse,[3] so that I may have herborow as for this nyght: and yf hit be so that I muste nedis fyght, spare me nat tomorne, whan I have rested me, for bothe I and myne horse be wery."

15

fol.143v

¶"Sir knyght," seyde the lady, "ye speke knyghtly and boldely; but wete you well the lorde of this castell lovyth nat Kynge Arthure, nother none of hys courte, for my lorde hath ever bene ayenste hym. And therefore thow were bettir nat to com within his castell:

20

¶"For and thou com in this nyght, thou muste com undir this fourme, that wheresomever thou mete hym, by [stygh] other by strete, thou muste yelde the to hym as presonere." "Madam," seyde Sir Gareth, "what is your lorde and what is his name?" "Sir, my lordys name is the Deuke de la Rouse."

25

¶"Well, madam," seyde Sir Gareth, "I shal promyse you in what place I mete youre lorde I shall yelde me unto hym and to his good grace, with[4] that I undirstonde that he woll do me no shame; and yf I undirstonde that he woll, I woll relece myself and I can with my spere and my swerde."

30

¶"Ye say wel," seyde the deuches.

¶Than she lette the drawbrygge downe; and so he rode into the halle and there he alyght, and the horse was ladde into the stable. And in the halle he unarmed hym and seyde, "Madam, I woll nat oute of this halle this nyght:

35

¶"And whan hit is daylyght, lat se who woll have ado with me; than he shall fynde me redy."

¶Than was he sette unto souper and had many good dysshis. Than Sir Gareth lyste well to ete, and full knyghtly he ete his mete— and egirly. Also there was many a fayre lady by hym, and som seyd they nevir sawe a goodlyer man—nothir so well of etynge.[5]

40

¶Than they made hym passynge good chere; and shortly, whan he had souped, his bedde was made there, and so he rested hym all nyght. And in the morne he herde Masse and brake hys faste, and toke his leve at the douches and at them all, and thanked hir goodly of hir lodgyng and of hir good chere.

45

¶And than she asked hym his name.

---

2. I.e., in return.
3. *Take no forse:* do not care.
4. I.e., provided.
5. *Nothir so well of etynge:* nor one so good at eating.

¶"Truly, madam," he seyde, "my name is Sir 𝕲areth of 𝕺rkeney—and som men call me 𝕭ewmaynes." Than knew she well hit was the same knyght that faught for Dame 𝕷yonesse. fol.144r

¶So Sir 𝕲areth departed and rode up unto a mountayne, and there mette hym a knyght; his name was Sir 𝕭endaleyne. And he seyde to Sir 𝕲areth, "Thou shalt nat passe this way, for other thou shalt juste with me othir ellys be my presonere." "Than woll I juste," seyde Sir 𝕲areth. And so they lette their horsis ren, and there Sir 𝕲areth smote hym thorowoute the body; and Sir 𝕭endelayne rode forth to his castell there besyde, and there dyed. 10

So Sir 𝕲areth wolde have rested hym fayne. So hit happed hym to com to Sir 𝕭endalaynes castell. Than his knyghtys and servauntys aspyed that hit was he that had slayne there lorde. Than they armed twenty good men and com oute and assayled Sir 𝕲areth; and so he had no spere, but his swerde, and so he put his shylde afore 15 hym, and there they brake ten sperys uppon hym. And they assayled hym passyngly sore, but ever Sir 𝕲areth defended hym as a knyght.

So whan they sawe they myght nat overcom hym, they rode [33] frome hym and toke their counceyle to sle his horse; and so they 20 cam in uppon Sir 𝕲areth, and so with hir sperys they slewe his horse—and than they assayled hym harde.

¶But whan he was on foote there was none that he raught but he gaff hym such a buffette that he dud never recover. So he slew hem by one-and-one tyll they were but foure; and there they fledde. 25

¶And Sir 𝕲areth toke a good horse that was one of theires and rode his way.

¶Than he rode a grete pace tyll that he cam to a castell, and there he herde muche mournyng of ladyes and jantyllwomen. So at the laste there cam by hym a payge; than he asked of hym, "What 30 noyse is this that I hyre within this castell?"

¶"Sir knyght," seyde the payge, "here be within this castell thirty ladyes, and all they be wydowys. For here is a knyght that waytyth fol.144v dayly uppon this castell, and he is callyd the Browne Knyght wythoute Pyté, and he is the perelust knyght that now lyvyth—and 35 therefore, sir," seyde the payge, "I rede you fle."

¶"Nay," seyde Sir 𝕲areth, "I woll nat fle, though thou be aferde of hym." Than the payge saw where cam the Browne Knyght, and sayde, "Lo, yondir he commyth!"

¶"Lat me dele with hym," seyde Sir 𝕲areth. And whan aythir of 40 othir had a syghte, they let theire horsis ren, and the Browne Knyght brake his spere, and Sir 𝕲areth smote hym thorow the body, that he overthrewe hym to the grounde sterke dede. So Sir 𝕲areth rode into the castell and prayde the ladyes that he myght repose hym. 45

¶"Alas!" seyde the ladyes, "ye may nat be lodged here."

¶"Yes, hardely,[6] make hym good chere," seyde the payge, "for 𝔑ow 𝔖ir 𝔊areth this knyght hath slayne your enemy." 𝔰lew the 𝔅rowne 𝔎nyght

¶Than they all made hym good chere as lay in theire power—

6. I.e., indeed.

but wete you well they made hym good chere, for they myght none other do, for they were but poore.

¶And so on the morne he wente to Masse, and there he sawe the thirty ladyes knele and lay grovelynge uppon dyverse toumbis, makynge grete dole and sorow. Than Sir Gareth knew well that in tho tombis lay their lordys. "Fayre ladyes," seyde Sir Gareth, "ye muste at the next feste be at the courte of Kynge Arthure, and sey that I, Sir Gareth, sente you thydir."

¶"Sir, we shall do your commaundemente," seyde the ladyes.

¶So he departed, and by fortune he cam to a mountayne; and there he founde a goodly knyght that bade hym, "Abyde, Sir knyght, and juste with me."

¶"What ar ye?" seyde Sir Gareth. "My name is," he seyde, "called Deuke de la Rowse." "A, sir, ye ar the same knyght that I lodged onys within your castell; and there I made promyse, unto youre lady that I sholde yelde me to you."

¶"A," seyde the deuke, "arte thou that proude knyght that pro-fyrde to fyght with my knyghtes? Therefore make the[7] redy, for I woll have ado wyth you."

¶So they let their horsis renne, and there Sir Gareth smote the deuke downe frome his horse; but the deuke lyghtly avoyded his horse and dressed his shylde and drew his swerde, and bade Sir Gareth alyght and fyght with hym. So he dud alyght, and they dud grete batayle togedyrs more than an houre, and eythir hurte other full sore; but at the laste Sir Gareth gate the deuke to the erthe, and wolde have slayne hym—and than he yelded hym.

¶"Than muste ye go," seyde Sir Gareth, "unto Kynge Arthure, my lorde, at the next hyghe feste, and sey that I, Sir Gareth, sente you thydir."

¶"We shall do this," seyde the deuke, "and I woll do you omage and feauté[8] wyth an hondredsom of knyghtes with me, and all the dayes of my lyff to do you servyse where ye woll commaunde me."

¶So the deuke departed, and Sir Gareth stoode there alone. And as he stoode he sey an armed knyght on horsebak commynge towarde hym.

¶Than Sir Gareth mownted uppon horsebak, and so withoute ony wordis they ran togedir as thundir. And there that knyght hurte Sir Gareth undir the syde with his spere; and than they alyght and drewe there swerdys and gaff grete strokys, that the bloode trayled downe to the grounde—and so they fought two owres.

¶So at the laste there com the damesell Lyonette that som men calle the Damesell Savyage. And she com rydynge uppon an ambe-lynge mule, and there she cryed all on hygh, "Sir Gawayne, leve thy fyghtynge with thy brothir, Sir Gareth!" And whan he herde hir sey so, he threwe away his shylde and his swerde, and ran to Sir Gareth and toke hym in his armys, and sytthen kneled downe and asked hym mercy.

7. thee.
8. On feudal custom, see n. 6, p. 9.

¶"What ar ye," seyde Sir Gareth, "that ryght now were so stronge and so myghty, and now so sodeynly is yelde to me?"

¶"A, Sir Gareth, I am your brother, Sir Gawayne, that for youre sake have had grete laboure and travayle."

¶Than Sir Gareth unlaced hys helme, and kneled downe to hym and asked hym mercy. Than they arose bothe, and braced eythir othir in there armys, and wepte a grete whyle or they myght speke; and eythir of them gaff other the pryse of the batayle, and there were many kynde wordys betwene them.

"Alas, my fayre brother," seyde Sir Gawayne, "I ought of ryght to worshyp you, and[9] ye were nat my brother; for ye have worshipte Kynge Arthure and all his courte, for ye have sente mo worshypfull knyghtes this twelvemonthe than fyve[1] the beste of the Rounde Table hath done, excepte Sir Launcelot." Than cam the Lady Savy-aige, that was the Lady Lyonet that rode with Sir Gareth so long; and there she dud staunche Sir Gareths woundis and Sir Gawaynes. "Now what woll ye do?" seyde the Damesell Saveaige. "Mesemyth hit were beste that Kynge Arthure had wetynge of you bothe, for your horsis ar so brused that they may not beare."

¶"Now, fayre damesell," seyde Sir Gawayne, "I pray you ryde unto my lorde, myne unkle Kynge Arthure, and tell hym what adventure is betydde me[2] here, and I suppose he woll nat tary longe."

¶Than she toke hir mule and lyghtly she rode to Kynge Arthure, that was but two myle thens.

¶And whan she had tolde hir tydynges to the Kynge, the Kynge bade, "Gete me a palferey!" And whan he was on horsebak he bade the lordys and ladyes com aftir and they wolde; and there was sadelyng and brydelyng of quenys and prynces horsis—and well was he that sonneste myght be redy.

¶So whan the Kynge cam there, he saw Sir Gawayne and Sir Gareth sitt uppon a lytyll hyllys syde.

¶Than the Kynge avoyded his horse, and whan he cam nye to Sir Gareth he wolde a[3] spokyn and myght nat—and therewyth he sanke downe in a sowghe for gladnesse. And so they sterte unto theire uncle and requyred hym of his good grace to be of good comforte. Wete you well the Kynge made grete joy; and many a peteuous complaynte he made to Sir Gareth—and ever he wepte as he had bene a chylde.

¶So with this com his modir, the Quene of Orkeney, Dame Morgawse; and whan she saw Sir Gareth redyly in the vysage she myght nat wepe, but sodeynly felle downe in a sowne and lay there a grete whyle lyke as she had bene dede. And than Sir Gareth recomforted hir in suche wyse that she recovirde and made good chere.

¶Than the Kynge commaunded that all maner of knyghtes that were undir his obeysaunce sholde make their lodgynge ryght there, for the love of his two nevewys. And so hit was done, and all maner

9. I.e., even if.
1. I.e., five of.
2. *Is betydde me*: has happened to me.
3. I.e., have.

of purveyans purveyde, that there lacked nothynge that myght be gotyn for golde nother sylver, nothir of wylde nor tame.[4]

¶And than by the meanys of the Damesell Saveaige, Sir Gawayne and Sir Gareth were heled of their woundys; and there they sug-geourned eyght dayes.

¶Than seyde Kynge Arthure unto the Damesell Saveaige, "I mer-vayle that youre sistyr, Dame Lyonesse, comyth nat hydir to me; and in especiall that she commyth nat to vysyte hir knyght, my nevewe, Sir Gareth, that hath had so muche travayle for hir love."

¶"My lorde," seyde the Damesell Lyonette, "ye muste of your good grace holde hir excused, for she knowyth nat that my lorde Sir Gareth is here."

¶"Go ye than for hir," seyde Kynge Arthure, "that we may be apoynted what is beste to done accordynge to the plesure of my nevewe."

¶"Sir," seyde the damesell, "hit shall be do." And so she rode unto hir sistir; and as lyghtly as she myght make hir redy she cam on the morne with hir brother, Sir Gryngamour, and with hir fourty knyghtes. And so whan she was com she had all the chere that myght be done bothe of the Kynge and of many other kynges, and also quenys.

¶And amonge all thes ladyes she was named the fayryst and pyereles.

¶Than whan Sir Gareth mette with hir, there was many a goodly loke and goodly wordys, that all men of worshyp had joy to beholde them.

¶Than cam Kynge Arthure and many othir kynges, and Dame Gwenyvere, and Quene Morgawse, his modir. And there the Kynge asked his nevew, Sir Gareth, whether he wolde have this lady as paramour, other ellys to have hir to his wyff.

¶"My lorde, wete you well that I love hir abovyn all ladyes lyvynge."

¶"Now, fayre lady," sayde Kynge Arthure, "what sey ye?"

¶"My moste noble Kynge," seyde Dame Lyonesse, "wete you well that my lorde Sir Gareth ys to me more lever to have and welde as my husbonde than ony kyng other prynce that is crystyned; and if I may nat have hym, I promyse you I woll never have none—for, my lorde Arthure," seyde Dame Lyonesse, "wete you well he is my fyrste love, and he shall be the laste; and yf ye woll suffir hym to have his wyll and fre choyse, I dare say he woll have me."

¶"That is trouthe," seyde Sir Gareth, "and I have nat you and welde you as my wyff, there shall never lady nother jantyllwoman rejoyse[5] me."

¶"What, nevew," seyde the Kynge, "is the wynde in that dore?[6]

¶"For wete you well I wolde nat for the stynte of my crowne to be causer to withdraw your hertys:

¶"And wete you well ye can nat love so well but I shall rather

---

4. *Nothir of wylde nor tame:* neither hunted nor domestic meat.
5. I.e., enjoy, possess.
6. *Is the wynde in that dore:* i.e., is that the way things are.

5

10

15

20

[35]

25

30

fol.146v

35

40

45

encrece hyt than discrece hit; and also ye shall have my love and
my lordeshyp in the uttirmuste wyse that may lye in my power."

¶And in the same wyse seyde Sir 𝔊aretḫys modir.

¶So anone there was made a provysion for the day of maryaige,
and by the Kynges advyse hit was provyded that hit sholde be at
Mychaelmasse folowyng, at 𝕶yngkenaḋowne, by the seesyde—for
there is a plenteuouse contrey—and so hit was cryed in all the
placis thorow the realme. And than Sir 𝔊areth sente his somons to
all tho knyghtes and ladyes that he had wonne in batayle tofore,
that they sholde be at his day of maryage at 𝕶yngkenaḋowne, by the
seesyde.

And than Dame 𝕷yoneße and the damesell 𝕷yonet wyth Sir 𝔊ryngamour rode to their castell; and a goodly and a ryche rynge she gaff
to Sir 𝔊areth; and he gaff hir another. And Kynge 𝕬rthure gaff hir a
ryche bye of golde; and so she departed. And Kynge 𝕬rthure and his
felyshyprode towarde 𝕶yngkenaḋowne; and Sir 𝔊areth brought his
lady on the way, and so cam to the Kynge agayne, and rode wyth
hym. Lorde, the grete chere that Sir 𝕷auncelot made of Sir 𝔊areth
and he of hym! For there was no knyght that Sir 𝔊areth loved so
well as he dud Sir 𝕷auncelot; and ever for the moste party he wolde
ever be in Sir 𝕷auncelottis company.

For evir aftir Sir 𝔊areth had aspyed Sir 𝔊awaynes conducions, he
wythdrewe hymself fro his brother Sir 𝔊awaynes felyshyp; for he
was evir vengeable, and where he hated he wolde be avenged with
murther—and that hated Sir 𝔊areth.[7]

So hit drew faste to Mychaelmas, that thydir cam the lady
Dame 𝕷yoneße, the lady of the Castell Perelus, and hir sistir, the
Damesell 𝕷yonet, with Sir 𝔊ryngamour, her brother with hem, for he
had the conduyte of thes ladyes. And there they were lodged at the
devyse of Kynge 𝕬rthure. And uppon Myghelmas day the Bysshop
of Caunturbyry[8] made the weddyng betwene Sir 𝔊areth and Dame
𝕷yoneße with grete solempnyté.

¶And Kynge 𝕬rthure made Sir 𝔊aḫerys to wedde the Damesell
Saveage, Dame 𝕷yonet. And Sir 𝕬ggrabayne Kynge 𝕬rthure made to
wedde Dame 𝕷yonesßeis neese, a fayre lady: hir name was Dame
𝕷awrell. And so whan this solempnyté was done—

¶Than com in the Grene Knyght, Sir 𝕻ertolope, with thirty
knyghtes; and there he dud omage and feauté to Sir 𝔊areth, and all
thes knyghtes to holde of hym for evermore.

¶Also Sir 𝕻ertolope seyde, "I pray you that at this feste I may be
your chambirlayne."

¶"With good wyll," seyde Sir 𝔊areth, "syth hit lyke you to take
so symple an offyce."

¶Than com in the Rede Knyght wyth three score knyghtes with

fol.147r

[36]

The weddynge of Sir
𝔊areth and of Sir
𝕬ggrabayne his
brother

---

7. The enmity between Gareth and Gawain is further documented in the next section, p. 416.
   With Gareth's opinion, Malory may be trying to smoothen out an awkward transition from
   one kind of Gawain to another as reflected in a change of source; for the current tale, his
   models for a "positive" Gawain probably derive from English tradition, which celebrated
   Gawain more thoroughly than the French tradition, from which he will take the next
   section.
8. On this ecclesiastical position, see n. 9, p. 7.

hym, and dud to Sir Gareth omage and feauté, and all tho knyghtes to holde of hym for evermore.

¶And than Sir Perimones prayde Sir Gareth to graunte hym to be his chyeff butler at the hygh feste. "I woll well," seyde Sir Gareth, "that ye have this offyce and hit were bettir."[9]

¶Than com in Sir Persaunte of Inde wyth an hondred knyghtes with hym, and there he dud omage and feauté, and all his knyghtes sholde do hym servyse and holde their londis of hym for evir. And there he prayde Sir Gareth to make hym his sewear-cheyff at that hyghe feste.

¶"I woll well," seyde Sir Gareth, "that ye have hit and hit were bettir."

¶Than com in the Deuke de la Rouse with an hondred knyghtes with hym, and there he dud omage and feauté to Sir Gareth, and so to holde there londis of hym for evermore. And he requyred Sir Gareth that he myght serve hym of the wyne that day of the hyghe feste. "I woll well," seyde Sir Gareth, "and hit were bettir."

¶Than cam the Rede Knyght of the Rede Laundis that hyght Sir Ironsyde, and he brought with hym three hondred knyghtes, and there he dud omage and feauté, and all tho knyghtes to holde their londys of hym for ever. And than he asked of Sir Gareth to be his kerver. "I woll well," seyde Sir Gareth, "and hit please you."

¶Than com into the courte thirty ladyes, and all they semed wydows; and tho ladyes brought with hem many fayre jantyll-women, and all they kneled downe at onys unto Kynge Arthure and unto Sir Gareth. And there all tho ladyes tolde the Kynge how that Sir Gareth had delyverde them fro the Dolorous Towre, and slew the Browne Knyght withoute Pyté—"and therefore all we and oure ayres for evermore woll do omage unto Sir Gareth of Orkeney."

¶So than the kynges, quenys, pryncis, erlys, barouns, and many bolde knyghtes wente to mete—and well may ye wete that there was all maner of plenté and all maner revels and game, with all maner of mynstralsy that was used tho dayes.

¶Also there was grete justys three dayes, but the Kynge wolde nat suffir Sir Gareth to juste, because of his new bryde—for, as the Freynsh boke seyth, that Dame Lyonesse desyred of the Kynge that none that were wedded sholde juste at that feste.

¶So the fyrste day there justed Sir Lameroke de Gelys; for he over-threwe thirty knyghtes and dud passyng mervelus dedis of armys. And than Kynge Arthure made Sir Persaunte and his bretherne knyghtes of the Rounde Table to their lyvys ende, and gaff hem grete landys.

¶Also the secunde day there justed Sir Trystrams beste; and he overthrew fourty knyghtes, and dud there mervelus dedis of armys. And there Kynge Arthure made Sir Ironsyde, that was the Rede Knyght of the Rede Laundys, a knyght of the Table Rounde to his lyvis ende, and gaff hym grete landis.

fol.147v

fol.148r

5

10

15

20

25

30

35

40

45

---

9. *And hit were bettir:* i.e., and would do so with an even higher office.

¶Than the thirde day there justed Sir Launcelot; and he overthrew fyfty knyghtes and dud many dedis of armys, that all men wondird.

¶And there Kynge Arthure made the Deuke de la Rowse a knyght of the Table Rounde to his lyvys ende, and gaff hym grete londis to spende.[1]

¶(But whan this justis[2] was done, Sir Lameroke and Sir Trystrams departed suddeynly and wolde nat be knowyn, for the whych Kyng Arthure and all the courte was sore dysplesid). And so they helde the courte fourty dayes with grete solempnyté.

¶And thus Sir Gareth of Orkeney was a noble knyght, that wedded Dame Lyonesse of the Castell Parelus.

¶And also Sir Gaheris wedded her sistir, Dame Lyonette, that was called the Damesell Saveaige.

¶And Sir Aggravayne wedded Dame Lawrell, a fayre lady wyth grete and myghty londys, wyth grete ryches i-gyffyn wyth them, that ryally they myght lyve tyll theire lyvis ende.

¶And I pray you all that redyth this tale to pray for hym that this wrote, that God sende hym good delyveraunce[3] sone, and hastely. Amen.

Here endyth the tale of Sir Gareth of Orkeney

1. I.e., make use of.
2. This: i.e, these. Justis: i.e, jousts.
3. I.e., deliverance presumably from the imprisonment Malory mentions at the end of Aftir Thes Questis, p. 112; cf. his prayers at p. 698.

The Fyrste and the Secunde Boke of Syr Trystrams de Lyones†

Here begynnyth the fyrste boke of **Syr Trystrams de Lyones**; and who was his fadir and hys modyr; and how he was borne and fostyrd; and how he was made knyght of Kynge **Marke of Cornuayle**.

fol.148v

There was a kynge that hyght **Melyodas**, and he was lorde of the contrey of Lyones; and this **Melyodas** was a lykly knyght as ony was that tyme lyvyng. And by fortune he wedded Kynge **Markis** sister of Cornuayle, and she was called **Elyzabeth**, that was called bothe good and fayre. And at that tyme Kynge **Arthure** regned, and he was hole kynge of Ingelonde, Walys, Scotlonde, and of many othir realmys, howbehit there were many kynges that were lordys of many contreyes; but all they helde their londys of Kynge **Arthure**: for in Walys were two kynges, and in the Northe were many kynges, and in Cornuayle and in the Weste were two kynges; also in **Irelonde** were two or three kynges—and all were undir the obeysaunce of Kynge **Arthure**; so was the Kynge of Fraunce and the Kyng of Bretayne, and all the lordshyppis unto **Roome**.

[VIII. 1]
5
10
15

¶So whan this Kynge **Melyodas** had bene with his wyff, wythin a whyle she wexed grete with chylde. And she was a full meke lady, and well she loved hir lorde, and he hir agayne; so there was grete joy betwyxte hem.

20

¶So there was a lady in that contrey that had loved Kynge **Melyodas** longe, and by no meane she never cowde gete his love. Therefore she let ordayne uppon a day as Kynge **Melyodas** rode an huntynge—for he was a grete chacer of dere—and there be enchauntemente she made hym chace an harte by hymself alone tyll that he com to an olde castell, and there anone he was takyn presoner by the lady that loved hym.

25

¶Whan **Elyzabeth**, Kynge **Melyodas** his wyff, myssed hir lorde, she was nyghe oute of hir wytte; and also, as grete with chylde as she was, she toke a jantylwoman with hir and ran into the fereste suddeynly to seke hir lorde.

30
fol.149r

¶And whan she was farre in the foreste she myght no farther; but ryght there she gan to travayle faste of hir chylde,[1] and she had many grymly throwys, but hir jantyllwoman halpe hir all that she myght. And so by myracle of Oure Lady of Hevyn she was delyverde with grete paynes; but she had takyn suche colde for the defaute of helpe that the depe draughtys of deth toke hir, that nedys she

35

---

† The title is editorial. Malory names what is by far the longest section of his work only by way of division into a first and second *Boke of Syr Trystram(s) de Lyones,* the division occurring in midspeech and not corresponding to a change of source. His use of *Book* may only represent a preoccupation with the physical division of a source MS into separate volumes (see n. 9, p. 337). The primary source for this section is the French prose *Tristan;* for illustrative selections, see p. 726.

1. *Travayle faste of hir chylde:* go quickly into labor.

muste dye and departe oute of thys worlde—there was none othir boote.

¶Whan this Quene **Elyzabeth** saw that she myght nat ascape, she made grete dole and seyde unto hir jantylwoman, "Whan ye se my lorde, Kynge **Melyodas**, recommaunde me unto hym and tell hym what paynes I endure here for his love, and how I muste dye here for his sake for defawte of good helpe, and lat hym wete that I am full sory to departe oute of this worlde fro hym:

¶"Therefore pray hym to be frende to my soule—

¶"Now lat me se my lytyll chylde, for whom I have had all this sorow." And whan she sye hym she seyde thus: "A, my lytyll son, thou haste murtherd thy modir! And therefore, I suppose, thou that arte a murtherer so yonge, thow arte full lykly to be a manly man in thyne ayge; and bycause I shall dye of the byrth of the,[2] I charge my jantyllwoman that she pray my lorde, the Kynge **Mely-odas**, that whan he is crystened let calle hym **Trystrams**, that is as muche to say as 'a sorowfull byrth.' "

¶And therewith the quene gaff up the goste and dyed. Than the jantyllwoman leyde hir undir an umbir of a grete tre, and than she lapped the chylde as well as she myght fro colde.

¶Ryght so there cam the barowns of Kynge **Melyodas** folowyng aftir the quene; and whan they sye that she was dede, and undir-stode none othir but that the kynge was destroyed—

¶Than sertayne of them wolde have slayne the chylde bycause they wolde have bene lordys of that contrey of **Lyonesse**. But than, thorow the fayre speche of the jantyllwoman and by the meanys that she made, the moste party of the barowns wolde nat assente thereto. But than they latte cary home the dede quene, and muche sorow was made for hir. Than this meanewhyle **Merlyon** had dely-verde Kynge **Melyodas** oute of preson on the morne aftir his quene was dede—and so whan the kynge was com home, the moste party of the barowns made grete joy.

¶But the sorow that the kynge made for his quene, there myght no tonge tell.

¶So than the kynge let entyre[3] hir rychely, and aftir he let crys-tyn his chylde as his wyff had commaunded byfore hir deth.

¶And than he lette calle hym **Trystrams**, "the sorowfull-borne chylde."

¶Than Kynge **Melyodas** endured aftir that seven yere withoute a wyff, and all this tyme **Trystrams** was forstred well.

¶Than hit befelle that the Kynge **Melyodas** wedded Kynge **How-ellys** of Bretaynes doughter; and anone she had chyldirne by Kynge **Melyodas**. Than was she hevy and wroth that hir chyldirne sholde nat rejoyse[4] the contrey of **Lyonesse**, wherefore this quene ordayned for to poyson yong **Trystrams**. So at the laste she let poyson be putt in a pees of sylver in the chambir where **Trystrams** and hir chyldir were togydyrs, unto that entente that whan **Trystrams** were thirsty

[2]

fol.149v

2. Thee.
3. I.e., inter.
4. I.e., enjoy possession of.

he sholde drynke that drynke. And so hit felle uppon a day, the quenys son, as he was in that chambir, aspyed the pyese with poyson, and he wente hit had bene good drynke; and because the chylde was thirsty he toke the pyese with poyson and dranke frely, and therewith the chylde suddaynly braste and was dede.

¶So whan the quene of Melyodas wyste of the deth of hir sone, wete you well that she was hevy—but yet the kynge undirstood nothynge of hir treson. Notwythstondynge, the quene wolde not leve by this, but effte she lette ordeyne more poyson and putt hit in a pyese. And by fortune Kyng Melyodas, hir husbonde, founde the pyese with wyne wherein was the poyson, and as he that was thirstelew toke the pyse for to drynke; and as he wolde have drunken thereof, the quene aspyed hym and ran unto hym and pulde the pyse from hym sodeynly.

¶The kynge mervayled of hir why she ded so, and remembred hym suddaynly how hir son was slayne with poyson. And than he toke hir by the honde, and sayde, "Thou false traytoures, thou shalt telle me what maner of drynke this is, other ellys I shall sle the!" And therewith he pulde oute his swerde and sware a grete othe that he sholde sle hir but yf she tolde hym the trouthe.

¶"A! mercy, my lorde," she seyde, and I shall telle you all." And than she tolde hym why she wolde have slayne Trystrams, because her chyldir sholde rejoyse his londe.

¶"Well" seyde the kynge, "and therefore ye shall have[5] the lawe." And so she was dampned by the assente of the barownes to be brente; and ryght as she was at the fyre to take hir execussion, this same yonge Trystrams kneled byfore his fadir Kynge Melyodas and besought hym to gyff hym a done. "I woll well," seyde the kynge. Than seyde yonge Trystrams, "Geff me the lyff of your quene, my stepmodir."

¶"That is unryghtfully asked," seyde the Kynge Melyodas, "for thou oughte of ryght to hate hir, for she wolde have slayne the with poyson—and for thy sake moste[6] is my cause that she sholde be dede."

¶"Sir," seyde Trystrams, "as for that, I beseche you of your mercy that ye woll forgyff hir; and as for my parte, God forgyff hir, and[7] I do. And hit lyked[8] so muche youre hyghenesse to graunte me my boone, for Goddis love I requyre you holde your promyse."

¶"Sytthen hit is so," seyde the kynge, "I woll that ye have hir lyff," and sayde, "I gyff hir you, and go ye to the fyre and take hir and do with hir what ye woll."

¶So thus Sir[9] Trystramps wente to the fyre, and by the commaundemente of the Kynge delyverde hir frome the deth.

¶But afftir that Kynge Melyodas wolde never have ado with hir

fol.150r

fol.150v

---

5. I.e., be subject to.
6. I.e., greatest.
7. I.e., if.
8. *And hit lyked:* since it pleased.
9. Tristram has yet to be knighted, but the error here—committed either by Malory himself or a later copyist—no doubt springs from Tristram's preexisting fame as a great knight of the Round Table.

as at bedde and at bourde. But by the meanys of yonge **Trystrams**, he made the kynge and hir accorded—but than the kynge wolde nat suffir yonge **Trystrams** to abyde but lytyll in his courte.

¶And than he lett ordayne a jantyllman that was well lerned and taught, and his name was **Governayle**; and than he sente yonge **Trys-trams** with **Governayle** into Fraunce to lerne the langage and nur-ture[1] and dedis of armys. And there was **Trystrams** more than seven yere.

¶So whan he had lerned what he myght in tho contreyes, than he com home to his fadir Kynge **Melyodas** agayne. And so **Trystrams** lerned to be an harper passyng all other, that there was none suche called in no contrey; and so in harpynge and on instrumentys of musyke in his youthe he applyed hym for to lerne. And aftir, as he growed in myght and strength, he laboured in huntynge and in hawkynge—never[2] jantylman more that ever we herde rede[3] of.

¶And as the booke seyth, he began good mesures of blowynge[4] of beestes of venery and beestes of chaace,[5] and all maner of ver-maynes, and all the tearmys we have yet[6] of hawkynge and hun-tynge. (And therefore the booke of [venery, of haukynge and huntynge is called "the book of] Sir **Trystrams**"[7]—wherefore, as me semyth, all jantyllmen that beryth olde armys[8] ought of ryght to honoure Sir **Trystrams** for the goodly tearmys that jantylmen have and use and shall do unto the Day of Dome, that thereby in a maner all men of worshyp may discover a jantylman frome a yoman and a yoman frome a vylayne. For he that jantyll is woll drawe hym to jantyll tacchis, and to folow the noble customys of jantylmen.)[9]

¶Thus **Trystrams** enduryd in **Lyonesse** unto that he was stronge and bygge, unto the ayge of eyghtene yere. And than Kyng **Melyodas** had grete joy of yonge **Trystrams**—and so had the quene, his wyff; for ever aftir in hir lyff, because Sir **Trystrams** saved hir frome the fyre, she ded never hate hym more afftir, but ever loved hym and gaff hym many grete gyfftys. For every astate loved hym, where[1] that he wente.

¶Than hit befelle that Kynge **Angwysh of Irelonde** sente unto Kynge **Marke of Cornuayle** for his trwayge that Cornuayle had payde many wyntyrs, and at that tyme Kynge **Marke** was behynde of the trwayge for seven yerys. And Kynge **Marke** and his barownes gaff

[3]

5

10

15

20

25

fol.151r   30

35

[4]

---

1. I.e., discipline.
2. I.e., never did.
3. I.e., read aloud in tales.
4. *Mesures of blowynge:* hunting-horn calls.
5. *Beestes of venery:* the hart, the hare, the boar, and the wolf. *Beestes of chaace:* the buck, the doe, the fox, the marten, and the roe deer.
6. I.e., still.
7. Tristram's identification as a source of wisdom on the arts of hunting appears to be an English tradition, also found, prior to Malory, in the Middle English romance of *Sir Tris-trem* (written in the late 13th century), and William Twiti's Anglo-Norman *Art de Venerie* (written c. 1327).
8. *Olde armys:* established heraldic credentials.
9. This parenthetical statement is one of Malory's relatively rare extemporary addresses to his readers, providing some of the most direct (though by no means complete) insights into his motivations behind writing; cf. pp. 137, 595, 625, and 680.
1. I.e., wherever.

unto the messyngers of Irelonde thes wordis and answere, that they wolde none pay, and bade the messyngers go unto their Kynge Angwysh, "and tell hym we woll pay hym no trwayge, but tell youre lorde, and[2] he woll allwayes have trwayge of us of Cornwayle, bydde hym sende a trusty knyght of his londe that woll fyght for his ryght, and we shall fynde another for to defende us."

¶So the messyngers departed into Irelonde; and whan Kynge Angwysh undyrstoode the answere of the messyngers, he was wrothe. And than he called unto hym Sir Marhalt, the good knyght that was nobly proved and a knyght of the Rounde Table—and this Marhaltt was brother unto the Quene of Irelonde. Than the kyng seyde thus: "Fayre brother, Sir Marhalt, I pray you go unto Cornewayle for my sake to do batayle for oure trwayge that we of ryght ought to have. And whatsomevir ye spende, ye shall have suffyciauntely more than ye shall nede." "Sir," seyde Sir Marhalte, "wete you well that I shall nat be loth to do batayle in the ryght of you and your londe with the beste knyght of Table Rounde, for I know them, for the moste party what bene their dedis; and for to avaunce my dedis and to encrece my worshyp, I woll ryght gladly go unto this journey."

¶So in all haste there was made purvyaunce for Sir Marhalte, and he had all thynge that hym neded, and so he departed oute of Irelonde and aryved up in Cornwayle evyn by Castell of Tyntagyll. And whan Kynge Marke undirstood that he was there aryved for to fyght for Irelonde, than made Kynge Marke grete sorow whan he undirstood that the good knyght Sir Marhalt was com; for they knew no knyght that durste have ado with hym, for at that tyme Sir Marhalte was called one of the famuste knyghtes of the worlde. And thus Sir Marhalte abode in the see, and every day he sente unto Kynge Marke for to pay the trwayge that was behynde seven yere, other ellys to fynde a knyght to fyght with hym for the trewayge. This maner of message Sir Marhalte sente unto Kynge Marke. Than they of Cornwayle lete make cryes that what knyght that wolde fyght for to save the trwayge of Cornwayle, he shold be rewarded to fare the bettir, terme of his lyff.

¶Than som of the barowns seyde to Kynge Marke, and counceyled hym to sende to the courte of Kynge Arthure for to seke Sir Launcelott du Lake that was that tyme named for the mervaylyste knyght of the worlde. Than there were other barownes, and seyde that hit was laboure in vayne bycause Sir Marhalte was a knyght of Rounde Table; therefore ony of hem wolde be loth to have ado with other, but[3] yf hit were so that ony knyght at his owne rekeyste wolde fyght disgysed and unknowyn.

¶So the Kynge and all his barownes assentyd that hit was no boote to seke aftir no knyght of the Rounde Table.

¶This meanewhyle cam the langayge and the noyse unto Kynge Melyodas how that Sir Marhalte abode faste by Tyntagyll, and

2. I.e., if.
3. I.e., unless.

fol.151v

how Kynge Marke cowde fynde no maner of knyght to fyght for hym.

¶So whan yonge **Trystrams** herde of thys he was wroth and sore ashamed that there durste no knyght in Cornwayle have ado with Sir **Marhalte** of Irelonde. Therewithall **Trystrams** wente unto his fadir, Kynge **Melyodas**, and asked hym counceyle what was beste to do for to recovir Cornwayle frome bondage. "For as me semyth," seyde **Trystrams**, "hit were shame that Sir **Marhalte**, the quenys brother of Irelonde, sholde go away onles that he were foughtyn withall."

"As for that," seyde Kynge **Melyodas**, "wete you well, sonne **Trys-tramys**, that Sir **Marhalte** ys called one of the beste knyghtes of the worlde; and therefore I know no knyght in this contrey is able to macche hym." "Alas," seyde Sir **Trystrams**, "that I were nat made knyght! And yf Sir **Marhalte** sholde thus departe into Irelonde, God let me never have worshyp.[4] And sir," seyde **Tristrams**, "I pray you, gyff me leve to ryde to Kynge **Marke**; and so ye woll nat be displesed, of Kynge **Marke** woll I be made knyght." "I woll well," seyde Kynge **Melyodas**, "that ye be ruled as youre corrage woll rule you."

¶Than **Trystrams** thanked his fadir, and than he made hym redy to ryde into Cornwayle.

¶So in the meanewhyle there com lettyrs of love fro Kynge **Far-amon of Fraunces** doughter unto Syr **Trystrams** that were peteuous lettyrs; but in no wyse **Trystrams** had no joy of hir lettyrs nor regarde unto hir. Also she sente hym a lytyll brachet that was passynge fayre. But whan the kynges doughter undirstoode that **Trystrams** wolde nat love hir, as the booke seyth, she dyed. And than the same squyre that brought the lettyrs and the brachet cam ayen unto Sir **Trystrams**—as aftir ye shall here in the tale folowynge.

So aftir this yonge **Trystrames** rode unto hys eme, Kynge **Marke** of Cornwayle, and whan he com there he herde sey that there wolde no knyght fyght with Sir **Marhalt**. "Sir," seyde **Trystrams**, "yf ye woll gyff me the ordir of knyghthode, I woll do batayle with Sir **Marhalte**." "What[5] ar ye?" seyde the kynge, "and frome whens be ye com?"

"Sir," seyde **Trystrames**, "I com frome Kynge **Melyodas** that wed-ded your systir—and a jantylman, wete you welle, I am." So Kyng **Marke** behylde **Trystrams** and saw that he was but a yonge man of ayge, but he was passyngly well made and bygge.

¶"Fayre sir," seyde the kynge, "what is your name and where were ye borne?" "Sir, my name is **Trystrams**, and in the contrey of **Lyonesse** was I borne." "Ye sey well," seyde the kynge, "and yf ye woll do this batayle I shall make you knyght." "Therefore cam I to you," seyde **Trystrams**, "and for none other cause." But than Kynge **Marke** made hym knyght; and therewithall, anone as he had made hym knyght, he sente unto Sir **Marhalte** that he had founde a yonge knyght redy for to take the batayle to the utteraunce.

4. I.e., honor.
5. I.e., Who.

[5]

fol.152r   5

10

15

How the Kynge of
Frauncis doughter
sente to Sir Tris-
trames a fayre
Brachete

25

30

fol.152v

35

40

45

¶"Hit may well be so," seyde Sir Marhalte, "but tell Kynge Marke I woll nat fyght with no knyght but he be of blood royall, that is to seye owther kynges son othir quenys son, borne of pryncis other of pryncesses."

¶Whan Kynge Marke undirstoode that, he sente for Sir Trystrams de Lyones and tolde hym what was the answere of Sir Marhalte. Than seyde Sir Trystrams, "Sytthen that he seyth so, lat hym wete that I am commyn of fadir syde and modir syde of as noble bloode as he is:

¶"For, sir, now shall ye know that I am Kynge Melyodas sonne, borne of youre owne sistir, Dame Elyzabeth, that dyed in the foreste in the byrth of me."

¶"A, Jesu!" seyde Kynge Marke, "ye ar welcom, fayre nevew, to me." Than in all the haste the kyng horsed Sir Trystrams, and armed hym on[6] the beste maner that myght be gotyn for golde othir sylver.

¶And than Kynge Marke sente unto Sir Marhalte, and dud hym to wete that a bettir man borne than he was hymself sholde fyght with hym—"and his name ys Sir Trystrams de Lyones, begotyn of Kynge Melyodas and borne of Kynge Markys sistir." Than was Sir Marhalte gladde and blyeth that he sholde feyght with suche a jantylman. And so by the assente of Kynge Marke they lete ordayne that they sholde fyght within an ilonde nyghe Sir Marhaltes shyppis; and so was Sir Trystrames put into a vessell, bothe his horse and he and all that to hym longed, bothe for his body and for his horse, that he lacked nothyng.

¶And, when Kynge Marke and his barownes of Cornwayle behelde how yonge Sir Trystrams departed with suche a caryage to feyght for the ryght of Cornwayle—

¶There was nother man nother woman of worshyp but they wepte to se and undirstonde so yonge a knyght to jouparté hymself for theire ryght.

¶So, to shortyn this tale, whan Syr Trystrams aryved within the ilonde he loked to the farther syde, and there he sawe at an ankyr six othir shyppis nyghe to the londe; and undir the shadow of the shyppys, upon the londe, there hoved the noble knyght Sir Marhalte of Irelonde. Than Sir Trystrams commaunded to have his horse upon the londe.

¶And than Governayle, his servaunte, dressed hys harneys at all maner of ryghtes,[7] and than Sir Trystrams mounted uppon his horse; and whan he was in his sadyll well apparayled, and his shylde dressed uppon his sholdir, so Sir Trystrams asked Governayle, "Where is this knyght that I shall have ado withall?" "Sir," seyde Governayle, "se ye hym nat? I wente that ye had sene hym, for yondir he hovyth undir the umbir of his shyppys, on horseback with his spere in his honde and his shylde uppon his sholdyr." "That is trouthe," seyde Sir Trystrams, "now I se hym."

¶Than he commaunded Governayle to go to his vessayle agayne—

---

6. I.e., in.
7. *At all maner of ryghtes*: in every respect.

"and commaunde me unto myne eme, Kynge **Marke**, and pray hym, yf that I be slayne in this batayle, for to entere my body as hym semyth beste. And as for me, lette hym wete I woll never be yoldyn for cowardyse; and if I be slayne and fle nat, they have loste no trewayge for me. And yf so be that I fle other yelde me as recreaunte, bydde myne eme bury me never in Crystyn buryellys. And uppon thy lyff," seyde Sir **Trystrams** unto **Govirnayle**, "that[8] thou com nat nyghe this ilonde tyll that thou see me overcom or slayne, other ellis that I wynne yondir knyght." So they departed,[9] sore wepyng.

And than Sir **Marhalte** avysed Sir **Trystrames**, and seyde thus: "Yonge knyght, Sir **Trystrams**, what doste thou here? Me sore repentys of thy corrayge, for wete thou well, I have bene assayede with many noble knyghtes, and the beste knyghtes of this londe have bene assayed of myne hondys—and also the beste knyghtes of the worlde, I have macched them; and therefore, be my counceyle, returne ayen unto thy vessell."

❡"A, fayre knyght and well proved," seyde Sir **Trystrams**, "thou shalt well wete I may nat forsake the in this quarell, for I am for thy sake made knyght, and thou shalt well wete that I am a kynges sonne borne, and gotyn uppon a quene. And suche promyse I have made at my nevewys requeste and myne owne sekynge, that I shall fyght with the unto the uttirmuste and delyvir Cornwayle frome the olde trewage—

❡"And also wete thou well, Sir **Marhalte**, that this ys the gretteste cause that thou coragyst me to have ado with the, for thou arte called one of the moste renomed knyghtes of the worlde. And bycause of that noyse and fame that thou haste, thou gevyst me corrayge to have ado with the—for never yett was I proved with good knyght. And sytthen I toke the order of knyghthode this day, I am ryght well pleased and to me moste worshyp that I may have ado wyth suche a knyght as thou arte. And now wete thou well, Syr **Marhalte**, that I caste me to geete worshyp on thy body; and yf that I be nat proved, I truste to God to be worshypfully proved uppon thy body, and to delyver the contrey of Cornwayle for ever fro all maner of trewayge frome Irelonde for ever."

❡Whan Sir **Marhalte** had herde hym sey what he wolde, he seyde thus agayne:[1] "Fayre knyght, sytthen hit is so that thou castyste to wynne worshyp of me, I lette the wete worshyp may thou none loose by me gyff thou may stonde me[2] three strokys—for I lat the wete, for my noble dedis proved and seyne, Kynge **Arthure** made me knyght of the Table Rounde."

❡Than they began to feauter there sperys, and they mette so fersly togydyrs that they smote aythir other downe, bothe horse and man.

❡But Sir **Marhalte** smote Sir **Trystrams** a grete wounde in the syde

---

8. I.e., make sure that.
9. I.e., separated.
1. I.e., in return.
2. *Stonde me:* withstand from me.

with his spere. And than they avoyded their horsis and pulde oute
their swerdys, and threwe their shyldis afore them—and than they
laysshed togydyrs as men that were wylde and corrageous.

¶And whan they had strykyn togydyrs longe, that there armys
fayled, than they leffte their strokys and foyned at brestys and   5
vysours; and whan they sawe that hit myght nat prevayle them,[3]
than they hurteled togedyrs lyke rammys to beare eythir othir
downe. Thus they fought stylle togydirs more than halffe a day,
and eythir of them were wounded passynge sore, that the blood
ran downe frome them uppon the grounde.   10

¶By than Sir Trystramps wexed more fyerser than he dud, and
Sir Marhalte fyebled,[4] and Sir Trystramps ever more well-wynded
and bygger. And with a myghty stroke he smote Sir Marhalte uppon
the helme suche a buffette that hit wente thorow his helme and   fol.154v
thorow the coyffe of steele and thorow the brayne-panne—and   15
the swerde stake so faste in the helme and in his brayne-panne
that Sir Trystramys pulled three tymes at his swerde or ever he
myght pulle hit oute frome his hede. And there Sir Marhalte felle
downe on his kneis, and the edge of his swerde leffte in hys brayne-
panne.   20

¶And suddeynly Sir Marhalte rose grovelynge[5] and threw his
swerde and his shylde frome hym, and so he ran to his shyppys
and fledde his way—and Sir Trystramps had ever his shelde and his
swerde.

¶And whan Sir Trystramps saw Sir Marhalte withdrow hym, he   25
seyde, "A! sir knyght of the Rounde Table, why withdrawyst thou
the? Thou doste thyself and thy kynne grete shame, for I am but a
yonge knyght—or[6] now I was never preved! And rather than I sholde
withdraw me frome the, I had rathir be hewyn in pyesemealys!"

¶Sir Marhalte answerde no worde, but yeode his way sore gron-   30
ynge. "Well, sir knyght," seyde Sir Trystrams, "I promyse the thy   [8]
swerde and thy shylde shall be myne; and thy shylde shall I were
in all placis where I ryde on myne adventures—and in the syght
of Kyng Arthure and all the Rounde Table."

¶So Sir Marhalte and hys felyshyp departed into Irelonde. And   35
as sone as he com to the kynge, his brother, they serched his woun-   Here is the deth of
dis, and whan his hede was serched, a pyese of Sir Trystrams swerde   Sir Marhalte, kinght
was therein founden, and myght never be had oute of his hede, for   of the Table Rounde,
no lechecraffte. And so he dyed of Sir Trystramps swerde; and that   by Sir Trystrames
pyse of the swerde the quene, his sistir, she kepte hit for ever with 40
hir, for she thought to be revenged and she myght.

¶Now turne we agayne unto Sir Trystrames, that was sore
wounded and sore for-bledde, that he myght nat within a lytyll
whyle stonde whan he had takyn colde, and unnethe styrre hym
of hys lymmes. And than he sette hym downe sofftely uppon a   45

3. *Prevayle them:* i.e., allow them to prevail.
4. I.e., (more) enfeebled.
5. I.e., headlong.
6. I.e., before.

lytyll hylle—and bledde faste. Than anone com Governayle, his man, with his vessell.

⁋And the kynge and the moste party of his barownes com with procession ayenst Sir Trystrames. And whan he was commyn unto the londe, Kynge Marke toke hym in his armys, and he and Sir Dynas the Senescyall lad Sir Tristrames into the castell of Tyntagyll; and than was he cerched in the beste maner, and leyde in his bed.

⁋And whan Kynge Marke saw his woundys he wepte hertely, and so dud all his lordys. "So God me helpe," seyde Kynge Marke, "I wolde nat for all my londys that my nevew dyed."

⁋So Sir Trystrames lay there a moneth and more; and ever he was lyke to dey of the stroke that Sir Marhalte smote hym fyrste wyth the spere—for, as the Frenshe booke seyth, the sperehede was invenymed, that Sir Trystrams myght nat be hole. Than was Kynge Marke and all hys barownes passynge hevy, for they demed none other but that Sir Trystrames sholde nat recover. Than the kynge lette sende for all maner of lechis and surgeons, bothe unto men and women; and there was none that wolde behote hym the lyff. Than cam there a lady that was a wytty[7] lady, and she seyde playnly unto the Kyng Marke and to Sir Trystrames and to all his barownes that he sholde never be hole but yf that Sir Trystrames wente into the same contrey that the venym cam fro, and in that contrey sholde he be holpyn, other ellys never.

⁋Thus seyde the lady unto the kynge. So whan the kynge undirstood hit, he lette purvey[8] for Syr Trystrames a fayre vessell and well vytayled, and therein was putt Sir Trystrames, and Governayle wyth hym; and Sir Trystrames toke his harpe with hym. And so he was putt into the see to sayle into Irelonde. And so by good fortune he aryved up in Irelonde evyn faste[9] by a castell where the kynge and the quene was. And at his aryvayle he sate and harped in his bedde a merry lay—suche one herde they never none in Irelonde before that tyme. And whan hit was tolde the kynge and the quene of suche a syke knyght that was suche an harper, anone the kynge sente for hym and lette serche hys woundys, and than he asked hym his name. Than he answerde and seyde, "I am of the contrey of Lyones, and my name is Tramtryste,[1] that was thus wounded in a batayle as I fought for a ladyes ryght."

⁋"So God me helpe," seyde Kynge Angwysh, ye shall have all the helpe in this londe that ye may have here. But in Cornwayle but late I had a grete losse as ever had kynge, for there I loste the beste knyght of the worlde; his name was Sir Marhalte, a full noble knyght and knyght of the Table Rounde." And there he tolde Sir Tramtryste wherefore Sir Marhalte was slayne.

⁋So Sir Tramtryste made sembelaunte as he had bene sory, and bettir he knew how hit was than the kynge. Than the kynge for grete favour made Tramtryste to be put in his doughtyrs awarde and

fol.155r

fol.155v

[9]

7. I.e., wise.
8. *Lette purvey:* caused to be provided.
9. *Evyn faste:* close.
1. Tristram here transposes the first and second syllables of his name to conceal his identity.

kepying, because she was a noble surgeon. And whan she had serched hym, she founde in the bottom of his wounde that therein
was poyson, and so she healed hym in a whyle—and therefore Sir
Tramtryste kyste grete love to **La Beale Isode**, for she was at that
tyme the fayrest lady and maydyn of the worlde. And there **Tram-** 5
tryste lerned[2] hir to harpe, and she began to have a grete fantasy[3]
unto hym. And at that tyme Sir **Palomydes** [the Sarasyn was in that
countrey, and wel cherysshed with the kynge and the quene; and
every day Sir **Palomydes**] drew unto **La Beale Isode** and profirde hir
many gyfftys, for he loved hir passyngly welle. 10

¶All that aspyed **Tramtryste**, and full well he knew **Palomydes** for
a noble knyght and a myghty man—and wete you well, Sir **Tram-**
tryste had grete despyte at Sir **Palomydes**, for La Beale **Isode** tolde
Tramtryste that **Palomydes** was in wyll[4] to be crystynde for hir sake.
Thus was ther grete envy betwyxte **Tramtryste** and Sir **Palomydes**. 15
Than hit befelle that Kynge **Angwysh** lett cry a grete justis and a   fol.156r
grete turnemente for a lady that was called the Lady of the Laun-
dys, and she was ny cosyn unto the kynge; and what man wanne
her, foure dayes after sholde wedde hir and have all hir londis.

¶This cry was made in Ingelonde, Walys, and Scotlonde, and 20
also in Fraunce and in Bretayne. So hit befelle upon a day, La
Beale **Isode** com unto **Tramtryste** and tolde hym of this turnemente.
He answerde and sayde, "Fayre lady, I am but a feeble knyght, and
but late I had bene dede, had nat your good ladyshyp bene—

¶"Now, fayre lady, what wolde ye that I sholde do in this mater? 25
Well ye wote, my lady, that I may nat juste." "A, **Tramtryste**," seyde
La Beale **Isode**, "why woll ye nat have ado at that turnamente? For
well I wote that Sir **Palomydes** woll be there and to do what he may.
And therefore, Sir **Tramtryste**, I pray you for to be there, for ellys
Sir **Palomydes** ys lyke to wynne the degré." 30

¶"Madam, as for that, hit may be so, for he is a proved knyght
and I am but a yonge knyght and late made—and the fyrste batayle
that ever I ded, hit myssehapped me to be sore wounded, as ye se.
But, and[5] I wyste that ye wolde be my bettir lady,[6] at that turnemente woll I be, on this covenaunte: so that ye woll kepe my coun- 35
ceyle and lette no creature have knowlech that I shall juste, but
yourself and suche as ye woll to kepe youre counceyle, my poure
person shall I jouparté there for youre sake, that peradventure Sir
Palomydes shall know whan that I com." Thereto seyde **La Beale**
Isode, "Do your beste—and as I can," seyde La Beale **Isode**, "I shall 40
purvey horse and armoure for you at my devyse." "As ye woll, so
be hit," seyde Sir **Tramtryste**. "I woll be at youre commaundemente."

¶So at the day of justys there cam Sir **Palomydes** with a blacke
shylde, and he ovirthrew many knyghtes, that all people had mer- 45

2. I.e., taught.
3. I.e., fancy, love.
4. *In wyll*: willing.
5. I.e., if.
6. *My bettir lady*: i.e., the lady I serve (in love).

vayle; for he put to the warre Sir Gawayne, Gaherys, Aggravayne, Bagdemagus, Kay, Dodynas le Savvaige, Sagramour le Desyrous, Gumrete le Petyte, and Gryfflet le Fyse de Du—all thes the fyrste day Sir Palomydes strake downe to the erthe. fol.156v

¶And than all maner of knyghtes were adrad of Sir Palomydes, and many called hym the Knyght with the Blacke Shylde. 5

¶So that day Sir Palomydes had grete worshyp. Than cam Kynge Angwyshe unto Tramtryste and asked hym why he wolde nat juste.

¶"Sir," he seyde, "I was but late hurte and as yett I dare nat aventure." Than there cam the same squyre that was sente frome the kynges doughter of Fraunce unto Sir Tramtryste, and whan he had aspyed Sir Trystrames he felle flatte to his feete—and that aspyed La Beale Isode, what curtesy the squyre made to Tramtryste—and therewithall suddeynly Sir Trystrames ran unto the squyre (his name was called Ebes le Renownys) and prayde hym hartely in no wyse to telle his name. 15

¶"Sir," seyde Hebes, "I woll nat discovir⁷ your name but yf ye commaunde me." Than Sir Trystramys asked hym what he dede in this contreys.

¶"Sir," he seyde, "I com hydir with Sir Gawayne for to be made knyght—and, yf hit please you, of your hondis that I may be made knyght." 20

¶"Well, awayte on me as⁸ tomorne secretly, and in the fylde I shall make you knyght."

¶Than had La Beale Isode grete suspeccion unto Tramtryste that he was som man of worshyp preved, and therewith she comforted herselfe and kyste more love unto hym, for well she demed he was som man of worshyp. And so, on the morne Sir Palomydes made hym redy to com into the fylde, as he dud the fyrste day, and there he smote downe the Kynge with the Hondred Knyghtes and the Kynge of Scottis. 25 30

¶Than had La Beale Isode ordayned and well arayde Sir Tramtryste with whyght horse and whyght armys, and ryght so she lette put hym oute at a prevy postren; and he cam so into the felde as⁹ hit had bene a bryght angell. And anone Sir Palomydes aspyed hym, and therewith he feautred hys spere unto Sir Trystramys, and he agayne unto hym, and there Sir Trystrams smote downe Sir Palomydes unto the erthe. And than there was a grete noyse of people: som seyde Sir Palomydes had a fall, som seyde "the Knyght with the Blacke Shylde hath a falle!"—and wete you well, La Beale Isode was passyng gladde. fol.157r 35 40

And than Sir Gawayne and his felowys nyne had mervayle who hit myght be that had smytten downe Sir Palomydes. Than wolde there none juste with Tramtryste, but all that there were forsoke hym, moste and leste. Than Sir Trystramys made Hebes a knyght and caused¹ to put hymself forth, and² dud ryght well that day; so 45

7. I.e., reveal.
8. I.e., until.
9. I.e., as if.
1. I.e., cause Hebes.
2. I.e., and Hebes.

aftir that Sir Hebes helde hym with Sir Trystrams. And whan Sir Palomydes had reseyved hys falle, wete ye well that he was sore ashamed, and as prevayly as he myght he withdrew hym oute of the fylde.

¶All that aspyed Sir Tramtryste, and lyghtly he rode aftir Sir Palomydes and overtoke hym and bade hym turne, for bettir he wolde assay hym or ever he departed.

¶Than Sir Palomydes turned hym, and eythir laysshed at other with their swerdys; but at the fyrste stroke Sir Trystrames smote downe Sir Palomydes and gaff hym suche a stroke upon the hede that he felle to the erthe.

¶So than Sir Trystrams bade hym yelde hym and do his commaundemente, other ellis he wolde sle hym.

¶Whan Sir Palomydes behylde hys countenaunce, he drad his buffettes so, that he graunted all his askynges.

¶"Well, seyde Sir Tramtryste, "this shall be youre charge: fyrst, uppon payne of youre lyff, that ye forsake my lady, La Beale Isode, and in no maner of wyse that ye draw no more to hir— fol.157v

¶"Also, this twelvemonthe and a day that ye bere none armys nother none harneys of werre. Now promyse me this, othir here shalt thou dye."

¶"Alas," seyde Sir Palomydes, "for ever I am shamed." Than he sware as Sir Trystrames had commaunded hym.

¶So for dispyte and angir Sir Palomydes kut of his harneyse and threw them awey. And so Sir Trystrames turned agayne to the castell where was La Beale Isode, and by the way he mette wyth a damesell that asked aftir Sir Launcelot that wan the Dolorous Garde;[3] and this damesell asked Sir Trystrames what he was, for hit was tolde her that hit was he that smote downe Sir Palomydes by whom the ten knyghtes of Arthures were smyttyn downe. Than the damesell prayde Sir Trystrames to telle her what he was, and whether that he were Sir Launcelot du Lake, for she demed that there was no knyght in the worlde that myght do suche dedis of armys but yf hit were Sir Launcelot.

"Wete you well that I am nat Sir Launcelot, fayre damesell, for I was never of suche proues. But in God is all; He may make me as good a knyght as that good knyght Sir Launcelot is."

"Now, jantyll knyght, put up thy vyser." And whan she behylde his vysage, she thought she sawe never a bettir mannys vysayge, nothir a bettir-farynge knyght.

¶So whan the damesell knew sertaynly that he was nat Sir Launcelot, than she toke hir leve and departed frome hym. And than Sir Trystrames rode prevayly unto the posterne where kepte[4] hym La

---

3. The story of Launcelot's conquest of the castle Dolorous Garde is not otherwise related in Malory; the story, describing Launcelot's first great adventure, holds that, after his capture of this formidable place from a tyrannical ruler, its name changed to Joyous Garde; this then became one of Launcelot's principal residences and is where he takes Gwenyvere after rescuing her from the stake (see p. 659 ff.). Launcelot renames the castle Dolerous Garde upon his expulsion from Arthur's court (see p. 670).
4. I.e., awaited.

Beale Isode, and there she made hym grete chere, and thanked
God of his good spede.

¶So anone within a whyle the kynge and the quene and all the
courte undirstood that hit was Sir Tramtryste that smote downe Sir
Palamydes, and than was he muche made of, more than he was
tofore.

¶Thus was Sir Tramtryste longe there well cherysshed with the
kynge and wyth the quene—and namely[5] with La Beale Isode. So
uppon a day the quene and La Beale Isode made a bayne for Sir
Tramtryste, and whan he was in his bayne, the quene and Isode, hir
doughter, romed up and downe in the chambir the whyles[6] Governayle and Hebes attendede uppon Tramtryste. The quene behelde
his swerde as hit lay uppon his bedde; and than at unhappis[7] the
quene drew oute his swerde and behylde hit a long whyle. And
bothe they thought hit a passynge fayre swerde; but within a foote
and an halff of the poynte there was a grete pyese thereof oute
brokyn of the edge. And whan the quene had aspyed that gappe in
the swerde, she remembirde hir of a a pyese of a swerde that was
founde in the brayne-panne of Sir Marhalte, that was hir brother.

¶"Alas," than seyde she unto hir doughter La Beale Isode, this is
the same traytoure knyght that slewe my brother, thyne eme!"

¶Whan Isode herde her sey so, she was passynge sore abaysshed,
for passynge well she loved Tramtryste, and full well she knew the
crewelnesse of hir modir the quene.

¶So anone therewithall the quene wente unto hir owne chambir
and sought hir cofyr, and there she toke oute the pyese of the
swerde that was pulde oute of Sir Marhaltys brayne-panne aftir that
he was dede. And than she ran wyth that pyese of iron unto the
swerde that laye uppon the bedde, [and whanne she putte that pyece
of stele and yron unto the swerd] hit was as mete as hit myght be
as whan hit was newe brokyn. And than the quene gryped that
swerde in hir honde fersely, and with all her myght she ran streyght
uppon Tramtryste where he sate in his bayne—and there she had
ryved hym thorowe, had nat Sir Hebes bene: he gate hir in his armys
and pulde the swerde frome her—and ellys she had thriste hym
thorowe.

¶So whan she was lette of[8] hir evyll wyll she ran to the kynge
her husbonde, and seyde, "A, my lorde!" On hir kneys knelynge,
she seyde, "Here have ye in your house that traytoure knyght that
slewe my brother and your servaunte, the noble knyght Sir Marhalte!" "Who is that?" seyde the kynge, "and where is he?" "Sir,"
she seyde, "hit is Sir Tramtryste, the same knyght that my doughter
helyd."

¶"Alas," seyde the kynge. "Therefore I am ryght hevy, for he is
a full noble knyght as ever I sawe in fylde. But I charge you," seyde

fol.158r

[11]

---

5. I.e., especially.
6. *The whyles:* while.
7. *At unhappis:* by ill-fortune.
8. *Lette of:* prevented from.

the kynge, "that ye have nat ado with that knyght, but lette me dele with hym."

¶Than the kynge wente into the chambir unto Sir Tramtryste; and than was he gone unto his owne chambir, and the kynge founde hym half redy armed to mownte uppon his horse.

¶So whan the kynge sawe hym all redy armed to go unto horsebacke, the kynge seyde, "Nay, Tramtryste, hit woll nat avayle to compare⁹ ayenste me. But thus muche I shall do, for my worshyp and for thy love—in so muche as thou arte wythin my courte, hit were no worship to sle the—therefore upon this conducion I woll gyff the¹ leve for to departe frome this courte in savyté: so thou wolte telle me who was thy fadir and what is thy name, and also yf thou slewe Sir Marhalte, my brother."

¶"Sir, seyde Tramtryste, "now I shall tell you all the trouthe. My fadyrs name ys Sir Melyodas, kyng of Lyonesse, and my modir hyght Elyzabeth, that was sister unto Kynge Marke of Cornwayle; and my modir dyed of me in the foreste, and because thereof she commaunded or she dyed that whan I was crystened they sholde crystyn me Trystrames. And because I wolde nat be knowyn in this contrey I turned my name and let calle me Tramtryste. And for the trwage of Cornwayle I fought, for myne emys sake and for the ryght of Cornwayle that ye had be possessed many yerys. And wete you well," seyde Sir Trystrames unto the kynge, "I dud the batayle for the love of myne uncle Kynge Marke, and for the love of the contrey of Cornwayle—and for to encrece myne honoure; for that same day that I fought with Sir Marhalte I was made knyght, and never or than dud I no batayle with no knyght. And fro me he wente alyve, and leffte his shylde and his swerde behynde hym."

¶"So God me helpe," seyde the kynge, "I may nat sey but ye dud as a knyght sholde do, and as hit was youre parte to do for your quarell, and to encrece your worshyp as a knyght sholde do. Howbehit I may nat mayntayne you in this contrey with my worship but that I sholde displese many of my barownes and my wyff and my kynne."

¶"Sir," seyde Sir Trystrames, "I thanke you of your good lordeship that I have had within here with you, and the grete goodnesse my lady your doughter hath shewed me. And therefore," seyde Sir Trystramys, "hit may so be that ye shall wynne² more be my lyff than be my deth; for in the partyes of Ingelonde hit may happyn I may do you servyse at som season,³ that ye shall be glad that ever ye shewed me your good lordshyp. Wyth more I promyse you, as I am trewe knyght, that in all placis I shall be my lady your doughtyrs servaunte and knyght in all ryght and in wronge, and I shall never fayle her to do as muche as a knyght may do. Also I beseche your good grace that I may take my leve at⁴ my lady youre doughter and at all the barownes and knyghtes." "I woll well," seyde the kynge.

[12]

fol.159r

---

9. I.e., contend.
1. Thee.
2. I.e., gain.
3. I.e., time, occasion.
4. I.e., from.

¶Than Sir Trystrames wente unto La Beale Isode and toke his leve. And than he tolde what he was, and how a lady tolde hym that he sholde never be hole "untyll I cam into this contrey where the poyson was made, wherethorow I was nere my deth, had nat your ladyshyp bene." "A, jantyll knyght!" seyde La Beale Isode, "full wo I am of thy departynge, for I saw never man that ever I ought so good wyll to"—and therewithall she wepte hertyly.

¶"Madam," seyde Sir Trystramps, "ye shall undirstonde that my name ys Sir Trystrames de Lyones, gotyn of a kynge and borne of a quene. And I promyse you faythfully, I shall be all the dayes of my lyff your knyght."

¶"Gramercy," seyde La Beale Isode, "and I promyse you there-agaynste I shall nat be maryed this seven yerys but by your assente; and whom that ye woll, I shall be maryed to hym and he woll have me, if ye woll consente thereto." And than Sir Trystrames gaff hir a rynge and she gaff hym another, and therewith he departed and com into the courte amonge all the barownes; and there he toke his leve at moste and leste, and opynly he seyde amonge them all, "Fayre lordys, now hit is so that I muste departe. If there be ony man here that I have offended unto, or that ony man be with me greved, lette hym complayne hym here afore me or that ever Y departe, and I shall amende hit unto my power:

¶"And yf there be ony man that woll proffir me[5] wronge, other sey me wronge other shame me behynde my backe, sey hit now or ellys never; and here is my body to make hit good, body ayenste body." And all they stood stylle; there was nat one that wolde sey one worde.

¶Yett were there som knyghtes that were of the quenys bloode and of Sir Marhaltys blood, but they wolde nat meddyll wyth hym. [13]

¶So Sir Trystramps departede and toke the see, and with good wynde he aryved up at Tyntagyll in Cornwayle. And whan Kynge Marke was hole in hys prosperité, there cam tydynges that Sir Trystrames was aryved, and hole of his woundis. Thereof was Kynge Marke passynge glad, and so were all the barownes.

¶And whan he saw hys tyme, he rode unto his fadir, Kynge Melyodas, and there he had all the chere that the kynge and the quene coude make hym. And than largely Kynge Melyodas and his quene departed[6] of their londys and goodys to Sir Trystrames. Than by the lysence of his fadir he returned ayen unto the courte of Kynge Marke. And there he lyved longe in grete joy longe tyme, untyll at the laste there befelle a jolesy and an unkyndenesse betwyxte Kyng Marke and Sir Trystrames, for they loved bothe one lady, and she was an erlys wyff that hyght Sir Segwarydes.[7] And this lady loved Sir Trystrames passyngly well, and he loved hir agayne; for she was a passynge fayre lady and that aspyed Sir Trystrames well. Than Kynge Marke undirstode that and was jeluse, for Kynge Marke loved hir passyngly welle.

¶So hit befelle uppon a day, this lady sente a dwarff unto Sir

---

5. *Proffir me*: attempt to do to me.
6. I.e., parted, distributed.
7. *She . . . hyght*: she was the wife of an earl named.

Trystrames and bade hym, as he loved hir, that he wolde be with hir the nexte nyght folowynge; "also she charged you that ye com nat to hir but yf ye be well armed"—for her lorde was called a good knyght.

¶Sir Trystrames answerde to the dwarff and seyde, "Recommaunde me unto my lady and tell hir I woll nat fayle, but I shall be with her the terme that she hath sette me." And therewith the dwarff departed.

¶And Kyng Marke aspyed that the dwarff was with Sir Trystrames uppon message frome Segwarydes wyff. Than Kynge Marke sente for the dwarff, and whan he was comyn he made the dwarff by force to tell hym all why and wherefore that he cam on message to Sir Trystrames, and than he tolde hym.

¶"Welle," seyde Kyng Marke, "go where thou wolte, and uppon payne of deth that thou sey no worde that thou spake with me."

¶So the dwarff departed. And that same nyght that the steavyn was sette betwyxte Segwarydes wyff and Sir Trystrames, so Kynge Marke armed and made hym redy, and toke two knyghtes of his counceyle with hym; and so he rode byfore for to abyde by the wayes for to wayte uppon Sir Trystrames. And as Sir Trystrames cam rydynge uppon his way with his speare in his hande, Kynge Marke cam hurlynge uppon hym, and hys two knyghtes, suddeynly, and all three smote hym with their sperys. And Kynge Marke hurt Sir Trystrames on the breste ryght sore.

¶And than Sir Trystrames feautred his spere and smote Kynge Marke so sore that he russhed hym to the erthe and brused hym, that he lay stylle in a sowne—and longe hit was or he myght welde hymselff. And than he ran to the one knyght and effte to the tothir, and smote hem to the colde erthe, that they lay stylle. And therewithall Sir Trystrames rode forth sore wounded to the lady, and founde hir abydynge hym at a postern; and there she welcommed hym fayre, and eyther halsed other in armys. And so she lette putt up his horse in the beste wyse, and than she unarmed hym; and so they soupede lyghtly and wente to bedde with grete joy and plesaunce—and so in hys ragynge[8] he toke no kepe of his grene wounde that Kynge Marke had gyffyn hym.

¶And so Sir Trystrames bledde[9] bothe the over-shete and the neyther-sheete, and the pylowes and the hede-shete. And within a whyle there cam one before, that warned her that hir lorde Sir Segwarydes was nerehonde, within a bowedrawght.

¶So she made Sir Trystrames to aryse, and he armed hym and toke his horse, and so departed.

¶So by than was Sir Segwarydes hir lorde com, and whan he founde hys bedde troubled and brokyn, he wente nere and loked by candyll-lyght and sawe that there had leyne a wounded knyght.

¶"A, false traytoures," he seyde, "why haste thou betrayde me?" And therewithall he swange oute a swerde and seyde, "But yf[1] thou telle me all [who hath ben here,] now shalt thou dey!"

5

10

fol.160v

20

[14]

25

30

35

40

45

---

8. I.e., passion.
9. I.e., bled on.
1. *But yf*: unless.

❡"A, my lorde, mercy!" seyde the lady, and helde up hir hondys, "and sle me nat, and I shall tell you all who hath bene here."

❡Than anone seyde **Segwarydes**, "Sey and tell me the trouthe." Anone for drede she seyde, "Here was Sir **Trystrames** with me, and by the way as he come to me-warde, he was sore wounded." fol.161r 5

❡"A, false traytoures! Where is he becom?" "Sir," she seyde, "he is armed and departed on horsebacke nat yett hens halff a myle."

❡"Ye sey well," seyde **Segwarydes**. Than he armed hym lyghtly and gate his horse and rode aftir Sir **Trystrames** the streyght wey unto **Tyntagyll**; and within a whyle he overtoke Sir **Trystrams**, and 10 than he bade hym, "Turne, false traytoure knyght!" And therewithall **Segwarydes** smote Sir **Trystrames** with a speare, that hit all to-braste; and than he swange oute hys swerde and smote faste at Sir **Trystrames**. "Sir knyght," seyde Sir **Trystrames**, "I counceyle you smyte no more; howbehit for the wrongys that I have done you 15 I woll forbere you as longe as I may."

❡"Nay," seyde **Segwarydes**, "that shall nat be, for other[2] thou shalt dye othir ellys I." Than Sir **Trystrames** drew oute his swerde and hurled his horse unto hym freysshely, and thorow the waste of the body he smote Sir **Segwarydes**, that he felle to the erthe in 20 sowne.

❡And so Sir **Trystrames** departed and leffte hym there. And so he rode unto **Tyntagyll** and toke hys lodgynge secretely, for he wolde nat be know that he was hurte.

❡Also Sir **Segwarydes** men rode afftir theire master and brought 25 hym home on his shylde; and there he lay longe or he were hole, but at the laste he recoverde.

❡Also Kynge **Marke** wolde nat be aknowyn[3] of that he had done unto Sir **Trystramys** whan he mette that nyght; and as for Sir **Trystramys**, he knew nat that Kynge **Marke** had mette with hym. And so 30 the kynge com ascawnce to Sir **Trystrames** to comforte hym as he lay syke in his bedde.

❡But as longe as Kynge **Marke** lyved, he loved never aftir Sir **Trystramys**. So aftir that, thoughe there were fayre speche, love was there none. And thus hit paste on many wykes and dayes, and all 35 was forgyffyn and forgetyn, for Sir **Segwarydes** durste nat have ado with Sir **Trystrames** because of his noble proues, and also because fol.161v he was nevew unto Kynge **Marke**. Therefore he lette hit over-slyppe—for he that hath a prevy hurte is loth to have a shame outewarde. 40

❡Than hit befelle upon a day that the good knyghte Sir **Bleo-** [15] **berys de Ganys**—brother unto Sir **Blamore de Ganys** and nye cosyne unto the good knyght Syr **Launcelot de Lake**—so this Sir **Bleoberys** cam unto the courte of Kyng **Marke**; and there he asked Kynge **Marke** to gyff hym a bone—"what[4] gyffte that I woll aske in this 45 courte."

❡Whan the kynge herde hym aske so, he mervayled of his

---

2. I.e., either.
3. *be aknowyn*: acknowledge.
4. I.e., whatever.

askynge, but bycause he was a knyght of the Rounde Table and of a grete renowne, Kynge Marke graunted hym his hole askynge.

¶Than seyde Sir Bleoberys, "I woll have the fayreste lady in your courte that me lyste to chose." "I may nat say nay," seyde Kynge Marke. "Now chose hir at your adventure." 5

¶And so Sir Bleoberys dud chose Sir Segwarydes wyff, and toke hir by the honde and so wente his way with her; and so he toke his horse, and made sette her behynde his squyer and rode uppon hys way.

¶Whan Sir Segwarydes herde telle that his lady was gone with a 10 knyght of Kynge Arthures courte, than he armed hym and rode after that knyght to rescow his lady.

¶So whan Sir Bleoberys was gone with this lady, Kynge Marke and all the courte was wroth that she was had away.

¶Than were there sertayne ladyes that knew that there was grete 15 love betwene Sir Trystrames and her—

¶And also that lady loved Sir Trystrames abovyn all othyr knyghtes. Than there was one lady that rebuked Sir Trystrams in the horrybelyst wyse, and called hym cowarde knyght, that he wolde for shame of hys knyghthode to se a lady so shamefully takyn away 20 fro his uncklys courte—but she mente that eythir of hem loved other with entyre herte. But Sir Trystrames answered her thus: fol.162r "Fayre lady, hit is nat my parte to have ado in suche maters whyle her lorde and husbonde ys presente here; and yf so be that hir lorde had nat bene here in this courte, than for the worshyp of this 25 courte peraventure I wolde have bene hir champyon:

¶"And yf so be Sir Segwarydes spede nat well, hit may happyn that I woll speke with that good knyght or[5] ever he passe far fro this contrey."

¶Than within a whyle com Sir Segwarydes squyres and tolde in 30 the courte that theyre master was betyn sore and wounded at the poynte of deth—"as he wolde have rescowed his lady, Sir Bleoberys overthrewe hym and sore hath wounded hym."

¶Than was Kynge Marke hevy thereof, and all the courte.

¶Whan Sir Trystrames herde of this he was ashamed and sore 35 agreved, and anone he armed hym and yeode to horsebacke—and Governayle, his servaunte, bare his shylde and his spere. And so as Syr Trystrames rode faste, he mette with Sir Andret, his cosyn, that by the commaundement of Kynge Marke was sente to brynge forth two knyghtes of Arthures courte that rode by the contrey to seke 40 their adventures.

¶Whan Sir Trystrames sawe Sir Andret he asked hym, "What tydynges?" "So God me helpe," seyde Sir Andret, "there was never worse with me, for here by the commaundemente of Kynge Marke I was sente to fecche two knyghtes of Kynge Arthurs courte, and 45 the tone bete me and wounded me, and sette nought be my messayge." "Fayre cosyn," seyde Sir Trystrames, "ryde on your way, and yf I may mete them hit may happyn I shall revenge you."

5. I.e., before.

¶So Sir Andret rode into Cornwayle and Sir Trystrames rode aftir the two knyghtes—whyche that one hyght Sir Sagramoure le Desyrous, and that othir hyght Sir Dodynas le Savyayge.

¶So within a whyle Sir Trystrames saw hem byfore hym, two lykly [16]   fol.162v
knyghtys. "Sir," seyde Governayle unto his maystir, "I wolde coun-   5
ceyle you nat to have ado with them, for they be two proved knyghtes of Arthures courte." "As for that," seyde Sir Trystrames, "have ye
no doute but I woll have ado with them bothe, to encrece my
worshyp—for hit is many day sytthen I dud any armys."[6] "Do as ye
lyste," seyde Governayle. And therewythall anone Sir Trystrames   10
asked them from whens they come and whothir they wolde, and
what they dud in those marchis.

¶So Sir Sagramoure loked upon Sir Trystrames and had scorne
of his wordys, and seyde to hym agayne, "Sir, be ye a knyght of
Cornwayle?" "Whereby askyste thou?" seyde Sir Trystrames. "For   15
hit is seldom seyne," seyde Sir Sagramoure, "that ye Cornysshe
knyghtes bene valyaunte men in armys; for within thes two owres
there mette with us one of you Cornysshe knyghtes, and grete
wordys he spake, and anone with lytyll myght he was leyde to the
erthe.   20

¶"And as I trow," seyde Sir Sagramoure, "that ye wolde have the
same hansell!"

¶Fayre lordys," seyde Sir Trystrames, "hit may so happe that I
may bettir wythstonde you than he ded; and whether ye woll or
nylle, I woll have ado with you, because he was my cosyn that ye   25
bete—and therefore here do your beste! And wete you well, but yf
ye quyte you[7] the bettir here uppon this grounde, one knyght of
Cornwayle shall beate you bothe."

¶Whan Sir Dodynas le Savyaige herde hym sey so, he gate a
speare in hys honde and seyde, "Sir knyght, kepe thyselff!" And   30
than they departed and com togydirs as hit had bene thundir; and
Sir Dodynas spere braste in sundir, but Sir Trystrames smote hym
with a more myght, that he smote hym clene over the horse croupyn, and nyghe he had brokyn his necke.

¶Whan Sir Sagramoure saw hys felow have suche a falle, he mer-   35
vayled what knyght he was. But so he dressed his speare with all   fol.163r
his myght, and Sir Trystrames ayenste hym, and so they cam togydir
as thundir; and there Sir Trystrames smote Sir Sagramour a stronge
buffette, that he bare hys horse and hym to the erthe—and in the
fallynge he brake his thyghe.   40

¶So whan this was done Sir Trystrames asked them, "Fayre
knyghtes, wyll ye ony more? Be there ony bygger knyghtys in the
courte of Kynge Arthure? Hit is to you shame to sey us knyghtes of
Cornwayle dishonour, for hit may happyn a Cornysh knyght may
macche you!"   45

¶"That is trouthe," seyde Sir Sagramoure, "that have we well
proved. But I requyre you," seyde Sir Sagramour, "telle us your

6. I.e., feats of arms.
7. *Quyte you:* acquit yourself.

name, be your feyth and trouthe that ye owghe to the hyghe order
of knyghthode."

⁋"Ye charge me with a grete thynge," seyde Sir Trystrames, "and
sytthyn ye lyste to wete, ye shall know and undirstonde that my
name ys Sir Trystrames de Lyones, Kynge Melyodas son, and nevew
unto Kynge Marke." Than were they two knyghtes fayne that they
had mette with Sir Trystrames, and so they prayde hym to abyde in
their felyshyp.

⁋"Nay," seyde Sir Trystrames, "for I muste have ado wyth one of
your felawys: his name is Sir Bleoberys de Ganys."

⁋"God spede yow well," seyde Sir Sagramoure and Sir Dodynas. [17]
So Sir Trystrames departed and rode onwarde on his way. And than
was he ware before hym in a valay where rode Sir Bleoberys wyth
Sir Segwarydes lady, that rode behynde his squyre upon a palfrey.
Than Sir Trystrames rode more than a pace untyll that he had over-
take hym.

⁋Than spake Sir Trystrames: "Abyde," he seyde, "knyght of Arthures courte; brynge agayne that lady, or delyver hir to me." "I woll
do neyther nother," seyde Sir Bleoberys, "for I drede no Cornysshe
knyght so sore that me lyste to delyver her."

⁋"Why," seyde Sir Trystrames, "may nat a Cornysshe knyght do
as well as another knyght?

⁋"Yes! This same day two knyghtes of youre courte wythin this fol.163v
three myle mette with me; and or ever we departed, they founde a
Cornysshe knyght good inowe for them bothe."

⁋"What were their namys?" seyde Sir Bleobrys. "Sir, they tolde
me that one hyght Sir Sagramoure le Desyrous and that other hyght
Sir Dodynas le Saveayge." "A!" seyde Sir Bleoberys, "have ye mette
with them?

⁋"So God me helpe, they were two good knyghtes and men of
grete worshyp; and yf ye have betyn them bothe ye muste nedis be
a good knyght. Yf hit be so ye have beatyn them bothe, yet shall
ye nat feare me, but ye shall beate me or ever ye have this lady."
"Than defende you!" seyde Sir Trystrames. So they departed and
com togydir lyke thundir, and eyther bare other downe, horse and
man, to the erthe.

⁋Than they avoyded their horsys and lasshed togydyrs egerly
with swerdys, and myghtyly, now here now there, trasyng and traversynge on the ryght honde and on the lyffte honde, more than
two owres; and somtyme they rowysshed togydir with suche a
myght that they lay bothe grovelynge on the erthe. Than Sir Bleoberys de Ganys sterte abacke and seyde thus:

⁋"Now, jantyll knyght, a whyle holde your hondes and let us
speke togydyrs." "Sey on what ye woll," seyde Sir Trystrames, "and
I woll answere you and[8] I can."

⁋"Sir," seyde Bleoberys, "I wolde wete of whens ye were, and of
whom ye be com, and what is your name." "So God me helpe,"
seyde Sir Trystrames, "I feare nat to telle you my name. Wete you

_____

8. I.e., if.

well, I am Kynge Melyodas son, and my mother is Kynge Markys
sistir, and my name is Sir Trystrames de Lyones, and Kynge Marke
ys myne uncle." "Truly," seyde Sir Bleoberys, "I am ryght glad of
you, for ye ar he that slewe [Marhalte] the knyght honde-for-honde
in the ilonde for the trwayge of Cornwayle: 5

☞"Also ye overcom Sir Palomydes, the good knyght, at the
turnemente in Irelonde where he bete Sir Gawayne and his nyne
felowys."

☞"So God me helpe," seyde Sir Trystrames, "wete you well I am   fol.164r
the same knyght: 10

☞"Now I have tolde you my name, telle me yourys with good
wyll." "Wete ye well that my name is Sir Bleoberys de Ganys, and
my brother hyght Sir Blamoure de Ganys, that is callyd a good
knyght—and we be sistyrs chyldyrn unto my lorde Sir Launcelot de
Lake, that we calle one of the beste knyghtes of the worlde." "That   15
is trouthe," seyde Sir Trystrames, "Sir Launcelot ys called pereles of
curtesy and of knyghthode—and for his sake," seyde Sir Trystramys,
"I wyll nat with my good wylle feyght no more with you, for the
grete love I have to Sir Launcelot."

"In good feyth," seyde Sir Bleoberys, "as for me, I wolde be loth   20
to fyght with you; but sytthen ye folow me here to have thys lady,
I shall proffir you kyndenes and curtesy ryght here uppon this
grounde. Thys lady shall be sette betwyxte us bothe, and who that
she woll go unto of you and me, lette hym have hir in pees." "I
woll well," seyde Sir Trystrames, "for as I deme, she woll leve you   25
and com to me." "Ye shall preve anone," seyde Sir Bleoberys.

So whan she was sette betwyxte them, she seyde thes wordys   [18]
unto Sir Trystrames: "Wete thou well, Sir Trystrames de Lyones, that
but late thou was the man in the worlde that I moste loved and
trusted, and I wente ye had loved me agayne above all ladyes; but   30
whan thou sawyste this knyght lede me away, thou madist no chere
to rescow me, but suffirdyst my lorde Sir Segwarydes to ryde after
me. But untyll that tyme I wente ye had loved me; and therefore
now I forsake the and never to love the more." And therewithall
she wente unto Sir Bleoberys.   35

☞Whan Sir Trystrames saw her do so, he was wondirly wroth with
that lady, and ashamed to com to the courte. But Sir Bleoberys
seyde unto Sir Trystrames, "Ye ar in the blame, for I hyre by this
ladyes wordis that she trusted you abovyn all erthely knyghtes, and,
as she seyth, ye have dysseyved hir. Therefore, wete you well, there   40
may no man holde that woll away; and rathir than ye sholde hertely   fol.164v
be displesed with me, I wolde ye had her, and she wolde abyde
with you."

☞"Nay," seyde the lady, "so Jesu me helpe, I woll never go wyth
hym, for he that I loved—and wente that he had loved me—forsoke   45
me at my nede.⁹ And therefore, Sir Trystrames," she seyde, "ryde as
thou com,¹ for though thou haddyste overcom this knyght, as thou

---

9. I.e., time of need.
1. *Ryde as thou com:* i.e., go back the way you came.

were lykly, with the[2] never wolde I have gone. And I shall pray thys knyght so fayre of[3] his knyghthode that, or evir he passe thys contrey, that he woll lede me to the abbey there my lorde Sir Segwarydes lyggys." 5

"So God me helpe," seyde Sir Bleoberys, "I latte you wete this, good knyght Sir Trystrames, because Kynge Marke gaff me the choyse of a gyffte in this courte, and so this lady lyked me beste (natwythstondynge she is wedded and hath a lorde), and I have also fulfylled my queste, she shall be sente unto hir husbande agayne—and in especiall moste for your sake, Sir Trystrames. And[4] 10 she wolde go with you, I wolde ye had her." "I thanke you," seyde Sir Trystrames, "but for her sake I shall beware what maner of lady I shall love or truste; for had her lorde Sir Segwarydes bene away from the courte, I sholde have bene the fyrste that sholde a folowed you: 15

¶"But syth ye have refused me, as I am a trew knyght, I shall know hir passyngly well that I shall love other truste."[5] And so they toke their leve and departed.

¶And so Sir Trystrames rode unto Tyntagyll, and Sir Bleoberys rode unto the abbey where Sir Segwarydes lay sore wounded; and 20 there he delyverde his lady and departed as a noble knyght. So whan Sir Segwarydes saw hys lady, he was gretly comforted. And than she tolde hym that Sir Trystrames had done grete batayle with Sir Bleoberys and caused hym to bryng her agayne—so that wordis[6] pleased Sir Segwarydes gretly, that Sir Trystrames wolde do so 25 muche; and so that lady tolde[7] all the batayle unto Kynge Marke   fol.165r betwexte Sir Trystramys and Sir Bleoberys.

So whan this was done, Kynge Marke caste all the wayes that he   [19] myght to dystroy Sir Trystrames, and than imagened in hymselff to sende Sir Trystramys into Irelonde for La Beale Isode; for Sir Trys- 30 trames had so preysed her for hir beauté and hir goodnesse that Kynge Marke seyde he wolde wedde hir—whereuppon he prayde Sir Trystramys to take his way into Irelonde for hym on message— and all this was done to the entente to sle Sir Trystramys. Natwiths- tondynge, he wolde nat refuse the messayge for no daunger nother 35 perell that myght falle, for the pleasure of his uncle.

¶So to go he made hym redy in the moste goodlyest wyse that myght be devysed, for he toke with hym the moste goodlyeste knyghtes that he myght fynde in the courte; and they were arayed aftir the gyse that was used that tyme in the moste goodlyeste 40 maner.

¶So Sir Trystrames departed and toke the see with all his fely- shyp. And anone as he was in the see a tempeste toke them and drove them into the coste of Ingelonde; and there they aryved faste

---

2. Thee.
3. *Fayre:* i.e., courteously. *Of:* i.e., for the sake of.
4. I.e., If.
5. *I shall know . . . love other truste:* i.e., I will henceforth much better know the woman I can love or trust.
6. *That wordis:* i.e., that utterance.
7. I.e., described.

by Camelot, and full fayne they were to take the londe. And whan
they were londed, Sir Trystrames sette up his pavylyon uppon the
londe of Camelot, and there he lete hange his shylde uppon the
pavylyon. And that same day cam two knyghtes of Kynge Arthures:
that one was Sir Ector de Marys, and that other was Sir Morganoure. 5
And thes two touched the shylde and bade hym com oute of the
pavylyon for to juste, and[8] he wolde.

"Anone ye shall be answeryd," seyde Sir Trystramys, "and ye woll
tary a lytyll whyle."

¶So he made hym redy; and fyrste he smote downe Sir Ector and 10
than Sir Morganoure, all with one speare, and sore brused them.
And whan they lay uppon the erthe, they asked Sir Trystramys what
he was and of what contrey he was knyght.

¶"Fayre lordis," seyde Sir Trystrames, "wete you well that I am
of Cornwayle." "Alas!" seyde Sir Ector, "now am I ashamed that 15
ever ony Cornysshe knyght sholde overcom me." And than for dispyte Sir Ector put of[9] his armoure fro hym, and wente on foot and
wolde nat ryde.

¶Than hit befelle that Sir Bleoberys and Sir Blamour de Ganys,
that were brethyrn, they had assomned Kynge Angwysshe of Ire- 20
londe for to com to Kynge Arthurs courte uppon payne of forfeture
of Kyng Arthurs good grace; and yf the Kynge of Irelonde come nat
in to that day assygned and sette—

¶The kynge sholde lose his londys.

¶So by Kynge Arthure hit was happened[1] that day that nother he 25
neythir Sir Launcelot myght nat be there where the jugemente
sholde be yevyn, for Kynge Arthure was with Sir Launcelot at Joyous
Garde. And so Kynge Arthure assygned Kynge Carados and the
Kynge of Scottis to be there that day as juges.

¶So whan thes kynges were at Camelot, Kynge Angwysshe of Ire- 30
londe was com to know hys accusers. Than was Sir Blamour de
Ganys there that appeled the Kynge of Irelonde of treson, that he
had slayne a cosyn of thers in his courte in Irelonde, by treson.

¶Than the kynge was sore abaysshed of his accusacion for why
he was at the sommons of Kyng Arthure—and or that he com at 35
Camelot, he wyste nat wherefore he was sente fore.

¶So whan the kynge herde hym sey his wyll, he undirstood well
there was none other remedy but to answere hym knyghtly; for the
custom was suche tho dayes that and ony man were appealed of
ony treson othir of murthure, he sholde fyght body-for-body,[2] other 40
ellys to fynde another knyght for hym—and alle maner of murthers
in tho dayes were called treson.

¶So whan Kynge Angwysshe undirstood his accusyng he was passynge hevy, for he knew Sir Blamoure de Ganys that he was a noble
knyght, and of noble knyghtes comyn. 45

¶So the Kynge of Irelonde was but symply purveyde of his

[20]

fol.165v

fol.166r

---

8. I.e., if.
9. *Put of:* removed.
1. *Hit was happened:* i.e., it was the circumstance.
2. I.e., man-to-man.

answere.[3] Therefore the juges gaff hym respyte, by the thirde day
to gyff his answere.

⁋So the Kynge departed unto his lodgynge.

⁋The meanewhyle there com a lady by Sir Trystrames pavylyon
makynge grete dole. "What aylyth you," seyde Sir Trystrames, "that
ye make suche dole?"

⁋"A! fayre knyght," seyde the lady, "I am shamed onles that som
good knyght helpe me, for a grete lady of worshyp sent by me a
fayre chylde[4] and a ryche unto Sir Launcelot; and hereby there mette
with me a knyght and threw me downe of[5] my palfrey and toke
away the chylde frome me."

⁋"Well, my lady," seyde Sir Trystramps, "and for my lorde Sir
Launcelotes sake, I shall gete you that chylde agayne, othir he[6] shall
beate me."

⁋And so Sir Trystramps toke his horse and asked the lady whyche
way the knyght yoode. Anone she tolde hym, and he rode aftir; so
within a whyle he overtoke that knyght and bade hym turne and
brynge agayne the chylde.

⁋Anone the knyght turned his horse and made hym redy to
fyght; and than Sir Trystramps smote hym with a swerde such a
buffet that he tumbled to the erthe—and than he yelded hym unto
Sir Trystramps. "Than com thy way," seyde Syr Trystrames, "and
brynge the chylde to the lady agayne." So he toke his horse weykely
and rode wyth Sir Trystrames—and so by the way he asked his
name.

⁋"Sir," he seyde, "my name is Breunys Sanze Pyté."[7] So whan he
had delyverde that chylde to the lady he seyde, "Sir, as in this the
chylde is well remedyed."

⁋Than Sir Trystramps lete hym go agayne—that sore repented[8]
hym aftir, for he was a grete foo unto many good knyghtes of Kyng
Arthures courte.

⁋Than whan Sir Trystrames was in his pavylyon, Governayle, his
man, com and tolde hym how that Kynge Angwysh of Irelonde was
com thydir, and he was in grete dystresse; and there he tolde hym
how he was somned and appeled of murthur.

⁋"So God me helpe!" seyde Sir Trystrames, "this is the beste
tydynges that ever com to me this seven yere, for now shall the
Kynge of Irelonde have nede of my helpe—for I dere say there is
no knyght in this contrey that is nat in Arthures courte that dare do
batayle wyth Sir Blamoure de Ganys—and for to wynne the love of
the Kynge of Irelonde I woll take the batayle uppon me. And
therefore, Governayle, bere me this worde, I charge the, to the
kynge." Than Governayle wente unto Kynge Angwyshe of Irelonde
and salewed hym full fayre.

[21]

fol.166v

3. *But symply purveyde of his answere:* i.e., was ill-prepared to give an answer.
4. I.e., a shield, *not* a child; Caxton's edition also presents a "c" spelling throughout this
    episode, and both texts may well preserve one of Malory's own variant spellings.
5. I.e., from.
6. I.e., the knight who stole the shield.
7. This is the same man as the Browne Knyghte wythoute Pyté, (p. 221). As is noted a few
    lines below, he will prove a persitent enemy to Arthur's knights.
8. I.e., regretted.

¶So the kynge welcommed hym and asked what he wolde.

¶"Sir," he seyde, "here is a knyght nerehonde that desyryth to speke wyth you, for he bade me sey that he wolde do you servyse."

¶"What knyght is he?" seyde the kynge.

¶"Sir, hit is Sir Trystrames de Lyones, that for the good grace ye shewed hym in your londys he woll rewarde you in thys contreys."

¶"Com on, felow," seyde the kynge, "with me anone, and brynge me unto Sir Trystramps." So the kynge toke a lytyll hackeney and but fewe felyshyp with hym, tyll that he cam unto Sir Trystramps pavylyon. And whan Sir Trystrames saw the kynge, he ran unto hym and wolde have holdyn his styrope; but the kynge lepe frome his horse lyghtly, and eythir halsed othir in armys.

¶"My gracious lorde," seyde Sir Trystrames, "grauntemercy of your grete goodnesse that ye shewed unto me in your marchys and landys. And at that tyme I promysed you to do you servyse and ever hit lay in my power."

¶"A, jantyll knyght," seyde the kynge unto Sir Trystrames, now have I grete nede of you—never had I so grete nede of no knyghtys helpe."

¶"How so, my good lorde?" seyde Sir Trystramps. "I shall tyll you," seyde the kynge. "I am assumned and appeled fro my contrey for the deth of a knyght that was kynne unto the good knyght Sir Launcelot; wherefore Sir Blamour de Ganys and Sir Bleoberys his brother hath appeled me to fyght wyth hym other for to fynde a knyght in my stede. And well I wote," seyde the kynge, "thes that ar comyn of Kynge Banys bloode, as Sir Launcelot and thes othir, ar passynge good harde knyghtes, and harde men for to wynne in batayle as ony that I know now lyvyng."

"Sir," seyde Sir Trystrames," for the good lordeshyp ye shewed unto me in Irelonde, and for my lady youre doughtirs sake, La Beale Isode, I woll take the batayle for you uppon this conducion, that ye shall graunte me two thynges: one is that ye shall swere unto me that ye ar in the ryght and that ye were never consentynge to the knyghtis deth:

¶"Sir, than," seyde Sir Trystramps, "whan I have done this batayle, yf God gyff me grace to spede, that ye shall gyff me a rewarde, what thynge resonable that I woll aske you."

¶"So God me helpe," seyde the kynge, "ye shall have whatsomever ye woll." "Ye sey well," seyde Sir Trystramps. "Now make your answere that your champyon is redy—for I shall dye in your quarell rathir than to be recreaunte." "I have no doute of you," seyde the kynge, "that and[9] ye sholde have ado with Sir Launcelot de Lake." "As for Sir Launcelot, he is called the noblyst or the worlde of knyghtes—and wete you well that the knyghtes of hys bloode ar noble men and drede shame. And as for Sir Bleoberys, brother unto Sir Blamour, I have done batayle wyth hym; therefore, uppon my hede, hit is no shame to calle hym a good knyght."

¶"Sir, hit is noysed," seyde the kynge, "that Sir Blamour is the

9. *That and:* i.e., even if.

hardyer knyght." "As for that, lat hym be. He shall nat be refused and[1] he were the beste knyght that beryth shylde or spere."

⁋So Kynge **Angwyssh** departed unto Kyng **Carados** and the kynges that were that tyme as juges, and tolde them how that he had founde his champyon redy. Than by the commaundementes of the kynges Sir **Blamour de Ganys** and Sir **Trystramys de Lyones** were sente fore to hyre their charge. And whan they were com before the juges, there were many kynges and knyghtes that behylde Sir **Trystrames**, and muche speche they had of hym because he slew Sir **Marhalte** the good knyght and because he forjusted Sir **Palomydes** the good knyght.

So whan they had takyn their charge, they withdrew hem to make hem redy to do batayle. Than seyde Sir **Bleoberys** to his brother Sir **Blamoure**, "Fayre dere brother," seyde he, "remembir of what kynne we be com of, and what a man is Sir **Launcelot de Lake**, nother farther ne nere but brethyrne chyldirne;[2] and there was never none of oure kynne that ever was shamed in batayle—but rathir, brothir, suffir deth than to be shamed."

⁋"Brothir," seyde Sir **Blamour**, "have ye no doute of me, for I shall never shame none of my bloode. Howbeit, I am sure, that yondir knyght ys called a passynge good knyght as of his tyme as ony in the worlde, yett shall I never yelde me nother sey the lothe worde:[3]

⁋"Well may he happyn to smyte me downe with his grete myght of chevalry, but rather shall he sle me than I shall yelde me recreaunte."

⁋"God spede you well," seyde Sir **Bleoberys**, "for ye shall fynde hym the myghtyest knyght that ever ye had ado withall—I knowe hym, for I have had ado with hym." "God me spede!" seyde Sir **Blamour**. And therewith he toke his horse at the one ende of the lystes, and Sir **Trystramys** at the othir ende of the lystes, and so they feautred their sperys and com togedyrs as hit had be thundir. And there Sir **Trystrames** thorow grete myght smote doune Sir **Blamour** and his horse to the erthe. Than anone Sir **Blamour** avoyded his horse and pulled oute his swerde and toke his shylde before hym, and bade Sir **Trystrames** alyght—"for thoughe my horse hath fayled, I truste to God the erthe woll nat fayle me!"

⁋And than Sir **Trystrames** alyght and dressed hym unto batayle; and there they laysshed togedir strongely, rasynge, foynynge and daysshynge many sad strokes, that the kynges and knyghtes had grete wondir that they myght stonde, for they evir fought lyke woode men. There was never seyne of two knyghtes that fought more ferselyer—for Sir **Blamour** was so hasty he wolde have no reste—that all men wondirde that they had brethe to stonde on their feete, that all the place was bloodé that they fought in. And at the laste Sir **Trystramys** smote Sir **Blamour** suche a buffette

fol.168r

---

1. I.e., if.
2. *Nother farther ne nere but brethyrne chyldirne:* no farther or nearer in blood (to us) than brothers' children.
3. *Sey the lothe worde:* i.e., speak the words that admit defeat.

uppon the helme that he there synked downe uppon his syde; and
Sir **Trystramps** stood stylle and behylde hym.

¶So whan Sir **Blamour** myght speke, he seyde thus: "Sir **Trystra-**
mes de Lyones, I requyre the, as thou art a noble knyght and the
beste knyght that ever I founde, that thou wolt sle me oute, for I
wolde nat lyve to be made lorde of all the erthe—for I had lever
dye here with worshyp than lyve here with shame—

¶"And nedis, Sir **Trystrames**, thou muste sle me, other ellys thou
shalt never wynne the fylde, for I woll never sey the lothe worde.
And therefore, yf thou dare sle me, sle me—I requyre the."

¶Whan Sir **Trystrames** herde hym sey so knyghtly, in his herte
he wyste nat what to do with hym—remembryng hym of bothe
partyes,[4] of what bloode he was commyn of, and for Sir **Launcelottis**
sake, he wolde be loth to sle hym; and in the other party, in no
wyse he myght nat chose but to make hym sey the lothe worde,
othir ellys to sle hym.

¶Than Sir **Trystrames** sterte abacke and wente to the kynges that
were Juges, and there he kneled downe tofore them and besought
them of their worshyppis, and for Kynge **Arthurs** love and for Sir
Launcellottis sake, that they wolde take this mater in their hondis—
"for, my fayre lordys," seyde Sir **Trystrames**, "hit were shame and
pyté that this noble knyght that yondir lyeth sholde be slayne; for
ye hyre well, shamed woll he nat be. And I pray to God that he
never be slayne nother shamed for me; and as for the kynge whom
I fyght fore, I shall requyre hym, as I am hys trew champyon and
trew knyght in this fylde, that he woll have mercy uppon this
knyght."

¶"So God me helpe," seyde Kyng **Angwyshe**, "I woll for your sake,
Sir **Trystrames**, be ruled as ye woll have me, and I woll hartely pray
the kynges that be here juges to take hit in there hondys."

¶Than the kynges that were juges called Sir **Bleoberys** to them
and asked his advyce. "My lordys," seyde Sir **Bleoberys**, "thoughe
my brother be beatyn and have the worse in his body thorow myght
of armys, [Sir **Trystramps**] hath nat beatyn his harte. And thanke
God he is nat shamed this day; and rathir than he be shamed, I
requyre you," seyde Sir **Bleoberys**, "lat Sir **Trystrames** sle hym oute."
"Hit shall nat be so," seyde the kynges. "For his parte, his adversary, bothe the kynge and the champyon, have pyté on Sir **Blamoure**
his knyghthode."

¶"My lordys," seyde Sir **Bleoberys**, "I woll ryght as ye woll."

¶Than the kynges called the Kynge of Irelonde and founde hym
goodly and tretable; and than, by all their advyces, Sir **Trystrames**
and Sir **Bleoberys** toke up Sir **Blamoure**, and the two bretherne were
made accorded wyth Kynge **Angwyshe**, and kyssed togydir and made
frendys for ever. And than Sir **Blamoure** and Sir **Trystrames** kyssed
togedirs; and there they made their othis that they wolde never
none of them two brethirne fyght wyth Sir **Trystrames**, and Sir

[23]

fol.168v

5

10

15

20

25

30

35

40

fol.169r

45

4. I.e., circumstances.

Trystramps made them the same othe. And for that jantyll batayle all the bloode[5] of Sir Launcelott loved Sir Tristrames for ever.

¶Than Kynge Angwyshe and Sir Trystrames toke their leve; and so he sayled into Irelonde wyth grete nobles[6] and joy.

¶So whan they were in Irelonde the Kynge lete make hit knowyn thorowoute all the londe how and in what maner Sir Trystrames had done for hym.

¶Than the quene and all that there were made the moste of hym that they myght—but the joy that La Beale Isode made of Sir Trystrames there myght no tunge telle, for of all men erthely[7] she loved hym moste.

¶Than uppon a day Kynge Angwyshe asked Sir Trystrames why he asked nat his bone. Than seyde Sir Trystrames, "Now hit is tyme. Sir, this is all that I woll desyre, that ye woll gyff La Beale Isode, youre doughter, nat for myself, but for myne uncle Kyng Marke shall have her to wyff, for so have I promysed hym." "Alas," seyde the Kynge, "I had lever than all the londe that I have that ye wolde have wedded hir yourself!" "Sir, and I dud so, I were shamed for ever in this worlde and false of my promyse. Therefore," seyde Sir Trystrames, "I requyre you, holde your promyse that ye promysed me, for this is my desyre, that ye woll gyff me La Beale Isode to go with me into Cornwayle for to be wedded unto Kynge Marke, myne uncle."

"As for that," Kynge Angwysshe seyde, "ye shall have her with yow to do with hir what hit please you: that is for to sey, if that ye lyste to wedde hir yourselff, that is me leveste;[8] and yf ye woll gyff hir unto Kyng Marke your uncle, that is in your choyse."

So, to make shorte conclusyon, La Beale Isode was made redy to go with Sir Trystrames, and Dame Brangwayne wente with hir for[9] hir chyff jantyllwoman, with many other. Than the quene, Isodes modir, gaff dame Brangwayne unto hir to be hir jantyllwoman. And also she and Governayle had a drynke of[1] the quene; and she charged them that where Kynge Marke sholde wedde, that same day they sholde gyff them that drynke that Kynge Marke sholde drynke to La Beale Isode[2]—"and than," seyde the quene, "ayther shall love other dayes of their lyff." So this drynke was gyvyn unto Dame Brangwayne and unto Governayle. So Sir Trystrames toke the see, and La Beale Isode. And whan they were in their caban, hit happed so they were thyrsty; and than they saw a lytyll flakette of golde stonde by them—and hit semed by the coloure and the taste that hit was noble wyne.

¶So Sir Trystrames toke the flaket in his honde, and seyde, "Madame Isode, here is a draught of good wyne that dame Brang-

[24]
fol.169v

---

5. I.e., blood relatives.
6. I.e., nobility.
7. *All men erthely:* i.e., all earthly men.
8. *Me leveste:* most desireable to me.
9. I.e., as.
1. I.e., from.
2. *Gyff them . . . drynke to La Beale Isode:* i.e. provide the couple with that drink for the wedding toast.

wayne, your maydyn, and **Governayle**, my servaunte, hath kepte for hemselff!" Than they lowghe and made good chere, and eyther dranke to other frely, and they thought never drynke that ever they dranke so swete nother so good to them. But by[3] that drynke was in their bodyes, they loved aythir other so well that never hir love departed, for well nother for woo.[4] And thus hit happed fyrst, the love betwyxte Sir **Trystrames** and La Beale **Isode**, the whyche love never departed dayes of their lyff.

¶So than they sayled tyll that by fortune they com nye a castell that hyght **Plewre**, and there they aryved for to repose them, wenynge to them to have had good herborow. But anone, as Sir **Trystrames** was within the castel, they were takyn presoners; for the custom of that castell was suche that who that rode by that castell and brought ony lady wyth hym, he muste nedys fyght with the lorde that hyght **Brewnour**. And yf hit so were that **Brewnor** wan the fylde, than sholde the knyght straunger and his lady be put to deth, what[5] that ever they were; and yf hit were so that the straunge knyght wan the fylde of Sir **Brewnor**, than sholde he dye and hys lady bothe. So this custom was used many wyntyrs, wherefore hit was called the Castell **Plewre**—that is to sey "the wepynge castell." Thus as Sir **Trystrames** and La Beale **Isode** were in preson, hit happynd a knyghte and a lady com unto them where they were to chere them.

¶Than seyde Sir **Trystrames** unto the knyght and to the lady, "What is the cause the lorde of this castell holdyth us in preson? For hit was never the custom of placis of worshyp that ever I cam in—

¶"Whan a knyght and a lady asked herborow, and they to receyve them and aftir to dystres them that be his gestys." "Sir," seyde the knyght, "this is the olde custom of this castell, that whan a knyght commyth here, he muste nedis fyght with oure lorde; and he that is the wayker muste lose his hede. And whan that is done, if his lady that he bryngyth be fowler than is oure lordys wyff, she muste lose hir hede; and yf she be fayrer preved than ys oure lady, than shall the lady of this castell lose her hede."

¶"So God me helpe," seyde Sir **Trystrames**, "this is a foule custom and a shamfull custom. But one avauntage have I," seyde Sir **Trystrames**: "I have a lady is fayre ynowe,[6] and I doute nat for lacke of beauté she shall nat lose her hede; and rathir than I shall lose myne hede, I woll fyght for hit on a fayre fylde:

¶"Sir knyght and your fayre lady, I pray you tell your lorde that I woll be redy as tomorne, wyth my lady and myselff, to do batayle, if hit be so I may have my horse and myne armoure."

¶"Sir," seyde the knyght, "I undirtake for[7] youre desyre shall be spedde; and therefore take your reste—and loke that ye be up

---

3. I.e., by the time.
4. I.e., woe, bad.
5. I.e., however noble.
6. *Is fayre ynowe:* who is exceedingly beautiful.
7. *Undirtake for:* i.e., take responsibility that.

betymes and make you redy, and your lady—for ye shall wante
nothynge that you behovyth."[8] And therewith he departed; and so
on the morne betymys that same knyght com to Sir Trystramys and
fecched hym oute, and his lady, and brought hym horse and
armoure that was his owne, and bade hym make hym redy to[9] the
fylde—for all the astatis and comyns of that lordshyp were there
redy to beholde that batayle and jugemente.

Than cam Sir Brewnor, the lorde of the castell, with his lady in
his honde, muffeled,[1] and asked Sir Trystrames where was his
lady—"for and[2] thy lady be feyrar than myne, with thy swerde
smyte of my ladyes hede; and yf my lady be fayrer than thyne, with
my swerde I muste stryke of hir hede—and if I may wynne the,
yette shall thy lady be myne, and thow shalt lese thy hede."

¶"Sir," seyde Sir Trystrames, "this is a foule custom and an horryble, and rather than my lady sholde lose hir hede, yett had I lever
lose myne hede."

¶"Nay, nay!" seyde Sir Brewnor, "the ladyes shall be fyrste
shewed togydir, and that one shall have hir jugemente." "Nay, I
wyll nat so," seyde Sir Trystrames, "for here is none that woll gyff
ryghtuous jugemente. But I doute nat," seyde Sir Trystrames, "my
lady is fayrer than youres, and that woll I make good with my
hondys—and who that woll sey the contrary, I woll preve hit on
his hede." And therewyth Sir Trystrames shewed forth La Beale
Isode and turned hir thryse aboute with his naked swerde in his
honde. And so dud Sir Brewnor the same wyse to his lady; but whan
Sir Brewnor behelde La Beale Isode, hym thought he saw never a
fayrer lady—and than he drad his ladyes hede sholde off.[3] And so
all the people that were there presente gaff jugement that La Beale
Isode was the fayrer lady, and the bettir made.

¶"How now?" seyde Syr Trystrames. "Mesemyth hit were pyté
that thy lady sholde lose hir hede; but bycause thou and she of
longe tyme have used this wycked custom—and by you bothe hath
many good knyghtes and fayre ladyes bene destroyed—for that
cause hit were no losse to destroy you bothe."

¶"So God me helpe," seyde Sir Brewnor, "for to sey the sothe,
thy lady is fayrer than myne, and that me sore repentys—and so I
hyre the people pryvyly sey—for of all women I sawe never none
so fayre; and therefore, and thou wolt sle my lady, I doute nat I
shall sle the and have thy lady."

¶"Well, thou shalt wyn her," seyde Sir Trystrames, "as dere as
ever knyght wanne lady. And bycause of thyne owne jugemente[4]
thou woldist have done to my lady if that she had bene fowler, and
bycause of the evyll custom, gyff me thy lady," seyde Syr Trystrames
—and therewithall Sir Trystrames strode unto hym and toke his

8. *You behovyth:* belongs to you.
9. I.e., for.
1. I.e., veiled.
2. I.e., if.
3. I.e., be cut off.
4. I.e., judgment concerning how.

lady frome hym, and with an awke stroke he smote of hir hede clene.

¶"Well, knyght," seyde Sir Brewnor, "now haste thou done me a grete dispyte. Now take thyne horse—and sytthen that I am ladyles, I woll wynne thy lady and I may." Than they toke their horsis and cam togydir as hit had bene thundir, and Sir Trystrames smote Sir Brewnor clene frome his horse; and lyghtly he rose up, and as Sir Trystrames com agayne by hym, he threste his horse thorowoute bothe shuldyrs, that his horse hurled here and there and felle dede to the grounde. And ever Sir Brewnor ran aftir to have slayne Sir Trystrames—but he was lyght and nymell and voyded his horse. [10]

¶Yett, or ever Sir Trystrames myght dresse his shylde and his swerde, he gaff hym three or foure strokys. Than they russhed togydyrs lyke two borys, trasynge and traversynge myghtyly and wysely as two noble knyghtes— [15]

¶For this Sir Brewnor was a proved knyght, and had bene or than[5] the deth of many good knyghtes.

¶Soo thus they fought, hurlynge here and there nyghe two owres, and aythir were wounded sore.

¶Than at the laste Sir Brewnor russhed uppon Sir Trystrames and toke hym in his armys, for he trusted much to[6] his strengthe. [20]

¶Than was Sir Trystrames called the strengyst knyght of the worlde, for he was called bygger than Sir Launcelotte (but Sir Launcelot was bettir brethid).[7]

¶So anone Sir Trystrames threste Sir Brewnor downe grovelyng; and than he unlaced his helme and strake of his hede. And than all they that longed to the castell com to hym and dud hym homage and feauté,[8] prayng hym that he wolde abyde stylle there a lytyll whyle to fordo that foule custom. So this Sir Trystrames graunted thereto. [25]

[26]
5
fol.171v
How Sir Trystrames slew Sir Brewnor and his wyff of Castel Pleure
30

¶So the meanewhyle one of the knyghtes rode unto Sir Galahalte the Haute Prynce, whyche was Sir Brewnors son, a noble knyght, and tolde hym what mysadventure his fadir had, and his modir.

Than cam Sir Galahalt and the Kynge with the Hondred Knyghtes with hym; and this Sir Galahalte profyrde to fyght wyth Sir Trystrames hande-for-hande. And so they made hem redy to go unto batayle on horsebacke wyth grete corrayge. [35]

¶So anone they mette togydyrs so hard that aythir bare othir adowne, horse and man, to the erthe. And whan they avoyded their horsis, as noble knythtes they dressed their shyldis and drewe their swerdys wyth ire and rancoure, and they laysshed togydyr many sad strokys—and one whyle strykynge and another whyle foynynge, tracynge and traversynge, as noble knyghtes. Thus they fought longe—nerehonde halff a day—and aythir were sore wounded. [40]

¶So at the laste Sir Trystrames wexed lyght and bygge, and [45]

[27]
fol.172r

---

5. *Or than*: before.
6. I.e., in.
7. *Bettir brethid*: in better condition.
8. On homage and fealty, see n. 6, p. 9.

doubled his strokys and drove Sir Galahalt abacke on the tone syde
and on the tothir, that he was nye myscheved, lyke to be slayne.

¶So wyth that cam the Kynge wyth the Hondred Knyghtes, and
all that felyshyp wente freyshly uppon Sir Trystrames. But whan Sir
Trystramys saw them comynge uppon hym, than he wyste well he   5
myght nat endure; so, as a wyse knyght of warre, he seyde unto Sir
Galahalt the Haute Prynce, "Syr, ye shew to me no kyndenesse for
to suffir all your men to have ado wyth me, and ye seme a noble
knyght of your hondys—hit is grete shame to you."

¶"So God me helpe," seyde Sir Galahalt, "there is none other   10
way but thou muste yelde the to me other ellys to dye, Sir Trystrames." "Sir, as for that, I woll rather yelde me to you than dye, for
hit is more for⁹ the myght of thy men than of thyne handys." And
therewithall Sir Trystrames toke his swerde by the poynte and put
the pomell in his¹ honde. And therewithall com the Kynge with   15
the Hondred Knyghtes, and harde began to assayle Sir Trystrames.
"Lat be," seyde Sir Galahalt, "that ye be nat so hardy to towche
hym, for I have gyffyn this knyght his lyff."

¶"That ys your shame," seyde the kynge, "for he hath slayne
youre fadir and your modir."   20

"As for that," seyde Sir Galahalte, "I may nat wyght hym gretly,
for my fadir had hym in preson and inforsed hym to do batayle
with hym; and my fadir hadde suche a custom—that was a shamefull custom—that what knyght and lady com thydir to aske herberow, his lady must nedis dye but yf she were fayrer than my   25
modir; and if my fadir overcom that knyght, he muste nedis dye.
Forsothe, this was a shamefull custom and usage—a knyght, for
his herborow askynge, to have suche herborage—and for this custom I wolde never draw aboute² hym."

¶"So God me helpe," seyde the kynge, "this was a shamefull   30
custom." "Truly," seyde Sir Galahalt, "so semyth me;³ and mesemyth hit had bene grete pyté that this knyght sholde have bene
slayne, for I dare sey he is one of the noblyst knyghtes that beryth
lyff, but yf hit be Sir Launcelot du Lake." "Now, fayre knyght," seyde
Sir Galahalte, "I requyre you, telle me youre name and of whens ye   35
ar and whethir thou wolte."

¶"Sir, he seyde, "my name is Sir Trystrames de Lyones, and frome
Kynge Marke of Cornwayle I was sente on messayge unto Kyng
Angwysh of Irelonde, for to fecche his doughtyr to be his wyff—
and here she is, redy to go wyth me into Cornwayle, and her name   40
is La Beale Isode." Than seyde Sir Galahalte unto Sir Trystramys,
"Well be ye founde⁴ in this marchis; and so⁵ ye woll promyse me
to go unto Sir Launcelot and accompany wyth hym, ye shall go where
ye woll, and youre fayre lady wyth you. And I shall promyse you

fol.172v

---

9. I.e., because of.
1. I.e., Galahalt's.
2. *Draw aboute*: approach, support.
3. So it seems to me.
4. I.e., You are welcome.
5. I.e., as long as, if.

never in all my dayes shall none suche custom be used in this castell as hath bene used heretofore."

❧"Sir, seyde Sir Trystrames, now I late you wete, so God me helpe, I wente ye had bene Sir Launcelot du Lake whan I sawe you fyrste, and therefore I dred you the more! And, sir, I promyse you," seyde Sir Trystrames, "as sone as I may, I woll se Sir Launcelot and infelyshyp me with hym, for of all the knyghtes in the worlde I moste desyre his felyshyp." And than Sir Trystramys toke his leve whan he sawe his tyme, and toke the see.

And meanewhyle worde com to Sir Galahalt and to Sir Trystramys that Kynge Carados, the myghty kynge that was made lyke a gyaunte, fought wyth Sir Gawayne and gaff hym suche strokys that he sowned in his sadyll—and after that he toke hym by the coler and pulled hym oute of his sadyll, and bounde hym faste to the sadyll-bowghe, and so rode his way with hym towarde his castell. And as he rode, Sir Launcelot by fortune mette with Kynge Carados— and anone he knew Sir Gawayne that lay bounde before hym. "A," seyde Syr Launcelot unto Sir Gawayne, "how stondyth hit wyth you?"

"Never so harde!" seyde Sir Gawayne, "onles that ye helpe me, for so God me helpe, withoute[6] ye rescow me I know no knyght that may, but you other Sir Trystrames"—wherefor Sir Launcelot was hevy at Sir Gawaynes wordys. And than Sir Launcelot bade Sir Cara- dos, "Ley downe that knyght and fyght with me."

❧"Thow arte but a foole," seyde Sir Carados, "for I woll serve the in the same wyse!"

❧"As for that," seyde Sir Launcelot, "spare me nat, for I warne the, I woll nat spare the." And than he bounde hym[7] hande and foote, and so threw hym to the grounde; and than he gate his speare in his honde of[8] his squyre and departed frome Sir Launcelot to fecche his course.[9] And so ayther mette with other and brake their speares to theire hondys; and than they pulled oute their swerdys and hurled togydyrs on horsebacke more than an owre— and at the laste Sir Launcelot smote Sir Carados suche a buffet on the helme that hit perysshed his brayne-panne.

❧So than Syr Launcelot toke Sir Carados by the coler and pulled hym undir his horse fete, and than he alyght and pulled of his helme and strake offe his hede.

❧Than Sir Launcelot unbownde Sir Gawayne. So this same tale was tolde to Sir Galahalte and to Syr Trystrames, and sayde,[1] "Now may ye hyre the nobles[2] that folowyth Sir Launcelot." "Alas," seyde Sir Trystrames, "and I had nat this messayge in hande with this fayre lady, truly I wolde never stynte or I had founde Sir Launcelot." Than Syr Trystrames and La Beale Isode yeode to the see and cam into Cornwayle, and anone all the barownes mette with hym.

fol.173r 5

[28]

10

15

20

25

30

fol.173v 35

How Sir Launcelot
slew Kyng Carados
of the Dolerous
Towre

40

---

6. I.e., unless.
7. I.e., Gawain.
8. I.e., from.
9. *Fecche his course*: make his charge.
1. I.e., the unnamed teller (of this brief tale in celebration of Launcelot) said.
2. *Hyre*: i.e., hear, acknowledge. *Nobles*: i.e., nobility.

Nd anone they[3] were rychely wedded wyth grete nobley. But evir, as the Frensche booke seyth, Sir Trystrames and La Beale Isode loved ever togedyrs. Than was there grete joustys and grete turnayynge, and many lordys and ladyes were at that feyste, and Sir Trystrames was moste praysed of all other.

⁋So thus dured the feste longe. And aftir that feste was done, within a lytyll whyle aftir, by the assente of two ladyes that were with the quene, they ordayned for hate and envye for to distroy Dame Brangwayne that was mayden and lady unto La Beale Isode. And she was sente into the foreste for to fecch herbys; and there she was mette and bounde honde and foote to a tre—and so she was bounden three dayes. And by fortune Sir Palomydes founde Dame Brangwayne, and there he delyverde hir from the deth, and brought hir to a nunry there besyde for to be recoverde.

Whan Isode the quene myssed hir mayden, wete you well she was ryght hevy as evir any quene myght be, for of all erthely women she loved hir beste—and moste cause why, she cam with her oute of her contrey. And so uppon a day Quene Isode walked into the foreste to put away hir thoughtes, and there she wente hirselff unto a welle and made grete moone. And suddeynly there cam Sir Pal- omydes unto her, and herde all hir complaynte, and seyde, "Madame Isode, and ye wolde graunte me my boone, I shall brynge agayne to you Dame Brangwayne sauff and sounde."

⁋Than the quene was so glad of his profyr that suddaynly unav- ysed she graunte all his askynge.

⁋"Well, madame," seyde Sir Palomydes, "I truste to youre pro- myse, and yf ye woll abyde halff an owre here I shall brynge hir to you." "Sir, I shall abyde you," seyde the quene. Than Sir Palomydes rode forth his way to that nunry, and lyghtly he cam agayne with Dame Brangwayne; but by hir good wylle she wolde nat have comyn to the quene, for cause she stoode in adventure[4] of hir lyff. Natwythstondynge, halff agayne hir wyll, she cam wyth Sir Palo- mydes unto the quene; and whan the quene sawe her she was pas- syng glad.

⁋"Now, madame," seyde Sir Palomydes, "remembir uppon your promyse, for I have fulfylled my promyse."

⁋"Sir Palomydes," seyde the quene, "I wote nat what is your desyre, but I woll that ye wete; howbehit that I profyrde you largely, I thought none evyll—nother, I warne you, none evyll woll I do."

⁋"Madame," seyde Sir Palomydes, "as at this tyme ye shall nat know my desyre." "But[5] byfore my lorde, myne husbonde, there shall ye know that ye shall have your desyre that I promysed you." And than the quene rode home unto the kynge, and Sir Palomydes rode with hir; and whan Sir Palomydes com before the kynge, he seyde, "Sir kynge, I requyre the, as thou arte ryghtuous kynge, that ye woll juge me the ryght."

[29]

5

10

15

20

fol.174r

25

30

35

40

45

---

3. I.e., Isode and King Mark.
4. I.e., danger.
5. Isode is speaking.

¶"Telle me your cause," seyde the kynge, "and ye shall have ryght."

¶"Sir," seyde Sir Palomydes, "I promysed youre quene, my lady Dame Isode, to brynge agayne Dame Brangwayne that she had loste, upon this covenaunte, that she sholde graunte me a boone that I wolde aske; and withoute grucchynge othir advysemente she graunted me." [30]

¶"What sey ye, my lady?" seyde the kynge.

¶"Hit is as he seyth, so God me helpe—to sey the soth," seyde the quene, "I promysed hym his askynge for[6] love and joy I had to se her."

¶"Welle, madame," seyde the kynge, "and yf [ye] were hasty to graunte what boone he wolde aske, I wolde well that [ye] perfourmed [your] promyse."

¶Than seyde Sir Palomydes, "I woll that ye wete that I woll have youre quene, to lede hir and to governe her whereas[7] me lyste." Therewyth the kynge stoode stylle, and unbethought hym[8] of Sir Trystrames, and demed that he wolde rescowe her. And than hastely the kynge answered and seyde, "Take hir to the, and the adventures withall that woll falle[9] of hit, for, as I suppose, thou wolt nat enjoy her no whyle."

¶"As for that," seyde Sir Palomydes, "I dare ryght well abyde the adventure."

¶And so, to make shorte tale, Sir Palomydes toke hir by the honde and seyde, "Madame, grucche nat to go with me, for I desyre nothynge but youre owne promyse."

¶"As for that," seyde the quene, "wete thou well, I feare nat gretely to go with the, howbehit thou haste me at avauntage upon my promyse—for I doute nat I shall be worshypfully rescowed fro the." "As for that," seyde Sir Palomydes, "be as hit be may." So Quene Isode was sette behynde Sir Palomydes and rode his way. And anone the kynge sente unto Sir Trystrames; but in no wyse he wolde nat be founde, for he was in the foreste an-huntynge—for that was allwayes hys custom, but yf he used armes,[1] to chace and to hunte in the forestes.

¶"Alas," seyde the kynge, "now am I shamed forever, that be myne owne assente my lady and my quene shall be devoured."[2]

¶Than cam there forth a knyght that hyght Lambegus, and he was a knyght of Sir Trystrames. "My lorde," seyde the knyght, "syth that ye have suche truste in my lorde Sir Trystrames, wete yow well for his sake I woll ryde aftir your quene and rescow her, other ellys shall I be beatyn." "Grauntemercy," seyde the Kynge. "And I lyve, Sir Lambegus, I shall deserve[3] hit." And than Sir Lambegus armed

fol.174v

fol.175r

6. I.e., out of.
7. I.e., wherever.
8. *Unbethought hym*: called to mind.
9. I.e., come.
1. *But yf he used armes*: unless he was performing deeds of arms.
2. I.e., destroyed.
3. I.e., reward.

hym and rode aftir them as faste as he myght, and than wythin a
whyle he overtoke hem; and than Sir Palompdes lefte the quene:

¶"What arte thou?" seyde Sir Palompdes, "arte thou Sir Trystrames?" "Nay," he seyde, "I am his servaunte, and my name is Sir
Lambegus." "That me repentys," seyde Sir Palompdes. "I had lever   5
thou had bene Sir Trystrames." "I leve you well," seyde Sir Lambegus,
"but whan thou metyste with Sir Trystrames, thou shalt have bothe
thy hondys full!" And than they hurteled togydyrs, and all to-braste
their sperys; and than they pulled oute their swerdys and hewed
on there helmys and hawbirkes. At the laste Sir Palompdes gaff Sir   10
Lambegus suche a wounde that he felle doune lyke a dede man to
the erthe. Than he loked aftir La Beale Isode, and than she was
gone, he woste nat where.

¶Wete you well that Sir Palompdes was never so hevy! So the
quene ran into the foreste, and there she founde a welle, and   15
therein she had thought to have drowned herselff. And as good
fortune wolde, there cam a knyght to her that had a castell there
besyde, and his name was Sir Adtherpe. And whan he founde the
quene in that myscheff, he rescowed her and brought hir to his
castell. And whan he wyste what he⁴ was, he armed hym and toke   20
his horse, and seyde he wolde be avenged uppon Sir Palompdes; and
so he rode unto the tyme he mette with hym, and there Sir Palompdes wounded hym sore. And by force he made hym to telle the
cause why he dud batayle wyth hym; and he tolde hym how he
ladde the quene La Beale Isode into hys owne castel.   25

"Now brynge me there" seyde Sir Palampdes, "or thou shalt of   fol.175v
myne handis die."

¶"Sir," seyde Sir Adtherpe, "I am so sore wounded I may nat
folow; but ryde you this way and hit shall bryng you to my castell,
and therein is the quene." Sir Palompdes rode tyll that he cam to   30
the castell, and at a wyndow La Beale Isode saw Sir Palompdes; than
she made the yatys to be shutte strongely.

¶And whan he sawe he myght nat entir into the castell, he put
of his horse brydyll and his sadyll, and so put his horse to pasture,
and sette hymselff downe at the gate, lyke a man that was oute of   35
his wytt that recked nat of hymselff.

¶Now turne we unto Sir Trystrames, that whan he was com home   [31]
and wyste that La Beale Isode was gone with Sir Palompdes, wete
you well he was wrothe oute of mesure. "Alas," seyde Sir Trystrames, "I am this day shamed!" Than he called Gabernaple, his man,   40
and seyde, "Haste⁵ the that I were armed and on horsebacke, for
well I wote Sir Lambegus hath no myght nor strength to wythstonde
Sir Palompdes—alas I had nat bene in his stede!"

¶So anone he was armed and horsed and rode aftir into the
foreyste, and within a whyle he founde his knyght Sir Lambegus   45
allmoste to deth wounded.

¶And Sir Trystrames bare hym to a foster and charged hym to
kepe hym welle. And than he rode forth and founde Sir Adtherpe

4. She.
5. I.e., hasten.

sore wounded—and he tolde all, and how "the quene had drowned
herselff had nat I bene, and how for her sake I tok uppon me to
do batayle with Sir Palomydes." "Where is my lady?" seyde Sir Trystrames. "Sir," seyde the knyght, "she is sure inowe wythin my castell—and she can holde her within hit." "Grauntemercy," seyde Sir
Trystrames, "of thy grete goodnesse." And so he rode tyll that he
cam nyghe his castell. And than Sir Palomydes sate at the gate and
sawe where Sir Trystrames cam; and he sate as he had slepe,[6] and
his horse pastured afore hym.

¶"Now go thou, Governayle," seyde Sir Trystrames, "and bydde
hym awake and make hym redy." So Governayle rode unto hym and
seyde, "Sir Palomydes, aryse and take to thyne harneys." But he was
in suche a study he herde nat what he seyde. So Governayle com
agayne to Sir Trystrames and tolde hym he slepe, or ellys he was
madde. "Go thou agayne," seyde Sir Trystrames, "and bydde hym
aryse, and telle hym I am here, his mortall foo." So Governayle rode
agayne, and putte uppon hym with the but of his spere, and seyde,
"Sir Palomydes, make the[7] redy, for wete thou welle Sir Trystrames
hovyth yondir and sendyth the worde he is thy mortall foo."

¶And therewithall Sir Palomydes arose stylly, withoute ony wordys, and gate hys horse anone, and sadylled hym and brydylled
hym; and lyghtly he lepe uppon hym and gate his spere in his
honde. And aythir feautred their spearys and hurled faste togedyrs;
and anone Sir Trystrames smote downe Sir Palomydes over his horse
tayle.

¶Than lyghtly Sir Palomydes put his shylde before hym and drew
his swerde; and there began stronge batayle on bothe partyes, for
bothe they fought for the love of one lady. And ever she lay on the
wallys and behylde them, how they fought oute of mesure—and
aythir were wounded passynge sore, but Sir Palomydes was muche
sorer wounded—for they fought thus, trasynge and traversynge,
more than two owres, that well-nyghe for doole and sorow La Beale
Isode sowned and seyde "Alas, that one I loved, and yet do, and the
other I love nat, that they sholde fyght—

¶"And yett hit were grete pyté that I sholde se Sir Palomydes
slayne, for well I know by[8] that the ende be done Sir Palomydes is
but a dede man[9] bycause that he is nat crystened—and I wolde be
loth that he sholde dye a Sarezen." And therewithall she cam
downe and besought hem for her love to fyght no more. "A,
madame!" seyde Sir Trystrames, "what meane you? Woll ye have
me shamed? For well ye know that I woll be ruled by you."

"A, myne awne lorde," seyde La Beale Isode, "full well ye wote I
wolde nat your dyshonour, but I wolde that ye wolde for my sake
spare this unhappy Sarezen, Sir Palomydes." "Madame," seyde Sir
Trystrames, "I woll leve[1] for youre sake."

¶Than seyde she to Sir Palomydes, "This shall be thy charge:

fol.176r

fol.176v

---

6. I.e., slept.
7. thee.
8. I.e., by the time.
9. *But a dede man:* i.e., a man who will not go to heaven.
1. I.e., leave off, desist.

thou shalt go oute of this contrey whyle I am quene theroff."
"Madame, I woll obey your commaundemente," seyde Sir Palomydes, "whyche is sore ayenste my wylle."

¶"Than take thy way," seyde La Beale Isode, "unto the courte of
Kynge Arthure, and there recommaunde me unto Quene Gwenyvere,   5
and tell her that I sende her worde that there be within this londe
but foure lovers, and that is Sir Launcelot and Dame Gwenyver, and
Sir Trystrames and Quene Isode." And so Sir Palomydes departed   [32]
with grete hevynesse. And Sir Trystrames toke the quene and
brought her agayne unto Kynge Marke; and than was there made   10
grete joy of hir homecommynge—than who was cheryshed but Sir
Trystrames!

Than Sir Trystrames latte fecche home Sir Lambegus, his knyght,
frome the forsters house; and hit was longe or[2] he was hole, but
so at the laste he recoverde. And thus they lyved with joy and play   15
a longe whyle—but ever Sir Andret, that was nye cosyn unto Sir
Trystrams, lay in a wayte betwyxte Sir Trystrames and La Beale Isode   fol.177r
for to take hym and devoure hym.

¶So upon a day Sir Trystrames talked with La Beale Isode in a
wyndowe, and that aspyed Sir Andred and tolde the kynge. Than   20
Kyng Marke toke a swerde in his honde and cam to Sir Trystrames
and called hym "false traytowre," and wolde have stryken hym; but
Sir Trystrames was nyghe hym and ran undir his swerde and toke
hit oute of his honde—and than the Kynge cryed, "Where ar my
knyghtes and my men? I charge you, sle this traytowre!" But at that   25
tyme there was nat one that wolde meve for his wordys.

¶Whan Sir Trystrames sawe there was none that wolde be ayenste hym, he shoke hys swerde to the kynge and made countenaunce
as he wolde have strykyn hym. And than Kynge Marke fledde—and
Sir Trystrames folowed hym, and smote hym fyve or six strokys fla-   30
tlynge in the necke, that he made hym falle on the nose. And than
Sir Trystrames yode his way, and armed hym and toke his horse and
his men, and so he rode into the foreste. And there uppon a day
Sir Trystrames mette with two bretherne that were knyghtes wyth
Kynge Marke; and there he strake of the hede of the tone brother   35
and wounded that other to the deth; and he made hym to bere the
hede[3] in his helme—and thirty mo he there wounded. And whan
that knyght com before the kynge to say hys message, he dyed there
before the kynge and the quene.

Than Kyng Marke called his counceyle unto hym and asked avyce   40
of his barownes, what were beste to do with Sir Trystrames. "Sir,"
seyde the barowns—and in especiall Sir Dynas the Senesciall—
"we woll gyff you counceyle for to sende for Sir Trystrames, for we
woll that ye wete many men woll holde with Sir Trystrames and he
were harde bestadde."[4]   45

¶"And, sir," seyde Sir Dynas the Seneseiall, "ye shall undirstonde
that Sir Trystrames ys called peereles and makeles of ony Crystyn   fol.177v

2. I.e., before.
3. I.e., the head of his brother.
4. *Harde bestadde:* hard pressed, attacked.

knyght, and of his myght and hardynes we know none so good a knyght but yf hit be Sir **Launcelot du Lake**. And yff he departe frome your courte and go to Kyng **Arthurs** courte, wete you well he woll so frende hym there that he woll nat sette by[5] your malyce; and therefore, sir, I counceyle you to take hym to your grace." "I woll well," seyde the kynge, "that he be sent fore, that we may be frendys."

¶Than the barounes sente for Sir **Trystrames** undir theire conduyte; and so whan Sir **Trystrames** com to the kynge, he was wellcom—and no rehersall[6] was made—and than there was game and play. And than the kynge and the quene wente an-huntynge, and [33] Sir **Trystrames**. So the Kynge and the quene made their pavylons and their tentes in that foreste besyde a ryver; and there was dayly justyng and huntyng, for there was ever redy thirty knyghtes to juste unto all that cam at that tyme. And there by fortune com Sir **Lamorak de Galis** and Sir **Dryaunte**; and there Sir **Dryaunte** justed well, but at the laste he had a falle.

¶Than Sir **Lamorak** profyrde,[7] and whan he began he fared so wyth the thirty knyghtes that there was nat one off them but he gaff a falle—and som of them were sore hurte. "I mervayle," seyde Kynge **Marke**, "what knyght he is that doth suche dedis of armys."

¶"Sir," seyde Sir **Trystrames**, "I know hym well for a noble knyght as fewe now be lyvynge, and his name is Sir **Lamerake de Galys**." "Hit were shame," seyde the kynge, "that he sholde go thus away onles that he were mannehandeled."[8] "Sir," seyde Sir **Trystrames**, "mesemyth hit were no worshyp for a nobleman to have ado with hym—

¶"And for this cause: for at this tyme he hath done overmuche for ony meane[9] knyght lyvynge. And as me semyth," seyde Sir **Trystrames**, "hit were shame to tempte hym ony more, for his horse is wery and hymselff both for the dedes of armes he hath done this day: fol.178r 30

¶"Welle concidered, hit were inow for Sir **Launcelot du Lake**." "As for that," seyde Kynge **Marke**, "I requyre you, as ye love me and my lady the quene La Beale **Isode**, take youre armys and juste with Sir **Lameroke de Galis**." "Sir," seyde Sir **Trystrames**, "ye bydde me do a thynge that is ayenste knyghthode—and well I can thynke that I shall gyff hym a falle, for hit is no maystry, for my horse and Y be freysshe, and so is nat his horse and he. And wete you well that he woll take hit for grete unkyndenes, for ever one good knyght is loth to take anothir at avauntage.[1] But bycause I woll nat displase, as ye requyre me, so muste I do, and obey youre commaundemente."

¶And so Sir **Trystrames** armed hym and toke his horse and putte hym forth. And there Sir **Lameroke** mette hym myghtyly; and what

5. *Sette by:* care about.
6. I.e., mention of what had happened.
7. I.e., entered the joust.
8. *Onles that he were mannehandeled:* without being handled roughly.
9. I.e., ordinary.
1. *Take anothir at avauntage:* i.e., take advantage of another.

with the myght of his owne spere and of Syr Trystrames spere, Sir
Lameroke his horse felle to the erthe, and he syttynge in the sadyll.

¶So as sone as he myght, he avoyded the sadyll and his horse,
and put his shylde afore hym, and drewe his swerde; and than he
bade Sir Trystrames, "alyght, thou knyght, and thou darste!"   5

¶"Nay, sir" seyde Sir Trystrames, "I woll no more have ado wyth
you, for I have done the² overmuche unto my dyshonoure and to
thy worshyppe."

¶"As for that" seyde Sir Lamerok, "I can the no thanke. Syn thou
haste forjusted me on horsebacke, I requyre the and I beseche the,   10
and thou be Sir Trystrames de Lyones, feyght with me on foote." "I
woll nat," seyde Sir Trystrames, "and wete you well my name is Sir
Trystrames de Lyones, and well I know that ye be Sir Lameroke de   fol.178v
Galis. And this have I done to you ayenst my wyll, but I was requyred thereto—but to sey that I woll do at your requeste as at this   15
tyme, I woll nat have no more ado with you at this tyme, for me
shamyth of that I have done."

¶"As for the shame," seyde Sir Lamerake, "on thy party or on
myne, beare thou hit and thou wyll:

¶"For thoughe a marys sonne³ hath fayled me now, yette a   20
quenys sonne⁴ shall nat fayle the! And therefore, and thou be
suche a knyght as men calle the, I requyre the alyght and fyght
with me." "Sir Lameroke," seyde Sir Trystrames, "I undirstonde your
harte is grete, and cause why⁵ ye have, to sey the soth, for hit wolde
greve me and⁶ ony good knyght sholde kepe hym freyssh and than   25
to stryke downe a wery knyght; for that knyght nother horse was
never fourmed that allway may endure—and therefore," seyde Sir
Trystrames, "I woll nat have ado with you, for me forthynkes of that
I have done." "As for that," seyde Sir Lameroke, "I shall quyte you
and ever I se my tyme."   30

¶So he departed frome hym with Sir Dryaunte, and by the way   [34]
they mette with a knyght that was sente fro Dame Morgan le Fay
unto Kynge Arthure; and this knyght had a fayre horne harneyste
with golde. And the horne had suche a vertu that there myght no
lady nothir jantyllwoman drynke of that horne but yf she were trew   35
to her husbande; and if she were false, she sholde spylle all the
drynke, and if she were trew to her lorde she myght drynke thereof
pesiblé. And because of the Quene Gwenyvere and in the dispyte of
Sir Launcelot, this horne was sente unto Kynge Arthure. And so by
forse Sir Lameroke made that knyght to telle all the cause why he   40
bare the horne; and so he tolde hym all hole.

¶"Now shalt thou bere this horne," seyde Sir Lamerok, to Kynge
Marke—othir chose to dye. For, in the dyspyte of Sir Trystrames,   fol.179r
thou shalt bere hit hym, that horne, and sey that I sente hit hym
for to assay his lady; and yf she be trew he shal preve her."   45

2. To thee.
3. A mare's son (i.e., Lamerok's horse).
4. I.e. Lamerok (as the son of King Pellynor).
5. *cause why*: good reason.
6. I.e., if.

¶So this knyght wente his way unto Kynge 𝕸arke and brought hym that ryche horne, and seyde that Sir 𝕷amerok sente hit hym; and so he tolde hym the vertu of that horne.

¶Than the kynge made his quene to drynke thereof, and an hondred ladyes with her; and there were but foure ladyes of all tho that dranke clene.[7] "Alas!" seyde Kynge 𝕸arke, "this is a grete dyspyte," and swore a grete othe that she sholde be brente, and the other ladyes also.

¶Than the barowns gadred them togedyrs and seyde playnly they wolde nat have tho ladyes brente for an horne made by sorsery that cam "frome the false sorseres and wycche moste that is now lyvyng"—for that horne dud never good, but caused stryff and bate, and allway in her dayes she was an enemy to all trew lovers.

¶So there were many knyghtes made their avowe that and ever they mette wyth 𝕸organ le 𝕱ay, that they wolde shew her shorte[8] curtesy.

¶Also Syr 𝕿rystrames was passyng wroth that Sir 𝕷ameroke sent that horne unto Kynge 𝕸arke, for welle he knew that hit was done in the dispyte of hym; and therefore he thought to quyte Sir 𝕷ameroke. Than Sir 𝕿rystrames used dayly and nyghtly to go to Quene 𝕵sode evir whan he myght—and ever Sir 𝕬ndret, his cosyn, wacched hym nyght by nyght for to take hym with 𝕷a 𝕭eale 𝕵sode. And so uppon a nyght Sir 𝕬ndret aspyed his owre and the tyme whan Sir 𝕿rystrames went to his lady.

¶Than Sir 𝕬ndret gate unto hym twelve knyghtis, and at mydnyght he sette uppon Sir 𝕿rystrames secretly and suddeynly; and there Sir 𝕿rystrames was takyn nakyd abed with 𝕷a 𝕭eale 𝕵sode, and so was he bounde hande and foote and kepte tyll day. And than by the assent of Kynge 𝕸arke and of Sir 𝕬ndret and of som of the barownes, Sir 𝕿rystramps was lad unto a chapell that stood uppon the see rockys, there for to take his jugemente. And so he was lad bounden with fourty knyghtes; and whan Sir 𝕿rystrames saw that there was none other boote but nedis he muste dye—

fol.179v

¶Than seyde he, "Fayre lordis, remembir what I have done for the contrey of Cornwayle, and what jouparté I have bene in for the wele of you all:

¶"For whan I fought with Sir 𝕸arhalte, the good knyght, I was promysed to be bettir rewarded, whan ye all refused to take the batayle. Therefore, as ye be good jantyll knyghtes, se me nat thus shamfully to dye, for hit is shame to all knyghthode thus to se me dye—

¶"For I dare sey," seyde Sir 𝕿rystrams, "that I mette never with no knyght but I was as good as he, or better."

¶Fye upon the," seyde Sir 𝕬ndrete, "false traytur thow arte; with thyne advauntage, for all thy boste, thou shalt dye this day!"

¶"A, 𝕬ndrete, 𝕬ndrete!" seyde Sir 𝕿rystrames, "thou sholdyst be my kynnysman, and now arte to me full unfrendely. But, and there

7. I.e., without spilling.
8. I.e., little.

were no more but thou and I, thou woldyst nat put me to deth."
"No?" seyde Sir Andred, and therewith he drew his swerde and
wolde have slayne hym.

¶So whan Sir Trystrames sye hym make that countenaunce, he
loked uppon bothe his hondis that were faste boundyn unto two
knyghtes, and suddeynly he pulde them bothe unto hym and
unwrayste his hondis, and lepe unto his cosyn Sir Andred and wroth
his swerde oute of his hondis. And than he smote Sir Andret, that
he felle downe to the erthe; and so he fought that he kylde ten
knyghtys.

So than Sir Trystrames gate the chapell and kepte hyt myghtyly.
Than the crye was grete, and peple drew faste unto Sir Andret, mo
than an hondred. So whan Sir Trystramys saw the peple draw unto
hym, he remembyrd he was naked, and sparde faste the chapell
dore and brake the barrys of a wyndow; and so he lepe oute and
felle uppon the craggys in the see. And so at that tyme Sir Andret
nothir none of his felowys myght nat gete hym.

But whan they were departed, Governayle and Sir Lambegus and
Sir Sentrayle de Lushon, that were Sir Trystrames men, sought sore
aftir their maystir whan they herde he was ascaped. And so on the
rokkys they founde hym, and with towels[9] pulde hym up. And than
Sir Trystrames asked where was La Beale Isode. "Sir," seyde Governayle, "she is put in a lazar-cote."

¶"Alas," seyde Sir Trystrames, "that is a full ungoodly place for
suche a fayre lady, and yf I may she shall nat be longe there." And
so he toke hys men and wente there as was La Beale Isode, and
fette her away, and brought hir into a fayre foreste to a fayre maner;
and so he abode there with hir.

¶So now this good knyght bade his men departe, for at that tyme
he myght nat helpe them; and so they departed, all save Governayle.
And so uppon a day Sir Trystrames yode into the foreste for to
disporte hym, and there he felle on slepe. And so happynde there
cam to Sir Trystrames a man that he had slayne his brothir.[1] And
so whan this man had founde hym, he shotte hym thorow the
sholdir [with an arow]—and anone Sir Trystrames sterte up and
kylde that man. And in the meanetyme hit was tolde unto Kynge
Marke how Sir Trystrames and La Beale Isode were in that same
maner, and thydir he cam with many knyghtes to sle Sir Trystrames;
and whan he cam there he founde hym gone. And anone he toke
La Beale Isode home with hym and kepte her strayte, that by no
meane she myght never wryght nor sende.[2]

¶And whan Sir Trystrames com toward the maner, he founde the
tracke of many horse—

¶And loked aboute in the place, and knew that his lady was
gone. And than Sir Trystrames toke grete sorow and endured with
grete sorow, and payne, longe tyme—for the arow that he was
hurte wythall was envenomed.

fol. 180r
[35]

9. I.e., rope made of tied cloths.
1. *That he had slayne his brothir*: i.e., whose brother he had slain.
2. I.e., send messages.

¶So by the meane of La Beale Isode she bade a lady that was cosyn unto Dame Brangwayne, and she cam unto Sir Trystrames and tolde hym that he myght nat be hole by no meanys—"for thy lady Isode may nat helpe the. Therefore she byddyth you, haste you into Bretayne unto Kynge Howell, and there shall ye fynde his doughter that is called Isode le Blaunche Maynes, and there shall ye fynde that she shall helpe you."

¶Than Sir Trystrames and Governayle gate them shyppyng, and so sayled into Bretayne.

¶And whan Kyng Howell knew that hit was Sir Trystrames, he was full glad of hym.

¶"Sir," seyde Sir Trystrames, "I am come unto this contrey to have helpe of youre doughter, [for hit is tolde me that there is none other may hele me but she."] And so [within a whyle] she heled hym.

There was an erle that hyght Grype, and thys erle made grete warre uppon the kynge and putte hym to the worse and beseged hym. And on a tyme Sir Keyhydyus that was sonne to the Kynge Howell, as he issewed oute he was sore wounded nyghe to the deth.

¶Than Governayle wente to the kynge and seyde, "Sir, I counceyle you to desyre my lorde Sir Trystrames as in your nede to helpe you."

¶"I woll do by youre counceyle," seyde the kynge; and so he yode unto Sir Trystrames and prayde hym as in his warrys to helpe hym—"for my sonne Sir Keyhidyus may nat go unto the fylde."

¶"Sir," seyde Sir Trystrames, "I woll go to the fylde and do what I may."

¶So Sir Trystrames issued oute of the towne wyth suche felyshyp as he myght make, and ded suche dedys that all Bretayne spake of hym. And than at the laste by grete force he slew the Erle Grype his owne hondys—and mo than an hondred knyghtes he slew that day. And than Sir Trystrames was resceyved into the cyté worshypfully with procession.

¶Than kyng Howell enbraced hym in his armys, and seyde, "Sir Trystrames, all my kyngedom I woll resygne to you."

¶"God defende!" seyde Sir Trystrames, "for I am beholdyn thereto for your doughtyrs sake to do for you more than that."

¶So by the grete meanes of the kynge and his sonne there grewe grete love betwyxte Isode and Sir Trystrames, for that lady was bothe goode and fayre, and a woman of noble bloode and fame—and for because that Sir Trystrames had suche chere and ryches and all other plesaunce, that he had allmoste forsakyn La Beale Isode. And so uppon a tyme Sir Trystrames aggreed to wed this Isode le Blaunche Maynes; and so at the laste they were wedded, and solemply hylde their maryayge.

¶And so whan they were abed bothe, Sir Trystrames remembirde hym of his olde lady, La Beale Isode, and than he toke suche a thoughte suddeynly that he was all dysmayde; and other chere made he none but with clyppynge and kyssynge. As for fleyshely lustys, Sir Trystrames had never ado with hir—suche mencion makyth the Freynshe booke:

¶Also hit makyth mencion that the lady wente[3] there had be no plesure but kyssynge and clyppynge. And in the meanetyme there was a knyght in Bretayne, his name was Sir Suppynabyles, and he com over the see into Inglonde; and so he com into the courte of Kynge Arthure. And there he mette with Sir Launcelot du Lake and tolde hym of the maryayge of Sir Trystrames.

Than seyde Sir Launcelot, "Fye uppon hym, untrew knyght to his lady! That so noble a knyght as Sir Trystrames is sholde be founde to his fyrst lady and love untrew, that is the Quene of Cornwayle! But sey ye to hym thus," seyde Sir Launcelot, "that of all knyghtes in the worlde I have loved hym [moost and had moost joye of hym], and all was for his noble dedys. And lette hym wete that the love betwene hym and me is done for ever, and that I gyff hym warnyng: from this day forthe I woll be his mortall enemy." So departed Sir Suppynabiles unto Bretayne agayne, and there he founde Sir Trystrames and tolde hym that he had bene in Kynge Arthures courte.

¶Than Sir Trystrames seyde, "Herd ye onythynge of me?" "So God me helpe," seyde Sir Suppynabyles, "there I harde Sir Launcelot speke of you grete shame, and that ye ar a false knyght to youre lady; and he bade me do you to wyte[4] that he woll be youre mortall foo in every place where he may mete you." "That me repentyth," seyde Sir Trystrames, "for of all knyghtes I loved moste to be in his felyshyp." Than Sir Trystrames was ashamed and made grete mone that ever any knyghtes sholde defame hym for the sake of his lady. And so in this meanewhyle La Beale Isode made a lettir unto Quene Gwenyvere complaynyng her of the untrouthe of Sir Trystrames, how he had wedded the kynges doughter of Bretayne.

¶So Quene Gwenyver sente hir another letter and bade her be of goode comforte, for she sholde have joy aftir sorow; for Sir Trystrames was so noble a knyght called, that by craftes of sorsery ladyes wolde make suche noble men to wedde them—"but the ende," Quene Gwenyver seyde, "shulde be thus: that he shall hate her and love you bettir than ever he dud."

¶So leve we Sir Trystrames in Bretayne, and speke we of Sir Lameroke de Galys, that as he sayled his shyppe felle on a rocke and disperysshed, all save Sir Lameroke and his squyer—for he swamme so myghtyly that fysshers of the Ile of Servayge toke hym up—and his squyer was drowned; and the shypmen had grete laboure to save Sir Lameroke his lyff, for all the comforte that they coude do. And the lorde of that ile hyght Sir Nabon le Noyre, a grete myghty gyaunte; and thys Sir Nabon hated all the knyghtes of Kynge Arthures, and in no wyse he wolde do hem no favoure. And thes fysshers tolde Sir Lameroke all the gyse of Syr Nabon, how there com never knyght of Kynge Arthurs but he distroyed hym. And the laste batayle that ever he ded was wyth Sir Nanowne le Petyte, and whan he had wonne hym he put hym to a shamefull deth in the despyte of Kynge Arthure: he was drawyn lym-meale.

[37]

5

10

fol.181v

15

20

25

30

35

fol.182r

40

45

3. I.e., believed.
4. *Do you to wyte*: let you know.

❡"That forthynkes me," seyde Sir **Lamerok**, "for that knyghtes deth, for he was my cosyn; and yf I were at myne ease[5] as well as ever I was, I wolde revenge his deth."

❡"Pease!" seyde the fysshers, "and make here no wordys; for or ever ye departe frome hens Sir **Nabon** muste know that ye have bene here, othir ellis we shall dye for your sake."

❡"So that I be hole," seyde Sir **Lameroke**, "of my mysse-ease that I have takyn in the see, I woll that ye telle hym that I am a knyght of Kynge **Arthurs**, for I was never ferde[6] to renayne my lorde."

Now turne we unto Sir **Trystrams**, that uppon a day he toke a lytyll barget and hys wyff **Isode le Blaunche Maynys** wyth Syr **Kehydyus**, her brother, to sporte hem on the costis. And whan they were frome the londe, there was a wynde that drove hem into the coste of Walys, uppon this Ile of Servage whereas was Sir **Lameroke**. And there the barget all to-rove, and there Dame **Isode** was hurte; and, as well as they myght, they gate into the forest.

And there by a welle he sye Sir **Segwarydes**, and a damesell with hym, and than aythir salewed other. "Sir," seyde Sir **Segwarydes**, "I know you well for Sir **Trystramys de Lyones**, the man in the worlde that I have moste cause to hate, bycause ye departed the love betwene me and my wyff. But as for that," seyde Sir **Segwarydes**, "I woll never hate a noble knyght for a lyght[7] lady; and therefore I pray you to be my frende, and I woll be yourys unto my power[8]— for wete you well, ye ar harde bestadde in this valey, and we shall have inowe ado aythir[9] to succoure other." And so Sir **Segwarydes** brought Sir **Trystrames** to a lady thereby that was borne in Cornwayle, and she tolde hym all the perels of that valay, how there cam never knyght there but he were takyn presonere or slayne.

❡"Wete you well, fayre lady," seyde Sir **Trystrames**, "that I slewe Sir **Marhalte** and delyverde Cornwayle frome the trewage of Irelonde; and I am he that delyverde the Kynge of Irelonde frome Sir **Blamoure de Ganys**; and I am he that bete Sir **Palomydes**; and wete you welle that I am Sir **Trystrames de Lyones**, that by the grace of God shall delyver this wofull Ile of Servage." So Sir Trystrames was wel eased that nyght. Than one[1] tolde hym there was a knyght of Kynge **Arthurs** that wrakked on the rockes. "What is his name?" seyde Sir **Trystrames**. "We wote nat," seyde the fysshers, "but he kepyth hit no counsel[2] that he is a knyght of Kynge **Arthurs**—and by the myghty lorde [of this yle] he settyth nought."

❡"I pray you," seyde Sir **Trystrames**, "and ye may, brynge hym hydir that I may se hym, and if he be ony of the noble knyghtes, I know hym." Than the good lady prayde the fysshers to brynge hym to hir place.

❡So on the morne they brought hym thydir in a fysshers

[38]
5
10
fol.182v
15
20
25
30
35
40
fol.183r

---

5. *At myne ease:* i.e., in good health.
6. I.e., afraid enough.
7. I.e., wanton.
8. *Unto my power:* i.e., to the best of my ability.
9. *Inowe ado aythir:* more than enough to occupy us both.
1. I.e., someone.
2. I.e., secret.

garmente, and as sone as Sir Trystrames sy hym he smyled uppon hym, and knew hym well—but he knew nat Sir Trystrams. "Fayre sir," seyde Sir Trystrams, "mesemyth be youre chere that ye have bene desesed but late—

¶"And also methynkyth I sholde know you heretoforne."

¶"I woll well," seyde Sir Lamerok, "that ye have seyne me, for the nobelyst knyghtes of the Table Rownde have seyne me and mette with me." "Fayre sir," seyde Sir Trystrames, "telle me youre name."

¶"Sir, uppon a covenaunte I woll tell you, so that ye telle me whether that ye be lorde of thys ilonde or no, that is callyd Sir Nabon le Noyre." "I am nat, nother I holde nat of hym, but I am his foo as well as ye be, and so shall I be founde or I departe of this ile."

¶"Well," seyde Sir Lamerok, "syn ye have seyde so largely unto me, my name is Syr Lamerok de Galys, son unto Kynge Pellynore." "Forsothe, I trow well," seyde Sir Trystrams, "for and³ ye seyde other, I know the contrary."

¶"What ar ye," seyde Sir Lamerok, "that knowith so me?" "Forsothe, sir, I am Sir Trystrames de Lyones." "A! sir, remembir ye nat of the fall ye dud gyff me onys—and aftir that ye refused to fyght on foote with me?"

¶"Sir, that was nat for no feare that I had of you, but me shamed at that tyme to have more ado with you—for as me semed, ye had inowe ado.⁴ But sir, wete you well, for my kyndenesse ye put many ladyes to a repreff whan ye sent the horne from Morgan le Fay unto Kynge Marke—and hit sholde have gone to Kynge Arthure, whereas ye dud that in dispyte of me."

¶"Well," seyde he, "and hit were to do agayne, so wolde I do, for I had lever stryff and debate felle in Kyng Markys courte rether than in Kynge Arthurs courte, for the honour of bothe courtes be nat lyke."

¶"As to that," seyde Sir Trystrams, "I know well:

¶"But that that was done was done for dispyte of me—but all youre malyce, I thanke God, hurte nat gretly. Therefore," seyde Sir Trystrames, "ye shall leve all youre malyce and so woll I, and lette us assay how we may wynne worshyp betwene you and me uppon this gyaunte Sir Nabon le Noyre, that is lorde of this ilonde, to destroy hym."

¶"Sir," seyde Sir Lameroke, "now I undirstonde youre knyghthode; hit may nat be false that all men sey, for of youre bounté, nobles, and worshyp, of all knyghtes ye ar pereles—and for your curtesy and jantylnes I shewed you unkyndnesse, and that now me repentyth."

So in the meanetyme cam worde that Sir Nabon had made a cry that all people sholde be at his castell the fifth day aftir; and the same day the sonne of Nabon sholde be made knyght, and all the knyghtes of that valey and thereaboute sholde be there to juste—

fol.183v

[39]

---

3. I.e., if.
4. As it seemed to me, you had had enough of fighting.

and all tho of the realme of Logrys sholde be there to juste wyth them of Northe Walys, and thydir cam fyve hondred knyghtes.

And so they of the contrey brought thydir Sir Lamerok and Sir Trystrames and Sir Keyhydyus and Sir Segwarydes, for they durste none otherwyse do. And than Nabon lente Sir Lamerok horse and armour at his owne desyre. And so Sir Lamerok justed and dud suche dedis of armys that Sir Nabon and all the people seyde there was never knyght that ever they sie that dud such dedis of armys— for, as the booke seyth, he forjusted all that were there, for the moste party of fyve hondred knyghtes, that none abode hym in his sadyll.

¶Than Sir Nabon profirde Sir Lamerok to play his play[5] with hym—"for I saw never one knyght do so muche uppon one day."

¶"I woll well," seyde Sir Lameroke, "play as I may, but I am wery and sore brused." And there aythir gate a speare; but this Sir Nabone wolde nat encountir with Sir Lameroke, but smote his horse in the forhede and so slew hym. And than Sir Lameroke yode on foote, and turned his shylde and drew his swerde, and there began stronge batayle on foote.

¶But Sir Lameroke was so sore brused and shorte brethid[6] that he traced and traversed somwhat abacke.

¶"Fayre felow," seyde Sir Nabone, "holde thy honde, and I shall shewe the more curtesy than ever I shewyd knyght, because I have sene this day thy noble knyghthode; and therefore stonde thou by, and I woll wete whethir ony of thy felowys woll have ado with me."

¶Whan Sir Trystrames harde that, he seyde, "Sir Nabone, lende me horse and sure armoure, and I woll have ado with you." "Well, felow," seyde Sir Nabone, "go thou to yondir pavylyon and arme the of the beste thou fyndyst there, and I shall play sone a mervayles pley wyth the." Than seyde Sir Trystrames, "Loke ye play well, other ellys peraventure I shall lerne you a new play!"

¶"That is well seyde," seyde Sir Nabone. So whan Sir Trystrames was armed as hym lyked beste, and well shylded and swerded,[7] he dressed to hym on foote—"for well I know that Sir Nabone wolde nat abyde a stroke with a speare, and therefore he woll sle all knyghtes horse."

¶"Now, fayre felow," seyde Sir Nabone, "latte us play!" And so they fought longe on foote, trasynge and traversynge, smytynge and foynynge longe, withoute ony reste.

¶So at the laste Sir Nabone prayde hym to tell hym his name.

¶"Sir," seyde he, "my name ys Sir Trystrames de Lyones, a knyght of Cornwayle, whyche am undir[8] Kynge Marke." "A, thou arte well-com!" seyde Sir Nabone, "for of all knyghtes I have moste desyred to fyght wyth the othir ellys wyth Sir Launcelot." And so they wente than egerly togydir, that at the laste Sir Trystrames slew Sir

fol.184r

How Sir Nabon and his son were slayne by the hondis of Sir Trystramps in the Isle of Serbage

fol.184v

---

5. *Play his play:* i.e., joust.
6. Short of breath.
7. *Shylded and swerded:* furnished with shield and sword.
8. I.e., in the service of.

Nabone—and so forthwithall he lepe to his sonne and strake of his
hede.

¶Than all the contrey seyde they wolde holde of[9] Sir Trystrames
all the whole valay of Servage. "Nay," seyde Sir Trystrames, "I woll
nat so, for here is a worshypfull knyght, Sir Lameroke de Galys, that   5
for me he shall be lorde of this ile—for he hath done here grete
dedis of armys."

¶"Nay," seyde Sir Lameroke, "I woll nat be lorde of this contrey,
for I have nat deserved hit as well as ye; therefore gyff ye hit where
ye woll, for I woll none have."   10

¶"Well," seyde Sir Trystrames, "syn ye nother I woll nat have hit,
lett us gyff hit unto hym that hath nat so well deserved hit."

¶"Sir, do as ye lyste, for the gyffte is yowres, for I woll none
and[1] I had deserved hit." And so by assente hit was yevyn unto Sir
Segwarydes. And he thanked them; and so was he lorde, and wor-   15
shypfully he dud governe hem. And than Sir Segwarydes delyvirde
all the presoners and sette good governaunce in that valey. And so
he turned into Cornwayle and tolde kynge Marke and La Beale
Isode how Sir Trystrames had avaunced hym in the Ile of Servayge.
And there he proclaymed in all Cornwayle of all the aventures of   20
thes two knyghtes; and so was hit opynly knowyn—but full wo was
La Beale Isode whan she herde telle that Sir Trystrames had with
hym Isode le Blaunche Maynys.

¶So turne we unto Sir Lamerok, that rode towarde Kynge Arthures   [40]
courte (and so Sir Trystramys, hys wyff, and Sir Keyhydyus toke a   25
vessell and sayled into Bretayne unto Kynge Howell, where they
were wellcom—and whan they herde of thes adventures they mervayled of his[2] noble dedys.)

¶Now turne we unto Sir Lameroke, that whan he was departed   fol.185r
frome Sir Trystrames he rode oute of the foreste tyll he cam to an   30
ermytage. And whan the ermyte sawe hym, he asked frome whens
he com. "Sir, I am com frome this valey."

¶"That mervayle we off,[3] for this twenty wyntir," seyde the
ermyte, "I saw never knyght passe this contrey but he was other
slayne other[4] vylansely wounded, or passe as a poore presonere."   35

¶"Sir, tho evyll customys are fordone," seyde Sir Lameroke, "for
Sir Trystrames hath slayne youre lorde Sir Nabone, and his sonne."

¶Than was the ermyte glade, and all his brethirne, for he seyde
there was never suche a tirraunte amonge Crystyn men. "And
therefore," seyde the ermyte, "this valey and fraunchyse shall ever   40
holde of Sir Trystrames." So on the morne Sir Lameroke departed;
and as he rode he sawe foure knyghtes fyght ayenste one—and
that one knyght defended hym well, but at the laste the foure
knyghtes had hym downe.

¶And than Sir Lameroke wente betwexte them and asked them   45

---

9. *Holde of*: hold as a feudal grant from (i.e., the people have proclaimed Trystram their new
   lord).
1. I.e., even if.
2. I.e., Trystram's.
3. I.e., of.
4. *other . . . other*: either . . . or.

why they wolde sle that one knyght, and seyde hit was shame, foure ayenste one.

¶"Thow shalt well wete," seyde the foure knyghtes, "that he is false." "So that is your tale," seyde Sir Lameroke, "and whan I here hym speke I woll sey as ye sey? Sir," seyde Sir Lameroke, "how sey you? Can ye nat excuse you none otherwyse but that ye ar a false knyght?"

¶"Sir, yett can I excuse me, bothe with my worde and with my hondys—and that[5] woll I make good uppon one of the beste of them, my body to his body."[6] Than spake they all at onys: "We woll nat jouparté oure bodyes—but wete thou welle," they seyde, "and Kynge Arthure were here hymselff, hit sholde nat lye in his power to save his[7] lyff." "That is seyde to largely,"[8] seyde Sir Lamerok, "but many[9] spekyth behynde a man more than he woll seye to his face. And for because of youre wordis, ye shall undirstonde that I am one of the symplyst[1] of Kynge Arthures courte—and in the worshyp of my lorde, now do your beste—and in the dispyte of you I shall rescow him!" And than they layshed all at onys to Syr Lameroke; but at two strokis he had slayne two of them—than the other two fled.

¶So than Sir Lamerok turned agayne unto that knyght and horsed hym, and asked hym his name.

¶"Sir, my name is Sir Froll of the Oute Ilys." And so he rode with Sir Lameroke and bare hym company; and as they rode by the way, they sawe a semely knyght rydynge and commynge ayenst them, and all in whyght.

¶"A," seyde Sir Froll, "yondir knyght justed but late wyth me and smote me downe; therefore I woll juste with hym."

¶"Ye shall nat do so," seyde Sir Lamerok, "be my counceyle. And ye woll tell me your quarell, where[2] ye justed at his requeste other he at youres." "Nay," seyde Sir Froll, "I justed with hym at my requeste." "Sir, than woll I counceyle you, deale no more with hym, for, lyke his countenaunce,[3] he sholde be a noble knyght and no japer—for methynkys he sholde be of the Rounde Table."

¶"As for that, I woll nat spare," seyde Sir Froll. Than he cryed and seyde, "Sir knyght, make the redy to juste!" "That nedyth nat," seyde the whyghte knyght, "for I have no luste to jape nother juste." So they feautred their sperys, and the whyght knyght overthrewe Sir Froll, and than he rode his way a soffte pace.[4]

¶Than Sir Lameroke rode aftir hym and prayde hym to telle his name—"for mesemyth ye sholde be of the felyshyp of the Rounde Table."

¶"Sir, upon a covenaunte, that ye woll nat telle my name, and also that ye woll tell me youres."

fol.185v

fol.186r

5. I.e., that assertion.
6. *My body to his body:* i.e., one-on-one.
7. I.e., the knight's.
8. *To largely:* too freely, too boastfully.
9. I.e., many a person.
1. I.e., lowest-ranking.
2. I.e., whether.
3. *Lyke his countenaunce:* i.e., as he appears.
4. *A soffte pace:* slowly.

¶"Sir, my name is Sir Lamerok de Galis." "And my name is Sir Launcelot du Lake." Than they putt up their swerdys and kyssed hertely togydirs, and aythir made grete joy of other. "Sir," seyde Sir Lameroke, "and hit please you, I woll do you servyse."

¶"God deffende, sir, that ony of so noble a blood as ye be sholde do me servyse." Than seyde Sir Launcelot, "I am in a queste that I muste do myselff alone." "Now God spede you," seyde Sir Lameroke. And so they departed.

¶Than Sir Lamerok com to Sir Froll and horsed hym agayne. "Sir, what knyght is that?" seyde Sir Froll. "Sir, hit is nat for you to know, nother is no poynte of youre charge."⁵

¶"Ye ar the more uncurteyse," seyde Sir Froll, "and therefore I woll departe felyshyp."

¶"Ye may do as ye lyste—and yett be⁶ my company ye have savid the fayryst floure of your garlonde."⁷

¶So they departed. Than wythin two or three dayes Sir Lamerok founde a knyght at a welle slepynge, and his lady sate with hym and waked. Ryght so com Sir Gawayne and toke the knyghtes lady and sette hir up behynde hys squyer.

¶So Sir Lamerok rode aftir Sir Gawayne and seyde, "Sir, turne ayen!" Than seyde Sir Gawayne, "What woll ye do with me? I am nevew unto Kynge Arthure." "Sir, for that cause I woll forbeare you; othir ellys⁸ that lady sholde abyde with me, [or els ye shold juste with me]." Than Sir Gawayne turned hym, and ran to hym that ought the lady with his speare; but the knyght wyth pure myght smote downe Sir Gawayne and toke his lady with hym—and all this sye Sir Lamerok, and seyde to hymselff, "but I revenge my felow,⁹ he woll sey me dishonoure in Kynge Arthurs courte." Than Sir Lamerok returned and profyrde that knyght to fyght.

¶"Sir, I am redy!" seyde he—and there they cam togedyrs with all theire myght.

¶And Sir Lamerok smote the knyght thorow bothe sydis, that he fylle to the erthe dede.

¶Than that lady rode to that knyghtis brothir, that hyght Sir Bellyaunce le Orgulus, that dwelled faste thereby, and tolde hym how his brother was slayne.

¶"Alas," seyde he, "I woll be revenged!" And so he horsed hym and armed hym, and within a whyle he overtoke Sir Lamerok, and bade hym turne—"and leve that lady, for thou and I muste play a new play; for thow haste slayne my brother Sir Froll that was a bettir knyght than ever was thou." "Ye may well sey hit," seyde Sir Lamerok, "but this day in the playne fylde¹ I was founde the bettir knyght!" So they rode togydyrs and unhorsed eche other, and turned their shyldis and drew their swerdys, and fought myghtyly

5. *Poynte of youre charge:* part of your request.
6. I.e., by way of, through.
7. *Ye have savid the fayryst floure of your garlonde:* i.e., you have preserved your life.
8. *Othir ellys:* i.e., in any other circumstance.
9. I.e., Gawayne.
1. *Playne fylde:* open field of battle.

as noble knyghtes preved, the space of two owres; so than Sir Bellyaunce prayde hym to telle hym his name.

¶"Sir, my name is Sir Lameroke de Galys." "A!" seyde Sir Bellyaunce, "thou arte the man in the worlde that I moste hate, for I
slew my sunnys for thy sake where I saved thy lyff—and now thou   5
haste slayne my brothir Sir Froll! Alas, how sholde I be accorded
with the? Therefore defende the—thou shalt dye; there is none
other way nor remedy."

¶Alas!" seyde Sir Lameroke, "full well me ought to know you, for
ye ar the man that moste have done for me."   10

¶And therewithall Sir Lamerok kneled adowne and besought hym
of grace.

¶"Aryse up," seyde Sir Bellyaunce, "othir ellys there as thou kne-
lyste I shall sle the!"

"That shal nat nede," seyde Sir Lameroke, "for I woll yelde me to   15
you, nat for no feare of you nor of youre strength, but youre goodnesse makyth me to lothe to have ado with you:

¶"Wherefore I requyre you, for Goddis sake and for the honour
of knyghthode, forgyff me all that I have offended unto you."   fol.187r

¶"Alas!" seyde Sir Bellyaunce, "leve thy knelynge, other ellys I   20
shall sle the withoute mercy."

¶Than they yode agayne to batayle, and aythir wounded othir,
that all the grounde was blody there as they fought; and at the laste
Sir Bellyaunce withdrew hym abacke and sette hym downe a lytyll
uppon an hylle, for he was faynte for bledynge, that he myght nat   25
stonde.

¶Than Sir Lameroke threw his shylde uppon his backe and cam
unto hym, and asked hym "What chere?"[2]

¶"Well," seyde Sir Bellyaunce. "A, sir, yett shall I shew you
favoure in youre male ease."[3] "A, knyght," seyde Sir Bellyaunce unto 30
Sir Lamerok, "thou arte a foole, for and I had the at suche avauntage
as thou haste me, I sholde sle the; but thy jantylnesse is so good
and so large that I muste nedys forgyff the myne evyll wyll."

¶And than Sir Lameroke kneled adowne and unlaced fyrst his
umbrere and than his owne.   35

¶And than aythir kyssed othir with wepynge tearys. Than Sir
Lamerok led Sir Bellyaunce to an abbey faste by; and there Sir Lamerok
wolde nat departe from Sir Bellyaunce tylle he was hole. And than
they were sworne togydyrs that none of hem sholde never fyght
ayenste other. So Sir Lamerok departed and wente to the courte of   40
Arthur.

Here levyth of[4] the tale of Sir Lamerok and of Syr Trystramys, and
here begynnyth the tale of Syr La Cote Male Taylé, that was a good
knyght.   45

2. *What chere?*: how are you doing?
3. *Male ease:* distress.
4. *Levyth of:* leaves off, breaks off.

To the courte of Kynge Arthure there cam a yonge man bygly made, and he was rychely beseyne, and he desyred to be made a knyght of the kynges—but his overgarmente sate over-thwartely, howbehit hit was ryche cloth of golde.

¶"What is youre name?" seyde Kynge Arthure. "Sir, my name is Brewnor le Noyre, and within shorte space ye shall know that I am comyn of goode kynne."

¶"Hit may well be," seyde Sir Kay the Senesciall, "but in mok-kynge ye shall be called 'La Cote Male Taylé'—that is as muche to sey 'The Evyll-Shapyn[5] Cote!' " "Hit is a grete thynge that thou askyste," seyde the Kynge—

¶"But for what cause weryst thou that ryche cote?" "Hit is for som cause, sir," he answerde. "I had a fadir, a noble knyght; and as he rode an-huntyng uppon a day, hit happed hym to ley hym downe to slepe. And there cam a knyght that had bene longe his enemy; and whan he saw he was faste on slepe, he all to-hew hym. And thys same cote had my fadir on[6] that tyme; and that makyth[7] this coote to sytte so evyll[8] uppon me, for the strokes be on hit as I founde hit—and never shall hit be amendid for me. Thus, to have my fadyrs deth in remembraunce, I were this coote tyll I be revenged—and because ye ar called the moste nobelyst kynge of the worlde, I com to you to make me a knyght."

¶"Sir," seyde Sir Lamerok and Sir Gaheris, "hit were well done to make hym knyght, for hym besemyth well of persone and of coun-tenaunce that he shall preve a good knyght and a myghty—for, sir, and ye be remembird,[9] evyn suche one was Sir Launcelot whan he cam fyrst into this courte, and full fewe of us knew from whens he cam. And now is he preved the man of moste worshyp in the worlde, and all your courte and Rounde Table is by Sir Launcelot worshypped and amended, more than by ony knyght lyvynge." "That is trouthe," seyde the Kynge, "and tomorow at youre requeste I shall make hym knyght."

¶So on the morne there was an harte founden, and thydir rode Kyng Arthure wyth a company of his knyghtes to sle that herte. And this yonge man that Sir Kay named La Cote Male Taylé was there leffte behynde wyth Quene Gwenyvere. And by a suddeyne adven-ture[1] there was an horryble lyon kepte in a towre of stoon, and he brake lowse and cam hurlyng before the quene and her knyghtes.

¶And whan the Quene sawe the lyon, she cryed oute and fledde and prayde hir knyghtes to rescow her—and there was none but twelve knyghtes that abode, and all the other fledde.

¶Than seyde La Cote Male Taylé, "Now I se that all cowherde knyghtes be nat dede!" And therewithall he drew his swerde and dressed hym before the lyon. And that lyon gaped wyde and cam uppon hym rawmpyng to have slayne hym; and he agayne smote

[IX.1]

fol.187v 5

10

15

20

25

30

fol.188r 35

40

45

---

5. I.e., badly-cut, ill-fitting.
6. *Had my fadir on:* i.e., my father had on.
7. I.e., causes.
8. I.e., poorly.
9. I.e., reminded.
1. I.e., chance event.

hym in the myddys of the hede, that hit claff in sundir and so dayshed downe to the erthe.

¶And anone hit was tolde the Quene how the yong man that Sir **Kay** named **La Cote Male Taylé** had slayne the lyon; and anone with that the Kynge com home and the Quene tolde hym of that adventure. He was well pleased, and seyde, "Uppon payne of myne hede, he shall preve a noble man and faythefull and trewe of his promyse." And so forthewithall the Kynge made hym knyght.

¶"Now, sir," seyde this yonge knyght, "I requyre you and all the knyghtes of the courte that ye calle me none other name but **La Cote Mele Taylé**: insomuche that Sir **Kay** hath so named me, so woll I be called." "I assente me thereto," seyde the Kynge. And so the same day there cam a damesell into the courte, and she brought wyth hir a grete blacke shylde with a whyght honde in the myddis holdynge a swerde; and other pyctoure was there none in that shylde.

Whan Kynge **Arthure** saw her, he asked her from whens she cam and what she wolde. "Sir," she seyde, "I have rydden longe and many a day with this shylde many wayes, and for this cause I am com to youre courte: for there was a good knyght that ought this shylde, and this knyght had undirtake a grete dede of armys to encheve hit. And so by myssefortune another stronge knyght mette with hym by suddeyne aventure, and there they fought longe, and aythir wounded othir passynge sore, and they were so wery that they lefft that batayle on evyn honde.²

¶So this knyght that ought the shylde sawe none other way but he muste dye; and than he commaunded me to bere this shylde to the courte of Kyng **Arthure**, he requyrynge and prayynge som good knyght to take his shylde, and that he wolde fulfylle the queste that he was in."

¶"Now what sey ye to this queste?" seyde Kynge **Arthure**. "Is there here ony of you that woll take uppon you to welde this shylde?" Than was there nat one that wolde speke a worde. Than Sir **Kay** toke the shylde in his hondis and lyfft hit up.

¶"Sir knyght," seyde the damesell, "what is your name?"

¶Wete you well my name is Sir **Kay** the Senesciall that wyde-where is knowyn."

¶"Sir, seyde the damesell, "lay downe that shylde, for wyte thou well hit fallyth nat for you, for he muste be a bettir knyght than ye that shall welde this chylde."³

¶"Damesell," seyde Sir **Kay**, "I toke youre shylde nat to that entente—but go whoso go woll, for I woll nat go with you."

¶Than the damesell stood styll a grete whyle and behylde many of the knyghtes.

¶Than spake this yonge knyght **La Cote Male Taylé** and seyde, "Fayre damesell, I woll take this shylde and the adventure uppon me, and⁴ I wyste whothirward my jurney myght be. For because I was this day made knyght, I wolde take this adventure uppon me."

2. *On evyn honde*: at a stalemate.
3. I.e., shield.
4. I.e., if.

¶"What is youre name, fayre yonge man?" seyde the damesell. "My name is," he seyde, "La Cote Male Taylé." Well may thou be callyd so," seyde the damesell, " 'the knyght wyth the evyll-shapyn coote!' But, and thou be so hardy to take on the to beare that shylde and to folowe me, wete thou well thy skynne shall be as well hewyn as thy cote." "As for that," seyde Sir La Cote Male Taylé, "whan I am so hewyn, I woll aske you[5] no salff to heale me withall!"

¶And forthwithall there com into the courte two squyers, and brought hym grete horsis and his armoure and spearys; and anone he was armed and toke his leve.

¶"Sir, I woll nat," seyde the Kynge, "be[6] my wyll that ye toke uppon you this harde adventure." "Sir," he seyde, "this adventure is myne, and the fyrste that ever I toke uppon me, and that woll I folow whatsomever com of me."

¶Than that damesell departed, and so Sir La Cote Male Taylé faste folowed afftir; and within a whyle he overtoke the damesell— and anone she mysseseyde hym in the fowlyst maner. Than Sir Kay ordayned Sir Dagonet, Kynge Arthurs foole, to folow aftir Sir La Cote Male Taylé; and there Sir Kay ordayned that Sir Dagonet was horsed and armed, and bade hym folow Sir La Cote Male Taylé and profyr hym to juste. And so he ded, and whan he sawe La Cote Male Taylé he cryed and bade make hym redy to juste; so Sir La Cote Male Taylé smote Sir Dagonet ovir his horse croupyn. Than the damesell mocked La Cote Male Taylé and seyde, "Fye for shame! Now arte thou shamed in Kynge Arthurs courte, whan they sende a foole to have ado with the, and specially at thy fyrste justys." Thus she rode longe and chydde.

¶And so within a whyle there cam Sir Bleoberys, the good knyght, and there he justed with Sir La Cote Male Taylé. And there Syr Bleoberys smote hym so sore that horse and all felle to the erthe. Than Sir La Cote Male Taylé arose up lyghtly and dressed his shylde and drew his swerde; and a wolde have done batayle to the uttraunce, for he was woode wroth.

"Nat so," seyde Sir Bleoberys de Ganys, "as at this tyme I woll nat fyght uppon foote." Than the Damesell Maledysaunte rebuked hym in the fowleste maner, and bade hym "turne agayne, cowarde!" "A, damesell," seyde he, "I pray you of mercy to myssesay me no more, for my gryff is inow, though ye gryff me no more. Yet I calle me never the worse knyght, though a marys sonne[7] hath fayled me—and also I counte myselff never the worse man for a falle of[8] Sir Bleoberys."

So thus he rode with her two dayes, and by fortune there he encountred wyth Sir Palomydes, the noble knyght; and in the same wyse Sir Palomydes served hym as ded Sir Bleoberys toforehonde. Than seyde the damesell, "What doste thou here in my felyship? For thou canste nat sytte no knyght nother wythstonde hym one

fol.189r

[3]

How La Cote Male
Taylé justed with
Sir Bleoberys and
had a falle

fol.189v

---

5. I.e., of you.
6. I.e., by.
7. *A marys sonne:* a mare's son (i.e., La Cote Male Taylé's horse).
8. *falle of:* a fall inflicted by.

buffette—but yf[9] hit were Sir **Dagonet**." "A, fayre damesell, I am
nat the worse to take a falle of Sir **Palomydes**; and yett grete dysworshyp have I none, for nother Sir **Bleoberys** nother yett Sir **Palomydes** woll not fyght with me on foote."

¶"As for that," seyde the damesell, "wete you welle they have
disdayne and scorne to alyght of their horsis to fyght with suche a
lewde knyght as thou arte." So in the meanewhyle there com Sir
Mordred, Sir **Gawaynes** brother, and so he felle in felyshyp with the
Damesell **Maledysaunte**.

And than they com before the Castell **Orgulus**; and there was
suche a custom that there myght com no knyght by the castell but
other he muste juste othir be presonere—othir at the leste to lose
his horse and harneyse. And there cam oute two knyghtes ayenste
them; and Sir **Mordred** justyd with the formyste, and that knyght of
the castell smote Sir **Mordred** downe of his horse. And than Sir **La
Cote Male Taylé** justed with that other, and ayther of hem smote
downe other horsis to the erthe; and anone they avoyded their
horsis and aythir of hem toke othirs horses. And than Sir **La Cote
Male Taylé** rode unto that knyght that smote downe Sir **Mordred**,
and there **La Cote Male Taylé** wounded hym passynge sore and putte
hym frome his horse—and he lay as he had bene dede.

¶So he turned unto hym that mette hym afore, and he toke the
flyght towarde the castell; and Sir **La Cote Male Taylé** rode aftir hym
into the Castell **Orgulus**, and there Sir **La Cote Male Taylé** slew hym.
And anone there cam an hondred knyghtys aboute hym, and all
assayled hym—and whan he sawe hys horse sholde be slayne, he
alyght and voyded his horse [and putte the brydel under his feete[1]]
and so put hym oute of the gate. And whan he had so done, he
hurled in amonge them and dressed his backe untyll a ladyes
chambir wall (thynkynge hymselff that he hadde lever dye there
with worshyp than to abyde the rebukes of the Damesell **Maledysaunte**). And so in the meanetyme, as he stood and fought, that lady
that hylde that chambir wente oute slyly at a posterne, and withoute[2] the gatys she founde Sir **La Cote Male Taylé** his horse; and
lyghtly she gate hym by the brydyll and tyed hym to the posterne.

¶And than she yode unto her chambir slyly agayne, for to
beholde how that one knyght faught ayenst an hondred knyghtes.

¶And whan she had beholde hym longe, she wente to a wyndow
behynde his backe and seyde, "Thou knyght that fyghtyst wondirly
well, but for all that at the laste thou muste nedys dye but yf thou
can thorow thy myghty prouesse wynne unto yondir posterne—for
there have I fastened thy horse to abyde the. But wete thou welle,
thou muste thynke on thy worshyp and thynke nat to dye, for thou
mayste nat wynne unto that posterne withoute thou do nobely and
myghtyly."

¶Whan Sir **La Cote Male Taylé** harde her sey so, he gryped his

---

9. *but yf:* unless.
1. *Putte the brydel under his feete:* i.e., made sure the bridle would not get tangled.
2. I.e., outside.

swerde in his honde and put his shylde fayre before hym; and
thorow the thyckyst pres he thryled thorow.

⸿And whan he cam to the posterne, he founde there redy foure
knyghtes; and at two the fyrste[3] strokys he slew two of the knyghtes,
and the other fledde—and so he wanne his horse and rode frome
them (and all hit was rehersed in Kynge Arthurs courte, how he
slew twelve knyghtes within the Castell Orgulus). And so he rode
on his way.

⸿And in the meanewhyle the damesell sayde unto Sir Mordred,
"I wene my foolyssh knyght be othir slayne or takyn presonere."
And than were they ware and saw hym com rydynge; and whan he
was com to them, he tolde all how he had spedde and escaped in
the dispyte of all the castell—"and som of the beste of hem woll
telle no talys." "Thow gabbyst falsely!" seyde the damesell, "that[4]
dare I make good, for as a foole and a dastarde to all knyghthode
they have latte the[5] passe."

⸿"That may ye preve," seyde La Cote Male Taylé. With that she
sente a corroure of hers that allway[6] rode with her; and so he rode
thydir lyghtly and spurred how and in what wyse that knyght ascaped oute of that castell.

⸿Than all the knyghtes cursed hym, and seyde he was a fende
and no man—"for he hath slayne here twelve of oure beste knyghtis, and we went unto[7] this day that hit had bene to muche for Sir
Trystrames de Lyones othir for Sir Launcelot de Lake—and in dyspyte
and magré of us all he is departed frome us." And so hir curroure
com agayne and tolde the damesell all how Sir La Cote Male Taylé
spedde at the Castell Orgulus. Than she smote[8] downe the hede
and seyde but lytyll.

"Be my hede," seyde Sir Mordred to the damesell, "ye ar gretly to
blame so to rebuke hym, for I warne you playnly he is a good
knyght, and I doute nat but he shall preve a noble man. But as
yette he may nat sytte sure on horsebacke; for he that muste be a
good horseman, hit muste com of usage and excercise. But whan
he commyth to the strokis of his swerde, he is than[9] noble and
myghty. And that saw Sir Bleoberys and Sir Palomydes—for wete
you well they were wyly men of warre, for they wolde know anone,
whan they sye a yonge knyght, by his rydynge, how they were sure
to gyffe hym a falle frome his horse othir a grete buffett; but for
the moste party they wyll nat lyght on foote with yonge knyghtes,
for they ar myghtyly and strongely armed. For in lyke wyse Syr
Launcelot du Lake, whan he was fyrste made knyght, he was oftyn
put to the worse on horsebacke; but ever uppon foote he recoverde
his renowne and slew and defowled many knyghtes of the Rounde
Table. And therefore the rebukes that Sir Launcelot ded unto many

fol.190v
5

10

15

20

25

30

35
fol.191r

40

---

3. *At two the fyrste*: i.e., at the two first.
4. I.e., that assertion.
5. Thee.
6. I.e., always.
7. *Went unto*: believed until.
8. I.e., bowed.
9. I.e., then.

knyghtes causyth them that be men of prouesse to beware, for oftyn tyme I have seyne the olde preved knyghtes rebuked and slayne by them that were but yonge begynners." Thus they rode sure, talkyng by the wey togydyrs.

5

❡Here this tale overlepyth a whyle unto Sir Launcelott—

That whan he was com to the courte of Kynge Arthure, than harde he telle of the yonge knyghte Sir La Cote Male Taylé, how he slew the lyon and how he toke uppon hym the adventures of the blacke shylde—whyche was named at that tyme the hardyest adventure of the worlde.

[5]

10

"So God me save!" seyde Sir Launcelot unto many of his felowys, "hit was shame to all the good noble knyghtes to suffir suche a yonge knyght to take so hyghe adventure on hym for his distruccion. For I woll that ye wyte," seyde Sir Launcelot, "that this damesell Maledysaunte hath borne that shylde many a day for to seche the moste proved knyghtes; and that was she that Sir Breunys Saunze Pité toke the shylde frome—[1]

15

❡"And aftir Sir Trystrames de Lyones rescowed that shylde frome hym and gaff hit to the damesell agayne, a lytyll afore that tyme that Sir Trystrames faught with my nevew Sir Blamoure de Ganys for a quarell that was betwyxte the Kynge of Irelonde and hym." Than many knyghtes were sory that Sir La Cote Male Taylé was gone forthe to that adventure.

20

fol.191v

25

"Truly," seyde Sir Launcelot, "I caste me to ryde aftir hym." And so within seven dayes Sir Launcelot overtoke Sir La Cote Male Taylé, and than he salewed hym and the damesell Maledysaunte; and whan Sir Mordred saw Launcelot, than he leffte their felyship, and so Sir Launcelot rode with hem all a day.[2] And ever that damesell rebuked Sir La Cote Male Taylé; and than Sir Launcelot answerde for hym; than she leffte of—and rebuked Sir Launcelot. So thys meanetyme Sir Trystramps sente by a damesell a lettir unto Sir Launcelot, excusynge hym[3] of the weddynge of Isod le Blaunche Maynes, and seyde in the lettir, as he was a trew knyght, he had never ado fleyshly with Isode le Blaunche Maynys. And passyng curteysly and jantely Sir Trystrames wrote unto Sir Launcelot, ever besechynge hym to be hys good frende and[4] unto La Beall Isod of Cornwayle, and that Sir Launcelot wolde excuse hym if that ever he saw her. And within shorte tyme, by the grace of God, Sir Trystramps seyd that he wolde speke with La Beall Isode and with hym ryght hastyly.

30

35

40

Than Sir Launcelot departed frome the damesell and frome Sir La Cote Male Taylé for to oversé that lettir and to wryte another lettir unto Sir Trystram. And in the meanewhyle Sir La Cote Male Talé rode with the damesel untyll they cam to a castell that hyght

45

---

1. *And that was she . . . the shylde frome*: Malory here appears to have confused the present shield with the one earlier sent to Launcelot by the Lady of the Lake (see p. 252).
2. *All a day*: daily.
3. I.e., himself.
4. I.e., and good friend.

Pendragon. And there were six knyghtes that stood afore hym, and one of them profirde to fyght or to juste with hym; and so Sir La Cote Male Taylé smote hym over hys horse croupe. And than the fyve knyghtes sette uppon hym all at onys with their spearys, and there they smote La Cote Male Taylé downe, horse and man; and than they ded alyght suddeynly and sette their hondis uppon hym all at onys and toke hym presonere, [and soo ledde hym unto the castel and kepte hym as prysoner.]

And on the morne Sir Launcelot arose and delyverde[5] the damesel with lettirs unto Sir Trystram, and than he toke hys way aftir Sir La Cote Male Taylé. And by the way uppon a brydge there was a knyght that profirde Sir Launcelot to juste; and Sir Launcelot smote hym downe. And than they faught uppon foote a noble batayle togydirs, and a myghty, and at the laste Sir Launcelot smote hym downe grovelynge uppon hys hondys and hys kneys; and than that knyght yelded hym, and Sir Launcelot resseyved hym.

❡"Fayre sir," seyde the knyght, "I requyre you, telle me youre name, for muche my harte yevith unto you."

❡"Nay," seyd Sir Launcelot, "as at thys tyme I woll nat telle you my name, onles that ye telle me youre name." "Sertaynly," seyde the knyght, "my name ys Sir Nerobeus, that was made knyght of my lorde Sir Launcelot du Lake." "A, Sir Nerobeus de Lyle!" seyde Sir Launcelot, "I am ryght glad that ye ar proved a good knyght, for now wyte you well my name ys Sir Launcelot." "Alas," seyde Sir Nerobeus, "what have I done?" And therewithall he felle flatlynge to hys feete and wolde have kyste them; but Sir Launcelot wolde nat suffir hym, and than aythir made grete joy of other. And than Sir Nerobeus tolde Sir Launcelot that he sholde nat go by the Castell of Pendragon— "for there ys a lorde, a myghty knyght, and many myghty knyghtes with hym, and thys nyght I harde sey that they toke a knyght pre- sonere that rode with a damesell—and they sey he ys a knyght of the Rounde Table."

"A," seyde Sir Launcelot, "that knyght ys my felow, and hym shall I rescowe and borow, or ellis lose my lyff therefore." And therewithall he rode faste tyll he cam before the Castell of Pen- drag[on; and][6] anone therewithall there cam six knyghtes, and all [made hem redy] to sette uppon Sir Launcelot at onys. Than Sir [Launcelot feutryd his] speare and smote the formyst, that he br[ake his bak in sonder]—and three of them smote hym, and three fa[yled. And thenne Sire Launcelot] passed thorow them; and lyghtly h[e torned in ageyne and smote] anothir knyght thorow the brest [and thorououte the bak,] more than an elle—and there[withalle his spere brak. Soo thenne] all the remenaunte of the foure k[nyghtes drewe their swerdes and lasshed] at Sir Launcelot; and at every s[troke Sire Launcelot bestowed so his] strokis that at foure

fol.192r

[6]

fol.192v

---

5. I.e., delivered to.
6. The lower outside corner of a leaf in the Winchester MS has been torn away at this point in the text, thus necessitating the frequent borrowings from Caxton's edition from here through the next page.

strokis sundry[7] they avoyded their sadyls passynge sore wounded—
and furthwithall he rode hurlynge into the castell.

And anone the lorde of that castell—which was called Sir Bryan
de Les Iles, whych was a noble man and a grete enemy to Kynge
Arthure—so within a whyle he was armed and on horsebacke; and
than they feautred their spearis and hurled togydirs so strongly that
bothe their horsys russhed to the erthe. And than they avoyded
their sadyls, and dressed their shyldis and drew their swerdis, and
flowe togydirs as wood[8] men—and there were many strokis [yeven
in] a whyle.

At the laste Sir Launcelot gaff Sir Bryan such a buffette that he
kneled uppon hys knees; and than Sir Launcelot russhed uppon
hym with grete force and pulled of his helme. And whan Sir Bryan
sy that he sholde be slayne, he yelded hym and put hym in hys
mercy and in hys grace. Than Sir Launcelot made hym to delyver
all hys presoners that he had within hys castell; and therein
Sir Launcelot founde of Kynge Arthurs knyghtes thirty knyghtes and
fourty ladyes—and so he delyverde hem and than he rode his way.

And anone as Sir La Cote Male Taylé was delyverde, he gate hys
horse and hys harneyse and hys damesell Maledysaunte. The meanewhyle Sir Neroveus, that Sir Launcelot had foughtyn withall before
at the brydge, he sente a damesell aftir Sir Launcelot to wete how
[he] had spedde at the castell of Pendragon. And than they in the
[castel mervey]led what knyght he was that was there whan [Sir
Bryan and his] knyghtes delyverde all tho presoners.

❡"Syr, [have ye no merveille,"] seyde the damesell, "for the beste
[knyghte in this world] was here and ded thys jurnay—and wyte
[ye wel," she said, "it was Sire Launc]elot." Than was Sir Bryan full
glad, [and soo was his lady and al]l hys knyghtes, that he sholde
wynne [them. And whan the damoy]sell and Sir La Cote Male Taylé
[understood that it was Syr La]uncelot that had rydden with hem
[in felauship, and that she reme]mbirde her how she had rebuked
hym and called hym cowarde, than she was passyng hevy.

❡So than they toke their horsis and rode forthe a great pace
aftir Sir Launcelot, and within two myle they overtoke hym, and
salewed hym and thanked hym—and anone the damesell cryed Sir
Launcelot mercy of hir evyll dede, and seyyng, "For now I know ye
ar the floure of all knyghthode of the worlde, and ye and Sir Trystram departe hit even betwene you. For God knowith, be my good
wyll," seyde the damesell, "that I have sought you, my lorde Sir
Launcelot and Sir Trystrams longe, and now I thanke God I have
mette with you. And onys at Camelot I mette with Sir Trystrams,
and there he rescowed thys blacke shylde with the whyght honde
holdyng a naked swerde, that Sir Brewnys Saunz Pité had takyn
frome me." "Now, fayre damesell," seyde Sir Launcelot, "who tolde
you my name?" "Sir," seyde she, "there cam a damesel frome a
knyght that ye fought withall at a brydge, and she tolde me that

fol.193r

[7]

7. Four separate strokes.
8. I.e., mad.

youre name was Sir Launcelot du Lake." "Blame have she therefore," seyde he, "but her lorde, Sir Neroveus, had tolde hir:

¶"But, damesell," seyde Sir Launcelot, "uppon thys covenaunte I woll ryde with you: so that ye wyll nat rebuke thys knyght Sir La Cote Male Taylé no more—for he ys a good knyght, and I doute nat but he shall preve a noble man; and for hys sake and pité, that he sholde nat be destroyed, I folowed hym to succour hym in thys grete nede." "A, Jesu thanke you!" seyde the damesell, "for now I woll sey unto you and to hym bothe, I rebuked hym never for none hate that I hated hym, but for grete love that I had to hym; for ever I supposed that he had bene to yonge and to tendur of ayge to take uppon hym thys aventure. And therefore be my wyll I wolde have dryvyn hym away for jelosy[9] that I had of hys lyff—for hit may be no yonge knyghtes dede that shall enchyve thys adventure to the ende."

"Perdé!" seyd Sir Launcelot, "hit ys well seyde of[1] you! And where ye ar called the Damesel Maledysaunt, I woll calle you the Damesell Byeau-Pansaunte." And so they rode forth togydirs a grete whyle unto they cam unto the contreye of Surluse, and there they founde a fayre vyllayge wyth a stronge brydge lyke a fortresse. And whan Sir Launcelot and they were at the brydge, there sterte forthe afore them of jantillmen and yomen many that seyde, "Fayre lordis, ye may nat passe thys brydge and thys fortresse because of that blacke shylde that I se one of you beare; and therefore there shall nat passe but one of you at onys—therefore chose you whych of you shall entir within thys brydge fyrst." Than Sir Launcelot profird hymselfe firste to juste and entir within thys brydge.

¶"Sir," seyde Sir La Cote Male Taylé, "I besech you to lette me entir within thys fortresse; and if I may spede well, I woll sende for you; and if hit so be that I be slayne, there hit goth;[2] and if I be takyn presonere, than may you rescow me."

¶"Sir, I am loth that ye sholde passe this passage first," seyde Sir Launcelot.

¶"Sir," seyde Sir La Cote Male Taylé, "I pray you lat me put my body in that adventure." "Now go youre way," seyde Sir Launcelot, "and Jesu be youre spede."

¶So he entird anone, and there mate[3] with hym two brethirne: the tone hyght Sir Playne de Fors and that othir hyght Sir Playne de Amoris. And anone they justed with Sir La Cote Male Taylé; and Sir La Cote Male Taylé smote downe Sir Playne de Fors, and aftir he smote downe Sir Playne de Amoris. And than they dressed their shyldis and swerdys and bade Sir La Cote Male Taylé alyght, and so he ded. And there was daysshynge and foynynge with swerdis, and so they began to assayle othir full harde; and they gaff Sir La Cote Male Taylé many grete woundis uppon hed and breste and uppon

fol.193v

How Sir La Cote Male Taylé strake adowne Sir Playne de Fors and Sir Playne de Amoris

9. I.e, concern.
1. I.e., by.
2. So it goes.
3. I.e., met.

shuldirs. And as he myght ever amonge⁴ he gaff sad strokis agayne; and than the two brethirne traced and traverced for to be of both hondis⁵ of Sir La Cote Male Talé—but he by fyne forse and knyghtly proues gate hem afore hym. And whan he felte hym so wounded, than he doubled hys strokis and gaffe them so many woundis that he felde hem to the erthe, and wolde have slayne them had they nat yelded them.

And ryght so Sir **La Cote Male Taplé** toke the beste horse that there was of the three, and so he rode forth hys way to the othir fortres and brydge. And there he mette with the thirde brother— hys name was Sir **Plenorpus**, a full noble knyght—and there they justed togydirs; and aythir smote other downe, horse and man, to the erthe. And than they avoyded their horsys and dressed their shyldis and swerdis, and than they gaff many sad strokis; and one whyle the one knyght was afore on the brydge, and another whyle the other. And thus they faught two owres and more and never rested—and ever Sir **Launcelot** and the damesell behylde them. "Alas," seyde the damesell, "my knyght fyghttyth passynge sore and overlonge!"

❡"Now may ye se," seyde Sir **Launcelot**, "that he ys a noble knyght, for to considir hys firste⁶ batayle and his grevous woundis —and evyn forthwithall, so wounded as he ys, hit ys mervayle that he may endure thys longe batayle with that good knyght." Thys meanewhyle Sir **La Cote Male Taplé** sanke ryght downe uppon the erthe, what for⁷ wounded and for-bled he myght nat stonde. Than the tothir knyght had pyté off hym and seyde, "Fayre knyght, dys- may you nat, for had ye bene freysshe whan ye mette with me as I was, I wote well that I coude nat have endured you; and therefore, for youre noble dedys of armys, I shall shew to you kyndenes and jantilnes all that I may." And furthewithall thys noble knyght Sir **Plenorpus** toke hym up in hys armys and ledde hym into hys towre. And than he commaunded hym the wyne and made to serch hym and to stop hys bledynge woundys.

❡"Sir," seyde Sir **La Cote Mal Taplé**, "withdraw you from me and hyghe you to yondir brydge agayne, for there woll mete with you another maner⁸ a knyght than ever was I."

❡"Why," seyde Sir **Plenorpus**, "ys there behynde⁹ ony mo of youre felyship?"

❡"Ye, sir, wyte you well there ys a muche bettir knyght than I am." "What ys hys name?" seyde Sir **Plenorpus**. "Sir, ye shall nat know for¹ me." "Well," seyde the knyght, "he shall be encountird withall, whatsomever he be." And anone he herde a knyght calle that seyde, "Sir **Plenorpus**, where arte thou? Othir thou muste dely- ver me that presoner that thou haste lad into thy towre, othir ellis

fol.194r

How Sir Plenorius
smote downe La
Cote Male Taplé

fol.194v

---

4. *Ever amonge:* every now and then.
5. *Of both hondis:* on both sides.
6. I.e., previous.
7. *What for:* i.e., what with being.
8. I.e., manner.
9. I.e., left behind.
1. I.e., because of.

com and do batayle with me!" Than Sir Plenorpus gate hys horse
and cam, with a speare in hys honde, waloppynge towarde Sir Launcelot; and than they began to feauter theire spearys, and cam togydir
as thundir, and smote aythir othir so myghtyly that their horsis
felle downe undir them. And than they avoyded their horsis and   5
pulled oute their swerdis, and lyke too bullis they laysshed togydirs
with grete strokis and foynys.

⁋But ever Sir Launcelot recoverde grounde uppon hym; and Sir
Plenorpus traced to have gone aboute hym, but Sir Launcelot wolde
nat suffir that, but bare hym backer and backer tylle he cam nye   10
hys towre gate. And than seyde Sir Launcelot, "I know you well for
a good knyght, but wyte thou well thy lyff and deth ys in my honde;
and therefore yelde the to me, and thy presonere."

⁋But he answerde no worde, but strake myghtyly uppon Sir
Launcelotis helme, that the fyre sprange oute of hys yen. Than Sir   15
Launcelot doubeled his strokes so thycke and smote at hym so mygh-
tyly that he made hym knele uppon his kneys; and therewithall Sir
Launcelot lepe uppon hym and pulled hym grovelynge downe.

⁋Than Sir Plenorpus yelded hym and hys towre and all his presoners at hys wylle; than Sir Launcelot receyved hym and toke hys   20
trowthe. And than he rode to the tothir brydge, and there Sir Launcelot justed with othir three of hys brethirn: that one hyght Sir
Pyllownes, and the othir hyght Sir Pellogres, and the thirde hyght
Sir Pelaundris. And first uppon horsebacke Sir Launcelot smote hem
doune, and aftirwarde he bete them on foote and made them to   25
yelde them unto hym. And than he returned ayen unto Sir Plenorpus; and there he founde in hys preson Kynge Carados of Scotlonde
and many other knyghtes, and all they were delyverde. And than   fol.195r
Sir La Cote Male Talé cam to Sir Launcelot, and than Sir Launcelot
wolde have gyvyn hym all thys fortresse and the brydges.   30

⁋"Nay, sir," seyde La Cote Male Taylé, "I woll nat have Sir Plenorpus lyvelode. With² that he wyll graunte you, my lorde Sir Launcelot, to com unto Kynge Arthurs house and to be hys knyght, and
all hys brethirne, I woll pray you, my lorde, to latte hym have hys
lyvelode."   35

⁋"I woll well," seyde Sir Launcelot, "with thys, that he woll com
to the courte of Kynge Arthure and bycom hys man, and hys brethern fyve—and as for you, Sir Plenorpus, I woll undirtake," seyde Sir
Launcelot, "at the nexte feste, so there be a place voyde, that ye shall
be knyght of the Rounde Table."   40

⁋"Sir," seyde Sir Plenorpus, "at the nexte feste of Pentecoste I
woll be at Kynge Arthurs courte, and at that tyme I woll be gyded
and ruled as Kynge Arthure and ye woll have me." Than Sir Launcelot
and Sir La Cote Male Taylé reposed them there untyll they were
hole of hir woundis; and there they had myry chere and good reste   45
and many good gamys—and there were many fayre ladyis. And so   [9]
in the meanewhyle cam Sir Kay the Senesciall and Sir Brandiles,
and anone they felyshipped with them.

2. I.e., provided.

And so within ten dayes they departed, the knyghtes of Kynge
Arthurs courte, from thes fortres.[3] And as Sir Launcelot cam by the
Castell of Pendragon, there he put Sir Bryan de Lese Iles from[4] his
londes, for because he wolde never be withholde with Kynge Arthur;
and all the castell of Pendragon and all the londis thereof he gaff   5
to Sir La Cote Male Taylé. And than Sir Launcelot sente for Sir Neroveus that he made onys knyght, and he made hym to have all the
rule of that castell and of that contrey undir Sir La Cote Male Taylé.
And so they rode unto Kynge Arthurs courte all hole togydirs; and
at Pentecoste nexte folowynge there was Sir Plenoryus and Sir La   10
Cote Male Taylé (called otherwyse be ryght[5] Sir Brewne le Noyre);
and bothe they were made knyghtes of the Rounde Table, and grete
londis Kynge Arthure gaff them.

And there Sir Breune le Noyre wedded that Damesell Maledy-   fol.195v
saunte—and aftir she was called the Lady Byeaue Ypbante. But ever   15
aftir for the more[6] party he was called La Cote Male Taylé; and he
preved a passyng noble knyght and a myghty, and many worshipfull
dedys he ded aftir in hys lyff. And Sir Plenoryus preved a good
knyght and was full of proues—and all the dayes of theyre lyff for
the moste party they awayted[7] uppon Sir Launcelot. And Sir Plenor-   20
yus brethirne were ever knyghtes of Kynge Arthurs—and also, as
the Freynshe booke makith mencion, Sir La Cote Male Taylé
revenged the deth of hys fadir.

Now leve we here Sir Launcelot de Lake and Sir La Cote Male   [10]
Taylé, and turne we unto Sir Trystram de Lyones that was in   25
Bretayne—

¶That whan La Beall Isode undirstood that he was wedded, she
sente to hym by hir maydyn, Dame Brangwayn, pyteuous lettirs as
coude be thought and made; and hir conclusyon was thus: that if
hit pleased Sir Trystram to com to hir courte and brynge with hym   30
Isode le Blaunche Maynys, and they shulde be kepte als well as herselff. Than Sir Trystram called unto hym Sir Keyhydyus and asked
hym whether he wolde go with hym into Cornwayle secretely; he
answerde hym and seyde that he was redy at all tymes. And than
he lete ordayne prevayly a lityll vessell, and therein they sayled, Sir   35
Trystram, Sir Keyhydyus, and Dame Brangwayne, and Governayle, Sir
Trystrams squyar. So whan they were in the see a contraryus wynde
blew them unto the costis of North Walis, ny the Foreyste Perelus.

Than seyde Sir Trystrames, "Here shall ye abyde me thes ten
dayes, and Governayle, my squyer, with you. And if so be I com   40
nat agayne by that day, take the nexte way into Cornwayle, for in
thys foreyste ar many strange adventures, as I have harde sey, and
som of hem I caste to preve[8] or that I departe—and whan I may,
I shall hyghe me aftir you."

Than Sir Trystrams and Sir Keyhydyus toke their horsis and   fol.196r   45
departed frome theire felyship. And so they rode within that

---

3. I.e., fortresses.
4. *put . . . from:* evicted.
5. *be ryght:* rightfully.
6. I.e., most.
7. I.e., attended.
8. *Caste to preve:* intend to put to the test.

foreyste a myle and more; and at the laste Sir Trystramps saw before
them a lykely knyght syttyng armed by a well, and a stronge myghty
horse stood passyng nyghe hym i-tyed to an oke, and a man hovyng
and rydynge by hym, ledynge an horse lode with spearys. And thys
knyght that sate at the well semyd by hys countenaunce to be   5
passyng hevy; than Sir Trystramps rode nere hym and seyde, "Fayre
knyght, why sitte you so droupynge? Ye seme to be a knyght
arraunte by youre armys and harneys; and therefore dresse you to
juste with one of us, other with bothe."

¶Therewithall that knyght made no wordes, but toke hys shylde   10
and buckeled hit aboute hys necke; and lyghtly he toke hys horse
and lepte uppon hym; and than he toke a grete speare of hys squyre
and departed hys way a furlonge.

¶Than Sir Keyhydyus asked leve of Sir Trystrames to juste firste.

¶"Sir," do your beste," seyde Sir Trystrames. So they mette togy-   15
dirs; and there Sir Keyhydius had a falle, and was sore wounded an
hyghe abovyn the pappis. Than Sir Trystramps seyde, "Knyght, that
ys well justed—now make you redy unto me!"

¶"Sir, I am redy," seyde the knyght. And anone he toke a grete
speare and encountird with Sir Trystramps. And there by fortune   20
and by grete force that knyght smote downe Sir Trystramps frome
hys horse, and had a grete falle. Than Sir Trystram was sore
ashamed, and lyghtly he avoyded hys horse, and put hys shylde
afore hys shulder and drew hys swerde.

¶And than Sir Trystramps requyred[9] that knyght of hys knygh-   25
thode to alyghte uppon foote and fyght with hym.

¶"I woll well," seyde the knyght. And so he alyght uppon foote
and avoyded hys horse, and kest hys shylde uppon hys shuldir and
drew oute hys swerde; and there they fought a longe batayle togydirs—nyghe two owrys. Than Sir Trystramps seyde, "Fayre knyght, 30
holde thyne honde a lityll whyle and telle me of whens thou arte   fol.196v
and what ys thy name." "As for that," seyde the knyght, "I woll be
avysed;[1] but, and ye woll telle me youre name, peradventure I woll
telle you myne."

¶"Now, fayre knyght," he seyde, "my name ys Sir Trystram de   [11]   35
Lyones." "Sir, and my name ys Sir Lamerok de Galys." "A! Sir Lamerok," seyde, Sir Trystram, "well be we mette! And bethynke the[2] now
of the despite thou dedist me of the sendynge of the horne[3] unto
Kynge Markis courte, to the entente to have slayne or dishonourde
my lady, Quene La Beall Isode—and therefore wyte thou well,"   40
seyde Sir Trystramps, "the tone of us two shall dy or[4] we departe."

¶"Sir," seyde Sir Lamerok, "that tyme that we were togydirs in
the Ile of Servage ye promysed me bettir frendeship."[5] So Sir Trystramps wolde make no lenger delayes, but laysshed at Sir Lamerok;

45

9. I.e., requested.
1. *Be avysed:* consider, think about it.
2. *Bethynke the:* think to yourself.
3. See p. 268.
4. I.e., before.
5. See p. 274.

and thus they faught longe, tylle aythir were wery of other. Than Sir Trystrams seyde unto Sir Lamorak, "In all my lyff mette I never with such a knyght that was so bygge and so well-brethed. Therefore," sayde Sir Trystramys, "hit were pité that ony of us bothe sholde here be myscheved." "Sir," seyde Sir Lamerok, "for youre renowne and your name I woll that ye have the worship, and therefore I woll yelde me unto you." And therewith he toke the poynte of hys swerde in hys honde to yelde hym.

"Nay," seyde Sir Trystrames, "ye shall nat do so, for well I know youre profirs are more of your jantilnes than for ony feare or drede ye have of me." And therewithall Sir Trystramys profferde hym hys swerde and seyde, "Sir Lamerak, as an overcom knyght I yelde me to you as a man of moste noble proues that I ever mette."

¶"Nay," seyde Sir Lamerok, "I woll do you jantylnes; I requyre you, lat us be sworne togydirs that never none of us shall aftir thys day have ado with other." And therewithall Sir Trystrames and Sir Lamorak sware that never none of hem sholde fyght agaynste othir, for well nother for woo. And thys meanewhyle com Sir Palomydes, the good knyght, folowyng the Questyng Beste[6] that had in shap lyke a serpentis hede and a body lyke a lybard, buttokked lyke a lyon and footed lyke an harte—and in hys body there was such a noyse as hit had bene twenty couple of houndys questynge,[7] and suche noyse that beste made wheresomever he wente.

And thys beste evermore Sir Palomydes folowed, for hit was called hys queste. And ryght so as he folowed this beste, hit cam by Sir Trystram, and sone aftir cam Sir Palomydes. And to breff thys mater, he smote downe Sir Trystramys and Sir Lamorak bothe with one speare—and so he departed aftir the Beste Glatyssaunte (that was called the Questynge Beste), wherefore thes two knyghtes were passynge wrothe that Sir Palomydes wold nat fyght with hem on foote.

¶(Here men may undirstonde, that[8] bene men of worshyp, that man was never fourmed that all tymes myght attayne, but somtyme he was put to the worse by malefortune; and at som tyme the wayker knyght put the byggar knyght to a rebuke.)[9]

Than Sir Trystrams and Sir Lamerok gate Sir Kayhydyus uppon a shylde betwyxte them bothe and led hym to a fosters lodge; and there they gaff hym in charge to kepe hym well—and with hym they abode three dayes. Than thes two knyghtes toke their horsys, and at a crosse they departed;[1] and than seyde Sir Trystramys to Sir Lamorak, "I requyre you, if ye hap to mete with Sir Palomydes, say to hym that he shall fynde me at the same welle there we mette tofore; and there I, Sir Trystramys, shall preve whether he be bettir knyght than I." And so ayther departed frome othir a sondry way; and Sir Trystramys rode nyghe there as was Sir Kayhydyus. And Sir

Here Sir Trystrams and Sir Lamorak faught tyll they were wery bothe; and so they lefte on evyn honde and were swore togydir   5

[12]
fol.197r   20

---

6. On this remarkable creature, see n. 9, p. 31.
7. I.e., hunting.
8. I.e., those that.
9. Another of Malory's few brief direct injunctions to the reader; cf. those occurring at pp. 137, 314, 595, 625, and 680.
1. *Crosse:* i.e., crossroads. *Departed:* i.e., separated.

Lamorak rode untyll he cam to a chapell, and there he put hys horse unto pasture; and anone there cam Sir Mellyagaunce that was Kynge Bagdemagus sonne, and he there put hys horse to pasture, and was nat ware of Sir Lamerok. And than thys knyght Sir Mellyagaunce made hys mone of the love that he had to Quene Gwenyver—and there he made a wofull complaynte.

fol.197v
5

¶All thys harde Sir Lamorak, and on the morne Sir Lamorake toke hys horse and rode unto the foreyste, and there he mette with two knyghtes hovyng undir the woodshaw. "Fayre knyghtes," seyde Sir Lamerok, "what do ye, hovyng here and wacchynge? And yff ye be knyghtes arraunte that wyll juste, lo I am redy." "Nay, Sir knyght," they seyde, "we abyde nat here for to juste with you, but we lye in a wayte uppon a knyght that slew oure brothir."

10

¶"What knyght was that," seyde Sir Lamorak, "that ye wolde mete withall?"

15

¶"Sir," they seyde, "hit ys Sir Launcelot, that we woll slee and he com thys way." "Ye take uppon you a grete charge," seyde Sir Lamorake, "for Sir Launcelot ys a noble proved knyght."

¶"As for that, sir, we doute[2] nat, for there ys none of us but we ar good inowghe for hym." "I woll nat beleve that, seyde Sir Lamerok, "for I harde never yet of no knyght dayes of oure lyff but Sir Launcelot was to bygge for hym." Ryght as they talked, Sir Lameroke was ware how Sir Launcelot com rydynge streyte towarde them. Than Sir Lamorak salewed hym, and he hym agayne; and than Sir Lamorak asked Sir Launcelot if there were onythynge that he myght do for hym in thys[3] marchis. "Nay," seyde Sir Launcelot, nat at thys tyme, I thanke you." Than ayther departed frome other; and Sir Lamorake rode ayen there as he leffte the two knyghtes, and than he founde them hydde in the leved woode.

20

[13]

25

¶"Fye on you" seyde, Sir Lamerak, "false cowardis!—that pité and shame hit ys that ony of you sholde take the hyghe order of knyghthode."

30

¶So Sir Lamerok departed fro them; and within a whyle he mette with Sir Mellyagaunce. And than Sir Lamorak asked hym why he loved Quene Gwenyver as he ded—"for I was nat far frome you whan ye made youre complaynte by the chapell." "Ded ye so?" seyde Sir Mellyagaunce. "Than woll I abyde[4] by hit: I love Quene Gwenyver." "What woll ye with hit?"[5] "I woll preve and make hit good that she ys the fayryste lady and moste of beauté in the worlde."

35

fol.198r

¶"As to that," seyde Sir Lamerok, "I say nay thereto, for Quene Morgause of Orkeney, modir unto Sir Gawayne, for she ys the fayryst lady that beryth the lyff." "That ys nat so!" seyde Sir Mellyagaunce, "and that woll I preve with my hondis."

40

¶"Wylle ye so?" seyde Sir Lamorak. "And in a bettir quarell kepe I nat to fyght!" So they departed ayther frome othir in grete wrathe; and than they com rydyng togydir as hit had bene thundir—

45

2. I.e., fear.
3. I.e., these.
4. I.e., stand.
5. *What woll ye with hit*: i.e., what will you do about your love.

and aythir smote other so sore that their horsis felle backewarde
to the erthe. And than they avoyded their horsys, and dressed their
shyldis and drew their swerdis, and than they hurteled togydirs as
wylde borys; and thus they fought a grete whyle—for Sir **Melly-**
agaunce was a good man and of grete myght, but Sir **Lamorak**   5
was harde byg[6] for hym and put hym allwayes abacke—but aythir
had wounded othir sore. And as they stood thus fyghtynge, by fortune com Sir **Launcelot** and Sir **Bleoberys**; and than Sir **Launcelot** rode
betwyxte them and asked them for what cause they fought so
togydirs—"and ye ar bothe of the courte of Kynge **Arthure!**"   10

¶"Sir," seyde Sir **Mellyagaunce**, "I shall telle you for what cause   [14]
we do thys batayle. I praysed my lady, Quene **Gwenyvere**, and seyde
she was the fayryste lady of the worlde; and Sir **Lameroke** seyde nay
thereto, for he seyde Quene **Morgause** of Orkeney was fayrar than
she and more of beauté."   15

¶"A!" seyde Sir **Launcelot**, "Sir **Lamorak**, why sayst thou so? Hit
ys nat thy parte to disprayse thy prynces that thou arte undir obeysaunce,[7] and we all."

¶And therewithall Sir **Launcelot** alyght on foote. "And therefore
make the[8] redy, for I woll preve uppon the that Quene Guenyver   20
ys the fayryst lady and most of bounté in the worlde." "Sir," seyde
Sir **Lamerok**, "I am lothe to have ado with you in thys quarell, for
every man thynkith hys owne lady fayryste, and thoughe I prayse
the lady that I love moste, ye sholde nat be wrothe—for thoughe
my lady Quene **Gwenyver** be fayryst in youre eye, wyte you well   25
Quene **Morgause of Orkeney** ys fayryst in myne eye—and so every
knyght thynkith hys owne lady fayryste. And wyte you well, sir, ye
ar the man in the worlde excepte Sir **Trystramys** that I am moste
lothyst to have ado withall; but, and ye woll nedys have ado with
me, I shall endure you as longe as I may."   30

¶Than spake Sir **Bleoberys** and seyde, "My lorde Sir **Launcelot**, I
wyste you never so mysseadvysed as ye be at thys tyme, for Sir
Lamerok seyth to you but reson and knyghtly. For I warne you, I
have a lady, and methynkith that she ys the fayryst lady of the
worlde: 35

¶"Were thys a grete reson that ye sholde be wrothe with me for
such langage?—

¶"And well ye wote that Sir **Lamorak** ys a noble knyght as I know
ony lyvynge, and he hath oughte you and all us ever good wyll;
therefore, I pray you, be fryndis!" Than Sir **Launcelot** seyde, "Sir, I   40
pray you, forgyve me myne offence and evyll wyll, and if I was
mysseadvysed I woll make amendis." "Sir," seyde Sir **Lamerok**, "the
amendis ys sone made betwyxte you and me." And so Sir **Launcelot**
and Sir **Bleoberys** departed; and Sir **Lamerok** and Sir **Mellyagaunce**
toke their horsis and aythir departed frome othir. And within a   45
whyle cam Kyng **Arthure** and mette with Sir **Lamorak** and justed with
hym; and there he smote downe Sir **Lamorak** and wounded hym

6. *Harde byg*: very strong.
7. *That thou arte undir obeysaunce*: whose rule you must follow.
8. Thee.

fol.198v

sore with a speare. And so he rode frome hym, wherefore Sir
Lamerok was wroth that he wolde nat fyght with hym on foote—
howbehit that Sir Lamerok knew nat Kynge Arthure.

Now levith of thys tale and spekith[9] of Sir Trystramps, that as   [15]
he rode he mette with Sir Kay the Senescyall; and there Sir   5
Kay asked Sir Trystramps of what contrey he was. He answerde and
seyde he was of the contrey of Cornwaile. "Hit may well be," seyde
Sir Kay, "for as yet harde I never that evir good knyght com oute   fol.199r
of Cornwayle."

"That ys yvell spokyn," seyde Sir Trystram, "but, and hit please   10
you, to telle me your name I pray you." "Sir, wyte you well that my
name ys Sir Kay the Senesciall." "A, sir, ys that youre name?" seyde
Sir Trystramps. "Now wyte you well that ye ar named the shame-
fullyst knyght of your tunge that now ys lyvynge—howbehit ye ar
called a good knyght, but ye ar called unfortunate and passyng   15
overthwart of youre tunge." And thus they rode togydirs tylle they
cam to a brydge.

And there was a knyght that wolde nat latte them passe tylle one
of them justed with hym. And so that knyght justed with Sir Kay,
and there he gaff Sir Kay a falle; and hys name was Sir Tor, Sir   20
Lamerokes halff-brothir. And than they two rode to their lodgynge,
and there they founde Sir Braundiles—and Sir Tor cam thydir
anone aftir. And as they sate at hir souper, thes foure knyghtes,
three of them spake all the shame by[1] Cornysh knyghtes that coude
be seyde. Sir Trystramps harde all that they seyde, and seyde but   25
lytyll—but he thought the more—but at that tyme he discoverde[2]
nat hys name. And upon the morne Sir Trystrams toke hys horse
and abode them uppon their way. And there Sir Brandiles profirde
to juste with Sir Trystram; and there Sir Trystram smote hym downe,
horse and all, to the erthe. Than Sir Tor le Fyze de Vaysshoure, he   30
encountird with Sir Trystram; and there Sir Trystram smote hym
downe. And than he rode hys way, and Sir Kay folowed hym, but
he wolde none of hys felyship.

Than Sir Brandiles com to Sir Kay and seyde, "I wolde wyte fayne
what ys that knyghtes name." Com one with me," seyde Sir Kay,   35
"and we shall pray hym to telle us hys name." So they rode togydirs
tyll they cam nyghe hym, and than they were ware where he sate
by a welle and had put of hys helme to drynke at the welle. And
whan that he saw them com, he laced on hys helme lyghtly, and
toke hys horse to profir hem to juste.   fol.199v   40

"Nay," seyde Sir Braundyles, "we justed late inowe with you! But
we com nat in that entente; but we requyre you of knyghthod to
telle us youre name." "My fayre lordys, sitthyn that hit ys youre
desyre; and now, for to please you, ye shall wyte that my name ys
Sir Trystram de Lyones, newev unto Kyng Mark of Cornwayle." "In   45
goode tyme," seyde Sir Brandiles, "and well be ye foundyn! And
wyte you well that we be ryght glad that we have founde you—and

9. I.e., speaks the tale.
1. Spoke of all of the shameful aspects of.
2. I.e., revealed.

we be of a felyship that wolde be ryght glad of youre company, for
ye ar the knyght in the worlde that the felyship of the Rounde
Table desyryth moste to have the company off."

¶"God thanke them all," seyde Sir Trystram, "of hir grete goodnes. But as yet I fele well that I am nat able to be of their felyship,
for I was never yet of[3] such dedys of worthynes to be in the com-
panye of such a felyship."

"A," seyde Sir Kay, "and ye be Sir Trystrams, ye ar the man called
now moste of proues excepte Sir Launcelot, for he beryth nat the
lyff crystynde nother hethynde[4] that canne fynde such anothir
knyght, to speke of hys proues and of his hondis[5] and hys trouthe
withall—for yet cowde there never creature sey hym dishonoure
and make hit good."[6] Thus they talked a grete whyle, and than they
departed ayther frome other such wayes as hem[7] semed beste.

Now shall ye here what was the cause that Kyng Arthure cam
into the Foreyste Perelous, that was in North Walis, by the meanys
of a lady—her name was Aunowre. And thys lady cam to Kynge
Arthure at Cardyeff; and she, by fayre promyses and fayre behestis,
made Kynge Arthure to ryde with her into that Foreyste Perelous.
And she was a grete sorseres; and many dayes she had loved Kynge
Arthure, and bycause she wolde have had hym to lye by her, she
cam into that contrey.

So whan the Kynge was gone with hir, many of hys knyghtes
folowed aftir hym whan they myste hym—as[8] Sir Launcelot, Sir
Brandiles, and many other. And whan she had brought hym to hir
towre she desired hym to ly by her; and than the Kynge remembird
hym of hys lady, and wolde nat for no crauffte that she cowde do.
Than every day she wolde make hym ryde into that foreyste with
hyr owne knyghtes, to the entente to have had hym slayne; for
whan thys Lady Aunowre saw that she myght nat have hym at her
wylle, than she laboured by false meanys to have destroyed Kynge
Arthure and slayne hym.

Than the Lady of the Lake, that was allwayes fryndely to Kynge
Arthure, she undirstood by hir suttyle craufftes that Kynge Arthure
was lykely to be destroyed; and therefore thys Lady of the Lake,
that hyght Nynyve, she cam into that foreyste to seke aftir Sir Launcelot du Lake othir ellis Sir Trystramys for to helpe Kynge Arthure—
for as that same day she knew well that Kynge Arthur sholde be
slayne onles that he had helpe of one of thes two knyghtes. And
thus she rode up and downe tyll she mette with Sir Trystram; and
anone as she saw hym she knew hym, and seyde, "A, my lorde Sir
Trystram, well be ye mette! And blyssed be the tyme that I have
mette with you—for thys same day, and within thys two owrys,
shall be done the dolefullyst dede that ever was done in thys
londe."

---

3. *Was never yet of:* have not yet done.
4. *He beryth . . . nother hethynde:* there is no one alive, neither Christian nor heathen.
5. I.e., strength of hand.
6. *Make hit good:* i.e., prove it.
7. I.e., to them.
8. I.e., such as.

"A, fayre damesell," seyde Sir Trystramps, "may I amende hit?"

¶"Yee, sir; therefore comyth on with me in all the haste ye may, for ye shall se the moste worshipfullyst knyght in the worlde harde bestadde." Than seyde Sir Trystramps, "I am redy, lo, to helpe you and suche a noble man as ye sey he ys." 5

¶"Sir, hit ys nother better ne worse," seyde the damesell, "but the noble Kynge Arthure hymselff." "God deffende," seyde Sir Trystramps, "that ever he shulde be in such distresse!" Than they rode togydirs a grete pace untyll they cam to a lityll turret in a castell; and undirnethe that castel they saw a knyght stondynge uppon 10 foote, fyghtyng with two knyghtes—and so Sir Trystramps behelde them. And at the laste thes two knyghtes smote downe that one knyght, and one of hem unlaced hys helme; and the Lady Aunowre gate Kynge Arthurs swerde in her honde to have strykyn of his hede. 15

And therewithall com Sir Trystramps, as faste as he myght, and seyyng, "Traytoures! Leve that knyght anone!" And so Sir Trystrams smote the tone of hem thorow the body that he felle dede; and than he russhed to the othir and smote hys backe in sundir—and in the meanewhyle the Lady of the Lake cryed to Kynge Arthur, 20 "Lat nat that false lady ascape!" Than Kynge Arthur overtoke hir, and with the same swerde he smote of her hede—and the Lady of the Lake toke up hir hede and hynge hit at hir sadill-bowe, by the heyre. And than Sir Trystramps horsed the Kynge agayne and rode forth with hym—but he charged the Lady of the Lake nat to dis- 25 cover hys name as at that tyme.

¶So whan the Kynge was horsed, he thanked hartely Sir Trys- tramps and desired to wyte hys name, but he wolde nat telle hym none other but that he was "a poure knyght aventures." And so he bare[9] Kynge Arthure felyship tylle he mette with som of hys knygh- 30 tes; and so within a whyle he mette with Sir Ector de Marys—and he knew nat Kynge Arthur nother yet Sir Trystram, and he desired to juste with one of them.

Than Sir Trystrams rode unto Sir Ector and smote hym frome hys horse; and whan he had done so, he cam agayne to the Kynge and 35 seyde, "My lorde, yondir ys one of youre knyghtes; he may beare you felyshyp. And anothir day, by that dede that I have done for you, I truste to God ye shall undirstonde that I wolde do you serv- yse." "Alas," seyde Kynge Arthure, "lat me wyte what ye ar!" "Nat at thys tyme," seyde Sir Trystramps. So he departed and leffte Kynge 40 Arthur and Sir Ector togydirs.

And than at a day sette, Sir Trystrams and Sir Lamerok mette at a welle; and than they toke Sir Keyhydyus at the fosters house; and so they rode with hym to the ship where they leffte Dame Brang- wayne and Governayle. And so they sayled into Cornuayle all hole 45 togydirs; and by assente and by enformacion of Dame Brangwayne, whan they were londed they rode unto Sir Dynas the Seneschall, a trusty frynde of Sir Trystramps. And so Sir Dynas and Dame Brang-

fol.200r

How Sir Trystrams rescowed Kyng Arthur fro the Lady Aunowre

[17]

fol.201r

9. I.e., provided, gave.

wayne rode to the courte of Kynge Marke and tolde the Quene La
Beall Isode that Sir Trystramps was nyghe hir in the contrey.

Than for verry pure joy La Beall Isode sowned; and whan she
myght speke, she seyde, "Jantyll senesciall, helpe that I myght
speke with hym othir my harte woll braste!" Than Sir Dynas and
Dame Brangwayne brought Sir Trystram and Sir Kayhidyus prevaly
into the courte, unto her chambir, whereas La Beall Isode assygned[1] them—and to telle the joyes that were betwyxte La Beall Isode
and Sir Trystramps, there ys no maker[2] can make hit, nothir no
harte can thynke hit, nother no penne can wryte hit, nother no
mowth can speke hit.

And, as the Freynshe booke makith mension, at the firste tyme
that ever Sir Kayhidius saw La Beall Isode, he was so enamered
uppon hir that for very pure love he myght never withdraw hit (and
at the laste, as ye shall hyre or the booke be ended, Sir Kayhydyus
dyed for the love of Isode). And than pryvaly he wrote unto her
lettris and baladis of the moste goodlyeste that were used in tho
dayes.

And whan La Beall Isode undirstoode hys lettris, she had pité of
hys complaynte, and unavised she wrote another lettir to comforte
hym withall. And Sir Trystram was all thys whyle in a turret, at the
commaundemente of La Beall Isode; and whan she myght, she
yeode and come to Sir Trystram. So on a day Kynge Marke played
at the chesse undir a chambir wyndowe; and at that tyme Sir Trystramps and Sir Kayhydyus were within the chambir over Kynge
Marke. And as hit myshapped, Sir Trystrams founde the lettir that
Sir Kayhydyus sente unto La Beall Isode.

¶Also he had founde the lettir that she had sente unto Sir Keyhydyus. And at the same tyme La Beall Isode was in the same chambir; than Sir Trystramps com unto La Beall Isode and seyde,
"Madame, here ys a lettir that was sente unto you; and here ys the
lettir that ye sente unto hym that sente you that lettir—

¶"Alas madame! The good love that I have lovyd you, and many
londis and grete rychesse have I forsakyn for youre love! And now
ye ar a traytouras unto me, whych dothe me grete payne. But as
for the, Sir Kayhydyus, I brought the oute of Bretayne into thys
contrey, and thy fadir, Kynge Howell, I wan[3] hys londis; howbehit
I wedded thy syster, Isode le Blaunche Maynes, for the goodnes she
ded unto me, and yet, as I am a trew knyght, she ys a clene[4] maydyn
for me:

¶"But wyte thou well, Sir Kayhydyus, for thys falshed and treson
thou hast done unto me, I woll revenge hit uppon the." And
therewithall Sir Trystram drew his swerde and seyde, "Sir Kayhidyus,
kepe the!"—and than La Beall Isode sowned to the erthe. And
whan Sir Kayhydyus saw Sir Trystrams com uppon hym, he saw none
other boote but lepte oute at a bay wyndow, evyn over the hede

fol.201v

1. I.e., had arranged with.
2. I.e., maker of poems, poet.
3. I.e., won the offer of (see p. 271).
4. I.e., virgin.

where sate Kynge Marke playyng at the chesse. And whan the kynge
saw one com hurlyng over hys hede he seyde, "Felow, what arte
thou, and what ys the cause thou lepe oute at that wyndow?" "My
lorde kynge," seyde Sir Kephydyus, "hit fortuned me that I was
aslepe in the wyndow abovyn youre hede, and as I slepte I slum-
birde,[5] and so I felle downe."

¶Thus Sir Kephydyus excused hym—and Sir Trystram drad hym   [18]
leste he were discoverde unto the kyng that he was there;
wherefore he drew hym to the strength[6] of the towre and armed
hym in such armour as he had for to fyght with hem that wolde
withstonde hym. And so, whan Sir Trystram saw that there was no
resistence agaynste hym, he sente Governayle for hys horse and
hys speare, and knyghtly he rode forth oute of the castell opynly
that was callyd the Castell of Tyntagyll. And evyn at the gate he
mette with Sir Gyngalyn, Gawaynes sonne; and anone Sir Gyngalyn
put hys speare in the reste and ran uppon Sir Trystram and brake
hys speare. And Sir Trystram at that tyme had but a swerde, and
gaff hym such a buffet uppon the helme that he fylle downe frome
hys sadill, and hys swerde slode adowne and carved asundir his
horse necke. And so Sir Trystramys rode hys way into the foreyste.

And all thys doynge saw Kynge Marke; and than he sente a squyer
unto the hurte knyght and commaunded hym to com to hym, and
so he ded. And whan Kynge Marke wyst that hyt was Sir Gyngalyn,
he wellcommyd hym and gaff hym anothir horse—and so he asked
hym what knyght was that encountyrde with hym. "Sir," seyde Sir
Gyngalyn," I wote nat what knyght hit was, but well I wote he syeth
and makith grete dole."

Than Sir Trystrames within a whyle mette with a knyght of hys
owne: hys name was Sir Fergus. And whan he had mette with hym,
he made such sorow that he felle downe of hys horse in a sowne—
and in such sorow he was inne three dayes and three nyghtes. Than
at the laste Sir Trystramys sente unto the courte by[7] Sir Fergus for
to spurre what tydyngis. And so, as he rode by the way, he mette
with a damesell that cam frome Sir Palomydes to know and seke
how Sir Trystramys ded. Than Sir Fergus tolde her how he was
allmoste oute of hys mynde. "Alas," seyde the damesell, "where
shall I fynde hym?"

¶"In suche a place," seyde Sir Fergus. Than Sir Fergus founde
Quene Isode syke in hir bedde, makynge the grettyste dole that
ever ony erthly woman made. And whan the damesell founde Sir
Trystramys she made grete dole, bycause she myght nat amende
hym; for the more she made of hym, the more was hys payne—
and at the laste Sir Trystram toke hys horse and rode awey frome
her. And than was hit three dayes or that she coude fynde hym;
and than she broute hym mete and drynke, but he wolde none.
And than another tyme Sir Trystramys ascaped away frome the
damesell, and hit happened hym to ryde by the same castell where

fol.202r

fol.202v

5

10

15

20

25

30

35

40

45

5. I.e., half awoke.
6. I.e., stronghold.
7. I.e., by way of.

Sir Palomydes and Sir Trystramps dyd batayle, whan La Beall Isode departed them.[8] And there by fortune the damesell mette with Sir Trystramps ayen, makynge the grettiste dole that ever erthely creature made—and she yode to the lady of that castell and tolde of the myssadventure of Sir Trystrames. "Alas," seyde the lady of that castell, "where ys my lorde Sir Trystramps?"

¶"Ryght here by youre castell," seyde the damesell. "In good tyme," seyde the lady, "ys he so nyghe me; he shall have mete and drynke of the beste—and an harpe I have of hys whereuppon he taught me, for of goodly harpyng he beryth the pryse of the worlde." So thys lady and damesell brought hym mete and drynke—but he ete lityll thereoff.

Than uppon a nyght he put hys horse frome hym and unlaced hys armour. And so he yeode unto the wyldirnes and braste downe the treys and bowis. And othirwhyle, whan he founde the harpe that the lady sente hym, than wolde he harpe and play thereuppon and wepe togydirs.[9] And somtyme, whan he was in the wood, the lady wyst nat where he was; than wolde she sette hir downe and play uppon the harpe, and anone Sir Trystramps wolde com to the harpe and harkyn thereto—and somtyme he wolde harpe hymselff. Thus he there endured a quarter off a yere; and so at the laste he ran hys way, and she wyst nat where he was becom—and than was he naked, and waxed leane and poore of fleyshe. And so he felle in the felyshyppe of herdemen and shyperdis, and dayly they wolde gyff hym som of their mete and drynke; and whan he ded ony shrewde[1] dede, they wolde beate hym with roddis. And so they clypped hym with sherys and made hym lyke a foole.

¶And so uppon a day Sir Dagonet, Kynge Arthurs foole, cam into Cornwayle with two squyers with hym; and as they rode thorow that foreyste they cam by a fayre welle where Sir Trystramps was wonte to be. And the weddir was hote, and they alyght to drynke of that welle—and in the meanewhyle theyre horsys brake lowse. Ryght so cam Sir Trystramps unto them; and firste he sowsed Sir Dagonet in that welle, and aftir that hys squyars—and thereat lowghe the shypperdis. And furthwithall he ran aftir their horsis and brought hem agayne, one by one;[2] and ryght so wete as they were, he made them lepe up and ryde their wayes.

Thus Sir Trystramps endured there an halff yere, naked, and wolde never com in towne. So the meanewhyle the damesell that Sir Palomydes sent to seke Sir Trystram, she yode unto Sir Palomydes and tolde hym off all the myschyff that Sir Trystram endured. "Alas," seyde Sir Palomydes, "hit ys grete pité that ever so noble a knyght sholde be so myscheved for the love of a lady. But nevertheles I woll go and seke hym and comforte hym, and[3] I may."

fol.203r

[19]

---

8. See p. 265.
9. I.e., at the same time.
1. I.e., mischievous.
2. *One by one:* i.e., to each man, individually.
3. I.e., if.

Than a lytyll before that tyme La Beall Isode had commaunded Sir Kayhydyus oute of the contrey of Cornwayle. So Sir Kayhydyus departed with a dolerous harte; and by aventure he mette with Sir Palomydes, and they felyshyppyd togydirs—and aythir complayned to other of there hote love that they loved La Beall Isode. "Now lat us," seyde Sir Palomydes, "seke Sir Trystramps, that lovyth her as well as we, and let us preve whether we may recover hym."

So they rode into the foreyste, and three dayes and three nyghtes they wolde never take lodgynge, but ever sought Sir Trystram. And upon a tyme, by adventure they mette with Kynge Marke that was rydden frome hys men all alone—and whan they saw hym, Sir Palomydes knew hym, but Sir Kayhydyus knew hym nat. "A, false knyght!" seyde Sir Palomydes, "hit ys pité thou haste thy lyff, for thou arte a destroyer of all worshipfull knyghtes—and by thy myschyff and thy vengeaunce thou haste destroyed that moste noble knyght, Sir Trystramps de Lyones. And therefore deffende the," seyde Sir Palomydes, "for thou shalt dye thys day!" "That were shame," seyde Kynge Marke, "for ye too[4] ar armed and I am unarmed."

"As for that," seyde Sir Palomydes, "I shall fynde a remedy therefore: here ys a knyght with me, and thou shalt have hys harneyse." "Nay," seyde Kynge Marke, "I woll nat have ado with you, for cause have ye none to[5] me, for all the mysse-ease that Sir Trystramps hath was for a lettir that he founde; for as for me, I ded to hym no displesure—and God knowith I am full sory for hys maledye and hys myssease." So whan the kynge had thus excused hymselff, they were fryndys, and Kynge Marke wolde have had them unto the Castell of Tyntagyll. But Sir Palomydes wolde nat, but turned unto the realme of Logrys; and Sir Kayhydyus seyde that he wolde[6] into Bretayne.

⁋Now turne we unto Sir Dagonet ayen, that whan he and hys squyers were uppon horsebacke, he demyd that the shyperdis had sente that foole to aray hem so bycause that they lawghed at them; and so they rode unto the kepers of the bestis and all to-bete them.

⁋Whan Sir Trystramps saw hem betyn that were wonte to gyff hym mete, he ran thydir and gate Sir Dagonet by the hede; and there he gaff hym such a falle to the erthe and brusede hym so that he lay stylle. And than he wraste hys swerde oute of hys honde, and therewith he ran to one of hys squyers and smote of hys hede— and hys othir squyer fled. And so Sir Trystramps toke his way with the swerde in hys honde, rennynge as he had bene wyld woode.[7]

⁋Than Sir Dagonet rode to Kynge Marke and tolde hym how he had spedde in the foreyste. "And therefore," seyde Sir Dagonet, "beware, Kynge Marke, that thou com nat aboute that well in the foreyste, for there ys a foole naked—and that foole and I, foole,[8] mette togydir, and he had allmoste slayne me!"

---

4. I.e., two.
5. I.e., with.
6. I.e., would go.
7. *Wyld woode*: stark mad.
8. Dagonet, as might be expected, here plays on the senses of *fool* as both "jester" and "idiot."

¶"A" seyde Kynge Marke, "that ys Sir Matto le Breune, that felle oute of hys wytte because he loste hys lady; for whan Sir Gaherys smote downe Sir Matto and wan hys lady of hym, never syns was he in his mynde—and that was grete pité, for he was a good knyght." [5]

¶Than Sir Andred, that was cousyn unto Sir Trystram, made a [20] lady that was hys paramour to sey and to noyse hit that she was with Sir Trystramys or ever he dyed. And thys tale she brought unto Kynge Markis house: that she buryed hym by a welle, and that or he dyed he besoughte Kynge Marke to make hys cousyn, Sir Andred, [10] kynge of the contrey of Lyonas, of the whych Sir Trystramys was lorde of—and all thys ded Sir Andred bycause he wolde have had Sir Trystramys londis.

And whan Kynge Mark harde telle that Sir Trystrames was dede, he wepte and made grete dole; but whan Quene Isode harde of [15] thes tydyngis, she made such sorow that she was nyghe oute of hir mynde. And so upon a day she thought to sle hirselff and never to lyve aftir the deth of Sir Trystramys; and so upon a day La Beall Isode gate a swerde pryvayly, and bare hit into her gardyne, and there she pyghte the swerde thorow a plum tre up to the hyltis so [20] that hit stake faste—and hit stoode breste-hyghe. And as she wolde have renne uppon the swerde and to have slayne hirselff, all thys aspyed Kynge Marke, how she kneled adowne and seyde, "Sweyte Lorde Jesu, have mercy uppon me, for I may nat lyve aftir the deth of Sir Trystram de Lyones, for he was my firste love, and shall be [25] the laste."

And with thes wordis cam Kynge Marke and toke hir in hys armys; and than he toke up the swerde and bare hir away with hym into a towre, and there he made hir to be kepte, and wacched hir surely. And aftir that she lay longe syke, nyghe at the poynte of [30] dethe.

¶So thys meanewhyle ran Sir Trystramys naked in the foreyste with the swerde in hys honde—and so he cam to an ermytayge, and there he layde hym downe and slepte. And in the meanewhyle the ermyte stale away the swerde and layde mete downe by hym. [35] Thus was he kepte there a[9] ten dayes; and at the laste he departed and com to the herdemen ayen.

And there was a gyaunte in that contrey that hyght Tauleas, and for feare of Sir Trystram more than seven yere he durste never muche go at large, but for the moste party he kepte hym in a sure [40] castell of hys owne. And so thys Tauleas harde telle that Sir Trystramys was dede, by[1] the noyse of the courte of Kynge Marke; than thys gyaunt Tauleas yode dayly at hys large.[2] And so he happyd uppon a day he cam to the herdemen wandrynge and langeryng; and there he sette hym dowme to reste amonge them. [45]

And in the meanewhyle there cam a knyght of Cornwayle that led a lady with hym, and hys name was Sir Dynaunte; and whan the

fol.204v

---

9. I.e., a stretch of.
1. I.e., according to.
2. *At hys large:* at will.

gyaunte saw hym, he wente frome the herdemen and hydde hym
under a tre. And so the knyght cam to the well and there he alyght
to repose hym. And as sone as he was frome hys horse, this gyaunte
Tauleas com betwyxte thys knyght and hys horse and [toke the hors
and] leped uppon hym; and so forthewith he rode unto Sir
Dynaunte, and toke hym by the coler, and pulled hym afore hym   5
uppon hys horse, and wolde have stryken of hys hede. Than the
herdemen seyde unto Sir **Trystram**, "Helpe yondir knyght!" "Helpe
ye hym!" seyde Sir **Trystram**. "We dare nat!" seyde the herdemen.

¶Than Sir **Trystram** was ware of the swerde of the knyght there   10
as hit lay, and so thydir he ran and toke up the swerde and smote
to Sir **Tauleas**, and so strake of hys hede; and so he yode hys way
to the herdemen.

Than Sir **Dynaunte** toke up the gyauntes hede and bare hit with
hym unto Kynge **Marke**, and tolde hym what adventure betydde   15
hym in the foreyste, and how a naked man rescowed hym frome
the grymly gyaunte, Sir **Tauleas**. "Where had ye thys aventure?"
seyde Kynge **Marke**. "Forsothe," seyde Sir **Dynaunte**, "at the fayre
fountayne in the foreyst, where many adventures[3] knyghtes mete—
and there ys the madde man."   20

"Well," seyde Kynge **Marke**, "I woll se that wood[4] man." So within
a day or too Kynge **Marke** commaunded hys knyghtes and his hunters to be redy, and seyde that he wolde hunte on the morn. And
so uppon the morne he wente into that foreyste; and whan the
kynge cam to that welle, he founde there lyyng a fayre naked man,   25
and a swerde by hym. Than Kynge **Marke** blew and straked, and
therewith hys knyghtes cam to hym; and than he commaunded hys
knyghtes to "take the naked man with fayrenes[5] and brynge hym
to my castell." And so they ded, savely and fayre, and keste mantels
uppon Sir **Trystramps**, and so lad hym unto Tyntagyll; and there   30
they bathed hym and wayshed hym, and gaff hym hote suppyngis
tylle they had brought hym well to hys remembraunce.[6] But all
thys whyle there was no creature that knew Sir **Trystramps** nothir
what maner man he was.

So hyt befelle uppon a day that the Quene La Beall **Isode** hard   35
of such a man that ran naked in the foreyst, and how the kynge
had brought hym home to the courte. Than La Beall **Isode** called
unto her **Dame Brangwayne** and seyde, "Com on with me, for we
woll go se thys man that my lorde brought frome the foreste the
laste day." So they passed forth and spirred where was the syke   40
man, and than a squyer tolde the quene that he was in the gardyne,
takyng hys reste to repose hym ayenst the sunne. So whan the
quene loked uppon Sir **Trystramps**, she was nat remembird of
hym—but ever she seyde unto Dame **Brangwayn**, "Mesemys I
shulde have sene thys man here before in many placis." But as   45

[21]

---

3. I.e., adventurous.
4. I.e., mad.
5. *With fayrenes:* gently.
6. *Brought hym well to hys remembraunce:* i.e., restored his memory.

some as Sir **Trystramys** sye her, he knew her well inowe—and than he turned away hys vysage and wepte.

Than the quene had allwayes a lytyll brachett that Sir **Trystramys** gaff hir the first tyme that ever she cam into Cornwayle—and never wold that brachet departe frome her but yf Sir **Trystram** were nyghe there as was La Beall **Isode**—and thys brachet was firste sente frome the Kynges doughter of Fraunce unto Sir **Trystrams** for grete love. And anone thys lityll brachet felte a savoure[7] of Sir **Trystram**; he[8] lepte uppon hym and lycked hys learys and hys earys, and than he[9] whyned and quested, and she smelled at hys feete and at hys hondis, and on all the partyes of hys body that she myght com to.

❡"A, my lady," seyde Dame **Brangwayne**, "alas, I se hit ys myne owne lorde, Sir **Trystramys**!" And thereuppon La Beall **Isode** felle downe in a sowne and so lay a grete whyle. And whan she myght speke, she seyde, "A, my lorde, Sir **Trystram**, blyssed be God ye have youre lyff! And now I am sure ye shall be discoverde by thys lityll brachet, for she woll never leve you; and also I am sure, as sone as my lorde Kynge **Marke** do know you, he woll banysh you oute of the contrey of Cornwayle—othir ellis he woll destroy you. And therefore, for Goddys sake, myne owne lorde, graunte Kynge **Marke** hys wyll and than draw you unto the courte off Kynge **Arthur**, for there ar ye beloved—and ever whan I may, I shall sende unto you. And whan ye lyste ye may com unto me; and at all tymys early and late I woll be at youre commaundement, to lyve as poore a lyff[1] as ever ded quyene or lady."

❡"A, madame!" seyde Sir **Trystramys**, "go frome me, for much angur and daunger have I ascaped[2] for youre love." Than the quene departed—but the brachet wolde nat frome hym. And therewithall cam Kynge **Marke**; and the brachet sate uppon hym[3] and bayed at them all—and therewithall Sir **Andred** spake and sayde, "Sir, thys ys Sir **Trystramys**—I se well by that brachet!"

❡"Nay," seyde the kynge, "I can nat suppose[4] that." Than the kyng asked hym uppon hys faythe what he was and what was hys name.

❡"So God me helpe," seyde he, "my name ys Sir **Trystramys** de Lyones. Now do by[5] me what ye lyst." "A!" sayde Kynge **Marke**, "me repentis of youre recoverynge." And so he lete calle hys barownes, to geve jugemente unto Sir **Trystramys** to the dethe; than many of hys barownes wolde nat assente thereto—and in especiall Sir **Dynas** the Senesciall and Sir **Fergus**. And so, by the avyse of them all, Sir **Trystramys** was banysshed oute of the contrey for ten yere; and thereuppon he toke hys othe uppon a booke[6] before the kynge

How the brachet of 5
La Beall Isode dis-
crebed Syr Trystra-
mys

10

15

20

fol.206r

25

[22]

30

35

40

---

7. *Felte a savoure*: caught the scent.
8. She.
9. She.
1. *As poore a lyff*: i.e., a life as much in the service of another.
2. I.e., escaped by being in the wilderness.
3. I.e., Trystram.
4. I.e., believe.
5. I.e., with.
6. I.e., Bible or missal.

and hys barownys. And so he was made to departe oute of the
contrey of Cornwayle; and there were many barownes brought[7]
hym unto hys shyp, that som were of hys frendis and som were of
hys fooys. And in the meanewhyle there cam a knyght of Kynge
Arthurs, and hys name was Sir Dynadan, and hys commyng was for
to seke aftir Sir Trystram; than they shewed hym where he was,
armed at all poyntis, goyng to the shyp.

⁋"Now, fayre knyght," seyde Sir Dynadan, "or ye passe thys
courte, that ye woll juste with me [I requyre the]."

⁋"With a good wyll," seyde Sir Trystramys, "and these lordes woll
gyffe me leve." Than the barownes graunted thereto. And so they
ranne togydir; and there Sir Trystramys gaff Sir Dynadan a falle—
and than he prayde Sir Trystram of hys jantylnes to gyff hym leve
to go in hys felyshyp.

⁋"Ye shall be ryght wellcom," seyd he. And than Sir Trystramys
and Sir Dynadan toke their horsys and rode to their shyppys togydir;
and whan Sir Trystramys was in the se, he seyde, "Grete well Kyng
Marke and all myne enemyes, and sey to hem I woll com agayne
whan I may. And sey hym well am I rewarded for the fyghtyng with
Sir Marhalt, and delyverd all hys contrey frome servayge; and well
am I rewarded for the fecchynge and costis[8] of Quene Isode oute
off Irelonde, and the daunger that I was in firste and laste—and,
by the way commyng home, what daunger I had[9] to brynge agayne
Quene Isode frome the Castell Pleure; and well am I rewarded whan
I fought with Sir Bleoberys for Sir Segwarydes wyff; and well am I
rewarded whan I faught with Sir Blamoure de Ganys for Kyng Angwysh, fadir unto La Beall Isode; and well am I rewarded whan I
smote down the good knyght Sir Lamerok de Galis at Kynge Markes
request; and well am I rewarded whan I faught with the Kynge
with the Hondred Knyghtes and the Kynge of North Galys—and
both thes wolde have put hys londe in servayge, and by me they
were put to a rebuke; and well am I rewarded for the sleyng of
Tauleas, the myghty gyaunte. And many othir dedys have I done
for hym—and now have I my waryson! And telle Kynge Marke that
many noble knyghtes of the Rounde Table have spared the barownes of thys contrey for my sake. And also, I am nat well rewarded
whan I fought with the good knyght Sir Palomydes and rescowed
Quene Isode frome hym—and at that tyme Kynge Marke seyde,
afore all hys barownes, I sholde have bene bettir rewarded." And
furthewithall he toke the see.

And at the nexte londynge, faste by the see there mette with
Sir Trystram and with Sir Dynadan Sir Ector de Marys and Sir
Bors de Ganys; and there Sir Ector justed with Sir Dynadan,
and he smote hym and hys horse downe. And than Sir Trystram
wolde have justed with Sir Bors; and Sir Bors seyde that he wolde
nat juste with no Cornyssh knyghtes—"for they ar nat called men
of worship." And all thys was done uppon a brydge. And with thys

5

10

fol.206v

15

20

25

30

35

40

[23]   fol.207r

45

---

7. I.e., who brought.
8. *The fecchynge and costis:* the expense of time and effort in rescuing.
9. I.e., experienced.

cam Sir Bleoberys and Sir Dryaunte; and Sir Bleoberys profird to juste
with Sir Trystram, and there Sir Trystram smote downe Sir Bleoberys.

Than seyde Sir Bors de Ganys, "I wyste never Cornysh knyght of
so grete a valure nor so valyaunte as that knyght that beryth the
trappours enbrowdred with crownys." And than Sir Trystram and
Sir Dynadan departed from them into a foreyst; and there mette
them a damesell that cam for the love of Sir Launcelot to seke aftir
som noble knyghtes of Kynge Arthurs courte for to rescow Sir Launcelot—for he was ordayned for, by the treson of Quene Morgan le
Fay, to have slayne hym, and for that cause she ordayned thirty
knyghtes to lye in wayte for Sir Launcelot. And thys damesell knew
thys treson.

And for thys cause she cam for to seke noble knyghtis to helpe
Sir Launcelot, for that nyght, other the day affter, Sir Launcelot
sholde com where thes thirty knyghtes were. And so thys damesell
mette with Sir Bors and Sir Bleoberys and Sir Ector and with Sir
Dryaunte, and there she tolde hem all foure of the treson of Morgan
le Fay. And than they promysed her that they wolde be nyghe her
whan Sir Launcelot shold mete with the thirty knyghtes—"and if so
be they sette upon hym, we woll do rescowis[1] as we can." So the
damesell departed, and by adventure she mette with Sir Trystram
and with Sir Dynadan; and there the damesell tolde hem of all the
treson that was ordayned for Sir Launcelot.

⁋"Now, fayre damesell," seyde Sir Trystram, "brynge me to that
same place where they shold mete with Sir Launcelot." Than seyde
Sir Dynadan, "What woll ye do? Hit ys nat for us to fyght with
thirty knyghtes! And wyte you well I woll nat thereoff;[2] as to macche o knyght, two, or three, ys inow, and[3] they be men—but for to
matche fiftene knyghtes, that I woll never undirtake."

⁋"Fy, for shame!" seyde Sir Trystram, "do but youre parte!"

⁋"Nay," seyde Sir Dynadan, "I woll nat thereoff, but iff ye woll
lende me your shylde—for ye bere a shylde of Cornwayle, and, for
the cowardyse that ys named[4] to the knyghtes of Cornwayle, by
youre shyldys ye bene ever forborne." "Nay" sayde Sir Trystram, "I
woll nat departe frome my shylde, for her sake that[5] gaff hit me—
but one thyng," seyde Sir Trystram, "I promyse the, Sir Dynadan:
but if thou wolte promyse me to abyde with me ryght here, I shall
sle the. For I desyre no more of the but answere one knyght—and
yf thy harte woll nat serve the, stonde by and loke uppon."[6]

⁋Sir seyde Sir Dynadan, "I woll promyse you to looke uppon and
to do what I may to save myselff—but I wolde I had nat mette with
you."[7] So than anone thes thirty knyghtes cam faste by thes foure

fol.207v

1. *Do rescowis*: perform a rescue.
2. *I woll nat thereoff*: I will not do that.
3. I.e., if.
4. I.e., reputed.
5. For the sake of she who.
6. *Loke uppon*: look out.
7. Given the acknowledgment just a few lines later of Dynadan's fine performance in combat,
his comments here are not intended to mark him out as a coward; rather he can be seen
as a kind of representative of what most men might reasonably think and do in his

knyghtes; and they were ware of them, and aythir of other. And so thes thirty knyghtes lette them passe for thys cause, that they wolde nat wratth them if case be they had ado with Sir Launcelot; and the foure knyghtes lette them passe to thys entente, that they wolde se and beholde what they wolde do with Sir Launcelot.

And so the thirty knyghtes paste on and cam by Sir Trystram and by Sir Dynadan; and than Sir Trystramps cryed on hyght, "Lo! here ys a knyght ayenste you for the love of Sir Launcelot!" And there he slew two with a speare and ten with hys swerde; and than cam in Sir Dynadan and he ded passyng welle. And so of the thirty knyghtes there yoode but ten away, and they fledde. And all thys batayle saw Sir Bors de Ganys and hys three felowys, and than they saw well hit was the same knyght that justed with hem at the brydge. Than they toke their horsys and rode unto Sir Trystramps and praysed hym and thanked hym of hys good dedys; and they all desyred Sir Trys-tram to go with them to their lodgynge, and he seyde he wold nat go to no lodgynge.

Than they foure knyghtes prayde hym to telle hys name. "Fayre lordys," seyde Sir Trystramps, "as at thys tyme I woll nat telle you my name." Than Sir Trystram and Sir Dynadan rode forthe their way tylle they cam to shyperdis and to herdemen; and there they asked them if they knew ony lodgyng there nerehonde. "Sir," seyde the herdemen, "hereby ys good herberow in a castell; but there ys such a custom that there shall no knyght herberow there but if he juste with two knyghtes, and if he be but o knyght he muste juste with two knyghtes—and as ye be,[8] sone shall ye be macched." "There ys shrewde herberow," seyde Sir Dynadan. "Lodge where ye woll, for I woll nat lodge there."

¶"Fye, for shame!" seyde Sir Trystramps, "ar ye nat a knyght of the Table Rounde?—wherefore ye may nat with your worship ref-fuse your lodgynge."

¶"Not so," seyde the herdemen, "for and ye be beatyn and have the warse, ye shall nat be lodged there; and if ye beate them, ye shall well be herberowed."

¶"A," seyde Sir Dynadan, "I undirstonde they ar two good knygh-tes." Than Sir Dynadan wolde nat lodge there in no maner but as Sir Trystramps requyred hym of hys knyghthode. And so they rode thydir; and to make shorte tale, Sir Trystram and Sir Dynadan smote hem downe bothe, and so they entirde into the castell and had good chere as they cowde thynke or devyse. And whan they were unarmed and thought to be myry and in good reste, there cam in at the yatis Sir Palomydes and Sir Gaherys, requyryng to have the custum of the castell.[9]

¶"What aray ys thys?"[1] seyde Sir Dynadan, "I wolde fayne have

---

situation. In that role, then, he demonstrates (with some degree of skeptical humor) how near-transcendent is the prowess and love of endeavor possessed by knights like Trystram and Launcelot.

8. *As ye be:* i.e., by the looks of you. Cf. Dynadan's comments about Trystram's shield, above.

9. *Requyryng to have the custum of the castell:* i.e., requiring that they also joust for the honor of their lodging.

1. *What aray ys thys?:* What is going on?

my reste." "That may nat be," seyde Sir Trystram. "Now muste we
nedis defende the custum of thys castell, insomuch as we have the
bettir of this lordes of thys castell—and therefor," seyde Sir Trystram, "nedis muste ye make you redy."

¶"In the devyls name," seyde Sir Dynadan, "cam I into youre   5
company!" And so they made them redy; and Sir Gaherys encountirde with Sir Trystram, and Sir Gaherys had a falle; and Sir Palomydes encountirde with Sir Dynadan, and Sir Dynadan had a falle:
than was hit falle-for-falle. So than muste they fyght on foote—
and that wolde nat Sir Dynadan, for he was sore brused of that falle   10
that Sir Palomydes gaff hym.

¶Than Sir Trystramys unlaced Sir Dynadans helme and prayde
hym to helpe hym. "I woll nat, seyde Sir Dynadan, "for I am sore
wounded of the thirty knyghtes that we had ado withall. But ye
fare," seyde Sir Dynadan, "as a man [that] were oute of hys mynde,   15
that wold caste hymselff away; and I may curse the tyme that ever
I sye you, for in all the worlde ar nat such two knyghtes that ar so
wood as ys Sir Launcelot and ye, Sir Trystram—for onys I felle in the
felyshyp of Sir Launcelot, as I have done now with you, and he sette
me so a-worke that a quarter of a yere I kept my bedde![2] Jesus   20
deffende me," seyde Sir Dynadan, "frome such two knyghtys, and
specially frome youre felyshyp!"

Than seyde Sir Trystram, "I woll fyght with hem bothe." And
anone Sir Trystram bade hem, "Com forthe bothe, for I woll fyght
with you." Than Sir Palomydes and Sir Gaherys dressed and smote   25
at hem bothe. Than Sir Dynadan smote at Sir Gaherys a stroke or
two, and turned frome hym. "Nay!" seyde Sir Palomydes, "hit ys to
much shame for us two knyghtes to fyght with one." And than he
ded bydde Sir Gaherys, "Stonde asyde with that knyght that hath
no lyste to fyght." Than they yode togydirs and fought longe; and   30
at the laste Sir Trystram doubled hys strokes and drove Sir Palomydes abak more than three stryddys—and than by one assente[3]
Sir Gaherys and Sir Dynadan wente betwyxt them and departed them
in sundir.

And than, by the assente of Sir Trystramys, they wolde have   35
lodged togydirs—but Sir Dynadan seyde he wold nat lodge in that
castell; and than he cursed the tyme that ever he com in theyre
felyship, and so he toke hys horse and hys harneyse and departed.
Than Sir Trystram prayde the lordys of that castell to lende hym a
man to brynge hym to a lodgyng. And so they ded, and overtoke   40
Sir Dynadan and rode to hir lodgynge, two myle thens, with a good
man in a pryory; and there they were well at ease. And that same
nyght Sir Bors and Sir Bleoberys and Sir Ector and Sir Dryaunt abode
stylle in the same place there as Sir Trystram faught with thirty
knyghtes. And there they mette with Sir Launcelot the same nyght,   45
and had made promyse to lodge with Sir Collgrevaunce the same
nyght.

---

2. *A quarter of a yere I kept my bedde:* i.e., I ended up bedridden for three months.
3. *One assente:* mutual agreement.

But anone, as Sir Launcelot harde of the shylde of Cornwayle, he [25]
wyste well hit was Sir Trystram that had fought with hys enemyes—
and than Sir Launcelot praysed Sir Trystram and called hym the man
of moste worshyp in the worlde.

¶So there was a knyght in that pryory that hyght Sir Pellynore, 5
and he desyred to wete the name of Sir Trystram, but in no wyse
he coude nat.

¶And so Sir Trystram departed and leffte Sir Dynadan in that
pryory, for he was so wery and so sore brused that he myght nat
ryde. Than thys knyght, Sir Pellynore, seyde unto Sir Dynadan, "Sith 10
ye woll nat telle me that knyghtes name, I shall ryde affter hym
and make hym to telle me hys name, other he shall dye therefore."

¶"Yet beware, sir knyght," seyde Sir Dynadan, "for and ye folow
hym, ye woll repente hit."

¶So that knyght, Sir Pellynor, rode aftir Sir Trystram and requy- 15
red hym of justis; than Sir Trystram smote hym downe and
wounded hym thorow the shulder, and so he paste on hys way. fol.209v
And on the nexte day folowynge Sir Trystram mette with pursyvauntis, and they tolde hym that there was made a grete crye of
turnemente betwene Kynge Carados of Scotlonde and the Kynge of 20
North Galys, and aythir shulde juste agayne othir afore the Castell
of Maydyns. And thes pursyvauntis sought all the contrey aftir
good knyghtes; and in especiall Kynge Carados lete make grete
sykynge for Sir Launcelot, and the Kynge of North Galis lete seke
specially for Sir Trystramps de Lyones. 25

And at that tyme Sir Trystramps thought to be at that justis. And
so by adventure they mette with Sir Kay the Seneseiall and Sir Sagramoure le Desirous; and Sir Kay requyred Syr Trystram to juste. And
Sir Trystram in a maner refused hym, bycause he wolde nat be
hurte nothir brused ayenste the grete justis that shuld be before 30
the Castell of Maydyns; and therefore he thought to reste hym and
to repose hym. And allway Sir Kay cryed, "Sir knyght of Cornwayle,
juste with me, othir ellys yelde the to me as recreaunte!"

¶Whan Sir Trystram herd hym sey so, he turned unto hym—and
than Sir Kay refused hym and turned hys backe. Than Sir Trystram 35
sayde, "As I fynde the, I shall take the!" Than Sir Kay turned with
evyll wyll, and Sir Trystram smote Sir Kay downe; and so he rode
forthe. Than Sir Sagramoure le Desirous rode aftir Sir Trystram and
made hym to juste with hym; and there Sir Trystram smote downe
Sir Sagramoure frome hys horse, and rode hys way. And the same 40
day he mette with a damesell that tolde hym that he sholde wynne
grete worshyp of a knyght aventures that ded much harme in all
that contrey.

¶Whan Sir Trystramps herde her sey so, he was glad to go with
her to wyn worshyp. And so Sir Trystram rode with that damesell fol.210r 45
a six myle; and than there mette with hym, Sir Gawayne, and
therewithall Sir Gawayne knew the damesell, that she was longynge
to Quyne Morgan le Fay. Than Sir Gawayne undirstood that she lad
that knyght to som myschyeff—

¶And sayde, "Fayre Knyght, whothir ryde ye now with that
damesell?"

¶ "Sir," seyde Sir **Trystram**, "I wote nat whothir I shall ryde, but as thys damesell woll lede me." "Sir," seyde Sir **Gawayne**, "ye shall nat ryde with her, for she and her lady ded never goode but yll." And than Sir **Gawayne** pulled oute hys swerde and seyde, "Damesell, but yf thou telle me anone for what cause thou ledyst thys knyght, thou shalt dye for hit ryght anone—for I know all youre ladyes treson, and yourys."

¶ "A, mercy, Sir **Gawayne!**" seyde she, "and yff ye woll save my lyff I woll telle you."

¶ "Say on," seyde Sir **Gawayne**, "and thou shalt have thy lyff." "Sir," she seyde, "Quene **Morgan**, my lady, hath ordayned a[4] thirty ladyes to seke and aspye aftir Sir **Launcelot** or aftir Sir **Trystram**; and by the traynys of thes ladyes, who that may fyrste mete ony of thes two knyghtes, they shulde turne hem unto **Morgan le Fayes** castell, sayyng that they sholde do dedys of worship. And yf ony of tho two knyghtes cam there, there be thirty knyghtes liyng and wacchyng in a towre to wayte uppon Sir **Launcelot** or uppon Sir **Trystramys**."

¶ "Fy, for shame," seyde **Sir Gawayne**, "that evir such false treson sholde be wrought or used in[5] a quene and a kyngys systir, and a kynge and a quenys doughtir."

"**S**ir," seyde Sir **Gawayne**, "wyll ye stonde with me, and we woll se the malyce of thes knyghtes?" "Sir," seyde Sir **Trystram**, "go ye to them and hit please you, and ye shall se I woll nat fayle you; for hit ys not longe ago syn I and a felow mette with thirty [knyghtes] of the quenys felyship—and God spede us so that we won away with worship." So than Sir **Gawayne** and Sir **Trystram** rode towarde the castell where **Morgan le Fay** was—and ever Sir **Gawayne** demed that he was Sir **Trystram de Lyones**, bycause he hard that two knyghtes had slayn and beatyn thirty knyghtes. And whan they cam afore the castell, Sir **Gawayne** spake on hyght[6] and seyde, "Quene **Morgan**, sende oute youre knyghtes that ye have layde in wacche for Sir **Launcelot** and for Sir **Trystram**:

"Now," seyde Sir **Gawayne**, "I know youre false treson, and all placis where that I ryde shall know of youre false treson—and now lat se,"[7] seyde Sir **Gawayne**, "whethir ye dare com oute of youre castell, ye thirty knyghtes." Than the quene spake, and all the thirty knyghtes at onys, and seyde, "A, Sir **Gawayne**, full well wotist thou what thou dost and seyst, for, pardé, we know the[8] passyng well; but all that thou spekyst and doyst, thou sayste hit uppon pryde of[9] that good knyght that ys there with the. For there be som of us know the hondys[1] of that good knyght overall well; and wyte thou well, Sir **Gawayne**, [hit is more for his sake than for thyn that we wylle not come oute of this castel—for wete ye wel, Sir **Gawayne**,] the knyght that beryth the armys of Cornwayle, we know hym and what he ys."

[26]

fol.210v

---

4. I.e., a group of.
5. I.e., by.
6. *On hyght:* on high, loudly.
7. Let us see.
8. Thee.
9. *Uppon pryde of:* out of pride for.
1. I.e., handiwork.

Than Sir Gawayne and Sir Trystram departed and rode on their wayes a day or two togydirs, and there by adventure they mette with Sir Kay and with Sir Sagramour le Desyrous. And than they were glad of Sir Gawayne, and he of them—but they wyst nat what he was with the shylde of Cornwayle but by demyng. And thus they rode togydirs a day or too; and than they were ware of Sir Breuse Saun3 Pité chasyng a lady for to have slayne her, for he had slayn her paramour afore. "Holde you all stylle," seyde Sir Gawayne, "and shew none of you forth, and ye shall se me rewarde yonder false knyght—for and he aspye you, he ys so well horsed that he woll ascape away." And than Sir Gawayne rode betwyxt Sir Breuse and the lady, and sayde, "False knyght, leve her and have ado with me!"

¶So whan Sir Brewse saw no man but Sir Gawayne, he feautred hys speare, and Sir Gawayne ayenste hym; and there Sir Breuse overthrew Sir Gawayne, and than he rode over hym and overtwarte hym twenty tymys to have destroyed hym. And whan Sir Trystram saw hym do so vylaunce a dede, he hurled oute ayenste hym.

¶And whan Sir Breuse hym saw with the shylde of Cornwayle, he knew hym well that hit was Sir Trystram; and than he fledde, and Sir Trystrams folowed hym—and so Sir Breuse was so horsed[2] that he wente hys way quyte. And Sir Trystram folowed hym longe affter, for he wolde fayne have bene avenged uppon hym; and so whan he had longe chaced hym, he saw a fayre well, and thydir he rode to repose hym, and tyed hys horse tylle a tre. And than he pulled of hys helme and waysshed hys vysayge and hys hondes— and so he felle on slepe.

And so in the meanewhyle cam a damesell that had sought Sir Trystram many wayes and dayes within thys londe. And whan she cam to the welle she loked uppon hym and had forgotyn hym as in remembraunce of Sir Trystrames; but by hys horse she knew hym, that hyght Passe-Brewell, that had ben hys hors many yerys (for whan he was madde in the foreyste, Sir Fergus kepte hym).

¶So thys lady, Dame Brangwayne, abode stylle tylle he was awake. And whan she saw hym awaked she salewed hym, and he her agayne, for aythir knew other of olde acqueyntaunce. Than she tolde Sir Trystram how she had sought hym longe and brode,[3] and there she tolde hym how she had lettirs frome the Quene La Beall Isode. Than anone [Sire Tristram redde them—and wete ye wel he was gladde, for thereyn was many a pyteous complaynte. Thenne Sir Tristram] seyde, "Lady, Dame Brangwayne, ye shall ryde with me tylle the turnemente be done at the Castell of Maydyns:

¶"And than shall ye beare lettirs and tydynges with you." And than Sir Trystram toke hys horse and sought lodgynge, and there he mette with a good aunciaunte knyght and prayde hym to lodge with hym (ryght so com Governayle unto Sir Trystram that was glad of the commyng of the lady). And thys olde knyghtes name was Sir Pellownes, and he tolde hym of the grete turnemente that shulde

---

2. *So horsed:* i.e., had such a good horse.
3. *Longe and brode:* far and wide.

fol.211r

[27]

fol.211v

be at the Castell of Maydyns—"and there Sir 𝕷𝖆𝖚𝖓𝖈𝖊𝖑𝖔𝖙 and two and twenty knyghtes of hys blood have ordayned shyldis of Corn-wayle."[4]

And ryght so there com one unto Sir 𝕻𝖊𝖑𝖑𝖔𝖜𝖓𝖊𝖘 and tolde hym that Sir 𝕻𝖊𝖗𝖘𝖎𝖉𝖊𝖘 𝖉𝖊 𝕭𝖑𝖔𝖞𝖘𝖊 was com home; than that knyght hylde up hys hondys and thanked God of hys commyng home-and there Sir 𝕻𝖊𝖑𝖑𝖔𝖜𝖓𝖊𝖘 tolde Sir 𝕿𝖗𝖞𝖘𝖙𝖗𝖆𝖒 that of two yere afore he had nat sene hys son, Sir 𝕻𝖊𝖗𝖘𝖞𝖉𝖊𝖘. "Sir," seyde Sir 𝕿𝖗𝖞𝖘𝖙𝖗𝖆𝖒𝖞𝖘, "I know youre son well inowgh for a good knyght." And so one tyme Sir 𝕿𝖗𝖞𝖘𝖙𝖗𝖆𝖒𝖞𝖘 and Sir 𝕻𝖊𝖗𝖘𝖞𝖉𝖊𝖘 com to their lodgyng both at onys; and so they unarmed hem and put uppon them such clothyng as they had.

And than thes two knyghtes ech wellcomyd other; and whan Sir 𝕻𝖊𝖗𝖘𝖎𝖉𝖊𝖘 undirstood that Sir 𝕿𝖗𝖞𝖘𝖙𝖗𝖆𝖒 was of Cornwayle, he seyde he was onys in Cornwayle—"and there I justed before Kynge 𝕸𝖆𝖗𝖐𝖊, and so hit happened me at that same day to overthrow ten knyghtis. And than cam to me Sir 𝕿𝖗𝖞𝖘𝖙𝖗𝖆𝖒𝖞𝖘 𝖉𝖊 𝕷𝖞𝖔𝖓𝖆𝖘 and over-threw me, and toke my lady fro me—and that shall I never forgete, but I shall remembir me and ever I se my tyme."[5]

❡"A," sayde Sir 𝕿𝖗𝖞𝖘𝖙𝖗𝖆𝖒, "now I undirstonde that ye hate Sir 𝕿𝖗𝖞𝖘𝖙𝖗𝖆𝖒. What deme you? [Wene ye] that Sir 𝕿𝖗𝖞𝖘𝖙𝖗𝖆𝖒 ys nat able to withstonde youre malyce?"

❡"Yes," seyde Sir 𝕻𝖊𝖗𝖘𝖞𝖉𝖊𝖘, "I know well that Sir 𝕿𝖗𝖞𝖘𝖙𝖗𝖆𝖒 ys a noble knyght and a muche bettir knyght than I am, yet I shall nat owghe hym my good wyll." Ryght as they stood thus talkynge at a bay wyndow of that castell, they sye many knyghtes ryde to and fro toward the turnemente. And than was Sir 𝕿𝖗𝖞𝖘𝖙𝖗𝖆𝖒 ware of a lykly knyght rydyng uppon a grete black horse, and a blacke coverde shylde.

❡"What knyght ys that," seyde Sir 𝕿𝖗𝖞𝖘𝖙𝖗𝖆𝖒, "with the blacke shylde and the blacke horse?" "I know hym well," seyde Sir 𝕻𝖊𝖗𝖘𝖎𝖉𝖊𝖘. "He ys one of the beste knyghtes of the worlde." "Than hit ys Sir 𝕷𝖆𝖚𝖓𝖈𝖊𝖑𝖔𝖙," seyde Sir 𝕿𝖗𝖞𝖘𝖙𝖗𝖆𝖒𝖞𝖘. "Nay," seyde Sir 𝕻𝖊𝖗𝖘𝖎𝖉𝖊𝖘, "hit ys Sir 𝕻𝖆𝖑𝖔𝖒𝖞𝖉𝖊𝖘, that ys yett oncrystynde." Than they saw muche people of the contrey salew Sir 𝕻𝖆𝖑𝖔𝖒𝖞𝖉𝖊𝖘, and seyde[6] with a lowde voice, "Jesu save the and kepe the, thou noble knyght Sir 𝕻𝖆𝖑𝖔𝖒𝖞-𝖉𝖊𝖘!" And within a whyle aftir there cam a squyer of that castell that tolde Sir 𝕻𝖊𝖑𝖑𝖔𝖜𝖓𝖊𝖘, that was lorde of that castell, that a knyght with a blacke shylde had smyttyn downe thirtene knyghtes.

❡"Now, fayre brother," seyde Sir 𝕿𝖗𝖞𝖘𝖙𝖗𝖆𝖒 unto Sir Persydes, "lat us caste on us lyght clokys, and lat us go se that play." "Not so," seyde Sir 𝕻𝖊𝖗𝖘𝖎𝖉𝖊𝖘, "we woll nat go lyke knavys thydir; but we woll ryde lyke men and as good knyghtes to withstonde oure enemyes." So they armed them and toke their horsys and grete spearys, and thydir they rode there as many knyghtes assayed themselff byfore the turnemente.

And anone Sir 𝕻𝖆𝖑𝖆𝖒𝖞𝖉𝖊𝖘 saw Sir 𝕻𝖊𝖗𝖘𝖎𝖉𝖊𝖘; and than he sente a squyar unto hym and seyde, "Go thou to the yondir knyght with

---

4. *Ordayned shyldis of Cornwayle*: arranged to carry shields sporting the arms of Cornwall.
5. *And ever I se my tyme*: i.e., if ever I see my chance for revenge.
6. I.e., who said.

the grene shyld and therein a lyon of gooldys, and say hym I
requyre hym to juste with me, and telle hym that my name ys Sir
Palomydes." Whan Sir Persides undirstood the rekeyst of Sir Palomydes, he made hym redy; and there anone they mette togydirs—
but Sir Persides had a falle. Than Sir Trystram dressed hym to be
revenged uppon Sir Palomydes. And that saw Sir Palomydes—that
was redy, and so was nat Sir Trystram—and toke hym at avauntayge[7] and smote hym over hys horse tayle, whan he had no speare
in· hys reste. Than sterte up Sir Trystram and toke horse lyghtly,
and was wrothe oute of mesure and sore ashamed of that falle.

How Sir Trystram
was takyn at abaun-
tage or he was redy
by Palomydes and
had a fall
fol.212v

Than Sir Trystramys sente unto Sir Palomydes by[8] Governayle,
and prayde hym to juste with hym at hys rekeyste. "Nay," seyde Sir
Palomydes, "as at thys tyme I woll nat juste with that knyght, for I
know hym bettir than he wenyth; and if he be wroth, he may ryght
hit tomorne at the Castell Maydyns, where he may se me and many
other knyghtes."

❡So with that cam Sir Dynadan, and whan he saw Sir Trystram
wroth, he lyste nat to jape, but seyde, "Lo, Sir Trystram, here may
a man preve, be he never so good, yet may he have a falle; and he
was never so wyse but he myght be oversayne—and he rydyth well
that never felle."[9]

❡So Sir Trystram was passyng wrothe, and seyde to Sir Persides
and to Sir Dynadan, "I woll revenge me!"

❡Ryght so as they stoode talkynge, there cam by Sir Trystram a
lykly knyght, rydyng passyng sobirly and hevyly, with a blacke
shylde.

❡"What knyght ys that?" seyde Sir Trystram unto Sir Persides. "I
know hym well," seyde Sir Persides, "for hys name ys Sir Bryaunte
of Northe Walis." And so he paste on amonge other knyghtes of
North Walis. And there com in Sir Launcelot de Lake with a shylde
of the armys of Cornwayle, and he sente a squyer unto Sir Bryaunte
and requyred hym to juste with hym. "Well," seyde Sir Bryaunte,
"sytthyn that I am requyred to juste, I woll do what I may." And
there Sir Launcelot smote downe Sir Bryaunte frome hys horse, a
grete falle—and than Sir Trystram mervayled what knyght he was
that bar the shylde of Cornwayle.

❡"Sir, whatsoever he be," seyde Sir Dynadan, "I warraunte he ys
of Kyng Bannys blode, whych bene knyghtes of the nobelyst proues
in the worlde, for to accompte so many for so many. Than there
cam in two knyghtes of North Galys, that one hyght Sir Hew de la
Mountayne, and the other Sir Madok de la Mountayne, and they chalenged Sir Launcelot footehote.

fol.213r

❡Sir Launcelot, not refusynge hem, but made hym redy, and with
one grete speare he smote downe bothe over their horse taylis—
and so Sir Launcelot rode hys way. "By the good Lorde," seyde Sir

---

7. At avauntayge: i.e., at a disadvantage.
8. I.e., by way of.
9. Here may a man preve . . . well that never felle: from this a man may learn that, no matter
   how proficient he is, he may still be thrown down; and no man was ever so wyse that he
   might not be proved wrong—and no one rides perfectly. (Cf. n. 9, p. 293.)

Trystrant, "he ys a good knyght that beryth the shylde of Cornwayle, and mesemyth he rydith on the beste maner that ever I saw knyght ryde." Than the Kynge of North Galis rode unto Sir Palomydes and prayed hym hartely for hys sake "to juste with that knyght that hath done us of North Galis dispite." "Sir," seyde Sir Palomydes, "I am full lothe to have ado with that knyght, and cause why as[1] tomorne the grete turnemente shall be; and therefore I wolde kepe myselff freyssh be my wyll."

¶"Nay," seyde the Kynge of North Galis, "I pray you, requyre hym of justis."

¶"Sir," seyde Sir Palomydes, "I woll juste at youre requeste and requyre that knyght to juste with me; and oftyn I have seyne a man at hys owne requeste have a grete falle." Than Sir Palomydes sente unto Sir Launcelot a squyre and requyred hym to juste.

¶"Fayre felow," seyde Sir Launcelot, "telle me thy lordis name." "Sir, my lordys name ys Sir Palomydes, the good knyght." "In good owre,"[2] seyde Sir Launcelot, "for there ys no knyght I saw thys seven yere that I had levir have ado withall." And so ayther knyghtes made them redy with two grete spearys.

¶"Nay," seyde Sir Dynadan, "ye shall se that Sir Palomydes woll quyte hym ryght well." "Hyt may be so," seyde Sir Trystram, "but I undirtake that knight with the shylde of Cornwayle shall gyff hym a falle." "I beleve hit nat," seyde Sir Dynadan. Ryght so they spurred their horsis and feautred their spearys, and aythir smote other; and Sir Palomydes brake a speare uppon Sir Launcelot, and he sate and meved nat. But Sir Launcelot smote hym so harde that he made hys horse to avoyde[3] the sadill; and the stroke brake hys shylde and the hawbarke, and had he nat fallyn he had be slayne.

¶"How now?" seyde Sir Trystram. "I wyst well by the maner of their rydynge bothe that Sir Palomydes shulde have a falle."

¶Ryght so Sir Launcelot rode hys way, and rode to a well to drynke and repose hym. And they of North Galis aspyed hym whother he wente; and than there folowed hym twelve knyghtes for to have myscheved hym for thys cause, that uppon the morne at the turnemente at the Castell of Maydyns that he sholde nat wyn the victory. So they com uppon Sir Launcelot suddeynly, and unnethe he myght put on hys helme and take hys horse but they were in hondis with[4] hym. And than Sir Launcelot gate hys speare in hys honde and ran thorow them; and there he slew a knyght, and brake hys speare in hys body. Than he drew hys swerde and smote uppon the ryght honde and uppon the lyffte honde, that within a few strokis he had slayne other three knyghtes; and the remenaunte that abode, he wounded hem sore, all that ded abyde.

Thus Sir Launcelot ascaped fro hys enemyes of Northe Walis. And than Sir Launcelot rode hys way tylle a frynde, and lodged hym tylle on the morowe—for he wolde nat the firste day have ado in the

---

1. *Cause why as*: because.
2. *In good owre*: at a good time.
3. I.e., throw off.
4. *In hondis with*: right upon.

turnemente bycause of hys grete laboure. And on the first day he
was with Kynge Arthur, there as he was sette on hye uppon a chafflet to discerne who was beste worthy of hys dedis—so Sir Launcelot
was with Kynge Arthur and justed nat the first day.

5

Here begynnyth the turnement of the castel maydyns, the fyrste day

NOw turne we unto Sir Trystramps de Lyones that commaunded
Governaple, hys servaunte, to ordayne hym a blacke shylde with
none other remembraunce[5] therein. And so Sir Persides and Sir
Trystramps departed from Sir Pellownes; and they rode erly toward
the turnemente, and than they drew them to Kynge Carydos syde
of Scotlonde. And anone knyghtes began the filde, what of the
Kynge of North Galys syde and of Kynge Carydos, and there began
a grete party.

¶Than there was hurlyng and russhyng; ryght so cam in Sir
Persides and Sir Trystram, and so they ded fare that day that they
put the Kyng of North Galis abacke. Than cam in Sir Bleoberys de
Ganys and Sir Gaherys with them of North Galis—and than was
Sir Persides smyttyn adowne and allmoste slayne, for mo than
fourty horsemen wente over hym—for Sir Bleoberys ded grete dedes
of armys, and Sir Gaherys fayled hym not.

¶Whan Sir Tristram behylde them and sye them do such dedis
of armys, he mervayled what they were.

¶Also Sir Trystram thought shame that Sir Persides was so done
to; and than he gate a grete speare in hys honde, and rode to Sir
Gaherys and smote hym down frome hys horse. And than Sir Bleoberys was wrothe, and gate a speare and rode ayenste Sir Trystram
in grete ire; and there Sir Trystram smote Sir Bleoberys frome hys
horse.

So than the Kynge with the Hondred Knyghtes was wrothe, and
he horsed Sir Bleoberys and Sir Gaherys agayne, and there began a
grete medlé; and ever Sir Trystram hylde them passyng shorte,[6] and
ever Sir Bleoberys was passyng bysy upon Sir Trystram. And there
cam in Sir Dynadan ayenst Sir Trystram—and Sir Trystram gaff hym
such a buffette that he sowned uppon hys horse; and so anone Sir
Dynadan cam to Sir Trystram and seyde, "Sir, I know the bettir than
thou wenyst, but here I promyse the my trouth, I woll never com
agaynst the more, for I promyse the that swerde of thyne shall
never com on my helme!" So with that com Sir Bleoberys; and Sir
Trystram gaff hym such a buffett that downe he abaysshed hys
hede, and than he raught hym so sore by the helme that he pulled
hym undir hys hors feete. And than Kyng Arthure blew to lodgyng.

Than Sir Trystram departed to hys pavylion, and Sir Dynadan rode
with hym, and Sir Persides. And Kynge Arthure than, and the kyngis
uppon bothe partyes, mervayled what knyght that was with the
blacke shylde. Many knyghtis seyde their avyse; and som knew hym

[30]

fol.214r

5

10

15

20

25

30

35

40

fol.214v

45

---

5. I.e., heraldic identification.
6. *Hylde them passyng shorte:* pressed them surpassingly hard.

for Sir Trystram and hylde their peace and wolde nat say. So that
firste day Kynge Arthure and all the kynges and lordis that were
juges gaff Sir Trystram the pryce, howbehyt they knew hym nat,
but named hym the Knyght with the Blacke Shylde. Than uppon   [31]
the morne Sir Palomydes returned from the Kynge of Northe Galis,   5
and rode to Kynge Arthurs syde, where was Kynge Carados and the
Kynge of Irelonde, and Sir Launcelottis kynne and Sir Gawaynes
kynne.

So Sir Palomydes sent the damesell unto Sir Trystram that he
sente to seke hym whan he was oute of hys mynde in the foreyst;   10
and this damesell asked Sir Trystramys what was hys name and
what he was. "As for that, telle Sir Palomydes that he shall nat wete
as at thys tyme, unto the tyme I have brokyn two spearis uppon
hym—but lat hym wete thys much, that I am the same knyght that
he smote downe in the over-evenynge at the turnemente—and   15
telle hym playnly, on what[7] party that he be, I woll be of the contrary party." "Sir," seyde the damesell, "ye shall undirstonde that
Sir Palomydes woll be on Kynge Arthurs party, where the moste
noble knyghtes of the worlde be."

❡"In the name of God," seyde Sir Trystram, "than woll I be with   20
the Kynge of Northe Galis, because of Sir Palomydes woll be on
Kynge Arthurs syde—and ellis I wolde nat, but for hys sake." So
whan Kyng Arthure was com they blew unto the fylde, and than
there began a grete party. And so Kynge Carados justed with the   fol.215r
Kynge with the Hondred Knyghtes, and there Kynge Carados had   25
a falle.

Than was there hurlyng and russhynge; and ryght so com in
knyghtes of Kyng Arthurs, and they bare on[8] bak the Kynge of North
Galis knyghtes. Than Sir Trystram cam in, and began so rowghly
and so bygly that there was none myght withstonde hym, and thus   30
he endured longe. And at the laste by fortune he felle amonge the
felyshyp of Kyng Ban; so there fylle uppon hym Sir Bors de Ganys,
and Sir Ector de Marys, and Sir Blamour de Ganys, and many othir
knyghtes. And than Sir Trystram smote on the ryght honde and on
the lyffte honde, that all lordis and ladyes spake of hys noble dedis.   35
But at the last Sir Trystram sholde have had the wars, had nat the
Kynge with the Hondred Knyghtes bene; and than he cam with
hys felyshyp and rescowed Sir Trystram, and brought hym away
frome the knyghtes that bare the shyldis of Cornwayle.

And than Sir Trystram saw another felyship by themselff, and   40
there was a[9] fourty knyghtes togydir; and Sir Kay le Senescial was
their governoure. Than Sir Trystram rode in amongyst them, and
there he smote downe Sir Kay frome hys horse, and there he fared
amonge tho knyghtis as a grehounde amonge conyes. Than Sir
Launcelot founde a knyght that was sore wounded uppon the hede.   45

❡"Sir," seyde Sir Launcelot, "who wounded you so sore?" "Sir, he
seyde, "a knyght that bearyth a blacke shylde—and I may curse

---

7. I.e., whatever.
8. *Bare on:* drove.
9. I.e., a group of.

the tyme that ever I mette with hym, for he ys a devyll and no
man." So Sir Launcelot departed frome hym, and thought to mete
with Sir Trystram. And so he rode with hys swerde i-drawyn in hys
honde to seke Sir Trystram; and than he aspyed hym hurlynge here
and there, and at every stroke Sir Trystram well-nyghe smote downe
a knyght.

¶"A, mercy Jesu!" seyde Sir Launcelot, "syth the firste tyme that
ever I bare armys saw I never one knyght do so mervaylous dedys
of armys—and if I sholde," seyde Sir Launcelot to hymselff, "sette
uppon thys knyght now, I ded shame to myselff." And therewithall
Sir Launcelot put up hys swerde. And than the Kynge with the Hondred Knyghtes, and an hondred mo of North Walis, sette uppon
the twenty knyghtes of Sir Launcelottes kynne; and they twenty
knyghtes hylde them ever togydir as wylde swyne, and none wolde
fayle other. So Sir Trystram, whan he behylde the nobles of thes
twenty knyghtes, he mervayled of their good dedys, for he saw by
their fare and rule that they had levyr dye than to avoyde the fylde.

¶"Now, Jesu," seyde Sir Trystram, "well may he be called
valyaunte and full of proues that hath such a sorte of noble knyghtes unto hys kynne, and full lyke ys he to be a nobleman that ys
their leder and governoure." He mente hit by[1] Sir Launcelot du Lake.

¶So whan Sir Trystram had beholde them longe, he thought
shame to se two hondred knyghtes batteryng uppon twenty knyghtes. Than Sir Trystram rode unto the Kynge with the Hondred
Knyghtes and seyde, "Sir, leve your fyghtynge with tho twenty
knyghtes, for ye wynne no worship of them, ye be so many and
they so feaw—and wyte you well, they woll nat oute of the fylde,
I se by their chere and countenaunce, that worship get you none
and ye sle them. Therefore leve your fyghtynge with them, for I,
to encrese my worship, I woll ryde unto the twenty knyghtes and
helpe them with all my myght and power."

"Nay," seyde the Kynge with the Hondred Knyghtes, "ye shall
nat do so. Now I se youre corayge and curtesye, I woll withdraw
my knyghtes for youre plesure—for evermore o good knyght woll
favoure another, and lyke woll draw to lyke." Than the Kynge with
the Hondred Knyghtes withdrew hys knyghtes. And all thys whyle
and longe tofore Sir Launcelot had wacched uppon Sir Trystram in
veary purpose to have felyshipped with hym—and than suddeynly
Sir Trystram, Sir Dynadan, and Governayle, hys man, rode their way
into the foreyste, that no man perceyved where they wente.

¶So than Kynge Arthure blew unto lodgynge, and gaff the Kynge
of North Galis the pryce, bycause Sir Trystram was uppon hys syde.

¶Than Sir Launcelot rode here and there as wode as a lyon that
faughted hys fylle, because he had loste Sir Trystram—and so he
returned unto Kynge Arthure. And than all the felde was in a noyse,
that with the wynde hit myght be harde two myle[2] how the lordys
and ladyes cryed, "The Knyght with the Blacke Shylde hath won
the fylde!"

---

1. *He mente hit by*: i.e., by that he meant.
2. *Harde two myle*: heard for two miles.

❡"Alas, seyde Kynge Arthure, "where ys that knyght becom? Hit
ys shame to all tho in the fylde so to lette hym ascape away frome
you; but with jantylnes and curtesye ye myght have brought hym
unto me, to thys Castell of Maydyns." Than Kynge Arthur wente to
hys knyghtes and comforted them and seyde, "My fayre felowis, be   5
nat dismayde thoughe ye have loste the fylde thys day." And many
were hurte and sore wounded, and many were hole. "My felowys,"
seyde Kyng Arthur, "loke that ye be of good chere, for tomorn I woll
be in the fylde with you and revenge you of youre enemyes."

So that nyght Kynge Arthure and hys knyghtes reposed themselff.   10
So the damesell that com frome La Beall Isod unto Sir Trystram,
all the whyle the turnement was a-doyng, she was with Quyene
Gwenyvere, and ever the Quene asked her for what cause she cam
into that contrey. "Madame," she answerde, "I com for none other
cause but frome my lady, La Beall Isode, to wete of youre well-   15
fare"—for in no wyse she wold nat telle the Quene that she cam   fol.216v
for Sir Trystramys sake.

So thys lady, Dame Brangwayn, toke hir leve of Quene Gwenyver,
and she rode aftir Sir Trystram. And as she rode thorow the foreyste, she harde a grete cry; than she commaunded hir squyar to   20
go into that foreyste to wyte what was that noyse. And so he cam
to a welle, and there he founde a knyght bounden tyll a tre, cryyng
as he had bene woode, and his horse and hys harneys stondyng by
hym; and whan he aspyed the squyar, with a brayde he brake hymselff lowse, and toke hys swerde in hys honde and ran to have   25
slayne that squyer.

Than he[3] toke hys horse and fledde to Dame Brangwayne and
tolde hir of hys adventure. Than she rode unto Sir Trystramys pavylon, and tolde Sir Trystram what adventure she had founde in the
foreyste. "Alas," seyde Sir Trystram, "uppon my hede, there ys som   30
good knyght at myschyff."[4] Than Sir Trystram toke hys horse and
hys swerde, and rode thyder; and there he harde how the knyght
complayned unto hymselff and sayde, "I, wofull knyght, Sir Palomydes, what mysseadventure befallith me that thus am defoyled
with falsehed and treson, thorow Sir Bors and Sir Ector? Alas!" he   35
seyde, "why lyve I so longe?" And than he gate his swerde in hys
honde and made many straunge sygnes and tokyns;[5] and so thorow[6]
the rageynge he threw hys swerd in that fountayne. Than Sir Palomydes wayled and wrange hys hondys—and at the laste, for pure
sorow, he ran into that fountayne and sought aftir hys swerde.   40

Than Sir Trystram saw that, and ran uppon Sir Palomydes and
hylde hym in hys armys faste. "What art thou," seyde Sir Palomydes,
"that holdith me so?" "I am a man of thys foreyste that wold the[7]
none harme." "Alas" seyde Sir Palomydes, "I may never wyn worship
where Sir Trystram ys; for ever where he ys and I be,[8] there gete I   fol.217r   45
no worshyp; and yf he be away, for the moste party I have the gré—

---

3. I.e., the squire.
4. At myschyff: in trouble.
5. Palomydes's strange gestures are perhaps to be identified with his non-Christian status.
6. I.e., through, by way of.
7. Thee.
8. Where he ys and I be: i.e., wherever he and I are in the same place.

onles that Sir Launcelot be there, othir ellis Sir Lamerok." Than Sir
Palomydes sayde, "Onys in Irelonde Sir Trystram put me to the wors,
and anothir tyme in Cornwayle, and in other placis in thys londe."
"What wolde ye do," seyde Sir Trystram, "and ye had Sir Trystram?"
"I wolde fyght with hym," seyde Sir Palomydes, "and ease my harte   5
uppon hym—and yet, to say the sothe, Sir Trystram ys the jantyl-
lyste knyght in thys worlde lyvynge."

⸿"Sir, what woll ye do," seyde Sir Trystram, "woll ye go with me
to youre lodgyng?"

⸿"Nay," he seyde, "to the Kynge with the Hondred Knyghtes,   10
for he rescowed me frome Sir Bors de Ganys and Sir Ector, and ellis
had I bene slayne traytourly." And Sir Trystram seyde hym such
kynde wordys that Sir Palomydes wente with hym to hys lodgynge.
Than Governayle wente tofore and charged Dame Brangwayne to
go oute of the way to hir lodgynge—"and byd ye Sir Persides that   15
he make hym no quarels." And so they rode togedirs tyll they cam
to Sir Trystramys pavylon; and there had Sir Palomydes all the chere
that myght be had all that nyght—but in no wyse Sir Trystram
myght nat be knowyn with⁹ Sir Palomydes. And so aftir souper they
yeode to reste, and Sir Trystram, for grete travayle, slepte tylle hit   20
was day.

⸿And Sir Palomydes myght nat slepe for angwysshe; and so in
the dawnyng of the day he toke hys horse prevaly and rode hys
way unto Gaherys and to Sir Sagramoure le Desirous, where they were
in their pavylons, for they three were felowis at the begynnynge of   25
the turnemente. And than uppon the morne the Kynge blew unto
the turnemente uppon the third day.

So the Kynge of Northe Galis and the Kynge of the Hondred   [33]
Knyghtes, they two encountird with Kynge Carados and the
Kynge of Irelonde; and there the Kynge with the Hondred Knygh-   30
tes smote downe Kynge Carados, and the Kyng of North Galis smote   fol.217v
downe the Kynge of Irelonde. So with that cam in Sir Palomydes,
and he made grete worke, for by hys endented shylde he was well
knowyn.¹ So there cam in Kynge Arthur and ded grete dedis of
armys togydirs, and put the Kynge of North Galis and the Kyng   35
with the Hondred Knyghtes to the wars.²

⸿So with this cam in Sir Trystram with hys blak shylde, and
anone he justed with Sir Palomydes; and there by fyne force Sir
Trystram smote Sir Palomydes over hys horse croupe. Than Kynge
Arthure cryed, "Knyght with the Blacke Shylde, make the³ redy to   40
me!"—and, in the same wyse, Sir Trystram smote Kynge Arthure.
And than, by forse of Kynge Arthurs knyghtes the Kynge and Sir
Palomydes were horsed agayne.

Than Kynge Arthur, with a grete egir harte, he gate a grete speare
in hys honde, and there uppon the one syde he smote Sir Trystram   45

---

9. I.e., to.
1. He was well known from the scalloped pattern in the coat of arms on his shield (see
   p. 324, line 42.
2. I.e., worse.
3. Thee.

over hys horse. Than footehote Sir Palomydes cam uppon Sir Trystram, as he was uppon foote, to have overryddyn hym; than Sir
Trystram was ware off hym, and stowped a lytyll asyde, and with
grete ire he gate hym by the arme and pulled hym downe frome
hys horse.

Than Sir Palomydes lyghtly arose; and they daysshed togydirs
with theire swerdys myghtyly, that many kynges, quenys, lordys,
and ladyes stoode and behelde them. And at the last Sir Trystram
smote Sir Palomydes uppon the helme three myghty strokes—and
at every stroke that he gaff he seyde, "Have thys for Sir Trystramys
sake!" And with that Sir Palomydes felle to the erthe grovelynge.
Than cam the Kynge of the Hondred Knyghtes and brought Sir
Trystram an horse, and so was he horsed agayne. And by that tyme
was Sir Palomydes horsed, and with grete ire he justed uppon Sir
Trystram with hys speare as hit was in the reyste, and gaff hym a
grete dayssh with hys swerde.

Than Sir Trystram avoyded hys speare, and gate hym by the nek
with hys bothe hondis and pulled hym clene oute of hys sadle; and
so he bare hym afore hym the lengthe of ten spearys, and than he
lete hym falle at hys adventure. Than Sir Trystram was ware of
Kynge Arthure with a naked swerde in hys honde, and with hys
speare Sir Trystram ran uppon Kyng Arthure; and than Kyng Arthure
boldely abode hym, and with hys swerde he smote a-to hys speare.

And therewithall Sir Trystram was astooned; and so Kynge Arthure
gaff hym three or foure strokis or he myght gete oute hys swerde—
and so Sir Trystram drew hys swerde, and aythir of them assayled
othir passyng harde. And with that the grete prease departed. Than
Sir Trystram rode here and there and ded hys grete payne, that a⁴
twelve of the good knyghtes of the bloode of Kynge Ban, that were
of Sir Launcelottis kyn, that day Sir Trystram smote downe, that all
the estatis mervayled of their grete dedis—and all people cryed
uppon the Knyght with the Blacke Shylde.

¶So thys cry was so large that Sir Launcelot harde hit, and than
he gate a grete speare in hys honde and cam towardis the cry.

¶Than Sir Launcelot cryed, "Knyght with the Blacke Shylde,
make ye redy to juste with me!"

¶Whan Sir Trystram harde hym sey so, he gate hys speare in hys
honde; and ayther abeysed their hedys downe lowe and cam togydir
as thundir, that Sir Trystrams speare brake in pecis. And Sir Launcelot by malefortune stroke Sir Trystram on the syde a depe wounde,
nyghe to the dethe; but yet Sir Trystram avoyded nat hys sadyll,
and so the speare brake therewithall—and yete Sir Trystram gate
oute hys swerde, and he russhed to Sir Launcelot and gaff hym three
grete strokes uppon the helme, that the fyre sprange oute, that Sir
Launcelot abeysed hys hede low toward hys sadyll-bow. And so
therewithall Trystram departed frome the fylde, for he felte hym so
wounded that he wente he sholde have dyed; and Sir Dynadan

fol.218r

[34]

4. I.e., a quantity of.

aspyed hym and folowed hym into the foreyste. Than Sir **Launcelot** abode[5] and ded mervaylous dedys.

¶So whan Sir **Trystram** was departed by the foreystis syde, he alyght and unlaced hys harneys and freysshid hys wounde. Than wente Sir **Dynadan** that he sholde have dyed, and wepte. "Nay, nay!" seyde Sir **Trystram**," never drede you, Sir **Dynadan**, for I am harte-hole,[6] and of thys wounde I shall sone be hole, by the mercy of God."

¶And anone Sir **Dynadan** was ware where cam Sir **Palomydes** rydynge streyte uppon them. Than Sir **Trystram** was ware that Sir **Palomydes** com to have destroyed hym—and so Sir **Dynadan** gaff hym warnynge and seyde, "Sir **Trystram**, my lorde, ye ar so sore wounded that ye may nat have ado with hym. Therefore I woll ryde agaynste hym and do to hym what I may—and yf I be slayne, ye may pray for my soule—and so in the meanewhyle ye may with-draw you and go into the castell or into the foreyste, that he shall nat mete with you." Sir **Trystram** smyled and seyde, "I thanke you, Sir **Dynadan**, [of your good wylle,] but ye shall undirstond that I am able to handyll hym." And anone hastely he armed hym, and toke hys horse and a grete speare in hys honde, and seyde to Sir **Dynadan** "Adew," and rode toward Sir **Palomydes** a soffte pace.

¶Whan Sir **Palomydes** saw hym, he[7] alyght and made a counten-aunce to amende hys horse,[8] but he ded hit for thys cause: for he abode Sir **Gaherys** that cam aftir hym—and whan he was com, he[9] rode towarde Sir **Trystram**. Than Sir **Trystram** sente unto Sir **Palo-mydes** and requyred hym to juste with hym; and if he smote downe Sir **Palomydes** he wolde do no more to hym, and if Sir **Palomydes** smote downe Sir **Trystram**, he bade hym do hys utteraunce.[1] And so they were accorded and mette togydirs; and Sir **Trystram** smote downe Sir **Palomydes**, that he had a vylaunce falle and lay stylle as he had bene dede. And than Sir **Trystram** ran uppon Sir **Gaherys**; and he wold nat have justed, but whethir he wolde or wolde nat, Sir **Trystram** smote hym over hys horse croupe, that he lay stylle. And Sir **Trystram** rode hys way, and lefft Sir **Persides** hys squyar within the pavelons.[2]

And Sir **Trystram** and Sir **Dynadan** rode to an olde knyghtes place to lodge them (and thys olde knyght had fyve sonnes at the turne-ment, that prayde God hartely for their commynge home; and so, as the Freynshe booke sayeth, they com home all fyve, well bea-tyn).[3] And whan Sir **Trystram** departed into the foreyste, Sir **Laun-celot** hylde allwayes the stowre lyke harde,[4] as a man araged that

---

5. I.e., stayed in the tournament.
6. I.e., not heart-broken, not dismayed.
7. I.e., Palomydes.
8. *Made a countenaunce to amende hys horse:* pretended to be repairing his horse's equip-ment.
9. I.e., Palomydes.
1. *Do hys utteraunce:* i.e., kill him.
2. *Within the pavelons:* i.e., back at Trystram's tent.
3. Indeed, three are brought back dead and the other two are "grevously wounded" (see p. 327). Malory's point would seem to be that one should be careful about what one asks for: dead or alive, all five knights *did* return home.
4. *Hylde allwayes the stowre lyke harde:* kept fighting tenaciously.

toke none hede to hymselff—and wyte you well, there was many
a noble knyght ayenste hym.

¶And whan Kyng Arthure saw Sir Launcelot do so mervaylous
dedis of armys, he than armed hym and toke hys horse and hys
armour, and rode into the fylde to helpe Sir Launcelot—and so many
knyghtes cam with Kynge Arthur. And to make shorte tale in conclusion, the Kyng of North Galis and the Kynge of the Hondred
Knyghtes were put to the wars.[5] And bycause Sir Launcelot abode
and was the laste in the fylde, the pryse was gyvyn hym.

But Sir Launcelot, nother for kynge, quene, nother knyght, wolde
thereoff; and where the cry was cryed thorow the fylde, "Sir Launcelot hath wonne the filde thys day," Sir Launcelot made another cry
contrary: "Sir Trystram hath won the fylde! For he began firste, and
lengyst hylde on—and so hathe he done the firste day, the secunde,
and the thirde day!" Than all the astatis and degrees, hyghe and
lowe, seyde of Sir Launcelot grete worship for the honoure that he
ded to Sir Trystram; and for the honour doyng[6] by Sir Launcelot, he
was at that tyme more praysed and renowmed than and he had
overthrowyn fyve hondred knyghtes. And all the peple hole, for
hys jantilnes—firste the astatis, hyghe and lowe, and after the
comynalté—at onys cryed, "Sir Launcelot hath won the gré, whosoever[7] sayth nay!"

Than was Sir Launcelot wrothe and ashamed; and so therewithall
he rode to Kynge Arthure. "Alas," seyde the Kynge, "we ar all dismayde that Sir Trystram ys thus departed frome us. Pardé," seyde
Kynge *Arthur,* "he ys one of the nobelyst knyghtes that ever I saw
holde speare in honde or swerde, and the moste curtayse knyght
in hys fyghtyng. For full harde I sye hym bestad," seyde Kynge
Arthure, "whan he smote Sir Palomydes upon the helme thryse, that
he abaysshed hys helme with hys strokis; and also he seyde 'here
ys a stroke for Sir Trystram'—and thus he seyde thryse." Than
Kynge Arthure and Sir Launcelot and Sir Dodynas le Saveage toke their
horsis to seke aftir Sir Trystram. And by the meanys of Sir Persides,
he had tolde Kynge Arthure where Sir Trystramys pavylyon was; but
whan they cam there, Sir Trystram and Sir Dynadan was gone. Than
Kynge Arthur and Sir Launcelot was hevy and returned ayen to the
Castell Maydyns, makyng grete dole for the hurte of Sir Trystram
and hys suddeyne departynge.

"So God me helpe," seyde Kynge Arthur, "I am more hevy that I
can nat mete with hym than I am for all the hurtys that all my
knyghtes have had at the turnement." And so furthwith cam Sir
Gaherys and told Kynge Arthur how Sir Trystram had smytten downe
Sir Palomydes, and hit was at hys owne requeste. "Alas" seyde Kynge
Arthur, "that was grete dishonoure to Sir Palomydes, inasmuch as
Sir Trystram was so sore wounded. And may we, all kyngis and
knyghtes and men of worship, sey that Sir Trystram may be called
a noble knyght—and one of the beste knyghtes that ever Y saw,

---

5. I.e., worse.
6. I.e., having been done to him.
7. I.e., regardless of whosoever.

dayes of my lyfe. For I woll that ye, all kyngis and knyghtes, know,"
seyde Kynge Arthur, "that I never saw knyght do so mervaylously
as he hath done thes three dayes; for he was the firste that began,
and the lengyst that hylde on, save thys laste day—and thoughe
he were hurte, hit was a manly adventure of two noble knyghtes.   fol.220r   5
And whan two noble men encountir, nedis muste the tone have
the worse, lyke as God wyll suffir at that tyme."

¶"Sir, as for me," seyde Sir Launcelot, "for all the londys that ever
my fadir leffte, I wolde nat have hurt Sir Trystram and I had knowyn
hym at that tyme that I hurte hym, for I saw nat hys shylde. For   10
and I had seyne hys blacke shylde, I wolde nat have medled with
hym for many causis," seyde Sir Launcelot, "for but late he ded as
muche for me as ever ded knyght—and that ys well knowyn that
he had ado with thirty knyghtes and no helpe only save Sir Dynadan.
And one thynge shall I promyse you," seyde Sir Launcelot, "Sir Pal-   15
omydes shall repente hit, as in hys unknyghtly delynge, so for to
folow that noble knyght that[8] I be mysfortune hurte hym thus." So
Sir Launcelot seyd all the worship that myght be spokyn by Sir Trystram. Than Kyng Arthure made a grete feste to[9] all that wolde com.

And thus we lat passe Kynge Arthure. And a lityll we woll turne   20
unto Sir Palomydes, that aftir he had a falle of Sir Trystram, he was
nyghehonde araged oute of hys wytte for despite of Sir Trystram,
and so he folowed hym by adventure. And as he cam by a ryver, in
hys woodnes he wolde have made hys horse to have lopyn over the
watir; and the horse fayled footyng and felle in the ryver, wherefore   25
Sir Palomydes was adrad leste he shulde have bene drowned. And
than he avoyded hys horse and swam to the londe, and lete hys
horse go downe by adventure. And whan he cam to the londe, he   [36]
toke of hys harnys and sate romynge and cryynge as a man oute of
hys mynde.   30

¶Ryght so cam a damessell evyn by Sir Palomydes, that was sente
fro Sir Gawayne and hys brothir unto Sir Mordred, that lay syke in
the same place with that olde knyght where Sir Trystram was (for,
as the booke seythe, Sir Persides hurte so Sir Mordred a ten dayes   fol.220v
afore, and, had hit nat bene for the love of Sir Gawayne and hys   35
brethirn, Sir Persides had slayne Sir Mordred). And so this damysell
cam by Sir Palomydes, and he and she had langage togyder whych
pleased neythir of them. And so thys damesell rode her wayes tyll
she cam to that olde knyghtes place, and there she tolde that olde
knyght how she mette with the woodist knyght by adventure that   40
ever she mette withall.

¶"What bare he in hys shylde?" seyde Sir Trystram. "Sir, hit was
endented with whyght and blacke," seyde the damesell. "A" seyde
Sir Trystram, "that was Palamydes, the good knyght. For well I know
hym," seyde Sir Trystram, "for one of the beste knyghtes lyvyng in   45
thys realme." Than that olde knyght toke a lityll hakeney and rode
for Sir Palomydes, and brought hym unto hys owne maner. And full

8. I.e., who.
9. I.e., for.

well knew Sir Trystram hym, but he sayde but lityll. For at that tyme Sir Trystram was walkyng uppon hys feete and well amended of his hurtis; and allwayes whan Sir Palomydes saw Sir Trystram he wolde beholde hym full mervaylously, and ever hym semed[1] that he had sene hym.

Than wolde he sey unto Sir Dynadan, "And ever I may mete with Sir Trystram, he shall nat escape myne hondis." "I mervayle," seyde Sir Dynadan, "that ye do boste behynde[2] Sir Trystram so, for hit ys but late that he was in youre hondys and ye in hys hondis. Why wolde ye nat holde hym whan ye had hym? For I saw myselff twyse or thryse that ye gate but lytyll worship of Sir Trystram." Than was Sir Palomydes ashamed. So leve we them a lityll whyle in the castell with the olde knyght, Sir Darras.

Now shall we speke of Kynge Arthure, that seyde to Sir Launcelot, "Had nat ye bene, we had nat loste Sir Trystram, for he was here dayly unto the tyme ye mette with hym; and in an evyll[3] tyme," seyde Kynge Arthure, "ye encountred with hym." "My lorde Arthure," seyde Sir Launcelot, "ye shall undirstonde the cause. Ye put now uppon me that I sholde be causer of hys departicion—God knowith hit was ayenste my wyll—but whan men bene hote in dedis of armys, oftyn hit ys seyne they hurte their frendis as well as their foys. And, my lorde," seyde Sir Launcelot, "ye shall undirstonde that Sir Trystram ys a man that I am ryght lothe to offende to, for he hath done more for me than ever Y ded for hym as yet."

But than Sir Launcelot mad brynge forthe a boke,[4] and than seyde Sir Launcelot, "Here we ar ten knyghtes that woll swere uppon thys booke never to reste one nyght where[5] we reste another thys twelvemonth, untyll that we fynde Sir Trystram. And as for me," seyde Sir Launcelot, "I promyse you uppon thys booke that, and I may mete with hym, other with fayrenes othir with fowlnes, I shall brynge hym to thys courte, other elles I shall dye therefore." And the namys of thes ten knyghtes that had undirtake thys queste [were these folowynge]: first was Sir Launcelot; Sir Ector de Marys, Sir Bors de Ganys, and Sir Bleoberys, Sir Blamour de Ganys, Sir Lucan de Butler, Sir Uwayne, Sir Galyhud, Sir Lyonel, and Sir Galyodyn.

So thes ten noble knyghtes departed frome the courte of Kynge Arthur; and so they rode uppon theire queste togydirs tyll they com to a crosse where departed foure wayes, and there departed the felyship in foure to seke Sir Trystram. And as Sir Launcelot rode, by adventure he mette with Dame Brangwayne that was sente into that contrey to seke Sir Trystram, and she fled as faste as her palfrey myght go. So Sir Launcelot mette with her and asked why she fled.

"A, fayre knyght," seyde Dame Brangwayne, "I fle for drede of my lyff, for here folowith me Sir Breuse Saunz Pité to sle me." "Holde you nyghe me," seyde Sir Launcelot. And whan he sye Sir Breuse

fol.221r

---

1. *Full mervaylously:* i.e., in wonder. *Hym semed:* it seemed to him.
2. I.e., behind the back of, in the absence of.
3. I.e., badly chosen.
4. I.e., Bible or missal.
5. I.e., in the same place where.

Saunz Pité he cryed unto hym and seyde, "False knyght, destroyer of ladyes and damesels, now thy laste dayes be com!" Whan Sir Breuse Saunce Pité saw Sir Launcelottis shylde he knew hit well (for at that tyme he bare nat the shylde of Cornwayle, but he bare hys owne). And than Sir Breuse returned and fled; and Sir Launcelot folowed aftir hym—but Sir Breuse was so well horsed that whan hym lyst to fle he myght fle whan he wolde and abyde whan he wolde.[6] And than Sir Launcelot returned unto Dame Brangwayne, and she thanked Sir Launcelot of hys curtesy and grete laboure.

Now woll we speke of Sir Lucan de Butlere, that by fortune he cam rydynge to the same place there as was Sir Trystram; and in he cam for none other entente but to aske herberow. Than the porter asked what was hys name.

❡"Sir, telle youre lorde that my name ys Sir Lucan de Butler, a knyght of the Rounde Table." So the porter yode unto Sir Darras, lorde of the place, and tolde hym who was there to aske herberow. "Nay, nay," seyde Sir Daname, that was nevew unto Sir Darras, "sey hym that he shall nat be lodged here; but lat hym wete that I, Sir Danam, woll mete with hym anone—and byd hym make hym redy." So Sir Danam com forthe on horseback, and there they met togydirs with spearys; and Sir Lucan smote downe Sir Danam over hys horse croupe, and than he fled into that place, and Sir Lucan rode aftir hym and asked aftir hym many tymys.

Than Sir Dynadan seyde to Sir Trystram, "Hit ys shame to se the lordys cousyne[7] of thys place defoyled." "Abyde," seyde Sir Trystram, "and I shall redresse hit." And in the meanewhyle Sir Dynadan was on horsebacke, and he justed with Sir Lucan; and he smote Sir Dynadan thorow the thycke of the thyghe, and so he rode hys way. And Sir Trystram was wroth that Sir Dynadan was hurte, and he folowed aftir and thought to avenge hym; and within a whyle he overtoke Sir Lucan and bade hym turne—and so they mette togydirs, and Sir Trystram hurte Sir Lucane passynge sore, and gaff hym a falle.

❡So with that com Sir Uwayne, a jantill knyght, and whan he saw Sir Lucan so hurte, he called to Sir Trystram to juste.

❡"Fayre knyght," seyde Sir Trystram, "telle me youre name, I requyre you."

❡"Sir knyght, wite you well my name ys Sir Uwayne le Fyze de Roy Ureyne." "A!" seyde Sir Trystram, "be my wylle, I wolde nat have ado with you at no tyme."

❡"Sir, ye shall nat do so," seyde Sir Uwayne, "but[8] ye shall have ado with me." And than Sir Trystram saw none other boote but rode ayenste hym, and overthrew Sir Uwayne and hurte hym in the syde; and so he departed unto hys lodgynge agayne. And whan Sir Danam undirstood that Sir Trystram had hurte Sir Lucan, he wolde

fol.221v

5

[37]   10

15

20

25

30

fol.222r   35

40

45

---

6. *So well horsed . . . abyde whan he wolde:* i.e., his horse was so fast that he could choose to fight or flee at will.
7. I.e., nephew.
8. *Ye shall nat do so . . . but:* you shall not do anything except.

have ryddyn aftir hym for to have slayne hym; but Sir Trystram wolde nat suffir hym.

Than Sir Uwayne lete ordayne an horse-litter, and brought Sir Lucan to the abbay of Ganys. And the castell thereby hyght the Castell off Ganys, of the whych Sir Bleoberys was lorde; and at that castell Sir Launcelot promysed all hys felowis there to mete in the queste of Sir Trystram. So whan Sir Trystram was com to hys lodgynge, there cam a damsell that tolde Sir Darras that three of his sunnys were slayne at that turnemente, and two grevously wounded so that they were never lyke to helpe themselff; and all thys was done by a noble knyght that bare a blacke shylde, and that was he that bare the pryce. Than cam one and tolde Sir Darras that the same knyght was within hys courte that bare the blacke shylde.

Than Sir Darras yode unto Sir Trystramys chambir, and there he founde hys shylde and shewed hit to the damesell. "A, sir," seyde the damesell, "thys same ys he that slewe youre three sunnys." Than withoute ony taryynge Sir Darras put Sir Trystram, Sir Palomydes, and Sir Dynadan within a stronge preson—and there Sir Trystram was lyke to have dyed of grete syknes. And every day Sir Palomydes wolde repreve[9] Sir Trystram of olde hate[1] betwyxt them; and ever Sir Trystram spake fayre and seyde lytyll.

¶But whan Sir Palomydes se that Sir Trystram was falle in syknes, than was he hevy for hym and comforted hym in all the beste wyse he coude. And, as the Freynshe booke sayth, there cam fourty knyghtes to Sir Darras that were of hys owne kynne; and they wolde have slayne Sir Trystram and hys felowis, but Sir Darras wolde nat but put[2] them in preson, and mete and drynke they had. So Sir Trystram endured there grete payne, for syknes had undirtake hym— and that ys the grettist payne a presoner may have, for all the whyle a presonere may have hys helth of body, he may endure undir the mercy of God and in hope of good delyveraunce;

¶But whan syknes towchith a presoners body, than may a presonere say all welth ys hym berauffte,[3] and than hath he cause to wayle and wepe—[4]

¶Ryght so ded Sir Trystram whan syknes had undirtake hym, for than he toke such sorow that he had allmoste slayne hymselff.

¶Now woll we leve Sir Trystram, Sir Palomydes, and Sir Dynadan in preson, and speke we of othir knyghtes that sought aftir Sir Trystram in many dyverse partyes of thys londe. And some yode

fol.222v

[38]

9. I.e., blame.
1. *Of olde hate:* for the long-lived enmity.
2. I.e., keep.
3. *All welth ys hym berauffte:* he is bereft of all wealth.
4. *That ys the grettist payne . . . cause to wayle and wepe:* this is perhaps the most personal and abject of Malory's rare extempory comments, here alluding to the imprisonment that (at p. 112) he says he himself endures at the time of writing. His implicit identification with Trystram might further be designed to create the impression of an extended allegorical autobiography, concerned with public and private identity and authority, conflicting moral obligation, and physical and, indeed, mental health. It is interesting that one of very few surviving records that reveal anything of Malory's activities while in prison (besides his writing the *Morte Darthur*) shows him witnessing the deathbed declaration of a fellow prisoner (see the chronology on p. 26). Cf. n. 9, p. 293.

into Cornwayle; and by adventure Sir Gaherys, nevew unto Kynge Arthure, cam unto Kynge Marke. And there he was well resseyved, and sate at Kynge Markys owne table and at hys owne messe.[5] Than Kynge Marke asked Sir Gaherys what tydynges there was within the realme of Logrys.

"Sir," seyde Sir Gaherys, "the Kynge regnys as a noble knyght. And now but late there was a grete justis and turnemente that ever Y saw within thys reallme of Logres, and the moste nobelyste knyghtes were at that justis; but there was one knyght that ded mervaylously three dayes, and he bare a blacke shylde, and on all the knyghtes that ever Y saw he preved the beste knyght." "That was," seyde Kynge Marke, "Sir Launcelot, other ellis Sir Palomydes the paynym." "Not so, seyde Sir Gaherys, "for they were both of the contrary party agaynste the Knyght with the Blacke Shylde."

¶ "Than was hit Sir Trystram de Lyones," seyde the kynge—and therewithall he smote downe hys hede, and in hys harte he feryd sore that Sir Trystram sholde gete hym[6] such worship in the realme of Logrys wherethorow hymselff shuld nat be able to withstonde hym. Thus Sir Gaherys had grete chere with Kynge Marke and with the quene. La Beall Isode was glad of his wordis, for well she wyste by hys dedis and maners that hit was Sir Trystram. And than the kynge made a feste royall, and to that feste cam Sir Uwayne le Fyze de Roy Urayne (and som called hym Sir Uwayne le Blaunche Maynes). And thys Sir Uwayne chalenged all the knyghtes of Cornwayle; than was the kynge wood wrothe that he had no knyghtes to answere hym.

Than Sir Andred, nevew unto Kynge Marke, lepe up and sayde, "I woll encountir with Sir Uwayne." Than he yode and armyd hym, and horsed hym in the beste maner. And there Sir Uwayne mette with Sir Andred and smote hym downe, that he sowned on the erthe.

Than was Kynge Marke sory and wrothe oute of mesure that he had no knyght to revenge hys nevew, Sir Andret. So the kynge called unto hym Sir Dynas le Seneschall, and prayde hym for hys sake to take uppon hym for to juste with Sir Uwayne. "Sir," seyd Sir Dynas, "I am full lothe to have ado with ony of the knyghtes of the Rounde Table." "Yet,[7] for my love, take uppon you for to juste!" So Sir Dynas made hym redy to juste, and anone they encountirde togydirs with grete spearys; but Sir Dynas was overthrowyn, horse and man—a grete falle.

Who was wroth than but Kynge Marke? "Alas," he seyde, "have I no knyght that woll encounter with yondir knyght?" "Sir," seyde Sir Gaherys, "for youre sake I woll just." So Sir Gaherys made hym redy, and whan he was armed he rode into the fylde. And whan Sir Uwayne saw Sir Gaherys shylde, he rode to hym and seyde, "Sir, ye do nat youre parte, for the firste tyme that ever ye were made knyght of the Rounde Table ye sware that ye shuld nat have ado with none of youre felyship wyttyngly. And, pardé, Sir Gaherys, ye

5
fol.223r
10
15
20
25
30
35
40
fol.223v
45

---

5. *At hys owne messe*: eating from the same food as that prepared for the king.
6. I.e., Trystram.
7. King Mark is speaking.

know me well inow by my shylde, and so do I know you by youre shylde; and thaughe ye wolde breke youre othe, I woll nat breke myne. For there ys nat one here, nother ye, that shall thynk I am aferde of you, but that I durst ryght well have ado with you—and yet we be syster sonnys." Than was Sir Gaherys ashamed. And so therewithall every knyght wente their way, and Sir Uwayne rode oute of the contrey.

Than Kynge Marke armed hym and toke hys horse and hys speare with a squyar with hym, and than he rode afore Sir Uwayne, and suddeynly, at a gap, he ran uppon hym as he that was nat ware of hym; and there he smote hym allmoste thorow the body, and so there leffte hym. So within a whyle there cam Sir Kay and founde Sir Uwayne, and asked hym how he was hurte. "I wote nat," seyde Sir Uwayne, "why nother wherefore, but by treson, I am sure, I gate thys hurte; for here cam a knyght suddeynly uppon me or that I was ware, and suddeynly hurte me." Than there was com Sir Andred to seke Kyng Marke. "Thou traytoure knyght!" seyde Sir Kay, "and I wyst hit were thou that thus traytourely haste hurte thys noble knyght, thou shuldist never passe my hondys." "Sir," seyde Sir Andred, "I ded never hurte hym, and that I reporte me to hymselff."

¶ "Fy on you, false knyghtes of Cornwayle," seyde Sir Kay, "for ye are naught worth."[8] So Sir Kay made cary Sir Uwayne to the Abbay of the Black Crosse, and there was he heled. Than Sir Gaherys toke hys leve of Kyng Marke—but or he departed he seyde, "Sir kynge, ye ded a fowle shame whan ye flemyd Sir Trystram oute of thys contrey, for ye nedid nat to have doughted no knyght and[9] he[1] had bene here." And so he departed. Than there cam Sir Kay the Senesciall unto Kynge Marke, and there he had god chere shewynge outewarde.[2]

¶ "Now, fayre lordys," seyde Kynge Marke, "woll ye preve ony adventure in this foreyste of Morrys, whych ys an harde adventure as I know ony?" "Sir" seyde Sir Kay, "I woll preve hit." And Sir Gaherys seyde he wolde be avysed,[3] for Kynge Marke was ever full of treson. And therewithall Sir Gaherys departed and rode hys way; and by the same way that Sir Kay sholde ryde, he leyde hym downe to reste, chargynge hys squyar to wayte uppon hym—"and yf Sir Kay comme, warne me whan he commyth."

So within a whyle Sir Kay com rydyng that way; and than Sir Gaherys toke hys horse and mette hym, and seyde, "Sir Kay, ye ar nat wyse to ryde at the rekeyste of Kynge Marke, for he delith all with treson." Than seyde Sir Kay, "I requyre you that we may preve well thys adventure." "I woll nat fayle you," seyde Sir Gaherys. And so they rode that tyme tylle a lake that was that tyme called the Perelous Lake, and there they abode under the shawe of the wood. The meanewhyle Kynge Marke within the castell of Tyntagyll

[39]
fol.224r

---

8. *Naught worth:* worth nothing.
9. I.e., if.
1. I.e., Trystram.
2. *He had god chere shewynge outewarde:* he received an outward show (i.e., a pretense) of a cordial welcome.
3. *Wolde be avysed:* would think about it.

avoyded all hys barownes, and all othir, save such as were prevy
with hym, were avoyded oute of the chambir. And than he let calle
hys nevew, Sir Andred, and bade arme hym and horse hym lyghtly,[4]
for by that tyme hit was nyghe mydnyght.

And so Kynge Marke was armed all in blacke, horse and all, and
so at a prevy postern they two yssued oute with their verlattes with
them, and so rode tylle they cam to that lake. Than Sir Kay aspyed
them firste, and gate hys speare in hys honde, and profirde to juste;
and Kynge Marke rode ayenst hym, and smote ech other full harde,
for the moone shone as the bryght day. And at that justis Sir Kayes
horse felle downe, for hys horse was nat so bygge as the kynges
horse was, and Sir Kayes horse brused hym full sore. Than Sir
Gaherys was wrothe that Sir Kay had a falle. Than he cryed,
"Knyght, sitte thou faste in thy sadle, for I wolle revenge my felow."

Than Kynge Marke was aferde of Sir Gaherys, and so with evyll
wylle Kynge Marke rode ayenste hym; and Sir Gaherys gaff hym such
a stroke that he felle downe. And so forthwithall Sir Gaherys ran
unto Sir Andred and smote hym frome hys horse quyte, that hys
helme smote in the erthe and nyghe had brokyn hys neke. And
therewithall Sir Gaherys alyght, and gate up Sir Kay; and than they
yeode both on foote to them, and bade them yelde them and telle
their namys, othir ellis they sholde dey. Than with grete payne Sir
Andred spake firste and seyde, "Hit ys Kynge Marke of Cornwayle—
therefore be ye ware what ye do—and I am Sir Andred, hys cousyn."

"Fy on you bothe!" seyde Sir Gaherys, "for ye ar false traytours,
and false treson have ye wrought undir youre semble chere that ye
made us. For hit were pité that ye sholde lyve ony lenger," seyde
Sir Gaherys. "Save my lyff," seyde Kynge Marke, "and I woll make
amendys—and concider that I am a kynge anoynted." "Hit were
the more shame," seyde Sir Gaherys, "to save thy lyff! For thou arte
a kynge anoynted with creyme;[5] and therefore thou sholdist holde
with all men of worship—and therefore thou arte worthy to dye."
And so with that he laysshed at Kynge Marke, and he coverde hym
with hys shylde and defended hym as he myght; and than Sir Kay
laysshed at Sir Andret. And therewithall Kynge Marke yelded hym
unto Sir Gaherys, and than he kneled adowne and made hys othe
uppon the crosse of the swerde that never whyle he lyved he wolde
be ayenste arraunte knyghtes; and also he sware to be good fryende
unto Sir Trystram, if ever he cam into Cornwayle. And by that tyme
Sir Andret was on the erthe, and Sir Kay wolde have slayne hym.

¶"Lat be," seyde Sir Gaherys, "sle hym nat, I pray you."

¶"Sir, hit were pité," seyde Syr Kay, "that he sholde lyve ony
lenger, for he ys cousyn nyghe unto Sir Trystram, and ever he hath
bene a traytoure unto hym, and by hym he was exhyled oute of
Cornwayle—and therefore I woll sle hym," seyde Sir Kay.

¶"Ye shall nat do so," seyde Sir Gaherys, "for sytthyn I have yevyn
the kynge hys lyff, I pray you gyff hym hys lyffe." And therewithall

4. I.e., quickly.
5. I.e., consecrated oil.

Sir 𝕶𝖆𝖞 lete hym go. And so they rode her wayes unto Sir 𝕯𝖞𝖓𝖆𝖘 le
Senesciall, for bycause they harde sey that he loved well Sir 𝕿𝖗𝖞𝖘𝖙𝖗𝖆𝖒. So they reposed them, and sone aftir they rode unto the
realme of Logrys. And so within a lityll while they mette with Sir
𝕷𝖆𝖚𝖓𝖈𝖊𝖑𝖔𝖙, that allwayes had Dame 𝕭𝖗𝖆𝖓𝖌𝖜𝖆𝖞𝖓𝖊 with hym, to that   5
entente he wente[6] to have mette the sunner with Sir 𝕿𝖗𝖞𝖘𝖙𝖗𝖆𝖒. And
Sir 𝕷𝖆𝖚𝖓𝖈𝖊𝖑𝖔𝖙 asked what tydynges in Cornwayle, and whethir they
harde of Sir 𝕿𝖗𝖞𝖘𝖙𝖗𝖆𝖒. Sir 𝕶𝖆𝖞 and Sir 𝕲𝖆𝖍𝖊𝖗𝖞𝖘 answerde that they
harde nat of hym, and so they tolde worde-by-worde of their adventure. Than Sir 𝕷𝖆𝖚𝖓𝖈𝖊𝖑𝖔𝖙 smyled and seyde, "Harde hit ys to take   10
oute off the fleysshe that ys bredde in the boone!"[7] And so they
made hem myrry togydirs.

    ¶Now leve we of thys tale and speke we of Sir 𝕯𝖞𝖓𝖆𝖘 that had   [40]
within the castell a paramour—and she loved anothir knyght bettir
than hym; and so whan Sir 𝕯𝖞𝖓𝖆𝖘 was oute an-huntynge, she slyp-   15
ped downe by a towell, and toke with hir two brachettis, and so
she yode to the knyght that she loved. And whan Sir 𝕯𝖞𝖓𝖆𝖘 cam
home and myste hys paramoure and hys brachettes, than was he
the more wrother for hys brachettis, more than for hys lady; so
than he rode aftir the knyghte that had hys paramoure, and bade   20
hym turne and juste.

    ¶So Sir 𝕯𝖞𝖓𝖆𝖘 smote hym downe, that with the falle he brake
hys legge and hys arme. And than hys lady and paramour cryed
and seyde "Sir 𝕯𝖞𝖓𝖆𝖘, mercy!" and she wolde love hym bettir than
ever she ded.   25

    ¶"Nay," seyde Sir 𝕯𝖞𝖓𝖆𝖘, "I shall never truste them that onys
betrayeth me; and therefore as ye have begunne, so ende, for I woll
nevir meddill with you." And so Sir 𝕯𝖞𝖓𝖆𝖘 departed and toke his
brachettis with hym, and so he rode to hys castell.

    ¶Now woll we turne unto Sir 𝕷𝖆𝖚𝖓𝖈𝖊𝖑𝖔𝖙, that was ryght hevy that   30
he cowth never hyre no tydynges of Sir 𝕿𝖗𝖞𝖘𝖙𝖗𝖆𝖒, for all this whyle
he was in preson with Sir 𝕯𝖆𝖗𝖗𝖆𝖘, Sir 𝕻𝖆𝖑𝖔𝖒𝖞𝖉𝖊𝖘, and Sir 𝕯𝖞𝖓𝖆𝖉𝖆𝖓.
Than Dame 𝕭𝖗𝖆𝖓𝖌𝖜𝖆𝖞𝖓𝖊 toke hyr leve to go into Cornwayle, and Sir
𝕷𝖆𝖚𝖓𝖈𝖊𝖑𝖔𝖙, Sir 𝕶𝖆𝖞 and Sir 𝕲𝖆𝖍𝖊𝖗𝖞𝖘 rode to seke the contrey of
Surluse.   35

    ¶Now spekith thys tale of Sir 𝕿𝖗𝖞𝖘𝖙𝖗𝖆𝖒 and of hys two felowis,
for every day Sir 𝕻𝖆𝖑𝖔𝖒𝖞𝖉𝖊𝖘 brawled and seyde langayge ayenste Sir
𝕿𝖗𝖞𝖘𝖙𝖗𝖆𝖒. Than seyde Sir 𝕯𝖞𝖓𝖆𝖉𝖆𝖓, "I mervayle of the, Sir 𝕻𝖆𝖑𝖔𝖒𝖞𝖉𝖊𝖘,
whethir and[8] thou haddyst Sir 𝕿𝖗𝖞𝖘𝖙𝖗𝖆𝖒 here, I trow thou woldiste
do none harme. For and a wolff and a sheepe were togydir in a   40
preson, the wolff wolde suffir the sheepe to be in pees. And wyte
thou well," seyde Sir 𝕯𝖞𝖓𝖆𝖉𝖆𝖓, "thys same ys Sir 𝕿𝖗𝖞𝖘𝖙𝖗𝖆𝖒, at[9] a
worde, and now mayst thou do thy beste with hym, and latte se
now [yf ye can] skyffte hit with youre handys." Than was Sir 𝕻𝖆𝖑𝖔𝖒𝖞𝖉𝖊𝖘 abaysshed, and seyde lityll. Than seyde Sir 𝕿𝖗𝖞𝖘𝖙𝖗𝖆𝖒 to Sir   45
𝕻𝖆𝖑𝖔𝖒𝖞𝖉𝖊𝖘, "I have harde muche of youre magré ayenste me, but I

fol.225v

---

6. I.e., expected.
7. I.e., it is hard to make King Mark go against his nature.
8. I.e., if.
9. I.e., in.

woll nat meddill with you at thys tyme, be my wylle, bycause [I drede] the lorde of this place that hath us in governaunce—for, and I dred hym nat more than I do the, sone hit sholde be skyffte." And so they peaced hemselff.

¶Ryght so cam in a damesell and seyde, "Knyghtes, be of good chere, for ye ar sure[1] of youre lyves, and that I harde my lorde Sir Darras sey." So than were they all glad, for dayly they wente to have dyed. Than sone after thys Sir Trystram fyll syke, that he wente to have dyed.

¶Than Sir Dynadan wepte, and so ded Sir Palomydes, undir[2] them bothe makynge grete sorow. So a damesell cam in to them and founde them mournynge; than she wente unto Sir Darras and tolde hym how the myghty knyght that bare the blacke shylde was lykly to dye. "That shall nat be," seyde Sir Darras, "for God deffende,[3] whan knyghtes com to me for succour, that I sholde suffir hem to dye within my preson—therefore," seyde Sir Darras, "go fecche me that syke knyght and hys felowis afore me."

And whan Sir Darras saw Sir Trystram i-brought afore hym, he seyde, "Sir knyght, me repentis of youre sykenes, for ye ar called a full noble knyght—and so hit semyth by you—and wyte you well that hit shall never be seyde that I, Sir Darras, shall destroy such a noble knyght as ye ar in preson, howbehit that ye have slayne three of my sunnes, wherefore I was gretely agreved. But now shalt thou go, and thy felowys, and take youre horse and youre armour, for they have bene fayre and clene kepte, and ye shall go where hit lykith you uppon this covenaunte, that ye, knyght, woll promyse me to be good frynde to my sunnys two that bene now on lyve, and also that ye telle me thy name."

¶"Sir, as for me, my name ys Sir Trystram de Lyones, and in Cornwayle was I borne, and nevew I am unto Kyng Marke. And as for the dethe of youre three sunnes, I myght nat do[4] withall; for and they had bene the nexte kyn that I have, I myght have done none othirwyse—and if I had slayne hem by treson other trechory, I had bene worthy to have dyed."

¶"All thys I consider," seyde Sir Darras, "that all that ye ded was by fors of knyghthode, and that was the cause I wolde nat put you to dethe. But sith ye be Sir Trystram the good knyght, I pray you hartyly to be my good frynde, and my sunnes." "Sir," seyde Sir Trystram, "I promyse you by the faythe of my body, ever whyle I lyve I woll do you servyse, for ye have done to us but as a naturall knyght ought to do." Than Sir Trystram reposed hym there a whyle tyll that he was amended of hys syknes; and whan he was bygge and stronge they toke their leve, and every knyght toke their horses and harneys, and so departed and rode togydirs tyll they cam to a crosseway.

¶"Now, felowis," seyde Sir Trystram, "here woll we departe in

fol.226r

fol.226v

---

1. I.e., secure, safe.
2. I.e., within, between.
3. I.e., forbid.
4. I.e., avoid.

sundir." And bycause Sir Dynadan had the firste adventure, of hym I woll begyn.

SO as Sir Dynadan rode by a well, he founde a lady makyng grete dole. [41]

¶"What aylith you?" seyde Sir Dynadan. "Sir knyght," seyde the lady, "I am the wofullyst lady of the worlde, for within thys fyve dayes here com a knyght called Sir Breuse Saunz Pité, and he slewe myne owne brothir; and ever syns he hath kepte me at hys owne wylle, and of all men in the worlde I hate hym moste—and therefore I requyre you of knyghthode to avenge me, for he woll nat tarry but be here anone."

¶"Lat hym com," seyde Sir Dynadan; "and bycause of the honoure of all women, I woll do my parte." So with this cam Sir Breuse, and whan he saw a knyght with his lady he was wood wrothe, and than he seyde, "Kepe the, Sir knyght, from me!" And so they hurled togydirs as the thundir, and aythir smote othir passynge sore; but Sir Dynadan put hym thorow the shuldir a grevous wounde—and or ever Sir Dynadan myght turne hym, Sir Breuse was gone and fledde. Than the lady prayde hym to brynge hyr to a castell there besyde but foure myle; and so Sir Dynadan brought her there and she was wellcom, for the lorde of that castell was hir uncle. And so Sir Dynadan rode hys way uppon hys adventure.

¶Now turnyth thys tale unto Sir Trystram, that by adventure he cam to a castell to aske lodgyng, wherein was Quene Morgan le Fay. fol.227r And so whan Sir Trystram was let into that castell, he had good chere all that nyght. And so uppon the morne, whan he wolde have departed, the quene seyde, "Wyte you well, ye shall nat departe lyghtly—for ye ar here as a presonere."

¶"Jesu deffende me!" seyde Sir Trystram, "for I was but late a presonere." "Now, fayre knyght," seyde the quene, "ye shall abyde with me tyll that I wyte what ye ar, and frome whens ye cam." And ever the quene wolde sette Sir Trystram on her one syde, and her paramour on hir other syde, and evermore the quene wolde beholde Sir Trystram. And thereat thys othir knyght was jeleous, and was in wyll suddeynly to have ronne uppon hym with a swerde, but he forbare for shame.

Than the quene seyde unto Sir Trystram, "Telle me your name, and I shall suffir you to departe whan ye wyll." "Uppon that covenaunte, madame, I woll telle you: my name ys Sir Trystram de Lyones." "A!" seyde quene Morgan le Fay, "and I had wyst that, thou sholdist nat have departed so sone as thou shalte; but sitthyn I have made a promyse, I wolde holde hit, with[5] that thou wolte promyse me to beare uppon the a shylde I shall delyver the, at the Castell of the Harde Roche, where Kynge Arthure hath cryed a grete turnemente. And there I pray you that ye woll be, and to do as much of dedys of armys for me as ye may do; for at the Castell of Maydyns, Sir Trystram, ye ded mervaylous dedis of armys as ever I harde knyght do."

5. I.e., provided.

"Madame," seyde Sir Trystram, "let me se the shylde that I shall beare." Than the shylde was brought forthe, and the fylde[6] was gouldes with a kynge and a quene therein paynted, and a knyght stondynge aboven them with hys one foote standynge uppon the kynges hede and the othir uppon the quenys hede. "Madame, seyde Sir Trystram, "thys ys a fayre shylde and a myghty, but what signyfyeth this kynge and this quene, and that knyght stondynge uppon bothe their hedis?"

¶"I shall telle you," seyde Morgan le Fay. "Hit signyfieth Kynge Arthure and Quene Gwenyver, and a knyght that holdith them bothe in bondage and in servage."

¶"Madame, who ys that knyght?" seyde Sir Trystram.

¶"Sir, that shall ye nat wyte as at thys tyme," seyde the quene. (But, as the Freynshe booke seyde, Quene Morgan loved Sir Launcelot beste, and ever she desired hym; and he wolde never love her nor do nothynge at her rekeyste, and therefore she hylde many knyghtes togydir to have takyn hym by strengthe. And bycause that she demed that Sir Launcelot loved Quene Gwenyver paramour, and she hym agayne, therefore Dame Morgan ordayned that shylde to put Sir Launcelot to a rebuke, to that entente that Kynge Arthure myght undirstonde the love betwene them.)

¶So Sir Trystram toke that shylde and promysed hir to beare hit at the turnemente of the Castell of Harde Roche; but Sir Trystram knew nat of that shylde that hit was ordayned ayenste Sir Launcelot—but aftirwarde he knew hit. So Sir Trystram toke hys leve of the quene, and toke the shylde with hym. Than cam the knyght that hylde Morgan le Fay, whos name was Sir Hemyson, and he made hym redy to folow Sir Trystram. "Now, fayre knyght," seyde Morgan, "ryde ye nat aftir that knyght, for ye shall wynne no worshyp of hym." "Fye on hym, coward knyght!" seyde Sir Hemyson. "For I wyste nevir good knyght com oute of Cornwayle, but yf hit were Sir Trystram de Lyones."

¶"Sir, what and[7] that be he?"

¶"Nay, nay," he seyde, "he ys with La Beall Isode, and thys ys but a daffysshe knyght." "Alas, my fayre frynde, ye shall fynde hym the beste knyght that ever ye mette withall, for I know hym bettir than ye do."

¶"Madame, for youre sake," seyde Sir Hemyson, "I shall sle hym." "A, fayre frynde," seyde the quene, "me repentith that ye woll folow that knyght, for I feare me sore of your agayne-commynge." And so with thys thys knyght rode hys way wood wrothe aftir Sir Trystram, as faste as he had be chaced with knyghtes.

¶So whan Sir Trystram harde a knyght com aftir hym so faste, he returned aboute and saw a knyght commynge agaynste hym. And whan he cam nyghe to Sir Trystram, he cryed on hyght and seyde, "Sir knyght, kepe the fro me! Than they russhed togydirs as hit had bene thundir; and Sir Hemyson brused hys speare uppon

fol.227v

[42]

fol.228r

6. I.e., background.
7. I.e., if.

Sir Trystram—but hys harneys was so good that he myght nat hurte hym. And Sir Trystram smote hym harder, and bare hym thorow the body, and fylle[8] over hys horse croupe. Than Sir Trystram turned to have done more with hys swerde, but he sy so much bloode go frome hym that hym semed lyckly to dye—and so he departed frome hym, and cam to a fayre maner to an olde knyght, and there Sir Trystram lodged.

¶Nowe leve we Sir Trystram and speke we of the knyght that was wounded to the dethe. Than hys varlette alyght, and toke of hys helme, and than he asked hys lorde whether there were ony lyff in hym.

¶"There ys in me lyff," seyde the knyght, "but hit ys but lytyll; and therefore lepe thou up behynde me whan thou haste holpyn me up, and holde me faste that I falle nat, and brynge me to Quene Morgan—for the deepe drawghtes of dethe drawith to my harte, that I may nat lyve. For I wolde speke with her fayne or I dyed, for my soule woll be in grete perell and I dye." For with grete payne hys varlet brought hym to the castell—and there Sir Hempson fylle downe dede.

¶Whan Morgan le Fay saw hym dede, she made grete sorow oute of reson. And than she lette dispoyle hym unto hys shurte, and so she lete put hym into a tombe; and aboute the tombe she lete wryte:

HERE LYETH SIR Hempson, SLAYNE BY THE HONDIS OF
SIR Trystram de Lyones

¶Now turne we unto Sir Trystram that asked the knyght, hys oste, if he saw late ony knyghtes aventures.[9]

¶"Sir," he seyde, "here lodged the laste nyght Sir Ector de Marys and a damesell with hym:

¶"And that damesell tolde me that he was one of the beste knyghtes of the worlde." "That ys nat so," seyde Sir Trystram, "for I know foure bettir knyghtes of his owne blood; and the firste ys Sir Launcelot du Lake—calle hym the beste knyght—and Sir Bors de Ganys, Sir Bleoberys de Ganys, and Sir Blamour de Ganys, and also Sir Gaherys." "Nay," seyde hys oste, "Sir Gawayne ys the bettir knyght." "That ys nat so," seyde Sir Trystram, "for I have mette with hem bothe, and I have felte Sir Gaherys for the bettir knyght—and Sir Lamorak, I calle hym as good as ony of them, excepte Sir Launcelot."

¶"Sir, why name ye nat Sir Trystram?" seyde hys oste. "For I accompte hym as good a knyght as ony of them." "I knowe nat Sir Trystram," seyde Sir Trystram.[1] Thus they talked and bourded as longe as them thought beste, and than wente to reste. And on the

---

8. I.e., Hemyson fell.
9. I.e., adventurous, errant.
1. *"I knowe nat Sir Trystram," seyde Sir Trystram.* The irony of the line is obvious, but one
   might pause to consider the degree to which it is true; recall Trystram's period of madness,
   his conflicting allegiances, the extended period during which he has gone incognito, and
   the restrictions imposed on him against working his own will. Cf. n. 4, p. 327.

morne, Sir **Trystram** departed and toke hys leve of hys oste, and rode towarde the Roche Deuré[2]—and none adventure [had Sire **Tristram**] but that. And so he rested nat tylle he cam to the castell, where he saw fyve hondred tentes.

❡So the Kynge of Scottes and the Kynge of Irelonde hylde agaynste Kynge **Arthurs** knyghtes, and there began a grete medlé. So there cam in Sir **Trystram** and ded mervaylous dedis of armys, for he smote downe many knyghtes—and ever he was before Kynge Arthure with that shylde;[3] and whan Kynge **Arthure** saw that shylde, he mervayled gretly in what entent hit was made. But Quene **Gwenyver** demed as hit was,[4] wherefore she was hevy.

Than was there a damesell of Quene **Morgan** in a chambir by Kynge **Arthure**; and whan she harde Kynge **Arthure** speke of that shylde, than she spake opynly unto Kynge **Arthure**: "Sir Kynge, wyte you well thys shylde was ordayned for you, to warn you of youre shame and dishonoure that longith to you and youre Quene." And than anone that damesell pycked her[5] away pryvayly, that no man wyste where she was becom. Than was Kynge **Arthure** sad and wrothe, and asked frome whens com that damesell; and there was nat one that knew her, nother wyste nat where she was becom. Than Quene **Gwenyvere** called to Sir **Ector de Marys**, and there she made hyr complaynte to hym and seyde, "I wote well thys shylde was made by **Morgan le Fay** in the dispite of me and of Sir **Launcelot**, wherefore I drede me sore leste I shall be distroyed."

And ever the Kynge behylde Sir **Trystram**, that ded so mervaylous dedis of armys that he wondred sore what knyght hit myght be— and well he wyste hit was nat Sir **Launcelot**. And also hit was tolde hym that Sir **Trystram** was in Bretayne with **Isode** le Blaunche Maynys—for, he[6] demed, and he had bene in the realme of Logrys, Sir **Launcelot** other som of hys felowis that were in the queste of Sir **Trystram**, that they sholde have founde hym or that tyme. So Kynge **Arthure** had mervayle what knyght he myght be—and ever Kynge **Arthurs** ye was on that shylde; and all that aspyed the Quene, and that made hir sore aferde. Than ever Sir **Trystram** smote downe knyghtes wondirly to beholde, what uppon the ryght honde and uppon the lyffte honde, that unnethe no knyght myght withstonde hym—and the Kynge of Scottes and the Kynge of Irelonde began to withdraw them.

❡Whan Kynge **Arthur** aspyed that, he thought the knyght with the straunge shylde sholde nat ascape hym. Than he called unto Sir **Uwayne** le Blaunche Maynes and bade hym arme hym and make hym redy. So anone Kyng **Arthure** and Sir **Uwayn** dressed them before Sir **Trystram** and requyred hym to telle where he hadde[7] that shylde. "Sir," he seyde, "I had hit of Quene **Morgan le Fay**, suster to Kynge **Arthure**."

fol.229r

2. I.e., the Castle of the Hard Rock.
3. *That shylde*: i.e., the shield given to him by Morgan le Fay.
4. *Demed as hit was*: recognized it for what it was.
5. *Pycked her*: took herself.
6. I.e., the person advising the king.
7. I.e., obtained.

So here levith of[8] this booke, for hit ys the firste booke of Sir 𝕿𝖗𝖞𝖘𝖙𝖗𝖆𝖒 𝖉𝖊 𝕷𝖞𝖔𝖓𝖊𝖘; and the secunde boke begynnyth where Sir 𝕿𝖗𝖞𝖘𝖙𝖗𝖆𝖒 smote downe Kynge 𝕬𝖗𝖙𝖍𝖚𝖗𝖊 and Sir 𝖀𝖜𝖆𝖞𝖓𝖊, bycause why he wolde nat telle hem wherefore that shylde was made—but to sey the soth, Sir 𝕿𝖗𝖞𝖘𝖙𝖗𝖆𝖒 coude nat telle the cause, for he knew hit nat—

"And yf hit be so[9] ye can dyscryve what ye beare, ye ar worthy to beare armys." "As for that," seyde Sir 𝕿𝖗𝖞𝖘𝖙𝖗𝖆𝖒, "I woll answere you. As for this shylde, hit was yevyn me, not desyred, of Quene 𝕸𝖔𝖗𝖌𝖆𝖓 𝖑𝖊 𝕱𝖆𝖞; and as for me, I can nat dyscryve this armys, for hit is no poynte of my charge[1]—and yet I truste to God to beare hit with worship." "Truly," seyde Kynge 𝕬𝖗𝖙𝖍𝖚𝖗𝖊, "ye ought nat to beare none armys but yf ye wyste what ye bare. But I pray you, telle me youre name." [X.1] fol.229v

❡"To what entente?" seyde Sir 𝕿𝖗𝖞𝖘𝖙𝖗𝖆𝖒. "For I wolde wete," seyde Kynge 𝕬𝖗𝖙𝖍𝖚𝖗𝖊. "Sir, ye shall nat wete for me at this tyme." "Than shall ye and I do batayle togydir."

❡"Why," seyde Sir 𝕿𝖗𝖞𝖘𝖙𝖗𝖆𝖒," woll ye do batayle with me but yf I telle you my name? Forsothe, that lytyll nedyth you? And ye were a man of worshyp, ye wolde nat have ado with me, for ye have sene me this day have had grete travayle; and therefore ye ar no valyaunte knyght to aske batayle of me, consyderynge my grete travayle. Howbehit, I woll nat fayle you—and have ye no doute that I feare nat you; though ye thynke ye have me at a grete avauntage, yet shall I ryght well endure you." And therewithall Kynge 𝕬𝖗𝖙𝖍𝖚𝖗𝖊 dressid his shylde and his speare, and Sir 𝕿𝖗𝖞𝖘𝖙𝖗𝖆𝖒 ayenst hym, and they come egirly togydyrs; and there Kynge 𝕬𝖗𝖙𝖍𝖚𝖗𝖊 brake his speare all to pecis on Sir 𝕿𝖗𝖞𝖘𝖙𝖗𝖆𝖒𝖘 shylde. But Sir 𝕿𝖗𝖞𝖘𝖙𝖗𝖆𝖒 smote Kynge 𝕬𝖗𝖙𝖍𝖚𝖗 agayne so sore that horse and man felle to the erthe—and there was Kynge 𝕬𝖗𝖙𝖍𝖚𝖗𝖊 woundid on the lyfte syde, a grete wounde and a perelous.

❡Whan Sir 𝖀𝖜𝖆𝖞𝖓𝖊 saw his lorde Kynge 𝕬𝖗𝖙𝖍𝖚𝖗 ly on the erthe sore woundid, he was passynge hevy; and than he dressid his shylde and his speare, and cryed alowde unto Sir 𝕿𝖗𝖞𝖘𝖙𝖗𝖆𝖒 and seyde, "Knyght, defende the!" So they come togydir as faste as their horse myght ren, and Sir 𝖀𝖜𝖆𝖞𝖓𝖊 brused his speare all to pecis uppon Sir 𝕿𝖗𝖞𝖘𝖙𝖗𝖆𝖒𝖘 shylde; and Sir 𝕿𝖗𝖞𝖘𝖙𝖗𝖆𝖒 smote hym harder and sorer with such a myght that he bare hym clene oute of his sadyll to the erthe. fol.230r

❡With that Sir 𝕿𝖗𝖞𝖘𝖙𝖗𝖆𝖒 turned hys horse aboute and sayde to them, "Fayre knyghtes, I had now no nede to juste with you, for I have had inowghe to do this day." Than arose up Kynge 𝕬𝖗𝖙𝖍𝖚𝖗𝖊

---

8. I.e., off.

9. *For he knew hit nat—"And yf hit be so*: this rather awkward transition between "books" could represent Malory's interpretation of a notation in his source text made by a scribe who has come to the end of the first physical volume of his copy text. King Arthur is the speaker in the opening sentence of this second book. In the Winchester MS the red three-line capital "A" appears at the beginning of the page, and is followed by a capital "N" filled in yellow; but the previous page is full to its bottom margin, and so there is little spatial sense of a major division.

1. *Hit is no poynte of my charge*: it is not part of my heraldic bearings.

and went to Sir Uwayne, and than he seyde to Sir Trystrams, "We have now as we have deservyd, for thorowe oure owne orgulyté we demaunded batayle of you, and yet youre name we know nat." "Neverthelesse, by Seynte Crosse," seyde Sir Uwayne, "he is a stronge knyght, at myne advyse,[2] as ony is lyvynge." 5

Than Sir Trystram departed, and in every place he asked aftir Sir Launcelot; but in no place he cowde hyre of hym whether he were dede other on lyve, wherefore Sir Trystram made grete dole and sorowe. So Sir Trystram rode by a foreyste, and than was he ware of a fayre toure by a marys on the tone syde, and on that other syde was a fayre medow, and there he sawe ten knyghtes fyghtynge togydyrs. And ever the nere he cam, he saw how there was but one knyght ded[3] batyle ayenst a nyne knyghtes; and that one knyght ded so mervaylousely that Sir Trystram had grete wondir that ever one knyght myght do so grete dedis of armys—and than within a lytyll whyle he had slayne halff theire horsys and unhorsid them, and their horsys ran into the feldys and forestes. 10 15

Than Sir Trystram had so grete pité of that one knyght that endured so grete payne, and ever hym thought hit sholde be Sir Palomydes, by his shylde. So he rode unto the knyghtys and cryed unto them and bade them sease of that batayle, for they ded themself grete shame, so many knyghtes to feyght wyth one. 20

Than answerde the maystir of tho knyghtes—hys name was called Sir Brunys Saunze Pyté, that was at that tyme the moste myschevuste knyght lyvynge—and seyde thus: "Sir knyght, what have ye ado with us to medyll? And therefore, and ye be wyse, departe on youre way as ye cam, for this knyght shall nat scape us." "That were grete pyté," seyde Sir Trystram, "that so good a knyght as he is sholde be slayne so cowardly; and therefore I make you ware I woll succour hym with all my puyssaunce." fol.230v 25 30

¶So Sir Trystram alyght of hys horse, because they were on foote, that they sholde nat sle his horse; and than Sir Trystram dressyd his shylde with hys swerde in his honde, and he smote on the ryght honde and on the lyffte honde passynge sore, that well-nye every stroke he strake downe a knyghte. And whan they aspyed his strokys they fledde, bothe Sir Brunys Saunze Pyté and hys felyshyp, unto the towre—and Sir Trystram folowed faste aftir wyth hys swerde in his honde; but they ascaped into the towre and shut Sir Trystram wythoute the gate. [2] 35

And whan Sir Trystram sawe that, he returned abacke unto Sir Palomydes and founde hym syttynge undir a tre, sore woundid. "A, fayre knyght," seyde Sir Trystram, "well be ye founde." "Gramercy," seyde Sir Palomydes, "of youre grete goodnesse, for ye have rescowed me of my lyff, and savyd me of my dethe." 40

¶"What is your name?" seyde Sir Trystram. "Sir, my name ys Sir Palomydes." "A, Jesu!" seyde Sir Trystram, "thou haste a fayre grace 45

2. *At myne advyse*: by my reckoning.
3. I.e., who did.

of me this day that I sholde rescowe the—and thou art the man in
the worlde that I moste hate! But now make the[4] redy, for I shall
do batayle with the." "What is your name?" seyde Sir **Palomydes**.
"My name is Sir **Trystram**, your mortall enemy."

⁋"Hit may be so," seyde Sir **Palomydes**, "but ye have done overmuche for me this day that I sholde fyght with you; for inasmuche
as ye have saved my lyff, hit woll be no worshyp for you to have
ado with me, for ye ar freyshe and I am sore woundid. And
therefore, and ye woll nedys have ado with me, assygne me a day,
and than shall I mete with you withoute fayle."

⁋"Ye say well," seyde Sir **Trystramys**. "Now I assygne you to mete
me in the medowe by the river of **Camelot**, where **Merlyon** sette the
perowne."[5]

⁋So they were agreed. Than Sir **Trystram** asked Sir **Palomydes**
why the nyne knyghtes ded batayle with hym. "For this cause,"
seyde Sir **Palomydes**. "As I rode uppon myne adventures in a foreyste here besyde, I aspyed where lay a dede knyght, and a lady
wepynge besydys hym; and whan I sawe her makynge suche doole,
I asked her who slew her lorde. 'Sir,' she seyde, 'the falsyste knyght
of the worlde, and moste he is of vylany—and his name is Sir
Brewnes Saunʒe Pité.' Than for pité I made the damesell to lepe on
her palferey, and I promysed her to be her waraunte and to helpe
to entyre[6] hir lorde. And suddeynly, as I cam rydyng by this towre,
there come oute Sir **Brewnys Saunce Pité**, and suddeynly he strake
me fro my horse; and or ever I myghte recovir my horse, this Sir
Brewnys slew the damesell. And so I toke my horse agayne—and I
was sore ashamyd—and so began this medlé betwyxte us; and this
is the cause wherefore we ded this batayle."

⁋"Well," seyde Sir **Trystram**, "now I undirstonde the maner of
your batayle. But in ony wyse, that[7] ye have remembraunce of your
promyse that ye have made with me to do batayle, this day fourtenyght."

⁋"I shall nat fayle you," sayde Sir **Palomydes**. "Well," seyde Sir
Trystram, "as at this tyme I woll nat fayle you tylle that ye be oute
of the damage of your enemyes." So they amowntid uppon their
horsys and rode togydyrs unto the foreyste; and there they founde
a fayre welle with clere watir burbelynge. "Fayre sir," seyde Sir
Trystramys, "to drynke of that water I have grete currage." And than
they alyght of their horsys; and than were they ware besyde them
where stoode a grete horse tyed tylle a tre, and ever he nayed. Than
they aspyed farthermore, and than were they ware of a fayre knyght
armed undir a tre, lackynge no pece of harnes, save hys helme lay
undir his hede.

⁋"By the good Lorde," seyde Sir **Trystram**, "yondir lyeth a well-
farynge knyght. What is beste to do?" seyde Sir **Trystram**. "Awake

How Sir Trystram
rescowed Sir Palo-
mydes from Sir
Brunes Saunʒ Pité
and from nine
knyghtis

fol.231r

fol.231v

---

4. Thee.
5. This is the tombstone of Sir Launceor mentioned earlier in the *Tale of Balyn and Balan*
   (p. 47) and on which Merlin had inscribed a prophecy of the great battle between Trystram
   and Launcelot to be fought on that spot: Malory recapitulates the story later (p. 343).
6. I.e., inter, bury.
7. *In ony wyse:* anyway. *That:* i.e., see that.

hym," seyde Sir Palomydes. So Sir Trystram awakyd hym wyth the
butte of hys speare. And so the knyght arose up hastely, and put
his helme uppon his hede, and mowntyd uppon his horse and gate
a grete speare in his honde; and withoute ony mo wordis he hurled
unto Sir Trystram and smote hym clene from his sadyll to the erthe,   5
and hurte hym on the lyffte syde. Than Sir Trystram lay stylle in
grete perell. Than he waloppyd further and fette his course,[8] and
come hurlynge uppon Sir Palomydes; and there he strake hym
aparte[9] thorow the body, that he felle frome hys horse to the erthe.
And than this straunge knyght lefte them there and toke his way   10
thorow the foreyste.

⁋So wyth this Sir Trystram and Sir Palomydes were on foote, and
gate their horsys agayne; and aythir asked counceyle of other what
was beste to done. "Be my hede," seyde Sir Trystram, "I woll folow
this stronge knyght that thus hath shamed us."   15

⁋"Well," seyde Sir Palomydes, "and I woll repose me here with a
frende of myne." "Beware," seyde Sir Trystram to Sir Palomydes,
"loke that ye fayle nat that day that ye have sette with me, for, as
I deme, ye woll nat holde your day, for I am muche bygger than
ye ar." "As for that," seyde Sir Palomydes, "be as be may, for I feare   20
you nat. For and I be nat syke nother presoner, I woll nat fayle
you—but I have more doute of you that ye woll nat mete with me,   fol.232r
for ye woll ryde aftir yondir stronge knyght; and yf ye mete with
hym, hit is in adventure[1] and ever ye scape his hondys." So Sir
Trystram and Sir Palomydes departyd, and ayther toke their wayes   25
dyverse.

And so Sir Trystram rode longe aftir this stronge knyght, and at   [3]
the laste he sye where lay a lady overtwarte a dede knyght. "Fayre
lady," seyde Sir Trystramys, "who hath slayne your lorde?" "Sir" she
seyde, "here came a knyght rydynge as my lorde and I restyd us   30
here, and askyd hym of whens he was, and my lorde seyde, 'of
Kynge Arthurs courte.' 'Therefore,' seyde the stronge knyght, 'I woll
juste with the, for I hate all tho that be of Arthurs courte.' And my
lorde that lyeth here dede amownted uppon hys horse; and the
stronge knyght and my lorde recountyrd togydir, and there he   35
smote my lorde thorowoute with his speare—and thus he hath
brought me in grete woo and damage."

"That me repentys," seyde Sir Trystram, "of youre grete hevynesse. But please hit you to tell me your husbondys name?" "Sir,
his name was Sir Galardonne, that wolde have prevyd a good   40
knyght." So departed Sir Trystram frome that dolorous lady, and
had muche evyll lodgynge. Than, on the thirde day, Sir Trystram
mette with Sir Gawayne and Sir Bleoberys in a foreyste at a lodge,
and ayther were sore wounded.

Than Sir Trystram askyd Sir Gawayne and Sir Bleoberys yf they   45
mette with suche a knyght with suche a conyssaunce, wyth a cov-

8. *Fette his course:* established enough distance for a charge.
9. I.e., partially.
1. I.e., doubt.

erde shylde. "Fayre knyght," seyde these wounded knyghtes, "such
a knyght mette with us, to oure damage—"

"And fyrste he smote downe my felowe, Sir **Bleoberys**, and sore
woundid hym, bycause he bade me I sholde nat have ado with hym
for why[2] he was over stronge for me. That stronge knyght[3] toke his
wordis at scorne, and seyde he seyde hit for mockery; and than
they rode togedyrs, and so he hurte my felowe. And whan he had
done so, I myght nat for shame but I muste juste wyth hym; and
at the fyrste course he smote me downe, and my horse, to the erthe.
And there he had allmoste slayne me; and frome us he toke his
horse and departed—and in an evyll tyme we mette with hym."

¶"Fayre knyghtes," seyde Sir **Trystram**, "so he mette wyth me
and with another knyght, Sir **Palomydes**, and he smote us bothe
downe with one speare and hurte us ryght sore." "Be my faythe,"
sayde Sir **Gawayne**, "be my counceyle ye shall lette hym passe and
seke hym no farther, for at the nexte feste of the Rounde Table,
upon payne of myne hede, ye shall fynde hym there."[4]

"Be my faythe," sayde Sir **Trystram**, "I shall never reste tyll that
I fynde hym." And than Syr **Gawayne** askyd hys name. [Thenne he
said, "My name is Sir **Tristram**." And so ayther told other their
names,] and so aythir departed. And so Sir **Trystram** rode his way;
and by fortune in a medowe he mette with Sir **Kay** the Senescyall
and with Sir **Dynadan**. "What tydynges," seyde Sir **Trystram**, "with
you knyghtes?" "Nat good," seyde these knyghtes. "Why so?" seyde
Sir **Trystram**. "I pray you tell me, for I ryde to seke a knyght." "What
conyssaunce beryth he?" seyde Sir **Kay**. "He beryth," seyde Sir
Trystram, "a shylde covyrde close."[5]

"Be my hede," seyde Sir **Kay**, "that is the same knyght that mette
with us! For this nyght we were lodged hereby in a wydows house,
and there was that knyght lodged; and whan he wyste we were of
Kynge **Arthurs** courte, he spake grete vylony by[6] the Kynge—and
specially by the Quene **Gwenyver**; and than on the morne was waged
batayle with hym for that cause. And at the fyrste recountir he
smote me downe," seyde Sir **Kay**, "fro myne horse, and hurte me
passyngly sore. And whan my felowe, Sir **Dynadan**, saw me smytten
downe and hurte sore, yet he wolde nat revenge me, but fledde fro
me; and thus is he departed from us."

And than Sir **Trystram** asked what was their namys, and so ayther
tolde other their namys. And so Sir **Trystram** departed from Sir **Kay**
and frome Sir **Dynadan**. And so he paste thorow a grete foreyste
into a playne tyll he was ware of a pryory; and there he reposyd
hym with a good man, six dayes. And than he sente his squyer,
Governayle, and commaunded hym to go to a cité thereby to fecche hym newe harneyse—for hit was longe tyme afore that Sir
Trystram had bene refreysshed, for his harneyse was brused and

fol.232v

fol.233r

[4]

---

2. *For why:* because.
3. I.e., Sir Gawayne.
4. *At the nexte feste . . . ye shall fynde hym there:* I.e., Gawain is promising to defeat the knight
and send him to King Arthur to acknowledge his sovereignty.
5. *Covyrde close:* covered up completely.
6. *Spake grete vylony by:* said villainous things about.

brokyn sore. And whan Governayle was com with his apparayle, he toke his leve at the wydow,[7] and mownted uppon his horse and rode his way, erly on the morne.

And by suddayne adventure he mette with Sir Sagramour le Desyrus and wyth Sir Dodynas le Saveayge. And this two knyghtes mette with Sir Trystram, and questyonde with hym and askyd hym yf he wolde juste wyth hem. "Fayre knyghtes," sayde Sir Trystram, "with good wyll I wolde juste with you, but I have promysed a day i-sette nerehonde to do batayle wyth a stronge knyght; and therefore am I loth to have ado with you, for and hit mysfortuned me to be hurte here, I sholde nat be able to do my batayle whyche I promysed." "As for that," sayde Sir Sagramour, "magré your hede[8] ye shal juste with us or ye passe frome us."

¶"Well, seyde Sir Trystram, "yf ye force me thereto, I muste do what I may." And than they dressed their shyldis and cam rennynge togydir with grete ire. But thorow Sir Trystrams grete force, he strake Sir Sagramoure frome his horse. Than he hurled his horse further[9] and seyde to Sir Dodynas, "Knyght, make the redy." And so, thorow fyne forse, Sir Trystram strake downe Sir Dodynas frome hys horse; and whan he sawe hem ly on the erthe, he toke his brydyll and rode furth on his way, and his man Governayle with hym.

And anone as Sir Trystram was paste, Sir Sagramour and Sir Dodynas gate their horsys and mownted up lyghtly and folowed aftir Sir Trystram; and whan Sir Trystram sawe them com so faste aftir hym, he returned his horse to them and asked them what they wolde. "Methynkyth hit is nat longe ago sytthen I smote you downe to the erthe at your owne desyre, and I wolde have ryddyn by you and ye wolde have suffyrd me; but now mesemyth ye wolde do more batayle with me." "That is trowthe," seyde Sir Sagramour and Sir Dodynas, "for we woll be revengyd of the dyspyte that ye have done to us."

"Fayre knyghtes," seyde Sir Trystram, "that shall lytyll nede you, for all that I ded to you, ye caused hit. Wherefore I requyre you of your knyghthode, leve me as at this tyme, for I am sure and I do batayle with you, I shall nat ascape withoute grete hurtes—and, as I suppose, ye shall nat ascape all lotles. And this is the cause why that I am so loth to have ado wyth you: for I muste fyght within this three dayes with a good knyght and a valyaunte as ony now is lyvynge—and yf I be hurte, I shall nat be able to do batayle with hym."

"What knyght is that," seyde Sir Sagramoure, "that ye shall fyght wythall?" "Sir, hit is a good knyght callyd Sir Palomydes." "Be my hede," seyde Sir Sagramour and Sir Dodynas, "ye have a cause to

fol.233v

---

7. Trystram was staying with a "good man," and the reference here to a widow (also found in Caxton's edition) suggests that Malory mistakenly recalled the widow that Kay and Dinadan reported lodging with just earlier.
8. *Magré your hede*: against your will, in spite of you.
9. *Hurled his horse further*: i.e., rushed his horse to a distance right for another charge.

drede hym, for ye shall fynde hym a passynge good knyght and a
valyaunte. And bycause ye shall have ado wyth hym, we woll forbeare you as at this tyme—and ellys ye sholde nat ascape us lyghtly.
But, fayre knyght," sayde Sir Sagramoure, "telle us your name."
"Syrrys, my name is Sir Trystram." "A!" sayde Sir Sagramoure and   5
Sir Dodynas, "well be ye founde, for muche worshyp have we harde
of you." And than aythir toke leve of other and departed on there
way.

　　And Sir Trystram rode streyte to Camelot to the perowne that   [5]
Merlyon had made tofore, where Sir Launceor, that was the Kynges   10
son of Irelonde, was slayne by the hondys of Sir Balyn; and in the
same place was the fayre lady Columbe slayne that was love unto   fol.234r
Sir Launceor, for aftir he was dede, she toke hys swerde and threste
hit thorow her body. And so by the crafte of Merlyon, he made to
entyre this knyght Launceor and his lady Columbe undir one stone—   15
and at that tyme Merlyon profecied that in that same place sholde
fyght two the beste knyghtes that ever were in Kynge Arthurs dayes,
and two of the beste lovers.

　　So whan Sir Trystram come to the towmbe of stone, he loked
aboute hym aftyr Sir Palomydes. Than was he ware where come a   20
semely knyght rydynge ayenst hym, all in whyght, and the coverde
shylde. Whan he cam nyghe Sir Trystram, he seyde on hyght, "Ye
be wellcom, sir knyght, and well and trewly have ye holdyn your
promyse." And than they dressid their shyldis and spearys, and cam
togydyrs with all her myghtes of their horsys. And they mette so   25
fersely that bothe the horsys and knyghtes felle to the erthe, and
as faste as they myght avoyde there horsys and put their shyldis
afore them; and they strake togedyrs wyth bryght swerdys as men
that were of myght—and aythir woundid othir wondirly sore, that
the bloode ran oute upon the grasse. And thus they fought the   30
space of foure owres, that never one wolde speke to other—and of
their harneys they had hewyn of many pecis.

　　"A, lorde Jesu!" seyde Governayle, "I mervayle gretely of the grete
strokis my maystir hath yevyn to youre maystir." "Be my hede,"
seyde Sir Launcelottis servaunte, "youre maystir hath not yevyn hym   35
so many, but your maystir hath resseyvede so many, or more." "A,
Jesu!" seyde Governayle, "hit is to muche for Sir Palomydes to suffir,
other Sir Launcelot; and yet pyté hit were that aythir of these good
knyghtes sholde dystroy otheris bloode." So they stoode and wepte
bothe, and made grete dole whan they sawe their swerdys over-   40
coverde with bloode of there bodyes.   fol.234v

　　Than at the laste Sir Launcelot spake and seyde, "Knyght, thou
fyghtyst wondir well as ever I sawe knyghte. Therefore, and hit
please you, tell me your name." "Sir, seyde Sir Trystram, "that is
me loth to telle ony man my name." "Truly," seyde Sir Launcelot,   45
"and I were requyred, I was never loth to tell my name." "Ye say
well," seyde Sir Trystram, "than I requyre you to tell me your name."
"Fayre knyght, my name is Sir Launcelot du Lake." "Alas," seyde Sir
Trystram, "what have I done? For ye ar the man in the worlde that

I love beste." "Now, fayre knyght," seyde Sir Launcelot, "telle me
your name." "Truly, sir, I hyght Sir Trystram de Lyones." "A, Jesu,"
seyde Sir Launcelot, "what aventure is befall[1] me!"

And therewyth Sir Launcelott kneled adowne and yeldid hym up
his swerde; and therewithall Sir Trystram kneled adowne and yeldid   5
hym up his swerde—and so aythir gaff other the gré. And than
they bothe forthwithall went to the stone and set hem downe
uppon hit, and toke of their helmys to keele them, and aythir kyste
other an hondred tymes. And than anone aftir, they toke their
horsis and rode to Camelot; and there they mette with Sir Gawayne   10
and with Sir Gaherys, that had made promyse to Kynge Arthure never
to com agayne to the courte tyll they had brought Sir Trystram with
hem.

¶"Returne agayne," seyde Sir Launcelot, "for youre queste is   [6]
done, for I have mette with Sir Trystram—lo, here is his owne   15
person!" Than was Sir Gawayne glad, and seyde to Sir Trystram, "Ye
ar wellcom, for now have ye easid me gretly of my grete laboure.

¶"For what cause," seyde Sir Gawayne, "com ye into this contrey?"

¶"Fayre sir," sayde Sir Trystram, "I come into this contrey   20
because of Sir Palomydes, for he and I assigned at this day to have   fol.235r
done batayle togydyrs at the peroune—and I mervayle I hyre nat
of hym[2]—and thus by adventure my lorde Syr Launcelot and I mette
togydirs." So wyth this come Kynge Arthure; and when he wyste Sir
Trystram was there, he yode unto hym and toke hym by the honde   25
and seyde, "Sir Trystram, ye ar as wellcom as ony knyght that ever
com unto this courte." And whan the Kynge herde how Sir Launcelot
and he had foughtyn, and aythir had wounded other wondirly sore,
then the Kynge made grete dole.

Than Sir Trystram tolde the Kynge how he com thydir to have   30
ado with Sir Palomydes; and than he tolde the Kynge how he had
rescowed hym from the nyne knyghtes and Sir Breunes Saunze Pité,
and how he founde a knyght lyynge by a welle—"and that knyghte
smote downe bothe Sir Palomydes and me, and hys shylde was coverde with a clothe. So Sir Palomydes leffte me, and I folowed aftir   35
that knyght, and in many placis I founde where he had slayne
knyghtes and forjustyd many." "Be my hede," seyde Sir Gawayne,
"that same knyght smote me downe, and Sir Bleoberys, and hurte
us sore bothe, he wyth the coverde shylde." "A!" sayde Sir Kay,
"that same knyght smote me downe and hurte me passynge sore."   40

¶"Jesu mercy!" seyde Kynge Arthure, "what knyght was that wyth
the coverde shylde?" "We knew hym not," seyde Sir Trystram—and
so seyde they all.

¶"No?" seyde Kynge Arthure. "Than wote I, for hit is Sir Launcelot." Than they all lokyd uppon Sir Launcelot and seyde, "Sir, ye   45
have begyled us all wyth youre coverde shylde?" "Hit is not the
fyrste tyme," seyde Kynge Arthure, "he hath done so!"

---

1. Has befallen.
2. It turns out that Palomydes is imprisoned in a castle (see p. 358).

❡"My lorde," seyde Sir Launcelot, "truly, wete you well I was the same knyght that bare the coverde shylde; and bycause I wolde nat be knowyn that I was of youre courte, I seyde no worshyp be youre house."[3] "That is trouthe," seyde Sir Gawayne, Syr Kay, and Sir Bleoberys. Than Kynge Arthure toke Sir Trystram by the honde and wente to the Table Rounde.

Than come Quene Gwenyver and many ladyes with her, and all tho ladyes seyde at one voyce, "Wellcom, Sir Trystram!" "Wellcom!" seyde damesels; ["Welcome!" sayd knyghtes;] "Wellcom," seyde Kynge Arthur, "for one of the beste knyghtes and the jentyllyst of the worlde, and the man of moste worship. For of all maner of huntynge thou beryste the pryce, and of all mesures of blowynge[4] thou arte the begynnynge; of all the termys of huntynge and haw-kynge ye ar the begynner; of all instirmentes of musyk ye ar the beste.[5] Therefore, jantyll knyghte," seyde Kynge Arthure, "ye ar well-com to this courte—and also, I pray you," seyde Kynge Arthure, "graunte me a done." "Sir, hit shall be at youre commaundemente," seyde Sir Trystram.

"Well," seyde Kynge Arthure, "I wyll desyre that ye shall abyde in my courte." "Sir," seyde Sir Trystram, "thereto me is lothe, for I have to do in many contreys." "Not so," seyde Kynge Arthure. "Ye have promysed me; ye may not say nay." "Sir," seyde Sir Trystram, "I woll as ye woll." Than wente Kynge Arthure unto the seges aboute the Rounde Table, and loked on every syege whyche were voyde that lacked knyghtes; and than the Kynge sye in the syege of Sir Marhalt lettyrs that seyde

This is the syege of the noble knyght
Sir Trystramys

And than Kynge Arthure made Sir Trystram a knyght of the Rounde Table wyth grete[6] nobeley and a feste as myght be thought. (For Sir Marhalte was slayne afore by the hondis of Sir Trystram in an ilonde—and that was well knowyn at that tyme in the courte of Kynge Arthure—for this Sir Marhalte was a worthy knyght, and for evyll dedis that he ded to the contreye of Cornwayle, Sir Trystram and he fought so longe tyll they felle bledynge to the erthe, for they were so sore wounded that they myght nat stonde for ble-dynge; and Sir Trystram by fortune recoverde, and Sir Marhalte dyed thorow the stroke he had in the hede.)

So leve we Sir Trystram and turne we unto Kynge Marke.

Than Kynge Marke had grete dispyte at Sir Trystram—and whan he chaced hym oute of Cornwayle, yette was he nevew unto Kynge Marke, but he had grete suspeccion unto Sir Trystram

fol.235v

fol.236r

[7]

---

3. *I seyde no worshyp be youre house:* I did not praise you or your court.
4. *Mesures of blowynge:* hunting-horn calls.
5. On Trystram's legendary status as an authority on hunting and as a great musician see n. 7, p. 231.
6. I.e., as great.

bycause of his quene, La Beal Isode, for hym semed that there was muche love betwene them twayne.

⁋So whan Sir Trystram was departed oute of Cornwayle into Ingelonde, Kynge Marke harde of the grete proues that Sir Trystram ded there, wyth the whyche he greved. So he sente on his party men to aspye what dedis he ded; and the quene sente pryvaly on hir party spyes to know what dedis he had done, for full grete love was there betwene them. So whan the messyngers were com home, they tolde the trouthe as they herde, and how he passed all other knyghtes, but yf hit were Sir Launcelot. Than Kynge Marke was ryght hevy of tho tydynges; and as glad was La Beale Isode.

Than grete dispyte Kynge Marke had at hym; and so he toke wyth hym two knyghtes and two squyers, and disgysed hymself, and toke his way into Ingelonde, to⁷ the entente to sle Sir Trystram (and one of tho knyghtes hyght Sir Bersules, and the other knyght was callyd Amaunte). So as they rode, Kynge Marke asked a knyght that he mette, where he myght fynde Kynge Arthure. "Sir," he seyde, "at Camelot." Also he asked that knyght aftir Sir Trystrams, whether he herde of hym in the courte of Kynge Arthure. "Wete you well," seyde that knyght, "ye shall fynde Sir Trystram there for a man of worshyp moste that is now lyvynge, for thorow his proues he wan the turnement at the Castell of Maydyns that stondyth by the Roche Dure. And sytthen he hath wonne⁸ wyth his hondys thirty knyghtes that were men of grete honoure; and the laste batayle that ever he ded, he fought with Sir Launcelot, and that was a mervaylus batayle:

⁋"And by love, and not by force, Sir Launcelotte brought Sir Trystram to the courte. And of hym Kynge Arthure made passynge grete joy, and so made hym knyght of the Table Rounde; and his seate is in the same place where Sir Marhalte the good knyghtes seate was." Than was Kynge Marke passynge sory whan he harde of the honour of Sir Trystram; and so they departed. Than seyde Kynge Marke unto his two knyghtes, "Now I woll tell you my counsel, for ye ar the men that I moste truste on lyve.⁹ And I woll that ye wete my commynge hydir is to this entente, for to destroy Sir Trystram by som wylys other by treson—and hit shal be harde and ever he ascape oure hondis."¹

⁋"Alas," seyde Sir Bersules, "my lorde, what meane you? For and ye be sette in such a way, ye ar disposed shamfully, for Sir Trystram is the knyght of worshyp moste that we knowe lyvynge. And therefore I warne you playnly, I woll not consente to the deth of hym—and therefore I woll yelde hym my servyse and forsake you." Whan Kynge Marke harde hym say so, suddeynly he drewe hys swerde and seyde, "A, traytoure!" and smote Sir Bersules on the hede, that the swerde wente to his teithe.

fol.236v

7. I.e., with.
8. I.e., defeated.
9. *On lyve:* alive.
1. *Hit shal be harde and ever he ascape oure hondis:* if he escapes us, it will be with great
   difficulty.

¶Whan Sir **Amant**, his felow, sawe hym do that vylaunce dede, and his squyers als, they seyde to the kynge, "Hit was foule done, and myschevously—wherefore we woll do you no more servyse; and wete you well we woll appele you of treson afore Kynge **Arthure**." Than was Kynge **Marke** wondirly wrothe, and wolde have slayne **Amaunte**; but he and the two squyers hylde them togydirs[2] and sette nought by his malyce.

So whan Kynge **Marke** sawe he myght nat be revenged on them, he seyde thus unto the knyght **Amante**: "Wyte thou well, and thou appeyche me of treson, I shall thereof defende me afore Kynge **Arthure**; but I requyre the that thou telle nat my name, that I am Kynge **Marke**, whatsomevir com of me." "As for that," seyde Sir **Amante**, "I woll nat discover your name." And so they departed; and Sir **Amante** and his felowys toke the body of Sir **Bersules** and buryed hit.

Than Kynge **Marke** rode tyll he com to a fountayne; and there he rested hym by that fountayne, and stoode in a dwere whether he myght ryde to Kynge **Arthurs** courte other none,[3] or to returne agayne to his contrey. And as he thus restyd hym by that fountayne, there cam by hym a knyght well armed on horsebacke; and he alyght and tyed his horse and sette hym downe by the brynke of the fountayne, and there he made grete langoure and dole. And so he made the dolefullyst complaynte of love that ever man herde; and all this whyle was he nat ware of Kynge **Marke**.

And this was a grete complaynte: he cryed and wepte and sayde, "O, thou fayre Quene of Orkeney,[4] Kynge **Lottys** wyff, and modir unto Sir **Gawayne** and to Sir **Gaherys**, and modir to many other, for thy love I am in grete paynys!" Than Kynge **Marke** arose and wente nere hym, and seyde, "Fayre knyght, ye have made a piteuos complaynte." "Truly," seyde the knyght, "hit is an hondred parte more rufullyer than myne herte can uttir." "I requyre you," seyde Kynge **Marke**, "telle me youre name." "Sir, as for my name, I wyll not hyde hit from no knyght that beryth a shylde. Sir, my name is Sir **Lameroke de Galys**."

But whan Sir **Lameroke** herde Kynge **Marke** speke, than wyste he well by his speche that he was a Cornysh knyght. "Sir knyght," seyde Sir **Lameroke**, "I undirstonde by your tunge that ye be of Cornewayle, wherein there dwellyth the shamfullist knyght of a kynge[5] that is now lyvynge, for he is a grete enemy to all good knyghtes— and that prevyth well, for he hath chased oute of that contrey Sir **Trystram**, that is the worshypfullyst knyght that now is lyvynge, and all knyghtes spekyth of hym worship—and for the jeleousnes of his quene he hath chaced hym oute of his contrey. Hit is pité," seyde Sir **Lameroke**, "that ony suche false kynge cowarde as Kynge **Marke** is shulde be macched with suche a fayre lady and a good as **La Beal Isode** is; for all the worlde of hym spekyth shame—and of

fol.237r

[8]

fol.237v

---

2. *Hylde them togydirs*: stood firm.
3. I.e., not.
4. I.e., Queen Morgause.
5. *knyght of a kynge*: i.e., man given the status of knight by a king.

her, grete worshyp as ony quene may have." "I have nat ado in this mater," seyde Kynge Marke, "but, sir, can you tell me ony tydyngis?"

❡"I can telle you," seyde Sir Lameroke, "there shall be a grete turnemente in haste bysyde Camelot, at the Castell of Jagent; and the Kynge wyth the Hondred Knyghtys and the Kynge of Irelonde, as I suppose, makyth that turnemente." Than cam there a knyght that was callyd Sir Dynadan, and salewed them bothe. And whan he wyste that Kynge Marke was a knyght of Cornwayle,[6] he repreved[7] hym—for the love of Kynge Marke—a thousandfolde more than ded Sir Lameroke; and so he profirde to juste with Kynge Marke. And he was full lothe thereto,[8] but Sir Dynadan egged hym so that he justed wyth Sir Lameroke; and Sir Lameroke smote Kynge Marke so sore that he bare hym on his speare ende over his horse tayle.

And than Kynge Marke arose, and gate his horse agayne and folowed aftir Sir Lameroke. But Sir Dynadan wolde nat juste with Sir Lameroke, but he tolde Kynge Marke that Sir Lameroke was Sir Kay the Senescyall. "That is nat so," seyde Kynge Marke, "for he is muche bygger than Sir Kay." And so he folowed and overtoke hym and bade hym abyde. "What woll ye do?" seyde Sir Lameroke. "Sir," he seyde, "I woll fyght wyth a swerde, for ye have shamed me with a speare."

And therewyth they daysshed togydyrs wyth swerdis; and Sir Lamerok suffyrde hym and forbare hym, and Kynge Marke was passyng besy and smote thycke strokys. Than Sir Lameroke saw he wolde nat stynte, he waxed somwhat wrothe, and doubled his strokys, for he was of the nobelyste of the worlde; and he beete hym so on the helme that his hede hynge nyghe on the sadyll-bowe.

❡Whan Sir Lameroke saw hym fare so, he sayde, "Knyght, what chere?[9] Mesemyth ye have nyghe youre fylle of fyghtynge. Hit were pyté to do you ony more harme, for ye ar but a meane[1] knyght; therefore I gyff you leve to go where ye lyst." "Gramercy," seyde Kynge Marke, "for ye and I be no macchis."

Than Sir Dynadan mocked Kynge Marke, and seyde, "Ye ar nat able to macche a good knyght!" "As for that," seyde Kynge Marke, "at the fyrste tyme that I justed with this knyght, ye refused hym." "Thynke ye that a shame?" seyde Sir Dynadan. "Nay, sir, hit is ever worshyp to a knyght to refuse that thynge that he may nat attayne.[2] Therefore your worshyp had bene muche more to have refused hym, as I ded; for I warne you playnly he is able to beate suche fyve as ye ar and I be[3]—for ye knyghtis of Cornwayle ar no men of worshyp as other knyghtes ar. And bycause ye ar nat of worshyp,

fol.238r

---

6. *He wyste that Kynge Marke was a knyght of Cornwayle*: i.e., Dynadan does not know that this is Mark, but does know that he is Cornish.
7. I.e., reproved, blamed.
8. *Lothe thereto*: reluctant to do so.
9. *What chere*: how are you doing.
1. I.e., ordinary, average.
2. On Dynadan as a less-than-idealistic knight, see n. 7, p. 307.
3. *Suche fyve as ye ar and I be*: five of our kind.

ye hate all men of worship, for never in your contrey was bredde
suche a knyght as Sir Trystram."

Than they rode furth all togydyrs—Kynge Marke, Sir Lameroke   [9]
and Sir Dynadan—tylle that they com to a brygge; and at the ende
thereof stood a fayre toure. Than saw they a knyght on horsebacke   5
well armed, braundisshynge a speare, cryynge,[4] and profyrde hymself to juste. "Now," seyde Sir Dynadan unto Kynge Marke, "yondir
ar too bretherne, that one hyght Alyne and that other hyght Tryan,
that woll juste with ony that passyth this passayge. Now profyr
youreself," seyde Sir Dynadan unto Kynge Marke, "for ever ye be   10
leyde to the erthe." Than Kynge Marke was ashamed, and therewith   fol.238v
he feautyrde hys speare and hurteled to Sir Tryan; and aythir brake
their spearys all to pecis, and passed thorow anone. Than Sir Tryan
sente Kyng Marke another speare to juste more, but in no wyse he
wolde nat juste no more.   15

Than they com to the castell, all thre knyghtes, and prayde the
lorde of that castell of herborow. "Ye ar ryght wellcom," seyde the
knyghtes of the castell, "for the love of the lorde of this towre,
the whyche hyght Sir Torre le Fyze Aryes." And than they com into
a fayre courte well repayred,[5] and so they had passynge good chere   20
tyll the lyefftenaunte of that castell, that hyght Berluse, aspyed
Kynge Marke of Cornwayle.

Than seyde Sir Berluse, "Sir knyght, I know you well better than   [10]
ye wene, for ye ar Kynge Marke, that slew my fadir afore myne owne
yghen; and me had ye slayn had I not ascapyd into a woode. But   25
wyte you well, for the love of my lorde, Sir Torre, whyche is lorde
of this castel, I woll nat at this tyme nother hurte nor harme you,
nothir none of your felyship—but wyte you well, whan ye ar paste
this loggynge, I shall hurte you and I may, for ye slew my fader
traytourly and cowardly. But fyrste, for my lorde Sir Torre, and for   30
the love of Sir Lameroke, the honorable knyght that here is lodgid,
ye sholde have none evyll lodgynge. For hit is pyté that ever ye
sholde be in the company of good knyghtes, for ye ar the moste
vylaunce knyght of a kynge that is now lyvynge—for ye ar a dystroyer of good knyghtes, and all that ye do is but by treson." Than   35
was Kynge Marke sore ashamyd and seyde but lytyll agayne.

But whan Sir Lameroke and Sir Dynadan wyste that he was Kynge
Marke, they were sory of his felyshyp. So aftir supper they went to
lodgynge. So on the morne they arose; and Kynge Marke and Sir
Dynadan rode togydyrs, and three myle of[6] there mette with hem   40
three knyghtes—and Sir Berluse was one, and other two of hys   fol.239r
cosyns.

⁋Whan Sir Berluse saw Kynge Marke, he cryed on hyghte, "Traytoure! kepe the from me, for wete thou well that I am Sir Berluse."
"Sir knyght," seyde Sir Dynadan, "I counceyle you as at this tyme   45
medyll nat wyth hym, for he is rydynge to Kynge Arthure; and
bycause I promysed to conduyte hym to my lorde Kynge Arthure,

---

4. I.e., calling out.
5. *Well repayred*: in good repair.
6. I.e., from.

nedis muste I take a parte[7] wyth hym—howbehit I love nat his condision[8] and fayne I wolde be from hym."

¶"Well, Sir Dynadan," seyde Sir Berluse, "me repentys that ye woll take party with hym—but now do youre beste!" Than he hurteled to Kynge Marke and smote hym sore uppon the shylde, that he bare hym clene oute of his sadil to the erthe. That saw Sir Dynadan, and he feautyrd hys speare and ran to one of his felowys and smote hym of hys sadyll. Than Sir Dynadan turned his horse and smote the thirde knyght in the same wyse, that he went to the erthe— for this Sir Dynadan was a good knyght on horsebacke.

¶And so there began a grete batayle, for Sir Berluse and hys felowys hylde them togydyrs strongely on foote. And so thorow the grete force of Sir Dynadan, Kynge Marke had Sir Berluse at the erthe—and his two felowys fled—and had nat Sir Dynadan bene, Kynge Marke wolde have slayne hym; and so Sir Dynadan rescowed hym of his lyff, for this Kynge Marke was but a murtherer. And than they toke their horsys and departed, and lefte Sir Berluse there sore woundid. Than Kynge Marke and Sir Dynadan rode forth a foure leagis Englyshe[9] tyll that they com to a brydge where hoved a knyght on horsebacke armyd, redy to juste.

¶"Lo," seyde Sir Dynadan unto Kynge Marke, "yonder hovyth a knyght that woll juste, for there shall none passe this brydge but he muste juste with that knyght."

¶"Ye say well," seyde Kynge Marke, "for this justys fallyth for you."

¶But Sir Dynadan knew the knyght for a noble knyght, and fayne he wolde have justyd, but he had levir that Kynge Marke had justed with hym; but by no meane Kynge Marke wolde nat juste. Than Sir Dynadan myght nat refuse hym in no maner; and so ayther dressed their spearys and their shyldys and smote togydyrs, that thorow fyne force Sir Dynadan was smyttyn to the erthe. And lyghtly he arose up and gate his horse, and requyred that knyght to do batayle with swerdys; and he answerde and seyde, "Fayre knyght, as at this tyme I may nat have ado with you no more, for the custom of this passage is suche." Than was Sir Dynadan passynge wrothe that he myght nat be revenged of that knyght, and so he departed. And in no wyse wolde that knyght telle hys name; but ever Sir Dynadan thought he sholde know hym by his shylde that he sholde be Sir Torre.

SO as they rode by the way, Kynge Marke than began to mocke Sir Dynadan, and seyde, "I wente you knyghtes of the Rounde Table myght in no wyse fynde youre macchis."

¶"Ye sey well," seyde Sir Dynadan. "As for you, on my lyff, I calle you none of the good knyghtes—but syth ye have such dispyte at me, I requere you to juste with me to preve my strengthe."

---

7. *Take a parte*: join, take sides.
8. I.e., character.
9. A distance of four English leagues (twelve miles; English measures were standardized by Malory's time, in contrast to those on the Continent).

¶"Nat so," seyde Kynge Marke, "for I woll nat have ado with you in no maner; but I requyre you of one thynge, that whan ye com to Kynge Arthures courte, discover nat my name, for I am sore there behatyd."

¶"Hit is shame to you," seyde Sir Dynadan, "that ye governe you so shamfully, for I se by you ye ar full of cowardyse—and ye ar also a murtherar, and that is the grettyst shame that ony knyght may have, for nevir had knyght murtherer worshyp, nother never shall have. For I sawe but late thorow my forse[1] ye wolde have slayne Sir Berluses, a better knyght than ever ye were or ever shall be, and more of proues." Thus they rode forth talkynge tyll they com to a fayre place where stoode a knyghte and prayde[2] them to take their lodgynge with hym. So at the requeste of that knyght they reposyd them there, and made them well at ease and had grete chere—for all araunte knyghtes to hym were welcom, and specially all tho of Kynge Arthurs courte.

¶Than Sir Dynadan demaunded his oste what was the knyghtes name that kepte the brydge.

¶"For what cause aske you?" seyde his oste. "For hit is nat longe ago," seyde Sir Dynadan, "sytthen he gaff me a falle."

¶"A, fayre knyght," seyde his oste, "thereof have ye no mervayle, for he is a passynge good knyght; and his name is Sir Torre, the sonne of Aryes le Vaysshere." "A!" seyde Sir Dynadan, "was that Sir Torre? Truly so ever me thought."

¶So ryght as they stood thus talkynge togydyrs, they saw com rydynge by them over a playne six knyghtes of the courte of Kynge Arthure, well armyd at all poyntys; and by their shyldys Sir Dynadan knew them well. The fyrste was the good knyght Sir Uwayne, the sonne of Kynge Uryen; the secunde was the noble knyght Sir Brandyles; the thirde was Ozanna le Cure Hardy; the fourth was Sir Uwayne les Adventurys; the fyfth was Sir Agravayne, the sixth, Sir Mordred, to[3] brethirne to Sir Gawayne.

Whan Sir Dynadan had aspyed thes six knyghtes, he thought to hymself he wolde brynge Kynge Marke by som wyle to juste with one of them. And than anone they toke their horsys and ran aftir these six knyghtes well-nye a three myle Englyshe.[4] Than was Kynge Marke ware where they sate, all six aboute a welle, and ete and dranke suche metys as they had, and their horsis walkynge and som tyed, and their shyldys hyng in dyverse placis about them.

¶"Lo," seyde Sir Dynadan, "yondir ar knyghtes arraunte that woll juste with us." "God forbede" seyde Kynge Marke, "for they be six, and we but two." "As for that," seyde Sir Dynadan, "lat us nat spare, for I woll assay the formyst." And therewith he made hym redy.

¶Whan Kynge Marke sawe hym do so, as faste as Sir Dynadan rode towardis them, Kynge Marke rode frowarde them with all his

fol.240r

fol.240v

5

10

15

20

25

30

35

40

45

---

1. I.e., success in battle.
2. I.e., who asked.
3. I.e., two.
4. A distance of three English miles.

mayneall mayné.[5] So whan Sir Dynadan saw that Kynge Marke was
gone, he sette the speare oute of the reaste and threwe hys shylde
uppon his backe and cam rydynge to the felyshyp of the Rounde
Table; and anone Sir Uwayne knew Sir Dynadan and welcomed hym,
and so ded all his felyshyp. And than they asked hym of aventures, [12]
and whether that he sawe of Sir Trystram othir Sir Launcelot. "So
God me helpe," seyde Sir Dynadan, "as for me, I sawe none of them
sytthyn we departed fro Camelot."

⁋"What knyght is that," seyde Sir Braundyles, "that so sodeynly
departed frome you and rode over yondir fylde?"

⁋"Sir, hit is a knyght of Cornwayle, and the moste orryble
cowarde that ever bestrode horse."

⁋"What is his name?" seyde all thos knyghtes. "I wote nat,"
seyde Sir Dynadan. So whan they had reposed them and spokyn
togydyrs, they toke there horsys and rode to a castell where dwellyd
an olde knyght that made all knyghtes arraunte good chere. So in
the meanewhyle that they were talkynge, com into the castell Sir
Gryfflet le Fyz de Deu, and there was he wellcom; and they all askyd
hym whethir he sye Sir Launcelot other Sir Trystram. He answerde
and seyde, "I sawe hem nat sytthyn they departed frome Camelot."

So as Sir Dynadan walked and behylde the castell, thereby in a
chambir he aspyed Kynge Marke; and than he rebuked hym and
asked why he departed so. "Sir, for I durst nat abyde, for they were
so many—but how ascaped ye?" seyde Kynge Marke. "Sir, they be
better frendis than I went they had ben." "Who is captayne of this
felyshyp?" seyde Kynge Marke. For to feare[6] hym, Sir Dynadan seyde
hit was Sir Launcelot.

"A, Jesu!" seyde Kynge Marke, "myght Y knowe Sir Launcelot by
his shylde?" "Ye," seyde Sir Dynadan, "for he beryth a shylde of
sylver and blacke bendis." All this he seyde to feare Kynge Marke,
for Sir Launcelot was nat in the felyshyp. "Now I pray you," seyde
Kynge Marke, "that ye woll ryde in my felyshyp." ["That is me lothe
to doo," said Syre Dynadan, "because ye forsoke my felauship."
Ryght soo Sir Dynadan went from Kyng Mark and wente to his own
felauship.] And so they mownted uppon there horsys and rode on
their wayes and talked of the Cornyshe knyght, for Sir Dynadan
tolde them that he was in the castell where they were lodged. "Hit
is well seyde," seyde Sir Gryfflet, "for here have I brought Sir Dagonet, Kynge Arthurs foole, that is the beste felow and the meryeste
in the worlde."

⁋"Woll ye than do well?"[7] seyde Sir Dynadan. "I have tolde the
Cornyshe knyght that here is Sir Launcelot, and the Cornyshe
knyght asked me what shylde he bare, and I tolde hym that he bare
the same shylde that Sir Mordred beryth." "Woll ye do well?" seyde
Sir Mordred. "I am hurte and may nat well beare my shylde nother
harneys; and therefore put my harneys and my shylde uppon Sir
Dagonet, and let hym sette uppon the Cornyshe knyght!" "That shall

fol.241r

---

5. *Mayneall mayné*: domestic retinue, servants.
6. I.e., frighten.
7. Would you do me a favor?

be done," seyde Sir Dagonet, "be my fayth." And so anone Sir Dagonet was armed in Sir Mordredis harneys and hys shylde, and he was
sette on a grete horse, and a speare in his honde.

"Now," seyde Sir Dagonet, "sette me to that knyght, and I trowe
I shall beare hym downe." So all thes knyghtes rode to a woodis
syde and abode tyll Kynge Marke cam by the way. Than they put
forth Sir Dagonet, and he cam on all the whyle his horse myght
renne uppon Kynge Marke; and whan he cam nye to Kynge Marke,
he cryed as he were woode, and sayde, "Kepe the, knyght of Cornwayle, for I woll sle the!" And anone, as Kynge Marke behylde his
shylde, he seyde to hymself, "Yondyr is Sir Launcelot! Alas, now am
I destroyed!" And therewithall he made his horse to ren, and fledde
as faste as he mygyht, thorow thycke and thorow thynne—and ever
Sir Dagonet folowed aftir Kynge Marke, cryynge and ratynge hym as
a woode man, thorow a grete foreste.

¶Whan Sir Uwayne and Sir Brandules saw Sir Dagonet so chace
Kynge Marke, they lawghed all as they were wylde; and than they
toke their horsys and rode aftir to se how Sir Dagonet spedde, for
theym behoved for no good[8] that Sir Dagonet were shente, for
Kynge Arthure loved hym passynge well and made hym knyght hys
owne hondys—and at every turnemente he began, to make Kynge
Arthure to lawghe.

Than the knyghtes rode here and there cryynge and chasynge
aftir Kynge Marke, that all the foreyste range of the noyse. So Kynge
Marke by fortune rode by a welle, in the way where stood a knyght
arraunte on horsebacke, armed at all poyntys, with a grete spere
in his honde. And whan he saw Kyng Marke com fleynge, he sayde
to the knyght, "Returne agayne for shame and stonde with me, and
I shall be thy waraunte." "A, fayre knyght," seyde Kynge Marke,
"lette me passe, for yondir commyth aftir me the beste knyght of
the worlde, wyth the blacke beanded shylde." "Fy, for shame,"
seyde the knyght, "for he is none of the worthy knyghtes; but, and
yf he were Sir Launcelot othir Sir Trystram, I shall nat doute to mete[9]
the bettyr of them bothe." Whan Kyng Marke harde hym sey that
worde, he returned his horse and abode by hym.

And than that stronge knyght bare a speare to Sir Dagonet and
smote hym so sore that he bare hym over his horse tayle, that nyghe
he had brokyn his necke. And anone aftir hym cam Sir Braundules;
and whan he sawe Sir Dagonette have that falle, he was passynge
wrothe, and seyde, "Kepe the, knyght!" And so they hurled togydyrs
wondir sore; but the knyghte smote Sir Braundules so sore that he
went to the erthe, horse and man. Sir Uwayne com aftir and sy all
this: "Jesu," he seyde, "yondyr is a stronge knyght!" And than they
feautred their spearys; and this knyght com so egirly that he smote
downe Sir Uwayne. Than cam Sir Ozanna wyth the Hardy Harte,
and he was smyttyn downe.

"Now," seyde Sir Gryfflet, "be my counceyle, lat us sende to
yondir arraunte knyghte and wete whether he be of Kynge Arthurs

fol.241v

[13]

fol.242r

---

8. *Theym behoved for no good:* it necessarily was no good for them.
9. *I shall nat doute to mete:* i.e., I doubt not that they will meet (in me).

courte—for, as I deme, hit is Sir Lameroke de Galys." So they sente[1]
unto hym and prayde that stronge knyght "to telle us his name,
and whethir he were of Kynge Arthurs courte other nat." "As for
my name, telle tho knyghtes I am a knyght arraunte, as they ar,
but my name they shall nat wete at this tyme; and lat them wete
that I am no knyght of Kynge Arthurs." And so the squyer rode ayen
and tolde as he seyde. "Be my hede," seyde Sir Aggravayne, "he is
one of the strongyst knyghtes that ever I saw, for he hathe overthrowyn three noble knyghtes, and nedis we muste encountyr with
hym for shame."

So Sir Aggravayne feautred his speare; and that othir was redy,
and smote hym downe over his horse tayle to the erthe—and in
the same wyse he smote Sir Uwayne les Avoutres, and also Sir Gryf-
flot. Than had he served them all but Sir Dynadan, for he was
behynde,[2] and Sir Mordrede, whyche Sir Dagonet had his harneys.
So whan this was done, this stronge knyght rode on his way a soffte
pace—and Kynge Marke rode aftir hym, praysynge hym mykyll. But
he wolde answere no wordys, but syghed wondirly sore, and hon-
gynge downe his hede, takynge no hyde to his wordys.

Thus they rode well-nye a three myle Englysh; and than this
knyght callyd to hym a varlet, and bade hym, "Ryde untyll yondir
fayre maner, and commaunde me to the lady of that castell and
place, and pray hir to sende me som refresshynge of good metys
and drynkys. And yf she aske the what I am, telle her that I am the
knyght that folowyth the Glatysaunte Beste" (that is in Englysh to
sey the "Questynge Beste," for the beste, wheresomever he yode,
he quested[3] in the bealy with suche a noyse as hit had bene a thirty
couple of howndis). Than the varlet wente his way and cam to the
maner, and salewed the lady and tolde her frome whens he come.
And whan he[4] undirstode that he cam fro the knyght that folowed
the Questynge Beste—

¶"A! swete Lorde Jesu," she seyde, "whan shall I se that jantyll
knyght, my dere sonne Sir Palomydes? Alas, woll he nat abyde with
me?" And therewith she sowned and wepte and made passynge
grete dole. But allso, sone as she myght, she gaff the varlet mete
all that he axed. And than the varlet returned unto Sir Palomydes.
For he was a varlet of Kynge Markis; and as sone as he cam he
tolde the knyghtes name was Sir Palomydes: "I am well pleased,"
seyde Kynge Marke, "but holde the[5] stylle and sey nothynge." Than
they alyght and sette them downe and reposed them a whyle; and
anone wythall Kynge Marke fylle on slepe. So whan Sir Palomydes
sawe hym sounde on slepe, he toke his horse and rode his way,
and seyde to them, "I woll nat be in the company of a slepynge
knyght." And so he rode a grete pace.

fol.242v

1. I.e., sent a squire.
2. I.e., delayed.
3. I.e., yelping.
4. She.
5. Thee.

Now turne we unto Sir Dynadan, that founde thes seven knyghtes [14]
passynge hevy; and whan he wyste how that they had sped, as hevy
was he. "Sir Uwayne," seyde Sir Dynadan, "I dare ley thereon my
hede, hit is Sir Lameroke de Galys. I promyse you all I shall fynde
hym, and he may be founde in this contrey." And so Sir Dynadan   5
rode aftir this knyght; and so ded Kynge Marke, that sought hym
thorow the foreyste. And so as Kynge Marke rode aftir Sir Palomydes,
he harde a noyse of a man that made grete dole; than Kynge Marke
rode as nye that noyse as he myght and as he durste. Than was he
ware of a knyght that was dissended of his horse, and he had putte   10
of his helme—and there he made a peteuous complaynte and a
dolerous, of love.

Now leve we off, and talke we of Sir Dynadan that rode to seke
Sir Palomydes; and as he cam wythin a foreyste, he mette with a
knyght, a chacer of deore. "Sir," seyde Sir Dynadan, "mette ye wyth   15
ony knyght wyth a shylde of sylver and lyons hedys?"

¶ "Ye, fayre knyght," seyde the other, "with suche a knyght mette   fol.243r
I wyth but a whyle agone, and streyte yondir way he yeode." "Gramercy," seyde Sir Dynadan, "for myght I fynde the tracke of his
horse, I sholde nat fayle to fynde that knyght." Ryght so, as Sir   20
Dynadan rode in the evenynge late, he harde a dolefull noyse as hit
were of a man.

Than Sir Dynadan rode towarde that noyse, and whan he cam
nyghe that noyse he alyght of his horse and wente nere hym on
foote. Than was he ware of a knyght that stoode undir a tre, and   25
his horse tyed by hym, and his helme off; and ever that knyght
made a dolefull complaynte as evir made knyght—and allwayes he
complayned of La Beale Isode, the Quene of Cornwayle, and sayde,
"A, fayre lady, why love I the? For thou arte fayryst of all othir;[6]
and as yet shewdyst thou never love to me, nother bounti, pardé—   30
and yet, alas, muste I love the. And I may nat blame the, fayre
lady, for myne eyen caused me this sorowe. And yet to love the I
am but a foole, for the beste knyght of the worlde lovyth the, and
ye hym agayne, that is Sir Trystram de Lyones. And the falsyst
knyght and kynge of[7] the worlde is your husbande, and the moste   35
cowarde and full of treson is youre lorde, Kynge Marke—and alas[8]
so beawteuous a lady and pereles of all othir sholde be matched
with the moste vylaunce knyght of the worlde!"

And all this langage harde Kynge Marke, what Sir Palomydes
seyde by hym—wherefore he was adrad, whan he sawe Sir Dynadan,   40
leste that he had aspyed hym, and that he wolde tell Sir Palomydes
that he was Kynge Marke; wherefore he wythdrewe hym, and toke
his horse and rode to his men where[9] he commaunded hem to
abyde. And so he rode as faste as he myght unto Camelot.

And the same day he founde there Sir Amant, the knyght, redy,   fol.243v   45
that afore Kynge Arthure had appelyd hym of treson. And so, lyghtly

6. I.e., other ladies.
7. I.e., in.
8. I.e., alas that.
9. I.e., in the place where.

the Kynge commaunded them to do batayle; and by mysadventure Kynge Marke smote Sir Amante thorow the body—and yet was Sir Amaunte in the ryghtuous quarell.[1] And ryght so he[2] toke his horse and departed frome the courte for drede of Sir Dynadan, that he wolde telle Sir Trystram and Sir Palomydes what he was.

Than was there damesels that La Beale Isode had sente to Sir Trystram that knew Sir Amante well. Than by the lycence of Kynge Arthure they wente to hym and spake with hym, for whyle the truncheon of the speare stake in his body he spake.[3] "A, fayre damesels," seyde Sir Amant, "recommaunde me unto La Beale Isode, and telle her that I am slayne for the love of her and of Syr Trystram." And there he tolde the damessels how cowardly Kyng Marke had slayne hym, and Sir Bersules, his felow—"and for that dede I appeled hym of treson, and here am I slayne in a ryghtuous quarell; and all was bycause Sir Bersules and I wolde nat consente by treson to sle the noble knyght Sir Trystram."

Than the two maydyns cryed alowde, that all the courte myght hyre, and seyde, "A, swete Jesu that knowyste all hydde thynges, why sufferyst Thou so false a traytoure to venqueyshe and sle a trewe knyght that faught in a ryghteuous quarell?" Than anone hit was spronge to the Kynge and the Quene and to all the lordis that hit was Kynge Marke that had slayne Sir Amante, and Sir Bersules aforehonde, wherefore they did there that batayle. Than was Kynge Arthure wrothe oute of mesure, and so was all other knyghtes.

¶But whan Sir Trystram wyst all, he wepte for sorow for the losse of Sir Bersules and of Sir Amante. Whan Sir Launcelot aspyed Sir Trystram wepe, he wente hastely to Kynge Arthure, and sayde, "Sir, I pray you, gyff me leve to returne ayen yondir false kynge and knyght." "I pray you," seyde Kynge Arthure, "fetche hym agayne— but I wolde nat ye slew hym, for my worshyp." Than Sir Launcelot armed hym in all haste, and mownted uppon a grete horse, and toke a spere in his honde and rode aftir Kynge Marke; and frome thens a three myle Englysh, Sir Launcelot overtoke hym and bade hym turne hym: "Recreaunte kynge and knyght! For whethir thou wylte othir nylt, thou shalt go with me to Kynge Arthurs courte."

Than Kynge Marke returned and loked uppon Sir Launcelot, and sayde, "Fayre sir, what is your name?" "Wyte you well, my name is Sir Launcelot—and therefore defende the!" And whan Kynge Marke knew that hit was Sir Launcelot, and cam so faste uppon hym with a speare, he cryed than alowde and seyde, "I yelde me to the, Sir Launcelot, honorable knyght." But Sir Launcelot wolde nat hyre[4] hym, but cam faste uppon hym.

¶Kynge Marke saw that, and made no deffence, but tumbeled adowne oute of his sadyll to the erthe as a sak; and there he lay stylle, and cryed, "Sir Launcelot, have mercy uppon me." "Aryse, recreaunte kynge and knyght!"

---

1. *In the ryghtuous quarell:* in the right in the dispute.
2. I.e., King Mark.
3. *Whyle the truncheon . . . stake . . . he spake:* i.e., as long as the broken portion of the spear stayed in his body, it prevented a sudden and fatal loss of blood.
4. I.e., hear.

[15]

5

10

15

20

25

fol.244r

30

35

40

45

❡"Sir, I woll nat fyght," seyde Kynge Marke, "but whother that ye woll I woll go wyth you."

❡"Alas, seyde Sir Launcelotte, "that I myght nat gyff the[5] one buffette for the love of Sir Trystram and of La Beale Isode, and for tho two knyghtes that thou haste slayne trayturly." And so he mownte uppon his horse and brought hym to Kynge Arthure; and there Kynge Marke alyght in that same place, and threwe his helme frome hym uppon the erthe, and his swerde, and felle flatte to the erthe at Kynge Arthurs feete, and put hym in his grace and mercy. "So God me helpe," seyde Kynge Arthure, "ye ar wellcom in a maner, and in a maner ye ar nat wellcom. In this maner ye ar wellcom: that ye com hydir magré your hede,[6] as I suppose." "That is trouthe," seyde Kynge Marke, "and ellys I had nat bene here now, for my lorde Sir Launcelot brought me hydir by fyne force, and to hym am I yoldyn to as recreaunte."

❡"Well," seyde Kynge Arthure, "ye ought to do me servyse, omayge, and feauté;[7] and never wolde ye do me none, but ever ye have bene ayenste me, and a dystroyer of my knyghtes. Now how woll ye acquyte you?"

❡"Sir," seyde Kynge Marke, "ryght as youre lordshyp woll requyre me, unto my power I woll make a large amendys"—

❡For he was a fayre speker, and false thereundir. Than for the grete plesure of Sir Trystram, to make them two accordid, the Kynge withhylde[8] Kynge Marke as at that tyme and made a brokyn love day[9] betwene them.

Now turne we agayne unto Sir Palomydes, how Sir Dynadan comfortyd hym in all that he myght frome his grete sorowe. "What knyght ar ye?" seyde Sir Palomydes. "Sir, I am a knyght arraunte as ye be, that have sought you longe by[1] your shylde." "Here is my shylde," seyde Sir Palomydes, "wete you well, and ye wolde ought therewith, I woll deffende hit." "Nay," seyde Sir Dynadan, "I woll nat have ado with you but in good[2] maner."

❡"And yf ye wyll, ye shall fynde me sone redy."

❡"Sir," seyde Sir Dynadan, "whotherwarde ryde ye this way?"

❡"Be my hede," seyde Sir Palomydes, "I wote nat whother, but as fortune ledyth me." "But harde ye other sawe ye ought of Sir Trystram?" "So God me helpe, of Sir Trystram I bothe herde and sawe, and natforthan we love nat inwardly well togydyrs, yet at my myscheffe Sir Trystram rescowed me fro my deth; and yet, or he and I departed, by bothe oure assentys we assygned a day that we sholde have mette at the stony grave that Merlyon sette besyde Camelot, and there to have done batayle togydyrs. Howbehit I was letted," seyde Sir Palomydes, "that I myght nat holde my day,

fol.244v

[16]

5. Thee.
6. *Magré your hede*: against your will.
7. On feudal obligations, see n. 6, p. 9.
8. I.e., retained (in feudal service).
9. *Brokyn love day*: day of reconciliation.
1. I.e., identifying you by.
2. I.e., appropriate.

fol.245r

whyche grevyth me sore. But I have a layrge excuse, for I was presonere with a lorde and many other mo; and that shall Sir Trystram well undirstonde, that I brake hit of no feare of[3] cowardyse." And than Sir Palomydes tolde Sir Dynadan the same[4] day that they sholde have mette.

"So God me helpe," seyde Sir Dynadan, "that same day mette Sir Launcelot and Sir Trystram at the same grave of stone; and there was the moste myghtyeste batayle that ever was sene in this londe betwyxte two knyghtes, for they fought more than fyve owres—and there they bothe bled so muche blood that all men mervayled that ever they myght endure hit. And so by bothe their assentys, they were made frendys and sworne brethirne for ever; and no man cowde juge the bettir knyght. And now is Sir Trystram made a knyght of the Rounde Table, and he syttyth in the syege of the noble knyght Sir Marhalte."

"Be my hede!" seyde Sir Palomydes, "Sir Trystram ys farre bygger than is Sir Launcelot, and the hardyer knyght." "Sir, have ye assayde them bothe?" seyde Sir Dynadan. "I have sayde[5] Sir Trystramys myght," seyde Sir Palomydes, "but never Sir Launcelot, to my wyttynge, but at the fountayne where lay Sir Launcelot on slepe; and there with one speare he smote downe Sir Trystram and me," seyde Sir Palomydes. "But at that tyme they knewe nat [eyther other], but aftyrwarde."

❡"Now, fayre knyght," seyde Sir Dynadan, "as for Sir Launcelot and Sir Trystram, lette them be, for the warre of them woll nat be lyghtly macchid of no knyghtes that I knowe lyvynge."

❡"No," seyde Sir Palomydes, "God deffende, but, and I hadde a quarell to the bettir of them bothe,[6] I wolde with as good a wyll fyght with hem as with you." "Sir, I requere you," seyde Sir Dynadan, "tell me your name, and in good fayth I shall holde you company tyll that we com to Camelot—and there shall ye have grete worshyp now at this grete turnemente, for there shall be Quene Gwenyver and La Beale Isode of Cornwayle."

❡"Wyte you well, sir knyght, for the love of La Beale Isode I woll be there, and ellis nat; but I woll nat have ado in Kynge Arthurs courte." "Sir," seyde Sir Dynadan, "I shall ryde with you and do you servyse, so ye woll tell me youre name." "Syr, ye shall undirstonde my name is Palomydes, brothir unto Sir Saphyre, the good knyght, and Sir Segwarydes—and were Sarezyns borne." "Sir, I thanke you," seyde Sir Dynadan, "for I am glad that I knowe your name. And by me ye shall nat be hurte but rathir avaunced, and I may, on my lyff; for ye shall wynne worshyp in the courte of Kynge Arthure and be ryghte wellcom." And so they dressed on their helmys and put on there shyldis, and mownted uppon their horsys and toke the brode way towarde Camelot; and than were they ware of a castell

fol.245v

---

3. I.e., stemming from.
4. *The same:* i.e., which.
5. I.e., assayed, put to the test.
6. *And I hadde a quarell to the bettir of them bothe:* if I had a rightful dispute with both of them.

that was fayre and ryche and also passynge stronge as ony was within this realme.

So Sir Palomydes seyde to Sir Dynadan, "here is a castell that I knowe well, and therein dwellyth Quene Morgan le Fay, Kynge Arthurs systyr. And Kynge Arthure gaff hir this castell, by the whyche he hath repented hym sytthyn a thousand tymes, for sytthen Kynge Arthur and she hath bene at debate and stryff—but this castell coude he never gete nother wynne of hir by no maner of engyne. And ever as she myght, she made warre on Kynge Arthure; and all daungerous knyghtes she wytholdyth with her for to dystroy all thos knyghtes that Kynge Arthure lovyth. And there shall no knyght passe this way but he muste juste with one knyght, other wyth two, other with three; and yf hit hap that Kynge Arthurs knyght be beatyn, he shall lose his horse and harnes and all that he hath, and harde yf that he ascape[7] but that he shall be presonere."

"So God me helpe," seyde Sir Palomydes, "this is a shamefull and a vylaunce usage for a quene to use—and namely to make suche warre uppon her owne lorde, that is called the floure of chevalry that is Crystyn othir hethyn[8]—and with all my harte I woll destroy that shamefull custom. And I woll that all the worlde wyte she shall have no servyse of me; and yf she sende oute ony knyghtes, as I suppose she woll, to juste, they shall have bothe there hondys full!" "And I shall nat fayle you," seyde Sir Dynadan, "unto my puyssaunce,[9] upon my lyff."

So as they stoode on horsebacke afore the castell, there cam a knyght[1] wyth a rede shylde, and two squyers aftir hym; and he cam strayte unto Sir Palomydes and sayde, "Fayre knyght arraunte, I requyre the for the love thou owyste unto knyghthode, that thou wylt not have ado here with this men of this castell"—thus Sir Lamerok seyde—"for I cam hydir to seke this dede, and hit is my rekeyste. And therefore I beseche you, knyght, lette me deale; and yf I be beatyn, revenge me." "In the name of God," seyde Sir Palomydes, "lat se how ye woll spede, and we shall beholde you."

Than anone come furth a knyght of the castell and profyrde to juste with the knyght wyth the rede shylde; and anone they encountyrd togydyrs, and he with the rede shylde smote hym so harde that he bare hym over to the erthe. And therewith anone cam another knyght of the castell; and he was smyttyn so sore that he avoyded hys sadyll. And furthwithall cam the thirde knyght; and the knyght with the rede shylde smote hym to the erthe. Than cam Sir Palomydes and besought hym that he myght helpe hym to juste.

¶ "Now, sir knyght," he seyde, "suffir me as at this tyme to have my wyll, for and they were twenty knyghtes I shall nat doute[2] them." And ever there were uppon the wallys of the castell many lordys [and ladyes] that cryed and seyde, "Well have ye justed,

---

7. *Harde yf that he ascape:* he will not easily escape.
8. *The floure of chevalry that is Crystyn othir hethyn:* i.e., the flower of all knighthood.
9. *Unto my puyssaunce:* to the best of my ability.
1. I.e., Sir Lamerok.
2. I.e., fear.

knyght with the rede shylde!" But as sone as the knyght had smyttyn hem downe, his squyers toke their horsys and avoyded there
sadyls and brydyls of the horsis, and turnede theym into the foreyste, and made the knyghtes to be kepte to the ende of the justys.

¶Ryght so cam forth of the castell the fourthe knyght, and
freyshly profyrde to juste wyth the knyght with the rede shylde;
and he was redy, and he smote hym so harde that horse and man
felle to the erthe—and the knyghtes backe brake with the falle,
and his necke also.

¶"A, Jesu!" seyde Sir Palomydes, "that yondir is a passynge good
knyght and the beste juster that ever I sawe."

¶"Be my hede," seyde Sir Dynadan, "he is as good as ever was
Sir Launcelot othir Sir Trystram, what knyght soever he be." Than
furthwithall cam a knyght oute of the castell with a shylde bended
with blak and with whyght; and anone the knyght wyth the rede
shylde and he encountyrd so harde that he smote the knyght of
the castell thorowoute the bended shylde and thorow the body,
and brake the horse backe.

¶"Fayre knyght," sayde Sir Palomydes, "ye have overmuche on
hande;[3] therefore I pray you, lette me juste, for ye had nede to be
reposed."

¶"Why, sir," seyde the knyght, "seme ye that I am weyke and
fyeble?

¶"A,[4] sir, methynkyth ye proffir me grete wronge and shame
whan I do well inowe; for I telle you now, as I tolde you arste, and
they were twenty knyghtes I shall beate theym; and yf I be beatyn
other slayne, than may ye revenge me. And yf ye thynke that I be
wery, and ye have an appetyte to juste with me, I shall fynde you
justynge inowghe."

¶"Syr," seyde he, "I sayde hit nat because that I wolde juste with
you, but mesemyth ye have overmuche on hande." "And therefore,
and ye were jantyll," sayde the knyght with the red shylde, "ye
wolde nat profyr me no shame; therefore I requyre you to juste
with me—and ye shall fynde that I am nat wery."

¶"Syth ye requyre me," seyde Sir Palomydes, "take kepe to[5]
youreselff." Than they two knyghtes com togydyrs as faste as their
horsys myght ren; and the knyght smote Sir Palomydes so sore on
the shylde that the speare wente into hys syde and hurte hym a
grete wounde and a perelous.

¶And therewith Sir Palomydes avoyded his sadyll. And that
knyght turned unto Sir Dynadan; and whan he sawe hym commynge, he cryed alowde and sayde, "Sir, I woll nat have ado with
you!" But for that he spared nat, but com strayte uppon hym; so
Sir Dynadan for shame put forth hys speare, and all to-shyvirde hit
uppon the knyght—but he smote Sir Dynadan agayne so harde that
he bare hym frome his horse (but he wolde nat suffyr his squyer

fol.246v   5

[18]

15

10

20

25

30

35

fol.247r   40

45

---

3. *Overmuche on hande*: too much to do.
4. Lamerok is still speaking.
5. *Take kepe to*: watch, look after.

to meddyll wyth there horsys, and bycause they were knyghtes arraunte).

Than he dressid hym agayne to the castell and justed with seven knyghtes mo; and there was none of hem that myght withstonde hym, but he bare them to the erthe. And of those a twelve knyghtes, he slewe in playne justys foure; and the eyght knyghtes, he made them to swere on the crosse of a swerde that they sholde never use the evyll customs of the castell; and whan he made them to swere that othe, he lete them passe. And stoode the lordis and the ladyes on the castell wallys, cryynge and seynge, "Knyght with the rede shylde, ye have mervaylously well done as ever we sawe knyght do!"

And therewith come a knyght oute of the castell unarmed, and seyde, "Knyght with the rede shylde, overmuche damage have ye done this same day; and therefore returne whother ye woll, for here ar no mo that woll have ado with the, for we repente sore that ever ye cam here—for by the is fordone all the olde customes of this castell." And with that worde he turned agayne into the castell, and shett the yatys.

Than the knyght wyth the rede shylde turned and called his squyers, and so paste forth on his way and rode a grete pace. And whan he was paste, Sir 𝔓𝔞𝔩𝔬𝔪𝔶𝔡𝔢𝔰 wente to Sir 𝔇𝔶𝔫𝔞𝔡𝔞𝔫 and seyde to hym, "I had never suche a shame of one knyght that ever I mette; and therefore I caste me to ryde aftir hym and to be revenged uppon hym with my swerde—for on horsebacke I deme I shall gete no worshyp of hym." ["Syre 𝔓𝔞𝔩𝔬𝔪𝔶𝔡𝔢𝔰," said 𝔇𝔶𝔫𝔞𝔡𝔞𝔫, "ye shalle not medle with hym, by my counceil, for ye shal gete no worship of hym,] and for this cause: that ye have sene hym this day have had ever muche to done and overmuche travayled."

⸿"Be Allmyghty Jesu," seyde Sir 𝔓𝔞𝔩𝔬𝔪𝔶𝔡𝔢𝔰, "I shall never be at ease tyll that I have had ado with hym." "Sir," seyde Sir 𝔇𝔶𝔫𝔞𝔡𝔞𝔫, "I shall gyff you my beholdynge!"[6] "Well," seyde Sir 𝔓𝔞𝔩𝔬𝔪𝔶𝔡𝔢𝔰, "than shall ye se how we shall redresse[7] oure myghtes!" So they toke there horsys of their varlettis and rode aftir the knyght with the rede shylde; and downe in a valay, besyde a fountayne, they were ware where he was alyght to repose hym, and had done of his helme for to drynke at the welle.

⸿Than Sir 𝔓𝔞𝔩𝔬𝔪𝔶𝔡𝔢𝔰 rode faste tyll he cam nyghe hym; and than he seyde, "Knyght, remembir ye me, and of the same dede that ye ded to me late at the castell? Therefore redresse the,[8] for I woll have ado with the."

⸿"Fayre knyght," seyde Sir 𝔏𝔞𝔪𝔢𝔯𝔬𝔨, "of me ye wynne no worshyp, for ye have sene this day that I have be travayled sore."

⸿"As for that," seyde Sir 𝔓𝔞𝔩𝔬𝔪𝔶𝔡𝔢𝔰, "I woll nat lette; for wyte you well, I woll be revenged." "Well," seyde the knyght, "I may happyn to endure you." And therewithall he mownted uppon his horse and toke a grete speare in his honde, redy to juste.

⸿"Nay," seyde Sir 𝔓𝔞𝔩𝔬𝔪𝔶𝔡𝔢𝔰, "I woll nat juste, for I am sure at

5

10

15

20

25

fol.247v

30

35

[19]

40

45

---

6. *I shall gyff you my beholdynge:* I will look on.
7. I.e., improve.
8. *Redresse the:* stand yourself up.

justynge I gete no pryce." "Now, fayre knyght," sayde he, "hit wolde
beseme a knyght to juste and to fyght on horsebacke."

❧"Ye shall se what I woll do" seyde Sir Palomydes. And therewith
he alyght downe uppon foote, and dressed his shylde afore hym
and pulled oute his swerde; than the knyght with the rede shylde
descended downe frome his horse and dressed his shylde afore
hym, and so he drewe oute his swerde. And than they come togydyrs a soffte pace, and wondirly they layshed togydyrs passynge
thycke, the mowntenaunce of an owre, or ever they breethid. Than
they trased and traverced and wexed wondirly wrothe; and aythir
behyght other deth. They hewe so faste wyth there swerdis that
they kutte downe halff their shyldis; and they hewe togydyrs on
helmys and mayles, that the bare fleysshe in som places stoode
abovyn there harneys. And whan Sir Palomydes behylde his felowys
swerde overheled with his blood, hit greved hym sore. And somwhyle they foyned and somwhyle they strake downe as wylde men.

❧But at the laste Sir Palomydes waxed wondir faynte, bycause of
his fyrste wounde that he had at the castell wyth a speare—for that
wounde greved hym wondirly sore.

❧"Now, fayre knyght," sayde Sir Palomydes, "mesemyth we have
assayed ayther other passyngly well; and yf hit may please you, I
requyre you of your knyghthode to tell me your name."

❧"Sir, he sayde, "that is me ryght loth, for ye have done me grete
wronge and no knyghthode to proffir me batayle, consyderynge my
grete travayle; but, and ye woll telle me youre name, I woll telle
you myne." "Sir, wyte you well, my name is Sir Palomydes." "Than,
sir, ye shall undirstonde my name is Sir Lameroke de Galys, sonne
and ayre unto the good knyght and kynge, Kynge Pellynore; and Sir
Torre, the good knyght, is my halff brothir."

When Sir Palomydes had herde hym sey so, he kneled adowne
and asked mercy—"for outrageously have I done to you this day,
consyderynge the grete dedis of armys I have sene you done, and
shamefully and unknyghtly I have requyred you to do batayle with
me."

❧"A, Sir Palomydes," seyde Sir Lamerok, "overmuche have ye done
and seyde to me." And therewyth he pulled hym up wyth his bothe
hondis, and seyde, "Sir Palomydes, the worthy knyght, in all this
londe is no bettir than ye be, nor more of proues, and me repentys
sore that we sholde fyght togydirs." "So hit doth nat me," seyde Sir
Palomydes, "and yett I am sorer wounded than ye be—but as for
that, I shall sone be hole. But sertaynly I wolde nat, for the fayryst
castell in this londe, but yf⁹ ye and I had mette, for I shall love you
dayes of my lyff afore all other knyghtes, excepte my brother, Sir
Saphir." "I say the same," seyde Sir Lameroke, "excepte my brother
Sir Torre." Than cam Sir Dynadan and he made grete joy of Sir
Lamerok. Than their squyers dressed bothe their shyldis and their
harnes, and stopped hir woundis. And thereby at a pryory they
rested them all nyght.

9. *I wolde nat . . . but yf:* I would not do anything else . . . unless.

¶Now turne we agayne, that whan Sir Uwayne and Sir Braundyles [20]
with his felowys cam to the courte of Kynge Arthure, and they tolde
the Kynge, Sir Launcelot, and Sir Trystram, how Sir Dagonet, the
foole, chaced Kynge Marke thorowoute the foreste, and how the
stronge knyght smote them downe, all seven, with one speare, than 5
there was grete lawghynge and japynge at Kynge Marke and at Sir
Dagonet. But all thos knyghtes coude nat telle what knyght hit was
that rescowed Kynge Marke.

Than they asked of Kynge Marke yf that he knewe hym, and he
answerde and sayde, "He named hymself 'the knyght that folowed 10
the Questynge Beste,' and in that name he sent oute one of my
varlettes to a place where was his modir; and whan she harde from
whens he cam, she made passyng grete dole—and so discoverde
to my varlette his name, and seyde, 'A, my dere son, Sir Palomydes,
why wolt thou nat se me?' And therefore, sir," seyde Kynge Marke, 15
"hit is to undirstonde his name is Sir Palomydes, a noble knyght."
Than were all the seven knyghtys passynge glad that they knewe
his name.

¶Now turne we agayne; for on the morne they toke their horsys,
bothe Sir Lameroke, Sir Palomydes, and Sir Dynadan, wyth their squy- 20
ers and varlettis, tylle they sawe a fayre castell that stoode on a
mountayne well closyd—and thydir they rode. And there they
founde a knyght that hyght Sir Galahalte, that was lorde of that fol.249r
castell; and there they had grete chere and were well eased. "Sir
Dynadan," seyde Sir Lameroke, "what woll ye do?" 25

"Sir, I woll tomorne to the courte of Kynge Arthure." "Be my
hede," seyde Sir Palomydes, "I woll nat ryde this three dayes, for I
am sore hurte and muche have I bledde; and therefore I woll
repose me here." "Truly," seyde Sir Lameroke, "and I woll abyde here
wyth you. And whan ye ryde, than woll I ryde—onles that ye tary 30
overlonge; than woll I take myne horse. Therefore I pray you, Sir
Dynadan, abyde ye and ryde with us."

¶"Faythfully," seyde Sir Dynadan, "I woll nat abyde, for I have
suche a talente[1] to se Sir Trystram that I may nat abyde longe from
hym." 35

¶"A, Sir Dynadan!" seyde Sir Palomydes, "now do I undirstonde
that ye love my mortall enemy—and therefore how sholde I truste
you?"

¶"Wyte you well," seyde Sir Dynadan, "I love my lorde Sir Trystram abovyn all othir knyghtes, and hym woll I serve and do 40
honoure."

¶"So shall I," seyde Sir Lameroke, "in all that I may with my
power." So on the morne Sir Dynadan rode unto the courte of Kynge
Arthur; and by the way as he rode he sawe where stoode an arraunte
knyght, and made hym redy for to juste. 45

¶"Nat so," seyde Sir Dynadan, "for I have no wyll to juste."

¶"Wyth me shall ye juste," seyde the knyght, "or that ye passe
this way."

1. I.e., desire.

¶"Sir, whether aske you justys of love othir of hate?"[2] The knyghte answerde and seyde, "Wyte you well I aske hit for loove and nat of hate." "Hit may well be," seyde Sir Dynadan, "but ye proffyr me harde love whan ye wolde juste with me wyth an harde speare! But, fayre knyght," seyde Sir Dynadan, "sytthyn ye woll juste with me, mete wyth me in the courte of Kynge Arthure, and there I shall juste wyth you." "Well," seyde the knyght, "sytthyn ye woll not juste wyth me, I pray you tell me your name."

"Sir Knyght, my name ys Sir Dynadan." "A, sir," seyde that knyght, "full well knowe I you for a good knyght and a jantyll—and wyte you well, sir, I love you hertyly." "Than shall here be no justys," seyde Syr Dynadan, "betwyxte us." So they departed, and the same day he com to Camelot where lay Kynge Arthure; and there he salewed the Kynge and the Quene, Sir Launcelot, and Sir Trystram. And all the courte was glad of Sir Dynadans commynge home, for he was jantyll, wyse, and a good knyght—and in aspeciall Sir Trystram loved Sir Dynadan passyngly well. Than the Kynge askyd Sir Dynadan what adventures he had sene. "Sir," seyde Sir Dynadan, "I have seyne many adventures, and of som Kynge Marke knowyth,[3] but nat all."

Than the Kynge herkened to Sir Dynadan, how he tolde that Sir Palomydes and he were byfore the castell of Morgan le Fay, and how Sir Lameroke toke the justys afore them, and how he forjusted twelve knyghtes, and of them foure he slew—and how aftir that "he smote downe Sir Palomydes and me bothe." "I may nat belyve that," seyde the Kynge, "for Sir Palomydes is a passynge good knyght." "That is verry trouthe," seyde Sir Dynadan, "but yett I sawe hym bettyr preved hande-for-hande."[4] And than he tolde the Kynge of all that batayle, and how Sir Palomydes was the more wayker and sorer was hurte, and more he loste of his blood than Sir Lameroke. "And withoute doute," seyde Sir Dynadan, "had the batayle lasted ony lenger, Sir Palomydes had be slayne." "A, Jesu," seyde Kynge Arthure, "this is to me a grete mervayle!"

¶"Sir," seyde Sir Trystram, "mervayle ye nothynge thereof, for, at myne advyce, there is nat a valyaunter knyght in the worlde lyvynge—for I know his myght. And now woll I say you, I was never so wery of knyght but yf hit were my lorde Sir Launcelot; and there is no knyght in the worlde excepte Sir Launcelot that I wolde ded so well as Sir Lamerok." "So God me helpe," seyde the Kynge, "I wolde fayne that knyght Sir Lamerok wolde com to this courte."

¶"Sir," serdde Sir Dynadan, "he woll be here in shorte space, and Sir Palomydes bothe, but I feare me that Sir Palomydes may nat yett travayle."

¶So wythin three dayes after, the Kynge lete make a justenynge at a pryory frome the justys,[5] and there made them redy many knyghtes of the Rounde Table. And Sir Gawayne and his bretherne,

---

2. *Of love othir of hate:* i.e., out of friendly sport or a desire to kill.
3. *And of som Kynge Marke knowyth:* and I know of some concerning King Mark.
4. *Bettyr preved hande-for-hande:* bettered in hand-to-hand combat.
5. *Frome the justys:* a distance away from the tournament.

they made them redy to juste; but Sir Launcelot, Syr Trystram, nother
Sir Dynadan wolde nat juste, but suffyrd Sir Gawayne for the love of
Kynge Arthure wyth his bretherne to wynne the degré yf they myght.
So on the morn they apparayled hem to juste. Sir Gawayne and his
foure bretherne, they ded grete dedis of armys, and Sir Ector de   5
Marys ded mervaylously well. But Sir Gawayne passed all that fely-
ship, wherefore Kynge Arthure and all the knyghtes gave Sir Gawayne
the honoure at the begynnynge.

   Ryght so was Kynge Arthure ware of a knyght and two squyers
that com oute of a foreystis syde wyth a covyrd shylde of lethir.[6]   10
Than he cam in [slyly], and hurled here and there; and anone with
one speare he had smyttyn downe two knyghtes of the Rounde
Table. And so wyth his hurtelynge he loste the coverynge of his
shylde; than was the Kynge and all ware that he bare a rede shylde.
"A, Jesu," seyde Kynge Arthure, "se where rydyth a strong knyght—   15
he wyth the rede shylde!" And there was a noyse and a grete cry:
"Beware the knyght with the rede shylde!"

   So wythin a lytyll whyle he had overthrowyn three bretherne of
Sir Gawaynes. "So God me helpe," seyde Kynge Arthur, "mesemyth
yondir is the beste juster that ever I sawe." So he loked aboute and   fol.250v   20
saw hym encountir with Sir Gawayne; and he smote hym downe
with so grete force that he made his horse to avoyde his sadyll.

   ⁋"How now?" seyde the Kynge to Sir Gawayne, "methynkyth ye have a falle! Well were me and[7] I knew what knyght he
were with the rede shylde." "I know hym well inowghe," seyde Sir   25
Dynadan, "but as at this tyme ye shall nat know his name." "Be my
hede," seyde Sir Trystram, "he justyth better than Sir Palomydes—
and yf ye lyste to know, his name is Sir Lameroke de Galys." And as
they stood thus, they saw Sir Gawayne and he encountyrd togedir
agayne; and there he smote Sir Gawayne from his horse and brused   30
hym sore—and in the syght of Kynge Arthure he smote downe
twenty knyghtes besyde Sir Gawayne; and so clyerly was the pryce
yevyn hym as a knyght piereles.

   Than, slyly and mervaylously,[8] Sir Lameroke wythdrewe hym from
all the felyshyp into the foreystys syde: all this aspyed Kynge   35
Arthure, for his yghe went never frome hym. Than the Kynge, Sir
Launcelot, and Sir Trystram and Sir Dynadan toke there hakeneyes
and rode streyte aftir the good knyght, Sir Lameroke de Galis, and
there founde hym. And thus seyde the Kynge: "A, fayre knyght,
well be ye founde!"   40

   ⁋Whan he sawe the Kynge, he put of his helme and salewed
hym. And whan he sawe Sir Trystram, he alyght adowne of his horse
and ran to [hym to] take hym by the [thyes].[9]

   ⁋But Sir Trystram wolde nat suffir hym, but he alyght or that he
cam, and ayther toke othir in armys and made grete joy of other.   45
Than the Kynge was gladde, and so was all the felyshyp of the

6. *Covyrd shylde of lethir:* a shield cloaked in leather.
7. I.e., if.
8. I.e., with marvelous stealth.
9. Lamerok here makes a gesture of submission.

Rounde Table, excepte Sir Gawayne and his bretherne—and whan
they wyste that hit was Sir Lameroke, they had grete despyte of hym,
and were wondirly wrothe wyth hym that he had put hym to such
a dishonoure that day.

⁋Than he called to hym prevaly in counceyle all his bretherne,
and to them seyde thus: "Fayre bretherne, here may ye se: whom
that we hate, Kynge Arthure lovyth, and whom that we love, he
hatyth.[1] And wyte you well, my fayre bretherne, that this Sir Lamerok woll nevyr love us, because we slew his fadir, Kynge Pellynor—
for we demed that he slew oure fadir, Kynge Lotte of Orkenay. And
for the deth of Kynge Pellynor, Sir Lameroke ded us a shame to oure
modir; therefore I woll be revenged." "Sir," seyde Sir Gawaynes
bretherne, "lat se;[2] devyse how ye woll be revenged, and ye shall
fynde us redy."

⁋"Well," seyde Sir Gawayne, "holde ye styll, and we shall aspye
oure tyme."

⁋Now passe we on oure mater, and leve we Sir Gawayne and
speke we of Kynge Arthure, that on a day seyde unto Kynge Marke,
"Sir, I pray you, gyff me a gyffte that I shall aske you."

⁋"Sir," seyde Kynge Marke, "I woll gyff you what gyffte I may
gyff you."

⁋"Sir, gramercy," seyde Kynge Arthure, "this woll I aske you: that
ye be good lorde[3] unto Sir Trystram, for he is a man of grete honoure; and that ye woll take hym with you into Cornwayle and lat
hym se his fryndis, and there cherysh hym for my sake."

⁋"Sir," seyde Kynge Marke, "I promyse you be my fayth and by
the fayth that I owe unto God and to you, I shall worship hym for
youre sake all that I can or may."

⁋Sir," seyde Kynge Arthure, "and I woll forgyff you all the evyll
wyll that ever I ought you, and ye swere that uppon a booke afore
me."

⁋"Wyth a good wyll," seyde Kynge Marke. And so he there sware
uppon a booke afore hym, and all his knyghtes; and therewith
Kynge Marke and Sir Trystram toke ayther othir by the hondis harde
knytte togydyrs. (But for all this, Kynge Marke thought falsely, as
hit preved aftir; for he put Sir Trystram in preson, and cowardly
wolde have slayne hym.)[4]

⁋Than, sone aftyr, Kynge Marke toke his leve to ryde into Cornwayle; and Sir Trystram made hym redy to ryde with hym—whereof
the moste party of the Rounde Table were wrothe and hevy. And
in especiall Sir Launcelot and Sir Lameroke and Sir Dynadan were
wrothe oute of mesure, for well they wyste that Kynge Marke wolde
sle or destroy Sir Trystram. "Alas," seyde Sir Dynadan, "that my lorde
Sir Trystram shall departe!" And Sir Trystram toke suche a sorow
that he was amased.[5]

fol.251r   5

10

15

[22]

20

25

30

35

fol.251v

40

45

1. Gawayne's speech marks a rift within the court of King Arthur, which will eventually lead
   to its downfall; cf. n. 7, p. 225, *The Tale of Sir Launcelot and Quene Gwenyvere* (p. 588)
   and *The Dethe of Arthur* (p. 646).
2. Let us see.
3. I.e., feudal superior and protector.
4. See p. 401.
5. I.e., out of his wits.

❡"Alas," seyde Sir **Launcelot** unto Kynge **Arthure**, "what have ye done? For ye shall lose the man of moste worshyp that ever cam into youre courte."

❡"Sir, hit was his owne desyre," seyde Kynge **Arthure**, "and therefore I myght nat do wythall,[6] for I have all that I can and made them at accorde."

❡"Acorde?" seyde Sir **Launcelotte**. "Now fye on that accorde! For ye shall here that he shall destroy Sir **Trystram** other put hym into preson, for he is the moste cowarde and the vylaunste kynge and knyght that is now lyvvynge." And therewith Sir **Launcelot** departed, and cam to Kynge **Marke** and sayde to hym thus: "Sir kynge, wyte thou well the good knyght Sir **Trystram** shall go with the. Beware, I rede the, of treson, for and thou myschyff that knyght by ony maner of falsehode or treson, by the fayth I awghe to God and to the order of knyghthode, I shall sle the myne[7] owne hondis!" "Sir **Launcelot**, overmuch have ye sayde unto me, and I have sworne and seyde over-largely afore Kynge **Arthure**, in hyrynge[8] of all hys knyghtes, [that I shal not sle nor bitraye hym; it were to me overmoche shame] to breke my promyse."

❡"Ye sey well," seyde Sir **Launcelot**, "but ye ar called so false and full of felony that no man may beleve you:

❡"Pardé, hit is knowyn well for what cause ye cam into this contrey, and for none other cause but to sle Syr[9] [Tristram." Soo with grete dole Kynge **Marke** and Sir **Tristram** rode togyders; for hit was by Sir Tristrams wil and his meanes to goo with Kyng **Marke**— and all was for the entente to see **La Beale Isoud**, for without the syghte of her Syr **Tristram** myght not endure.

Now torne we ageyne unto Sire **Lamorak** and speke we of his bretheren: Syr **Tor**, whiche was Kynge **Pellenors** fyrst sone and bygoten of **Aryes** wyf, the couherd, for he was a bastard; and Sire **Aglovale** was his fyrste sone begoten in wedlok; Syre **Lamorak**, **Dornar**, **Percyvale**, these were his sones to[1] in wedlok. [23]

❡Soo whanne Kynge **Marke** and Sire **Tristram** were departed from the courte there was made grete dole and sorowe for the departynge of Sir **Tristram**. Thenne the Kynge and his knyghtes made no manere of joyes eyghte dayes after. And atte eyghte dayes ende ther cam to the courte a knyghte with a yonge squyer with hym; and whanne this knyghte was unarmed, he went to the Kynge and requyred hym to make the yonge squyer a knyghte. "Of what lygnage is he come?" said Kynge **Arthur**. "Syre," sayd the knyght, "he is the sone of Kyng **Pellenore**, that dyd you somtyme good servyse, and he is broder unto Syr **Lamorak de Galys**, the good knyghte." "Wel," sayd the Kynge, "for what cause desyre ye that of me, that I shold make hym knyghte?" "Wete you wel, my lord the kynge, that this yonge squyer is broder to me as wel as to Sir **Lamorak**, and my name is **Aglavale**." "Syre **Aglovale**," sayd **Arthur**, "for the love of

---

6. *I myght nat do wythall:* i.e., I could not do anything.
7. I.e., with my.
8. I.e., the hearing.
9. A folio is missing from the Winchester MS at this point, requiring a moderately extensive substitution from Caxton.
1. I.e., too, also.

Sire Lamorak and for his faders love, he shalle be made knyghte tomorowe.

⸿"Now telle me," said Arthur, "what is his name?" "Syre," sayd the knyght, "his name is Percyvale de Galys." Soo on the morne the Kynge made hym knyght in Camelott—but the Kynge and alle the knyghtes thoughte hit wold be longe or² that he preved a good knyghte.

⸿Thenne at the dyner, whanne the Kynge was set at the table, and every knyght after he was of prowesse,³ the Kyng commaunded hym to be sette amonge meane knyghtes; and soo was Sire Percyvale sette as the Kynge commaunded. Thenne was there a mayden in the Quenes court that was come of hyhe blood, and she was domme and never spak word. Ryght so she cam streyght into the halle, and went unto Sir Percyvale, and toke hym by the hand and said alowde, that the Kyng and all the knyghtes myght here hit, "Aryse, Syr Percyvale, the noble knyght—and Goddes knyght—and go with me." And soo he dyd; and there she broughte hym to the ryght syde of the Sege Perillous⁴ and said, "Fair knyghte, take here thy sege, for that sege apperteyneth to the and to none other." Ryght soo she departed and asked⁵ a preste; and as she was confessid and houseld, thenne she dyed. Thenne the Kynge and alle the courte made grete joye of Syr Percyvale.⁶

Now torne we unto Sir Lamorak, that moche was there preysed. [24] Thenne by the meane of Sir Gawayn and his bretheren, they sente for her⁷ moder there besydes, fast by a castel besyde Camelot; and alle was to that entente to slee Sir Lamorak. The Quene of Orkeney was there but a whyle, but Sir Lamorak wyst of their beynge⁸ and was ful fayne; and for to make an ende of this matere, he sente unto her, and ther betwixe them was a nyght assygned that Sir Lamorak shold come to her. Therof] was ware Sir Gaherys, fol.253r and rode afore the same nyght, and wayted uppon Sir Lamerok; and than he sy where he cam rydynge all armed, and where he alyght and tyed his horse to a prevay postren, and so he wente into a parler and unarmed hym. And than he wente unto the quenys bed, and she made of hym passynge grete joy, and he of her agayne, for ayther lovid other passynge sore. So whan Sir Gaherys sawe his tyme, he cam to there beddis syde all armed, wyth his swerde naked, and suddaynly he gate his modir by the heyre and strake of her hede.

⸿Whan Sir Lameroke sawe the blood daysshe uppon hym all hote—whyche was the bloode that he loved passyng well—wyte

2. I.e., before.
3. *After he was of prowesse:* (seated) according to his prowess.
4. For Merlin's early prophecy concerning the occupancy of this seat, see p. 65.
5. I.e., requested.
6. The authority of the dumb maiden in effecting this change in the court's opinion comes from her evident proximity to divine power: first, in miraculously gaining the power of speech; second, in speaking exclusively of Perceval's status once given that power; and third, in preparing for her death, which comes immediately, as if to suggest that she had satisfactorily completed God's mission.
7. I.e., their.
8. I.e., being there.

you well he was sore abaysshed and dismayed of that dolerous syght. And therewithall Sir Lamerok lepte oute of the bed in his shurte as a knyght dismayed, saynge thus: "A, Sir Gaherys! Knyght of the Table Rounde, fowle and evyll have ye done, and to you grete shame! Alas, why have ye slayne youre modir that bare you? For with more ryght ye shulde have slayne me I"

¶"The offence haste thou done" seyde Sir Gaherys, "natwithstondynge a man is borne to offir his servyse;[9] but yett sholdyst thou beware with whom thou medelyst, for thou haste put my bretherne and me to a shame. And thy fadir slew oure fadir; and thou to ly by oure modir is to muche shame for us to suffir—and as for thy fadir, Kynge Pellynor, my brothir Sir Gawayne and I slew hym."

¶"Ye ded the more wronge," seyde Sir Lamerok, "for my fadir slew nat your fadir: hit was Balyn le Saveage.[1] And as yett my fadyrs deth is nat revenged."

¶"Leve tho wordys!" seyde Sir Gaherys, "for and thou speke vylaunsly, I woll sle the; but bycause thou arte naked I am ashamed to sle the. But wyte thou well, in what place I may gete the, I woll sle the. And now is my modir quytte of[2] the, for she shal never shame her chyldryn—and therefore hyghe the and wythdrawe the and take thyne armour, that thou were gone."

¶So Sir Lameroke saw there was none other boote, but faste armed hym and toke his horse and roode his way, makynge grete sorow. But for shame and sorowe he wolde nat ryde to Kynge Arthurs courte, but rode another way. But whan hit was knowyn that Sir Gaherys had slayne his modir, the Kynge was wrothe and commaunded hym to go oute of his courte. Wyte you well Sir Gawayne was wrothe that Sir Gaherys had slayne his modir and lete Sir Lamerok ascape. And for this mater was the Kynge passynge wrothe, and many other knyghtes.

¶"Sir," seyde Sir Launcelot, "here is a grete myscheff fallyn by fellony and by forecaste[3] [treason], that your syster is thus shamfully i-slayne; and I dare say hit was wrought by treson—and I dare say also that ye shall lose that good knyght, Sir Lamerok. And I wote well, and Sir Trystram wyste hit, he wolde never com within your courte." "God deffende," seyde Kynge Arthur, "that I sholde lese Sir Lamerok [or Sir Tristram, for thenne tweyne of my chyef knyghtes of the Table Round were gone."] "Yes," seyde Sir Launcelot, ["I am sure ye shalle lese Sir Lamerok,] for Sir Gawayne and his bretherne woll sle hym by one meane other by another." "That shall I lette,"[4] seyde Kynge Arthur.

¶Now leve we of Sir Lamerok, and speke we of Sir Gawayne his[5] bretherne, Sir Aggravayne and Sir Mordred. As they rode on their

---

9. I.e., homage as a lover.
1. Lamerok is mistaken; according to Malory's own account earlier (p. 65), Lamerok's father, Pellinore, does in fact kill King Lot.
2. *Quytte of*: repaid for.
3. I.e., premeditated.
4. I.e., prevent, hinder.
5. *Sir Gawayne his*: Sir Gawain's.

adventures they mette wyth a knyght flyynge sore wounded, and
they asked hym what tydynges.

¶"Fayre knyghtes," sayde he, "here commyth a knyght aftir me
that woll sle me!" So wyth that come Sir Dynadan fast rydynge to
them, by adventure,[6] but he wolde promyse them none helpe; but
Sir Aggravayne and Sir Mordred promysed to rescowe hym. And
therewithall come that knyght streyte unto them, and anone he
profyrde to juste. That sawe Sir Mordred, and rode to hym and
strake hym; but he smote Sir Mordred over his horse tayle. That
sawe Sir Aggravayne, [and streyghte he rode toward that knyght;]   fol.254r   10
and ryght so as he served Sir Mordred, so he served Sir Aggravayne—
and [said], "Wyte you well, syrrys bothe, that I am Sir Brewnys
Saunje Pité that hath done thus to you." And yet he rode over Sir
Aggravayne fyve or six tymes.

¶Whan Sir Dynadan saw this, he muste nedis juste with hym for   15
shame. And so Sir Dynadan and he encountyrd togydyrs; but wyth
pure strengthe Sir Dynadan smote hym over hys horse tayle. Than
he toke his horse and fledde, for he was on foote one of the
valyaunte knyghtes in Arthurs dayes, and a grete dystroyer of all
good knyghtes. Than rode Sir Dynadan unto Sir Mordred and unto   20
Sir Aggravayne. "Sir knyght, well have ye done, and well have ye
revenged us, wherefore we pray you tell us your name."

¶"Fayre syrs, ye ought to knowe my name, whyche is called Sir
Dynadan." Whan they undirstode that hit was Sir Dynadan, they
were more wrothe than they were before, for they hated hym oute   25
of mesure bycause of Sir Lameroke (for Sir Dynadan had suche a
custom that he loved all good knyghtes that were valyaunte, and
he hated all tho that were destroyers of good knyghtes—and there
was none that hated Sir Dynadan but tho that ever were called
murtherers).   30

Than spake the hurte knyght that Brewnes Saunje Pité had chaced—his name was Dalan—and sayde, "Yf thou be Sir Dynadan,
thou slewe my fadir." "Hit myght well be so," seyde Sir Dynadan,
"but than hit was in my deffence and at his requeste." "Be my
hede," seyde Dalyn, "thou shalt dye therefore!" And therewith he   35
dressed his speare and his shylde; and, to make shorte tale, Sir
Dynadan smote hym downe of his horse, that his necke was nye
brokyn—and in the same wyse he smote Sir Mordred and Sir Aggravayne. (And aftir, in the Queste of the Sankgreal, cowardly and   fol.254v
felonsly they slew Sir Dynadan, whyche was a [grete dammage, for   40
he was a] grete bourder and a passynge good knyght.)[7]

And so Sir Dynadan rode to a castall that hyght Beal Valet, and
there he founde Sir Palamydes, that was nat hole of the wounde
that Sir Lamerok gaff hym; and there Sir Dynadan tolde Sir Palomydes
all the tydynges that he harde and sawe of Sir Trystram, and how   45
he was gone with Kynge Marke—"and wyth hym he hath all his
wyll and desyre." Therewith Sir Palomydes wexed wrothe, for he

---

6. *By adventure:* by chance, as it happened.
7. Malory does not mention Dynadan's death again.

loved **La Beale Isode**, and than he wyste well that Sir **Trystram** enjoyed her.

¶Now leve we Sir **Palomydes** and Sir **Dynadan** in the castell of **Beale Valet**, and turne we agayne unto Kynge **Arthure**. There cam a knyght oute of Cornwayle—his name was Sir **Fergus**, a felow of the Rounde Table—and there he tolde the Kynge and Sir **Launcelot** good tydyngis of Sir **Trystram** (and there was brought goodly letters), and how he leffte hym in the castell of **Tyntagyll**. Than cam a damesell that brought goodly lettyrs unto Kynge **Arthure** and unto Sir **Launcelot**; and there she had passynge good chere of the Kynge and of the Quene and of Sir **Launcelot**—and so they wrote goodly lettyrs agayne.[8] But Sir **Launcelot** bade ever Sir **Trystram** beware of Kynge **Marke**, for ever he called hym in hys lettirs Kynge **Foxe**, as who[9] saythe, he faryth allwey with wylys and treson.

¶Whereof Sir **Trystram** in his herte thanked Sir **Launcelot**. Than the damesell wente unto La Beale **Isode** and bare hir lettirs frome the Kyng and from Sir **Launcelot**—whereof she was in grete joy. "Fayre "damesell," seyde **Isode**, "how faryth my lorde **Arthure** and Quene **Gwenyver** and the noble knyght Sir **Launcelot**?" She answerd, and to make shorte tale, "Muche the bettir that ye and Sir **Trystram** bene in joy." "God rewarde them," seyde **Isode**, "for Sir **Trystram** hath suffirde grete payne for me, and I for hym."

¶So the damesell departed and brought the lettirs to Kynge **Marke**; and whan he had rad them and undirstonde them, he was wroth wyth Sir **Trystram**, for he demed that he had sente the damesell to Kynge **Arthure**. For Kynge **Arthure** and Sir **Launcelot** in a maner thretned Kynge **Marke** in his letters, and as Kynge **Marke** red this lettyrs he demede treson by Sir **Trystram**. "Damesell," seyde Kynge **Marke**, "woll ye ryde agayne and beare lettyrs frome me unto Kynge **Arthure**?" "Sir" she seyde, "I woll be at youre commaundement to ryde whan ye wyll."

¶"Ye sey well," seyde the kynge. "Com ye agayne tomorne and fecche youre lettyrs." Than she departed and cam to La Beall **Isode** and to Sir **Trystram** and tolde hem how she sholde ryde agayne with lettyrs to Kynge **Arthure**. "Than we pray you," seyde they, "that whan ye have resceyved youre lettyrs, that ye wolde com by us, that we may se the prevyté of youre lettirs." "All that I may do, madame, ye wote well I muste do for Sir **Trystram**, for I have be longe his owne maydyn."

¶So on the morne the damesell wente unto Kynge **Marke** to have resceyved his lettyrs and to departe.

¶"Damesell, I am nat avysed," seyde Kynge **Marke**, "as at this tyme to sende my lettyrs." But so pryvayly and secretely he sente lettirs unto Kynge **Arthure** and unto Quene **Gwenyver** and unto Sir **Launcelot**. So the varlet departed, and founde the Kynge and the Quene in Walys, at **Carlyon**. And as the Kynge and the Quene was at Masse the varlet cam wyth the lettyrs; and whan Masse was

8. I.e., in reply.
9. I.e., whoever.

done the Kynge and the Quene opened the lettirs prevayly. And to
begyn, the kyngis lettirs spake wondirly shorte[1] unto Kynge Arthur,
and bade hym entermete with hymself and wyth hys wyff, and of
his knyghtes, for he was able to rule his wyff and his knyghtes.[2]

¶Whan Kynge Arthure undirstode the lettir, he mused of many
thynges, and thought of his systyrs wordys, Quene Morgan le Fay,
that she had seyde betwyxte Quene Gwenyver and Sir Launcelot;[3] and
in this thought he studyed a grete whyle.

¶Than he bethought hym agayne how his owne sistir was his
enemy, and that she hated the Quene and Sir Launcelot to the deth,
and so he put that all oute of his thought. Than Kynge Arthur rad
the letter agayne, and the lattir clause seyde that Kynge Marke toke
Sir Trystram for his mortall enemy; wherefore he put Kynge Arthure
oute of doute he wolde be revenged of Sir Trystram.

Than was Kynge Arthure wrothe wyth Kynge Marke. And whan
Quene Gwenyver rad hir lettir and undirstode hyt, she was wrothe
oute of mesure, for the letter spake shame by her and by Sir Launcelot; and so prevayly she sente the lettir unto Sir Launcelot. And
whan he wyste the entente of the letter, he was so wrothe that he
layde hym downe on his bed to slepe—whereof Sir Dynadan
was ware, for hit was his maner to be prevy with[4] all good knyghtes;
and as Sir Launcelot slepte, he stale the lettir oute of his honde
and rad hit worde by worde, and than he made grete sorow for
angir.

And Sir Launcelot so wakened, and wente to a wyndowe and redde
the letter agayne, whyche made hym angry. "Syr," seyde Sir Dynadan, "wherefore be ye angry? I pray you, discover your harte to me,
for, pardé, ye know well that I wolde you but well, for I am a poore
knyght and a servyture unto you and to all good knyghtes. For
though I be nat of worship myself, I love all tho that bene of worship." "Hit is trouthe," seyde Sir Launcelot, "ye ar a trusty knyght,
and for grete truste I wol shewe you my counceyle."

And whan Sir Dynadan undirstoode hit well, he seyde, "Sir, thus
is my counceyle: sette you ryght naught by thes thretenynges, for
Kynge Marke is so vylaunce a knyght that by fayre speche shall
never man gete ought[5] of hym. But ye shall se what I shall do: I
woll make a lay for hym, and whan hit is made I shall make an
harpere to syng hit afore hym." And so anone he wente and made
hit, and taught hit to an harpere that hyght Elyot; and whan he
cowde hit, he taught hit to many harpers. And so by the wyll of
Kynge Arthure and of Sir Launcelot, the harpers wente into Walys
and into Cornwayle to synge the lay that Sir Dynadan made by
Kynge Marke—whyche was the worste lay that ever harper songe
with harpe or with ony other instrument!

fol.255v

[27]

5

10

15

20

25

fol.256r

30

35

40

---

1. I.e., curtly.
2. *Entermete with hymself . . . to rule his wyff and his knyghtes:* i.e., mind his own business.
3. For Morgan's accusation that Gwenyvere and Launcelot, as lovers, have deceived Arthur,
   see p. 336.
4. *prevy with:* in the confidence of.
5. I.e., any satisfaction.

Now turne we agayne unto Sir Trystram and to Kynge Marke. Now as Sir Trystram was at a justys and at a turnemente, hit fortuned he was sore hurte bothe with a speare and with a swerde (but yet allwayes he wan the gré). And for to repose hym, he wente to a good knyght that dwelled in Cornwayle in a castell, whos name was Sir Dynas the Senesciall. So by myssefortune there come oute of Syssoyne a grete numbre of men of armys, and an hedeous oste, and they entyrd nye the castell of Tyntagyll; and hir captens name was Sir Elyas, a good man of armys.

¶Whan Kynge Marke undirstood his enemyes were entyrd into his londe, he made grete dole and sorow—for in no wyse by his good wylle Kynge Marke wolde nat sende for Sir Trystram, for he hated hym dedly. So whan his counceyle was com, they devysed and caste many perellys of the grete strengthe of hir enemyes; and than they concluded all at onys, and seyde thus unto Kynge Marke: "Sir, wyte you well ye muste sende for Sir Trystram, the good knygyht, other ellys they woll never be overcom; for by Sir Trystram they muste be foughtyn withall—other ellys we rowe ayenste the streme."

¶"Well," seyde Kynge Marke, "I woll do by youre counceyle." But yette he was full lothe thereto, but nede constrayned hym to sende for hym; and so he was sente fore in all haste that myght be, that he sholde com to Kynge Marke. And whan he undirstoode that he had sente for hym, he bestrode a soffte ambular and rode to Kynge Marke; and whan he was com the kynge seyde thus: "Fayre nevew, Sir Trystram, this is all: here be com oure enemyes off Sessoyne that ar here nyhonde; and withoute taryynge they muste be mette wyth shortly, other ellys they woll destroy this contrey."

¶"Sir," seyde Sir Trystram, "wyte you well, all my power is at your commaundement:

¶"But, sir, this[6] eyght dayes I may beare none armys, for my woundis be nat hole; and by that day I shall do what I may."

¶"Ye say well," seyde Kynge Marke. "Than go ye agayne and repose you and make you freysh; and I shall go mete the Sessoynes with all my power." So the kynge departed unto Tyntagyll, and Sir Trystram wente to repose hym. And the kynge made a grete oste and departed them in three: the fyrste parte ledde Sir Dynas the Senescyall, and Sir Andret led the secunde parte, and Sir Arguys led the thirde parte—and he was of the bloode of Kynge Marke. And the Sessoynes had three grete batayles[7] and many good men of armys. And so Kynge Marke, by the advyce of his knyghtes, yssued oute of the castell of Tyntagyll upon his enemyes. And Sir Dynas, the good knyght, rode oute afore and slewe two good knyghtes his[8] owne hondis.

And than began the batayles; and there was mervaylous brekynge of spearys and smytynge of swerdys, and kylled downe many good knyghtes—and ever was Sir Dynas the Senesciall beste of

[28]

fol.256v

fol.257r

6. I.e., for the next.
7. I.e., battalions.
8. I.e., with his.

Kynge Markys party. And thus the batayle endured longe with grete
mortalyté; but at the laste Kynge Marke and Sir Dynas—were they
never so loth—they were dryvyn to the castall of Tyntagyll with
grete slaughter of people. And the Syssoynes folowed on faste, that
ten of them were getyn[9] wythin the yatys, and foure slayne wyth   5
the portecolyes.[1] Than Kynge Marke sente for Sir Trystram by a
varlet agayne that tolde hym of all the mortalyté. Than he sente
the varlet agayne and bade hym, "Telle Kynge Marke that I woll
com as sone as I am hole, for arste I may do hym no goode."

Than Kynge Marke hadde hys answere; and therewith cam Elyas,   10
and bade the kynge yelde up the castell—"for ye may not holde hit
nowhyle." "Sir Elyas," seyde Kynge Marke, "and yf I be nat the
sonner rescowed, I muste yelde up this castell."

¶And anone the kynge sente ayen for rescow to Sir Trystram.
And by that tyme Sir Trystram was nyghe hole, and he had getyn   15
hym ten good knyghtes of Kynge Arthurs; and wyth hem he rode
unto Tyntagyll. And whan he sawe the grete oste of Sessoynes, he
mervayled wondir gretly. And than Sir Trystram rode by the woddys
and by the dychis as secretely as he myght, tyll he cam ny the gatis.
And anone there dressed a knyght to hym—   20

¶Whan he sawe that Sir Trystram wolde have entird: than Sir
Trystram ran to hym and smote hym downe dede; and so he served
three mo—and everyche of these ten knyghtes slewe a man of
armys. So Sir Trystram entyrde into the yatys of Tyntagyll; and whan
Kynge Marke wyste that Sir Trystram was com, he was glad of his   25
commynge, and so was all the felyship, and of hym they made grete
joy. And on the morne Elyas the captayne cam and bade Kynge
Marke, "Com oute and do batayle, for now the good knyght Sir
Trystram is entyrd—and hit woll be shame," seyde Elyas, "for to
kepe[2] thy wallys."   30

¶Whan Kynge Marke undirstoode this, he was wrothe and seyde
no worde, but wente to Sir Trystram and axed hym his counceyle.
"Sir," seyde Sir Trystram, "woll ye that I gyff hym his answere?"

¶"I woll well," seyde Kynge Marke. Than Sir Trystram seyde thus
to the messengere: "Beare thy lorde worde frome the kynge and   35
me, and sey how that we woll do batayle tomorne wyth hym in the
playne fylde."

¶"Sir, what is your name?" seyde the messyngere. "Sir, wyte
thou well my name is Sir Trystram de Lyones." So therewithall the
messyngere departed and tolde his lorde, Elyas.   40

¶"Sir," seyde Sir Trystram, "I pray of you, gyff me leve to have
the rule[3] of youre oste tomorowe." "Sir, I pray you take the rule,"
seyde Kynge Marke. Than Sir Tristram lete devyse the batayle[4] in
what maner that they sholde be; so he lete his oste be departed in
six batayles, and ordayned Sir Dynas the Seneschall to have the   45

---

9. *Were getyn:* had gotten.
1. *Slayne wyth the portecolyes:* i.e., crushed by the sliding grille of the gateway.
2. I.e., stay within.
3. I.e., command.
4. *Lete devyse the batayle:* had the army divided strategically.

voward, and other good knyghtes to rule the remenaunte. And the
same nyght Sir **Trystram** gart bren[5] all the **Sessoynes** shyppis unto
the colde water; and anone, as **Elyas** wyst that, he seyde hit was of
Sir **Trystrams** doynge—"for he castyth that we shall never ascape,
modyrs sonne[6] of us! Therefore, fayre felowys, fyght frely tomorow,
and myscomfort you nought for one knyght, for though he be the
beste knyght of the worlde he may nat have ado with us all."

Than they ordayned their batayles in foure partyes, wondirly well
apparayled and garnysshed with men of armys. Thus they wythin
issued oute, and they wythoute sette frely uppon them; and there
Sir **Dynas** ded grete dedis of armys. Natforthan Sir **Dynas** and his
felyshyp were put to the wors. So with that cam Sir **Trystram** and
slew two knyghtes with one speare; than he slew on the ryght
honde and on the lyffte honde, that men mervayled that ever he
myght do suche dedis of armys. And than he myght se somtyme
the batayle was dryvyn a bow-draught frome the castell, and somtyme hit was at the yatys of the castell.

Than cam **Elyas** the captayne, russhynge here and there, and
smote Kynge **Marke** so sore uppon the helme that he made hym to
avoyde his sadyll—and than Sir **Dynas** gate Kynge **Marke** agayne to
horsebacke. And therewyth cam Syr **Trystram** lyke a lyon, and there
he mette wyth Sir **Elyas**, and he smote hym so sore on the helme
that he avayded his sadyll. And thus they fought tylle hit was nyght;
and for grete slaughtir of peple and for wounded peple, every party
withdrew to theire resseyte.

¶And whan Kynge **Marke** was com wythin the castell of **Tyntagyll**
he lacked of his knyghtes an hondred; and they withoute lacked
two hondred. Than they serched the wounded men on bothe partyes, and than they wente to counceyle—and wyte you well, eythir
party were loth to fyght more, so that aythir myght ascape with
their worshyp.

¶Whan **Elyas** the captayne undirstoode the deth of his men, he
made grete dole; also, whan he knew that they were loth to go to
batayle agayne, he was wrothe oute off mesure. Than Elyas sente
unto Kynge **Marke** in grete dispyte uppon hede whether[7] he wolde
fynde a knyght that wolde fyght with hym body-for-body; and yf
that he myght sle Kynge **Markis** knyght, he to have the trewayge of
Cornwayle yerely—"and yf that his knyght sle myne, I fully releace
my clayme for ever." Than the messyngre departed unto Kynge
Marke and tolde hym how that his lorde **Elyas** had sent hym worde
to fynde a knyght to do batayle wyth hym body-for-body.

¶Whan Kynge **Marke** undirstood the messynge, he bade hym
abyde and he sholde have his answere. Than callyd he all the [bar-
onage] togydir to wyte what was beste counceyle, and they seyde
all at onys, "To fyght in a fylde we have no luste, for had nat bene
the proues of Sir **Trystram**, hit hadde bene lykly that we never
sholde have scaped; and therefore, sir, as we deme, hit were well

fol.258r

fol.258v

5. *Gart bren*: caused to have burned.
6. *Modyrs sonne*: i.e., not one.
7. *Uppon hede*: malice aforethought. *Whether*: i.e., asking whether.

done to fynde a knyght that wolde do batayle wyth hym, for he knyghtly proferyth."[8]

¶Natforthan, whan all this was seyde, they coude fynde no knyght that wolde do batayle with hym.

¶"Sir kynge," seyde they all, "here is no knyght that dare fyght with Elyas." "Alas," seyde Kynge Marke, "than am I shamed and uttirly distroyed—onles that my nevew Sir Trystram wolde take the batayle uppon hym." "Sir, wyte you well," they seyde all, "he had yesterday overmuche on hande, and he is wery and travayled, and sore wounded."

¶"Where is he?" seyde Kynge Marke. Than one answeryd and sayde, "Sir, he lyeth in his bedde for to repose hym." "Alas," seyde Kynge Marke, "but I have the succour of my nevew Sir Trystram, I am utterly destroyed for ever!" And therewithall one wente to Sir Trystram there he lay, and tolde hym what Kynge Marke seyde; and therewith Sir Trystram arose lyghtly and put on hym a longe gowne, and cam afore the kynge and the lordis. And whan he saw them so dismayed, he axed them what tydynges.

¶"Never worse," seyde the kynge—and therewyth he tolde hym all as ye have herde aforehonde. "And as for you," seyde the kynge, "we may aske no more of you for shame, for thorow youre hard-ynesse yestirday ye saved all oure lyvys."

¶"Sir," seyde Sir Trystram, "now I undirstonde ye wolde have my succour, and reson wolde[9] that I sholde do all that lyyth in me to do, savynge[1] my worshyp and my lyff, howbehit that I am sore brused and hurte; and sytthyn Sir Elyas proferyth so largely, I shall fyght with hym. Other ellys I woll be slayne in the fylde, othir ellys delyver Cornwayle of the olde trewage. And therefore lyghtly calle his messyngere, and he shall be answerde—for as yett my woundis bene grene, and they woll be sorer hereaftir sevennyght[2] than they be now—and therefore he shal have his answere, that I woll do batayle tomorne." Than was the messyngere brought before Kynge Marke.

"Now herkyn, my felow," seyde Sir Trystram, "go faste unto thy lorde, and bid hym make trewe assurance on his party for the trwayge,[3] as the kynge here shall on his party; and than tell thy lorde that Sir Trystram, Kynge Arthurs knyght and knyght of the Table Rounde, wyll as tomorne mete with thy lorde on horsebak to do batayle as longe as I may endure, and aftir that to do batayle with hym on foote to the uttraunce."[4]

The messyngere behylde Sir Trystram frome the top to the too, and therewythall he departed; and so he cam to his lorde and tolde hym how he was answered of Sir Trystram. And therewithall was

[30]

5

fol.259r

15

25

30

35

40

fol.259v

8. *For he knyghtly proferyth:* because Elyas makes his offer in an honorable fashion.
9. *Reson wolde:* i.e., reason dictates.
1. I.e., save losing.
2. I.e., a week from now.
3. *Make trewe assurance on his party for the trwayge:* make a binding agreement on his part concerning the tribute (should he lose).
4. I.e., to the death.

made ostage[5] on bothe partyes, and made hit as sure as hit myght
be, that whethirsomever party had the victory, so for to ende.[6] And
than were bothe ostys assembeled on bothe partyes the fylde
wythoute the castell of Tyntagyll; and there was none that bare
armys but Sir Trystram and Sir Elyas. So whan all the poyntemente
was made, they departed in sundir and cam togydirs wyth all the
myght that there horsys myght ren, that ayther knyght smote othir
so harde that bothe horsis and knyghtes wente to the erthe.

¶Natforthan they bothe arose lyghtly, and dressed their shyldis
on their sholdyrs with naked swerdys in their hondis; and they
daysshed togydirs so that hit semed a flamynge fyre aboute them.
Thus they traced and traversced, and hewe on helmys and hawberkes, and cut away many cantellys of their shyldis; and aythir
wounded othir passynge sore, that the hoote blood ran freyshly
uppon the erthe—and by than they had foughtyn the mowntenaunce of an owre.

¶Sir Trystram waxed faynte and wery, and bled sore, and gaff
sore abak.[7]

¶That sawe Sir Elyas, and folowed fyersly uppon hym, and
wounded hym in many placis. And ever Sir Trystram traced and
traverced and wente froward hym here and there, and coverde hym
with his shylde as he myght, all waykely, that all men sayde he was
overcom—for Sir Elyas had gyvyn hym twenty strokes ayenste one.
Than was there lawghynge amonge the Sessoynes party, and grete
dole on Kynge Markis party.

"Alas," seyde the kynge, "we ar all shamed and destroyed for
ever!" For, as the booke seyth, Sir Trystram was never so macched
but yf hit were of Sir Launcelot. Thus, as they stode and behylde
bothe partyes, that one party laughynge and the othir party
wepynge, Sir Trystram remembird hym of his lady, La Beale Isode,
that loked uppon hym, and how he was never lykly to com in hir
presence; than he pulled up his shylde that before hynge full lowe,
and than he dressed hym unto Sir Elyas and gaff hym many sad
strokys—twenty ayenst one—and all to-brake his shylde and his
hawberke, that the hote bloode ran downe as hit had bene rayne.

Than began Kynge Marke and all Cornyshemen to lawghe, and
the other party to wepe. And ever Sir Trystram seyde to Sir Elyas,
"Yelde the!" And whan Sir Trystram saw hym so stakir on the
grounde, he seyde, "Sir Elyas, I am ryght sory for the, for thou arte
a passynge good knyght as ever I mette withall, excepte Sir Launcelot"—and therewithall Sir Elyas fell to the erthe and there dyed.

¶"Now what shall I do?" seyde Sir Trystram unto Kynge Marke,
for this batayle ys at an ende." Than they [of Elyas party] departed;
and Kynge Marke toke of hem many presoners to redresse[8] the
harmys and the scathis, and the remenaunte he sente into her

5
10
15
20
25

fol.260r

30
35
40
45

---

5. I.e., exchange of hostages.
6. I.e., end the conflict.
7. *Gaff sore abak*: painfully gave way.
8. I.e., repay through their ransom.

contrey to borow oute their felowys. Than was Sir **Trystram** serched and well healed.

¶Yett for all this Kynge **Marke** wolde have slayne Sir **Trystram**; but for all that ever Sir **Trystram** saw other herde by Kynge **Marke**, he wolde never beware of his treson—but evir he wolde be there as La Beale **Isode** was.   5

¶Now woll we passe over this mater and speke we of the harpers that Sir **Launcelot** and Sir **Dynadan** had sente into Cornwayle. And at the grete feste that Kynge **Marke** made for the joy that the Sessoynes were put oute of his contrey, than cam **Elyot**⁹ the harper   10
with the lay that Sir **Dynadan** had made, and secretly brought hit unto Sir **Trystram** and tolde hym the lay that Sir **Dynadan** had made by Kynge **Marke**. And whan Sir **Trystram** harde hit, he sayde, "O   fol.260v
Lord Jesu! That Sir **Dynadan** can make wondirly well—and yll there he sholde make evyll!"¹ "Sir," seyde **Elyot**, "dare I synge this songe   15
afore Kynge **Marke**?" "Yee, on my perell," seyde Sir **Trystram**, "for I shall be thy waraunte."

¶So at the mete in cam **Elyot** the harper, amonge other mynstrels, and began to harpe; and because he was a coryous harper, men harde hym synge the same lay that Sir **Dynadan** made, whyche   20
spake the moste vylany by Kynge **Marke** and of his treson that ever man herde.

¶And whan the harper had sunge his songe to the ende, Kynge **Marke** was wondirly wrothe and sayde, "Harper, how durste thou be so bolde, on thy hede, to synge this songe afore me?" "Sir,"   25
seyde **Elyot**, "wyte thou well I am a mynstrell, and I muste do as I am commaunded of thos lordis that I beare the armys of;² and, sir, wyte you well that Sir **Dynadan**, a knyght of the Table Rounde, made this songe and made me to synge hit afore you."

"Thou seyste well," seyde Kynge **Marke**, "and bycause thou arte   30
a mynstrell thou shalt go quyte—but I charge the, hyghe the faste oute of my syght!"

So **Elyot** the harper departed and wente to Sir **Trystram** and tolde hym how he had sped. Than Sir **Trystram** let make lettyrs as goodly as he cowde to Camelot and to Sir **Dynadan**, and so he let conduyte   35
the harper oute of the contrey. But to sey that Kynge **Marke** was wondirly wrothe, [he was], for he demed that the lay that was songe afore hym was made by Sir **Trystrams** counceyle—wherefore he thought to sle hym and all his well-wyllers in that contrey.

Now turne we to another mater that felle betwene Kyng **Marke**   [32] 40
and his brother, that was called the good Prynce **Bodwyne**, that all the peple of the contrey loved hym passyng well. So hit befelle on a tyme that the myscreauntys Sarezynes londid in the contrey   fol.261r
of Cornwayle sone aftir these **Sessoynes** were departed.

---

9. This portion of the text confuses the name of the harper Elyot (see p. 372, line 39) with Elyas, the knight who has just been slain by Trystram; all such instances have been silently emended.

1. *Sir Dynadan can make . . . evyll:* i.e., Dynadan is such a good composer that he can also write badly when he has to.

2. *Thos lordis that I beare the armys of:* i.e. the lords in whose service I work. It was common in the later Middle Ages for servants to wear the livery of their superior, typically a variation of the lord's coats of arms.

¶And whan the good prynce Sir Bodwyne was ware of them where they were londed, than at the londynge he areysed the peple pryvayly and hastyly. And or hit were day he let put wylde-fyre[3] in three of his owne shyppis; and suddeynly he pulled up the sayle, and wyth the wynde he made tho shyppis to be drevyn amonge the navy of the Sarezynes—and to make a short tale, tho three shyppis sett on fyre all the shyppis, that none were saved. And at the poynte of the day[4] the good Prynce Bodwyne with all his felyship set on the myscreauntys with showtys and cryes, and slew the numbir of fourty thousand, and lefft none on lyve.

¶Whan Kynge Marke wyste this, he was wondirly wrothe that his brother sholde wynne suche worship and honour; and bycause this prynce was bettir beloved than he in all that contrey—and also this Prynce Bodwyne lovid well Sir Trystram—and therefore he thought to sle hym. And thus, hastely and uppon hede,[5] as a man that was full of treson, he sente for Prynce Bodwyne, and Anglydes, his wyff, and bade them brynge their yonge sonne with hem, that he myght se hym—and all this he ded to the entente to sle the chylde, as well as his fadir, for he was the falsist traytour that ever was borne. (Alas, for the goodnes and for hys good dedis, this jantyll Prynce Bodwyne was slayne.) So whan he cam wyth his wyff Anglydes, the kynge made them fayre semblaunte[6] tylle they had dyned.

¶And whan they had dyned, Kynge Marke sente for his brother, and seyde thus: "Brothir, how sped you whan the myscreauntes aryved by you?

¶"Mesemyth hit had bene your parte to have sente me worde, that I myght have bene at that journey;[7] for hit had bene reson that I had had the honoure, and nat you."

¶"Sir," seyde Prince Bodwyne, "hit was so that, and I had [taryed tyl that I had] sente for you, tho myscreauntes had distroyed my contrey."

¶"Thou lyeste, false traytoure!" seyde Kynge Marke. "For thou arte ever aboute[8] to wynne worship from me and put me to dishonoure—and thou cherysht that[9] I hate!" And therewith he stroke hym to the herte wyth a dagger, that he never aftir spake worde. Than the lady Anglydes made grete dole and sowned, for she saw her lorde slayne afore her face.

Than was there no more to do, but Prynce Bodwyne was dispoyled and brought to his buryellys—but his lady Anglydes pryvaly gate hir husbandis dubled and his shurte, and that she kepte secretly. Than was there muche sorow and cryynge, and grete dole made betwyxt Sir Trystram, Sir Dynas, and Sir Fergus—and so ded all knyghtes that were there, for that prynce was passyngly well beloved. So La Beall Isode sente for Anglydes, his wyff, and bade her avoyde

fol.261v

---

3. *Wylde-fyre*: a highly flammable compound used in warfare.
4. *Poynte of the day*: break of day.
5. *Uppon hede*: with malice aforethought.
6. *Fayre semblaunte*: a pretense of hospitality.
7. I.e., day's fighting.
8. I.e., seeking about.
9. I.e., that which.

delyverly,[1] other ellys hir yonge sonne, **Alysaundir le Orphelyne**, sholde be slayne.

¶Whan she harde this, she toke her horse and hir chylde and rode away with suche poore men as durste ryde with hir. Notwyth-stondynge—[2]

¶Whan Kynge **Marke** had done this dede, yet he thought to do more vengeaunce. And with his swerde in his honde he sought frome chambir to chambir for **Anglydes** and hir yonge sonne. And whan she was myst, he called a good knyght to hym that hyght Sir **Sadoke**, and charged hym in payne of dethe to fette agayne **Anglydes** and hir yonge sonne.

So Sir **Sadoke** departed and rode aftir **Anglydes**; and within ten myle he overtoke her, and bade hir turne ayen and ryde with hym to Kynge **Marke**. "Alas, fayre knyght!" she seyde, "what shall ye wynne be my sunnys deth, other ellys by myne? For I have over-muche harme, and to grete a losse." "Madame," seyde Sir **Sadoke**, "for your losse is grete dole and pité—but, madame," seyde Sir **Sadoke**, "wolde ye departe oute of this contrey wyth youre sonne, and kepe hym tyll he be of ayge, that he may revenge his fadyrs deth? Than wolde I suffir you to departe frome me, so ye promyse me to revenge the deth of Prynce **Bodwyne**."

¶"A, jantyll knyght, Jesu thanke the! And yf ever my sonne **Aly-saundir le Orphelyne** lyve to be a knyght, he shall have his fadirs dublet and his shurte, with the blody markes, and I shall gyff hym suche a charge that he shall remember hit whylys he lyvyth." And therewithall departed Sir **Sadoke** frome her, and ayther [bytoke other to God]. And whan Sir **Sadoke** cam unto Kynge **Marke**, he tolde hym faythfully that he had drowned yonge **Alysaundir**, her sonne; and thereof Kynge **Marke** was full glad.

¶Now turne we unto **Anglydes**, that rode bothe nyght and day by adventure oute off Cornwayle; and sylden and in feaw placis she rested, but ever she drewe southwarde to the seesyde, tyll by for-tune she cam to a castell that is called **Magowns**, that now is called **Arundell**, in Southsex. And the conestable of that castell welcomed **Anglydes**, and seyde she was wellcom to her owne castell—and so she was there worshypfully resceyved, for the conestable his wyff was her ny cousyn—and the conestablys name was Sir **Bellyngere**, and he tolde **Anglydes** that the same castell was hers by ryght iner-ytaunce.

Thus **Anglydes** endured yerys and wyntyrs, tyll **Alysaundir** was bygge and stronge, and there was none so wyghty in all that con-trey, that there was no man myght do no maner of maystry afore hym.[3] Than uppon a day Sir **Bellyngere** the constable cam to **Angly-des** and seyde, "Madame, hit were tyme my lorde Sir **Alysaundir** were made knyght, for he is a stronge yonge man."

¶"Sir," seyde she, "I wolde he were made knyght—but than

---

1. *Avoyde delyverly:* leave quickly.
2. I.e., nevertheless, despite this.
3. *Do no maner of maystry afore hym:* overpower him.

muste I gyff hym the moste[4] charge that ever synfull modir gaff to
hir childe." "As for that, do as ye lyste, and I shall gyff hym warnynge that he shall be made knyght; and hit woll be well done that
he be made knyght at Oure Lady Day, in Lente."[5]

¶"Be hit so," seyde Anglydes, "and I pray you, make ye redy
therefore." So cam the conestable to Alysaundir, and tolde hym that
he sholde at Oure Lady of Lente be made a knyght. "Sir, I thanke
God and you," seyde Alysaundir "for this is the beste tydynges that
ever cam to me." Than the conestable ordayned twenty of the grettyste jantylmennes sunnys and the beste borne men of that contrey
whyche sholde be made knyghtes the same day that Alysaundir was
made knyght.

And so on the same day that he and his twenty felowys were
made knyghtes, at the offerynge of the Masse there cam this lady
Anglydes unto her sonne, and seyde thus: "A, my fayre swete sonne,
I charge the uppon my blyssynge, and of the hyghe order of chevalry that thou takyste here this day, to take hede what I shall sey
and charge the wythall." And therewithall she pulled oute a blody
dublet and a blody shurte that was be-bled with olde bloode.

¶Whan Alysaundir saw this, he sterte abak and waxed paale, and
sayde, "Fayre moder, what may this be or meane?" "I shall tell the,
fayre son: this was thyne owne fadyrs doublet and shurte that he
ware uppon hym that same tyme that he was slayne." And there
she tolde hym why and wherefore—"and for hys good dedis Kynge
Marke slew hym with his dagger, afore myne owne yghen. And
therefore this shall be youre charge that I gyff you at thys tyme:
"Now I requere the, and I charge the, uppon my blyssynge and
uppon the hyghe order of knyghthode, that thou be revenged
uppon Kynge Marke for the deth of thy fadir." And therewythall
she sowned; than Alysaundir lepte to his modir, and toke her up in
his armys, and sayde, "Fayre modir, ye have gyvyn me a grete
charge, and here I promyse you I shall be avenged uppon Kynge
Marke whan that I may, and that I promyse to God and to you." So
this feste was ended, and the conestable, by the avyce of Anglydes
let purvey[6] that Alysaundir were well horsed and harneyste. Than
he justed with his twenty felowys, that were made knyghtes with
hym; but for to make a shorte tale, he overthrewe all tho twenty,
that none myght withstonde hym[7] a buffet. Than one of tho knyghtes departed unto Kynge Marke, and tolde all how Alysaundir was
made knyght, and all the charge that his modir gaff hym, as ye
have harde aforetyme.

¶"Alas, false treson!" seyde Kynge Marke. "I wente that yonge
traytoure had bene dede—alas, whom may I truste?" And
therewithall Kynge Marke toke a swerde in his honde, and sought
Sir Sadoke from chambir to chambir, to sle hym.

---

4. I.e., greatest.
5. The Feast of the Annunciation of the Virgin Mary (March 25), held during Lent (a season
   of penitence, the forty weekdays before Easter).
6. *Let purvey*: arranged.
7. I.e., from him.

¶Whan Sir Sadoke saw Kynge Marke com with his swerde in his honde,

¶"Syr," he seyde, "beware, Marke, and com nat to nyghe me! For wyte thou well that I saved Alysaundir his lyff, of the whyche I never repente me, for thou falsely and cowardly slew his fadir, Prynce Bodwyne, traytourly for his good dedis. Wherefore I pray Allmyghty Jesu sende Alysaundir myght and power to be revenged upon the; and now beware, Kynge Marke, of yonge Alysaundir, for he is made a knyght."

"Alas," seyde Kynge Marke, "that ever I sholde hyre a traytoure sey so afore me!" And therewith foure knyghtes of Kynge Markes drew their swerdis to sle Sir Sadoke; but anone Kynge Marke his knyghtes were slayne afore hym. And Sir Sadoke paste forthe into his chambir, and toke his harneys and his horse and rode on his way—for there was nother Sir Trystram, Sir Dynas, nother Sir Fergus, that wolde Sir Sadoke ony evyll wyll. Than was Kynge Marke wood wrothe, and thought to destroy Sir Alysaundir, for hym he dradde and hated moste of any man lyvynge.

¶Whan Sir Trystram undirstood that Alysaundir was made knyght, anone furthwithall he sent hym a lettir, prayynge and chargynge hym that he draw[8] hym to the courte of Kynge Arthure, and that he put hym in the rule and in the hondis of Sir Launcelot. So this lettyr was sente unto Sir Alysaundir from his cousyne, Sir Trystram; and at that tyme he thought to do after his commaundemente. Than Kynge Marke called a knyght that brought hym the tydynges frome Alysaundir, and bade hym abyde stylle in that contrey. "Sir," seyde the knyght, "so muste I do, for in my nowne contrey dare I nat com."

¶"No force,"[9] seyde Kynge Marke, "for I shall gyff the here double as muche londis as ever thou haddyste of thyne owne." But within shorte space Sir Sadoke mette wyth that false knyght and slew hym. Than was Kynge Marke wood wrothe oute of mesure; than he sente unto Quene Morgan le Fay and to the Quene of Northe Galys, prayynge them in his lettyrs that they two sorserers wolde sette all the contrey envyrone with ladyes that were enchauntours, and by suche that were daungerous knyghtes, as Sir Malagryne and Sir Brewnys Saunȝe Pyté, that by no meane Alysaundir le Orphelyne shulde never ascape, but other he sholde be takyn or slayne. And all this ordynaunce made Kynge Marke to distroy Sir Alysaunder.

Now turne we unto Sir Alysaundir, that, at his departyng his modir, toke with hym his fadyrs blody sherte; and so he bare hit with hym tyll his deth day, in tokenynge to thynke uppon his fadyrs deth. So was Alysaundir purposed to ryde to London, by the counceyle of Sir Trystram, to Sir Launcelot. And by fortune he went aftir the seesyde,[1] and rode wronge;[2] and there he wan at a turne-

fol.263v 15

20

25

30

35

40

[36]

fol.264r 45

---

8. I.e., withdraw.
9. *No force*: that does not matter.
1. *Went aftir the seesyde*: i.e., followed the coast.
2. I.e., the wrong way.

mente the gré, that Kynge Carados made, and there he smote downe
Kynge Carados and twenty of his knyghtes, and also Sir Saffir, a
good knyght that was Sir Palomydes brother. And all this sawe a
damesell, and went to Morgan le Fay, and tolde hir how she saw
the beste knyght juste that ever she sawe; and ever as he smote   5
downe knyghtes, he made them to swere to were none harneyse
of³ a twelvemonthe and a day.

¶ "This is well seyde," seyde Morgan le Fay, "for that is the knyght
that I wolde fayne se." And so she toke her palfrey and rode a grete
whyle; and than she rested her in her pavylyon. So there cam foure   10
knyghtes—two of them were armed, and two were unarmed—and
they tolde Morgan le Fay there namys: the fyrste was Elyas de Gomeret, the secunde Car de Gomeret (tho two were armed), and the other
two were of Camylarde, cousyns unto Quene Gwenyver; and that
one hyght Sir Gye, and that othir hyght Sir Garaunte (tho two were   15
unarmed). And this foure knyghtes tolde Morgan le Fay how a yonge
knyght had smyttyn them downe afore a castell—"for the maydyn
of that castell seyde that he was but late made knyght, and yonge;
but as we suppose, but yf hit were Sir Trystram othir Sir Launcelot,
other ellys Sir Lameroke the good knyght, [there is none] that myght 20
sytte hym⁴ a buffette with a speare."

¶ "Well," seyde Morgan le Fay, "I shall mete wyth that knyght or
hit be longe tyme, and he dwelle in that contrey."

¶ So turne we to the damesell of the castell, that whan Alysaundir
le Orphelyne had forjusted the foure knyghtes, she called hym to her 25
and seyde thus: "Sir knyght, wolte thou for my sake juste and fyght
wyth a knyght of this contrey, that is and hath bene longe an evyll
neyghboure to me? His name is Sir Malegryne, and he woll nat suffir
me to be maryde in no maner." "Damesell," seyde Sir Alysaundir,   fol.264v
"and he com the whyle that I am here, I woll fyght with hym."   30

And therewithall she sente for hym, for he was at her commaundemente. And whan ayther had a syght of other, they made
hem redy for to juste; and so they cam togydyr egirly, and this Sir
Malegryne brused his speare uppon Sir Alysaundir—and he⁵ smote
hym agayne so harde that he bare hym quyte from his horse [to   35
the erthe]. But this Malegryne devoyded, and lyghtly arose and
dressed his shylde, and drew his swerde and bade hym alyght—
"for wyte thou well, sir knyghte, thoughe thou have the bettir on
horsebacke, thou shalt fynde that I shall endure the lyke a knyght
on foote."   40

¶ "Ye sey well," seyde Sir Alysaundir; and so he avoyded his horse
and bytoke hym⁶ to his varlet. And than they russhed togydyrs lyke
two boorys, and leyde on their helmys and shyldis longe tyme—by
the space of three owrys—that never man coude sey whyche was
the bettir knyght. (And in the meanewhyle cam Morgan le Fay to   45
the damesell of the castell, and they behylde the batayle.) But this

3. I.e., for.
4. *Sytte hym:* withstand from him.
5. I.e., Alysaundir.
6. I.e., his horse.

Sir Malagryne was an olde-rooted[7] knyght, and he was called one
of the daungerous knyghtes of the worlde to do batayle on foote—
but on horsebacke there was many bettir.

⁋And ever this Malagryne awayted to sle Sir Alysaundir, and so
wounded hym wondirly sore that hit was mervayle that ever he   5
myght stonde, ror he had bled so muche—for this Sir Alysaundir
fought ever wyldely and nat wyttyly, and that othir was a felonous
knyght and awayted[8] hym and smote hym sore. And somtyme they
russhed togydyrs with their shyldis lyke two boorys other rammys,
and felle grovelynge bothe to the erthe.   10

⁋"Now, sir knyght," seyde Sir Malegryne, "holde thyne honde a
whyle, and telle me what thou arte." "That woll I nat," seyde Sir
Alysaundir, "but yf me lyst well; but tell me thy name, and why   fol.265r
thou kepyste thys contrey, other ellys thou shalt dye of my hondis."
"Sir, wyte thou well," seyde Sir Malagryne, "that for this maydyns   15
love, of this castell, I have slayne ten good knyghtes by myssehap,
and by outerage and orgulyté of myselff I have slayne othir ten
knyghtes."

"So God helpe me," seyde Sir Alysaundir, "this is the fowlyste
confession that ever I harde knyght make, and hit were pité that   20
thou sholdiste lyve ony lenger—and therefore kepe the,[9] or, as I
am a trewe knyght, other thou shalt sle me, other ellys I shall sle
the. Than they laysshed togydyrs fyersely; and at the laste Sir Alysaundir smote hym to the erthe—and than he raced of his helme
and smote of his hede. And whan he had done this batayle, he toke   25
his horse and wolde have mownted uppon his horse, but he myght
nat for faynte.

⁋And than he seyde, "A, Jesu, succoure me!" So by that com
Morgan le Fay, and bade hym be of good comforte. And so she
layde hym, this Alysaundir, in an horse-lettir, and so led hym into   30
the castell, for he had no foote to stonde uppon the erthe—for he
had sixtene grete woundis, and in especiall one of them was lyke
to be his deth. Than Quene Morgan le Fay serched his woundis   [37]
and gaff hym suche an oynement that he sholde have dyed. And
so on the morne whan she cam to hym agayne, he complayned   35
hym sore; and than she put another oynemente uppon hym, and
than he was oute of his payne.

⁋Than cam the damesell of the castell, and seyde unto Morgan
le Fay, "I pray you helpe me that this knyght myght wedde me, for
he hath wonne me with his hondis."   40

⁋"Ye shall se," seyde Morgan le Fay, "what I shall sey." Than this
quene Morgan le Fay wente to Sir Alysaundir and bade hym in ony
wyse that he shulde "refuse this lady, and she desyre to wed you;
for she is nat for you." So this damesell cam and desired of hym   fol.265v
maryage.   45

⁋"Damesell," seyde Sir Alysaundir, "I thanke you, but as yet I
caste me nat to mary in this contrey."

---

7. *Olde-rooted:* firm-footed.
8. I.e., watched shrewdly.
9. *Kepe the:* defend yourself.

❡"Sir" she seyde, "sytthyn ye woll nat mary me, I pray you, inso-muche as ye have wonne me, that ye woll gyff me to a knyght of this contrey that hath bene my frende and loved me many yerys.

❡"Wyth all myne herte," seyde Sir Alysaundir, "I woll assente thereto."

❡Than was the knyght sente fore, and his name was Sir Geryne le Grose; and anone he made them honde-faste and wedded them. Than cam Quene Morgan le Fay to Sir Alysaundir and bade hym aryse, and so put hym in an horse-lytter; and so she gaff hym suche a drynke that of three dayes and three nyghtes he waked never, but slepte. And so she brought hym to hir owne castell, that at that tyme was called La Beale Regarde. Than Morgan le Fay com to Sir Alysaundir and axed hym yf he wolde fayne be hole. "Madame, who wolde be syke and he myght be hole?"

❡"Well," seyde Morgan, "than shall ye promyse me by youre knyghthode that this twelvemonthe and a day ye shall nat passe the compace of this castell, and ye shall lyghtly be hole."

❡"I assent me," seyde Sir Alysaundir; and there he made hir a promyse and was sone hole. And whan Sir Alysaundir was hole, he repented hym of his othe, for he myght nat be revenged uppon Kynge Marke. Ryght so there cam a damesell that was cousyn nyghe to the Erle of Pase, and she was cousyn also unto Morgan le Fay; and by ryght that castell of La Beale Regarde sholde have bene hers by trew enherytaunce. So this damesell entyrd into this castell where lay Sir Alysaundir, and there she founde hym uppon his bedde, passynge hevy and all sad.

❡"Sir knyght," seyde the damesell, "and ye wolde be myrry, I cowde tell you good tydyngis." "Well were me," seyde Sir Alysaundir, "and I myght hyre of good tydynges, for now I stonde as a presonere be my promyse." "Sir," she seyde, "wyte you well that ye be a presonere—and wors than ye wene, for my lady, my cousyn, Quene Morgan, kepyth you here for none other entente but for to do hir plesure whan hit lykyth hir."

❡"A, Jesu defende me," seyde Sir Alysaundir, "frome suche pleasure—for I had levir kut away my hangers[1] than I wolde do her ony suche pleasure!" "As Jesu me helpe," seyde the damesell, "and ye wolde love me and be ruled by me, I shall make your delyveraunce with your worship."[2] "Telle me now by what meane, and ye shall have my love." "Fayre knyght," sayde she, "this castell ought of ryght to be myne. And I have an uncle that is a myghty erle, and he is Erle of the Pace; and of all folkis he hatyth [moost] Morgan le Fay. And I shall sende unto hym and pray hym for my sake to destroy this castell for the evyll customys that bene used therein; and than woll he com and sette fyre on every parte with wylde-fyre—and so shall I gete you at a prevy postren, and there shall ye have your horse and youre harneis."

[38]
fol.266r

---

1. I.e., testicles.
2. *With your worship:* i.e., while retaining your honor.

"Fayre damesell, ye sey passynge well." "And than may ye kepe the rome[3] of this castell this twelvemonthe and a day, and than breke ye nat youre othe." "Truly, fayre damesell," seyde Sir Alysaundir, "ye say sothe" (and than he kyssed hir and ded to her plesaunce as hit pleased them bothe at tymes and leysers). So anone she sente unto hir uncle and bade hym com to destroy that castell—for, as the booke seyth, he wolde have destroyed that castell aforetyme, had nat that damesell bene.

¶Whan the erle undirstode hir letteris, he sente her worde on suche a day he wolde com and destroy that castell. So whan that day cam, Sir Alysaundir yode to a postren where he sholde fle into the gardyne, and there he sholde fynde his armoure and his horse.

¶So whan the day cam that was sette, thydir cam the Erle of the Pase wyth foure hondred knyghtes, and sette on fyre all the partyes of the castell, that or they seased they leffte nat one stone stondynge. And all this whyle that this fyre was in the castell, he[4] abode in the gardyne; and whan the fyre was done, he let crye that he wolde kepe that pyce of erthe, there as the castell of La Beale Regarde was, a twelvemonthe and a day, frome all maner of knyghtes that wolde com.

¶So hit happed there was a deuke, Aunsyrus, and he was of the kynne of Sir Launcelot. And this knyght was a grete pylgryme, for every thirde yere he wolde be at Jerusalem; and bycause he used all his lyff to go in pylgrymage, men called hym Deuke Aunserus the Pylgryme. And this deuke had a doughter that hyght Alys, that was a passynge fayre woman; and bycause of her fadir she was called Alys le Beall Pylgryme.

And anone, as she harde of this crye, she wente unto Kyng Arthurs courte and seyde opynly, in hyrynge of many knyghtes, that "what knyght may overcom that knyght that kepyth the pyce of erthe shall have me and all my londis." Whan knyghtes of the Rounde Table harde hir sey thus, many of them were glad, for she was passynge fayre and ryche, and of grete rentys. Ryght so she lete crye in castellys and townys as faste on her syde as Sir Alysaundir ded on his syde. Than she dressed hir pavylion streyte by the pyese of erthe that Sir Alysaundir kepte.

So she was nat so sone there but there cam a knyght of Kynge Arthurs courte that hyght Sir Sagramour le Desyrous. And he profyrde to juste wyth Sir Alysaundir; and so they encountyrd, and he brused his speare uppon Sir Alysaundir—but Sir Alysaundir smote hym so sore that he avoyded his arson of his sadyll to the erthe. Whan La Beale Alys sawe hym juste so well, she thought hym a passyng goodly knyght on horsebacke; and than she lepe oute of hir pavylyon and toke Sir Alysaundir by the brydyll, and thus she seyde: "Fayre knyght, of thy knyghthode, shew me thy vysayge."

"That dare I well," seyde Sir Alysaundir, "shew my vysayge." And than he put of his helme; and whan she sawe his vysage she seyde, "A, swete Fadir Jesu! The I muste love, and never othir!" "Than

---

3. *Kepe the rome:* stay in the confines.
4. I.e., Alisaundir.

shewe me youre vysage," seyde he. And anone she unwympeled [39]
her;[5] and whan he sawe her, he seyde, "A, Lorde Jesu! Here have
I founde my love and my lady! And therefore, fayre lady, I promyse
you to be youre knyght, and none other that beryth the lyff."

"Now, jantyll knyghte," seyde she, "telle me youre name." 5
"Madame, my name is Sir Alysaundir le Orphelyne. [Now damoysel,
telle me your name," sayd he.] "A, sir," seyde she, "syth ye lyst to
know my name, wyte you well my name is Alys la Beale Pellaron;
and whan we be more at oure hartys ease, bothe ye and I shall telle
of what bloode we be com." So there was grete love betwyxt them; 10
and as they thus talked, there cam a knyght that hyght Sir Harleuse
le Berbuse,[6] and axed parte of Sir Alysaundirs spearys.[7]

Than Sir Alysaundir encountred with hym, and at the fyrste Sir
Alysaundir smote hym over his horse croupe. And than there cam
another knyght that hyght Sir Hewgon, and Sir Alysaundir smote hym 15
downe, as he ded that othir. Than Sir Hewgan profirde batayle on
foote; and anone Sir Alysaundir overthrewe hym within three
strokys—and than he raced of his helme and there wolde have
slayne hym, had he nat yelded hym. So than Sir Alysaundir made
bothe tho knyghtes to swere to were none armour of a twelvemon- 20
the and a day. Than Sir Alysaundir alyght, and wente to reste hym
and to repose hym.

Than the damesell that halpe Sir Alysaundir oute of the castell, fol.267v
in her play tolde Alys alltogydir how he was presonere in the castell
of La Beall Regarde; and there she tolde her how she gate hym 25
oute of preson. "Sir," seyde Alys la Beall Pillaron, "mesemyth ye ar
muche beholdynge to this mayden."

¶"That is trouthe," seyde Sir Alysaundir. And there Alys tolde of
what bloode she was com and seyde, "Sir, wyte you well that I am
of the bloode of Kynge Ban, that was fadir unto Sir Launcelot." 30
"Iwys, fayre lady," seyde Sir Alysaundir, "my modir tolde me my fadir
was brothir unto a kynge, and I am nye cousyn unto Sir Trystram."

So this meanewhyle cam three knyghtes: that one hyght Sir
Vayns, and that other hyght Harvis le Marchis, and the thirde hyghte
Peryne de la Mountayne—and with one speare Sir Alysaundir smote 35
them downe, all three, and gaff them suche fallys that they had no
lyst to fyght uppon foote. So he made them to swere to were none
armys of a twelvemonthe. So whan they were departed, Sir Alysaundir behylde his lady Alys on horsebak as she stoode in hir pavylion; and than was he so enamered uppon her that he wyst nat 40
whether he were on horsebacke other on foote. Ryght so cam the
false knyght Sir Mordred, and sawe Sir Alysaundir was so afonned
uppon his lady; and therewithall he toke hys horse by the brydyll
and lad hym here and there, and had caste to have lad hym oute
of that place to have shamed hym. 45

---

5. *Unwympeled her*: removed her veil.
6. This knight has already been killed once (p. 53), something Malory has evidently forgotten;
   had he remembered, he would have presumably changed the name here or in the earlier
   passage. On such inconsistencies in Malory, cf. n. 1, p. 34.
7. *Axed parte of Sir Alysaundirs spearys*: asked to borrow some of Alysaundir's lances (i.e.,
   challenged him to joust).

So whan the damesell that halpe hym oute of that castell sawe
how shamefully he was lad, anone she lete arme her and sette a
shylde uppon her shuldir; and therewith she amownted uppon his
horse, and gate a naked swerde in hir honde, and she threste unto
Alysaundir with all hir myght—and she gaff hym suche a buffet that
hym thought the fyre flowe oute of his yghen.

¶And whan Sir Alysaundir felte that stroke, he loked aboute hym
and drew his swerde; and whan she sawe that, she fledde—and so
ded Sir Mordred—into the foreyste; and the damesell fled into the
pavylyon.

So whan Sir Alysaundir undirstood hymselff how the false knyght
wolde have shamed hym had nat the damesell bene, than was he
wroth with hymselff that Sir Mordred had so ascaped his hondis—
but than Sir Alysaundir and his lady Alys had good game at[8] the
damesell, how sadly[9] she smote hym upon the helme!

Than Sir Alysaundir justed thus, day be day, and on foote ded
many batayles with many knyghtes of Kynge Arthurs courte and
with many knyghtes straungers, that for to tell batayle by batayle
hit were overmuche to reherse. For every day in that twelvemonthe
he had to do wyth one knyght owther wyth another, and som day
with three or foure; and there was never knyght that put hym to
the warre.[1] And at the twelvemonthes ende, he departed with his
lady La Beall Pyllerowne—and the damesell wolde never go frome
hym—and so they wente into their contrey of Benoy, and lyved
there in grete joy.

¶But, as the booke tellyth, Kynge Marke wolde never stynte tylle
he had slayne hym by treson. And by Alis he gate a chylde that
hyght Bellengerus le Beuse; and by good fortune he cam to the
courte of Kynge Arthure and preved a good knyght. And he revenged
his fadirs deth,[2] for this false Kynge Marke slew bothe Sir Trystram
and Sir Alysaundir falsely and felonsly. And hit happed so that Sir
Alysaunder had never grace ne fortune to com to Kynge Arthurs
courte; for and he had com to Sir Launcelot, all knyghtes seyde that
knew hym that he was one of the strengyste knyghtes that was in
Kynge Arthurs dayes—and grete dole was made for hym.

So lette we hym passe, and turne we to another tale.

¶So hit befelle that Sir Galahalte the Haute Prynce was lorde of
the contrey of Surluse, whereof cam oute many good knyghtes;
and this noble prince was a passynge good man of armys, and ever
he hylde a noble felyship togydirs. And than he cam to Kynge
Arthurs courte and tolde hym his entente, how this was his wyll:
he wolde let cry[3] a justys in the contrey of Surluse, the whyche

fol.268r

[40]

fol.268v

---

8. *Had good game at:* were greatly amused by.
9. I.e., soundly.
1. I.e., worse.
2. This conception of Mark's demise is likely to be Malory's own. Malory's immediate sources
are unlikely to have mentioned how Mark died, and nowhere else is he recorded as having
been killed by the son of Alysaundir the Orphan. In other stories Mark is killed by Launcelot, or Pamlart (a descendant of King Ban), or even kept in a cage and overfed to death.
Malory's conception alone provides for revenge by a close blood relative (Alysaunder, like
Trystram, is Mark's nephew).
3. *Let cry:* cause to be proclaimed.

contrey was within the bandis of Kynge Arthur, and there he asked leve to crye a justys. "I woll gyff you leve," seyde Kynge Arthur, "but wyte you well I may not be there myselff."

¶"Sir," seyde Quene Gwenyver, "please hit you to gyff me leve to be at that justis?" "Wyth ryght a good wyll," seyde Kynge Arthur, "for Sir Galahalte the good prynce shall have you in governaunce." "Sir, as ye wyll, so be hit." Than the Quene seyde, "I woll take with me suche knyghtes as lykyth me beste." "Do as ye lyste," seyde Kynge Arthure.

So anone she commaunded Sir Launcelot to make hym redy with suche knyghtes as hym thought beste. So in every goode towne and castell off this londe was made a crye that in the contrey of Surluse Sir Galahalte shulde make a justis that sholde laste seven dayes, and how the Hawte Prince, with the helpe of Quene Gwenyvers knyghtes, sholde juste agayne all maner of men that commyth. Whan this crye was knowyn, kynges and prynces, deukes, erlys, and barownes and noble knyghtes made them redy to be at that justys.

And at the day of justenynge there cam in Sir Dynadan, disgysed, and ded many grete dedis of armys. Than at the requeste of Quene Gwenyver and of Kynge Bagdemagus, Sir Launcelot com into the thrange—but he was disgysed, that was the cause that feaw folke knew hym—and there mette wyth hym Sir Ector de Marys, his owne brother; and ayther brake their spearys uppon other to their handis. And than aythir gate another speare; and than Sir Launcelot smote downe Sir Ector, his owne brother. That sawe Sir Bleoberys, and he smote Sir Launcelot uppon the helme suche a buffet that he wyste nat well where he was.

¶Than Sir Launcelot smote Sir Bleoberys so sore uppon the helme that his hed bowed downe bakwarde; and he smote hym efft another stroke, and therewith he avoyded his sadyll. And so he rode by and threste in amonge the thykkyst.

¶Whan the Kynge of North Galys saw Sir Ector and Sir Bleoberys ley on the grounde, than was he wrothe, for they cam on his party agaynste them of Surluse. So the Kynge of North Galys ran unto Sir Launcelot and brake a speare uppon hym all to pecis; and therewith Sir Launcelot overtoke the Kynge of North Galys and smote hym such a buffet on the helme with his swerde that he made hym to avoyde the arson of his sadyll. And anone the kynge was horsed agayne; so Kynge Bagdemagus and the Kynge of Northe Galys, aythir party hurled to other, and than began a stronge medlé—but they of Northe Galys were muche bygger than the other.

¶So whan Sir Launcelot saw his party go so to the warre,[4] he thrange oute to the thyckyst with a bygge swerde in his honde; and there he smote downe on the ryght honde and on the lyffte hond, and pulled downe knyghtes and russhed of helmys, that all men had wondir that ever knyght myght do suche dedis of armys.

[41]

fol.269r

5

10

15

20

25

30

35

40

45

4. I.e., worse.

¶Whan Sir Mellyagaunce, that was sonne unto Kynge Bagdemagus, saw how Sir Launcelot fared, [he merveiled gretely;] and whan he undirstood that hit was he, he wyste well that he was disgysed for his sake. Than Sir Mellyagaunce prayde a knyght to sle Sir Launcelotes horse, other with swerde or speare. And at that tyme, Kynge Bagdemagus mett with another knyght that hyght Sauseyse, a good knyght, and sayde, "Now, fayre knyght Sir Sauseyse, encountir with my sonne, Sir Mellyagaunce, and gyff hym layrge pay;[5] for I wolde that he were well beatyn of thy hondis, that he myght departe oute of this felyship." And than Sir Sauseyse encountyrd with Sir Mellyagaunce, and aythir smote other adowne; and than they fought on foote—and there Sir Sauseyse had wonne Sir Mellyagaunce, had there nat com rescowys. So than the Haute Prynce blewe to lodgynge,[6] and every knyght unarmed hym and wente to the grete feyste.

Than in the meanewhyle there came a damesell to the Haute Prynce and complayned that there was a knyght that hyght Sir Gonereyes that withhylde all her londis; and so the knyght was there presente, and keste his glove[7] to hir or to ony that wolde fyght in hir name. So the damesell toke up the glove all hevyly, for the defaute of a champyon. Than there cam a varlet to her and seyde, "Damesell, woll ye do aftir me?"[8] "Full fayne," seyde the damesell.

"Than go ye unto suche a knyght that lyeth here besyde in an ermytage—and that knyght folowyth the Questynge Beeste—and pray hym to take the batayle uppon hym, and anone he woll graunte you." So anone she toke her palferey, and within a whyle she founde that knyght, whyche was called Sir Palompdes; and whan she requyred[9] hym, he armed hym and rode with her and made her go to the Haute Prynce and to aske leve for hir knyght to do batayle.

"I woll well," seyde the Haute Prynce. Than the knyghtes made them redy and cam to the fylde to juste on horsebacke; and aythir gate a grete speare in his honde, and so mette togydirs so hard that theire spearis all to-shevird. And anone they flange oute their swerdis; and Sir Palompdes smote Sir Gonereyse downe to the erthe—and than he raced of his helme and smote of his hede.

Than they wente to souper. And this damesell loved Sir Palompdes as her paramour; but the booke seyth she was of his kynne. So than Sir Palompdes disgysed hymselff in this maner: in his shylde he bare[1] the Questynge Beste, and in all his trapours. And whan he was thus redy, he sente to the Haute Prynce to gyff hym leve to juste with othir knyghtes—but he was adouted of Syr Launcelot; than the Haute Prynce sente hym worde agayne that he sholde be

fol.269v

fol.270r

---

5. *Layrge pay*: generous satisfaction.
6. *Blewe to lodgynge*: had a trumpet sounded to summon the knights to their lodging.
7. *Keste his glove*: i.e., threw down the gauntlet. A chivalric custom that is the literal antecedent of the modern expression. The throwing down of the gauntlet—the gauntlet being seen as a symbol of its owner's martial authority—constitutes a challenge to combat.
8. *Aftir me*: according to my instructions.
9. I.e., made request of.
1. I.e., bore as his coat of arms.

wellcom, and that Sir Launcelot sholde nat juste wyth hym. Than
Sir Galahalte the Haute Prynce lete cry that what knyght somever[2]
smote downe Sir Palomydes sholde have his damesell to hymselff
to his demaynes.[3]

Ere begynnyth the secunde day. And anone as Sir Palomydes [42] 5
came into the fylde, Sir Galahalte the Haute Prynce was at the
raunge ende, and mette wyth Sir Palomydes, and he with hym, with
two grete spearys; and they cam so harde togydyrs that their
spearys all to-shevirde. But Sir Galahalte smote hym so harde that
he bare hym bakwarde over his horse—but yet he loste nat his 10
styroppis.[4] Than they pulled oute their swerdis, and laysshed togydirs many sad strokis, that many worshypfull knyghtes leffte their
busynes to beholde them; but at the laste Sir Galahalte smote a
stroke of myght unto Sir Palomydes sore uppon the helme—but the
helme was so harde that the swerde myght nat byghte, but slypped 15
and smote of the hede of his horse. But whan Sir Galahalte saw the
good knyght Sir Palomydes fall to the erthe, he was ashamed of that
stroke; and therewithall he alyght adowne of his owne horse, and
prayde Sir Palomydes to take that horse of[5] his gyffte and to forgyff
hym that dede. 20

¶ "Sir," seyde Sir Palomydes, "I thanke you of youre grete goodnes—for ever of[6] a man of worship a knyght shall never have disworshyp." And so he mownted uppon that horse, and the Haute
Prynce had another horse anone.

"Now, seyde the Haute Prynce, "I releace to you that maydyn, 25
for ye have wonne her." "A," sayde Sir Palomydes, "the damesell
and I be at youre commaundement." So they departed. And Sir
Galahalte ded grete dedis of armys; and ryght so cam Sir Dynadan
and encountyrd wyth Sir Galahalte—and aythir cam on other so
faste that their spearys brake to there hondis. But Sir Dynadan had 30
wente the Haute Prynce had bene more weryar than he was, and fol.270v
than he smote many sad strokes at the Haute Prynce; but whan
Sir Dynadan saw he myght nat gete hym to the erthe, he seyde, "My
lorde, I pray you, leve me and take anothir."

So the Haute Prynce knew nat Sir Dynadan, but leffte hym goodly 35
for his fayre wordis; and so they departed—but another knyght
there cam and tolde the Haute Prynce that hit was Sir Dynadan.
"Iwys!" seyde the Haute Prynce, "therefore am I hevy that he is so
ascaped fro me, for with his mokkis and his japys[7] now shall I never
have done with hym." And than Sir Galahalte rode faste aftyr hym 40
and bade hym, "Abyde, Sir Dynadan, for Kynge Arthurs sake!"

"Nay," seyde Sir Dynadan, "so God me helpe, we mete no more
togydyrs this day!" Than in that haste Sir Galahalte mett with Sir
Mellyagaunce; and he smote hym so in the throte that, and he had

2. *what . . . somever:* whatever.
3. *To his demaynes:* within his estates.
4. *Loste nat his styroppis:* i.e., was not unhorsed.
5. I.e., as.
6. I.e., from.
7. *His mokkis and his japys:* his mockery and his jesting. On Sir Dynadan's character, see
   n. 7, p. 307.

fallyn, his necke had be brokyn—and with the same speare he
smote downe anothir knyght. Than cam in they of the Northe
Galys, and many straungers with them, and were lyke to have put
them of Surluse to the worse, for Sir Galahalte the Haute Prynce
had overmuche in honde. So there cam the good knyght Sir Sym-
ounde the Valyaunte with fourty knyghtes, and bete them all abacke.
Than Quene Gwenyver and Sir Launcelot let blow to lodgynge; and
every knyght unarmed hym and dressed them to the feste.

¶So whan Sir Palomydes was unarmed, he axed lodgynge for
hymselff and the damesell, and anone the Haute Prynce commaunded them to lodgynge; and he was nat so sone in his lodgynge
but there cam a knyght that hyght Archade: he was brothir unto Sir
Gomoryes that Sir Palomydes slewe afore in the damesels quarell.
And this knyght Archede called Sir Palomydes traytoure, and appeled
hym for the deth of his brother. "By the leve of the Haute Prynce,"
seyde Sir Palomydes, "I shall answere the."

¶Whan Sir Galahalte undirstood there quarell, he bade them go
to the dyner—"and as sone as ye have dyned, loke that aythir
knyght be redy in the fylde." So whan they had dyned, they were
armed bothe and toke their horsys; and the Quene and the prynce
and Sir Launcelot were sette to beholde them. And so they let ren
their horsis; and there Sir Palomydes and Sir Archade mette, and he
bare Sir Archade on his speare ende over his horse tayle. And than
Sir Palomydes alyght and drewe his swerde; but Sir Archade myght
nat aryse—and there Sir Palomydes raced of his helme and smote
of his hede.

¶Than the Haute Prynce and Quene Gwenyver went to souper.
Than Kynge Bagdemagus sente away his sonne, Mellyagaunce,
bycause Sir Launcelot sholde nat mete with hym—for he hated Sir
Launcelot, and that knewe he nat.

Now begynnyth the thirde day of justis. And at that day Kynge
Bagdemagus made hym redy; and there cam agaynste hym
Kynge Marsyll that had in[8] gyffte an ilonde of Sir Galahalte the
Haute Prynce—and this ilonde was called Pomytayne. Than hit
befelle thus that Kynge Bagdemagus and Kynge Marsyll of Pomytayne mett togydir wyth spearys; and Kynge Marsyll had suche a
buffet that he felle over his horse croupe. Than cam therein a
knyght of Kynge Marsyls to revenge his lorde; and Kynge Bagdemagus smote hym downe, horse and man, to the erthe. So there
came an erle that hyght Sir Arrowse, and Sir Breuse, and an hondred
knyghtes wyth hem of Pometaynes—and the Kynge of Northe
Galys was with hem, and all they were agaynste them of Surluse.

And than there began a grete batayle; and many knyghtes were
caste undir their horse fyete. And ever Kynge Bagdemagus ded
beste, for he fyrste began and ever he was lengyste that helde on;
but Sir Gaherys, Gawaynes brother, smote ever at the face of Kynge
Bagdemagus—and at the laste he smote downe Sir Gaherys, horse
and man. And by aventure Sir Palomydes mette with Sir Blamour de

[43]

5

10

fol.271r

15

20

25

[44]

30

35

40

45

fol.271v

8. I.e., as a.

Ganys, brother unto Sir Bleoberys; and ayther smote other with grete spearis, that bothe horse and men felle to the erthe—but Sir Blamour had [suche a falle that he had] allmoste broke his necke, for the blood braste oute at the nose, mowthe, and earys.

Than cam in Deuke Chalens of Claraunce, and undir his governaunce there cam a knyght that hyght Sir Elys la Noyre; and there encountyrd with hym Kynge Bagdemagus, and he smote Sir Elys, that he made hym to avoyde his arson of his sadyll. So this Deuke Chalence of Claraunce ded there grete dedis of armys, and, so late as he cam in the thirde day, there ded no man so well, excepte Kynge Bagdemagus and Sir Palomydes. And the pryce was gyvyn that day unto Kynge Bagdemagus; and than they blew unto lodgyng and unarmed them and wente to the feyste.

Ryght so cam in Sir Dynadan and mocked and japed wyth Kynge Bagdemagus, that all knyghtes lowghe at hym, for he was a fyne japer and lovynge unto all good knyghtes. So anone as they had dyned, there cam a varlet beerynge foure spearys on his backe; and he cam to Sir Palomydes and seyde thus: "Here is a knyght by that hath sente the[9] choyse of foure spearys, and requyryth you for youre ladyes sake to take that one halff of thes spearys and juste with hym in the fylde." "Telle hym," seyde Sir Palomydes, " 'I woll nat fayle you.' " So Sir Galahalte seyde, "Make you redy!"

¶So Quene Gwenyver, the Haute Prynce, and Sir Launcelot, they were sette in scaffoldis [to gyve the jugement of these two knyghtes]. Than Sir Palomydes and the straunge knyght ran togydirs and brake there spearys to their hondys; and anone aythir of them toke another speare and shyvyrd them in pecis. And than ayther toke a gretter speare; and than the knyght smote downe Sir Palomydes, horse and man—and as he wolde have passed over hym, the knyghtes horse stombeled and felle downe uppon Sir Palomydes. Than they drewe theire swerdis, and laysshed togydirs wondirly sore. Than the Haute Prynce and Sir Launcelot seyde they saw never two knyghtes fyght bettir. But ever the straunge knyght doubled his strokys and put Sir Palomydes abak—and therewithall the Haute Prynce cryed "Whoo!"

¶And than they wente to lodgynge; and whan they were unarmed, anone they knew hym for Sir Lamerok. And whan Launcelot knew Sir Lamerok, he made muche of hym, for of all erthely men he loved hym beste, excepte Sir Trystram. Than Quene Gwenyver commended hym, and so did all good knyghtes, and made muche of hym—excepte Sir Gawaynes brethirne. Than Quene Gwenyvir seyde unto Sir Launcelot, "Sir, I requyre you that, and ye juste ony more, that ye juste wyth none of the blood[1] of my lorde Kynge Arthur." And so he promysed he wolde nat as at that tyme.

Ere begynnyth the fourth day. Than cam into the fylde the Kynge with the Hondred Knyghtes, and all they of Northe Galys, and Deuke Chalens of Claraunce, and Kynge Marsyll of

Pometayne. And there cam Sir Saphir, Sir Palomydes brother, and he tolde hym tydynges of hys fadir and of his modir—"and his name was called [the] Erle,[2] and so I appeled hym afore the Kynge, for he made warre uppon oure fadir and modir; and there I slewe hym in playne batayle."

So they two wente into the fylde—and the damesell wyth hem. And there cam to encounter agayne them Sir Bleoberys de Ganys and Sir Ector de Marys. And Sir Palomydes encountyrd wyth Sir Bleoberys, and aythir smote other downe; in the same wyse ded Sir Saphir and Sir Ector, and tho two couplys ded batayle on foote. Than cam in Sir Lamerok; and he encountyrd with the Kynge of the Hondred Knyghtes and smote hym quyte over his horse tayle. And in the same wyse he served the Kynge of Northe Galys, and also he smote downe Kynge Marsyll—and so, or ever he stynte, he smote downe wyth his speare and with his swerde thirty knyghtys.

Whan Deuke Chalens saw Sir Lamerok do so grete proues, he wolde nat meddyll with hym for shame; and than he charged all his knyghtes in payne of deth that "none of you towche hym, for hit were shame to all goode knyghtes and that knyght were shamed." Than the two kynges gadird them togydirs; and all they sett uppon Sir Lameroke—and he fayled them nat, but russhed here and there and raced of many helmys, that the Haute Prince and Quene Gwenyver seyde they sawe never knyght do suche dedis of armys on horsebacke.

❡"Alas," seyde Sir Launcelot to Kynge Bagdemagus, "I woll arme me and helpe Sir Lamerok." "And I woll ryde wyth you," seyde Kynge Bagdemagus. And whan they two were horsed, they cam to Sir Lamerok, that stood amonge thirty knyghtes; and well was hym that myght reche hym a buffet, and ever he smote agayne myghtyly.

Than cam there into the pres Sir Launcelot; and he threwe downe Sir Mador de la Porte—and with the troncheon of that speare he threwe downe many knyghtes. And Kynge Bagdemagus smote on the lyffte honde and on the ryght honde mervaylusly well; and than tho three kynges[3] fledde abak. And therewithall Sir Galahalte lat blow to lodgynge; and all herrowdis gaff Sir Lamerok the pryce.

And all this whyle fought Sir Palomydes, and Sir Bleoberys, and Sir Safer, and Sir Ector on foote; and never was there foure knyghtes more evynner macched. And anone they were departed,[4] and had[5] unto their lodgynge, and unarmed[6]—and so they wente to the grete feste. But whan Sir Lamerok was com unto the courte, Quene Gwenyver enbraced hym in her armys and seyde, "Sir, well have ye done this day!" Than cam the Haute Prynce, and he made of hym grete joy—and so ded Sir Dynadan, for he wepte for joy; but the joy that Sir Launcelot made of Sir Lamerok, there myght no tonge telle.

fol.272v

fol.273r

---

2. Neither the Winchester MS nor Caxton provide a proper name for this earl; in Malory's likely source, the prose *Tristan*, he is styled the Earl *de la Planche*.
3. I.e., the three kings first encountered by Sir Lamerok (in the previous paragraph).
4. I.e., separated.
5. I.e., made way.
6. I.e., disarmed.

Than they wente unto reste. And so on the morne the Haute Prynce Sir **Galahalte** blew unto the fylde.

HEre begynnyth the fyfth day. So hit befell that Sir **Palomydes** cam in the morne-tyde, and profyrde to juste there as Kynge **Arthur** was in a castell there besydys Surluse; and there encountyrd with hym a worshypfull deuke that hyght **Adrawns**, and there Sir **Palomydes** smote hym over his horse croupyn. And this deuke was uncle unto Kynge **Arthure**. [46]

Than Sir **Elyce**, his sonne, rode unto Sir **Palomydes**—and so he servid Sir **Elyce** in the same wyse. Whan Sir **Gawayne** sawe this, he was wrothe. Than he toke his horse and encountird with Sir **Palomydes**; and Sir **Palomydes** smote hym so harde that he wente to the erthe, horse and man—and, for to make a short tale, he smote downe his three bretherne, that is for to say Sir **Mordred**, Sir **Gaherys**, and Sir **Aggravayne**.

"A, Jesu!" seyde Kynge Arthure, "this is a grete dispyte that suche a Saryson shall smyte downe my blood!" And therewithall Kynge **Arthure** was wrothe and thought to have made hym redy to juste. That aspyed Sir **Lamerok**, that Kynge **Arthure** and his blood was so discomfite; and anone he was redy and axed Sir **Palomydes** if he wolde ony more juste. "Why sholde I nat juste?" seyde Sir **Palomydes**. So they hurled togydirs and brake their spearys, and all to-shyvird them, that all the castell range of their dyntys. fol.273v

¶Than aythir gate a gretter speare, and they cam so fyersly togydir that Sir **Palomydes** speare brake, and Sir **Lamerokes** hylde; and therewythall Sir **Palomydes** loste his styroppis, and so he lay upryght[7] on his horse backe. But Sir **Palomydes** recoverde agayne, and toke his damesell—and so Sir **Saffir** and he wente their way. So whan he was departed, the Kynge cam to Sir **Lamerok** and thankyd hym of his goodnes, and prayde hym to tell hym his name. "Syr," seyde Sir **Lamerok**, "wyte you well I owghe you my servyse; but as at this tyme I woll nat abyde here, for I se off myne enemyes many aboute you." "Alas," seyde Kynge **Arthure**, "nowe wote I well hit is Sir **Lamerok** de Galys!

¶"A, Sir **Lamerok**, abyde wyth me! And, be[8] my crowne, I shall never fayle the—and nat so hardy in Sir **Gawaynes** hede, nothir none of his bretherne, to do the[9] wronge." "Sir, grete wronge have they done me and you bothe." "That is trouthe," seyde Kynge **Arthur**, "for they slew their owne modir, my sistir. Hit had bene muche fayrer and bettir that ye hadde wedded her, for ye ar a kynges sonne as well[1] as they."

¶"A, Jesu, mercy!"[2] seyde Sir **Lamerok**. "Her deth shall I never forgete; and if hit were nat at the[3] reverence of youre hyghnes, I

---

7. I.e., flat on his back.
8. I.e., (I swear) by.
9. *And nat so . . . of his bretherne:* and let not Gawain, on pain of his head, nor any of his brothers, be so bold. *The:* thee.
1. I.e., much.
2. I.e., thank you.
3. *At the:* i.e., out of.

sholde be revenged uppon Sir Gawayne and his bretherne." "Truly,"
seyde Kynge Arthour, "I woll make you at acorde."

¶"Sir," seyde Sir Lamerok, "as at this tyme I may nat abyde with
you, for I muste to the justis where is Sir Launcelot and the Haute
Prynce, Sir Galahalte." So there was a damesell that was doughtir
unto kynge Baudas; and there was a Sarazen knyght that hyght Sir
Corsabryne, and he loved the damesell. And in no wyse he wolde
suffir her to be maryed, for ever this Corsabryne noysed her and
named[4] her that she was oute of her mynde—and thus he lette her
that she myght nat be maryed.

¶So by fortune this damesell harde telle that Sir Palomydes ded
muche for damesels; and anone she sente hym a pensell[5] and
prayde hym to fyght with Sir Corsabroyne for her love, and he sholde
have her and all her londis, and of her fadirs that sholde falle[6] aftir
hym. Than the damesell sente unto Sir Corsabryne and bade hym
go unto Sir Palomydes—that was a paynym as well as he—and she
gaff hym warnynge that she had sente hym her pensell; and yf he
myght overcom Sir Palomydes, she wolde wedde hym.

¶Whan Sir Corsabryne wyste of her dedis, than was he wood
wrothe. And anone he rode unto Surluse where the Haute Prynce
was; and there he founde Sir Palomydes redy, the whyche had the
pensell. And so there they waged batayle aythir with othir, afore
Sir Galahalte. "Well," seyde the Haute Prynce, "this day muste
noble knyghtes juste; and at aftir dyner we shall se how ye[7] can
do." Than they blew to justys. And in cam Sir Dynadan and mette
with Sir Geryne, a good knyght, and he threw hym downe over his
horse croupen.

And Sir Dynadan overthrew foure knyghtes mo—and there he
dede grete dedis of armys, for he was a good knyght. But he was a
grete skoffer and a gaper, and the meryste knyght amonge felyship
that was that tyme lyvynge; and [he hadde suche a customme[8] that]
he loved every good knyght and every good knyght loved hym. So
whan the Haute Prynce saw Sir Dynadan do so well, he sente unto
Sir Launcelot and bade hym stryke hym adowne—"and [whan that
ye have done] so, brynge hym afore me and Quene Gwenyver." Than
Sir Launcelot ded as he was requyred.

Than cam Sir Lamorak and smote downe many knyghtes, and
raced of helmys, and droff all the knyghtes afore hym. And Sir
Launcelot smote adowne Sir Dynadan and made his men to unarme
hym, and so brought hym to the Quene and the Haute Prynce,
[and they] lowghe at Sir Dynadan that they myght nat stonde.
"Well," seyde Sir Dynadan, "yet have I no shame, for the olde shrew
Sir Launcelot smote me downe."

So they wente to dyner, all the courte, and had grete disporte at
Sir Dynadan. So whan the dyner was done, they blew to the fylde
to beholde Sir Palomydes and Sir Corsabryne. Syr Palomydes pyght

[47]
fol.274r

fol.274v

---

4. I.e., reputed of.
5. Presumably bearing the lady's heraldic insignia, and offered to the knight as a request for
   his service in arms.
6. I.e., descend to her.
7. I.e., Corsabryne and Palomydes alone.
8. I.e., manner, disposition.

his pensell in myddys of the fylde; and than they hurled togydirs
with her spearys as hit were thundir, and they smote aythir other
to the erthe. And than they pulled oute there swerdis and dressed
their shyldis and laysshed togydirs myghtyly as myghty knyghtes,
that well-nyghe there was no pyse of harneyse wolde holde⁹ them—   5
for this **Corsabryne** was a passynge felownse knyght.

¶Than **Corsabryne** seyde, "Sir **Palomydes**, wolt thou release me¹
yondir damesell, and the pensell?"

¶Than was he wrothe oute of mesure, and gaff Sir **Palomydes**
suche a buffet that he kneled on his kne; than Sir **Palomydes** arose   10
lyghtly and smote hym uppon the helme, that he fell upryght to
the erthe—and therewithall he raced of his helme, and seyde,
"Yelde the, **Corsabryne**, or thou shalt dye."

¶"Fye on the!" seyde Sir **Corsabryne**, "and do thy warste!" Than
he smote of his hede—and therewithall cam a stynke of his body,   15
whan the soule departed, that there myght nobody abyde the
savoure.² So was the corpus had away and buryed in a wood,
bycause he was a paynym.

Than they blew unto lodgyng, and Sir **Palomydes** was unarmed.
Than he wente unto Quene **Gwenyver**, to the Haute Prynce, and to   20
Sir **Launcelot**. "Sir," seyde the Haute Prynce, "here have ye seyne
this day a grete myracle by **Corsabryne**, what savoure was there whan
the soule departed frome the body; therefore we all requyre you to
take the baptyme uppon you—and than all knyghtes woll sette the
more be³ you."   25

¶"Sir," seyde Sir **Palomydes**, "I woll that ye all knowe that into
this londe I cam to be crystyned, and in my harte I am crystynde,   fol.275r
and crystynde woll I be; but I have made suche a vowe that I may
nat be crystynde tyll I have done seven trewe bataylis for Jesus
sake. And than woll I be crystynde; and I truste that God woll take⁴   30
myne entente, for I meane truly." Than Sir **Palomydes** prayde
Quene **Gwenyver** and the Haute Prynce [to soupe with hym]; and
so he ded bothe⁵ Sir **Launcelot** and Sir **Lamerok** and many other good
knyghtes. So on the morne they herde there Masse, and blewe to
the felde; and than many worshipfull knyghtes made them redy.   35

HEre begynnyth the syxth day. Than cam therein Sir **Gaherys**;   [48]
and there encountyrd with hym Sir **Ossayse** of **Surluse**, and Sir
Gaherys smote hym over his horse croupe. And than ayther party
encountyrd with othir, and there were many [speres, broken and
many] knyghtes caste undir fyete. So there cam in Sir **Darnarde** and   40
Sir **Agglovale**, that were bretherne unto Sir **Lamerok**, and they mette
with other two knyghtes; and aythir smote other so harde that all
foure knyghtes and horsis fell to the erthe.

¶Whan Sir **Lamerok** saw his two bretherne downe, he was wrothe

---

9. I.e., protect.
1. I.e., to me.
2. The stench of Corsabryne's body is a sign of the corruption and damnation of his soul;
   conversely, as is still commonly reported of the corpses of saints and holy people, a sweet
   smell is a sign of divine election.
3. I.e., by.
4. I.e., accept.
5. I.e., as well as.

oute of mesure; and than he gate a grete speare in his honde, and therewithall he smote downe foure good knyghtes—and than his speare brake.

¶Then he pulled oute his swerde and smote aboute hym on the ryght honde and on the lyffte honde, and raced of helmys and pulled downe knyghtes, that all men mervayled of suche dedis of armys as he ded, for he fared so that many knyghtes fledde.

¶Than he horsed his bretherne agayne and sayde, "Bretherne, ye ought to be ashamed to falle so of your horsis! What is a knyght but whan he is on horsebacke? For I sette nat by a knyght whan he is on foote, for all batayles on foote ar but pyllours batayles— for there sholde no knyght fyghte on foote but yf hit were for tre-son, or ellys he were dryvyn by forse to fyght on foote. Therefore, bretherne, sytte faste in your sadyls, or ellys fyght never more afore me!"

So with that cam in the Deuke Chalence of Claraunce; and there encountyrd with hym the Erle of Ulbawys of Surluse, and aythir of hem smote other downe. Than the knyghtes of bothe partyes horsed their lordis agayne—for Sir Ector and Sir Bleoberys were on foote waytynge on the Deuke Chalence, and the Kynge with the Hondred Knyghtes was with the Erle of Ulbawes. So wyth that cam Sir Gaherys and laysshed to the Kynge wyth the Hondred Knyghtes, and he to hym agayne; than cam the Deuke Chalence and departed them.

So they blew to lodgynge; and the knyghtes unarmed them and drewe them to there dyner. And at the myddys of this dynar in cam Sir Dynadan and began to rayle. And than he behelde the Haute Prynce that hym[6] semed wrothe with som faute that he sawe—for he had a condission that he loved no fysshe—and bycause he was served with fysshe, and hated hit, therefore he was nat myrry.

¶And whan Sir Dynadan had aspyed the Haute Prynce, he aspyed where was a fysshe with a grete hede; and anone that he gate betwyxte two disshis, and served the Haute Prynce with that fysshe—and than he sayde thus: "Sir Galahalte, well may I lykkyn you to a wolff, for he woll never ete fysshe, but fleysshe." And anone the Haute Prynce lowghe at his wordis.

¶"Well, well," seyde Sir Dynadan to Sir Launcelot, "what devyll do ye in this contrey? For here may no meane knyghtes wynne no worship for the:

¶"I ensure the," Sir Dynadan seyde, "Sir Launcelot, I shall no more mete with the, nother with thy grete speare; for I may nat sytte in my sadyll when thy speare hittyth me—and[7] I be happy, I shall beware of thy boysteous body that thou beryst!"

¶"Well," seyde Sir Launcelot, "make good wacche:[8]

¶"Over God[dis] forbode[9] that ever we mete but hit be at a

fol.275v

6. I.e., to him.
7. I.e., if.
8. *Make good wacche:* be very vigilant.
9. *Over God[dis] forbode:* Against God's forbidding. Both Winchester and Caxton have the nonpossessive form *God,* but this may represent the "correction" in this or an earlier copy by a scribe confused by the preterite form of *forbid* in what was, even in the 15th century,

dysshe of mete!" Than lowghe the Quene and the Haute Prynce,
that they myght nat sytte at their table—and thus they made grete
joy tyll on the morne. And than they harde Masse, and blew to the
fylde; and Quene Gwenyver and all astatys were sette as jouges,
armed clene[1] with their shyldis, to kepe the ryghtes.

Now begynnyth the sevynth batayle. Here cam in the Deuke
Cambynes; and there encountyrd with hym Sir Arystaunce, that
was cownted a good knyght, and they mette so harde that aythir
bare other adowne, horse and man. Than there cam in the Erle
Lambayle and halpe the deuke agayne to horsebacke; than there
cam in Sir Ossayse of Surluse, and he smote the Erle Lambayle
downe frome his horse. And so they began grete dedis of armys;
and many spearys were brokyn, and many knyghtes were caste to
the erthe. Than the Kynge of Northe Galys and the Erle Ulbawes
smote togydyrs, that all the jouges thought hit was mortall deth.

This meanewhyle, Quene Gwenyver and the Haute Prynce and
Sir Launcelot made there Sir Dynadan to make hym redy to juste. "I
woll, seyde Sir Dynadan, "ryde into the fylde—but than one of you
twayne woll mete with me!" "Perdeus!" seyde the Haute Prynce
and Sir Launcelot, "ye may se how we sytte here as jouges with oure
shyldis, and allway may ye beholde where[2] we sytte here or nat."

¶So Sir Dynadan departed and toke his horse, and mette with
many knyghtes and ded passyngly well; and as he was departed,
Sir Launcelot disgysed hymselff and put uppon his armour a maydyns garmente freysshely attyred.

¶Than Sir Launcelot made Sir Galyhodyn to lede hym thorow the
raunge—and all men had wondir what damesell was that. And so
as Sir Dynadan cam into the raunge, Sir Launcelot, that was in the
damesels aray, gate Sir Galyhodyns speare and ran unto Sir Dynadan.
And allwayes he loked up there as Sir Launcelot was—and than he
sawe one sytte in the stede of Sir Launcelot armed—but whan Sir
Dynadan saw a maner of a damesell, he dradde perellys lest hit
sholde be Sir Launcelot disgysed. But Sir Launcelot cam on hym so
faste that he smote Sir Dynadan over his horse croupe—and anone
grete coystrons gate Sir Dynadan, and[3] into the foreyste there
besyde; and there they dispoyled hym unto his sherte and put
uppon hym a womans garmente, and so brought hym into fylde.
And so they blew unto lodgyng, and every knyght wente and
unarmed them.

¶And than was Sir Dynadan brought in amonge them all; and
whan Quene Gwenyver sawe Sir Dynadan i-brought in so amonge
them all, than she lowghe, that she fell downe—and so dede all
that there was.

¶"Well," seyde Sir Dynadan, "Sir Launcelot, thou arte so false that
I can never beware of the!"

fol.276r

[49]

fol.276v

---

an old and conventional phrase—but rarer than "God forbid"; alternatively, a small abbreviation for the possessive inflexion on *God* may not have been noticed in copying.

1. I.e., only.
2. I.e., whether.
3. I.e., and took him.

¶Than by all the assente they gaff Sir Launcelot the pryce; the next was Sir Lameroke de Galys, and the thirde was Sir Palomydes; the fourth was Kynge Bagdemagus. So thes foure knyghtes had the pryce, and there was grete joy and grete nobelay in all the courte. And on the morne Quene Gwenyver and Sir Launcelot departed unto Kynge Arthur—but in no wyse Sir Lamerok wolde nat go wyth them.

¶"Sir, I shall undirtake", seyde Sir Launcelot, "that, and ye woll go wyth us, Kynge Arthure shall charge Sir Gawayne and his bretherne never to do you hurte."

¶"As for that," sayde Sir Lamerok, "I woll nat truste to Sir Gawayne, nother none of his bretherne—and wyte you well, Sir Launcelot, and hit were nat for my lorde Kynge Arthurs sake, I shuld macche Sir Gawayne and his bretherne well inowghe. But for to sey that I shall truste them, that shall I never; and therefore I pray you recommaunde me unto Kynge Arthure and all my lordys of the Rounde Table—and in what place that ever I com, I shall do you all servyse to my power. And, sir, yet hit is but late[4] that I revenged them whan they were put to the wors by Sir Palomydes." Than Sir Lameroke departed frome Sir Launcelot and all the felyship, and aythir of them wepte at her departynge.

Now turne we from this mater and speke of Sir Trystram, of whom this booke is pryncipall[5] off, and leve we the Kynge and the Quene, and Sir Launcelot and Sir Lamerok.

¶And here begynneth the treson of Kynge Marke that he ordayned agayne Sir Trystram. And there was cryed by the costys of Cornwayle a grete turnemente and justus, and all was done by Sir Galahalt the Haute Prynce and Kynge Bagdemagus, to the entente to sle syr Launcelot, other ellys uttirly to destroy hym and shame hym, bycause Sir Launcelot had evermore the hygher degré.

¶Therefore this prince and this kynge made this justys ayenst Sir Launcelot. And thus her counceyle was discoverde unto Kynge Marke, whereof he was glad; than Kynge Marke unbethought hym that he wolde have Sir Trystram unto the turnemente disgysed, that no man sholde knowe hym, to that entente that the Haute Prynce sholde wene that Sir Trystram were Sir Launcelot. And so at that justys cam in Sir Trystram; and at that tyme Sir Launcelot was not there.

¶But whan they sawe a knyght disgysed do suche dedis of armys, they wente hit had bene Sir Launcelot—and in especiall Kynge Marke seyde hit was Sir Launcelot playnly. Than they sette uppon hym, bothe Kynge Bagdemagus and the Haute Prynce; and there knyghtes seyde that hit was wondir that ever Sir Trystram myght endure that payne. Notwythstondynge for all the payne that they ded hym, he wan the degri at that turnemente—and there he hurte many knyghtes and brused them; [and they hurte hym and brused hym] wondirly sore. So whan the justys was all done, they knewe

5

10

15

fol.277r
20

[50]

25

30

35

40

45

---

4. I.e., recently.
5. I.e., principally.

well that he was Sir **Trystram de Lyones**; and all they that were on
Kynge **Markis** party were glad that Sir **Trystram** was hurte, and all
the remenaunte were sory of his hurte—

¶For Sir **Trystrams** was nat so behated as was Sir **Launcelot**, nat
wythin the realme of Ingelonde. Than cam Kynge **Marke** unto Sir   fol.277v   5
Trystrams, and sayde, "Fayre nevew, I am hevy of your hurtys."

¶"Gramercy, my lorde," seyde Sir **Trystram**. Than Kynge **Marke**
made hym to be put in an horse-letter in grete tokenynge of love,
and sayde, "Fayre cousyne, I shall be your leche myselff." And so
he rode forth wyth Sir **Trystram** and brought hym into a castell by   10
daylyght. And than Kynge **Marke** made Sir **Trystram** to ete, and aftir
that he gaff hym a drynke; and anone as he hadde drunke he felle
on slepe. And whan hit was nyght, he made hym to be caryed to
another castell; and there he put hym in a stronge preson—

¶And[6] a man and a woman to gyff hym his mete and his drynke.   15
So there he was a grete whyle.

¶Than was Sir **Trystram** myssed, and no creature wyst where he
was becam.

¶And whan La Beall **Isode** harde how he was myste, pryvayly
she wente unto Sir **Sadocke** and prayde hym to aspye where was Sir   20
Trystram. And whan Sir **Sadocke** knew how Sir **Trystram** was myste,
he sought and made spyes for hym; and than he aspyed that Kynge
Marke had put the good knyght in preson by his owne assente and
the traytoures of **Magouns**.[7] Than Sir **Sadocke** toke with hym too of
his cousyns, and he layde them and hymself anone in a bushe-   25
mente faste by the castell of Tyntagyll, in armys; and as by fortune
there cam rydyng Kynge **Marke** and foure of his nevewys, and a
sertayne[8] of the traytoures of Magouns.

¶So whan Sir **Sadocke** aspyed them, he brake oute of bushemente and sette there uppon them.   30

¶And whan that Kynge **Marke** aspyed Sir **Sadocke** he fledde as
faste as he myght; and there Sir **Sadocke** slew all the foure nevewys
of Kynge **Marke**, his cousyns.[9] But these traytoures of **Magouns**
smote one of Sir **Sadockes** cousyns a grete wounde in the necke—
but Sir **Sadocke** smote other twayne to the deth. Than Sir **Sadocke**   35
rode uppon his way unto the castell that was called **Lyonas**, and   fol.278r
there he aspyde of the treson and felony of Kynge **Marke**. So off[1]
that castell they rode wyth Sir **Sadocke** tyll they cam to a castel that
hyght **Arbray**; and there in the towne they founde Sir **Dynas** the
Senesciall, that was a good knyght.   40

¶But whan Sir **Sadock** had tolde Sir **Dynas** of all the treson of
Kynge **Marke**, than he defyed suche a kynge, and seyde he wolde
gyff up all his londis that [he] hylde of hym; and whan he seyde
thes wordis, all maner[2] knyghtes seyde as Sir **Dynas** sayde.

¶Than by his advyse, and of Sir **Sadockes**, he let stuff all the   45

---

6. I.e., with.
7. *Traytoures of Magouns:* traitors from the castle of Magouns.
8. I.e., certain number.
9. I.e., close relatives.
1. I.e., from.
2. I.e., manner of.

townys and castels wythin the contrey of Lyones, and assemble all that they cowde make.

Now turne [we] unto Kynge Marke, that whan he was ascaped frome Sir Sadocke he rode unto the castell of Tyntagyll; and there he made a grete cry and noyse, and cryed unto harneyse[3] all that myght bere armys. Than they sought and founde where was dede foure cousyns of Kynge Marke, and the traytoure of Magouns; than the kynge lette entyre[4] them in a chapell. Than Kynge Marke lette cry in all the contrey that hylde of[5] hym to go unto armys, for he undirstood that to the warre he muste nedis.

¶So whan Kynge Marke harde and undirstood how Sir Dynas and Sir Sadok were arysyn in the contrey of Lyones, he remembird of treson and wyeles; and so thus he ded lete make and countirfete lettirs from the Pope, and dede make a straunge clarke to brynge tho lettyrs unto Kynge Marke, the whyche lettyrs specifyed that Kynge Marke sholde make hym redy, uppon payne of cursynge,[6] wyth his oste to com to the Pope to helpe hym to go to Jerusalem for to make warre upon the Saresyns.

¶So whan this clarke was com, by the meane of the kynge, anone therewyth Kynge Marke sente that clarke unto Sir Trystram and bade hym sey thus: that, and he wolde go warre upon the myscreauntes, he sholde go oute of preson and have all his power with hym.

¶Whan Sir Trystram undirstood this lettir, than he sayde thus to the clerke:

¶"A, Kynge Marke, ever haste thou bene a traytoure, and ever wolt be! But thou, clerke," seyde Sir Trystram, "sey thou thus unto Kynge Marke: syne the Pope hath sente for hym, bid hym go thidir hymselff—for, telle hym, traytoure kynge as he is, I woll nat go at his commaundement, gete oute of preson as well as I may, for I se I am well rewarded for my trewe servyse."

¶Than the clarke returned agayne unto Kynge Mark and tolde hym of the answere of Sir Trystram. "Well," seyde Kynge Marke, "yet shall he be begyled." And anone he wente unto hys chambir and countirfeted lettyrs, and the lettyrs specifyed that the Pope desyred Sir Trystram to com hymself to make warre uppon the myscreauntes.

¶So whan the clerke cam agayne unto Sir Trystram and toke hym thes lettyrs, he aspyed they were of Kynge Markes countirfe-tynge, and sayde, "A, Kynge Marke, false hast thou ever bene, and so wolt thou ende."

¶Than the clarke departed frome Sir Trystram and cam unto Kynge Marke agayne. And so by than there was com foure wounded knyghtes within the castell of Tyntagyll; and one of them his necke was nyghe brokyn in twayne, and another had his arme nyghe stry-kyn away; the thirde was boren thorow with a speare; the fourthe

[51]

5

10

15

20

fol.278v

25

30

35

40

45

---

3. *Cryed unto harneyse:* ordered to arms.
4. I.e., inter.
5. *Hylde of:* held land from (as feudal tenants).
6. I.e., excommunication.

had his thyghe stryken in twayne. And whan they cam afore Kynge
Marke, they cryed and sayde, "Kynge, why fleyste thou nat? For all
this contrey ys clyerly arysen ayenste the." Than was Kynge Marke
wrothe oute of mesure. And so in the meanewhyle there cam into
the contrey Sir Percivale de Galys to seke aftir Sir Trystram; and whan   5
Sir Percivale harde that Sir Trystram was in preson, he made clerly
the delyveraunce of hym by his knyghtly meanys. And whan he was
so delyverde, he made grete joy of Sir Percivale, and so ded ech one
of other.

⁋Than Sir Trystram seyde unto Sir Percivale, "And ye woll abyde   10
in this marchis, I woll ryde with you." "Nay," seyde Sir Percivale,   fol.279r
"in thes contreyes I may nat tary, for I muste nedis into Wales."
So Sir Percivale departed frome Sir Trystram, and streyte he rode
unto Kynge Marke and tolde hym how he had delyvered Sir Trystram; and also he tolde the kynge that he had done hymselff grete   15
shame for to preson Sir Trystram so—"for he is now the knyght of
moste reverence in the worlde lyvynge. And wyte you well that the
noblyste knyghtes of the worlde lovyth Sir Trystram; and yf he woll
make warre uppon you, ye may nat abyde hit."

⁋"That is trouthe," seyde Kynge Marke, "but I may nat love Sir   20
Trystram, bycause he lovyth my quene, La Beall Isode." "A, fy, for
shame!" seyde Sir Percivale. "Sey ye never so more! For ar nat ye
uncle unto Sir Trystram, and he youre neveaw? Ye sholde never
thynke that, so noble a knyght as Sir Trystram is, that he wolde do
hymselff so grete vylany to holde his unclys wyff. Howbehit," seyde   25
Sir Percivale, "he may love youre quene synles,[7] because she is
called one of the fayryst ladyes of the worlde." Than Sir Percivale
departed frome Kynge Marke—but yet he bethought hym of more
treson.

Notwithstondynge, he graunted unto Sir Percivale never by no   30
maner of meanys to hurte Sir Trystram. So anone Kynge Marke
sente unto Sir Dynas the Senesciall that he sholde put downe[8] all
the people that he had raysed, for he sente hym an othe[9] that he
wolde go hymselff unto the Pope of Rome to warre uppon the
myscreauntes—"and I trow that is fayrer warre than thus to areyse   35
people agaynste youre kynge." And anone as Sir Dynas undirstood
that he wolde go uppon the myscreauntys, than Sir Dynas, in all
the haste that myght be, he putte downe all his people. And whan
the people were departed every man to his home—

⁋Than Kynge Marke aspyed where was Sir Trystram wyth La   40
Beall Isode; and there by treson Kynge Marke lete take hym and put
hym in preson, contrary to his promyse that he made unto Sir
Percivale.

⁋Whan Quene Isode undirstode that Sir Trystram was in preson   fol.279v
agayne, she made grete sorow as ever made lady or jantyllwoman.   45
Than Sir Trystram sente a lettir unto La Beall Isode and prayde hir
to be his good lady, and sayde, yf hit pleased her to make a vessell

---

7. I.e., platonically, at a distance.
8. *Put downe:* i.e., put at rest, send home.
9. I.e., a promise.

redy for her and hym, he wolde go wyth her unto the realme of Logrys (that is this londe).[1]

¶Whan La Beall Isode undirstood Sir Trystrams [letters] and his entente, she sente hym another and bade hym be of good comforte, for she wolde do make the vessell redy and all maner of thynge to purpose. Than La Beall Isode sente unto Sir Dynas and to Sir Sadok and prayde hem in ony wyse to take Kynge Marke and put hym in preson unto the tyme that she and Sir Trystram were departed unto the realme of Logrys.

¶Whan Sir Dynas the Senesciall undirstood the treson of Kynge Marke, he promysed her to do her commaundemente, and sente her worde agayne that Kynge Marke sholde be put in preson; and so as they devysed hit was done. And than Sir Trystram was delyverde oute of preson; and anone in all haste Quene Isode and Sir Trystram wente and toke there counceyle,[2] and so they toke wyth them what them lyste beste, and so they departed.

Than La Beall Isode and Sir Trystram toke their vessell, and cam by watir into this londe. And so they were nat foure dayes in this londe but there was made a crye of a justys and turnement that Kynge Arthure let make. Whan Sir Trystram harde tell of that turnement, he disgysed hymselff and La Beall Isode and rode unto that turnemente. And whan he cam there, he sawe many knyghtes juste and turney; and so Sir Trystram dressed hym to the raunge[3]— and, to make shorte conclusyon, he overthrewe fourtene knyghtes of the Rounde Table.

¶Whan Sir Launcelot saw thes knyghtes of the Rounde Table thus overthrowe, he dressed hym to Sir Trystram.

¶And that sawe La Beall Isode, how Sir Launcelot was commyn into the fylde; than she sente unto Sir Launcelot a rynge to lat hym wete hit was Sir Trystram de Lyones.

¶Whan Sir Launcelot undirstood that he was Sir Trystram, he was full glad and wolde nat juste. And than Sir Launcelot aspyed whydir Syr Trystram yeode, and aftir hym he rode; and than aythir made grete joy of other. And so Sir Launcelot brought Sir Trystram and Isode unto Joyus Garde, that was his owne castell, and he had wonne hit with his owne hondis; and there Sir Launcelot put them in, to welde hit for their owne.

¶And wyte you well, that castell was garnyshed and furnysshed for a kynge and a quene royall there to have suggeourned. And Sir Launcelot charged all his people to honoure them and love them as they wolde do hymselff.

¶So Sir Launcelot departed unto Kynge Arthure; and than he tolde Quene Gwenyver how he that justed so well at the laste turnemente was Sir Trystram—and there he tolde her how that he had with hym La Beall Isode, magré Kynge Marke. And so Quene Gwenyvere tolde all this to Kynge Arthure; and whan Kynge Arthure wyste that Sir Trystram was ascaped and commyn from Kynge Marke and had

[52]

fol.280r

1. *This londe:* i.e., England, one of Arthur's kingdoms.
2. *Toke there counceyle:* i.e., consulted with one another.
3. *Dressed hym to the raunge:* entered the tournament.

brought La Beall Isode with hym, than was he passyng glad. So, bycause of Sir Trystram, Kynge Arthure let make a cry that on May-day shulde be a justis byfore the castell of Lonezep—and that castell was faste by Joyus Garde.

¶And thus Kynge Arthure devysed that all the knyghtes of this londe, of Cornwayle, and of North Walys, shulde juste ayenste all thes contreyis: Irelonde and Scotlonde and the remenaunte of Walys, and the contrey of Goore and Surluse, and of Lystenoyse, and they of Northumbirlonde, and all those that hylde londis of Kynge Arthurs a this halff[4] the se.

¶So whan this crye was made, many knyghtes were glad and many were sad. "Sir," seyde Sir Launcelot unto Kynge Arthure, "by this cry that ye have made ye woll put us that bene aboute you in grete jouparté, for there be many knyghtes that hath envy to us:

¶"Therefore whan we shall mete at the day of justis there woll be harde skyffte for us."

¶"As for that, seyde Kynge Arthure, "I care nat; there shall we preve whoo shall be beste of his hondis."

¶So whan Sir Launcelot undirstood wherefore Kynge Arthure made this justenynge, than he made suche purvyaunce that La Beall Isode sholde beholde the justis in a secrete place that was honeste[5] for her astate.

¶Now turne we unto Sir Trystram and to La Beall Isode, how they made joy togydrys dayly with all maner of myrthis that they coude devyse. And every day Sir Trystram wolde go ryde an-huntynge, for he was called that tyme the chyeff chacer of the worlde, and the noblyst blower of an horne of all maner of mesures. (For, as bookis reporte, of Sir Trystram cam all the good termys of venery and of huntynge,[6] and all the syses and mesures of all blow-yng wyth an horne; and of hym we had fyrst all the termys of hawkynge, and whyche were bestis of chace and bestis of venery, and whyche were vermyns; and all the blastis that longed to all maner of game: fyrste to the uncoupelynge, to the sekynge, to the fyndynge, to the rechace, to the flyght, to the deth, and to strake, and many other blastis and termys, that all maner jantylmen hath cause to the worldes ende to prayse Sir Trystram and to pray for his soule—"Amen," sayde Sir Thomas Malleorré.)[7]

¶So on a day La Beall Isode seyde unto Sir Trystram, "I mervayle me muche that ye remembir nat youreselff how ye be here in a straunge contrey, and here be many perelous knyghtes—and well ye wote that Kynge Marke is full of treson; and that ye woll ryde thus to chace and to hunte unarmed, ye myght be sone destroyed."

¶"My fayre lady and my love, mercy.[8] I woll no more do so." So

5

fol.280v

15

20

25

30

35

[53]

40

fol.281r

---

4. I.e., side of.
5. I.e., decent.
6. On Trystram's legendary status as a founder of the arts of hunting, see n. 7, p. 231.
7. *Prayse Sir Trystram and . . . pray for his soule—"Amen!" sayde Sir Thomas Malleorré*: i.e., Malory is being identified, either by himself or by a later scribe, as saying amen to any such prayer said for Trystram, or even just to the proposition that such prayers should be said for him. On *amen*, cf. n. 8, p. 112.
8. I.e., thank you.

than Sir Trystram rode dayly an-huntynge armed, and his men berynge his shylde and his speare.

¶So on a day, a lytil afore the moneth o May, Sir Trystram chaced an harte passynge egirly; and so the harte passed by a fayre welle.

¶And than Sir Trystram alyght and put of his helme to drynke of that burbely welle, and ryght so he harde and sawe the Questynge Beste commynge towarde the welle.

¶So whan Sir Trystram saw that beste, he put on his helme, for he demed he sholde hyre of Sir Palomydes—for that beste was hys queste.

¶Ryght so, Sir Trystram saw where cam a knyghte armed uppon a noble courser, and so he salewed hym.

¶So they spake of many thynges; and this knyghtes name was Sir Brewnys Saunz Pité. And so anone with that there cam unto them Sir Palomydes, and aythir salewed other and spake fayre to other. "Now, fayre knyghtes," seyde Sir Palomydes, I can tell you tydynges."

¶"What is that?" seyde tho knyghtes.

¶"Sirris, wyte you well that Kynge Marke of Cornwayle is put in preson by his owne knyghtes. And all was for the love of Sir Trystram; for Kynge Marke had put Sir Trystram twyse in preson, and onys Sir Percivale delyverde hym, and at the laste tyme La Beall Isode delyverde Sir Trystram and wente clyerly away wyth hym into this realme. And all this whyle Kynge Marke is in preson. And[9] this be trouthe," seyde Sir Palomydes, "we shall hyre hastely of Sir Trystram. And as for to say that I love La Beall Isode paramoures, I dare make good that I do, and that she hath my servyse abovyn all other ladyes, and shall have, all the terme of my lyff."

¶And ryght so as they stoode thus talkynge, they sawe afore them where cam a knyght all armed on a grete horse; and his one man bare hys shylde, and the othir his speare. And anone as that knyght aspied hem, he gate his shylde and his speare and dressed hym to juste. "Now, fayre felowys," seyde Sir Trystram, "yondir ys a knyghte woll juste wyth us; now lette us se whyche of us shall encountir wyth hym—for I se well he is of the courte of Kynge Arthur." "Hit shall nat be longe ar he be mette wythall," seyde Sir Palomydes, "for I fonde never no knyght in my queste of this Glatissynge Beste but, and he wolde juste, I never yet refused hym." "Sir, as well may I," seyde Sir Brewnes Saunz Pité, "folow that beste as ye." "Than shall ye do batayle wyth me," seyde Sir Palomydes.

So Sir Palomydes dressed hym unto that othir knyght—whyche hyght Sir Bleoberis, that was a noble knyght and nygh kynne unto Sir Launcelot; and so they mette so harde that Sir Palomydes felle to the erthe, horse and man. Than Sir Bleoberys cryed alowde and seyde thus: "Make redy, thou false traytoure knyght, Sir Brewnys Saunze Pité! For I woll have ado wyth the to the uttraunce, for the noble knyghtes and ladyes that thou haste betrayde."

¶Whan Sir 𝔅𝔯𝔢𝔴𝔫𝔶𝔰 harde hym sey so, he toke his horse by the brydyll and fledde his way [as faste as ever his hors myghte renne].

¶Whan Sir 𝔅𝔩𝔢𝔬𝔟𝔢𝔯𝔶𝔰 saw hym fle, he folowed faste after, thorow thycke and thorow thynne. And by fortune, as Sir 𝔅𝔯𝔢𝔴𝔫𝔶𝔰 fled, he saw evyn afore hym three knyghtes of the Table Rounde: that one hyght Sir 𝔈𝔠𝔱𝔬𝔯 𝔡𝔢 𝔐𝔞𝔯𝔶𝔰 and the othir hyght Sir 𝔓𝔢𝔯𝔠𝔦𝔟𝔞𝔩𝔢 𝔡𝔢 𝔊𝔞𝔩𝔶𝔰; the thirde hyght Sir 𝔥𝔞𝔯𝔯𝔶 𝔩𝔢 𝔍𝔶𝔷𝔢 𝔏𝔞𝔨𝔢, a good knyght and an hardy——and as for Sir 𝔓𝔢𝔯𝔠𝔦𝔟𝔞𝔩𝔢, he was called that tyme as of his ayge one of the beste knyghtes of the worlde and the beste assured.[1] So whan Sir 𝔅𝔯𝔢𝔴𝔫𝔶𝔰 saw these knyghtes, he rode strayte unto them and cryed and prayde them of rescowys.

¶"What nede have ye?" seyde Sir 𝔈𝔠𝔱𝔬𝔯. "A, fayre knyghte," seyde Sir 𝔅𝔯𝔢𝔴𝔫𝔶𝔰, "here folowyth me the moste traytour knyght, and the moste coward, and moste of vylany—and his name is Sir 𝔅𝔯𝔢𝔴𝔫𝔶𝔰 𝔖𝔞𝔲𝔫𝔷𝔢 𝔓𝔦𝔱é—and if he may gete me, he woll sle me wythoute mercy and pyté." "Than abyde ye with us," seyde Sir 𝔓𝔢𝔯𝔠𝔦𝔟𝔞𝔩𝔢, "and we shall warraunte you." And anone were they ware of Sir 𝔅𝔩𝔢𝔬𝔟𝔢𝔯𝔶𝔰 whyche cam rydyng all that[2] he myght. Than Sir 𝔈𝔠𝔱𝔬𝔯 put hymselff fyrste forthe to juste afore them all.

¶And whan Sir 𝔅𝔩𝔢𝔬𝔟𝔢𝔯𝔶𝔰 saw that they were foure knyghtes and he but hymselff, he stoode in a dwere whethir he wolde turne other holde his way.

¶Than he seyde to hymselff, "I am a knyght of the Table Rounde, and rathir than I sholde shame myne othe[3] and my bloode, I woll holde my way, whatsomever falle thereoff." And than Sir 𝔈𝔠𝔱𝔬𝔯 dressed his speare, and smote aythir other passyng sore— but Sir 𝔈𝔠𝔱𝔬𝔯 felle to the erthe. That saw Sir 𝔓𝔢𝔯𝔠𝔦𝔟𝔞𝔩𝔢; and he dressed his horse towarde hym all that he myght dryve—but Syr 𝔓𝔢𝔯𝔠𝔶𝔳𝔞𝔩𝔢 had[4] suche a stroke that horse and man felle bothe to the erthe.

¶Whan Sir 𝔥𝔞𝔯𝔯𝔶 saw that they were bothe to the erthe—

¶Than he seyde to hymselff, "Never was Sir 𝔅𝔯𝔢𝔴𝔫𝔢𝔰 of suche proues." So Sir 𝔥𝔞𝔯𝔯𝔶 dressed his horse; and they mette togydyrs so strongly that bothe the horsys and the knyghtes felle to the erthe—but Sir 𝔅𝔩𝔢𝔬𝔟𝔢𝔯𝔶𝔰 horse began to recover agayne.

¶That saw Sir 𝔅𝔯𝔢𝔴𝔫𝔶𝔰 and cam hurtelynge, and smote hym over and over, and wolde have slayne hym as he lay on the grounde.

¶Than Sir 𝔥𝔞𝔯𝔯𝔶 arose lyghtly and toke the brydyll of Sir 𝔅𝔯𝔢𝔴𝔫𝔶𝔰 horse, and sayde, "Fy, for shame! Stryke never a knyght whan he is at the erthe! For this knyght may be called no shamefull knyght of his dedis, for on this grounde he hath done worshypfully, and put to the warre passynge good knyghtes." "Therefore woll I nat let," seyde Sir 𝔅𝔯𝔢𝔴𝔫𝔶𝔰. "Thou shalt nat chose,"[5] seyde Sir 𝔥𝔞𝔯𝔯𝔶, "as at this tyme!" So whan Sir 𝔅𝔯𝔢𝔴𝔫𝔶𝔰 saw that he myght nat have hys wylle, he spake fayre.[6] Than Sir 𝔥𝔞𝔯𝔯𝔶 let hym go; and than

fol.282r

---

1. *Beste assured:* i.e., most confident.
2. *All that:* i.e., as fast as.
3. I.e., sworn duty. On the sworn prerogatives of knighthood, see n. 6, p. 77.
4. I.e., received.
5. I.e., decide this.
6. *Spake fayre:* i.e., spoke as if agreeable.

anone he made his horse to renne over Sir Bleoberys, and rosshed hym to the erthe, lyke to have slayne hym.

⁋Whan Sir Harry saw hym do so vylaunsly, he cryed and sayde, "Traytoure knyght! leve of, for shame!"

⁋And as Sir Harry wolde have takyn his horse to fyght wyth Syr Brewnys, than Sir Brewnys [ranne upon hym] as he was halff uppon his horse, and smote hym downe, horse and man, and had slayne nere Sir Harry, the good knyght.

⁋That saw Sir Percyvale, and than he cryde, "Traytur knyght! what doste thou?"

⁋And whan Sir Percyvale was uppon his horse, Sir Brewnys toke his horse and fledde all that ever he myght—and Sir Percyvale and Sir Harry folowed hym faste; but ever the lenger they chaced, the farther were they behynde. Than they turned agayne and cam to Sir Ector de Marys and to Sir Bleoberys. Than sayde Sir Bleoberys, "Why have ye so succoured that false traytoure knyght?"

⁋"Why," sayde Sir Harry, "what knyght is he? For well I wote hit is a false knyght," seyde Sir Harry, "and a cowarde and a felons knyght." "Sir," seyde Sir Bleoberys, "he is the moste cowarde knyght, and a devowrer of ladyes, and also a distroyer of Kynge Arthurs knyghtes as grete as ony ys now lyvynge."

⁋"Sir, what is youre name?" seyde Sir Ector. "My name is", he seyde, "Sir Bleoberys de Ganys." "Alas, fayre cousyn!" seyde Sir Ector, "forgyff me, for I am Sir Ector de Marys." Than Sir Percyvale and Sir Harry made grete joy of Sir Bleoberys—but all they were hevy that Sir Brewnys Saunze Pité had ascaped them, whereof they made grete dole.

⁋Ryght so as they stood there cam Sir Palomydes; and whan he saw the shylde of Sir Bleoberys ly on the erthe, than sayde Sir Palomydes, "He that owyth that shylde, lette hym dresse hym to me, for he smote me downe here faste by at a fountayne—and therefore I woll fyght wyth hym on foote."

⁋"Sir, I am redy," seyde Sir Bleoberys, "here to answere the; for wyte thou well, Sir knyght, hit was I—and my name ys Sir Bleoberys de Ganys." "Well art thou mette," seyde Sir Palomydes—"and wyte thou well my name ys Sir Palomydes the Saresyn." (And aythir of them hated other to the dethe.)

⁋"Sir Palomydes," seyde Sir Ector, "wyte thou well there is nother thou nothir no knyght that beryth the lyff that sleyth ony of oure bloode but he shall dye for hit. Therefore, and thou lyst to fyght, go and syke Sir Launcelot othir ellys Sir Trystram, and there shalt thou fynde thy matche."

⁋"Wyth them have I mette," seyde Sir Palomydes, "but I had never no worshyp of them."

⁋"Was there never no maner of knyght," seyde Sir Ector, "but they too⁷ that ever matched you?"

⁋"Yes," seyde Sir Palomydes, "there was the thirde—as good a knyght as ony of them—and of his ayge he was the beste, for yet

---

7. I.e., two.

founde I never his pyere; for, and he myght have lyved tyll he had
bene more of ayge, an hardyer man there lyvith nat than he wolde
have bene—and his name was Sir **Lamorak de Galys**. And as he had
justed at a turnemente, there he overthrewe me and thirty knyghtes
mo, and there he wan the gré; and at his departynge there mette
hym Sir **Gawayne** and his bretherne, and wyth grete payne they
slewe hym felounsly, unto all good knyghtes grete damage."[8]

¶And anone as Sir **Percyvale** herde that his brothir was dede, Sir
Lamerok, he felle over his horse mane sownynge; and there he made
the grettyste dole and sorow that ever made any noble knyght.

¶And whan Sir **Percyvale** arose, he seyde, "Alas, my good and
noble brother, Sir **Lamorak**, now shall we never mete! And I trowe
in all the wyde worlde may nat a man fynde suche a knyght as
he was of his ayge. And hit is to muche to suffir the deth of oure
fadir, Kynge **Pellynor**, and now the deth of oure good brother Sir
Lamorak."

¶So in this meanewhyle there cam a varlet frome the courte of
Kynge **Arthure**, and tolde hem of the grete turnemente that sholde
be at **Lonezep**, and how this londis, Cornwayle and Northe Galys,
shulde juste ayenst all that wolde com of other contereyes.

NOw turne we unto Sir **Trystram**, that as he rode an-huntynge
he mette wyth Sir **Dynadan**, that was commyn[9] into the contrey
to seke Sir **Trystram**. And anone Sir **Dynadan** tolde Sir **Trystram** his
name—but Sir **Trystram** wolde nat tell his name. Wherefore Sir
Dynadan was wrothe—"for suche a folyshe knyght as ye ar," seyde
Sir **Dynadan**, "I saw but late this day lyynge by a welle: and he fared
as he slepte, and there he lay lyke a fole, grennynge, and wolde nat
speke—and his shylde lay by hym, and his horse also stood by
hym—and well I wote he was a lovear." "A, fayre sir," seyde Sir
Trystram, "ar nat ye a lovear?"

¶"Mary, fye on that craufte!" seyde Sir **Dynadan**. "Sir, that is
yevell seyde," seyde Sir **Trystram**, "for a knyght may never be of
proues but yf he be a lovear." "Ye say well," seyde Sir **Dynadan**.
"Now I pray you telle me youre name, syth ye be suche a lovear;
othir ellys I shall do batayle with you."

¶"As for that," seyde Sir **Trystram**, "hit is no reson to fyght wyth
me but yf I telle you my name; and as for my name, ye shall nat
wyte as at this tyme for me."

¶"Fye, for shame! Ar ye a knyght and dare nat telle youre name
to me? Therefore, sir, I woll fyght with you."

¶"As for that," seyde Sir **Trystram**, "I woll be avysed, for I woll
nat do batayle but yf me lyste—and yf I do batayle wyth you," seyde
Sir **Trystram**, "ye ar nat able to withstonde me." "Fye on the,
cowarde," seyde Sir **Dynadan**. And thus as they hoved stylle, they
saw a knyght com rydynge agaynste them.

¶"Lo," seyde Sir **Trystram**, "se where commyth a knyght rydynge
whyche woll juste wyth you." Anone, as Sir Dynadan behylde hym,

[55]

fol.283v

8. *Grete damage*: a matter of great pity.
9. *Was commyn*: had come.

he seyde, "Be my fayth, that same is the doted knyght that I saw lye by the welle, nother slepynge nother wakynge."

❡"Well," seyde Sir Trystram, "I know that knyght well, wyth the coverde shylde of assure, for he is the Kynges sonne of Northumbirlonde: his name is Sir Epynogrys, and he is as grete a lover as I know, and he lovyth the Kynges doughter of Walys, a full fayre lady—

❡"And now I suppose," seyde Sir Trystram, "and ye requyre hym, he woll juste wyth you—and than shall ye preve whether a lover be bettir knyght, or ye that woll nat love no lady."

❡"Well," seyde Sir Dynadan, "now shalt thou se what I shall do." And therewythall Sir Dynadan spake on hyght and sayde, "Sir knyght, make the[1] redy to juste wythe me, for juste ye muste nedis, for hit is the custom of knyghtes arraunte." "Sir," seyde Sir Epynogrys "ys that the rule and custom of you [arraunt knyghtes, for to make a knyght to juste will he or nyll he?"][2] "As for that," seyde Sir Dynadan, "make the redy—for here is for me!"[3] And therewythall they spurred their horsys, and mette togydirs so harde that Sir Epynogrys smote downe Sir Dynadan. And anone Sir Trystram rode to Sir Dynadan, and sayde, "How now? Mesemyth the lover hath well sped."

❡"Fye on the, cowarde," seyde Sir Dynadan. "And yf thou be a good knyght, revenge me!"

❡"Nay," seyde Sir Trystram, "I woll nat juste as at this tyme; but take youre horse and let us go hens."

❡"God defende me," seyde Sir Dynadan, "frome thy felyshyp, for I never spedde well syns I mette wyth the." And so they departed. "Well," seyde Sir Trystram, "peraventure I cowde tell you tydynges of Sir Trystram?" "Godde save me," seyde Sir Dynadan, "from thy felyshyp! For Sir Trystram were mykyll the warre and[4] he were in thy company." And they departed.

❡"Sir," seyde Sir Trystram, "yet hit may happyn that I may mete wyth yow in othir placis."

❡So rode Sir Trystram unto Joyus Garde, and there he harde in that towne grete noyse and cry.

❡"What is this noyse?" seyde Sir Trystram. "Sir," seyde they, "here is a knyght of this castell that hath be longe amonge us; and ryght now he is slayne wyth[5] two knyghtes, and for none other cause but that oure knyght seyde that Sir Launcelot was bettir knyght than Sir Gawayne." "That was a symple[6] cause," seyde Sir Trystram, "for to sle a good knyght for seyynge well by his maystir." "That is lytyll remedy to us," seyde the men of the towne, "for and Sir Launcelot had bene hyre, sone we sholde have bene revenged uppon tho false knyghtes."

fol.284r

1. Thee.
2. The emendation here is made on the model of Caxton, though the words are from the Winchester MS, where they appear to have been mistakenly copied, through eye-skip error on "knyghtes arraunte," at the end of Dynadan's challenge immediately preceding.
3. *Here is for me*: i.e., here I come.
4. *Mykyll the warre and*: much the worse off if.
5. I.e., by.
6. I.e., trivial.

❡Whan Sir **Trystram** harde them sey so, he sente for his shylde
and his speare; and lyghtly so wythin a whyle he had overtake them,
and made them turne and amende that they had myssedone.

❡"What amendis woldiste thou have?" seyde the one knyght.
And therewyth they toke there course;[7] and aythir mette other so
harde that Sir **Trystram** smote downe that knyght over his horse
tayle. Than the othir knyght dressed hym to Sir **Trystram**, and in
the same wyse he served the othir knyght; and than they gate of
their horsis as well as they myght and dressed their swerdis and
their shyldis to do batayle to the utteraunce.

❡"Now, knyghtes," seyde Sir **Trystram**, "woll ye telle me of whens
ye be and what is youre namys? For suche men ye myght be ye
shulde harde ascape my hondis; and also ye myght be suche men
and of such a cuntré that for all youre yevell dedis ye myght passe
quyte."

❡"Wyte thou well, sir knyght," seyde they, "we feare nat muche
to telle the oure namys—for my name is Sir **Aggravayne**—and my
name is Sir **Gaherys**—brethirne unto the good knyght Sir **Gawayne**;
and we be nevewys unto Kynge **Arthure**." "Well," seyde Sir **Trystram**,
"for Kynge **Arthurs** sake I shall lette you passe as at this tyme—but
hit is shame," seyde Sir **Trystram**, "that Sir **Gawayne** and ye be commyn of so grete blood, that ye foure bretherne be so named as ye
be: for ye be called the grettyste distroyers and murtherars of good
knyghtes that is now in the realme of Ingelonde. And as I have
harde say, Sir **Gawayne** and ye, his brethirne, amonge you slew a
bettir knyght than ever any of you was, whyche was called the
noble knyght Sir **Lamorak de Galys**. And hit had pleased God," seyde
Sir **Trystram**, "I wolde I had bene by hym at his deth day." "Than
shuldist thou have gone the same way," seyde Sir **Gaherys**. "Now,
fayre knyghtes, than muste there have bene many mo good knyghtes than ye of youre bloode."

❡And therewythall Sir **Trystram** departed frome them towarde
Joyus Garde.

❡And whan he was departed they toke there horsis, and the tone
seyde to the tothir, "We woll overtake hym and be revenged uppon
hym in the despyte of Sir **Lamerok**." So whan they had overtakyn
Sir **Trystram**, Sir **Aggravayne** bade hym, "Turne, traytoure knyght!"

❡"Ye sey well," seyde Sir **Trystram**; and therewythall he pulled
oute his swerde and smote Sir **Aggravayne** suche a buffet uppon the
helme that he tumbeled downe of his horse in a sowne, and he
had a grevous wounde. And than he turned to Sir **Gaherys**; and Sir
Trystram smote hys swerde and his helme togydir wyth suche a
myght that Sir **Gaherys** felle oute of his sadyll. And so Sir **Trystram**
rode unto Joyus Garde; and there he alyght and unarmed hym. So
Sir **Trystram** tolde La Beall **Isode** of all this adventure, as ye have
harde toforne. And whan she harde hym tell of Sir **Dynadan**, "Sir,
she seyde, "is nat that he that made the songe by[8] Kynge **Marke**?"
"That same is he," seyde Sir **Trystram**, "for he is the beste bourder

fol.284v   5

10

15

20

25

30

35

[56]

fol.285r   40

45

---

7. *Toke there course:* i.e., made their charge.
8. I.e., about.

and japer that I know, and a noble knyght of his hondis, and the beste felawe that I know—and all good knyghtis lovyth his felyship."

¶"Alas, sir," seyde she, "why brought ye hym nat wyth you hydir?"

¶"Have ye no care," seyde Sir Trystram, "for he rydyth to seke me in this contrey, and therefore he woll nat away tyll he have mette wyth me." And there Sir Trystram tolde La Beall Isode how Sir Dynadan hylde[9] ayenste all lovers.

¶Ryght so cam in a varlette and tolde Sir Trystram how there was com an arraunte knyght into the towne, wyth suche a coloures[1] uppon his shylde.

¶"Be my fayth, that is Sir Dynadan," seyde Sir Trystram. "Therefore, madame, wote ye what ye shall do: sende ye for hym, and I woll nat be seyne. And ye shall hyre the myrryeste knyght that ever ye spake wythall, and the maddyst talker—and I pray you hertaly that ye make hym good chere."

¶So anone La Beall Isode sente unto the towne, and prayde Sir Dynadan that he wolde com into the castell and repose hym there wyth a lady.

¶"Wyth a good wyll!" seyde Sir Dynadan; and so he mownted uppon his horse and rode into the castell, and there he alyght and was unarmed and brought into the halle.

¶And anone La Beall Isode cam unto hym, and aythir salewed other.

¶Than she asked hym of whens that he was. "Madame," seyde Sir Dynadan, "I am of the courte of Kynge Arthure, and a knyght of the Table Rounde; and my name is Sir Dynadan." "What do ye in this contrey?" seyde La Beall Isode. "Forsothe, madame, I seke after Sir Trystram, the good knyght, for hit was tolde me that he was in this contrey." "Hit may well be," seyde La Beall Isode, "but I am nat ware of hym." "Madame," seyde Sir Dynadan, "I mervayle at Sir Trystram and mo other suche lovers: fol.285v

¶"What aylyth them to be so madde and so asoted uppon women?"

¶"Why," seyde La Beall Isode, "ar ye a knyght and ar no lovear? Forsothe, hit is grete shame to you; wherefore ye may nat be called a good knyght by reson but yf ye make a quarell for a lady."

¶"God deffende me!" seyde Sir Dynadan, "for the joy of love is to shorte, and the sorow thereof, [and what cometh thereof,] is duras over longe."

¶"A," sayde La Beall Isode, "say ye nevermore so! For hyre faste by was the good knyght Sir Bleoberys de Ganys, that fought wyth three knyghtes at onys for a damesell; and he wan her afore the Kynge off Northumbirlonde—and that was worshypfully done," seyde La Beall Isode. "Forsothe, hit was so," seyde Sir Dynadan, "for I knowe hym well for a good knyght and a noble; and commyn he

9. I.e., held an opinion.
1. *A coloures:* heraldic colors.

is of noble bloode—and all be noble knyghtes of the blood of Sir
Launcelot de Lake." "Now I pray you, for my love," seyde La Beall
Isode, "wyll ye fyght for me wyth three knyghtes that doth me grete
wronge? And insomuche as ye bene a knyght of Kynge Arthurs, I
requyre you to do batayle for me." 5

¶Than Sir Dynadan seyde, "I shall sey you ye be as fayre a lady
as evir I sawe ony—and much fayrer than is my lady Quene Gwenyver—but wyte you well, at one worde, I woll nat fyght for you
wyth three knyghtes—Jesu me defende!" Than Isode lowghe, and
had good game at hym. So he had all the chyre that she myght 10
make hym, and there he lay all that nyght. And on the morne early
Sir Trystram armed hym, and La Beall Isode gaff hym a good helme;
and than he promysed her that he wolde mete wyth Sir Dynadan.
And so they two wolde ryde togedyrs unto Lonezep, where the turnemente sholde be—"and there shall I make redy for you, where ye 15
shall se all the seyght."

¶So departed Sir Trystram wyth two squyers that bare his shylde [57]   fol.286r
and his speares that were grete and longe.

¶So aftir that Sir Dynadan departed and rode his way a grete
shake untyll he had overtakyn Sir Trystram; and whan Sir Dynadan 20
had overtakyn hym, he knew hym anone, and hated the felyshyp
of hym of all othir knyghtes.

¶"A!" seyde Sir Dynadan, "arte thou that cowherd knyght that I
mette wyth yestirday? Well, kepe the, for thou shalt juste wyth me,
magré thyne hede."[2] 25

¶"Well," seyde Sir Trystram, "and I am passynge lothe to juste."
And so they lette there horsis renne; and Sir Trystram myste of hym
a[3] purpose, and Sir Dynadan brake his speare al to-shyvyrs—and
therewythall Sir Dynadan dressed hym to drawe oute his swerde.
"Not so, sir!" seyde Sir Trystram. "Why ar ye so wrothe? I am nat 30
disposid to fyght at this tyme."

¶"Fye on the, cowarde," seyde Sir Dynadan, "thou shamyste all
knyghts!"

¶"As for that," seyde Sir Trystram, "I care nat, for I woll wayte
uppon you and be undyr youre proteccion, for cause ye ar so good 35
a knyght that ye may save me."

¶"God delyver me of the!" seyde Sir Dynadan. "For thou arte as
goodly a man of armys and of thy persone as ever I sawe—and also
the moste cowarde that ever I saw. What wolt thou do wyth grete
spearys and suche wepen as thou caryeste with the?" "Sir, I shall 40
yeff them," seyde Sir Trystram, "to som good knyght whan I com
to the turnemente; and yf I se that you do beste, sir, I shall gyff
them to you."

¶So thus as they rode talkynge, they saw where cam an arraunte
knyght afore them that dressed hym to juste. 45

¶"Lo," seyde Sir Trystram, "yondir is one that woll juste: now
dresse you to hym." "A, shame betyde the!" seyde Sir Dynadan.

---

2. *Magré thyne hede:* despite you, regardless of what you want.
3. I.e., on.

"Nay, nat so," seyde Sir Trystram, "for that knyght semyth a shrewe."[4] "Than shall I," seyde Sir Dynadan. And so they dressed there shyldis and there spearys; and there they mett togydirs so harde that the othir knyght smote downe Sir Dynadan frome his horse.

¶"Lo," seyde Sir Trystram, "hit had bene bettir ye had lefft!" "Fye on the, cowarde," seyde Sir Dynadan. And than he sterte up and gate his swerde in his honde, and proffyrd to do batayle on foote.

¶"Whether in love[5] other in wrathe?" seyde the other knyght.

¶"Sir, lat us do batayle in love," seyde Sir Dynadan.

¶"What is youre name?" seyde that knyght. "I pray you telle me."

¶"Sir, wyte you well my name is Sir Dynadan." "A, Sir Dynadan," seyde that knyght, "and my name is Sir Gareth, yongyst brothir unto Sir Gawayne." Than aythir made of other grete chere, for this Sir Gareth was the beste knyght of all the brethirne, and he preved a good knyght. Than they toke their horsys, and there they spoke of Sir Trystram, how suche a cowarde he was—and every worde Sir Trystram harde, and lowgh them to scorne.[6] Than were they ware where cam a knyght afore them well horsed and well armed, and he made hym redy to juste.

¶"Now, fayre knyght," sayde Sir Trystram, "loke betwyxte you who shall juste wyth yondir knyght, for I warne you I woll nat have ado wyth hym." "Than shall I," seyde Sir Gareth. And so they encountyrd togydyrs; and there that knyght smote downe Sir Gareth over his horse croupe.

¶"How now?" seyde Sir Trystram unto Sir Dynadan. "Now dresse you and revenge the good knyght Sir Gareth." "That shall I nat," seyde Sir Dynadan, "for he hath strykyn downe a muche bygger knyght than I am." "A, Sir Dynadan," seyde Sir Trystram, "now I se and fele that youre harte faylyth you—and therefore now shall ye se what I shall do." And than Sir Trystram hurtelyd unto that knyght and smote hym quyte frome his horse.

¶And whan Sir Dynadan saw that, he mervayled gretly—and than he derned that hit was Sir Trystram. And anone this knyght that was on foote pulled oute his swerde to do batayle.

¶"Sir, what is youre name?" seyde Sir Trystram.

¶"Wyte you well," seyde that knyght, "my name is Sir Palomydes." "A, sir knyght, whyche knyght hate ye moste in the worlde?" seyde Sir Trystram.

¶"Forsothe," seyde he, "I hate Sir Trystram moste—to the deth—for, and I may mete wyth hym, the tone of us shall dye."

¶"Ye sey well," seyde Sir Trystram. "And now wyte you well that my name is Sir Trystram de Lyones—and now do your warste!"

¶Whan Sir Palomydes herd hym sey so he was astoned. And than he seyde thus: "I pray you, Sir Trystram, forgyff me all my evyll wyll! And yf I lyve, I shall do you servyse afore all other knyghtes that bene lyvynge; and there as I have owed you evyll wyll, me sore

fol.286v

fol.287r

---

4. I.e., dangerous one.
5. *In love*: i.e., not to the death.
6. *Lowgh them to scorne*: i.e., laughed in spite of them.

repentes. I wote nat what eylyth me, for mesemyth that ye ar a
good knyght; and that ony other knyght that namyth hymselff a
good knyght sholde hate you, me sore mervaylyth. And therefore I
requyre you, Sir Trystram, take none displaysure at myne unkynde
wordis."   5

"Sir Palomydes," seyde Sir Trystram, "ye sey well. And well I wote
ye ar a good knyght, for I have seyne you preved; and many grete
entirpryses ye have done, and well enchyeved them. Therefore,"
seyde Sir Trystrams, "and ye have ony yevyll wyll to me, now may
ye ryght hit, for I am redy at youre hande."[7]   10

☞"Nat so, my lorde Sir Trystram, for I woll do you knyghtly servyse in all thynge as ye woll commaunde me."

☞"Sir, ryght so I woll take you," seyde Sir Trystram. And so they
rode forthe on their wayes, talkynge of many thynges.

☞Than seyde Sir Dynadan, "A, my lorde Sir Trystram, fowle have   15
ye mocked me, for God knowyth I came into this contrey for youre
sake—and by the advyce of my lorde Sir Launcelot; and yet wolde
he nat tell me the sertaynté of you where I sholde fynde you."

☞"Truly!" seyde Sir Trystram, "and Sir Launcelot wyste beste
where I was—for I abyde in his owne castell." And thus they rode   [58]   20
untyll they were ware of the coste of Lonezep, and than were they
ware of foure hondred tentes and pavelouns, and mervaylous grete   fol.287v
ordynaunce. "So God me helpe," seyde Sir Trystram, "yondir I se
the grettyste ordynaunce that ever I sawe." "Sir," seyde Sir Palomydes, "mesemyth that there [was as] grete ordynaunce at the Cas-   25
tell of Maydyns uppon the roche, where ye wan the pryce—for I
saw myself where ye forjusted thirty knyghtes."

☞"Sir," seyde Sir Dynadan, "and in Surluce, at the turnemente
that Sir Galahalte of the Longe Iles made, whyche there dured seven
dayes; for there was as grete a gaderynge as is hyre, for there were   30
many nacions."

☞"Syr, who was the beste there?" seyde Sir Trystram. "Sir,
hit was Sir Launcelot du Lake, and the noble knyght Sir Lamerok de
Galys."

☞"Be my fayth," sayde Sir Trystram, "and[8] Sir Launcelot were   35
there, I doute nat," seyde Sir Trystram, "but he wan the worshyp,
so he had nat bene overmacched wyth many knyghtes. And of the
deth of Sir Lamorak," seyde Sir Trystram, "hit was over grete pité,
for I dare say he was the clennyst-myghted man and the beste-
wynded of his ayge that was on lyve. For I knew hym, that he was   40
one of the best knyghtes that ever I mette wythall, but yf hit were
Sir Launcelot." "Alas," seyde Sir Dynadan and Sir Trystram, "that full
wo is us for his deth! And yf they were nat the cousyns of my lorde
Kynge Arthure that slew hym, they sholde dye for hit, all that were
concentynge to his dethe." "And for suche thynges," seyde Sir Trys-   45
trams, "I feare to drawe unto the courte of Kynge Arthure: sir, I woll
that ye wete hit," seyde Sir Trystram unto Sir Gareth.

7. *I am redy at youre hande*: i.e., I am ready to fight.
8. I.e., if.

¶"As for that, I blame you nat," seyde Sir Gareth, "for well I undirstonde the vengeaunce of my brethirne, Sir Gawayne, Sir Aggravayne, Sir Gaherys, and Sir Mordred. But as for me," seyde Sir Gareth, "I meddyll nat of their maters; and therefore there is none that lovyth me of them.[9] And for cause that I undirstonde they be murtherars of good knyghtes, I lefte there company—and wolde God I had bene besyde Sir Gawayne whan that moste noble knyght Sir Lamorake was slayne."

¶"Now, as Jesu be my helpe," seyde Sir Trystram, "hit is passyngly well sayde of you, for I had lever," seyde Sir Trystrams, "than all the golde betwyxte this[1] and Rome I had bene there." "Iwysse," seyde Sir Palompdes, "so wolde I—and yet had I never the gré at no justis nothir turnemente and that noble knyght Sir Lamorak had be there, but other on horsebak othir ellys on foote he put me ever to the wars.[2] And that day that Sir Lamorak was slayne he ded the moste dedis of armys that ever I saw knyght do in my lyeff. And whan he was gyvyn the gré be my lorde Kynge Arthure, Sir Gawayne and his three bretherne, Sir Aggravayne, Sir Gaherys, and Sir Mordred, sette uppon Sir Lamorak in a pryvy place. And there they slew his horse, and so they faught with hym on foote more than three owrys, bothe byfore hym and behynde hym; and so Sir Mordrede gaff hym his dethis wounde behynde hym at his bakke, and all tohewe hym—for one of his squyers tolde me that sawe hit." "Now fye uppon treson!" seyde Sir Trystram, "for hit sleyth mine harte to hyre this tale."

¶"And so hit dothe myne," seyde Sir Gareth, "bretherne as they be myne."

¶"Now speke we of othir dedis," seyde Sir Palompdes, "and let hym be; for his lyff ye may nat gete agayne." "That is the more pité" seyde Sir Dynadan, "for Sir Gawayne and his bretherne—excepte you, Sir Gareth—hatyth all good knyghtes of the Rounde Table for the moste party. For well I wote, and[3] they myght, prevayly they hate my lorde Sir Launcelot and all his kyn, and grete pryvay dispyte they have at hym—and sertaynly that is my lorde Sir Launcelot well ware of, and that causyth hym the more to have the good knyghtes of his kynne aboute hym."

¶"Now, sir, seyde Sir Palompdes, "let us leve of this mater, and let us se how we shall do at this turnemente—and, sir, by myne advyce, lat us foure holde togydyrs ayenst all that woll com."

¶"Nat be my counceyle," seyde Sir Trystram, "for I se by their pavylouns there woll be foure hondred knyghtes; and doute ye nat," seyde Sir Trystram, "but there woll be many good knyghtes, and be a man never so valyaunte nother so bygge but he may be overmatched. And so have I seyne knyghtes done many; and whan they wente beste to have wonne worshyp, they loste hit—for manhode is nat worthe but yf hit be medled with wysdome: and as for me," seyde Sir Trystram, "hit may happen I shall kepe myne owne hede

fol.288r

[59]

fol.288v

9. *None that lovyth me of them:* i.e., none of them that love me.
1. I.e., this place.
2. I.e., worse.
3. I.e., whenever.

as well as[4] another." So thus they rode untyll they cam to Humbir banke, where they harde a crye and a dolefull noyse.

¶Than were they ware in the wynde where cam a ryche vessell heled over with rede sylke, and the vessell londed faste by them. Therewith Sir Trystram alyght, and his knyghtes; and so Sir Trystram wente afore and entird into that vessell. And whan he cam in, he saw a fayre bedde rychely coverde, and thereuppon lay a semely dede knyght, all armed sauff the hede, and was all bloody wyth dedly woundys uppon hym, whych semed to be a passynge good knyght.

¶"Jesu, how may this be," seyde Sir Trystram, "that this knyght is thus slayne?" And anone Sir Trystram was ware of a lettir in the dede knyghtes honde.

¶"Now, maystir marynars,"[5] seyde Sir Trystram, "what meanyth this lettir?"

¶"Sir," seyde they, in that lettir shall ye hyre and knowe how he was slayne, and for what cause, and what was his name. But, sir," seyde the marynars, "wyte you well that no man shall take that lettir and rede hit but yf he be a good knyght, and that he woll faythfully promyse to revenge his dethe, and ellis shall there no knyght se that lettir opyn." "And wyte you well," seyde Sir Trystram, "that som of us may revenge his dethe as well as another; and yf hit so be as ye marynars sey, his dethe shall be revenged."

¶And therewythall Sir Trystram toke the lettir oute of the knyghtes honde. And than he opened hit and rad hit, and thus hit specifyed:

Harmaunce, kyng and lorde of the Rede Cité, I sende to all knyghtes arraunte, recommaundynge[6] unto you noble knyghtes of Arthurs courte. I beseche them all amonge them to fynde one knyght that woll fyght for my sake with two bretherne that I brought up off nought,[7] and felounsly and traytourly they slewe me.

   ¶Wherefore I beseche one good knyght to revenge my dethe; and he that revengyth my dethe, I woll that he have my Rede Cité and all my castels.

fol.289r

"Sir," seyde the marynars, "wyte you well, this knyght and kynge that hyre lyeth was a full worshypfull man and of grete proues, and full well he loved all maner of knyghtes arraunte."

¶"So God me helpe," seyde Sir Trystram, "here is a pyteuous case, and full fayne I wolde take this entirpryse, but I have made suche a promyse that nedis I muste be at this grete justys and turnement, othir ellys I am shamed. For well I wote for my sake in aspeciall my lorde Kynge Arthure made this justis and turnemente in this contrey—and well I wote that many worshypfull people woll be hyre at this turnemente for to se me—and therefore I

4. *As well as:* i.e., no better than.
5. Trystram is now speaking to the ship's crew.
6. I.e., commending myself.
7. *Off nought:* for nothing, uselessly.

feare to take this entirpryse uppon me, that I shall nat com agayne
betyme to this iustys."

¶ "Sir, seyde Sir Palomydes, "I pray you gyff me this entirpryse,
and ye shall se me enchyeve hit worshypfully; other ellys I shall
dye in this quarell." 5

¶ "Well," seyde Sir Trystram, "and this entirpryse I gyff hit you,
wyth this,[8] that ye be with me at this turnemente, whyche shall be
as this day sevennyght."

¶ "Sir, seyde Sir Palomydes, "I promyse you I shall be wyth you
by that day, and I be unslayne and unmaymed." 10

¶ So departed Sir Trystram, Sir Gareth, and Sir Dynadan, and so   [60]
leffte Sir Palomydes in the vessell. And so Sir Trystram behylde the
marynars, how they sayled overlonge Humbir; and whan Sir Palomydes was oute of there syght they toke their horsys and loked
aboute them. And than were they ware of a knyght that cam 15
rydynge agaynste them unarmed, and nothynge but a swerde
aboute hym; and whan he cam nyghe, this knyght salewed them
and they hym agayne.

¶ "Now, fayre knyghtes," seyde that knyght, "I pray you, inso-   fol.289v
muche as ye be knyghtes arraunte, that ye woll com and se my 20
castall and take suche as ye fynde there—I pray you hertely."
"Wyth a good wyll," seyde Sir Trystram. And so they rode with hym
untyll his castell; and there they were brought into the halle, whyche was well apparayled, and so they were there unarmed and sette
at a borde. And whan this knyght sawe Sir Trystram, anone he knew 25
hym, and wexed passynge pale and wrothe at Sir Trystram; and
whan Sir Trystram sawe his oste make suche chere, he mervayled
and sayde, "Sir, myne oste, what chere make you?"

¶ "Wyte thou well," sayde he, "I fare muche the warre that I se
the! For I know the for Sir Trystram de Lyones, for thou slewyste 30
my brother—and therefore I gyff the warnynge that I woll sle the
and ever I may gete the at large."[9]

¶ "Sir knyght," seyde Sir Trystram, "I am never advysed that ever
I slew ony brother of yourys, and yf ye say that I ded hit, I woll
make amendys unto my power." 35

¶ "I woll no mendys have," seyde the knyght. "But kepe the
frome me."

¶ So whan he hadde dyned, Sir Trystram asked his armys and
departed. And so they rode on there wayes; and wythin a myle way
Sir Dynadan saw where cam a knyght armed and well horsed, wyth 40
a whyghte shylde. "Sir Trystram," seyde Sir Dynadan, "take kepe to
youreselff, for I dare undirtake yondir commyth your oste that woll
have ado wyth you."

¶ "Lat hym com," seyde Sir Trystram. "I shall abyde hym as I
may." And whan the knyght cam nyghe to Sir Trystram, he cryed 45
and bade hym abyde and kepe hym. And anone they hurteled togydyrs; but Sir Trystram smote the other knyght so sore that he bare

---

8. *Wyth this:* i.e., with this condition.
9. At liberty.

hym over his horse croupen. Than the knyght arose lyghtly and
toke his horse agayne and rode fyersly to Sir Trystram, and smote
hym twyse other thryse harde uppon the helme.

¶"Sir knyght," seyde Sir Trystram, "I pray you leve of and smyte
me no more, for I wolde be lothe to deale with you and I myght
chose, for I have of your mete and drynke in my body." And for all
that he wolde nat leve; than Sir Trystram gaff hym suche a buffette
uppon the helme that he felle up-so-downe from his horse, that
the bloode braste oute at the ventrayles of his helme—and so he
lay stylle, lykly to be dede. Than Sir Trystram sayde, "Me repentys
of this buffette that I smote so sore, for as I suppose, he is dede."
And so they lefft hym and rode on their wayes.

¶So whan they had ryddyn awhyle, they sawe com rydynge agay-
enst them two full lyckely knyghtes, well armed and well horsed,
and goodly servauntes aboute them. And that one knyght hyght
Sir Berraunt le Apres (and he was called the Kynge with the Hondred
Knyghtes), and the other was Sir Segwarydes, that were renomed
two noble knyghtes. So as they cam aythir by other, the kynge loked
uppon Sir Dynadan; and at that tyme Sir Dynadan had Sir Trystrams
helme uppon his shuldir, whyche the kynge had seyne tofore with
the Quene of Northe Galys. And that quene the kynge loved as
paramour; and that helme the Quene of Northe Galys gaff to La
Beall Isode; and Quene Isode gaff hit to Sir Trystram.

¶"Sir knyght," seyde Sir Berraunte, "where had ye that helme?"
"What wolde ye?" seyde Sir Dynadan. "For I woll have ado wyth
you," seyde the kynge, "for the love of her that ought this helme—
and therefore kepe you!" So they cam togydir wyth all there myghtes of their horsis; and there the Kynge with the Hondred Knyghtes
smote downe Sir Dynadan and his horse. And than he commaunded
his servaunte to take that helme off and kepe hit. So the varlet
wente to unbuckyll his helme.

¶"What wolt thou do?" seyde Sir Trystrams. "Leve that helme!"

¶"To what entente," seyde the kynge, "wyll ye meddyll with that
helme?"

¶"Wyte you well," seyde Sir Trystram, "that helme shall nat
departe fro me tyll hit be derrer bought." "Than make you redy!"
seyde Sir Berraunte unto Sir Trystram. So they hurteled togydyrs;
and there Sir Trystram smote hym downe over his horse tayle. And
than the kynge arose lyghtly and gate his horse agayne, and than
he strake fyersly at Sir Trystram many grete strokys; and than he
gaff Sir Berraunte such a buffette uppon the helme that he felle
downe over his horse, sore astonyed.

¶"Lo!" seyde Sir Dynadan, "that helme is unhappy to us twayne,
for I had a falle for hit, and now, sir kynge, have ye another falle!"
Than Sir Segwarydes asked, "Who shall juste wyth me?" "I pray
you," seyde Sir Gareth unto Sir Dynadan, "let me have this justys."
"Sir," seyde Sir Dynadan, "I pray you hertely take hit, as for me."
"That is no reson!" seyde Sir Trystram, "for this justys shulde have
bene youres."

¶"At a worde," seyde Sir Dynadan, "I woll nat thereof."

❡Than Sir **Gareth** dressed hym unto Sir **Segwarydes**; and there Sir **Segwarydes** smote Sir **Gareth** and his horse to the erthe.

❡"Now," seyde Sir **Trystram** unto Sir **Dynadan**, "juste ye with yondir knyght." "I woll nat thereof," seyde Sir **Dynadan**. "Than woll I," seyde Sir **Trystram**; and than Sir **Trystram** ranne unto hym and gaff hym a falle—and so they leffte hem on foote. And Sir **Trystram** rode unto Joyus Garde. And there Sir **Gareth** wolde nat of his curtesy have gone into his castell; but Sir **Trystram** wolde nat suffir hym to departe, and so they alyght and unarmed them and had grete chere. But whan Sir **Dynadan** cam afore La Beall **Isode**, he cursed her that ever he bare Sir **Trystrams** helme—and there he tolde her how Sir **Trystram** had mocked hym. Than there was lawghynge and japynge at Sir **Dynadan**, that they wyste nat what to do wyth hym.

❡Now woll we leve them myrry wythin Joyus Garde, and speke we of Sir **Palomydes**, the whyche sayled evynlongis Humbir untyll that he came unto the see costys; and thereby was a fayre castell, and at that tyme hit was erly in the mornynge, afore day. Than the marynars wente unto Sir **Palomydes**, that slepte faste.

"Sir knyght," seyde the marynars, "ye muste aryse, for here is a castell that ye muste go into." "I assente me," seyde Sir **Palomydes**. And therewithall he aryved, and than he blew his horne, that the marynars had yevyn hym; and whan they in the castell harde that horne, they put oute many knyghtes. And there they stood uppon the wallys, and sayde with one voyse, "Wellcom be ye to this castell!" And than hit waxed clyere day, and Sir **Palomydes** entyrde into the castell; and within a whyle he was served with many dyverse metys. Than Sir **Palomydes** harde aboute hym muche wepyng and grete dole.

❡"What may this meane?" seyde Sir **Palomydes**. "For I love nat to hyre suche a sorowfull noyse; and therefore I wolde knowe what hit meaned." Than there cam a knyght afore hym—his name was Sir **Ebell**—that seyde thus: "Wyte you well, sir knyght, this dole and sorow is made here every day, and for this cause. We had a kynge that hyght **Harmaunce**, and he was Kynge of the Rede Cité, and this kynge that was oure lorde was a noble knyght, layrge and lyberall of his expence. And in all the worlde he loved nothynge so muche as he ded arraunte knyghtes of Kyng **Arthurs** courte, and all justynge, huntynge, and all maner of knyghtly gamys—for so good a kynge and knyght had never the rewle of poore peple. And bycause of his goodnes and jantyll demeanys we bemoone hym, and ever shall:

❡"And all kyngis and astatys may beware by oure lorde, for he was destroyed in his owne defaute:[1] for had he cheryshed his owne bloode,[2] he had bene a lyvis kynge, and lyved with grete ryches and reste. But all astatys may beware by owre kynge—but alas," seyde Sir **Ebell**, "that ever we sholde gyff all other[3] warnynge by his

fol.291r

[61]

fol.291v

---

1. *In his owne defaute:* through his own fault.
2. I.e., blood relatives.
3. I.e., other people.

dethe." "Telle me," seyde Sir Palomydes, "how and in what maner was your lorde slayne, and by whom." "Sir," seyde Sir Ebell, "oure kynge brought up of chyldir[4] two men that now ar perelous knyghtes; and thes two knyghtes, oure kynge had them so in favour that he loved no man, nother trusted no man of his owne bloode, nother none other that was aboute hym. And by thes two knyghtes oure kynge was governed; and so they ruled hym peasably[5]—and his londys—and never wolde they suffir none of his bloode to have no rule with oure kynge:

❡"And also he was so fre and so jeantyll, and they so false and so dysseyvable, that they ruled hym peasabely; and that aspyed the lordis of oure kynges bloode, and departed frome hym unto their owne lyeffloode:[6]

❡"And whan this traytours undirstood that they had dryvyn all the lordis of his bloode frome hym, than were they nat pleased wyth suche rewle, but ever thought to have more—

❡"And as ever hit is an olde sawe, 'Gyeff a chorle rule and thereby he woll nat be suffysed,'[7] for whatsomever he be that is rewled by a vylayne borne,[8] and the lorde of the soyle be a jantylman born, that same vylayne shall destroy all the jeauntylmen aboute hym. Therefore all the astatys and lordys, of what astate ye be, loke ye beware whom ye take aboute you. And therefore, sir, and ye be a knyght of Kynge Arthurs courte, remembir this tale, for this is the ende and conclusyon: my lorde and kynge rode unto the foreyste hereby by the advyse of thes two traytoures; and there he chaced at the rede deare, armed at all peacis full[9] lyke a good knyght; and so for labour he waxed drye, and than he alyght and dranke at a well; and whan he was alyght, by the assente of thes two traytoures, the tone, whyche hyght Helyus, he suddeynly smote oure kynge thorow the body wyth a speare. And so they leffte hym there; and whan they were departed, than by fortune I cam to the welle and founde my lorde and kynge, wounded to the deth:

❡"And whan I harde his complaynte, I lat brynge hym to the watirs syde; and in that same shyppe I put hym on lyve. And whan my lorde Kynge Harmaunce was in that vessell, he requyred me, for the trewe feythe I owed unto hym, for to wryte a lettir, in this maner:

❡Recommaunde me unto Kynge Arthure and to all his noble knyghtys arraunte, besechynge them all that, insomuche as I, Kynge Harmaunce, Kynge of the Rede Cité, thus am slayne by felony and treson thorow two knyghtes of myne owne bryngynge up and of myne owne makynge, [that som worshipful knyght wil] revenge my dethe, insomuch as I have bene ever

---

4. *Of chyldir*: as children (i.e., as if they were his children).
5. I.e., without opposition.
6. *Departed frome hym unto their owne lyeffloode*: i.e., left him to make their own way in the world because he would not support them.
7. *Gyeff a chorle rule and thereby he woll nat be suffysed*: give a churl power, and he will never have enough.
8. *A vylayne borne*: a low-born man.
9. *At all peacis full*: fully equipped.

to my power well-wyllynge unto Kynge Arthurs courte. And who that woll adventure his lyff for my sake to revenge my deth and sle thes two traytoures in one batayle, I, Kynge Harmaunce, Kynge of the Red Cité, frely woll gyff hym all my londis and rentes that ever I welded in my lyeff.[1]

"And this lettir," seyde Sir Ebell, "I wrote be my lordis commaundemente; and than he resceayved his Creature.[2] And whan he was dede, he commaunded me, or ever he were colde, to put that lettir faste in his honde; and than he commaunded me to sende forthe that same vessell downe by Humbir streyme, and that I sholde gyeff thes marynars in commaundemente never to stynte tyll they cam unto Lonezep, where all the noble knyghtes shall assemble at this tyme—'and there shall som good knyght have pité of me and revenge my deathe, for there was never knyght nother lorde falselyar nothir traytourlyar slayne than I am hyere, wounded unto my dethe.' Thus was the complaynte of oure Kynge Harmaunce.

"Now," seyde Sir Ebell, "ye knowe all how oure lorde was betrayed; and therefore we requyre you for Goddis sake have pité uppon his dethe, and worshypfully than may ye welde all his londis; for we all wyte well, and ye may sle tho two traytours, the Rede Cité and all that be therein woll take you for their kyndely lorde."

"Truly," seyde Sir Palompdes, "hit grevyth myne harte for to hyre you tell this dolefull tale; and, to say the trouthe, I saw that same lettir that ye speke of, and one of the beste knyghtes of the worlde rad that same lettir to me that ye speake of, and by his commaundemente I cam hydir to revenge your kynges deathe. And therefore have done[3] and let me wyte where I shall fynde tho traytoures—for I shall never be at ease in my harte tyll I be in handis wyth[4] them."

¶"Sir," seyde Ebell, "than take youre shyppe agayne, and that shyppe muste brynge you unto the Delectable Ile, faste by the Rede Cité. And we in this castell shall pray for you and abyde youre agayne-commynge—for this same castell, and ye sped well, muste nedis be youres. For oure Kynge Harmaunce lette make this castell for the love of tho two traytoures, and so we kepte hit with stronge honde;[5] and therefore full sore ar we thretened."

¶"Wote ye what ye shall do," seyde Palompdes. "Whatsomevir com of me, loke ye kepe well thys castell, for and hit myssefortune me so to be slayne in this queste, I am sure there woll com one of

fol.292v

---

1. The differences between this quotation of the letter and that given earlier (p. 417) should not be taken as evidence of guile on Sir Ebell's part. There is probably a combination of reasons for the differences: (1) Malory is following the pattern of his source, and medieval literary tradition generally, which is not bound by modern conceptions of absolute consistency—the letters are, after all, fundamentally "the same" and provide independent corroboration of Harmaunce's intentions; (2) the second quotation is understood to be from memory (cf. Ebell's *in this maner*) and is thus susceptible to change, and in this case perhaps deliberately provides Malory with the advantage of poignant emotional embellishment.
2. I.e., Creator, God.
3. *Have done:* cease, stop.
4. *In handis wyth:* right upon, in close combat.
5. *Stronge honde:* (military) force.

the beste knyghtis of the worlde for to revenge my dethe: and that
is Sir Trystram de Lyones, othir ellis Sir Launcelot de Lake." Than Sir
Palomydes departed frome that castell; and as he cam nyghe the
shyppe, there cam oute of a shyppe a goodly knyght armed ayenste
hym, wyth his shylde on his shuldir and his honde uppon his
swerde. And anone as he cam nyghe unto Sir Palomydes, he seyde,
"Sir knyght, what seke you hyre? Leeve this queste, for hit is
myne—and myne hit was or hit were youres, and therefore I woll
have hit."

¶"Sir knyght," seyde Sir Palomydes, "hit may well be that this
queste was youres or hit was myne; but whan the lettir was takyn
oute of the dede knyghtes honde, at that tyme by lyklyhode[6] there
was no knyght had undirtake to revenge the kynges dethe. And so
at that tyme I promysed to avenge his dethe, and so I shall—other
ellys I am shamed."

¶"Ye say well," seyde the knyght, "butte wyte you well, than woll
I fyght wyth you; and whether of us be bettir knyght, lat hym take
the batayle on honde."

¶"I assente me," seyde Sir Palomydes. And than they dressed
their shyldis and pulled oute their swerdis, and laysshed togydyrs
many sad strokys as men of myght. And this fyghtynge lasted more
than an owre; but at the laste Sir Palomydes waxed bygge and bettir-
wynded, and than he smote that knyght suche a stroke that he
kneled on his kneis. Than that knyght spake on hyght and sayde,
"Jeantyll knyght, holde thy honde!" And therewyth Sir Palomydes
wythdrewe his honde.

¶Than thys knyght seyde, "Sir, wyte you well ye ar bettir worthy
to have this batayle than I; and I requyre you of knyghthode, telle
me youre name." "Sir, my name is Sir Palomydes, a knyght of Kynge
Arthurs and of the Table Rounde, whyche am com hydir to revenge
[the dethe of] thys same dede kynge." "Sir, well be ye founde,"
seyde the knyght to Sir Palomydes, "for of all knyghtes that bene
on lyve, excepte three, I had levyste have you: and the fyrste is Sir
Launcelot du Lake, and the secunde ys Sir Trystram de Lyones, and
the thyrde is my nyghe cousyn, the good knyght Sir Lamorak de
Galys. And I am brothir unto Kynge Harmaunce that is dede; and my
name is Sir Hermynde."

"Ye sey well," seyde Sir Palomydes, "and ye shall se how I shall
spyede; and yff I be there slayne, go ye unto my lorde Sir Launcelot,
other ellys to my lorde Sir Trystram, and pray them to revenge my
dethe. For as for Sir Lamorak, hym shall ye never se in this worlde."

¶"Alas!" seyde Sir Hermynde, "how may that be that he is slayne?"
"By Sir Gawayne and his bretherne," seyde Sir Palomydes. "So God
me helpe," seyde Sir Hermynde, "there was nat one-for-one[7] that
slew hym?" "That is trouthe," seyde Sir Palomydes, "for they were
foure daungerus knyghtes that slew hym: that was Sir Gawayne, Sir
Aggravayne, Sir Gaherys, and Sir Mordred. But Sir Gareth, the fifth

fol.293r

[63]

fol.293v

---

6. *By lyklyhode:* i.e., the odds were that.
7. I.e., one engaged in single combat.

brothir, was awey, the beste knyght of them all." And so Sir Palomydes tolde Sir Hermynde all the maner and how they slew Sir Lamorak, all only by treson.

So Sir Palomydes toke his shyppe and drove up to the Delectable
Ile. And in the meanewhyle Sir Hermynde, the kynges brothir, he
aryved up at the Rede Cité, and there he tolde them how there
was com a knyght of Kynge Arthurs to avenge Kynge Harmaunce
dethe: "and his name ys Sir Palomydes, the good knyght, that for
the moste party he folowyth the Beste Glatyssaunte."

Than all the cité made grete joy, for muche had they harde of
Sir Palomydes and of his noble prouesse. So they lette ordayne a
messyngere, and sente unto the two bretherne and bade them to
make them redy, for there was a knyght com that wolde fyght wyth
them bothe. So the messyngere wente unto them where they were
at a castell there besyde, and there he tolde them how there was
a knyght comyn of Kynge Arthurs to fyght with them bothe at onys.
"He is wellcom," seyde they, "but is hit Sir Launcelot other ony of
his bloode?" "Sir, he is none of that bloode," seyde the messyngere.

⁋"Than we care the lesse," seyde the two brethirne, "for none
of the bloode of Sir Launcelot we kepe⁸ nat to have ado wythall."

⁋"Sir, wyte you well," seyde the messyngere, "his name is Sir
Palomydes, that yet is uncrystened, a noble knyght."

⁋"Well," seyde they, "and he be now uncrystynde, he shall never
be crystynde." So they appoynted to be at the cité within two dayes.
And whan Sir Palomydes was comyn to the cité, they made pas-
saynge grete joy of hym; and than they behylde hym, and thought
he was well made and clenly⁹ and bygly, and unmaymed of his
lymmys, and neyther to yonge nother to olde—and so all the people
praysed hym. And though he were nat crystynde, yet he belyved in
the beste maner and was full faythefull and trew of his promyse,
and well-condyssyonde; and bycause he made his avow that he
wolde never be crystynde unto the tyme that he had enchyeved the
Beste Glatysaunte (the whyche was a full wondirfull beyste and a
grete sygnyfycasion; for Merlyon prophesyed muche of that
byeste).¹ And also Sir Palomydes avowed never to take full Crystyndom untyll that he had done seven batayles within lystys.

So wythin the thirde day, there cam to the cité thes two brethirne: the tone hyght Sir Helyus and the other hyght Helake, the
whyche were men of grete prouesse; howbehit that they were falsse
and full of treson, and but poore men born, yet were they noble
knyghtes of their handys. And with them they brought fourty
knyghtes, of theire hondis noble men, to that entente that they
shulde be bygge inowghe for the Rede Cité.

Thus cam the two bretherne wyth grete bobbaunce and pryde,
for they had put the Rede Cité in grete feare and damage.² Than

fol.294r

---

8. I.e., care.
9. I.e., fully (formed).
1. In the French *Suite de Merlin,* Merlin prophecies that Pellinor's son Percival will capture
the beast during the Grail Quest. About the Questing Beast, see n. 9, p. 31.
2. I.e., regret.

they were brought to the lystes; and Sir Palomydes cam into the place and seyde thus: "Be ye the two brethirne, Helyus and Helake, that slew youre kynge and lorde Sir Harmaunce by felony and treson—

¶For whom that I am comyn hydir to revenge his dethe? Wyte thou well," seyde Sir Helyus and Sir Helake, "that we ar the same knyghtes that slewe Kynge Harmaunce—and wyte thou well, thou Sir Palomydes, Sarezyn, that we shall so handyll the or that thou departe that thou shalt wysshe that thou haddyst be crystynde!" "Hit may well be," seyde Sir Palomydes, "but as yet I wolde nat dye or that I were full crystynde; and yette so aferde am I nat of you bothe but that I shall dye a bettir Crystyn man than ony of you bothe. And doute ye nat," seyde Sir Palomydes, "ayther ye other I shall be leffte dede in this place."

¶So they departed in grete wreath; and the two bretherne cam ayenst Sir Palomydes, and he ayenste them, as faste as their horsis myght ren. And by fortune Sir Palomydes smote Sir Helake thorow his shylde and thorow his breste more than a fadom. All this whyle Sir Helyus hylde up his speare, and for pryde and orgule he wolde nat smyte Sir Palomydes wyth his speare. But whan he saw his brothir lye on the erthe, and saw he myght nat helpe hymselff, than he seyde unto Sir Palomydes, "Kepe the!" And therewyth he cam hurtelynge unto Sir Palomydes with his speare, and smote hym quyte frome his horse.

So Sir Helyus rode over Sir Palomydes twyse or thryse. And therewyth Sir Palomydes was ashamed, and gate the horse of Sir Helyus by the brydyll; and therewithall the horse arered, and Sir Palomydes halpe aftir, and so they felle to the erthe. But anone Sir Helyus starte up lyghtly, and there he smote Sir Palomydes a grete stroke uppon the helme, that he kneled uppon his kne; and than they laysshed togydyrs many sad strokis and trased and traversed, now bakwarde, now sydelynge, hurtelynge togydyrs lyke two borys—and that same tyme they felle bothe grovelynge to the erthe.

¶Thus they fought stylle withoute ony reposynge two owres, and never brethid;[3] and than Sir Palomydes wexed faynte and wery, and Sir Helyus waxed passynge stronge and doubeled his strokes and drove Sir Palomydes ovirtwarte and endelonge all the fylde. Than whan they of the cité saw Sir Palomydes in this case, they wepte and cryed and made grete dole—and the other party made as grete joy.

¶"Alas!" seyde the men of the cité, "that this noble knyght shulde thus be slayne for oure kynges sake." And as they were thus wepynge and cryynge, Sir Palomydes—whyche had suffyrde an hondred strokes, and wondir hit was that he stoode on his fyete—so at the laste Sir Palomydes loked aboute as he myght, waykely, unto the comyn people, how they wepte for hym; and than he seyde to

How Sir Palomydes revenged the deth of Kyng Harmaunce of the Rede Cité

fol.294v

[64]

fol.295r

3. I.e., stopped to catch (their) breath.

hymselff, "A, fye for shame, Sir Palomydes! Why hange ye youre hede so lowe?"

And therewith he bare up his shylde and loked Sir Helyus in the vysoure and smote hym a grete stroke uppon the helme, and aftir that anothir, and anothir; and than he smote Sir Helyus with suche a myght that he felde hym to the erthe grovelynge—and than he raced of hys helme frome his hede and so smote of his hede from the body. And than were the people of the cité the myryest people that myght be. So they brought hym to his lodgynge with grete solempnyé; and there all the people becam his men.[4]

And than Sir Palomydes prayde them all to take kepe unto[5] all the lordeship of Kyng Harmaunce—"for, fayre sirrys, wyte you well, I may nat as at this tyme abyde with you, for I muste in all haste be wyth my lorde Kynge Arthure at the castel of Lonezep." Than were people full hevy at his departynge, for all the cité profyrd Sir Palomydes the thirde parte of their goodis so that he wolde abyde wyth hem—but in no wyse as at that tyme he ne wolde abyde. And so Sir Palomydes departed, and cam unto the castell there as Sir Ebell was lyefftenaunte; and whan they in the castell wyste how Sir Palomydes had sped, there was a joyfull mayné.

And so Sir Palomydes departed and cam to the castell of Lonezep; and when he knew that Sir Trystram was nat there, he toke hys way over Humbir and cam unto Joyus Garde, where was Sir Trystram and La Beall Isode. So Sir Trystram had commaunded that what knyght arraunte cam within Joyus Garde, as in the towne, that they sholde warne Sir Trystram. So there cam a man of the towne and tolde Sir Trystram how there was a knyght in the towne, a passyng goodly man.

¶ "What maner of man ys he?" seyde Sir Trystram, "and what sygne beryth he?" And anone he tolde hym all the tokyns of hym. "Be my fayth, that ys Sir Palomydes!" seyde Sir Dynadan. "Forsothe hit may well be," seyde Sir Trystram. "Than go ye, Sir Dynadan, and fecche hym hydir." Than Sir Dynadan wente unto Sir Palomydes, and there aythir made othir grete chere; and so they lay togydirs that nyght; and on the morn erly cam Sir Trystram and Sir Gareth and toke them in their beddis.[6] And so they arose and brake their faste.

¶ And than Sir Trystram dressed Sir Palomydes unto the fyldis and woodis; and so they were accorded to repose them in the foreyste. And when they had played them a grete whyle, they rode unto a fayre well; and anone they were ware of an armed knyght cam rydynge agaynste them—and there ayther salewed other. Than this armed knyght spake to Sir Trystram and asked what were those knyghtes that were lodged in Joyus Garde.

fol.295v

[65]

4. On the expediencies of feudalism see n. 6, p. 9.
5. Take kepe unto: look after.
6. So they lay togydirs . . . toke them in their beddis: one could see a mirror of homosexual life here or simply note that the asexual sharing of beds was common in the Middle Ages (lawyers at the Inns of Court, for instance, had appointed bedfellows) and that Dynadan and Palomydes have been "upgraded" to the presumably more comfortable beds of the higher-ranking knights, Trystram and Gareth.

❡"I wote nat what they ar," seyde Sir Trystram. "But what knyghtes be ye? For mesemyth ye be no knyghtes arraunte, because ye
ryde unarmed."

❡"Sir, whethir we be knyghtes or nat, we lyste nat to telle the
oure name."

❡"Why wolt thou nat tell me thy name?" seyde that knyght.
"Than kepe the, for thou shalt dye of myne hondis!" And
therewithall he gate his speare and wolde have ronne Sir Trystram
thorow. That saw Sir Palomydes, and smote his horse traverse in
myddys the syde, that he smote horse and man spyteuously to the
erthe; and therewyth Sir Palomydes alyght and pulled oute his
swerde to have slayne hym.

❡"Lat be," seyde Sir Trystram, "sle hym nat, for the knyghte is
but a foole, and hit were shame to sle hym. But take away his
speare," seyde Sir Trystram, "and lat hym take his horse and go
where that he wyll." So whan this knyght arose, he groned sore of
the falle; and so he gate his horse, and whan he was up he turned
his horse and requyred Sir Trystram and Sir Palomydes to telle hym
what knyghtes they were. "Now wyte thou well," seyde Sir Trystram,
"my name is Sir Trystram de Lyones, and this knyghtes name is Sir
Palomydes." Whan he wyste what he hyght, he toke his horse wyth
the spurrys, bycaus[7] they shulde nat aske hym his name; and so he
rode faste away thorow thicke and thorow thynne.

Than cam there by them a knyght with a bended shylde of
assure;[8] his name was Sir Epynogrys, and he cam a grete walop.
"Whother ar ye away?" sayde Sir Trystram. "My fayre lordis," seyde
Sir Epynogrys, "I folow the falsiste knyght that beryth the lyeff—
wherefore I requyre you telle me whethyr ye sye hym, for he beryth
a shylde with a case of rede over hit." "So God me helpe," seyde
Sir Trystram, "suche a knyght departed frome us nat a quarter of
an owre agone—and therefore we pray you to telle us his name."

"Alas," seyde Sir Epynogrys, "why let ye hym ascape from you?
And he is so grete a foo untyll all arraunte knyghtys, whos name
is Sir Brewnys Saunze Pieté." "A, fy, for shame!" seyde Sir Palomydes,
"and alas that ever he ascapyd myne hondis, for he ys the man in
the worlde whom I hate moste." Than eviry knyght made grete
sorow to othir; and so Sir Epynogrys departed and folowed the chace
aftir hym. Than Sir Trystram and hys three felowys rode towarde
Joyus Garde. And there Sir Trystram talked unto Sir Palomydes of
his batayle, and how that he had sped at the Rede Cité. And as ye
have harde afore, so was hyt ended.

❡"Truly," seyde Sir Trystram, "I am glad ye have well sped, for
ye have done worshypfully.

❡"Well," seyde Sir Trystram, "we muste forwarde as tomorne."
And than he devysed how hit shulde be: and there Sir Trystram
devysed to sende his two pavelons to set hem faste by the well of
Lonezep—"and therein shall be the quene La Beall Isode." "Ye sey

fol.296r

fol.296v

---

7. *Toke his horse wyth the spurrys:* spurred his horse. *Bycaus:* i.e., so that.
8. *A bended shylde of assure:* a shield with a coat of arms with blue bands.

well," seyde Sir Dynadan. But whan Sir Palomydes herde of that his harte was ravysshed oute of mesure.

¶Notwythstondynge, he seyde but lytyll. So whan they cam to Joyus Garde, Sir Palomydes wolde nat have gone into the castell, but as Sir Trystram lad hym by the honde into Joyus Garde. And whan Sir Palomydes saw La Beall Isode, he was so ravysshed that he myght unnethe speke.

So they wente unto mete; but Sir Palomydes myght nat ete, and there was all the chire that myght be had. And so on the morn they were apparayled for to ryde towarde Lonezep: so Syr Trystram had three squyars, and La Beall Isode had three jantyllwomen—and bothe the quene and they were rychely apparayled—and other peo-ple had they none with them but varlettes to beare their shyldis and their spearys. And thus they rode forthe; and as they rode, they saw afore them a route of knyghtes—and that was Sir Galyhodyn with twenty knyghtes with hym.

¶"Now, fayre fealowys," seyde Sir Galyhodyn, "yondir commyth foure knyghtes and a ryche and a well fayre lady—and I am in wyll to take that fayre lady from them."

"Sir, that is nat beste," seyde one of them, "but sende ye to them and a-wyte what they woll say." And so they ded; and anone there cam a squyer unto Sir Trystram and asked them whether they wolde juste other ellys to lose that lady.

¶"Nat so," seyde Sir Trystram, "but telle your lorde and bydde hym com, as many as we bene,[9] and wynne her and take her."

¶"Sir," seyde Sir Palomydes, "and hit please you, lat me have this dede, and I shall undirtake them, all foure." "Sir, I woll that ye have hit," seyde Sir Trystram, "at youre pleasure."

¶"Now go and telle your lorde Sir Galyhodyn that this knyght woll encountir with hym and his felowys." So this squyer departed and tolde Sir Galyhodyn. Than he dressed his shylde and put forth a speare, and Sir Palomydes [another; and there Sire Palomydes] smote Sir Galyhodyn so harde that horse and man bothe yode to the erthe—and there he had an horryble falle. And than cam another knyght, and the same wyse[1] he served hym; and so he served the thirde and the fourthe, that he smote them over their horse croupes—and allwayes Sir Palomydes speare was hole.

Than cam there six knyghtes mo of Sir Galyhodynes men, and wolde have bene avenged uppon Sir Palomydes. "Lat be!" seyde Sir Galyhodyn, "nat so hardy! None of you all meddyll with this knyght, for he is a man of grete bounté and honoure—and yf he wolde do his uttermuste, ye ar nat all able to deale wyth hym." And ryght so they hylde them styll—and ever Sir Palomydes was redy to juste; and whan he sawe they wolde no more, he rode unto Sir Trystram.

¶"A, Sir Palomydes! Ryght well have ye done and worshypfully, as a good knyght sholde."

¶So this Sir Galyhodyn was nyghe kyn unto Sir Galahalte the

fol.297r

[66]

---

9. *As many as we bene:* i.e., in numbers equal to ours.
1. In the same manner.

Haute Prynce, and this Sir 𝕲𝖆𝖑𝖕𝖍𝖔𝖉𝖞𝖓 was a kynge within the contrey of Surluse. So as Sir 𝕿𝖗𝖞𝖘𝖙𝖗𝖆𝖒 with his three felowys and La Beall Isode rode, they saw afore them foure knyghtes, and every knyght had his speare in his honde. The fyrst was Sir 𝕲𝖆𝖜𝖆𝖞𝖓𝖊; the secunde was Sir Uwayne; the thirde was Sir 𝕾𝖆𝖌𝖗𝖆𝖒𝖔𝖚𝖗 𝖑𝖊 𝕯𝖊𝖘𝖞𝖗𝖚𝖘; and the fourthe was Sir 𝕯𝖔𝖉𝖞𝖓𝖆𝖘 𝖑𝖊 𝕾𝖆𝖛𝖊𝖆𝖌𝖊. And whan Sir 𝕻𝖆𝖑𝖔𝖒𝖞𝖉𝖊𝖘 behylde them, that the foure knyghtes were redy to juste, he prayde Sir 𝕿𝖗𝖞𝖘𝖙𝖗𝖆𝖒 to gyff hym leve to have ado with them also longe as he myght holde hym on horsebak—"and yf that I be smyttyn downe, I pray you revenge me."

𝕮"Well," seyde Syr 𝕿𝖗𝖞𝖘𝖙𝖗𝖆𝖒, "and ye ar nat so fayne to have worship but I wolde as fayne encrease youre worshyp."[2] And wythall Sir 𝕲𝖆𝖜𝖆𝖞𝖓𝖊 put forthe his speare, and Sir 𝕻𝖆𝖑𝖔𝖒𝖞𝖉𝖊𝖘 another.

𝕮And so they cam egirly togydyrs, that Sir 𝕻𝖆𝖑𝖔𝖒𝖞𝖉𝖊𝖘 smote hym so harde that Sir 𝕲𝖆𝖜𝖆𝖞𝖓𝖊 felle to the erthe, horse and all. And in the same wyse he served Sir 𝖀𝖜𝖆𝖞𝖓𝖊 and Sir 𝕯𝖔𝖉𝖞𝖓𝖆𝖘 and Sir 𝕾𝖆𝖌𝖗𝖆-mour; and all thes foure knyghtes Sir 𝕻𝖆𝖑𝖔𝖒𝖞𝖉𝖊𝖘 smote them downe with dyverse spearys.

𝕮And than Sir 𝕿𝖗𝖞𝖘𝖙𝖗𝖆𝖒 departed towarde 𝕷𝖔𝖓𝖊𝖟𝖊𝖕. And whan they were departed, than cam thydir Sir 𝕲𝖆𝖑𝖕𝖍𝖔𝖉𝖞𝖓 with his twenty knyghtes unto Sir 𝕲𝖆𝖜𝖆𝖞𝖓𝖊; and there he tolde hym all how he had sped.

𝕮"Be my trouthe," seyde Sir 𝕲𝖆𝖜𝖆𝖞𝖓𝖊, "I mervayle what knyghtes they ben—that ar so arayed all in grene."[3] "And that knyght upon the whyghte horse smote me downe," seyde Sir 𝕲𝖆𝖑𝖕𝖍𝖔𝖉𝖞𝖓, "and three of my felowys." "So ded he me," seyde Sir 𝕲𝖆𝖜𝖆𝖞𝖓𝖊, "and my three felowys—and well I wote," seyde Sir 𝕲𝖆𝖜𝖆𝖞𝖓𝖊, "that other he uppon the whyghte horse ys Sir 𝕿𝖗𝖞𝖘𝖙𝖗𝖆𝖒 othir ellys Sir 𝕻𝖆𝖑𝖔𝖒𝖞𝖉𝖊𝖘, and that well-beseyne lady is Quene Isode." And as they talked thus of one thynge and of other, and in the meanewhyle Sir 𝕿𝖗𝖞𝖘-tram passed on tyll that he cam to the welle where his pavylyons were sette; and there they alyghted, and there they sawe many pavylons and grete aray.

Than Sir 𝕿𝖗𝖞𝖘𝖙𝖗𝖆𝖒 leffte there Sir 𝕻𝖆𝖑𝖔𝖒𝖞𝖉𝖊𝖘 and Sir 𝕲𝖆𝖗𝖊𝖙𝖍 with 𝕷𝖆 𝕭𝖊𝖆𝖑𝖑 𝕴𝖘𝖔𝖉𝖊; and Sir 𝕿𝖗𝖞𝖘𝖙𝖗𝖆𝖒 and Sir 𝕯𝖞𝖓𝖆𝖉𝖆𝖓 rode unto 𝕷𝖔𝖓𝖊𝖟𝖊𝖕 to herkyn tydynges—and Sir 𝕿𝖗𝖞𝖘𝖙𝖗𝖆𝖒 rode uppon Sir 𝕻𝖆𝖑-𝖔𝖒𝖞𝖉𝖊𝖘 whyghte horse. And whan he cam into the castell, Sir 𝕿𝖗𝖞𝖘-tram harde a grete horne blowe, and to the horne drewe many knyghtes.

𝕮Than Sir 𝕿𝖗𝖞𝖘𝖙𝖗𝖆𝖒𝖘 asked a knyght, "What meanyth the blaste of that horne?" "Sir," seyde that knyght, "hit is for all tho that shall holde ayenste Kynge 𝕬𝖗𝖙𝖍𝖚𝖗𝖊 at this turnemente:

𝕮"The fyrst ys the Kynge of Irelonde, and the Kynge of Surluse, and the Kynge of Lystenoyse, the Kynge of Northumbirlonde, and the kynge of the beste parte of Walys, with many other contreys."

fol.297v

---

2. *Ye ar nat so fayne . . . encrease youre worshyp*: i.e., I will gladly honor you more than you would honor yourself.

3. I.e., Trystram and his comrades are all equipped in green, disguising their usual heraldic insignia.

And all thes drewe them to a counceyle to undirstonde what governaunce they shall be of.

¶But the Kyng of Irelonde—his name was Sir Marhalte,[4] that was fadir unto the good knyght, Sir Marhalte, that Sir Trystram slew—and he had the speache,[5] that Sir Trystram myght hyre: "Now, lordis and felowis, lat us loke to oureselff; for wyte you well, Kynge Arthure ys sure[6] of many good knyghtes—other ellys he wolde nat with feaw knyghtes have ado with us. Therefore, be my rede,[7] lat every kynge have a standarde[8] and a cognyssaunce by hymselff, that every knyght may draw to his naturall lorde; and than may every kynge and captayne helpe his knyght yf he have nede."

¶Whan Sir Trystram had harde all their counceyle, he rode unto Kynge Arthure, for to hyre his counceyle.

¶But Sir Trystram was nat so sone com unto the place but Sir Gawayne and Sir Galyhodyn wente unto Kynge Arthure, and tolde hym that "that same grene knyght[9] in the grene harneyse with the whyghte horse smote us two downe—and six of oure felowys—this same day!"

¶"Well?" seyde Kynge Arthure, and than he called Sir Trystram to hym and asked what was his name.

¶"As for that," seyde Sir Trystram, "ye shall holde me excused; as at this tyme ye shall nat know my name." And there Sir Trystram returned and rode his way. "I have mervayle," seyde Kynge Arthure, "that yondir knyght woll nat tell me his name. But go ye, Sir Gryfflet, and pray hym to speke with me betwyxt us twayne."

¶Than Sir Gryfflet rode aftir hym and overtoke hym, and seyde that Kynge Arthure prayde hym to speke with hym.

¶"Sir, uppon this covenaunte," seyde Sir Trystram, "I woll turne agayne: so that ye woll ensure me that the Kynge woll nat desyre to hyre my name." "I shall undirtake hit,"[1] seyde Sir Gryfflet, "that he woll nat gretly desyre of you." So they rode togydirs tyll they cam to Kynge Arthure. "Now, fayre sir," seyde Kynge Arthure, "what is the cause ye woll nat tell me your name?" "Sir," seyde Sir Trystram, "withoute a cause I wolde nat hyde my name."

¶"Well, uppon what party woll ye holde?" seyde Kynge Arthure. "Truly, my lorde," seyde Sir Trystram, "I wote nat yet on what party I woll be on untyll I com to the fylde—and there as my harte gyvyth[2] me, there woll I holde me—but tomorow ye shall se and preve on what party I shall com." And therewithall he returned and went to his pavelons. And uppon the morne they armed them all in grene and cam into the fylde. And there yonge knyghtys began to juste and ded many worshypfull dedis.

---

4. I.e., Marhalte the elder, father of Sir Marhalte.
5. *Had the speache:* i.e., was speaking to the assembly.
6. I.e., secure.
7. *Be my rede:* by my advice.
8. I.e., flag.
9. I.e., Trystram.
1. *Undirtake hit:* take it upon myself (to say).
2. I.e., inclines.

¶Than spake Sir Gareth unto Sir Trystram, and prayde hym to gyff hym leve to breake his speare,[3] for hym thought shame to beare his speare hole agayne.

¶Whan Sir Trystram had harde hym sey so, he lowghe and sayde, "I pray you, do youre beste!"

¶Than Sir Gareth gate his speare and profirde to juste; and that sawe a knyght that was neveaw unto the Kynge with the Hondred Knyghtes: his name was Sir Selyses, a good knyght and a good man of armys. So this Selyses dressed hym unto Sir Gareth, and they two mette togydirs so harde that ayther smote other downe, horse and man, to the erthe. And so they were bothe hurte and brused, and there they lay tyll the Kynge with the Hondred Knyghtes halpe up Sir Selyses; and Sir Trystram and Sir Palompdes halpe up Sir Gareth ayen—and so they rode wyth hym to their pavylons.

And than they pulled of his helme, and whan La Beall Isode sawe Sir Gareth brused so in the face, she asked hym what ayled hym. "Madame," sayde Sir Gareth, "I had a grete buffette, and I suppose I gaff anothir—but none of my fealowys, God thanke hem, wolde rescowe me!" "Perdeus," seyde Sir Palompdes, "hit longyth nat to none of us at this day to juste, for there hath nat this day justed no proved knyghtes. [And nedely ye wold juste;] and whan the other party saw that ye profyrd yourself to juste, they sente a passyng good knyght unto you—for I know hym well: his name is Sir Selyses. And worshypfully ye mette with hym, and neyther of you ar dishonoured; and therefore refreyshe yourselff, that ye may be redy and hole to juste tomorne." "As for that," seyde Sir Gareth, "I shall nat fayle you—and[4] I may bestryde myne horse!"

¶"Now, sirs, uppon what party is hyt beste," seyde Sir Trystram, "to be withall tomorne?"

¶"Sir," seyde Sir Palompdes, "ye shall have myne advyse to be ayenst Kynge Arthure as tomorne, for on his party woll be Sir Launcelot, and many good knyghtes of his blood with hym; and the mo men of worship that they be, the more worshyp shall we wynne."

¶"That is full knyghtly spokyn," seyde Sir Trystram, "and so shall hit be ryght as ye counceyle me."

¶"In the name of God," seyde they all. So that nyght they were reposed with the beste. And in the morne whan hit was day, they were arayed all in grene trapurs, bothe shyldis and spearys, and La Beall Isode in the same coloure, and her three damesels. And ryght so thes foure knyghtes cam into the fylde endlynge and thorow;[5] and so they lad La Beall Isode thidir as she sholde stande and beholde all the justes in a bay wyndow (but allwayes she was wympled, that no man myght se her vysayge). And than thes foure knyghtes rode streyte unto the party of the Kynge of Scottis.

¶Whan Kynge Arthure had seyne hem do all this, he asked Sir Launcelot what were this knyghtes and this quene.

[68]
fol.299r

---

3. *Breake his speare:* i.e., enter the fray, fight.
4. I.e., if.
5. *Endlynge and thorow:* (riding) through from end to end.

¶"Sir, seyde Sir Launcelot, "I can nat tell you for no sertayne; but yf Sir Trystram be in this contrey, or Sir Palomydes—

¶"Sir, wyte you well hit be they, and there is Quene La Beall Isode." Than Kynge Arthure called unto hym Sir Kay, and seyde, "Go ye lyghtly and wyte how many knyghtes there bene hyre lack-ynge of the Table Rounde, for by the segis ye may know." So went Sir Kay and saw by the wrytynge in the syeges that there lacked ten knyghtes, and thes were hir namys: Sir Trystram, Sir Palomydes, Sir Percivall, Sir Gareth, Sir Gaherys, Sir Epynogrys, Sir Mordred, Sir Dynadan, Sir La Cote Male Taylé, and Sir Pelleas, the noble knyght.

¶"Well," seyde Kynge Arthur, "som of thes, I dare undirtake, ar here this day ayenste us."

¶Than cam therein two bretherne, cousyns unto Sir Gawayne: that one hyght Sir Edwarde and that other hyght Sir Sadok, the whyche were two good knyghtes. And they asked of Kynge Arthure that they myght have the fyrste justis, for they were of Orkeney. "I am pleased," seyde Kynge Arthure.

Than Sir Edwarde encountirde with the Kynge of Scottis, in whos party was Sir Trystram and Sir Palomydes. And this Sir Edwarde of Orkeney smote the Kynge of Scottis quyte frome his horse, a grete falle; and Sir Sadoke smote the Kynge of Northe Walys downe and gaff hym a wondir grete falle, that there was a grete cry on Kynge Arthurs party. And that made Sir Palomydes passyngly wrothe; and so Sir Palomydes dressed his shylde and his speare, and wyth all hys myght he mette with Sir Edwarde of Orkeney and smote hym so harde that his horse had no myght to stonde on his fyete, and so he hurled downe to the erthe. And than with the same speare Sir Palomydes smote downe Sadok over his horse croupe. "A, Jesu!" seyde Kyng Arthure, "what knyght ys that arayed so, all in grene? For he justyth myghtyly."

¶"Wyte you well," seyde Sir Gawayne, "he ys a good knyght, and yet shall ye se hym juste bettir or he departe—and yet shall ye se a more bygger knyght in the same colour than he is; for that same knyght," seyde Sir Gawayne, "that smote downe ryght now my two cousyns, he smote me downe within thes two dayes, and seven felowys mo."

¶This meanewhyle, as they stood thus talkynge, there cam into the place Sir Trystram upon a blacke horse; and or ever he stynte he smote downe with one speare foure good knyghtes of Orkeney that were of the kynne of Sir Gawayne. And Sir Gareth and Sir Dyna-dan, everyche of them smote downe a good knyght. "A, Jesu!" seyde Arthure, "yondir knyght uppon the blacke horse dothe myghtyly and mervaylously."

¶"Well, abyde you," seyde Sir Gawayne. "That knyght on the blak horse began nat yet." Than Sir Trystrams made to horse the two knyghtes agayne that Sir Edwarde and Sir Sadok had unhorsed at the begynnynge. And than Sir Trystram drew his swerde and rode unto the thyckyst prease ayenste them of Orkeney; and there he smote downe knyghtes and raced off helmys and pulled away their shyldis and hurteled downe many of their knyghtes. And so he

fol.299v

fol.300r

fared that Kynge Arthure and all knyghtes had grete mervayle to se ony o knyght do so muche dedis of armys.

And Sir Palompdes fayled nat uppon the other syde, that he so mervaylously ded, and well, that all men had wondir; for Kynge Arthure lykened Sir Trystram, that was on the blak horse, unto a wood[6] lyon; and he lykened Sir Palompdes, uppon the whyght horse, unto a wood lybarde, and Sir Gareth and Sir Dynadan unto egir wolvis.

But the custom was suche amonge them that none of the kyngys wolde helpe other,[7] but all the felyshyp of every standarde to helpe other as they myght. But ever Sir Trystram ded so muche dedis of armys that they of Orkeney wexed wery of hym, and so withdrew them unto Lonezep. Than was the cry of herowdys and all maner of comyn people, "The grene knyght hathe done mervaylously and beatyn all them of Orkeney!" And there herowdis numbird[8] that Sir Trystram, that was uppon the blacke horse, had smytten downe with spearys and swerdis thirty knyghtes; and Sir Palompdes had smyttyn downe twenty knyghtes; and the moste party of thes fyfty knyghtes were of the house of Kynge Arthure and proved knyghtes.

❡"So God me helpe," seyde Kynge Arthur unto Sir Launcelotk, "this is a grete shame [to us] to se foure knyghtes beate so many knyghtes of myne; and therefore make you redy, for we woll have ado with them."

❡"Sir," seyde Sir Launcelot, "wyte you well that there ar two passynge good knyghtes, and grete worship were hit nat to us now to have ado with them, for they ar gretly travayled." "As for that," seyde Kynge Arthure, "I woll be avenged; and therefore take with you Sir Bleoberys and Sir Ector de Marys—and I woll be the fourthe," seyde Kynge Arthure.

❡"Well, sir," seyde Sir Launcelot, "ye shall fynde me redy, and my brother Sir Ector and my cousyn Sir Bleoberys." And so whan they were redy and on horsebacke, "Now chose," seyde Kynge Arthure unto Sir Launcelot, "whom that ye woll encountir wythall."

❡"Sir," seyde Sir Launcelot, "I woll counter wyth the grene knyght uppon the blacke horse" (that was Sir Trystram); "and my cousyn Sir Bleoberys shall macche the grene knyght uppon the whyght horse" (that was Sir Palompdes); "and my brother Sir Ector shall macche wyth the grene knyght uppon the dunne horse" (that was Sir Gareth). "Than muste I," seyde Kynge Arthur, "have ado with the grene knyght uppon the gresylde horse" (and that was Sir Dynadan). "Now every man take kepe to his felow," seyde Sir Launcelot. And so they trotted on togydyrs.

❡And there encountirde Sir Launcelot ayenst Sir Trystram; [soo Syr Launcelot] smote [Sir Tristram] so sore [upon the shelde] that horse and man yeode to the erthe. But Sir Launcelot wente that hit had be Sir Palompdes, and so he passed utter.[9] And than Sir

5

[69]

10

15

20

25

30

fol.300v

35

40

How Sir Trystram had a falle

---

6. I.e., angry, fierce, mad.
7. *Helpe other*: i.e., help another to the exclusion of all others.
8. I.e., counted.
9. *Passed utter*: moved completely away.

Bleoberys encountyrd wyth Sir Palomydes; and he smote hym so harde uppon the shylde that Sir Palomydes and his whyght horse rosteled to the erthe.

⁋Than Sir Ector smote Sir Gareth so harde that downe he felle frome his horse. And than noble Kynge Arthure, he encountyrd wyth Sir Dynadan; and Kynge Arthure smote hym quyte frome his horse. And than the noyse turned a whyle and seyde the grene knyghtes were felde downe.

⁋Whan the Kyng of Northe Galys saw that Sir Trystram was on foote, and than he remembyrd hym how grete dedis of armys they had done, than he made redy many knyghtes. For the custom and the cry was suche that, what knyght were smytten downe and myght nat be horsed agayne by his felowys othir by his owne strengthe, that as that day he sholde be presonere unto the party that smote hym downe.

⁋So there cam in the Kynge of Northe Galys, and he rode streyte unto Sir Trystram; and whan he cam nyghe hym, he alyght delyvirly and toke Sir Trystram hys horse, and seyde thus: "Noble knyght, I know ye nat, nothir of what contrey ye be, but for the noble dedis that ye have done this day, take there my horse—and let me do as well as I may, for, as Jesu be my helpe, ye ar bettir worthy to have myne horse than myselff."

⁋"Grauntemercy," seyde Sir Trystram. "And yf I may, I shall quyte you; and loke that ye go nat far frome us, and as I suppose I shall wynne you sone another horse." And therewythall Sir Trystram mounte uppon his horse. And anone he mette wyth Kynge Arthure, and he gaff hym suche a buffet that Kynge Arthure had no power to kepe his sadyll; and than Sir Trystram gaff the Kynge of Northe Galys Kynge Arthurs horse. Than was there grete prease aboute Kynge Arthure for to horse hym agayne. [But Sire Palomydes wold not suffre Kynge Arthur to be horsed ageyne,] but ever Sir Palomydes smote on the ryght honde and on the lyffte honde, and raced of helmys myghtyly as a noble knyght.

And this meanewhyle Sir Trystram rode thorow the thyckyste prece and smote downe knyghtes on the ryght honde and on the lyffte honde, and raced of helmys—and so passed forthe unto his pavelouns, and leffte Sir Palomydes on foote. And than Sir Trystram chonged his horse and disgysed hymselff all in rede, horse and harnes. And whan Quene Isode saw Sir Trystram unhorsed, and she wyst nat where he was becom, than she wepte hartely.

⁋But Sir Trystram, whan he was redy, cam daysshynge lyghtly into the fylde.

⁋And than La Beall Isode aspyed hym; and so he ded grete dedis of armys wyth one speare that was grete, for Sir Trystram smote downe fyve knyghtes or ever he stynted. Than Sir Launcelot aspyed hym redyly that hit was Sir Trystram, and than he repented hym of that[1] he had smyttyn hym downe; and so Sir Launcelot wente oute of the prees to repose hym (and lyghtly he cam agayne). And so

How Sir Palomydes had a fal

How Sir Gareth had a falle   5

How Sir Dynadan had a fal

10

15

fol.301r   20

25

30

35

[70]

40

45

---

1. *Repented hym of that:* regretted that.

whan Sir Trystram was com into the prees, thorow his grete forse
he put Sir Palomydes uppon his horse, and Sir Gareth and Sir Dynadan; and than they began to do mervaylously.

¶But Sir Palomydes nothir none of his two felowys knew nat who
had holpen them to horsebak; but ever Sir Trystram was nyghe
them and knew them, and they nat hym, because he had chonged
into rede armour. And all this whyle Sir Launcelot was away.

¶So whan La Beall Isode aspyed Sir Trystram agayne uppon his
horse bak, she was passynge glad, and than she lowghe and made
good chere. And as hit happened, Sir Palomydes loked up toward
her; she was in the wyndow, and Sir Palomydes aspyed how she
lawghed. And therewyth he toke suche a rejoysynge that he smote
downe, what wyth his speare and wyth hys swerde, all that ever he
mette; for thorow the syght of her he was so enamered in her love
that he semed at that tyme, that and bothe Sir Trystram and Sir
Launcelot had bene bothe ayenste hym, they sholde have wonne no
worshyp of hym. And in his harte, as the booke saythe, Sir Palomydes wysshed that wyth his worshyp he myght have ado wyth Sir
Trystram before all men, bycause of La Beall Isode.

¶Than Sir Palomydes began to double his strengthe, and he ded
so mervaylously all men had wondir—and ever he kaste up his yee
unto La Beall Isode.

¶And whan he saw her make suche chere he fared lyke a lyon,
that there myght no man wythstonde hym. And than Sir Trystram
behylde hym, how he styrred aboute, and seyde unto Sir Dynadan,
"So God me helpe, Sir Palomydes ys a passynge [good knyghte and
a] well endurynge! But suche dedis sawe I hym never do, nother
never erste herde I tell that ever he ded so muche in one day."
"Sir, hit is his day," seyde Sir Dynadan—and he wolde sey no more
unto Sir Trystram; but to hymself he seyde thus: "And Sir Trystram
knew for whos love he doth all this dedys of armys, sone he wolde
abate his corrage."

"Alas," seyde Sir Trystram, "that Sir Palomydes were nat crystynde." So seyde Kynge Arthur, and so seyde all that behylde them;
than all people gaff hym the pryse as for the beste knyght that day,
and he passed[2] Sir Launcelot othir ellys Sir Trystram. "Well," seyde
Sir Dynadan to hymselff, "all this worshyp that Sir Palomydes hath
here thys day, he may thanke the quene Isode; for had she bene
away this day, had nat Sir Palomydes gotyn the pryse."

Ryght so cam into the fylde Sir Launcelot du Lake, and sawe and
harde the grete noyse and the grete worshyp that Sir Palomydes
had. He dressed hym ayenst Sir Palomydes wyth a grete speare and
a longe, and thought to have smyttyn hym downe; and whan Sir
Palomydes saw Sir Launcelot com uppon hym so faste, he toke his
horse wyth the spurrys and ran uppon hym as faste wyth his
swerde; and as Sir Launcelot sholde have strykyn hym, he smote the
speare on syde[3] and smote hit a-too wyth his swerde. And

2. I.e., surpassed.
3. *On syde:* aside.

therewyth Sir Palomydes russhed unto Sir Launcelot and thought to
have put hym to shame, and wyth his swerde he smote of his horse
nek that Sir Launcelot rode uppon. And than Sir Launcelot felle to
the erthe.

Than was the cry huge and grete, how "Sir Palomydes the Saresyn
hath smyttyn downe Sir Launcelots horse!" Ryght so there were
many knyghtes wrothe wyth Sir Palomydes bycause he had done
that dede, and helde there ayenste hit, and seyde hyt was unknyghtly done in a turnemente to kylle an horse wylfully, othir ellys
that hit had bene done in playne batayle, lyff-for-lyff.[4]

⁋Whan Sir Ector de Marys saw Sir Launcelot, his brothir, have
suche a dispyte and so sette on foote, than he gate a speare egirly
and ran ayenst Sir Palomydes; and he smote hym so harde that he
bare Sir Palomydes quyte frome his horse. That sawe Sir Trystram,
and he smote downe Sir Ector de Marys quyte frome his horse.

Than Sir Launcelot dressed his shylde uppon his shuldir, and wyth
his swerde naked in his honde, and so he cam streyte uppon Sir
Palomydes: "Wyte thou well, thou haste done me this day the grettyste dispyte that ever ony worshipfull knyght ded me in
turnemente othir in justys! And therefore I woll be avenged uppon
the—and therefore take kepe to youreself." "A, mercy,[5] noble
knyght," seyde Sir Palomydes, "of"[6] my dedis! And, jantyll knyght,
forgyff me myne unknyghtly dedis, for I have no power nothir
myght to wythstonde you—

⁋"And I have done so muche this day that well I wote I ded
never so muche, nothir never shall do so muche in my dayes:

⁋"And therefore, moste noble knyght of the worlde, I requyre
the[7] spare me as this day, and I promyse you I shall ever be youre
knyght whyle I lyve—for, and yf ye put me from my worshyp now,
ye put me from the grettyst worship that ever I had or ever shall
have." "Well," seyde Sir Launcelot, "I se. For to say the sothe, ye
have done mervaylously well this day, and I undirstonde a parte[8]
for whos love ye do hit—and well I wote that love is a grete maystry:

⁋"And yf my lady were here—as she is nat—

⁋"Wyte you well, Sir Palomydes, ye shulde nat beare away the
worshyp! But beware youre love be nat discoverde, for and Sir
Trystram may know hit, ye woll repente hit. And sytthyn my quarell
is nat here, ye shall have this day the worshyp as for me; consyderynge the grete travayle and payne that ye have had this day, hit
were no worship for me to put you frome hit."

⁋And therewythall Sir Launcelot suffyrd Sir Palomydes to departe.
Than Sir Launcelot by grete forse and myght gate his horse agayne
magré twenty knyghtes.

⁋So whan Sir Launcelot was horsed, he ded many mervaylouse
dedis of armys—and so ded Sir Trystram and Sir Palomydes in lyke

[71]

fol.302v

5

10

15

20

25

30

35

40

45

---

4. *In playne batayle, lyff-for-lyff:* in open mortal combat.
5. I.e., have mercy.
6. I.e., for.
7. thee.
8. *A parte:* in part, implicitly.

wyse. Than Sir 𝕷auncelot smote adowne wyth a speare Sir 𝕯ynadan, and the Kynge off Scotlonde, and the Kynge of Northe Walys, and the Kynge of Northumbirlonde, and the Kynge of Lystenoyse.

⟨So than Sir 𝕷auncelot and his felowys smote downe well-nye a fourty knyghtes. Than cam the Kynge of Irelonde and the Kynge of the Streyte Marchis to rescowe Sir 𝕿rystram and Sir 𝕻alomydes; and there began a grete medlé, and many knyghtys were smyttyn downe on bothe partyes. And allwayes Sir 𝕷auncelot spared Sir 𝕿rystram, and he spared hym; and Sir 𝕻alomydes wolde nat meddyll wyth Sir 𝕷auncelot. And so there was hurlynge here and there, and than Kynge 𝕬rthure sente oute many knyghtes of the Table Rounde; and Sir 𝕻alomydes was ever in the formyste frunte;[9] and Sir 𝕿rystram ded so strongly that the Kynge and all othir had mervayle.

And than the Kynge let blowe to lodgynge; and bycause Sir 𝕻alomydes beganne fyrste, and never he wente nor rode oute of the fylde to repose hym, but ever he was doynge on horsebak othir on foote, and lengyst durynge, Kynge 𝕬rthure and all the kynges gaff Sir 𝕻alomydes the honoure and the gré as for that day. Than Sir 𝕿rystram commaunded Sir 𝕯ynadan to fecche the quene 𝕷a 𝕭eall 𝕴sode and brynge her to his two pavelons by the well.

⟨And so Sir 𝕯ynadan ded as he was commaunded. But whan Sir 𝕻alomydes undirstoode and knew that Sir 𝕿rystram was he that was in the rede armour and on the rede horse, wyte you well that he was glad, and so was Sir 𝕲areth and Sir 𝕯ynadan, for all they wente that Sir 𝕿rystram had be takyn presonere. And than every knyght drew to his inne. And than Kynge 𝕬rthure and every knyghte spake of tho knyghtes; but of all men they gaff Sir 𝕻alomydes the pryce, and all knyghtes that knew Sir 𝕻alomydes had wondir of his dedis.

"Sir," seyde Sir 𝕷auncelot unto Kynge 𝕬rthure, "as for Sir 𝕻alomydes, and he be the grene knyght, I dare say as for this day he is beste worthy to have the gré, for he reposed hym never, nor never chaunged hys wedis, and he began fyrste and lengyste hylde on— and yet well I wote," seyde Sir 𝕷auncelot, "that there was a better knyght than he, and that ye shall preve or we departe fro them, [upon payne] of my lyff." Thus they talked on aythir party, and so Sir 𝕯ynadan rayled wyth Sir 𝕿rystram, and sayde, "What the devyll ys uppon the this day? For Sir 𝕻alomydes strengthe fyeblede never this day, but ever he doubled; and Sir 𝕿rystram fared all this day as he had bene on slepe—and therefore I calle hym a coward."

⟨"Well, Sir 𝕯ynadan," seyde Sir 𝕿rystram, "I was never called cowarde or now of earthely knyght in my lyff. And wyte thou well, Sir 𝕯ynadan, [I calle myselfe never the more coward] though Sir 𝕷auncelot gaff me a falle, for I outecepte hym of all knyghtes. And doute ye nat, Sir 𝕯ynadan, and[1] Sir 𝕷auncelot have a quarell good, he is to over good for ony knyght that now ys lyvynge, and yet[2] of his sufferaunce, larges, bounté, and curtesy, I calle hym a knyght pyerles." And so Sir 𝕿rystram was in maner wrothe wyth Sir

fol.303r

fol.303v
[72]

5

10

15

20

25

30

35

40

45

---

9. *Formyste frunte*: very front of the line of battle.
1. I.e., if.
2. I.e., still.

Dynadan; but all this langayge Sir Dynadan sayde because he wolde angur Sir Trystram for to cause hym to wake hys speretes, for well knew Sir Dynadan that, and Sir Trystram were thorowly wrothe, Sir Palompdes shulde wynne no worship uppon the morne. And for thys entente Sir Dynadan seyde all this raylynge langage ayenste Sir Trystram.

"Truly," seyde Sir Palompdes, "as for Sir Launcelot, of noble knyghthode and of his curtesy, proues, and jantylnes, I know nat his piere. For this day," seyde Sir Palompdes, "I ded full uncurteysly unto Sir Launcelot, and ful unknyghtly—

¶"And full knyghtly and curteysly he ded to me agayne; for and he had bene so unjantyll to me as I was to hym, this day had I wonne no worshyp—and therefore," seyde Sir Palompdes, "I shall be Sir Launcelottis knyght whyles that I lyve."

And all this was talkynge off³ in all the howsis of the kynges; and all kynges and lordis and knyghtes seyde, of clyere knyghthode and of pure strengthe and of bounté and of curtesy Sir Launcelot and Sir Trystram bare the pryce of all knyghtes that ever were in Kyng Arthurs dayes. And there were no knyghtes in Kynge Arthurs dayes that ded halff so many dedis of armys as they two ded; as the booke seyth, no ten knyghtes ded nat halff the dedis that they ded, and there was never knyght in there dayes that requyred Sir Launcelot othir ellys Sir Trystram of ony queste, so⁴ hit were nat to there shame, but they parformed there desyre.⁵

¶So on the morne Sir Launcelot departed. And Sir Trystram was redy, and La Beall Isode wyth Sir Palompdes and Sir Gareth; and so they rode all in grene, full freysshely besayne, unto the foreyste— and Sir Trystram laffte Sir Dynadan slepynge in his bedde. And so as they rode, hit happened the Kynge and Sir Launcelot stode in a wyndow and saw Sir Trystram ryde, and La Beall Isode.

"Sir," seyde Sir Launcelot, "yondir rydyth the fayreste lady of the worlde excepte youre Quene, Dame Gwenyver." "Who ys that?" seyde Kynge Arthure. "Sir," seyde he, "hit is Quene Isode that, out-etake my lady youre Quene, she ys makeles." "Take youre horse," seyde Kynge Arthure, and aray you at all ryghtes,⁶ as I woll do. And I promyse you," seyde the Kynge, "I woll se her." And anone they were armed and horsed, and aythir toke a speare and rode unto the foreyste.

¶"Sir," seyde Sir Launcelot, "hit is nat good that ye go to nyghe them, for wyte you well there ar two as good knyghtes⁷ as ony now ar lyvynge—and therefore, sir, I pray you, be nat to hasty:

¶"For peradventure there woll be som knyghtes that woll be displeased and we com suddeynly uppon them." "As for that" seyde Kynge Arthure, "I woll se her, for I take no forse whom I gryeve." "Sir," seyde Sir Launcelot, "ye put youreselff in grete jupardé." "As

[fol.304r] [20]

[73] [25]

---

3. *Talkynge off*: being talked of.
4. *Queste*: i.e., request. *So*: i.e., as long as.
5. *Parformed there desyre*: did what they asked.
6. *At all ryghtes*: in every respect.
7. *Two as good knyghtes*: i.e., two knights as good.

for that," seyde the Kynge, "we woll take the adventure." Ryght so anone the Kynge rode evyn to her and [salewed her and] seyde, "God you save!"

¶ "Sir," she seyde, "ye ar wellcom." Than the Kynge behylde her, and lyked her wondirly well.

¶ So wyth that cam Sir Palomydes unto Kynge Arthure and seyde, "Thou uncurteyse knyght, what sekyst thou here? For thou art uncurteyse to com uppon a lady thus suddeynly. Therefore wythdrawe the."

¶ But Kynge Arthure toke none hede of Sir Palomydes wordys, but ever he loked stylle uppon Quene Isode. Than was Sir Palomydes wrothe; and therewyth he toke a speare and cam hurtelynge uppon Kynge Arthure and smote hym downe with a speare—a grete falle.

¶ Whan Sir Launcelot saw that despyte of Sir Palomydes, he seyde to hymselff, "I am lothe to have ado wyth yondir knyght—and nat for his owne sake, but for Sir Trystrams; and of one thynge I am sure of hym: yf I smyte downe Sir Palomydes, I muste have ado wyth Sir Trystram, and that were to muche to macche them bothe for me alone, for they ar two noble knyghtes. Natwythstondynge, whethir I lyve or dye, nedys muste I revenge my lorde Arthure—and so I woll, whatsomever befalle me." And [therewith Sir Launcelot cryed to Sir Palomydes, "Kepe the from me!" And] therewythall Sir Launcelot and Sir Palomydes russhed togydyrs wyth two spearys strongly. But Sir Launcelot smote Sir Palomydes so harde that he wente quyte oute of his sadyll, and had a grete falle.

¶ Whan Sir Trystram saw Sir Palomydes have that falle, he seyde to Sir Launcelot, "Sir knyght, kepe the, for I muste juste wyth the." "As for to juste wyth me," seyde Sir Launcelot, "I woll nat fayle you for no drede that I have of you; but I am lothe to have ado wyth you, and I myght chose, for I woll that ye wyte that I muste revenge my speciall lorde and my moste bedrad frynde, that was unhorsed unwarely and unknyghtly. And therefore, sir, thoughe I revenge that falle, take ye no displesure, for he is to me suche a frynde that I may nat se hym shamed."

¶ Anone Sir Trystram undirstood by hys persone and by his knyghtly wordis hit was Sir Launcelot du Lake; and truly Sir Trystram demed that hit was Kynge Arthure that Sir Palomydes had smyttyn downe. And than Sir Trystram put hys speare frome hym, and gate Sir Palomydes agayne on his horse backe; and Sir Launcelot gate Kynge Arthure agayne to horsebacke, and so departed.

"So God me helpe," seyde Sir Trystram unto Sir Palomydes, "ye ded nat worshypfully whan ye smote downe that knyght so suddeynly as ye ded; and wyte you well ye ded youreselff grete shame, for the knyghtes came hyddir of there jantylnes to se a fayre lady— and that ys every good knyghtes parte, to beholde a fayre lady— and ye had nat ado to play suche maystryes for my lady. Wyte thou well hit woll turne to angir; for he that ye smote downe was Kynge Arthure, and that othir was the good knyght Sir Launcelot. But I shall nat forgete," seyde Sir Trystram, "the wordys of Sir Launcelot, whan that he called hym a man of grete worshyp; and thereby I wyste

fol.304v

fol.305r

that hit was Kynge Arthure. And as for Sir Launcelot, and there had
bene an hondred knyghtes in the medow, he wolde nat a refused
them—and yet he seyde he wolde refuse me; and by that agayne I
knew that hit was Sir Launcelot, for ever he forberyth me in every
place, and shewyth me grete kyndenes. And of all knyghtes—I
outetake none, say what men wyll say—he bearyth the floure: assay
hym whosomever wyll, and he[8] be well angred and that hym lyst
to do his utteraunce wythoute ony favoure, I know hym nat on lyve
but Sir Launcelot ys over[9] harde for hym, take hym bothe on
horsebacke and on foote."

¶"Sir, I may never belyeve," seyde Sir Palompdes, "that Kynge
Arthure woll ryde so pryvaly as a poure arraunte knyght." "A," sayd
Sir Trystrams, "ye know nat my lorde Kynge Arthure! for all knyghtes
may lerne to be a knyght of hym—and therefore ye may be sory,"
seyde Sir Trystram, "of youre unknyghtly dedys done to so noble a
knyght."

"And a thynge, sir, be done, hit can nat be undone," seyde Sir
Palompdes. Than Sir Trystram sente Quene Isode unto her lodgynge
into the pryory, there to beholde all the turnemente.

Than there was a cry unto all knyghtes made, that whan they
herde the horne blow they sholde make justes as they ded
the fyrste day; and lyke as the brethirne Sir Edwarde and Sir Sadok
began the justys the fyrste day, Sir Uwayne, the Kyngis son Uryen,
and Sir Lucanere de Butlere, began the justis the secunde day. And
at the fyrste encountir, Sir Uwayne smote downe the Kynge of Scottys; and Sir Lucanere ran ayenste the kynge of Walys, and they brake
there spearys all to pecis—and they were so fyrse bothe that they
hurteled there horsys togydir that bothe felle to the erthe.

¶Than they off Orkeney horsed agayne Sir Lucanere; and than
cam in Syr Trystram de Lyones and smote downe Sir Uwayne and
Sir Lucanere. And Sir Palompdes smote downe othir two knyghtes.
And than cam Sir Gareth and smote downe othir two good knyghtes.
Than seyde Kynge Arthure unto Sir Launcelott, "A, se yondir three
knyghtes do passyngly well, and namely the fyrste that justed."

¶"Sir," seyde Sir Launcelot, "that knyght began nat yet—but ye
shall se hym do mervaylously!" And than cam into the place the
knyghtes of Orkeney, and than they began to do many dedys of
armys.

¶Whan Sir Trystram saw them so begyn, he seyde to Sir Palompdes, "How feele ye youreselff? May ye do this day as ye ded
yestirday?"

¶"Nay," seyde Sir Palompdes, "I feele myselff so wery and so sore
brused of the dedis of yestirday that I may nat endure as I ded."

¶"That me repentyth," seyde Sir Trystram, "for I shall lacke you[1]
this day." "But helpe youreselff," seyde Sir Palompdes, "and truste
nat to me, for I may nat do as I ded." (And all thes wordis seyde

fol.305v

[74]

---

8. I.e., he who would test Launcelot in battle.
9. I.e., too.
1. *Lacke you:* notice your diminished presence.

Sir Palomydes but to begyle Sir Trystram.) Than seyde Sir Trystram
unto Sir Gareth, "Than muste I truste upon you; wherefore I pray
you be nat farre fro me to rescow me and nede be."

⁋"Sir, I shall nat fayle you," seyde Sir Gareth, "in all that I may
do."

⁋Than Sir Palomydes rode by hymselff; and than in despyte of
Sir Trystram he put hymselff in the thyckyst prees amonges them
of Orkeney. And there he ded so mervaylous dedis of armys that
all men had wondir of hym—for there myght none stonde hym a
stroke. Whan Sir Trystram saw Sir Palomydes do suche dedys, he
mervayled and sayde to hymselff, "Methynkyth he is wery of my
company."

⁋So Sir Trystram behylde hym a grete whyle and ded but lytyll
ellys, for the noyse and cry was so grete that Sir Trystram mervayled
frome whens cam the strengthe that Sir Palomydes had there.

⁋"Sir," seyde Sir Gareth unto Sir Trystram, "remembir ye nat of
the wordis that Sir Dynadan seyde to you yestirday, whan he called
you cowarde? Pardé, sir, he seyde hit for none ylle, for ye ar the
man in the worlde that he lovyth beste, and all that he seyde was
for youre worshyp:

⁋"And therefore," seyde Sir Gareth, "lat me know this day what
ye be²—and wondir ye nat so uppon Sir Palomydes, for he forsyth
hymselff to wynne all the honoure frome you."

⁋"I may well beleve hit," seyde Sir Trystram, "and sytthyn I
undirstonde his yevil wyll and hys envy, ye shall se, yf that I enforce
myselff, that the noyse shall be leffte³ that is now uppon hym."
Than Sir Trystram rode into the thyckyst of the prees; and than he
ded so mervaylously well and ded so grete dedis of armys that all
men seyde that Sir Trystram ded dowble so muche dedys of armys
as ded Sir Palomydes aforehande. And than the noyse wente clene
frome Sir Palomydes, and all the people cryed uppon Sir Trystram
and seyde, "A, Jesu, a! Se how Sir Trystram smytyth wyth hys speare
so many knyghtes to the erthe—and se," seyde they all, "how many
knyghtes he smytyth downe wyth his swerde, and how many knyghtes he racith of there helmys and there shyldys!" And so he bete
all of Orkeney afore hym.

⁋"How now?" seyde Sir Launcelot unto Kynge Arthure. "I tolde
you that thys day there wolde a knyght play his pageaunte:⁴ for
yondir rydyth a knyght. Ye may se he dothe all knyghtly, for he
hath strengthe and wynde⁵ inowe."

⁋"So God me helpe," seyde Kynge Arthure to Sir Launcelot, "ye
sey sothe, for I sawe never a bettir knyght—for he passyth farre
Sir Palomydes."

⁋"Sir, wyte you well," seyde Sir Launcelot, "hit muste be so of
ryght, for hit is hymselff that noble knyght Sir Trystram." "I
may ryght well belyeve hit," seyde Kynge Arthure. But whan Sir

fol.306r

fol.306v

2. *What ye be:* i.e., what you are made of.
3. I.e., gone.
4. *Play his pageaunte:* i.e., play out his part.
5. I.e., stamina.

Palomydes harde the noyse and the cry was turned frome hym, he rode oute on the tone syde and behylde Sir Trystram. And whan he saw hym do so mervaylously well, he wepte passyngly sore for dispyte, for he wyst well than he sholde wyn no worshyp that day; for well knew Sir Palomydes, whan Sir Trystram wolde put forthe his strengthe and his manhode, that he sholde gete but lytyll worshyp that day.

¶Than cam Kynge Arthure and the Kynge of Northe Galys and Sir Launcelot du Lake. And Sir Bleoberys and Sir Bors de Ganys and Sir Ector de Marys, thes three knyghtes cam into the fylde wyth Sir Launcelot; and so they foure ded so grete dedys of armys that all the noyse began uppon Sir Launcelot. And so they bete the Kynge of Walys and the Kynge of Scottys far abacke, and made them to voyde the fylde. But Sir Trystram and Sir Gareth abode stylle in the fylde and endured all that ever there cam, that all men had wondir that ever ony knyght endured so many grete strokys; but ever Sir Launcelot and hys kynnesmen forbare Sir Trystram and Sir Gareth. Than seyde Kynge Arthure, "Ys that Sir Palomydes that enduryth so well?"

"Nay," seyde Sir Launcelot, "wyte you well hit ys the good knyght Sir Trystram, for yondir ye may se Sir Palomydes beholdyth and hovyth, and doth lytyll or naught. And, sir, ye shall undirstonde that Sir Trystram wenyth this day to beate us all oute of the fylde—and as for me," seyde Sir Launcelot, "I shall nat mete hym, mete hym whoso wyll. But, sir," seyde Sir Launcelot, "ye may se how Sir Palomydes hovyth yondir as thoughe he were in a dreame; and wyte you well he ys full hevy that Sir Trystram doyth suche dedys of armys."

"Than ys he but a foole," seyde Kynge Arthure, "for never yet was Sir Palomydes suche a knyght, nor never shall be of suche proues. And yf he have envy at Sir Trystram," seyde Kynge Arthure, "and commyth in wyth hym uppon his syde, he ys a false knyght." And as the Kynge and Sir Launcelot thus spake, Sir Trystram rode pryvayly oute of the prees, that no man aspyed hym but La Beall Isode and Sir Palomydes—for they two wolde nat leve off there yghesyght of hym.

¶And whan Sir Trystram cam to his pavylons, he founde Sir Dynadan in hys bedde aslepe. "Awake!" seyde Sir Trystram, "for ye ought to be ashamed so to slepe whan knyghtes have ado in the fylde."

¶Than Sir Dynadan arose lyghtly and sayde, "Sir, what wyll ye do?" "Make you redy," seyde Sir Trystram, "to ryde wyth me into the fylde."

¶So whan Sir Dynadan was armed, he loked uppon Sir Trystrames helme and on hys shylde, and whan he saw so many strokys uppon his helme and uppon hys shylde, he seyde, "In good tyme was I thus aslepe, for had I bene wyth you I muste nedys for shame have folowed wyth you—more for shame than for any proues that ys in me!—for I se well now be thy strokys that I sholde have bene truly beatyn, as I was yestirday."

❡"Leve youre japys," seyde Sir **Trystram**, "and com of,[6] that we were in the fylde agayne." "What?" sayde Sir **Dynadan**, "ys youre harte up now? Yestirday ye fared as ye had dremed."

❡So than Sir **Trystram** was arayed all in blacke harneys. "A, Jesu!" seyde Sir **Dynadan**, "what ayleth you thys day? Mesemyth that ye be more wyldar than ye were yestirday."

❡Than smyled Sir **Trystram** and seyde to Sir **Dynadan**, "Awayte well uppon me yf ye se me ovirmacched, and loke that ever ye be byhynde me, and I shall make you redy way,[7] by Goddys grace."

❡So they toke there horsys. And all thys aspyed Sir **Palomydes**, bothe the goynge and the comynge; and so ded La Beall Isode, for she knew Sir **Trystram** passynge well.

❡Than Sir **Palomydes** sawe that Sir **Trystram** was disgysed, and thought to shame hym; and so he rode unto a knyght that was sore wounded, that sate undir a thorne a good way frome the fylde.

❡"Syr knyght," seyde Sir **Palomydes**, "I pray you to lende me youre armour and youre shylde, for myne ys overwell knowyn in thys fylde, and that hath done me grete damayge; and ye shall have myne armour and my shylde that ys as sure as youres." "I woll well," seyde the knyght, "that ye have myne armoure and also my shylde. Yf they may do you ony avayle, I am well pleased."

❡So Sir **Palomydes** armed hym hastely in that knyghtes armour and hys shylde, that shone lyke ony crystall or sylver. And so he cam rydynge into the fylde; and than there was nothir Sir **Trystram** nothir none of hys party, nothir of Kynge **Arthurs**, that knew Sir **Palomydes**. And as sone as he was com into the fylde, Sir **Trystram** smote downe three knyghtes—evyn in the syght of Sir **Palomydes**; and than he rode ayenste Sir **Trystram**, and aythir mette othir wyth grete spearys, that they all to-braste to there hondys. And than they daysshed togedir wyth swerdys egirly.

❡Than Sir **Trystram** had mervayle what knyght he was that ded batayle so myghtyly wyth hym.

❡Than was Sir **Trystram** wrothe, for he felte hym passynge stronge, and he demed that he cowde nat have ado wyth the remenaunte of the knyghtes bycause of the strengthe of Sir **Palomydes**. So they laysshed togydyrs and gaff many sad strokys togydyrs; and many knyghtys mervayled what knyght he was that so encountred wyth the blak knyght, Sir **Trystram**. And full well knew La Beall **Isode** that hit was Sir **Palomydes** that faught wyth Sir **Trystram**, for she aspyed all in her wyndow where that she stood, how Sir **Palomydes** chaunged hys harnes wyth the wounded knyght; and than she began to wepe so hertely for the dyspyte of Sir **Palomydes** that well-nyghe there she sowned.

❡Than cam in Sir **Launcelot** wyth the knyghtes of Orkeney; and whan the todir party had aspyed Sir **Launcelot**, they cryed and seyde, "Returne, for here commyth Sir **Launcelot**!" So there cam in a knyght unto Sir **Launcelot**, and seyde, "Sir, ye muste nedis fyght

fol.307v

[76]

fol.308r

---

6. *Com of*: i.e., get moving.
7. *Redy way*: easy going.

wyth yondyr knyght in the blak harneyes" (whyche was Sir Trystram) "for he hath allmoste overcom that good knyghte that fyghtyth wyth hym wyth the sylver shylde" (whyche was Sir Palompdes).
Than Sir Launcelot rode betwyxte them, and Sir Launcelot seyde unto
Sir Palompdes, "Sir knyghte, let me have this batayle, for ye have
nede to be reposed."

¶Sir Palompdes knew well Sir Launcelot, and so ded Sir Trystram,
but bycause Sir Launcelot was farre hardyer knyght and bygger than
Sir Palompdes, he was ryght glad to suffir Sir Launcelot to fyght wyth
Sir Trystram—for well wyste he that Sir Launcelot knew nat Sir Trystram, and therefore he hoped that Sir Launcelot sholde beate other
shame Sir Trystram; and thereof Sir Palompdes was full fayne.

And so Sir Launcelot laysshed at Sir Trystram many sad strokys—
but Sir _Launcelot_ knew nat Sir Trystram—but Sir Trystram knew
well Sir Launcelot. And thus they faught longe togydyrs, whyche
made La Beall Isode well-nyghe oute of her mynde for sorow. Than
Sir Dynadan tolde Sir Gareth how that knyght in the blak harneys
was there lorde, Sir Trystram—"and that othir ys Sir Launcelot that
fyghtyth wyth hym, that muste nedys have the bettyr of hym, for
Sir Trystram hath had overmuche travayle this day."

"Than lat us smyte hym downe," seyde Sir Gareth. "So hit is beste
that we do," seyde Sir Dynadan, "rathir than Sir Trystrams sholde
be shamed—for yondir hovyth the straunge knyghte wyth the
sylver shylde to falle uppon Sir Trystram, yf nede be." And so furthwythall Sir Gareth russhed uppon Sir Launcelot and gaff hym a
grete stroke uppon the helme, that he was astoned. And than cam
in Sir Dynadan wyth hys speare, and he smote Sir Launcelot suche a
buffet that horse and man yode to the erthe and had a grete falle.

¶"Now, fye for shame!" seyde Sir Trystram unto Sir Gareth and
Sir Dynadan, "why ded ye so to-smyte adowne soo good a knyght as
he ys, and namely whan I had ado wyth hym? A, Jesu! ye do youreselff grete shame, and hym no disworshyp, for I hylde hym resonabely hote,[8] though ye had nat holpyn me." Than cam Sir
Palompdes, whyche was disgysed, and smote downe Sir Dynadan
frome hys horse.

Than Sir Launcelot, bycause Sir Dynadan had smyttyn hym downe
aforehonde, therefore he assayled Sir Dynadan passynge sore. And
Sir Dynadan deffended hym myghtyly; but well undirstood Sir Trystram that Sir Dynadan myght nat endure ayenste Sir Launcelot,
wherefore Sir Trystram was sory. Than cam Sir Palompdes freysshe
uppon Sir Trystram; and whan he saw Sir Palompdes com so
freyshly, he thought to delyver hym at onys, bycause that he wolde
helpe Sir Dynadan that stoode in perell wyth Sir Launcelot.

Than Sir Trystram hurteled unto Sir Palompdes and gaff hym a
grete buffet; and than Sir Trystram gate Sir Palompdes and pulled
hym downe undirnethe [hym—and so felle Sir Tristram with hym;]
and than Sir Trystram lyghtly lepe up and leffte Sir Palompdes, and

fol.308v

fol.309r

---

8. _Hylde hym resonabely hote:_ was pressing him reasonably hard.

wente betwyxte Sir Launcelot and Sir Dynadan. And than they began
to do batayle togydyrs.

¶And ryght so Sir Dynadan gate Sir Trystrams horse, and seyde
on hyght, that Sir Launcelot myght hyre,

¶"My lorde Sir Trystram, take youre horse!" And whan Sir Launcelot harde hym name Sir Trystram, "A, Jesu! what have I done?"
seyde Sir Launcelot, "for now am I dishonoured"—and seyde, "A,
my lorde Sir Trystram, why were ye now disgysed? Ye have put
youreselff this day in grete perell! But I pray you to pardon me, for
and I had knowyn you, we had nat done this batayle."

¶"Sir, seyde Sir Trystrams, "this is nat the fyrste kyndenes and
goodnes that ye have shewed unto me." And anone they were
horsed bothe agayne. So all the peple on that one syde gaff Sir
Launcelot the honoure and the gré; and all the people on the othir
syde gaff Sir Trystram the honoure and the gré. But Sir Launcelot
seyde nay thereto—"for I am nat worthy to have this honoure, for
I woll reporte me to all knyghtes that Sir Trystram hath bene lenger
in the fylde than I, and he hath smyttyn downe many mo knyghtes
this day than I have done. And therefore I woll gyff Sir Trystram
my voyse and my name;[9] and so I pray all my lordys and felowys
so to do." Than there was the hole voyse of kyngys, deukes, and
erlys, barons and knyghtes, that Sir Trystram de Lyones "thys day ys
preved the beste knyght."

Than they blewe unto lodgynge. And Quene Isode was lad unto
her pavelons; but wyte you well she was wrothe oute of mesure
wyth Sir Palompdes, for she saw all his treson, frome the begynnynge to the endynge. And all thys whyle neythir Sir Trystram, Sir
Gareth, nothir Sir Dynadan knew nat of the treson of Sir Palompdes;
but aftirward ye shall hyre how there befelle the grettyst debate
betwyxte Sir Trystram and Sir Palompdes that myght be.

¶So whan the turnemente was done Sir Trystram, Sir Gareth and
Sir Dynadan rode wyth La Beall Isode to his pavelons; and ever Sir
Palompdes rode wyth them in there company, disgysed as he was.

¶But whan Sir Trystram had aspyed hym, that he was the same
knyght wyth the shylde of sylver that hylde hym so hote that day,
than seyde Trystram, "Sir knyght, wyte thou well here ys none that
hath nede of youre felyshyp, and therefore I pray you departe frome
us."

¶Than Sir Palompdes answered agayne, as though he had nat
knowyn Sir Trystram, "Wyte you well, sir knyght, that frome this
felyshyp woll I nat departe, for one of the beste knyghtys of the
worlde commaunded me to be in this company, and tyll that he
discharge me of my servyse I woll nat be discharged."

¶So by his langayge Sir Trystram knew that hit was Sir Palompdes,
and seyde, "A, sir, ar ye such a knyght? Ye have be named wronge,
for ye have ben called ever a jantyll knyght; and as this day ye have
shewed me grete unjantylnes, for ye had allmoste brought me to

fol.309v

[77]

---

9. *My voyse and my name*: my recommendation and support.

my dethe. But as[1] for you, I suppose I sholde have done well
inowghe; but Sir **Launcelot** with you was overmuche, for I know no
knyght lyvynge but Sir **Launcelot** ys to over good for hym, and he
woll do hys utteryst." "Alas," seyde Sir **Palomydes**, "ar ye my lorde
Sir **Trystram**?" "Yee, sir, and that know you well inow."

"Be my knyghthod," seyde Sir **Palomydes**, "untyll now I knew you
nat, for I wente that ye had bene the Kynge off Irelonde—for well
I wote that ye bare his armys." "I bare his armys," seyde Sir **Trys-**
tram, "and that woll I abyde bye, for I wanne them onys in a fylde
of a full noble knyght whos name was Sir **Marhalte**; and wyth grete
payne I wan that knyght, for there was none othir recover. But Sir
Marhalte dyed thorow false[2] lechis; and yet was he never yoldyn to
me." "Sir," seyde Sir **Palomydes**, "I wente that ye had bene turned
uppon Sir **Launcelottys** party, and that caused me to turne."

⁋"Ye sey well," seyde Sir **Trystram**, "and so I take you and forgyff
you."

⁋So than they rode to there pavelons. And whan they were
alyght they unarmed them and wysshe there facis and there hondys, and so yode unto mete and were set at there table.

⁋But whan La Beall Isode saw Sir **Palomydes**, she chaunged than
her coloures—for wrathe she myght nat speake. Anone Sir **Trys-**
tram aspyed her countenaunce, and seyde, "Madame, for what
cause make ye us such chere? We have bene sore travayled all thys
day."

⁋"Myne owne lorde," seyde La Beall Isode, "for Goddys sake,
be ye nat displeased wyth me, for I may none othirwyse do:

⁋"I sawe thys day how ye were betrayed and nyghe brought unto
youre dethe. Truly, sir, I sawe every dele, how and in what wyse.
And therefore, sir, how sholde I suffir in youre presence suche a
felonne and traytoure as ys Sir **Palomydes**? For I saw hym wyth
myne yen, how he behylde you whan ye wente oute of the fylde—
for ever he hoved stylle uppon his horse tyll that he saw you com
agaynewarde; and than furthwythall I saw hym ryde to the hurte
knyght, and chaunged hys harneys with hym; and than streyte I
sawe hym, how he sought you all[3] the fylde; and anone as he had
founde you, he encountred wyth you, and wylfully Sir **Palomydes**
ded batayle wyth you. And as for hym, sir, I was nat gretly aferde;
but I drad sore Sir **Launcelot**, whyche knew nat you."

⁋"Madame," seyde Sir **Palomydes**, "ye may say what ye woll—I
may nat contrary you—but, be my knyghthod, I knew nat my lorde
Sir **Trystram**." "No forse,"[4] seyde Sir **Trystram** unto Sir **Palomydes**,
"I woll take youre exscuse—but well I wote ye spared me but a
lytyll—but no forse, all ys pardoned as on my party." Than La Beall
Isode hylde downe her hede and seyde no more at that tyme. And
therewythall two knyghtes armed come unto the pavelon; and
there they alyght bothe and cam in armed at all pecis.[5]

1. *But as*: except.
2. I.e., incompetent.
3. I.e., throughout.
4. *No forse*: No matter.
5. *Armed at all pecis*: fully armed.

fol.310r

fol.310v

[78]

¶"Fayre knyghtes," seyde Sir Trystram, "ye ar to blame to com thus armed at all pecis uppon me whyle we ar at oure mete; and yf ye wolde onythynge⁶ wyth us, whan we were in the fylde, there myght ye have eased youre hertys." "Not so, sir," seyde the tone of tho knyghtes. "We com nat for that entente, but wyte you well, Sir Trystram, we be com as youre frendys; and I am comyn hydir for to se you, and this knyght ys comyn for to se youre quene Isode." Than seyde Sir Trystram, "I requyre you, do of your helmys, that I may se you."

¶"Sir, that woll we do at youre desyre," seyde the knyghtes. And whan their helmys were of, Sir Trystram thought that he sholde know them. Than spake Sir Dynadan prevaly unto Sir Trystram, "That is my lorde Kynge Arthure; and that other that spake to you fyrst ys my lorde Sir Launcelot." "A, madame, I pray you aryse," seyde Sir Trystram, "for here ys my lorde, Kynge Arthure." Than the Kynge and the quene kyssed, and Sir Launcelot and Sir Trystram enbraced aythir other in armys—and than there was joy wythoute mesure; and at the requeste of La Beall Isode, the Kynge and Sir Launcelot were unarmed, and than there was myry talkynge.

¶"Madame," seyde Kynge Arthur, "hit is many a day ago sytthyn I desyred fyrst to se you, for ye have bene praysed so fayre a lady. And now I dare say ye ar the fayryste that ever I sawe, and Sir Trystram ys as fayre and as good a knyght as ony that I know—and therefore mesemyth ye ar well besett togydir."

¶"Sir, God thanke you," seyde Sir Trystram and La Beall Isode. "Of youre goodnes and of youre larges ye ar pyerles." And thus they talked of many thyngys, and of all the hole justes. "But for what cause," seyde Kynge Arthure, "were ye, Sir Trystram, ayenst us? And ye ar a knyght of the Table Rounde, and of ryght ye sholde have bene with us." "Sir," seyde Sir Trystram, "here ys Sir Dynadan and Sir Gareth, youre owne nevew, caused me to be ayenst you."

¶"My lorde Arthure," seyde Sir Gareth, "I may well beare the blame, for my bak ys brode inowghe—but, forsothe, hit was Sir Trystrams awne dedis." "Be God, that may I repente," seyde Sir Dynadan, "for thys unhappy Sir Trystram brought us to this turnemente—and many grete buffettys he hath caused us to have! Than the Kynge and Sir Launcelot lowghe, that unnethe they myght sytte.

¶"But what knyght was that," seyde Kynge Arthure, "that hylde you so shorte,⁷ [this with the sheld of sylver?]"

¶"Sir," seyde Sir Trystram, "here he syttyth at this table."

¶"What?" seyde Kynge Arthure, "was hit Sir Palomydes?"

¶"Sir, wyte you well that hit was he," seyde La Beall Isode. "So God me helpe," seyde Kyng Arthure, "that was unknyghtly done of you as of so good a knyght, for I have harde many people calle you a curtayse knyght."

¶"Sir," seyde Sir Palomydes, "I knew nat Sir Trystram, for he was so disgysed." "So God helpe me," seyde Sir Launcelot, "hit may well

---

6. *Wolde onythynge:* wished to settle anything.
7. *Hylde you so shorte:* pressed you so hard.

be, for I knew hym nat myselff." "But[8] I mervayled whye ye turned on oure party." "Sir, hit was done for the same cause," seyde Sir Launcelot.

¶"Syr, as for that," seyde Sir Trystram, "I have pardouned hym, and I wolde be ryght lothe to leve hys felyshyp, for I love ryght well hys company." And so they leffte of and talked of other thynges; and in the evenynge, Kynge Arthure and Sir Launcelot departed unto their lodgyng. But wyte you well, Sir Palomydes had grete envy hartely, for all that nyght he hid never reste in his bed, but wayled and wepte oute of mesure.

¶So on the morne Sir Trystram, Sir Gareth and Sir Dynadan arose early and went unto Sir Palomydes chambir, and there they founde hym faste aslepe, for he had all nyght wacched—and it was sene uppon his chekes that he had wepte full sore. "Say ye nothynge," seyde Sir Trystram, "for I am sure he hath takyn angir and sorow for the rebuke that I gaff hym, and La Beall Isode."

Than Sir Trystram let calle Sir Palomydes and bade hym make redy, for hit was tyme to go to the fylde. And anon they armed them, and clothed them all in rede—bothe La Beall Isode and all the felyshyp—and so they lad her passynge freysshly thorow the fylde into the pryory where was hir lodgynge. And anone they harde three blastes blowe; and every kynge and knyght dressed hym to the fylde.

And the fyrste that was redy to juste was Sir Palomydes and Sir Kaynes le Straunge, a knyght of the Table Rounde. And so they two encountyrd togydyrs; but Sir Palomydes smote Sir Kaynes so harde that he bare hym quyte over his horse croupe. And furthewithall Sir Palomydes smote downe anothir knyght and brake his speare, and than pulled oute hys swerde and ded wondirly well—and than the noyse began gretly uppon Sir Palomydes. "Lo," seyde Kynge Arthure, "yondir Sir Palomydes begynnyth to play his play!"

"So God me helpe," seyde Kynge Arthur, "he is a passynge goode knyght." And ryght as they stood talkynge thus, in cam Sir Trystram as thundir, and he encountird wyth Sir Kay le Seneschall; and there he smote hym downe quyte frome his horse. And wyth that same speare he smote downe three knyghtes more; and than he pulled oute his swerde and ded mervaylously. Than the noyse and the cry chonged fro Sir Palomydes and turned unto Sir Trystram— and than all the people cryed, "A, Trystram! A, Trystram!" And than was Sir Palomydes clene forgotyn. "How now?" seyde Sir Launcelot unto Kynge Arthure, "yondyr rydyth a knyght that playyth his pageauntes."[9]

¶"So God me help," seyde Kynge Arthure, "ye shall se this day that yondir two knyghtes shall do here wondirs." "Sir," seyde Sir Launcelot, "the tone knyghte waytyth upon the tother and enfor-syth hymselff thorow envy to passe Sir Trystram—and he knowyth nat the prevy envy of Sir Palomydes; for, sir, all that Sir Trystram doth is thorow clene knyghthod."

fol.311v

[79]

fol.312r

---

8. Arthur is speaking.
9. *Playyth his pageauntes:* plays his parts, fulfills his roles.

And than Sir Gareth and Sir Dynadan ded ryght well that day, that
Kynge Arthure spake of them grete worshyp; and the kynges and
the knyghtes on Sir Trystrams syde ded passynge well and hylde
them truly togydyrs. Than Kynge Arthure and Sir Launcelot toke their
horsys and dressed them to the fylde amonge the thyckeste of the   5
prees. And there Sir Trystram unknowyng smote downe Kynge
Arthur; and than Sir Launcelot wolde have rescowed hym, but there
were so many uppon Sir Launcelot that they pulled hym downe from
his horse—and than the Kynge of Irelonde and the Kynge of Scottes with their knyghtes ded their payne to take Kynge Arthure and   10
Sir Launcelot presoners.

Whan Sir Launcelot harde them sey so, he fared as hit had bene
an hungry lyon, for he fared so that no knyght durst nyghe hym.
Than cam Sir Ector de Marys, and he bare a speare ayenst Sir Palomydes and braste hit uppon hym all to shyvyrs. And than Sir Ector   15
cam agayne and gaff Sir Palomydes suche a daysshe with a swerde
that he stowped adowne uppon his sadyll-bowe; and forthwythall
Sir Ector pulled downe Sir Palomydes undir his horse fyete, and than
he [gate] Sir Launcelot [an hors and brought hit to hym, and badde
hym mounte upon hym]—but Sir Palomydes lepe before and gate   20
the horse by the brydyll and lepe into the sadyll.

⸿"So God me helpe," seyde Sir Launcelot, "ye ar bettir worthy to
have that horse than I!"

⸿Than Sir Ector brought Sir Launcelot another horse. "Grauntemercy," seyde Sir Launcelot unto his brother. And so, when he was   25
horsed agayne, with one speare he smote downe foure good knyghtes; and than Sir Launcelot gate Kynge Arthure a good horse.

⸿Than Kyng Arthure and Sir Launcelot wyth a feawe of his knygh-   fol.312v
tes of Sir Launcelottis kynne ded mervaylouse dedis of armys; for
that tyme, as the booke recordyth, Sir Launcelot smote downe and   30
pulled downe thirty knyghtes. Natwithstondynge, the other parté
hylde them so faste togydir that Kynge Arthure and his knyghtes
were overmacched.

⸿And whan Sir Trystram saw that, what laboure Kynge Arthure
and his knyghtes, and in especiall the grete noble dedis that Sir   35
Launcelott ded with hys owne hondis, [he merveylled gretely.]

⸿Than Sir Trystram called unto hym Sir Palomydes, Sir Gareth   [80]
and Sir Dynadan, and seyde thus to them: "My fayre fealowys, wyte
you well that I woll turne unto Kynge Arthures party, for I saw never
so feawe men do so well—and hit woll be shame unto us that bene   40
knyghtes of the Rounde Table to se oure lorde Kynge Arthure and
that noble knyght, Sir Launcelot, to be dishonoured." "Sir, hit wyll
be well do,"[1] seyde Sir Gareth and Sir Dynadan. "Sir, do your beste,"
seyde Sir Palomydes, "for I woll nat chaunge my party that I cam
in wythall." "That is for envy of me," seyde Sir Trystram, "but God   45
spede you well in your journey!" And so departed Sir Palomydes
frome them.

⸿Than Sir Trystram, Sir Gareth and Sir Dynadan turned with Sir
Launcelot. And than Sir Launcelot smote downe the Kynge of Irelonde

---

1. I.e., done.

quyte frome his horse; and he smote downe the Kyng of Scottes
and the Kynge of Walys. And than the Kynge Arthure ran unto Sir
Palomydes and smote hym quyte frome his horse. And than Sir
Trystram bare downe all that ever he mette wythall; and Sir Gareth
and Sir Dynadan ded there as noble knyghtes. And anone all the 5
todir party began to fle.

⁋"Alas," seyde Sir Palomydes, "that ever I sholde se this day! For
now I have loste all the worshyp that I wan." And than Sir Palomydes wente hys way, waylynge, and so wythdrewe hym tylle he
cam to a welle; and there he put his horse from hym and ded of 10
his armoure, and wayled and wepte lyke as he had bene a wood
man. Than many knyghtes gaff the pryce unto Sir Trystram; and
there were many mo that gaff the pryce unto Sir Launcelot. fol.313r

⁋"Now, fayre lordys, I thanke you of youre honoure that ye
wolde gyff me, but I pray you hartely that ye woll gyff youre voyce 15
unto Sir Launcelot—for, be my fayth, I woll gyff Sir Launcelot my
voyce," seyde Sir Trystram. But Sir Launcelot wolde none of hit; and
so the pryce was gyffyn betwyxte them bothe. And so every man
rode to his lodgynge; and Sir Bleoberys and Sir Ector rode wyth Sir
Trystram and La Beall Isode unto her pavelons. Than as Sir Palo- 20
mydes was at the welle, waylynge and wepynge, there cam fleynge
the Kynge of Walys, and of Scotlonde; and they sawe Sir Palomydes
in that rayge.

⁋"Alas," seyde they, "so noble a man as ye be sholde be in this
aray." And than the kynges gate Sir Palomydes horse agayne, and 25
made hym to arme hym and mownte uppon his horse agayne; and
so he rode wyth them, makyng grete dole.

⁋So whan Sir Palomydes cam nygh Sir Trystram and La Beall
Isode pavelons, than Sir Palomydes prayde the two kynges to abyde
hym there the whyle that he spake wyth Sir Trystram. And whan 30
he cam to the porte of the pavelon, Sir Palomydes seyde an hyghe,
"Where art thou, Sir Trystram de Lyones?" "Sir," seyde Sir Dynadan,
"that ys Sir Palomydes."

⁋"What, Sir Palomydes, woll ye nat com nere amonge us?"

⁋"Fye on the, traytoure!" seyde Sir Palomydes, "for wyte thou 35
well, and hit were daylyght as hit is nyght,[2] I sholde sle the my
nawne[3] hondis—and yf ever I may gete the," seyde Sir Palomydes,
"thou shalt dye for this dayes dede."

⁋"Sir Palomydes," seyde Sir Trystram, "ye wyte me wyth wronge,
for, had ye done as I ded, ye sholde have had worshyp. But sytthyn 40
ye gyff me so large warnynge, I shall be well ware of you."

⁋"Fye on the, traytoure!" seyde Sir Palomydes—and therewythall
he departed.

⁋Than on the morne Sir Trystram and La Beall Isode, Sir Bleo-
berys, Sir Ector de Marys, Sir Gareth, and Sir Dynadan, what by londe fol.313v 45
and by watir, they brought La Beall Isode unto Joyus Garde; and
there they reposed them a sevennyght, and made all the myrthis

2. *And hit were daylyght as hit is nyght:* night or day.
3. *My nawne:* (with) my own.

and desportys that they cowde devyse. And Kynge **Arthure** and his knyghtes drew unto **Camelot**. And Sir **Palomydes** rode wyth the two kynges—and ever he made the grettyst dole that ony man cowde thynke, for he was nat all only so dolorous for the departynge frome La Beall Isode, but he was as sorowful aparte to go frome the felyshyp of Sir **Trystram**; for he was so kynde and so jantyll that whan Sir **Palomydes** remembyrd hym [therof] he myght never be myrry.

So at the sevennyghtes ende, Sir **Bleoberys** and Sir **Ector** departed frome Sir **Trystram** and frome the quene; and thes two knyghtes had[4] grete gyfftys. And ever Sir **Gareth** and Sir **Dynadan** abode wyth Sir **Trystram**. And whan Sir **Bleoberys** and Sir **Ector** were comyn there as Quene **Gwenybere** was lodged, in a castell by the sesyde (and thorow the grace of God the Quene was recovirde of hir malady), than she asked the two knyghtes fro whens they cam. And they seyde they cam frome Sir **Trystram** and frome La Beall **Isode**. "How doth Sir **Trystram**," seyde the Quene, "and La Beall **Isode**?"

"Truly, madame," seyde tho knyghtes, "he doth as a noble knyght shulde do; and as for the Quene, she is pyerles of all ladyes—for to speake of her beauté, bounté, and myrthe, and of hir goodnes, we sawe never hir macche as far as we have ryddyn and gone."

"A, mercy Jesu!" seyde Quene **Gwenybir**, "thus seyth all folkys that hath sene her and spokyn wyth her. God wolde," seyde she, "that I had parte of her condycions! And was now myssefortuned me of my syknesse[5] whyle that turnemente endured, for, as I suppose, I shall never se in all my lyff such asemblé of noble knyghtes and fayre ladyes." And than the knyghtes tolde the Quene how Sir **Palomydes** wan the gré the fyrste day wyth grete nobles—"and the secunde day Sir **Trystram** wan the gré, and the thirde day Sir **Launcelot** wan the gré."

❡"Well," seyde Quene **Gwenybir**, "who ded beste all three dayes?" "So God me help," seyde thes knyghtes, "Sir **Launcelot** and Sir **Trystram** had there leste dishonour. And wyte you well Sir **Palomydes** ded passyngly well and myghtyly, but he turned ayenste the party that he cam in wythall, and that caused hym to loose a grete parte of his worshyp—for hit semed that Sir **Palomydes** ys passynge envyous." "Than shall he never wynne worshyp," seyde the Quene, "for and hyt happyn an envyous man onys to wynne worshyp, he shall be dishonoured twyse therefore—and for this cause: all men of worshyp hate an envyous man, and woll shewe hym no favoure; and he that ys curteyse and kynde and jantil hath favoure in every place."

❡Now leve we of this mater and speke we of Sir **Palomydes**, that rode and lodged wyth the two kynges all that nyght. And on the morne Sir **Palomydes** departed frome the two kynges, whereof they were hevy. Than the Kynge of Irelonde sente a man of his to Sir **Palomydes** and gaff hym a grete courser; and the Kynge of

---

4. I.e., received.
5. *Was now myssefortuned me of my syknesse*: my sickness brought misfortune to me.

Scotlonde gaff hym grete gyfftes—and fayne they wolde have had hym abyde wyth them, but he wolde nat in no wyse.

And so he departed and rode as adventures wolde gyde hym tyll hitte was nyghe none; and than in a foreyste by a well Sir Palomydes saw where lay a fayre wounded knyght, and his horse bounden by hym. And that knyght made the grettyst dole that ever he herde man make, for ever he wepte and therewyth syghed as he wolde dye.

¶Than Sir Palomydes rode nere hym, and salewed hym myldely and sayde, "Fayre knyght, why wayle you so? Lat me lye downe by you and wayle also—

¶"For dowte ye nat, I am muche more hevyar than ye ar—for I dare say," seyde Sir Palomydes, "that my sorow ys an hondred-folde more than youres ys. And therefore lat us complayne aythir to other."

¶"Fyrst," seyde the woundid knyght, "I requyre you, telle me youre name. For and thou be none of the noble knyghtes [of the Round Table,] thou shalt never know my name, whatsomever com of me."

¶"Fayre knyght," seyde Sir Palomydes, "suche as I am, be hit bettir be hit worse, wyte thou well that my name ys Sir Palomydes, sunne and ayre unto Kynge Asclabor; and Sir Saphir and Sir Seg-warydes ar my two brethirne—and wyte thou well, as for myselff, I was never crystynde, but my two brethirne ar truly crystynde."

¶"A, noble knyght," seyde that woundid knyght, "well ys me that I have mette wyth you. And wyte you well that my name ys Sir Epynogrys, the Kynges sonne of Northumbirlonde—

¶"Now sytte ye downe," seyde Sir Epynogrys, "and let us aythir complayne to othir." Than Sir Palomydes alyght and tyed his horse faste. And thus Sir Palomydes began hys complaynte, and sayde, "Now shall I tell you what wo I endure. I love the fayryst quene and lady that ever bare lyff: and wyte you well her name ys La Beall Isode, Kynge Markes wyff of Cornwayle." "That ys grete foly," seyde Sir Epynogrys, "for to love Quene Isode, for one of the beste knygh-tes of the worlde lovyth her, that ys Sir Trystram de Lyones."

"That ys trouthe," seyde Sir Palomydes, "for no man knowyth that mater bettir than I do. For I have bene in Sir Trystrams felyshyp this moneth and more, and wyth La Beall Isode togydyrs. And, alas," seyde Sir Palomydes, "unhappy man that I am, now have I loste the felyshyp of Sir Trystram and the love of La Beall Isode for ever; and I am never lykly to se her more, and Sir Trystram and I bene aythir to othir mortall enemyes."

¶"Well," seyde Sir Epynogrys, "syth that ye loved La Beall Isode, loved she ever you agayne[6] by onythynge that ye cowde wyte,[7] othir ellys ded ye ever rejoyse[8] her in ony plesure?"

¶"Nay, be my knyghthode," seyde Sir Palomydes, "for I never aspyed that ever she loved me more than all the worlde ded, nor

___

6. I.e., in return.
7. *By onythynge that ye cowde wyte:* in any way that you could discern.
8. I.e., enjoy, possess.

never had I pleasure wyth her; but the laste day she gaff me the grettyst rebuke that ever I had, whyche shall never go fro my harte—and yet I well deservyd that rebuke, for I ded nat knyghtly— and therefore I have loste the love of her, and of Sir Trystram, for ever. And I have many tymes enforsed myselff to do many dedis of armys for her sake, and ever she was the causer of my worship- wynnynge. And, alas, now have I loste all the worshyp that ever I wanne, for never shall befalle me suche proues as I had in the felyshyp of Sir Trystram."

"Nay, nay!" seyde Sir Epynogrys, "youre sorow ys but japys to[9] my sorow; for I rejoysed my lady, and wan her wyth myne hondis, and loste her agayne—alas that day! [83]

¶ "And fyrst thus I wan her: my lady was an erlys doughtir, and as the erle and two knyghtes cam home fro the turnement of Lone- zep, for her sake I sette uppon this erle myselff and on his two knyghtes, and my lady there beynge presente; and so by fortune there I slew the erle and one of the knyghtes, and the othir knyght fledde—and so that nyght I had my lady. And on the morne, as she and I reposed us at this wellesyde, than cam there to me an arraunte knyght—his name was Sir Helyor le Prewse, an hardy knyght—and he chalenged me to fyght for my lady. And than we wente to batayle, fyrst uppon horsebacke and aftir uppon foote.

¶ "But at the laste Sir Helyor wounded me so that he lefft me for dede; and so he toke my lady with hym. And thus my sorow ys more than youres; for I have rejoysed, and ye nevir rejoysed." "That ys trouthe," seyde Sir Palomydes, "but syth I can nat recover myselff, I shall promyse you, yf I can mete with Sir Helyor, that I shall gete to you your lady agayne, other ellys he shall beate me." Than Sir Palomydes made Sir Epynogrys to take his horse; and so they rode untyll an ermytage, and there Sir Epynogrys rested hym. fol.315v

And in the meanewhyle Sir Palomydes walked prevayly oute to reste hym under the levis. And there besydes he sawe a knyght com rydynge wyth a shylde that he had sene Sir Ector de Marys beare aforehonde; and there cam aftir hym a ten knyghtes—and so thes knyghtes hoved undir the levys for hete. And anone aftir, there cam a knyght with a grene shylde and therein a whyght lyon, ledynge a lady uppon a palfrey. Than this knyght with the shylde, he semed to be maystir of the ten knyghtes; and he rode fyersly aftir Sir Helyor (for hit was he that hurte Sir Epynogrys). And whan he cam nygh Sir Helyor, he bade hym deffende his lady.

"I woll deffende her," seyde Sir Helyor, "unto my power!" And so they ran togydirs so myghtyly that ayther smote other downe, horse and all, to the erth; and than they wan[1] up lyghtly, and drewe swerdys and dressed their shyldis, and laysshed togydyrs wondir fyersly more than an owre—and all this Sir Palomydes saw and behylde. But ever at the laste, the knyght with Sir Ectors shylde was far bigger, and at the laste he smote downe Sir Helyor. And

9. I.e., compared to.
1. I.e., rose.

than that knyght unlaced his helme to have strykyn off his hede; and than he cryed mercy and prayed hym to save his lyff, and bade hym take his lady.

Than Sir Palomydes dressed hym up, bycause he wyste well that that same lady was Sir Epynogrys lady, and he had promysed hym to helpe hym. Than Sir Palomydes went streyte to that lady and toke her by the honde, and asked her whether she knew a knyght why-che was called Sir Epynogrys. "Alas," she seyde, "that evir I knew hym other he me! For I have for his sake loste my worshyp, and also hys lyff—that greveth me moste of all."   fol.316r   10

❡"Nat so, fayre lady," sayde Sir Palomydes. "Commyth on with me, for here ys Sir Epynogrys in this ermytage." "A, well ys me," seyde that lady, "and he be on lyve!"

❡Than cam the tother knyght and seyde, "Whythir wolt thou with that lady?"   15

❡"I woll do wyth her what me lyste," seyde Sir Palomydes.

❡"Wyte thou well," seyde that knyght, "thou spekyst over large, thoughe thou semyst thou haste me at avauntayge bycause thou sawyst me do batayle but late. Thou wenyst, sir knyght, to have that lady away frome so lyghtly? Nay! thynke hit never; and thou   20 were as good a knyght as ys Sir Launcelot or Sir Trystram, other ellys Sir Palomydes, but thou shalt wyn her more derar than ever ded I." And so they wente unto batayle uppon foote; and there they gaff many sad strokys togydir, and aythir wounded other wondirly sore—and thus they faught togydir styll more than an owre. Than   25 Sir Palomydes had mervayle what knyght he myght be that was so stronge and so well-brethid durynge,[2] and at the laste thus seyde Sir Palomydes: "Knyght, I requyre the telle me thy name." "Wyte thou well," seyde that knyght, "I dare telle the my name, so that thou wolt tell me thy name."   30

❡"I woll," seyde Sir Palomydes. "Truly," seyde that knyght, "and my name ys Sir Saphir, sonne of Kynge Asclabor, and Sir Palomydes and Sir Segwarydes ar my bretherne."

❡"Now, and wyte thou well, my name ys Sir Palomydes!" Than Sir Saphir kneled adowne uppon his kneis and prayde hym of   35 mercy; and than they unlaced their helmys and aythir kyssed other, wepynge. And the meanewhyle Sir Epynogrys rose of his bedde and harde them by the strokys,[3] and so he armed hym to helpe Sir Palomydes, yf nede were. Than Sir Palomydes toke the lady by the   [84] honde and brought her to Sir Epynogrys; and there was grete joy   40 betwyxte them, for aythir sowned for joy whan they were mette.

"Now, fayre knyght and lady," sayde Sir Saphir, "hit were pité   fol.316v to departe you too; and therefore Jesu sende you joy, ayther of othir." "Grauntemercy, jantyll knyght," seyde Sir Epynogrys, "and muche more thanke to my lorde Sir Palomydes that thus hath tho-   45 row his proues made me to gete my lady." Than Sir Epynogrys requyred Sir Palomydes and Sir Saffir, his brother, to ryde with hym unto his castell, for the sauffgarde of his persone.

---

2. *So well-brethid durynge*: of such fit endurance.
3. I.e., strokes of their weapons.

¶"Syr," seyde Sir Palomydes, "we woll be redy to conduyte[4] you, because that ye ar sore woundid." And so was Sir Epynogrys and hys lady horsed uppon a soffte ambler. And than they rode unto his castell; and there they had grete chere and grete joy as ever Sir Palomydes and Sir Saffir had in their lyvys. So on the morne Sir Saphir and Sir Palomydes departed and rode—

¶But[5] as fortune lad them, and so they rode all that day untyll aftir noone; and at the laste they harde a grete wepyng and a grete noyse downe in a maner.

¶"Sir," seyde Sir Saffir, "lette us wyte what noyse this ys." "I woll well," seyde Sir Palomydes. And so they rode tyll that they com to a fayre gate of a maner—and there sate an olde man, sayynge his prayers and beadis. Than Sir Palomydes and Sir Saphir alyght and leffte their horsis and wente within the gatys; and there they saw full many goodly men wepynge.

¶"Now, fayre sirrys," seyde Sir Palomydes, "wherefore wepe ye and make thys sorow?" And anone one of tho knyghtes of the castel behylde Sir Palomydes and knew hym; and than he wente to his felowys and sayde, "Fayre fealowys, wyte you well all, we have within this castell the same knyght that slew oure lorde at Lonezep, for I know hym well for Sir Palomydes."

Than they wente unto harneys, all that myght beare harneys, som on horsebak and som uppon foote, to the numbir of three score; and whan they were redy, they cam freysshly uppon Sir Palomydes and uppon Sir Saphir wyth a grete noyse, and sayde thus: "Kepe the, Sir Palomydes, for thou arte knowyn! And be[6] ryght thou muste be dede, for thou haste slayne oure lorde; and therefore wyte thou well we may do the[7] none other favoure but sle the—and therefore deffende the!"

Than Sir Palomydes and Sir Saphir, the tone sette his bak to the todir and gaff many sad strokes, and also toke many grete strokes; and thus they faught wyth twenty knyghtes and fourty jantyllmen and yomen nyghe a two owres. But at the laste, though they were never so lothe, Sir Palomydes and Sir Saphir were takyn and yoldyn and put in a stronge preson. And within three dayes twelve knyghtes passed[8] uppon hem; and they founde Sir Palomydes gylty, and Sir Saphir nat gylty, of the lordis deth.

¶And whan Sir Saphir shulde be delyverde, there was grete dole betwyxte his brother and hym, and many peteous complayntis that was made at her departicion—there ys no maker can reherse the tenthe parte.

¶"Now, fayre brother, lat be youre doloure," seyde Sir Palomydes, "and youre sorow, for and I be ordeyned to dy a shamfull dethe, wellcom be hit. But, and I had wyste of this deth that I am derned unto, I sholde never have bene yoldyn."

fol.317r

4. I.e., provide safe conduct for.
5. I.e., only.
6. I.e., by.
7. Thee.
8. I.e., passed judgment.

❡So departed Sir Saphir, his brother, with the grettyst sorow that
ever made knyght. And on the morne they of the castell ordayned
twelve knyghtes for to ryde wyth Sir Palomydes unto the fadir of
the same knyght that Sir Palomydes slew. And so they bounde his
leggys undir an olde steedis bealy, and than they rode wyth Sir
Palomydes unto a castell by the seesyde that hyght Pylownes;
and there Sir Palomydes shulde have his justise—thus was their
ordynaunce.

And so they rode wyth Sir Palomydes faste by the castell of Joyus
Garde; and as they passed by that castell, there cam rydynge one
of that castell by them that knew Sir Palomydes. And whan that
knyght saw hym lad bounden uppon a croked courser, than the
knyght asked Sir Palomydes for what cause he was so lad.

❡"A, my fayre felow and knyght," seyde Sir Palomydes, "I ryde
now towarde my dethe for the sleynge of a knyght at the turnemente of Lonezep. And yf I had [not] departed frome my lorde, Sir
Trystram, as I ought [not] to have done, now myght I have bene
sure to have had my lyff saved. But I pray you, sir knyght, recommaunde me unto my lorde Sir Trystram, and unto my lady Quene
Isode, and sey to them, yf ever I trespast to⁹ them, I aske them
forgyffnes—and also, I beseche you, recommaunde me unto my
lorde Kynge Arthure and to all the felyshyp of the Rounde Table,
unto my power."¹

Than that knyght wepte for pité, and therewyth he rode unto
Joyus Garde as faste as his horse myght renne; and lyghtly that
knyght descended downe of his horse and went unto Sir Trystram,
and there he tolde hym all as ye have harde—and ever the knyght
wepte as he were woode.

❡Whan Sir Trystram knew how Sir Palomydes wente to his dethward,² he was hevy to hyre thereof, and sayde, "Howbehit that I
am wrothe wyth hym, yet I woll nat suffir hym to dye so shamefull
a dethe, for he ys a full noble knyght." And anone Sir Trystram
asked his armys; and whan he was armed he toke his horse and
two squyars wyth hym, and rode a grete pace thorow a foreyste
aftir Sir Palomydes, the nexte way unto the castell Pelownes where
Sir Palomydes was jowged to his dethe.

And as the twelve knyghtes lad hym byfore them, there was the
noble knyght Sir Launcelot whyche was alyght by a welle, and had
tyed hys horse tyll a tre, and had takyn of hys helme to drynke of
that welle. And whan he sawe suche a route whyche semed knyghtes, Sir Launcelot put on his helme and suffyrd them to passe by
hym—and anone he was ware of Sir Palomydes bounden and lad
shamfully towarde his dethe.

❡"A, Jesu!" seyde Sir Launcelot, "what mysseadventure ys befallyn
hym that he ys thus lad towarde hys dethe?

❡"Yet, pardeus," seyde Sir Launcelot, "hit were shame to me to
suffir this noble knyght thus to dye and I myght helpe hym; and

fol.317v

[85]

fol.318r

---

9. I.e., against.
1. *Unto my power:* i.e., to my utmost.
2. *To his dethward:* toward his death.

therefore I woll helpe hym whatsomever com of hit, other ellys I shall dye for hys sake."

¶And than Sir Launcelot mounted on hys horse and gate hys speare in hys honde, and rode aftyr the twelve knyghtes whyche lad Sir Palomydes. "Fayre knyghtes," seyde Sir Launcelot, "whother lede ye that knyght? For hit besemyth hym full evyll to ryde bounden." Than thes twelve knyghtes returned suddeynly there horsis, and seyde to Sir Launcelot, "Sir knyght, we counceyle you nat to meddyll of this knyght, for he hath deserved deth, and unto deth he ys jouged." "That me repentyth," seyde Sir Launcelot, "that I may nat borow hym wyth fayrenes, for he ys over good a knyght to dye such a shamefull dethe—and therefore, fayre knyghtes," seyde Sir Launcelot, "than kepe you as well as ye can, for I woll rescow that knyght, othir ellys dye for hit."

¶Than they began to dresse there spearys; and Sir Launcelot smote the formyste downe, horse and man—and so he served three mo wyth one spere. And than that speare braste, and therewythall Sir Launcelot drewe his swerde; and than he smote on the ryght honde and on the lyffte honde. And so wythin a whyle he leffte none of tho knyghtes but he had leyde them to the erthe—and the moste party of them were sore wounded. And than Sir Launcelot toke the beste horse, and lowsed Sir Palomydes and sette hym uppon that horse; and so they returned agayne unto Joyus Garde. And than was Sir Palomydes ware of Sir Trystram, how he cam rydynge; and whan Sir Launcelot sy hym, he knew hym well; but Sir Trystram knew nat hym, because he had on his shuldir a gylden shylde.

So Sir Launcelot made hym redy to juste wyth Sir Trystram, because he sholde nat wene that he were Sir Launcelot. Than Sir Palomydes cryed on lowde to Sir Trystram and seyde, "A, my lorde, I requyre you, juste nat wyth this knyght, for he hath saved me frome my dethe."

¶Whan Sir Trystram harde hym sey so, he cam a soffte trottynge pace towarde hym.

¶And than Sir Palomydes seyde, "My lorde, Sir Trystram, muche am I beholdynge unto you of youre grete goodnes, that wolde proffir youre noble body to rescow me undeserved, for I have greatly offended you. Natwythstondynge," seyde Sir Palomydes, "here mette we wyth this noble knyght that worshypfully and manly rescowed me frome twelve knyghtes, and smote them downe all, and sore wounded hem."

¶"Fayre knyght," seyde Sir Trystram unto Sir Launcelot, "of whens be ye?" "I am a knyght arraunte," seyde Sir Launcelot, "that rydyth to seke many dedis."

¶"Sir, what ys youre name?" seyde Sir Trystram. "Sir, as at this tyme I woll nat telle you."

¶Than Sir Launcelot seyde unto Sir Trystram and to Sir Palomydes, "Now ar ye mette togydirs aythir wyth other, and now I woll departe frome you."

¶"Nat so," seyde Sir Trystram, "I pray you and requyre you of knyghthod to ryde wyth me unto my castell." "Wyte you well,"

seyde Sir Launcelot, "I may nat ryde wyth you, for I have many dedis
to do in other placys, that at this tyme I may nat abyde wyth you."
"A, mercy Jesu!" seyde Sir Trystram, "I requyre you, as ye be a trewe
knyght to the order of knyghthode, play[3] you wyth me this nyght."   5

⁊Than Sir Trystram had a graunte[4] of Sir Launcelot; howbehit,
thoughe he had nat desyred[5] hym, he wolde have rydden with hem,
other sone a com aftir hym, for Sir Launcelot cam for none other
cause into that contrey but for to se Sir Trystram. And whan they
were com wythin Joyus Garde they alyght, and there horsis were   10
lad into a stable. And than they unarmed them; for Sir Launcelot,
as sone as his helme was of, Sir Trystram and Sir Palomydes knew
hym.

⁊Than Sir Trystram toke Sir Launcelot in his armys—and so ded   fol.319r
La Beall Isode—and Sir Palomydes kneled downe uppon his kneis   15
and thanked Sir Launcelot. And whan he sawe Sir Palomydes knele,
he lyghtly toke hym up and seyde thus: "Wyte thou well, Sir Palomydes, that I, and ony knyght in this londe of worshyp, muste of
verry ryght succoure and rescow so noble a knyght as ye ar preved
and renowmed, thorougheoute all this realme, enlonge and over-   20
twarte."[6] Than was there grete joy amonge them. And the ofter
that Sir Palomydes saw La Beall Isode, the hevyar he waxed day be
day.

⁊Than Sir Launcelot wythin three or foure dayes departed, and
wyth hym rode Sir Ector de Marys and Sir Dynadan; and Sir Palomydes   25
was leffte there wyth Sir Trystram a[7] two monethis and more. But
ever Sir Palomydes faded and mourned, that all men had merveyle
wherefore he faded so away. So uppon a day, in the dawnynge, Sir
Palomydes wente into the foreste by hymselff alone; and there he
founde a welle, and anone he loked into the well and in the watir   30
he sawe his owne vysayge, how he was discolowred and defaded,
a nothynge lyke as he was.

⁊"Lorde Jesu, what may this meane?" seyde Sir Palomydes. And
thus he seyde to hymselff: "A, Palomydes, Palomydes! Why arte thou
thus defaded, and ever was wonte to be called one of the fayrest   35
knyghtes of the worlde? Forsothe, I woll no more lyve this lyff, for
I love that[8] I may never gete nor recover. And therewythall he leyde
hym downe by the welle, and so began to make a ryme of La Beall
Isode and [hym]. And so in the meanewhyle Sir Trystram was ryddyn into the same foreyste to chace an harte of grece[9] (but Sir   40
Trystram wolde nat ryde an huntynge nevermore unarmed bycause   fol.319v
of Sir Brewnys Saunze Pité).

And so Sir Trystram rode into the foreyste up and downe, and as
he rode he harde one synge mervaylowsly lowde; and that was Sir
Palomydes whyche lay by the welle. And than Sir Trystram rode

3. I.e., pass the time.
4. *A graunte:* consent.
5. I.e., invited.
6. *Enlonge and overtwarte:* i.e., the length and breadth.
7. I.e., for a period of.
4. I.e., that which.
9. *Harte of grece:* fat deer.

sofftly thydir, for he demed that there was som knyght arraunte whyche was at the welle.

¶And whan Sir Trystram cam nyghe, he descended downe frome hys horse and tyed his horse faste tyll a tre; and so he cam nere on foote, and sone aftir he was ware where lay Sir Palomydes by the welle, and sange lowde and myryly. And ever the complayntys were of La Beall Isode—whyche was mervaylously well seyde, and pyteuously and full dolefully made—and all the hole songe Sir Trystram harde, worde by worde; and whan he had herde all Sir Palomydes complaynte, he was wrothe oute of mesure, and thought for to sle hym there as he lay.

¶Than Sir Trystram remembyrde hymselff that Sir Palomydes was unarmed, and of so noble a name that Sir Palomydes had, and also the noble name that hymselff had. Than he made a restraynte of his angir; and so he wente unto Sir Palomydes a soffte pace[1] and seyde, "Sir Palomydes, I have harde youre complaynte, and of youre treson that ye have owed me longe, and wyte you well, therefore ye shall dye. And yf hit were nat for shame of knyghthode, thou sholdyst nat ascape my hondys, for now I know well thou haste awayted me wyth treson—and therefore," seyde Sir Trystram, "tell me how thou wolt acquyte the."

"Sir, I shall acquyte me thus: as for Quene La Beall Isode, thou shalt wyte that I love her abovyn all other ladyes in this worlde; and well I wote hit shall befalle by me as for her love as befelle on the noble knyght Sir Kayhydyus, that dyed for the love of La Beall Isode. And now, Sir Trystram, I woll that ye wyte that I have loved La Beall Isode many a longe day, and she hath bene the causer of my worshyp—and ellys I had bene the moste symplyste knyght in the worlde, for by her, and bycause of her, I have wonne the wor-shyp that I have. For whan I remembred me of Quene Isode, I wanne the worshyp wheresomever I cam, for the moste party; and yet I had never rewarde nother bounté of[2] her dayes of my lyff—and yet I have bene her knyght longe gwardonles. And therefore, Sir Trystram, as for ony dethe I drede nat, for I had as lyeff dye as lyve; and yf I were armed as ye ar, I shulde lyghtly do batayle with the."

¶"Sir, well have ye uttyrd youre treson," seyde Sir Trystram. "Sir, I have done to you no treson," seyde Sir Palomydes, "for love is fre for all men; and thoughe I have loved your lady, she ys my lady as well as youres. Howbehyt that I have wronge—if ony wronge be, for ye rejoyse her and have youre desyre of her, and so had I nevir, nor never am lyke to have—and yet shall I love her to the utter-muste dayes of my lyff as well as ye."

¶Than seyde Sir Trystram, "I woll fyght with you to the utteryste."[3] "I graunte," seyde Sir Palomydes, "for in a bettir quarell kepe I never to fyght; for and I dye off youre hondis, of a bettir knyghtes hondys

---

1. *A soffte pace*: quietly, slowly.
2. I.e., from.
3. Utmost (i.e., to the death).

myght I never be slayne. And sytthyn I undirstonde that I shall never
rejoyse La Beall Isode, I have as good wyll to dye as to lyve.”

¶“Than sette ye a day,” seyde Sir Trystram, “that we shall do
batayle.” “Sir, this day fyftene dayes,” seyde Sir Palompdes, “I woll
mete with you hereby, in the medow undir Joyus Garde.”

¶“Now fye, for shame!” seyde Sir Trystram. “Woll ye sette so
longe a day? Lat us fyght tomorne.”

¶“Nat so,” seyde Sir Palompdes, “for I am megir, and have bene
longe syke for the love of La Beall Isode. And therefore I woll
repose me tyll I have my strengthe agayne.”

¶So than Sir Trystram and Sir Palompdes promysed faythefully to
mete at the welle that day fyftene dayes. “But now I am remembred,” seyde Sir Trystram to Sir Palompdes, “that ye brake me onys
a promyse whan that I rescowed you frome Sir Brewnys Saunze Pité
and nyne knyghtes; and than ye promysed to mete me at the perowne and the grave besydis Camelot, where as that tyme ye fayled
of youre promyse.” “Wyte you well,” seyde Sir Palompdes unto Sir
Trystram, “I was at that day in preson, that I myght nat holde my
promyse. But wyte you well,” seyde Sir Palompdes, “I shall promyse
you now and kepe hit.”

¶“So God me helpe,” seyde Sir Trystram, “and ye had holden
youre promyse, this worke had nat bene here now at this tyme.”

¶Ryght so departed Sir Trystram and Sir Palompdes. And so Sir
Palompdes toke his horse and hys harneys, and so he rode unto
Kynge Arthurs courte; and there he gate hym foure knyghtes and
foure sargeauntes of armys,[4] and so he returned agayne unto Joyus
Garde. And so in the meanewhyle Sir Trystram chaced and hunted
at all maner of venery; and aboute three dayes afore the batayle
that shulde be, as Sir Trystram chaced an harte, there was an archer
shotte at the harte, and by mysfortune he smote Sir Trystram in
the thyk of the thyghe—and the same arrow slew Sir Trystrams
horse undir hym.

Whan Sir Trystram was so hurte he was passynge hevy—and wyte
you well he bled passynge sore—and than he toke another horse
and rode unto Joyus Garde with grete hevynes, more for the promyse that he had made unto Sir Palompdes to do batayle with hym
wythin three dayes aftir [than for ony hurte of his thygh].

¶Wherefore there was nother man nother woman that coude
chere hym [with onythynge that they coude make to hym, neyther
Quene La Beale Isoud;] for ever he demed that Sir Palompdes had
smytten hym so because he sholde nat be able to do batayle with
hym at the day appoynted. But in no wyse there was no knyght
aboute Sir Trystram that wolde belyeve that Sir Palompdes wolde
hurte hym, nother by his owne hondis nothir by none other
consentynge.[5]

And so whan the fyftenth day was com, Sir Palompdes cam to the
welle wyth foure knyghtes wyth hym of Kynge Arthurs courte and

fol.320v

5

10

15

20

25

30

35

fol.321r

[88]

40

45

---

4. *Sargeauntes of armys*: officers appointed to keep order.
5. *None other consentynge*: i.e., anyone else agreeing (to do it for him).

three sargeauntes of armys. And for this entente Sir Palomydes brought tho knyght[es] with hym, and the sargeauntes of armys: for they sholde beare recorde of the batayle betwyxt Sir Trystram and hym; and one sargeaunte brought in his helme, and the tother his speare, and the thirde his swerde. 5

¶So Sir Palomydes cam into the fylde, and there he abode nyghe two owres; and than he sente a squyar unto Sir Trystram and desyred hym to com into the fylde to holde his promyse.

¶Whan the squyar was com unto Joyus Garde, anone as Sir Trystram harde of his commynge he commaunded that the squyar 10 shulde com to his presence there as he lay in his bedde.

¶"My lorde Sir Trystram," seyde Sir Palomydes squyar, "wyte you well, my lorde Sir Palomydes abydyth you in the fylde, and he wolde wyte whether ye wolde do batayle or nat." "A, my fayre brother," seyde Sir Trystram, "wyte you well that I am ryght hevy for this 15 tydyngis. But telle youre lorde Sir Palomydes, and I were well at ease I wolde nat lye here, nothir he sholde have had no nede to sende for me and I myght othir ryde or go—and for thou shalt se that I am no lyar"—Sir Trystram shewed hym his thyghe, and the depnes of the wounde was syx inchis depe: 20

¶"And now thou haste sene my hurte, telle thy lorde that this is no fayned mater, and tell hym that I had levir than all the golde that Kynge Arthure hath that I were hole; and lat hym wyte that as fol.321v for me, as sone as I may ryde I shall seke hym endelonge and overtwarte this londe—and that I promyse you as I am a trew 25 knyght. And yf ever I may mete hym, telle youre lorde Sir Palomydes he shall have of me hys fylle of batayle." And so the squyar departed.

And whan Sir Palomydes knew that Sir Trystram was hurte, than he seyde thus: "Truly, I am glad of his hurte, and for this cause: 30 for now I am sure I shall have no shame—for I wote well, and we had medled, I sholde have had harde handelynge of hym; and by lyklyhode I muste nedys have had the worse, for he is the hardyeste knyght in batayle that now ys lyvynge, excepte Sir Launcelot."

And than departed Sir Palomydes whereas fortune lad hym. And 35 within a moneth Sir Trystram was hole of his hurte; and than he toke hys horse and rode frome contrey to contrey. And all straunge adventures he encheved wheresomever he rode—and allwayes he enquyred for Sir Palomydes; but off all that quarter⁶ of somer, Sir Trystram coude never mete with Sir Palomydes. 40

But thus as Sir Trystram soughte and enquyred aftir Sir Palomydes, Sir Trystram enchevyd many grete batayles, wherethorow all the noyse and brewte felle to Sir Trystram, and the name⁷ ceased of Sir Launcelot. And therefore Sir Launcelottis bretherne and his kynnysmen wolde have slayne Sir Trystram bycause of his fame; 45 but whan Sir Launcelot wyste how hys kynnysmen were sette, he seyde to them opynly, "Wyte you well that and ony of you all be

6. I.e., season.
7. I.e., renown.

so hardy to wayte my lorde Sir Trystram wyth ony hurte, shame, or vylany, as I am trew knyght, I shall sle the beste of you all myne owne hondis—

⁅"Alas, fye for shame, sholde ye for his noble dedys awayte to sle hym! Jesu defende," seyde Sir Launcelot, "that ever ony noble knyght as Sir Trystram ys sholde be destroyed wyth treson."   5

⁅So of this noyse and fame sprange into Cornwayle and unto them of Lyones, whereof they were passynge glad and made grete joy.   fol.322r

⁅And than they of Lyones sente lettyrs unto Sir Trystram of recommendacion,[8] and many greate gyfftys to mayntene Sir Trys-trams astate.[9] And ever betwene Sir Trystram resorted unto Joyus Garde whereas La Beall Isode was, that lovid hym ever.   10

Ow leve we Sir Trystram de Lyones, and speke we of Sir Launcelot du Laake, and of Sir Galahad,[1] Sir Launcelottis sonne, how he was begotyn and in what maner, as the booke of Frenshe makyth mencion. Afore the tyme that Sir Galahad was begotyn or borne, there cam in an ermyte unto Kynge Arthure uppon Whitsunday,[2] as the knyghtes sate at the Table Rounde. And whan the ermyte saw the Syege Perelous, he asked the Kynge and all the knyghtes why that syege was voyde.   [XI.1]   15   20

⁅Than Kynge Arthure for all the knyghtes answerde and seyde, "There shall never none sytte in that syege but one, but if he be destroyed."   25

⁅Than seyde the ermyte, "Sir, wote ye what he ys?"

⁅"Nay," seyde Kynge Arthure and all the knyghtes, "we know nat who he ys yet that shall sytte there."

⁅"Than wote I," seyde the ermyte. "For he that shall sytte there ys yet unborne and unbegotyn, and this same yere he shall be bygotyn that shall sytte in that Syege Perelous; and he shall wynne the Sankgreall."[3]   30

⁅Whan this ermyte had made this mencion he departed frome the courte of Kynge Arthure. And so aftir this feste, Sir Launcelot rode on his adventure tyll on a tyme by adventure he paste over the Pounte de Corbyn; and there he saw the fayryste towre that ever he saw, and thereundir was a fayre lytyll towne full of people. And all the people, men and women, cryed at onys, "Wellcom, Sir Laun-celot, the floure of knyghthode, for by the[4] we shall be holpyn oute of daungere!"   35   fol.322v   40

---

8. I.e., recommendation of themselves. Cf. the conventional way medieval letters are pref-aced at pp. 760 and 766.
9. I.e., way of life.
1. This section of Malory's story of Trystram, in common with some of his French *Tristan* sources, looks back to the earlier period of Arthur's reign, and functions, among other things, as a kind of prophetic introduction to the next major story, concerning the quest for the Holy Grail. Before returning to Sir Trystram very near the end of this "book" (p. 49), this section also invites comparison between Launcelot and Trystram (and Launcelot and his son Galahad) by examining the fragility of Launcelot's sanity and knightly identity when complicated by his secret loves.
2. On Whitsunday, see n. 1, p. 10.
3. I.e., the Holy Grail (about which, see n. 7, p. 464).
4. Thee.

¶"What meane ye," seyde Sir Launcelot, "that ye cry thus uppon me?"

¶"A, fayre knyght," seyde they all, "here is wythin this towre a dolerous lady that hath bene there in paynes many wyntyrs and dayes; for ever she boyleth in scaldynge watir. And but late," seyde all the people, "Sir Gawayne was here, and he myght nat helpe her, and so he leffte her in payne stylle." "Peradventure so may I," seyde Sir Launcelot, "leve her in payne as well as Sir Gawayne." "Nay," seyde the people, "we know well that hit ys ye, Sir Launcelot, that shall delyver her."

¶"Well," seyde Sir Launcelot, "than telle me what I shall do." And so anone they brought Sir Launcelot into the towre; and whan he cam to the chambir there as this lady was, the doorys of iron unlo-ked and unbolted, and so Sir Launcelot wente into the chambir, that was as hote as ony styew. And there Sir Launcelot toke the fayryst lady by the honde that ever he sawe—and she was as naked as a nedyll. And by enchauntemente Quene Morgan le Fay and the Quene of Northe Galys had put her there in that paynes, bycause she was called the fayryst lady of that contrey; and there she had bene fyve yere, and never myght she be delyverde oute of her pay-nes unto the tyme the beste knyght of the worlde had takyn her by the honde.

¶Than the people brought her clothis; and whan sche was arayed, Sir Launcelot thought she was the fayryst lady that ever he saw, but yf hit were Quene Gwenyver. Than this lady seyde to Sir Launcelot, "Sir, if hit please you, woll ye go wyth me hereby into a chapel, that we may gyff lovynge[5] to God?"

¶"Madame," seyde Sir Launcelot, "commyth on wyth me, and I woll go with you." So whan they cam there, they gaff thankynges to God, all the people bothe lerned and lewde,[6] and seyde, "Sir knyght, syn ye have delyverde this lady, ye muste delyver us also frome a serpente whyche ys here in a tombe."

¶Than Sir Launcelot toke hys shylde, and seyde, "Sirrys, brynge me thydir, and what that I may do to the plesure of God and of you I shall do." So whan Sir Launcelot com thydir, he saw wrytten uppon the tombe wyth lettyrs of golde that seyde thus:

HERE SHALL COM A LYBARDE OF KYNGES BLOOD AND HE SHALL
SLE THIS SERPENTE: AND THIS LYBARDE SHALL ENGENDIR A
LYON IN THIS FORAYNE CONTREY WHYCHE LYON SHALL PASSE
ALL OTHER KNYGHTES

Soo whan Sir Launcelot had lyffte up the tombe, there came oute an orryble and a fyendely dragon spyttynge wylde-fyre oute of hys mowthe. Than Sir Launcelotte drew his swerde and faught wyth that dragon longe; and at the laste, wyth grete payne, Sir Launcelot slew

fol.323r

5. I.e., praise.
6. *Lerned and lewde*: educated and uneducated (i.e., everyone).

that dragon. And therewythall com Kynge Pelles, the good and
noble kynge, and salewed Sir Launcelot, and he hym agayne.

¶"Now, fayre knyght," seyde the kynge, "what is youre name? I
requyre you of youre knyghthode, telle ye me."

¶"Sir," seyde Sir Launcelot, "wyte you well my name ys Sir Laun-   [2]   5
celot du Lake." "And my name ys Kynge Pelles, kynge of the forayne
contré, and cousyn nyghe unto Joseph of Aramathy."[7] And than
aythir of them made muche of othir; and so they wente into the
castell to take there repaste. And anone there cam in a dove[8] at a
wyndow, and in her mowthe there semed a lytyll senser of golde;   10
and therewythall there was suche a savour as all the spycery of the   fol.323v
worlde had bene there; and furthwythall there was uppon the table
all maner of meates and drynkes that they coude thynke uppon.

So there came in a damesell, passynge fayre and yonge, and she
bare a vessell of golde betwyxt her hondis; and thereto the kynge   15
kneled devoutly and seyde his prayers, and so ded all that were
there. "A, Jesu!" seyde Sir Launcelot, "what may this meane?"

¶"Sir," seyde the kynge, "this is the rychyst thynge that ony man
hath lyvynge; and whan this thynge gothe abrode, the Rounde
Table shall be brokyn for a season. And wyte you well," seyde the   20
kynge, "this is the Holy Sankgreall that ye have here seyne."

¶So the kynge and Sir Launcelot lad there lyff the moste party of
that day togydir. And fayne wolde Kynge Pelles have found the
meane that Sir Launcelot sholde have ley by his doughter, fayre
Eleyne, and for this entente: the kynge knew well that Sir Launcelot   25
shulde gete a pusyll uppon his doughtir, whyche shulde be called
Sir Galahad, the good knyght by whom all the forayne cuntrey
shulde be brought oute of daunger; and by hym the Holy Grayle
sholde be encheved.

¶Than cam furth a lady that hyght Dame Brusen, and she seyde   30
unto the kynge, "Sir, wyte you well Sir Launcelot lovyth no lady in
the worlde but all only Quene Gwenyver; and therefore worche ye be
my counceyle, and I shall make hym to lye wyth youre doughter—
and he shall nat wyte but that he lyeth by Quene Gwenyver."

¶"A, fayre lady," sayde the kynge, "hope ye that ye may brynge   35
this mater aboute?"

¶"Sir," seyde she, "uppon payne of my lyff, latte me deale." For
thys Dame Brusen was one of the grettyst enchaunters that was   fol.324r
that tyme in the worlde; and so anone by Dame Brusens wytte, she
made one to com to Sir Launcelot that he knew well, and this man   40
brought a rynge frome Quene Gwenyver lyke as hit had com frome

---

7. In the New Testament, Joseph is "a good man, and a just" (Luke 23:50) who requested
the body of Christ from Pilate, deposed the body, and provided it with a tomb (for these
details, see John 19.38–42). According to legends of the later Middle Ages, a soldier of
Pilate's gave Joseph the Holy Grail, a vessel (more like a dish or bowl than a cup) reputedly
used at the Last Supper and with which Joseph collected some of the deposed Christ's
blood. According to a variety of other legends, Joseph brought the Grail to Britain. For
Malory's account of the legend, see *The Noble Tale of the Sankgreal*, esp. pp. 507–9.

8. The dove is a conventional symbol of the Holy Spirit and of God's messengers. (Cf. Luke
3:22–23: "And the Holy Ghost descended in a bodily shape like a dove upon [Jesus], and
a voice came from heaven, which said, Thou art my beloved Son; in thee I am well
pleased.")

her, [and suche one as she was wonte for the moost parte to were]—and whan Sir **Launcelot** saw that tokyn, wyte you well he was never so fayne.

❡"Where is my lady?" seyde Sir **Launcelot**. "In the castell of **Case**, seyde the messyngere, "but fyve myle hens." Than thought Sir **Launcelot** to be there the same nyght. And than this Dame **Brusen**, by the commaundemente of Kynge **Pelles**, he let sende **Elayne** to this castell wyth fyve and twenty knyghtes, unto the castell of **Case**. Than Sir **Launcelot** ayenst nyght[9] rode unto the castell; and there anone he was receyved worshypfully wyth suche people, to his semynge, as were aboute Quene **Gwenyver** secrete.[1] So whan Sir **Launcelot** was alyght, he asked where the Quene was.

❡So Dame **Brusen** seyde she was in her bed. And than people were avoyded,[2] and Sir **Launcelot** was lad into her chambir. And than Dame **Brusen** brought Sir **Launcelot** a kuppe of wyne; and anone as he had drunken that wyne, he was so asoted and madde[3] that he myght make no delay, but wythoute ony let he wente to bedde. And so he wente that mayden **Elayne** had bene Quene **Gwenyver**—and wyte you well that Sir **Launcelot** was glad—and so was that lady **Eleyne**, that she had gotyn Sir **Launcelot** in her armys; for well she knew that that same nyght sholde be bygotyn Sir **Galahad** upon her, that sholde preve the beste knyght of the worlde. And so they lay togydir untyll underne of the morne; and all the wyndowys and holys of that chambir were stopped, that no maner of day myght be seyne.

❡And anone Sir **Launcelot** remembryd hym and arose up and wente to the wyndow.

❡And anone, as he had unshutte the wyndow, the enchauntemente was paste.

❡Than he knew hymselff that he had done amysse. "Alas," he seyde, "that I have l[y]ved[4] so longe, for now am I shamed." And anone he gate his swerde in his honde and seyde, "Thou traytoures! What arte thou that I have layne bye all this nyght? Thou shalt dye ryght here of myne hondys." Than this fayre lady **Elayne** skypped oute of her bedde, all naked, and seyde, "Fayre curteyse knyght, Sir **Launcelot**,"—knelynge byfore hym—"ye ar comyn of kynges bloode; and therefore I requyre you have mercy uppon me; and as thou arte renowmed the moste noble knyght of the worlde, sle me nat, for I have in my wombe bygetyn of the that[5] shall be the moste nobelyste knyght of the worlde."

❡"A, false traytoures, why haste thou betrayed me? Telle me anone," seyde Sir **Launcelot**, "what thou arte."

❡"Sir," she seyde, "I am Elayne, the daughter of Kynge **Pelles**."

---

9. I.e., the coming of night.
1. *Aboute Quene Gwenyver secrete:* servants to the Queen in confidential matters.
2. I.e., cleared out.
3. I.e., passionate.
4. The Winchester MS reading is *loved* and presumably reflects at least a scribe's perception of Launcelot as critically aware of the perils of his love for Gwenyvere. The Caxton reading has been adopted here, however, because it more closely represents the likely French source, which has Launcelot contemplating death without confession.
5. *Bygetyn of the that:* i.e., the one conceived by you who.

"Well," seyde Sir Launcelot, "I woll forgyff you." And therewyth he
toke her up in his armys and kyssed her (for she was a fayre lady
and thereto lusty and yonge—and wyse as ony was that tyme
lyvynge). "So God me helpe," seyde Sir Launcelot, "I may nat wyte
you; but her that made thys enchauntemente uppon me, and   5
betwene you and me, and I may fynde her, that same lady Dame
Brusen shall lose her hede for her wycchecrauftys—for there was
never knyght disceyved as I am this nyght."

¶Than she seyde, "My lorde, Sir Launcelot, I beseche you, se me
as sone as ye may, for I have obeyde me unto the prophesye that   10
my fadir tolde me. And by hys commaundemente to fullfyll this
prophecie I have gyvyn the the grettyst ryches and the fayryst floure
that ever I had, and that is my maydynhode that I shall never have   fol.325r
agayne—and therefore, jantyll knyght, owghe me youre good wyll."

And so Sir Launcelot arayed hym and armed hym, and toke hys   15
leve myldely at that yonge Lady Eleyne; and so he departed and
rode to the castell of Corbyn where her fadir was. And as faste as
her tyme cam, she was delyverde of a fayre chylde; and they crystynd hym Galahad. And wyte yow well, that chylde was well kepte
and well norysshed. (And he was so named Galahad bycause Sir   20
Launcelot was so named at the fountayne[6] stone; and aftir that the
Lady of the Lake confermed hym Sir Launcelot du Lake.)[7] Than, aftir
the lady was delyverde and churched,[8] there cam a knyght unto
her; hys name was Sir Bromell la Pleche, the whyche was a grete
lorde, and he had loved that lady Eleyne longe, and he evermore   25
desyred to wedde her—and so by no meane she coude put hym
off—

¶Tylle on a day she seyde to Sir Bromell, "Wyte you well, sir
knyght, I woll nat love you, for my love ys sette uppon the beste
knyght of the worlde."   30

¶"Who ys that?" seyde Sir Bromell. "Sir," she seyde, "hit ys Sir
Launcelot du Lake that I love, and none other; and therefore wowe
ye me no lenger." "Ye sey well," seyde Sir Bromell, "and sytthyn ye
have tolde me so muche, ye shall have lytyll joy of Sir Launcelot, for
I shall sle hym wheresomever I mete hym."   35

¶"Sir," seyde this lady Elayne, "do to hym no treson, and God
forbede that ye spare hym."[9]

¶"Well, my lady," seyde Sir Bromell, "and I shall promyse you
this twelvemonthe and a day I shall kepe Le Pounte Corbyn for Sir
Launcelot sake, that he shall nothir com nother go unto you but I   40
shall mete wyth hym."

Than as hit fell by fortune and adventure, Sir Bors de Ganys, that   [4]
was nevew unto Sir Launcelot, com over that brydge. And there Sir
Bromell and Sir Bors justed; and Sir Bors smote Sir Bromell suche
a buffette that he bare hym over his horse croupe. And than Sir   fol.325v   45

---

6. I.e., (baptismal) font.
7. On Launcelot's first having been named Galahad see p. 79.
8. I.e., commemorated at a service offered in thanks for her safe delivery.
9. *and God forbede that ye spare hym*: i.e., and if you do act treacherously, God forbid that
   he lives to take vengeance on you.

Bromell, as an hardy man, pulled oute his swerde and dressed hys shylde to do batayle wyth Sir Bors; and anone Sir Bors alyght and voyded his horse, and there they daysshed togydyrs many sad strokys. And longe thus they faught; and at the laste Sir Bromell was leyde to the erthe—and there Sir Bors began to unlace his helme to sle hym; than Sir Bromell cryed hym mercy and yeldyd hym. "Uppon this covenaunte thou shalt have thy lyff," seyde Sir Bors, "so thou go unto my lorde Sir Launcelot uppon Whytsonday nexte commynge and yelde the unto hym as a knyght recreaunte."

¶"Sir, I woll do hit," seyde Sir Bromell—and so he sware uppon the crosse of the swerde; and so he lete hym departe. And Sir Bors rode unto Kynge Pelles that was wythin Corbyne. And whan the kynge and Elayne, hys doughter, knew that Sir Bors was nevew unto Sir Launcelot they made hym grete chere. Than seyde Dame Elayne, "We mervayle where Sir Launcelot ys, for he cam never here but onys that ever I sawe."

¶"Madame, mervayle ye nat," seyde Sir Bors, "for this halff yere he hath bene in preson wyth[1] Quene Morgan le Fay, Kynge Arthurs systir." "Alas," seyde Dame Elayne, "that me sore repentyth." And ever Sir Bors behylde that chylde in her armys, and ever hym semed hit was passynge lyke Sir Launcelot. "Truly," seyde Dame Elayne, "wyte you well, this chylde he begate uppon me." Than Sir Bors wept for joy, and there he prayde to God that hit myght preve as good a knyght as hys fadir was.

And so there cam in a whyght dowve, and she bare a lytyll sensar of golde in her mowthe, and there was all maner of metys and drynkis. And a mayden bare that Sankgreall; and she seyde there opynly, "Wyte you well, Sir Bors, that this chylde, Sir Galahad, shall sytte in the Syege Perelous and enchyve the Sankgreall—and he shall be muche bettir than ever was Sir Launcelot, that ys hys owne fadir." And than they kneled adowne and made there devocions; and there was suche a savoure as all the spycery in the worlde had bene there; and as the dowve had takyn her flyght, the mayden vanysshed wyth the Sankgreall as she cam.

"Sir," seyde Sir Bors than unto kynge Pelles, "this castell may be named the Castell Adventures, for here be many stronge adventures!" "That is sothe," seyde the kynge, "for well may thys place be called the adventures place. For there com but feaw knyghtes here that goth away wyth ony worshyppe—be he never so stronge, here he may be preved. And but late ago Sir Gawayne, the good knyght, gate lytyll worshyp here; for I lat you wyte," seyde Kynge Pelles, "here shall no knyght wynne worshyp but yf he be of worshyp hymselff and of good lyvynge, and that lovyth God and dredyth God—and ellys he getyth no worshyp here, be he never so hardy a man."

¶"That is a wondir thynge," seyde Sir Bors, "what ye meane in thys contrey, for ye have many straunge adventures—and therefore woll I lye in thys castell thys nyght."

fol.326r

---

1. I.e., under the power of.

❡"Sir, ye shall nat do so," seyde Kynge Pelles, "be my counceyle, for hit ys harde and ye ascape wythoute a shame."

❡"Sir, I shall take the adventure that woll fall," seyde Sir Bors. "Than I counceyle you," seyde the kynge, "to be clene confessed."

❡"As for that," seyde Sir Bors, "I woll be shryvyn wyth a good wyll."   5

❡So Sir Bors was confessed. (And for all women Sir Bors was a vergyne, sauff for one, that was the doughter of Kynge Braundegorys; and on her he gate a chylde whyche hyght Elayne, and sauff for her, Sir Bors was a clene mayden.) And so Sir Bors was lad unto bed in a fayre large chambir, and many durres were shutte   10 aboute the chambir.

❡Whan Sir Bors had aspyde all tho durrys, he avoyded all the   fol.326v people, for he myght have nobody wyth hym. But in no wyse Sir Bors wolde unarme hym, but so he leyde hym downe uppon the   15 bed; and ryght so he saw a lyght com, that he myght well se a speare grete and longe that cam streyte uppon hym poyntelynge— and Sir Bors semed[2] that the hede of the speare brente lyke a tapir—and anone, or Sir Bors wyste, the speare smote hym in the shuldir, an hande-brede in depnes. And that wounde grevid Sir   20 Bors passyng sore, and than he layde hym downe for payne; and anone therewythall cam a knyght armed wyth hys shylde on hys shuldir and hys swerde in hys honde, and he bade Sir Bors, "Aryse, sir knyght, and fyght wyth me!"

❡"I am sore hurte, but yet I shall nat fayle the." And than Sir   25 Bors sterte up and dressed his shylde; and than they laysshed togydyrs myghtyly a grete whyle, and at the laste Sir Bors bare hym bakwarde tyll that he cam to a chambir dore; and there that knyght yode into that chambir and rested hym a grete whyle. And whan he had reposed hym, he cam oute fyersly agayne and began new   30 batayle wyth Sir Bors myghtyly and strongely; than Sir Bors   [5] thought he sholde no more go into that chambir to reste hym, and so Sir Bors dressed hym betwyxte the knyght and the chambir dore, and there Sir Bors smote hym downe; and than that knyght yelded hym.   35

❡"What ys youre name?" seyde Sir Bors. "Sir, my name ys Sir Bedyvere of the Streyte Marchys." So Sir Bors made hym to swere at Whytsonday nexte commynge to com to the courte of Kynge Arthure—"and yelde you there as presonere and as an overcom knyght[3] by the hondys of Sir Bors." So thus departed Sir Bedyvere   40 of the Strayte Marche. And than Sir Bors layde hym downe to reste. And anone he harde muche noyse in that chambir.

❡And than Sir Bors aspyed that there cam in—he wyst nat whethir at durrys or at wyndowys—shotte of arowys and of quar   fol.327r ellys so thyk that he mervayled, and many felle uppon hym and   45 hurte hym in the bare placys. And than Sir Bors was ware where cam in an hedyous lyon; so Sir Bors dressed hym to that lyon, and

2. *Sir Bors semed*: it seemed to Sir Bors.
3. *An overcom knyght*: i.e., a knight overcome.

anone the lyon beraufte hym hys shylde—and with hys swerde Sir
Bors smote of the lyons hede.

¶Ryght so furthwythall he sawe a dragon in the courte, passynge
parelous and orryble; and there semyd to hym that there were lettyrs off golde wryttyn in hys forhede: and Sir **Bors** thought that the   5
lettyrs made a sygnyfycacion of "Kynge **Arthure**;" and ryght so there
cam an orryble lybarde and an olde; and there they faught longe
and ded grete batayle togydyrs; and at the laste the dragon spytte
oute of hys mowthe as hit had bene an hondred dragons; and
lyghtly all the smale dragons slew the olde dragon and tore hym   10
all to pecys.[4]

¶And anone furthwythall there cam an olde man into the halle,
and he sette hym downe in a fayre chayre—and there semed to be
two addirs[5] aboute hys nek; and than the olde man had an harpe,
and there he sange an olde lay of **Joseph of Aramathy**, how he cam   15
into this londe; and whan he had sungen, this olde man bade Sir
Bors go frome thens—"for here shall ye have no mo adventures;
yet full worshypfully have ye encheved this—and bettir shall ye do
hyreaftir."[6]

And than Sir **Bors** semed that there cam the whyghtyst dowve   20
that ever he saw, wyth a lytyll goldyn sensar in her mowthe; and
anone therewythall the tempeste ceased and passed away that
afore was mervaylous to hyre; so was all that courte full of good
savoures. Than Sir **Bors** saw foure fayre chyldren berynge foure
fayre tapirs, and an olde man in the myddys of this chyldyrn wyth   25
a sensar in hys one honde and a speare in hys othir honde: and
that speare was called the Speare of Vengeaunce.

¶"Now," seyde that olde man to Sir **Bors**, "go ye to youre cousyn
Sir **Launcelot** and telle hym this adventure had be moste convenyent[7] for hym of all earthely[8] knyghtes; but synne ys so foule in   30
hym that he may nat enchyve none suche holy dedys, for had nat
bene hys synne, he had paste all the knyghtes that ever were in
hys dayes. And telle thou Sir **Launcelot**, of all worldly adventures he
passyth in manhode and proues all othir, but in this spyrytuall
maters he shall have many hys bettyrs."[9]   35

And than Sir **Bors** sawe foure jantyllwomen com by hym, pourely
beseyne; and he saw where that they entirde into a chambir where
was grete lyght, as hit were a somers lyght; and the women kneled
downe before an auter of sylver wyth foure pyloures; and as hit
had bene a bysshop kneled[1] afore the table of sylver. And as Sir   40

fol.327v

[6]

---

4. The vision of the dragon is clearly prophetic: the leopard that fights with Arthur is Launcelot (cf. the inscription on the tomb, above), and the smaller dragons represent the
rebellion of Mordred and his followers over Launcelot's affair with Gwenyvere. Although
Launcelot remains loyal to Arthur, it is he who lies at the source of Arthur's destruction
at the hands of his own kindred, Gawayne and Mordred.

5. The significance of the snakes is not certain, but cf. Mark 16: 15–18: "And [Jesus] said
unto them, . . . these signs shall follow them that believe; . . . They shall take up serpents;
and if they drink any deadly thing, it shall not hurt them."

6. Bors will achieve the Grail; see p. 581 ff.

7. I.e., suitable.

8. On the resonances of this word, as they apply to Launcelot and Galahad, see n. 6, p. 507.

9. *He shall have many hys bettyrs:* there will be many who prove to be his better.

1. *As hit had bene a bysshop kneled:* someone who looked like a bishop kneeled.

Bors loked over hys hede, he saw a swerde lyke sylver, naked, hovynge over hys hede, and the clyernes thereof smote in hys yghen,
that as at that tyme Sir Bors was blynde; and there he harde a
voyce whyche seyde, "Go hens, thou Sir Bors, for as yet thou arte
nat worthy for to be in thys place." And than he yode bakwarde 5
tylle hys bedde tylle on the morne.

¶And so on the morne Kyng Pelles made grete joy of Sir Bors.
And than he departed and rode unto Camelot; and there he founde
Sir Launcelot and tolde hym of the adventures that he had sene wyth
Kynge Pelles at Corbyn. And so the noyse sprange in Kynge Arthurs 10
courte that Sir Launcelot had gotyn a chylde uppon Elayne, the
doughter of Kynge Pelles—wherefore Quene Gwenyver was wrothe,
and she gaff many rebukes to Sir Launcelot and called hym false
knyght. And than Sir Launcelot tolde the Quene all, and how he
was made to lye by her "in the lyknes of you, my lady the Quene." 15
And so the Quene hylde Sir Launcelot exkused.

And as the booke seythe, Kynge Arthure had bene in Fraunce and
hadde warred uppon the myghty Kynge Claudas and had wonne   fol.328r
muche of hys londys; and whan the Kynge was com agayne, he
lete cry a grete feste, that all lordys and ladyes of all Ingelonde 20
shulde be there but yf hit were suche as were rebellyous agaynste
hym.

¶And whan Dame Elayne, the doughter of Kynge Pelles, harde [7]
of thys feste she yode to her fadir and requyred hym that he wolde
gyff her leve to ryde to that feste. 25

¶The kynge answerde and seyde, "I woll that ye go thydir; but
in ony wyse, as ye love me and woll have my blyssynge, loke that
ye be well beseyne in the moste rychest wyse, and loke that ye
spare nat for no coste. Aske and ye shall have all that nedyth unto
you." 30

¶Than by the advyce of Dame Brusen, her mayden, all thynge
was appareyled unto the purpose, that there was never no lady
rychelyar beseyne.

¶So she rode wyth twenty knyghtes and ten ladyes and jantyllwomen, to the numbir of an hondred horse; and whan she cam to 35
Camelott, Kynge Arthure and Quene Gwenyver seyde wyth all the
knyghtes that Dame Elayne was the beste beseyne lady that ever
was seyne in that courte.

¶And anone as Kynge Arthure wyste that she was com, he mette
her and salewed her—and so ded the moste party of all the knygh- 40
tes of the Rounde Table, both Sir Trystram, Sir Bleoberys, and Sir
Gawayne, and many mo that I woll nat reherse. But whan Sir Launcelot sye her he was so ashamed that, bycause he drew hys swerde
to her on the morne aftir that he had layne by her, that he wolde
nat salewe her nother speke wyth her—and yet Sir Launcelot 45
thought that she was the fayrest woman that ever he sye in his
lyeff dayes.

But whan Dame Elayne saw Sir Launcelot wolde nat speke unto
her, she was so hevy she wente her harte wolde have to-braste; for
wyte you well, oute of mesure she loved hym. And than Dame 50

Elayne seyde unto her woman, Dame Brusen, "The unkyndenes of Sir Launcelot sleyth myne harte nere."

¶"A, peas, madame," seyde Dame Brusen, "I shall undirtake that this nyght he shall lye wyth you, and ye woll holde you stylle."[2] "That were me lever," seyde Dame Elayne, "than all the golde that ys abovyn erthe!" "Lat me deale," seyde Dame Brewsen. So whan Dame Eleyne was brought unto the Quene, aythir made other goode chere as by countenaunce,[3] but nothynge wyth there hartes. But all men and women spake of the beauté of Dame Elayne. And than hit was ordayned that Dame Elayne shulde slepe in a chambir nygh by the Quene, and all undir one rooff; and so hit was done as the Kynge commaunded.

¶Than the Quene sente for Sir Launcelot and bade hym com to her chambir that nyght—"Other ellys," seyde the Quene, "I am sure that ye woll go to youre ladyes bedde, Dame Elayne, by whome ye gate Galahad." "A, madame!" seyde Sir Launcelot, "never say ye so, for that I ded was ayenste my wylle." "Than," seyde the Quene, "loke that ye com to me whan I sende for you."

¶"Madame," seyde Sir Launcelot, "I shall nat fayle you, but I shall be redy at youre commaundement."

¶So this bargayne was nat so sone done and made betwene them but Dame Brusen knew hit by her crauftes, and tolde hit unto her lady Dame Elayne.

¶"Alas," seyde she, "how shall I do?"

¶"Lat me deale," seyde Dame Brusen, "for I shall brynge hym by the honde evyn to youre bedde, and he shall wyne[4] that I am Quene Gwenyvers messyngere."

¶"Than well were me," seyde Dame Elayne, "for all the worlde I love nat so muche as I do Sir Launcelot."

¶So whan tyme com that all folkys were to bedde, Dame Brusen cam to Sir Launcelottes beddys syde and seyde, "Sir Launcelot du Lake, slepe ye? My lady Quene Gwenyver lyeth and awaytyth uppon you."

¶"A, my fayre lady," seyde Sir Launcelot, "I am redy to go wyth you whother ye woll have me."

¶So Launcelot threwe uppon hym a longe gowne, and so he toke his swerde in hys honde. And than Dame Brusen toke hym by the fyngir and lad hym to her ladyes bedde, Dame Elayne, and than she departed and leaffte them there in bedde togydyrs. And wyte you well this lady was glad—and so was Sir Launcelot, for he wende that he had had another in hys armys.

¶Now leve we them kyssynge and clyppynge, as was a kyndely[5] thynge. And now speke we of Quene Gwenyver, that sente one of her women that she moste trusted unto Sir Launcelotys bedde; and whan she cam there, she founde the bedde colde, and he was nat therein—and so she cam to the Quene and tolde her all.

[8]

fol.329r

2. *Holde you stylle:* remain calm.
3. I.e., appearances.
4. I.e., believe.
5. I.e., natural.

¶"Alas!" seyde the Quene, "where is that false knyght becom?"

¶So the Quene was nyghe oute of her wytte, and than she wrythed and waltred as a madde woman, and myght nat slepe a foure or a fyve owres.

¶Than Sir Launcelot had a condicion, that he used of custom to clatir in his slepe and to speke oftyn of hys lady, Quene Gwenyver. So Sir Launcelot had awayked as longe as hit had pleased hym, and so by course of kynde he slepte and Dame Elayne bothe. And in his slepe he talked and claterde as a jay of the love that had bene betwyxte Quene Gwenyver and hym; and so as he talked so lowde the Quene harde hym there as she lay in her chambir. And whan she harde hym so clattir she was wrothe oute of mesure, [and for anger and payne wist not what to do.]

¶And than she cowghed so lowde that Sir Launcelot awaked. And anone he knew her hemynge, and than he knew welle that he lay not by the Quene—and therewyth he lepte oute of hys bedde as he had bene a wood man, in hys shurte.

¶And anone the Quene mette hym in the floure, and thus she seyde: "A, thou false traytoure knyght, loke thou never abyde in my courte, and lyghtly that thou voyde my chambir! And nat[6] so hardy, thou false traytoure knyght, that evermore thou com in my syght." "Alas," seyde Sir Launcelot; and therewyth he toke suche an hartely sorow at her wordys that he felle downe to the floure in a sowne. And therewythall Quene Gwenyver departed.

And whan Sir Launcelot awooke oute of hys swoghe, he lepte oute at a bay wyndow into a gardyne—and there wyth thornys he was all to-cracched of his vysage and hys body—and so he ranne furth he knew nat whothir, and was as wylde [woode][7] as ever was man; and so he ran two yere, and never man had grace to know hym.

¶Now turne we unto Quene Gwenyver and to the fayre lady Elayne, that, when Dame Elayne harde the Quene so rebuke Sir Launcelot, and how also he sowned and how he lepte oute of the bay wyndow, than she seyde unto Quene Gwenyver, "Madame, ye ar gretly to blame for Sir Launcelot, for now have ye loste hym, for I saw and harde by his countenaunce that he ys madde for ever. And therefore—alas, madame—ye have done grete synne, and youreselff grete dyshonoure, for ye have a lorde royall of youre owne; and therefore hit were youre parte for to love hym, for there ys no quene in this worlde that hath suche another kynge as ye have. And yf ye were nat,[8] I myght have getyn the love of my lorde Sir Launcelot; and a grete cause I have to love hym, for he hadde my maydynhode, and by hym I have borne a fayre sonne whose name ys Sir Galahad—and he shall be in hys tyme the beste knyght of the worlde."

¶"Well, Dame Elayne," seyde the Quene, "as sone as hit ys daylyght I charge you to avoyde my courte. And for the love ye owghe unto Sir Launcelot, discover not hys counceyle, for and ye do, hit

---

6. I.e., be not.
7. *Wylde woode:* mad as a wild man. Cf. Trystram's period as an insane wild man, p. 301.
8. *Yf ye were nat:* i.e., if you had not existed.

woll be hys deth." "As for that," seyde Dame **Elayne**, "I dare undirtake he ys marred for ever—and that have you made—for nother
ye nor I ar lyke to rejoyse hym, for he made the moste pyteuous
gronys whan he lepte oute at yondir bay wyndow that ever I harde
man make. Alas," seyde feyre **Elayne**; and "Alas," seyde the Quene,
"for now I wote well that we have loste hym forever."[9]

¶So on the morne Dame **Elayne** toke her leve to departe and
wolde no lenger abyde. Than Kynge **Arthur** brought her on her way
wyth mo than an hondred knyghtes thorowoute a foreyste; and by
the way she tolde Sir **Bors de Ganys** all how hit betydde that same
nyght, and how Sir **Launcelot** lepte oute at a wyndow araged oute
of hys wytte.

¶"Alas," than seyde Sir **Bors**, "where ys my lorde Sir **Launcelot**
becom?"

¶"Sir," seyde Dame **Elayne**, "I wote nere."[1]

¶"Now, alas," seyde Sir **Bors**, "betwyxt you bothe ye have
destroyed a good knyght."

¶"As for me, sir," seyde Dame **Elayne**, "I seyde nevir nother[2] dede
thynge that shulde in ony wyse dysplease hym. But wyth the
rebuke, sir, that Quene **Gwenyver** gaff hym, I saw hym sowne to the
erthe; and whan he awoke he toke hys swerde in hys honde, naked
save hys shurte, and lepe oute at a wyndow wyth the greselyest
grone that ever I harde man make."

¶"Now farewell, Dame **Elayne**," seyde Sir **Bors**, "and holde my
lorde Kynge **Arthure** wyth a tale[3] as longe as ye can, for I woll turne
agayne unto Quene **Gwenyver** and gyff her an hete. And I requyre
you, as ever ye woll have my servyse, make good wacche and aspye
yf ever hit may happyn you to se my lorde Sir **Launcelot**."

"Truly," seyde Dame **Elayne**, "I shall do all that I may do, for I
wolde lose my lyff for hym rathir than he shulde be hurte."

¶"Madame," seyde Dame **Brusen**, "lat Sir **Bors** departe and
hyghe hym as faste as he may to seke Sir **Launcelot**, for I warne you,
he ys clene oute of hys mynde—and yet he shall be welle holpyn,
and but by[4] myracle."

¶Than wepte Dame **Elayne**, and so ded Sir **Bors de Ganys**, and
anone they departed. And Sir **Bors** rode streyte unto Quene **Gwenyver**, and whan she saw Sir **Bors** she wepte as she were wood.

¶"Now fye on youre wepynge!" seyde Sir **Bors de Ganys**, "for ye
wepe never but whan there ys no boote.

¶Alas," seyde Sir **Bors**, "that ever Sir **Launcelot** or ony of hys blood
ever saw you, for now have ye loste the beste knyght of oure blood,

fol.330r

5

10

15

20

25

30

35

fol.330v 40

---

9. *And yf ye were nat . . . we have loste hym forver:* this vituperative exchange appears to be
of Malory's own devising, independent of his sources. If it can be seen as the most direct
criticism on his part of the love between Launcelot (his favorite knight) and Gwynyvere,
it perhaps also should be seen both as a testament to Launcelot's worthiness for being
loved and as a reminder of his transcendant legacy through his son Galahad. The anger
here directed at Gwenyvere is also not to be underestimated; cf. the apparently unique
passage remarked on at n. 7, p. 474; note also, however, Malory's own comments at p. 625.

1. *Wote nere:* know not where.
2. *Nevir nother:* nor ever.
3. *Holde . . . wyth a tale:* keep occupied with some story.
4. *And but by:* if only by.

and he that was all oure leder and oure succoure. And I dare say
and make hit good[5] that all kynges, crystynde nother hethynde,[6]
may nat fynde suche a knyght, for to speke of his noblenes and
curtesy, wyth hys beauté and hys jantylnes—

¶"Alas!" seyde Sir Bors, "what shall we do that ben of hys
bloode?"[7] "Alas," seyde Sir Ector de Marys, and "Alas," seyde Sir
Lyonell. And whan the Quene harde hem sey so, she felle to the
erthe in a dede sowne.

¶And than Sir Bors toke her up and dawed her, and whan she
awaked she kneled afore tho three knyghtes and hylde up bothe
her hondys and besought them to seke hym—"and spare nat for
no goodys but that he be founden, for I wote well that he ys oute
of hys mynde."

¶And Sir Bors, Sir Ector, and Sir Lyonell departed frome the
Quene, for they myght nat abyde no lenger for sorow. And than
the Quene sente them tresoure inowe for there expence; and so
they toke there horsys and there armour and departede. And than
they rode frome contrey to contrey, in forestes and in wyldirnessys
and in wastys, and ever they leyde waycche bothe at forestes and
at all maner of men as they rode, to harkyn and to spare afftir hym,
as he that was a naked man, in his shurte, wyth a swerde in hys
honde. And thus they rode nyghe a quarter of a yere, endelonge
and overtwarte,[8] and never cowde hyre worde of hym—and wyte
you well, these three knyghtes were passynge sory.

And so at the laste Sir Bors and hys felowys mette wyth a knyght
that hyght Sir Melyon de Tartare. "Now, fayre knyght," seyde Sir
Bors, "whothir be ye away?" (for they knew aythir other aforetyme).
"Sir," seyde Sir Mellyon, "I am in the way to the courte of Kynge
Arthure." "Than we pray you," seyde Sir Bors, "that ye woll telle my
lorde Arthure and my lady Quene Gwenyver, and all the felyshyp of
the Rounde Table, that we can nat in no wyse here[9] telle where
Sir Launcelot ys becom." Than Sir Mellyon departed from them, and
seyde that he wolde telle the Kynge and the Quene and all the
felyshyp of the Rounde Table as they had desyred hym.

¶And whan Sir Mellyon cam to the courte, he tolde the Kynge
and the Quene and all the felyship as they had desyred hym, how
Sir Bors had seyde of Sir Launcelot. Than Sir Gawayne, Sir Uwayne,
Sir Sagramoure le Desyrous, Sir Agglovale and Sir Percyvale de Galys
toke uppon them by the grete desyre of the Kynge, and in especiall
by the Quene, to seke all Inglonde, Walys, and Scotlonde to fynde
Sir Launcelot; and wyth them rode eyghtene knyghtes mo to beare
them felyshyppe—and wyte you well they lakked no maner of spendynge—and so were they three and twenty knyghtes.

¶Now turne we unto Sir Launcelot and speke we of hys care
and woo, and what payne he there endured; for colde, hungir and

---

5. *Make hit good:* i.e., prove it in combat.
6. *Crystynde nother hethynde:* neither Christian nor heathen.
7. *And whan she saw Sir Bors . . . that ben of hys bloode?* As with the exchange above between
    Elayne and Gwynyvere, this passage is not matched in Malory's known sources. Cf. also
    the passage remarked on at n. 5, p. 475.
8. I.e., the breadth of the country.
9. I.e., hear.

thyrste he hadde plenté. And thus as these noble knyghtes rode togydyrs, they by assente departed;[1] and than they rode by two and by three, and by foure and by fyve, and ever they assygned where they sholde mete.

And so Sir **Agglovale** and Sir **Percyvale** rode togydir unto there modir, whyche was a quene in tho dayes; and whan she saw her two sunnes, for joy she wepte tendirly, and than she seyde, "A, my dere sonnes! Whan youre fadir was slayne he leffte me foure sonnes, of the whyche now be two slayne—and for the dethe of my noble sonne, Sir **Lamorak**, shall myne harte never be glad." And than she kneled downe uppon her knees to fore Sir **Agglov-ale** and Sir **Percyvale** and besought them to abyde at home wyth her.

❡"A, my swete modir," seyde Sir **Percyvale**, "we may nat, for we be comyn of kynges bloode of bothe partis.[2] And therefore, modir, hit ys oure kynde to haunte[3] armys and noble dedys."

❡"Alas, my swete sonnys," than she seyde, "for youre sakys I shall fyrste lose my lykynge and luste,[4] and than wynde and wedir I may nat endure, what for the dethe of Kynge **Pellynor**, youre fadir, that was shamefully slayne by the hondys of Sir **Gawayne** and hys brothir, Sir **Gaherys**—and they slew hym nat manly, but by treson. And alas, my dere sonnes, thys ys a pyteuous complaynte for me off youre fadyrs dethe, conciderynge also the dethe of Sir **Lamorak**, that of knyghthod had but feaw fealowys. And now, my dere son-nes, have this in youre mynde." And so there was but wepynge and sobbynge in the courte whan they sholde departe; and she felle in sownynge in the myddys of the courte.[5]

❡And whan she was awaked, aftir them she sente a squyar wyth spendynge inowghe; and so whan the squyar had overtake them, they wolde nat suffir hym to ryde wyth them, but sente hym home agayne to comforte there modir, prayynge her mekely of her blys-synge. And so he rode agayne, and so hit happened hym to be benyghtyd; and by mysfortune he cam to a castel where dwelled a barowne. And whan the squyar was com into the castell, the lorde asked hym from whens he cam and whom he served.

❡"My lorde," seyde the squyar, "I serve a good knyght that ys called Sir **Agglovale**." The squyar sayde hit to good entente, wen-ynge unto hym[6] to have be more forborne for Sir **Agglovales** sake than and[7] he seyde he had served the quene, hys modir.

❡"Well, my felow," seyde the lorde of the castell, "for Sir **Agglov-alys** sake thou shalt have evyll lodgyng, for Sir **Agglovale** slew my

fol.331v

[11]

---

1. I.e., separated.
2. I.e., sides of the family.
3. *Kynde*: i.e., nature. *Haunte*: ie.; attend to, frequent.
4. *Lykynge and luste*: i.e., capacity for joy and lust for life.
5. *And than she kneled . . . sownynge in the myddys of the courte*: Like the two passages remarked on at n. 9, p. 473 and n. 7, p. 474, this appears to have been written by Malory independently of his sources; like the previous two passages, it presents a stolid vindication of chivalric obligation, despite the personal infelicities brought about by it, especially for women.
6. *Wenynge unto hym*: i.e., expecting from him.
7. I.e., if.

brother; and therefore thou shalt have thy dethe in party of paymente." And than that lorde commaunded hys men to have hym
away and to sle hym; and so they ded, and than they pulled hym
oute of the castell, and there they slewe hym, wythoute mercy.

¶And ryght so on the morne com Sir Agglovale and Sir Percyvale   5
rydynge by a churche-yearde—

¶Where men and women were busy and behylde the dede   fol.332r
squyar, and so thought to bury hym. "What ys that there," seyde
Sir Agglovale, "that ye beholde so faste?"

¶Anone a good woman sterte furth and seyde, "Fayre knyght,   10
here lyeth a squyar slayne shamefully this nyght."

¶"How was he slayne, fayre modir?" sayde Sir Agglovale. "My
fayre lorde," seyde the woman, "the lorde of thys castell lodged this
squyar thys nyght, and because he seyde he was servaunte unto a
good knyght whyche is wyth Kynge Arthure, whos name ys Sir   15
Agglovale, therefore the lorde commaunded to sle hym—and for
thys cause ys he slayne."

¶"Gramercy," seyde Sir Agglovale, "and ye shall se hys deth
lyghtly revenged, for I am that same knyght for whom thys squyar
was slayne."   20

¶Than Sir Agglovale called unto hym Sir Percyvale and bade hym
alyght lyghtly. And anone they betoke there men their horsys, and
so they yode on foote into the castell; and as sone as they were
wythin the castell gate Sir Agglovale bade the porter go unto hys
lorde and tell his lorde "that I am here, Sir Agglovale, for whom my   25
squyar was slayne thys nyght." And anone, as this porter had tolde
hys lorde, "He ys welcom!" seyde Sir Goodwyne; and anone he armed
hym and cam into the courte, and seyde, "Whyche of you ys Sir
Agglovale?"

¶"Here I am, loo. But for what cause slewyst thou thys nyght   30
my modyrs squyar?"

¶"I slew hym," seyde Sir Goodwyne, "bycause of the, for thou
slewyste my brother, Sir Gawdelyne." "As for thy brother," seyde Sir
Agglovale, "I avow I slew hym, for he was a false knyght and a
betrayer of ladyes and of good knyghtes—and for the dethe of my   35
squyar," seyde Sir Agglovale, [thow shalt dye." "I defye the!" said
Sir Goodewyn;] and anone they laysshed togydyrs as egirly as hit had
bene two lyons (and Sir Percyvale, he faught wyth all the remenaunte that wolde fyght; and wythin a whyle Sir Percyvale had slayne
all that wolde withstonde hym, for Sir Percyvale deled so hys strokys   fol.332v   40
that were so rude[8] that there durste no man abyde hym.)

And wythin a whyle Sir Agglovale had Sir Goodwyne at the erthe;
and there he unlaced hys helme and strake of hys hede. And than
they departed and toke their horsys; and than they let cary the
dede squyar unto a pryory, and there they entered hym. And whan   45
thys was done, they rode in many contreys, ever inquyrynge aftir   [12]
Sir Launcelot; but they coude never hyre of hym. And at the laste
they com to a castell that hyght Cardycan, and there Sir Percyvale
and Sir Agglovale were lodged togydyrs. And prevaly, aboute myd-

---

8. I.e., violent.

nyght, Sir 𝔓𝔢𝔯𝔠𝔶𝔟𝔞𝔩𝔢 com to Sir 𝔄𝔤𝔤𝔩𝔬𝔟𝔞𝔩𝔢𝔰 squyar, and seyde, "Aryse
and make the[9] redy, for ye and I woll ryde away secretely."

¶"Sir," seyde the squyar, "I wolde full fayne ryde with you where
ye wolde have me; but, and my lorde, youre brother, take me, he
woll sle me." "As for that, care not, for I shall be youre warraunte."
And so Sir 𝔓𝔢𝔯𝔠𝔶𝔟𝔞𝔩𝔢 rode tyll hyt was aftir none, and than he cam
uppon a brydge of stone; and there he founde a knyght whyche
was bounden wyth a chayne faste aboute the waste unto a pylloure
of stone. "A, my fayre knyght," seyde that boundyn knyght, "I
requyre the of knyghthode, lowse my bondys of!"

¶"Sir, what knyght ar ye?" seyde Sir 𝔓𝔢𝔯𝔠𝔶𝔟𝔞𝔩𝔢. "And for what
cause ar ye bounden?"

¶"Sir, I shall telle you," seyde that knyght. "I am a knyght off
the Table Rounde, and my name ys Sir 𝔓𝔢𝔯𝔰𝔶𝔡𝔢𝔰. And thus by
adventure I cam thys way, and here I lodged in thys castell at the
brydge foote. And therein dwellyth an uncurteyse lady; and
bycause she proffyrd me to be her paramoure and I refused her,
she sette her men upon me suddeynly or ever I myght com to my
wepyn: thus they toke me and bounde me—and here I wote well
I shall dye but yf som man of worshyp breke my bondys."

¶"Sir, be ye of good chere," seyde Sir 𝔓𝔢𝔯𝔠𝔶𝔟𝔞𝔩𝔢. "And bycause ye
ar a knyght of the Rounde Table as well as I, I woll truste to God
to breke youre bondys." And therewyth Sir 𝔓𝔢𝔯𝔠𝔶𝔟𝔞𝔩𝔢 pulled oute
hys swerde and strake at the chayne wyth suche a myght that he
cutte a-to the chayne and thorow Sir 𝔓𝔞𝔯𝔰𝔶𝔡𝔢𝔰 hawbirke, and hurte
hym a lytyll.

¶"A, Jesu!" seyde Sir 𝔓𝔞𝔯𝔰𝔶𝔡𝔢𝔰, "that was a myghty stroke as ever
I felte of mannes hande, for had nat the chayne be, ye had slayne
me!" And therewithall Sir 𝔓𝔞𝔯𝔰𝔶𝔡𝔢𝔰 saw a knyght whyche cam oute
of the castell as faste as ever he myght flynge.

¶"Sir, beware! For yondyr commyth a knyght that woll have ado
with you." "Lat hym com," seyde Sir 𝔓𝔢𝔯𝔠𝔶𝔟𝔞𝔩𝔢, and so mette that
knyght in myddys the brydge; and Sir 𝔓𝔢𝔯𝔠𝔶𝔟𝔞𝔩𝔢 gaff hym suche a
buffette that he smote hym quyte frome hys horse and over a parte
of the brydge, that, and there had nat bene a lytyll vessell undir
the brydge, that knyght had bene drowned. And than Sir 𝔓𝔢𝔯𝔠𝔶𝔟𝔞𝔩𝔢
toke the knyghtes horse and made Sir 𝔓𝔢𝔯𝔰𝔶𝔡𝔢𝔰 to mounte uppon
hym. And so they two rode unto the castell, and bade the lady
delyver Sir 𝔓𝔢𝔯𝔰𝔶𝔡𝔢𝔰 servauntys—othir ellys he wolde sle all that
ever he founde. And so for feare she delyverde them all.

¶Than was Sir 𝔓𝔢𝔯𝔠𝔶𝔟𝔞𝔩𝔢 ware of a lady that stoode in that towre.

¶"A, madame," seyde Sir 𝔓𝔢𝔯𝔠𝔶𝔟𝔞𝔩𝔢, "what use and custom ys that
in a lady to destroy good knyghtes but yf they woll be youre paramour? Perdé, this is a shamefull custom of a lady; and yf I had nat
a grete mater to do in my honde[1] I shulde fordo all youre false
customys." And so Sir 𝔓𝔞𝔯𝔰𝔶𝔡𝔢𝔰 brought Sir 𝔓𝔢𝔯𝔠𝔶𝔟𝔞𝔩𝔢 unto hys owne
castell, and there he made hym grete chere all that nyght.

And on the morne, whan Sir 𝔓𝔢𝔯𝔠𝔶𝔟𝔞𝔩𝔢 had harde a Masse and

fol.333r

9. Thee.
1. I.e., in hand.

broke hys faste, he bade Sir Parsydes ryde unto Kynge Arthure—   fol.333v
"and telle ye the Kynge how that ye mette wyth me, and telle you
my brother, Sir Agglovale, how I rescowed you. And byd hym seke
nat aftir me, for I am in the queste to syke Sir Launcelot du Lake;
and thoughe he seke me, he shall nat fynde me; and tell hym I woll   5
never se hym nothir the courte tylle that I have founde Sir Launcelot.
Also telle Sir Kay the Senescyall and Syr Mordred that I truste to
Jesu to be of as grete worthynes as aythir of them; for tell them
that I shall never forgete their mokkys and scornys that day that I
was made knyght—and telle them I woll never se that courte tylle   10
men speke more worshyp of me than ever they ded of ony of them
bothe."

And so Sir Parsydes departed frome Sir Percyvale; and than he
rode unto Kynge Arthure and tolde of Sir Percyvale. And whan Sir
Agglovale harde hym speke of hys brothir Sir Percyvale, "Forsothe,"   15
he seyde, "he departed fro me unkyndly."

¶"Sir," seyde Sir Parsydes, "on my lyff, he shall preve a noble   [13]
knyght as ony now ys lyvynge." And whan he saw Sir Kay and Sir
Mordred, Sir Parsydes sayde thus: "My fayre lordys, Sir Percyvale
gretyth you well bothe, and he sente you worde by me that he   20
trustyth to God or ever he com to courte agayne to be of as grete
nobles as ever were you bothe, and mo men to speke of his noble-
nesse than ever spake of youres."

¶"Hyt may well be," seyde Sir Kay and Sir Mordred, "but at that
tyme he was made knyght he was full unlykly to preve a good   25
knyght."

¶"As for that," seyde Kynge Arthure, "he muste nedys preve a
good knyght, for hys fadir and hys bretherne were noble knyghtes
all."

¶And now woll we turne unto Sir Percyvale, that rode longe. And   30
in a foreyste he mette wyth a knyght wyth a brokyn shylde and a
brokyn helme. And as sone as aythir saw other they made them   fol.334r
redy to juste; and so they hurled togydyrs wyth all [the] myghtes
[of theyr horses,] and they mette togydyrs so hard that Sir Percyvele
was smyttyn to the erthe—and than Sir Percyvale arose delyverly,   35
and keste hys shylde on hys shuldir and drew hys swerde, and bade
the other knyght alyght and do batayle unto the uttirmuste.

¶"Well, sir, wyll ye more yet?" seyde that knyght. And therewyth
he alyght, and put hys horse from hym. And than they cam togydir
an easy pace and laysshed togydyrs with noble swerdys; and som-   40
tyme they stroke and somtyme they foyned, that ayther gaff other
many sad strokys and woundys. And thus they faught nerehande
halffe a day and never rested but lytyll; and there was none of them
bothe that hadde leste woundys but he had fyftene—and they
bledde so muche that hyt was mervayle they stoode on their feete.   45
But thys knyght that faught wyth Sir Percyvale was a proved knyght
and a wyse-fyghtynge knyght, and Sir Percyvale was yonge and
stronge, nat knowynge in fyghtynge as the othir was.

¶Than Sir Percyvale spake fyrste and seyde, "Sir knyght, holde
thy honde a whyle, for we have foughtyn over longe for a symple   50

mater and quarell. And therefore I requyre the tell me thy name, for I was never ar thys tyme thus macched."

¶"So God me helpe," seyde that knyght, "and never or this tyme was there never knyght that wounded me so sore as thou haste done, and yet have I foughtyn in many batayles; and now shall thou wyte that I am a knyght of the Table Rounde, and my name ys Sir Ector de Marys, brother unto the good knyght Sir Launcelot du Lake." "Alas!" sayde Sir Percyvale, "and my name ys Sir Percyvale de Galys, whyche hath made my queste to seke Sir Launcelott; and now am I syker that I shall never fenyshe my queste, for ye have slayne me with youre hondys."

¶"Hit is nat so," seyde Sir Ector, "for I am slayne by youre hondys, and may not lyve—and therefore I requyre you," seyde Sir Ector unto Sir Percyvale, "ryde ye here faste by to a pryory, and brynge me a preste, that I may resseyve my Savyoure, for I may nat lyve. And whan ye com to the courte of Kynge Arthure tell nat my brother, Sir Launcelot, how that ye slew me, for than woll he be youre mortall enemy; but ye may sey that I was slayne in my queste as I sought hym."

¶"Alas," seyde Sir Percyvale, "ye sey that thynge that never woll be, for I am so faynte for bledynge that I may unnethe stonde. How sholde I than take my horse?" Than they made bothe grete dole oute of mesure. "This woll nat avayle," seyde Sir Percyvale; and than he kneled downe and made hys prayer devoutely unto Allmyghty Jesu, for he was one of the beste knyghtes of the worlde at that tyme, in whom the verrey fayth stoode moste in.

¶Ryght so there cam by the holy vessell, the Sankegreall, wyth all maner of swetnesse and savoure—but they cowde nat se redyly who bare the vessell.

¶But Sir Percyvale had a glemerynge of the vessell and of the mayden that bare hit, for he was a parfyte mayden.[2] And furthwithall they were as hole of hyde and lymme as ever they were in their lyff. Than they gaff thankynges to God with grete myldenesse.

¶"A, Jesu!" seyde Sir Percyvale, "what may thys meane, that we be thus heled, and ryght now we were at the poynte of dyynge?"

¶"I woote full well," seyde Sir Ector, "what hit is. Hit is an holy vessell that is borne by a mayden, and therein ys a parte of the bloode of Oure Lorde Jesu Cryste. But hit may nat be sene," seyde Sir Ector, "but yff hit be by [a parfyte] man."

¶"So God me helpe," seyde Sir Percyvale, "I saw a damesell, as me thought, all in whyght, with a vessell in bothe her hondys—and furthwithall I was hole."

¶So than they toke their horsys and their harneys, and mended hyt as well as they myght that was brokyn. And so they mounted up and rode talkynge togydyrs; and there Sir Ector de Marys tolde Sir Percyvale how he had sought hys brother, Sir Launcelot, longe, and never cowde hyre wytynge of hym; "In many harde adventures

fol.334v

[14]

fol.335r

---

2. *For he was a parfyte mayden:* i.e., Percyvale's perfect virginity allows him a glimpse of the Grail.

have I bene in thys queste." And so aythir tolde othir of there grete adventures.

And now leve we of a whyle of Sir Ector and of Sir Percyvale, and speke we of Sir Launcelot that suffird and endured many sharpe³ showres, that ever ran wylde woode frome place to place, and lyved by fruyte and suche as he myght gete, and dranke watir two yere; and other clothynge had he but lytyll, but in his shurte and his breke. And thus as Sir Launcelott wandred here and there, he cam into a fayre medow where he founde a pavelon; and thereby uppon a tre hynge a whyght shylde, and two swerdys hynge thereby, and two spearys lened thereby to a tre. [XII.1]

And whan Sir Launcelot saw the swerdys, anone he lepte to the tone swerde, and clyched that swerde in hys honde and drew hitte oute; and than he laysshed at the shylde, that all the medow range of the dyntys, that he gaff such a noyse as ten knyghtes hadde fought togydyrs. Than cam furth a dwarff, and lepe unto Sir Launcelot, and wolde have had the swerde oute of his honde; and than Sir Launcelot toke hym by the bothe shuldrys and threw hym unto the grounde, that he felle uppon hys nek and had nygh brokyn hit—and therewythall the dwarff cryede helpe.

¶Than there com furth a lykly knyght, and well apparaylede in scarlet furred with menyvere. And anone as he saw Sir Launcelot he demed that he shulde be oute of hys wytte; and than he seyde wyth fayre speche, "Good man, ley downe that swerde, for as mesemyth thou haddyst more nede of a slepe and of warme clothis than to welde that swerde."

¶"As for that," seyde Sir Launcelot, "com nat to nyghe, for and thou do, wyte thou well I woll sle the!" And whan the knyght of the pavylon saw that, he starte bakwarde into hys pavylon. And than the dwarffe armed hym lyghtly; and so the knyght thought by force and myght to have takyn the swerde fro Sir Launcelot—and so he cam steppynge uppon hym. And whan Sir Launcelot saw hym com so armed wyth hys swerde in hys honde— fol.335v

¶Than Sir Launcelot flowghe to hym wyth suche a myght, and smote hym uppon the helme suche a buffet, that the stroke troubled his brayne—and therewythall the swerde brake in three. And the knyght felle to the erthe and semed as he had bene dede, the bloode brastynge oute of his mowthe, nose, and eares. And than Sir Launcelot ran into the pavelon, and russhed evyn into the warme bedde; and there was a lady that lay in that bedde. And anone she gate her smokke, and ran oute of the pavylon; and whan she sawe her lorde lye at the grounde lyke to be dede, than she cryed and wepte as she had bene madde.

¶And so wyth her noyse the knyght awaked oute of his sowghe, and loked up weykly wyth his yen; and than he asked where was that madde man whyche had yevyn hym suche a buffette—"for suche a one had I never of mannes honde!"

---

3. I.e., bitter, harsh.

❡"Sir," seyde the dwarff, "hit is nat youre worshyp to hurte hym, for he ys a man oute of his wytte; and doute ye nat he hath bene a man of grete worshyp, and for som hartely sorow that he hath takyn he ys fallyn madde—and mesemyth," seyde the dwarff, "that he resembelyth muche unto Sir Launcelot, for hym I sawe at the turnemente of Lonezep."

"Jesu defende," seyde that knyght, "that ever that noble knyght Sir Launcelot sholde be in suche a plyght! But whatsomever he be," seyde that knyght, "harme woll I none do hym." And this knyghtes name was Sir Blyaunte, the whyche seyde unto the dwarff, "Go thou faste on horsebak unto my brother, Sir Selyvaunte, whyche ys in the Castell Blanke, and telle hym of myne adventure, and byd hym brynge wyth hym an horse-lytter; and than woll we beare thys knyght unto my castell."

❡So the dwarff rode faste, and he cam agayn and brought Sir Selyvaunte wyth hym, and six men wyth an horse-lytter; and so they toke up the fethir bedde wyth Sir Launcelot, and so caryed all away wyth hem unto the Castell Blanke. And he never awaked tylle he was wythin the castell; and than they bounde hys handys and hys feete, and gaff hym good metys and good drynkys, and brought hym agayne to hys strengthe and his fayrenesse. But in hys wytte they cowde nat brynge hym [ageyn,] nother to know hymselff. And thus was Sir Launcelot there more than a yere and an halff, hones-tely⁴ arayed and fayre faryn⁵ wythall.

Than uppon a day thys lorde of that castell, Sir Blyaunte, toke hys armys on horsebak wyth a speare to seke adventures. And as he rode in a foreyste there mette hym to knyghtes adventures: that one was Sir Brewnys Saunze Pité, and hys brother, Sir Bartelot. And thes two ran bothe at onys on Sir Bleaunte and brake theyre spearys uppon hys body; and than they drewe there swerdys and made grete batayle, and foughte longe togydyrs. But at the laste Sir Blyaunte was sore wounded and felte hymselffe faynte, and anone he fledde on horsebak towarde hys castell. And as they cam hurlyng undir the castell, there was Sir Launcelot at a wyndow, and saw how two knyghtes layde uppon Sir Blyaunte wyth there swerdys.

❡And whan Sir Launcelot saw that, yet as woode as he was, he was sory for hys lorde, Sir Blyaunte. And than in a brayde Sir Laun-celot brake hys chaynes of hys leggys and of hys armys (and in the breakynge he hurte hys hondys sore); and so Sir Launcelot ran oute at a posterne, and there he mette wyth tho two knyghtes that cha-ced Syr Blyaunte. And there he pulled downe Sir Bartelot wyth his bare hondys frome hys horse, and therewythall he wrothe oute the swerde oute of hys honde; and so he lepe unto Sir Brewse⁶ and gaff hym suche a buffette upon the hede that he tumbeled bakwarde over hys horse croupe. And whan Sir Bartelot saw hys brother have suche a buffet, he gate a speare in hys honde, and wolde have renne Sir Launcelot thorow.

5

fol.336r

[2]   15

20

25

30

35

fol.336v   40

45

---

4. I.e., decently.
5. *Fayre faryn:* well treated.
6. I.e., Brewnys.

¶And that saw Sir Blyaunte and strake of the hande of Sir Bartelot; and than Sir Brewse and Sir Bartelot gate there horsis and fledde away as faste as they myght.

¶So whan Sir Selyvaunte cam and saw what Sir Launcelot had done for hys brother, than he thanked God, and so ded hys brother, that ever they ded hym ony good. But whan Sir Blyaunte sawe that Sir Launcelot was hurte wyth the brekynge of hys irons, than was he hevy that ever he bounde hym:

¶"I pray you, brother Sir Selyvaunte, bynde hym no more, for he ys happy and gracyous."[7]

¶Than they made grete joy of Sir Launcelot; and [they bound hym no more, and] so he bode thereafftir an halff yere and more. And so on a morne Sir Launcelot was ware where cam a grete bore wyth many houndys afftir hym; but the boore was so bygge ther myght no houndys tary hym—and so the hunters cam aftir, blowynge there hornys, bothe uppon horsebacke and som uppon foote. And than Sir Launcelot was ware where one alyght and tyed hys horse tylle a tre, and lened hys speare ayenst the tre.

¶So there cam Syr Launcelot and founde the horse [bounden tyl a tree, and a spere lenyng ageynst a tree,] and a good swerde tyed to the sadyll bowe; and anone Sir Launcelot lepe into the sadyll and gate that speare in hys honde, and than he rode faste aftir the boore. And anone he was ware where he set his ars to a roche, faste by an ermytayge; and than Sir Launcelot ran at the boore wyth hys speare and all to-shyvird his speare. And therewyth the boore turned hym lyghtly, and rove oute the longys and the harte of the horse, that Sir Launcelot felle to the erthe—and, or ever he myght gete frome hys horse, the bore [rafe] hym on the brawne of the thyghe up unto the howghe-boone; and than Sir Launcelot was wrothe, and up he gate uppon hys feete, and toke hys swerde and smote of the borys hede at one stroke.

¶And therewythall cam oute the ermyte and saw hym have suche a wounde. Anone he meaned hym, and wolde have had hym home unto his ermytage.

¶But whan Sir Launcelot harde hym speake, he was so wrothe wyth hys wounde that he ran uppon the ermyte to have slayne hym; than the ermyte ran away, and whan Sir Launcelot myght nat overgete hym, he threw his swerde aftir hym, for he myght no farther for bledynge.

¶Than the ermyte turned agayne and asked Sir Launcelot how he was hurte. "A, my fealow," seyde Sir Launcelot, "this boore hath byttyn me sore." "Than com ye wyth me," seyde the ermyte, "and I shall heale you." "Go thy way," seyde Sir Launcelot, "and deale nat wyth me." Than the ermyte ran his way, and there he mette wyth a goodly knyght [wyth many men].

¶"Sir," seyde the ermyte, "here is faste by my place the goodlyest man that ever I sawe, and he ys sore wounded wyth a boore—and yet he hath slayne the bore. But well I wote," seyde the good man,

---

7. *Happy and gracyous:* i.e, fortunate and blessed.

"and he be nat holpyn, he shall dye of that wounde, and that were grete pité."

¶Than that knyght at the desyre of the ermyte gate a carte, and therein he put the boore and Sir **Launcelot**; for he was so fyeble that thei myght ryght easyly deale with hym. And so Sir **Launcelot** was brought unto the ermytayge. And there the ermyte healed hym of hys wounde; but the ermyte myght nat fynde hym his sustenaunce,[8] and so he empeyred and wexed fyeble bothe of body and of hys wytte: for defaute of sustenaunce he waxed more wooder than he was aforetyme.

And than uppon a day Sir **Launcelot** ran his way into the foreyste; and by the adventure he com to the cité of **Corbyn** where Dame **Elayne** was, that bare **Galahad**, Sir **Launcelottys** sonne. And so whan he was entyrde into the towne, he ran thorow the towne to the castell; and than all the yonge men of that cité ran aftir Sir **Launcelot**, and there they threwe turvis at hym and gaff hym many sad strokys. And ever as Sir **Launcelot** myght reche ony of them, he threw them so that they wolde never com in hys hondes no more, for of som he brake the leggys and armys. And so he fledde into the castell.

¶And than cam oute knyghtes and squyars and rescowed Sir **Launcelot**. Whan they behylde hym and loked uppon hys persone, they thought they never sawe so goodly a man. And whan they sawe so many woundys uppon hym, they demed that he had bene a man of worshyp; and than they ordayned hym clothis to hys body, and straw and lytter undir the gate of the castell to lye in. And so every day they wolde throw hym mete and set hym drynke; but there was but feaw that wolde brynge hym mete to hys hondys.

¶So hit befelle that Kyng **Pelles** had a neveaw whos name was **Castor**; and so he desyred of the kynge to be made knyght, and at hys owne rekeyste the kynge made hym knyght at the feste of Candylmasse.[9] And whan Sir **Castor** was made knyght, that same day he gaff many gownys; and than Sir **Castor** sente for the foole— whych was Sir **Launcelot**—and whan he was com afore Sir **Castor**, he gaff Sir **Launcelot** a robe of scarlet and all that longed unto hym. And whan Sir **Launcelot** was so arayed lyke a knyght, he was the semelyeste man in all the courte, and none so well made.

¶So whan he sye hys tyme, he wente into the gardyne, and there he layde hym downe by a welle and slepte. And so at aftir none Dame **Elayne** and her maydyns cam into the gardyne to sporte them; and as they romed up and downe, one of Dame **Elaynes** may-dens aspyed where lay a goodly man by the welle slepynge, [and anone shewed hym to Dame **Elayne**:]

¶"Peas," seyde Dame **Elayne**, "and sey no worde, but shew me that man where he lyeth." So anone she brought Dame **Elayne** where he lay. And whan that she behylde hym, anone she felle in remembraunce of hym, and knew hym veryly for Sir **Launcelot**; and

---

8. *Myght nat fynde hym his sustenaunce*: could not find enough food for him.
9. On this date, see n. 9, p. 10.

therewythall she felle on wepynge so hartely that she sanke evyn
to the erthe. And whan she had thus wepte a grete whyle, than she
arose and called her maydyns and seyde she was syke.

And so she yode oute of the gardyne as streyte to her fadir as
she cowde, and there she toke hym by herselff aparte; and than   5
she seyde, "A, my dere fadir, now I have nede of your helpe, and
but yf that ye helpe me now, farewell my good dayes forever!"

❡"What ys that, doughter?" seyde Kynge Pelles. "In¹ youre gardyne I was to sporte me, and there, by the welle, I founde Sir
Launcelot du Lake slepynge." "I may nat byleve hit," seyde Kynge   10
Pelles. "Truly, sir, he ys there," she seyde. "And mesemyth he
shulde be yet distracke oute of hys wytte." "Than holde you stylle,"
seyde the kynge, "and lat me deale."

❡Than the kynge called unto hym suche as he moste trusted, a²
foure persones, and Dame Elayne, hys doughter, and Dame Brusen,   15
her servaunte. And whan they cam to the welle and behylde Sir
Launcelot, anone Dame Brusen seyde to the kynge, "We muste be
wyse how we deale wyth hym, for thys knyght ys oute of hys mynde;
and yf we awake hym rudely, what he woll do we all know nat. And
therefore abyde ye a whyle, and I shall throw an inchauntemente   20
uppon hym, that he shall nat awake of an owre." And so she ded;
and than the kynge commaunded that all people shulde avoyde,   fol.338v
that none shulde be in that way there as the kyng wolde com.

❡And so whan thys was done, thes foure men and thes ladyes
layde honde on Sir Launcelot, and so they bare hym into a towre,   25
and so into a chambir where was the holy vessell of the Sankgreall;
and byfore that holy vessell Sir Launcelot was layde. And there cam
an holy man and unhylled that vessell; and so by myracle and by
vertu of that holy vessell Sir Launcelot was heled and recoverde.
And as sone as he was awaked, he groned and syghed, and com-   30
playned hym sore of hys woodnes and strokys that he had had.

And as sone as Sir Launcelot saw Kynge Pelles and Dame Elayne,   [5]
he waxed ashamed and seyde thus: "A, Lorde Jesu, how cam I
hydir? For Goddys sake, my fayre lorde, lat me wyte how that I
cam hydir."   35

❡"Sir," seyde Dame Elayne, "into thys contrey ye cam lyke a
mased man, clene oute of youre wytte. And here have ye ben kepte
as a foole; and no cryature here knew what ye were, untyll by
fortune a mayden of myne brought me unto you whereas ye lay
slepynge by a well. And anone as I veryly behylde you [I knewe   40
yow.] Than I tolde my fadir; and so were ye brought afore thys holy
vessell, and by the vertu of hit thus were ye healed."

❡"A, Jesu, mercy!" seyde Sir Launcelot. "Yf this be sothe, how
many be there that knowyth of my woodnes?"

❡"So God me helpe," seyde Dame Elayne, "no mo but my fadir,   45
and I, and Dame Brusen." "Now, for Crystes love," seyde Sir
Launcelot, "kepe hit counceyle³ and lat no man knowe hit in the

---

1. Elayne is speaking.
2. I.e., a group of.
3. I.e., secret.

worlde—for I am sore ashamed that I have be myssefortuned, for I am banysshed[4] the contrey of [Logrys for ever" (that is for to saye, the countrey of] Inglonde). And so Sir Launcelot lay more than a fourtenyght or ever that he myght styrre, for sorenes. And than uppon a day he seyde unto Dame Elayne thes wordis:

"Fayre lady Elayne, for youre sake I have had muche care and angwyshe—hit nedyth nat to reherse hit, ye know how. Natwythstondynge I know well I have done fowle to you, whan that I drewe my swerde to you to have slayne you uppon the morne aftir whan that I had layne wyth you; and all was for the cause that ye and Dame Brusen made me for to lye be you magry myne hede[5]—and, as ye say, Sir Galahad your sonne, was begotyn."

❡"That ys trouthe," seyde Dame Elayne. "Than woll ye for my sake," seyde Sir Launcelot, "go unto youre fadir and gete me a place of hym wherein I may dwelle? For in the courte of Kynge Arthure may I never com. "Sir," seyde Dame Eleyne, "I woll lyve and dye wyth you, only for youre sake; and yf my lyff myght nat avayle you and my dethe myght avayle you, wyte you well I wolde dye for youre sake. And I woll to my fadir; and I am ryght sure there ys nothynge that I can desyre of hym but I shall have hit. And wher ye be, my lorde Sir Launcelot, doute ye nat but I woll be wyth you, wyth all the servyse that I may do."

❡So furthwythall she wente to her fadir and sayde, "Sir, my lorde Sir Launcelot desyreth to be hyre by you in som castell off youres."

❡"Well, doughter," seyde the kynge, "sytthyn hit is his desyre to abyde in this marchis, he shall be in the castell of Blyaunte. And there shall ye be wyth hym, and twenty of the fayryste yonge ladyes that bene in thys contrey, and they shall be all of the grettyst blood in this contrey, and ye shall have twenty knyghtes wyth you; for, doughter, I woll that ye wyte we all be honowred by the blood of Sir Launcelot." Than wente Dame Elayne unto Sir Launcelot and tolde hym all how her fadir had devysed.

❡Than cam a knyght whyche was called Sir Castor, that was neveaw unto Kynge Pelles, and he cam unto Sir Launcelot and asked hym what was hys name.

❡"Sir," seyde Sir Launcelot, "my name ys Le Shyvalere Ill Makeete—that ys to sey 'The Knyght That Hath Trespassed'." "Sir," seyde Sir Castor, "hit may well be so:

❡"But ever mesemyth youre name shulde be Sir Launcelot du Lake, for or now I have seyne you." "Sir," seyde Sir Launcelot, "ye ar nat jantyll, for I put a case[6] that my name were Sir Launcelot and that hyt lyste me nat to dyscover my name; what shulde hit greve you here to kepe my counsell, and ye nat hurte thereby? But wyte you well, and ever hit lye in my power, I shall greve you, and ever I mete with you in my way!"

❡Than Sir Castor kneled adowne and besought Sir Launcelot of

4. I.e., banished from.
5. *Magry myne hede:* against my will.
6. *I put a case:* i.e., let us suppose.

Margin notes:
fol.339r
[6]
fol.339v

Line numbers: 5, 10, 15, 20, 25, 30, 35, 40, 45

mercy—"for I shall never uttir what ye be whyle that ye ar in thys
partyes."

¶Than Sir Launcelot pardowned hym. And so kynge Pelles wyth
twenty knyghtes and Dame Elayne wyth her twenty ladyes rode unto
the castel of Blyaunte, that stood in an ilonde beclosed envyrowne[7]
wyth a fayre watir, depe and layrge. And whan they were there
Sir Launcelot lat calle hit the Joyus Ile; and there was he called
none otherwyse but Le Shyvalere Mafete, "The Knyght That Hath
Trespast."

¶Than Sir Launcelot lete make hym a shylde all of sable, and a
quene crowned in the myddis, of sylver, and a knyght clene[8] armed
knelynge afore her. And every day onys—for[9] ony myrthis that all
the ladyes myght make hym—he wolde onys every day loke towarde
the realme of Logrys, where Kynge Arthure and Quene Gwenyver was;
and than wolde he falle uppon a wepyng as hys harte shulde
to-braste.

¶So hit befelle that tyme Sir Launcelot harde of a justynge faste
by, wythin three leagis. Than he called unto hym a dwarff, and he
bade hym go unto that justynge—"and or ever the knyghtes
departe, loke that thou make there a cry, in hyrynge[1] of all knyghtes, that there ys one knyght in Joyus Ile, whyche ys the castell of
Blyaunte, and sey that hys name ys Le Shyvalere Mafete, that woll
juste ayenst knyghtes, all that woll com. And who that puttyth that
knyght to the wars,[2] he shall have a fayre maydyn and a jarfawcon."
So whan this cry was cryed—

¶Unto Joyus Ile drew the numbir of fyve hondred knyghtes. And
wyte you well, there was never seyne in Kynge Arthurs dayes one
knyght that ded so muche dedys of armys as Sir Launcelot ded tho
three dayes togydyrs; for, as the boke makyth truly mencyon, he
had the bettir of all the fyve hondred knyghtes—and there was nat
one slayne of them. And aftir that Sir Launcelot made them all a
grete feste. And in the meanewhyle cam Sir Percyvale de Galys and
Sir Ector de Marys undir that castell whyche was called the Joyus
Ile; and as they behylde that gay castell, they wolde have gone to
that castell, but they myght nat for the brode watir, and brydge
coude they fynde none. Than were they ware on the othir syde
where stoode a lady wyth a sparhawke on her honde, and Sir Percyvale called unto her and asked that lady who was in that castell.

"Fayre knyghtes," she seyde, "here wythin thys castell ys the
fayryste lady in thys londe, and her name is Dame Elayne. Also we
have in thys castell one of the fayryste knyghtes and the myghtyest
man that ys, I dare sey, lyvynge, and he callyth hymselff Le Shyvalere Mafete."

¶"How cam he into thys marchys?" seyde Sir Percyvale.

_____

7. *beclosed envyrowne*: enclosed around.
8. I.e., fully.
9. I.e., despite.
1. I.e., hearing.
2. I.e., worse.

¶"Truly," seyde the damesell, "he cam into thys contrey lyke a madde man, wyth doggys and boyes chasynge hym thorow the cyté of **Corbyn**; and by the holy vessell of the **Sankgreall** he was brought into hys wytte agayne. But he woll nat do batayle wyth no knyght but by undirne or noone. And yf ye lyste to com into the castell," seyde the lady, "ye muste ryde unto the farther syde of the castell, and there shall ye fynde a vessell that woll beare you and youre horse."

Than they departed and cam unto the vessell; and than Sir **Per-cyvale** alyght, and sayde unto Sir **Ector de Marys**, "Ye shall abyde me hyre untyll that I wyte what maner a knyght he ys; for hit were shame unto us, inasmuche as he ys but one knyght, and we shulde bothe do batayle wyth hym."

"Do as ye lyste," seyde Syr **Ector**, "and here I shall abyde you untyll that I hyre off you." Than passed Sir **Percyvale** the water, and whan he cam to the castell gate he seyde unto the porter, "Go thou to the good knyght of this castell and telle hym hyre ys com an arraunte knyght to juste wyth hym."

¶Than the porter yode in and cam agayne, and bade hym ryde "into the comyn place, there as the justynge shall be, where lordys and ladyes may beholde you." And so anone as Sir **Launcelot** had a warnynge, he was sone redy; and there Sir **Percyvale** and Sir **Laun-celot** were com bothe. They encountirde wyth suche a myght, and there spearys were so rude, that bothe the horsys and the knyghtys fell to the grounde. Than they avoyded there horsys, and flange oute there noble swerdys, and hew away many cantels of there shyldys, and so hurteled togydyrs lyke two borys; and aythir wounded othir passynge sore—and so at the laste Sir **Percyvale** spake fyrste, whan they had foughtyn there longe, more than two owres.

¶"Now, fayre knyght," seyde Sir **Percyvale**, "I requyre you of youre knyghthode to telle me youre name, for I mette never wyth suche another knyght."

¶"Sir, as for my name," seyde Sir **Launcelot**, "I woll nat hyde hyt frome you, but my name ys Le Shyvalere Mafete. Now telle me your name," seyde Sir **Launcelot**, "I requyre you." "Truly," seyde Sir **Percyvale**, "my name ys Sir **Percyvale de Galys**, that was brothir unto the good knyght Sir **Lamorak de Galys**; and Kynge **Pellynor** was oure fadir, and Sir **Agglovale** ys my brothir." "Alas!" seyde Sir **Launcelot**, "what have I done to fyght wyth you, whyche ar a knyght of the Table Rounde?—and somtyme I was youre felawe." And there-wythall Sir **Launcelot** kneled downe uppon hys kneys and threwe away hys shylde and hys swerde frome hym.

¶Whan Sir **Percyvale** sawe hym do so, he mervayled what he meaned, and than he seyde thus: "Sir knyght, whatsomever ye be, I requyre you uppon the hyghe order of knyghthode to telle me youre trewe name." Than he answerde and seyde, "So God me helpe, my name ys Sir **Launcelot du Lake**, Kynge **Bannys** son of **Benoy**."

fol.340v

fol.341r

[8]

¶"Alas!" than seyde Sir Percyvale, "what have I now done? For I was sente by the Quene for to seke you, and so I have sought you nygh thys two yere—and yondir ys Sir Ector de Marys, youre brothir, whyche abydyth me on the yondir syde of the watyr—and therefore, for Goddys sake," seyde Sir Percyvale, "forgyffe me myne offencys that I have here done."

¶"Sir, hyt ys sone forgyvyn," seyde Sir Launcelot. Than Sir Percyvale sente for Sir Ector de Marys; and whan Sir Launcelot had a syght of hym he ran unto hym and toke hym in hys armys. And than Sir Ector kneled downe, and aythir wepte uppon othir, that all men had pité to beholde them.

¶Than cam forthe Dame Elayne; and she made them grete chere as myght be made. And there she tolde Sir Ector and Sir Percyvale how and in what maner Sir Launcelot cam into that contrey, and how he was heled.

¶And there hyt was knowyn how longe Sir Launcelot was with Sir Blyaunte and wyth Sir Selyvaunte, and how he fyrste mette wyth them, [and how he] departed frome them bycause he was hurte wyth a boore; and how the ermyte healed hym off hys grete wounde, and how that he cam to the cité of Corbyn.

Now leve we Sir Launcelot in Joyus Ile wyth hys lady, Dame Elayne, and Sir Percyvayle and Sir Ector playynge wyth them; and now turne we unto Sir Bors de Ganys and unto Sir Lyonell, that had sought Sir Launcelot long, nye by the space of two yere, and never coude they hyre of hym. And as they thus rode, by adventure they cam to the house of Kynge Brandegorys; and there Sir Bors was well knowyn, for he had gotyn a chylde uppon the kynges doughtir fyftene yere tofore, and hys name was Elyne le Blanke. And whan Sir Bors sawe that chylde, he lyked hym passynge well; and so thoo knyghtes had good chere of Kynge Brandegorys. [And on the morne Syre Bors came afore Kynge Brandegore,] and seyde, "Here ys my sonne Elyne le Blanke; and syth hyt ys so, I wyll that ye wyte I woll have hym wyth me unto the courte of Kynge Arthur."

"Sir," seyde the kynge, "ye may well take hym wyth you, but he ys as yet over tendir of ayge." "As for that," seyde Sir Bors, "yet I woll have hym wythe me, and brynge hym to the howse of moste worshyp in the worlde."

¶So whan Sir Bors shulde departe, there was made grete sorow for the departynge of Helyne le Blanke. But at the laste they departed, and wythin a whyle they cam unto Camelot whereas was Kynge Arthure. And so whan Kynge Arthure undirstoode that Helyne le Blanke was Sir Bors son, and neveaw unto Kynge Brandegorys, than Kynge Arthure let make hym knyghte of the Rounde Table— and so he preved a good knyghte and an adventurus.

¶And now woll we to oure mater of Sir Launcelot. So hyt befelle on a day that Sir Ector and Sir Percyvale cam unto Sir Launcelot and asked of hym what he wolde do, and whethir he wolde go wyth them unto Kynge Arthure.

[9]

fol.341v

¶"Nay," seyde Sir Launcelott, "that may I nat do by no meane, for I was so vengeabely deffended the courte³ that I caste me never to com there more." fol.342r

¶"Sir," seyde Sir Ector, "I am youre brothir, and ye ar the man in the worlde that I love moste; and yf I undirstoode that hyt were youre dysworshyp,⁴ ye may undirstonde that I wolde never counceyle you thereto:

¶"But Kynge Arthure and all hys knyghtes—and in especiall Quene Gwenyver—makyth suche dole and sorow for you that hyt ys mervayle to hyre and se. And ye muste remembir the grete worshyp and renowne that ye be off, how that ye have bene more spokyn of than ony othir knyght that ys now lyvynge—for there ys none that beryth the name now but ye and Sir Trystram. And therefore, brother," seyde Sir Ector, "make you redy to ryde to the courte wyth us—and I dare sey and make hyt good," seyde Sir Ector, "hyt hath coste my lady the Quene twenty thousand pounde, the sekynge of you!"

¶"Welle, brothir," seyde Sir Launcelot, "I woll do aftir youre counceyle and ryde wyth you."

¶So than they toke there horses and made redy, and anone they toke there leve at Kynge Pelles and at Dame Elayne. And whan Sir Launcelot shulde departe, Dame Elayne mad grete sorow. "My lorde, Sir Launcelot," seyde Dame Elayne, "thys same feste of Pentecoste shall youre sonne and myne, Galahad, be made knyght, for he ys now fully fyftene wynter olde."

¶"Madame, do as ye lyste," seyde Sir Launcelot, "and God gyff hym grace to preve a good knyght." "As for that," seyde Dame Elayne, "I doute nat he shall preve the beste man of hys kynne—except one."⁵

¶"Than shall he be a good man inowghe," seyde Sir Launcelot.

¶So anone they departed, and wythin fyftene dayes journey they cam unto Camelot, that ys in Englyshe called Wynchester. And whan Sir Launcelot was com amonge them, the Kynge and all the knyghtes made grete joy of hys homecommynge. [10] fol.342v

¶And there Sir Percyvale and Sir Ector de Marys began and tolde the hole adventures: how Sir Launcelot had bene oute of hys mynde in the tyme of hys abcence, and how he called hymselff Le Shyvalere Mafete, "The Knyght That Had Trespast"; and in three dayes wythin Joyus Ile Sir Launcelot smote downe fyve hondred knyghtes. And ever as Sir Ector and Sir Percyvale tolde thes talys of Sir Launcelot, Quene Gwenyver wepte as she shulde have dyed.

¶Than the Quene made hym grete chere.

¶"A, Jesu!" seyde Kynge Arthure, "I mervayle for what cause ye, Sir Launcelot, wente oute of youre mynde. For I and many othir deme hyt was for the love of fayre Elayne, the doughtir of kynge Pelles, by whom ye ar noysed that ye have gotyn a chylde: and hys

---

3. *Vengeabely deffended the courte*: strictly forbidden access to the court.
4. I.e., to your dishonor.
5. I.e., except you. This is a diplomatic underestimation of Galahad's prophesied excellence.

name ys 𝔊alahad, and men sey that he shall do many mervaylouse
thyngys."

⸿"My lorde," seyde Sir 𝔏auncelot, "yf I ded ony foly, I have that
I sought."[6] And therewythall the Kynge spake no more. But all Sir
𝔏auncelottys kynnesmen knew for whom he wente oute of hys
mynde. And than there was made grete feystys, and grete joy was
there amonge them; and all lordys and ladyes made grete joy whan
they harde how Sir 𝔏auncelot was com agayne unto the courte.

𝔑ow woll we leve of thys mater, and speke we off Sir 𝔗rystram   [11]
and of Sir 𝔓alompdes that was the Sarezen uncrystynde.
Whan Sir 𝔗rystram was com home unto Joyus Garde frome hys
adventures—

⸿And all thys whyle that Sir 𝔏auncelot was thus myste, two yere
and more, Sir 𝔗rystram bare the brewte and renowne thorow all
the realme of 𝔏ogprs, and many stronge adventures befelle hym,   fol.343r
and full well and worshypfully he brought hem to an ende—

⸿So whan he was com home, La Beall Isode tolde hym off the
grete feste that sholde be at 𝔓entecoste nexte folowynge. And there
she tolde hym how Sir 𝔏auncelot had bene myssed two yere, and all
that whyle he had bene oute of hys mynde, and how he was holpyn
by the holy vessell of the 𝔖ankgreall.

⸿"Alas," seyde Sir 𝔗rystram, "that caused som debate betwyxte
hym and Quene 𝔊wenyver!"

⸿"Sir," seyde Dame Isode, "I knowe hyt all, for Quene 𝔊wenyver
sente me a lettir all how hyt was done, for because I sholde requyre
you to seke hym. And now, blessyd be God," seyde La Beall Isode,
"he ys hole and sounde and comyn ayen to the courte."

⸿"A, Jesu, thereof am I fayne," seyde Sir 𝔗rystram. "And now
shall ye and I make us redy, for bothe ye and I woll be at that
feste."

⸿"Sir," seyde Dame 𝔍sode, "and hyt please you, I woll nat be
there, for thorow me ye bene marked of many good knyghtes, and
that causyth you for to have muche more laboure for my sake.than
nedyth you to have."

⸿"Than woll I nat be there," seyde Sir 𝔗rystram, "but yf ye be
there."

⸿"God deffende," seyde La Beall Isode, "for than shall I be spokyn of shame amonge all quenys and ladyes of astate; for ye that
ar called one of the nobelyste knyghtys of the worlde and a knyght
of the Rounde Table, how may ye be myssed at that feste? For
what shall be sayde of you amonge all knyghtes?—

⸿" 'A! se how Sir 𝔗rystram huntyth, and hawkyth, and cowryth
wythin a castell wyth hys lady, and forsakyth us'—

⸿" 'Alas!' shall som sey, 'hyt ys pyté that ever he was knyght, or
ever he shulde have the love of a lady!'

⸿"Also, what shall quenys and ladyes say of me?—'Hyt ys pyté

6. *That I sought*: what I asked for.

that I have my lyff, that I wolde holde[7] so noble a knyght as ye ar frome hys worshyp.' "

"So God me helpe," seyde Sir Trystram unto La Beall Isode, "hyt ys passyngly well seyde of you, and nobely counceyled:

"And now I well undirstonde that ye love me. And lyke as ye have counceyled me, I woll do a parte thereaftir, but there shall no man nor chylde ryde wyth me but myselff alone:

❡"And so I woll ryde on Tewysday next commynge, and no more harneyse of warre but my speare and my swerde."

❡And so whan the day come Sir Trystram toke hys leve at La Beall Isode; and she sente wyth hym foure knyghtys; and wythin halff a myle he sente them agayne. And within a myle way aftir, Sir Trystram sawe afore hym where Sir Palomydes had stryken downe a knyght and allmoste wounded hym to the dethe.

❡Than Sir Trystram repented hym that he was nat armed, and therewyth he hoved stylle.

❡And anone as Sir Palomydes saw Sir Trystram, he cryed on hyght, "Sir Trystram, now be we mette, for or we departe we shall redresse all oure olde sorys!"

❡"As for that," seyde Sir Trystram, "there was never yet no Crystyn man that ever myght make hys boste that ever I fledde from hym—and wyte thou well, Sir Palomydes, thou that arte a Sarezen shal never make thy boste that ever Sir Trystram de Lyones shall fle fro the!"

❡And therewyth Sir Trystram made hys horse to ren, and wyth all hys myght he cam streyte uppon Sir Palomydes and braste hys speare uppon hym at an hondred pecis; and furthwythall Sir Trystram drewe hys swerde, and than he turned hys horse and stroke togydyrs six grete strokys uppon hys helme.

❡And than Sir Palomydes stode stylle and byhylde Sir Trystram, and mervayled gretely at hys woodnes and of hys foly.

❡And than Sir Palomydes seyde unto hymselff, "And thys Sir Trystram were armed, hyt were harde to cese hym frome hys batayle; and yff I turne agayne and sle hym, I am shamed wheresomevir I go."

❡Than Sir Trystram spake and seyde, "Thou cowarde knyght, what castyste thou to do? And why wolt thou nat do batayle wyth me? For have thou no doute I shall endure the and all thy malyce."

❡"A, Sir Trystram," seyde Sir Palomydes, "full well thou wotyste I may nat have ado wyth the for shame, for thou arte here naked[8] and I am armede, and yf that I sle the, dyshonoure shall be myne— and well thou wotyste," seyde Sir Palomydes unto Sir Trystram, "I knowe thy strengthe and thy hardynes to endure ayenste a goode knyght."

❡"That ys trouthe," seyde Sir Trystram, "I undirstonde thy valyauntenesse."

---

7. I.e., keep.
8. I.e., not wearing armor.

❡"Ye say well," seyde Sir 𝔓𝔞𝔩𝔬𝔪𝔶𝔡𝔢𝔰. "Now, I requyre you, telle⁹ me a questyon that I shall sey unto you."

❡"Than telle me what hyt ys," seyde Sir 𝔗𝔯𝔶𝔰𝔱𝔯𝔞𝔪, "and I shall answere you of the trouthe, as God me helpe."

❡"Sir, I put a case,"¹ seyde Sir 𝔓𝔞𝔩𝔬𝔪𝔶𝔡𝔢𝔰, "that ye were armed at all ryghtes² as well as I am, and I naked as ye be, what wolde ye do to me now, be youre trewe knyghthode?"

❡"A," seyde Sir 𝔗𝔯𝔶𝔰𝔱𝔯𝔞𝔪, "now I undirstonde the well, Sir 𝔓𝔞𝔩-𝔬𝔪𝔶𝔡𝔢𝔰, for now muste I sey myne owne jugemente—and, as God me blysse, that³ I shal sey shall nat be seyde for no feare that I have of the, Sir 𝔓𝔞𝔩𝔬𝔪𝔶𝔡𝔢𝔰. But thys ys all: wyte thou well, Sir 𝔓𝔞𝔩-𝔬𝔪𝔶𝔡𝔢𝔰, as at thys tyme thou sholdyst departe from me, for I wolde nat have ado wyth the."

❡"No more woll I," seyde Sir 𝔓𝔞𝔩𝔬𝔪𝔶𝔡𝔢𝔰. "And therefore ryde furth on thy way."

❡"As for that," seyde Sir 𝔗𝔯𝔶𝔰𝔱𝔯𝔞𝔪, "I may chose othir to ryde othir to go.⁴

❡"But, Sir 𝔓𝔞𝔩𝔬𝔪𝔶𝔡𝔢𝔰," seyde Sir 𝔗𝔯𝔶𝔰𝔱𝔯𝔞𝔪, "I mervayle greatly of one thynge, that⁵ thou arte so good a knyght: that thou wolt nat be crystynde—and thy brothir, Sir 𝔖𝔞𝔣𝔣𝔦𝔯, hath bene crystynde many a day."

❡"As for that," seyde Sir 𝔓𝔞𝔩𝔬𝔪𝔶𝔡𝔢𝔰, "I may nat yet be crystyned for a vowe that I have made many yerys agone. Howbehyt, in my harte and in my soule I have had many a day a good beleve in Jesu Cryste and hys mylde modir Mary; but I have but one batayle to do, and were that onys done I wolde be baptyzed." [13]   fol.344v

❡"Be my hede," seyde Sir 𝔗𝔯𝔶𝔰𝔱𝔯𝔞𝔪, "as for one batayle, thou shalt nat seke hyt longe—for God deffende," seyde Sir 𝔗𝔯𝔶𝔰𝔱𝔯𝔞𝔪, "that thorow my defaute thou sholdyste lengar lyve thus a Sarazyn! For yondyr ys a knyght that ye have hurte and smyttyn downe:

❡"Now helpe me than that I were armed in hys armoure, and I shall sone fullfyll thyne avowys."

❡"As ye wyll," seyde Sir 𝔓𝔞𝔩𝔬𝔪𝔶𝔡𝔢𝔰, "so shall hyt be."

❡So they rode bothe unto that knyght that sate uppon a banke, and than Sir 𝔗𝔯𝔶𝔰𝔱𝔯𝔞𝔪 salewed hym, and he waykely salewed hym agayne.

❡"Sir knyght," seyde Sir 𝔗𝔯𝔶𝔰𝔱𝔯𝔞𝔪, "I requyre you telle me youre ryght name."

❡"Syr," he seyde, "my ryght name ys Sir 𝔊𝔞𝔩𝔩𝔢𝔯𝔬𝔫 off 𝔊𝔞𝔩𝔬𝔴𝔢𝔶, and a knyght of the Table Rounde."

❡"So God me helpe," seyde Sir 𝔗𝔯𝔶𝔰𝔱𝔯𝔞𝔪, "I am ryght hevy of youre hurtys. But thys ys all: I muste pray you to leane me youre hole armoure, for ye se that I am unarmed, and I muste do batayle wyth thys knyght."

❡"Sir, ye shall have hyt wyth a good wyll. But ye muste beware,

9. I.e., answer.
1. *I put a case:* supposing.
2. *At all ryghtes:* fully.
3. I.e., that which.
4. I.e., walk.
5. I.e., given that.

for I warne you, that knyght ys an hardy knyght as ever I mette wythall—

¶"But, sir," seyde Sir Galeron, "I pray you, telle me youre name, and what ys that knyghtes name that hath beatyn me?"

¶"Sir, as for my name, wyte you well yt ys Sir Trystram de Lyones; and as for hym, hys name ys Sir Palomydes, brothir unto the good knyght Sir Sapher—and yet ys Sir Palomydes uncrystynde."

¶"Alas," seyde Sir Galleron, "that ys grete pyté that so good a knyght and so noble a man off armys sholde be uncrystynde."

¶"So God me helpe," seyde Sir Trystram, "owthyr he shall sle me, othir I hym, but that[6] he shall be crystynde or ever we departe in sundir."

¶"My lorde, Sir Trystram," seyde Sir Galleron, "youre renowne and worshyp ys well knowyn thorow many realmys, and God save you thys day frome senshyp and shame."

¶Than Sir Trystram unarmed Sir Galleron, the whyche was a noble knyght and had done many dedys of armys—and he was a large knyght of fleyshe and boone. And whan he was unarmed he stood on hys feete, for he was sore brused in the backe wyth a speare.

¶Yet as well as Sir Galleron myght, he armed Sir Trystram. And than Sir Trystram mounted uppon hys horse, and in hys honde he gate Sir Galleron hys speare. And therewythall Sir Palomydes was redy; and so they cam hurtelynge togydyrs, and aythir smote othir in myddys off there shyldys—and therewythall Sir Palomydes speare brake, and Sir Trystram smote downe Sir Palomydes, horse and man, to the erthe. And than Sir Palomydes, as sone as he myght, avoyded hys horse, and dressed hys shylde, and pulled oute hys swerde.

That sawe Sir Trystram, and therewythall he alyght and tyed hys horse to a tre. And than they cam togydyrs egirly as two wylde borys; and so they layshed togydyrs, trasynge and traversynge as noble men that offten had bene well proved in batayle—but ever Sir Palomydes dred passynge sore the myght of Sir Trystram, and therefore he suffyrd hym to breeth hym,[7] and thus they faught more than two owrys. But oftyntymes Sir Trystram smote suche strokys at Sir Palomydes that he made hym to knele.

¶And Sir Palomydes brake and kutte many pecis of Sir Trystrams shylde.

¶And than Sir Palomydes wounded Sir Trystram passynge sore, for he was a well-fyghtynge man.

¶Than Sir Trystram waxed wood wrothe oute off mesure, and russhed uppon Sir Palomydes wyth suche a myght that Sir Palomydes felle grovelynge to the erthe—and therewythall he lepe up lyghtly uppon hys feete.

¶And than Sir Trystram wounded sore Sir Palomydes thorow the shuldir—and ever Sir Trystram fought stylle inlyke harde; and Sir Palomydes fayled hym nat but gaff hym many sad strokys agayne.

fol.345r

fol.345v

[14]

---

6. I.e., (God help me) that.
7. *Suffyrd hym to breeth hym:* allowed him to catch his breath.

And at the laste Sir Trystram doubeled hys strokys uppon hym, and by fortune Sir Trystram smote Sir Palomydes swerde oute of hys honde—and yf Sir Palomydes had stouped for hys swerde, he had bene slayne.

⸿And than Sir Palomydes stood stylle and behylde hys swerde wyth a sorowfull harte.

⸿"How now?" sayde Sir Trystram. "For now I have the at avauntayge," seyde Sir Trystram," as thou haddist me thys day. But hyt shall never be seyde in no courte nor amonge no good knyghtes that Sir Trystram shall sle ony knyght that ys wepynles; and therefore take thou thy swerde, and lat us make an ende of thys batayle."

⸿"As for to do thys batayle," seyde Sir Palomydes, "I dare ryght well ende hyt. But I have no grete luste to fyght no more—and for thys cause," seyde Sir Palomydes: "myne offence ys to you nat so grete but that we may be fryendys, for all that I have offended ys and was for the love of La Beall Isode. And as for her, I dare say she ys pyerles of all othir ladyes; and also I profyrd her never no maner of dyshonoure—and by her I have getyn the moste parte of my worshyp—and sytthyn I offended never as to her owne persone:

⸿"And as for the offence that I have done, hyt was ayenste youre owne persone; and for that offence ye have gyvyn me thys day many sad strokys—and som I have gyffyn you agayne—and now I dare sey I felte never man of youre myght nothir so well-brethed, but yf hit were Sir Launcelot du Laake. Wherefore I requyre you, my lorde, forgyff me all that I have offended unto you:

⸿"And thys same day have me to the nexte churche, and fyrste lat me be clene conffessed, and aftir that se youreselff that I be truly baptysed. And than woll we all ryde togydyrs unto the courte of Kynge Arthure, that we may be there at the nexte hyghe feste folowynge."

⸿"Than take youre horse," seyde Sir Trystram, "and as ye sey, so shall hyt be; and all my evyll wyll[8] God forgyff hyt you, and I do. And hereby wythin thys myle ys the suffrygan of Carlehylle whyche shall gyff you the sacramente of baptyme." And anone they toke there horsys—and Sir Galleron rode wyth them—and whan they cam to the suffrygan, Sir Trystram tolde hym there desyre.

Than the suffrygan let fylle a grete vessell wyth watyr, and whan he had halowed hyt he than conffessed clene Sir Palomydes. And Sir Trystram and Sir Galleron were hys two godfadyrs. And than sone afftyr they departed and rode towarde Camelot where that Kynge Arthure and Quene Gwenyvir was, and the moste party of all the knyghtes of the Rounde Table were there also.

⸿And so the Kynge and all the courte were ryght glad that Sir Palomydes was crystynde.

⸿And at that same feste in cam Sir Galahad that was son unto Sir Launcelot du Lake, and sate in the Syge Perelous. And so

fol.346r

5

10

15

20

25

30

35

40

45

---

8. *All my evyll wyll:* i.e., all the ill will you directed toward me.

therewythall they departed and dysceyvirde, all the knyghtys of the   fol.346v
Rounde Table.

¶And than Sir Trystram returned unto Joyus Garde; and Sir Palomydes folowed aftir the Questynge Beste.

¶Here endyth the secunde boke off Syr Trystram de Lyones,   5
whyche drawyn[9] was oute of Freynshe by Sir Thomas Malleorré,
knyght, as Jesu be hys helpe. Amen.

¶But here ys no rehersall of the thirde booke; but here folowyth
the noble tale off the Sankegreall,[1] whyche called ys the holy vessell
and the sygnyfycacion of blyssed bloode off Oure Lorde Jesu   10
Cryste, whyche was brought into thys londe by Joseph off Aramathye.
Therefore on all synfull, blyssed Lorde, have—on thy knyght—
mercy.[2] Amen.

9. I.e., translated.
1. *But here ys no rehersall . . . the Sankegreall:* the third book to which Malory refers was probably a third volume of a single copy text of his source, the French *Tristan* (cf. n. 9, p. 337). That portion of the source would have contained its own version of the Grail quest; but, either through choice or because the third volume was not available to him, Malory's *Noble Tale of the Sankegreal* translates instead from the French *Queste del Saint Graal*. Malory does not substantially return to Trystram beyond this point, except to provide an elaboration on the circumstances of his death (see p. 641).
2. *On all synfull . . . have—on thy knyght—mercy:* i.e. on all sinful people—on your knight—have mercy.

The Noble Tale of the Sankgreal†

AT the vigyl of Pentecoste,[1] whan all the felyship of the Table Rownde were com unto Camelot and there harde hir servyse, so at the laste the tablys were sette redy to the meete, ryght so entird into the halle a full fayre jantillwoman on horsebacke that had ryddyn full faste—for hir horse was all beswette. Than she there alyght and com before the Kynge and salewed hym; and he seyde, "Damesell, God you blysse!"

¶"Sir," seyde she, "for Goddis sake telle me where ys Sir Launcelot." "He ys yondir: ye may se hym," seyde the Kynge.

¶Than she wente unto Sir Launcelot and seyde, "Sir Launcelot, I salew you on Kynge Pelles behalff, and I also requyre you to com with me hereby into a foreste." Than Sir Launcelot asked her with whom she dwelled. "I dwelle," she seyde, "with Kynge Pelles." "What woll ye with me?" seyde Sir Launcelot. "Ye shall know," she seyde, "whan ye com thydir." "Well," seyde he, "I woll gladly go with you."

¶So Sir Launcelot bade hys squyre sadyll hys horse and brynge hys armys in haste. So he ded hys commandemente. Than com the Quene unto Sir Launcelot, and seyde, "Woll ye leve us now alone at thys hyghe feste?"

¶"Madam," seyde the jantyllwoman, "wyte you well he shall be with you tomorne by dyner tyme."

¶"If I wyste," seyde the Quene, "that he sholde nat be here with us tomorne, he sholde nat go with you be my goodwyll."

Ryght so departed Sir Launcelot, and rode untyll that he com into a foreste and into a grete valey, where they sye an abbey of nunnys; and there was a squyre redy, and opened the gatis, and so they entird and descended of their horsys. And anone there cam a fayre felyship aboute Sir Launcelot and wellcomed hym; and than they ladde hym unto the abbas chambir and unarmed hym. And ryght so he was ware uppon a bed lyynge two of hys cosyns, Sir Bors and Sir Lyonell; and anone he waked them, and whan they syghe hym they made grete joy. "Sir," seyde Sir Bors unto Sir Launcelot, "what adventure hath brought you hidir? For we wende to have founde you tomorne at Camelot."

¶"So God me helpe," seyde Sir Launcelot, "a jantillwoman brought me hydir, but I know nat the cause."

¶So in the meanewhyle that they thus talked togydir, there com in twelve nunnes that brought with hem Galahad, the whych was

---

† The title is taken editorially from the colophon to the previous section (p. 495). Malory's principal source for this section is the French *Queste del Saint Graal;* for illustrative selections, see p. 733. In the Winchester MS, this section begins on a new gathering (i.e. one of the several booklets of paper sewn together to form a book). The last four and a half pages of the previous gathering, however, have been left blank, after the conclusion of the *Books of Sir Trystram,* making this, on a visual level at least, the most significant division in the MS. The floriated initial "A" is dark blue with red sprays, and the capital "T" which follows is touched in yellow. On the history of the Grail as assumed by this tale, see n. 7, p. 464.
1. On the feast of Pentecost, see n. 1, p. 10.

passynge fayre and welle made, that unneth in the worlde men myght nat fynde hys macche—and all tho ladyes wepte.

¶"Sir," seyd they all, "we brynge you hyre thys chylde the whycch we have norysshed; and we pray you to make hym knyght, for of a more worthyer mannes honde may he nat resceyve the order of knyghthode."

¶Sir Launcelot behylde thys yonge squyer and saw hym semely and demure as a dove, with all maner of goode fetures, that he wende of hys ayge never to have seene so fayre a fourme of a man. Than seyde Sir Launcelot, "Commyth thys desyre of hymselff?" He and all they seyde, "Yes."

¶"Than shall he," seyde Sir Launcelot, "resseyve the order of knyghthode at the reverence of[2] the hyghe feste." So that nyght Sir Launcelot had passyng good chere; and on the morne at the howre of pryme, at Galahaddis desyre, he made hym knyght, and seyde, "God make you a good man, for of beauté faylith you none as ony that ys now lyvynge:

¶"Now, fayre Sir," seyde Sir Launcelot, "woll ye com with me unto the courte of Kynge Arthure?" "Nay," seyde he, "I woll nat go with you at thys tyme." Than he departed frome them, and toke hys two cosynes with hym. And so they com unto Camelot by the owre of undirne on Whytsonday. So by that tyme the Kynge and the Quene was gone to the mynster to here their servyse. Than the Kynge and the Quene were passynge glad of Sir Bors and Sir Lyonel, and so was all the felyshyp.

¶So whan the Kynge and all the knyghtes were com frome serv- yse, the barownes aspyed in the segys of the Rounde Table all aboute wretyn with golde lettirs,

Here ought to sitte he

—and

He ought to sitte hyre

And thus they wente so longe[3] tylle that they com to the Sege Perelous, where they founde lettirs newly wrytten of golde whych seyde,

Foure hondred wyntir and foure and fyffty[4]
acomplyvysshed aftir the Passion of Oure Lorde Jesu
Cryst oughte thys syege to be fulfylled

Than all they seyde, "Thys ys a mervaylous thynge, and an adven- tures." "In the name of God," seyde Sir Launcelot—and than accounted the terme of the wrytynge, frome the byrth of Oure

Here Galahad was made knyght

[2]

fol.350r

2. *at the reverence of*: out of respect for.
3. *Wente so longe*: i.e., kept going (seat to seat).
4. *Foure hondred wyntir and foure and fyffty*: 454 years.

Lorde untyll that day—"hit semyth me," seyd Sir Launcelot, "that thys syge oughte to be fulfylled thys same day! For thys ys the Pentecoste after the foure hondred and foure and fyffty yere. And if hit wolde please all partyes, I wolde none of thes lettirs were sene thys day tyll that he be com that ought to enchyve thys adventure."

Than made they to ordayne a cloth of sylke for to cover thes lettirs in the Syege Perelous. Than the Kynge bade haste[5] unto dyner. "Sir," seyde Sir Kay the Stywarde, "if ye go now unto youre mete ye shall breke youre olde custom of youre courte, for ye have nat used on thys day to sytte at your mete or that ye have sene some adventure."

¶"Ye sey sothe," seyde the Kynge, "but I had so grete joy of Sir Launcelot and of hys cosynes whych bene com to the courte hole and sounde, that I bethought me nat of none olde custom."

¶So as they stood spekynge, in com a squyre that seyde unto the Kynge, "Sir, I brynge unto you mervaylous tydynges."

¶"What be they?" seyde the Kynge. "Sir, there ys here bynethe[6] at the ryver a grete stone whych I saw fleete abovyn the watir, and therein I saw stykynge a swerde."[7] Than the Kynge seyde, "I woll se that mervayle." So all the knyghtes wente with hym; and whan they cam unto the ryver they founde there a stone fletynge, as hit were of rede marbyll, and therein stake a fayre ryche swerde, and the pomell thereof was of precious stonys wrought with lettirs of golde subtylé.

¶Than the barownes redde the lettirs, whych seyde in thys wyse:

NEVER SHALL MAN TAKE ME HENSE
BUT ONLY HE BY WHOS SYDE I OUGHT TO HONGE:
AND HE SHALL BE THE BESTE KNYGHT OF THE WORLDE

¶So whan the Kynge had sene the lettirs, he seyde unto Sir Launcelot, "Fayre sir, thys swerde ought to be youres, for I am sure ye be the beste knyght of the worlde."

¶Than Sir Launcelot answerde full sobirly, "Sir, hit ys nat my swerde. Also, I have no hardines to sette my honde thereto, for hit longith nat to hange be my syde. Also, who that assayth to take hit and faylith of[8] that swerde, he shall resseyve a wounde by that swerde that he shall nat be longe hole afftir. And I woll that ye weyte that thys same day shall the adventure of the Sankgreall begynne, that ys called the holy vessell."

¶"Now, fayre nevew," seyde the Kynge unto Sir Gawayne, "assay ye for my love." "Sir," he seyde, "sauff youre good grace, I shall nat do that."

¶"Sir," seyde the Kynge, "assay to take the swerde for my love, and at my commaundemente."

---

5. I.e., make haste.
6. I.e., below.
7. This is Balyn's sword, which Merlin placed in the stone after the mutual fratricide of Balyn and Balan (p. 61).
8. *Faylith of*: fails to take.

¶"Sir, youre commaundemente I woll obey." And therewith he toke the swerde by the handyls, but he myght nat stirre hit. "I thanke you," seyde the Kynge.

"My lorde Sir Gawayne," seyde Sir Launcelot, "now wete you well, thys swerde shall touche you so sore that ye wolde nat ye had sette youre honde thereto, for the beste castell of thys realme."

¶"Sir," he seyde, "I myght nat withsey myne unclis wyll." But whan the Kynge herde thys, he repented hit much, and seyde unto Sir Percyvall, "Sir, woll ye assay for my love?"

¶And he assayed gladly, for to beare Sir Gawayne felyship; and therewith he sette to hys honde on the swerde and drew at hit strongely, but he myght nat meve hytte. Than were there no mo that durste be so hardy to sette their hondis thereto. "Now may ye go to youre dyner," seyde Sir Kay unto the Kynge, "for a mervalous adventure have ye sene."

¶So the Kynge and all they wente unto the courte, and every knyght knew hys owne place and sette hym therein; and yonge men that were good knyghtes served them.

¶So whan they were served and all syegis fulfylled—sauff only the Syege Perelous—

¶Anone there befelle a mervaylous adventure, that all the doorys and wyndowes of the paleyse shutte by themselff.

¶Natforthan the halle was nat gretly durked, and therewith they abaysshed bothe one and other.[9]

¶Than Kynge Arthure spake fyrste and seyde, "Be God, fayre felowis and lordis, we have sene this day mervayles! But or nyght I suppose we shall se gretter mervayles." In the meanewhyle com in a good olde man and an awnciente, clothed all in whyght—and there was no knyght knew from whens he com.

¶And with hym he brought a yonge knyght (and bothe on foote), in rede armys, withoute swerde other shylde sauff a scawberd hangynge by hys syde. And thes wordys he seyde: "Pees be with you, fayre lordys!"[1]

¶Than the olde man seyde unto Kynge Arthure, "Sir, I brynge you here a yonge knyght the whych ys of kynges lynage and of the kynrede of Joseph of Aramathy,[2] whereby the mervayles of this courte and of stronge realmys shall be fully complevysshed."

¶The Kynge was ryght glad of hys wordys and seyde unto the good man, "Sir, ye be ryght wellcom, and the yonge knyght with you."

¶Than the olde man made the yonge man to unarme hym; and he was in a cote of rede sendell, and bare a mantell uppon hys sholder that was furred with ermyne,[3] and put that uppon hym.

¶And the olde knyght seyde unto the yonge knyght, "Sir, swith me." And anone he lad hym to the Syege Perelous, where besyde

Marginal notes:
- 5
- 10
- 15
- 20
- 25 / fol.351r
- 30
- 35
- [4]
- 40
- How Sir Galahad sate in Seege Perelous / 45

9. *Abaysshed bothe one and other*: were all astonished.
1. Cf. John 20:19: "where the disciples were assembled . . . came Jesus and stood in the midst, and saith unto them, Peace be unto you."
2. On Joseph of Arimathea (a town located about twenty miles northwest of Jerusalem) see n. 7, p. 464.
3. On ermine, see n. 2, p. 206. White (the predominant color of ermine) and red are the symbolic colors of Christ.

sate Sir Launcelot; and the good man lyffte up the clothe and founde
there the lettirs that seyde thus:

THYS YS THE SYEGE OF SIR Galahad, THE HAWTE[4] PRYNCE

"Sir," seyde the olde knyght, "weyte you well that place ys youres;"
and than he sette hym downe surely in that syge. And than he
seyde unto the olde man, "Now may ye, sir, go youre way, for well
have ye done in that that[5] ye were commaunded. And recommaunde me unto my grauntesyre, Kynge Pelles, and unto my lorde
Kynge Pecchere, and sey hem on my behalff I shall com and se hem
as sone as ever Y may."

¶So the good man departed; and there mette hym twenty noble
squyers, and so toke their horsys and wente their wey.

¶Than all the knyghtes of the Table Rounde mervayled gretly
of Sir Galahad, that he durst sitte there and was so tendir of ayge,
and wyst nat frome whens he com but all only be God.

¶All they seyde, "Thys ys he by whom the Sankgreall shall
be encheved, for there sate never none but he there but he were
myscheved."[6]

¶Than Sir Launcelot behylde hys sonne and had grete joy of hym.

¶Than Sir Bors tolde hys felowis, "Uppon[7] payne of my lyff, thys
yonge knyght shall com to grete worship." So thys noyse was grete
in all the courte, that hit cam unto the Quene; and she had mervayle what knyght hit myght be that durste adventure hym to sytte
in that Sege Perelous.

¶Than som seyde he resembled much unto Sir Launcelot. "I may
well suppose," seyde the Quene, "that Sir Launcelot begate hym on
Kynge Pelles doughter, whych made hym to lye by her by enchauntemente: and hys name ys Galahad. I wolde fayne se hym," seyde
the Quene, "for he muste nedys be a noble man—for so hys fadir
ys that hym begate, I reporte me unto all the Table Rounde."

¶So whan the mete was done, that the Kynge and all were rysen,
the Kyng yode to the Sege Perelous and lyfft up the clothe and
founde there the name of Sir Galahad. And than he shewed hit unto
Sir Gawayne and seyde, "Fayre nevew, now have we amonge us Sir
Galahad, the good knyght that shall worship us all. And uppon
payne of my lyff he shall encheve the Sankgreall, ryght as Sir Launcelot had done us to undirstonde."

Than cam Kynge Arthure unto Sir Galahad and seyde, "Sir, ye be
ryght wellcom, for ye shall meve many good knyghtes to the Queste
of the Sankgreall; and ye shall enchyve that[8] many other knyghtes
myght never brynge to an ende." Than the Kynge toke hym by the

fol.351v

---

4. The designation of Galahad as the High Prince possibly results from confusion of his
   name with that of Galahalt, though it is not inaccurate as an anticipation of his status
   after achieving the Grail (for which, see pp. 582–86).
5. *That that*: i.e., that which.
6. *There sate never . . . he were myscheved*: no one except him ever sat there who was not
   brought to harm.
7. I.e., I swear upon.
8. I.e., that which.

honde and wente downe frome the paleyes to shew 𝕲𝖆𝖑𝖆𝖍𝖆𝖉 the
adventures of the stone.

⁋Than the Quene harde thereof and cam aftir with many ladyes,
and[9] shewed her the stone where hit hoved on the watir.

⁋"Sir," seyde the Kynge unto Sir 𝕲𝖆𝖑𝖆𝖍𝖆𝖉, "here ys a grete mervayle as ever Y sawe—and ryght good knyghtes have assayde and
fayled." "Sir," seyde Sir 𝕲𝖆𝖑𝖆𝖍𝖆𝖉, "hit ys no mervayle, for thys adventure ys nat theyrs but myne; and for the sureté of thys swerde I
brought none with me, but here by my syde hangith the scawberte." And anone he leyde hys honde on the swerde, and lyghtly
drew hit oute of the stone, and put hit in the sheethe, and seyde
unto the Kynge, "Now hit goth [better than hit dyd aforehand!"]
"Sir," seyde the Kynge, "a shylde God may sende you!"

⁋"Now have I the swerde that somtyme was the good knyghtes,
𝕭𝖆𝖑𝖞𝖓𝖘 𝖑𝖊 𝕾𝖆𝖚𝖊𝖆𝖎𝖌𝖊, and he was a passynge good knyght of hys hondys; and with thys swerde he slew hys brothir 𝕭𝖆𝖑𝖆𝖓—and that was
grete pité, for he was a good knyght—and eythir slew othir thorow
a Dolerous Stroke[1] that 𝕭𝖆𝖑𝖞𝖓 gaff unto Kynge 𝕻𝖊𝖑𝖑𝖊𝖘, the whych
ys nat yett hole—nor naught shall be, tyll that I hele hym."

⁋So therewith the Kynge had aspyed com rydynge downe the
ryver a lady on a whyght palferey a grete paace towarde them. Than
she salewed the Kynge and the Quene and asked if that Sir 𝕷𝖆𝖚𝖓𝖈𝖊𝖑𝖔𝖙 were there; and than he answerd hymselff and seyde, "I am
here, my fayre lady." Than she seyde all with wepynge chere, "A,
Sir 𝕷𝖆𝖚𝖓𝖈𝖊𝖑𝖔𝖙, how youre grete doynge ys chonged sytthyn thys day
in the morne!"

⁋"Damesell, why sey ye so?"

⁋"Sir, I say you sothe," seyde the damesell, "for ye were thys day
in the morne the best knyght of the worlde; but who sholde sey so
now, he sholde be a lyer, for there ys now one bettir than ye be.
And well hit ys preved by the adventure of the swerde—

⁋"Whereto ye durst nat sette to your honde: and that ys the
change of youre name[2] and levynge—

⁋"Wherefore I make unto you a remembraunce that ye shall nat
wene frome hensforthe that ye be the best knyght of the worlde."

⁋"As towchyng unto that," seyde Sir 𝕷𝖆𝖚𝖓𝖈𝖊𝖑𝖔𝖙, "I know well I was
never none of the beste."

⁋"Yes," seyde the damesell, "that were ye, and ar yet, of ony
synfull man of the worlde—

⁋"And, Sir Kynge, 𝕹𝖆𝖈𝖎𝖊𝖓 the eremeyte sendeth the[3] worde that
the shall befalle the grettyst worship that ever befelle kynge in
Bretayne—and I sey you wherefore: for thys day the 𝕾𝖆𝖓𝖐𝖊𝖌𝖗𝖊𝖆𝖑𝖑
appered in thy house and fedde the and all thy felyship of the
Rounde Table." So she departed and wente the same way that she
cam.

⁋"Now," seyde the Kynge, "I am sure at this Quest of the 𝕾𝖆𝖓𝖐𝖊𝖌𝖗𝖊𝖆𝖑𝖑 shall all ye of the Rownde Table departe, and nevyr shall I

[5]

𝕳𝖔𝖜 𝕾𝖎𝖗 𝕲𝖆𝖑𝖆𝖍𝖆𝖉
𝖕𝖚𝖑𝖑𝖊𝖉 𝖙𝖍𝖊 𝖘𝖜𝖊𝖗𝖉𝖊   5
𝖔𝖚𝖙 𝖔𝖋 𝖙𝖍𝖊 𝖕𝖊𝖗𝖔𝖓

10

fol.352r

15

20

25

30

35

40

45

[6]

---

9. I.e., and who.
1. On the Dolerous Stroke, see the *Tale of Balyn and Balan* (p. 56).
2. I.e., reputation.
3. Thee.

se you agayne holé[4] togydirs. Therefore ones[5] shall I se you togydir
in the medow, all holé togydirs—therefore I woll se you all holé
togydir in the medow of **Camelot** to juste and to turney, that aftir
youre dethe men may speke of hit that such good knyghtes were
here, such a day, holé togydirs."[6]   fol.352v   5

As unto that counceyle, and at the Kynges rekeyst, they accorded
all, and toke on the harneyse that longed unto joustenynge. But
all thys mevynge of the Kynge[7] was for thys entente, for to se **Gala-**
had preved; for the Kynge demed he sholde nat lyghtly com agayne
unto the courte aftir thys departynge.   10

¶So were they assembled in the medowe, both more and lasse.[8]

¶Than Sir **Galahad**, by the prayer of the Kynge and the Quene,
dud[9] on a noble jesseraunte uppon hym, and also he dud on hys
helme; but shylde wolde he take none, for no prayer of the Kynge.

¶So than Sir **Gawayne** and othir knyghtes prayde hym to take a   15
speare; ryght so he dud.

¶So the Quene was in a towure with all hir ladyes for to beholde
that turnement. Than Sir **Galahad** dressed hym in myddys of the
medow and began to breke spearys mervaylously, that all men had
wondir of hym; for he there surmownted all othir knyghtes, for   20
within a whyle he had defowled many good knyghtes of the Table
Rounde sauff all only tweyne, that was Sir **Launcelot** and Sir
Persyvale.

Than the Kynge at the Quenys desyre made hym to alyght and   [7]
to unlace hys helme, that the Quene myght se hym in the   25
vysayge. Whan she avysed hym[1] she seyde, "I dare well sey sothely
that Sir **Launcelot** begate hym, for never two men resembled more
in lyknesse. Therefore hit ys no mervayle thoughe he be of grete
proues." So a lady that stood by the Quene seyde, "Madam, for
Goddis sake, ought he of ryght to be so good a knyght?"   30

¶"Ye, forsothe," seyde the Quene, "for he ys of all partyes[2]
comyn of the beste knyghtes of the worlde, and of the hyghest
lynage; for Sir **Launcelot** ys com but of the eyghth degré frome Oure
Lord Jesu Cryst, and thys Sir **Galahad** ys the nyneth degré frome
Oure Lorde Jesu Cryst: 35

¶"Therefore I dare sey they be the grettist jantillmen of the
worlde." And than the Kynge and all the astatis wente home unto
Camelot, and so wente unto evynsong to the grete monester;[3] and
so aftir uppon that to sowper—and every knyght sette in hys owne

                                                                        40

---

4. I.e., wholly.
5. I.e., once more, one last time.
6. *Holé togydirs . . . togydir . . . holé togydir . . . holé togydir . . . holé togydirs*: (the King's distraction in anticipation of great loss is clear enough; cf. the closing of *Le Morte Darthur*,
   p. 697, lines 35–37).
7. *All thys mevynge of the Kynge*: all that the King had done. (Rubrication of "aftir" later in
   the sentence follows "of Kynge," crossed through in the manuscript, and probably reflects
   the scribe's mistaken anticipation of "Arthur.")
8. *More and lasse*: i.e., people of all ranks.
9. I.e., put.
1. *Avysed hym*: looked him in the face.
2. *Of all partyes*: in every respect.
3. I.e., monastery church.

place, as they were toforehonde. Than anone they harde crakynge and cryynge of thundir, that hem thought the palyse sholde all to-dryve.

¶So in the myddys of the blast entyrde a sonnebeame, more clerer by seven tymys than ever they saw day, and all they were alyghted of[4] the grace of the Holy Goste. Than began every knyght to beholde other; and eyther saw other, by their semyng, fayrer than ever they were before. Natforthan there was no knyght that myght speke one worde a grete whyle; and so they loked every man on other as they had bene doome.[5]

Than entird into the halle the Holy Grayle coverde with whyght samyte, but there was none that myght se hit, nother whom that bare hit. And there was all the halle fulfylled with good odoures, and every knyght had such metis and drynkes as he beste loved in thys worlde.[6] And whan the Holy Grayle had bene borne thorow the hall, than the holy vessell departed suddeynly, that they wyst nat where hit becam. Than had they all breth to speke, and than the Kyng yelded thankynges to God of Hys good grace that He had sente them.

¶"Sertes," seyde the Kynge, "we ought to thanke Oure Lorde Jesu Cryste gretly that he hath shewed us thys day at the reverence of thys hygh feste of Pentecost." "Now," seyde Sir Gawayne, "we have bene servyd thys day of what metys and drynkes we thought on—

¶"But one thyng begyled us, that we myght nat se the Holy Grayle: hit was so preciously coverde. Wherefore I woll make here a vow that tomorne, withoute longer abydynge, I shall laboure in the Queste of the Sankgreall—and that I shall holde me oute a twelvemonth and a day or more if nede be—and never shall I returne unto the courte agayne tylle I have sene hit more opynly than hit hath bene shewed here. And iff I may nat spede, I shall returne agayne, as he that may nat be ayenst the wylle of God."

¶So whan they of the Table Rounde harde Sir Gawayne sey so, they arose up the moste party and made such avowes as Sir Gawayne hathe made. Anone as Kynge Arthur harde thys, he was gretly dysplesed, for he wyst well he myght nat agaynesey their avowys.

"Alas," seyde Kynge Arthure unto Sir Gawayne, "ye have nygh slayne me for the avow that ye have made; for thorow you ye have berauffte me the fayryst and the trewyst of knyghthode that ever was sene togydir in ony realme of the worlde. For whan they departe frome hense, I am sure they all shall never mete more togydir in thys worlde; for they shall dye many in the Queste. And so hit forthynkith me nat a litill, for I have loved them as well as my lyff—wherefore hit shall greve me ryght sore, the departicion

---

4. *Alyghted of:* illuminated with.
5. I.e., without speech (cf. the description of Pentecost, Acts 2:1–4, and see n. 1, p. 10).
6. The miraculous provision of food is a traditional sign of God's blessing: cf. Exodus 16 and Psalm 78 (God provides manna), Wisdom 16:20–21 (God provides bread that changes to suit everyone's taste), John 2:9 (Jesus changes water into wine), and Matthew 14:13–21 (Jesus feeds the five thousand). Consider also Christ's words in John 6:35: "I am the bread of life: he that cometh to me shall never hunger; and he that believeth on me shall never thirst." Ancient non-Judeo-Christian legends that tell of vessels, such as the Cornucopia, that produce food of their own accord may also inform this aspect of the Grail.

of thys felyship, for I have had an olde custom to have hem in my felyship." And therewith the teerys felle in hys yen; and than he seyde, "[A,] Gawayne, [Gawayne!] Ye have sette me in grete sorow, for I have grete doute[7] that my trew felyshyp shall never mete here more agayne." [8]

"A, sir," sayde Sir Launcelot, "comforte youreself; for hit shall be unto us a grete honoure, and much more than[8] we dyed in other placis, for of deth we be syker."

¶"A, Launcelot," seyde the Kynge, "the grete love that I have had unto you all the dayes of my lyff makith me to sey such dolefull wordis. For there was never Crysten kynge that ever had so many worthy men at hys table as I have had thys day at the Table Rounde. And that ys my grete sorow."

¶Whan the Quene, ladyes, and jantillwomen knew of thys tydynges, they had such sorow and hevynes that there myght no tunge telle, for tho knyghtes had holde them in honoure and charité. But aboven all othir, Quene Gwenyver made grete sorow: "I mervayle," seyd she, "that my lorde woll suffir hem to departe fro hym." Thus was all the courte trowbled for the love of[9] the departynge of these knyghtes. And many of tho ladyes that loved knyghtes wolde have gone with hir lovis—and so had they done, had nat an olde knyght com amonge them in relygious clothynge, and spake all on hyght and seyde, "Fayre lordis whych have sworne in the Queste of the Sankgreall:

¶"Thus sendith you Nacien the eremyte worde that none in thys Queste lede lady nother jantillwoman with hym, for hit ys nat to do[1] in so hyghe a servyse as they laboure in. For I warne you playne, he that ys nat clene of hys synnes, he shall nat se the mysteryes of Oure Lorde Jesu Cryste." And for thys cause they leffte thes ladyes and jantilwomen. So aftir thys the Quene com unto Sir Galahad and asked hym of whens he was and of what contrey. Than he tolde hir of whens he was. "And sonne unto Sir Launcelot?" [she said:] as to that, [he] seyde nother yee nother nay. "So God me helpe," seyde the Quene, "ye dare nat shame! For he ys the goodlyest knyght, and of the beste men of the worlde commyn— fol.354r

¶"And of the strene of all partyes of kynges;[2]

¶"Wherefore ye ought of ryght to be of youre dedys a passyng good man—and sertayne," she seyde, "ye resemble hym much."

¶Than Sir Galahad was a lityll ashamed, and seyde, "Madame, sithyn ye know in sertayne, wherefore do ye aske hit me? For he that ys my fadir shall be knowyn opynly and all betymys."[3] And than they wente unto reste them. And in honoure of the hyghnes of knyghthod, Sir Galahad he was ledde into kynge Arthures chambir, and there rested in hys owne bedde. And as sone as hit was day the Kynge arose, for he had no reste of all that nyght for sorow. 45

---

7. I.e., fear.
8. I.e., than if.
9. *For the love of:* i.e., on account of.
1. *Nat to do:* i.e., not done.
2. *Of the strene of all partyes of kynges:* from the stock of kings on all sides (of his ancestry).
3. *All betymys* : soon enough.

¶Than he wente unto Sir Gawayne and unto Sir Launcelot that were arysen for to hyre Masse; and than the Kynge agayne seyde, "A, Gawayne, Gawayne, ye have betrayed me! For never shall my courte be amended by you. But ye woll never be so sory for me as I am for you." And therewith the tearys began to renne downe by hys vysayge—and therewith the kynge seyde, "A, curteyse knyght, Sir Launcelot, I requyre you that ye counceyle me, for I wolde that thys Queste were at an ende and⁴ hit myght be."

¶"Sir," seyde Sir Launcelot, "ye saw yestirday, so many worthy knyghtes there were sworne that they may nat leve hit in no maner of wyse."

¶"That wote I well," seyde the Kynge, "but hit shall so hevy me at their departyng that I wote well there shall no maner of joy remedy me." And than the Kynge and the Quene wente unto the mynster.

¶So anone Sir Launcelot and Sir Gawayne commaunded hir men to brynge hir armys; and whan they all were armed sauff hir shyldys and her helmys, than they com to their felyship, whych were all redy in the same wyse, for to go to the monastery to hyre their Masse and servyse.

Than aftir servyse the Kynge wolde wete how many had undirtake the Queste of the Holy Grayle. Than founde they be tale an hondred and fiffty—and all tho were knyghtes ofthe Rounde Table. And than they put on their helmys and departed, and recommaunded them all hole unto the Kynge and Quene; and there was wepyng and grete sorow. Than the Quene departed into the chambir and holde hir there, that no man shold perceyve hir grete sorowys.

¶Whan Sir Launcelot myssed the Quene he wente tyll hir chambir, and whan she saw hym she cryed alowde and seyde, "A, Sir Launcelot, Launcelot, ye have betrayde me and putte me to the deth, for to leve thus my lorde!"

¶"A, madam, I pray you be nat displeased, for I shall com agayne as sone as I may with my worship."

¶"Alas," seyde she, "that ever I syghe you! But He that suffird dethe upon the Crosse for all menkynde, He be unto you good conduyte and saufté, and all the hole felyshyp."

¶Ryght so departed Sir Launcelot and founde hys felyship that abode hys commyng; and than they toke their horsys and rode thorow the strete of Camelot. And there was wepyng of ryche and poore—and the Kynge turned away and myght nat speke for wepyng.

¶So within a whyle they rode all togydirs tyll that they com to a cité and a castell that hyght Vagon. And so they entird into the castell; and the lorde thereof was an olde man and good of hys lyvyng, and sette opyn the gatis and made hem all the chere that he myght. And so on the morne they were all accorded that they sholde departe everych from othir; and on the morne they

fol.354v

4. I.e., if.

departed, with wepyng chere, and than every knyght toke the way
that hym lyked beste.

Ow rydith Galahad yet withouten shylde, and so rode foure [9]
dayes withoute ony adventure, and at the fourthe day aftir
evynsonge he com to a whyght abbay;[5] and there was he resceyved 5
with grete reverence and lad untyll a chambir, and there was he
unarmed. And than was he ware of two knyghtes of the Table
Rounde—one was Sir Bagdemagus, and Sir Uwayne—and whan they
sy hym they went to Sir Galahad and made of hym grete solace. fol.355r
And so they wente unto supper. 10

"Sirs," seyde Sir Galahad, "what adventure brought you hydir?"
"Sir," they seyde, "hit ys tolde us that in thys place ys a shylde, that
no man may bere hit aboute his necke but he be myscheved other
dede within three dayes, other maymed for ever." "But, sir," seyde
Kynge Bagdemagus, "I shall beare hit tomorne for to assay thys 15
adventure." "In the name of God!" seyde Sir Galahad. "Sir," seyde
Bagdemagus, "and I may nat encheve the adventure of thys shylde,
ye shall take hit uppon you, for I am sure ye shall nat fayle."

❡"Sir, I ryght well agré me thereto, for I have no shylde." So on
the morne they arose and herde Masse. Than Syr Bagdemagus asked 20
where the adventures shylde was. Anone a munke ledde hym
behynde an awter where the shylde hynge, as whyght as ony snowe,
but in the myddys was a rede crosse. "Syrres," seyde the monke,
"thys shylde oughte nat to be honged aboute the nek of no knyght
but he be the worthyest knyght of the worlde; therefore I counceyle 25
you, knyghtes, to be well avysed."

❡"Well," seyde Sir Bagdemagus, "I wote well I am nat the beste
knyght, but I shall assay to bere hit"—and so bare hit oute of the
monaster. Than he seyde unto Sir Galahad, "And hit please you to
abyde here styll, tylle that ye wete how that I spede?" 30

❡"Sir, I shall abyde you," seyde Sir Galahad. Than Kynge Bagdemagus toke with hym a good squyre, to brynge tydynges unto Sir
Galahad how he spedde. Than they rode two myle and com to a
fayre valey before an ermytayge; and than they saw a knyght com
frome that partyes in whyght armour, horse and all—and he com 35
as faste as hys horse myght renne, and hys speare in hys reeste.

Than Sir Bagdemagus dressed hys speare ayenste hym and brake
hit upon the whyght knyght; but the othir stroke hym so harde
that he braste the mayles and threste hym thorow the ryght sholdir—for the shylde coverde hym nat as at that tyme—and so he 40
bare hym frome hys horse. And therewith he alyght and toke hys
whyght shylde frome hym, saynge, "Knyght, thou hast done thy- fol.355v
selff grete foly, for thys shylde ought nat to be borne but by hym
that shall have no pere that lyvith." And than he com to Bagdemagus
squyre and bade hym, "Bere thys shylde to the good knyght Sir 45
Galahad that thou leffte in the abbey, and grete hym well by me."

❡"Sir, seyde the squyre, "what ys youre name?" "Take thou none

5. A whyght abbay: i.e., an abbey of Cistercian monks (who wear white habits).

hede of my name," seyde the knyghte, "for hit ys nat for the to know, nother none erthely[6] man."

¶"Now, fayre sir," seyde the squyre, "at the reverence of Jesu Cryst, telle me be what cause thys shylde may nat be borne but if the berer thereof be myscheved."

¶"Now syn thou hast conjoured[7] me so," seyde the knyght, "thys shelde behovith unto no man but unto Sir **Galahad**." Than the squyre wente unto **Bagdemagus** and asked hym whethir he were sore wounded or none.

¶"Ye forsoth," seyde he, "I shall ascape harde frome the deth." Than he fette hys horse and ledde hym with a grete payne tylle they cam unto the abbay. Than he was takyn downe sofftely and unarmed, and leyde in hys bedde and loked there to[8] hys woundys —and, as the booke tellith, he lay there longe and ascaped hard with the lyff.

¶"Sir **Galahad**," seyde the squyre, "that knyght that wounded **Bagdemagus** sende you gretyng, and bade that ye sholde bere thys shylde, wherethorow grete adventures sholde befalle." "Now blyssed be good fortune," seyde Sir **Galahad**. And than he asked hys armys and mownted uppon hys horse backe, and hanged the whyght shylde aboute hys necke and commaunded hem unto God. So Sir **Uwayne** seyde he wolde beare hym felyshyp if hit pleased hym.

¶"Sir, seyde Sir **Galahad**, "that may ye nat, for I must go alone— save thys squyre shall bere me felyship." And so departed Sir **Uwayne**. Than within a whyle cam Sir **Galahad** there as the whyght knyght abode hym by the ermytayge, and everych salewed other curteysly.

¶"Sir," seyde Sir **Galahad**, "by thys shylde bene many mervayles fallen?"

¶"Syr," seyde the knyght, "hit befelle aftir the Passion of Oure Lorde Jesu Cryste, two and thirty yere, that **Joseph of Aramathy**, that jantyll knyght the whych toke downe Oure Lorde of the Holy Crosse, at that tyme he departed frome Jerusalem with a grete party of hys kynrede with hym. And so he labourde tyll they com to a cité whych hyght **Sarras**; And that same owre that **Joseph** com to **Sarras**, there was a kynge that hyght **Evelake** that had grete warre ayenst the Sarezens—and in especiall ayenste one Sarezyn the whych was Kynge **Evelakes** cousyn, a ryche kynge and a myghty, whych marched nyghe hys londe: and hys name was called **Tholomé la Feyntis**. So on a day thes two mette to do batayle.

"Than **Joseph**, the sonne of [**Joseph of**] **Aramathy**, wente to Kyng **Evelake** and tolde hym he sholde be discomfite and slayne but he leffte hys beleve of the Olde Law[9] "and beleeve uppon the New

---

6. I.e., worldly, of this world. The implication is that Galahad is not of this world; often Malory will use this word to describe Launcelot, usually in a way which allows him to be seen as imperfect beside Galahad and yet still the best knight of *this* world.
7. I.e., constrained.
8. *Loked there to:* attended to, treated.
9. I.e., the religion of the Jews, who were considered by medieval Christians (followers of the "New Law") to have accepted the persuasion of the devil not to convert.

Law;" and anone he shewed hym the ryght beleve of the Holy Trynyté, for the whyche he agreed unto with all hys herte. And there thys shylde was made for Kyng **Evelake**, in the name of Hym that dyed on the Crosse. And than, thorow hys goodly belyeve, he had the bettir of Kynge **Tholomé**: for whan Kynge **Evelake** was in the batayle there was a clothe sette afore the shylde, and whan he was in the grettist perell he lett put awey the cloth; and than hys enemyes saw a vigoure[1] of a man on the crosse, wherethorow they all were discomfite:

¶ "And so hit befelle that a man of Kynge **Evelakes** was smytten hys honde off,[2] and bare that honde in hys other honde. And **Joseph** called that man unto hym and bade hym with good devocion touche the crosse; and as sone as that man had towched the crosse with hys honde, hit was as hole as ever hit was tofore. Than sone afftir there felle a grete mervayle, that the crosse of the shylde at one tyme vanysshed, that no man wyste where hit becam. And than Kynge **Evelake** was baptyzed, and the moste party of all the people of that cité:

¶ "So sone aftir **Joseph** wolde departe, and Kynge **Evelake** wolde nedys go with hym whethir he wolde or nolde. And so by fortune they com into thys londe, that at that tyme was called Grete Bretayne; and there they founde a grete felon paynym that put **Joseph** into preson. And so by fortune that[3] tydynges com unto a worthy man that hyght **Mondrames**, and he assembled all hys people for the grete renowne he had herde of **Joseph**; and so he com into the londe of Grete Bretaygne and disheryted thys fellon paynym, and confounded hym, and therewith delyverde **Joseph** oute of preson. And after that all the people withturned to the Crystyn feythe:

"So nat longe afftir, **Joseph** was leyde in hys dedly bedde;[4] and whan Kyng **Evelake** saw that, he had muche sorow, and seyde, 'For thy love I leffte my contrey, and syth ye sholl departe frome me oute of thys worlde, leve me som tokyn that I may thynke on you.' **Than Joseph** seyde, 'That woll I do full gladly. Now brynge me youre shylde that I toke[5] you whan ye wente into batayle ayenst Kyng **Tholomé**.'

"Than **Joseph** bledde sore at the nose, that he myght nat by no meane be staunched; and there uppon that shylde he made a crosse of hys owne bloode, and seyd, 'Now may ye se a remembraunce that I love you, for ye shall never se thys shylde but ye shall thynke one me—and hit shall be allwayes as freysh as hit ys now. And never shall no man beare thys shylde aboute hys necke but he shall repente hit, unto the tyme that **Galahad**, the good knyght, beare hit, and—laste of my lynayge—have hit aboute hys necke, that shall do many mervaylous dedys.'

¶ " 'Now,' seyde Kyng **Evelake**, 'where shall I put thys shylde, that thys worthy knyght may have hit?'

fol.356v 20

[11]

---

1. I.e., figure.
2. *Was smytten hys honde off:* had his hand cut off.
3. I.e., those.
4. *Dedly bedde:* deathbed.
5. I.e., gave.

¶" 'Sir, ye shall leve hit there as Nacien the ermyte shall put hit afftir hys dethe; for thydir shall that good knyght com, the fiftenth day afftir that he shall reseyve the order of knyghthode.' And so that day that they sette ys thys tyme that he have hys shylde; and in the same abbay lyeth Nacien the eremyte." And than the whyght knyght vanyshed. Anone, as the squyre had herde thes wordis, he alyght of hys hakeney and kneled downe at Galahadys feete, and prayde hym that he myght go [with hym] tyll he had made hym knyght.

¶"If I wolde [have felyship I wolde]⁶ nat refuse you."

¶"Than woll ye make me a knyght?" seyde the squyre. "And that order, by the grace of God, shall be well besette in me."

¶So Sir Galahad graunted hym and turned ayen unto the abbay there they cam fro; and there men made grete joy of Sir Galahad. And anone, as he was alyght, there was a munke brought⁷ hym unto a tombe in a chirche-yarde—"where ys such a noyse that who hyryth hit veryly shall nyghe be madde, other lose hys strengthe— and, sir, we deme hit ys a fyende." "Now lede me thydir," seyd Sir Galahad. And so they dud, all armed sauff hys helme. "Now," seyde the good man, "go to the tombe and lyffte hit up." And so he dud, and herde a grete noyse: and pyteuously he seyde, that all men myght hyre,

¶"Sir Galahad, the servaunte of Jesu Crist, com thou nat nyghe me, for thou shalt make me go agayne there where I have bene so longe."

¶But Sir Galahad was nothynge aferde, but heve up the stone; and there com oute a fowle smoke, and aftir that he saw the fowlyst vygoure lepe thereoute that ever he saw, in the lyknes of a man. And than he blyssed hym⁸ and wyst well hit was a fyende.

¶Than herde he a voyce sey, "Sir Galahad, I se there envyrowne aboute the so many angels that my power may nat deare⁹ the!"

¶Ryght so Sir Galahad saw a body all armed lye in that tombe, and besyde hym a swerde. "Now, fayre brothir," seyde Sir Galahad, "lette remeve thys body, for he ys nat worthy to lye within thys chyrche-yarde—for he was a false Crysten man." And therewithall they departed and wente to the abbay. And anone, as he was unarmed, a good man cam and set hym downe by hym—

¶And seyd, "Sir, I shall telle you what betokenyth of that ye saw in the tombe. Sir, that that¹ coverde the body, hit betokenyth the duras of the worlde, and the grete synne that Oure Lorde founde in the worlde. For there was suche wrecchydnesse that the fadir loved nat the sonne, nother the sonne loved nat the fadir. And that was one of the causys that Oure Lorde toke fleysh and bloode of

fol.357r

Here Galahad coni-
oure a devil out of
a tombe

[12]

---

6. The phrase is omitted from both the Winchester and Caxton versions, and is supplied on the model of Vinaver's similar emendation, using the likely text of Malory's French source as a guide (O³, p. 1549). An alternative, also consistent with the French, and first suggested by A. W. Pollard, is to change *If* to *Yes*. The current emendation seems preferable, however, inasmuch as Galahad has already agreed to the squire's "felyship" (p. 507, line 25) while declining Uwayne's.

7. I.e., who brought.

8. *Blyssed hym:* crossed himself.

9. I.e., harm.

1. *That that:* that which.

a clene maydyn; for oure synnes were so grete at that tyme that   fol.357v
well-nyghe all was wyckednesse."

¶"Truly," seyde Sir Galahad, "I beleve you ryght well." So Sir
Galahad rested hym there that nyght. And uppon the morne he
made the squyre a knyght, and asked hym hys name and of what   5
kynred he was com. "Sir," he seyde, "men calle me Melyas de Lyle,
and I am the sonne of the Kynge of Denmarke."

¶"Now, fayre sir," seyde Galahad, "sitthyn that ye be com of kynges and quenys, now lokith that knyghthode be well sette in you,
for ye ought to be a myrroure unto all chevalry." "Sir," seyde Sir   10
Melyas, "ye sey soth. But, sir, sytthyn ye have made me a knyght,
ye muste of ryght graunte me my first desyre that ys resonable."

¶"Ye say soth," seyde Galahad, "I graunte hit you." "Grauntmercy, myne owne lorde," seyde he—"and that ye woll suffir me
to ryde with you in thys Queste of the Sankgreall tyll that som   15
adventure departe us?" "I graunte you, sir." Than men brought Sir
Melias hys armour and his speare and hys horse; and so Sir Galahad
and he rode forth all that wyke or ever they founde ony adventure.
And than uppon a Munday, in the mornynge, as they were
departed frome an abbay, they com to a crosse whych departed   20
two wayes; and in that crosse were letters wretyn that seyd thus:

¶NOW YE KNYGHTES ARRAUNTE WHICH GOTH TO SEKE
KNYGHTES ADVENTURYS, SE HERE TWO WAYES: THAT ONE WAY
DEFENDITH[2] THE THAT THOU NE GO THAT WAY, FOR HE SHALL   25
NAT GO OUTE OF THE WAY AGAYNE BUT IF HE BE A GOOD MAN
AND A WORTHY KNYGHT; AND IF THOU GO ON THE LYFFTE
HONDE THOU SHALL NAT THERE LYGHTLY WYNNE PROUESSE,
FOR THOU SHALT IN THYS WAY BE SONE ASSAYDE.

"Sir," seyde Melyas unto Sir Galahad, "if hit lyke you to suffir me to
take the way on the lyffte honde [telle me,] for I shall well preve
my strength." "Hit were bettir," seyde Sir Galahad, "ye rode nat that
way, for I deme I sholde bettir ascape in that way—better than
ye."

¶"Nay, my lorde, I pray you lette me have that adventure." "Take
hit in Goddys name," seyde Sir Galahad.

Now turnyth the tale unto Syr Melyas de Lyle.[3]

2. I.e., forbid.
3. The cross in the margin appears at the same relative location (in the outside margin, with
its base aligned just below *Now turnyth* . . .) and at the same line height as it does in the
Winchester MS. The image presented here is a copy of the freehand drawing in the MS,
but has been rendered more symmetrical along its vertical axis; the original also leans
rather to the left. The drawing, done in red ink, is as likely to be an independent scribal
addition as it is part of Malory's original plan; whatever the case, it does provide a strikingly
apposite "landmark" for readers as they enter into the account of the Grail Quest in
earnest. Clearly, the drawing is meant to represent the *crosse whych departed two wayes*,
and its base and shaft are not dissimilar to the form of actual stone crosses of the period
(though its upper proportions as drawn would make a real stone cross precariously top
heavy). In emblematic terms the three steps of the pedestal are a definitive feature of
"Graded" (or "Calvary") crosses, and are traditionally held to represent the three graces
of Faith, Hope, and Charity, as well as—perhaps most significantly for the story of the
Grail Quest—the process of death, resurrection, and ascension.

And than rode Sir Melyas into an olde foreyste, and therin he roode two dayes and more. And than he cam into a fayre medow, and there was a fayre lodge of bowys; and than he aspyed in that lodge a chayre wherein was a crowne of golde, ryche and subtyly wrought—also there was clothys coverde uppon the erthe, and many delycious metis sette thereon.

¶ So Sir Melyas behylde thys adventure and thought hit mervaylous. But he had no hungir, but of the crowne of golde he toke much kepe; and therewith he stowped downe and toke hit up, and rode hys way with hit. And anone he saw a knyght com rydyng aftir hym that seyde, "Knyght, sette downe that crowne, whych ys nat youres—and therefore defende you!"

¶ Than Sir Melyas blyssed hym and seyde, "Fayre Lorde of Hevyn, helpe and save thy new-made knyght." And than they lette their horses renne as faste as they myght, and so they smote togydirs; but the othir knyght smote Sir Melyas thorow hawbirke and thorow the lyfft syde, that he felle to the erth nyghe dede. And than he toke hys crowne and yode hys way; and Sir Melyas lay stylle and had no power to styrre hym.

¶ So in the meanewhyle by fortune com Sir Galahad and founde hym there in perell of dethe; and than he seyde, "Sir Melyas, who hath wounded you? Therefore hit had bene bettir to have ryddyn the other way." And whan Sir Melyas herde hym speke, "Sir," he seyde, "for Goddys love, lat me nat dye in thys foreyst, but brynge me to the abbey here besyde, that I may be confessed and have my ryghtes."[4] "Hit shall be done," seyde Sir Galahad. "But where ys he that hath wounded you?"

¶ So with that Sir Galahad herde on[5] amonge the levys cry on hyght, "Knyght, kepe the from me!" "A, sir!" seyde Sir Melyas, "beware, for that ys he that hath slayne me." Sir Galahad answerde and seyde, "Sir knyght, com on your perell."

Than aythir dressed to other and com as fast as they myght dryve; and Sir Galahad smote hym so that hys speare wente thorow his shuldir, and smote hym downe of hys horse—and in the fallyng Sir Galahaddis speare brake.

¶ So with that com oute another knyght oute of the grene levys and brake a spere uppon Sir Galahad or ever he myght turne hym.

¶ Than Sir Galahad drew oute hys swerde and smote the lyffte arme off, that hit felle to the erthe; and than he fledde, and Sir Galahad sewed faste aftir hym—and than he turned agayne unto Sir Melyas. And there he alyght and dressed hym softely on hys horse tofore hym—for the truncheon of hys speare was in hys body. And Sir Galahad sterte up behynde hym and hylde hym in hys armys, and so brought hym to the abbay, and there unarmed hym and brought hym to hys chambir. And than he asked hys Saveoure,[6] and whan he had reseyved Hym, he seyde unto Sir Galahad, "Syr, latte Dethe com whan hit pleasith hym." And therewith he

[13]
fol.358r
How Sir Melyas
toke up the crowne of
golde

5

10

15

20

25

30

35

fol.358v

40

45

4. I.e., last sacraments.
5. I.e., someone.
6. *Asked hys Saveoure*: i.e., requested the last sacraments.

drew the truncheon of the speare oute of hys body, and than he sowned.

Than com there an olde monke whych somtyme had bene a knyght, and behylde Sir Melyas; and anone he ransaked hym,[7] and than he seyde unto Sir Galahad, "I shall heale hym of hys play, by the grace of God, within the terme of seven wykes."

¶Than was Sir Galahad glad, and unarmed hym and seyde he wolde abyde there stylle all that nyght. Thus dwelled he there three dayes; and than he asked Sir Melyas how hit stood with hym.

¶Than he seyde he was turned into helpynge[8]—"God be thanked." "Now woll I departe," Sir Galahad seyde, "for I have much on honde,[9] for many good knyghtes be fulle bysy aboute hit; and thys knyght and I were in the same Quest of the Sankgreal."

"Sir," seyde a good man, "for hys synne he was thus wounded. And I mervayle," seyde the good man, "how ye[1] durste take uppon you so rych a thynge as the hyghe order of knyghthode ys, withoute clene confession: that was the cause that ye were bittirly wounded, for the way on the ryght hande betokenyd the hygheway of Oure Lorde Jesu Cryst, and the way of a good trew lyver; and the othir way betokenyth the way of synnars and of myssebelevers, and whan the devyll saw your pryde and youre presumpcion for to take you to the Queste of the Sankgreal, that made you to be overthrowyn—for hit may nat be encheved but by vertuous lyvynge.

"Also, the wrytyng on the crosse was a significacyon of hevynly dedys, and of knyghtly dedys in Goddys workys, and no knyghtes dedys in worldly workis. And pryde ys hede of every synne: that caused thys knyght to departe frome Sir Galahad—and where thou toke the crowne of golde, thou ded syn in covetyse and in theffte. All this was no knyghtly dedys. And so, Sir Galahad, the holy knyght which fought with the two knyghtes, the two knyghtes signyfyeth the two dedly synnes whych were holy[2] in thys knyght, Sir Melias; and they myght nat withstonde you, for ye ar withoute dedly synne." So now departed Sir Galahad frome thens and betaughte hem all unto God.

¶Than Sir Melias seyde, "My lorde Syr Galahad, as sone as I may ryde I shall seke you."

¶"God sende you helthe," seyde Sir Galahad. And so he toke hys horse and departed, and rode many journeyes forewarde and bakwarde; and departed frome a place that hyght Abblasoure and had harde no Masse.

¶Than Sir Galahad com to a mowntayne where he founde a chapell passyng olde, and founde therein nobody, for all was desolate; and there he kneled before the awter and besought God of good counceyle.

¶And so as he prayde, he harde a voyce that seyd, "Go thou

[5]

[14]

[10]

[15]

[20]

fol.359r

[25]

[30]

[35]

[40]

[45]

---

7. *Ransaked hym*: examined his wounds.
8. *Turned into helpynge*: recovering.
9. *On honde*: in hand, to do.
1. The "good man" is now speaking to Melyas, but later speaks of him in the third person, as if turning to address Galahad and others, and then ends by speaking directly to Galahad.
2. I.e., wholly.

now, thou adventurus knyght, to the Castell of Maÿdyns, and there do thou away[3] the wycked customes."

⸿Whan Sir Galahad harde thys, he thanked God and toke hys horse; and he had nat ryddyn but a whyle but he saw in a valey before hym a stronge castell with depe dychys, and there ran besyde hyt a fayre ryver that hyght Sebarne. And there he mette with a man of grete ayge, and ayther salewed other, and Sir Galahad asked hym the castels name.

⸿"Fayre sir," seyde he, "hit ys the Castell of Maydyns, that ys a cursed castell, and all they that be conversaunte therein; for all pité ys oute[4] thereoff, and all hardynes and myschyff ys therein. Therefore I counceyle you, sir knyght, to turne agayne." "Sir," Sir Galahad seyde, "wete you welle that I shall nat turne agayne." Than loked Sir Galahad on hys armys that nothyng fayled hym,[5] and than he putte hys shylde before hym.

⸿And anone there mette hym seven fayre maydyns, the whych seyde unto hym, "Sir knyght, ye ryde here in grete foly, for ye have the watir to passe over."

⸿"Why shold I nat passe the watir?" seyde Sir Galahad. So rode he away frome hem and mette with a squyre that seyde, "Knyght, thoo knyghtes in the castel defyeth you and defendith[6] you ye go no farther tyll that they wete what ye wolde."

⸿"Fayre sir," seyde Sir Galahad, "I com for to destroy the wycked custom of thys castell." "Sir, and ye woll abyde by that, ye shall have inowghe to do!"

⸿"Go ye now," seyde Sir Galahad, "and hast my nedys."[7] Than the squyre entird into the castell; and anone aftir there com oute of the castell seven knyghtes—and all were brethirne. And whan they saw Sir Galahad, they cryed, "Knyght, kepe the, for we assure you nothyng but deth!"

⸿"Why," seyd Galahad, "woll ye all have ado with me at onys?"

⸿"Yee," seyde they, "thereto mayste thou truste."[8]

⸿Than Galahad put forth hys speare and smote the formyst to the erthe, that nerehonde he brake hys necke; and therewithall the other six smote hym on hys shylde grete strokes, that their sperys brake. Than Sir Galahad drew oute hys swerde and sette uppon hem so harde that hit was mervayle; and so thorow grete force he made hem for to forsake the fylde—and Sir Galahad chased hem tylle they entird into the castell, and so passed thorow the castell at another gate.

⸿And anone there mette Sir Galahad an olde man clothyd in relygyous clothynge, and seyde, "Syr, have here the kayes of thys castell." Than Sir Galahad openyd the gatis and saw so muche people in the stretys that he myght nat numbir hem—and all they

[15]
5

10

fol.359v

20

25

30

35

40

---

3. *Do thou away:* do away with.
4. I.e., driven out.
5. *Loked . . . on hys armys that nothyng fayled hym:* checked his equipment to make sure that none of it would malfunction.
6. I.e., warn.
7. *Hast my nedys:* i.e, hasten the completion of my mission.
8. *Thereto mayste thou truste:* i.e., trust us.

seyde, "Sir, ye be wellcom, for longe have we abydyn here oure delyveraunce." Than com to hym a jantillwoman, and seyde, "Sir, thes knyghtes be fledde, but they woll com agayne thys nyght, and here to begyn agayne their evyll custom."

⁋"What woll ye that I do?" seyde Sir Galahad. "Sir," seyde the jantilwoman, "that ye sende aftir all the knyghtes hydir that holde their londys of thys castell:

⁋"And make hem all to swere for to use the customs that were used here of olde tyme." "I woll well," seyde Sir Galahad. And there she brought hym an horne of ivery boundyn with golde rychely, and seyde, "Sir, blow thys horne, which woll be harde two myles aboute." Whan Sir Galahad had blowyn the horne, he sette hym downe uppon a bedde.

⁋Than com a pryste to Galahad, and seyde, "Sir, hit ys past a seven yere agone that thes seven brethirne com into thys castell and herberowde with the lorde of this castell, that hyght the Dyuke Lyanowre—and he was lorde of all this contrey. And whan they had aspyed the dyukes doughter, that was a full fayre woman, than by there false covyn they made a bate betwyxte hemselff;[9] and the deuke of hys goodnes wolde have departed them, and there they slew hym and hys eldyst sonne:

⁋"And than they toke the maydyn and the tresoure of the castell; and so by grete force they helde all the knyghtes of the contrey undir grete servayge and trewayge. So on a day the deukes doughter seyde to them, 'Ye have done grete wronge to sle my fadir and my brothir, and thus to holde oure londys. Natforthan,' she seyde, 'ye shall nat holde thys castell many yerys, for by one knyght ye shall all be overcom.'

⁋"Thus she prophecyed seven yerys agone.

⁋" 'Well,' seyde the seven knyghtes, 'sythyn ye sey so, there shall never lady nother knyght passe thys castell but they shall abyde magré their hedys[1] other dye therefore, tyll that knyght be com by whom we shall lose thys castell.' And therefore hit ys called the Maydyns Castell, for they have devoured[2] many maydyns." "Now," seyde Sir Galahad, "ys she here for whom thys castell was loste?" "Nay, sir," seyde the pryste, "she was dede within three nyghtes aftir that she was thus forsed; and sytthen have they kepte hir yonger syster whych enduryth grete payne, with mo other ladyes." By thys[3] were the knyghtes of the contrey com, and than he made hem to do omage and feawté[4] to the dukes doughter, and sette them in grete ease of harte.

And in the morne there com one and tolde Sir Galahad how that Sir Gawayne, Sir Gareth, and Sir Uwayne had slayne the seven brethirne. "I supposse well," seyde Sir Galahad, and toke hys armoure and hys horse, and commaunded hem unto God.

fol.360r

fol.360v

---

9. *By there false covyn they made a bate betwyxte hemselff*: through their treacherous conspiracy they concocted a quarrel amongst themselves.
1. *Magré their hedys*: against their will.
2. I.e., destroyed.
3. *By thys*: i.e., by this time.
4. On declarations of feudal loyalty, see n. 6, p. 9.

Here levith the tale of Sir Galahad, and spekith of Sir Gawayne.

Now seyth the tale, aftir Sir Gawayne departed, he rode many [16] journeys both towarde and frowarde;[5] and at the last he com to the abbey where Sir Galahad had the whyght shylde. And there Sir Gawayne lerned the way to sewe aftir Sir Galahad; and so he rode 5 to the abbey where Melyas lay syke—and there Sir Melyas tolde Sir Gawayne of the mervaylous adventures that Sir Galahad dud. "Sertes," seyde Sir Gawayne, "I am nat happy that I toke nat the way that he wente, for and I may mete with hym I woll nat departe from hym lyghtly; for all mervaylous adventures Sir Galahad 10 enchevith." "Sir," seyde one of the munkes, "he woll nat of youre felyship."

¶ "Why so?" seyde Sir Gawayne. "Sir," seyd he, "for ye be wycked and synfull, and he ys full blyssed." So ryght as they thus talked there com in rydynge Sir Gareth, and than they made grete joy aythir 15 of other. And on the morne they herde Masse and so departed; and by the way they mett with Sir Uwayne le Avowtres, and there Sir Uwayne tolde Sir Gawayne that he had mette with none adventures syth he departed frome the courte. "Nother yet we," seyd Sir Gawayne. And so ayther promysed othir of tho three knyghtes nat 20 to departe whyle they were in that Queste but if suddayne fortune caused hyt.

So they departed and rode by fortune tyll that they cam by the Castell of Maydyns; and there the seven brethirn aspyed the three knyghtes, and seyde, "Sytthyn we be flemyd by one knyght from 25 thys castell, we shall destroy all the knyghtes of Kyng Arthurs that we may overcom, for the love of[6] Sir Galahad." And therewith the seven knyghtes sette uppon hem three knyghtes; and by fortune Sir Gawayne slew one of the brethren; and ech one of hys felowys overthrew anothir, and so slew all the remenaunte. fol. 361r 30

And than they toke the wey undir the castell; and there they loste the way that Sir Galahad rode—and there everych of hem departed from other. And Syr Gawayne rode tyll he com to an ermytayge; and there he founde the good man seyynge hys evynsonge of Oure Lady. And there Sir Gawayne asked herberow for charité, 35 and the good man graunted hym gladly; than the good man asked hym what he was.

¶ "Sir," he seyde, "I am a knyght of Kynge Arthures that am in the Queste of the Sankgreall, and my name ys Sir Gawayne." "Sir," seyde the good man, "I wolde wete how hit stondith betwyxte God 40 and you."

¶ "Sir," seyd Sir Gawayne, "I wyll with a good wyll shew you my lyff[7] if hit please you." There he tolde the eremyte how a monke of an abbay "called me wycked knyght." "He myght well sey hit," seyde the eremyte, "for whan ye were made first knyght ye sholde 45 have takyn you to knyghtly dedys and vertuous lyvyng; and ye have done the contrary, for ye have lyved myschevously many wyntirs.

5. *Towarde and frowarde:* to and fro.
6. *For the love of:* i.e., on account of.
7. I.e., allow you to hear my confession.

"And Sir Galahad ys a mayde and synned never; and that ys the cause he shall enchyve where he goth that ye nor none suche shall never attayne—nother none in youre felyship—for ye have used[8] the moste untrewyst lyff that ever I herd knyght lyve. For sertes, had ye nat bene so wycked as ye ar, never had the seven brethirne be slayne by you and youre two felowys; for Sir Galahad hymself alone bete hem all seven the day toforne, but hys lyvyng ys such that he shall sle no man lyghtly. Also I may sey you that the Castell of Maydyns betokenyth the good soulys that were in preson before the Incarnacion of Oure Lorde Jesu Cryste:

¶"And the seven knyghtes betokenyth the seven dedly synnes that regned that tyme in the worlde; and I may lyckyn the good knyght Galahad unto the Sonne of the Hyghe Fadir that lyght within a maydyn and bought[9] all the soules oute of thralle:[1] so ded Sir Galahad delyver all the maydyns oute of the woofull castell. Now, Sir Gawayne," seyde the good man, "thou muste do penaunce for thy synne." "Sir, what penaunce shall I do?"

¶"Such as I woll gyff the," seyde the good man. "Nay," seyd Sir Gawayne, "I may do no penaunce, for we knyghtes adventures many tymes suffir grete woo and payne." "Well," seyde the good man, and than he hylde hys pece. And on the morne than Sir Gawayne departed frome the ermyte and bytaught hym unto God. And by adventure he mette wyth Sir Agglovale and Sir Gryfflet, two knyghtes of the Rounde Table; and so they three rode foure dayes withoute fyndynge of ony adventure. And at the fifth day they departed, and everych hylde as felle them[2] by adventure.

¶Here levith the tale of Syr Gawayne and hys felowys and spekith of Sir Galahad.

So whan Sir Galahad was departed frome the Castell of Maydyns he rode tyll he com to a waste forest; and there he mette with Sir Launcelot and Sir Percivale—but they knew hym nat,[3] for he was new dysgysed.

¶Ryght so hys fadir, Sir Launcelot, dressed hys speare and brake hit uppon Sir Galahad; and Sir Galahad smote hym so agayne that he bare downe horse and man. And than he drew his swerde and dressed hym unto Sir Percyvall, and smote hym so on the helme that hit rooff to the coyff of steele; and had nat the swerde swarved, Sir Percyvale had be slayne—and with the stroke he felle oute of hys sadyll. So thys justis was done tofore the ermytayge where a recluse dwelled. And whan she saw Sir Galahad ryde, she seyde, "God be with the, beste knyght of the worlde! A, sertes," seyde she all alowde—that Sir Launcelot and Percyvall myght hyre—"and yon-

[17]

fol.361v

---

8. I.e., lived.
9. I.e., ransomed.
1. *The good soulys . . . oute of thralle:* the story of the Harrowing of Hell, dependent largely on the apocryphal *Gospel of Nicodemus,* achieved wide popularity in the Middle Ages. According to the story, Christ descended to Hell upon His crucifixion and reclaimed many souls, including the necessarily pre-Christian souls of Adam, Eve, and Moses.
2. *Hylde as felle them:* attended to whatever befell them.
3. Cf. Luke 24:15–16 on the journey to Emmaus after the Crucifixion: "Jesus himself drew near, and went with them. But their eyes were holden that they should not know him."

dir two knyghtes had knowyn the as well as I do, they wolde nat
have encountird with the."

Whan Sir Galahad herde hir sey so, he was adrad to be knowyn;
and therewith he smote hys horse with his sporys and rode a grete
pace froward them. Than percyved they bothe that he was Sir Galahad, and up they gate on their horsys and rode faste aftir hym—
but within a whyle he was oute of hir syght, and than they turned
agayne wyth hevy chere, and seyde, "Lat us spyrre som tydynges,"
seyde Percyvale, "at yondir rekles." "Do as ye lyst," seyde Sir Launcelot. So whan Sir Percyvale com to the recluse, she knew hym well
ynoughe, and Sir Launcelot both.

But Syr Launcelot rode overthwarte and endelonge a wylde foreyst, and hylde no patthe but as wylde adventure lad hym. And at
the last he com to a stony crosse whych departed two wayes in
waste londe; and by the crosse was a stone that was a marble[4]—
but hit was so durke that Sir Launcelot myght nat wete what hyt
was.

⁋Than Sir Launcelot loked besyde hym and saw an olde chapell,
and there he wente to have founde people, and anone Sir Launcelot
fastenyd hys horse tylle a tre, and there he dud of hys shylde and
hynge hyt uppon a tre. And than he wente to the chapell dore and
founde hit waste and brokyn; and within he founde a fayre awter
full rychely arayde with clothe of clene sylke, and there stoode a
clene fayre candyllstykke whych bare six grete candyls therein—
and the candilstyk was of sylver.

⁋And whan Sir Launcelot saw thys lyght, he had grete wylle for to
entir into the chapell; but he coude fynde no place where he myght
entir. Than was he passyng hevy and dysmayed, and returned ayen
and cam to hys horse, and dud of hys sadyll and brydyll and leete
hym pasture hym, and unlaced hys helme and ungerde hys
swerde, and layde hym downe to slepe uppon hys shylde, tofore
the crosse.

⁋And so he felle on slepe; and half wakyng and half slepynge,
he saw commyng by hym two palfreyes all fayre and whyght, whych
bare a lytter, and therein lyyng a syke knyght—and whan he was
nyghe the crosse, he there abode stylle. All thys Sir Launcelot sye
and behylde hit—for he slepte nat veryly—and he herde hym sey,
"A, sweete Lorde, whan shall thys sorow leve me, and whan shall
the holy vessell com by me wherethorow I shall be heled? For I
have endured thus longe for litill trespasse."[5] A full grete whyle
thus complayned the knyght, and allways Sir Launcelot harde hit.

So with that Sir Launcelot sye the candyllstyk with the six tapirs
cam before the crosse, and he saw nobody that brought hit. Also
there cam a table of sylver, and the holy vessell of the Sankgreall,
which Sir Launcelot had sene toforetyme in Kynge Pecchers house.[6]
And therewith the syke knyght sette hym up, and hylde up both
hys hondys, and seyde, "Fayre swete Lorde, whych ys here within

fol.362r

5

10

15

20

25

30

[18]

35

fol.362v

40

45

4. I.e., a stone with an inscription.
5. I.e., sin.
6. I.e., the house of Peccher's grandson, King Pelles (see p. 464).

the holy vessell, take hede unto me, that I may be hole of thys malody." And therewith on hys hondys and kneys he wente so nyghe that he towched the holy vessell and kyst hit, and anone he was hole. And than he seyde, "Lorde God, I thanke The, for I am helyd of thys syknes."

⁋So whan the holy vessell had bene there a grete whyle, hit went unto the chapell with the chaundeler and the lyght, so that Sir **Launcelot** wyst nat where hit was becom; for he was overtakyn with synne, that he had no power to ryse agayne[7] the holy vessell (wherefore aftir that many men seyde hym shame—but he toke repentaunce aftir that). Than the syke knyght dressed hym up and kyssed the crosse; anone hys squyre brought hym hys armys and asked hys lorde how he ded.

⁋"Sertes," seyde he, "I thanke God, ryght well. Thorow the holy vessell I am heled—

⁋"But I have mervayle of thys slepyng knyght, that he had no power to awake whan thys holy vessell was brought hydir."

⁋"I dare well sey," seyde the squyre, "that he dwellith in som dedly synne whereof he was never confessed."

⁋"Be my fayth," seyde the knyght, "whatsomever he be, he ys unhappy; for, as I deme, he ys of the felyship of the Rounde Table whych ys entird in the Queste of the **Sankgreall**." "Sir," seyde the squyre, "here I have brought you all youre armys, save youre helme and youre swerde; and therefore, be myne assente, now may ye take thys knyghtes helme and his swerde." And so he dud; and whan he was clene armed, he toke there Sir **Launcelottis** horse, for he was bettir than hys, and so departed they frome the crosse.

Than anone Sir **Launcelot** waked and sett hym up, and bethought hym what he had sene there, and whether hit were dremys or nat; ryght so harde he a voyse that seyde, "Sir **Launcelot**,[8] more harder than ys the stone,[9] and more bitter than ys the woode, and more naked and barer than ys the lyeff of the fygge tre; therefore go thou from hens, and withdraw the from thys holy places!" And whan Sir **Launcelot** herde thys, he was passyng hevy and wyst nat what to do, and so departed sore wepynge and cursed the tyme that he was bore, for than he demed never to have worship more—for tho wordis wente to hys herte, tylle that he knew wherefore he was called so.

⁋Than Sir **Launcelot** wente to the crosse and founde hys helme, hys swerde, and hys horse away. And than he called hymselff a verry wrecch, and moste unhappy of all knyghtes; and there he seyde, "My synne and my wyckednes hath brought me unto grete dishonoure. For whan I sought worldly adventures for worldely desyres, I ever encheved them and had the bettir in every place—and never was I discomfite in no quarell, were hit ryght, were hit wronge. And now I take upon me the adventures to seke of holy thynges, now I se and undirstonde that myne olde synne hyndryth

---

7. I.e., in front of, before.
8. I.e., Sir Launcelot, who is.
9. I.e., seed.

me and shamyth me, that I had no power to stirre nother speke whan the holy bloode appered before me."

¶So thus he sorowed tyll hit was day, and harde the fowlys synge; than somwhat he was comforted.

¶But whan Sir Launcelot myssed his horse and hys harneyse, than he wyst well God was displesed with hym. And so he departed frome the crosse on foote into a fayre foreyste; and so by pryme[1] he cam to an hyghe hylle and founde an ermytage, and an ermyte therein whych was goyng unto Masse. And than Sir Launcelot kneled downe and cryed on Oure Lorde mercy for hys wycked workys.

¶So whan Masse was done Sir Launcelot called hym, and prayde hym for seynte charité for to hyre hys lyff. "With a good wylle," seyde the good man, and asked hym whethir he was of Kyng Arthurs and of the felyship of the Table Rounde.

¶"Ye, forsoth, sir, and my name ys Sir Launcelot du Lake, that hath bene ryght well seyde off[2]—and now my good fortune ys chonged, for I am the moste wrecch of the worlde." The ermyte behylde hym, and had mervayle whye he was so abaysshed.

"Sir," seyde the ermyte, "ye ought to thanke God more than ony knyght lyvynge, for He hath caused you to have more worldly worship than ony knyght that ys now lyvynge. And for youre presumpcion to take uppon you in dedely synne for to be in Hys presence where Hys fleyssh and Hys blood was, which caused you ye myght nat se hyt with youre worldely yen: for He woll nat appere where such synners bene, but if hit be unto their grete hurte other unto their shame. And there is no knyght now lyvynge that ought to yelde God so grete thanke as ye, for He hath yevyn you beauté, bownté, semelynes, and grete strengthe, over all other knyghtes. And therefore ye ar the more beholdyn unto God than ony other man to love Hym and drede Hym, for youre strengthe and your manhode woll litill avayle you and[3] God be agaynste you."

¶Than Sir Launcelot wepte with hevy harte, and seyde, "Now I know well ye sey me sothe." "Sir, seyde the good man, "hyde none olde synne frome me." "Truly," seyde Sir Launcelot, "that were me full lothe to discover,[4] for thys fourtene yere I never discoverde one thynge that I have used—and that may I now wyghte my shame and my disadventure." And than he tolde there the good man all hys lyff, and how he had loved a quene unmesurabely and oute of mesure[5] longe. "And all my grete dedis of armys that I have done, for the moste party was for the Quenys sake, and for hir sake wolde I do batayle were hit ryght other wronge; and never dud I batayle all only for Goddis sake, but for to wynne worship and to cause me the bettir to be beloved—and litill or nought I thanked never God of hit."

¶Than Sir Launcelot seyde, "Sir, I pray you counceyle me."

---

1. On prime, see n. 4, p. 86.
2. *That hath bene ryght well seyde off*: who has been very favorably spoken of.
3. I.e., if.
4. *Me full lothe to discover*: very loathsome to me to reveal.
5. *Oute of mesure*: unrestrainedly.

¶"Sir, I woll counceyle you," seyde the ermyte, "[yf] ye shall ensure me by youre knyghthode ye shall no more com in that quenys felyship as much as ye may forbere." And than Sir **Launcelot** promysed hym that he nolde, by the faythe of hys body.

¶"Sir, loke that your harte and youre mowth accorde," seyde the good man, "and I shall ensure you ye shall have the more worship than ever ye had."

¶"Holy fadir," seyde Sir **Launcelot**, "I mervayle of the voyce that seyde to me mervayles wordes, as ye have herde toforehonde."

¶"Have ye no mervayle," seyde the good man, "thereoff, for hit semyth well God lovith you. For men may undirstonde a stone ys harde of kynde,[6] and namely one more than another; and that ys to undirstonde by the, Sir **Launcelot**, for thou wolt nat leve thy synne for no goodnes that God hath sente the. Therefore thou arte more harder than ony stone, and woldyst never be made neyssh nother by watir nother by fyre[7]—and that ys the hete of the Holy Goste may nat entir in the. Now take hede: in all the worlde men shall nat fynde one knyght to whom Oure Lorde hath yevyn so much of grace as He hath lente the, for He hathe yeffyn the[8]—fayrenes with semelynes; also He hath yevyn the wytte and discression to know good frome ille; he hath also yeven prouesse and hardinesse, and gevyn the to worke so largely that thou hast had the bettir all thy dayes of thy lyff wheresomever thou cam. And now Oure Lorde wolde suffir the no lenger but that thou shalt know Hym, whether thou wolt other nylt. And why the voyce called the bitterer than the woode: for wheresomever much synne dwellith, there may be but lytyll swettnesse—wherefore thou art lykened to an olde rottyn tre:

¶"Now have I shewed the why thou art harder than the stone and bitterer than the tre; now shall I shew the why thou art more naked and barer than the fygge tre:

¶"Hit befelle that Oure Lorde on Palme Sonday[9] preched in Jerusalem, and there He founde in the people that all hardnes was herberowd in them, and there He founde in all the towne nat one that wolde herberow Hym. And than He wente oute of the towne and founde in myddis the way a fygge tre which was ryght fayre and well garnysshed of levys, but fruyte had hit none. Than Oure Lorde cursed the tre that bare no fruyte; that betokenyth the fyg tre unto Jerusalem, that had levys and no fruyte. So thou, Sir **Launcelot**, whan the Holy Grayle was brought before the, He founde in the no fruyte nother good thought nother good wylle, and defouled with lechory."

¶"Sertes," seyde Sir **Launcelot**, "all that ye have seyde ys trew,

5

10

15

20

25

30

fol.364v

35

40

---

6. *Of kynde* : by nature.
7. *Nother by watir nother by fyre*: i.e., neither by the water of baptism nor by the fire of the Holy Spirit. Cf. Matthew 24:32–33: "Now learn a parable of the fig tree; When his branch is yet tender, and putteth forth leaves, ye know that summer is nigh: so likewise ye, when ye shall see all these things, know that [God] is near, even at the doors."
8. Thee.
9. For the episode of Christ's entry into Jerusalem on Palm Sunday and His cursing of the fig tree, see Matthew 21.1–19.

and frome hensforewarde I caste me, by the grace of God, never
to be so wycked as I have bene but as to sew knyghthode and to
do fetys of armys." Than thys good man joyned[1] Sir Launcelot suche
penaunce as he myght do, and to sew knyghthode, and so assoyled
hym, and prayde hym to abyde with hym all that day. "I woll well,"
seyde Sir Launcelot, "for I have nother helme, horse, ne swerde."
"As for that," seyde the good man, "I shall helpe you or tomorne
at evyn of an horse[2] and all that longith unto you." And than Sir
Launcelot repented hym gretly of hys myssededys.

Here levith the tale of Sir Launcelot and begynnyth of Sir Percyvale
de Galis.

Now seyth the tale that whan Sir Launcelot was ryddyn aftir Sir
Galahad, the whych had all thes adventures aboven seyd, Sir
Percivale turned agayne unto the recluse, where he demed to have
tydynges of that knyght that Sir Launcelot folowed; and so he kneled
at hir wyndow and the recluse opened hit and asked Sir Percivale
what he wolde.

¶"Madam," he seyde, "I am a knyght of Kyng Arthurs courte and
my name ys Sir Percivale de Galis."

¶Whan the recluse herde his name she had grete joy of hym,
for mykyll she loved hym toforn passyng ony other knyght (she
ought so to do, for she was hys awnte). And than she commaunded
the gatis to be opyn, and there he had grete chere, as grete as she
myght make hym, or ly in hir power. So on the morne Sir Percyvale
wente to the recluse and asked her if she knew that knyght with
the whyght shylde.

¶"Sir," seyde she, "why woll ye wete?" "Truly, madam," seyde
Sir Percyvale, "I shall never be well at ease tyll that I know of that
knyghtes felyship, and that I may fyght with hym—for I may nat
leve hym so lyghtly, for I have the shame as yette."

¶"A, Sir Percyvale," seyde she, "wolde ye fyght with hym? I se
well ye have grete wyll to be slayne, as youre fadir was thorow
outerageousnes[3] slayne."

¶"Madam, hit semyth by your wordis that ye know me."

¶"Yee," seyde she, "I well oughte to know you, for I am youre
awnte, allthoughe I be in a poore place. For som men called me
somtyme the Quene of the Wast Landis, and I was called the
quene of moste rychesse in the worlde; and hit pleased me never
so much, my rychesse, as doth my poverté."

¶Than Percyvale wepte for verry pité whan he knew hit was hys
awnte. "A, fayre nevew," seyde she, "whan herde you tydynges of
youre modir?"

¶"Truly," seyde he, "I herde none of hir, but I dreme of hir
muche in my slepe; and therefore I wote nat whethir she be dede
other alyve."

---

1. I.e., enjoined, assigned.
2. *Helpe you or tomorne at evyn of an horse:* provide you before tomorrow evening with a
   horse.
3. I.e., recklessness.

⁋"Sertes, fayre nevew, youre modir ys dede. For aftir youre departynge frome her she toke such a sorow that anone as she was confessed, she dyed." "Now God have mercy on hir soule!" seyde Sir Percyvale. "Hit sore forthynkith me[4]—but all we muste change the lyff.[5] Now, fayre awnte, what ys that knyght?[6] I deme hit be he that bare the rede armys on Whytsonday."

⁋"Wyte you well," seyde she, "that this ys he, for othirwyse ought he nat to do but to go in rede armys; and that same knyght hath no peere, for he worchith all by myracle, and he shall never be overcom of none erthly mannys hande. Also Merlyon made the Rounde Table in tokenyng of rowndnes of the worlde, for men sholde by the Rounde Table undirstonde the rowndenes signyfyed by ryght.[7] For all the worlde, crystenyd and hethyn, repayryth unto the Rounde Table; and whan they ar chosyn to be of the felyshyp of the Rounde Table, they thynke hemselff more blessed and more in worship than they had gotyn halff the worlde—and ye have sene that they have loste hir fadirs and hir modirs, and all hir kynne, and hir wyves and hir chyldren, for to be of youre felyship:

"Hit ys well seyne be you; for synes ye departed from your modir, ye wolde never se her, ye founde such felyship at the Table Rounde. Whan Merlyon had ordayned the Rounde Table, he seyde, 'By them whych sholde be felowys of the Rounde Table the trouth of the Sankegreall sholde be well knowyn.' And men asked hym how they myght know them that sholde best do and to encheve the Sankgreall. Than he seyde, 'There sholde be three whyght bullis sholde encheve hit: and the two sholde be maydyns[8] and the thirde sholde be chaste—and one of thos three shold passe hys fadir as much as the lyon passith the lybarde, both of strength and of hardines.'

⁋"They that herde Merlion sey so seyde thus: 'Sitthyn there shall be such a knyght, thou sholdyst ordayne by thy craufftes a syge, that no man shold sytte in hit but he all only that shold passe all other knyghtes.' Than Merlyon answerde that he wold so do, and than he made the Syge Perelous in whych Galahad sate at hys mete on Whyttsonday last past."

⁋"Now, madam," seyde Sir Percyvale, "so much have I herde of you that, be my good wyll, I woll never have ado with Sir Galahad but by wey of goodnesse. And for Goddis love, fayre awnte, can ye teche me where I myght fynde hym? For much I wolde love the felyship of hym."

⁋"Fayre nevew," seyde she, "ye muste ryde unto a castell, the whych ys called Gooth, where he hath a cousyn jermayne,[9] and there may ye be lodged thys nyght. And as he techith you, sewith afftir as faste as ye can; and if he can telle you no tydynges of hym,

[2]

10

fol.365v   15

20

25

30

35

40

---

4. *Sore forthynkith me*: sorely causes me regret.
5. *Change the lyff*: i.e., pass on, die.
6. Malory seems to have forgotten that Percyvale has already identified this knight as Galahad (p. 517).
7. *By ryght*: truly.
8. I.e., virgins.
9. *Cousyn jermayne*: first cousin.

ryde streyte unto the castell of **Carbonek** where the Maymed Kyng
ys lyyng, for there shall ye hyre trew tydynges of hym."

Than departed Sir **Percivale** frome hys awnte, aythir makyng grete   [3]   fol.366r
sorow. And so he rode tyll aftir evynsonge, and than he herde a
clock smyte;[1] and anone he was ware of an house closed well with   5
wallys and depe dyches, and there he knocke at the gate. And
anone he was lette in, and [he alyght and] was ledde unto a chamber and sone onarmed.

¶And there he had ryght good chere all that nyght. And on the
morne he herde hys Masse; and in the monestery he founde a   10
preste redy at the awter, and on the ryght syde he saw a pew closed[2]
with iron, and behynde the awter he saw a ryche bedde and a fayre,
as of cloth of sylke and golde. Than Sir **Percivale** aspyed that therein
was a man or a woman, for the visayge was coverde. Than he leffte
of hys lokynge and herd hys servyse. And whan hit cam unto the   15
sakarynge,[3] he that lay within the perclose dressyd[4] hym up and
uncoverde hys hede; and than hym besemed a passyng olde man,
and he had a crowne of golde uppon hys hede, and hys shuldirs
were naked, and unhylled unto hys navyll. And than Sir **Percyvale**
aspyed hys body was full of grete woundys, both on the shuldirs,   20
armys, and vysayge—and ever he hylde up hys hondys agaynst
Oure Lordis body[5] and cryed, "Fayre swete Lorde Jesu Cryste, forgete nat me." And so he lay nat downe, but was allway in hys
prayers and orysons; and hym semed to be of the ayge of three
hondred wynter.   25

¶And whan the Masse was done the pryste toke Oure Lordys
Body and bare hit unto the syke kynge; and whan he had used hit,
he ded of[6] hys crowne and commaunded the crowne to be sett on
the awter.

¶Than Sir **Percyvale** asked one of the brethirn what he was. "Sir,"   30
seyde the good man, "ye have herde much of **Joseph of Aramathy**,
how he was sent [by Jhesu Cryst] into thys londe for to teche and
preche the holy Crysten faythe; and therefor he suffird many per-
secucions, the whych the enemyes of Cryst ded unto hym. And in
the cité of **Sarras** he converted a kynge whos name was **Evelake**;[7]   35
and so the kyng cam with **Joseph** into thys londe—and ever he was   fol.366v
bysy to be there as the **Sankgreall** was; and on a tyme he nyghed
hit so nyghe that Oure Lorde was displeased with hym, but ever
he folowed hit more and more, tyll God stroke hym allmoste
blynde. Than thys kynge cryed mercy, and seyde, 'Fayre Lorde, lat   40
me never dye tyll the good knyght of my blood of the nyneth degré[8]
be com, that I may se hym opynly that shall encheve the **Sankgreall**,
and that I myght kysse hym.'

---

1. I.e., strike the hour.
2. I.e., enclosed.
3. I.e., consecration (of the bread and wine).
4. I.e., sat.
5. *Agaynst Oure Lordis body*: i.e., against a crucifix.
6. *Used hit*: i.e., received the sacrament. *Ded of*: took off.
7. In Malory's French source, the king is renamed Mordrains upon his baptism; Malory later
   uses the new name (p. 580) without accounting for the change.
8. *Nyneth degré*: ninth generation.

"Whan the kynge thus had made hys prayers, he herde a voyce [4]
that seyde, 'Herde ys thy prayers, for thou shalt nat dye tylle he
hath kyssed the; and whan that knyght shall com the clerenes of
youre yen shall com agayne, and thou shalt se opynly, and thy
woundes shall be heled—and arst shall they never close.' And thus 5
befelle of Kynge Evelake, and thys same kynge hath lyved foure
hondred yerys thys holy lyff—and men sey the knyght ys in thys
courte that shall heale hym:

¶"Sir," seyde the good man, "I pray you telle me what knyght
that ye be, and if that ye be [of Kyng Arthurs courte and] of the 10
Rownde Table. "Yes, forsoth, and my name ys Sir Percyvale de
Galis." And whan the good man undirstood hys name, he made
grete joy of hym.

And than Sir Percyvale departed and rode tylle the owre of none.
And he mette in a valey aboute twenty men of armys whych bare 15
in a beere a knyght dedly slayne. And whan they saw Sir Percyvale,
they [asked] hym of whens he was; and he seyde, "Of the courte of
Kynge Arthur." Than they cryed all at onys, "Sle hym!" Than Sir
Percivale smote the firste to the erth, and hys horse uppon hym;
and than seven of the knyghtes smote uppon hys shylde at onys— 20
and the remenaunte slew hys horse, that he felle to the erth, and
had slayne hym ore takyn hym, had nat the good knyght Sir Galahad, with the rede armys, com there by adventure into tho partys.
And whan he saw all tho knyghtes uppon one knyght—

¶He [cryed], "Save me that knyghtes lyve!" And than he dressed 25
hym towarde the twenty men of armys as faste as hys horse myght
dryve, with hys speare in hys reaste, and smote the formyste, horse fol.367r
and man, to the erth. And whan his speare was brokyn, he sette
hys honde to hys swerde and smote on the ryght honde and on the
lyffte honde, that hit was mervayle to se. 30

And at every stroke he smote downe one or put hym to a rebuke,
so that they wolde fyght no more, but fledde to a thyk foreyst—
and Sir Galahad folowed them. And whan Sir Percyvale saw hym
chace them so, he made grete sorow that hys horse was away—
and than he wyst well hit was Sir Galahad, and cryed alowde and 35
seyde, "Fayre knyght, abyde and suffir me to do you thankynges,
for much have ye done for me!" But ever Sir Galahad rode fast, that
at the last he past oute of hys syght—and as fast as Sir Percyvale
myght, he wente aftir hym on foote, cryyng. And than he mette
with a yoman rydyng uppon an hakeney which lad in hys ryght 40
honde a grete steede, blacker than ony [beré.]

"A, fayre frende," seyde Sir Percivale, "as ever Y may do for you,
and to be youre knyght in the first place ye woll requyre me, that
ye woll lende me that blacke steed, that I myght overtake a knyght
which rydeth before me." 45

¶"Sir," seyde the yoman, "that may I nat do, for the horse is
such a mannys horse that he wolde sle me."

¶"Alas, seyde Sir Percivale, "I had never so grete sorow as I have
for losyng of yondir knyght." "Sir," seyde the yoman, "I am ryght
hevy for you, for a good horse wolde beseme you well, but I dare 50
nat delyver you thys horse but if ye wolde take hym frome me."

¶"That woll I nat," seyde Sir 𝔓𝔢𝔯𝔠𝔦𝔟𝔞𝔩𝔢. And so they departed, and Sir 𝔓𝔢𝔯𝔠𝔦𝔟𝔞𝔩𝔢 sette hym downe under a tre and made sorow oute of mesure; and as he sate, there cam a knyght rydynge on the horse that the yoman lad, and he was clene armyd.

¶And anone the yoman com rydynge and pryckyng aftir as fast as he myght, and asked Sir 𝔓𝔢𝔯𝔠𝔦𝔟𝔞𝔩𝔢 if he saw ony knyght rydyng on hys blacke steede.

¶"Ye, sir, forsothe—

¶"Why aske ye me, sir?"

"A, sir! that steede he hath benomme me with strengthe,[9] wherefore my lorde woll sle me in what place somever he fyndith me." "Well," seyde Sir 𝔓𝔢𝔯𝔠𝔶𝔟𝔞𝔩𝔢, "what woldist thou that I ded? Thou seest well that I am on foote; but, and I had a good horse, I sholde soone brynge hym agayne."

¶"Sir," syde the yoman, "take my hakeney and do the beste ye can, and I shall sew you on foote to wete how that ye shall spede."

¶Than Sir 𝔓𝔢𝔯𝔠𝔦𝔟𝔞𝔩𝔢 bestrode the hakeney and rode as faste as he myght; and at the last he saw that knyght, and than he cryde, "Knyght, turne agayne!" And he turned and set hys speare ayenst Sir 𝔓𝔢𝔯𝔠𝔦𝔟𝔞𝔩𝔢, and he smote the hackeney in myddis the breste, that he felle downe [dede] to the erthe—and there he had a grete falle; and the other rode hys way. And than Sir 𝔓𝔢𝔯𝔠𝔦𝔟𝔞𝔩𝔢 was wood wrothe and cryed, "Abyde, wycked knyght—cowarde and false-harted knyght!—turne ayen, and fyght with me on foote." But he answerd nat, but past on hys way.

¶Whan Sir 𝔓𝔢𝔯𝔠𝔦𝔟𝔞𝔩𝔢 saw he wolde nat turne, he kest away shylde, helme, and swerde, and seyde, "Now am I a verry wreche, cursed and moste unhappy of all other knyghte." So in thys sorow there he abode all that day tyll hit was nyght; and than he was faynte and leyde hym downe and slepte tyll hit was mydnyght. And than he awaked and saw before hym a woman whych seyde unto hym ryght fyersely, "Sir 𝔓𝔢𝔯𝔠𝔦𝔟𝔞𝔩𝔢, what dost thou here?"

¶"I do nother good nother grete ille."

¶"If thou wolt ensure me," seyde she, "that thou wolt fulfylle my wylle when I somon the, I shall lende the myne owne horse whych shall bere the whother thou wolt." Sir 𝔓𝔢𝔯𝔠𝔦𝔟𝔞𝔩𝔢 was glad of hir profer, and ensured hir to fulfylle all hir desire. "Than abydith me here, and I shall go fecche you an horse." And so she cam sone agayne and brought an horse with her (that was [inly] black).[1]

¶Whan Sir 𝔓𝔢𝔯𝔠𝔶𝔟𝔞𝔩𝔢 behylde that horse, he mervaylde that he was so grete and so well apparayled; and natforthan he was so hardy, he lepte uppon hym and toke none hede off hymselff.

¶And anone as he was uppon hym he threst to hym with hys spurres, and so rode by a foreste (and the moone shoone clere); and within an owre and lasse he bare hym foure dayes journey thense, untyll he com to a rowghe watir whych rored—and that horse wolde have borne hym into hit.

¶And when Sir 𝔓𝔢𝔯𝔠𝔦𝔟𝔞𝔩𝔢 cam nye the brymme, he saw the watir

---

9. *Benomme me with strengthe:* taken from me by force.
1. *Inly black:* inwardly black (i.e., fiendish).

so boysteous he doutted to passe over hit; and than he made a
sygne of the crosse in hys forehed.

¶Whan the fende felte hym so charged he shooke of Sir Percivale,
and he wente into the watir cryynge [and roryng] and makyng grete
sorowe—and hit semed unto hym that the watir brente.   5

¶Than Sir Percivale perceyved hit was a fynde, the whych wolde
have broughte hym unto perdicion. Than he commended hymselff
unto God, and prayde Oure Lorde to kepe hym frome all sucche
temptacions; and so he prayde all that nyght tylle on the morne
that hit was day. And anone he saw he was in a wylde mounteyne   10
whych was closed[2] with the se nyghe all aboute, that he myght se
no londe aboute hym whych myghte releve hym, but wylde bestes.

¶And than he wente downe into a valey; and there he saw a
serpente brynge a yonge lyon by the necke, and so he cam by Sir
Percivale. So with that com a grete lyon[3] cryynge and romyng[4] aftir   15
the serpente. And as fast as Sir Percivale saw thys, he hyghed hym
thydir; but the lyon had overtake the serpente and began batayle
with hym.

¶And than Sir Percivale thought to helpe the lyon, for he was
the more naturall beste of the two; and therewith he drew hys   20
swerde and sette hys shylde afore hym, and there he gaff the serpente suche a buffett that he had a dedely wounde.

¶Whan the lyon saw that, he made no sembelaunte to fyght
with hym, but made[5] hym all the chere that a beest myghte make[6]
a man.   25

¶Whan Sir Percivale perceyved hit, he kyst downe his shylde,
whych was brokyn, and than he dud of hys helme for to gadir
wynde, for he was gretly chaffed with the serpente. And the lyon
wente allwey aboute hym fawnynge as a spaynell; and than he
stroked hym on the necke and on the sholdirs and thanked God   30
of the feliship of that beste. And aboute noone the lyon toke hys
lityll whelpe and trussed hym and bare hym there he com fro.   fol.368v

Than was Sir Percivale alone. And as the tale tellith, he was at
that tyme one of the men of the worlde whych moste beleved in
Oure Lorde Jesu Cryste, for in tho dayes there was but fewe folkes   35
at that tyme that beleved perfitely—for in tho dayes the sonne
spared nat the fadir no more than a straunger; and so Sir Percivale
comforted hymselff in Oure Lorde Jesu and besought Hym that
no temptacion sholde brynge hym oute of Goddys servys, but to
endure as His trew champyon.   40

¶Thus whan Sir Percyvale had preyde, he saw the lyon com
towarde hym and cowched downe at his feet; and so all that nyght
the lyon and he slepte togydirs. And whan Sir Percivale slepte he
dremed a mervaylous dreme: that two ladyes mette with hym, and
that one sate uppon a lyon, and that other sate uppon a serpente,   45

2. I.e., enclosed, surrounded.
3. Cf. the description of Christ in Revelation 5:5 as "the Lion of the tribe of Judah."
4. I.e., roaring.
5. I.e., showed.
6. I.e., show.

and that one of hem was yonge, and that other was olde—and the
yongist, hym thought, seyde, "Sir Percyvale, my lorde salewith the
and sendeth the worde thou aray the and make the redy, for
tomorne thou muste fyght with the strongest champion of the
worlde:

¶"And if thou be overcom, thou shalt nat be quytte for losyng
of ony of thy membrys,[7] but thou shalt be shamed for ever to the
worldis ende." And than he asked her what was hir lorde; and she
seyde, "the grettist lorde of the worlde." And so she departed suddeynly, that he wyst nat where.

¶Than com forth the tothir lady, that rode uppon the serpente,   [7]
and she seyde, "Sir Percyvale, I playne unto you of that ye haye done
unto me, and I have nat offended unto you."

¶"Sertes, madam," seyde he, "unto you nor no lady I never
offended."

¶"Yes," seyde she, "I shall sey you why. I have norysshed in thys
place a grete whyle a serpente whych pleased me much [and
whych[8] served me a grete whyle;] and yestirday ye slew hym as he
gate hys pray.

¶"Sey me for what cause ye slew hym, for the lyon was nat
youres."

¶"Madam, I know well the lyon was nat myne. But for the lyon
ys more of jantiller nature than the serpente, therefore I slew   fol.369r
hym—and mesemyth I dud nat amysse agaynst you, Madam,"
seyde he—

¶"What wolde ye that I dud?" "I wolde," seyde she, "for the
amendis of my beste that ye becam my man." And than he
answerde and seyde, "That woll I nat graunte you." "No?" seyde
she. "Truly, ye were never but my servaunte syn ye resseyved the
omayge[9] of Oure Lorde Jesu Cryste. Therefore I you ensure, in
what place that I may fynde you withoute kepyng,[1] I shall take you
as he that somtyme was my man." And so she departed fro Sir
Percivale and leffte hym slepynge, whych was sore travayled of hys
avision. And on the morne he arose and blyssed hym—and he was
passynge fyeble.

¶Than was Sir Percivale ware in the see where com a shippe
saylyng toward hym; and Sir Percivale wente unto the ship and
founde hit coverde within and withoute with whyght samyte. And
at the [bord] stoode an olde man clothed in a surplyse, in lyknes
of a pryste.

¶"Sir," seyde Sir Percivale, "ye be wellcom." "God kepe you,"
seyde the good man. "And of whense be ye?"

¶"Sir, I am of Kynge Arthurs courte and a knyght of the Rounde
Table, whych am in the Queste of the Sankgreall; and here I am in
grete duras and never lyke to ascape oute of thys wyldernes."

---

7. *Be quytte for losyng of ony of thy membrys:* be acquitted by losing any of your limbs.
8. *And whych:* is not in Caxton but is supplied editorially as the likely cause of an eye-skip
   error there (where the phrase *whych pleased me much* is missing) and in the Winchester
   MS (where its missing phrase begins with *and*).
9. I.e., homage by way of sacrament (in baptism and communion).
1. *Withoute kepyng:* i.e., off guard.

"Doute ye nat," seyde the good man, "and ye be so trew a knyght as the order of shevalry requyrith, and of herte as ye ought to be, ye shold nat doute that none enemy shold slay you."

¶"What ar ye?" seyde Sir Percyvale. "Sir, I am of a strange contrey, and hydir I com to comforte you."

¶"Sir," seyde Sir Percivale, "what signifieth my dreme that I dremed thys nyght?" And there he tolde hym all togydir:

¶"She which rode uppon the lyon, hit betokenyth the New Law of Holy Chirche, that is to undirstonde fayth, good hope, belyeve, and baptyme; for she semed yonger than that othir hit ys grete reson, for she was borne in the Resurreccion and the Passion of Oure Lorde Jesu Cryste. And for grete love she cam to the to warne the of thy grete batayle that shall befalle the."

¶"With whom," seyde Sir Percivale, "shall I fyght?" "With the moste douteful[2] champion of the worlde, for, as the lady seyde, but if thou quyte the[3] welle thou shalt nat be quytte by losyng of one membir, but thou shalt be shamed to the worldis ende. And she that rode on the serpente signifieth the Olde Law,[4] and that serpente betokenyth a fynde. And why she blamed the that thou slewyst hir servaunte: hit betokenyth nothynge but the serpente ye slewe, that betokenyth the devyll that thou rodist on to the roche; and whan thou madist a sygne of the crosse, there thou slewyst hym and put away hys power. And whan she asked the[5] amendis and to becom hir man, than thou saydist nay, that was to make the beleve on her and leve thy baptym."

¶So he commaunded Sir Percivale to departe; and so he lepte over the boorde, and the shippe and all wente away, he wyste nat whydir.

¶Than he wente up into the roche and founde the lyon whych allway bare hym felyship, and he stroked hym uppon the backe and had grete joy of hym. Bi that Sir Percivale had byddyn there tyll mydday, he saw a shippe[6] com saylyng in the see as all the wynde of the worlde had dryven hit; and so hit londid undir that rocche. And whan Sir Percivale saw thys, he hyghed hym thydir and founde the shippe coverde with sylke more blacker than ony [beré]; and therein was a jantillwoman of grete beauté, and she was clothed rychly—there myght be none bettir.

¶And whan she saw Sir Percivale she asked hym who brought hym into thys wyldernesse, "where ye be never lyke to passe hense, for ye shall dye here for hunger and myscheff." "Damesell," seyde Sir Percivale, "I serve the beste man of the worlde, and in Hys servyse He woll nat suffir me to dye: for who that knockith shall entir, and who that askyth shall have, and who that sekith Hym, He hydyth Hym not unto hys wordys."[7]

¶But than she seyde, "Sir Percivale, wote ye what I am?"

5

fol.369v 10

15

20

25

30 [8]

35

40

fol.370r

45

2. I.e., fearsome.
3. Thee.
4. On the Old Law, see n. 9, p. 507.
5. Of thee.
6. On the symbolic possibilities of ships and boats in Malory, see n. 1, p. 616.
7. *For who that . . . unto hys wordys:* a close paraphrase of Matthew 7:7–8.

¶"Who taught you my name now?" seyde Sir Percivale. "I[8] knowe you bettir than ye wene: I com but late oute of the Waste Foreyste where I founde the rede knyght with the whyghte shylde." "A, fayre damesell," seyde he, "that knyght wolde I fayne mete withall." "Sir knyght," seyde she, "and ye woll ensure me by the fayth that ye owghe unto knyghthode that ye shall do my wyll what tyme I somon you, and I shall brynge you unto that knyght."

¶"Yes," he seyde, "I shall promyse you to fullfylle youre desyre."

¶"Well, seyde she, "now shall I telle you. I saw hym in the Waste Foreyste chasyng two knyghtes unto the watir whych ys callede Mortayse, and they drove into that watir for drede of dethe; and the two knyghtes passed over, and the Rede Knyght passed aftir, and there hys horse was drowned, and he thorow grete strengthe ascaped unto the londe." Thus she tolde hym, and Sir Percivale was passynge glad thereoff.

¶Than she asked hym if he had ete ony mete late.

¶"Nay, madam, truly I yeete no mete nyghe thes three dayes— but late here I spake with a good man that fedde me with hys good wordys and refreyshed me gretly."

¶"A, sir knyght, that same man," seyde she, "ys an inchaunter and a multiplier of wordis! For and ye belyve hym, ye shall be playnly shamed and dye in thys roche for pure hunger, and be etyn with[9] wylde bestis—and ye be a yonge man and a goodly knyght, and I shall helpe you and ye woll."

¶"What ar ye," seyde Sir Percivale, "that proferyth me thus so grete kyndenesse?" "I am," seyde she, "a jantillwoman that am diseryte, whych was the rychest woman of the worlde." "Damesell," seyde Sir Percivale, "who hath disheryte you? For I have grete pité of you."

¶"Sir," seyde she, "I dwelled with the grettist man of the worlde, and he made me so fayre and so clere that there was none lyke me. And of that grete beawté I had a litill pryde, more than I oughte to have had; also I sayde a worde that plesed hym nat. And than he wolde nat suffir me to be no lenger in his company, and so he drove me frome myne herytayge and disheryted me for ever—and he had never pité of me, nother of none of my counceyle nother of my courte.[1] And sitthyn, sir knyght, hit hath befallyn me to be so overthrowyn, and all myne; yet I have benomme hym som of hys men and made hem to becom my men, for they aske never nothynge of me but I gyff hem that and much more. Thus I and my servauntes were[2] ayenste hym nyght and day; therefore I know no good knyght nor no good man but I gete hem on my syde, and I may. And for that I know that ye ar a good knyght, I beseche you to helpe me—and for ye be a felowe of the Rounde Table, wherefore ye ought nat to fayle no jantillwoman which ys disherite and she besought you of helpe."

fol.370v

8. The lady is speaking.
9. I.e., by.
1. I.e., courtiers.
2. I.e., make war.

❡Than Sir **Percivale** promysed her all the helpe that he myght, [9] and than she thanked hym. And at that tyme the wedir was hote; than she called unto her a jantillwoman and bade hir brynge forth a pavilion. And so she ded, and pyghte hit uppon the gravell.

❡"Sir," seyde she, "now may ye reste you in thys hete of thys 5 day." Than he thanked her, and she put of hys helme and hys shylde, and there he slepte a grete whyle. And so he awoke and asked her if she had ony mete, and she seyde, "Yee, ye shall have inowghe." And anone there was leyde a table, and so muche meete was sette thereon that he had mervayle, for there was all maner of 10 meetes that he cowde thynke on. Also he dranke there the stren- gyst wyne that ever he dranke, hym thought, and therewith he was chaffett a lityll more than he oughte to be. With that he behylde that jantilwoman, and hym thought she was the fayryst creature fol.371r that ever he saw. 15

❡And than Sir **Percivale** profird hir love, and prayde hir that she wolde be hys. Than she refused hym in a maner whan he requyred her, for cause he sholde be the more ardente on hir; and ever he sesed nat to pray hir of love. And whan she saw hym well enchaf- fed, than she seyde, "Sir **Percivale**, wyte you well I shall nat fulfylle 20 youre wylle but if ye swere frome henseforthe ye shall be my trew servaunte, and to do nothynge but that I shall commaunde you—

❡"Woll ye ensure me thys, as ye be a trew knyght?"

❡"Yee," seyde he, "fayre lady, by the feythe of my body!"

❡"Well," seyde she, "now shall ye do with me what ye wyll—and 25 now, wyte you well, ye ar the knyght in the worlde that I have moste desyre to." And than two squyres were commaunded to make a bedde in myddis of the pavelon, and anone she was unclothed and leyde therein.

❡And than Sir **Percivale** layde hym downe by her, naked; and by 30 adventure and grace he saw hys swerde ly on the erthe, naked, where in the pomell was a rede crosse and the sygne of the crucifixe therin, and bethought hym on hys knyghthode and hys promyse made unto the good man tofornehande; and than he made a sygne [of the crosse in his forehede:] and therewith the pavylon turned 35 up-so-downe, and than hit chonged unto a smooke and a blak clowde. And than he drad sore, and cryed alowde, "Fayre swete [10] Lorde Jesu Cryste, ne lette me nat be shamed, which was nyghe loste had nat Thy good grace bene!" And than he loked unto her shippe and saw her entir therein, which seyde, "Syr **Percivale**, ye 40 have betrayde me." And so she wente with the wynde, rorynge and yellynge, that hit semed all the water brente after her.[3]

❡Than Sir **Percivale** made grete sorow, and drew hys swerde unto hym and seyde, "Sitthyn my fleyssh woll be my mayster, I shall punyssh hit." And therewith he rooff hymselff thorow the thygh,[4] fol.371v 45 that the blood sterte aboute hym, and seyde, "A, good Lord, take

---

3. Cf. the departure of the demon horse, p. 526.
4. On a possible (and, for the Middle Ages, not unconventional) interpretation of this wound, see below, n. 6, p. 563.

thys in recompensacion of that I have myssedone ayenste The, Lorde."

¶So than he clothed hym and armed hym and called hymself "wrecche of all wrecchis—how nyghe I was loste, and to have lost that I sholde never have gotyn agayne, that was my virginité, for that may never be recoverde aftir hit ys onys loste." And than he stopped hys bledyng woundes with a pece of hys sherte.

¶Thus as he made hys mone, he saw the same shippe com fro the oryente that the good man was in the day before. And thys noble knyght was sore ashamed of hymselff, and therewith he fylle in a sowne. And whan he awooke he wente unto hym waykely, and there he salewed the good man.

¶And than he asked Sir Percivale, "How haste thou done syth I departed?"

¶"Sir," seyde he, "here was a jantillwoman, and ledde me into dedly synne." And there he tolde hym all togidirs. "Knew ye nat that mayde?" seyde the good man.

¶"Sir," seyde he, "nay—but well I wote the fynde sente hir hydir to shame me." "A, good knyght," seyde he, "thou arte a foole; for that jantillwoman was the mayster fyende of helle, which hath pousté over all other devyllis—and that was the olde lady that thou saw in thyne avision rydyng on the serpente!"

¶Than he tolde Sir Percivale how "Oure Lorde Jesu Cryste bete hym oute of hevyn for hys synne, whycch was the moste bryghtist angell of hevyn[5]—and therefore he loste hys heritaige—and that was the champion that thou fought withall, whych had overcom the, had nat the grace of God bene:

¶"Now, Sir Percivale, beware and take this for an insample."[6] And than the good man vanysshed. Than Sir Percivale toke hys armys, and entirde into the shippe, and so he departed from thens.

¶So levith thys tale, and turnyth unto Sir Launcelot.

Whan the eremyte had kepte Sir Launcelot three dayes, than the eremyte gate hym an horse, a helme, and a swerde; and than he departed and rode untyll the owre of none. And than he saw a litill house, and whan he cam nere he saw a lityll chapell; and there besyde he sye an olde man which was clothed all in whyght full rychely. And than Sir Launcelot seyde, "Sir, God save you!"

¶"Sir, God kepe you," seyde the good man, "and make you a good knyght."

¶Than Sir Launcelot alyght and entird into the chapell, and there he saw an olde man, dede, and in a whyght sherte of passyng fyne clothe. "Sir," seyde the good man, "this man ought nat to be in such clothynge as ye se hym in, for in that he brake the othe of hys order, for he hath bene more than an hondred wynter a man

[XV.1]

fol.372r

---

5. On the rebellion of Satan and the other fallen angels, see Revelation 13:7–17. Cf. the gentlewoman's (now clearly allegorical) story of herself, on p. 529.

6. I.e., moral lesson.

of religion."[7] And than the good man and Sir Launcelot [went into the chapell;] and the good man toke a stole aboute hys neck, and a booke, and than he conjoured[8] on that booke. And with that they saw the fyende in an hydeous fygure, that there was no man so hardé-herted in the worlde but he sholde a bene aferde.

¶Than seyde the fyende, "Thou haste travayle me gretly! Now telle me what thou wolte with me." "I woll," seyde the good man, "that thou telle me how my brothir becam dede, and whether he be saved or dampned."

¶Than he seyde with an horrible voice, "He ys nat lost, but he ys saved."

¶"How may that be?" seyde the good man. "Hit semyth me that he levith nat well, for he brake hys order for to were a sherte where he ought to were none; and who that trespassith ayenst oure order doth nat well." "Nat so," seyde the fyende. "Thys man that lyeth here was com of grete lynage. And there was a lorde that hyght the Erle de Vale that hylde grete warre ayenste thys mannes nevew, which hyght Aguaurs; and so thys Aguaurs saw the erle was bygger than he:

¶"Than he wente for to take counceyle of hys uncle, which lyeth dede here [as ye may se,] and than he wente oute of hys ermytaige for to maynteyne his nevew ayenste the myghty erle. And so hit happed that thys man that lyeth dede, ded so muche by hys wyse-dom and hardines that the erle was take, and three of hys lordys, by force of thys dede man:

¶"Than was there pees betwyxte thys erle and thys Aguaurs, and grete sureté that the erle sholde never warre agaynste hym more. Than this dede man that here lyeth cam to thys ermytayge agayne. And than the erle made two of hys nevews for to be avenged uppon this man; so they com on a day and founde thys dede man at the sakerynge of hys Masse, and they abode hym tyll he had seyde Masse, and than they sette uppon hym and drew oute their swerdys to have slayne hym—but there wolde no swerde byghte on hym more than uppon a gadde of steele, for the Hyghe Lorde which he served, He hym preserved:

¶"Than made they a grete fyre and dud of all hys clothys and the heyre[9] of hys backe. And than thys dede man ermyte seyde unto them, 'Wene ye to bren me? Hit shall nat lyghe in youre power, nother to perish me[1] as much as a threde, and there were ony on my body.'

¶" 'No?' seyde one of them. 'Hit shall be assayde.' And than they dispoyled hym, and put uppon hym hys sherte, and kyste hym in a fyre; and there he lay all that day tyll hit was nyght in that fyre, and was nat dede. And so in the morne than com I and founde hym—dede—but I founde neyther threde nor skynne tamed. So

[2]

fol.372v

---

7. I.e., a religious order.
8. I.e., began an exorcism.
9. I.e., hair shirt (a course haircloth shirt worn to mortify the flesh and remind the wearer of the vanity of worldly comforts).
1. *Perish me:* destroy of me.

toke they hym oute of the fyre, with grete feare, and leyde hym here as ye may se—

⸿"And now may ye suffir me to go my way, for I have seyde you the sothe." And than he departed with a grete tempest. Than was the good man and Sir Launcelot more gladder than they were tofore. And than Sir Launcelot dwelled with that good man that nyght. "Sir," seyde the good man, "be ye nat Sir Launcelot du Lake?" "Ye, sir," seyde he.

⸿"Sir, what seke you in thys contrey?"

⸿"I go, sir, to seke the adventures of the Sankgreall." "Well," seyde he, "seke ye hit ye may well:

⸿"But thoughe hit were here, ye shall have no power to se hit— no more than a blynde man that sholde se a bryght swerde—and that ys longe on² youre synne, and ellys ye were more abeler than ony man lyvynge." And than Sir Launcelot began to wepe. Than seyde the good man, "Were ye confessed synne ye entred into the Queste of the Sankgreall?" "Ye, sir," seyde Sir Launcelot. Than uppon the morne, whan the good man had songe hys Masse, than they buryed the dede man.

⸿"Now," seyde Sir Launcelot, "fadir, what shall I do?" "Now," seyde the good man, "I requyre you take thys hayre that was thys holy mannes and put hit nexte thy skynne, and hit shall prevayle the³ gretly."

⸿"Sir, than woll I do hit," seyde Sir Launcelot. "Also, sir, I charge the that thou ete no fleysshe as longe as ye be in the Queste of Sankgreall, nother ye shall drynke no wyne, and that ye hyre Masse dayly and ye may com thereto. So he toke the hayre and put hit uppon hym, and so departed at evynsonge, and so rode into a for- eyste; and there he mette with a jantillwoman rydyng uppon a whyght palferey, and than she asked hym, "Sir knyght, whother ryde ye?"

⸿"Sertes, damesell," seyde Sir Launcelot, "I wote nat whothir I ryde but as fortune ledith me."

⸿"A, Sir Launcelot," seyde she, "I wote what adventure ye seke, for ye were beforetyme nerar than ye be now—and yet shall ye se hit more opynly than ever ye dud, and that shall ye undirstonde in shorte tyme."

⸿Than Sir Launcelot asked her where he myght be harberowde that nyght. "Ye shall none fynde thys day nor nyght; but tomorne ye shall fynde herberow goode, and ease of that⁴ ye bene in doute off." And than he commaunded hir unto God, and so he rode tylle that he cam to a crosse, and toke that for hys oste as for that nyght.

⸿And so he put hys horse to pasture, and ded of hys helme and hys shylde, and made hys prayers unto the crosse that he never falle in dedely synne agayne; and so he leyde hym downe to slepe. And anone as he was on slepe, hit befylle hym there a vision, that there com a man afore hym all bycompast with sterris; and that

5

10

15

20

25 fol.373r

30

35

40

[3]

The avision of Sir Launcelot

---

2. *Longe on:* owing to.
3. Thee.
4. I.e., that which.

man had a crowne of golde on hys hede, and that man lad in hys felyship seven kynges and two knyghtes; and all thes worshipt the crosse, knelyng uppon their kneys, holdyng up their hondys towarde the hevyn, and all they seyde, "Swete Fadir of Hevyn, com and visite us, and yelde unto everych of us as we have deserved."

¶Than loked Sir Launcelot up to the hevyn, and hym semed the clowdis ded opyn, and an olde man com downe with a company of angels and alyghte amonge them and gaff unto everych hys blys-synge and called them hys servauntes and hys good and trew knyghtes. And whan thys olde man had seyde thus, he com to one of the knyghtes, and seyde, "I have loste all that I have besette in the, for thou hast ruled the ayenste me as a warryoure and used wronge warris with vayneglory for the pleasure of the worlde more than to please me; therefore thou shalt be confounded withoute⁵ thou yelde me my tresoure." All thys avision saw Sir Launcelot at the crosse. And on the morne he toke hys horse and rode tylle mydday.

¶And there by adventure he mette the same knyght that toke hys horse, helme, and hys swerde whan he slepte, whan the Sank-greall appered afore the crosse.

¶So whan Sir Launcelot saw hym, he salewede hym nat fayre, but cryed on hyght, "Knyght, kepe the! For thou deddist me grete unkyndnes." And than they put afore them their spearis; and Sir Launcelot com so fyersely that he smote hym and hys horse downe to the erthe, that he had nyghe brokyn hys neck. Than Sir Launcelot toke the knyghtes horse that was hys owne beforehonde, and descended frome the horse he sate uppon and mownted uppon hys horse, and tyed the knyghtes owne horse to a tre, that he myght fynde that horse whan he was rysen.

¶Than Sir Launcelot rode tylle nyght; and by adventure he mette an ermyte, and eche of hem salewd other. And there he reste with that good man all nyght, and gaff hys horse suche as he myght gete. Than seyde the good man unto Sir Launcelot, "Of whens be ye?" "Sir," seyde he, "I am of Arthurs courte, and my name ys Sir Launcelot de Lake, that am in the Queste of the Sankegreall—and therefor, sir, I pray you counceile me of a vision that I saw thys nyght." And so he tolde hym all.

"Lo, Sir Launcelot," seyde the good man, "there myght thou undir-stonde the hyghe lynayge that thou arte com off, that thyne avision betokenyth. Aftir the Passion of Jesu Cryste, fourty yere, Joseph of Aramathy preched of the victory of Kynge Evelake, that he had in hys batayles the bettir of hys enemyes.⁶ And of the seven kynges and the two knyghtes, the firste of hem ys called Nappus, an

5. I.e., unless.
6. The relationship between this and the next sentence is not at all clear without reference to the (rather labyrinthine) French, and may represent a passage that was either beyond Malory's translational will to follow or that confused a subsequent copyist into rendering a text beyond repair; the former seems more likely insofar as the first account of Laun-celot's dream also appears to have been abridged: (see n. 9, p. 535). For the corresponding passage from the French, see p. 734. In short, Launcelot is descended from the grand-father of the visionary Nacien, who was brother-in-law to Evelake (who later took the baptized name of Mordrains).

fol.373v

holy man; and the secunde hyght **Nacien** in remembraunce of hys grauntesyre—and in hym dwelled Oure Lord Jesu Cryst; and the third was called **Hellyas le Grose**; and the fourth hyght **Lysays**:

"And the fifth hyght **Jonas**; he departed oute of hys contrey and wente into Walis and toke there the doughter of **Manuell**, whereby he had the londe **Gaule**; and he com to dwelle in thys contrey, and of hym com Kynge **Launcelot**, thy grauntesyre, whych were wedded to the Kynges doughter of Irelonde—and he was as worthy a man as thou arte; and of hym cam kynge **Ban**, thy fadir, whych was the laste of the seven kynges. And by the, Sir **Launcelot**, hit signyfieth that the angels seyde thou were none of the seven felysship:[7]

❡"And the last was the nyneth knyght; he was signyfyed to a lyon,[8] for he sholde passe all maner of erthely knyghtes: that ys Sir **Galahad**, whych thou gate on Kynge **Pelles** doughter. And thou ought to thanke God more than ony othir man lyvyng, for of a synner erthely thou hast no pere as in knyghthode, nother never shall have;[9] but lytyll thanke hast thou yevyn to God for all the grete vertuys that God hath lente the."

❡"Sir," seyde Sir **Launcelot**, "ye sey that good knyght ys my sonne?"

"That ought thou to know," seyde the good man, "for thou knew the doughter of Kyng **Pelles** fleyshly, and on her thou begatist Sir **Galahad**, and that was he that at the feste of Pentecoste sate in the Syge Perelous; and therefore make thou hit to be knowyn opynly that he ys of thy begetynge. And [I counceyle the,] in no place prees nat uppon hym to have ado with hym, for hit woll nat avayle no knyght to have ado with hym."

❡"Well," seyde Sir **Launcelot**, "mesemyth that good knyght shold pray for me unto the Hyghe Fadir, that I falle nat to synne agayne." "Truste thou well," seyde the good man, "thou faryst muche the better for hys prayer. For the sonne shall nat beare the wyckednesse of the [fader, nor the fader shalle not bere the wyckednes of the] sonne, but every man shall beare hys owne burdon; and therefore beseke thou only God, and He woll helpe the in all thy nedes."

And than Sir **Launcelot** and he wente to supere, and so leyde hem to reste; and [the] heyre prycked faste [Syr **Launcelots** skynne] and greved hym sore, but he toke hyt mekely and suffirde the payne. And so on the morne he harde hys Masse and toke hys armys and so toke hys leve, and mownted uppon hys horse and rode into a foreyst and helde no hygheway. And as he loked before hym he sye a fayre playne, and besyde that a fayre castell, and before the castell were many pavelons of sylke and of dyverse hew.

fol.374r   5

10

15

20

25

30

35

[5]   40
fol.374v

---

7. *Thou were none of the seven felysship*: i.e., you were not one of the seven kings, but you were one of the two knights.
8. This detail does not occur in Malory's foregoing account, but does occur in his source.
9. *For of a synner . . . never shall have*: here Malory mitigates the critique of his favorite knight's failings endemic to his French model, which at this point stresses that Galahad cannot be matched in chivalry by anyone (cf., n. 1, p. 543). On Malory's use of *erthely*, see n. 6, p. 507.

And hym semed that he saw there fyve hondred knyghtes rydynge on horsebacke, and there was two partyes: they that were of the castell were all on black horsys, and their trappoures black; and they that were withoute were all on whyght horsis and trappers. So there began a grete turnemente, and everyche hurteled with other, that hit mervayled Sir Launcelot gretly; and at the laste hym thought they of the castell were putt to the wars.[1]

¶Than thought Sir Launcelot for to helpe there the wayker party, in incresyng of hys shevalry.

¶And so Sir Launcelot threste in amonge the party of the castell, and smote downe a knyght, horse and man, to the erthe; and than he russhed here and there and ded many mervaylous dedis of armys. And than he drew oute hys swerde and strake many knyghtes to the erth, that all that saw hym mervayled that ever one knyght myght do so grete dedis of armys.

¶But allwayes the whyght knyghtes hylde them nyghe aboute Sir Launcelot for to tire hym and wynde hym; and at the laste [—as a man may not ever endure—] Sir Launcelot [waxed so faynt of— fyghtyng and travaillyng, and] was so wery of hys grete dedis, that he myght nat lyffte up hys armys for to gyff one stroke, that he wente never[2] to have borne armys.

¶And than they all toke and ledde hym away into a foreyste and there made hym to alyght to reeste hym. And than all the felyship of the castell were overcom for the defaughte of hym. Than they seyd all unto Sir Launcelot, "Blessed be God that ye be now of oure felyship, for we shall holde you in oure preson."[3] And so they leffte hym with few wordys.

¶And than Sir Launcelot made grete sorowe—"for never or now was I never at turnemente nor at justes but I had the beste; and now I am shamed, and am sure that I am more synfuller than ever I was." Thus he rode sorowyng, and halff a day oute of dispayre, tyll that he cam into a depe valey. And whan Sir Launcelot sye he myght nat ryde up unto the mountayne, he there alyght undir an appyll tre. And there he leffte hys helme and hys shylde, and put hys horse unto pasture; and than he leyde hym downe to slepe. And than hym thought there com an olde man afore hym whych seyde, "A, Launcelot, of evill wycked fayth and poore beleve!

¶"Wherefore ys thy wyll turned so lyghtly toward dedly synne?" And whan he had seyde thus he vanysshed away, and Sir Launcelot wyst nat where he becom.

¶Than he toke hys horse and armed hym; and as he rode by the hygheway he saw a chapell where was a recluse, which had a wyndow that she myght se up to the awter.[4] And all aloude she called Sir Launcelot, for that he semed a knyght arraunte. And than he

fol.375r

---

1. I.e., worse.
2. I.e., never again.
3. I.e., the forest, the mock prison of the tournament.
4. This recluse, like the famous English author and anchoress, Julian of Norwich, is enclosed in a cell within a church. The cell could have a number of windows, at least one of which would provide a view of the high altar so that the recluse could follow the Mass. People would regularly visit the recluse for spiritual guidance and to request prayers.

cam, and she asked hym what he was, and of what place, and where aboute he wente to seke.

And than he tolde hir alltogydir worde by worde, and the trouth [6] how hit befelle hym at the turnemente; and aftir that he tolde hir hys avision that he had that nyght in hys slepe [and prayd her to 5 telle hym what hit myght mene, for he was not wel contente with hit.] "A, Launcelot," seyde she, "as longe as ye were knyght of erthly[5] knyghthode ye were the moste mervayloust man of the worlde, and moste adventurest.

"Now," seyde the lady, "sitthen ye be sette amonge the knyghtis 10 of hevynly adventures, if aventure falle [the contrary at that turnement,] have ye no mervayle; for that turnamente yestirday was but a tokenynge of Oure Lorde. And natforethan there was none enchauntemente, for they at the turnemente were erthely knyghtes: the turnamente was tokyn to se who sholde have moste knygh- 15 tes, Eliazar, the sonne of Kynge Pelles, or Argustus, the sonne of Kynge Harlon. But Eliazar was all clothed in whyght, and Argustus fol.375v were coverde in blacke:

❡"And what thys betokenyth I shall telle you. The day of Pentecoste, whan Kynge Arthure hylde courte, hit befelle that erthely 20 kynges and erthely knyghtes toke a turnemente togydirs, that ys to sey the Queste of the Sankgreall. Of thes [the] erthely knyghtes [were they] which were clothed all in blake; and the coveryng betokenyth the sy[n]nes whereof they be nat confessed. And they with the coverynge of whyght betokenyth virginité, and they that hath 25 chosyn chastité; and thus was the Queste begonne in them. Than thou behelde the synners and the good men; and whan thou saw the synners overcom, thou enclyned to that party for bobbaunce and pryde of the worlde, and all that muste be leffte in that Queste; for in thys Queste thou shalt have many felowis, and thy bettirs. 30 For thou arte so feble of evyll truste and good beleve,[6] thys made hit[7] whan thou were [there] where they toke the and ladde the into the foreyste:

"And anone there appered the Sankgreall unto the whyght knyghtes, but thou were so fyeble of good [byleve and] fayth that thou 35 myght nat abyde hit, for all the techyng of the good man before. But anone thou turned to the synners; and that caused thy mysseaventure, that thou sholde know good frome vayneglory of the worlde—hit[8] ys nat worth a peare. And for grete pryde thou madist grete sorow that thou haddist nat overcom all the whyght knyghtes; 40 therefore God was wrothe with you, for in thys Queste God lovith no such dedis. And that made the avision to say to the that thou were of evyll faythe and of poore bylyeve, the which woll make the to falle into the depe pitte of helle, if thou kepe the nat the better:

❡"Now have I warned the of thy vayneglory and of thy pryde, 45 that thou haste many tyme arred ayenste thy Maker. Beware of fol.376r

---

5. On Malory's use of this word in connection with Launcelot, see n. 6, p. 507.
6. *Feble of evyll truste and good beleve*: i.e., weakened by poor faith and in sound belief.
7. *Thys made hit*: i.e., this was signified.
8. I.e., vainglory.

everlastynge payne, for of all erthly knyghtes I have moste pité of
the, for I know well thou haste nat thy pere of ony erthly synfull
man."

And so she commaunded Sir Launcelot to dyner. And aftir dyner
he toke hys horse and commaunde her to God, and so rode into a
depe valey; and there he saw a ryver that hyght Mortays. And thorow the watir he muste nedis passe, the whych was hedyous; and
than, in the name of God, he toke hit with good herte. And whan
he com over he saw an armed knyght, horse and man all black as
a beré.⁹ Withoute ony worde he smote Sir Launcelottis horse to the
dethe; and so he paste on, and wyst nat where he was becom. And
than he toke hys helme and hys shylde, and thanked God of hys
adventure.

Here levith the tale of Sir Launcelot and spekith of Sir Gawayne.

Whan Sir Gawayne was departed frome hys felyship he rode [XVI.1]
longe withoute ony adventure, for he founde nat the tenthe
parte of aventures as they were wonte to have; for Sir Gawayne rode
frome Whytsontyde tylle Mychaellmasse,¹ and founde never
adventure that pleased hym. So on a day hit befelle that Gawayne
mette with Sir Ector de Maris, and aythir made grete joy of othir;
and so they tolde everyche othir and complayned them gretely that
they coude fynde none adventure.

❡"Truly," seyde Sir Gawayne, "I am ny wery of thys Queste, and
lothe I am to folow further in straunge contreyes." "One thynge
mervaylith me muche," seyde Sir Ector: "I have mette with twenty
knyghtes that be felowys of myne, and all they complayne as I do."

❡"I have mervayle," seyd Sir Gawayne, "where that Sir Launcelot,
your brothir, ys." "Truly," seyde Sir Ector, "I can nat hyre of hym,
nother of Sir Galahad, Sir Percivale, and Sir Bors."

❡"Lette hem be," seyde Sir Gawayne, "for they foure have no
peerys. And if one thynge² were nat [in] Sir Launcelot, he had none
felow of an erthely man; but he ys as we be, but if he take the more
payne uppon hym. But, and these foure be mette togydyrs, they
woll be lothe that ony man mete with hem; for and they fayle of
the Sankgreall, hit ys in waste of all the remenaunte³ to recover
hit."

Thus Sir Ector and Sir Gawayne rode more than eyght dayes; and
on a Satirday they founde an auncyant chapell which was wasted,
that there semed no man nor woman thydir repayred.⁴ And there
they alyght and sette their sperys at the dore; and so they entirde
into the chapell and there made their orysons a grete whyle. And

---

9. The Winchester MS and Caxton both have *beare*, but, as in an earlier passage (see p. 524,
line 41, where Caxton's probably more authentic spelling *beré* is adopted), the French
source draws a comparison to a mulberry; that Malory did originally indicate a berry is
further suggested by the unequivocal spelling *byry* in the same phrase later (p. 549, line
14). The earlier Caxton spelling is adopted here.
1. I.e., from the week beginning with Whitsunday (Pentecost, the seventh Sunday after
Easter) until the festival of the archangel Michael (September 29).
2. *One thynge*: i.e., his illicit love of Guenevere.
3. *In waste of all the remenaunte*: useless for the rest (of us).
4. I.e., dwelled.

than they sette hem downe in the segys of the chapell, and as they spake of one thynge and of othir, for hevynesse they felle on slepe—and there befelle hem bothe mervaylous adventures.

⁋Sir Gawayne hym semed he cam into a medow full of herbis and floures, and there he saw a rake of bullis, an hundrith and fyffty, that were proude and black, save three of hem was[5] all whyght; and one had a blacke spotte, and the othir two were so fayre and so whyght that they myght be no whytter. And thes three bullis which were so fayre were tyed[6] with two stronge cordis. And the remnaunte of the bullis seide amonge them, "Go we hens to seke bettir pasture." And so som wente, and som com agayne, but they were so megir that they myght nat stonde upryght; and of the bullys that were so whyght, that one com agayne, and no mo.

⁋But whan thys whyght bulle was com agayne and amonge thes other, there rose up a grete crye for lacke of wynde [that] fayled them; and so they departed, one here and anothir there. Thys avision befelle Sir Gawayne that nyght.

But to Sir Ector de Mares befelle another avision, the contrary. For hit semed hym that hys brothir, Sir Launcelot, and he alyght oute of a chayre and lepte uppon two horsis; and the one sayde to the othir, "Go we to seke that we shall nat fynde." And hym thought thatt a man bete Sir Launcelot and dispoyled hym, and clothed hym in another aray whych was all fulle of knottis, and sette hym uppon an asse. And so he rode tylle that he cam unto the fayryst welle that ever he saw, and there Sir Launcelot alyght and [wolde have dronke] of that welle; and whan he stowped to drynke of that watir, the watir sanke frome hym. And whan Sir Launcelot saw that, he turned and wente thidir as he com fro.

⁋And in the meanewhyle he trowed that hymself, Sir Ector, rode tylle that he com to a ryche mannes house, where there was a weddynge; and there he saw a kynge whych seyd, "Sir knyght, here ys no place for you." And than he turned agayne unto the chayre that he cam fro. And so within a whyle both Sir Gawayne and Sir Ector awaked, and ayther tolde other of their avision, whych mervayled hem gretly. "Truly," seyde Sir Ector, "I shall never be myrry tyll I hyre tydynges of my brothyr Sir Launcelot." So as they sate thus talkynge, they saw an honde shewynge[7] unto the elbow—and was coverde with rede samyte, and uppon that a brydill nat ryght[8] ryche—that hylde within the fyste a grete candill whych brenned ryght clere—and so passed before them and entird into the chapell, and than vanysshed away, they wyste nat whydir.

And anone com downe a voice which seyde, "Knyghtes full of evyll fayth and of poore beleve, thes three[9] thynges have fayled you; and therefore ye may nat com to the aventures of the

The avision of Sir Gawayne

[2]
fol.377r

5. I.e., which were.
6. I.e., tied together.
7. I.e., revealed.
8. I.e., very.
9. The MS here reads "ii" (two; so Caxton), but the French source, and the hermit Nacien's interpretation (p. 543), indicates three ("iii").

Sankgreall." Than first spake Sir Gawayne and seyde, "Sir Ector, have ye herde thes wordys?"

¶"Ye, truly," seyde Sir Ector, "I herde all. Now go we," seyde Sir Ector, "unto som ermyte that woll telle us of oure avision, for hit semyth me we laboure all in waste." And so they departe and rode into a valey; and there they mette with a squyre which rode on an hakeney, and anone they salew hym fayre.

¶"Sir," seyde Sir Gawayne, "can thou teche us to ony ermyte?"

¶"Sir, here ys one in a litill mowntayne; but hit ys so rowghe there may no horse go thydir, and therefore ye muste go on foote. And there ye shall fynde a poore house; and therein ys Nacien the ermyte, whych ys the holyeste man in thys contrey." And so they departed eythir frome othir. And than in a valey they mette with a knyght all armed, which profirde hem to fyght and juste as sone as he saw them. "In the name of God," seyde Gawayne, "for sitthyn I departed frome Camelot there was none that profirde me to juste but onys, and now."

¶"Sir," seyde Sir Ector, "lat me juste with hym." "Nay, ye shall nat, but if I be betyn. Hit shall nat than forthynke me[1] if ye go to hym [after me]." And than aythir enbraced other to juste; and so they cam togydirs as faste as [their horses] myght renne, that they braste their shyldis and mayles—and that one more than the tother: but Sir Gawayne was wounded in the lyffte syde, and thys other knyght was smytten thorow the breste, that the speare com oute on that other syde. And so they felle bothe oute of their sadyls, and in the fallynge they brake both their spearys. And anone Sir Gawayne arose and sette hys honde to hys swerde and caste hys shylde before hym; but all for naught was hit, for the knyght had no power to aryse agayne hym.

¶Than seyde Sir Gawayne, "Ye muste yelde you as an overcom man, other ellis I muste sle you." "A, sir knyght!" he seyde, "I am but dede. Therefore, for Goddys sake and of youre jantilnes, lede me here unto an abbay, that I may resceyve my Creature."[2]

¶"Sir," seyde Sir Gawayne, "I know no house of religion here nyghe."

¶"Sir, sette me on an horse tofore you, and I shall teche you."

¶So Sir Gawayne sette hym up in the sadyll, and he lepe up behynde hym to sustayne hym. And so they cam to the abbay, and there were well resceyved. And anone he was unarmed and resceyve hys Creature; than he prayde Sir Gawayne to drawe oute the truncheon of the speare oute of hys body.

¶Than Sir Gawayne asked hym what he was.

¶"Sir," he seyde, "I am of Kynge Arthurs courte, and was a felow of the Rounde Table, and we were sworne togydir—and now, Sir Gawayne, thou hast slayne me. And my name ys Sir Uwayne[3] that

fol.377v

5

10

15

20

25

30

35

fol.378r

40

Here Sir Gawayne slew Sir Uwayne his cousyn germayne

1. *Forthynke me*: cause me regret.
2. I.e., Creator. The knight wishes to gain access to heaven by having received last rites from a priest.
3. The MS (and Caxton) identifies the knight more fully as Uwayne le Avoutres, but he is in fact Uwayne le Fitz Uryen, Gawain's first cousin; this identity is confimed by the marginal annotation.

somtyme[4] was sone unto Kynge **Uryen**; and I was in the Queste of the **Sankgreall**. And now forgyff the[5] God, for hit shall be ever rehersed that the tone sworne brother hath slayne the other."

¶"Alas," seyde Sir **Gawayne**, "that ever thys mysadventure befelle me."

¶"No force,"[6] seyde Sir **Uwayne**, "sytthyn I shall dye this deth, of a much more worshipfuller mannes hande myght I nat dye. But whan ye com to the courte, recommaunde me unto my lorde **Arthur**, and to all them that be leffte on lyve. And for olde brothir-hode thynke on me."

¶Than began Sir **Gawayne** to wepe, and also **Sir Ector**. And than Sir **Uwayne** bade hym draw oute the truncheon of the speare; and than Sir **Gawayne** drew hit oute, and anone departed the soule frome the body. Than Sir **Gawayne** and Sir **Ector** buryed hym as them ought to bury a kynges sonne, and made hit wrytyn uppon hys tombe what was hys name and by whom he was slayne.

¶Than departed Sir **Gawayne** and Sir **Ector**, as hevy as they myght for their mysseadventure, and so rode tyl that they com to the rowghe mountayne; and there they tyed their horsis and wente on foote to the ermytayge. And whan they were com up they saw a poore house, and besyde the chapell a litill courtelayge—

¶Where **Nacien** the ermyte gadred wortis to[7] hys mete, as he whych had tasted none other mete of a grete whyle. And whan he saw the arraunte knyghtes, he cam to them and salewed them, and they hym agayne.

¶"Fayre lordis," seyde he, "what adventure brought you hydir?" Than seyde Sir **Gawayne**, "to speke with you for to be confessed."

¶"Sir," seyde the ermyte, "I am redy." Than they tolde hym so muche that he wyste welle what they ware, and than he thought to counceyle them if he myght. Than began Sir **Gawayne**, and tolde hym of hys avision that he had in the chapell; and Ector tolde hym all as hit ys before reherced.

¶"Sir," seyde the ermyte unto Sir **Gawayne**, "the fayre medow and the rak: therein ought to be undirstonde the Rounde Table, and by the medow oughte to be undirstonde humilité and paciens; tho be the thynges which bene allwey grene and quyk. For that men mowe no tyme overcom humilité and pacience, therefore was the Rounde Table founden, and the shevalry hath ben at all tymes so hyghe[8] by the fraternité which was there that she[9] myght nat be overcom; for men seyde she was founded in paciens and in humi-lité. At the rack ete an hondred and fyffty bullys, but they ete nat in the medowe, for if they had, their hartes sholde have bene sette in humilité and paciens. And the bullis were proude and blacke, sauff only three:

[3]

5

10

15

20

25

fol.378v

30

35

40

45

---

4. I.e., Uwayne describes himself as one who has died.
5. Thee.
6. *No force*: that does not matter.
7. I.e., for.
8. *So hyghe*: held in such high regard.
9. I.e., chivalry.

¶"And by the bullys ys undirstonde the felyshyp of the Rounde
Table, whych for their synne and their wyckednesse bene blacke:
blackenes ys as much to sey withoute good vertues or workes. And
the three bulles whych were whyght, sauff only one had bene spot-
ted: the too whyght betokenythe Sir 𝕲𝖆𝖑𝖆𝖍𝖆𝖉 and Sir 𝕻𝖊𝖗𝖈𝖎𝖛𝖆𝖑𝖊, for   5
they be maydyns and clene withoute spotte, and the thirde, that
had a spotte, signifieth Sir 𝕭𝖔𝖗𝖘 𝖉𝖊 𝕲𝖆𝖞𝖓𝖊𝖘, which trespassed but
onys in hys virginité—but sithyn be kepyth hymselff so wel in chastité that all ys forgyffyn hym and hys myssededys.[1] And why tho
three were tyed by the neckes: they be three knyghtes in virginité   10
and chastité, and there ys no pryde smytten[2] in them. And the
blacke bullis whych seyde, 'go we hens,' they were tho whych at
Pentecoste at the hyghe feste toke uppon hem to go in the Queste
of the 𝕾𝖆𝖓𝖐𝖌𝖗𝖊𝖆𝖑𝖑 withoute confession: they myght nat entir in the
medow of humilité and paciens.   15

"And therefore they turned into waste contreyes that signifieth
dethe, for there shall dye many off them; for everych of them shall
sle othir for synne—and they that shall ascape shall be so megir
that hit shall be mervayle to se them. And of the three bullis withoute spotte, the one shall com agayne, and the other two never."   20

¶Than spake 𝕹𝖆𝖈𝖎𝖊𝖓 unto Sir 𝕰𝖈𝖙𝖔𝖗: "Soth hit ys that Sir 𝕷𝖆𝖚𝖓𝖈𝖊𝖑𝖔𝖙   [4]   fol.379r
and ye com downe of one chayre; the chayer betokenyth mayster-
ship and lordeship which ye too cam downe fro. But ye two knyghtes," sayde the ermyte, "ye go to seke that ye shall nat fynde, that
ys the 𝕾𝖆𝖓𝖐𝖌𝖗𝖊𝖆𝖑𝖑, for hit ys the secrete thynges of Oure Lorde Jesu   25
Cryste—

¶"But what ys to meane that Sir 𝕷𝖆𝖚𝖓𝖈𝖊𝖑𝖔𝖙 felle doune of hys
horse? He hath leffte hys pryde and takyn to humilité, for he hath
cryed mercy lowde for hys synne and sore repented hym; and Oure
Lorde hath clothed hym in Hys clothynge, whych ys full of knottes   30
—that ys the hayre that he werith dayly:

¶"And the asse that he rode uppon ys a beest of humilité—for
God wolde nat ryde uppon no styede nother uppon no palferey[3]—
in an exemple that an asse betokenyth mekenes, that thou saw Sir
𝕷𝖆𝖚𝖓𝖈𝖊𝖑𝖔𝖙 ryde in thy slepe. At the welle whereat the watir sanke   35
frome hym when he sholde have takyn thereoff, and whan he saw
he myght nat have hit he returned from whens he cam: for the
welle betokenyth the hyghe grace of God, for the more men desyre
hit to take hit, the more shall be their desire:

¶"So whan he cam nyghe the 𝕾𝖆𝖓𝖐𝖌𝖗𝖊𝖆𝖑𝖑 he meked hym so that   40
he hylde hym nat the man worthy to be so nyghe the holy vessell,
for he had be so defoyled in dedly synne by the space of many yere.
Yett whan he kneled downe to drynke of the welle, there he sawe
grete prevydence of the 𝕾𝖆𝖓𝖐𝖌𝖗𝖊𝖆𝖑𝖑. And for he hath served so longe
the devyll he shall have [vengeaunce] foure and twenty dayes, for   45
that he hath bene the devillis servaunte foure and twenty yerys;

1. On Bors's one trespass, see p. 468, lines 7–10.
2. I.e., impressed.
3. *God wolde nat . . . uppon no palferey*: so Matthew 21.5 (the account of Christ's entry into
   Jerusalem): "Behold, thy King cometh unto thee, meek, and sitting upon an ass."

and than sone aftir he shall returne to **Camelot** oute of thys contrey, and he shall sey a party[4] such thyngis as he hath founde:

¶"Now woll I telle you what betokenyth the hande with the candill and the brydyll: that ys to undirstonde the Holy Goste where charité ys ever; and the brydyll signifieth abstinens, for whan she[5] ys brydeled in a Crysten mannes herte, she holdith hym so shorte that he fallith nat in dedly synne. And the candyll which shewith clernesse and lyght signyfieth the ryght way of Jesu Cryste—

"And whan they[6] wente, He seyde, 'Knyghtes of pore fayth and of wycked beleve, thes three thynges fayled'—charité, abstinaunce and trouthe—[7] 'therefore ye may nat attayne thys adventure of the **Sankgreall**.' " "Sertes," seyde Sir **Gawayne**, "full sothly have ye seyde, that I se hit opynly. Now I pray you telle me why we mette nat with so many adventures as we were wonte to do."

"I shall telle you gladly," seyde the good man. "The adventure of the **Sankgreall** whych be in shewynge now, [ye and many other have undertake the Quest of it and fynde it not,] for hit apperith nat to no synners—wherefore mervayle ye nat though ye fayle thereoff, and many othir, for ye bene an untrew knyght and a grete murtherar—and to good men signifieth othir thynges than murthir. For I dare sey, as synfull as ever Sir **Launcelot** hath byn, sith that he wente into the Queste of the **Sankgreal** he slew never man, nother nought shall, tylle that he com to **Camelot** agayne; for he hath takyn [upon] hym to forsake synne. And ne were[8] that he ys nat stable—but by hys thoughte he ys lyckly to turne agayne—he sholde be nexte to encheve hit sauff Sir **Galahad**, hys sonne; but God knowith hys thought and hys unstablenesse. And yett shall he dye ryght an holy man, and no doute he hath no felow[9] of none erthly synfull man lyvyng."[1]

"Sir," seyde Sir **Gawayne**, "hit semyth me by youre wordis that for oure synnes hit woll nat avayle us to travayle in thys Queste." "Truly," seyde the good man, "there bene an hondred such as ye bene shall[2] never prevayle, but to have shame." And whan they had herde thes wordis they commaunded hym unto God.

¶Than the good man called Sir **Gawayne**, and seyde, "Hit ys longe tyme passed sith that ye were made knyght and never synnes servyd thou thy Maker; and now thou arte so olde a tre that in the ys neythir leeff, nor grasse, nor fruyte. Wherefore bethynke the that thou yelde to Oure Lorde the bare rynde, sith the fende hath the levis and the fruyte."

¶"Sir," seyde **Sir Gawayne**, "and I had leyser I wolde speke with

---

4. *Sey a party:* describe in part.
5. I.e., charity.
6. I.e., the hand and candle.
7. In the midst of his quotation of the voice, Nacien adds this interpretive elaboration.
8. *Ne were:* if it were not.
9. I.e., peer.
1. *For I dare sey . . . synfull man lyvyng:* this passage is not matched in Malory's known source, and reflects Malory's characteristic tendency to mitigate the shortcomings of his favorite knight; cf., n. 9, p. 535.
2. I.e., who shall.

you, but my felow Sir Ector ys gone, and abithe me yondir bynethe the hylle."

¶"Well," seyde the good man, "thou were better to be counceyled."

¶Than departed Sir Gawayne and cam to Sir Ector, and so toke their horsis and rode tylle that they com to a fosters house, which herberowde them ryght welle. And on the morne [they] departed frome hir oste and rode longe or they cowthe fynde ony adventure.

Now turnyth thys tale unto Syr Bors de Ganys, et cetera.[3]

When Sir Bors was departed frome Camelot he mette with a religious man rydynge on an asse, and anone Sir Bors salewed hym. And anone the good man knew that he was one of the knyghtes arraunte that was in the Queste of the Sankgreall. "What ar ye?" seyde the good man. "Sir," seyde he, "I am a knyght that fayne wolde be counceyled, that ys entirde into the Queste of the Sankgreall—for he shall have much erthly worship that may bryng hit to an ende."

"Sertes," seyde the good man, "that ys sothe, withoute fayle, for he shall be the beste knyght of the worlde and the fayryst of the felyship. But wyte you welle, there shall none attayne hit but by clennes, that ys pure confession." So rode they togydir tyll that they com unto a litill ermytayge, and there he prayde Sir Bors to dwelle all that nyght. And so he [alyghte and] put of hys armoure and prayde hym that he myght be confessed, [and soo they wente into the chappel and there he was clene confessid.]

And so they ete brede and dranke watir togydir. "Now, seyde the good man, "I pray the[4] that thou ete none other tyll that thou sitte at the table where the Sankgreall shall be."

¶"Sir," seyde he, "I agré me thereto—but how know ye that I shall sytte there?"

¶"Yes," seyde the good man, "that know I well; but there shall be but fewe of youre felowis with you." "All ys wellcomme," seyde Sir Bors, "that God sendith me." "Also," seyde the good man, "insteede of a shurte, and in sygne of chastisemente,[5] ye shall were a garmente.[6] Therefore I pray you do of all your clothys and youre shurte." And so he dud; and than he toke hym a scarlet cote so that sholde be hys instede of hys sherte tylle he had fulfilled the Queste of the Sankgreall. And thys good man founde hym in so mervales a lyffe and so stable that he felte he was never gretly correpte in fleysshly lustes, but in one tyme that he begat Elyan le Blanke.[7]

Than he armyd hym and toke hys leve, and so departed. And so a litill frome thens he loked up into a tre, and there he saw a passynge grete birde uppon that olde tre—and hit was passyng

fol.380r

[6]

fol.380v

---

3. I.e., and others.
4. Thee.
5. I.e., mortificatin (of the flesh).
6. I.e., overcoat.
7. See p. 468, lines 7–10.

drye, withoute leyffe—so he sate above, and had birdis whiche were dede for hungir. So at the laste he smote hymselffe with hys beke, which was grete and sherpe, and so the grete birde bledde so faste that he dyed amonge hys birdys; and the yonge birdys toke lyff by the bloode of the grete birde.[8]

¶Whan Sir 𝕭𝖔𝖗𝖘 saw thys, he wyste well hit was a grete token-ynge. For whan he saw the grete birde arose nat, than he toke hys horse and yode hys way. And so by aventure, by evynsonge tyme, he cam to a stronge towre and an hyghe, and there was he her-berowde gladly. And whan he was unarmed they lad hym into an hyghe towre where was a lady, yonge, lusty and fayre; and she resceyved hym with grete joy and made hym to sitte down by her. And anone he was sette to supper with fleyssh[9] and many deyntees.

¶But whan Sir 𝕭𝖔𝖗𝖘 saw that, he bethought hym on hys pen-aunce and bade a squyre to brynge hym watir. And so he brought hym, and he made soppis therein and ete them. "A," seyde the lady, "I trow ye lyke nat youre mete." "Yes, truly," seyde Sir 𝕭𝖔𝖗𝖘, "God thanke you, madam, but I may nat ete none other mete today." Than she spake no more as at that tyme, for she was lothe to displease hym.

¶Than aftir supper they spake of one thynge and of othir. So with that there cam a squyre and seyde, "Madam, ye muste pirvey you tomorne for a champion, for ellis youre syster woll have thys castell and also youre londys, excepte ye can fynde a knyght that woll fyght tomorne in youre quarell ayenste 𝕾𝖎𝖗 𝕻𝖗𝖞𝖉𝖆𝖒 𝖑𝖊 𝕹𝖔𝖞𝖗𝖊. Than she made grete sorow, and seyde, "A, Lorde God, wherefore graunted ye me to holde my londe whereof I sholde now be dis-herited withoute reson and ryght?"

And whan Sir 𝕭𝖔𝖗𝖘 herde hir sey thus, he seyde, "I shall comforte you." "Sir," seyde she, "I shall telle you. There was here a kynge that hyghte 𝕬𝖓𝖞𝖆𝖜𝖘𝖊 whych hylde all thys londe in hys kepynge. So hit myssehapped he loved a jantillwoman a grete dele elder than I; and so he toke[1] her all this londe in hir kepynge, and all hys men to governe, and she brought up many evyll custums whereby she put to dethe a grete party of his kynnesmen. And whan he saw that, he [lete chace] her oute of this londe and bytoke hit me, and all thys londe in my demenys. But anone as that worthy kynge was dede, thys other lady began to warre uppon me, and hath destroyed many of my men and turned hem ayenste me, that I have well-nyghe no man leffte me; and I have naught ellis but thys hyghe towre that she leffte me—

¶"And yet she hath promysed me to have[2] thys towre withoute[3] I can fynde a knyght to fyght with her champion."

[7]

5

10

15

20

25

30 fol.381r

35

40

8. The image is closely reminiscent of the widespread medieval motif of the "pelican in its piety." It was believed that the pelican pierced its own breast with its bill in order to feed its young with the blood; in so doing the pelican was even able, it was thought, to revive dead chicks. The analogy to Christ is obvious enough; cf. the abbot's interpretation of the dream p. 552.
9. I.e., meat.
1. I.e., gave, entrusted.
2. I.e., take back.
3. I.e., unless.

❡"Now telle me," seyde Sir **Bors**, "what ys that **Prydam le Noyre**?" "Sir, he ys the moste douted[4] man of thys londe." "Than may ye sende hir worde that ye have founde a knyght that shall fyght with that **Prydam le Noyre**, in Goddis quarelle and youres." So that lady was than [not a lytel] glad and sente her worde that she was purveyde.[5]

❡And so that nyght Sir **Bors** had passyng good chere, but in no bedde he wolde com but leyde hym on the floore—nor never wolde do otherwyse tyll that he had mette with the Queste of the **Sankegreall**. And anone as he was aslepe hym befelle a vision, that there cam two birdis, that one whyght as a swanne and that other was merveylous blacke—but he was nat so grete as was that other, but in the lyknes of a raven. Than the whyght birde cam to hym and seyde, "And thou woldist gyff me mete and serve me, I sholde gyff the all the ryches of the worlde, and I shall make the as fayre and as whyght as I am."

So the whyght birde departed; and than cam the blacke birde to hym, and seyde, "And thou serve me tomorow and have me in no dispite, thoughe I be blacke, for wyte thou well that more avaylith myne blaknesse than the odirs whyghtnesse." And than he departed. Than he had anothir vision: [hym thoughte] that he cam to a grete place which semed a chapell, and there he founde a chayre sette, on the lyffte syde which[6] was a worme-etyn and fyeble tre besyde hit, and on the ryght honde were two floures lyke a lylye: and that one wolde a benomme[7] the tother hir whyghtnes.

❡But a good man departed them, that they towched none othir; and than oute of eche floure com oute many floures and fruyte grete plenté.

❡Than hym thought the good man seyde, "Sholde nat he do grete foly that wolde lette thes two floures perishe for to succoure the rottyn tre, that[8] hyt felle nat to the erthe?"

❡"Sir," seyde he, "hit semyth me that thys wood myght nat avayle."[9] "Now kepe the," seyde the good man, "that thou never se such adventure befalle the." Than he awaked and made a sygne of the crosse in myddys of the forehede, and so he arose and clothed hym. And anone there cam the lady of the place, and she salewed hym, and he her agayne, and so wente to a chapell and herd their servyse. And anone there cam a company of knyghtes that the lady had sente for to lede Sir **Bors** unto the batayle.

❡Than asked he his armys; and whan he was armed, she prayde hym to take a lytyll morsell to dyne.

❡"Nay, madam," seyde he, "that shall I nat do tylle I have done my batayle, by the grace of God." And so he lepe uppon hys horse and departed, and all the knyghtes and men with hym. And as sone as thes two ladyes mette togydir, she which Sir **Bors** sholde fyght

[8]

The avysion of Sir
Bors whan he fought
with Sir Prydam

fol.381v

---

4. I.e., feared.
5. I.e., provided with a champion.
6. I.e., of which.
7. *A benomme:* have taken from.
8. I.e., so that.
9. *Myght nat avayle:* is useless.

for, she playned hir and seyde, "Madam, ye have done grete wronge to beryve me my landis that Kyng 𝔄𝔫𝔶𝔞𝔴𝔰 gaff me, and full lothe I am there sholde be ony batayle."

¶"Ye shall nat chose," seyde the other, "othir ellis lat your knyght withdraw hym." Than there was the cry made, which party had the bettir of tho two knyghtes, that hys lady sholde rejoyse all the londys. Than departed the one knyght here and the other there.

Than they cam togydirs with such raundom that they perced their shildes and their habergeons, and their spearis flye in pecis, and they sore wounded. Than hurteled they togydyrs so that they beete eche other to the erthe, and[1] theire horsis betwene their leggis; and anone they arose, and sette handis to their swerdys and smote eche one other uppon their hedys, that they made grete woundis and depe, that the blode wente oute of hyre bodyes. For there founde Sir 𝔅𝔬𝔯𝔰 gretter deffence in that knyght more than he wente; for thys Sir 𝔓𝔯𝔶𝔡𝔞𝔪 was a passyng good knyght and wounded Sir 𝔅𝔬𝔯𝔰 full evyll—and he hym agayne, but ever Sir 𝔓𝔯𝔦-𝔡𝔞𝔪 hylde the stowre inlyche harde. That perceyved Sir 𝔅𝔬𝔯𝔰, and suffird hym tylle he was nyghe ataynte, and than he ranne uppon hym more and more; and the other wente backe for drede of dethe.

¶So in hys withdrawyng he felle upryght; and Sir 𝔅𝔬𝔯𝔰 drew hys helme so strongly that he rente hit frome hys hede, and gaff hym many sadde strokes with the flatte of hys swerde uppon the visayge, and bade hym yelde hym or he sholde sle hym.

¶Than he cryed hym mercy, and seyde, "Fayre knyght, for God-dis love, sle me nat, and I shall ensure the never to warre ayenste thy lady, but be allway towarde hir." So Sir 𝔅𝔬𝔯𝔰 gaffe hym hys lyff, and anone the olde lady fledde with all hir knyghtes.

Than called Sir 𝔅𝔬𝔯𝔰 all tho that hylde landis of[2] hys lady, and seyde he sholde destroy them but if they dud such servyse unto her as longed to their londys. So they dud her omayge;[3] and they that wolde nat were chaced oute of their londis, that hit befelle that the yonge lady com to her astate agayne be the myghty prouesse of Sir 𝔅𝔬𝔯𝔰 𝔡𝔢 𝔊𝔞𝔫𝔶𝔰. So whan all the contrey was well sette in pease, than Sir 𝔅𝔬𝔯𝔰 toke hys leve and departed; and she thanked hym gretly and wolde have gyffyn hym grete gyfftes, but he refused hit. Than he rode all that day tylle nyght; and so he cam to an herberow, to a lady which knew hym well inowghe and made of hym grete joy.

So on the morne, as sone as the day appered, Sir 𝔅𝔬𝔯𝔰 departed from thens, and so rode into a foreyste unto the owre of mydday—and there befelle hym a mervaylous aventure. So he mette at the departynge of the two wayes two knyghtes that lad Sir 𝔏𝔶𝔬𝔫𝔢𝔩𝔩, hys brothir, all naked, bowndyn uppon a stronge hakeney, and his hon-dis bounden tofore hys breste. And everych of them helde in theyre hondis thornys wherewith they wente betynge hym so sore that the bloode trayled downe more than in an hondred placis of hys body,

---

9

1. I.e., with.
2. I.e., from.
3. On feudal homage, see n. 6, p. 9.

so that he was all bloodé tofore and behynde—but he seyde never
a worde, as he whych was grete of herte suffird all that they ded
to hym as thoughe he had felte none angwysh.

And anone Sir Bors dressed hym to rescow hym that was his
brothir; and so he loked uppon the other syde of hym, and sawe a
knyght which brought a fayre jantillwoman, and wolde a sette her
in the thycke[st place] of the foreyste for to have be the more surer
oute of the way from hem that sought her. And she whych was
nothynge assured[4] cryde with an hyghe voice, "Seynte Mary, succour youre mayde!" And anone as she syghe Sir Bors, she demed
hym a knyght of the Rounde Table.

Than she conjoured hym, by the faythe that he ought "unto Hym
in whos servyse thou arte entred, [and] for Kynge Arthures sake,
which I suppose made the[5] knyght, that thou helpe me and suffir
me nat to be shamed of this knyght."

⁋Whan Sir Bors herde hir say thus, he had so much sorow that
he wyst nat what to do—"for if I latte my brothir be in adventure[6]
he muste be slayne, and that wold I nat for all the erthe; and if I
helpe nat the mayde, she ys shamed, and shall lose hir virginité
which she shall never gete agayne."

Than lyffte he up hys yghen and seyde, wepynge, "Fayre swete
Lorde Jesu Cryst, whos [lyege man] I am, kepe me[7] Sir Lyonell, my
brothir, that thes knyghtes sle hym nat; and for pité of You[8] and
for mylde Maryes sake, I shall succour thys mayde." Than dressed
he hym unto the knyght which had the jantillwoman, and than he
cryed, "Sir knyght, let youre honde of youre maydyn, or ye be but
dede." And than he sette downe the mayden, and was armed at all
pycis,[9] sauff he lacked his speare.

Than he dressed hys shylde and drew oute his swerde—and Sir
Bors smote hym so harde that hit wente thorow hys shylde and
habirgeon on the lyffte sholdir; and thorow grete strengthe he bete
hym downe to the erthe. And at the pullyng oute of Sir Bors spere,
he there sowned. Than cam Sir Bors to the mayde, and seyde,
"How semyth hit you?[1] Of thys knyght be ye delyverde at thys
tyme." "Now, sir," seyde she, "I pray you lede me there as this
knyght had[2] me." "So shall I do gladly"—and toke the horse of the
wounded knyght and sette the jantilwoman uppon hym, and so
brought hir as she desired.

⁋"Sir knyght," seyde she, "ye have bettir spedde than ye wente,
for and I had loste my maydynhode, fyve hondred men sholde have
dyed therefore."

⁋"What knyght was he that had you in the foreyst?" "Be my
fayth, he ys my cosyne. So wote I never with what engyne the fynde

fol.383r

[10]

4. *Nothynge assured:* i.e., without safety.
5. Thee.
6. *In adventure:* at risk.
7. I.e., for me.
8. *Pité of You:* by your mercy.
9. *At all pycis:* fully.
1. *How semyth hit you:* i.e., how does it look to you.
2. I.e., captured.

enchaffed hym, for yestirday he toke me fro my fadir privayly—for
I, nother none of my fadirs men, myssetrusted hym nat—and iff
he had had my maydynhode, he had dyed for the synne of hys
body, and shamed and dishonoured for ever."

¶Thus as she stood talkyng with hym, there cam twelve knyghtes
sekyng aftir hir, and anone she tolde hem all how Sir **Bors** had
delyverde hir. Than they made grete joy and besought hym to com
to her fadir, a grete lorde, and he sholde be ryght wellcom.

¶"Truly," seyde Sir **Bors**, "that may nat be at thys tyme, for I
have a grete aventure to do in this contrey." So he commaunde
hem to God, and departed. Than Sir **Bors** rode after Sir **Lyonell**,
hys brothir, by the trace of their horsis. Thus he rode sekyng a
grete whyle; and anone he overtoke a man clothed in a religious
wede, and rode on a stronge blacke horse, blacker than a byry, and
seyde, "Sir knyght, what seke you?" "Sir," seyde he, "I seke my
brother that I saw erewhyle betyn with two knyghtes." "A, Sir **Bors**,
discomforte you nat, nor falle nat into no wanhope, for I shall telle
you tydyngis such as they be—for truly he ys dede." Than shewed
he hym a new-slayne body, lyyng in a buyssh, and hit semed hym
well that hyt was the body of Sir **Lyonell**, hys brothir. And than he
made suche sorow that he felle to the erthe in a sowne, and so lay
a grete whyle there.

And whan he cam to hymselff, he seyde, "Fayre brother! Sytthe
the company of you and me ar departed,[3] shall I never have joy in
my herte—and now He whych I have takyn unto my mayster, He[4]
be my helpe." And whan he had seyde thus, he toke the body
lyghtly in hys armys and put hit upon the harson of hys sadyll.

¶And than he seyde to the man, "Can ye shew me ony chapell
nyghe where that I may bury thys body?" "Com one," seyde he,
"here ys one faste bye." And so longe they rode tylle they saw a
fayre towre, and afore hit there semed an olde fyeble chapell; and
than they alyght bothe, and put hym in the tombe of marble.

¶"Now leve we hym here," seyde the good man, "and go we to
oure herberow, tylle tomorow we com hyre agayne to do hym
servyse."

¶"Sir," seyd Sir **Bors**, "be ye a pryest?" "Ye, forsothe," seyde he.
"Than I pray you telle[5] me a dreme that befelle me the laste nyght."

¶"Say on," seyde he. So he begon so much to telle hym of the
grete birde in the foreyste, and aftir tolde hym of hys birdys, one
whyght and another blacke, and of the rottyn tre and of the whyght
floures.

¶"Sir, I shall telle you a parte now, and the othir dele tomorow.
The whyght fowle betokenyth a jantillwoman fayre and ryche
whych loved the[6] paramours and hath loved the longe:

¶"And if that thou warne[7] hir love she shall dy anone—if thou

fol.383v

fol.384r

5

10

15

20

25

30

[11]

35

40

45

---

3. *Ar departed*: i.e., is at an end.
4. I.e., may He.
5. I.e., explain.
6. Thee.
7. I.e., refuse.

have no pité on her. That signifieth the grete birde which shall make the to warne hir. Now, for no feare that thou haste, ne for no drede that thou hast of God, thou shalt nat warne hir; for thou woldist nat do hit for to be holdyn chaste, for to conquere the [loos] of the vaynglory of the worlde;[8] for that shall befalle the now, and thou warne hir, that Sir Launcelot, the good knyght—thy cousyn— shall dye. And than shall men sey that thou arte a man-sleer, both of thy brothir Sir Lyonell and of thy cousyn Sir Launcelot, whych thou myght have rescowed easyly, but thou wentist to rescow a mayde which perteyned nothynge to the:

¶"Now loke thou whether hit had bene gretter harme, of thy brothers dethe, other ellis to have suffirde her to have loste hir maydynhode." Than seyde he, "Now hast thou harde the tokyns[9] of thy dreme?"

¶"Ye," seyd Sir Bors. "Than ys hit in thy defaughte if Sir Launcelot thy cousyn dye." "Sir," seyde Sir Bors, "that were me lothe,[1] for there ys nothynge in the worlde but I had levir do hit than to se my lorde Sir Launcelot dye in my defaught." "Chose ye now the tone or that other." Than he ladde hym into the hygh towre. And there he founde knyghtes and ladyes that seyde he was welcom; and so they unarmed hym, and whan he was in his dublette they brought hym a mantell furred with ermyne[2] and put hit aboute hym. So they made hym such chere that he had forgotyn hys sorow; and anone cam oute of a chambir unto hym the fayryst lady that ever he saw, and more rycher beseyne than ever was Quene Guenyver or ony other astate.

¶"Lo," seyde they, "Sir Bors, here ys the lady unto whom we owghe all oure servyse; and I trow she be the rychyst lady and the fayryste of the worlde—whych lovith you beste aboven all other knyghtes, for she woll have no knyght but you." And whan he undirstood that langayge, he was abaysshed.

Notforthan she salewed hym, and he her; and than they sate downe togydirs and spake of many thyngis, insomuch that she besought hym to be hir love, for she had loved hym aboven all erthly men, and she sholde make hym rycher than evyr was man of hys ayge.[3] Whan Sir Bors undirstood hir wordis he was ryght evyll at ease; but in no wyse he wolde breke his chastité, and so he wyst nat how to answere her. "Alas, Sir Bors!" seyde she—

¶"Woll ye nat do my wylle?" "Madam," seyde he, "there ys no lady in thys worlde whos wylle I wolde fullfylle as of[4] thys thynge. She ought nat desire hit, for my brothir lyeth dede, which was slayne ryght late."

¶"A, Sir Bors," seyde she, "I have loved you longe for the grete beauté I have sene in you and the grete hardynesse that I have

8. *For thou woldist nat . . . vaynglory of the worlde:* i.e., you would not take pity on her out of true chastity but out of a worldly desire for being famous for your chastity.
9. *Harde the tokyns:* understood the symbolism.
1. *Me lothe:* loathsome to me.
2. On ermine, see n. 2, p. 206.
3. I.e., time.
4. *As of:* concerning.

herde of you, that nedys ye muste lye be me tonyght—therefore I pray you graunte me." "Truly," seyde he, "I shall do hit in no maner wyse." Than anone she made hym such sorow as thoughe she wolde have dyed.

¶"Well, Sir Bors," seyd she, "unto thys have ye brought me, nyghe to myne ende." And therewith she toke hym by the hande and bade hym beholde her—"and ye shall se how I shall dye for youre love." And he seyd than, "I shall hit never se." Than she departed and wente up into an hyghe batilment, and lad with her twelve jantilwomen; and whan they were above, one of the jantill-women cryed,

"A, Sir Bors, jantill knyght, have mercy on us all, and suffir my lady to have hir wyll; and if ye do nat, we muste suffir dethe with oure lady, for to falle downe of this hyghe towre—and if ye suffir us thus to dye for so litill a thynge, all ladys and jantillwomen woll sey you dishonoure."

Than loked he upwarde and saw they semed all ladyes of grete astate, and rychely and well beseyne. Than had he of hem grete pité—nat for that he was nat uncounceyled in hymselff[5] that levir he had they all had loste their soules[6] than he hys soule. And with that they felle all at onys unto the erthe; and whan he saw that, he was all abaysshed and had thereof grete mervayle—and with that he blyssed[7] hys body and hys vysayge. And anone he harde a grete noyse and a grete cry, as all the fyndys of helle had bene aboute hym; and therewith he sawe nother towre, lady, ne jantill-women, nother no chapell where he brought hys brothir to.

Than hylde he up both hys hondis to the hevyn, and seyde, "Fayre swete Lorde, Fadir and God in hevyn, I am grevously asca-ped!" And than he toke hys armys and hys horse and set hym on hys way. And anone he herde a clocke smyte on hys ryght honde; and thydir he cam to an abbay which was closed with hyghe wallis. And there was he lette in; and anone they supposed that he was one of the knyghtes of the Rounde Table that was in the Queste of the Sankgreall, so they led hym into a chambir and unarmed hym.

"Sirs," seyde Sir Bors, "if there be ony holy man in thys house, I pray you lette me speke with hym." Than one of hem lad hym unto the abbotte, which was in a chapell; and than Sir Bors salewed hym, and he hym agayne. "Sir," seyde Sir Bors, "I am a knyght arraunte," and tolde hym the adventures whych he had sene.

"Sir knyght," seyde the abbotte, "I wote nat what ye be, for I went that a knyght of youre ayge myght nat have be so stronge in the grace of Oure Lorde Jesu Cryste. Natforthan, ye shall go unto youre reste, for I woll nat counceyle thys day—hit ys to late—and tomorow I shall counceyle you as I can." And that nyght was Sir Bors served rychely; and on the morne erly he harde Masse. And than the abbot cam to hym and bade hym good morow, and Sir

fol.385r

[13]

5. *Nat for that he was nat uncounceyled in hymselff*: not that he had changed his mind.
6. I.e., by committing the mortal sin of suicide.
7. I.e., made the sign of the cross over.

Bors to hym agayne; and than he tolde hym he was felow of the Queste of the Sangreall, and how he had charge of the holy man to ete brede and watir.

"Than[8] Oure Lorde shewed Hym unto you in the lyknesse of a fowle, that suffirde grete anguysshe for us whan He was putte upon the Crosse, and bledde Hys herte blood for mankynde: there was the tokyn and the lyknesse of the Sankgreall that appered afore you, for the blood that the grete fowle bledde reysyd the chykyns[9] frome dethe to lyff. And by the bare tre betokenyth the worlde, whych ys naked and nedy, withoute fruyte, but if hit com of Oure Lorde. Also, the lady for whom ye fought for, and Kyng Anyaws, whych was lorde thereto, betokenyth Jesu Cryste, which ys Kyng of the worlde.

"And that ye fought with the champion for the lady, thus hit betokenyth: whan ye toke the batayle for the lady, by her shall ye undirstonde the Newe Law of Oure Lord Jesu Cryst and Holy Chirche; and by the othir lady ye shall undirstonde the Olde Lawe[1] and the fynde, which all day warryth ayenst Holy Chirch. Therefore ye dud youre batayle with ryght, for ye be Jesu Crystes knyghtes— therefore ye oughte to be defenders of Holy Chirche. [And by the black byrd myghte ye understande Holy Chirche,] whych seyth, 'I am blacke,' but he ys fayre.[2] And by the whyght birde may men undirstonde the fynde, and I shall telle you how the swan ys whyght withoutefurth and blacke within:

¶"Hit ys ipocresye, which ys withoute[3] yalew or pale, and[4] semyth withouteforth the servauntis of Jesu Cryste; but they be withinfurthe so horrible of fylth and synne, and begyle the worlde so evyll. Also, whan the fynde apperith to you in lyknesse of a man of religion and blamed the that thou lefft thy brothir for a lady, and he lede the where thou semed thy brothir was slayne—but he ys yette on lyve!—and all was for to putte the in erroure, and to brynge the into wanhope and lechery; for he knew thou were tendir-herted, and all was for thou sholdist nat fynde the aventure of the Sankgreall. And the thirde fowle betokenyth the stronge batayle ayenste the fayre ladyes whych were all devyls. Also, the dry tre and the whyght lylyes:

"The sere tre betokenyth thy brothir, Sir Lyonell, whych ys dry withoute vertu; and therefore men oughte to calle hym the rotyn tre, and the worme-etyn tre, for he ys a murtherer, and doth contrary to the order off knyghthode. And the two whyght floures signifieth two maydyns: the one ys a knyght which ye wounded the other day, and the other is the jantillwoman whych ye rescowed. And why the other floure drew nye the tother, that was the knyght

fol.385v

fol.386r

---

8. The abbot is speaking.
9. I.e., chicks.
1. On the Old Law and the New Law, see n. 9, p. 507.
2. I.e., white Cf. the lover's declaration in the Song of Solomon, 1.5: "I am black but comely, O ye daughters of Jerusalem." Traditional Christian interpretation of the Old Testament understands this phrase allegorically to refer to the Church of the New Law as loved by Christ.
3. I.e., on the outside.
4. I.e., and whose representatives.

which wolde have defowled her and hymselff bothe. And, Sir Bors, ye had bene a grete foole and in grete perell for to have sene tho two flowris perish for to succoure the rottyn tre, for and they had synned togydir,[5] they had be dampned; and for ye rescowed them bothe, men myght calle you a verry knyght and the servaunte of Jesu Cryste."

¶Than wente Sir Bors frome thens and commaunded the abbotte to God. And than he rode all that day, and herberowde with an olde lady; and on the morne he rode to a castell in a valey, and there he mette with a yoman goyng a grete pace toward a foreyste.

"Sey me," seyde Sir Bors, "canst thou telle me of ony adventure?" "Sir," seyde he, "here shall be undir thys castell a grete and a mervaylous turnemente." "Of what folkys shall hit be?" seyde Sir Bors. "The Erle of Playns shall be on the tone party, and the Ladyes nevew off Herbyn on the todir party." Than Sir Bors thought to be there, to assay iff he myght mete with hys brothir Sir Lyonell, or ony other of hys felyship whych were in the Queste of the Sankgreall. Than he turned to an ermytayge that was in the entré of the foreysst; and whan he was com thydir he founde there Sir Lyonell, his brother, which sate all unarmed at the entré of the chapell dore, for to abyde there herberow[6] tylle on the morne that the turnement sholde be. And whan Sir Bors saw hym he had grete joy of hym, that no man cowde telle of gretter joy.

¶And than he alyght of his horse, and seyde, "Fayre swete brothir, whan cam ye hydir?" And as Sir Lyonell saw hym he seyde, "A, Sir Bors, ye may nat make none avaunte, but as for you I myght have bene slayne: whan ye saw two knyghtes lede me away beatynge me, ye leffte me to succour a jantillwoman, and suffird me in perell of deth—for never arste ne ded no brothir to another so grete an untrouthe—and for that myssedede I ensure you now but dethe, for well have ye deserved hit. Therefor kepe you frome me frome hensforewarde—and that shall ye fynde as sone as I am armed."

¶Whan Sir Bors undirstode his brothirs wratth, he kneled downe tofore hym to the erthe, and cryed hym mercy, holdyng up both hys hondis, and prayde hym to forgyff hym hys evyll wylle.

"Nay, nay," seyde Sir Lyonell, "that shall never [be] and[7] I may have the hygher[8] hande—that I make myne avow to God. Thou shalt have dethe, for hit were pité ye leved any lenger." Ryght so he wente in and toke hys harneyse, and lyghte upon his horse and cam tofore hym, and seyde, "Sir Bors, kepe the fro me, for I shall do to the as I wolde do to a felon other a traytoure; for ye be the untrewyst knyght that ever cam oute of so worthy an house as was Kyng Bors de Ganis, which was oure fadir. Therefore

---

5. By medieval standards, it was possible to argue that the gentlewoman could have sinned if she allowed herself to be raped; committing suicide in this instance might not have been considered a mortal sin, given the alternative.
6. *Abyde there herberow*: lodge there.
7. I.e., if.
8. I.e., upper.

sterte uppon thy horse—and so shalt thou be moste at thyne avauntayge—and but if[9] thou wylt, I woll renne uppon the there as thou arte, on foote. And so the shame shall be myne, and the harme youres—but of that shame recke I nought."

Whan Sir **Bors** sye that he must fyght with his brothir othir ellis to dye, he wyst nat what to do; so hys herte counceyled hym nat thereto, inasmuch as Sir **Lyonell** was hys elder brothir, wherefore he oughte to bere hym reverence. Yette kneled he adowne agayne tofore Sir **Lyonelles** horse feete, and seyde, "Fayre swete brothir, have mercy uppon me and sle me nat, and have in remembraunce the grete love which oughte to be betwene us two."

¶So whatsomever Sir **Bors** seyde to Sir **Lyonell**, he rought nat, for the fynde had brought hym in suche a wylle that he sholde sle hym.

¶So when Sir **Lyonell** saw he wolde none other do, nor wolde nat ryse to gyff hym batayle, he russhed over hym so that he smote Sir **Bors** with his horse feete upwarde to the erthe, and hurte hym so sore that he sowned for distresse which he felte in hymselff to have dyed withoute confession.

¶So when Sir **Lyonell** saw thys, he alyght of hys horse to have smytten of hys hede; and so he toke hym by the helme and wolde have rente hit frome hys hede.

¶Therewith cam the ermyte rennynge unto hym, which was a good man and of grete ayge, and well had herde all the wordis [that were betwene them]. He lepe betwene them, and so felle downe uppon Sir **Bors**, and seyde unto Sir **Lyonell**, "A, jantyll knyght, have mercy uppon me and uppon thy brothir, for if thou sle hym thou shalt be dede of that synne—and that were grete sorow, for he ys one of the worthyest knyghtes of the worlde and of beste condicions." "So God me helpe, 'sir'[1] pryste, but if ye fle from hym I shall sle you, and he shall never the sunner be quytte."[2]

¶"Sertes," seyde the good man, "I had levir ye sle me than hym, for as for my dethe shall nat be grete harme, nat halff so much as for his woll be."

¶"Well," seyd Sir **Leonell**, "I am agreed!"—and sette his honde to his swerde and smote hym so harde that hys hede yode off bacwarde. And natforthan he [restrayned] hym nat of hys evyll wyll, but toke hys brothir by the helme and unlaced hit to have smytten off hys hede—and had slayne hym, had nat a felowe of hys of the Rounde Table com, whos name was called Sir **Collegrevaunce**, a felow of the Rounde Table that com thydyr as Oure Lordis wyll wolde. And whan he saw the good man slayne, he mervayled much what hit myght be.

And than he behylde Sir **Lyonell** that wolde have slayne hys brothir, [and knewe] Sir **Bors**, which he loved ryght well. Than sterte he adowne and toke Sir **Lyonell** by the shuldirs, and drew hym strongely abacke frome Sir **Bors**, and seyde to Sir **Lyonell**, "Woll ye

How Sir Lyonell wolde have slayne his brother Sir Bors

ep

10

15

fol.387r

20

[15]

25

30

35

40

45

---

9. *But if:* unless.
1. I.e., Lyonell mocks the old priest's ability in fighting.
2. *Never the sunner be quytte:* i.e., still not escape.

sle youre brothir, the worthyest knyght one[3] of the worlde? That sholde no good man suffir."

¶"Why so?" seyde Sir **Lyonell**, "woll ye lette[4] me thereoff? For if ye entirmete thereoff, I shall sle you to, and hym thereafftir."

¶"Why," seyde Sir **Colgrevaunce**, "ys thys sothe that ye woll sle hym?"

¶"Yee, sle hym woll I, whoso seyth the contrary, for he hath done so muche ayenst me that he hath well deserved hit"—and so ran uppon hym, and wolde have smytten of the hede. And so Sir **Colgrevaunce** ran betwixte them, and seyde, "And ye be so hardy to do so more, we two shall meddyll togidirs!"

¶So whan Sir **Lyonell** undirstood his wordis, he toke his shylde tofore hym and asked hym what that he was.

¶"Sir, my name ys Sir **Collgrevaunce**, one of his felowis."

¶Than Sir **Lyonell** defyed hym, and so he sterte uppon hym and gaff hym a grete stroke thorow the helme. Than he drew his swerde—for he was a passyng good knyght—and defended hym ryght manfully. And so longe dured there the batayle that Sir **Bors** sate up all angwyshlye and behylde Sir **Collegrevaunce**, the good knyght, that fought with his brother for his quarell. Thereof he was full hevy, and thought if Sir **Collgrevaunce** slew hys brothir that he sholde never have joy—

¶Also, and if hys brothir slew Sir **Collgrevaunce**, "the same shame sholde ever be myne." Than wolde he have rysen to have departed them, but he had nat so much myght to stonde one foote.

¶And so he abode so longe that Sir **Collgrevaunce** was over-throwyn, for thys Sir **Lyonell** was of grete chevalry, and passyng hardy; for he had perced the hawbirke and the helme so sore that he abode but deth—for he had lost much blood, that hit was mer-vayle that he myght stonde upryght. Than behylde he Sir **Bors** whych sate dressyng[5] upward hymselff, [and] seyde, "A, Sir **Bors**! Why cam ye nat to rescowe me oute of perell of dethe, wherein I have putte me to succour you which were ryght now nyghe dethe?" "Sertes," seyde Sir **Lyonell**, "that shall nat avayle you! For none of you shall be othirs warraunte, but ye shall dye both of my honde."

¶Whan Sir **Bors** herde that he seyde so muche, he arose and put on hys helme—and than he perceyved first the ermyte pryste whych was slayne; than made he a mervaylous sorow uppon hym.

¶Than Sir **Collgrevaunce** cryed offtyn uppon Sir **Bors** and seyde, "Why woll ye lat me dye here for your sake? No forse, sir, if hit please you that I shall dy; the deth shall please me the bettir, for to save a worthyer man myght I never ressayve the dethe."

¶With that worde Sir **Lyonell** smote of the helme frome hys hede. And whan Sir **Collgrevaunce** saw that he myght nat ascape, than he seyde, "Fayre swete Jesu Cryste, that I have myssedo, have mercy uppon my soule. For such sorow that my harte suffirthe for

Marginal notes:
fol.387v

How Sir Lyonell slewe the ermyte and Collgrevaunce for the rescowe of his brother Syr Bors

[16]

fol.388r

---

3. *The worthyest knyght one:* one of the worthiest knights.
4. I.e., stop, hinder.
5. I.e., propping.

goodnes and for almesdede that I wolde have done here, be to me alyegemente of penaunce unto my sowle helthe."[6]

And so at thes wordis Sir **Lyonell** smote hym so sore that he bare hym dede to the erthe. And whan he had slayne Sir **Collgrevaunce,** he ran uppon hys brothir as a fyndely man, and gaff hym such a stroke that he made hym stoupe; and [he,] as he that was full of humilité, prayde hym for Goddis love to leve his batayle—"for if hit befelle, fayre brothir, if that I sle you other ye me, we both shall dye for that synne."

"So God me helpe, I shall never have othir mercy, and I may have the bettir honde." "Well," seyde Sir **Bors**—and drew hys swerde, all wepyng—and seyde, "fayre brother, God knowith myne entente, for ye have done full evyll thys day to sle an holy pryste which never trespasced. Also ye have slayne a jantill knyght, and one of oure felowis. And well wote ye that I am nat aferde of you gretely; but I drede the wratthe of God—and thys ys an unkyndely[7] werre—therefore God shew His myracle uppon us bothe, and God have mercy uppon me, thoughe I defende my lyff ayenst my bro-thir!" And so with that Sir **Bors** lyffte up hys honde, and wolde have smyttyn hys brothir. And with that he harde a voice whych seyde, "Fle, Sir **Bors,** and towche hym nat, othir ellis thou shalt sle hym!"

¶Ryght so alyght a clowde betwyxte them in lykenes of a fayre and a mervaylous flame, that bothe hir two shyldis brente. Than were they sore aferde and felle both to the erthe, and lay there a grete whyle in a sowne.

¶And whan they cam to themselff, Sir **Bors** saw that hys brothir had none harme—than he hylde up both his hondys, for he drad last God had takyn vengeaunce uppon hym. So with that he harde a voyce that seyde, "Sir **Bors,** go hens and beare felyship no lenger with thy brothir, but take thy way anone ryght to the see, for Sir **Percivale** abydith the there."

¶Than he seyde to his brother, "For Goddis love, fayre swete brothir, forgyff me my trespasse!" Than he answerd and seyde, "God forgyff you, and I do gladly." So Sir **Bors** departed frome hym, and rode the next way to the se; and at the last by fortune he cam to an abbay which was nyghe the see, and that nyght he rested hym there. And as he slepte, there cam a voyse [to hym] and bade hym go to the see. Than he sterte up and made a signe of the crosse [in the myddes of his forhede,] and toke hym to hys harnes, and made redy hys horse, [and mounted upon hym;] and at a bro-kyn wall he rode oute, and by fortune he cam to the see. And uppon the see stronde he founde a shyppe that was coverde all with whyght samyte.

¶Than he alyghte and betoke hym to Jesu Cryste. And as sone as he was entird, the shippe departed into the see and [wente so fast that] to hys semyng hit wente fleyng. But hit was sone durked,

---

6. *Be to me alyegemente of penaunce unto my sowle helthe:* (Jesus) be to me the alleviation of penance paid for the health of my soul.
7. I.e., unnatural.

that he myght know no man; than he layde hym downe and slept tyll hit was day. And whan he was waked, he sawe in myddis of the shippe a knyght lye all armed, sauff hys helme; and anone he was ware hit was Sir Percivale de Galys. And than he made of hym ryght grete joy.

But Sir Percivale was abaysshed of hym and asked what he was. "A, fayre sir," seyde Sir Bors, "know ye me nat?" "Sertes," seyde he, "I mervayle how ye cam hydir, but if Oure Lorde brought you hydir Hymselff." Than Sir Bors smyled, and ded off hys helme, and anone Sir Percyvale knew hym—and ayther made grete joy of othir, that hit was mervayle to hyre. Than Sir Bors tolde hym how he cam into the ship, and by whos amonyshment. And aythir told other of their temptacions, as ye have herde toforehonde. So wente they dryvyng in the see, one whyle backwarde, another while fore-warde; and every man comforted other, and ever they were in theyre prayers. Than seyde Sir Percivale, "We lak nothynge but Sir Galahad, the good knyght."

Now turnyth the tale unto Sir Galahad.

Now seyth the tale, whan Sir Galahad had rescowed Sir Percyvale frome the twenty knyghtes, he rode tho into a waste foreyste wherein he dud many journeyes and founde many adventures which he brought all to an ende, whereof the tale makith here no mencion.

❡Than he toke hys way to the see. And on a day, as hit befelle, as he passed by a castell there was a wondir turnemente. But they withoute[8] had done so much that they within were put to the worse, and yet were they within good knyghtes inow.

❡So whan Sir Galahad saw tho within were at so grete myschyff that men slew hem at the entré of the castell, than he thought to helpe them, and put a speare furthe, and smote the firste, that he flowe to the erthe and the speare yode in pecis. Than he drew hys swerde and smote there as they were thyckyst. And so he dud won-dirfull dedys of armys, that all they mervayled; and so hyt happynde that Sir Gawayne and Sir Ector de Marys were with the knyghtes withoute.

❡But than they aspyed the whyght shylde with the rede crosse; and anone that one seyde to that othir, "Yondir ys the good knyght Sir Galahad, the haute prynce. Now, forsothe, methynkith he shall be a grete foole that shall mete with hym to fyght!"—but at the last by aventure he cam by Sir Gawayne and smote hym so sore that he clave hys helme and the coyff of iron unto the hede—

❡That Sir Gawayne felle to the erthe; but the stroke was so grete that hit slented downe and kutte the horse sholdir in too. So whan Sir Ector saw Sir Gawayne downe, he drew hym asyde, and thought hit no wysedom for to abyde hym—and also for naturall love, for because he was hys uncle.

❡Thus thorow hys hardynesse he bete abacke all the knyghtes withoute; and than they within cam oute and chaced them all

fol.389r

[XVII.1]

Here Sir Galahad hurte Sir Gawayne lyke as Sir Launce-lot made mencion tofore at Camelot

fol.389v

5

10

15

20

25

30

35

45

8. I.e., from outside the castle.

aboute. But whan Sir Galahad saw there wolde none turne agayne, he stale away prevayly, and no man wyste where he was becom. "Now, be my hede," seyde Sir Gawayne unto Sir Ector, "now ar the wondirs trew that was seyd of Sir Launcelot, that the swerd which stake in the stone shulde gyff me such a buffette that I wold nat have hit for the beste castell in the worlde;[9] and sothely now hit ys preved trew, for never ar had I such a stroke of mannys honde." "Sir," seyde Sir Ector, "mesemyth youre queste ys done—and myne is nat done."

¶"Well," seyde he, "I shall seke no farther." Than was Sir Gawayne borne into the castell, and unarmed hym and leyde hym in a rych bedde, and a leche was founde to hele hym [and to be hole within a moneth. Thus Gawayne and Ector abode togyder,] and Sir Ector wolde nat departe frome hym tyll he was nyghe hole.

¶And so this good knyght Sir Galahad rode so faste that he cam that nyght to the castell[1] of Carbonecke; and so hit befelle hym that he was benyghted, and cam unto an armytayge.

¶So the good man was fayne whan he saw he was a knyght arraunte.

¶So whan they were at reste, there befelle a jantillwoman com and cnokkede at the dore and called Sir Galahad; and so the good man cam to the dore to wete what she wolde. Than she called the ermyte, Sir Ulphyne, and seyde, "I am a jantillwoman that wolde fayne speke with the knyght which ys within you."[2] Than the good man awaked Sir Galahad and bade hym aryse, "and speke with a jantyllwoman that semyth she hath grete nede of you." Than Sir Galahad wente to hir and asked hir what she wolde.

¶"Sir Galahad," seyde she, "I woll that ye arme you and lyght uppon your horse and sew me, for I shall shew you within thys three dayes the hyghest adventure that ever ony knyght saw." So anone Sir Galahad armed hym and toke hys horse, and commended the ermyte to God. And so he bade the jantillwoman to ryde, and he wolde folow there as she lyked.

¶So she rode as faste as hir palferey myght bere her tyll that she cam to the see, whych was called Collybye. And by nyght they com unto a castell in a valey closed[3] with a rennyng watir, whych had stronge wallis and hyghe. And so she entird into the castell with Sir Galahad—and there had he grete chere, for the lady of that castell was the damesels lady. So was he unarmed.

¶Than seyde the damesell, "Madame, shall we abyde here all thys day?" "Nay," seyde she, "but tylle he hath dyned and slepte a litill." And so he ete and slepte a whyle; and this mayde than called hym and armed hym by torchelyght. And whan the mayden was horsed and he bothe, the lady toke Sir Galahad a fayre shylde and ryche, and so they departed frome the castell and rode tylle they

_____

9. For the prediction, see p. 499, lines 4–6.
1. I.e., the environs of the castle.
2. *Within you*: with you within.
3. I.e., enclosed.

cam to the see; and there they founde the shippe that Sir 𝔅𝔬𝔯𝔰 and
Sir 𝔓𝔢𝔯𝔠𝔦𝔟𝔞𝔩𝔢 was in, whych seyde on the shipbourde—[4]

❡"Sir 𝔊𝔞𝔩𝔞𝔥𝔞𝔡, ye be wellcom, for we have abydyn you longe."
And whan he herde them, he asked them what they were. "Sir,"
seyde she, "leve youre horse hyre, and I shall leve myne also"—   5
and toke hir sadils and hir brydyls with them, and made a crosse
on them, and so entird into the ship. And the two knyghtes resceyved them bothe with grete joy, and everych knew other. And so
the wynde arose and drove hem thorow the see into a mervayles
place; and within a whyle hit dawed. Than dud Sir 𝔊𝔞𝔩𝔞𝔥𝔞𝔡 of hys   10
helme and hys swerde, and asked of hys felowis from whens com
that fayre shippe.

❡"Trewly," seyde they, "ye wote as well as we, but[5] hit com of
Goddis grace." And than they tolde everych to othir of all theyre
harde aventures, and of her grete temptacions. "Truly," seyd Sir   15
𝔊𝔞𝔩𝔞𝔥𝔞𝔡, "ye ar much bounden to God, for ye have escaped ryght
grete adventures—

❡"Sertes, had nat this jantillwoman bene, I had nat come hydir
at thys tyme; for as for you two, I wente never to have founde you
in thys straunge contreys." "A, Sir 𝔊𝔞𝔩𝔞𝔥𝔞𝔡," seyde Sir 𝔅𝔬𝔯𝔰, "if Sir   20
𝔏𝔞𝔲𝔫𝔠𝔢𝔩𝔬𝔱 your fadir were here, than were we well at ease, for than   fol.390v
mesemed we fayled nothynge."

❡"That may nat be," seyd Sir 𝔊𝔞𝔩𝔞𝔥𝔞𝔡, "but if hit pleased Our
Lorde." By than the shipp had renne frome the londe of 𝔏𝔬𝔤𝔯𝔶𝔰
many myles. So by adventure hit aryved up bytwyxte two rocchis,   25
passynge grete and mervaylous; but there they myght nat londe,
for there was a swalowe of the see—

❡Save[6] there was another shippe, and uppon hit they myght go
withoute daungere.

❡"Now go we thydir," seyde the jantillwoman, "and there shall   30
we se adventures, for so ys Oure Lordys wylle." And wan they com
thyder, they founde the shippe ryche inowghe, but they founde
nother man nor woman therein. But they founde in the ende of
the shippe two fayre lettirs wrytten, which seyde a dredefull worde
and a mervaylous: 35

❡THOU MAN WHYCH SHALT ENTIR INTO THYS SHIPPE,
BEWARE THAT THOU BE IN
STEDEFASTE BELEVE, FOR I AM FAYTHE.

                                                                                 40

AND THEREFORE BEWARE HOW THOU ENTIRST BUT IF THOU BE
STEDFASTE, FOR AND THOU FAYLE THEREOF
I SHALL NAT HELPE THE.

And than seyde the jantillwoman, "Sir 𝔓𝔢𝔯𝔠𝔦𝔟𝔞𝔩𝔢," seyde she, "wote   45
ye what I am?" "Sertes," seyde he, "nay; unto my wytynge I saw

---

4. *On the shipbourde*: from on board the ship.
5. I.e., unless.
6. I.e., except.

you never arst." "Wyte ye well," seyde she, "I am thy syster, whych was doughter unto Kynge Pellynor—and therefore wete you welle ye ar the man that I moste love. And if ye be nat in perfite belyve of Jesu Cryste, entir nat in no maner of wyse: for than sholde ye perish[7] the shippe, for he[8] ys so perfite he woll suffir no synner within hym."

¶So whan Sir Percyvale undirstode she was hys verry syster, he was inwardly[9] glad, and seyde, "Fayre sister, I shall entir in, for if I be a myssecreature other an untrew knyght, there shall I perische."

¶So in the meanwhyle Sir Galahad blyssed hym[1] and entirde [3] thereinne, and so nexte the jantillwoman, and than Sir Bors, and than Sir Percyvale. And whan they were in, hit was so mervaylous fayre and ryche [that they merveylled]. And amyddis the shippe was a fayre bedde; and anone Sir Galahad wente thereto and founde fol.391r thereon a crowne of sylke. And at the feete was a swerde, rych and fayre, and hit was drawyn oute of the sheeth [half] a foote and more. And the swerde was of dyverse fassions: and the pomell was of stoone, and there was in hym all maner of coloures that ony man myght fynde, and every of the coloures had dyverse vertues;[2] and the scalis of the hauffte were of two rybbis of two dyverse bestis: that one was a serpente whych ys coversaunte in Calydone and ys called there the serpente of the fynde—and the boone of hym ys of such vertu that there ys no hande that handelith hym shall never be wery nother hurte; and the other bone ys of a fyssh whych ys nat ryght grete, and hauntith the floode[3] of Eufrate, and that fyssh ys called Ertanax—and the bonys be of such maner of kynde that who that handelyth hym shall have so muche wyll that he shall never be wery, and he shall nat thynke on joy nother sorow that he hath had, but only that thynge that he beholdith before hym. (And as for thys swerde, there shall never man begrype hym—that ys to sey, the handils—but one; and he shall passe all othir.)

"In the name of God," seyde Sir Percivale, "I shall assay to handyll hit." So he sette hys honde to the swerde, but he myght nat begrype hit. "Be my faythe," seyde he, "now have I fayled." Than Sir Bors sette to hys hande, and fayled.

¶Than Sir Galahad behylde the swerde, and saw lettirs lyke bloode that seyde:

LAT SE WHO DARE DRAW ME OUTE OF MY SHEETH
BUT IF HE BE MORE HARDYER THAN ONY OTHER.
FOR WHO THAT DRAWITH ME OUTE, WETE YOU WELLE
HE SHALL NEVER BE SHAMED OF HYS BODY,
NOTHER WOUNDED TO THE DETHE.

---

7. I.e., destroy.
8. I.e., the ship.
9. I.e., thoroughly, fully.
1. *Blyssed hym:* i.e., crossed himself.
2. I.e., powers.
3. I.e., river.

¶"Perfay," seyde Sir Galahad, "I wolde draw thys swerde oute of the sheethe, but the offendynge ys so grete that I shall nat sette my hande thereto."

¶"Now, sirs," seyde the jantillwoman, "the drawynge of thys swerde ys warned[4] to all, sauff all only to you. Also thys shippe aryved into the realme of Logrys, and that tyme was dedly warre betwene Kyng Labor, which was fadir unto the Maymed Kynge, and Kynge Hurlaine, whych was a Saresyn. But than was he newly crystened, and so aftirwarde hylde hym one of the worthyest men of the worlde. And so upon a day hit befelle that Kynge Labor and Kynge Hurlaine had assembeled theire folke uppon the see, where thys shippe was aryved. And there Kynge Hurlaine was discomfite, and hys men slayne; and he was aferde to be dede and fledde to thys shippe, and there founde this swerde, and drew hit—

¶"And cam oute and founde Kynge Labor, the man of the worlde of all Crystyn in whom there was the grettist faythe—and whan Kynge Hurlaine [saw Kynge Labor, he dressid this suerd] and smote hym uppon the helme so harde that he clave hym and hys horse to the erthe with the firste stroke of hys swerde. And hit was in the realme of Logris, and so befelle there grete pestilence, and grete harme to bothe reallmys; for there encresed nother corne, ne grasse, nother well-nye no fruyte, ne in the watir was founde no fyssh.

"Therefore men calle hit—the londys of the two marchys—the Waste Londe, for that dolerous stroke. And whan Kynge Hurleine saw thys swerde so kerveyynge, he turned agayne to fecch the scawberd, and so cam into thys shippe and entird, and put up the swerde in the sheethe; and as sone as he had done hit he felle downe dede afore the bedde. Thus was the swerde preved that never man drew hit but he were dede or maymed.

¶"So lay he here tyll a maydyn cam into the shippe and caste hym oute, for there was no man so hardy in the worlde to entir in that shippe for the defens."[5]

¶And than behylde they the scawberte: hit besemyd to be of a serpentis skynne, and thereon were lettirs of golde and sylver (and the gurdyll was but porely to com to, and nat able to susteyne such a ryche swerde) and the lettirs seyde:

HE WHYCH SHALL WELDE ME OUGHT TO BE MORE HARDY THAN
ONY OTHER, IF HE BEARE ME
AS TRULY AS ME OUGHTE TO BE BORNE.
¶FOR THE BODY OF HYM WHICH I OUGHT TO HANGE BY, HE
SHALL NAT BE SHAMED IN NO PLACE WHYLE HE YS GURDE WITH
THE GURDYLL. NOTHER NEVER NONE BE SO HARDY TO DO AWAY
THYS GURDYLL, FOR HIT OUGHT NAT TO BE DONE AWAY

---

4. I.e., forbidden.
5. *For the defens:* because of the prohibition (of the two letters, see p. 559).

BUT BY THE HONDIS OF A MAYDE, AND THAT SHE BE A KYNGIS
DOUGHTER AND A QUENYS; AND SHE MUST BE A MAYDE ALL
THE DAYES OF HIR LYFF, BOTH IN WYLL AND IN WORKE;
AND IF SHE BREKE HIR VIRGINITÉ, SHE SHALL DY THE MOSTE
VYLAYNES DETH THAT EVER DUD ONY WOMAN.   5

¶ "Sir, seyde Sir Percivale, "turne thys swerde that we may se what
ys on the other syde." And hit was rede os bloode, with blacke
lettirs as ony cole that seyde:

HE THAT SHALL PRAYSE ME MOSTE, MOSTE SHALL HE FYNDE ME
TO BLAME AT A GRETE NEDE;[6] AND TO WHOM I SHOLDE BE
MOSTE DEBONAYRE[7] SHALL BE MOST FELON[8]—AND THAT
SHALL BE AT ONE TYME ONLY.

"Fayre brother," seyde she to Sir Percyvale, "hit befelle afftir a fourty
yere aftir the Passion of Oure Lorde Jesu Cryste, that Nacien, the
brothir-in-law of Kyng Mordrayns,[9] was bore in a towne, more than
fourtene dayes journey frome his contray, by the commaundemente of Oure Lorde, into an yle into the partyes[1] of the Weste   20
that men clepith the Ile of Turnaunce.

"So befelle hit, he founde thys shippe at the entré of a roche,
and he founde the bedde and the swerde, as we have herd now;
natforthan he had nat so much hardynesse to draw hit. And there
he dwelled an[2] eyght dayes, and at the nynyth day there felle a   25
grete wynd whych departed hym oute of the ile, and brought hym
to another ile by a roche; and there he founde the grettist gyaunte
that ever man myght see. And therewith cam that horrible gyaunte
to sle hym; and than he loked aboute hym, and myght nat fle—
also he had nothyng wherewith to defende hym. But at the laste   30
he ran to the swerde, and whan he saw hit naked he praysed hit
muche, and than he shooke hit—and therewith hit brake in the   fol.392v
myddys.

" 'A!' seyde Nacien, the thynge that I moste praysed ought I now
moste to blame.' And therewith he threw the pecis of this swerde   35
over hys bedde; and aftir that he lepe over the bourde to fyght with
the gyaunte, and slew hym. And anone he entirde into the shyppe
agayne, and the wynde arose and drove hym thorow the see, that
by adventure he cam to another shippe, where Kynge Mordrayns
was, whych had bene tempted full evyll with[3] the fynde, in the   40
porte of Perelous Roche. And whan that one saw that other they
made grete joy aythir of othir; and so they tolde eche other of their
adventure—and how the swerde fayled hym at hys moste nede:

6. I.e., time of need.
7. I.e., gracious.
8. I.e., treated as a felon.
9. Cf. n. 6, p. 534.
1. I.e., regions.
2. I.e., a period of.
3. I.e., by.

¶ "So whan 𝕸ordrayns saw the swerde, he praysed hit muche—
'but the brekyng was do by wyckednesse of thyselff-ward,[4] for thou
arte in som synne.' And there he toke the swerde and sette the
pecis togydirs: and they were as fayre i-sowdred as ever they were
tofore. And than he put the swerde in the sheeth ayen, and leyde
hit downe on the bedde:

¶ "Than herde they a voyce that seyde, 'Go ye oute of thys shippe
a litill whyle and entir into that othir for drede ye falle in dedly
synne—for and ye be founde in dedely synne ye may nat ascape,
but perishe.' And so they wente into the othir shippe; and as 𝕹acyen
wente over the bourde, he was smytten with a swerde on the ryght
foote, that he felle downe noselynge to the shippebourde.

"And therewith he seyde, 'A, Good Lorde, how am I hurte?' Than
there cam a voice that seyde, 'Take thou that for thy forfette that
thou dyddist in drawynge of this swerde; therefore thou hast ressayved a wounde, for thou were never worthy to handyll hit: the
wrytynge makith mencion.' " "In the name of God," seyde Sir 𝕲alahað, "ye ar ryght wyse of thes workes."[5] "Sir," seyde she, "there
was a kynge that hyght 𝕻elleaus, which men called the Maymed
Kynge, and whyle he myght ryde he supported much Crystyndom
and Holy Chyrche. So upon a day he hunted in a woode of hys
owne whych lasted unto the see, so at the laste he loste hys howndys and hys knyghtes, sauff only one. And so he and his knyght
wente tyll that they cam toward Irelonde, and there he founde the
shippe.

"And whan he saw the lettirs and undirstood them, yet he entird,
for he was ryght perfite of lyff (but hys knyght had no hardynes to
entir). And there founde he thys swerde, and drew hit oute as much
as ye may se:

¶ "So therewith entirde a spere wherewith he was smytten thorow both thyghes—and never sith myght he be heled, ne nought
shall tofore we com to hym.[6] Thus," seyde she, "was Kyng 𝕻elles,
youre grauntesyre, maymed for hys hardynes." "In the name of
God, damesell," seyde Sir 𝕲alahað. So they wente towarde the
bedde to beholde all aboute hit; and abovyn the bed there hynge

[5]

fol.393r

4. *Of thyselff-ward*: coming from you.
5. *Wyse of thes workes*: i.e., knowledgeable of these events.
6. *Pelleaus . . . the Maymed Kynge . . . tofore we com to hym*: Pelleaus, or Pelles, is elsewhere
in Malory the *father* of the actual Maimed King, Pellam of Lystenoyse, and therefore the
great-grandfather of Galahad, not his grandfather as claimed just below—and the method
of maiming is different from that about to be described (see p. 56). In the French source
at this point a new and unrelated Maimed King is introduced, named Parlan. In an effort
to simplify the immediate narrative, Malory has thus introduced an awkward cluster of
inconsistencies when viewed against the totality of his work. As in Malory's source, the
present account is a partial recollection of stories of the Fisher King and the Waste Land
in which the king's health is directly linked to the health of his land; as such those stories
probably reflect ancient fertility myth—a dimension perhaps implicit in the present
account in the form of the wound through the thighs, potentially to be understood as a
euphemism for castration (cf. Percyvale's self-wounding in the interests of greater spiritual
purity on p. 530). In Malory's *Tale of Balyn and Balan*, the Dolerous Stroke, which Balyn
levels at Pellam and which lays waste to his lands (p. 56) is another partially recollected
manifestation of such mythic material.

two swerdys. Also there were spyndelys whych were whyght as
snowe, and othir that were rede as bloode, and othir abovyn[7] grene
as ony emerawde—of these three colowres were thes spyndyls, and
of naturall coloure within, and withoute ony payntynge.

"Thes spyndyls," seyde the damesell—"was[8] whan synfull Eve   5
cam to gadir fruyte, for which Adam and she were put oute of
Paradyse; she toke with her the bowgh whych the appyll hynge on.
Then perseyved she that the braunche was freysh and grene, and
she remembird of the losse which cam of the tre.

"Than she thought to kepe the braunche as longe as she myght;   10
and, for she had no coffir to kepe hit in, she put hit in the erthe.
So by the wylle of Oure Lorde the braunche grew to a grete tre
within a litill whyle—and was as whyght as ony snowe, braunchis,
bowis, and levys: that was a tokyn that a maydyn planted hit. But
affter that, Oure Lorde com to Adam and bade hym know hys wyff   15
fleyshly, as nature requyred:

❡"So lay Adam with hys wyff, undir the same tre; and anone the
tre which was whyght felle[9] to grene os ony grasse, and all[1] that
com oute of hit. And in the same tyme that they medled[2] togydirs,
Abell was begotyn.   20

"Thus was the tre longe of grene coloure. And so hit befelle many
dayes aftir, undir the same tre, Cayme slew Abell—whereof befelle   fol.393v
grete mervayle; for as Abell had ressayved dethe undir the grene
tre, he[3] loste the grene colour and becam rede: and that was in
tokenyng of blood. And anone all the plantis dyed thereoff, but the   25
tre grewe and waxed mervaylusly fayre, and hit was the moste fayryst tre and the most delectable that ony man myght beholde and
se (and so ded the plantes that grewe oute of hit tofore that Abell
was slayne undir hit). And so longe dured the tre tyll that Salamon,
Kynge Davythys sonne, regned and hylde the londe aftir his fadir.   30
So thys Salamon was wyse, and knew all the vertues of stonys and
treys; also he knew the course of the stirres, and of many other
dyvers thynges:

❡"So this Salamon had an evyll wyff, wherethorow he wente[4]
there had be no good woman borne; and therefore he dispysed   35
them in hys bookis.[5] So there answerde a voice that seyde to hym
thus: 'Salamon, if hevynesse com to a man by a woman,[6] ne rek
thou never, for yet shall there com a woman[7] whereof there shall

---

7. I.e., at the top.
8. I.e., it was.
9. I.e., changed.
1. I.e., all subsequent trees.
2. I.e., lay.
3. I.e., the tree.
4. I.e., believed.
5. Solomon was reputed to have written the Books of Proverbs, Canticles, Ecclesiastes, and
   the Wisdom of Solomon. Most famous of passages from these which were traditionally
   seen as misogynistic is Ecclesiastes 7:26–29, which begins, "I find more bitter than death
   the woman, whose heart is snares and nets, and her hands as bands: whoso pleaseth God
   shall escape from her; but the sinner shall be taken by her." Cf. Proverbs 7:5–27, 9:13–
   18, 22:14, and 23:27.
6. I.e., not just his wife, but the legacy of Eve.
7. I.e., the Virgin Mary.

com gretter joy to a man an hondred tymes than thys hevynesse gyvith sorow—and that woman shall be borne of thy lynayge.'

❡"So whan Salamon harde thes wordis, he hylde hymself but a foole—that preff had he by[8] olde bookis—the trouthe. Also the Holy Goste shewed hym the commynge of the glorius Virgyne Mary. Than asked he the voyce if hit sholde be in the yarde[9] of hys lynayge. 'Nay,' seyde the voyce, 'but there shall com a man which shall be a mayde, and laste of youre bloode, and he shall be as good a knyght as deuke Josue, thy brother-in-law:

" 'Now have I sertefyed the of that[1] thou stondist in doute.' Than was Salamon gladde that there shulde com ony suche of hys lynayge; but ever he mervayled and studyed who that sholde be, and what hys name myght be. So hys wyff perceyved that he studyed, and thought she wolde know at som season; and so she wayted hir tyme, and cam to hym and asked hym, and there he tolde her alltogydir how the voice had tolde hym—

❡" 'Well,' seyde she, 'I shall lette make a shippe of the beste wood and moste durable that ony man may fynde.' So Salamon sente for carpenters, of all the londe the beste. And whan they had made the shippe, the lady seyde to Salamon, 'Sir, syn hit ys so that thys knyght oughte to passe all knyghtes of chevalry whych hath bene tofore hym and shall com afftir hym, moreover I shall lerne[2] you,' seyde she: 'ye shall go into Oure Lordis temple, where ys Kyng Davith his swerde, youre fadir, whych ys the mervaylouste and the sherpyste that ever was takyn in ony knyghtes hondys. Therefore take ye that, and take off the pomelle, and thereto make ye a pomell of precious stonys; late hit be so suttelly made that no man perceyve hit but that they beth all one.[3]

" 'And aftir make there an hylte so mervaylously that no man may know hit; and aftir that make a mervaylous sheethe. And whan ye have made all thys, I shall lette make a gurdyll thereto, such one as shall please me.'

❡"So all thys Kyng Salamon ded lat make as she devised, bothe the shippe and all the remenaunte. And whan the shippe was redy in the see to sayle, the lady lete make a grete bedde and mervaylous ryche, and sette hir uppon the beddis hede coverde with sylke, and leyde the swerde at the feete. And the gurdyls were of hempe[4]—and therewith the kynge was ryght angry:

❡" 'Sir, wyte you welle that I have none so hyghe a thynge whych were worthy to susteyne [soo hyhe a suerd. And a mayde shall brynge other knyghtes thereto, but I wote not whanne hit shalle be, ne what tyme.'] And there she lete make a coverynge to the shippe of clothe of sylke, that sholde never rotte for no manner of wedir. Than thys lady wente and made a carpynter to com to the tre whych Abelle was slayne undir. 'Now,' seyde she, 'carve me oute

---

8. *That preff had he by:* he had proof of that by reference to.
9. I.e., branch, tribe.
1. *Sertefyed the of that:* clarified for you that which.
2. I.e., instruct.
3. *Perceyve hit but that they beth all one:* recognize that it is anything but one piece.
4. I.e., of rope.

of thys tre as much woode as woll make me a spyndill.' 'A, madam,'
seyde he, 'thys ys the tre which oure firste modir planted.'

" 'Do hit,' sayd she, 'other ellis I shall destroy the.' Anone as he
began to worke, there com oute droppis of blood; and than wolde
he a[5] leffte, but she wolde nat suffir hym. And so he toke as muche
woode as myght make a spyndyll, and so she made hym to take as
muche of the grene tre, and so of the whyght[6] tre. And whan thes
three spyndyls were shapyn, she made hem to be fastened uppon
the syler of the bedde.

"So whan 𝕾alamon saw thys, he seyde to hys wyff, 'Ye have done
mervaylously, for thoughe all the worlde were here ryght now, they
cowde nat devise wherefore all thys was made but Oure Lorde
Hymselff—and thou that haste done hit wote nat what hit shall
betokyn.' 'Now lat hyt be,' seyde she, 'for ye shall here peraventure
tydynges sonner than ye wene—' "

𝕹ow here ys a wondir tale of 𝕶yng 𝕾alamon and of hys wyff—

"𝕿hat nyght lay 𝕾alamon before the shippe with litill felyship.
And whan he was on slepe, hym thought there com from
hevyn a grete company of angels, and alyght into the shippe, and
toke water whych was brought by an angell in a vessell of sylver,
and besprente all the shippe. And aftir, he cam to the swerde and
drew lettirs on the hylte, and aftir wente to the shippebourde and
wrote there other lettirs whych seyde,

THOU MAN THAT WOLTE ENTIR WITHIN ME,
BEWARE THAT THOU BE FULLE IN THE FAYTHE,
FOR I NE AM BUT[7] FAYTH AND BELYVE.

¶"Whan 𝕾alamon aspyed thos lettirs, he was so abaysshed that
he dirst nat entir; and so he drew hym abacke, and the shippe was
anone shovyn in the see. He[8] wente so faste that he had loste the
syght of hym within a litill whyle—and than a voyce seyde, '𝕾alamon, the laste knyght of thy kynred shall reste in thys bedde.' Than
wente 𝕾alamon and awaked hys wyff, and tolde her the adventures
of thys shipp."

Now seyth the tale that a grete whyle the three felowis behylde
the bed and the three spyndyls. Than they were at a sertayne that
they were of naturall coloures, withoute ony payntynge. Than they
lyfft up a cloth which was above the grounde, and there founde a
rych purse be semyng;[9] and Sir Percivale toke hit and founde
therein a wrytte, and so he rad hit, and devysed the maner of the
spyndils and of the ship, whens hit cam, and by whom hit was
made.

---

5. I.e., have.
6. According to the French, the saplings that grew from the tree before the death of Abel
   retained the parent tree's original white color.
7. *Ne am but*: am nothing less than. This is the same inscription as that quoted on p. 559;
   the differences of wording are attributable to similar differences in the French. Cf. n. 1,
   p. 422.
8. I.e., the ship.
9. *A rych purse be semyng*: what appeared to be a rich purse.

"Now," seyde Sir Galahad, "where shall we fynde the jantillwoman that shall make new gurdyls to the swerde?" "Fayre sirres,"   fol.395r
seyde Percivallis syster, "dismay you nat, for by the leve of God I
shall lette make a gurdyll to the swerde, such one as scholde longe
thereto." And than opynde she a boxe and toke oute gurdils which   5
were semely wrought with goldyn thredys, and uppon that were
sette full precius stonys, and a ryche buckyll of golde. "Lo, lordys,"
she seyde, "here ys a gurdill that ought to be sette aboute the
swerde—and wete you well, the grettist parte of thys gurdyll was
made of my hayre, whych somme tyme I loved well, whyle that I   10
was woman of the worlde:

¶"But as sone as I wyste that thys adventure was ordayned me,
I clipped off my heyre and made thys gurdyll." "In the name of
God, ye be well i-founde!" seyde Sir Bors, "for serteyse ye have put
us oute off grete payne wherein we scholde have entirde,[1] ne had   15
your tydyngis ben."

¶Than wente the jantillwoman and sette hit on the gurdyll of
the swerde.

¶"Now," seyde the felyship, "what ys the name of the swerde,
and what shall we calle hit?" "Truly," seyde she, "the name of the   20
swerde ys the 'Swerde with the Straunge Gurdyls;' and the sheeth,
'Mevear of Blood'—for no man that hath blood in hym ne shall
never see that one party of the sheth whych was made of the tree
of lyff."[2] Than they seyde, "Sir Galahad, in the name of Jesu Cryste,
we pray you to gurde you with thys swerde which hath bene desy-   25
red so much in the realme of Logrys." "Now latte me begynne,"
seyde Galahad, "to grype thys swerde for to gyff you corrayge—

¶"But wete you well, hit longith no more to me than hit doth to
you." And than he gryped aboute hit with his fyngirs a grete dele,
and than she gurte hym aboute the myddyll with the swerde: "Now   30
recke I nat though I dye, for now I holde me one of the beste
blyssed maydyns of the worlde, whych hath made the worthyest
knyght of the worlde." "Damesell," seyde Sir Galahad, "ye have done
so muche that I shall be your knyght all the dayes of my lyff." Than
they wente frome that ship and wente to the other. And anone the   35
wynde droff hem into the see a grete pace—but they had no
vytayle.

So hit befelle that they cam on the morne to a castell that men   fol.395v
calle Cartelople, that was in the marchys of Scotlonde. And whan
they had passed the porte, the jantillwoman seyde, "Lordys, here   40
be men aryven that, and they wyst that ye were of Kynge Arthurs
courte, ye shulde be assayled anone." "Well, damesell, dismay you
nat," seyde Sir Galahad, "for He that cast us oute of the rocche shall
delyver us frome hem."

¶So hit befelle, as they talked thus togydir, there cam a squyre   [8]   45
by them and asked what they were. "Sir, we ar of Kyng Arthurs
howse." "Ys that sothe?" seyde he. "Now, be my hede," seyd he,
"ye be evyll arayde." And than turned agayne unto the chyff

---

1. *Put us oute . . . sholde have entirde:* prevented us from suffering should we have entered.
2. So-called because, according to popular legend, from this tree descended the trees used
to make the Cross—the tree, or wood, so to speak, of everlasting life.

fortresse, and within a whyle they harde an horne blow. Than a
jantillwoman cam to hem and asked them of whens they were;
anone they tolde her. "Now, fayre lordys," she seyde, "for Goddys
love, turnyth agayne if ye may, for ye be com to youre dethe."

¶ "Nay, forsoth," they seyde, "we woll nat turne agayne, for He   5
shulde helpe us into whos servyse we were entred in."

¶ So as they stoode talkynge, there cam ten knyghtes well armed,
and bade hem yelde othir ellis dye.

¶ "That yoldyng," seyde they, "shall be noyous unto you." And
therewith they lete their horsis renne, and Sir Percivale smote the   10
firste that he bare hym to the erth, and toke hys horse and bestrode
hym; and the same wyse dud Sir Galahad, and also Sir Bors served
another so; for they had no horse in that contrey, for they lefft
their horsys whan they toke their shippe. And so whan they were
horsed, than began they to sette uppon them; and they of the cas-   15
tell fledde into stronge fortressis—and thes three knyghtes aftir
them into the castell, and so alyght on foote, and with their swerdis
slew them downe, and gate into the halle. Than whan they behelde
the grete multitude of the people that they had slayne, they helde
themself grete synners.   20

"Sertes," seyde Sir Bors, "I wene, and God had loved them, that
we sholde nat have had power to have slayne hem thus; but they   fol.396r
have done so muche agaynst³ Oure Lorde that He wolde nat suffir
hem to regne no lenger." "Yee, say nat so," seyde Galahad, "for if
they mysseded ayenst God, the vengeaunce ys nat owris, but to   25
Hym which hath power thereoff."

So cam there oute of a chambir a good man which was a preste,
and bare Goddis body in a cuppe.⁴ And whan he saw hem whych
lay dede in the halle, he was abaysshed. Anone Sir Galahad ded of
hys helme and kneled adowne, and so dud hys two felowis.   30

¶ "Sir," seyde they, "have ye no drede of us, for we bene of Kynge
Arthurs courte." Than asked the good man how they were slayne so
suddaynly, and they tolde hym. "Truly," seyde the good man, "and
ye myght lyve as longe as the worlde myght endure, ne myght ye
have done so grete almys-dede as this."   35

"Sir," seyde Sir Galahad, "I repente me gretely inasmuch as they
were crystynde."

"Nay, repente you nat," seyde he, "for they were nat crystynde.
And I shall telle you how that I know of⁵ thys castell. Here was a
lorde erle whos name was Hernox, nat but⁶ one yere; and he had   40
three sonnys, good knyghtes of armys, and a doughter, the fayrist
jantillwoman that men knew. So tho three knyghtes loved their
syster so sore that they brente in love; and so they lay by her, magré
her hede⁷—and, for she cryed to hir fadir, they slew her, and toke
their fadir and put hym in preson and wounded hym nye to the   45

3. I.e., against.
4. *Goddis body in a cuppe:* i.e., the Eucharist in a chalice.
5. I.e., about.
6. *Nat but:* not more than.
7. *Magré her hede:* against her will.

deth; but a cosyn of hers rescowed hym. And than ded they grete untrouthe,[8] for they slew clerkis and prestis, and made[9] bete downe chapellis, that Oure Lordys servyse myght nat be seyde:

¶"And thys same day her fadir sente unto me for to be confessed and howseled. But such shame had never man as I had thys same day with the three bretherne; but the olde erle made me to suffir, for he seyde they shold nat longe endure, for three servauntes of Oure Lorde sholde destroy them. And now hit ys brought to an ende; and by thys may you wete that Oure Lorde ys nat displesed with youre dedis."

¶"Sertes, seyde Sir Galahad, land hit had nat pleased Oure Lorde, never sholde we have slayne so many men in so litill a whyle." And they brought the Erle Hernox oute of preson into the myddis of the hall, the which knew well Sir Galahad, and yet he sye hym never before but by revelacion of Oure Lorde.

¶Than began he to wepe ryght tendirly, and seyde, "Longe have I abyddyn youre commynge! But for Goddis love, holdith me in youre armys, that my soule may departe oute of my body in so good a mannys armys as ye be."[1] "Full gladly," seyde Sir Galahad. And than one seyde on hyght, that all folke harde, "Sir Galahad, well hast thou ben avenged on Goddis enemyes. Now behovith the to go to the Maymed Kynge as sone as thou mayste, for he shall ressavve by the[2] helth whych he hath abyddyn so longe." And therewith the soule departed frome the body; and Sir Galahad made hym to be buryed as hym ought to be.

¶Ryght so departed the three knyghtes, and Sir Percivallis syster with them. And so they cam into a waste foreyst, and there they saw afore them a whyght herte which foure lyons lad. Than they toke[3] hem to assente for to folow aftir to know whydir they repayred. And so they rode aftir a grete pase tyll that they cam to a valey; and thereby was an ermytayge where a good man dwelled, and the herte and the lyons entirde also. Whan they saw all thys, they turned to the chapell and saw the good man in a religious wede and in the armour of Oure Lorde,[4] for he wolde synge Masse of the Holy Goste. And so they entird in and herde Masse; and at the secretis of the Masse they three saw the herte becom a man, which mervayled hem, and sette hym uppon the awter in a ryche sege, and saw the foure lyons were chaunged:

fol.396v

[9]

---

8. I.e., acts of betrayal.
9. I.e., caused to.
1. Cf. the words of Simeon, guided "by the Spirit" to the infant Jesus (Luke 2:28–30): "Then he took him up in his arms, and blessed God, and said, 'Lord, now lettest thou thy servant depart in peace, according to thy word: For mine eyes have seen thy salvation.' " From this point in the narrative, the number of implicit comparisons of Galahad to Christ will increase.
2. thee.
3. I.e., betook.
4. *The armour of Oure Lorde:* cf. Ephesians 6:13–17: "take unto you the whole armour of God, that ye may be able to withstand in the evil day, and having done all, to stand. Stand therefore, having your loins girt about with truth, and having on the breastplate of righteousness; And your feet shod with the preparation of the gospel of peace; Above all, taking the shield of faith, wherewith ye shall be able to quench all the fiery darts of the wicked. And take the helmet of salvation, and the sword of the Spirit, which is the word of God."

¶One to the fourme of man, and another to the fourme of a lyon, and the thirde to an egle, and the fourth was changed to an oxe. Than toke they her sege where the harte sate, and wente out thorow a glasse wyndow; and there was nothynge perisshed nother brokyn.

And they harde [a voyce] say. "In such maner entred the Sonne of God into the wombe of Maydyn Mary, whos virginité ne was perished, ne hurte." And whan they harde thes wordis they felle downe to the erthe and were astoned. And therewith was a grete clerenesse;[5] and whan they were com to theirselff agayne, they wente to the good man and prayde hym that he wolde sey them the trouthe of that vision.

¶"Why, what thynge have ye sene?" Anone they tolde hym all. "A, lordys," seyde he, "ye be wellcom, for now wote I well ye beth the good knyghtes whych shall brynge the Sankgreall to an ende; for ye bene they unto whom Oure Lorde shall shew grete secretis. And well ought Oure Lorde be signifyed to an harte—

¶"For the harte, whan he ys olde, he waxith yonge agayne in his whyght skynne: ryght so commyth agayne Oure Lorde, for He lost erthely fleysshe, that was the dedly fleyssh whych He had takyn in the wombe of the Blyssed Virgyne Mary, and for that cause appered Oure Lorde as a whyght harte withoute spot. And the foure that were with hym ys to undirstonde the foure Evaungelistis, which sette in wrytynge a parte of Jesu Crystes dedys, that He dud somtyme whan He was amonge you an erthely[6] man. For wete you welle, never arst ne myght no knyght knowe the trouthe; for oftyn-tymes or thys hath Oure Lorde shewed Hym unto good men and to good knyghtes in lyknesse of an herte—

¶"But I suppose frome henseforthe ye shall se hit no more." And than they joyed much, and dwelled there all day; and uppon the morne, whan they had herde Masse, they departed and com-mended the good man to God. And so they cam to a castell, and passed; so there cam a knyght armed aftir them, and seyde, "Lordys, thys jantillwoman that ye lede with you, ys she a mayde?" "Ye, sir," seyde she, "a mayde I am." Than he toke hir by the brydyll, and seyde, "By the Holy Crosse, ye shall nat ascape me tofore ye have yolden the custum of thys castell."

"Lat her go!" seyde Sir Percivale. "Ye be nat wyse, for a mayde, in what place she commythe, ys fre."

¶So in the meanewhyle there cam oute a ten or twelve knyghtes armed oute of the castell, and with hem cam jantillwomen, the which hylde a dyssh of sylver; and than they seyde, "Thys jantill-woman muste yelde us the custom of thys castell."

¶"Why," seyde Sir Gallahad, "what ys the custom of thys castell?" "Sir," seyde a knyght, "what mayde passith hereby, sholde hylde thys dyshe full of bloode of hir ryght arme." "Blame have he," seyde Galahad, "that brought up such customs! And so God save me, also

fol.397r

[10]

fol.397v

---

5. I.e., brightness, splendor.
6. On Malory's use of this word in connection with Galahad and, especially, Launcelot, see n. 6, p. 507.

sure mow ye be that of this jantillwoman shall ye fayle whyle that
I have hele."

¶ "So God me helpe," seyde Sir Percivale, "I had lever be slayne."
"And I also," seyde Sir Bors.

"Be my fayth," seyde the knyght, "than shall ye dye, for ye mow
nat endure ayenste us, thoughe ye were the beste knyghtes of the
worlde." Than lette they ren ech horse to other; and thes three
knyghtes bete the ten knyghtes, and than set their hondis to their
swerdis and bete them downe. Than there cam oute of the castell
a sixty knyghtes armed. "Now, fayre lordis," seyde thes three
knyghtes, "have mercy on youreselff, and have nat ado with us."
"Nay, fayre lordes," seyde the knyghtes of the castell, "we counceyle you to withdrawe you, for ye ben the beste knyghtes of the
worlde; and therefore do no more, for ye have done inow:

¶ "We woll lat you go with thys harme, but we muste nedys have
the custum." "Sertes," seyde Sir Galahad, "for noughte speke ye."

¶ "Well," seyd they, "woll ye dye?"

¶ "Sir, we be nat yet com thereto," seyde Sir Galahad. Than began
they to meddyll togydirs; and Sir Galahad, with the Straunge Gurdyls, drew his swerde and smote on the ryght honde and on the
lyffte honde, and slew whom that ever abode hym, and dud so
mervaylously that [there was none that sawe hym, they wend[7] he
had ben none erthely man but a monstre]. And hys two felowis
holpe hym passyngly well; and so they helde their journey everych
inlycke harde[8] tyll hit was nyghe nyght. Than muste they nedis
departe.

¶ So there cam a good knyght and seyde to thes three [felawes],
"If ye woll com in tonyght and take such herberow as here ys, ye
shall be ryght wellcom—and we shall ensure you by the fayth of
oure bodyes, and as we be trew knyghtes, to leve you in such astate
tomorow as here we fynde you, withoute ony falsehode—and as
sone as ye know of the custom, we dare sey ye woll accorde
therefore." "For Goddis love," seyde the Jantyllwoman, "go we thydir, and spare nat for me."

¶ "Well, go we," seyde Sir Galahad. And so they entird into the
castell, and whan they were alyght they made grete joy of hem.

¶ So within a whyle the three knyghtes asked the custom of the
castell, and wherefore hit was used. "Sir, what hit ys, we woll sey
you the sothe. There ys in this castell a jantillwoman, whych both
we and thys castell ys hers, and many other. So hit befelle many
yerys agone there happened on her a malodye, and whan she had
lyene a grete whyle she felle unto a mesell,[9] and no leche cowde
remedye her; but at the laste an olde man sayde, 'And she myght
have a dysshfulle of bloode of a maydyn and a clene virgyne in
wylle and in worke, and a kynges doughter, that bloode sholde be

fol.398r

[11]

---

7. *None that sawe hym they wend:* no one who saw him who did not believe.
8. *Helde their journey everych inlycke harde:* each sustained their day's fight with utter
   severity.
9. I.e., leprosy (a traditional sign of sin).

her helth,[1] for to anoynte her withall.' And for thys thynge was thys custom made."

¶"Now" seyde Sir **Percivallis** sister, "fayre knyghtes, I se well that this jantillwoman ys but dede withoute helpe—and therefore lette me blede." "Sertes," seyde Sir **Galahad**, "and ye blede so muche ye mon dye." "Truly," seyd she, "and I dye for the helth of her, I shall gete me grete worship and soule helthe, and worship to my lynayge—and better ys one harme than twayne; and therefore there shall no more batayle be, but tomorne I shall yelde you youre custom of this castell." And than there was made grete joy over there[2] was made tofore—for ellis had there bene mortall warre uppon the morne (natwithstondynge, she wolde none other, whether they wolde or nolde).

So that nyght were thes three felowis eased with the beste. And on the morne they harde Masse, and Sir **Percivallis** sister bade them brynge forth the syke lady; so she was brought forth, whych was full evyll at ease.

¶Than seyde she, "Who shall lette me bloode?"

¶So one cam furthe and lette her bloode; and she bled so muche that the dyssh was fulle. Than she lyfft up her honde and blyssed her,[3] and seyde to thys lady, "Madame, I am com to my dethe for to hele you; therefore, for Goddis love, prayeth for me." And with that she felle in a sowne. Than Sir **Galahad** and his two felows sterte up to her, and lyffte hir up, and staunched hir blood—but she had bled so muche that she myght nat lylve.

So whan she was awaked, she seyde, "Fayre brothir Sir **Percivale**, I dye for the helynge of this lady. And whan I am dede, I requyre you that ye burye me nat in thys contrey, but as sone as I am dede putte me in a boote[4] at the nexte haven, and lat me go as aventures woll lede me; and as sone as ye three com to the cité of **Sarras**, there to enchyeve the Holy Grayle, ye shall fynde me undir a towre aryved. And there bury me in the spirituall palyse—for I shall telle you for trouthe, there Sir **Galahad** shall be buryed, and ye bothe, in the same place." Whan Sir **Percivale** undirstoode thes wordis, he graunted hir all wepyngly. And than seyde a voice unto them, "Lordis [and felawes], tomorow at the owre of pryme ye three shall departe everych frome other, tylle the aventure brynge you unto the Maymed Kynge."

Than asked she her Saveoure;[5] and as sone as she had reseyved Hym, the soule departed frome the body. So the same day was the lady heled, whan she was anoynted with hir bloode. Than Sir **Percivale** made a lettir of all that[6] she had holpe them as in stronge aventures, and put hit in hir ryght honde—and so leyde hir in a barge, and coverde hit with blacke sylke. And so the wynde arose

fol.398v   15

The deth of Sir Percivalis syster

1. I.e., remedy.
2. I.e., that which there.
3. *Blyssed her*: i.e., crossed herself.
4. On the possible significance of boats and ships in Malory, see n. 1, p. 616.
5. I.e., the last sacraments.
6. *Of all that*: i.e., describing all those things with which.

and droff the barge frome the londe; and all maner of knyghtes behylde hit tyll hit was oute of ther syght.

⸤Than they drew all to the castell, and furthewith there fylle a suddeyne tempeste of thundir and lyghtnynge and rayne, as all the erthe wolde a brokyn.

⸤So halff the castell turned up-so-downe. So hyt passyd evynsonge or the tempest were seased; than they saw tofore hem a knyght armed, and wounded harde in the body and in the hede, whych seyde, "A, Good Lorde, succour me, for now hit ys nede." So after thys knyght there cam another knyght and a dwarff, which cryed to hem afarre, "Stonde, ye may nat ascape!" Than the wounded knyght hylde up hys hondys, and prayde God he myght nat dye in suche tribulacion.

"Truly," seyde Sir Galahad, "I shall succour hym, for His sake[7] that he callith on."

⸤"Sir, seyde Sir Bors, "I shall do hit, for hit ys nat[8] for you, for he ys but one knyght." "Sir," seyde he, "I graunte you." So Sir Bors toke hys [horse] and commaunded hym to God, and rode after to rescow the wounded knyght.

Now turne we to [the two felawes.

Now saith the] tale [that] Sir Galahad and Sir Percivall were in a chapell all nyght in hir prayers, for to save hem Sir Bors. So on the morow they dressed them in their harneys toward the castell, to wete what was fallyn of[9] them therein. And whan they cam there, they founde nother man nother woman that he ne was dede by the vengeaunce of Oure Lorde. So with that they harde a voice that seyde, "Thys vengeaunce ys for bloode-shedynge of maydyns." Also they founde at the ende of the [chappel] a chirche-yarde, and therein they myght se a sixti fayre tumbis; and that place was fayre and so delectable that hit semed hem there had bene no tempeste.

And there lay the bodyes of all the good maydyns which were martirde for the syke lady. Also they founde there namys of ech lady, and of what bloode they were com off; and all were of kyngys bloode, and twelve of them were kynges doughtirs.

⸤Than departed they and wente into a foreyste. "Now," seyde Sir Percivale unto Sir Galahad, "we muste departe, and therefore pray we Oure Lorde that we may mete togydirs in shorte tyme." Than they ded of their helmys and kyssed togydir, and sore wepte at theyre departynge.

Now turnyth thys tale unto Sir Launcelott.

Now seyth the tale that whan Sir Launcelot was com to the watir of Mortays, as hit ys reherced before, he was in grete perell. And so he leyde hym downe and slepte, and toke the aventure that God wolde sende hym. So whan he was aslepe, there cam a vision unto hym that seyde, "Sir Launcelot, aryse up and take thyne

---

7. *For His sake:* i.e., for the sake of He.
8. I.e., not necessary.
9. *Was fallyn of:* had befallen.

armour, and entir into the firste shippe that thou shalt fynde." And whan he herde thes wordys, he sterte up and saw grete clerenesse aboute hym; and than he lyffte up hys honde and blyssed hym—

¶And so toke hys armys and made hym redy. And at the laste he cam by a stronde and founde a shippe withoute sayle other ore; and as sone as he was within the shippe, there he had the moste swettnes that ever he felte, and he was fulfylled with all thynge that he thought on other desyred.

¶Than he seyde, "Swete Fadir, Jesu Cryste, I wote natt what joy I am in, for thys passith all erthely joyes that ever I was in." And so in thys joy he leyde hym downe to the shippebourde and slepte tyll day. And whan he awooke he founde there a fayre bed, and therein lyynge a jantillwoman, dede, which was Sir Percivalles sister; and as Sir Launcelot avised her, he aspyed in hir ryght honde a wrytte, whych he rad, that tolde hym all the aventures that ye have herde before, and of what lynayge she was com. So with thys jantillwoman Sir Launcelot was a moneth and more. If ye wold aske how he lyved, for He that fedde the chyldirn of Israel with manna in deserte, so was he fedde:[1]

¶For every day, whan he had seyde hys prayers, he was susteyned with the grace of the Holy Goste.

¶And so on a [nyghte] he wente to play hym by the watirs syde, for he was somwhat wery of the shippe. And than he lystened and herde an hors com, and one rydyng uppon hym; and whan he cam nyghe, hym semed a knyght. And so he late hym passe and wente there as the ship was; and there he alyght, and toke the sadyll and the brydill, and put the horse frome hym, and so wente into the shyppe.

And than Sir Launcelot dressed hym unto the shippe, and seyde, "Sir, ye be wellcom." And he answerd and salewed hym agayne, and seyde, "Sir, what ys youre name? For much my herte gevith unto you." "Truly," seyde he, "my name ys Sir Launcelot du Lake." "Sir," seyde he, "than be ye wellcom, for ye were the begynner of me in thys worlde." "A, sir, ar ye Sir Galahad?"

"Ye, forsothe." And so he kneled downe and askyd hym hys blyssynge, and aftir that toke of hys helme and kyssed hym; and there was grete joy betwyxte them, for no tunge can telle what joy was betwyxte them. And there every of them tolde othir the aventures that had befalle them syth that they departed frome the courte.

And anone, as Sir Galahad saw the jantillwoman dede in the bedde, he knew her well, and seyde grete worship of hir, that she was one of the beste maydyns lyvyng and hit was grete pité of hir dethe. But whan Sir Launcelot herde how the mervayles swerde was gotyn, and who made hit, and all the mervayles rehersed afore, than he prayd Sir Galahad that he wolde shew hym the swerde; and so he brought hit forth, and kyssed the pomell and the hiltis and the scawberde.

fol.400r

1. On this miraculous feeding, cf. n. 8, p. 545. Cf. also Exodus 16:35: "the children of Israel did eat manna forty years, until they came to a land inhabited."

¶"Truly," seyde Sir Launcelot, "never arste knew I of so hyghe adventures done, and so mervalous stronge."

¶So dwelled Sir Launcelot [and Sir][2] Galahad within that shippe halff [a yere, and served God dayly and] nyghtly with all their power. [And often they aryved in yles ferre] frome folke, where th[ere repayred none but wylde beestes, and ther] they founde many [straunge adventures and peryllous whiche they] brought to an end; [but for tho adventures were with wylde beestes,] and nat in the q[uest of the Sancgreal, therfor the tale ma]kith here no menci[on therof, for it wolde be to longe to telle of alle tho adven]tures that befelle] them.

¶So aftir, [on a Mondaye, hit befelle that they aryved in the] edge of a forey[ste, tofore a crosse. And thenne sawe they a knyghte] armed all in [whyte, and was rychely horsed, and ledde in his] ryght hond [a whyte hors; and soo he cam to the shyp and] salewed the two knyghtes in the hyghe Lordis behalff, and seyde unto Sir Galahad, "Sir, ye have bene longe inowe with youre fadir. Therefor com oute of the shippe, and take thys horse, and go where the aventures shall lede you in the Queste of the Sankgreall." Than he wente to hys fadir and kyste hym swetely, and seyde, "Fayre swete fadir, I wote nat whan I shall se you more tyll I se the body of Jesu Cryste."

"Now, for Goddis love," seyde Sir Launcelot, "pray to the [Hyghe] Fadir that He holde me stylle in Hys servyse." And so he toke hys horse; and there they hard a voyce that seyde, "Every of you thynke for to do welle, for nevermore shall one se another off you before the dredefull day of doome."[3]

¶"Now, my sonne, Sir Galahad, sith we shall departe and nother of us se other more, I pray to that Hyghe Fadir conserve me and you bothe." "Sir," seyde Sir Galahad, "no prayer avaylith so much as youres." And therewith Sir Galahad entird into the foreyste. And the wynde arose and drove Sir Launcelot more than a moneth thorow the se, where he sleped but litill, but prayde to God that he myght se som tydynges of the Sankgreall.

So hit befelle on a nyght, at mydnyght, he aryved before a castell, on the backe [syde, whiche was ry]ch and fayre, and there was a posterne [opened toward the see, and was open] withoute ony kepynge, save two [lyons kept the entré; and the moon]e shone ryght clere. A[none Sir Launcelot herd a voyce that] seyde, "Launcelot, go oute [of this shyp and entre into the castel,] where thou shalte [see a grete parte of thy desyre." Thenne he ran] to hys armys and [soo armed hym, and soo wente to the gate and] saw the lyons.

¶[Thenne sette he hand to his suerd and dr]ew hit. So there cam [a dwerf sodenly and smote hym on th]e arme so sore [that the suerd felle oute of his hand; thenne] herde he a voice [say, "O,

fol.400v

[14]

2. The lower outside corner of a leaf in the Winchester Manuscript has been torn away at this point in the text, thus necessitating most of the frequent borrowings from Caxton's edition over the next page or so. In the current reading *Sir* is not found in Caxton but is supplied as inevitable, given the amount of space that would have been left in the line in the MS.

3. I.e., judgment.

man of evylle feyth and poure byleve,] wherefore trustist thou more
on thy harneyse than in thy Maker? For He myght more avayle the
than thyne armour in what servyse that thou arte sette in."

¶Than seyde Sir **Launcelot**, "Fayre Fader, Jesu Cryste! I thanke
The of Thy grete mercy that Thou reprevyst me of my myssedede;
now se I that Thou holdiste me for one of Thy servauntes." Than
toke he hys swerde agayne and put hit up in hys sheethe, and made
a crosse in hys forehede, and cam to the lyons. And they made
sembelaunte to do hym harme.

Natwithstondynge, he passed by them withoute hurte, and
entird into the castell to the chyeff fortresse. And there were they[4]
all at reste. Than Sir **Launcelot** entred so armed, for he founde no
gate nor doore but hit was opyn; and at the laste he founde a
chambir whereof the doore was shutte, and he sett hys honde
thereto to have opened hit, but he myght nat. Than he enforced
hym myckyll to undo the doore. Than he lystened, and herde a
voice whych sange so swetly that hit semede none erthely thynge—
and hym thought the voice seyde, "Joy and honoure be to the Fadir
of Hevyn." Than Sir **Launcelot** kneled adowne tofore the chambir
dore, for well wyst he that there was the **Sankgreall** within that
chambir.

Than seyde he, "Fayre swete Fadir, Jesu Cryste, if ever I dud
thynge that plesed The, Lorde, for Thy pité ne have me nat in
dispite for my synnes done byforetyme, and that Thou shew me
somthynge of that[5] I seke." And with that he saw the chambir dore
opyn, and there cam oute a grete clerenesse, that the house was
as bryght as all the tourcheis of the worlde had bene there.

¶So cam he to the chambir doore and wolde have entird; and
anone a voice seyde unto hym, "Sir **Launcelot**, flee and entir nat, for
thou ought nat to do hit, for and if thou entir, thou shalt forthynke
hit." Than he withdrew hym aback ryght hevy.

¶Than loked he up into the myddis of the chambir and saw a
table of sylver, and the holy vessell coverde with rede samyte, and
many angels aboute hit, whereof one hylde a candyll of wexe brennynge, and the other hylde a crosse and the ornementis of an
awter. And before the holy vessell he saw a good man clothed as
a pryste, and hit semed that he was at the sakerynge of the Masse;
and hit semed to Sir **Launcelot** that above the prystis hondys were
three men, whereof the two put the yongyste by lyknes[6] betwene
the prystes hondis; and so he lyffte them up ryght hyghe, and hit
semed to shew so to the peple.

And than **Sir Launcelot** mervayled nat a litill, for hym thought
the pryste was so gretly charged of the vygoure[7] that hym semed
that he sholde falle to the erth; and whan he saw none aboute hym
that wolde helpe hym, than cam he to the dore a grete pace, and

---

4. I.e., the inhabitants of the castle.
5. I.e., that which.
6. *By lyknes*: apparently. Launcelot is witnessing an absolute realization of the Host, the
sanctified bread raised by the priest during the Eucharist; it is no less than the body of
Christ, sent by the Father and the Holy Spirit.
7. *Charged of the vygoure*: burdened by the figure.

fol.401r

5

10

[15]

15

20

25

fol.401v   30

35

The signification of
the Sankgreal that
ys called the holy
vessel, the which
appered to Sir Laun-
celot

45

seyde, "Fayre Fadir, Jesu Cryste, ne take hit for no synne if I helpe the good man whych hath grete nede of helpe."

Ryght so entird he into the chambir and cam toward the table of sylver; and whan he cam nyghe hit he felte a breeth that hym thought hit was entromedled with fyre, which smote hym so sore in the vysayge that hym thought hit brente hys vysayge—and therewith he felle to the erthe, and had no power to aryse, as he that had loste the power of hys body, and hys hyrynge and syght.[8]

¶Than felte he many hondys whych toke hym up and bare hym oute of the chambir doore and leffte hym there, semynge dede to all people. So uppon the morow whan hit was fayre day, they within were rysen, and founde Sir **Launcelot** lyynge before the chambir doore; all they mervayled how that he com in. And so they loked uppon hym, and felte hys powse to wete whethir were ony lyff in hym; and so they founde lyff in hym, but he myght nat stonde nother stirre no membir that he had. And so they toke hym by every parte of the body and bare hym into a chambir and leyde hym in a rych bedde, farre frome folke; and so he lay foure dayes.

¶Than one seyde he was on lyve, and another seyde nay, he was dede.

¶"In the name of God," seyde an olde man, "I do you veryly to wete he ys nat dede, but he ys as fulle of lyff as the strengyst of [you] all; therefore I rede you all that he be well kepte tylle God sende lyff in hym agayne." So in such maner they kepte Sir **Launcelot** foure and twenty dayes and also[9] many nyghtis, that ever he lay stylle as a dede man. And at the fyve-and-twentythe day befylle hym aftir mydday that he opened hys yen; and whan he saw folke he made grete sorow and seyde, "Why have ye awaked me? For I was more at ease than I am now.

"A, Jesu Cryste, who myght be so blyssed that myght se opynly Thy grete mervayles of secretnesse, there where no synner may be?" "[What] have ye sene?" seyde [they aboute hym. "I have sene," seyde] he, "grete mervayles that no tunge may telle, and more than ony herte can thynke—and had nat my synne bene beforetyme, ellis I had sene muche more." Than they tolde hym how he had layne there foure and twenty dayes and nyghtes. Than hym thought hit was ponyshemente for the foure and twenty yere that he had bene a synner—

¶Wherefore Oure Lorde put hym in penaunce the foure and twenty dayes and nyghtes. Than loked **Launcelot** tofore hym and saw the hayre[1] whych he had borne nyghe a yere; for that he forthoughte hym ryght muche that he had brokyn his promyse unto the ermyte whych he had avowed to do.

¶Than they asked how hit stood with hym. "Forsothe," seyde he, "I am hole of body, thanked be Oure Lorde. Therefore, for Goddis love, telle me where I am." Than seyde they all that he was in the castell of **Carbonek**. Therewith com a jantillwoman and

---

8. On this blinding, cf. the story of King Evelake on p. 563.
9. I.e., as.
1. I.e., hair shirt (cf. n. 9, p. 532).

brought hym a shirte of small² lynen clothe; but he chaunged nat   fol.402v
there, but toke the hayre to hym agayne.

¶"Sir," seyde they, "the Queste of the 𝕾ankgreall ys encheved³
now ryght in you—and never shall ye se of 𝕾ankgreall more than
ye have sene." "Now I thanke God," seyde Sir 𝕷auncelot, "for Hys   5
grete mercy of that I have sene, for hit suffisith me. For, as I suppose, no man in thys worlde have lyved bettir than I have done to
enchyeve that I have done." And therewith he toke the hayre and
clothed hym in hit, and aboven that he put a lynen shirte, and aftir
that a roobe of scarlet, freyssh and new.   10

And whan he was so arayed they mervayled all, for they knew
hym well that he was Sir 𝕷auncelot, the good knyght—and than they
seyde all, "A, my lorde Sir 𝕷auncelott, ye be he!" And he seyde, "Yee
truly, I am he." Than cam worde to the Kynge 𝕻elles that the
knyght that had layne so longe dede was the noble knyght Sir 𝕷aun-   15
celot. Than was the kynge ryght glad and wente to se hym; and
whan Sir 𝕷auncelot saw hym com, he dressed hym ayenste hym,⁴
and than made the kynge grete joy of hym. And there the kynge
tolde hym tydynges, how his fayre doughter was dede.

¶Than Sir 𝕷auncelot was ryght hevy, and seyde, "Me forthynkith   20
of the deth of youre doughter, for she was a full fayre lady, freyshe
and yonge—and well I wote she bare the beste knyght that ys now
on erthe, or that ever was syn God⁵ was borne."

So the kynge hylde hym there foure dayes, and on the morow
he toke hys leve at Kynge 𝕻elles and at all the felyship, and thanked   25
them of the grete laboure. Ryght so as they sate at her dyner in
the chyff halle, hit befylle that the 𝕾angreall had fulfylled the table
with all metis that ony harte myght thynke. And as they sate, they
saw all the doorys of the paleyse and wyndowes shutte withoute
mannys honde—so were they all abaysshed.   30

¶So a knyght whych was all armed cam to the chyeff dore, and   fol.403r
knocked, and cryed, "Undo!"⁶ But they wolde nat; and ever he
cryed, "Undo!" So hit noyed hem so much that the kynge hymselff
arose and cam to a wyndow there where the knyght called. Than
he seyde, "Sir knyght, ye shall nat enter at thys tyme—   35

¶"Whyle the 𝕾ankgreall ys hyre; and therefore go ye into anothir
fortresse, for ye be none of the knyghtes of the Quest, but one of
them whych have servyd the fyende, and haste leffte the servyse
of Oure Lorde." Than was he passynge wroth at the kynges wordis.

¶"Sir knyght," seyde the kynge, "syn ye wolde so fayne entir,   40
telle me of what contrey ye be."

¶"Sir," he seyde, "I am of the realme of 𝕷ogrys, and my name ys
Sir 𝕰ctor de 𝕸arys, brother unto my lorde Sir 𝕷auncelot." "In the
name of God," seyde the kynge, "me forthynkis [of that I have]
seyde, for youre brother ys hereinne."   45

2. I.e., fine.
3. I.e., expended. Launcelot has not "achieved" the Grail in the transcendent sense usually
   intended with the word.
4. *Dressed hym ayenste hym:* rose at his coming.
5. I.e., Jesus.
6. I.e., Open up.

¶Whan Sir **Ector** undirstood that hys brother was there—for he was the man in the worlde that he moste drad[7] and loved—than he seyde, "A, good lorde, now dowblith my sorow and shame! Full truly seyde the good man of the hylle, unto Sir **Gawayne** and to me, of oure dremys."

¶Than wente he oute of the courte as faste as hys horse myght, and so thorowoute the castell. Than Kyng **Pelles** cam to Sir **Launcelot** and tolde hym tydynges of hys brothir—anone he was sory therefore, that he wyst nat what to do. So Sir **Launcelot** departed and toke hys armys, and seyde he wold go se the realme of **Logris**, whych he had nat sene afore in a yere, and therewith commaunded the kynge to God—and so rode thorow many realmys; and at the laste he com to a whyght[8] abbay, and there they made hym that nyght grete chere. And on the morne he arose and hard Masse; and afore an awter he founde a ryche tombe which was newly made. And than he toke hede and saw the sydys wryten with golde which seyde,

HERE LYETH KYNG **Bagdemagus** of Gore, WHICH KYNGE **Arthurs** NEVEW SLEW—

and named hym—

SIR **Gawayne**.

Than was he nat a litill sory, for Sir **Launcelot** loved hym muche more than ony other (and had hit bene ony other than Sir **Gawayne**, he sholde nat ascape frome the dethe), and seyde to hymselff,

"A, Lorde God, thys ys a grete hurte unto Kynge **Arthurs** courte, the losse of suche a man." And than he departed and cam to the abbey where Sir **Galahad** dud the aventure of the tombis and wan the whyght shylde with the rede crosse; and there had he grete chere all that nyght. And on the morne he turned to **Camelot**, where he founde Kynge **Arthure** and the Quene. But many of the knyghtes of the Rounde Table were slayne and destroyed—more than halff. And so three of them were com home, Sir **Ector, Gawayne, and Lyonell**, and many other that nedith nat now to reherce.

And all the courte were passyng glad of Sir **Launcelot**, and the Kynge asked hym many tydyngis of hys sonne Sir **Galahad**. And there Sir **Launcelot** tolde the Kynge of hys aventures that befelle hym syne he departed. And also he tolde hym of the aventures of Sir **Galahad**, Sir **Percivale**, and Sir **Bors**, whych that he knew by the lettir of the ded mayden, and also as Sir **Galahad** had tolde hym. "Now God wolde," seyde the Kynge, "that they were all three here."

"That shall never be," seyde Sir **Launcelot**, "for two of hem shall ye never se. But one of them shall com home agayne."

¶**Now levith thys tale and spekith of Sir Galahad.**

---

7. I.e., respected.
8. I.e., Cistercian (cf. n. 5, p. 506).

[18]

ℕOw seyth the tale that Sir 𝔊alahad rode many journeys in vayne; and at the last he com to the abbay where Kynge 𝔐ordrayns⁹ was. And whan he harde that, he thoughte he wolde abyde to se hym. And so uppon the morne, whan he had herd Masse, Sir 𝔊alahad com unto Kynge 𝔐ordrayns.

And anone the kyng saw hym, whych had layne blynde of longe tyme, and than he dressed hym ayenste hym, and seyde, "Sir 𝔊alahad, the servaunte of Jesu Cryste and verry knyght, whos commynge I have abyddyn longe, now enbrace me and lette me reste on thy breste, so that I may reste betwene thyne armys. For thou arte a clene virgyne above all knyghtes, as the floure of the lyly in whom virginité is signified; and thou arte the rose which ys the floure of all good vertu, and in colour of fyre—for the fyre of the Holy Goste ys takyn so in the that my fleyssh, whych was all dede of oldenes, ys becom agayne yonge."

¶Whan Sir 𝔊alahad harde thes wordys, than he enbraced hym and all hys body. Than seyde he,¹ "Fayre Lorde Jesu Cryste, now I have my wylle; now I requyre The, in thys poynte² that I am in, that Thou com and visite me." And anone Oure Lorde herde his prayere, and therewith the soule departed frome the body. And than Sir 𝔊alahad put hym in the erthe as a kynge oughte to be— and so departed, and cam into a perelous foreyste where he founde the welle which boyled with grete wawis, as the tale tellith tofore.

¶And as sone as Sir 𝔊alahad sette hys honde thereto, hit seased, so that hit brente no more, and anone the hete departed away: and cause why that hit brente, hit was a sygne of lechory that was that tyme muche used—but that hete myght nat abyde hys pure virginité. And so thys was takyn in the contrey for a miracle, and so ever afftir was hit called 𝔊alahaddis Welle.

So by aventure he com unto the contrey of 𝔊ore, and into the abbey where Sir 𝔏auncelot had bene toforehonde and founde the tombe of Kynge 𝔅agdemagus—but he was [nat only] fownder³ thereoff; for there was the tombe of 𝔍oseph of 𝔄ramathyys son and the tombe of 𝔖ymyan, where Sir 𝔏auncelot had fayled.

Than he loked into a croufte undir the mynstir, and there he sawe a tombe which [brent] full mervaylously. Than asked he the brethirne what hit was. "Sir", seyde they, "a mervalous aventure that may nat be brought to an ende but by hym that passith of bounté and of knyghthode all them of the Rounde Table."

¶"I wolde," seyde Sir 𝔊alahad, "that ye wolde brynge me thereto." "Gladly," seyde they, and so ledde hym tyll a cave; and so he wente downe uppon grecis and cam unto the tombe; and so the flamyng fayled, and the fyre staunched, which many a day had bene grete.

¶Than cam there a voice whych seyde, "Much ar ye beholde to

5

10

fol.404r

15

20

25

30

35

40

---

9. This is in actuality King Evelake, blinded in the presence of the Grail at p. 523; in Malory's sources the King receives the name of *Mordrains* after his baptism.
1. I.e., the king.
2. I.e., position.
3. *Nat only*: the emendation is conjectural, based on Vinaver's suggestion (O³, p. 1581); Caxton agrees with Winchester's *was fownder*. Fownder: i.e., finder.

thanke God which hath gyven you a good owre,[4] that ye may draw
oute the soulis of[5] erthely payne and to putte them into the joyes
of Paradyse:

  ❡"Sir, I am of youre kynred,[6] which hath dwelled in thys hete
thys three hondred wyntir and four-and-fifty, to be purged of the
synne[7] that I ded ayenste **Aramathy Joseph**." Than Sir **Galahad** toke
the body in his armys and bare hit into the mynster. And that nyght
lay Sir **Galahad** in the abbay; and on the morne he gaff hym hys
servyse[8] and put hym in the erthe byfore the hyghe awter. So
departed he frome thens, and commended the brethirn to God;
and so he rode fyve dayes, tylle that he cam to the Maymed Kynge.
And ever folowed Sir **Percivale** the fyve dayes [askynge] where he
had bene; and so one tolde hym how the aventures of **Logrus** were
encheved. So on a day hit befelle that [they][9] cam oute of a grete
foreyste, and there mette they at travers with Sir **Bors** which rode
alone—

  ❡Hit ys no rede[1] to aske if they were glad! And so he salewed
them, and they yelded to hym honoure and good aventure,[2] and
everych tolde other how they had spedde.

  ❡Than seyde Sir **Bors**, "Hit ys more than a yere and a halff that
I ne lay ten tymes where men dwelled, but in wylde forestis and in
mownteaynes—but God was ever my comforte."

  ❡Than rode they a grete whyle tylle they cam to the castell of
Carbonek. And whan they were entirde within, Kynge **Pelles** knew
hem; so there was grete joy, for he wyste well by her commynge
that they had fulfylled the [Quest of the] **Sankgreall**. Than **Elyazar**,
Kynge **Pelles** sonne, brought tofore them the brokyn swerde
wherewith **Josephe** was stryken thorow the thyghe. Than Sir **Bors**
sette his honde thereto to say[3] if he myght have sowded hit agayne,
but hit wolde nat be.

  Than he toke hit to Sir **Percivale**, but he had no more power
thereto than he. "Now have ye hit agayne," seyde Sir **Percivale** unto
Sir **Galahad**, "for and hit be ever encheved by ony bodily man, ye
muste do hit." And than he toke the pecis and set hem togydirs,
and semed to them as hit had never be brokyn, and as well as hit
was firste forged. And whan they within aspyed that the aventure
of the swerde was encheved, than they gaff the swerde to Sir **Bors**,
for hit myght no bettir be sette, for he was so good a knyght, and
a worthy man.

  And a litill before evyn the swerde arose, grete and merevaylous,
and was full of grete hete, that many men felle for drede; and

fol.404v

5

[19]

10

15

20

25

30

fol.405r

35

40

---

4. I.e., fortune.
5. I.e., from.
6. In the French source, the voice identifies itself as that of Simeon; the sin he had committed
    against Joseph and his kin relationship is not made clear.
7. The sin is not specified in the French source.
8. I.e., burial service.
9. The Winchester MS reads *he,* but it is evident by the end of the sentence that, as in the
    French source, Perceval has already caught up with Galahad.
1. *Ys no rede:* serves no purpose.
2. I.e., fortune.
3. I.e., test, prove.

anone alyghte a voyce amonge them, and seyde, "They that ought nat to sitte at the table of Oure Lorde Jesu Cryste, avoyde hens! For now there shall verry knyghtes be fedde." So they wente thense, all sauf Kyng Pelles and Elyazar hys sonne, which were holy men, and a mayde whych was hys nyce: and so thes three [felawes] and thes three [were there]—elles were no mo.

¶And anone they saw knyghtes all armed that cam in at the halle dore, and ded of their helmys and armys, and seyde unto Sir Galahad, "Sir, we have hyghed ryght muche for to be with you at thys table where the holy mete shall be departed."[4]

¶Than seyde he, "Ye be wellcom. But of whens be ye?"

¶So three of them seyde they were of Gaule, and other three seyde they were of Irelonde, and other three seyde they were of Danemarke.

¶And so as they sate thus, there cam oute a bedde of tre of[5] a chambir—

¶Which foure jantillwomen broughte; and in the bedde lay a good man, syke, and had a crowne of golde uppon his hede. And there in the myddis of the paleyse they sette hym downe, and wente agayne. Than he lyffte up hys hede and seyde, "Sir Galahad, good knyght, ye be ryght wellcom, for much have I desyred your commyng. For in such payne and in such angwysh as I have suffird longe. But now I truste to God the terme ys com that my payne shall be alayed and [I] sone passe oute of thys worlde, so as hit was promysed me longe ago." And therewith a voice seyde, "There be two amonge you that be nat in the Queste of the Sankgreall—and therefore departith."

Than Kynge Pelles and hys sunne departed. And therewithall besemed[6] them that there cam an olde man and foure angelis frome hevyn, clothed in lyknesse of a byshop, and had a crosse in hys honde; and thes foure angels bare hym up in a chayre and sette hym downe before the table of sylver—

¶Whereuppon the Sankgreall was. And hit semed that he had in myddis of hys forehede lettirs which seyde

[20] fol.405v

SE YOU HERE Joseph, THE FIRSTE BYSSHOP OF CRYSTENDOM,
THE SAME WHICH OURE LORDE SUCCOURED IN THE CITÉ OF
Sarras IN THE SPIRITUALL PALLEYS.

Than the knyghtes mervayled, for that bysshop was dede more than three hondred yere tofore. "A, knyghtes," seyde he, "mervayle nat, for I was somtyme an erthely man."

So with that they harde the chambir dore opyn, and there they saw angels; and two bare candils of wexe, and the thirde bare a towell, and the fourth a speare which bled mervaylously, that the droppis felle within a boxe which he hylde with hys othir hande.

---

4. *The holy mete shall be departed*: i.e., the Eucharist will be divided.
5. *Tre*: i.e., wood. *Of*: i.e., from.
6. I.e., it seemed to.

And anone they sette the candyls uppon the table, and the thirde
the towell uppon the vessell, and the fourth the holy speare evyn
upryght uppon the vessell. And than the bysshop made sembelaunte as thoughe he wolde have gone to the sakeryng of a Masse,
and than he toke an obley which was made in lyknesse of brede; 5
and at the lyftyng up there cam a vigoure in lyknesse of a chylde.

And the vysayge was as rede and as bryght os ony fyre, and smote
hymselff into the brede, that all they saw hit that the brede was
fourmed of a fleyshely man.[7] And than he[8] put hit into the holy
vessell agayne, and than he ded that[9] longed to a preste to do 10
Masse. And than he wente to Sir Galahad and kyssed hym, and
bade hym go and kysse hys felowis; and so he ded anone.

"Now," seyde he, "the servauntes of Jesu Cryste, ye shull be
fedde afore thys table with swete metis that never knyghtes yet
tasted"—and whan he had seyde, he vanysshed away. And they 15
sette hem at the table in grete drede and made their prayers.

Than loked they and saw a man com oute of the holy vessell that
had all the sygnes of the Passion of Jesu Cryste bledynge all opynly,
and seyde, "My knyghtes and my servauntes and my trew chyldren,
which bene com oute of dedly lyff into the spirituall lyff, I woll no 20
lenger cover[1] me frome you, but ye shall se now a parte of my
secretes and of my hydde thynges:

¶"Now holdith and resseyvith the hyghe order and mete whych
ye have so much desired."

¶Than toke He Hymselff the holy vessell and cam to Sir Galahad; 25
and he kneled adowne and resseyved hys Saveoure. And aftir hym
so ressayved all hys felowis, and they thought hit so sweete that
hit was mervaylous to telle. Than seyde He to Sir Galahad, "Sonne,
wotyst thou what I holde betwyxte my hondis?" "Nay," seyde he,
"but if ye telle me." 30

"Thys ys," seyde He, "the holy dysshe wherein I ete the lambe
on Estir Day,[2] and now hast thou sene that thou moste desired to
se. But yet hast thou nat sene hit so opynly as thou shalt se hit in
the cité of Sarras, in the spirituall paleyse. Therefore thou must
go hense and beare with the thys holy vessell, for this nyght hit 35
shall departe frome the realme of Logrus, and hit shall nevermore
be sene here. And knowyst thou wherefore? For he ys nat served
nother worshipped to hys ryght[3] by hem of thys londe, for they be
turned to evyll lyvyng; and therefore I shall disherite them of the
honoure whych I have done them. And therefore go ye three 40
[tomorowe] unto the see, where ye shall fynde youre shippe redy;
and with you take the Swerde with the Stronge Gurdils, and no

---

7. This is a realization of the doctrine of transubstantiation, in which it is believed that the
whole substance of the bread and wine of the Eucharist is converted into the whole
substance of the body and blood of Christ, with only the appearance of bread and wine
remaining.
8. I.e., the bishop.
9. I.e., that which.
1. I.e., conceal.
2. I.e., the Last Supper, which would most likely have been held at Passover time, and of
course before the historical institution of the Christian Easter.
3. To hys ryght: rightfully.

mo with you but Sir Percivale and Sir Bors. Also I woll that ye take
with you off thys bloode of thys speare for to anoynte the Maymed
Kynge, both his legges and hys body, and he shall have hys heale."

"Sir," seyde Galahad, "why shall nat thys other felowis go with
us?" "For thys cause: for ryght as I departe[4] my postels, one here
and anothir there, so I woll that ye departe. And two of you shall
dy in my servyse, and one of you shall com agayne and telle tydynges." Than gaff He hem Hys blyssynge and vanysshed away. And
Sir Galahad wente anone to the speare which lay upon the table
and towched the bloode with hys fyngirs, and cam aftir to the
Maymed Kynge and anoynted his legges and hys body. And
therewith he clothed hym anone, and sterte uppon hys feete oute
of hys bedde as an hole man, and thanked God that He had heled
hym; and anone he leffte the worlde[5] and yelded hymselffe to a
place of religion of whyght monkes, and was a full holy man.

And that same nyght, aboute mydnyght, cam a voyce amonge
them which seyde, "My sunnes, and nat my chyeff sunnes, my
frendis, and nat my enemyes, go ye hens where ye hope beste to
do, and as I bade you do."

¶"A, thanked be Thou, Lorde, that Thou wolt whyghtsauff to
calle us Thy sunnes! Now may we well preve that we have nat lost
oure paynes."[6] And anone in all haste they toke their harneyse and
departed; but the three knyghtes of Gaule—one of hem hyght
Claudyne, Kynge Claudas sonne, and the other two were grete
jantillmen—than prayde Sir Galahad to every of them that, and they
com to Kynge Arthurs courte, "to salew my lorde Sir Launcelot, my
fadir, and hem all of the Rounde Table"—if they com on that party,
nat to forgete hit.

Ryght so departed Sir Galahad, and Sir Percivale and Sir Bors with
hym. And so they rode three dayes, and than they com to a ryvage
and founde the shippe whereof the tale spekith of tofore; and whan
they com to the bourde they founde in the myddys of [the bedde][7]
the table of sylver, whych they had lefft with the Maymed Kynge,
and the Sankgreall whych was coverde with rede samyte.

Than were they glad to have such thyngis in their felyship; and
so they entred and made grete reverence thereto. And Sir Galahad
felle on hys kneys and prayde longe tyme to Oure Lorde, that at
what tyme that he asked, he myght passe oute of this worlde—and
so longe he prayde tyll a voice seyde, "Sir Galahad, thou shalt have
thy requeste:

¶"And whan thou askyst the deth of thy body, thou shalt have
hit—and than shalt thou have the lyff of thy soule." Than Sir
Percivale harde hym a litill, and prayde hym of felyship that was
betwene them wherefore he asked such thynges.

¶"Sir, that shall I telle you," seyde Sir Galahad. "Thys othir day,

---

4. I.e., separated.
5. I.e., the secular world.
6. I.e., efforts.
7. The reading is not present in either the Winchester MS or Caxton and is that supplied by
   Vinaver, (O³ p. 1032, line 5), as suggested by Malory's likely French source, by the reference to the bed a few lines below, and by the unanswered *of* in the Winchester text.

whan we sawe a parte of the adventures of the Sangreall, I was in
such joy of herte that I trow never man was[8] [that was] erthely;
and therefore I wote well, whan my body ys dede, my soule shall
be in grete joy to se the Blyssed Trinité every day, and the majesté
of Oure Lorde Jesu Cryste."

And so longe were they in the shippe that they seyde to Sir
Galahad, "Sir, in thys bedde ye oughte to lyghe, for so seyth the
lettirs." And so he layde hym downe and slepte a grete whyle. And
whan he awaked, he loked tofore hym and saw the cité of Sarras—
and as they wolde have londed, they saw the shyp wherein Sir
Percivall had putte hys syster in. "Truly," seyde Sir Percivall, "in the
name of God, well hath my syster holden us covenaunte!"[9]

Than toke they oute of the shyppe the table of sylver; and he
toke[1] hit to Sir Percivale and to Sir Bors to go tofore, and Sir Galahad
com behynde, and ryght so they wente into the cité. And at the
gate of the cité they saw an olde man croked; and anone Sir Galahad
called hym and bade hym "helpe to bere thys hevy thynge."

"Truly," seyde the olde man, "hit ys ten yere ago that I myght
nat go but with crucchis." "Care thou nat," seyde Sir Galahad,
"aryse up and shew thy good wyll." And so he assayde, and founde
hymselff as hole as ever he was. Than ran he to the table and toke
one parte ayenst[2] Sir Galahad. Anone rose there a grete noyse in
the cité that a crypple was made hole by knyghtes merveylous that
entird into the cité.

¶Than anone aftir, the three knyghtes wente to the watir and
brought up into the paleyse Sir Percivallis syster, and buryed her
as rychely as them oughte a kynges doughter. And whan the kynge
of that contrey knew that and saw that felyship (whos name was
Estoranse), he asked them of whens they were, and what thynge hit
was that they had brought uppon the table of sylver. And they told
hym the trouth of the Sankgreall, and the power whych God hath
sette there. Than thys kynge was a grete tirraunte, and was com
of the lyne of paynymes, and toke hem and put hem in preson, in
a depe hole—but as sone as they were there, Our Lord sente them
the Sankgreall, thorow whos grace they were allwey fullfylled whyle
they were in preson.

¶So at the yerys ende hit befelle that thys kynge lay syke and
felte that he sholde dye. Than he sente for the three knyghtes, and
they cam afore hym; and he cryed hem mercy of that he had done
to them, and they forgave hym goodly, and he dyed anone. Whan
the kynge was dede all the cité stoode dyssemayde, and wyst nat
who myght be her kynge. Ryght so as they were in counceyle, there
com a voice downe amonge them and bade hem chose the yongyst
knyght of three to be her kynge—"for he shall well maynteyne you
and all youris."

8. I.e., was so joyful.
9. *Holden us covenaunte:* kept (her) promise to us.
1. I.e., gave.
2. I.e., beside.

So they made Sir 𝕲𝖆𝖑𝖆𝖍𝖆𝖉 kynge by all the assente of the hole cité (and ellys they wolde have slayne hym). And whan he was com to hys [land], he lete make abovyn the table of sylver a cheste of golde and of precious stonys that coverde the holy vessell; and every day erly thes three [felawes] wolde com before hit and make their prayers. Now at the yerys ende, and the selff Sonday aftir that Sir 𝕲𝖆𝖑𝖆𝖍𝖆𝖉 had borne the crowne of golde, he arose up erly, and hys felowis, and cam to the paleyse, and saw tofore hem the holy vessell, and a man knelyng on his kneys in lyknesse of a bysshop, that had aboute hym a grete feliship of angels—as hit had bene Jesu Cryste hymselff. And than he arose and began a Masse of Oure Lady; and so he cam to the sakerynge, and anone made an ende.

⸿He called Sir 𝕲𝖆𝖑𝖆𝖍𝖆𝖉 unto hym and seyde, "Com forthe, the servaunte of Jesu Cryste, and thou shalt se that thou hast much desired to se." And than he began to tremble ryght harde whan the dedly[3] fleysh began to beholde the spirituall thynges. Than he hylde up his hondis towarde hevyn, and seyde, "Lorde, I thanke The, for now I se that that hath be my desire many a day. Now, my Blyssed Lorde, I wold nat lyve in this wrecched worlde no lenger, if hit myght please The, Lorde." And therewith the good man toke Oure Lordes Body[4] betwyxte hys hondis and profird hit to Sir 𝕲𝖆𝖑𝖆𝖍𝖆𝖉, and he resseyved hit ryght gladly and mekely.

⸿"Now wotist thou what I am?" seyde the good man. "Nay, sir," seyde Sir 𝕲𝖆𝖑𝖆𝖍𝖆𝖉. "I am Joseph, the sonne of 𝕵𝖔𝖘𝖊𝖕𝖍 𝖔𝖋 𝕬𝖗𝖆𝖒𝖆𝖙𝖍𝖞, which Oure Lorde hath sente to the to bere the[5] felyship. And wotyst thou wherefore He hathe sente me more than ony other? For thou hast resembled me in to thynges: that thou hast sene the merveyles of the 𝕾𝖆𝖓𝖐𝖌𝖗𝖊𝖆𝖑𝖑; and for that thou hast bene a clene mayde, as I have be and am."

And whan he had seyde thes wordis [Sir 𝕲𝖆𝖑𝖆𝖍𝖆𝖉] wente to Sir 𝕻𝖊𝖗𝖈𝖎𝖛𝖆𝖑𝖊 and kyssed hym and commended hym to God; and so he wente to Sir 𝕭𝖔𝖗𝖘 and kyssed hym and commended hym to God, and seyde, "My fayre lorde, salew me unto my lorde Sir 𝕷𝖆𝖚𝖓𝖈𝖊𝖑𝖔𝖙, my fadir, and as sone as ye se hym, bydde hym remembir of this worlde unstable." And therewith he kneled downe tofore the table and made hys prayers; and so suddeynly departed hys soule to Jesu Cryste, and a grete multitude of angels bare hit up to hevyn evyn in the syght of hys two felowis. Also thes two [felawes] saw com frome hevyn an hande, but they sy nat the body; and so hit cam ryght to the vessell and toke hit, and the speare, and so bare hit up into hevyn—and sythen was there never man so hardy to sey that he hade seyn the 𝕾𝖆𝖓𝖐𝖌𝖗𝖊𝖆𝖑.

So whan Sir 𝕻𝖊𝖗𝖈𝖎𝖛𝖆𝖑𝖊 and Sir 𝕭𝖔𝖗𝖘 saw Sir 𝕲𝖆𝖑𝖆𝖍𝖆𝖉 dede they made as much sorow as ever ded men—and if they had nat bene good men they myght lyghtly have falle in dispayre—and so people of the contrey and cité, they were ryght hevy. But so he was buryed;

fol.408r

[23]

---

3. I.e., mortal.
4. I.e., the Host of the Eucharist.
5. Thee.

and as sone as he was buryed Sir **Percivale** yelded[6] hym to an ermytayge oute of the cité, and toke religious clothyng. And Sir **Bors**
was allwey with hym, but he chonged never hys seculer clothyng,
for that he purposed hym to go agayne into the realme of Logrus.
Thus a yere and two monethis lyved Sir **Percivale** in the ermytayge
a full holy lyff, and than passed oute of the worlde. Than Sir **Bors**
lat bury hym by hys syster and by Sir **Galahad** in the spiritualités.[7]

¶So whan Sir **Bors** saw that he was in so farre[8] contreyes as in
the partis of **Babilonye**, he departed frome the cité of **Sarras** and
armed hym and cam to the see, and entird into a shippe. And so
hit befelle hym, by good adventure, he cam unto the realme of
Logrus; and so he rode a pace tylle he com to **Camelot** where the
Kynge was. And than was there made grete joy of hym in all the
courte, for they wente he had bene loste, for as much as he had
bene so longe oute of the contrey. And whan they had etyn, the
Kynge made grete clerkes to com before hym, for cause they shulde
cronycle of the hyghe adventures of the good knyghtes.

¶So whan Sir **Bors** had tolde hym of the hyghe aventures of the
Sankgreall such as had befalle hym and his three felowes, which
were Sir **Launcelot**, **Percivale**, and Sir **Galahad** and hymselff, than Sir
Launcelot tolde the adventures of the **Sangreall** that he had sene.
And all thys was made in grete bookes, and put up in almeryes at
Salysbury.[9]

¶And anone Sir **Bors** seyde to Sir **Launcelot**, "Sir **Galahad**, youre
owne sonne, salewed you by[1] me, and aftir you my lorde Kynge
Arthure and all the hole courte; and so ded Sir **Percivale**, for I buryed
them both myne[2] owne hondis in the cité of **Sarras**. Also, Sir **Launcelot**, Sir **Galahad** prayde you to remembir of thys unsyker worlde,
as ye behyght hym whan ye were togydirs more than halffe a yere."

¶"Thys ys trew," seyde Sir **Launcelot**, "now I truste to God hys
prayer shall avayle me." Than Sir **Launcelot** toke Sir **Bors** in hys
armys, and seyde, "Cousyn, ye ar ryght wellcom to me, for [alle
that ever I maye doo for yow and for yours, ye shall fynde my poure
body redy atte all tymes whyles the spyryte is in hit, and that I
promyse yow feythfully, and never to fayle—and wete ye well, gen-
tyl cosyn Syre **Bors**, that] ye and I shall never departe in sundir
whylis oure lyvys may laste." "Sir, seyde he, "as ye woll, so woll I."

Thus endith the tale of the **Sankgreal** that was breffly drawyn
oute[3] of Freynshe—which ys a tale cronycled for one of the trewyst
and of the holyest that ys in thys worlde—by Sir **Thomas Maleorré,
knyght. ☩ blessed Jesu, helpe hym thorow Hys myght.**[4] **Amen.**

fol.409r

---

6. I.e., withdrew.
7. I.e., consecrated grounds.
8. I.e., distant.
9. Salisbury was an important center of ecclesiastical learning during the Middle Ages.
1. I.e., through.
2. I.e., with my.
3. *Breffly drawyn oute:* i.e., translated with abridgment.
4. Note the unevenly spaced rhyme within the rubricated text: *knyght . . . myght* (and cf. the
   same effect in the closing prayer of p. 698). If the rhyme is deliberate, its purpose may be
   to give additional formality and gravity to the prayer.

The Tale of Sir Launcelot and
Quene Gwenyvere†

SO afftir the Quest of the Sankgreall was fulfylled, [XVIII.1] fol.409v
and all knyghtes that were leffte on lyve were
com home agayne unto the Table Rownde—as
the Booke of the Sankgreall makith mencion—
than was there grete joy in the courte, and en 5
especiall[1] Kynge Arthure and Quene Gwenyvere made grete joy of the
remenaunte that were com home. And passyng gladde was the
Kynge and the Quene of Sir Launcelot and of Sir Bors, for they had
bene passynge longe away in the Queste of the Sankgreall.

Than, as the booke seyth, Sir Launcelot began to resorte unto 10
Quene Gwenivere agayne, and forgate the promyse and the perfeccion that he made in the Queste; for, as the booke seyth, had nat
Sir Launcelot bene in his prevy thoughtes and in hys myndis so sette
inwardly to the Quene as he was in semynge outewarde to God,
there had no knyght passed hym in the Queste of the Sankgreall. 15
But ever his thoughtis prevyly were on the Quene, and so they
loved togydirs more hotter than they dud toforehonde, and had
many such prevy draughtis togydir that many in the courte spake
of hit—and in especiall Sir Aggravayne, Sir Gawaynes brothir, for he
was ever opynne-mowthed. 20

So hit befelle that Sir Launcelot had many resortis of ladyes and
damesels which dayly resorted unto hym, [that besoughte hym] to
be their champion. In all such maters of ryght Sir Launcelot applyed
hym dayly to do for the plesure of Oure Lorde Jesu Cryst; and ever
as much as he myght he withdrew hym fro the company of Quene 25
Gwenyvere for to eschew the sclawndir and noyse[2]—wherefore the
Quene waxed wrothe with Sir Launcelot.

So on a day she called hym to hir chambir, and seyd thus: "Sir
Launcelot, I se and fele dayly that youre love begynnyth to slake, for
ye have no joy to be in my presence, but ever ye ar oute of thys 30
courte; and quarels and maters ye have nowadayes for ladyes, fol.410r
madyns, and jantillwomen, more than ever ye were wonte to have
beforehande."

❡"A, madame," seyde Sir Launcelot, "in thys ye must holde me
excused, for dyvers causis. One ys, I was but late in the Quest of 35
the Sankgreall, and I thanke God of Hys grete mercy, and never of
my deservynge, that I saw in that my queste as much as ever saw

---

† The title is partly taken from the colophon to this section (p. 645), with the addition,
according to editorial custom, of "and Quene Gwenyvere" to distinguish this section from
the one with a similar title, beginning on p. 151. Malory's principal sources for this section
are the French prose *Mort le Roi Artu* and the Middle English stanzaic *Morte Arthur* (for
illustrative selections, see p. 740 and p. 747). In the Winchester MS this section begins
on a new page, with half of the previous page left blank after the end of the *Tale of the
Sankgreall*; those features, along with the floriated "S" make this one of the major divisions
of the MS. The floriated "S" is red with sprays in brown and some of the smallest com-
partments of its decoration filled in yellow; the capital "O" which follows is also filled in
yellow, and yellow is used to highlight the "th" in the first "the" of the line.
1. *En especiall:* especially.
2. I.e., rumor, scandal.

ony synfull man lyvynge—and so was hit tolde me. And if that I
had nat had my prevy thoughtis to returne to youre love agayne as
I do, I had sene as grete mysteryes as ever saw my sonne Sir Galahad, Percivale, other Sir Bors.

"And therefore, madam, I was but late in that Queste; and wyte
you well, madam, hit may nat be yet lyghtly forgotyn, the hyghe
servyse in whom I dud my dyligente laboure. Also, madame, wyte
you well that there be many men spekith of oure love in thys courte
and have you and me gretely in awayte,[3] as thes Sir Aggravayne and
Sir Mordred. And, madam, wyte you well I drede them more for
youre sake than for ony feare I have of them myselffe, for I may
happyn to ascape and ryde myselff in a grete nede, where, madame,
ye muste abyde all that woll be seyde unto you—

¶"And than, if that ye falle in ony distresse thorowoute wyllfull
foly, than ys there none [other remedy] other helpe but by me and
my bloode[4]—and wyte you well, madam, the boldenesse of you
and me woll brynge us to shame and sclaundir; and that were me
lothe, to se you dishonoured. And that is the cause I take uppon
me more for to do for damesels and maydyns than ever Y ded
toforne, that men sholde undirstonde my joy and my delite ys my
plesure to have ado for damesels and maydyns."

All thys whyle the Quene stoode stylle and lete Sir Launcelot sey
what he wolde. And whan he had all seyde, she braste oute on
wepynge; and so she sobbed and a-wepte a grete whyle. And whan
she myght speke, she seyde, "Sir Launcelot, now I well understonde
that thou arte a false, recrayed knyght and a comon lechourere,
and lovyste and holdiste othir ladyes, and of me thou haste dys-
dayne and scorne:

¶"For wyte thou well, now I undirstonde thy falsehede, I shall
never love the[5] more, and loke thou be never so hardy to com in
my syght; and ryght here I dyscharge the thys courte, that thou
never com within hit, and I forfende the my felyship, and uppon
payne of thy hede that thou se me nevermore."

¶Ryght so Sir Launcelot departed with grete hevynes, that unneth
he myght susteyne hymselff for grete dole-makynge. Than he
called Sir Bors, Ector de Maris, and Sir Lyonell, and tolde hem how
the Quene had forfende hym the courte, and so he was in wyll to
departe into hys owne contrey.

"Fayre Sir," seyde Bors de Ganys, "ye shall not departe oute of
thys londe, by myne advyce, for ye muste remembir you what ye
ar, and renomed the moste nobelyst knyght of the worlde, and
many grete maters ye have in honde. And women in their hasty-
nesse woll do oftyntymes that, aftir, hem sore repentith. And
therefore, be myne advyce, ye shall take youre horse and ryde to
the good ermyte here besyde Wyndesore, that somtyme was a good
knyght—hys name ys Sir Brascias—and there shall ye abyde tyll
that I sende you worde of bettir tydynges."

3. *In awayte:* under insidious watch.
4. I.e., blood relatives.
5. Thee.

¶"Brother," seyde Sir Launcelot, "wyte you well I am full loth to departe oute of thys reallme, but the Quene hath defended me so hyghly[6] that mesemyth she woll never be my good lady as she hath bene." "Sey ye never so," seyde Sir Bors, "for many tymys or this she hath bene wroth with you, and aftir that she was the firste repented[7] hit."

¶"Ye sey well," seyde Sir Launcelot, "for now woll I do by your counceyle and take myne horse and myne harneyse and ryde to the ermyte Sir Brastias; and there woll I repose me tille I hyre som maner of tydynges frome you. But, fayre brother, in that ye can, gete me the love of my lady Quene Gwenyvere. "Sir," seyde Sir Bors, "ye nede nat to meve me of such maters, for well ye wote I woll do what I may to please you.

And than Sir Launcelot departed suddeynly, and no creature wyst where he was becom but Sir Bors. So whan Sir Launcelot was departed, the Quene outewarde made no maner of sorow in shewyng to none of his bloode nor to none other; but wyte ye well, inwardely, as the booke seythe, she toke grete thought—but she bare hit oute with a proude countenaunce, as thoughe she felte no thought nother daungere.

So the Quene lete make a pryvy dynere in London unto the knyghtes of the Rownde Table, and all was for to shew outwarde that she had as grete joy in all other knyghtes of the Rounde Table as she had in Sir Launcelot. So there was all only at that dyner Sir Gawayne and his brethern, that ys for to sey, Sir Aggravayne, Sir Gaherys, Sir Gareth and Sir Mordred. Also there was Sir Bors de Ganis, Sir Blamour de Ganys, Sir Bleobris de Ganys, Sir Galihud, Sir Eliodyn, Sir Ector de Maris, Sir Lyonell, Sir Palamydes, Sir Safyr, his brothir, Sir La Cote Male Taylé, Sir Persaunte, Sir Ironsyde, Sir Braundeles, Sir Kay le Senysciall, Sir Madore de la Porte, Sir Patrise (a knyght of Irelonde), Sir Alyduke, Sir Ascamoure, and Sir Pynell le Saveayge, whych was cosyne to Sir Lameroke de Galis, the good knyght that Sir Gawayne and hys brethirn slew by treson. And so thes foure and twenty knyghtes sholde dyne with the Quene in a prevy place by themselff, and there was made a grete feste of all maner of deyntees. But Sir Gawayne had a custom that he used dayly at mete and at supper, that he loved well all maner of fruyte, and in especiall appyls and pearys. And therefore whosomever dyned other fested Sir Gawayne wolde comonly purvey for good fruyte for hym.

And so ded the Quene: for to please Sir Gawayne she lette purvey for hym all maner of fruyte, for Sir Gawayne was a passyng hote[8] knyght of nature. And thys Sir Pyonell hated Sir Gawayne bycause of hys kynnesman Sir Lamorakes dethe; and therefore, for pure envy

fol.411r

[3]

6. *Defended*: i.e., forbidden. *Highly*: i.e., seriously.
7. I.e., who repented.
8. I.e., of a choleric humor. In the Middle Ages one's condition was often estimated in terms of an equilibrium between four elemental fluids: blood, yellow bile, phlegm, and black bile; the fluids were considered to be linked with the four elements, air, fire, water, and earth, respectively; a predominance of any one of the fluids accounted for a disposition that was, respectively, sanguine, choleric, phlegmatic, or melancholic. Fruit was considered a "cool" food (as opposed, for instance, to "hot" meat or wine) and would be an appropriate choice for Gawain.

fol.411v

and hate, Sir Pyonell enpoysonde sertayn appylls for to enpoysen Sir Gawayne. So thys was well yet unto the ende of mete, and so hit befylle by myssefortune a good knyght, Sir Patryse, which was cosyn unto Sir Mador de la Porte, toke an appyll, for he was enchaffed with hete of wyne, and hit myssehapped hym to take a poy-sonde apple. And whan he had etyn hit he swall sore tylle he braste, and there Sir Patryse felle downe suddeynly dede amonge hem.

Than every knyght lepe frome the bourde ashamed and araged for wratthe oute of hir wittis, for they wyst nat what to sey; con-siderynge Quene Guenyvere made the feste and dyner, they had all suspeccion unto hir. "My lady, the Quene," seyde Sir Gawayne, "madam; wyte you that thys dyner was made for me and my felowis, for all folkes that knowith my condicion undirstonde that I love well fruyte—and now I se well I had nere be slayne! Therefore, madam, I drede me leste ye woll be shamed."

Than the Quene stood stylle, and was so sore abaysshed that she wyst nat what to sey. "Thys shall nat so be ended," seyde Sir Mador de la Porte, "for here have I loste a full noble knyght of my bloode; and therefore uppon thys shame and dispite I woll be revenged to the utteraunce."[9] And there opynly Sir Mador appeled the Quene of the deth of hys cousyn Sir Patryse. Than stood they all stylle, that none wolde speke a worde ayenste hym, for they all had grete suspeccion unto the Quene bycause she lete make that dyner. And the Quene was so abaysshed that she cowde none oth-erwayes do but wepte so hartely that she felle on a swowghe. So with thys noyse and crye cam to them Kynge Arthure, and whan he wyste of the trowble he was a passyng hevy man.

¶And ever Sir Madore stood stylle before the Kynge and appeled the Quene of treson; for the custom was such at that tyme that all maner of shamefull deth was called treson. "Fayre lordys," seyd Kynge Arthure, "me repentith of thys trouble, but the case ys so I may nat have ado in thys mater, for I muste be a ryghtfull juge[1]— and that repentith me that I may nat do batayle for my wyff, for, as I deme, thys dede com[2] never by her. And therefor I suppose she shall nat be all distayned, but that somme good knyght shall put hys body in jouperté for my quene rather than she sholde be brente in a wronge quarell. And therefore, Sir Madore, be nat so hasty, for, perdé, hit may happyn she shall nat be all frendeles; and therefore desyre thou thy day of batayle, and she shall purvey hir of som good knyght that shall answere you—other ellis hit were to me grete shame, and to all my courte."

¶"My gracious lorde," seyde Sir Madore, "ye muste holde me excused, for thoughe ye be oure Kynge, in that degré[3] ye ar but a knyght as we ar, and ye ar sworne unto knyghthode als welle as we be. And therefore I beseche you that ye be nat displeased, for there

[4]

fol.412r

9. I.e., death.
1. Arthur's sworn duty as King is to uphold the laws and the welfare of his realm before all other considerations (cf. his coronation vows, p. 11).
2. I.e., originated.
3. *In that degré:* in the present situation.

ys none of all thes foure and twenty knyghtes that were bodyn to thys dyner but all they have grete suspeccion unto the Quene—

⁋ "What sey ye, all my lordys?" seyde Sir Madore. Than they answerde by and by and seyde they coude nat excuse the Quene for why she made the dyner, and other hit[4] muste com by her other by her servauntis. "Alas," seyde the Quene—

⁋ "I made thys dyner for a good entente, and never for none evyll; so Allmyghty Jesu helpe me in my ryght, as I was never purposed to do such evyll dedes, and that I reporte me[5] unto God."

⁋ "My lorde the Kynge," seyde Sir Madore, "I requyre you as ye beth a ryghteuous kynge, gyffe me my day that I may have justyse." "Well," seyde the Kynge, "thys day fiftene dayes, loke thou be redy armed on horsebak in the medow besydes Wynchestir; and if hit so falle that there be ony knyght to encountir ayenste you, there may you do youre beste, and God spede the ryght—and if so befalle that there be no knyght redy at that day, than muste my quene be brente; and there she shall be redy to have hir jugemente." "I am answerde," seyde Sir Madore. And every knyght yode where hym lyked.

⁋ So whan the Kyng and the Quene were togidirs, the Kynge asked the Quene how this case befelle. Than the Quene seyde, "Sir—as Jesu be my helpe"—she wyst nat how, nother in what manere.

⁋ "Where ys Sir Launcelot?" seyde Kynge Arthure. "And he were here he wolde nat grucche to do batayle for you." "Sir," seyde the Quene, "I wote nat where he ys, but hys brother and hys kynessmen deme that he be nat within thys realme."

⁋ "That me repentith," seyde Kyng Arthure, "for and he were here he wolde sone stynte thys stryffe.

⁋ "Well, than I woll counceyle you," seyde the Kyng, "that ye go unto Sir Bors and pray hym for to do batayle for you for Sir Launcelottis sake; and uppon my lyff he woll nat refuse you. For well I se," seyde the Kynge, "that none of the foure and twenty knyghtes that were at your dyner where Sir Patryse was slayne woll do batayle for you, nother none of hem woll sey well of you, and that shall be grete sclaundir to you in thys courte." "[Allas," said the Quene, "and I maye not doo withall,][6] but now I mysse Sir Launcelot, for and he were here he wolde sone putte me in my hartis ease."

⁋ "What aylith you," seyde the Kynge, "that ye can nat kepe Sir Launcelot uppon youre syde? For wyte you well," seyde the Kynge, "who that hath Sir Launcelot uppon his party hath the moste man of worship in thys worlde uppon hys syde. Now go youre way," seyde the Kynge unto the Quene, "and requyre Sir Bors to do batayle for you for Sir Launcelottis sake."

⁋ So the Quene departed frome the Kynge, and sente for Sir Bors into the chambir; and whan he cam she besought hym of succour.

fol.412v   20

[5]   45

How Quene Gwenyvere besought Sir Bors to fyght for her

---

4. *Other hit:* i.e., either the crime.
5. *Reporte me:* declare.
6. *And I maye not doo withall:* if I can not bring it about.

❡"Madam," seyde he, "what wolde ye that I ded? For I may nat with my worship have ado in thys mater, because I was at the same dyner, for drede [that] ony of tho knyghtes wolde have [me] in suspeccion—

❡"Also, madam," seyde Sir Bors, "now mysse ye Sir Launcelot, for he wolde nat a fayled you in youre ryght nother in youre wronge:

❡"For whan ye have bene in ryght grete daungers he hath suc-coured you. And now ye have drevyn hym oute of thys contrey by whom ye and all we were dayly worshipped by. Therefore, madame, I mervayle how ye dare for shame to requyre me to do onythynge for you, insomuche ye have enchaced oute of your courte by whom we were up borne and honoured."

❡"Alas, fayre knyght," seyde the Quene, "I put me holé in youre grace, and all that ys amysse I woll amende as ye woll counceyle me." And therewith she kneled downe upon both hir kneys and besought Sir Bors to have mercy upon her—"other ellis I shall have a shamefull dethe, and thereto I never offended."

❡Ryght so cam Kynge Arthure and founde the Quene knelynge [afore Sir Bors]. And than Sir Bors toke hir up and seyde, "Madam, ye do me grete dishonoure." "A, jantill knyght," seyde the Kynge, "have mercy uppon my quene, curteyse knyght, for I am now in sertayne she ys untruly[7] defamed. And therefore, curteyse knyght," the Kynge seyde, "promyse her to do batayle for her, I requyre you, for the love ye owghe unto Sir [Launcelot." "My lord," sayd Syr] Bors, "ye requyre me the grettist thynge that ony man may requyre me—

"And wyte you well, if I graunte to do batayle for the Quene I shall wretth many of my felyship of the Table Rounde. But as for that," seyde Sir Bors, "I woll graunte—for my lorde Sir Launcelottis sake and for youre sake—I woll at that day be the Quenys cham-pyon, onles that there com by adventures a better knyght than I am to do batayle for her."

❡"Woll ye promyse me this," seyde the Kynge, "by youre fayth?" "Yee, sir," seyd Sir Bors, "of that I shall nat fayle you nother her—but if there com a bettir knyght than I am: than shall he have the batayle." Than was the Kynge and the Quene passynge gladde, and so departed and thanked hym hertely.

❡Than Sir Bors departed secretly uppon a day and rode unto Sir Launcelot there as he was with Sir Brascias, and tolde hym of all thys adventure. "A, Jesu," Sir Launcelot seyde, "thys ys com happely[8] as I wolde have hit; and therefore I pray you make you redy to do batayle, but loke that ye tarry tylle ye se me com as longe as ye may. For I am sure Sir Madore ys an hote knyght whan he ys inchaf-fed, for the more ye suffyr hym the hastyer woll he be to batayle."

❡"Sir, seyde Sir Bors, "latte me deale with hym. Doute ye nat ye shall have all youre wylle."

❡So departed Sir Bors frome hym and cam to the courte agayne. Than was hit noysed in all the courte that Sir Bors sholde do

---

7. I.e., falsely.
8. I.e., by a lucky chance.

batayle for the Quene—wherefore many knyghtes were displeased
with hym that he wolde take uppon hym to do batayle in the
Quenys quarell, for there were but fewe knyghtes in all the courte
but they demed the Quene was in the wronge and that she had
done that treson. So Sir Bors answered thus to hys felowys of the   5
Table Rounde: "Wete you well, my fayre lordis, hit were shame to
us all and we suffird to se the moste noble quene of the worlde to
be shamed opynly, consyderyng her lorde and oure lorde ys the
man of moste worship crystynde, and he hath ever worshipped us
all in all placis."   10

¶Many answerd hym agayne: "As for oure moste noble Kynge
Arthure, we love hym and honoure hym as well as ye do; but as for
Quene Guenyver, we love hir nat, because she ys a destroyer of good
knyghtes."

"Fayre lordis," seyde Sir Bors, "mesemyth ye sey nat as ye sholde   15
sey, for never yet in my dayes knew I never ne harde sey that ever
she was a destroyer of good knyghtes; but at all tymes, as far as
ever I coude know, she was a maynteyner of good knyghtes—and
ever she hath bene large and fre of hir goodis to all grood knyghtes,
and the moste bownteuous lady of hir gyfftis and her good grace   20
that ever I saw other harde speke off. And therefore hit were shame
to us all and to oure moste noble kynges wyff whom we serve [and
we suffred her] to be shamefully slayne—and wete you well," seyde
Sir Bors, I woll nat suffir hit, for I dare sey so much, for the Quene
ys nat gylty of Sir Patryseys dethe: for she ought hym never none   25
evyll wyll, nother none of the foure and twenty knyghtes that were
at that dyner, for I dare sey for good love she bade us to dyner and
nat for no male engyne.[9] And that, I doute nat, shall be preved
hereafftir—for howsomever the game goth, there was treson   fol.414r
amonge us."   30

¶Than som seyde to Sir Bors, "We may well belyve youre wordys." And so somme were well pleased and som were nat. So the   [6]
day com on faste untyll the evyn[1] that the batayle sholde be.

¶Than the Quene sente for Sir Bors and asked hym how he was
disposed. "Truly, madame," seyde he, "I am disposed in lyke wyse   35
as I promysed you, that ys to sey I shall natt fayle you onles there
by aventure com a bettir knyght than I am to do batayle for you;
than, madam, I am of you discharged of my promyse."

¶"Woll ye," seyde the Quene, "that I telle my lorde the Kyng
thus?" "Doth as hit pleasith you, madam." Than the Quene yode   40
unto the Kyng and tolde the answere of Sir Bors.

¶"Well, have ye no doute," seyde the Kynge, "of Sir Bors, for I
calle hym now that ys lyvynge one of the nobelyst knyghtes of the
worlde, and moste perfitist man."

¶And thus hit paste on tylle the morne; and so the Kynge and   45
the Quene and all maner of knyghtes that were there at that tyme
drewe them unto the medow bysydys Wynchester where the

9. *Male engyne*: evil scheme.
1. I.e., evening before.

batayle sholde be. And so whan the Kynge was com with the Quene
and many knyghtes of the Table Rounde, so the Quene was than
put in the conestablis awarde,[2] and a grete fyre made aboute an
iron stake, that an[3] Sir Mador de la Porte had the bettir, she sholde
there be brente. (For such custom was used in tho dayes, for   5
favoure, love, nother affinité there sholde be none other but ryghtuous jugemente, as well uppon a Kynge as uppon a knyght, and
as well uppon a quene as uppon another poure lady.)[4]

So thys meanewhyle cam in Sir Mador de la Porte and toke hys
othe before the Kynge, how that the Quene ded thys treson untill   10
hys cosyn Sir Patryse—"and unto myne othe I woll preve hit with
my body, honde for hande, who[5] that woll sey the contrary."

¶Ryght so cam in Sir Bors de Ganys, and seyde that as for Quene
Gweniver, "she ys in the ryght, and that woll I make good that she
ys nat culpable of thys treson that is put uppon her."   15

¶"Than make the redy," seyde Sir Madore, "and we shall preve   fol.414v
whethir thou be in the ryght or I." "Sir Madore," seyde Sir Bors,
"wete you well, I know you for a good knyght; natforthan I shall
nat feare you so gretly, but I truste to God I shall be able to withstonde youre malyce. But thus much have I promised my lorde   20
Arthure and my lady the Quene, that I shall do batayle for her in
thys cause to the utteryste—onles that there com a bettir knyght
than I am and discharge me."

¶"Is that all?" seyde Sir Madore. "Othir com thou off[6] and do
batayle with me, other elles sey nay." "Take youre horse," seyde   25
Sir Bors, "and, as I suppose, [ye] shall nat tarry long but ye shall
be answerde." Than ayther departed to their tentis and made hem
redy to horsebacke as they thought beste. And anone Sir Madore
cam into the fylde with hys shylde on hys shulder and hys speare
in hys honde—   30

¶"And so rode aboute the place, cryyng unto Kyng Arthure, "Byd
youre champyon com forthe, and he dare!"

¶Than was Sir Bors ashamed, and toke hys horse and cam to
the lystis ende—and than was he ware where cam frome a woode
there fast by a knyght all armed uppon a whyght horse, with a   35
straunge shylde of straunge armys, and he cam dryvyng all that[7]
hys horse myght renne; and so he cam to Sir Bors and seyd thus:
"Fayre knyght, I pray you be nat displesed, for here muste a bettir   How Sir Launcelot
knyght than ye ar have thys batayle. Therefore I pray you withdraw   rescowed Quene
you, for wyte you well I haye had thys day a ryght grete journey,   Gwenyvere from the
and thys batayle ought to be myne—and so I promysed you whan   deth   40

<hr>

2. *In the Conestablis awarde:* under the Constable's guard.
3. I.e., if.
4. Another of Malory's relatively rare meditations on his own times (cf. his comments on
   pp. 137, 625, and 680). The period leading up to and during the Wars of the Roses was
   characterized by legal conflicts beween magnates who regularly corrupted judicial procedure (not to mention the principles of legal royal succession); cf. the selections from
   the Paston letters (p. 763) and Berkeley letters (p. 759).
5. I.e., despite who.
6. *com . . . off:* proceed.
7. *All that:* i.e., as fast as.

I spake with you laste—and with all my herte I thanke you of youre good wylle."

¶Than Sir **Bors** rode unto Kynge **Arthure** and tolde hym how there was a knyght com that wolde have the batayle to fyght for the Quene.

¶"What knyght ys he?" seyde the Kyng. "I wote nat," seyde Sir **Bors**, "but suche covenaunte he made with me to be here thys day:

¶"Now, my lorde," seyde Sir **Bors**, "here I am discharged."

Than the Kynge called to that knyght and asked hym if he wolde fyght for the Quene. Than he answerd and seyde, "Sir, therefore com I hyddir; and therefore, Sir Kynge, tarry me no lenger, for anone as I have fynysshed thys batayle I muste departe hens, for I have to do many batayles elswhere. For wyte you well," seyde that knyght, "thys ys dishonoure to you and to all knyghtes of the Rounde Table to se and know so noble a lady and so curteyse [a quene] as Quene **Gwenyvere** ys, thus to be rebuked and shamed amongyst you." Than they all mervayled what knyght that myght be that so toke [the bataille] uppon hym, for there was nat one that knew hym but if hit were Sir **Bors**.

Than seyde Sir **Madore de la Porte** unto the Kynge, "Now lat me wete with whom I shall have ado." And than they rode to the lystes ende. And there they cowched their spearis and ran togydirs with all their myghtes; and anone Sir **Madors** speare brake all to pecis, but the othirs speare hylde and bare Sir **Madors** horse and all backwarde to the erthe, a grete falle. But myghtyly and delyverly he avoyded his horse from hym, and put hys shylde before hym and drew hys swerde, and bade the othir knyght alyght and do batayle with hym on foote.

¶Than that knyght descended downe frome hys horse, and put hys shylde before hym and drew hys swerde. And so they cam egirly unto batayle; and aythir gaff othir many sadde strokes, trasyng and traversyng, [racynge] and foynyng, [and hurtlyng] togydir with their swerdis as hit were wylde boorys, thus fyghtyng nyghe an owre—for thys Sir **Madore** was a stronge knyght and myghtyly proved in many strange batayles. But at the laste thys knyght smote Sir **Madore** grovelynge uppon the erthe, and the knyght stepte nere hym to have pulde Sir **Madore** flatlynge uppon the grounde; and therewith Sir **Madore** arose, and in hys rysyng he[8] smote that knyght thorow the thyk of the thyghes, that the bloode braste oute fyersly. And whan he felte hymself so wounded and saw hys bloode, he lete hym aryse uppon hys feete.

And than he gaff hym such a buffette uppon the helme that he felle to the erthe flatlyng. And therewith he strode to hym to have pulled of hys helme of hys hede; and so Sir **Madore** prayde that knyght to save hys lyff: and so he yeldyd hym as overcom, and releaced the Quene of hys quarell.

¶"I woll nat graunte the thy lyff," seyde that knyght, "only[9] that thou frely relees the Quene for ever, and that no mencion be made

[7]

10

fol.415r

15

20

25

30

35

40

fol.415v

45

---

8. I.e., the disguised knight.
9. I.e., except.

uppon Sir 𝕻atryseys tombe that ever Quene 𝕲wenyver consented to that treson."

"All thys shall be done," seyde Sir 𝕸adore. "I clerely discharge my quarell for ever." Than the knyghtes parters[1] of the lystis toke up Sir 𝕸adore and led hym tylle hys tente. And the othir knyght wente strayte to the stayre-foote where sate Kynge 𝕬rthure—and by that tyme was the Quene com to the Kyng, and aythir kyssed othir hartely.

And whan the Kynge saw that knyght, he stowped downe to hym and thanked hym, and in lyke wyse ded the Quene. And the Kynge prayde hym to put of his helmet and to repose hym and to take a soppe of wyne.[2] And than he putte of hys helmette to drynke—and than every knyght knew hym, that hit was Sir 𝕷auncelot. And anone as the Kyng wyst that, he toke the Quene in hys honde and yode unto Sir 𝕷auncelot, and seyde, "Sir, grauntemercy of youre grete travayle that ye have had this day for me and for my quyene."

❡"My lorde," seyde Sir 𝕷auncelot, "wytte you well Y ought of ryght ever to be in youre quarell and in my ladyes the Quenys quarell to do batayle; for ye ar the man that gaff me the hygh order of knyghthode. And that day my lady, youre Quene, ded me worshyp—and ellis had I bene shamed—for that same day that ye made me knyght, thorow my hastynes I loste my swerde, and my lady, youre Quene, founde hit, and lapped hit in her trayne, and gave me my swerde whan I had nede thereto; and ells had I bene shamed amonge all knyghtes. And therefore, my lorde 𝕬rthure, I promysed her at that day ever to be her knyght, in ryght othir in wronge."[3]

❡"Grauntemercy," seyde the Kynge, "for this journey[4]—and wete you well," seyde the Kynge, "I shall acquyte youre goodnesse."

❡And evermore the Quene behylde Sir 𝕷auncelot, and wepte so tendirly that she sanke allmoste to the grownde for sorow that he had done to her so grete kyndenes where she shewed hym grete unkyndenesse. Than the knyghtes of hys bloode drew unto hym, and there aythir of them made grete joy of othir—and so cam all the knyghtes of the Table Rounde that were there at that tyme, and wellcommed hym. And than Sir 𝕸adore was [had to] lechecrauffte, and Sir 𝕷auncelot was heled of hys play. And so there was made grete joy, and many merthys there was made in that courte.

And so hit befelle that the Damesell of the Lake that hyght 𝕹ynyve, whych wedded the good knyght Sir 𝕻elleas, and so she cam to the courte, for ever she ded grete goodnes unto Kynge 𝕬rthure and to all hys knyghtes thorow her sorsery and enchauntementes. And so whan she herde how the Quene was greved for the dethe

fol.416r

[8]

---

1. *Knyghtes parters:* marshals.
2. *Soppe of wyne:* wine with bread dipped in it.
3. Mention of these events surrounding Launcelot's investiture as knight is not made elsewhere in Malory; they are, however, paralleled in the French Prose *Launcelot*, one of Malory's sources for other parts of his work. There, after being knighted, Launcelot is distracted from receiving his sword by the compulsion to aid a wounded knight; soon thereafter he agrees to champion the Lady of Nohaut and leaves the court without his rightful sword. The Queen later sends Launcelot the sword (Lacy, II, Chapters 22–23).
4. I.e., day's fighting.

of Sir Patryse, than she tolde hit opynly that she was never gylty, and there she disclosed by whom hit was done, and named hym, Sir Pynel, and for what cause he ded hit; there hit was opynly knowyn and disclosed, and so the Quene was excused.

And thys knyght Sir Pynell fledde unto hys contrey, and was opynly knowyn that he enpoysynde the appyls at that feste to that entente to have destroyed Sir Gawayne, bycause Sir Gawayne and hys brethirne destroyed Sir Lamerok de Galys, which Sir Pynell was cosyn unto.

¶Than was Sir Patryse buryed in the chirche of Westemynster in a towmbe, and thereuppon was wrytten:

HERE LYETH SIR Patryse OF IRELONDE,
SLAYNE BY SIR Pynell le Sabeaige THAT ENPOYSYNDE APPELIS
TO HAVE SLAYNE SIR Gawayne;
AND BY MYSSEFORTUNE SIR Patryse ETE
ONE OF THE APPLIS, AND THAN SUDDEYNLY HE BRASTE.

Also there was wrytyn uppon the tombe that Quene Gwenyvere was appeled of treson of the deth of Sir Patryse by Sir Madore de la Porte; and there was made mencion how Sir Launcelot fought with hym for Quene Gwenyvere and overcom hym in playne batayle. All thys was wretyn uppon the tombe of Sir Patryse in excusyng of the Quene. And than Sir Madore sewed dayly and longe to have the Quenys good grace; and so by the meanys of Sir Launcelot he caused hym to stonde in the Quenys good grace, and all was forgyffyn.

Thus hit passed untyll Oure Lady Day of the Assumpcion.[5] Within a fiftene dayes of[6] that feste the Kynge lete crye a grete justyse and a turnement that sholde be at that day at Camelott, otherwyse callyd Wynchester;[7] and the Kyng lete cry that he and the Kynge of Scottes wolde juste ayenst all the worlde.

¶And whan thys cry was made, thydir cam many good knyghtes; that ys to sey the Kynge of North Galls, and Kynge Angwysh of Irelonde, and the Kynge with the Hondred Knyghtes, and Syr Galahalte the Haute Prynce, and the Kynge of Northumbirlonde, and many other noble deukes and erlis of other dyverse contreyes.

¶So Kynge Arthure made hym redy to departe to hys justis, and wolde have had the Quene with hym; but at that tyme she wolde nat, she seyde, for she was syke and myght nat ryde. "That me repentith," seyde the Kynge, "for thys seven yere ye saw nat such a noble felyship togydirs excepte the Whytsontyde whan Sir Galahad departed frome the courte."

"Truly," seyde the Quene, "ye muste holde me excused; Y may nat be there." And many demed the Quene wolde nat be there because of Sir Launcelot, for he wolde nat ryde with the Kynge, for

fol.416v

---

5. About this feast day, see n. 6, p. 212.
6. *Within a fiftene dayes of:* fifteen days before.
7. On Malory's identification of Camelot with Winchester, see n. 5, p. 61.

he seyde he was nat hole of the play[8] of Sir **Madore**—wherefore the Kynge was hevy and passynge wroth; and so he departed towarde Wynchestir with hys felyship. And so by the way the Kynge lodged at a towne that was called **Ascolot**, that ys in Englysh **Gylforde**, and there the Kynge lay in the castell. So whan the Kynge was departed, the Quene called Sir **Launcelot** unto her, and seyde thus: "Sir, ye ar gretly to blame thus to holde you behynde[9] my lorde. What woll youre enemyes and myne sey and deme?—

¶" 'Se how Sir **Launcelot** holdith hym ever behynde the Kynge, and so the Quene doth also, for that they wolde have their plesure togydirs'—and thus woll they sey," seyde the Quene.

¶"Have ye no doute, madame," seyde Sir **Launcelot**, "I alow[1] youre witte; hit ys of late com syn ye were woxen so wyse.[2] And therefore, madam, at thys tyme I woll be ruled by youre counceyle: and thys nyght I woll take my reste, and tomorow betyme I woll take my way towarde Wynchestir. But wytte you well," seyde Sir **Launcelot** unto the Quene, "at that justys I woll be ayenste the Kynge and ayenst all hys felyship."

¶"Sir, ye may there do as ye lyste," seyde the Quene, "but be my counceyle ye shall nat be ayenst youre Kynge and your felyshyp, for there bene full many hardé knyghtes of youre bloode."

¶"Madame," seyde Sir **Launcelot**, "I shall take the adventure that God woll gyff me." And so uppon the morne erly he harde Masse and [brake his fast], and so he toke hys leve of the Quene and departed. And than he rode so muche unto the tyme he com to **Ascolott**, and there hit happynd hym that in the evenyng-tyde he cam to an olde barownes place that hyght Sir **Barnarde** of Ascolot; and as Sir **Launcelot** entird into hys lodgynge, Kynge **Arthure** aspyed hym as he dud walke in a gardeyne besyde the castell—he knew hym welle inow.

¶"Well, sirs," seyde Kynge **Arthure** unto hys knyghtes that were by hym besyde the castell, "I have now aspyed one knyght," he seyde, "that woll play hys play at the justys, I undirtake."

¶"Who ys that?" seyde the knyghtes.

¶"At thys tyme ye shall nate wyte for me," seyde the Kynge, and smyled, and wente to hys lodgynge.

¶So whan Sir **Launcelot** was in hys lodgyng and unarmed in hys chambir, the olde barown Sir **Barnarde** com to hym and wellcomed hym in the beste maner—but he knew nat Sir **Launcelot**. "Fayre Sir," seyde Sir **Launcelot** tylle hys oste, "I wolde pray you to lende me a shylde that were nat opynly knowyn, for myne ys well knowyn." "Sir," seyde hys oste, "ye shall have youre desire, for mesemyth ye bene one of the lyklyest knyghtes that ever Y sawe— and therefore, sir, I shall shew you freynship"—and seyde, "Sir, wyte you well I have two sunnes that were but late made knyghtes, and the eldist hyght Sir **Tirry**; and he was hurte that same day he

8. I.e., wound.
9. *Holde you behynde:* stay back from.
1. I.e., acknowledge.
2. *Hit ys of late com syn ye were woxen so wyse:* it is only lately that you have grown so shrewd.

was made knyght, and he may nat ryde, and hys shylde ye shalle
have, for that ys nat knowyn I dare sey but here, and in no place
else."

And hys yonger sonne "hyght Sir Lavayne; and if hit please you,
he shall ryde with you unto that justis, for he ys of hys ayge stronge
and wyght. For much my herte gyvith unto you that ye sholde be
a noble knyght; and therefore I praye you to telle me youre name,"
seyde Sir Barnarde. "As for that," seyd Sir Launcelot, "ye muste holde
me excused as at thys tyme; and if God gyff me grace to spede well
at the justis, I shall com agayne and telle you my name. But I pray
you in ony wyse lete me have your sonne Sir Lavayne with me, and
that I may have hys brothers shylde."

"Sir, all thys shall be done," seyde Sir Barnarde. So thys olde
barown had a doughtir that was called that tyme the Fayre Maydyn
off Ascolot; and ever she behylde Sir Launcelot wondirfully—and, as
the booke sayth, she keste such a love unto Sir Launcelot that she
cowde never withdraw hir loove, wherefore she dyed—and her
name was Elayne le Blanke.

So thus as she cam to and fro she was so hote in love that she
besought Sir Launcelot to were uppon hym at the justis a tokyn of
hers. "Damesell," seyde Sir Launcelot, "and if I graunte you that, ye
may sey that I do more for youre love than ever Y ded for lady or
jantillwoman." Than he remembird hymselff that he wolde go to
the justis disgysed; and because he had never aforne borne no
maner of tokyn of no damesell, he bethought hym to bere a tokyn
of hers, that none of hys bloode thereby myght know hym. And
than he seyde, "Fayre maydyn, I woll graunte you to were a tokyn
of youres uppon myne helmet. And therefore what ys hit? Shewe
ye hit me." "Sir," she seyde, "hit ys a rede sleve of myne, of scarlet,
well embrowdred with grete perelles." And so she brought hit hym.

¶So Sir Launcelot resseyved hit and seyde, "Never dud I erste so
much for no damesell." Than Sir Launcelot betoke the fayre mayden
hys shylde in kepynge, and prayde her to kepe hit untill tyme that
he com agayne. And so that nyght he had myrry reste and grete
chere, for thys damesell Elayne was ever aboute Sir Launcelot all the
whyle she myght be suffirde.

¶So uppon a day, on the morne, Kynge Arthure and all hys knyghtis departed, for there the Kyng had tarryed three dayes to abyde
hys noble knyghtes.

¶And so whan the Kynge was rydden, Sir Launcelot and Sir
Lavayne made them redy to ryde, and aythir of them had whyght
shyldis—and the rede sleve Sir Launcelot lete cary with hym; and
so they toke their leve at Sir Barnarde, the olde barowne, and at hys
doughtir, the fayre mayden. And than they rode so longe tylle that
they cam to Camelot, that tyme called Wynchester; and there was
grete pres of kyngis, deukes, erlis, and barownes, and many noble
knyghtes.

¶But there Sir Launcelot was lodged pryvaly by the meanys of Sir
Lavayne with a ryche burgeyse, that no man in that towne was ware
what they were; and so they reposed them there tyll Oure Lady
Day of the Assumpcion, that the grete justes sholde be.

¶So whan trumpettis blew unto the fylde[3] and Kynge Arthur was
sette on hyght uppon a chafflet to beholde who ded beste—but,
as the Freynshe booke seyth, the Kynge wold nat suffir Sir Gawayne
to go frome hym, for never had Sir Gawayne the bettir and Sir Launcelot were in the fylde, and many tymes was Sir Gawayne rebuked
so whan Sir Launcelot was in the fylde in ony justis dysgysed—than
som of the kyngis, as Kynge Angwysh of Irelonde and the Kynge of
Scottis, were that tyme turned to be uppon the syde of Kynge
Arthur. And than on the othir party was the Kynge of North Galis,
and the Kynge with the Hondred Knyghtis, and the Kynge of
Northhumbirlonde, and Sir Galahalte the Halte Prynce—but thes
three kyngis and thys duke was passynge wayke to holde ayenste
Arthurs party, for with hym were the nobelyst knyghtes of the worlde.

¶So than they withdrew them, aythir party frome othir, and
every man made hym redy in his beste maner to do what he myght.

¶Than Sir Launcelot made hym redy, and put the rede slyeve
uppon hys helmette and fastened hit faste; and so Sir Launcelot and
Sir Lavayne departed oute of Wynchestir pryvayly and rode untyll
a litill leved woode behynde the party that hylde ayenste Kynge
Arthure party. And there they hylde hem stylle tylle the partyes
smote togydirs. And than cam in the Kynge of Scottis and the
Kynge of Irelonde on Kynge Arthurs party, and ayenste them cam
in the Kynge of Northumbirlonde and the Kynge with the Hondred
Knyghtes; and there began a grete medlé, and there the Kynge of
Scottis smote downe the Kynge of Northumbirlonde, and the
Kynge with the Hondred Knyghtes smote downe Kynge Angwysh of
Irelonde.

¶Than Sir Palamydes, that was one Arthurs party, he encountird
with Sir Galahalte, and ayther of hem smote downe othir—and
aythir party halpe their lordys on horseback agayne. So there began
a stronge assayle on bothe partyes: and than com in Sir Braundyles,
Sir Sagramoure le Desyrous, Sir Dodynas le Saveayge, Sir Kay la
Senesciall, Sir Gryffelet le Fyze de Dieu, Sir Lucan de Butlere, Sir
Bedwere, Sir Aggravayne, Sir Gaherys, Sir Mordred, Sir Melyot de
Logrys, Sir Ozanna le Cure Hardy, Sir Saphyr, Sir Eppynogrys, Sir
Gallerowne of Galeway—all thes fiftene knyghtes, that were knygh-
tes of the Rounde Table. So thes, with mo other, cam in togydir
and bete abacke the Kynge off Northumbirlonde and the Kynge of
North Walys.

¶Whan Sir Launcelot saw thys, as he hoved in the lytyll leved
wood, than he seyde unto Sir Lavayne, "Se yondir ys a company of
good knyghtes, and they holde them togydirs as borys that were
chaced with doggis." "That ys trouth," seyde Sir Lavayne. "Now,"
seyde Sir Launcelot, "and ye woll helpe a lityll, ye shall se the yonder
felyship that chacith now thes men on oure syde, that they shall
go as faste backwarde as they wente forewarde!" "Sir, spare ye nat
for my parte," seyde Sir Lavayne, "for I shall do what I may."

¶Than Sir Launcelot and Sir Lavayne cam in at the thyckyst of
the prees; and there Sir Launcelot smote downe Sir Brandeles, Sir

fol.418v

10

15

20

25

30

35

fol.419r

40

[11]

45

---

3. *Blew unto the fylde*: i.e., called knights to the contest.

Sagramour, Sir Dodynas, Sir Kay, Sir Gryfflet—and all thys he ded
with one speare; and Sir Lavayne smote downe Sir Lucan de Butlere
and Sir Bedwere. And than Sir Launcelotgate another grete speare,
and there he smote downe Sir Aggravayne and Sir Gaherys, Sir Mordred, Sir Melyot de Logrys—and Sir Lavayne smote downe Sir Ozanna   5
le Cure Hardy.

And than Sir Launcelot drew hys swerde; and there he smote on
the ryght honde and on the lyft honde, and by grete forse he
unhorsed Sir Safir, Sir Epynogrys, and Sir Galleron—and than the
knyghtes of the Table Rounde withdrew them abacke, aftir they   10
had gotyn their horsys as well as they myght. "A, mercy Jesu!" seyde
Sir Gawayne. "What knyght ys yondir that doth so mervaylous dedys
in that fylde?"

¶"I wote what he ys," seyde the Kyng, "but as at thys tyme I woll
nat name hym." "Sir," seyde Sir Gawayne, "I wolde sey hit were Sir   15
Launcelot, by hys rydynge and hys buffettis that I se hym deale; but
ever mesemyth hit sholde nat be he, for that he beryth the rede
slyve uppon hys helmet—for I wyst hym never beare tokyn at no
justys of lady ne jantillwoman."

¶"Lat hym be," seyde Kynge Arthure, "for he woll be bettir   20
knowyn and do more or ever he departe." Than the party that was
ayenst Kynge Arthur were well comforted, and than they hylde hem
togydirs that befornhande were sore rebuked.

¶Than Sir Bors, Sir Ector de Marys, and Sir Lyonell, they called
unto them the knyghtes of their blood, as Sir Blamour de Ganys, Sir   fol.419v   25
Bleoberys, Sir Alyduke, Sir Galyhud, Sir Galyhodyn, Sir Bellyngere le
Bewse. So thes nyne knyghtes of Sir Launcelottis kynne threst in
myghtyly, for they were all noble knyghtes; and they, of grete hate
and despite [that they had unto hym,] thought to rebuke Sir Launcelot and Sir Lavayne, for they knew hem nat; and so they cam hur-   30
lyng togydirs and smote downe many knyghtes of North Walys and
of Northumbirlonde. And whan Sir Launcelot saw them fare so, he
gate a grete speare in hys honde; and there encountird with hym,
all at onys, Sir Bors, Sir Ector, and Sir Lyonell, and they three smote
hym at onys with their spearys, and with fors of themselff they   35
smote Sir Launcelottis horse revers to the erthe. And by mysbefore-
tune Sir Bors smote Sir Launcelot thorow the shylde into the syde,
and the speare brake, and the hede leffte stylle in the syde.

¶Whan Sir Lavayne saw hys mayster lye on the grounde, he ran
to the Kynge of Scottis and smote hym to the erthe; and by grete   40
forse he toke hys horse and brought hym to Sir Launcelot, and magré
them all he made hym to mownte uppon that horse.

¶And than Sir Launcelot gate a speare in hys honde, and there
he smote Sir Bors, horse and man, to the erthe, and in the same
wyse he served Sir Ector and Sir Lyonell—and Sir Lavayne smote   45
downe Sir Blamour de Gaynys. And than Sir Launcelot drew hys
swerde, for he felte hymselff so sore hurte that he wente there to
have had hys deth; and than he smote Sir Bleoberis such a buffet
on the helmet that he felle downe to the erthe in a sowne, and in
the same wyse he served Sir Alyduke and Sir Galyhud.   50

❡And Sir **Labayne** smote downe Sir **Bellyngere**, that was sone to **Alysaunder le Orphelyn**; and by thys was done, was Sir **Bors** horsed agayne and in cam with Sir **Ector** and Sir **Lyonell**, and all they three smote with their swerdis uppon Sir **Launcelottis** helmet. And whan he felte their buffettis—and with that hys wounde greved hym grevously—than he thought to do what he myght whyle he cowde endure; and than he gaff Sir **Bors** such a buffette that he made hym bowghe hys hede passynge lowe—and therewithall he raced of hys helme, and myght have slayne hym, but whan he saw his vysayge, so pulde hym downe.

And in the same wyse he served Sir **Ector** and Sir **Lyonell**; for, as the booke seyth, he myght have slayne them, but whan he saw their visages, hys herte myght nat serve hym thereto, but leffte hem there. [And thenne afterward he hurled into the thyckest prees of them alle, and dyd there the merveyloust dedes of armes that ever man sawe or herde speke of]—and ever Sir **Labayne** with hym. And there Sir **Launcelot** with hys swerde smote downe and pulled downe, as the Freynsh booke seyth, mo than thirty knyghtes, and the moste party were of the Table Rounde; and there Sir **Labayne** dud full well that day, for he smote downe ten knyghtes of the Table Rounde.

❡"Mercy Jesu!" seyde Sir **Gawayne** unto Kynge **Arthur**, "I mervayle what knyght that he ys with the rede sleve." "Sir," seyde Kyng **Arthure**, "he woll be knowyn or ever he departe." And than the Kynge blew unto lodgynge;[4] and the pryce was gyvyn by herowdis unto the knyght with the whyght shylde that bare the rede slyve.

❡Than cam the Kynge of North Galys, and the Kynge of North-humbirlonde, and the Kynge with the Hondred Knyghtes, and Sir **Galahalte** the Haute Prince, and seyde unto Sir **Launcelot**, "Fayre knyght, God you blysse, for muche have ye done for us thys day; and therefore we pray you that ye woll com with us, that ye may resceyve the honour and the pryce as ye have worshypfully deserved hit."

❡"Fayre lordys," seyde Sir **Launcelot**, "wete you well, gyff I have deserved thanke I have sore bought hit—and that me repentith, for I am never lyke to ascape with the lyff. Therefore, my fayre lordys, I pray you that ye woll suffir me to departe where me lykith, for I am sore hurte—and I take no forse of[5] none honoure, for I had levir repose me than to be lorde of all the worlde." And therewithall he groned pyteuously and rode a grete walop awaywarde from them untyll he cam undir a woodys evyse.

And whan he saw that he was frome the fylde nyghe a myle, that he was sure he myght nat be seyne, than he seyde with an hyghe voyce and with a grete grone, "A, jantill knyght, Sir **Labayne**, helpe me that thys truncheoune were oute of my syde, for hit stykith so sore that hit nyghe sleyth me." "A, myne owne lorde," seyde Sir **Labayne**, "I wolde fayne do that myght please you, but I drede me

---

4. *Blew unto lodgynge:* i.e., had a trumpet call blown to summon the contestants to their lodgings.
5. *Take no forse of:* care not for.

sore and I pulle oute the truncheoune that ye shall be in perelle of dethe."

"I charge you," seyde Sir Launcelot, "as ye love me, draw hit oute." And therewithall he descended frome hys horse, and ryght so ded Sir Labayne; and forthwithall he drew the truncheoune oute of hys syde, and gaff a grete shryche and a gresly grone, that the blood braste oute—nyghe a pynte at onys—that at the laste he sanke downe uppon hys arse, and so sowned downe pale and dedly.

¶"Alas," seyde Sir Labayne, "what shall I do?" And than he turned Sir Launcelot into the wynde, and so he lay there nyghe halff an owre as he had bene dede. And so at the laste Sir Launcelot caste up hys yghen, and seyde, "A, Sir Labayne, helpe me that I were on my horse, for here ys faste by, within thys two myle, a jantill ermyte that somtyme was a full noble knyght and a grete lorde of possessyons:

"And for grete goodnes he hath takyn hym to wyllfull poverté and forsakyn myghty londys—and hys name ys Sir Bawdwyn of Bre-tayne, and he ys a full noble surgeon and a good leche. Now lat se and helpe me up that I were there, for ever my harte gyvith me[6] that I shall never dye of my cousyne jermaynes[7] hondys." And than with grete payne Sir Labayne holpe hym uppon hys horse, and than they rode a grete walop togydirs—and ever Sir Launcelot bled, that hit ran downe to the erthe. And so by fortune they cam to an ermytayge [whiche] was undir a woode, and a grete clyff on the othir syde, and a fayre watir rennynge undir hit.

And than Sir Labayne bete on the gate with the but of hys speare, and cryed faste, "Lat[8] in, for Jesus sake!" And anone there cam a fayre chylde to hem and asked them what they wolde.

¶"Fayre sonne," seyde Sir Labayne, "go and pray thy lorde the ermyte for Goddys sake to late in here a knyght that ys full sore wounded—and thys day, telle thy lorde, I saw hym do more dedys of armys than ever I herde sey that ony man ded."

¶So the chylde wente in lyghtly, and than he brought the ermyte whych was a passynge lycly man. fol.421r

¶Whan Sir Labayne saw hym he prayde hym for Goddys sake of succour.

¶"What knyght ys he?" seyde the ermyte. "Ys he of the house of Kynge Arthure, or nat?"

¶"I wote nat," seyde Sir Labayne, "what he ys, nother what ys hys name, but well I wote I saw hym do mervaylously thys day as of dedys of armys." "On whos party was he?" seyde the ermyte.

¶"Sir," seyde Sir Labayne, "he was thys day ayenste Kynge Arthure, and there he wanne the pryce of all the knyghtis of the Rounde Table."

¶"I have seyne the day," seyde the ermyte, "I wolde have loved hym the worse bycause he was ayenste my lorde Kynge Arthure, for

---

6. *Gyvith me:* inclines me to feel.
7. *Cousyne jermaynes:* first cousin's.
8. I.e., Let us.

sometyme I was one of the felyship, but now I thanke God I am othirwyse disposed—

¶"But where ys he? Lat me se hym." Than Sir **Labayne** brought the ermyte to hym.

¶And whan the ermyte behylde hym as he sate leenynge uppon hys sadyll-bowe, ever bledynge spiteuously, and ever the knyght ermyte thought that he sholde know hym; but he coude nat brynge hym to knowlech[9] bycause he was so pale for bledyng. [13]

¶"What knyght ar ye?" seyde the ermyte, "and where were ye borne?"

¶"My fayre lorde," seyde Sir **Launcelot**, "I am a straungere and a knyght aventures that laboureth thorowoute many realmys for to wynne worship." Than the ermyte avysed hym[1] bettir, and saw by a wounde on hys chyeke that he was Sir **Launcelot**. "Alas," seyde the ermyte, "myne owne lorde! Why layne you youre name from me? Perdeus, I ought to know you of ryght, for ye ar the moste nobelyst knyght of the worlde—for well I know you for Sir **Launcelot**." "Sir," seyde he, "syth ye know me, helpe me, and ye may, for Goddys sake, for I wolde be oute of thys payne at onys, othir to deth othir to lyff."

¶"Have ye no doute," seyde the ermyte, "for ye shall lyve and fare ryght well." And so the ermyte called to hym two of hys servauntes, and so they bare hym into the ermytayge, and lyghtly unarmed hym and leyde hym in hys bedde. And than anone the ermyte staunched hys bloode and made hym to drynke good wyne, that he was well refygowred and knew hymselff.

¶(For in thos dayes hit was nat the gyse as ys nowadayes; for there were none ermytis in tho dayes but that they had bene men of worship and of prouesse, and tho ermytes hylde grete houseHoldis and refreysshed people that were in distresse.)[2] fol.421v

Now turne we unto Kynge **Arthure** and leve we Sir **Launcelot** in the ermytayge. So whan the Kyngis were [comen] togydirs on both partyes, and the grete feste sholde be holdyn, Kynge **Arthure** asked the Kynge of North Galis and their felyshyp where was that knyght that bare the rede slyve: "Lat brynge hym before me, that he may have hys lawde and honoure and the pryce, as hit ys ryght." Than spake Sir **Galahalte** the Haute Prynce and the Kynge with the Hondred Knyghtes, and seyde, "We suppose that knyght ys myscheved so that he ys never lyke to se you nother none of us all—and that ys the grettyst pyté that ever we wyste of ony knyght."

¶"Alas," seyde Kynge **Arthure**, "how may thys be? Ys he so sore hurte?—

---

9. *Brynge hym to knowlech:* identify him.
1. *Avysed hym:* looked him in the face.
2. It is difficult to say whether Malory's aside here is meant to be as much a criticism of hermits in his own day as it is an invention of a better class of hermit for the Arthurian past; certainly, since the 14th century at least, there had been a tradition of complaint against false hermits: cf. the prologue to William Langland's *Piers Plowman:* "A heap of hermits with hooked staffs / Went of to Walsingham, with their wenches behind them" (trans. E. T. Donaldson, as printed in the *Norton Anthology of English Literature,* 7th ed. 1:320).

¶"But what ys hys name?" seyde Kynge Arthure. "Truly," seyde
they all, "we know nat hys name, nother frome whens he cam,
nother whother he wolde." "Alas," seyde the Kynge, "thys ys the
warste tydyngis that cam to me thys seven yere, for I wolde nat for
all the londys I welde to knowe and wyte hit were so that that noble   5
knyght were slayne."

¶"Sir, knowe ye ought of hym?" seyde they all. "As for that,"
seyde Kynge Arthure, "whethir I know hym other none, ye shall nat
know for me what man he ys—but Allmyghty Jesu sende me good
tydyngis of hym." And so seyde they all.   10

¶"Be my hede," seyde Sir Gawayne, "gyff hit so be that the good
knyght be so sore hurte, hit ys grete damage and pité to all thys
londe, for he ys one of the nobelyst knyghtes that ever I saw in a
fylde handyll speare or swerde—and iff he may be founde, I shall
fynde hym, for I am sure he ys nat farre frome thys contrey." "Sir,   15
ye beare you well," seyde Kynge Arthure, "and ye [maye] fynde hym,
onles that he be in such a plyte that he may nat welde hymselff."
"Jesu defende,"[3] seyde Sir Gawayne. "But wyte well, I shall know
what he ys and[4] I may fynde hym."

¶Ryght so Sir Gawayne toke a squyre with hym uppon hakeneyes   fol.422r   20
and rode all aboute Camelot within six or seven myle, but so he
com agayne and cowde here no worde of hym. Than within two
dayes Kynge Arthure and all the felyshyp returned unto London
agayne; and so as they rode by the way, hyt happened Sir Gawayne
at Ascolot to lodge with Sir Barnarde, there as was Sir Launcelot   25
lodged. And so as Sir Gawayne was in hys chamber to repose hym,
Sir Barnarde, the olde barowne, cam in to hym, and hys doughtir
Elayne, to chere hym and to aske hym what tydyngis, and who ded
beste at the turnemente of Wynchester.

¶"So God me helpe," seyde Sir Gawayne, "there were two knygh-   30
tes that bare two whyght shyldys, but one of them bare a rede sleve
uppon hys hede, and sertaynly he was the beste knyght that ever I
saw juste in fylde. For I dare sey," seyde Sir Gawayne, "that one
knyght with the rede slyve smote downe fourty knyghtes of the
Rounde Table—and his felow ded ryght well and worshipfully."   35
"Now blyssed be God," seyde thys Fayre Maydyn of Ascolate, that
that knyght sped so welle! For he ys the man in the worlde that I
firste love—and truly he shall be the laste that ever I shall love."

¶"Now, fayre maydyn," seyde Sir Gawayne, "ys that good knyght
youre love?" "Sertaynly, sir," she seyde, "he ys my love." "Than   40
know ye hys name?" seyde Sir Gawayne. "Nay, truly, sir," seyde the
damesell, "I know nat hys name nothir frome whens he com; but
to sey that I love hym, I promyse God and you I love hym." "How
had ye knowlecch of hym firste?" seyde Sir Gawayne. Than she tolde   [14]
hym, as ye have harde before, and how hir fadir betoke hym her   45
brother to do hym servyse, and how hir fadir lente hym her brothirs, Sir Tyrryes, shylde; "and here with me he leffte hys owne
shylde."

3. I.e., forbid.
4. I.e., if.

❡"For what cause ded he so?" seyde Sir Gawayne. "For thys cause," seyde the damesell, "for hys shylde was full well knowyn amonge many noble knyghtes." "A, fayre damesell," seyde Sir Gawayne, "please hit you to lette me have a syght of that shylde?"

❡"Sir," she seyde, "hit ys in my chambir, coverde wyth a case, and if ye woll com with me ye shall se hit." _{fol.422v} 5

❡"Nat so," seyde Sir Barnarde to hys doughter, "but sende ye for that shylde." So whan the shylde was com, Sir Gawayne toke of the case; and whan he behylde that shylde he knew hyt anone that hit was Sir Launcelottis shylde and hys owne armys. 10

❡"A, Jesu mercy!" seyde Sir Gawayne, "now ys my herte more hevyar than ever hit was tofore."

❡"Why?" seyde thys mayde Elayne. "For I have a grete cause," seyde Sir Gawayne. "Ys that knyght that owyth thys shylde youre love?" 15

❡"Yee truly," she sayde, "my love ys he—

❡"God wolde that I were hys love!"

❡"So God me spede," seyde Sir Gawayne, "fayre damesell, ye have ryght, for and he be youre love, ye love the moste honorabelyst knyght of the worlde, and the man of moste worship." "So 20 methought ever," seyde the damesell, "for never ar that tyme no knyght that ever I saw loved I never none arste." "God graunte," seyde Sir Gawayne, "that aythir of you may rejoyse[5] othir, but that ys in a grete aventure[6]—

❡"But truly," seyde Sir Gawayne unto the damesell, "ye may sey 25 ye have a fayre grace, for why I have knowyn that noble knyght thys foure and twenty yere, and never or that day I (nor none othir knyght, I dare make good),[7] saw never nother herde say that ever he bare tokyn or sygne of no lady, jantillwoman, nor maydyn, at no justis nother turnemente. And therefore, fayre maydyn, ye ar 30 much beholdyn to hym to gyff hym thanke. But I drede me," seyde Sir Gawayne, "that ye shall never se hym in thys worlde, and that ys as grete pité as ever was of ony erthely man."

"Alas!" seyde she, "how may thys be? Ys he slayne?" "I say nat so," seyde Sir Gawayne, "but wete you well he ys grevously wounded, 35 by all maner of sygnys,[8] and by [mens] syght[9] more lycklyer to be dede than to be on lyve. And wyte you well, he ys the noble knyght Sir Launcelot—for by thys shylde I know hym."

❡"Alas!" seyde thys Fayre Maydyn of Ascolat, "how may thys be? And what was hys hurte?" 40

❡"Truly," seyde Sir Gawayne, "the man in the worlde that loved _{fol.423r} beste hym hurte hym—and I dare sey," seyde Sir Gawayne, "and that knyght that hurte hym knew the verry sertaynté that he had hurte Sir Launcelot, hit were the moste sorow that ever cam to hys herte." "Now, fayre fadir," seyde than Elayne, "I requyre you gyff 45 me leve to ryde and seke hym; othir ellis I wote well I shall go oute

---

5. I.e., enjoy.
6. I.e., state of jeopardy.
7. *Make good*: i.e. prove it.
8. *By all maner of sygnys*: judging by all the signs.
9. I.e., estimation, reckoning.

of my mynde, for I shall never stynte tyll that I fynde hym, and my brothir Sir Lavayne."

¶"Do ye as hit lykith you," seyde hir fadir, "for sore me repentis of the hurte of that noble knyght."

¶Ryght so the mayde made hyr redy and departed before Sir Gawayne, makynge grete dole. Than on the morne Sir Gawayne com to Kynge Arthure and tolde hym all how he had founde Sir Launce-lottis shylde in the kepynge of the Fayre Mayden of Ascolat. "All that knew I aforehande," seyde Kynge Arthure, "and that caused me I wolde nat suffir you to have ado at the grete justis; for I aspyed hym whan he cam untyll hys lodgyng, full late in the evenyng, into Ascolat. But grete mervayle have I," seyde Kynge Arthure, "that ever he wolde beare ony sygne of ony damesell, for ar now I never herde sey nor knew that ever he bare ony tokyn of none erthely woman." "Be my hede, sir," seyde Sir Gawayne, "the Fayre Maydyn of Ascolat lovith hym mervaylously well—what hit meanyth I cannat sey— and she ys ryddyn aftir to seke hym."

¶So the Kynge and all com to London, and there Gawayne all opynly disclosed hit to all the courte that hit was Sir Launcelot that justed beste. And whan Sir Bors harde that, wyte you well he was an hevy man, and so were all hys kynnysmen. But whan the Quy-ene wyst that hit was Sir Launcelot that bare the rede slyve of the Fayre Maydyn of Ascolat, she was nygh ought of her mynde for wratthe; and than she sente for Sir Bors de Ganys in all haste that myght be. So whan Sir Bors was com before the Quyene, she seyde, "A, Sir Bors, have ye nat herde sey how falsely Sir Launcelot hath betrayed me?" "Alas, madame," seyde Sir Bors, "I am aferde he hath betrayed hymselff and us all." "No forse,"[1] seyde the Quene, "though he be distroyed, for he ys a false traytoure knyght."

¶"Madame," seyde Sir Bors, "I pray you sey ye no more so, for wyte you well I may nat here no such langayge of hym."

¶"Why so, Sir Bors?" seyde she. "Shold I nat calle hym traytoure whan he bare the rede slyve uppon hys hede at Wynchester at the grete justis?" "Madame," seyde Sir Bors, "that slyeve-berynge repentes[2] me, but I dare say he dud beare hit to none evyll entent; but for thys cause he bare the rede slyve, that none of hys blood shold know hym. For or than[3] we, nother none of us all, never knew that ever he bare tokyn or sygne of maydyn, lady, nothir jantillwoman."

¶"Fy on hym!" seyde the Quene. "Yet for all hys pryde and bob-baunce, there ye proved youreselff better man than he." "Nay, madam, sey ye nevermore so, for he bete me and my felowys, and myght have slayne us and he had wolde."

¶"Fy on hym!" seyde the Quene. "For I harde Sir Gawayne say before my lorde Arthure that hit were mervayle to telle the grete love that ys betwene the Fayre Maydyn of Ascolat and hym."

[15]

fol.423v

---

1. *No forse*: it does not matter.
2. I.e., regret.
3. *Or than*: before then.

¶"Madam," seyde Sir Bors, "I may nat warne[4] Sir Gawayne to sey what hit pleasith hym, but I dare sey, as for my lorde Sir Launcelot, that he lovith no lady, jantillwoman, nother mayden, but as he lovith all inlyke muche. And therefore, madam," seyde Sir Bors, "ye may sey what ye wyll, but wyte you well I woll hast me to syke hym and fynde hym wheresumever he be—and God sende me good tydyngis of hym."

¶And so leve we them there, and speke we of Sir Launcelot that lay in grete perell.

¶And so as thys fayre madyn Elayne cam to Wynchester, she sought there all aboute; and by fortune Sir Lavayne hir brothir was ryddyn to sporte hym to enchaff hys horse. And anone as thys maydyn Elayne saw hym she knew hym, and than she cryed on lowde tylle hym; and whan he herde her he com to her, and anone with that she asked hir brother, "How dothe my lorde Sir Launcelot?" "Who tolde you, syster, that my lordys name was Sir Launcelot?"

Than she tolde hym how Sir Gawayne by hys shylde knew hym. So they rode togydirs tyll that they cam to the ermytayge, and anone she alyght. So Sir Lavayne brought her in to Sir Launcelot; and whan she saw hym ly so syke and pale in hys bed, she myght nat speke, but suddeynly she felle downe to the erthe in a sowghe. And there she lay a grete whyle; and when she was releved,[5] she shryked and seyde, "My lord, Sir Launcelot! Alas, whyghe lye ye in thys plyte?"And than she sowned agayne; and than Sir Launcelot prayde Sir Lavayne to take hir up, "and brynge hir hydir to me."

¶And whan she cam to herselff, Sir Launcelot kyste her and seyde, "Fayre maydyn, why fare ye thus? For ye put me to more payne; wherefore make ye no such chere, for and ye be com to comforte me, ye be ryght wellcom—and of thys lytyll hurte that I have, I shall be ryght hastely hole, by the grace of God—

¶"But I mervayle," seyde Sir Launcelot, "who tolde you my name." And so thys maydyn tolde hym all how Sir Gawayne was lodged with hir fader, "and there by youre shylde he dyscoverde[6] youre name."

¶"Alas," seyde Sir Launcelot, "that repentith me that my name ys knowyn, for I am sure hit woll turne untyll angir."

¶And than Sir Launcelot compaste in hys mynde that Sir Gawayne wolde telle Quene Gwenyvere how he bare the rede slyve, and for whom; that he wyst well wolde turne unto grete angur. So thys maydyn Elayne never wente frome Sir Launcelot, but wacched hym day and nyght, and dud such attendaunce to hym that the Freynshe booke seyth there was never woman dyd never more kyndlyer for man.

¶Than Sir Launcelot prayde Sir Lavayne to make aspyes[7] in Wynchester for Sir Bors if he cam there, and tolde hym by what tokyns he sholde know hym: by a wounde in hys forehede. "For I

---

4. I.e., forbid.
5. I.e., revived.
6. I.e., revealed.
7. *Make aspyes*: have watch kept.

am sure," seyde Sir Launcelot, "that Sir Bors woll seke me, for he
ys the same good knyght that hurte me."

¶Now turne we unto Sir Bors de Ganys, that cam untyll Wynchestir to seke aftir hys cosyne Sir Launcelot. And whan he cam to
Wynchester, Sir Lavayne leyde wacche for Sir Bors; and anone he
had warnyng of hym, and so he founde hym, and anone he salewed
hym and tolde hym frome whens he com.

¶"Now, fayre knyght," seyde Sir Bors, "ye be wellcom, and I
requyre you that ye woll brynge me to my lorde Sir Launcelot."

¶"Sir," seyde Sir Lavayne, "take youre horse, and within thys
owre ye shall se hym." So they departed and com to the ermytayge.

¶And whan Sir Bors saw Sir Launcelot lye in hys bedde, dede pale
and discoloured, anone Sir Bors loste hys countenaunce,[8] and for
kyndenes and pité he myght nat speke but wepte tendirly a grete
whyle. But whan he myght speke he seyde thus: "A, my lorde Sir
Launcelot, God you blysse and sende you hasty recoveryng! For full
hevy am I of my mysfortune and of myne unhappynesse[9]—for now
I may calle myselff unhappy; and I drede me that God ys gretely
displeasyd with me, that He wolde suffir me to have such a shame
for to hurte you that ar all[1] oure ledar and all oure worship: and
therefore I calle myselff unhappy. Alas, that ever such a caytyff
knyght as I am sholde have power by unhappines to hurte the
moste noblyst knyght of the worlde! Where I so shamefully sette
uppon you and overcharged you, and where ye myght have slayne
me, ye saved me; and so ded nat I, for I and all oure bloode ded
to you their utteraunce. I mervayle," seyde Sir Bors, "that my herte
or my bloode wolde serve me—

¶"Wherefore, my lorde Sir Launcelot, I aske you mercy.

¶"Fayre cousyn," seyde Sir Launcelot, "ye be ryght wellcom; and
wyte you well, overmuche ye sey for the plesure of me—

¶"Whych pleasith me nothynge, for why I have the same i-
sought;[2] for I wolde with pryde have overcom you all—and there
in my pryde I was nere slayne, and that was in myne owne
defaughte; for I myght have gyffyn you warnynge of my beynge
there, and than had I had no hurte. For hit ys an olde-seyde sawe,
'there ys harde batayle there as kynne and frendys doth batayle
ayther ayenst other; for there may be no mercy, but mortall warre.'
Therefore, fayre coosyn," seyde Sir Launcelot, "lat thys langage overpasse, and all shall be wellcom that God sendith. And latte us leve
of thys mater and speke of som rejoysynge, for thys that ys done
may nat be undone; and lat us fynde a remedy how sone that I may
be hole."

¶Than Sir Bors lenyd uppon hys beddys syde and tolde Sir Launcelot how the Quene was passynge wrothe with hym, "because ye
ware the rede slyve at the grete justes." And there Sir Bors tolde
hym all how Sir Gawayne discoverde hit—"by youre shylde"—that

[16]

5

10

15

20

25

30

fol.425r

35

40

45

---

8. I.e., composure.
9. I.e., ill fortune.
1. I.e., of us all.
2. *For why I have the same i-sought:* because I have sought the same thing (as you).

he leffte with the Fayre Madyn of Ascolat. "Than ys the Quene wrothe?" seyde Sir Launcelot. "Therefore am I ryght hevy—but I deserved no wrath, for all that I ded was bycause I wolde nat be knowyn."

⁋"Sir, ryght so excused I you," seyde Sir Bors, "but all was in vayne, for she seyde more largelyer to me than I to you sey now. But sir, ys thys she," seyde Sir Bors, "that ys so busy aboute you, that men calle the Fayre Maydyn of Ascolat?" "Forsothe, she hit ys," seyde Sir Launcelot, "that by no meanys I can nat put her fro me." "Why sholde ye put her frome you?" seyde Sir Bors, "for she ys a passyng fayre damesell, and well besayne and well taught— and God wolde, fayre cousyn," seyde Sir Bors, "that ye cowde love her; but as to that I may nat nother dare nat counceyle you. But I se well," seyde Sir Bors, "by her dyligence aboute you that she lovith you intyerly."

⁋"That me repentis," seyde Sir Launcelot. "Well," seyde Sir Bors, "she ys nat the firste that hath loste hir payne uppon you, and that ys the more³ pyté." And so they talked of many mo thynges. And so within three or foure dayes Sir Launcelot wexed bygge and lyght. Than Sir Bors tolde Sir Launcelot how there was sworne⁴ a grete turnement betwyxt Kyng Arthure and the Kynge of North Galis, that sholde be uppon All Halowmasse Day,⁵ besydes Wynchestir.

⁋"Is that trouth?" seyde Sir Launcelot. "Than shall ye abyde with me stylle a lityll whyle untyll that I be hole, for I fele myself resonabely bygge and stronge."

⁋"Blessed be God," seyde Sir Bors. Than they were there nyghe a moneth togydirs, and ever thys maydyn Elayne ded ever hir dyligence and labour both nyght and day unto Sir Launcelot, that there was never chylde nother wyff more mekar tyll fadir and husbande than was thys Fayre Maydyn of Ascolat—

⁋Wherefore Sir Bors was gretly pleased with her.

⁋So uppon a day, by the assente of Sir Lavayne, Sir Bors, and Sir Launcelot, they made the ermyte to seke in woodys for diverse erbys, and so Sir Launcelot made fayre Elayne to gadir erbys for hym to make hym a bayne. So in the meanewhyle Sir Launcelot made Sir Lavayne to arme hym at all pecis,⁶ and there he thought to assay hymselff uppon horsebacke with a speare, whether he myght welde hys armour and hys speare for hys hurte or nat. And so whan he was uppon hys horse he steyrred hym freyshly, and the horse was passyng lusty and frycke because he was nat laboured of⁷ a moneth before.

⁋And than Sir Launcelot bade Sir Lavayne gyff hym that grete speare, and so Sir Launcelot cowchyd that speare in the reeste. The courser lepte myghtyly whan he felte the spurres, and he that was uppon hym, [whiche] was the nobelyst horseman of the worlde,

[17]
fol.425v   20

3. I.e., greater.
4. I.e., agreed on oath.
5. *All Halowmasse Day:* All Saints' Day (November 1).
6. *At all pecis:* fully.
7. *Was nat laboured of:* had not been worked for.

strayned hym[8] myghtyly and stabely, and kepte stylle the speare in the reeste. And therewith Sir Launcelot strayned hymselff so straytly, with so grete fors to gete the courser forewarde, that the bottom of hys wounde braste both within and withoute, and therewithall the bloode cam oute so fyersely that he felte hymselff so feble that he myght nat sitte uppon hys horse. And than Sir Launcelot cryed unto Sir Bors, "A, Sir Bors and Sir Lavayne, helpe, for I am com unto myne ende."

¶And therewith he felle downe on the one syde to the erth lyke a dede coorse. And than Sir Bors and Sir Lavayne cam unto hym with sorow-makynge oute of mesure. And so by fortune thys mayden, Elayne, harde their mournynge; and than she cam, and whan she founde Sir Launcelot there armed in that place she cryed and wepte as she had bene wood.

¶And than she kyssed hym and ded what she myght to awake hym; and than she rebuked her brothir and Sir Bors, and called hem false traytours, and seyde, "Why wolde ye take hym oute of hys bed?—for and he dye, I woll appele you of hys deth!" And so with that cam the ermyte, Sir Bawdewyn of Bretayne, and whan he founde Sir Launcelot in that plyte he seyde but lityll—but wyte you well he was wroth—but he seyde, "Lette us have hym in," and anone they bare hym into the ermytage and unarmed hym, and leyde hym in hys bedde; and evermore hys wounde bled spiteuously, but he stirred no lymme off hym.

Than the knyght armyte put a thynge[9] in hys nose and a litill dele of watir in hys mowthe, and than Sir Launcelot waked of hys swowghe. And than the ermyte staunched hys bledyng, and whan Sir Launcelot myght speke, he asked why he put his lyff so in jouperté. "Sir," seyde Sir Launcelot, "because I wente I had be stronge inowghe, and also Sir Bors tolde me that there sholde be at Halowmasse a grete justis betwyxte Kynge Arthure and the Kynge of Northe Galys; and therefore I thought to assay myselff, whether I myght be there or not."

"A, Sir Launcelot," seyde the ermyte, "youre harte and youre currayge woll never be done untyll youre laste day. But ye shall do now be my counceyle: lat Sir Bors departe frome you, and lat hym do at that turnemente what he may—and, by the grace of God," seyde the knyght ermyte, "be[1] that the turnemente be done and he comyn hydir agayne, sir, ye shall be hole, so[2] that ye woll be governed by me."

Than Sir Bors made hym redy to departe frome hym; and Sir Launcelot seyde, "Fayre cousyn, Sir Bors, recommaunde me unto all tho ye owght recommaunde me unto, and I pray you enforce youreselff at that justis that ye may be beste, for my love—and here shall I abyde you, at the mercy of God, tyll youre agaynecommynge." And so Sir Bors departed and cam to the courte of

fol.426r

[18]
fol.426v

---

8. Exerted himself.
9. *A thynge:* i.e., something.
1. I.e., by the time.
2. I.e., provided.

Kynge Arthure, and tolde hem in what place he leffte Sir Launcelot.
"That me repentis!" seyde the Kynge. "But syn he shall have hys
lyff, we all may thanke God." And than Sir Bors tolde the Quene
what jouperté Sir Launcelot was in whan he wolde asayde[3] hys
horse—"And all that he ded was for the love of you, because he   5
wolde a bene at thys turnemente."

¶"Fy on hym, recreayde knyght!" seyde the Quene, "for wyte
you well I am ryght sory and he shall have hys lyff."

¶"Madam, hys lyff shall he have," seyde Sir Bors, "and who that
wolde otherwyse—excepte you, madame—we that ben of hys   10
blood wolde helpe to shortyn their lyves. But, madame," seyde Sir
Bors, "ye have ben oftyntymes displeased with my lorde Sir Launcelot, but at all tymys at the ende ye founde hym a trew knyght."
And so he departed.

And than every knyght of the Rounde Table that were there that   15
tyme presente made them redy to that justes at All Halowmasse;
and thidir drew many knyghtes of diverse contreyes. And as Halowmasse drew nere, thydir cam the Kynge of North Galis and the
Kynge with the Hondred Knyghtes, and Sir Galahalt the Haute
Prynce of Surluse; and thider cam Kynge Angwysh of Irelonde, and   20
the Kynge of Northumbirlonde, and the Kynge of Scottis: so thes
three Kynges com to Kynge Arthurs party.

And so that day Sir Gawayne ded grete dedys of armys and began
first, and the herowdis nombirde that Sir Gawayne smote downe
twenty knyghtes. Than Sir Bors de Ganys cam in the same tyme,   25
and he was numbirde he smote downe twenty knyghtes; and
therefore the pryse was gyvyn betwyxt them bothe, for they began
firste and lengist endured.

Also Sir Gareth, as the boke seyth, ded that day grete dedis of   fol.427r
armys, for he smote downe and pulled downe thirty knyghtes; but   30
whan he had done that dedis he taryed nat, but so departed, and
therefore he loste hys pryse. And Sir Palampydes ded grete dedis of
armys that day, for he smote downe twenty knyghtes—but he
departed suddeynly; and men demed that he and Sir Gareth rode
togydirs to som maner adventures.   35

¶So whan thys turnement was done, Sir Bors departed, and rode
tylle he cam to Sir Launcelot, hys cousyne. And than he founde hym
walkyng on hys feete—and there aythir made grete joy of other—
and so he tolde Sir Launcelot of all the justys, lyke as ye have herde.
"I mervayle," seyde Sir Launcelot, "that Sir Gareth, whan he had done   40
such dedis of armys, that he wolde nat tarry."

¶"Sir, thereof we mervayled all," seyde Sir Bors, "for but if hit
were you, other the noble knyght Sir Trystram, other the good
knyght Sir Lamorake de Galis, I saw never knyght bere so many
knyghtes and smyte downe in so litill a whyle as ded Sir Gareth—   45
and anone as he was gone we all wyst nat where he becom."

"Be my hede," seyde Sir Launcelot, "he ys a noble knyght and a
myghty man and well-brethed; and yf he were well assayed," seyd

3. I.e., have tested.

Sir Launcelot, "I wolde deme he were good inow for ony knyght that beryth the lyff—and he ys jantill, curteyse and ryght bownteuous, meke and mylde, and in hym ys no maner of male engynne, but playne,[4] faythfull an trew." So than they made hem redy to departe frome the ermytayge.

And so uppon a morne they toke their horsis, and this **Elayne le Blanke** with hem. And whan they cam to **Ascolat**, there were they well lodged and had grete chere of Sir **Barnarde** the olde baron, and of Sir **Tirré**, hys sonne. And so uppon the morne, whan Sir **Launcelot** sholde departe, fayre **Elayne** brought hir fadir with her, and Sir **Lavayne**, and Sir **Tyrré**, and than thus she sayde: "My lorde, Sir **Launcelot**, now I se ye woll departe frome me. Now, fayre knyght, and curtayse knyght," seyde she, "have mercy uppon me, and suffir me nat to dye for youre love."

¶"Why, what wolde you that I dud?" seyde Sir **Launcelot**. "Sir, I wolde have you to my husbande," seyde **Elayne**. "Fayre damesell, I thanke you hartely," seyde Sir **Launcelot**, "but truly," seyde he, "I caste me never to be wedded man."

¶"Than, fayre knyght," seyde she, "woll ye be my paramour?" "Jesu deffende me," seyde Sir **Launcelot**, "for than I rewarded youre fadir and youre brothir full evyll for their grete goodnesse."

¶"Alas than!" seyde she, "I muste dye for youre love."

¶"Ye shall nat do so," seyde Sir **Launcelot**, "for wyte you well, fayre mayden, I myght have bene maryed and I had wolde, but I never applyed me yett to be maryed; but bycause, fayre damesell, that ye love me as ye sey ye do, I woll for youre good wylle and kyndnes shew to you som goodnesse: that ys thys, that wheresomever ye woll besette youre herte uppon som good knyght that woll wedde you, I shall gyff you togydirs a thousand pounde yerly, to you and to youre ayris. This muche woll I gyff you, fayre mayden, for youre kyndnesse; and allweyes whyle I lyve to be youre owne knyght."

¶"Sir, of all thys," seyde the maydyn, "I woll none, for but yff ye woll wedde me, other to be my paramour at the leste, wyte you well, Sir **Launcelot**, my good dayes ar done." "Fayre damesell," seyde Sir **Launcelot**, "of thes two thynges ye muste pardon me." Than she shryked shirly and felle downe in a sowghe; and than women bare hir into her chambir, and there she made overmuche sorowe. And than Sir **Launcelot** wolde departe, and there he asked Sir **Lavayne** what he wolde do.

¶"Sir, what sholde I do," seyde Sir **Lavayne**, "but folow you, but if ye dryve me frome you or commaunde me to go frome you?" Than cam Sir **Barnarde** to Sir **Launcelot**, and seyde to hym, "I cannat se but that my doughtir woll dye for youre sake." "Sir, I may nat do withall." seyde Sir **Launcelot**. "For that me sore repentith, for I reporte me to youreselff that my profir ys fayre. And me repentith," seyde Sir **Launcelot**, "that she lovith me as she dothe, for I was never

4. *Male engynne*: evil contrivance. *Playne*: i.e., honest.

the causer of hit; for I reporte me unto[5] youre sonne, I never erly
nother late profirde her bownté nother fayre behestes—

"And as for me," seyde Sir Launcelot, "I dare do that a knyght
sholde do, and sey that she ys a clene mayden for me, bothe for
dede and wylle.[6] For I am ryght hevy of hir distresse, for she ys a
full fayre maydyn, goode and jentill, and well i-taught." "Fadir,"
seyde Sir Lavayne, "I dare make good she ys a clene maydyn as for
my lorde Sir Launcelot—but she doth as I do; for sythen I saw first
my lorde Sir Launcelot, I cowde never departe frome hym, nother
nought I woll and[7] I may folow hym."

¶Than Sir Launcelot toke hys leve, and so they departed and cam
to Wynchestir. And whan Kynge Arthur wyst that Sir Launcelot was
com hole and sownde, the Kynge made grete joy of hym; and so
ded Sir Gawayne and all the knyghtes of the Rounde Table—excepte
Sir Aggravayne and Sir Mordred; also Quene Gwenyver was woode
wrothe with Sir Launcelot, and wolde by no meanys speke with hym,
but enstraunged herselff frome hym.

¶And Sir Launcelot made all the meanys that he myght for to
speke with the Quene, but hit wolde nat be.

¶Now speke we of the Fayre Maydyn of Ascolat that made such
sorow day and nyght that she never slepte, ete, nother dranke, and
ever she made hir complaynte unto Sir Launcelot. So whan she had
thus endured a ten dayes, that she fyebled so that she muste nedis
passe oute of thys worlde, than she shrove her clene and resseyved
hir Creature[8]—and ever she complayned stylle upon Sir Launcelot.
Than hir gostly fadir[9] bade hir leve such thoughtes.

Than she seyde, "Why sholde I leve such thoughtes? Am I nat
an erthely woman? And all the whyle the brethe ys in my body I
may complayne me, for my belyve ys that I do none offence, though
I love an erthely man, unto God; for He fourmed me thereto—and
all maner of good love comyth of God, and othir than good love
loved I never Sir Launcelot du Lake. And I take God to recorde, I
loved never none but hym, nor never shall, of erthely creature; and
a clene maydyn I am for hym and for all othir. And sitthyn hit ys
the sufferaunce of God that I shall dye for so noble a knyght, I
beseche the Hyghe Fadir of Hevyn, have mercy uppon me and my
soule, and uppon myne unnumerable paynys that I suffir may be
alygeaunce of parte of my synnes. For, Swete Lorde Jesu," seyde
the fayre maydyn, "I take God to recorde I was never to The grete
offenser, nother ayenste Thy lawis, but that I loved thys noble
knyght Sir Launcelot oute of mesure. And of myselff, Good Lorde,
I had no myght to withstonde the fervent love, wherefore I have
my deth." And than she called hir fadir, Sir Bernarde, and hir brothir, Sir Tirry, and hartely she prayd hir fadir that hir brothir myght
wryght a lettir lyke as she ded endite.

fol.428r

fol.428v

---

5. *Reporte me unto:* i.e., ask confirmation of.
6. *For me, bothe for dede and wylle:* with respect to me, both in deed and in (my) intention.
7. *Nother nought I woll and:* I wish nothing more if.
8. *Shrove her clene and resseyved hir Creature:* i.e., took confession and communion.
9. *Gostly fadir:* spiritual father, confessor.

And so hir fadir graunted her. And whan the lettir was wryten, worde by worde lyke as she devised hit, than she prayde hir fadir that she myght be wacched untylle she were dede—"and whyle my body ys hote, lat thys lettir be put in my ryght honde, and my honde bounde faste to the letter untyll that I be colde; and lette me be put in a fayre bed with all the rychyste clothys that I have aboute me, and so lat my bed and all my rychyst clothis be ledde with me in a charyat unto the nexte place where the Temmys ys; and there lette me be put within a barget, and but one man with me, such as ye truste, to stirre me thidir; and that my barget be coverde with blacke samyte over and over. And thus, fadir, I beseche you, lat hit be done."

So hir fadir graunte her faythfully all thynge sholde be done lyke as she had devised. Than hir fadir and hir brothir made grete dole for her. And whan thys was done, anone she dyed. And whan she was dede, the corse and the bedde all was lad the nexte way unto the Temmys; and there a man and the corse, and all thynge as she had devised, was put in the Temmys. And so the man stirred the bargett unto Westmynster; and there hit rubbed and rolled too and fro a grete whyle or ony man aspyed hit.[1]

So by fortune Kynge **Arthure** and Quene **Gwenyver** were talkynge togydirs at a wyndow, and so as they loked into the Temmys they aspyed that blacke barget, and had mervayle what hit mente. Than the Kynge called Sir **Kay** and shewed hit hym. "Sir," seyde Sir **Kay**, "wete you well, there ys som new tydynges." "Therefore go ye thidir," seyde the Kynge to Sir **Kay**, "and take with you Sir **Braundiles** and Sir **Aggravayne**, and brynge me redy worde what ys there."

¶Than thes three knyghtes departed and cam to the barget and wente in; and there they founde the fayryst corse lyyng in a ryche bed that ever he saw, and a poore man syttynge in the bargettis ende, and no worde wolde [he] speke. So thes three knyghtes returned unto the Kynge agayne and tolde hym what they founde.

"That fayre corse woll I se," seyde the Kynge. And so the Kynge toke the Quene by the honde and wente thydir. Than the Kynge made the barget to be holde faste, and than the Kynge and the Quene wente in with sertayne knyghtes with them; and there he saw the fayryst woman ly in a ryche bed, coverde unto her myddyll with many rych clothys, and all was of cloth of golde—and she lay as she had smyled. Than the Quene aspyed the lettir in hir ryght hande and tolde the Kynge; than the Kynge toke hit and seyde, "Now am I sure thys lettir woll telle us what she was, and why she ys com hyddir."

So than the Kynge and the Quene wente oute of the bargette, and so commaunded a sertayne[2] to wayte uppon the barget. And

[20]   fol.429r

---

1. Ships and boats often figure in medieval literature as symbols of the salvific protection afforded by the Church (cf. the derivation of *nave*—the central part of a church—from latin *navis*, "ship"); they also figure (often concurrently) as symbols of abandonment to (or trust in) the viscissitudes of fate and fortune, this latter symbolism ultimately related to Celtic myths of heroes set adrift in rudderless boats. For other examples in Malory, see pp. 39, 250, 528, and 572.
2. I.e., certain number of men.

so whan the Kynge was com to hys chambir, he called many knyghtes aboute hym and seyde that he wolde wete opynly what was
wryten within that lettir. Than the Kynge brake hit[3] and made a
clerke to rede hit, and thys was the entente of the lettir:

¶Moste noble knyght, my lorde Sir Launcelot, now hath
dethe made us two at debate for youre love. And I was youre
lover, that men called the Fayre Maydyn of Ascolate—therefore unto all ladyes I make my mone—yet for my soule ye[4]
pray and bury me at the leste, and offir ye my masse-peny: thys
ys my laste requeste. And a clene maydyn I dyed, I take God
to wytnesse. And pray for my soule, Sir Launcelot, as thou arte
pereles.

¶Thys was all the substaunce in the lettir. And whan hit was
rad, the Kynge, the Quene, and all the knyghtes wepte for pité of
the dolefull complayntes. Than was Sir Launcelot sente for, and
whan he was com Kynge Arthure made the lettir to be rad to hym.
And whan Sir Launcelot harde hit worde by worde, he seyde, "My
lorde Arthur, wyte you well I am ryght hevy of the deth of thys fayre
lady; and God knowyth I was never causar of her deth be my wyllynge, and that woll I reporte me unto her owne brothir that here
ys, Sir Lavayne. I woll nat say nay," seyde Sir Launcelot, "but that
she was both fayre and good, and much I was beholdyn unto her,
but she loved me oute of mesure."

¶"Sir," seyde the Quene, "ye myght have shewed hir som bownté
and jantilnes whych myght have preserved hir lyff."

¶"Madame," seyde Sir Launcelot, "she wolde none other wayes
be answerde but that she wolde be my wyff othir ellis my paramour,
and of thes two I wolde not graunte her; but I proffird her, for her
good love that she shewed me, a thousand pounde yerely to her
and to her ayres, and to wedde ony maner of knyght that she coude
fynde beste to love in her harte. For, madame," seyde Sir Launcelot,
"I love nat to be constrayned to love, for love muste only aryse of
the harte[5] selff, and nat by none constraynte."

¶"That ys trouth, sir," seyde the Kynge, "and with many knyghtes love ys fre in hymselffe, and never woll be bonde; for where he
ys bonden he lowsith hymselff." Than seyde the Kynge unto Sir
Launcelot, "Sir, hit woll be youre worshyp that ye oversé that she be
entered[6] worshypfully."

¶"Sir," seyde Sir Launcelot, "that shall be done as I can beste
devise." And so many knyghtes yode thyder to beholde that fayre
dede mayden. And so uppon the morn she was entered rychely;
and Sir Launcelot offird her masse-peny—and all tho knyghtes of
the Table Rounde that were there at that tyme offerde with Sir
Launcelot. And than the poure man wente agayne wyth the barget.

¶Than the Quene sent for Sir Launcelot and prayde hym of mercy

fol.429v

fol.430r

3. *Brake hit:* I.e. broke its seal.
4. I.e., (I ask that) you (Launcelot).
5. I.e., heart's.
6. I.e., interred.

for why that she had ben wrothe with hym causeles. "Thys ys nat
the firste tyme," seyde Sir Launcelot, "that ye have ben displese with
me causeles, but, madame, ever I muste suffir you—but what
sorow that I endure, ye take no forse." So thys passed on all that
wynter, with all maner of huntynge and hawkynge; and justis and   5
turneyes were many betwyxte many grete lordis. And ever in all
placis Sir Lavayn gate grete worshyp, that he was nobely defamed[7]
amonge many knyghtis of the Table Rounde.

    ¶Thus hit past on tylle Crystemasse, and than every day there   [21]
was justis made for a dyamonde: who that justed best shulde have   10
a dyamounde. But Sir Launcelot wolde nat juste but if hit were a
grete justes cryed;[8] but Sir Lavayne justed there all the Crystemasse
passyngly well, and was beste praysed, for there were but feaw that
ded so well; wherefore all maner of knyghtes demed that Sir Lavayn
sholde be made knyght of the Table Rounde at the next feste of   15
Pentecoste.

    ¶So at afftir Crystemas Kynge Arthure lete calle unto hym many
knyghtes, and there they avysed togydirs to make a party and a
grete turnemente and justis. And the Kynge of North Galys seyde
to Kynge Arthure he wolde have on hys party Kyng Angwysh of Ire-   20
londe and the Kynge wyth the Hondred Knyghtes and the Kynge
of Northhumbirlonde and Sir Galahalt the Haute Prynce. So thes
foure Kynges and this myghty deuke toke party ayenste Kynge
Arthure and the knyghtes of the Rounde Table. And the cry was
made that the day off justys shulde be besydes Westemynster,   25
uppon Candylmasse[9] day, whereof many knyghtes were glad and
made them redy to be at that justys in the freysshyste maner.

    Than Quene Gwenyver sent for Sir Launcelot, and seyd thus: "I   fol.430v
warne you that ye ryde no more in no justis, nor turnementis but
that youre kynnesmen may know you, and at thys justis that shall   30
be ye shall have of me a slyeve of golde. And I pray you for my
sake to force[1] yourselff there, that men may speke you worshyp.
But I charge you, as ye woll have my love, that ye warne your
kynnesmen that ye woll beare that day the slyve of golde upon
your helmet."   35

    ¶"Madame," seyde Sir Launcelot, "hit shall be done." And eythir
made grete joy of othir. And whan Sir Launcelot saw hys tyme, he
tolde Sir Bors that he wolde departe, and no mo wyth hym but Sir
Lavayne, unto the good ermyte that dwelled in the foreyst of Wyndesore, whos name was Sir Brascias. And there he thought to   40
repose hym and to take all the reste that he myght, because he
wolde be freysh at that day of justis. So Sir Launcelot and Sir Lavayne
departed, that no creature wyste where he was becom but the
noble men of hys blood. And whan he was com to the ermytayge,
wyte you well he had grete chyre. And so dayly Sir Launcelot used   45

---

7. I.e., famed.
8. *A grete justes cryed*: a grand joust proclaimed (by heralds).
9. On this day, see n. 9, p. 10.
1. I.e., exert.

to go to a welle by the ermytage, and there he wolde ly downe and
se the well sprynge and burble, and somtyme he slepte there.

¶So at that tyme there was a lady that dwelled in that foreyste,
and she was a grete hunteresse, and dayly she used to hunte; and
ever she bare her bowghe with her, and no men wente never with   5
her, but allwayes women—and they were all shooters and cowde
well kylle a dere at the stalke and at the treste.[2] And they dayly
beare bowys, arowis, hornys and wood-knyves; and many good doggis they had, bothe for the strenge and for abate.

¶So hit happed the lady, the huntresse, had abated her dogge   10
for the bowghe at a barayne hynde,[3] and so [this barayne hynde]
toke the flyght over hethys and woodis. And ever thys lady and
parte of her women costed the hynde, and checked hit by the noyse   fol.431r
of the hounde to have mette with the hynde at som watir; and so
hit happened that that hynde cam to the same welle there as Sir   15
Launcelot was by that welle slepynge and slumberynge.

¶And so the hynde, whan he cam to the welle, for heete she
wente to soyle, and there she lay a grete whyle; and the dogge cam
aftir and umbecaste aboute, for she had lost the verray parfyte
fewte of the hynde. Ryght so cam that lady, the hunteres, that knew   20
by her dogge that the hynde was at the soyle in that welle, and
thyder she cam streyte and I founde the hynde; and anone as she
had spyed [her][4] she put a brode[5] arow in her bowe and shot at
the hynde—and so she overshotte the hynde, and so by myssefortune the arow smote Sir Launcelot in the thycke of the buttok, over   25
the barbys.[6]

¶Whan Sir Launcelot felte hym so hurte, he whorled up woodly,
and saw the lady that had smytten hym; and whan he knew she
was a woman he sayde thus: "Lady, or damesell, whatsomever ye
be, in an evyll tyme bare ye thys bowe—the devyll made you a   30
shoter!" "Now, mercy, fayre sir," seyde the lady, "I am a jantill-   [22]
woman that usyth[7] here in thys foreyste huntynge—and God
knowyth I saw you nat but as here was a barayne hynde at the
soyle in thys well—and I wente I had done welle, but my hande
swarved."   35

¶"Alas," seyde Sir Launcelot, "ye have myscheved me." And so
the lady departed. And Sir Launcelot, as he myght, pulled oute the
arow, and leffte the hede stylle in hys buttok; and so he wente
waykely unto the ermytayge, evermore bledynge as he wente. And
whan Sir Labayne and the ermyte aspyed that Sir Launcelot was so   40
sore hurte, wyte you well they were passyng hevy. But Sir Labayne
wyst nat how that he was hurte nothir by whom, and than were
they wrothe oute of mesure. And so wyth grete payne the ermyte

2. *At the stalke and at the treste*: in stalking and when awaiting a deer that has been driven
    to her.
3. *Abated her dogge for the bowghe at a barayne hynde*: sent her dog to chase an unpregnant
    hind within range of her bow.
4. The reading is supplied editorially against the Winchester MS's *hym*; Caxton lacks the
    host phrase.
5. I.e., wide-tipped.
6. *Over the barbys*: i.e., deep enough to set the barbs.
7. I.e., practices.

gate oute the arow-hede oute of Sir **Launcelottis** buttoke, and muche   fol.431v
of hys bloode he shed—and the wounde was passynge sore and
unhappyly smytten, for hit was on such a place that he myght nat
sytte in no sadyll.

⁋"A, mercy Jesu!" seyde Sir **Launcelot**, "I may calle myselff the   5
moste unhappy man that lyvyth, for ever whan I wolde have faynyst
worshyp there befallyth me ever som unhappy thynge—

⁋"Now, so Jesu me helpe," seyde Sir **Launcelot**, "and if no man
wolde but God, I shall be in the fylde on Candilmas day at the
justys, whatsomever falle of hit." So, all that myght be gotyn to   10
hele Sir **Launcelot** was had.

⁋So whan the day was com, Sir **Launcelot** lat devise that he was
arayed, and Sir **Labayne** and he and their horsis, as they had ben
Sarasyns; and so they departed and cam nyghe to the fylde. So the
Kynge of North Galys, he had an hondred knyghtes with hym, and   15
the Kynge of Northehumbirlonde brought with hym an hondred
good knyghtes, and Kynge **Angwysh** of Irelonde brought with hym
an hondred good knyghtes redy to juste; and Sir **Galahalte** the Haute
Prynce brought with hym an hondred good knyghtes, and the
Kynge wyth the Hondred Knyghtes brought with hym as many,   20
and all these were proved good knyghtes.

⁋Than cam in Kynge **Arthurs** party; and in cam wyth hym the
Kynge of Scottes, and an hondred knyghtes with hym; and Kynge
Uryence of Goore brought with hym an hondred knyghtes; and
Kynge **Howell** of Bretayne, he brought wyth hym an hondred   25
knyghtes, and Deuke **Chalaunce of Claraunce** brought with hym an
hondred **knyghtes**. And Kynge **Arthure** hymselff cam into the fylde
with two hondred knyghtes, and the moste party were knyghtes of
the Rounde Table that were all proved noble men. And there were
olde knyghtes set on skaffoldys for to jouge with the Quene who   30
ded beste.

Than they blew unto the fylde.[8] And there the Kynge off North   [23]
Galis encountred wyth the Kynge of Scottes, and there the   fol.432r
Kynge of Scottis had a falle; and the Kynge of Irelonde smote
downe Kynge **Uryence**; and the Kynge of Northhumbirlonde smote   35
downe Kynge **Howell** of Bretayne; and Sir **Galahalte** the Haute
Prynce smote downe Deuke **Chalaunce** of **Claraunce**. And than Kynge
Arthure was wood wrothe, and ran to the Kynge wyth the Hondred
Knyghtes, and so Kynge Arthure smote hym downe; and aftir, wyth
that same speare, he smote downe other three knyghtes (and than   40
hys speare brake) and ded passyngly well.

⁋So therewith cam in Sir **Gawayne** and Sir **Gaherys**, Sir **Aggravayne**
and Sir **Mordred**, and there everych of them smote downe a
knyght—and Sir **Gawayne** smote downe foure knyghtes. And than
there began a grete medlé, for than cam in the knyghtes of Sir   45
Launcelottys blood, and Sir **Gareth** and Sir **Palomydes** wyth them, and

---

8. This part of Malory's text, through to its concluding comments on love (p. 625) has no
   known direct source and may well be of Malory's own devising.

many knyghtes of the Rounde Table; and they began to holde the foure Kynges and the myghty deuke so harde that they were ny discomfyte.

But thys Sir Galahalte the Haute Prynce was a noble knyght, and by hys myghty proues of armys he hylde the knyghtes of the Rounde Table strayte.[9] So all thys doynge saw Sir Launcelot; and than he cam into the fylde wyth Sir Labayne with hym, as hit had bene thunder. And than anone Sir Bors and the knyghtes of hys bloode aspyed Sir Launcelot anone, and seyde unto them all, "I warne you, beware of hym with the slyve of golde uppon hys hede, for he ys hymselff my lorde Sir Launcelot." And for grete goodnes Sir Bors warned Sir Gareth.

"Sir, I am well payde," seyde Sir Gareth, "that I may know hym." "But who ys he," seyde they all, "that rydith with hym in the same aray?"

❡ "Sir, that ys the good and jantyll knyght Sir Labayne," seyde Sir Bors. So Sir Launcelot encountred with Sir Gawayne, and there by force Sir Launcelot smote downe Sir Gawayne and his horse to the erthe; and so he smote downe Sir Aggrabayne and Sir Gaherys, and also he smote downe Sir Mordred—and all this was wyth one speare. Than Sir Labayne mette with Sir Palompdes, and aythir mette other so harde and so fersely that both theire horsis felle to the erthe; and than were they horsed agayne.

And than mette Sir Launcelot with Sir Palompdes, and there Sir Palompdes had a falle; and so Sir Launcelot, or ever he stynte, and as faste as he myght gete spearys, he smote downe thirty knyghtes, and the moste party were knyghtes of the Rounde Table—and ever the knyghtes of hys bloode wythdrew them, and made hem ado in othir placis where Sir Launcelot cam nat. And than Kynge Arthure was wrotthe whan he saw Sir Launcelot do suche dedis; and than the Kynge called unto hym Sir Gawayne, Sir Gaherys, Sir Aggrabayne, Sir Mordred, Sir Kay, Sir Grpfflet, Sir Lucan de Butlere, Sir Bedpvere, Sir Palompdes, and Sir Safpre, hys brothir—and so the Kynge wyth thes nyne knyghtes made them redy to sette uppon Sir Launcelot and uppon Sir Labayne. And all thys aspyed Sir Bors and Sir Gareth. "Now I drede me sore," seyde Sir Bors, "that my lorde Sir Launcelot woll be harde macched."

❡ "Now, be my hede," seyde Sir Gareth, "I woll ryde unto my lorde Sir Launcelot for to helpe hym whatsomever me betyde—for he ys the same man that made me knyght."

❡ "Sir, ye shall nat do so," seyde Sir Bors, "be my counceyle, onles that ye were disgysed."

❡ "Sir, ye shall se me sone disgysed," seyde Sir Gareth. And therewithall he had aspyed a Waylshe knyght where he was to repose hym, for he was sore hurte before of Sir Gawayne; and unto hym Sir Gareth rode and prayde hym of hys knyghthode to lende hym hys shylde for hys. "I woll well," seyde the Waylshe knyght.

fol.432v

9. *Hylde . . . strayte:* pressed (them) hard.

And whan Sir Gareth had hys shylde—the booke seythe hit was gryne, wyth a maydyn whych semed[1] in hit—than Sir Gareth cam dryvynge unto Sir Launcelot all that ever he myght, and seyde, "Sir knyght, take kepe to[2] thyselff, for yondir commyth Kynge Arthur with nyne noble knyghtes wyth hym, to put you to a rebuke—and so I am com to beare you felyshyp for the olde love ye have shewed unto me."

¶"Grauntemercy," seyde Sir Launcelot.

¶"But, sir," seyde Sir Gareth, "encountir ye with Sir Gawayne, and I shall encountir with Sir Palomydes, and lat Sir Lavayne macche with the noble Kynge Arthur; and whan we have delyverde them lat us three holde us sadly[3] togydirs."

¶So than cam in Kynge Arthure wyth hys nyne knyghtes with hym. And Sir Launcelot encountred with Sir Gawayne and gaff hym suche a buffette that the arson of hys sadyll braste, and Sir Gawayne felle to the erthe. Than Sir Gareth encountred with Sir Palomydes, and he gaff hym such a buffet that bothe hys horse and he days- shed to the erthe. Than encountred Kynge Arthure wyth Sir Lavayne, and there aythir of them smote other to the erthe, horse and all, that they lay bothe a grete whyle.

¶Than Sir Launcelot smote downe Sir Aggravayne, and Sir Gaherys, and Sir Mordred; and Sir Gareth smote downe Sir Kay, Sir Safir, and Sir Gryfflet. And than Sir Lavayne was horsed agayne, and he smote downe Sir Lucan de Butlere and Sir Bedyvere—and than there began grete thrange of good knyghtes. Than Sir Launcelot hurled here and there, and raced and pulled of helmys, that at that tyme there myght none sytte[4] hym a buffette with speare nothir with swerde. And Sir Gareth ded such dedys of armys that all men mervayled what knyght he was with the gryne shylde, for he smote downe that day and pulled downe mo than thirty knyghtes; and, as the Freynshe booke sayth, Sir Launcelot mervayled, whan he behylde Sir Gareth do such dedis, what knyght he myght be. And Sir Lavayne smote and pulled downe mo than twenty knyghtes.

¶And yet, for all thys, Sir Launcelot knew nat Sir Gareth; for and Sir Trystram de Lyones other Sir Lamorak de Galys had ben on lyve, Sir Launcelot wolde have demed he had bene one of them twayne.

¶So ever as Sir Launcelot, Sir Gareth, and Sir Lavayne fought on the tone syde, Sir Bors, Sir Ector de Marys, Sir Lyonell, Sir Bleoberys, Sir Galyhud, Sir Galyhodyn, and Sir Pelleas and many mo other of Kynge Banys blood faught uppon another party, and hylde the Kynge wyth the Hondred Knyghtes and the Kynge of Northhum- birlonde ryght strayte.

¶So thys turnemente and justis dured longe, tylle hit was nere nyght, for the knyghtes of the Rounde Table releved ever unto Kynge Arthure; for the Kyng was wrothe oute of mesure that he and hys knyghtes myght nat prevayle that day.

fol.433r

5

10

15

20

25

30

fol.433v

[24]

35

40

45

1. I.e., appeared.
2. *Take kepe to*: i.e., watch out for.
3. I.e., closely, firmly.
4. I.e., withstand from.

¶Than sayde Sir Gawayne to the Kynge, "Sir, I mervayle where ar all thys day Sir Bors de Ganys and hys felyshyp of Sir Launcelottis blood, that of all thys day they be nat aboute you; and therefore I deme hit ys for som cause," seyde Sir Gawayne. "Be my hede," seyde Sir Kay, "Sir Bors ys yondir all thys day upon the ryght honde of thys fylde, and there he and his blood dothe more worshypfully than we do."

¶"Hit may well be," seyde Sir Gawayne, "but I drede me ever of gyle; for on payne of my lyff, that same knyght with the rede slyve of golde ys hymselff Sir Launcelot, for I se well by hys rydynge and by hys greate strokis. And the othir knyght in the same colowres ys the good yonge knyght Sir Labayne; and that knyght with the grene shylde ys my brothir Sir Gareth—and yet he hath disgysed hymselff, for no man shall make hym be ayenste Sir Launcelot, bycause he made hym knyght." "By my hede," seyde Kynge Arthure, "neveaw, I belyeve you; and therefore now telle me what ys youre beste counceyle."

¶"Sir," seyde Sir Gawayne, "my counceile ys to blow unto lod- gynge, for and he be Sir Launcelot du Lake, and my brothir Sir Gareth wyth hym, wyth the helpe of that goode yonge knyght, Sir Labayne, truste me truly, hit woll be no boote to stryve wyth them but if we sholde falle ten or twelve uppon one knyght—and that were no worshyp, but shame."

¶"Ye say trouthe," seyde the Kynge, "hit were shame for us, so many as we be, to sette uppon them ony more. For wyte you well," seyde Kynge Arthure, "they be three good knyghtes, and namely[5] that knyght with the slyve of golde." And anone they blew unto lodgyng; but furthwithall Kynge Arthure lete sende[6] unto the foure Kyngis and to the myghty deuke, and prayde hem that the knyght with the slyve of golde departe nat frome them, but that the Kynge may speke with hym. Than furthwithall Kynge Arthur alyght and unarmed hym, and toke a lytyll hakeney and rode after Sir Launcelot, for ever he had a spy uppon hym. And so he founde hym amonge the foure Kyngis and the deuke, and there the Kynge prayde hem all unto suppere, and they seyde they wolde with good wyll; and whan they were unarmed, Kynge Arthure knew Sir Launcelot, Sir Gareth and Sir Labayne.

¶"A, Sir Launcelot," seyde Kynge Arthure, "thys day ye have heted me and my knyghtes."

¶And so they yode unto Kynge Arthurs lodgynge all togydir, and there was a grete feste and grete revell; and the pryce was yevyn unto Sir Launcelot, for by herowdys they named hym that he had smytten downe fyfty knyghtys—and Sir Gareth fyve and thirty knyghtes, and Sir Labayne foure and twenty.

Than Sir Launcelot tolde the Kynge and the Quene how the lady hunteras shotte hym in the foreyste of Wyndesore, in the buttok, wyth a brode arow, and how the wounde was at that tyme six inchys

5. I.e., especially.
6. *Lete sende:* i.e., had messages sent.

depe and inlyke longe. Also Kynge Arthure blamed Sir Gareth   fol.434v
because he leffte hys felyshyp and hylde with Sir Launcelot. "My
lorde," seyde Sir Garethe, "he made me knyght, and whan I saw hym
so hard bestad, methought hit was my worshyp to helpe hym. For
I saw hym do so muche dedis of armys, and so many noble knyghtes   5
ayenste hym, that whan I undirstode that he was Sir Launcelot du
Lake, I shamed to se so many good knyghtes ayenste hym alone."

¶"Now, truly," seyde Kynge Arthur unto Sir Gareth, "ye say well,
and worshypfully have ye done, and to youreselff grete worshyp.

¶"And all the dayes of my lyff," seyde Kynge Arthure unto Sir   10
Gareth—

¶"Wyte you well I shall love you and truste you the more bettir.
For ever hit ys," seyde Kynge Arthure, "a worshypfull knyghtes dede
to help and succoure another worshypfull knyght whan he seeth
hym in daungere. For ever a worshypfull man woll be lothe to se   15
a worshypfull man shamed, and he that ys of no worshyp and med-
elyth with cowardise, never shall he shew jantilnes nor no maner
of goodnes where he seeth a man in daungere, for than woll
a cowarde never shew mercy—and allwayes a good man woll do
ever to another man as he wolde be done to hymselff." So than   20
there were made grete festis unto kyngis and deukes, and revell,
game, and play, and all maner of nobeles was used—and he
that was curteyse, trew, and faythefull to hys frynde was that tyme
cherysshed.   [25]

And thus hit passed on frome Candylmas untyll after Ester, that   25
the moneth of May was com, whan every lusty harte begynnyth to
blossom and to burgyne. For, lyke as trees and erbys burgenyth
and florysshyth in May, in lyke wyse every lusty harte that ys ony
maner of lover spryngith, burgenyth, buddyth, and florysshyth in   fol.435r
lusty dedis. For hit gyvyth unto all lovers corrayge, that lusty   30
moneth of May, in somthynge to constrayne hym to som maner of
thynge more in that moneth than in ony other monethe, for
dyverce causys: for than all erbys and treys renewyth a man and
woman, and in lyke wyse lovers callyth to their mynde olde jantylnes and olde servyse, and many kynde dedes that was forgotyn by   35
neclygence.

For, lyke as wynter rasure dothe allway arace and deface grene
summer, so faryth hit by unstable love in man and woman: for in
many persones there ys no stabylité, for we may se all day, for a
lytyll blaste of wyntres rasure, anone we shall deface and lay aparte   40
trew love, for lytyll or nowght, that coste muche thynge. Thys ys
no wysedome nother no stabylité, but hit ys fyeblenes of nature
and grete disworshyp, whosomever usyth[7] thys. Therefore, lyke as
May moneth flowryth and floryshyth in every mannes gardyne, so
in lyke wyse lat every man of worshyp florysh hys herte in thys   45
worlde, firste unto God, and nexte unto the joy of them that he
promysed hys feythe unto. For there was never worshypfull man
nor worshypfull woman, but they loved one bettir than anothir;
and worshyp in armys may never be foyled. But firste reserve the

7. I.e., practices.

honoure to God, and secundely thy quarell muste com of thy lady—and such love I calle vertuouse love.

¶But nowadayes men can nat love seven nyght but they muste have all their desyres. That love may nat endure by reson; for where they[8] bethe sone accorded and hasty, heete sone keelyth. And ryght so faryth the love nowadayes, sone hote, sone colde: thys ys no stabylyté. But the olde love was nat so; for men and women coude love togydirs seven yerys, and no lycoures lustis was betwyxte them—and than was love trouthe and faythefulnes.

¶And so in lyke wyse was used such love in Kynge **Arthurs** dayes. Wherefore I lykken love nowadayes unto sommer and wynter: for, lyke as the tone ys colde and the othir ys hote, so faryth love nowadayes. And therefore all ye that be lovers, calle unto youre remembraunce the monethe of May, lyke as ded Quene **Gwenyver**, for whom I make here a lytyll mencion, that whyle she lyved she was a trew lover, and therefor she had a good ende.[9]

SO hit befelle in the moneth of May, Quene **Gwenyver** called unto her ten knyghtes of the Table Rounde, and she gaff them warnynge that early uppon the morn she wolde ryde on mayynge into woodis and fyldis besydes Westemynster: "And I warne you that there be none of you but he be well horsed, and that ye all be clothed all in gryne, othir in sylke othir in clothe; and I shall brynge with me ten ladyes, and every knyght shall have a lady be hym; and every knyght shall haye a squyar and two yomen—and I woll that all be well horsed."

¶So they made hem redy in the freysshyst maner, and thes were the namys of the knyghtes:

¶Sir **Kay** le Senesciall, Sir **Aggravayne**, Sir **Braundyles**, Sir **Sagramour** le Desyrous, Sir **Dodynas** le Savayge, Sir **Ozanna le Cure Hardy**, Sir **Ladynas** of the Foreyst Savayge, Sir **Persaunte** of Inde, Sir **Ironsyde** that was called the Knyght of the Rede Laundes, and Sir **Pelleas**, the lovear. And thes ten knyghtes made them redy in the freysshyste maner to ryde wyth the Quyne; and so uppon the morne or hit were day, in a May mornynge, they toke their horsys wyth the Quene and rode on mayinge in wodis and medowis as hit pleased hem, in grete joy and delytes (for the Quene had caste to have bene agayne with Kynge **Arthur** at the furthest[1] by ten of the clok, and so was that tyme her purpose).

fol.435v

[XIX.1]

---

8. I.e., lovers.
9. *But nowadayes . . . she had a good ende:* coming at the end of a section with no known direct source (see n. 8, p. 620), this is another of Malory's relatively rare meditations on conditions in his own time as they compare to those of the Arthurian past (for other such passages, see pp. 231, 595, and 680). The spirit of this passage, however, even in Malory's time, had an old heritage; it is, for instance, reminiscent of the lament for the loss of true courtly love (and its components of integrity, generosity, and honor), which opens one of the earliest of all Arthurian romances, *Yvain*, written by Chrétien de Troyes c. 1177. Malory's equation of love with *trouthe and faythefulnes* is further reminiscent of *Ywain and Gawain*, the Middle English translation of Chrétien's poem, which emphasizes *trewth* over love (for the ME text and a modern translation of Chrétien, see MER, p. 76, lines 33–40, and p. 411, respectively). Malory's *lytyll mencion* of Gwenyvere as *a trew lover* likely contemplates the steadfastness of her love for Launcelot and the steadfastness in love she received from him—something put to its greatest test in the subsequent sections of Malory's text.
1. I.e., latest.

Than there was a knyght whych hyght Sir Mellyagaunce, and he was sonne unto Kynge Bagdemagus; and this knyght had that tyme a castell of the gyffte of Kynge Arthure within seven myle of Westemynster. And thys knyght Sir Mellyagaunce loved passyngly well Quene Gwenyver—and so had he done longe and many yerys—and the booke seyth he had layn in awayte for to stele away the Quene; but evermore he forbare for bycause of Sir Launcelot, for in no wyse he wolde meddyll with the Quene and[2] Sir Launcelot were in her company, othir ellys and[3] he were nerehonde.

(And that tyme was such a custom that the Quene rode never wythoute a grete felyshyp of men of armys aboute her, and they were many good knyghtes; and the moste party were yonge men that wolde have worshyp, and they were called the Quenys Knyghtes. And never in no batayle, turnement nother justys they bare none of hem no maner of knowlecchynge of their owne armys, but playne whyght shyldis, and thereby they were called the Quenys Knyghtes. And whan hit happed ony of them to be of grete worshyp by hys noble dedis, than at the nexte feste of Pentecoste, gyff there were ony slayne or dede—as there was none yere that there fayled but there were som dede—than was there chosyn in hys stede that was dede[4] the moste men of worshyp that were called the Quenys Knyghtes: and thus they cam up firste or they were renowmed men of worshyp, both Sir Launcelot and all the remenaunte of them.)[5]

¶But thys knyght, Sir Mellyagaunce, had aspyed the Quene well and her purpose, and how Sir Launcelot was nat wyth her, and how she had no men of armys with her but the ten noble knyghtis all rayed in grene for maiynge. Than he purveyde hym a twenty men of armys and an hondred archars for to destresse the Quene and her knyghtes, for he thought that tyme was beste seson to take the Quene.

¶So as the Quene was oute on mayynge wyth all her knyghtes— whych were bedaysshed wyth erbis, mossis, and floures in the freysshyste maner—

¶Ryght so there cam oute of a wood Sir Mellyagaunte with an eyght score men, all harneyst as they shulde fyght in a batayle of areste,[6] and bade the Quene and her knyghtis abyde, for magré their hedis they shulde abyde.

2. I.e., if.
3. *othir ellys and:* or if.
4. *In hys stede that was dede:* in place of he who was dead.
5. Evidently the Queen's Knights are not those attending Gwenyvere on this day, although the ten knights who are with her are presumably alumni of the worthy order. Malory's purpose in mentioning this order would seem, first, to establish further grounds for explaining Mellyagaunce's unwillingness to approach the Queen and, second, to augment the credentials of his favorite knight, Launcelot. For his account of the order, Malory has modified his likely sources, the prose *Lancelot* and the *Suite de Merlin,* which describe the order as one in which the knights were seekers of adventure, not bodyguards, and who sported their own coats of arms. Examining these changes, P. J. C. Field has suggested that Malory may have intended to allude to "the Queen's gallants," a group of intrepid knights who fought on behalf of Queen Margaret of Anjou at the battle of Blore Heath, September 23, 1459 (*Malory: Texts and Sources,* pp. 62–64); if this is the case, then Malory has also with this passage implicitly provided a reminder of the potential of his own times to configure institutions of an Arthurian caliber.
6. *Batayle of areste:* raid.

fol.436r

[2]

fol.436v

¶"Traytoure knyght," seyd Quene Gwenyver, "what caste thou to do? Wolt thou shame thyselff? Bethynke the[7] how thou arte a kyngis sonne and a knyght of the Table Rounde—and thou thus to be aboute to dishonoure the noble Kyng that made the[8] knyght! Thou shamyst all knyghthode and thyselffe and me. And I lat the[9] wyte thou shalt never shame me, for I had levir kut myne owne throte in twayne rather than thou sholde dishonoure me."

¶"As for all thys langayge," seyde Sir Mellyagaunte, "be as hit be may; for wyte you well, madame, I have loved you many a yere, and never ar now cowde I gete you at such avayle—and therefore I woll take you as I fynde you." Than spake all the ten noble knyghtes at onys, and seyde, "Sir Mellyagaunte, wyte thou well thou ar aboute to jouparté thy worshyp to dishonoure, and also ye caste to jouparté youre persones. Howbehit we be unarmed and ye have us at a grete avauntayge—for hit semyth by you that ye have layde wacch uppon us—but rather than ye shulde put the Quene to a shame, and us all, we had as lyff[1] to departe frome owre lyvys; for and we othyrwayes ded, we were shamed for ever."

Than seyde Sir Mellyagaunt, "Dresse you as well as ye can, and kepe[2] the Quene!" Than the ten knyghtis of the Rounde Table drew their swerdis, and thes othir lat ren at them wyth their spearys; and the ten knyghtes manly abode them and smote away their spearys, that no speare ded them no harme.

¶Than they laysshed togydirs wyth swerdis, and anone Sir Kay, Sir Sagramoure, Sir Aggravayne, Sir Dodynas, Sir Ladynas, and Sir Ozanna were smytten to the erthe with grymly woundis; than Sir Braundiles and Sir Persaunte, Sir Ironsyde, and Sir Pelleas faught longe—and they were sore wounded, for thes ten knyghtes, or ever they were leyde to the grounde, slew fourty men of the boldyste and the beste of them.

¶So whan the Quene saw her knyghtes thus dolefully wounded, and nedys muste be slayne at the laste, than for verry pyté and sorow she cryed and seyde, "Sir Mellyagaunte, sle nat my noble knyghtes and I woll go with the,[3] uppon thys covenaunte: that thou save them and suffir hem no more to be hurte, wyth thys[4] that they be lad with me wheresomever thou ledyst me, for I woll rather sle myselff than I woll go wyth the,[5] onles that thes noble knyghtes may be in my presence." "Madame," seyde Sir Mellyagaunt, "for your sake they shall be lad wyth you into myne owne castell, with that ye woll be reuled and ryde with me."

¶Than the Quene prayde the foure knyghtes to leve their fyghtynge, and she and they wolde nat departe.[6]

fol.437r

---

7. Thee.
8. Thee.
9. Thee.
1. *As lyff:* sooner, preferably.
2. I.e., guard.
3. Thee.
4. *Wyth thys:* provided.
5. Thee.
6. I.e., separate.

❡"Madame, seyde Sir Pelleas, "we woll do as ye do, for as for me, I take no force of my lyff nor deth"—for, as the Freynshe booke seyth, Sir Pelleas gaff such buffettis there that none armoure myght holde[7] hym. Than by the Quenys commaundemente they leffte batayle and dressed the wounded knyghtes on horsebak, som syttyng and som overtwarte their horsis, that hit was pité to beholde. And than Sir Mellyagaunt charged the Quene and all her knyghtes that none of hir felyshyp shulde departe frome her; for full sore he drad Sir Launcelot du Lake, laste he shulde have ony knowlecchynge—and all this aspyed the Quene, and pryvaly she called unto her a chylde of her chambir whych was swyfftely horsed, of a grete avauntayge.[8]

❡"Now go thou," seyde she, "whan thou seyst thy tyme, and beare thys rynge unto Sir Launcelot du Laake, and pray hym as he lovythe me that he woll se me and rescow me, if ever he woll have joy of me—and spare nat thy horse," seyde the Quyene, "nother for watir nother for londe."

❡So thys chyld aspyed hys tyme, and lyghtly he toke hys horse with spurres and departed as faste as he myght. And wan Sir Mellyagaunte saw hym so fle, he undirstood that hit was by the Quyenys commaundemente for to warne Sir Launcelot; than they that were beste horsed chaced hym and shotte at hym, but frome hem all the chylde wente delyverly.

And than Sir Mellyagaunte sayde unto the Quyne, "Madame, ye ar aboute to betray me, but I shall ordayne for Sir Launcelot that he shall nat com lyghtly at you." And than he rode wyth her and all the felyshyp in all the haste that they myght; and so by the way Sir Mellyagaunte layde in buyshemente of the beste archars that he had, of a thirty, to awayte uppon Sir Launcelot, chargynge them that yf they saw suche a maner a knyght com by the way uppon a whyght horse, "that in ony wyse ye sle hys horse, but in no maner have ye ado wyth hym bodyly, for he ys over hardé to be overcom."

❡So thys was done, and they were com to hys castell; but in no wyse the Quene wolde never lette none of the ten knyghtes and her ladyes oute of her syght, but allwayes they were in her presence; for the booke sayth Sir Mellyagaunte durste make no mastryes for drede of Sir Launcelot, insomuche he demed that he had warnynge. So whan the chylde was departed fro the felyshyp of Sir Mellyagaunte, wythin a whyle he cam to Westemynster, and anone he founde Sir Launcelot. And whan he had tolde hys messayge and delyverde hym the Quenys rynge—

❡"Alas!" seyde Sir Launcelot, "now am I shamed for ever, onles that I may rescow that noble lady frome dishonour." Than egirly he asked hys armys. And ever the chylde tolde Sir Launcelot how the ten knyghtes faught mervaylously, and how Sir Pelleas, Sir Ironsyde, Sir Braundyles and Sir Persaunte of Inde fought strongly, but namely[9] Sir Pelleas, there myght none harneys holde hym; and how

[3]

5

10

fol.437v

15

20

25

30

35

40

45

---

7. I.e., resist.
8. *Swyfftely horsed, of a grete avauntayge:* i.e., placed on a horse of extraordinary swiftness.
9. I.e., especially.

they all faught tylle they were layde to the erthe, and how the   fol.438r
Quene made apoyntemente[1] for to save their lyvys and to go wyth
Sir Mellyagaunte. "Alas," seyde Sir Launcelot, "that moste noble lady,
that she shulde be so destroyed! I had lever," seyde Sir Launcelot,
"than all Fraunce that I had bene there well armed."   5

¶So whan Sir Launcelot was armed and uppon hys horse, he
prayde the chylde of the Quynys chambir to warne Sir Lavayne how
suddeynly he was departed, and for what cause—"And pray hym,
as he lovyth me, that he woll hyghe hym aftir me, and that he
stynte nat untyll he com to the castell where Sir Mellyagaunt   10
abydith—for there," seyde Sir Launcelot, "he shall hyre of me, and
I be a man lyvynge."

¶Than Sir Launcelot rode as faste as he myght, and the booke   [4]
seyth he toke the watir at Westmynster Brydge and made hys horse
swymme over the Temmys unto Lambyth. And so within a whyle   15
he cam to the same place there as the ten noble knyghtes fought
with Sir Mellyagaunte; and than Sir Launcelot folowed the trak untyll
that he cam to a woode, and there was a strayte way: and there
the thirty archers bade Sir Launcelot, "turne agayne and folow no
longer that trak."   20

¶"What commaundemente have ye," seyde Sir Launcelot, "to
cause me, that am a knyght of the Rounde Table, to leve my ryght
way?"

¶"Thys wayes shalt thou leve, othir ellis thou shalte go hit on
thy foote; for wyte thou well thy horse shall be slayne." "That ys   25
lytyll maystry," seyde Sir Launcelot, "to sle myne horse; but as for
myselff, whan my horse ys slayne I gyff ryght nought of[2] you, nat
and ye were fyve hundred mo." So than they shotte Sir Launcelottis
horse, and smote hym with many arowys. And than Sir Launcelot
avoyded hys horse and wente on foote; but there were so many   30
dychys and hedgys betwyxte hem and hym that he myght nat meddyll with none of hem.

¶"Alas, for shame," seyde Sir Launcelot, "that ever one knyght
shulde betray anothir knyght. But hyt ys an olde-seyde saw: 'A good   fol.438v
man ys never in daungere but whan he ys in the daungere[3] of a   35
cowhard.' " Than Sir Launcelot walked on a whyle, and was sore
acombird of hys armoure, hys shylde, and hys speare—wyte you
well he was full sore anoyed, and full lothe he was for to leve
onythynge that longed unto hym, for he drad sore the treson of Sir
Mellyagaunce.   40

¶Than by fortune there cam [by hym] a charyote that cam thydir
to feche wood. "Say me, carter," seyde Sir Launcelot, "what shall I
gyff the[4] to suffir me to lepe into thy charyote, and that thou wolte
brynge me unto a castell within thys two myle?" "Thou shalt nat
entir into thys charyot," seyde the carter, "for I am sente for to   45
fecche wood."

1. I.e., agreement.
2. *Gyff ryght nought of*: care nothing about.
3. I.e., power.
4. Thee.

¶ "Unto whom?" seyde Sir Launcelot. "Unto my lorde, Sir Melly-agaunce," seyde the carter. "And with hym wolde I speke," seyde Sir Launcelot.

¶ "Thou shalt nat go with me!" seyde the carter. [Thenne] Sir Launcelot lepe to hym and gaff hym backwarde with hys gauntelot a reremayne that he felle to the erthe starke dede. Than the tothir carter, hys felow, was aferde and wente to have gone the same way; and than he sayde, "Fayre lorde, sauff my lyff, and I shall brynge you where ye woll." "Than I charge the,"[5] seyde Sir Launcelot, "that thou dryve me and thys charyote unto Sir Mellyagaunce yate."

¶ "Than lepe ye up into the charyotte," seyde the carter, "and ye shall be there anone." So the carter drove on a grete walop—and Sir Launcelottes hors folowed the charyot, with mo than fourty arowys in hym. And more than an owre and an halff Quene Gwe-nyver was awaytyng in a bay wyndow; than one of hir ladyes aspyed an armed knyght stondyng in a charyote.

¶ "A, se madam," seyde the lady, "where rydys in a charyot a goodly armed knyght—and we suppose he rydyth unto hangynge."[6]

¶ "Where?" seyde the Quene. Than she aspyed by hys shylde that hit was Sir Launcelot—and than was she ware where cam hys horse after the charyotte, and ever he trode hys guttis and hys paunche undir hys feete.

¶ "Alas," seyde the Quene, "now I may preve and se that well ys that creature that hath a trusty frynde. A-ha!" seyde Quene Gwe-nyver, "I se well that ye were harde bestad whan ye ryde in a char-yote." And than she rebuked that lady that lykened Sir Launcelot to ryde in a charyote to hangynge: "Forsothe, hit was fowle-mowthed," seyde the Quene, "and evyll lykened, so for to lyken the moste noble knyght of the worlde unto such a shamefull dethe. A, Jesu deffende hym and kepe hym," sayde the Quene, "frome all myschevous ende."

¶ So by thys was Sir Launcelot comyn to the gatis of that castell; and there he descended down and cryed, that all the castell myght rynge, "Where arte thou, thou false traytoure Sir Mellyagaunte, and knyght of the Table Rownde? Com forth, thou traytour knyght, thou and all thy felyshyp with the,[7] for here I am, Sir Launcelot du Lake, that shall fyght with you all!" And therewithall he bare the gate wyde opyn upon the porter, and smote hym undir the ere wyth hys gauntelot, that hys nekke braste in two pecis.

¶ Whan Sir Mellyagaunce harde that Sir Launcelot was comyn, he ranne unto the Quene and felle upon hys kne, and seyde, "Mercy, madame, for now I putte me holé in your good grace." "What ayles you now?" seyde Quene Gwenyver. "Pardé, I myght well wete that some good knyght wolde revenge me, thoughe my lorde Kynge Arthure knew nat of thys your worke."

fol.439r

[5]

---

5. Thee.
6. The lady's assumption derives from the medieval (and later) custom of bringing con-demned felons to the gallows in a cart—for a knight this would be an especially ignomin-ious mode of transport.
7. Thee.

¶"A, madame," seyde Sir Mellyagaunte, "all thys that ys amysse on my party shall be amended ryght as youreselff woll devyse— and holy I put me in youre grace."

¶"What wolde ye that I ded?" seyde the Quene.

¶"Madame, I wolde no more," seyde Sir Mellyagaunt, "but that ye wolde take all in youre owne hondys, and that ye woll rule my lorde Sir Launcelot; and such chere as may be made hym in thys poure castell, ye and he shall have untyll tomorn, and than may ye and all they returne ayen unto Westmynster—and my body and all that I have I shall put in youre rule." fol.439v

¶"Ye sey well," seyde the Quene, "and bettir ys pees than ever-more warre—and the lesse noyse[8] the more ys my worshyp."

¶Than the Quene and hur ladyes wente downe unto Sir Launcelot, that stood wood wrothe oute of mesure [in the inner courte] to abyde batayle; and ever he seyde, "Thou traytour knyght, com forthe!" Than the Quene cam unto hym, and seyde, "Sir Launcelot, why be ye so amoved?"

¶"A, madame," seyde Sir Launcelot, "why aske ye me that ques-tyon? For mesemyth ye oughte to be more wrotther than I am, for ye have the hurte and the dishonour—for wyte you well, madame, my hurte ys but lytyll in regard for the sleyng of a marys[9] sonne, but the despite grevyth me much more than all my hurte."

"Truly," seyde the Quene, "ye say trouthe, but hartely I thanke you," seyde the Quene. "But ye muste com in with me pesyblé, for all thynge ys put in myne honde, and all that ys amysse shall be amended; for the knyght full sore repentys hym of thys mysadven-ture that ys befallyn hym." "Madame," seyde Sir Launcelot, "syth hit ys so that ye be accorded with hym, as for me I may nat agaynesay hit, howbehit Sir Mellyagaunte hath done full shamefully to me, and cowardly. And, madame," seyde Sir Launcelot, "and I had wyste that ye wolde have bene so lyghtly accorded with hym, I wolde nat a made such haste unto you."

¶"Why say ye so?" seyde the Quene. "Do ye forthynke youreselff of youre good dedis?

¶"Wyte you well," seyde the Quene, "I accorded never with hym for no favoure nor love at I had unto hym, but of every shamefull noyse of wysedom to lay adoune."[1]

¶"Madame," seyde Sir Launcelot, "ye undirstonde full well I was never wyllynge nor glad of shamefull sclaundir nor noyse; and there ys nother kynge, quene, ne knyght that beryth the lyffe, excepte my lorde Kynge Arthur and you, madame, that shulde lette[2] me but I shulde make Sir Mellyagaunce harte full colde or ever I departed frome hense." "That wote I well," seyde the Quene, "but what woll ye more? Ye shall have all thynge ruled as ye lyste to have hit." fol.440r

¶"Madame," seyde Sir Launcelot, "so ye be pleased, as for my parte, ye shall sone please me." Ryght so the Quene toke Sir

---

8. I.e., rumor, scandal.
9. I.e., mare's.
1. *Of wysedom to lay adoune:* out of wisdom to suppress.
2. I.e., hinder.

Launcelot by the bare honde, for he had put of hys gauntelot, and
so she wente wyth hym tyll her chambir; and than she commaunded hym to be unarmed. And than Sir Launcelot asked the
Quene where were hir ten knyghtes that were wounded with her.

Than she shewed them unto hym, and there they made grete joy
of the commyng of Sir Launcelot; and he made grete sorow of their
hurtis. And there Sir Launcelot tolde them how cowardly and traytourly he sette archers to sle hys horse, and how he was fayne to
put hymselff in a charyotte. And thus they complayned everyche
to other—and full fayne they wolde have ben revenged, but they
kepte the pees bycause of the Quene.

¶Than, as the Freynsh booke saythe, Sir Launcelot was called
many dayes aftyr "le Shyvalere de Charyotte," and so he ded many
dedys and grete adventures—and so we leve of here of la Shyvalere
le Charyote, and turne³ we to thys tale.

So Sir Launcelot had grete chere with the Quene; and than he
made a promyse with the Quene that the same nyght he sholde
com to a wyndow outewarde⁴ towarde a gardyne—and that wyndow was barred with iron—and there Sir Launcelot promysed to
mete her whan all folkes were on slepe.

¶So than cam Sir Lavayne dryvynge to the gatis, seyyng "Where
ys my lorde Sir Launcelot?" And anone he was sente fore, and whan
Sir Lavayne saw Sir Launcelot, he seyde, "A, my lorde, I founde howe
ye were harde bestadde, for I have founde your hors that ys slayne
with arowys." "As for that" seyde Sir Launcelot, "I praye you, Sir
Lavayne, speke ye of othir maters, and lat thys passe, and ryght hit
anothir tyme and we may."

¶Than the knyghtes that were hurt were serched, and soffte
salves were layde to their woundis; and so hit passed on tyll souper-
tyme—and all the chere that myght be made them there was done
unto the Quene and all her knyghtes. And whan season⁵ was they
wente unto their chambirs; but in no wyse the Quene wolde nat
suffir her wounded knyghtes to be fro her, but that they were layde
in wythdraughtes by hur chambir, upon beddis and paylattes, that
she myght herselff se unto them that they wanted nothynge.

¶So whan Sir Launcelot was in hys chambir whych was assygned
unto hym, he called unto hym Sir Lavayne and tolde hym that nyght
he must speke with hys lady, Quene Gwenyver. "Sir," seyde Sir
Lavayne, "let me go with you, and hyt please you, for I drede me
sore of the treson of Sir Mellyagaunte."

¶"Nay," seyde Sir Launcelot, "I thanke you, but I woll have
nobody wyth me." Than Sir Launcelot toke hys swerde in hys honde
and prevaly wente to the place where he had spyed a ladder toforehande; and that he toke undir hys arme, and bare hit thorow the
gardyne and sette hit up to the wyndow—and anone the Quene
was there redy to mete hym. And than they made their complayntes
eyther to othir of many dyverce thyngis.

3. I.e., return.
4. I.e., facing outward.
5. I.e., the appropriate time.

❡And than Sir Launcelot wysshed that he myght have comyn in to her.

❡"Wyte you well," seyde the Quene, "I wolde as fayne as ye that ye myght com in to me."

❡"Wolde ye so, madame," seyde Sir Launcelot, "wyth youre harte, that I were with you?"

❡"Ye, truly," seyde the Quene.

❡"Than shall I prove my myght," seyde Sir Launcelot, "for youre love." And than he sette hys hondis upon the barrys of iron and pulled at them with suche a myght that he braste hem clene oute of the stone wallys—and therewithall one of the barres of iron kutte the brawne of hys hondys thorowoute, to the bone—and than he lepe into the chambir to the Quene.

❡"Make ye no noyse," seyde the Quene, "for my wounded knyghtes lye here fast by me." So, to passe uppon thys tale, Sir Launcelot wente to bedde with the Quene and toke no force of hys hurte honde, but toke hys plesaunce and hys lykynge[6] untyll hit was the dawnyng of the day—for wyte you well, he slept nat, but wacched. And whan he saw hys tyme that he myght tary no lenger, he toke hys leve and departed at the wyndowe, and put hit togydir as well as he myght agayne, and so departed untyll hys owne chambir; and there he tolde Sir Labayne how that he was hurte. Than Sir Labayne dressed hys honde and staunched hit and put uppon hit a glove, that hit sholde nat be aspyed. And so [the Quene] lay longe [in her] bed in the mornynge tylle hit was nyne of the clok.

❡Than Sir Mellyagaunte wente to the Quenys chambir and founde her ladyes there redy clothed. "A, Jesu mercy," seyde Sir Mellyagaunte, "what ayles you, madame, that ye slepe thys longe?" And therewithall he opened the curtayn for to beholde her; and than was he ware where she lay, and all the hede-sheete, pylow, and over-shyte was all be-bled of the bloode of Sir Launcelot and of hys hurte honde.

❡Whan Sir Mellyagaunt aspyed that blood, than he demed in her that she was false to the Kynge and that som of the wounded knyghtes had lyene by her all that nyght. "A-ha, madame!" seyde Sir Mellyagaunte, "now I have founde you a false traytouras unto my lorde Arthur, for now I preve well hit was nat for nought that ye layde thes wounded knyghtis within the bondys of youre chambir. Therefore I [wille] calle[7] you of treson afore my lorde Kynge Arthure. And now I have proved you, madame, wyth a shamefull dede; and that they[8] bene all false, or som of them, I woll make hit good, for a wounded knyght thys nyght hath layne by you."

"That ys false," seyde the Quene, "that I woll report[9] me unto them." But whan the ten knyghtes harde Sir Mellyagaunteys wordys, than they spake all at onys and seyd, "Sir Mellyagaunte, thou falsely

6. This is the only point in Malory where the adulterous nature of Launcelot's relationship with Qwenyvere is materially confirmed. For a sense of Malory's moral conception of this relationship, cf. n. 3, p. 152; n. 9, p. 625; and n. 6, p. 638.
7. I.e., accuse.
8. I.e., the knights in the recesses.
9. I.e., appeal for confirmation.

belyest my lady the Quene, and that we woll make good uppon the,[1] any of us. Now chose whych thou lyste of us, whan we ar hole of the woundes thou gavyst us."

❡"Ye shall nat—away with youre proude langayge!—for here ye may all se that a wounded knyght thys nyght hath layne by the Quene." Than they all loked, and were sore ashamed whan they saw that bloode—and wyte you well, Sir Mellyagaunte was passyng glad that he had the Quene at suche avauntayge, for he demed by that to hyde hys owne treson. And so in thys rumour com in Sir Launcelot, and fownde them at a grete affray.

❡"What aray ys thys?"[2] seyde Sir Launcelot. Than Sir Mellyagaunce tolde hem what he had founde; and so he shewed hym the Quenys bed.

❡"Now truly," seyde Sir Launcelot, "ye ded nat youre parte, nor knyghtly, to touche a Quenys bed whyle hit was drawyn,[3] and she lyyng therein—and I dare say," seyde Syr Launcelot, "my lorde Kynge Arthur hymselff wolde nat have displayed[4] hir curtaynes, she beyng within her bed, onles that hit had pleased hym to have layne hym downe by her; and therefore, Sir Mellyagaunce, ye have done unworshypfully and shamefully to youreselff."

❡"Sir, I wote nat what ye meane," seyde Sir Mellyagaunce, "but well I am sure there hath one of hir hurte knyghtes layne with her thys nyght; and that woll I prove with myne hondys,[5] that she ys a traytoures unto my lorde Kynge Arthur." "Beware what ye do," seyde Sir Launcelot, "for and ye say so and wyll preve hit, hit woll be takyn at youre handys."[6] "My lorde, Sir Launcelot," seyde Sir Mellyagaunce, "I rede you beware what ye do; for thoughe ye ar never so good a knyght—as I wote well ye ar renowmed the beste knyght of the worlde—yet shulde ye be avysed[7] to do batayle in a wronge quarell, for God woll have a stroke in every batayle.

"As for that," seyde Sir Launcelot, "God ys to be drad. But as to that I say nay, playnly, that thys nyght there lay none of thes ten knyghtes wounded with my lady, Quene Gwenyver; and that woll I prove with myne hondys, that ye say untrewly in that.

❡"Now what sey ye?" seyde Sir Launcelot.

❡"Thus I say," seyde Sir Mellyagaunce: "here ys my glove[8] that she ys a traytoures unto my lorde Kynge Arthur, and that thys nyght one of the wounded knyghtes lay wyth her."

❡"Well, sir, and I resceyve youre glove," seyde Sir Launcelot. And anone they were sealed with their synattes, and delyverde unto the ten knyghtes.[9] "At what day shall we do batayle togydirs?" seyde

fol.441v

[7]

fol.442r

---

1. Thee.
2. What is going on here?
3. I.e., with its curtains drawn closed.
4. I.e., drawn open.
5. *Prove with myne hondys:* i.e., prove in trial by combat.
6. *Hit woll be takyn at youre handys:* i.e., that challenge will be taken up.
7. *Be avysed:* think carefully.
8. I.e., gauntlet held out in a challenge to combat. See n. 7, p. 390.
9. *They were sealed . . . the ten knyghtes:* they sealed a written agreement with their signet rings and delivered it to the ten knights as witnesses.

Sir Launcelot. "Thys day eyght dayes," seyde Sir Mellyagaunce, "in the fylde besydys Westemynster." "I am agreed," seyde Sir Launcelot.

¶"But now," seyde Sir Mellyagaunce, "sytthyn hit ys so that we muste nedys fyght togydirs, I pray you, as ye betthe a noble knyght, awayte me wyth no treson nother no vylany the meanewhyle, nother none for you."[1]

¶"So God me helpe," seyde Sir Launcelot, "ye shall ryght well wyte that I was never of no such condusions. For I reporte me to all knyghtes that ever have knowyn me, I fared never wyth no treson, nother I loved never the felyshyp of hym that fared with treson."

¶"Than lat us go unto dyner," seyde Sir Mellyagaunce, "and aftir dyner the Quene and ye may ryde all unto Westemynster." "I woll well," seyde Sir Launcelot. Than Sir Mellyagaunce seyde unto Sir Launcelot, "Sir, pleasyth you to se esturys of thys castell?" "With a good wyll," seyde Sir Launcelot. And than they wente togydir frome chambir to chambir; for Sir Launcelot drad no perellis—for ever a man of worshyp and of proues dredis but lytyll of perels, for they wene that every man be as they bene.

But ever he that faryth with treson puttyth oftyn a trew man in grete daungere. And so hit befelle uppon Sir Launcelot, that no perell dred: as he wente with Sir Mellyagaunce he trade on a trappe, and the burde rolled, and there Sir Launcelot felle downe more than ten fadom into a cave full off strawe. And than Sir Mellyagaunce departed and made no fare,[2] no more than he that wyste nat where he was. And whan Sir Launcelot was thus myssed, they mervayled where he was becomyn; and than the Quene and many of them demed that he was departed, as he was wonte to do, suddaynly— for Sir Mellyagaunce made suddaynly to put on syde[3] Sir Labaynes horse, that they myght all undirstonde that Sir Launcelot were departed suddaynly, so that hit passed on tyll afftir dyner.

And than Sir Labayne wolde nat stynte untyll that he had horse- lytters for the wounded knyghtes, that they myght be caryed in them; and so with the Quene, bothe ladyes and jantylwomen and [other] rode unto Westemynster. And there the knyghtes tolde how Sir Mellyagaunce had appeled the Quene of hyghe treson, and how Sir Launcelot resceyved the glove of hym, "and thys day eyght dayes they shall do batayle before you."

"Be my hede," seyde Kynge Arthure, "I am aferde Sir Mellyagaunce hath charged hymselff with a grete charge. But where is Sir Laun- celot?" seyde the Kynge. "Sir, we wote nat where he ys, but we deme he ys ryddyn to som adventure, as he ys offtyntymes wonte to do, for he had Sir Labaynes horse." "Lette hym be," seyde the Kynge, "for he woll be founden, but if he be be-trapped wyth som treson."

¶Thus leve we Sir Launcelot liyng within that cave in grete payne; and every day there cam a lady and brought hys mete and hys drynke—and wowed hym every day to have layne by her; and ever

Here Sir Launcelot felle into a depe pytte by the treson off Sir Melly- agaunce ten fadum

fol.442v

[8]

---

1. *Nother none for you:* i.e., nor no treason will be worked against you.
2. I.e., commotion.
3. *Put on syde:* i.e., hide away.

Sir Launcelot seyde her nay. Than seyde she, "Sir, ye ar nat wyse, for ye may never oute of this preson but if ye have my helpe. And also youre lady, Quene Gwenyver, shall be brente in youre defaute onles that ye be there at the day of batayle."

¶"God deffende," seyde Sir Launcelot, "that she shulde be brente in my defaught. And if hit be so," seyde Sir Launcelot, "that I may nat be there, hit shall be well undirstonde, bothe at the Kynge and the Quene and with all men of worship, that I am dede, syke, othir in preson; for all men that know me woll say for me that I am in som evyll case and I be nat that day there. And thus well I undir-stonde that there ys som good knyght, othir of my blood other som other that lovys me, that woll take my quarell in honde—and therefore," seyde Sir Launcelot, "wyte you well, ye shall nat feare⁴ me; and if there were no mo women in all thys londe but ye, yet shall nat I have ado with you."

¶"Than ar ye shamed," seyde the lady, "and destroyed for ever." "As for worldis shame, now Jesu deffende me; and as for my dis-tresse, hit ys welcom, whatsomever hit be that God sendys me." So she cam to hym agayne, the same day that the batayle shulde be, and seyde, "Sir Launcelot, bethynke you, for ye ar to hard-harted; and therefore, and ye wolde but onys kysse me, I shulde delyver you and your armoure, and the beste horse that was within Sir Mellyagaunce stable."

"As for to kysse you," seyde Sir Launcelot, "I may do that and lese no worshyp—and wyte you well, and I undirstood there were ony disworshyp for to kysse you, I wold nat do hit." And than he kyssed hir; and anone she gate hym up untyll hys armour, and whan he was armed she brought hym tylle a stable where stoode twelve good coursers, and bade hym to chose of the beste.

¶Than Sir Launcelot loked uppon a whyght courser and that lyked hym beste, and anone he commaunded hym to be sadeled with the beste sadyll of warre, and so hit was done. Than he gate hys owne speare in hys honde and hys swerde by hys syde; and than he commaunded the lady unto God, and sayde, "Lady, for thys dayes dede I shall do you servyse, if ever hit lye in my power."

¶Now leve we here Sir Launcelot, all that ever he myght walop,⁵ and speke we of Quene Gwenyver that was brought tyll a fyre to be brente; for Sir Mellyagaunce was sure, hym thought, that Sir Laun-celotte sholde nat be at that batayle, and therefore he ever cryed uppon Sir Arthur to do hym justyse, othir ellys brynge forth Sir Launcelot. Than was the Kynge and all the courte full sore abays-shed and shamed that the Quene shulde have be brente in the defaute of Sir Launcelot.

¶"My lorde Kynge Arthur," seyde Sir Lavayne, "ye may undir-stonde that hit ys nat well with my lorde Sir Launcelot, for and he were on lyve, so he be nat syke other in preson, wyte you well he wolde have bene here; for never harde ye that ever he fayled yet

---

4. I.e., frighten.
5. *All that ever he myght walop*: i.e., galloping as fast as he can.

hys parte for whom he sholde do batayle fore. And therefore,"
seyde Sir Lavayne," my lorde Kynge Arthur, I beseche you that ye
woll gyff me lycence to do batayle here thys day for my lorde and
mayster, and for to save my lady the Quene."

"Grauntemercy, jantill Sir Lavayne," seyde Kynge Arthur, "for I
dare say all that Sir Mellyagaunce puttith uppon my lady the Quene
ys wronge. For I have spokyn with all the ten wounded knyghtes,
and there ys nat one of them, and he were hole and able to do
batayle, but he wolde prove uppon Sir Mellyagaunce body [that it is
fals that he putteth uppon my Quene]." "And so shall I," seyde Sir
Lavayne, "in the deffence of my lorde Sir Launcelot, and ye woll gyff
me leve."

¶"And I gyff you leve," seyde Kynge Arthur, "and do youre
beste—for I dare well say there ys som treson done to Sir Launcelot."

¶Than was Sir Lavayn armed and horsed, and delyverly at the
lystes ende he rode to perfourme hys batayle—and ryght as the
herrowdis shuld cry, "Lechés les alere!"[6] ryght so com Sir Launcelot
dryvyng with all the myght of hys horse—and than Kynge Arthure
cryed, "Whoo!" and "Abyde!" And than was Sir Launcelot called
tofore Kynge Arthur, and there he tolde opynly tofor the Kynge all
how that Sir Mellyagaunce had served[7] hym firste and laste. And
whan the Kynge and Quene and all the lordis knew off the treson
of Sir Mellyagaunte, they were all ashamed on hys behalffe.

Than was the Quene sente fore, and sette by the Kynge in the
grete truste of hir champion. And than Sir Launcelot and Sir Mellyagaunte dressed them togydir wyth spearys as thunder; and there
Sir Launcelot bare hym quyte over hys horse croupe. And than Sir
Launcelot alyght and dressed hys shylde on hys shuldir and toke hys
swerde in hys honde; and so they dressed to eche other and smote
many grete strokis togydir.

And at the laste Sir Launcelot smote hym suche a buffet uppon
the helmet that he felle on the tone syde to the erthe; and than he
cryed uppon hym lowde and seyde, "Moste noble knyght Sir Launcelot, save my lyff, for I yelde me unto you, and I requyre you, as
ye be a knyght and felow of the Table Rounde, sle me nat, for I
yelde me as overcomyn—and whethir I shall lyve or dey, I put me
in the Kynges honde and youres."

¶Than Sir Launcelot wyst nat what to do, for he had lever than
all the good in the worlde that he myght be revenged uppon hym.
So Sir Launcelot loked uppon the Quene, gyff he myght aspye by
ony sygne or countenaunce what she wolde have done: and anone
the Quene wagged hir hede uppon Sir Launcelot, as ho[8] seyth "sle
hym." And full well knew Sir Launcelot by her sygnys that she wolde
have hym dede. Than Sir Launcelot bade hym, "Aryse, for shame,
and perfourme thys batayle with me to the utteraunce."[9] "Nay,"

fol.444r

6. *Lechés les alere:* let them go. French is employed as a heraldic custom.
7. I.e., treated.
8. I.e., she who.
9. I.e., death.

seyde Sir Mellyagaunce, "I woll never aryse untyll that ye take me as yolden and recreaunte."

¶"Well, I shall proffir you a large[1] proffir," seyde Sir Launcelot, "that ys for to say I shall unarme my hede and my lyffte quarter of my body, all that may be unarmed as for that quarter, and I woll lette bynde my lyfft honde behynde me there hit shall nat helpe me, and ryght so I shall do batayle with you."

¶Than Sir Mellyagaunce sterte up and seyde on hyght, "Take hede, my lorde Arthur, of thys proffir, for I woll take hit; and lette hym be dissarmed and bounden accordynge to hys proffir."

¶"What sey ye?" seyde Kynge Arthur unto Sir Launcelot. "Woll ye abyde by youre proffir?"

¶"Ye, my lorde," seyde Sir Launcelot, "for I woll never go fro that[2] I have onys sayde." Than the knyghtes parters of the fylde disarmed Sir Launcelot, firste hys hede and than hys lyffte arme and hys lyffte syde, and they bounde his lyffte arme to hys lyffte syde fast behynde hys bak, withoute shylde or onythynge—and anone they yode togydirs.

¶Wyte you well there was many a lady and many a knyght mer-   fol.444v
vayled [that] Sir Launcelot wolde jouparté hymselff in suche wyse. Than Sir Mellyagaunce com wyth swerde all on hyght, and Sir Launcelot shewed hym opynly hys bare hede and the bare lyffte syde. And whan he went to have smytten hym uppon the bare hede—

¶Than lyghtly he devoyded[3] the lyffte legge and the lyffte syde and put hys honde and hys swerde to that stroke, and so put hit on syde[4] wyth grete slyght; and than with grete force Sir Launcelot smote hym on the helmet such a buffett that the stroke carved the hed in two partyes. Than there was no more to do, but he was drawyn oute of the fylde. And at the grete instaunce of the knygh-tes of the Table Rounde, the Kynge suffird hym to be entered, and the mencion made uppon hym[5] who slewe hym and for what cause he was slayne. And than the Kynge and the Quene made more of Sir Launcelot, and more was he cherysshed than ever he was aforehande.

Than, as the Freynshe boke makith mencion,[6] there was a good   [10]
knyght in the londe of Hungré whos name was Sir Urré; and he was an adventurys knyght, and in all placis where he myght here of ony adventures dedis and of worshyp, there wold he be.

---

1. I.e., generous.
2. I.e., that which.
3. I.e., concealed.
4. *Put hit on syde:* i.e., deflected it.
5. I.e., his tomb.
6. Contrary to the appeal to a French authority, it would appear that this part of the text, through to p. 644, has no known direct source and is probably of Malory's own devising. The episode, which involves Launcelot's miraculous healing of Sir Urry, bestows upon Launcelot a measure of divine approbation reminiscent of the most successful knights of the Grail Quest—Galahad, Bors, and Percival—and this very soon after Malory's most revealing portrayal of the nature of Launcelot's relationship with Gwenyvere (cf. n. 6, p. 633). The episode also gives Malory the opportunity to present, on the eve, as it were, of the downfall of Arthur's world, an extensive and largely sequential list of Round Table knights that, supported with its occasional parenthetical elaborations and digressions (not to mention its rubrication, as presented in the Winchester MS), suggests a sense of cumulative achievement (cf. n. 9, p. 119). On Malory's listing of names, cf. n. 3, p. 216.

¶So hit happened in Spayne there was an erle, and hys sunnes name was called Sir Alpheus. And at a grete turnemente in Spayne thys Sir Urry, knyght of Hungré, and Sir Alpheus of Spayne encoun-tred togydirs for verry envy—and so aythir undirtoke other to the utteraunce. And by fortune thys Sir Urry slew Sir Alpheus, the erlys son of Spayne; but thys knyght that was slayne had yevyn Sir Urry, or ever he were slayne, seven grete woundis, three on the hede and three on hys body, an one uppon hys lyffte honde. And thys Sir Alpheus had a modir [whiche] was a grete sorseras; and she, for the despyte of hir sunnes deth, wrought by her suttyle craufftis that Sir Urry shulde never be hole, but ever his woundis shulde one tyme fester and another tyme blede, so that he shulde never be hole untyll the beste knyght of the worlde had serched hys woundis—and thus she made her avaunte, wherethorow hit was knowyn that this Sir Urry sholde never be hole.

Than hys[7] modir lete make an horse-lytter and put hym therein, with two palfreyes caryyng hym; and than she toke wyth hym hys syster, a full fayre damesell whos name was Fyleloly, and a payge wyth hem to kepe their horsis, and so they lad Sir Urry thorow many contreyes—for, as the Freynshe booke saythe, she lad hym so seven yere thorow all londis crystened[8] and never cowde fynde no knyght that myght ease her sunne.

So she cam unto Scotlonde and into the bondes of Inglonde; and by fortune she com [nyghe] the feste of Pentecoste untyll Kynge Arthurs courte, that at that tyme was holdyn at Carlehylle. And whan she cam there, she made hit to be opynly knowyn how that she was com into that londe for to hele her sonne.

¶Than Kynge Arthur lette calle that lady and aske her the cause why she brought that hurte knyght into that londe. "My moste noble kynge," seyde that lady, "wyte you well I brought hym hyddir to be heled of hys woundis, that of all thys seven yere myght never be hole." And thus she tolde the Kynge, and where he was wounded and with whom, and how hys[9] modir discoverde[1] hit in her pryde how she had wrought by enchauntemente that he sholde never be hole untyll the beste knyght of the worlde had serched hys woundis. "And so I have passed all the londis crystynde thorow to have hym healed, excepte thys londe, and gyff I fayle here in thys londe I woll never take more payne uppon me—and that ys grete pité, for he was a good knyght and of grete nobeles."

¶"What ys hys name?" seyde Kynge Arthure. "My good and gra-cious lorde," she seyde, "his name ys Sir Urré of the Mounte." "In good tyme," seyde the Kynge, "and sythyn ye ar com into thys londe, ye ar ryght wellcom; and wyte you welle, here shall youre son be healed and ever ony Crystyn man [may] heale hym. And for to gyff all othir men off worshyp a currayge,[2] I myselff woll asay to

fol.445r

fol.445v

---

7. I.e., Urry's.
8. I.e., Christian.
9. I.e., Alpheus's.
1. I.e., revealed.
2. A currayge: i.e., encourage.

handyll your sonne, and so shall all the kynges, dukis, and erlis
that ben here presente at thys tyme—nat presumyng uppon me
that I am so worthy to heale youre son be my dedis—but I woll
corrayge othir men of worshyp to do as I woll do."

And than the Kynge commaunded all the kynges, dukes, and
erlis, and all noble knyghtes of the Rounde Table that were there   5
that tyme presente, to com into the medow of Carlehyll. And so at
that tyme there were but an hondred an ten of the Rounde Table—
for forty knyghtes were that tyme away—and so here we muste
begynne at Kynge Arthur, as is kyndely[3] to begynne at hym that was
that tyme the moste man of worshyp crystynde. Than Kynge Arthur   10
loked uppon Sir Urré, and he thought he was a full lykly man whan   [11]
he was hole; and than the Kynge made to take hym downe of the
lyttar and leyde hym uppon the erth, and anone there was layde a
cussheon of golde that he shulde knele uppon.   15

And than Kynge Arthur sayde, "Fayre knyght, me rewyth of thy
hurte, and for to corrayge all other knyghtes I woll pray the[4] sofftely
to suffir me to handyll thy woundis." "My moste noble crystynd   fol.446r
kynge, do ye as ye lyste," seyde Sir Urré, "for I am at the mercy of
God and at youre commaundemente." So than Kynge Arthur softely   20
handeled hym; and than som of hys woundis renewed uppon ble-
dynge. Than Kynge Claryaunce of Northumbirlonde serched, and
hit wolde nat be; and than Sir Barraunte le Apres, that was called
the Kynge with the Hundred Knyghtes, he assayed and fayled.

¶So ded Kynge Uryence of the londe of Gore; so ded Kynge Ang-   25
wysh of Irelonde, and so ded Kynge Nentrys of Garloth; so ded
Kynge Carydos of Scotlonde; so ded the duke Sir Galahalt, the Haute
Prynce; so ded Sir Constantyne that was Kynge Cadors son of Cornwayle. So ded duke Chalaunce of Claraunce.

¶So ded the Erle of Ulbawys; so ded the Erle Lambayle; so ded   30
the Erle Arystanse. Than cam in Sir Gawayne wyth hys three sunnes,
Sir Gyngalyn, Sir Florence, and Sir Lovell (thes two were begotyn
uppon Sir Braundeles syster), and all they fayled. Than cam in Sir
Aggravayne, Sir Gaherys, and Sir Mordred, and the good knyght Sir
Gareth that was of verry knyghthod worth all the brethirn. So cam   35
in the knyghtes of Sir Launcelottis kyn (but Sir Launcelot was nat that
tyme in the courte, for he was that tyme uppon hys adventures),
than Sir Lyonell, Sir Ector de Marys, Sir Bors de Ganys, Sir Blamoure
de Ganys, Sir Bleoberys de Gaynys, Sir Gahalantyne, Sir Galyhodyn, Sir
Menaduke, Sir Vyllars the Valyaunte, Sir Hebes le Renowné—all thes   40
were of Sir Launcelottis kynne—and all they fayled. Than cam in Sir
Sagramour le Desyrus, Sir Dodynas le Saveage, Sir Dynadan, Sir Brewne
le Noyre (that Sir Kay named La Cote Male Taylé),[5] and Sir Kay le
Senesciall, Sir Kay d'Estraunges, Sir Mellyot de Logris, Sir Petipace of
Wynchylsé, Sir Galleron of Galway, Sir Melyon of the Mountayne,   45
Sir Cardoke, Sir Uwayne les Avoutres, and Sir Ozanna le Cure Hardy.   fol.446v
Than cam in Sir Ascamour, and Sir Grummor Grummorson, Sir Cros-

---

3. I.e., natural.
4. Thee.
5. See p. 280.

seleme, Sir **Severause le Brewse** (that was called a passynge stronge
knyght, for as the booke seyth, the chyff lady of the Lady off the
Lake fested Sir **Launcelot** and Sir **Severause le Brewse**, and whan she
had fested them both at sundry tymes, she prayde hem to gyff her
a done, and anone they graunted her; and than she prayde Sir
Severause that he wolde promyse her never to do batayle ayenste
Sir **Launcelot**, and in the same wyse she prayde Sir **Launcelot** never
to do batayle ayenste Sir **Severause**; and so aythir promysed her—
for the Freynshe booke sayth that Sir **Severause** had never corayge
nor grete luste to do batayle ayenste no man but if hit were ayenste
gyauntis, and ayenste dragons and wylde bestis).[6]

¶So leve we thys mater and speke we of them that at the Kynges
rekeyste were [there] at the hyghe feste, as knyghtes of the Rounde
Table, for to serche Sir **Urré**. And to thys entente the Kynge ded
hit: to wyte whych was the moste nobelyste knyght amonge them
all. Than cam in Sir **Agglovale**, Sir **Durnor** and Sir **Tor** (that was
begotyn uppon the cowardis[7] wyff—but he was begotyn afore **Aryes**
wedded her—and Kynge **Pellynore** begate them all: firste Sir **Tor**,
Sir **Agglovale**, Sir **Durnor**, Sir **Lamorak** the moste nobeleste knyght
one of them that ever was in Kynge **Arthurs** dayes as for a worldly
knyght, and Sir **Percivale** that was pyerles, excepte Sir **Galahad**, in
holy dedis—but they dyed in the Queste of the **Sangreall**). Than
cam in Sir **Gryfflet** le Fyze de Du, Sir **Lucan the Butlere**, Sir **Bedyvere**,
hys brothir, Sir **Braundeles**, Sir **Constantyne** (Sir **Cadors** son of Cornwayle that was Kynge aftir **Arthurs** dayes),[8] and Sir **Clegis**, Sir **Sadok**,
Sir **Dynas** le Senesciall de Cornwayle, Sir **Fergus**, Sir **Dryaunte**, Sir
Lambegus, Sir **Clarrus** off Cleremownte, Sir **Cloddrus**, Sir **Hectymere**,
Sir **Edwarde** of Carnarvan, Sir **Pryamus** (whych was crystynde by the
meanys of Sir **Trystram**, the noble knyght),[9] and thes three were
brethirn; Sir **Helayne le Blanke** (that was son unto Sir **Bors**, for he
begate hym uppon Kynge **Brandygorys** doughter), and Sir **Bryan
de Lystenoyse**; Sir **Gauter**, Sir **Raynolde**, Sir **Gyllymere** (were three
brethirn whych Sir **Launcelot** wan uppon a brydge, in Sir **Kayes**
armys);[1] Sir **Gwyarte le Petite**, Sir **Bellyngere le Bewse** (that was son
to the good knyght Sir **Alysaundir** le Orphelyn, that was slayne by
the treson of Kynge **Marke**[2]—

¶Also that traytoure kynge slew the noble knyght Sir **Trystram**,[3]
as he sate harpynge afore hys lady, La Beall Isode, with a tren-
chaunte glayve, for whos dethe was the moste waylynge of[4] ony
knyght that ever was in Kynge **Arthurs** dayes, for there was never
none so bewayled as was Sir **Trystram**—and Sir **Lamerok**—for they
were with treson slayne: Sir **Trystram** by Kynge **Marke**, and Sir **Lamorake** by Sir **Gawayne** and hys brethirn. And thys Sir **Bellynger**

fol.447r

6. The source of this story is not known.
7. I.e., Ayres the cowherd's (see pp. 63–65).
8. See p. 119.
9. See p. 147 (though Gawayne is the agent of conversion).
1. See pp. 168–69.
2. See p. 388.
3. What follows is the most substantial account of Trystram's death in Malory; cf. the
   accounts at pp. 388 and 654.
4. *Waylynge of*: i.e., wailing of grief for.

revenged the deth of hys fadir, Sir **Alysaundir**, and Sir **Trystram**, for he slewe Kynge **Marke**. And La Beall **Isode** dyed sownyng uppon the crosse[5] of Sir **Trystram**—whereof was grete pité. And all that were with Kynge **Marke** whych were of assente of the dethe of Sir **Trystram** were slayne—as Sir **Andred**, and many othir). Than cam Sir **Hebes**, Sir **Morganoure**, Sir **Sentrayle**, Sir **Suppynabiles**, Sir **Belyaunce** le Orgulus (that the good knyght Sir **Lamorak** wan in playne batayle),[6] Sir **Neroveus** and Sir **Plenoryus** (two good knyghtes that Sir **Launcelot** wanne),[7] Sir **Darras**, Sir **Harry** le Fyze Lake, Sir **Ermynde** (brother to Kyng **Hermaunce**, for whom Sir **Palomydes** faught at the Rede Cité with two brethirn);[8] and Sir **Selyses** of the Dolerous Towre, Sir **Edward** of Orkeney, Sir **Ironsyde** (that was called the noble Knyght of the Rede Laundis, that Sir **Gareth** wan for the love of Dame **Lyones**);[9] Sir **Arrok**, Sir **Degrevaunt**,[1] Sir **Degrave** Saunze Vylony (that faught wyth the gyaunte of the Blak Lowe);[2]

¶ Sir **Epinogrys** (that was the Kynges son of Northumbirlonde), Sir **Pelleas** (that loved the lady **Ettarde**—and he had dyed for her sake, had nat bene one of the ladyes of the lake whos name was Dame **Nynyve**; and she wedde Sir **Pelleas**, and she saved hym ever aftir, that he was never slayne by her dayes, and he was a full noble knyght),[3] and Sir **Lampell** of Cardyff (that was a grete lovear);[4] Sir **Playne de Fors**, Sir **Melyaus de Lyle**, Sir **Boarte le Cure Hardy** (that was Kynge **Arthurs** son), Sir **Madore de la Porte**, Sir **Collgrevaunce**, Sir **Hervyse** de la Foreyst Saveayge, Sir **Marrok** (the good knyght that was betrayed with his wyff, for he[5] made hym seven yere a warwolff);[6] Sir **Persaunt**, Sir **Pertolope**, hys brothir (that was called the Grene Knyght), and Sir **Perymones**, brother unto them bothe (whych was called the Rede Knyght, that Sir **Gareth** wanne whan he was called **Bewmaynes**).[7] All thes hondred knyghtes and ten serched Sir **Urryes** woundis by the commaundemente of Kynge **Arthur**.

"Mercy Jesu," seyde Kynge **Arthur**, "where ys Sir **Launcelot** du Lake, that he ys nat here at thys tyme?" And thus, as they stood and spake of many thyngis, there one aspyed Sir **Launcelot** that com

5. Although Caxton's edition supports *crosse* at this point, indicating Trystram's grave and implying Isode's death by grief, the reading of the Winchester MS is somewhat ambiguous, showing signs of scribal correction to or from *corsse* ("body"—although Winchester's spelling for the word has only one "s" in every other instance). The latter reading brings the account of Isode's death into line with that of Malory's usual Tristan source, the French prose *Tristan*, where Iseult is crushed in the arms of the dying Tristan.

6. See p. 279.

7. See pp. 286 and 290.

8. See p. 417 ff.

9. See p. 200.

1. Not otherwise mentioned in this text, this knight may owe his presence here to Malory's familiarity with the Middle English romance of *Sir Degrevaunt*.

2. The origin of this story is not clear, but Vinaver argues (O[3], p. 1613) that it may ultimately be based on an episode in the French *Livre d'Artus*.

3. See pp. 102–6.

4. Lamyell is not otherwise mentioned in Malory; the reference to him as a great lover may identify him with Sir Launfal, the knight with a fairy mistress, whose story is told in a number of Middle English romances (for editions of two of these, *Sir Launfal* and its source, *Sir Landevale*, see *MER*).

5. She.

6. The precise details of this story are not matched in known texts; but cf. *Bisclavret* (*The lay of the Werewolf*), written in the late 12th century by Marie de France.

7. See p. 190.

rydynge towarde them, and anone they tolde the Kynge. "Pees," seyde the Kynge, "lat no man say nothyng untyll he be com to us."

⁋So whan Sir Launcelot had aspyed Kynge Arthur, he descended downe frome hys horse and cam to the Kynge and salewed hym and them all. And anone as the damesell, Sir Urryes syster, saw Sir Launcelot, she romed to her brothir there as he lay in hys lyttar, and seyde, "Brothir, here ys com a knyght that my harte gyveth⁸ gretly unto."

"Fayre syster," seyde Sir Urré, "so doth my harte lyghte⁹ gretly ayenste hym,¹ and my harte gyvith me more unto hym than to all thes that hath serched me." Than seyde Kynge Arthur unto Sir Launcelot, "Sir, ye muste do as we have done," and tolde hym what they had done, and shewed hym them all that had serched hym. "Jesu defende me," seyde Sir Launcelot, "whyle so many noble kyngis and knyghtes have fayled, that I shulde presume uppon me to enchyve that all ye, my lordis, myght nat enchyve."

⁋"Ye shall nat chose," seyde Kynge Arthur, "for I commaunde you to do as we all have done." "My moste renowmed lorde,"seyde Sir Launcelot, "I know well I dare nat, nor may nat, disobey you; but, and I myght or durste, wyte you well I wolde nat take uppon me to towche that wounded knyght in that entent that I shulde passe all othir knyghtes—Jesu deffende me frome that shame."

⁋"Sir, ye take hit wronge," seyde Kynge Arthur, "for ye shall nat do hit for no presumpcion, but for to beare us felyshyp, insomuche as ye be a felow of the Rounde Table; and wyte you well," seyde Kynge Arthur, "and ye prevayle nat and heale hym, I dare sey there ys no knyght in thys londe that may hele hym—and therefore, I pray you, do as we have done." And than all the kyngis and knyghtes for the moste party prayed Sir Launcelot to serche hym.

And than the wounded knyght Sir Urré set hym up waykely, and seyde unto Sir Launcelot, "Now, curteyse knyght, I requyre the, for Goddis sake, heale my woundis—for methynkis ever sytthyn ye cam here my woundis grevyth me nat so muche as they ded." "A, my fayre lorde," seyde Sir Launcelot, "Jesu wolde that I myght helpe you. For I shame sore with myselff that I shulde be thus requyred; for never was I able in worthynes to do so hyghe a thynge."

⁋Than Sir Launcelot kneled downe by the wounded knyght, saiyng, "My lorde Arthure, I muste do youre commaundemente, whych ys sore ayenste my harte." And than he hylde up hys hondys and loked unto the este,² saiynge secretely unto hymselff,

"Now, Blyssed Fadir and Son and Holy Goste, I beseche The of Thy mercy that my symple worshyp and honesté be saved, and Thou Blyssed Trynyté, Thou mayste yeff me power to hele thys syke knyght by the grete vertu and grace of The—but, Good Lorde, never of³ myselff."

8. I.e., inclines.
9. I.e., lift up.
1. *Ayenste hym:* at his coming.
2. I.e., the direction of the Holy Land.
3. I.e., from.

And than Sir Launcelot prayde Sir Urré to lat hym se hys hede.
And than, devoutly knelyng, he ransaked[4] the three woundis, that
they bled a lytyll; and forthwithall the woundis fayre heled, and
semed as they had bene hole a seven yere.[5] And in lyke wyse he
serched hys body of other three woundis, and they healed in lyke
wyse. And than the laste of all he serched hys honde, and anone
hit fayre healed.

fol.448v

5

Than Kynge Arthur and all the kynges and knyghtes kneled
downe and gave thankynges and lovynge unto God and unto Hys
Blyssed Modir—and ever Sir Launcelote wepte, as he had bene a
chylde that had bene beatyn.

10

Than Kyng Arthure lat ravyshe[6] prystes and clarkes in the moste
devoutiste wyse to brynge in Sir Urré into Carlyle with syngyng and
lovyng to God. And whan thys was done, the Kynge lat clothe hym
in ryche maner; and than was there but feaw bettir made knyghtes
in all the courte, for he was passyngly well made and bygly. Than
Kynge Arthur asked Sir Urré how he felte hymselff. "A, my good
and gracious lorde, I felte myselffe never so lusty."

15

¶"Than woll ye juste and do ony armys?" seyd Kynge Arthur. "Sir,
and I had all[7] that longed unto justis, I wolde be sone redy." Than
Kynge Arthur made a party of a hondred knyghtes to be ayenste an
hondred; and so uppon the morn they justed for a dyamounde—
but there justed none of the daungerous knyghtes. And so, for to
shortyn this tale, Sir Urré and Sir Labayne justed beste that day, for
there was none of them but he overthrew and pulled down a thirty
knyghtes.

[13]

20

25

And than by assente of all the kynges and lordis, Sir Urré and
Sir Labayne were made knyghtes of the Table Rounde. And than
Sir Labayne keste hys love unto Dame Fyleloly, Sir Urré syster, and
than they were wedded with grete joy, and so Kynge Arthur gaff to
every[8] of them a barony of londis. And this Sir Urré wolde never
go frome Sir Launcelot, but he and Sir Labayne awayted evermore
uppon hym, and they were in all the courte accounted for good
knyghtes and full desyrous[9] in armys; and many noble dedis they
ded, for they wolde have no reste but ever sought uppon their
dedis. Thus they lyved in all that courte wyth grete nobeles and joy
longe tymes.

30

fol.449r
35

But every nyght and day Sir Aggravayne, Sir Gawaynes brother,
awayted[1] Quene Gwenyver and Sir Launcelot to put hem bothe to a
rebuke and a shame.

40

¶And so I leve here of this tale, and overlepe grete bookis of Sir
Launcelot, what grete adventures he ded whan he was called le Shyvalere de Charyot. For, as the Freynshe booke sayth, because of
dispyte that knyghtes and ladyes called hym "the Knyght that rode

---

4. I.e., searched.
5. A seven yere: for a period of seven years (i.e., for a long time).
6. Lat ravyshe: had fetched.
7. I.e., all the equipment.
8. I.e., each.
9. I.e., eager.
1. I.e., lay in wait upon.

in the Charyot," lyke as he were juged to the jubett, therefore in
the despite of all them that named hym so, he was caryed in a
charyotte a twelvemonethe; for but lytill aftir that he had slayne
Sir 𝕸ellyagaunte in the Quenys quarell, he never of a twelvemoneth
com on horsebak—and, as the Freynshe booke sayth, he ded that
twelvemoneth more than fourty batayles.

And bycause I have loste the very mater[2] of *Shevalere de Charyot*,
I departe frome the tale of Sir 𝕷aunrelot; and here I go unto the
Morte 𝕬rthur—and that caused Sir 𝕬ggrabayne.[3] And here on the
othir syde[4] folowyth the moste pyteuous tale of the *Morte 𝕬rthure
𝕾aunz 𝕲werdon, par le 𝕾hyvalere 𝕾ir 𝕿homas 𝕸alleorré*, knyght. 𝕵esu,
ayede ly pur voutre bone mercy.[5] 𝕬men.

---

2. *The very mater:* the full story. Here, as in the previous sentence, Malory seems to be
   acknowledging his inability to acquire or to have maintained possession of MSS containing
   the additional adventures of Lancelot that are known to exist in the French prose *Lancelot*,
   and with which his readership might already have been familiar; cf. his conclusion to the
   books of Sir Trystram, p. 495. This may, however, simply be a rhetorical stratagem to
   conceal a deliberate reduction.
3. I.e., and Sir Aggravayne instigated that death.
4. *Here on the othir syde:* on the other side of this page. Although in the Winchester MS the
   next section begins on the same page, Malory must have intended in his original MS to
   begin the next section on a fresh page—as indeed it does in Caxton's edition.
5. *the Morte Arthure . . . voutre bone mercy:* the *Death of Arthur without Recompense*, by the
   Knight Sir Thomas Malory. Jesus assist him of Your good mercy. *Morte Arthure* is a conventional title for the impending story, and so the French is retained; but the use of French
   for the rest of the colophon is likely intended to reflect the prestige and gravity of the
   narrative, as French remained the language of the noble elite in Malory's England, even
   if its use was progressively more artificial and irregular. The French also suggests Malory's
   direct access to an authoritative French source, though in fact Malory's main source for
   the next section is an English poem.

THE DETH OF ARTHUR†

[XX.1]

N May, whan every harte floryshyth and burgenyth—for, as the season ys lusty[1] to beholde and comfortable,[2] so man and woman rejoysyth and gladith of somer commynge with his freyshe floures, for wynter wyth hys rowghe wyndis and blastis causyth lusty men and women to cowre and to syt by fyres—

¶So thys season hit befelle in the moneth of May a grete angur and [unhap] that stynted nat tylle the floure of chyvalry of [alle] the worlde was destroyed and slayne. And all was longe uppon[3] two unhappy knyghtis whych were named Sir **Aggravayne** and Sir **Mordred**, that were brethirn unto Sir **Gawayne**; for thys Sir **Aggravayne** and Sir **Mordred** had ever a prevy hate unto the Quene, Dame **Gwenyver**, and to Sir **Launcelot**—and dayly and nyghtly they ever wacched uppon Sir **Launcelot**.

So hyt myssefortuned Sir **Gawayne** and all hys brethirne were in Kynge **Arthurs** chambir; and than Sir **Aggravayne** seyde thus opynly, and nat in no counceyle,[4] that manye knyghtis myght here, "I mervayle that we all be nat ashamed bothe to se and to know how Sir **Launcelot** lyeth dayly and nyghtly by the Quene—and all we know well that hit ys so—and hit ys shamefully suffird of us all that we shulde suffir so noble a kynge as Kynge Arthur ys to be shamed." Than spake Sir **Gawayne**, and seyde, "Brothir, Sir **Aggravayne**, I pray you and charge you, meve no such maters no more afore me; for wyte you well, I woll nat be of youre counceyle."

¶"So God me helpe," seyde Sir **Gaherys** and Sir **Gareth**, "we woll nat be knowyn of your dedis." "Than woll I!" seyde Sir **Mordred**. "I lyve[5] you well," seyde Sir **Gawayne**, "for ever unto all unhappynes, sir, ye woll graunte; and I wolde that ye leffte [alle this,] and make you nat so bysy—for I know," seyde Sir **Gawayne**, "what woll falle[6] of hit."

¶"Falle whatsumever falle may," seyde Sir **Aggravayne**, "I woll disclose hit to the Kynge."

¶"Nat be my counceyle," seyde Sir **Gawayne**, "for, and there aryse warre and wrake betwyxte Sir **Launcelot** and us, wyte you well, brothir, there woll many kynges and grete lordis holde with Sir **Launcelot**. Also, brothir Sir **Aggravayne**," seyde Sir **Gawayne**, "ye muste remembir how oftyntymes Sir **Launcelot** hath rescowed the Kynge

fol.449v

† The title is taken editorially from the colophon to the end of this section (p. 697, lines 37–38). Malory's principal sources for this section are the Middle English sMA and, to a lesser extent, the French *Mort le Roi Artu*; for illustrative selections, see pp. 740 and 747. In the Winchester MS this section begins after a two-line blank space on the same page as the colophon to the previous section; however, in that colophon Malory appears to indicate that he intended this section to begin on a fresh page (*on the othir syde*), which direction is followed here. The seven-line-high red initial (I), followed by a yellow-filled "N," and combined with the large rubricated textura font of the opening line, is reminiscent of the beginning of *The Weddyng of Kyng Arthur* (p. 62), which presents the appearance of a major textual division.
1. I.e., delightful.
2. I.e., comforting.
3. *Longe uppon*: owing to.
4. I.e., secrecy.
5. I.e., believe.
6. I.e., befall, become.

and the Quene; and the beste of us all had bene full colde at the
harte-roote[7] had nat Sir Launcelot bene bettir than we, and that
hathe he preved hymselff full ofte. And as for my parte," seyde Sir
Gawayne, "I woll never be ayenste Sir Launcelot for one dayes dede:
that was whan he rescowed me frome Kynge Carados of the Dolerous Towre and slew hym and saved my lyff.[8] Also, brother Sir
Aggravayne and Sir Mordred, in lyke wyse Sir Launcelot rescowed you
bothe, and three score and two, frome Sir Tarquyne.[9] And therefore,
brothir, methynkis suche noble dedis and kyndnes shulde be
remembirde." "Do ye as ye lyste," seyde Sir Aggravayne, "for I woll
layne hit no lenger."

¶So wyth thes wordis cam in Sir Arthur. "Now, brothir," seyde
Sir Gawayne, "stynte youre stryff." "That woll I nat," seyde Sir Aggravayne and Sir Mordred.

¶"Well, woll ye so?" seyde Sir Gawayne. "Than God spede you,
for I woll nat here of youre talis, nothir be of youre counceile."
"No more woll I," seyde Sir Gaherys. "Nother I," seyde Sir Gareth,
"for I shall never say evyll by that man that made me knyght." And
therewythall they three departed, makynge grete dole.

¶"Alas," seyde Sir Gawayne and Sir Gareth, "now ys thys realme
holy destroyed and myscheved, and the noble felyshyp of the
Rounde Table shall be disparbeled." So they departed; and than
Kynge Arthure asked them what noyse they made.

¶"My lorde," seyde Sir Aggravayne, "I shall telle you, for I may
kepe hit no lenger:

¶"Here ys I and my brothir Sir Mordred brake unto[1] my brothir
Sir Gawayne, Sir Gaherys and to Sir Gareth—for thys ys all, to make
hit shorte: we know all that Sir Launcelot holdith youre Quene, and
hath done longe; and we be your syster-sunnes, we may suffir hit
no lenger. And all we wote that ye shulde be above Sir Launcelot—
and ye ar the Kynge that made hym knyght—and therefore we woll
preve hit that he is a traytoure to youre person."

¶"Gyff hit be so," seyde the Kynge, "wyte you well, he ys non
othir. But I wolde be lothe to begyn such a thynge but I myght
have prevys of hit:

¶"For Sir Launcelot ys an hardy knyght, and all ye know that he
ys the beste knyght amonge us all; and but if he be takyn with the
dede[2] he woll fyght with hym that bryngith up the noyse, and I
know no knyght that ys able to macch hym. Therefore, and hit be
sothe as ye say, I wolde that he were takyn with the dede." For, as
the Freynshe booke seyth, the Kynge was full lothe that such a
noyse shulde be uppon Sir Launcelot and his Quene; for the Kynge
had a demyng of hit, but he wold nat here thereoff, for Sir Launcelot
had done so much for hym and for the Quene so many tymes that,
wyte you well, the Kynge loved hym passyngly well.

---

7. *Full colde at the harte-roote*: i.e., dead.
8. See p. 261.
9. See p. 162.
1. *Brake unto*: broken up with, at odds with.
2. *Takyn with the dede*: i.e., caught in the act.

¶"My lorde," seyde Sir Aggravayne, "ye shall ryde tomorne an-huntyng—and doute ye nat, Sir Launcelot woll nat go wyth you—and so whan hit drawith towarde nyght, ye may sende the Quene worde that ye woll ly oute all that nyght, and so may ye sende for your cookis. And than, uppon payne of deth, that nyght we shall take hym wyth the Quene, and we shall brynge hym unto you, quycke or dede."

¶"I woll well," seyde the Kynge. "Than I counceyle you to take with you sure³ felyshyp." "Sir," seyde Sir Aggravayne, "my brothir Sir Mordred and I woll take wyth us twelve knyghtes of the Rounde Table."

¶"Beware," seyde Kynge Arthure, "for I warne you, ye shall fynde hym wyght."⁴

¶"Lat us deale," seyde Sir Aggravayne and Sir Mordred. So on the morne Kynge Arthure rode an-huntyng, and sente worde to the Quene that he wolde be oute all that nyght. Than Sir Aggravayne and Sir Mordred gate to them twelve knyghtes and hyd hemselff in a chambir in the castell of Carlyle—and thes were their namys: Sir Collgrevaunce, Sir Mador de la Porte, Sir Gyngalyne, Sir Mellyot de Logris, Sir Petipace of Wynchylsé, Sir Galleron of Galoway, Sir Melyon de la Mountayne, Sir Ascomore, Sir Gromore Somer Joure,⁵ Sir Curse-salyne, Sir Florence, and Sir Lovell. So thes twelve knyghtes were with Sir Mordred and Sir Aggravayne—and all they were of Scotlonde,⁶ other ellis of Sir Gawaynes kynne, other well-wyllers to hys brothir. So whan the nyght cam, Sir Launcelot tolde Sir Bors how he wolde go that nyght and speke wyth the Quene.

¶"Sir," seyde Sir Bors, "ye shall nat go thys nyght be my counceyle." "Why?" seyde Sir Launcelot. "Sir, for I drede me ever of Sir Aggravayne, that waytith uppon you dayly to do you shame, and us all. And never gaff my harte ayenste no goynge that ever ye wente to the Quene so much as now, for I mystruste that the Kynge ys oute thys nyght frome the Quene [bycause peradventur he hath layne somme watche for yow and the Quene]—therefore I drede me sore of som treson." "Have ye no drede," seyde Sir Launcelot, "for I shall go and com agayne and make no taryynge."

¶"Sir," seyde Sir Bors, "that me repentis, for I drede me sore that youre goyng thys nyght shall wratth⁷ us all."

¶"Fayre neveawe," seyd Sir Launcelot, "I mervayle me much why ye say thus, sytthyn the Quene hath sente for me; and wyte you well, I woll nat be so much a cowarde, but she shall undirstonde I woll se her good grace." "God spede you well," seyde Sir Bors, "and sende you sounde and sauff aggayne." So Sir Launcelot departed and toke hys swerde undir hys arme—and so he walked in hys mantell,⁸ that noble knyght, and put hymselff in grete jou-parté. And so he past on tylle he cam to the Quenys chambir; and

5

10

fol.451r   15

20

25

30

35

40

[3]

fol.451v

---

3. I.e., strong.
4. I.e., strong.
5. On this character, follow the references in n. 1, p. xxviii.
6. I.e., supporters of Aggravayne, the son of King Lot of Orkney and Lothian, in Scotland.
7. I.e., injure.
8. I.e., not in his armor.

so lyghtly he was had into the chambir, for, as the Freynshe booke
seyth, the Quene and Sir Launcelot were togydirs.

And whether they were abed other at other maner of disportis,
me lyste nat thereof make no mencion, for love that tyme was nat
as love ys nowadayes;[9] but thus as they were togydir, there cam Sir
Aggravayne and Sir Mordred wyth twelve knyghtes with them of the
Rounde Table. And they seyde with grete cryyng and scaryng
voyce, "Thou traytoure, Sir Launcelot, now ar thou takyn!" And thus
they cryed wyth a lowde voyce, that all the courte myght hyre hit.
And thes fourtene knyghtes all were armed at all poyntis,[1] as they
shulde fyght in a batayle.

¶"Alas," seyde Quene Gwenyver, "now ar we myscheved bothe!"

¶"Madame," seyde Sir Launcelot, "ys there here ony armour
within you[2] that myght cover my body wythall? And if there be ony,
gyff hit me, and I shall sone stynte their malice, by the grace of
God."

¶"Now, truly," seyde the Quyne, "I have none armour nother
helme, shylde, swerde, nother speare—wherefore I dred me sore
oure longe love ys com to a myschyvus ende; for I here by their
noyse there be many noble knyghtes, and well I wote they be surely
armed, and ayenst them ye may make no resistence, wherefore ye
ar lykly to be slayne, and than shall I be brente:

¶"For and ye myght ascape them," seyde the Quene, "I wolde
nat doute but that ye wolde rescowe me in what daunger that I
ever stood in." "Alas," seyde Sir Launcelot, "in all my lyff thus was
I never bestad, that I shulde be thus shamefully slayne for lake of
myne armour." But ever Sir Aggravayne and Sir Mordred cryed,
"Traytour knyght! Com oute of the Quenys chambir, for wyte thou
well thou arte besette so that thou shalt nat ascape!"

¶"A, Jesu mercy!" seyd Sir Launcelot, "thys shamefull cry and
noyse I may nat suffir, for better were deth at onys than thus to
endure thys payne." Than he toke the Quene in hys armys and
kyssed her, and seyde, "Moste nobelest Crysten Quene, I besech
you, as ye have ben ever my speciall good lady, and I at all tymes
your poure knyght and trew unto my power, and as I never fayled
you in ryght nor in wronge sytthyn the firste day Kynge Arthur made
me knyght, that ye woll pray for my soule if that I be slayne. For
well I am assured that Sir Bors, my nevewe, and all the remenaunte
of my kynne, with Sir Labayne and Sir Urré, that they woll nat fayle
you to rescow you from the fyer. And therefore, myne owne lady,
recomforte youreselff, whatsomever com of me, that ye go with Sir
Bors, my nevew, and they all woll do you all the plesure that they
may, and ye shall lyve lyke a Quene upon my londis."

¶"Nay, Sir Launcelot, nay!" seyde the Quene. "Wyte thou well
that I woll never lyve longe aftir thy dayes.[3] But, and ye be slayne,

fol.452r

---

9. Cf. Malory's comments at p. 625 and his less diplomatic sources at this point at pp. 740
   and 750.
1. *At all poyntis:* in every respect, fully.
2. *Within you:* i.e., in your chamber.
3. *Wyte thou well . . . aftir thy dayes:* as D. S. Brewer observed in his edition of Malory, this
   is only one of two occasions when, apparently riven by the stress of the moment, Gwenyvere resorts to "familiar" second-person singular pronouns (*thee* forms rather than the

I woll take my dethe as mekely as ever ded marter take hys dethe for Jesu Crystes sake."

¶"Well, madame," seyde Sir Launcelot, "syth hit ys so that the day ys com that oure love muste departe, wyte you well I shall selle my lyff as dere as I may—and a thousandfolde," seyde Sir Launcelot, "I am more hevyar for you than for myselff— 5

¶"And now I had levir than to be lorde of all Crystendom that I had sure armour uppon me, that men myght speke of my dedys or ever I were slayne."

¶"Truly," seyde the Quene, "and hit myght please God, I wolde that they wolde take me and sle me and suffir you to ascape." "That 10 shall never be," seyde Sir Launcelot. "God deffende me frome such a shame! But, Jesu Cryste, be Thou my shylde and myne armoure." [4] And therewith Sir Launcelot wrapped hys mantel aboute hys arme fol.452v well and surely; and by than they had getyn a grete fourme oute 15 of the halle, and therewith[4] they all russhed at the dore.

"Now, fayre lordys," seyde Sir Launcelot, "leve youre noyse and youre russhynge, and I shall sette opyn thys dore, and than may ye do with me what hit lykith you." "Com of, than," seyde they all, "and do hit, for hit avaylyth the[5] nat to stryve ayenste us all; and 20 therefore lat us into thys chambir, and we shall save thy lyff— untyll thou com to Kynge Arthur."

Than Sir Launcelot unbarred the dore, and with hys lyffte honde he hylde hit opyn a lytyll, that but one man myght com in at onys. And so there cam strydyng a good knyght—a much man and a 25 large, and hys name was called Sir Collgrevaunce of Goore—and he wyth a swerde strake at Sir Launcelot myghtyly; and so he[6] put asyde the stroke, and gaff hym such a buffette upon the helmet that he felle grovelyng[7] dede wythin the chambir dore. Than Sir Launcelot with grete myght drew the knyght within the chambir dore; and 30 than Sir Launcelot, wyth helpe of the Quene and her ladyes, he was lyghtly armed in Collgrevaunce armoure—and ever stood Sir Aggravayne and Sir Mordred cryyng, "Traytoure knyght! Come forthe oute of the Quenys chambir!"

¶"Sires, leve youre noyse," seyde Sir Launcelot, "for wyte you well, 35 Sir Aggravayne, ye shall nat preson me thys nyght; and therefore, and ye do be my counceyle, go ye all frome thys chambir dore and make you no suche cryyng and such maner of sclaundir as ye do. For I promyse you be my knyghthode, and ye woll departe and make no more noyse, I shall as tomorne appyere afore you all and 40 before the Kynge; and than lat hit be sene whych of you all, other ellis ye all, that woll deprave[8] me of treson. And there shall I answere you, as a knyght shulde, that hydir I cam to the Quene fol.453r

---

more formal and "polite" plural *you* forms) when addressing Launcelot (see also p. 692, lines 3–19). Launcelot's usage is, by contrast, consistently formal.
4. I.e., using the bench as a battering ram.
5. Thee.
6. I.e., Launcelot.
7. I.e., facedown.
8. I.e., accuse.

for no maner of male engyne;[9] and that woll I preve and make hit good uppon you wyth my hondys."

¶"Fye upon the, traytour!" seyde Sir Aggravayne and Sir Mordred, "for we woll have the magré thyne hede, and sle the and[1] we lyste! For we let the wyte, we have the choyse of[2] Kynge Arthure to save the other sle the."

"A, sirres," seyde Sir Launcelot, "ys there none other grace with you? Than kepe youreselff!" And than Sir Launcelot sette all opyn the chambir dore, and myghtyly and knyghtly he strode in amonge them; and anone at the firste stroke he slew Sir Aggravayne—and anone aftir twelve of hys felowys; within a whyle he had layde them down colde to the erthe, for there was none of the twelve knyghtes myght stonde Sir Launcelot one buffet. And also he wounded Sir Mordred, and therewithall he fled with all hys myght. And than Sir Launcelot returned agayne unto the Quene and seyde, "Madame, now wyte you well, all oure trew love ys brought to an ende, for now wyll Kyng Arthur ever be my foo. And therefore, madam, and hit lyke you that I may have you with me, I shall save you frome all maner adventures daungers."

¶"Sir, that ys nat beste," seyde the Quene, "mesemyth, for now ye have don so much harme hit woll be beste that ye holde you styll with this. And if ye se that as tomorne they woll putte me unto dethe, than may ye rescowe me as ye thynke beste."

¶"I woll well," seyde Sir Launcelot, "for have ye no doute, whyle I am a man lyvyng I shall rescow you." And than he kyste her— and ayther of hem gaff othir a rynge—and so the Quene he leffte there and wente untyll hys lodgynge.

¶Whan Sir Bors saw Sir Launcelot, he was never so glad of hys homecomynge.

¶"Jesu mercy," seyde Sir Launcelot, "why be ye all armed? What meanyth thys?" "Sir," seyde Sir Bors, "aftir ye were departed frome us, we all that ben of youre blood and youre well-wyllars were so [dretched] that som of us lepe oute of oure beddis naked, and som in their dremys caught naked swerdys in their hondis. And therefore," seyde Sir Bors, "we demed there was som grete stryff on honde, and so we demed that ye were betrapped with som treson; and therefore we made us thus redy, what nede that ever ye were in."

¶"My fayre nevew," seyde Sir Launcelot unto Sir Bors, "now shall ye wyte all that thys nyght I was more harde bestad than ever I was dayes of my lyff; and thanked be God, I am myselff ascaped their daungere"—and so he tolde them all how and in what maner, as ye have harde toforehande. "And therefore, my felowys," seyde Sir Launcelot, "I pray you all that ye woll be of harte good, and helpe me in what nede that ever I stonde—for now ys warre comyn to us all."

¶"Sir," seyde Sir Bors, "all ys wellcom that God sendyth us, and as we have takyn much weale with you and much worshyp, we woll

---

9. *Male engyne:* ill purpose, evil scheme.
1. I.e., if.
2. I.e., on the authority of.

take the woo with you as we have takyn the weale." "And
therefore," they seyde, all the good knyghtes, "loke ye take no discomforte; for there ys no bondys of knyghtes undir hevyn but we
shall be able to greve them as much as they [may] us, and therefore discomforte nat youreselff by no maner. And we shall gadir   5
togyder all that we love and that lovyth us, and what that ye woll
have done shall be done—and therefore lat us take the wo and the
joy togydir."

"Grauntmercy," seyde Sir Launcelot, "of youre good comforte, for
in my grete distresse, fayre nevew, ye comforte me gretely. But   10
thus, my fayre nevew, I wolde that ye ded, in all haste that ye may,
[or] hit ys far dayes paste: that ye woll loke in their lodgynge that
ben lodged nyghe here aboute the Kynge, whych woll holde with
me and whych woll nat, for now I wolde know whych were my
frendis fro my fooes." "Sir," seyde Sir Bors, "I shall do my payne;   15
and or hit be seven of the clok, I shall wyte of such as ye have done
fore,[3] who that woll holde with you."

⁋Than Sir Bors called unto hym Sir Lyonel, Sir Ector de Marys,
Sir Blamour de Ganys, Sir Gahalantyne, Sir Galyhodyn, Sir Galyhud, Sir
Menaduke, Sir Vyllyers the Valyaunte, Syr Hebes le Renowné, Sir   20
Lavayne, Sir Urré of Hungry, Sir Neroveus, Sir Plenoryus (for thes two
were knyghtes that Sir Launcelot wan uppon a brydge, and therefore
they wolde never be ayenst hym), and Sir Harry le Fyz Lake, and
Sir Selyses of the Dolerous Towre, Sir Mellyas de Lyle, and Sir
Bellangere le Bewse (that was Sir Alysaundir le Orphelyne sone;   25
bycause hys modir was kyn unto Sir Launcelot, he hylde wyth hym).
So cam Sir Palomydes and Sir Saphir, hys brothir; Sir Clegis, Sir
Sadok, Sir Dynas and Sir Clarryus of Cleremount.

So thes two and twenty knyghtes drew hem togydirs, and by than
they were armed and on horsebak, they promysed Sir Launcelot to   30
do what he wolde. Than there felle to[4] them, what of Northe Walys
and of Cornwayle, for Sir Lamorakes sake and for Sir Trystrames
sake, to the numbir of a foure score knyghtes.

⁋Than spake Sir Launcelot: "Wyte you well, I have bene ever syns
I cam to thys courte well-wylled unto my lorde Arthur and unto my   35
lady Quene Gwenyver unto my power. And thys nyght, bycause my
lady the Quene sente for me to speke with her—I suppose hit was
made by treson, howbehit I dare largely excuse her person—
natwithstondynge I was there by [a forecaste][5] nerehonde slayne,
but as Jesu provyded for me."   40

And than that noble knyght Sir Launcelot tolde hem how he was
harde bestad in the Quenys chambir, and how and in what maner
he ascaped from them—"And therefore wyte you well, my fayre
lordis, I am sure there nys but warre unto me and to myne, and
for cause I have slayne thys nyght Sir Aggravayne, Sir Gawaynes bro-   45
thir, and at the leste twelve of hys felowis. And for thys cause now

fol.454r

fol.454v

---

3. *Done fore:* helped.
4. *Felle to:* i.e., fell in with.
5. I.e., design, scheme.

am I sure of mortall warre, for thes knyghtes were sente by Kynge
Arthur to betray me; and therefore the Kyng woll in thys hete[6] and
malice jouge the Quene unto brennyng, and that may nat I suffir
that she shulde be brente for my sake. For and I may be harde and
suffirde and so takyn,[7] I woll feyght for the Quene, that she ys a
trew lady untyll her lorde. But the Kynge, in hys hete, I drede woll
nat take me as I ought to be takyn."

"My lorde, Sir Launcelot," seyde Sir Bors, "be myne advyce, ye
shall take the woo wyth the weall; and sytthyn hit ys fallyn as hit
ys, I counceyle you to kepe youreselff—for and ye woll youreselffe,
there ys no felyshyp of knyghtes crystynde that shall do you
wronge. And also I woll counceyle you, my lorde, that my lady
Quene Gwenyver, and she be in ony distres, insomuch as she ys in
payne for youre sake, that ye knyghtly rescow her; for and ye ded
ony other wyse, all the worlde wolde speke you shame to the
worldis ende. Insomuch as ye were takyn with her, whether ye ded
ryght othir wronge, hit ys now youre parte to holde wyth the
Quene, that she be nat slayne and put to a myschevous deth—for
and she so dye, the shame shall be evermore youres."

¶"Now Jesu deffende me from shame," seyde Sir Launcelot, "and
kepe and save my lady the Quene from vylany and shamefull dethe,
and that she never be destroyed in my defaute:

¶"Wherefore, my fayre lordys, my kyn and my fryndis," seyde
Sir Launcelot, "what woll ye do?" And anone they seyde all with one
voyce, "We woll do as ye woll do." "Than I put thys case unto you,"
seyde Sir Launcelot: "that my lorde Kynge Arthure, by evyll counceile,
woll tomorn in hys hete put my lady the Quene unto the fyre and
there to be brente. Than, I pray you, counceile me what ys beste
for me to do." Than they seyde all at onys with one voice, "Sir, us
thynkis beste that ye knyghtly rescow the Quene. Insomuch as she
shall be brente, hit ys for youre sake—and hit ys to suppose, and
ye myght be handeled, ye shulde have the same dethe, othir ellis
a more shamefuller dethe. And, sir, we say all that ye have rescowed her frome her deth many tymys for other mennes quarels;
therefore us semyth hit ys more youre worshyp that ye rescow the
Quene from thys quarell, insomuch that she hath hit for your
sake."

Than Sir Launcelot stood stylle, and sayde, "My fayre lordis, wyte
you well I wolde be lothe to do that thynge that shulde dishonour
you or my bloode; and wyte you well I wolde be full lothe that my
lady the Quene shulde dye such a shamefull deth. But, and hit be
so that ye woll counceyle me to rescow her, I must do much harme
or I rescow her, and peradventure I shall there destroy som of my
beste fryndis. And if so be that I may wynne the Quene away,
where shall I kepe her?"

¶"Sir, that shall be the leste care of us all," seyde Sir Bors, "for
how ded the moste noble knyght Sir Trystram? By youre good wyll,

---

6. I.e., anger.
7. *Harde and suffirde and so takyn:* permitted to be heard and so understood.

kept nat he with hym La Beall Isode nere three yere in Joyous
Garde, the whych was done by youre althers avyce?[8] And that same
place ys youre owne, and in lyke wyse may ye do, and ye lyst, and
take the Quene knyghtly away with you if so be that the Kynge
woll jouge her to be brente. And in Joyous Garde may ye kepe her   5
longe inowe untyll the hete be paste of the Kynge, and than hit
may fortune you to brynge the Quene agayne to the Kynge with
grete worshyp; and peradventure ye shall have than thanke for
youre bryngyng home where othir[9] may happyn to have magré."[1]

¶ "That ys hard for to do," seyde Sir Launcelot, "for by Sir Trystram   fol.455v   10
I may have a warnynge: for whan by meanys of tretyse Sir Trystram
brought agayne La Beall Isode unto Kynge Marke from Joyous
Garde, loke ye now what felle on the ende, how shamefully that
false traytour Kyng Marke slew hym as he sate harpynge afore hys
lady, La Beall Isode. Wyth a grounden glayve he threste hym in   15
behynde, to the harte—whych grevyth sore me," seyde Sir Launcelot, "to speke of his dethe, for all the worlde may nat fynde such
another knyght."

"All thys ys trouthe," seyde Sir Bors, "but there ys one thyng
shall corrayge you and us all: ye know well that Kynge Arthur and   20
Kynge Marke were never lyke of conducions, for there was never
yet man that ever coude preve Kynge Arthure untrew of hys promyse." But so, to make shorte tale, they were all condiscended that,
for bettir othir for wars, if so were that the Quene were brought
on that morne to the fyre, shortely they all wolde rescow her. And   25
so, by the advyce of Sir Launcelot they put hem all in a wood as
nyghe Carlyle as they myght, and there they abode stylle to wyte
what the Kynge wold do.

¶ Now turne we agayne, that whan Sir Mordred was ascaped   [7]
frome Sir Launcelot, he gate hys horse and cam to Kynge Arthur sore   30
wounded and all for-bled; and there he tolde the Kynge all how hit
was, and how they were all slayne save hymselff alone. "A, Jesu,
mercy! how may thys be?" seyde the Kynge. "Toke ye hym in the
Quenys chambir?"

¶ "Yee, so God me helpe," seyde Sir Mordred, "there we founde   35
hym unarmed, and anone he slew Sir Collgrevaunce and armed hym
in hys armour." And so he tolde the Kynge frome the begynnyng
to the endynge. "Jesu mercy," seyde the Kynge, "he ys a mervaylous
knyght of proues. And alas," seyde the Kynge, "me sore repentith
that ever Sir Launcelot sholde be ayenste me, for now I am sure the   fol.456r   40
noble felyshyp of the Rounde Table ys brokyn for ever, for wyth
hym woll many a noble knyght holde. And now hit ys fallen so,"
seyde the Kynge, "that I may nat with my worshyp[2] but my Quene
muste suffir dethe—and was sore amoved.

¶ So than there was made grete ordynaunce in thys ire, and the   45
Quene muste nedis be jouged to the deth; and the law was such

---

8. *Youre althers avyce:* the advice of all of you.
9. I.e., others.
1. *Have magré:* receive (the King's) ill-will.
2. *I may nat with my worshyp:* I can honorably do nothing else.

in tho dayes that whatsomever they were, of what astate or degré, if they were founden gylty of treson there shuld be none other remedy but deth, and othir the menour other the takynge wyth the dede[3] shulde be causer[4] of their hasty jougement. And ryght so was hit ordayned for Quene Gwenyver: bycause Sir Mordred was ascaped sore wounded, and the dethe of thirtene knyghtes of the Rounde Table, thes previs and experyenses caused Kynge Arthure to commaunde the Quene to the fyre and there to be brente.

¶Than spake Sir Gawayn and seyde, "My lorde Arthure, I wolde counceyle you nat to be over hasty, but that ye wolde put hit in respite, thys jougemente of my lady the Quene, for many causis. One ys thys: thoughe hyt were so that Sir Launcelot were founde in the Quenys chambir, yet hit myght be so that he cam thydir for none evyll. For ye know, my lorde," seyde Sir Gawayne, "that my lady the Quene hath oftyntymes ben gretely beholdyn unto Sir Launcelot, more than to ony othir knyght; for oftyntymes he hath saved her lyff and done batayle for her whan all the courte refused the Quene. And peradventure she sente for hym for goodnes and for none evyll, to rewarde hym for his good dedys that he had done to her in tymes past. And peraventure my lady the Quene sente for hym to that entente, that Sir Launcelot sholde a com prevaly to her, wenyng that hyt had be beste in eschewyng of slaundir; for oftyntymys we do many thynges that we wene for the beste be, and yet peradventure hit turnyth to the warste—for I dare sey," seyde Sir Gawayne, "my lady, your Quene, ys to you both good and trew. And as for Sir Launcelot, I dare say he woll make hit good uppon ony knyght lyvyng that woll put uppon hym vylany or shame, and in lyke wyse he woll make good for my lady the Quene."

¶"That I beleve well," seyde Kynge Arthur, "but I woll nat that way worke with[5] Sir Launcelot, for he trustyth so much uppon hys hondis and hys myght that he doutyth[6] no man; and therefore for my Quene he shall nevermore fyght, for she shall have the law— and if I may gete Sir Launcelot, wyte you well he shall have as shamefull a dethe." "Jesu defende me," seyde Sir Gawayne, "that I never se hit nor know hit."

¶"Why say you so?" seyde Kynge Arthur. "For, perdé, ye have no cause to love hym, for thys nyght last past he slew youre brothir Sir Aggravayne, a full good knyght! And allmoste he had slayne youre othir brother, Sir Mordred; and also there he slew thirtene noble knyghtes—and also remembir you, Sir Gawayne, he slew two sunnes of youres, Sir Florens and Sir Lovell."

"My lorde," seyde Sir Gawayne, "of all thys I have a knowleche, whych of her dethis sore repentis me. But insomuch as I gaff hem warnynge and tolde my brothir and my sonnes aforehonde what wolde falle on the ende, and insomuche as they wolde nat do be

fol.456v

---

3. *Othir the menour other the takynge wyth the dede:* either being caught in overwhelmingly incriminating circumstances or being caught in the act.
4. I.e., grounds.
5. *Worke with:* i.e., behave toward.
6. I.e., fears.

my counceyle, I woll nat meddyll me thereoff, nor revenge me
nothynge of their dethys; for I tolde them there was no boote to
stryve with Sir Launcelot. Howbehit, I am sory of the deth of my
brothir and of my two sunnes; but they ar the causars of their owne
dethe, for oftyntymes I warned my brothir Sir Aggrabayne, and I   fol.457r   5
tolde hym of the perellis."

    ¶Than seyde Kynge Arthur unto Sir Gawayne, "Make you redy, I   [8]
pray you, in youre beste armour, wyth youre brethirn, Sir Gaherys
and Sir Gareth, to brynge my quene to the fyre and there to have
her jougement."   10

    ¶"Nay, my moste noble Kynge," seyde Sir Gawayne, "that woll I
never do. For wyte you well I woll never be in that place where so
noble a quene as ys my lady Dame Gwenyver shall take such a shamefull ende—

    ¶"For wyte you well," seyde Sir Gawayne, "my harte woll nat serve   15
me for to se her dye; and hit shall never be seyde that ever I was
of youre counceyle for her deth." "Than," seyde the Kynge unto
Sir Gawayne, "suffir your brethirn Sir Gaherys and Sir Gareth to be
there."

    ¶"My lorde," seyde Sir Gawayne, "wyte you well they wyll be lothe   20
to be there present bycause of many adventures that ys lyke to
falle; but they ar yonge and full unable to say you nay." Than spake
Sir Gaherys and the good knyght Sir Gareth unto Kynge Arthur: "Sir,
ye may well commaunde us to be there, but wyte you well hit shall
be sore ayenste oure wyll. But, and we be there by youre strayte   25
commaundement, ye shall playnly holde us there excused: we woll
be there in pesyble wyse, and beare none harneyse of warre upon
us." "In the name of God," seyde the Kynge, "than make you redy,
for she shall have sone her jugemente."

    ¶"Alas," seyde Sir Gawayne, "that ever I shulde endure to se this   30
wofull day." So Sir Gawayne turned hym and wepte hartely, and so
he wente into hys chambir. And so the Quene was lad furthe withoute Carlyle, and anone she was dispoyled into her smokke. And
than her gostely fadir[7] was brought to her to be shryven of her
myssededis. Than was there wepyng and waylynge and wryngyng   35
of hondis of many lordys and ladyes; but there were but feaw in   fol.457v
comparison that wolde beare ony armoure for to strengthe the
dethe of the Quene.

    Than was there one that Sir Launcelot had sente unto that place,
whych wente to aspye what tyme the Quene shulde go unto her   40
deth; and anone as he saw the Quene dispoyled into her smok and
shryvyn, than he gaff Sir Launcelot warnynge anone. Than was
there but spurryng and pluckyng up of horse, and ryght so they
cam unto the fyre; and who that stoode ayenste them, there were
they slayne. [There myghte none withstande Sir Launcelot; so all   45
that bare armes and withstoode hem, there were they slayne], full
many a noble knyght: for there was slayne Sir Bellyas le Orgulus,
Sir Segwarydes, Sir Gryfflet, Sir Braundyles, Sir Agglovale, Sir Tor; Sir

---

7. *Gostely fadir*: priest, confessor.

Gauter, Sir Gyllymer, Sir Raynold, three brethirn; and Sir Damas, Sir Priamus, Sir Kay le Straunge, Sir Dryaunt, Sir Lambegus, Sir Hermynde; Sir Pertolyp, Sir Perymones, two brethern whych were called the Grene Knyght and the Rede Knyght.

And so in thys russhynge and hurlynge, as Sir Launcelot thrange here and there, hit mysfortuned hym to sle Sir Gaherys and Sir Gareth, the noble knyght, for they were unarmed[8] and unwares. As the Freynshe booke sayth, Sir Launcelot smote Sir Gaherys and Sir Gareth uppon the brayne-pannes, wherethorow that they were slayne in the felde—howbehit, in very trouth, Sir Launcelot saw them [nat]. And so were they founde dede amonge the thyckyste of the prees. Than Sir Launcelot, whan he had thus done, and slayne and put to flyght all that wolde wythstonde hym, than he rode streyt unto Quene Gwenyver and made [to be] caste a kurdyll and a gown uppon her, and than he made her to be sette behynde hym and prayde her to be of good chere. Now wyte you well the Quene was glad that she was at that tyme ascaped frome the deth.

And than she thanked God, and Sir Launcelot. And so he rode hys way wyth the Quene, as the Freynshe booke seyth, unto Joyous Garde, and there he kepte her as a noble knyght shulde. And many grete lordis and many good knyghtes were sente hym, and many full noble knyghtes drew unto hym. Whan they harde that Kynge Arthure and Sir Launcelot were at debate, many knyghtes were glad, and many were sory of their debate.

¶Now turne we agayne unto Kynge Arthure, that whan hit was tolde hym how and in what maner the Quene was taken away frome the fyre, and whan he harde of the deth of his noble knyghtes, and in especiall Sir Gaherys and Sir Gareth, than he sowned for verry pure sorow. And whan he awooke of hys swoughe, than he sayde, "Alas, that ever I bare crowne uppon my hede, for now have I loste the fayryst felyshyp of noble knyghtes that ever hylde Crystyn kynge togydirs. Alas, my good knyghtes be slayne and gone away fro me, that now within thys two dayes I have loste nygh fourty knyghtes—and also the noble felyshyp of Sir Launcelot and hys blood, for now I may nevermore holde hem togydirs with my worshyp. Now, alas, that ever thys warre began!

¶"Now, fayre felowis," seyde the Kynge, "I charge you that no man telle Sir Gawayne of the deth of hys two brethirne, for I am sure," seyde the Kynge, "whan he hyryth telle that Sir Gareth ys dede, he wyll go nygh oute of hys mynde. Merci Jesu!" seyde the Kynge, "why slew he Sir Gaherys and Sir Gareth? for I dare sey, as for Sir Gareth, he loved Sir Launcelot of all men erthly." "That ys trouth," seyde som knyghtes, "but they were slayne in the hurlynge, as Sir Launcelot thrange in the thyckyst of the prees; and as they were unarmed, he smote them and wyst nat whom that he smote— and so unhappely they were slayne."

¶"Well," seyde Arthure, "the deth of them woll cause the grettist mortall warre that ever was, for I am sure that whan Sir Gawayne

5

10

15

fol.458r

20

[9]   25

30

35

40

45

fol.458v

---

8. I.e., not just without arms, but without their heraldic coats of arms which, would identify them more readily in the commotion.

knowyth hereoff that Sir Gareth ys slayne, I shall never have reste of hym tyll I have destroyed Sir Launcelottys kynne and hymselff bothe—othir ellis he to destroy me. And therefore," seyde the Kynge, "wyte you well, my harte was never so hevy as hit ys now. And much more I am soryar for my good knyghtes losse than for the losse of my fayre quene; for quenys I myght have inow, but such a felyship of good knyghtes shall never be togydirs in no company. And now I dare sey," seyde Kynge Arthur, "there was never Crystyn kynge that ever hylde such a felyshyp togydyrs. And alas, that ever Sir Launcelot and I shulde be at debate! A, Aggravayne, Aggravayne," seyde the Kynge, "Jesu forgyff hit thy soule, for thyne evyll wyll that thou haddist, and Sir Mordred thy brothir, unto Sir Launcelot hath caused all this sorow." And ever amonge thes complayntes the Kynge wepte and sowned.

Than cam there one to Sir Gawayne and tolde hym how the Quene was lad away with Sir Launcelot, and nygh a foure and twenty knyghtes slayne. "A, Jesu, save me my two brethirn," seyde Sir Gawayne. "For full well wyst I," sayde Sir Gawayne, "that Sir Launcelot wolde rescow her, othir ellis he wolde dye in that fylde; and to say the trouth, he were nat of worshyp but if he had rescowed the Quene, insomuch as she shulde have be brente for his sake. And as in that," seyde Sir Gawayne, "he hath done but knyghtly, and as I wolde have done myselff and I had stonde[9] in lyke case. But where ar my brethirn?" seyde Sir Gawayne, "I mervayle that I se nat of them." Than seyde that man, "Truly, Sir Gaherys and Sir Gareth be slayne."

❡"Jesu deffende!" seyd Sir Gawayne. "For all thys worlde I wolde nat that they were slayne—and in especiall my good brothir Sir Gareth." "Sir," seyde the man, "he ys slayne, and that ys grete pité."

❡"Who slew hym?" seyde Sir Gawayne. "Sir Launcelot," seyde the man, "slew hem both."

❡"That may I nat beleve," seyde Sir Gawayne, "that ever he slew my good brother Sir Gareth, for I dare say my brothir loved hym bettir than me and all hys brethirn and the Kynge bothe. Also I dare say, an Sir Launcelot had desyred my brothir Sir Gareth with hym, he wolde have ben with hym ayenste the Kynge and us all. And therefore I may never belyeve that Sir Launcelot slew my brethern."

❡"Veryly, sir," seyde the man, "hit ys noysed that he slew hym."

❡"Alas," seyde Sir Gawayne, "now ys my joy gone!" And than he felle downe and sowned, and longe he lay there as he had ben dede. And whan he arose oute of hys swoughe he cryed oute sorowfully and seyde, "Alas!" And forthwith he ran unto the Kynge, criyng and wepyng, and seyde, "A, myne uncle Kynge Arthur, my good brothir Sir Gareth ys slayne, and so ys my brothir Sir Gaherys, whych were two noble knyghtes."

Than the Kynge wepte and he bothe, and so they felle on sownynge. And whan they were revyved, than spake Sir Gawayne and

9. I.e., stood.

seyde, "Sir, I woll goo and se my brother Sir 𝕲aret𝕳." "Sir, ye may
nat se hym," seyde the Kynge, "for I caused hym to be entered and
Sir 𝕲a𝕳ery𝕤 bothe, for I well undirstood that ye wolde make overmuche sorow, and the syght of Sir 𝕲aret𝕳 shulde have caused youre
double sorow." "Alas, my lorde," seyde Sir 𝕲awayne, "how slew he
my brothir Sir 𝕲aret𝕳? I pray you telle me." "Truly," seyde the
Kynge, "I shall tell you as hit hath bene tolde me: Sir 𝕷auncelot slew
hym and Sir 𝕲a𝕳ery𝕤 both."

"Alas," seyde Sir 𝕲awayne, "they beare none armys ayenst hym,
neyther of them bothe?" "I wote nat how hit was," seyde the Kynge,
"but as hit ys sayde, Sir 𝕷auncelot slew them in the thyk prees and
knew them nat—and therefore lat us shape a remedy for to revenge
their dethys."

❡"My kynge, my lorde, and myne uncle," seyde Sir 𝕲awayne,
"wyte you well, now I shall make you a promyse whych I shall holde
be my knyghthode, that frome thys day forewarde I shall never
fayle[1] Sir 𝕷auncelot untyll that one of us have slayne that othir. And
therefore I requyre[2] you, my lorde and kynge, dresse you unto the
warres, for wyte you well, I woll be revenged uppon Sir 𝕷auncelot;
and therefore, as ye woll have my servyse and my love, now haste
you thereto and assay[3] youre frendis. For I promyse unto God,"
seyde Sir 𝕲awayn, "for the deth of my brothir, Sir 𝕲aret𝕳, I shall
seke Sir 𝕷auncelot thorowoute seven kynges realmys, but I shall sle
hym, other ellis he shall sle me."

"Sir, ye shall nat nede to seke hym so far," seyde the Kynge, "for
as I here say, Sir 𝕷auncelot woll abyde me and us all wythin the
castell of Joyous Garde—and muche peple drawyth unto hym, as
I here say." "That may I ryght well belyve," seyde Sir 𝕲awayne. "But
my lorde," he sayde, "assay your fryndis and I woll assay myne."
"Hit shall be done," seyde the Kyng, "and as I suppose I shall be
bygge inowghe to dryve hym oute of the bygyst toure of hys castell."

So than the Kynge sente lettirs and wryttis thorowoute all
Inglonde, both the lengthe and the brede, for to assomon all hys
knyghtes. And so unto Kynge 𝕬rt𝕳ure drew many knyghtes, deukes,
and erlis, that he had a grete oste; and whan they were assembeled,
the Kynge enfourmed hem how Sir 𝕷auncelot had beraffte hym hys
Quene. Than the Kynge and all hys oste made hem redy to ley
syege aboute Sir 𝕷auncelot, where he lay within Joyus Garde.

And anone Sir 𝕷auncelot harde thereof, and purveyde hym off
many good knyghtes; [for with hym helde many knyghtes,] som for
hys owne sake and som for the Quenys sake. Thus they were on
bothe partyes well furnysshed and garnysshed of all maner of
thynge that longed unto the warre.

❡But Kynge 𝕬rt𝕳ur𝕤 oste was so grete that Sir 𝕷auncelotti𝕤 oste
wolde nat abyde hym in the fylde; for he was full lothe to do batayle
ayenste the Kynge. But Sir 𝕷auncelot drew hym unto hys stronge

fol.459v

fol.460r

---

1. I.e., fail to strive against.
2. On the feudal obligations of an overlord, such as Arthur, to his vassals, see n. 6, p. 9.
3. I.e., test the loyalty of.

castell with all maner of vytayle plenté, and as many noble men as he myght suffyse within the towne and the castell. Than cam Kynge Arthure with Sir Gawayne wyth a grete oste and leyde syge all aboute Joyus Garde, both the towne and the castell. And there they made stronge warre on bothe partyes; but in no wyse Sir Launcelot wolde ryde oute [nor go out] of the castell of longe tyme, and nother he wold nat suffir none of hys good knyghtes to issew oute, nother of the towne nother of the castell, untyll fiftene wykes were paste.

So hit felle upon a day [in hervest tyme] that Sir Launcelot loked over the wallys and spake on hyght unto Kynge Arthure and to Sir Gawayne: "My lordis bothe, wyte you well all thys ys in vayne that ye make at thys syge, for here wynne ye no worshyp, but magré and dishonoure—for and hit lyste me to com myselff oute, and my good knyghtes, I shulde full sone make an ende of thys warre."

"Com forth," seyde Kynge Arthur unto Sir Launcelot, "and thou darste, and I promyse the I shall mete the in myddis of thys fylde." "God deffende me," seyde Sir Launcelot, "that ever I shulde encounter wyth the moste noble kynge that made me knyght." "Now fye uppon thy fayre langayge!" seyde the Kynge, "for wyte thou well and truste hit, I am thy mortall foo and ever woll to my deth day; for thou haste slayne my good knyghtes and full noble men of my blood, that shall I never recover agayne. Also thou haste layne be my quene and holdyn her many wynters, and sytthyn, lyke a traytoure, taken her away fro me by fors."

⁋"My moste noble lorde and kynge," seyde Sir Launcelot, "ye may sey what ye woll, for ye wote well wyth youreselff I woll nat stryve. But there as ye say that I have slayne youre good knyghtes, I wote well that I have done so, and that me sore repentith; but I was forced to do batayle with hem in savyng of my lyff, othir ellis I muste have suffirde hem to have slayne me. And as for my lady Quene Gwenyver, excepte youre person of your hyghnes and my lorde Sir Gawayne, there nys no knyght undir hevyn that dare make hit good uppon me[4] that ever I was traytour unto youre person. And where hit please you to say that I have holdyn my lady, youre Quene, yerys and wynters, unto that I shall ever make a large answere,[5] and prove hit uppon ony knyght that beryth the lyff, excepte your person and Sir Gawayne, that my lady Quene Gwenyver ys as trew a lady unto youre person as ys ony lady lyvynge unto her lorde—and that woll I make good with my hondis. Howbehyt, hit hath lyked her good grace to have me in favoure and cherysh me more than ony other knyght; and unto my power agayne I have deserved her love, for oftyntymes, my lorde, ye have concented that she sholde have be brente and destroyed in youre hete, and than hit fortuned me to do batayle for her, and or I departed from her adversary they confessed there untrouthe, and she full worsshypfully excused. And at suche tymes, my lorde Arthur," seyde Sir Laun-

[11]

5

10

fol.460v

15

20

25

30

35

40

45

---

4. *Make hit good uppon me*: i.e., put to trial by combat.
5. An answer consisting of an open challenge.

celot, "ye loved me and thanked me whan I saved your Quene frome the fyre, and than ye promysed me for ever to be my good lorde; and now methynkith ye rewarde me evyll for my good servyse. And, my lorde, mesemyth I had loste a grete parte of my worshyp in my knyghthod and I had suffird my lady, youre quene, to have ben brente, insomuche as she shulde have bene brente for my sake; for sytthyn I have done batayles for youre Quene in other quarels than in myne owne quarell, mesemyth now I had more ryght to do batayle for her in her ryght quarell. And therefore, my good and gracious lorde," seyde Sir Launcelot, "take your quene unto youre good grace, for she ys both tru and good."

¶"Fy on the, false recreayed knyght!" seyde Sir Gawayn, "for I lat the wyte, my lorde, myne uncle Kynge Arthur, shall have hys Quene and the[6] bothe magré thy vysayge,[7] and sle you bothe and save you whether hit please hym."

¶"Hit may well be," seyde Sir Launcelot, "but wyte thou well, my lorde Sir Gawayne, and me lyste to com oute of thys castell ye shuld wyn me and the Quene more harder than ever ye wan a stronge batayle."

¶"Now, fy on thy proude wordis!" seyde Sir Gawayne. "As for my lady the Quene, wyte thou well I woll never say her shame. But thou, false and recrayde knyght," seyde Sir Gawayne, "what cause haddist thou to sle my good brother Sir Gareth that loved the more than me and all my kynne? And alas, thou madist hym knyght thyne owne hondis! Why slewest thou hym that loved the so well?"

¶"For to excuse me," seyde Sir Launcelot, "hit boteneth me nat; but by Jesu, and by the feyth that I owghe unto the hyghe order of knyghthode, I wolde with as good a wyll have slayne my nevew, Sir Bors de Ganys, [at that tyme]—and alas, that ever I was so unhappy," seyde Sir Launcelot, "that I had nat seyne Sir Gareth and Sir Gaherys."

"Thou lyest, recrayed knyght," seyde Sir Gawayne. "Thou slewyste hem in the despite of me; and therefore wyte thou well, Sir Launcelot, I shall make warre uppon the, and all the whyle that I may lyve be thyne enemy." "That me repentes," seyde Sir Launcelot, "for well I undirstonde hit boteneth me nat to seke none accordemente whyle ye, Sir Gawayne, ar so myschevously sett. And if ye were nat, I wolde nat doute to have the good grace of my lorde Kynge Arthure." "I[8] leve well, false recrayed knyght, for thou haste many longe dayes overlad me and us all, and destroyed many of oure good knyghtes."

¶"Sir, ye say as hit pleasith you," seyde Sir Launcelot, "yet may hit never be seyde on me and opynly preved that ever I be forecaste[9] of treson slew no goode knyght, as ye, my lorde Sir Gawayne, have done—and so ded I never but in my deffence, that I was dryven thereto in savyng of my lyff." "A, thou false knyght," seyde Sir

fol.461r

fol.461v

---

6. Thee.
7. *Magré thy vysayge:* i.e., despite you, against your will.
8. Gawain is speaking.
9. *Be forecaste:* by design.

Gawayne, "that thou menyst by Sir Lamorak.[1] But wyte thou well, I slew hym!"

"Sir, ye slew hym nat youreselff,"[2] seyde Sir Launcelot, "for hit had ben overmuch for you, for he was one of the beste knyghtes crystynde of his ayge—and hit was grete pité of hys deth."

¶ "Well, well, Sir Launcelot," seyde Sir Gawayne, "sytthyn thou enbraydyst me of Sir Lamorak, wyte thou well I shall never leve the tyll I have the at suche avayle that thou shalt nat ascape my hondis." "I truste you well inowgh," seyde Sir Launcelot, "and ye may gete me,[3] I gett but lytyll mercy."

But the Freynsh booke seyth Kynge Arthur wolde have takyn hys quene agayne and to have bene accorded with Sir Launcelot, but Sir Gawayne wolde nat suffir hym by no maner of meane. And so Sir Gawayne made many men to blow[4] uppon Sir Launcelot; and so all at onys they called hym "false recrayed knyght!"

But whan Sir Bors de Ganys, Sir Ector de Marys, and Sir Lyonell harde thys outecry, they called unto them Sir Palomydes, and Sir Lavayne an Sir Urré, wyth many mo knyghtes of their bloode, and all they wente unto Sir Launcelot, and seyde thus: "My lorde, wyte you well we have grete scorne of the grete rebukis that we have harde Sir Gawayne sey unto you; wherefore we pray you and charge you, as ye woll have oure servyse, kepe us no lenger wythin thys wallis—for we lat you wete playnly, we woll ryde into the fylde and do batayle wyth hem. For ye fare as a man that were aferde; and for all [your] fayre speche hit woll nat avayle you, for wyte you well, Sir Gawayne woll nevir suffir you to accorde wyth Kynge Arthur—and therefore fyght for youre lyff and ryght, and ye dare."

¶ "Alas," seyde Sir Launcelot, "for to ryde oute of thys castell and to do batayle I am full lothe."

¶ Than Sir Launcelot spake on hyght unto Kyng Arthur and Sir Gawayne: "My lorde, I requyre you and beseche you, sytthyn that I am thus requyred and conjoured to ryde into the fylde, that neyther you, my lorde Kyng Arthur, nother you, Sir Gawayne, com nat into the fylde."

¶ "What shall we do than?" seyde Sir Gawayne. "Is nat thys the Kynges quarel to fyght wyth the? And also hit ys my quarell to fyght wyth the because of the dethe of my brothir Sir Gareth."

"Than muste I nedys unto batayle," seyde Sir Launcelot. "Now wyte you well, my lorde Arthur and Sir Gawayne, ye woll repent hit whansomever I do batayle wyth you." And so than they departed eythir frome othir; and than aythir party made hem redy on the morne for to do batayle, and grete purveyaunce was made on bothe sydys. And Sir Gawayne lat purvey many knyghtes for to wayte uppon Sir Launcelot for to oversette hym and to sle hym; and on the morn at underne Kynge Arthure was redy in the fylde with three grete ostys.

1. On the oft-lamented death of Lamorak, see pp. 411, 416, 590, and 598.
2. I.e., on your own.
3. *I truste you . . . and ye may gete me:* I am sure enough that, if you can catch me.
4. I.e., cry out against, defame.

And than Sir Launcelottis felyshyp com oute at the three gatis in full good aray; and Sir Lyonell cam in the formyst batayle,[5] and Sir Launcelot cam in the myddyll, and Sir Bors com oute at the thirde gate. And thus they cam in order and rule as full noble knyghtes— and ever Sir Launcelot charged all hys knyghtes in ony wyse to save Kynge Arthure and Sir Gawayne. Than cam forth Sir Gawayne frome the Kyngis oste, and [came before and] profirde to juste. And Sir Lyonel was a fyers knyght, and lyghtly he encountred with hym; and there Sir Gawayne smote Sir Lyonell thorowoute the body, that he daysshed to the erth lyke as he had ben dede.

And than Sir Ector de Marys and other mo bare hym into the castell. And anone there began a grete stowre and much people were slayne. And ever Sir Launcelot ded what he myght to save the people on Kynge Arthurs party; for Sir Bors and Sir Palomydes and Sir Saffir overthrew many knyghts—for they were dedely knyghtes —and Sir Blamour de Ganys and Sir Bleoberys, wyth Sir Bellyngere le Bewse, thes six knyghtes ded much harme. And ever was Kynge Arthur aboute Sir Launcelot to have slayne hym, and ever Sir Launcelot suffird hym and wolde nat stryke agayne. So Sir Bors encountirde wyth Kynge Arthur, and Sir Bors smote hym [doun;] and so he alyght and drew hys swerde, and seyd to Sir Launcelot, "Sir, shall I make an ende of thys warre?"—for he mente to have slayne hym.

"Nat[6] so hardy," seyde Sir Launcelot, "uppon payne of thy hede, that thou touch hym no more! For I woll never se that moste noble kynge that made me knyght nother slayne nor shamed." And therewithall Sir Launcelot alyght of hys horse and toke up the Kynge and horsed hym agayne, and seyd thus: "My lorde the Kynge, for Goddis love, stynte thys stryff, for ye gette here no worshyp and I wolde do myne utteraunce.[7] But allwayes I forbeare you, and ye nor none off youres forberyth nat me; and therefore, my lorde, I pray you remembir what I have done in many placis, and now am I evyll rewarded."

⁋So whan Kynge Arthur was on horsebak, he loked on Sir Launcelot; than the teerys braste oute of hys yen, thynkyng of the grete curtesy that was in Sir Launcelot more than in ony other man. And therewith the Kynge rod hys way and myght no lenger beholde hym, saiyng to hymselff, "Alas, alas, that [ever] yet thys warre began!" And than aythir party of the batayles wythdrew them to repose them, and buryed the dede and serched the wounded men—

⁋And leyde to their woundes soffte salves; and thus they endured that nyght tylle on the morne. And on the morne by undirn they made them redy to do batayle, and than Sir Bors lad the vawarde; so uppon the morn there cam Sir Gawayne, as brym as ony boore, wyth a grete spere in hys honde.

fol.462v

[13]

fol.463r

---

5. I.e., battalion.
6. I.e., be not.
7. *ye gette here . . . do myne utteraunce:* i.e., you would receive no honor here if I were to kill you.

¶And whan Sir Bors saw hym, he thought to revenge hys brother Sir Lyonell of the despite Sir Gawayne gaff hym the other day. And so, as they that knew aythir other, feautred their spearis, and with all their myght of their horsis and themselff, so fyersly they mette togydirs and so felonsly that aythir bare other thorow; and so they felle bothe to the bare erthe. And than the batayle joyned, and there was much slaughter on bothe partyes.

¶Than Sir Launcelot rescowed Sir Bors and sent hym into the castell; but neyther Sir Gawayne nother Sir Bors dyed nat of their woundis, for they were well holpyn. Than Sir Labayne and Sir Urré prayde Sir Launcelot to do hys payne—"and feyght as they do, for we se that ye forbeare and spare, and that doth us much harme; and therefore we pray you spare nat youre enemyes no more than they do you." "Alas," seyde Sir Launcelot, "I have no harte to fyght ayenste my lorde Arthur, for ever mesemyth I do nat as me ought to do."

"My lorde," seyde Sir Palomydes, "thoughe ye spare them never so[8] much all thys day, they woll [never] can you thanke;[9] and yf they may gete you at avayle, ye ar but a dede man." So than Sir Launcelot undirstoode that they seyde hym trouthe. Than he stray-ned hymselff more than he ded toforehonde; and bycause of hys nevew Sir Bors was sore wounded, he payned hymselff the more.

And so within a lytyll whyle, by evynsong tyme, Sir Launcelottis party the bettir stood, for their horsis wente[1] in blood paste the fyttlokkes, there were so many people slayne. And than, for verry pité, Sir Launcelot withhylde hys knyghtes, and suffird Kynge Arthurs party to withdraw them on syde. And so he withdrew hys meyny into the castell; and aythir partyes buryed the dede and put salve unto the wounded men. So whan Sir Gawayne was hurte, they on Kynge Arthurs party were nat so orgulus as they were toforehonde to do batayle.

¶So of thys warre that was betwene Kynge Arthure and Sir Laun-celot hit was noysed thorow all Crystyn realmys; and so hit cam at the laste by relacion unto the Pope. And than the Pope toke a consideracion of the grete goodnes of Kynge Arthur and of the hyghe proues off Sir Launcelot, that was called the moste nobelyst knyght of the worlde. Wherefore the Pope called unto hym a noble clerke that at that tyme was there presente (the Freynshe boke seyth hit was the Bysshop of Rochester), and the Pope gaff hym bulles undir leade,[2] and sente hem unto the Kynge, chargyng hym uppon payne of entirdytynge[3] of all Inglonde that he take hys quene agayne and accorde with Sir Launcelot.

So whan thys Bysshop was com unto Carlyle he shewed the Kynge hys bullys; and whan the Kynge undirstode them, he wyste nat what to do. But full fayne he wolde have bene acorded with Sir Launcelot, but Sir Gawayn wolde nat suffir hym; but to have the

---

8. *Never so:* i.e., no matter.
9. *Can you thanke:* know how to thank you.
1. I.e., walked.
2. *Bulles undir leade:* official documents with lead seals.
3. I.e., interdiction, excommunication with suspension of all church functions.

Quene he thereto agreed—but in no wyse he wolde suffir the
Kynge to accorde with Sir Launcelot—but as for the Quene, he
consented. So the Bysshop had of the Kynge hys grete seale and
hys assuraunce,[4] as he was a trew and anoynted kynge, that Sir
Launcelot shulde go sauff and com sauff, and that the Quene shulde   5
nat be seyde unto of[5] the Kynge, nother of none[6] other, for
nothynge done of tyme paste. And of all thes appoyntementes[7]
the Bysshop brought with hym sure wrytynge to shew unto Sir
Launcelot.

So whan the Bysshop was com to Joyus Garde, there he shewed   10
Sir Launcelot how he cam frome the Pope with wrytynge unto Kyng
Arthur and unto hym. And there he tolde hym the perelis, gyff he
wythhelde the Quene frome the Kynge.

❡"Sir, hit was never in my thought," seyde Sir Launcelot, "to withholde the Quene frome my lorde Arthur. But I kepe her for thys   15
cause: insomuche as she shulde have be brente for my sake,
mesemed hit was my parte to save her lyff and put her from that
daungere tyll bettir recover myght com. And now I thanke God,"
seyde Sir Launcelot, "that the Pope hathe made her pease. For God
knowyth," seyde Sir Launcelot, "I woll be a thousandefolde more   20
gladder to brynge her agayne than ever I was of her takyng away—
wyth thys[8] I may be sure to com sauff and go sauff, and that the   fol.464v
Quene shall have her lyberté [as she had before,] and never for
nothyng that hath be surmysed afore thys tyme that she never
frome thys stonde in no perell.[9] For ellis," seyde Sir Launcelot, "I   25
dare adventure me to kepe her frome an harder showre[1] than ever
yet I had."

❡"Sir, hit shall nat nede you," seyde the Bysshop, "to drede thus
muche; for wyte yow well, the Pope muste be obeyed, and hit were
nat the Popes worshyp, nother my poure honesté, to know you   30
distressed nother the Quene, nother in perell nother shamed." And
than he shewed Sir Launcelot all hys wrytynge, bothe frome the
Pope and Kynge Arthure.

"Thys ys sure ynow," seyde Sir Launcelot, "for full well I dare
truste my lordys owne wrytyng and hys seale, for he was never   35
shamed[2] of hys promyse. Therefore," seyde Sir Launcelot unto the
Bysshop, "ye shall ryde unto the Kynge afore and recommaunde
me unto hys good grace, and lat hym have knowlecchynge that this
same day eyght dayes, by the grace of God, I myselff shall brynge
the Quene unto hym. And than sey ye to my moste redouted Kynge   40
that I woll sey largely for the Quene,[3] that I shall none excepte for

---

4. *Hys grete seale and hys assuraunce:* i.e., a document attesting to the agreement, with the
   king's own seal.
5. *Seyde unto of:* reprimanded by.
6. *Of none:* i.e., by no one.
7. I.e., arrangements.
8. *Wyth thys:* provided that.
9. *and never for . . . in no perell:* and henceforth that she not be endangered because of
   speculation about the past.
1. I.e., conflict.
2. *Never shamed:* i.e., always honorable.
3. *Sey largely for:* declare an open challenge on behalf of.

drede nother for feare but the Kynge hymselff, and my lorde Sir
Gawayne—and that ys for the Kyngis love more than for hymselff."[4]
So the Bysshop departed and cam to the Kynge to Carlehyll, and
tolde hym all how Sir Launcelot answerd hym; so that made the
teares falle oute at the Kyngis yen. ⁵

Than Sir Launcelot purveyed hym an hondred knyghtes, and all
well clothed in grene velvet, and their horsis trapped in the same
to the heelys, and every knyght hylde a braunche of olyff in hys
honde in tokenyng of pees; and the Quene had foure and twenty
jantillwomen folowyng her in the same wyse. And Sir Launcelot had ¹⁰
twelve coursers folowyng hym, and on every courser sate a yonge
jantylman, and all they were arayed in whyght velvet, with sarpis   fol.465r
of golde aboute their quarters, and the horse trapped in the same
wyse down to the helys, wyth many owchys, i-sette with stonys and
perelys in golde, to the numbir of a thousande. And in the same   ¹⁵
wyse was the Quene arayed, and Sir Launcelot in the same, of
whyght clothe of golde tyssew. And ryght so as ye have harde, asthe
Freynshe booke makyth mencion, he rode with the Quene frome
Joyus Garde to Carlehyll. And so Sir Launcelot rode thorowoute
Carlehylle, and so into the castell, that all men myght beholde   ²⁰
hem—and there was many a wepyngg ien.

And than Sir Launcelot hymselff alyght and voyded hys horse, and
toke adowne the Quene, and so lad her where Kyng Arthur was in
hys seate; and Sir Gawayne sate afore hym, and many other grete
lordys. So whan Sir Launcelot saw the Kynge and Sir Gawayne, than   ²⁵
he lad the Quene by the arme, and than he kneled downe and the
Quene bothe.

⁋Wyte you well, than was there many a bolde knyght wyth
Kynge Arthur that wepte as tendirly as they had seyne all their
kynne dede afore them. So the Kynge sate stylle and seyde no   ³⁰
worde.

⁋And whan Sir Launcelot saw hys countenaunce, he arose up and
pulled up the Quene with hym, and thus he seyde full knyghtly:
"𝕸y moste redouted Kynge, ye shall undirstonde, by the Popis   [15]
commaundemente and youres I have brought to you my lady   ³⁵
the Quene, as ryght requyryth. And if there be ony knyght, of what
degré that ever he be off, except your person, that woll sey or dare
say but that she ys trew and clene to you, I here myselff, Sir Launcelot du Lake, woll make hit good uppon hys body that she ys a trew
lady unto you.[5] But, sir, lyars ye have lystened, and that hath   ⁴⁰
caused grete debate betwyxte you and me. For tyme hath bene, my
lorde Arthur, that ye were gretly pleased with me whan I ded batayle   fol.465v
for my lady, youre Quene; and full well ye know, my moste noble
Kynge, that she hathe be put to grete wronge or thys tyme. And
sytthyn hyt pleased you at many tymys that I shulde feyght for her,   ⁴⁵
therefore mesemyth, my good lorde, I had more cause to rescow
her from the fyer whan she sholde have ben brente for my sake.

---

4. I.e., Gawain.
5. *And if there be . . . a trew lady unto you:* this sentence is not matched in Malory's known
   sources.

For they that tolde you tho talys were lyars, and so hit felle uppon them; for by lyklyhode, had nat the myght of God bene with me, I myght never have endured with fourtene knyghtes, and they armed and afore purposed, and I unarmed—

❡ "And nat purposed: for I was sente for unto my lady, youre Quyne, I wote nat for what cause, but I was nat so sone within the chambir dore but anone Sir Aggravayne and Sir Mordred called me traytoure and false recrayed knyght."

❡ "Be my fayth, they called the[6] ryght!" seyde Sir Gawayne. "My lorde, Sir Gawayne," seyde Sir Launcelot, "in their quarell they preved nat hemselff the beste, nother in the ryght."

❡ "Well, well, Sir Launcelot, seyde the Kynge, "I have gyvyn you no cause to do to me as ye have done, for I have worshipt you and youres more than ony othir knyghtes."

"My lorde," seyde Sir Launcelot, "so ye be nat displeased, ye shall undirstonde that I and myne have done you oftyntymes bettir serv- yse than ony othir knyghtes have done, in many dyverce placis; and where ye have bene full hard bestadde dyvers tymes, I have res- cowed you frome many daungers—and ever unto my power I was glad to please you and my lorde Sir Gawayne. In justis and in tur- nementis and in batayles set, bothe on horsebak and on foote, I have oftyn rescowed you—and you, my lorde Sir Gawayne—and many mo of youre knyghtes in many dyvers placis. For now I woll make avaunte," seyde Sir Launcelot, "I woll that ye all wyte that as yet I founde never no maner of knyght but that I was over harde for hym and I had done myne utteraunce, God graunte mercy! Howbehit I have be macched with good knyghtes, as Sir Trystram and Sir Lamorak, but ever I had favoure unto them and a demyng what they were; and I take God to recorde, I never was wrothe nor gretly hevy wyth no good knyght and I saw hym besy and aboute to wyn worshyp, and glad I was ever whan I founde a good knyght that myght onythynge endure me on horsebak and on foote. How- behit, Sir Carados of the Dolerous Toure was a full noble knyght and a passynge stronge man—and that wote ye, my lorde Sir Gawayne; for he myght well be called a noble knyght whan he be fyne fors pulled you oute of your sadyll and bounde you over- thwarte afore hym to hys sadyll-bow.[7] And there, my lorde Sir Gawayne, I rescowed you and slew hym afore your syght. Also I founde youre brothir, Sir Gaherys, and Sir Terquyn ledyng hym bounden afore hym; and there also I rescowed youre brothir and slew Sir Terquyn and delyverde three score and foure of my lorde Arthurs knyghtes oute of hys preson.[8] And now I dare sey," seyde Sir Launcelot, "I mette never wyth so stronge a knyght nor so well- fyghtyng as was Sir Carados and Sir Tarquyn, for they and I faught to the uttermest. And therefore," seyde Sir Launcelot unto Sir Gawayne, "mesemyth ye ought of ryght to remembir this; for, and I

fol.466r

6. Thee.
7. See p. 261.
8. See p. 162.

myght have youre good wyll, I wold truste to God for to have my
lorde Arthurs good grace."

¶"Sir,[9] the Kynge may do as he wyll," seyde Sir Gawayne, "but [16]
wyte thou well, Sir Launcelot, thou and I shall never be accorded
whyle we lyve, for thou hast slayne three of my brethyrn—and two 5
of hem thou slew traytourly and piteuously, for they bare none
harneys ayenste the, nother none wold do." fol.466v

¶"Sir, God wolde they had ben armed," seyde Sir Launcelot, "for
than had they ben on lyve. And [as] for Gareth, I loved no kynnesman I had more than I loved hym; and ever whyle I lyve," seyde 10
Sir Launcelot, "I woll bewayle Sir Gareth hys dethe, nat all only for
the grete feare I have of you, but for many causys whych causyth
me to be sorowfull. One is that I made hym knyght; another ys, I
wote well he loved me aboven all othir knyghtes; and the third ys,
he was passyng noble and trew, curteyse and jantill and well- 15
condicionde; the fourth ys, I wyste well, anone as I harde that Sir
Gareth was dede, I knew well that I shulde never aftir have youre
love, my lorde Sir Gawayne, but everlastyng warre betwyxt us—and
also I wyste well, that ye wolde cause my noble lorde Kynge Arthur
for ever to be my mortall foo. 20

"And as Jesu be my helpe, and be my knyghthode, I slewe never
Sir Gareth nother hys brother be my wyllynge—but alas that ever
they were unarmed that unhappy day! But this much I shall offir
me to you," seyde Sir Launcelot, "if hit may please the Kyngis good
grace and you, my lorde Sir Gawayn: I shall firste begyn at Sand- 25
wyche, and there I shall go in my shearte, barefoote, and at every
ten myles ende I shall founde and gar make[1] an house of religious,
of what order that ye woll assygne me, with an hole covente, to
synge and rede day and nyght in especiall for Sir Gareth sake and
Sir Gaherys; and thys shall I perfourme [from Sandwyche unto Car- 30
leil; and every hows[2] shal have suffycyent lyvelode. And this shal I
performe] whyle that I have ony lyvelod in Crystyndom, and there
ys none of all thes religious placis but they shall be perfourmed,[3]
furnysshed, and garnysshed with all thyngis as an holy place ought
to be. And thys were fayrar and more holyar and more perfyte to fol.467r 35
their soulis than ye, my moste noble Kynge, and you, Sir Gawayne,
to warre uppon me, for thereby shall ye gete none avayle."

Than all the knyghtes and ladyes that were there wepte as they
were madde, and the tearys felle on Kynge Arthur hys chekis. "Sir
Launcelot," seyde Sir Gawayne, "I have ryght well harde thy langayge 40
and thy grete proffirs. But wyt thou well, lat the Kynge do as hit
pleasith hym, I woll never forgyff the my brothirs dethe, and in
especiall the deth of my brothir Sir Gareth. And if myne uncle
Kynge Arthur wyll accorde wyth the, he shall loose my servys—for
wyte thou well," seyde Sir Gawayne, "thou arte bothe false to the 45

---

9. From here to p. 670, line 16 (*I shall delyver you*): most of this extended dialogue is not
   matched in Malory's known sources.
1. *Gar make:* have established.
2. I.e., house of religion.
3. I.e., completed.

Kynge and to me." "Sir," seyde Sir Launcelot, "he beryth nat the lyff
that may make hit good![4] And ye, Sir Gawayne, woll charge me with
so hyghe a thynge, ye muste pardone me, for than nedis must I
answere you."

¶"Nay, nay," seyde Sir Gawayne, "we ar paste that as at thys tyme, [5]
and that causyth the Pope, for he hath charged myne uncle the
Kynge that he shall take agayne his quene and to accorde wyth
the, Sir Launcelot, as for thys season, and therefore thou shalt go
sauff as thou com. But in this londe thou shalt nat abyde paste a
fiftene dayes, such somons[5] I gyff the; for so the Kynge and we [10]
were condescended and accorded ar thou cam. And ellis," seyde
Sir Gawayn, "wyte thou well, thou shulde nat a comyn here but if
hit were magré thyne hede. And if hit were nat for the Popis commaundement," seyde Sir Gawayne, "I shulde do batayle with the
myne[6] owne hondis, body for body, and preve hit uppon the that [15]
thou haste ben both false unto myne uncle Kynge Arthur and to
me bothe; and that shall I preve on thy body, whan thou arte
departed fro hense, wheresomever that I fynde the."

Than Sir Launcelotte syghed, and therewith the tearys felle on hys [17] fol.467v
chekys, and than he seyde thus: "Moste nobelyst Crysten realme, [20]
whom I have loved aboven all othir realmys, and in the I have gotyn
a grete parte of my worshyp! And now that I shall departe in thys
wyse, truly me repentis that ever I cam in thys realme, that I shulde
be thus shamefully banysshyd, undeserved and causeles. But fortune ys so varyaunte, and the wheele[7] so mutable, that there ys no [25]
constaunte abydynge—and that may be preved by many olde cronycles, as of noble Ector of Troy and Alysaunder the myghty conquerroure, and many mo other:

¶"Whan they were moste in her royalté, they alyght passyng
lowe. And so faryth hit by me," seyde Sir Launcelot, "for in thys [30]
realme I had worshyp, and be me and myne all the hole Rounde
Table hath bene encreced more in worshyp—by me and myne—
than ever hit was by ony of you all. And therefore wyte thou well,
Sir Gawayne, I may lyve uppon my londis as well as ony knyght that
here ys; and yf ye, my moste redoutted Kynge, woll com uppon my [35]
londys with Sir Gawayne to warre uppon me, I muste endure you
as well as I may—but as to you, Sir Gawayne, if that ye com there,
I pray you charge me nat wyth treson nother felony, for and ye do,
I muste answere you."

"Do thou thy beste," seyde Sir Gawayne, "and therefore hyghe [40]
the[8] faste that thou were gone. And wyte thou well, we shall sone
com aftir, and breke thy strengyst castell that thou hast uppon thy
hede."

4. *He beryth nat the lyff that may make hit good:* there is no one alive who (in trial by combat)
   can prove that.
5. I.e., terms.
6. I.e., with my.
7. In the Middle Ages, Fortune was commonly envisaged as a goddess turning a wheel to
   which people, usually legendary rulers, were fixed, their welfare being determined by the
   position of the wheel—either rising into glory or falling to ignominy. Cf. Arthur's dream
   at p. 683; see also pp. 743 and 754.
8. Thee.

❡"Hyt shall nat nede that,"⁹ seyde Sir Launcelot, "for and I were as orgulous sette¹ as ye ar, wyte you well I shulde mete you in myddys of the fylde." "Make thou no more langayge," seyde Sir Gawayne, "but delyvir the Quene from the, and pyke the lyghtly oute of thys courte."

❡"Well," seyde Sir Launcelot, "and I had wyste of thys shortecomyng, I wolde a advysed me twyse or that I had com here. For and the Quene had be so dere unto me as ye noyse her, I durste have kepte her frome the felyshyp of the beste knyghtes undir hevyn."

And than Sir Launcelot seyde unto Quene Gwenyver, in hyryng of the Kynge and hem all, "Madame, now I muste departe from you and thys noble felyshyp for ever; and sytthyn hit ys so, I besech you to pray for me, and I shall pray for you. And telle ye me and if ye be harde bestad by ony false tunges; but lyghtly, my good lady, sende me worde, and if ony knyghtes hondys undir the hevyn may delyver you by batayle, I shall delyver you."

And therewithall Sir Launcelot kyssed the Quene, and than he seyde all opynly, "Now lat se whatsomever he be in thys place that dare sey the Quene ys nat trew unto my lorde Arthur, lat se who woll speke and he dare speke." And therewith he brought the Quene to the Kynge. And than Sir Launcelot toke hys leve and departed; and there was nother kynge, duke, erle, barowne, nor knyght, lady nor jantyllwoman, but all they wepte as people oute of mynde, excepte Sir Gawayne.

And whan thys noble knyght Sir Launcelot toke his horse to ryde oute of Carlehyll, there was sobbyng and wepyng for pure dole of hys departynge. And so he toke his way to Joyus Garde—and than ever afftir he called hit the "Dolerous Garde"²—and thus departed Sir Launcelot frome the courte for ever. And so whan he cam to Joyus Garde, he called hys felyshyp unto hym and asked them what they wolde do. Than they answerde all holé togydirs with one voyce, they wold do as he wolde do.

❡"Than, my fayre felowys," seyde Sir Launcelot, "I muste departe oute of thys moste noble realme; and now I shall departe, hit grevyth me sore, for I shall departe with no worship, for a fleymed man departith never oute of a realme with no worship. And that ys to me grete hevynes, for ever I feare aftir my dayes that men shall cronycle uppon me that I was fleamed oute of thys londe—and ellis, my fayre lordis, be ye sure, and I had nat drad shame, my lady Quene Gwenyvere and I shulde never have departed."

❡Than spake noble knyghtes, as Sir Palomydes and Sir Saffyr, hys brothir, and Sir Bellynger le Bewse, and Sir Urré with Sir Lavayne, with many other: "Sir, and ye woll so be disposed to abyde in thys londe we woll never fayle you; and if ye lyste nat abyde in thys londe, there ys none of the good knyghtes that here be that woll

fol.468r — 5

10

15

20

25

30

fol.468v

35

40

45

---

9. *Hyt shall nat nede that:* i.e., that will not be necessary.
1. *Orgulous sette:* arrogantly disposed.
2. I.e., Launcelot restores the name the castle had before he captured it from its tyrannical owner; see n. 3, p. 240.

fayle you, for many causis. One ys, all we that[3] be nat of your
bloode shall never be wellcom unto the courte; and sytthyn hit
lyked us to take a parte with you in youre distres in this realme,
wyte you well hit shall lyke us as well to go in othir contreyes with
you and there to take suche parte as ye do." 5

¶"My fayre lordys," seyde Sir Launcelot, "I well undirstond you,
and as I can, I thanke you. And ye shall undirstonde, suche lyvelode as I am borne unto I shall departe with you in thys maner of
wyse: that ys for to say, I shall departe all my lyvelode and all my
londis frely amonge you, and myselff woll have as lytyll as ony of 10
you; for, have I sufficiaunte that may longe unto my person, I woll
aske none other ryches nother aray—and I truste to God to maynteyne you on my londys as well as ever ye were maynteyned."

Than spake all the knyghtes at onys: "Have he shame that woll
leve you! For we all undirstonde, in thys realme [wyll be now no 15
quyete], but ever debate and stryff, now the felyshyp of the Rounde
Table ys brokyn. For by the noble felyshyp of the Rounde Table
was Kynge Arthur upborne, and by their nobeles the Kynge and all
the realme was ever in quyet and reste; and a grete parte," they
sayde all, "was because of youre moste nobeles, Sir Launcelot." 20

¶"Now, truly I thanke you all of youre good sayinge, howbehit
I wote well that in me was nat all the stabilité of thys realme, but
in that I myght, I ded my dever. And well I am sure, I knew many
rebellyons in my dayes that by me and myne were peased—and
that I trow we all shall here of in shorte space, and that me sore 25
repentith; for ever I drede me," seyde Sir Launcelot, "that Sir Mordred
woll make trouble, for he ys passyng envyous and applyeth hym
muche to trouble."

And so they were accorded to departe wyth Sir Launcelot to hys
landys. And to make shorte thys tale, they trussed and payed all 30
that wolde aske them; and holé an hondred knyghtes departed with
Sir Launcelot at onys, and made their avowis they wolde never leve
hym for weale ne for woo. And so they shypped at Cardyff, and
sayled unto Benwyke (som men calle hit Bayan, and som men calle
hit Beawme, where the wyne of Beawme ys). But to say the sothe, 35
Sir Launcelott and hys neveawis was lordes of all Fraunce and of all
the londis that longed unto Fraunce; he and hys kynrede rejoysed[4]
hit all thorow Sir Launcelottis noble proues. And than he stuffed[5]
and furnysshed and garnysshed all his noble townys and castellis.
Than all the people of tho landis cam unto Sir Launcelot on foote 40
and hondis.[6]

And so whan he had stabelysshed all those contreyes, he shortly
called a parlement; and there he crowned Sir Lyonell Kynge off
Fraunce; and Sir Bors he crowned hym Kynge of all Kyng Claudas
londis; and Sir Ector de Marys, Sir Launcelottis yonger brother, he 45
crowned hym Kynge of Benwyke and Kynge of all Gyan, whych

---

3. *All we that:* i.e., even those of us who.
4. I.e., enjoyed.
5. I.e., furnished with men and provisions for defense.
6. *On foote and hondis:* i.e., in a gesture of submission.

was Sir Launcelottis owne londys, and he made Sir Ector prynce of
them all. And thus he departed hys londis and avaunced all hys
noble knyghtes. And firste he avaunced them off hys blood, as Sir
Blamour, he made hym Duke of Lymosyn in Gyan; and Sir Bleoberys, he made hym Duke of Payters; and Sir Gahalantyne, he made   5
hym Deuke of Overn; and Sir Galyodyn, he made hym Deuke of
Sentonge; and Sir Galyhud, he made hym Erle of Perygot; and Sir
Menaduke, he made hym Erle of Roerge; and Sir Vyllars the Valyaunt,
he made hym Erle of Bearne; and Sir Hebes le Renownes, he made
hym Erle of Comange; and Sir Lavayne, he made hym Erle of Army-   10
nake; and Sir Urré, he made hym Erle of Estrake; and Sir Neroveus,
he made hym Erle of Pardyak; and Sir Plenoryus, he made hym Erle
of Foyse; and Sir Selyses of the Dolerous Toure, he made hym Erle
of Mausank; and Sir Melyas de le Ile, he made hym Erle of Tursanke; and Sir Bellyngere le Bewse, he made hym Erle of the Lawun-   15
dis; and Sir Palomydes, he made hym Deuke of Provynce; and Sir
Saffir, he made hym Deuke of Landok; and Sir Clegys, he gaff hym
the erledome of Agente; and Sir Sadok, he gaff hym the erledom
of Sarlat; and Sir Dynas le Senesciall, he made hym Deuke of
Angeoy; and Sir Clarrus, he made hym Duke of Normandy. Thus   20
Sir Launcelot rewarded hys noble knyghtes, and many mo that mesemyth hit were to longe to rehers.

So leve we Sir Launcelot in hys londis and hys noble knyghtes   [19]
with hym, and returne we agayne unto Kynge Arthure and unto Sir   fol.470r
Gawayne that made a grete oste aredy to the numbir of three score   25
thousande; and all thynge was made redy for shyppyng to passe
over the see, to warre uppon Sir Launcelot and uppon hys londis.
And so they shypped at Cardyff; and there Kynge Arthur made Sir
Mordred chyeff ruler of all Ingelonde, and also he put the Quene
undir hys governaunce: bycause Sir Mordred was Kynge Arthurs son,   30
he gaff hym the rule off hys londe and off hys wyff. And so the
Kynge passed the see and landed uppon Sir Launcelottis londis; and
there he brente and wasted, thorow the vengeaunce of Sir Gawayne,
all that they myght overrenne.

❡So whan thys worde was com unto Sir Launcelot, that Kynge   35
Arthur and Sir Gawayne were landed uppon hys londis and made
full grete destruccion and waste, than spake Sir Bors and seyde,
"My lorde, Sir Launcelot, hit is shame that we suffir hem thus to
ryde over oure londys. For wyte you well, suffir ye hem as longe as
ye wyll, they woll do you no favoure and they may handyll[7] you."   40
Than seyde Sir Lyonell that was ware and wyse, "My lorde, Sir
Launcelot, I woll gyff you thys counceyle: lat us us kepe oure stronge-
walled townys untyll they have hunger and colde, and blow on their
nayles;[8] and than lat us fresshly set uppon them and shrede hem
downe as shepe in a folde, that ever aftir alyauntis may take ensam-   45
ple how they lande uppon oure londys!"

Than spake Kynge Bagdemagus to Sir Launcelot and seyde, "Sir,

---

7. I.e., get hold of.
8. *Blow on their nayles:* i.e., try to keep their hands warm.

youre curtesy woll shende us all, and youre curtesy hath waked all
thys sorow; for and they thus overryde oure londis, they shall by
proces brynge us all to nought whyle we thus in holys us hyde."
Than seyde Sir Galyhud unto Sir Launcelot, "Sir, here bene knyghtes
com of kyngis blod that woll nat longe droupe and dare[9] within
thys wallys. Therefore gyff us leve, lyke as we ben knyghtes, to
mete hem in the fylde, and we shall so deale wyth them that they
shall curse the tyme that ever they cam into thys contrey." Than
spake seven brethirn of Northe Walis whych were seven noble
knyghtes—for a man myghte seke seven kyngis londis or he myght
fynde such seven knyghtes—and thes seven noble knyghtes seyde
all at onys, "Sir Launcelot, for Crystis sake, late us ryde oute with
Sir Galyhud, for we were never wonte to coure in castels nother in
noble townys."

Than spake Sir Launcelot, that was mayster and governoure of
hem all, and seyde, "My fayre lordis, wyte you well I am full lothe
to ryde oute with my knyghtes for shedynge of Crysten blood; and
yet my londis I undirstonde be full bare for to sustayne any oste
awhyle for[1] the myghty warris that whylom made Kyng Claudas
uppon thys contrey and uppon my fadir, Kyng Ban, and on myne
uncle, Kynge Bors. Howbehit, we woll as at this tyme kepe oure
stronge wallis; and I shall sende a messyngere unto my lorde Arthur
a tretyse for to take, for better ys pees than allwayes warre."

¶So Sir Launcelot sente forthe a damesel wyth a dwarff with her,
requyryng Kynge Arthur to leve hys warryng uppon hys londys. And
so he[2] starte uppon a palferey, and the dwarffe ran by her syde,
and whan she cam to the pavelon of Kynge Arthur, there she alyght.
And there mette her a jantyll knyght, Sir Lucan the Butlere, and
seyde, Fayre damesell, com ye frome Sir Launcelot du Lake?"

¶"Yee, sir," she seyde, "therefore cam I hyddir, to speke with my
lorde the Kynge." "Alas," seyde Sir Lucan, "my lorde Arthure wolde
accorde with Sir Launcelot, but Sir Gawayne woll nat suffir hym."
And than he seyde, "I pray to God, damesell, that ye may spede
[wel], for all we that bene aboute the Kynge wolde that Launcelot
ded beste of ony knyght lyvynge." And so with thys Sir Lucan lad
the damesell to the Kynge, where he sate with Syr Gawayne, for to
hyre what she wolde say.

¶So whan she had tolde her tale, the watir ran oute of the Kyngis
yen. And all the lordys were full glad for to advyce the Kynge to be
accorded with Sir Launcelot—save all only Sir Gawayne; and he
seyde, "My lorde, myne uncle, what woll ye do? Woll ye now turne
agayne, now ye ar paste thys farre uppon youre journey? All the
worlde woll speke of you vylany and shame."

"Now," seyde Kynge Arthur, "wyte you well, Sir Gawayne, I woll
do as ye advyse me; and yet mesemyth", seyde Kynge Arthur, hys
fayre proffers were nat good[3] to be reffused. But sytthyn I am com

9. *Droupe and dare:* lie low and hide.
1. I.e., because of.
2. She.
3. I.e., suitable.

fol.470v

fol.471r

so far uppon thys journey, I woll that ye gyff the damesell her answere—for I may nat speke to her for pité, for her profirs ben so large."[4]

¶Than Sir Gawayne seyde unto the damesell, "Thus sey ye to Sir Launcelot, that hyt ys waste laboure now to sew to[5] myne uncle; for telle hym, and he wolde have made ony laboure for pease, he sholde have made hit or thys tyme, for telle hym now hit ys to late—and say to hym that I, Sir Gawayne, so sende hym word that I promyse hym, by the faythe that I owghe to God and to knyghthode, I shall never leve hym tylle he hathe slayne me or I hym."

¶So the damesell wepte and departed—and so there was many a wepyng yghe. And than Sir Lucan brought the damesell to her palffrey, and so she cam to Sir Launcelot where he was, amonge all hys knyghtes.

¶And whan Sir Launcelot had harde hir answere, than the tearys ran downe by hys chekys. And than hys noble knyghtes com aboute hym, and seyde, "Sir Launcelot, wherefore make ye suche chere? Now thynke what ye ar and what men we ar, and lat us noble knyghtis macche hem in myddis of the fylde."

¶"That may be lyghtly done," seyde Sir Launcelot, "but I was never so lothe to do batayle; and therefore I pray you, sirres, as ye love me, be ruled at thys tyme as I woll have you. For I woll allwayes fle that noble kynge that made me knyght; and whan I may no farther, I muste nedis deffende me—and that woll be more worshyp for me and us all than to compare[6] with that noble kynge whom we have all served." Than they hylde their langayge, and as that nyght they toke their reste. And uppon the mornyng erly, in the dawnynge of the day, as knyghtes loked oute, they saw the cité of Benwyke besyged rounde aboute, and[7] gan faste to sette up laddirs.[8] And they within kepte them oute of the towne and bete hem myghtyly frome the wallis.

¶Than cam forthe Sir Gawayne, well armede, uppon a styff steede, and he cam before the chyeff gate with hys speare in hys honde, cryynge, "Where arte thou, Sir Launcelot? Ys there none of all your proude knyghtes that dare breake a speare with me?"

¶Than Sir Bors made hym redy and cam forth oute of the towne; and there Sir Gawayne encountred with Sir Bors, and at that tyme he smote hym downe frome hys horse, and allmo'ste he had slayne hym. And so Sir Bors was rescowed and borne into the towne.

¶Than cam forthe Sir Lyonell and thoughte to revenge hym; and aythir feawtred their spearys and so ran togydirs, and there they mette spiteously—but Sir Gawayne had such a grace that he smote Sir Lyonell downe and wounded hym there passyngly sore. And than Sir Lyonell was rescowed and borne into the towne. And thus Sir Gawayne com every day, and fayled nat but that he smote downe

[20]

5

10

15

fol.471v

20

25

30

35

40

45

4. I.e., generous.
5. *Sew to:* make formal requests of.
6. I.e., contend.
7. I.e., and the besiegers.
8. I.e., ladders to scale the walls.

one knyght or othir. So thus they endured halff a yere, and muche
slaughter was of people on bothe partyes.

¶Than hit befelle uppon a day that Sir Gawayne cam afore the
gatis, armed at all pecis, on a noble horse, with a greate speare in
hys honde; and than he cryed with a lowde voyce and seyde,
"Where arte thou now, thou false traytour, Sir Launcelot? Why hol-
dyst thou thyselff within holys and wallys lyke a cowarde? Loke
oute, thou false traytoure knyght, and here I shall revenge uppon
thy body the dethe of my three brethirne."

And all thys langayge harde Sir Launcelot, every deale; than hys
kynne and hys knyghtes drew aboute hym, and all they seyde at
onys unto Sir Launcelot, "Sir, now muste you deffende you lyke a
knyght, othir ellis ye be shamed for ever—for now ye be called
uppon treson, hit ys tyme for you to styrre, for ye have slepte over
longe, and suffirde overmuche."

¶"So God me helpe," seyde Sir Launcelot, "I am ryght hevy at Sir
Gawaynes wordys, for now he chargith me with a grete charge; and
therefore I wote as well as ye I muste nedys deffende me, other
ellis to be recreaunte."

¶Than Sir Launcelot bade sadyll hys strongest horse and bade let
fecche hys armys and brynge all to the towre of the gate. And than
Sir Launcelot spake on hyght unto the Kynge, and seyde, "My lorde
Arthur, and noble kynge that made me knyght, wyte you well, I am
ryght hevy for youre sake that ye thus sewe uppon me. And allwayes
I forbeare you; for and I wolde be vengeable, I myght have mette
you in myddys the fylde or thys tyme and thereto have made your
boldiste knyghtes full tame. And now I have forborne you and suffirde you halff a yere, and Sir Gawayne, to do what ye wolde do.
And now I may no lenger suffir to endure, but nedis I muste deffende myselff, insomuch as Sir Gawayn hathe becalled me of treson; whych ys gretly ayenste my wyll that ever I shulde fyghte
ayenste ony of youre blood. But now I may nat forsake hit—for I
am dryvyn thereto as beste tylle a bay."[9]

Than Sir Gawayne seyde unto Sir Launcelotte, "And thou darste do
batayle, leve thy babelynge and com off, and lat us ease oure
hartis!" Than Sir Launcelot armed hym and mownted uppon hys
horse, and aythir of them gate greate spearys in their hondys. And
so the oste withoute stoode stylle all aparte; and the noble knyghtes
of the cité cam a greate numbir, that whan Kynge Arthur saw the
numbir of men and knyghtes he mervaylde and seyde to hymself,
"Alas, that ever Sir Launcelot was ayenst me, for now I se that he
hath forborne me." And so the covenaunte was made: there sholde
no man nyghe hem nother deale wyth them tylle the tone were
dede other yolden.

Than Sir Launcelot and Sir Gawayne departed a greate way in sundir;[1] and than they cam togydirs with all their horse myghtes as
faste as they myght renne, and aythir smote othir in myddis of their

9. *As beste tylle a bay:* as is a cornered animal forced to defend itself.
1. *In sundir:* apart, at a distance.

fol.472r

5

10

15

20

25

30

fol.472v

35

40

[21]

45

shyldis. But the knyghtes were so stronge and their spearys so bygge that their horsis myght nat endure their buffettis, and so their horsis felle to the erthe. And than they avoyded their horsys, and dressed their shyldis afore them.

Than they cam togydirs and gaff many sad[2] strokis on dyverse placis of their bodyes, that the bloode braste oute on many sydis. Than had Sir Gawayne suche a grace and gyffte that an holy man had gyvyn hym, that every day in the yere, frome undern tyll hyghe noone, hys myght encresed tho[3] three owres as much as thryse hys strength. And that caused Sir Gawayne to wynne grete honoure; and for hys sake Kynge Arthur made an ordynaunce that all maner off batayles for ony quarels that shulde be done afore Kynge Arthur shulde begynne at undern; and all was done for Sir Gawaynes love, that by lyklyhode if Sir Gawayne were on the tone parté, he shulde have the bettir in batayle whyle hys strengthe endured three owrys. But there were that tyme but feaw knyghtes lyvynge that knewe thys advauntayge that Sir Gawayne had, but Kynge Arthure all only.

¶So Sir Launcelot faught wyth Sir Gawayne; and whan Sir Launcelot felte hys myght evermore encrese, Sir Launcelot wondred and drad hym sore to be shamed—for, as the Freynshe booke seyth, he wende, whan he felte Sir Gawaynes double hys strengthe, that he had bene a fyende and none earthely man. Wherefore Sir Launcelot traced and traverced, and coverde hymselff with hys shylde, and kepte hys myght and hys brethe duryng three owrys.

And that whyle Sir Gawayne gaff hym many sad bruntis [and many sadde strokes,] that all knyghtes that behylde Sir Launcelot mervayled how he myght endure hym; but full lytyll undirstood they that travayle that Sir Launcelot had to endure hym. And than whan hit was paste noone, Sir Gawaynes strengthe was gone and he had no more but hys owne myght.

¶Whan Sir Launcelot felte hym so com downe, than he strecched hym up and strode nere Sir Gawayne, and seyde thus: "Now I fele ye have done youre warste; and now, my lorde Sir Gawayn, I muste do my parte, for many grete and grevous strokis I have endured you thys day with great payne." And so Sir Launcelot doubled hys strokis and gaff Sir Gawayne suche a stroke uppon the helmet that sydelynge he felle downe uppon hys one syde—and Sir Launcelot withdrew hym frome hym.

¶"Why wythdrawyst thou the?" seyde Sir Gawayne. "Turne agayne, false traytoure knyght, and sle me oute! For and thou leve me thus, anone as I am hole I shall do batayle with the agayne."

¶"Sir," seyde Sir Launcelot, "I shall endure you, be Goddis grace! But wyte thou well, Sir Gawayne, I woll never smyte a felde knyght." And so Sir Launcelot departed and wente unto the cité; and Sir Gawayne was borne unto Kynge Arthurs pavylon, and anone lechys were brought unto hym of the beste, and serched and salved hym with souffte oynementis. And than Sir Launcelot seyde, "Now have

fol.473r

fol.473v

2. I.e., grievous.
3. I.e., during those.

good day, my lorde the Kynge, for wyte you welle ye wynne no
worshyp at thes wallis; for and I wolde my knyghtes outebrynge,
there shulde many a douty man dye—and therefore, my lorde
Arthur, remembir you of olde kyndenes, and howsomever I fare,
Jesu be youre gyde in all placis."   5

¶"Now, alas," seyde the Kynge, "that ever thys unhappy warre   [22]
began! For ever Sir Launcelot forbearyth me in all placis, and in lyke
wyse my kynne; and that ys sene well thys day, what curtesy he
shewed my neveawe, Sir Gawayne." Than Kynge Arthur felle syke
for sorow of Sir Gawayne, that he was so sore hurte, and bycause   10
of the warre betwyxte hym and Sir Launcelot.

So aftir that, they on Kynge Arthurs party kepte the sege with
lytyll warre wythouteforthe, and they withinforthe kepte their wallys and deffended them whan nede was. Thus Sir Gawayne lay syke
and unsounde three wykes in hys tentis with all maner of leche-   15
crauffte that myght be had. And as sone as Sir Gawayne myght go
and ryde, he armed hym at all poyntis and bestroode a styff courser
and gate a grete speare in hys honde, and so he cam rydynge afore
the chyeff gate of Benwyke; and there he cryed on hyght and seyde,
"Where arte thou, Sir Launcelot? Com forth, thou false traytoure   20
knyght and recrayed, for I am here, Sir Gawayne, that woll preve
thys that I say uppon the!"

And all thys langayge Sir Launcelot harde, and sayde thus: "Sir
Gawayne, me repentis of youre fowle sayinge, that ye woll nat cease
your langayge. For ye wote well, Sir Gawayne, I know youre myght   fol.474r 25
and all that ye may do; and well ye wote, Sir Gawayne, ye may nat
greatly hurte me." "Com downe, traytoure knyght," seyde he, "and
make hit good[4] the contrary wyth thy hondys! For hit myssehapped
me the laste batayle to be hurte of thy hondis; therefore, wyte thou
well, I am com thys day to make amendis—for I wene this day to   30
ley the as low as thou laydest me." "Jesu deffende me," seyde Sir
Launcelot, "that ever I be so farre in youre daunger as ye have bene
in myne, for than my dayes were done—

¶"But, Sir Gawayne," seyde Sir Launcelot, "ye shall nat thynke that
I shall tarry longe; but sytthyn that ye unknyghtly calle me thus of   35
treson, ye shall have bothe youre hondys fulle of me." And than
Sir Launcelot armed hym at all poyntis and mounted uppon his
horse, and gate a grete speare in hys honde and rode oute at the
gate. And bothe their ostis were assembled, of them withoute and
within, and stood in aray full manly; and bothe partyes were   40
charged to holde hem stylle to se and beholde the batayle of thes
two noble knyghtes. And than they layde their spearys in their
restis and so cam togydir as thundir; and Sir Gawayne brake hys
speare in an hondred peces to hys honde, and Sir Launcelot smote
hym with a gretter myght, that Sir Gawaynes horse feete reysed, and   45
so the horse and he felle to the erthe.

Than Sir Gawayne delyverly devoyded hys horse and put hys
shylde afore hym, and egirly drew hys swerde—and bade Sir

4. *Make hit good:* i.e., prove.

Launcelot, "Alyght, traytoure knyght!"—and seyde, "Gyff a marys sonne[5] hath fayled me, wyte thou well a kyngis sonne and a quenys sonne[6] shall nat fayle the!"

Than Sir Launcelot devoyded hys horse and dressed hys shylde afore hym and drew hys swerde; and so cam [they] egirly togydirs and gaff many sad strokis, that all men on bothe partyes had wondir. But whan Sir Launcelot felte Sir Gawaynes myght so mervaylously encres, he than wythhylde hys corayge and hys wynde, and so he kepte hym undir coverte of hys myght and of hys shylde; he traced and traverced here and there to breake Sir Gawaynys strokys and hys currayge—and ever Sir Gawayne enforced hymselff wyth all hys myght and power to destroy Sir Launcelot, for, as the Freynshe booke saythe, ever as Sir Gawaynes myght encresed, ryght so encreced hys wynde and hys evyll wyll. And thus he ded grete payne unto Sir Launcelot, three owres, that he had much ado to defende hym; and whan the three owres were paste, that he felte Sir Gawayne was com home to his owne propir strengthe, than Sir Launcelot sayde, "Sir, now I have preved you twyse that ye ar a full daungerous knyght and a wondirfull man of [your] myght; and many wondir dedis have ye done in youre dayes, for by youre myght encresyng ye have desceyved many a full noble knyght. And now I fele that ye have done youre myghty dedis, now, wyte you well, I muste do my dedis."

And than Sir Launcelot strode nere Sir Gawayne and doubled hys strokys; and ever Sir Gawayne deffended hym myghtyly, but nevertheles Sir Launcelot smote such a stroke upon hys helme and upon the olde wounde that Sir Gawayne sanke downe and sowned—and anone, as he ded awake, he waved and foyned at Sir Launcelot as he lay, and seyde, "Traytoure knyght, wyte thou well I am nat yet slayne. Therefore com thou nere me, and [perfourme] thys batayle to the utteraunce!"

¶"I woll no more do than I have done," seyde Sir Launcelot. "For whan I se you on foote I woll do batayle upon you all the whyle I se you stande upon youre feete; but to smyte a wounded man that may nat stonde, God defende me from such a shame." And than he turned [hym and wente] hys way towarde the cité, and Sir Gawayne evermore callyng hym "traytoure knyght," and seyde, "Traytoure knyght! Wyte thou well, Sir Launcelot, whan I am hole I shall do batayle with the agayne, for I shall never leve the tylle the tone of us be slayne."

Thus as thys syge endured and as Sir Gawayne lay syke nerehande a moneth, and whan he was well recovirde and redy within three dayes to do batayle agayne with Sir Launcelot, ryght so cam tydyngis unto Kynge Arthur frome Inglonde that made Kynge Arthur and all hys oste to remeve.

fol.474v

fol.475r

---

5. I.e., a horse.
6. *Kyngis sonne and a quenys sonne*: i.e., Gawayne himself, as son of King Lot and Queen Morgause.

As Sir 𝔐ordred was rular of all Inglonde, he lete make lettirs as thoughe that they had com frome beyonde the see, and the lettirs specifyed that Kynge 𝔄rthur was slayne in batayle with Sir 𝔏auncelot.   [XXI.1]

⸿Wherefore Sir 𝔐ordred made a parlemente, and called the lordys togydir, and there he made them to chose [hym] Kynge; and so was he crowned at Caunturbyry, and hylde a feste there fiftene dayes. And aftirwarde he drew hym unto Wynchester, and there he toke Quene 𝔊wenyver, and seyde playnly that he wolde wedde her—which was hys unclys wyff and hys fadirs wyff. And so he made redy for the feste, and a day prefyxte that they shulde be wedded—wherefore Quene Gwenyver was passyng hevy; but she durst nat discover her harte, but spake faayre, and aggreed to Sir 𝔐ordredys wylle.

And anone she desyred of Sir 𝔐ordred to go to London to byghe all maner thynges that longed to the brydale; and bycause of her fayre speche, Sir 𝔐ordred trusted her and gaff her leve. And so whan she cam to London, she toke the Towre of London, and suddeynly in all haste possyble she stuffed hit with all maner of vytayle, and well garnysshed hit with men, and so kepte hit.

⸿And whan Sir 𝔐ordred wyst thys, he was passynge wrothe oute of mesure; and shorte tale to make, he layde a myghty syge aboute the Towre and made many assautis, and threw engynnes[7] unto them, and shotte grete gunnes.[8] But all myght nat prevayle, for Quene 𝔊wenyver wolde never—for fayre speache nother for foule—never to truste unto Sir 𝔐ordred to com in hys hondis agayne. Than cam the Bysshop of Caunturbyry,[9] whych was a noble clerke and an holy man, and thus he seyde unto Sir 𝔐ordred: "Sir, what woll ye do? Woll ye firste displease God, and sytthyn shame youreselff and all knyghthode?—

⸿For ys nat Kynge 𝔄rthur youre uncle, and no farther but youre modirs brothir, and uppon her he hymselffe begate you, uppon hys owne syster? Therefore how may ye wed youre owne fadirs wyff? And therefor, sir," seyde the Bysshop, "leve thys opynyon, other ellis I shall curse you with booke, belle, and candyll."[1]

⸿"Do thou thy warste," seyde Sir 𝔐ordred, "and I defyghe the!"

⸿"Sir," seyde the Bysshop, "wyte you well I shall nat feare me to do that me ought to do. And also ye noyse that my lorde 𝔄rthur ys slayne, and that ys nat so—and therefore ye woll make a foule warke in thys londe." "Peas, thou false pryste," seyde Sir 𝔐ordred,

[fol.475v]

---

7. *Threw engynnes:* i.e., fired siege engines (such as catapults).
8. I.e., cannon. This is an apparent innovation of Malory's and may, according to P. J. C. Field, represent his recollection of the only time in history before the completion of the *Morte Darthur* that cannon were in fact used against the Tower: in 1460 the Yorkists beseiged the Lancastrian garrison there. It is difficult to say whether the innovation is meant to invoke a kind of pro-Lancastrian allegory or is simply an evocation of historical verisimilitude.
9. On this ecclesiastical position, see n. 9, p. 7.
1. *Curse you with booke, belle, and candyll:* i.e., excommunicate you. Like the modern phrase "bell, book, and candle" Malory's alludes to certain solemn and prescribed effects used either in the Mass or the rite of excommunication.

"for and thou chauffe me ony more, I shall [make] stryke of thy hede."

¶So the Bysshop departed, and ded the cursynge[2] in the moste orguluste wyse that myght be done; and than Sir Mordred sought the Bysshop off Caunturbyry for to have slayne hym. Than the Bysshop fledde, and tooke parte of hys good with hym, and wente nyghe unto Glassyngbyry; and there he was a preste-ermyte in a chapel, and lyved in poverté and in holy prayers—for well he undirstood that myschevous warre was at honde. Than Sir Mordred soughte uppon Quene Gwenyver by lettirs and sondis, and by fayre meanys and foule meanys, to have her to com oute of the Towre of London; but all thys avayled nought, for she answerd hym shortely, opynly and pryvayly, that she had levir sle herselff than to be maryed with hym.

Than cam there worde unto Sir Mordred that Kynge Arthure had areysed the syge frome Sir Launcelot and was commynge homwarde wyth a greate oste to be avenged uppon Sir Mordred; wherefore Sir Mordred made wryttes unto all the baronny of thys londe. And muche people drew unto hym; for than was the comyn voyce amonge them that with Kynge Arthur was never othir lyff but warre and stryff, and with Sir Mordrede was grete joy and blysse. Thus was Kynge Arthur depraved,[3] and evyll seyde off—and many there were that Kynge Arthur had brought up of nought,[4] and gyffyn them londis, that myght nat than say hym a good worde.

¶Lo, ye, all Englysshemen, se ye nat what a myschyff here was? For he that was the moste kynge and nobelyst knyght of the worlde, and moste loved the felyshyp of noble knyghtes—and by hym they all were upholdyn—and yet myght nat thes Englyshemen holde them contente with hym. Lo, thus was the olde custom and usayges of thys londe; and men say that we of thys londe have nat yet loste that custom. Alas, thys ys a greate defaughte of us Englysshemen, for there may no thynge us please no terme. And so fared the peple at that tyme: they were better pleased with Sir Mordred than they were with the noble Kynge Arthur, and muche people drew unto Sir Mordred and seyde they wold abyde wyth hym for bettir and for wars.[5] And so Sir Mordred drew with a greate oste to Dovir, for there he harde sey that Kyng Arthur wolde aryve, and so he thought to beate hys owne fadir fro hys owne londys. And the moste party of all Inglonde hylde wyth Sir Mordred, for the people were so new-fangill.[6] And so, as Sir Mordred was at Dovir with hys oste—

¶So cam Kyng Arthur wyth a greate navy of shyppis and galyes and carykes. And there was Sir Mordred redy awaytyng uppon hys

2. I.e., rite of excommunication.
3. I.e., defamed, discredited.
4. *Brought up of nought:* raised from nothing.
5. I.e., worse.
6. *Lo, ye, all Englysshemen . . . so new-fangill.* This is the most famous of Malory's direct addresses to his readers concerning the political upheavals and reversals of his own day—and quite possibly those of his own life choices, given his use of *we.* For some historical contexts, see the chronology on p. xix as well as p. 759 ff. and p. 819. For Malory's other extemporary comments, see pp. 137, 231, 293, 314, 327, 595, and 625.

5

10

fol.476r

15

20

25

30

35

[2] 40

fol.476v

londynge—to lette[7] hys owne fadir to londe uppon the londe that
he was Kynge over. Than there was launchyng of greate botis and
smale, and full of noble men of armys; and there was muche
slaughtir of jantyll knyghtes, and many a full bolde barown was
layde full lowe on bothe partyes.

¶But Kynge Arthur was so currageous that there myght no maner
of knyght lette hym to lande, and hys knyghtes fyersely folowed
hym; and so they londed magré Sir Mordredis hede and all hys
power, and put Sir Mordred abak, [that he fledde] and all hys
people.

¶So whan thys batayle was done, Kynge Arthure let serche hys
people that were hurte and dede. And than was noble Sir Gawayne
founde in a greate boote, liynge more than halff dede.

¶Whan Kyng Arthur knew that he was layde so low, he wente
unto hym and so fownde hym; and there the Kynge made greate
sorow oute of mesure, and toke Sir Gawayne in hys armys, and
thryse he there sowned. And than whan he was waked, Kyng Arthur
seyde, "Alas, Sir Gawayne, my syster-son, here now thou lyghest,
the man in the worlde that I loved moste. And now ys my joy gone,
for now, my nevew Sir Gawayne, I woll discover[8] me unto you, that
in youre person and in Sir Launcelot I moste had my joy and myne
affyaunce. And now have I loste my joy of you bothe, wherefore
all myne erthely joy ys gone fro me."

¶"A, myn uncle," seyde Sir Gawayne, "now I woll that ye wyte
that my deth-dayes be com; and all I may wyte[9] myne owne hastynes and my wylfulnesse, for thorow my wylfulnes I was causer
of myne owne dethe. For I was thys day hurte and smytten uppon
myne olde wounde that Sir Launcelot gaff me—and I fele myselff
that I muste nedis be dede by the owre of noone. And thorow me
and my pryde ye have all thys shame and disease, for had that noble
knyght Sir Launcelot ben with you, as he was[1] and wolde have ben,
thys unhappy warre had never ben begunne; for he, thorow hys
noble knyghthode and hys noble bloode, hylde all youre cankyrde
enemyes in subjeccion and daungere. And now," seyde Sir Gawayne,
"ye shall mysse Sir Launcelot. But alas that I wolde nat accorde with
hym! And therefore, fayre unkle, I pray you that I may have paupir,
penne, and inke, that I may wryte unto Sir Launcelot a letter wrytten
with myne owne honde."

¶So whan pauper, penne, and inke was brought, than Sir
Gawayne was sette up waykely[2] by Kynge Arthure—for he was shryven a lytyll afore—and than he toke hys penne and wrote thus, as
the Freynshe booke makith mencion:

> ¶Unto the, Sir Launcelot, floure of all noble knyghtes that
> ever I harde of or saw be my dayes, I, Sir Gawayne, Kynge Lottis
> sonne of Orkeney, and systirs sonne unto the noble Kynge

fol.477r

How Sir Gawayn
wrote a letter to Sir
Launcelot at the tyme
of his dethe

7. I.e., hinder.
8. I.e., reveal.
9. *All I may wyte:* I can blame everything on.
1. I.e., once was.
2. I.e., in his weakness.

Arthur, sende the[3] gretynge, lattynge the to have knowlecche that the tenthe day of May I was smytten uppon the olde wounde that thou gaff me afore the cité of Benwyke, and thorow that wounde I am com to my dethe-day.

¶And I woll that all the worlde wyte that I, Sir Gawayne, knyght of the Table Rounde, soughte my dethe, and nat thorow thy deservynge, but myne owne sekynge. Wherefore I beseche the, Sir Launcelot, to returne agayne unto thys realme and se my toumbe and pray som prayer more other les for my soule. And thys same day that I wrote this same sedull I was hurte to the dethe, whych wounde was fyrste gyffyn of thyn honde, Sir Launcelot; for of a more nobelar man myght I nat be slayne. Also, Sir Launcelot, for all the love that ever was betwyxte us, make no taryyng, but com over the see in all the goodly haste that ye may wyth youre noble knyghtes, and rescow that noble kynge that made the[4] knyght, for he ys full straytely bestad wyth an false traytoure whych ys my halff-brothir Sir Mordred. For he hath crowned hymselff Kynge, and wolde have wedded my lady Quene Gwenyver; and so had he done, had she nat kepte the Towre of London with stronge honde.[5] And so the tenthe day of May last paste, my lorde Kynge Arthur and we all londed uppon them at Dover; and there he put that false traytoure Sir Mordred to flyght—and so hit there mysfortuned me to be smytten uppon the strooke that ye gaff me of olde. And the date of thys lettir was wrytten but two owrys and an halff afore my dethe, wrytten with myne owne honde and subscrybed[6] with parte of my harte blood. And therefore I requyre the, moste famous knyght of the worlde, that thou wolte se my tumbe.

fol.477v

And than he wepte and Kynge Arthur both, and sowned. And whan they were awaked bothe, the Kynge made Sir Gawayne to resceyve hys sacrament.[7] And than Sir Gawayne prayde the Kynge for to sende for Sir Launcelot and to cherysshe hym aboven all othir knyghtes. And so at the owre of noone Sir Gawayne yelded up the goste. And than the Kynge lat entere hym in a chapell within Dover castell; and there yet all men may se the skulle of hym, and the same wounde is sene that Sir Launcelot gaff in batayle.[8]

¶Than was hit tolde the Kynge that Sir Mordred had pyght a new fylde[9] uppon Bireon Downe. And so uppon the morne Kynge Arthur rode thydir to hym, and there was a grete batayle betwyxt hem, and muche people were slayne on bothe partyes; but at the laste

3. Thee.
4. Thee.
5. *Stronge honde*: i.e., military force.
6. I.e., signed.
7. I.e., last rites.
8. Caxton also mentions the presence of Gawain's skull at Dover Castle (see p. 816), and it is quite possible that such a "relic," however inauthentic it may have been, was indeed kept there. Cf. Caxton's account of the Round Table at Winchester (p. 816), and n. 5, p. 61.
9. *Pyght a new fylde*: established positions at a new prospective battlefield.

Kynge Arthurs party stoode beste, and Sir Mordred and hys party fledde unto Caunturbyry. And than the Kynge let serche all the downys for hys knyghtes that were slayne and entered[1] them, and salved them with soffte salvys that full sore were wounded.

⁋Than much people drew unto Kynge Arthur, and than they sayde that Sir Mordred warred uppon Kynge Arthure wyth wronge. And anone Kynge Arthure drew hym wyth his oste downe by the seesyde westewarde towarde Salusbyry; and there was a day, assygned betwyxte Kynge Arthur and Sir Mordred, that they shulde mete uppon a downe besyde Salesbyry and nat farre frome the seesyde. And thys day was assygned on Monday aftir Trynyté Sonday,[2] whereof Kynge Arthur was passyng glad that he myght be avenged uppon Sir Mordred. Than Sir Mordred arraysed muche people aboute London, for they of Kente, Southsex and Surrey, Esax, Suffolke and Northefolke[3] helde the moste party with Sir Mordred. And many a full noble knyght drew unto hym and also to the Kynge— but they that loved Sir Launcelot drew unto Sir Mordred.

⁋So uppon Trynyté Sunday at nyght Kynge Arthure dremed a wondirfull dreme, and in hys dreme hym semed that he saw uppon a chafflet a chayre, and the chayre was faste to a whele,[4] and thereuppon sate Kynge Arthure in the rychest clothe of golde that myght be made. And the Kynge thought there was undir hym, farre from hym, an hydeous depe blak watir, and therein was all maner of serpentis and wormes and wylde bestis, fowle and orryble. And suddeynly the Kynge thought that the whyle turned up-so-downe, and he felle amonge the serpentes, and every beste toke hym by a lymme. And than the Kynge cryed as he lay in hys bed, "Helpe! helpe!" And than knyghtes, squyars, and yomen awaked the Kynge; and than he was so amased that he wyste nat where he was. And than so he awaked untylle hit was nyghe day, and than he felle on slumberynge agayne, nat slepynge nor thorowly wakynge:

⁋So the Kyng semed verryly that there cam Sir Gawayne unto hym with a numbir of fayre ladyes wyth hym. So whan Kyng Arthur saw hym, he seyde, "Wellcom, my systers sonne! I wende ye had bene dede; and now I se the on lyve, much am I beholdyn unto Allmyghty Jesu. A, fayre nevew, what bene thes ladyes that hyder be com with you?"

⁋"Sir," seyde Sir Gawayne, "all thes be ladyes for whom I have foughten for, whan I was man lyvynge, and all thes ar tho that I ded batayle fore in ryghteuous quarels; and God hath gyvyn hem

[3]
fol.478r

fol.478v

1. I.e., interred, buried.
2. The first Sunday after Pentecost, instituted to honor the Holy Trinity. On Pentecost, see n. 1, p. 10.
3. These are the counties stretching to the south and east of London, with Kent—and therefore Dover, where Mordred first awaits Arthur—roughly in the middle. Cf. the *sMA*, one of Malory's main sources at this point, which says that Mordred gained the support of great men "on ylke a (i.e., each) side" of Dover (line 3046). His likely source aside, it has been argued that in naming these counties, Malory may well have been recalling centers of Yorkist loyalty during the Wars of the Roses.
4. *Was faste*: i.e., fixed fast. On the Wheel of Fortune, see n. 7, p. 669. Arthur's dream is, of course, prophetic but, after the model of the *sMA*, is not as philosophical as Malory's other main source, the French *Mort le Roi Artu*. For the corresponding source passages, see pp. 743 and 754.

that grace at their grete prayer, bycause I ded batayle for them for
their ryght, that they shulde bryng me hydder unto you. Thus much
hath gyvyn me leve God for to warne you of youre dethe; for, and
ye fyght as tomorne with Sir 𝕸𝖔𝖗𝖉𝖗𝖊𝖉, as ye bothe have assygned,
doute ye nat ye shall be slayne, and the moste party of youre people   5
on bothe partyes. And for the grete grace and goodnes that All-
myghty Jesu hath unto you, and for pyté of you and many mo other
good men there shall be slayne, God hath sente me to you of Hys
speciall grace to gyff you warnyng that in no wyse ye do batayle as
tomorne, but that ye take a tretyse for a moneth-day, and proffir   10
you largely[5] so that tomorne ye put in a delay. For within a moneth
shall com Sir 𝕷𝖆𝖚𝖓𝖈𝖊𝖑𝖔𝖙 with all hys noble knyghtes, and rescow you
worshypfully, and sle Sir 𝕸𝖔𝖗𝖉𝖗𝖊𝖉 and all that ever wyll holde wyth
hym."

⁋Than Sir 𝕲𝖆𝖜𝖆𝖞𝖓𝖊 and all the ladyes vanysshed. And anone the   15
Kynge called uppon hys knyghtes, squyars, and yomen, and
charged them wyghtly to fecche hys noble lordis and wyse bysshoppis unto hym; and whan they were com, the Kynge tolde hem
of hys avision, that Sir 𝕲𝖆𝖜𝖆𝖞𝖓𝖊 had tolde hym and warned hym
that and he fought on the morn he sholde be slayne. Than the   20
Kynge commaunded Sir 𝕷𝖚𝖈𝖆𝖓 𝖙𝖍𝖊 𝕭𝖚𝖙𝖑𝖊𝖗𝖊 and hys brothir Sir 𝕭𝖊𝖉𝖞-
𝖛𝖊𝖗𝖊 the bolde, with two bysshoppis wyth hem, and charged them   fol.479r
in ony wyse to take a tretyse for a moneth-day wyth Sir 𝕸𝖔𝖗𝖉𝖗𝖊𝖉—
"and spare nat: proffir hym londys and goodys as much as ye thynke
resonable."   25

So than they departed and cam to Sir 𝕸𝖔𝖗𝖉𝖗𝖊𝖉 where he had a
grymme oste of an hondred thousand, and there they entretyd Sir
𝕸𝖔𝖗𝖉𝖗𝖊𝖉 longe tyme. And at the laste Sir 𝕸𝖔𝖗𝖉𝖗𝖊𝖉 was aggreed for
to have Cornwale and Kente by Kynge 𝕬𝖗𝖙𝖍𝖚𝖗𝖘 dayes, and afftir that
all Inglonde, after the dayes of Kynge 𝕬𝖗𝖙𝖍𝖚𝖗. Than were they con-   [4]   30
descende that Kynge 𝕬𝖗𝖙𝖍𝖚𝖗𝖊 and Sir 𝕸𝖔𝖗𝖉𝖗𝖊𝖉 shulde mete betwyxte
bothe their ostis, and everych of them shulde brynge fourtene persons. And so they cam wyth thys worde unto 𝕬𝖗𝖙𝖍𝖚𝖗; than seyde he,
"I am glad that thys ys done." And so he wente into the fylde.

And whan Kynge 𝕬𝖗𝖙𝖍𝖚𝖗 shulde departe, he warned all hys oste   35
that and they se ony swerde drawyn, "loke ye com on fyersely and
sle that traytoure Sir 𝕸𝖔𝖗𝖉𝖗𝖊𝖉, for [I] in no wyse truste hym." In
lyke wyse Sir 𝕸𝖔𝖗𝖉𝖗𝖊𝖉 warned hys oste, that "and ye se ony maner
of swerde drawyn, loke that ye com on fyersely and so sle all that
ever before you stondyth, for in no wyse I woll nat truste for thys   40
tretyse." And in the same wyse seyde Sir 𝕸𝖔𝖗𝖉𝖗𝖊𝖉 unto hys oste,
"for I know well my fadir woll be avenged uppon me." And so they
mette as their poyntemente was, and were agreed and accorded
thorowly. And wyne was fette, and they dranke togydir.

Ryght so cam oute an addir[6] of a lytyll hethe buysshe, and hit   45
stange a knyght in the foote. And so whan the knyght felte hym so
stonge, he loked downe and saw the adder; and anone he drew hys

5. *Proffir you largely:* make generous offers.
6. Cf. n. 5, p. 469.

swerde to sle the addir, and thought[7] none othir harme. And whan
the oste on bothe partyes saw that swerde drawyn, than they blewe
beamys, trumpettis, and hornys, and shoutted grymly, and so bothe
ostis dressed hem togydirs.[8] And Kynge **Arthur** toke hys horse, and
seyde, "Alas, this unhappy day!" and so rode to hys party— fol.479v 5

❡And Sir **Mordred** in lyke wyse: and never syns was there seyne
a more dolefuller batayle in no Crysten londe, for there was but
russhynge and rydynge, foynynge and strykynge, and many a grym
worde was there spokyn of aythir to othir, and many a dedely
stroke. But ever Kynge **Arthure** rode thorowoute the batayle[9] of Sir 10
Mordred many tymys and ded full nobely, as a noble kynge shulde
do, and at all tymes he fayntted[1] never. And Sir **Mordred** ded hys
devoure that day and put hymselffe in grete perell. And thus they
fought all the longe day, and never stynted tylle the noble knyghtes
were layde to the colde erthe. And ever they fought stylle tylle hit 15
was nere nyght, and by than was there an hondred thousand leyde
dede uppon the erthe.

Than was Kynge **Arthure** wode wroth[2] oute of mesure, whan he
saw hys people so slayne frome hym. And so he loked aboute hym
and cowde se no mo of all hys oste and good knyghtes leffte no 20
mo on lyve but two knyghtes: the tone was Sir **Lucan de Buttler** and
hys brother, Sir **Bedwere**—and yette they were full sore wounded.

"Jesu mercy!" seyde the Kynge, "where ar all my noble knyghtes
becom? Alas, that ever I shulde se thys doleful day! For now", seyde
Kynge **Arthur**, "I am com to myne ende. But wolde to God," seyde 25
he, "that I wyste now where were that traytoure Sir **Mordred** that
hath caused all thys myschyff." Than Kynge **Arthur** loked aboute
and was ware where stood Sir **Mordred** leanyng uppon hys swerde
amonge a grete hepe of dede men. "Now gyff me my speare," seyde
Kynge **Arthure** unto Sir **Lucan**, "for yondir I have aspyed the tray- 30
toure that all thys woo hath wrought."

❡"Sir, latte hym be," seyde Sir **Lucan**, "for he ys unhappy;[3] and
yf ye passe this unhappy day ye shall be ryght well revenged. And,
[good lord, remember ye of your nyghtes dreme and] what the
spyryte of Sir **Gawayne** tolde you tonyght, and yet God of Hys grete fol.480r 35
goodnes hath preserved you hyddirto. And for Goddes sake, my
lorde, leve of thys, for blyssed be God, ye have won the fylde: for
yet we ben here three on lyve, and with Sir **Mordred** ys nat one on
lyve. And therefore if ye leve of now, thys wycked day of desteny
ys paste." 40

❡"Now tyde me dethe, tyde me lyff," seyde the Kyng, "now I se
hym yondir alone, he shall never ascape myne hondes—for at a
bettir avayle shall I never have hym."

❡"God spyede you well," seyde Sir **Bedyvere**. Than the Kynge gate
his speare in bothe hys hondis, and ran towarde Sir **Mordred**, cryyng 45

---

7. I.e., intended.
8. *Dressed hem togydirs:* arrayed themselves against each other.
9. I.e., battalion.
1. I.e., faltered, gave way.
2. *Wode wroth:* wildly angry.
3. I.e., dangerously ill-fortuned.

and saying, "Traytoure, now ys thy dethe-day com!" And whan Sir
Mordred saw Kynge Arthur, he ran untyll hym with hys swerde
drawyn in hys honde; and there Kyng Arthur smote Sir Mordred
undir the shylde, with a foyne of hys speare, thorowoute the body
more than a fadom. And whan Sir Mordred felte that he had hys   5
dethys wounde, he threste hymselff with the myght that he had
upp to the burre of Kyng Arthurs speare; and ryght so he smote hys
fadir, Kynge Arthure, with hys swerde holdynge in both hys hondys,
uppon the syde of the hede, that the swerde perced the helmet
and the tay of the brayne. And therewith Mordred daysshed downe   10
starke dede to the erthe. And noble Kynge Arthure felle in a
swoughe to the erthe, and there he sowned oftyntymys; and Sir
Lucan and Sir Bedwere offtetymys hove hym up, and so waykly
betwyxte them they lad hym to a lytyll chapell nat farre frome the
see—and whan the Kyng was there, he thought hym resonabely   15
eased. Than harde they people crye in the fylde.

⁋"Now go thou, Sir Lucan," seyde the Kyng, "and do me to wyte
what betokyns that noyse in the fylde."

⁋So Sir Lucan departed, for he was grevously wounded in many
placis; and so as he yode he saw and harkened by the moonelyght   20
how that pyllours and robbers were com into the fylde to pylle and
to robbe many a full noble knyght of brochys and bees and of many   fol.480v
a good rynge and many a ryche juell. And who that were nat dede
all oute, there they slewe them for their harneys and their ryches.

⁋Whan Sir Lucan undirstood thys warke, he cam to the Kynge   25
as sone as he myght, and tolde hym all what he had harde and
seyne. "Therefore be my rede," seyde Sir Lucan, "hit ys beste that
we brynge you to som towne." "I wolde hit were so," seyde the   [5]
Kynge, "but I may nat stonde, my hede worchys⁴ so—

⁋"A, Sir Launcelot!" seyde Kynge Arthure, "thys day have I sore   30
myssed the! And alas, that ever I was ayenste the, for now have I
my dethe, whereof Sir Gawayne me warned in my dreame."

⁋Than Sir Lucan toke up the Kynge the tone party, and Sir Bedwere the othir parté, and in the lyfftyng up the Kynge sowned; and
in the lyfftynge Sir Lucan felle in a sowne, that parte of hys guttis   35
felle oute of hys body, and therewith the noble knyght hys harte
braste. And whan the Kynge awoke, he behylde Sir Lucan, how he
lay fomyng at the mowth, and parte of his guttes lay at hys fyete.

⁋"Alas," seyde the Kynge, "thys ys to me a fulle hevy syght, to
se thys noble deuke so dye for my sake, for he wold have holpyn   40
me that had more nede of helpe than I. Alas, that he wolde nat
complayne hym, for hys harte was so sette to helpe me. Now Jesu
have mercy uppon hys soule!" Than Sir Bedwere wepte for the deth
of hys brothir.

⁋"Now leve thys mournynge and wepyng, jantyll knyght," seyde   45
the Kyng, "for all thys woll nat avayle me. For wyte thou well, and
I myght lyve myselff, the dethe of Sir Lucan wolde greve me evermore. But my tyme passyth on faste," seyde the Kynge:

4. I.e., hurts.

¶"Therefore," seyde Kynge **Arthur** unto Sir **Bedwere**, "take thou here **Excaliber**, my good swerde, and go wyth hit to yondir watirs syde; and whan thou commyste there, I charge the throw my swerde in that water, and com agayne and telle me what thou syeste there."

¶"My lorde," seyde Sir **Bedwere**, "youre commaundement shall be done, and lyghtly brynge you worde agayne." So Sir **Bedwere** fol.481r departed, and by the way he behylde that noble swerde, and the pomell and the hauffte was all precious stonys; and than he seyde to hymselff, "If I throw thys ryche swerde in the water, thereof shall never com good, but harme and losse." And than Sir **Bedwere** hyd **Excalyber** undir a tre, and so as sone as he myght he cam agayne unto the Kynge, and seyde he had bene at the watir and had throwen the swerde into the watir.

¶"What sawe thou there?" seyde the Kynge.

¶"Sir," he seyde, "[I] saw nothyng but wawis and wyndys." "That ys untruly seyde of the," seyde the Kynge. "And therefore go thou lyghtly agayne, and do my commaundemente; as thou arte to me lyff and dere, spare nat, but throw hit in."

¶Than Sir **Bedwere** returned agayne and toke the swerde in hys honde; and yet hym thought synne and shame to throw away that noble swerde. And so effte he hyd the swerde, and returned agayne and tolde the Kynge that he had bene at the watir and done hys commaundement. "What sawist thou there?" seyde the Kynge.

¶"Sir, he seyde, "I sy nothynge but watirs wap and wawys wanne."[5] "A, traytour unto me and untrew," seyde Kyng **Arthure**, "now hast thou betrayed me twyse! Who wolde wene that thou that hast bene to me so leve and dere, and also named so noble a knyght, that thou wolde betray me for the ryches of thys swerde? But now go agayn lyghtly; for thy longe taryynge puttith me in grete jouperté of my lyff—for I have takyn colde—and but if thou do now as I bydde the, if ever I may se the, I shall sle the myne[6] owne hondis, for thou woldist for my rych swerde se me dede."

Than Sir **Bedwere** departed and wente to the swerde and lyghtly toke hit up. And so he wente unto the watirs syde; and there he bounde the gyrdyll aboute the hyltis, and threw the swerde as farre fol.481v into the watir as he myght. And there cam an arme and an honde above the watir, and toke hit and cleyght hit, and shoke hit thryse and braundysshed, and than vanysshed with the swerde into the watir.

¶So Sir **Bedyvere** cam agayne to the Kynge and tolde hym what he saw.

¶"Alas," seyde the Kynge, "helpe me hens, for I drede me I have taryed over longe."

¶Than Sir **Bedwere** toke the Kynge uppon hys bak, and so wente with hym to the watirs syde. And whan they were there, evyn faste by the banke hoved a lytyll barge wyth many fayre ladyes in hit;

5. *Watirs wap and wawys wanne:* the waters lap and the waves grow dark.
6. I.e., with my.

and amonge hem all was a quene, and all they had blak hoodis, and all they wepte and shryked whan they saw Kynge Arthur.

❡"Now put me into that barge," seyde the Kynge. And so he ded, sofftely; and there resceyved hym three ladyes, with grete mournyng. And so they sette hem downe, and in one of their lappis Kyng Arthure layde hys hede. And than the quene seyde, "A, my dere brothir, why have ye taryed so longe frome me? Alas, thys wounde on youre hede hath caught overmuch coulde." And anone they rowed fromward the londe. And Sir Bedivere behylde all tho ladyes go frowarde hym; than Sir Bedivere cryed and seyde, "A, my lorde Arthur, what shall becom of me, now ye go frome me and leve me here alone amonge myne enemyes?"

❡"Comforte thyselff," seyde the Kynge, "and do as well as thou mayste, for in me ys no truste for to truste in. For I [wyl] into the vale of *Avylyon* to hele me of my grevous wounde—and if thou here nevermore of me, pray for my soule." But ever the quene and ladyes wepte and shryked, that hit was pité to hyre. And as sone as Sir Bedivere had loste the syght of the barge, he wepte and wayled, and so toke the foreste and wente all that nyght. And in the mornyng he was ware, betwyxte two holtis hore,[7] of a chapell and an ermytage.

❡Than was Sir Bedivere fayne, and thyder he wente; and whan he cam into the chapell, he saw where lay an ermyte grovelynge on all foure faste there by a tumbe was[8] newe gravyn.

❡Whan the ermyte saw Sir Bedivere he knewe hym well, for he was but lytyll tofore Bysshop of Caunturbery, that Sir Mordred fleamed.

❡"Sir," seyde Sir Bedivere, "what man ys there here entyred that ye pray so faste fore?"

❡"Fayre sunne," seyde the ermyte, "I wote nat veryly but by demynge. But thys same nyght, at mydnyght, here cam a numbir of ladyes, and brought here a dede corse and prayde me to entyre hym—and here they offird an hondred tapers, and they gaff me a thousande besauntes."

❡"Alas," seyde Sir Bedivere, "that was my lorde Kynge Arthur, whych lyethe here gravyn in thys chapell."

❡Than Sir Bedivere sowned; and whan he awooke, he prayde the ermyte that he myght abyde with hym stylle, there to lyve with fastynge and prayers. "For from hens woll I never go," seyde Sir Bedivere, "be my wyll, but all the dayes of my lyff here to pray for my lorde Arthur."

"Sir, ye ar wellcom to me," seyde the ermyte, "for I know you bettir than ye wene that I do: for ye ar Sir Bedivere the bolde, and the full noble duke Sir Lucan de Butlere was your brother." Than Sir Bedivere tolde the ermyte all as ye have harde tofore, and so he belaffte with the ermyte that was beforehande Bysshop of Caunturbyry; and there Sir Bedivere put uppon hym poure clothys, and served the ermyte full lowly in fastyng and in prayers.

fol.482r

[6]

---

7. *Holtis hore:* (old) gray woods.
8. I.e., which was.

¶Thus of **Arthur** I fynde no more wrytten in bokis that bene auctorysed, nothir more of the verry sertaynté of hys dethe harde I never rede,[9] but thus was he lad away in a shyp wherein were three quenys: that one was Kynge **Arthur** syster, Quene **Morgan le Fay**, the tother was the Quene of North Galis, and the thirde was the Quene of the Waste Londis. Also there was Dame **Nynyve**, the chyff lady of the laake, whych had wedded Sir **Pellyas**, the good knyght; and thys lady had done muche for Kynge **Arthure**. (And thys Dame **Nynyve** wolde never suffir Sir **Pelleas** to be in no place where he shulde be in daungere of hys lyff, and so he lyved unto the uttermuste of hys dayes with her in grete reste.)

¶Now more of the deth of Kynge **Arthur** coude I never fynde, but that thes ladyes brought hym to hys grave, and such one was entyred there whych the ermyte bare wytnes that sometyme was Bysshop of Caunturbyry. But yet the ermyte knew nat in sertayne that he was veryly the body of Kynge **Arthur**; for thys tale Sir **Bed-were**, a knyght of the Table Rounde, made hit to be wrytten.

Yet som men say in many partys of Inglonde that Kynge **Arthure** ys nat dede, but had by the wyll of Oure Lorde Jesu into another place; and men say that he shall com agayne, and he shall wynne the Holy Crosse.[1]

¶Yet I woll nat say that hit shall be so; but rather I wolde sey, here in thys worlde he chaunged hys lyff.[2] And many men say that there ys wrytten uppon the tumbe thys [vers]:[3]

Hic iacet Arthurus, rex quondam rexque futurus.

And thus leve I here Sir **Bedyvere** with the ermyte that dwelled that tyme in a chapell besydes Glassyngbyry, and there was hys ermy-tage; and so they lyved in prayers and fastynges and grete abstyn-aunce. And whan Quene **Gwenyver** undirstood that Kynge **Arthure** was dede, and all the noble knyghtes, Sir **Mordred** and all the remanaunte, than she stale away with fyve ladyes with her, and so she wente to Amysbyry. And there she lete make herselff a nunne, and wered whyght clothys and blak, and grete penaunce she toke uppon her as ever ded synfull woman in thys londe. And never

fol.482v

5

10

15

[7]

20

25

30

fol.483r

---

9. I.e., read of.
1. I.e., recover the Holy Land for Christendom. On crusading concerns in Malory's day, see n. 5, p. 149; cf. his closing comments about some of Launcelot's survivors, at p. 697.
2. *He chaunged hys lyff:* this is one of Malory's most ambiguous statements; it could mean simply that Arthur died (cf. n. 5, p. 522), or could refer to his passing on to a new condition of living elsewhere in this world (not unlike Gwenyvere, as soon noted below).
3. *Vers:* as supplied from Caxton, it may not be an authentic reading, but it does accurately describe the famous epitaph that follows (which can be translated "Here lies Arthur, king once, king to be"); it is written in an internally rhyming six-stress form popular in Latin poetry of the Middle Ages and known as a leonine hexameter (the origin of the first part of the term is obscure, perhaps named after a poet who was well known for his use of the meter). Among other purposes, the form was commonly employed for single-line proverbs and mnemonic tags, functions at least partially served in the present instance, as the epitaph appears to have been widely known, a response perhaps to a popular legend of ancient (Celtic) origins that envisioned a king's transport to a magical otherworld. The epitaph appears in a number of other medieval texts, most notably in nearly identical form as a later addition to the end of the *aMA* and, as John Withrington has pointed out, in some MSS of John Lydgate's *Fall of Princes,* a "best-seller," that Malory may well have known. The epitaph comes at the end of a sequence of statements not matched in Malory's immediate sources and that defer certification of Arthur's death and allow for the possi-bility of his return—even if only in terms of the perdurability of fame.

creature coude make her myry, but ever she lyved in fastynge, prayers, and almes-dedis, that all maner of people mervayled how vertuously she was chaunged.

Now leve we the Quene in Amysbery, a nunne in whyght clothys and blak (and there she was abbas and rular, as reson wolde), and now turne we from her and speke we of Sir Launcelot du Lake— [5]

That whan he harde in hys contrey that Sir Mordred was [8] crowned kynge in Inglonde and made warre ayenst Kyng Arthur, hys owne fadir, and wolde lette[4] hym to londe in hys[5] owne londe—also hit was tolde hym how Sir Mordred had leyde a syge aboute the Towre of London, bycause the Quene wold nat wedde hym—than was Sir Launcelot wrothe oute of mesure, and seyde to hys kynnesmen, "Alas, that double traytoure Sir Mordred, now me repentith that ever he ascaped my hondys, for much shame hath he done unto my lorde Arthure. For I fele by thys dolefull letter that Sir Gawayne sente me—on whos soule Jesu have mercy—that my lorde Arthur ys full harde bestad. Alas," seyde Sir Launcelot, "that ever I shulde lyve to hyre of that moste noble kynge that made me knyght thus to be oversette with[6] hys subjette in hys owne realme. And this dolefull lettir that my lorde Sir Gawayne hath sente me afore hys dethe, praynge me to se hys tumbe, wyte you well hys doleffull wordes shall never go frome my harte—for he was a full noble knyght as ever was born; and in an unhappy owre was I born, that ever I shulde have that myssehappe to sle firste Sir Gawayne, Sir Gaherys the good knyght, and myne owne frynde Sir Gareth that was a full noble knyght. Now, alas, I may sey I am unhappy that ever I shulde do thus—and yet, alas, myght I never have hap to sle that traytoure, Sir Mordred."

"Now leve youre complayntes," seyde Sir Bors, "and firste revenge you of the dethe of Sir Gawayne, on whos soule Jesu have mercy; and hit woll be well done that ye se hys tumbe, and secundly that ye revenge my lorde Arthur and my lady Quene Gwenyver." "I thanke you," seyde Sir Launcelot, "for ever ye woll my worshyp." Than they made hem redy in all haste that myght be, with shyppis and galyes, with hym and hys oste to pas into Inglonde. And so at the laste he cam to Dover; and there he landed with seven kyngis, and the numbir[7] was hedeous to beholde.

¶Than Sir Launcelot spyrred of men of Dover where was the Kynge becom. And anone the people tolde hym how he was slayne, and Sir Mordred to, with an hondred thousand that dyed upon a day; and how Sir Mordred gaff Kynge Arthur the first batayle there at hys londynge, and there was Sir Gawayne slayne; and upon the morne Sir Mordred faught with the Kynge on Baram Downe, and there the Kyng put Sir Mordred to the wars.[8] "Alas," seyde Sir Launcelot, "thys is the hevyest tydyngis that ever cam to my harte!

fol.483v

4. I.e., prevent.
5. I.e., Arthur's.
6. I.e., by.
7. I.e., number of troops.
8. I.e., worse.

❡"Now, fayre sirres," seyde Sir **Launcelot**, "shew me the tumbe
of Sir **Gawayne**." And anone he was brought into the castel of Dover,
and so they shewed hym the tumbe. Than Sir **Launcelot** kneled
downe by the tumbe and wepte, and prayde hartely for hys soule.
And that nyght he lete make a dole of⁹ all that wolde com of the   5
towne or of the contrey. They had as much fleyssh and fysshe and
wyne and ale, and every man and woman he dalt to twelve pence,
com whoso wolde. Thus with hys owne honde dalte he thys money,
in a mournyng gown; and ever he wepte hartely, and prayde the
people to pray for the soule of Sir **Gawayne**. And on the morn all   10
the prystes and clarkes that myght be gotyn in the contrey and in
the town were there, and sange Massis of requiem. And there offird
first Sir **Launcelot**, and he offird an hondred pounde; and than the
seven kynges offirde, and every of them offirde fourty pounde; also
there was a thousand knyghtes, and every of them offirde a pounde;   15
and the offeryng dured fro the morne to nyght.

And there Sir **Launcelot** lay two nyghtes uppon hys tumbe in
prayers and in dolefull wepynge. Than on the thirde day, Sir **Launcelot** called the kyngis, deukes, and erlis, with the barownes and all
hys noble knyghtes, and seyde thus: "My fayre lordis, I thanke you   20
all of youre comynge into thys contrey with me. But wyte you well,
all we ar com to late—and that shall repente me whyle I lyve—but
ayenste deth may no man rebell. But sytthyn hit ys so," seyde Sir
Launcelot, "I woll myselffe ryde and syke my lady, Quene **Gwenyver**;
for, as I here sey, she hath had grete payne and muche disease,¹   25
and I here say that she ys fledde into the weste. And therefore ye
all shall abyde me here; and but if I com agayne within thes fyftene
dayes, take youre shyppis and youre felyship and departe into youre
contrey, for I woll do as I sey you."

Than cam Sir **Bors** and seyde, "My lorde Sir **Launcelot**, what   30
thynke ye for to do, now for to ryde in thys realme? Wyte you well
ye shall do fynde feaw fryndis." "Be as be may as for that," seyde
Sir **Launcelot**, "kepe you stylle here, for I woll furthe on my journey,
and no man nor chylde shall go with me." So hit was no boote to
stryve,² but he departed and rode westirly; and there he sought a   35
seven or eyght dayes, and at the laste he cam to a nunry. And anone
Quene **Gwenyver** was ware of Sir **Launcelot** as she walked in the
cloyster. And anone as she saw hym there, she sowned thryse, that
all ladyes and jantyllwomen had worke inowghe to hold the Quene
frome the erthe.   40

❡So whan she myght speke, she called her ladyes and jantillwomen to her, and than she sayde thus: "Ye mervayle, fayre ladyes,
why I make thys fare. Truly," she seyde, "hit ys for the syght of
yondir knyght that yondir stondith, wherefore I pray you calle hym
hyddir to me."   45

Than Sir **Launcelot** was brought before her; than the Quene seyde
to all tho ladyes, "Thorow thys same man and me hath all thys

9. *A dole of*: a (memorial) distribution of gifts for.
1. I.e., hardship.
2. *Hit was no boote to stryve*: there was nothing to be gained in arguing.

warre be wrought, and the deth of the moste nobelest knyghtes of
the worlde; for thorow oure love that we have loved togydir ys my
moste noble lorde slayne. Therefore, Sir Launcelot, wyte thou well   fol.484v
I am sette in suche a plyght to gete my soule [hele].³ And yet I
truste, thorow Goddis grace and thorow Hys Passion of Hys woun-   5
dis wyde, that aftir my deth I may have a syght of the blyssed face
of Cryste Jesu, and on Doomesday to sytte on Hys ryght syde;⁴ for
as synfull as ever I was, now ar seyntes in hevyn.⁵ And therefore,
Sir Launcelot, I requyre the and beseche the hartily, for all the love
that ever was betwyxt us, that thou never se me no more in the   10
visayge. And I commaunde the, on Goddis behalff, that thou forsake my company, and to thy kyngedom loke thou turne agayne,
and kepe well thy realme frome warre and wrake. For as well as I
have loved the heretofore, myne harte woll nat serve now to se the;
for thorow the and me ys the floure of kyngis and knyghtes   15
destroyed. And therefore go thou to thy realme, and there take ye
a wyff and lyff with hir wyth joy and blys—and I pray the hartely
to pray for me to the everlastynge Lorde that I may amende my
mysselyvyng."

❡"Now, my swete madame," seyde Sir Launcelot, "wolde ye that   20
I shuld turne agayne unto my contrey and there to wedde a lady?
Nay, madame, wyte you well, that shall I never do, for I shall never
be so false unto you of that⁶ I have promysed; but the selff⁷ desteny
that ye have takyn you to, I woll take me to, for the pleasure of
Jesu, and ever for you I caste me specially to pray."   25

❡"A, Sir Launcelot, if ye woll do so and holde thy promyse! But I
may never beleve you," seyde the Quene, "but that ye woll turne
to the worlde agayne."

❡"Well, madame," seyde he, "ye say as hit pleasith you, for yet
wyste ye me never false of my promyse. And God deffende but that   30
I shulde forsake the worlde as ye have done; for in the Queste of
the Sankgreall I had that tyme forsakyn the vanytees of the worlde,
had nat youre love bene. And if I had done so at that tyme with
my harte, wylle, and thought, I had passed all the knyghtes that
ever were in the Sankgreall except Sir⁸ [Galahad, my sone. And ther- 35
fore, lady, sythen ye have taken you to perfeccion, I must nedys
take me to perfection, of ryght. For I take recorde of God, in you
I have had myn erthly joye; and yf I had founden you now so
dysposed, I had caste me to have had you into myn owne royame:
"But sythen I fynde you thus desposed, I ensure you faythfully,   [10]   40
I wyl ever take me to penaunce and praye whyle my lyf las-
teth, yf that I may fynde ony heremyte, other graye or whyte,⁹ that

---

3. *Soule hele:* soul's health (i.e., redemption).
4. I.e., on the side of those who are saved.
5. *for as . . . in hevyn:* for there are now saints in heaven who were once as sinful as I ever
   was.
6. I.e., that which.
7. I.e., same.
8. At this point the Winchester MS breaks off, having lost its final gathering, some sixteen
   folio sides. Text corresponding to that which is missing is supplied from Caxton's edition.
9. *Graye or whyte:* i.e., Franciscan or Carmelite (the latter distinguished from white monks,
   or Cistercians).

wyl receyve me. Wherfore, madame, I praye you kysse me, and
never no more."

"Nay," sayd the Quene, "that shal I never do, but absteyne you
from suche werkes." And they departed; but there was never so
harde an herted man but he wold have wepte to see the dolour
that they made, for there was lamentacyon as they had be stungyn
wyth sperys, and many tymes they swouned; and the ladyes bare
the Quene to hir chambre; and Syr Launcelot awok, and went and
took his hors, and rode al that day and al nyght in a forest, wepyng.
And atte last he was ware of an ermytage and a chappel stode
betwyxte two clyffes, and than he herde a lytel belle rynge to
Masse, and thyder he rode, and alyght and teyed his hors to the
gate, and herd Masse—and he that sange Masse was the Bysshop
of Caunterburye. Bothe the Bysshop and Sir Bedwer knewe Syr
Launcelot, and they spake togyders after Masse. But whan Syr Bedwere had tolde his tale al hole, Syr Launcelottes hert almost braste
for sorowe, and Sir Launcelot threwe hys armes abrode, and sayd,
"Alas, who may truste thys world?"

And than he knelyd doun on his knee and prayed the Bysshop
to shryve hym and assoyle[1] hym; and than he besought the Bysshop
that he myght be hys brother.[2] Than the Bysshop sayd, "I wyll
gladly," and there he put an habyte upon Syr Launcelot. And there
he servyd God day and nyght with prayers and fastynges.

Thus the grete hoost abode at Dover. And than Sir Lyonel toke
fyftene lordes with hym and rode to London to seke Sir Launcelot;
and there Syr Lyonel was slayn, and many of his lordes. Thenne
Syr Bors de Ganys made the grete hoost for to goo hoome ageyn;
and Syr Boors, Syr Ector de Maris, Syr Blamour, Syr Bleoberis, with
moo other of Syr Launcelottes kynne, toke on hem to ryde al Englond
overthwart and endelonge to seek Syr Launcelot.

So Syr Bors by fortune rode so longe tyl he came to the same
chapel where Syr Launcelot was. And so Syr Bors herde a lytel belle
knylle that range to Masse, and there he alyght and herde Masse.
And whan Masse was doon, the Bysshop, Syr Launcelot, and Sir
Bedwere came to Syr Bors; and whan Syr Bors sawe Sir Launcelot in
that maner clothyng, than he prayed the Bysshop that he myght
be in the same sewte.[3] And so there was an habyte put upon hym,
and there he lyved in prayers and fastyng. And wythin halfe a yere,
there was come Syr Galyhud, Syr Galyhodyn, Sir Blamour, Syr Bleoberis, Syr Wyllyars, Syr Clarrus, and Sir Gahallantyne. So al these
seven noble knyghtes there abode styll; and whan they sawe Syr
Launcelot had taken hym to suche perfeccion, they had no lust to
departe, but toke such an habyte as he had.

Thus they endured in grete penaunce syx yere, and than Syr
Launcelot took th'abyte of preesthode of the Bysshop; and a twelvemonthe he sange Masse. And there was none of these other
knyghtes but they redde in bookes and holpe for to synge Masse,

---

1. *Shryve hym and assoyle:* hear his confession and absolve.
2. I.e., brother hermit.
3. *In the same sewte:* dressed in the same manner.

and range bellys, and dyd lowly[4] al maner of servyce. And soo their
horses wente where they wolde, for they toke no regarde of no
worldly rychesses; for whan they sawe Syr Launcelot endure suche
penaunce in prayers and fastynges, they toke no force[5] what payne
they endured, for to see the nobleste knyght of the world take such
abstynaunce that he waxed ful lene.

And thus upon a nyght there came a vysyon to Syr Launcelot and
charged hym, in remyssyon of his synnes, to haste hym unto Almys-
bury: "And by thenne thou come there, thou shalt fynde Quene
Guenever dede. And therfore take thy felowes with the, and purvey
them of an hors-bere, and fetche thou the cors of hir, and burye
hir by her husbond, the noble Kyng Arthur." So this avysyon came
to Launcelot thryse in one nyght.

THan Syr Launcelot rose up or day and tolde the heremyte. "It [11]
were wel done," sayd the heremyte, "that ye made you redy
and that ye dyshobeye not the avysyon." Than Syr Launcelot toke
his eyght felowes with hym, and on fote they yede from Glastynburye to Almysburye, the whyche is lytel more than thirty myle—
and thyder they came within two dayes, for they were wayke and
feble to goo.

And whan Syr Launcelot was come to Almysburye within the
nunerye, Quene Guenever deyed but halfe an oure afore. And the
ladyes tolde Syr Launcelot that Quene Guenever tolde hem al or she
passyd that Syr Launcelot had ben preest nere a twelvemonthe—
"and hyder he cometh as faste as he may to fetche my cors, and
besyde my lord Kyng Arthur he shal berye me." Wherefore the
Quene sayd in heryng of hem al, "I beseche Almyghty God that I
may never have power to see Syr Launcelot wyth my worldly eyen."
"And thus," said al the ladyes, "was ever hir prayer these two dayes
tyl she was dede."

Than Syr Launcelot sawe hir vysage, but he wepte not gretelye,
but syghed. And so he dyd al the observaunce of the servyce hymself, bothe the dyryge and on the morne he sange Masse. And there
was ordeyned an hors-bere; and so wyth an hondred torches ever
brennyng aboute the cors of the Quene, and ever Syr Launcelot with
his eyght felowes wente aboute the hors-bere, syngyng and redyng
many an holy oryson, and frankensens upon the corps encensed.

Thus Syr Launcelot and his eyght felowes wente on foot from
Almysburye unto Glastynburye; and whan they were come to the
chapel and the hermytage, there she had a dyryge wyth grete devocyon. And on the morne the heremyte that somtyme was Bysshop
of Canterburye sange the Masse of requyem wyth grete devocyon;
and Syr Launcelot was the fyrst that offeryd, and than al his eyght
felowes. And than she was wrapped in cered clothe of Raynes, from
the toppe to the too, in thirtyfolde; and after she was put in a
webbe[6] of leed, and than in a coffyn of marbyl.

And whan she was put in th'erth Syr Launcelot swouned, and laye

4. I.e., humbly.
5. I.e., care.
6. I.e., wrapping.

longe stylle, whyle the hermyte came and awaked hym, and sayd,
"Ye be to blame, for ye dysplese God with suche maner of sorow-
makyng." "Truly," sayd Syr Launcelot, "I trust I do not dysplese God,
for He knoweth myn entente; for my sorow was not, nor is not, for
ony rejoysyng of synne—but my sorow may never have ende. For   5
whan I remembre of hir beaulté and of hir noblesse, that was bothe
wyth hyr kyng and wyth hyr, so whan I sawe his corps and hir corps
so lye togyders, truly myn herte wold not serve to susteyne my
careful[7] body. Also whan I remembre me how by my defaute and
myn orgule and my pryde that they were bothe layed ful lowe, that   10
were pereles that ever was lyvyng of Cristen people, wyt you wel,"
sayd Syr Launcelot, "this remembred, of their kyndenes and myn
unkyndenes, sanke so to myn herte that I myght not susteyne
myself." So the Frensshe book maketh mencyon.

Henne Syr Launcelot never after ete but lytel mete, nor dranke,   [12] 15
tyl he was dede; for than he seekened more and more, and
dryed and dwyned awaye—for the Bysshop nor none of his felowes
myght not make hym to ete, and lytel he dranke, that he was waxen
by a kybbet shorter than he was, that the peple coude not knowe
hym. For evermore, day and nyght, he prayed, but somtyme he   20
slombred a broken slepe: ever he was lyeng grovelyng on the tombe
of Kyng Arthur and Quene Guenever, and there was no comforte that
the Bysshop, nor Syr Bors, nor none of his felowes coude make
hym—it avaylled not.

Soo wythin syx wekys after, Syr Launcelot fyl seek and laye in his 25
bedde, and thenne he sente for the Bysshop that there was
heremyte, and al his trewe felowes. Than Syr Launcelot sayd wyth
drery steven, "Syr Bysshop, I praye you gyve to me al my ryghtes
that longeth to a Crysten man." "It shal not nede[8] you," sayd the
heremyte and al his felowes. "It is but hevynesse of your blood. Ye 30
shal be wel mended by the grace of God tomorne."

"My fayr lordes" sayd Syr Launcelot, "wyt you wel my careful body
wyll into th'erthe—I have warnyng more than now I wyl say; therfore gyve me my ryghtes." So whan he was howselyd and enelyd[9]
and had al that a Crysten man ought to have, he prayed the Bys-   35
shop that his felowes myght bere his body to Joyous Garde (somme
men say it was Anwyk, and somme men say it was Bamborow).[1]
"Howbeit," sayd Syr Launcelot, "me repenteth sore, but I made myn
avowe somtyme that in Joyous Garde I wold be buryed; and
bycause of[2] brekyng of myn avowe, I praye you all, lede me thyder." 40

Than there was wepyng and wryngyng of handes among his
felowes. So at a seson of the nyght they al wente to theyr beddes,
for they alle laye in one chambre. And so after mydnyght, ayenst[3]

7. I.e., troubled.
8. I.e., be necessary for.
9. *Howselyd and enelyd:* given the Eucharist and had received extreme unction (the sacrament in which a priest prays for and anoints one near death).
1. *Anwyk . . . Bamborow:* there is nothing to match the details of this aside in Malory's
   sources, and it is possible that he is recalling his own involvement in military action against
   these two castles; see the entry for October 1462 in the chronology on p. xxvi.
2. *Bycause of:* i.e., for fear of.
3. I.e., shortly before.

day, the Bysshop that was hermyte, as he laye in his bedde aslepe, he fyl upon a grete laughter—and therwyth al the felyshyp awoke and came to the Bysshop and asked hym what he eyled. "A, Jesu mercy,"sayd the Bysshop, "why dyd ye awake me? I was never in al my lyf so mery and so wel at ease." "Wherfore?" sayd Syr Bors. "Truly," sayd the Bysshop, "here was Syr Launcelot with me, with mo angellis than ever I sawe men in one day. And I sawe the angellys heve up Syr Launcelot unto heven, and the yates of heven opened ayenst hym." "It is but dretchyng of swevens," sayd Syr Bors, "for I doubte not Syr Launcelot ayleth nothynge but good." "It may wel be," sayd the Bysshop. "Goo ye to his bedde, and than shall ye preve the soth."

So whan Syr Bors and his felowes came to his bedde, they founde hym starke dede; and he laye as he had smyled, and the swettest savour⁴ aboute hym that ever they felte. Than was there wepynge and wryngyng of handes, and the grettest dole they made that ever made men. And on the morne the Bysshop dyd his Masse of requyem, and after the Bysshop and al the nyne knyghtes put Syr Launcelot in the same hors-bere that Quene Guenevere was layed in tofore that she was buryed. And soo the Bysshop and they al togyders wente wyth the body of Syr Launcelot dayly, tyl they came to Joyous Garde—and ever they had an hondred torches brennyng aboute hym. And so within fyftene dayes they came to Joyous Garde; and there they layed his corps in the body of the quere, and sange and redde many saulters and prayers over hym and aboute hym. And ever his vysage was layed open and naked, that al folkes myght beholde hym; for suche was the custom in tho dayes that al men of worshyp shold so lye wyth open vysage tyl that they were buryed.

And ryght thus as they were at theyr servyce, there came Syr Ector de Maris that had seven yere sought al Englond, Scotlond, and Walys, sekyng his brother, Syr Launcelot.

And whan Syr Ector herde suche noyse and lyghte in the quyre [13] of Joyous Garde, he alyght and put his hors from hym and came into the quyre; and there he sawe men synge and wepe— and al they knewe Syr Ector, but he knewe not them. Than wente Syr Bors unto Syr Ector and tolde hym how there laye his brother Syr Launcelot, dede; and than Syr Ector threwe hys shelde, swerde, and helme from hym, and whan he behelde Syr Launcelottes vysage, he fyl doun in a swoun.

And when he waked it were harde ony⁵ tonge to telle the doleful complayntes that he made for his brother. "A, Launcelot!" he sayd, "thou were hede of al Crysten knyghtes. And now I dare say," sayd Syr Ector, "thou Sir Launcelot, there thou lyest, that thou were never matched of erthely knyghtes hande; and thou were the curtest⁶ knyght that ever bare shelde; and thou were the truest frende to

4. *Swettest savour*: sweetest odor. On its significance, see n. 2, p. 397.
5. I.e., for any.
6. I.e., most courteous.

thy lovar that ever bestrade hors; and thou were the trewest lover,
of[7] a synful man, that ever loved woman; and thou were the kyndest
man that ever strake wyth swerde; and thou were the godelyest
persone that ever cam emonge prees of knyghtes; and thou was
the mekest man and the jentyllest that ever ete in halle emonge
ladyes; and thou were the sternest knyght to thy mortal foo that
ever put spere in the reeste." Than there was wepyng and dolour
out of mesure.

Thus they kepte Syr Launcelots corps on-lofte fyftene dayes, and
than they buryed it with grete devocyon. And than at leyser they
wente al with the Bysshop of Canterburye to his ermytage, and
there they were togyder more than a monthe. Than Syr Constantyn
that was Syr Cadores sone of Cornwayl was chosen Kyng of
Englond; and he was a ful noble knyght, and worshypfully he rulyd
this royame. And than thys Kyng Constantyn sent for the Bysshop
of Caunterburye, for he herde saye where he was; and so he was
restored unto his bysshopryche and lefte that ermytage—and Syr
Bedwere was there ever stylle heremyte to his lyves ende.

Than Syr Bors de Ganys, Syr Ector de Maris, Syr Gahalantyne, Syr
Galyhud, Sir Galyhodyn, Syr Blamour, Syr Bleoberys, Syr Wyllyars le
Valyaunt, Syr Clarrus of Cleremounte, al these knyghtes drewe them
to theyr contreyes—howbeit Kyng Constantyn wold have had them
wyth hym, but they wold not abyde in this royame—and there they
al lyved in their cuntreyes as holy men. And somme Englysshe
bookes maken mencyon that they wente never oute of Englond
after the deth of Syr Launcelot; but that was but favour of makers,[8]
for the Frensshe book maketh mencyon—and is auctorysed[9]—that
Syr Bors, Syr Ector, Syr Blamour, and Syr Bleoberis wente into the
Holy Lande, there as Jesu Cryst was quycke and deed.[1] And anone
as they had stablysshed theyr londes—for the book saith, so Syr
Launcelot commaunded them for to do or ever he passyd oute of
thys world—these foure knyghtes dyd many bataylles upon the
myscreantes or Turkes; and there they died upon a Good Fryday
for Goddes sake.

Here is the ende of *The Hoole Book of Kyng Arthur and of His Noble
Knyghtes of the Rounde Table,* that whan they were holé togyders
there was ever an hondred and [fifty].[2] And here is the ende of *The
Deth of Arthur.*

I praye you all, jentylmen and jentylwymmen that redeth this book
of Arthur and his knyghtes from the begynnyng to the endynge,

---

7. I.e., having the condition of.
8. *Favour of makers*: authorial bias.
9. There is indeed no record of such an authority, French or otherwise; the crusading story
   is likeley to have originated with Malory. Cf. n. 1, p. 689.
1. *Was quycke and deed*: i.e., had lived and died.
2. Caxton prints *xl* (forty) here, but consistency with the number Malory reports elsewhere
   requires ten more knights; cf. King Lodegreauns's account, p. 63.

praye for me whyle I am on lyve that God sende me good delyver-
aunce;[3] and whan I am deed, I praye you all praye for my soule.
For this book was ended the ninth yere of the reygne of Kyng
Edward the Fourth,[4] by Syr 𝕿𝖍𝖔𝖒𝖆𝖘 𝕸𝖆𝖑𝖊𝖔𝖗𝖾́, 𝖐𝖓𝖞𝖌𝖍𝖙, 𝖆𝖘 𝕵𝖊𝖘𝖚 𝖍𝖊𝖑𝖕𝖊
𝖍𝖞𝖒, 𝖋𝖔𝖗 𝕳𝖞𝖘 𝖌𝖗𝖊𝖙𝖊 𝖒𝖞𝖌𝖍𝖙, 𝖆𝖘 𝖍𝖊 𝖎𝖘 𝖙𝖍𝖊 𝖘𝖊𝖗𝖛𝖆𝖚𝖓𝖙 𝖔𝖋 𝕵𝖊𝖘𝖚 𝖇𝖔𝖙𝖍𝖊 𝖉𝖆𝖞 𝖆𝖓𝖉 𝖓𝖞𝖌𝖍𝖙.   5
𝕬𝖒𝖊𝖓.][5]

3. Cf. Malory's comments at the end of *The Tale of Sir Gareth of Orkeney*, p. 227.
4. Edward IV's reign officially began on March 4, 1461, making his ninth regnal year extend
   from March 4, 1469, to March 3, 1470. For an estimation of Malory's situation at that
   time, see the chronology on p. 26.
5. Note the unevenly spaced rhyme within the rubricated text: *knyght . . . myght . . . nyght*
   (and cf. the same effect in the closing prayer of *The Noble Tale of the Sankgreal* on p. 587).
   The spacing above each of the last two paragraphs is editorial (i.e., not Caxton's); so too
   the imposition of paragraph breaks. The rubrication of the closing line is modeled editorially on that which appears, again, at the end of the *The Noble Tale of the Sankgreal*; the
   closing *Amen* is not found in Caxton, but is supplied on the basis of its appearance in
   Malory's other concluding prayers (e.g., pp. 112, 227, and 495). Caxton adds a colophon
   to this conclusion: see p. 819.

SOURCES AND BACKGROUNDS

By modern standards, Malory's alleged propensity for criminal activity might seem to apply to his handling of sources:[1] sometimes without acknowledgment he relates tales that he did not create; at other times he proclaims the authority of a "French book" when there is none; and more often than not he adapts the work of earlier writers in ways that surely violate their original intentions. As a medieval writer, however, Malory proceeds according to tradition, his "originality" at least as much an index of covert adaptation as it is of outright creation:

> [T]he different meanings of the word "original" are the dividing line between the traditional writer and the modern novelist. For a traditional writer, borrowings are not so many skeletons in the cupboard he will seek to conceal; they are the bare bones of his narrative. If there is anything he might wish to hide, it is precisely those parts which he has added himself and which cannot be traced back to an authoritative original.[2]

Since the later nineteenth century, much work has gone into establishing the identities of Malory's sources; with that have come increasingly sophisticated appreciations of the complex translational and redactive strategies Malory employed in his reinscription of those sources. Fundamental to much recent study is an awareness that Malory's skills and perhaps his motivations developed as he wrote, such that uniquely nuanced hermeneutic principles may have to be adduced for the study of each tale in turn; generalizations about Malory's methods—including those that will be offered below—can be useful, but not at the expense of examining local detail.[3]

Known major sources for each of the eight main divisions or "tales" of the *Morte Darthur* are named in the table below. Malory tends to use one source text as the principal "template" for each tale, accounting for the majority of his source information—a practice suggesting perhaps a serial borrowing of source manuscripts not inconsistent with Malory's confinement in prison. Unless otherwise noted, the template source is listed first. Brief acknowledgment is also given in the table to the most well known of those passages that are evidently unique to Malory (further such notices are made in the footnotes to the text).

Sources for Malory's Tales

Tale	Major Source(s)
Uther unto Arthur	The French prose *Suite de Merlin* (from the Vulgate Cycle)
Arthure and Lucius	• The alliterative *Morte Arthure* (in English; Malory does not, however, incorporate its tragic ending)

1. The rhetoric of this statement is not intended to be entirely facetious and stands in part as an invitation to explore further the relationship between Malory's work, his life, and 15th-century conceptions of law; cf. Catherine Batt's essay on Malory and rape (p. 797 herein) and Elizabeth Edwards, *The Genesis of Narrative in Malory's "Morte Darthur"* (Cambridge: Brewer, 2001), esp. pp. 155–166 (with helpful references to additional studies).
2. Terence McCarthy, "Malory and His Sources," in *A Companion to Malory*, p. 78.
3. A further complication arises from a degree of uncertainty over the precise order of the tales' composition. Although for most purposes the only practical recourse is to assume that the order of composition matches the order of presentation confirmed by both Caxton and the Winchester MS, it is important to be aware of challenges to the assumption: for a brief survey of the main discussions, see P. J. C. Field, "Author, Scribe and Reader in Malory: The Case of Harleuse and Peryne," in *Malory: Texts and Sources*, p. 74, n. 9.

Tale	Major Source(s)
	• John Hardyng's verse *Chronicle* (in English; a probable influence for Malory's triumphant conclusion to the tale)
Sir Launcelot du Lake	• The French prose *Lancelot* (from the Vulgate Cycle; Malory selects three noncontiguous episodes only from a much longer work)
	• *Perlesvaus* (French, in prose; a source for the "Chapel Perilous" episode, p. 171)
Sir Gareth of Orkeney	There is no known direct source for this tale, suggesting its original composition by Malory. However, the story of *La Cote Mal Taillé*, which Malory later translates from the French prose *Tristan*, is an obvious analogue from which Malory may have drawn inspiration; such could also be the case with romances in the "Fair Unknown" tradition, such as the French *Le Bel Inconnu* or its English counterpart, *Lybeaus Desconus*. P. J. C. Field has postulated Malory's use of a now-lost Middle English romance, possibly alliterative, and based on folkloric material that may well derive from the sources of the analogous texts just cited.*
Syr Trystrams de Lyones	The French prose *Tristan* (about six times the length of Malory's rendition)
The Sankgreal	The French prose *Queste del Saint Graal* (from the Vulgate Cycle)
Launcelot and Gwenyvere	• The stanzaic *Morte Arthur* (in English)
	• The French prose *Mort le Roi Artu* (from the Vulgate Cycle)
	• A now-lost version, perhaps, of the prose *Launcelot*, providing the episode of "The Knight of the Cart" (ultimately derived from Chrétien de Troyes's *Chevalier de la Charrette*)
	Malory's use of the first two sources is concurrent, but the English text appears to provide the model for his choice of episodes. There is, however, much in this tale that appears unique to Malory, including the Maid of Ascolat's vindication of her love for Launcelot (p. 615), the tournament at Westminster (p. 620), and Launcelot's healing of Sir Urry (p. 638).
The Dethe of Arthur	• The stanzaic *Morte Arthur*
	• The French prose *Mort le Roi Artu*
	Malory's use of these two sources is similar in relative disposition to that of the previous tale. Ector's remarkable threnody for Launcelot (p. 696) is probably inspired by Mordred's threnody for Gawain in the alliterative *Morte Arthure*.

---

*See P. J. C. Field, "The Source of Malory's 'Tale of Gareth,' " in *Malory: Texts and Sources*, pp. 246–260.

If there is any agreement about general patterns in Malory's handling of sources, it is that he abbreviated extensively, removed the interdispersing of multiple story lines—the *entrelacement*—characteristic of some of his French sources, suppressed expressions of (amorous) sentiment and psychological introspection, reduced passages of religious allegory and other expressions of doctrine, and reduced accounts of magical phenomena; at the same time he emphasized accounts of martial endeavor and knightly values of loyalty and honor, and drew greater attention to the (tragic) heroism of certain characters— in particular Launcelot. Sometimes, however, he produced virtual word-for-word translations or incorporated words and phrases verbatim from his English sources. Most of these procedures and others are evident in the selections printed in this section when compared with the corresponding passages in Malory and enable a degree of informed speculation about Malory's intentions.[4] There is no substitute, of course, for examining the entirety of a source text against the entirety of Malory's response to it, and readers are encouraged to consult the editions and translations from which the selections printed below are taken; and an invaluable complement to such study is the Commentary in the third volume of O[3], the most detailed running exposition of Malory's use of sources available.

It is worth keeping in mind that none of the source manuscripts that Malory actually used have survived; those witnesses to his sources that do survive are likely to provide close reflections in most instances, but we must always be aware that a reading apparently unique to Malory, or an interpolation apparently from another source, or even a substantial omission, might in fact have come directly from his source manuscript.[5] A further complication for studies of Malory's sources is that his text bears the conjecturable impress of many other texts (sometimes referred to as "minor sources") but whose influence cannot finally be proved. A case in point is Malory's depiction of Trystram's wilderness exploits during the period of his madness, where details such as the forced parting that attends his recognition of Isode and the consolation he takes in harping do not correspond strongly with the French source but do present some similarity with the condition of the harpist-hero Orfeo's period of wilderness distraction in the Middle English *Sir Orfeo*.[6] The correspondences are compelling but not close enough in detail or conception to afford proof of direct influence. The same can be said of a host of other Middle English poems—*Ipomadon, Sir Degrevant, Sir Launfal, Syre Gaweyne and the Carle of Carelyle, The Jeaste of Syr Gawayne, the Awntyrs off Arthure, Ywain and Gawain, Torrent of Portyngale, The Franklin's Tale, Troilus and Criseyde,* and others[7]—where the sheer volume of possible correspondences (and the very casualness with which they are deployed) is enough to mitigate for Malory's familiarity with a wide literary corpus, but from which a precise itinerary of his literate engagement cannot be charted.

A literary restriction on what constitutes a "source" is in itself problematic as it overlooks what might be called the empirical component of Malory's work, evident for instance in his extemporary meditations on his times, on the proper

4. As Terence McCarthy has noted ("Malory and his Sources," pp. 94–95), many of these procedures are also evident in a wide variety of Middle English romances and should encourage further study of Malory's somewhat neglected relation to English narrative tradition; cf. the discussion of Malory's minor sources below.
5. For illustrations of such circumstances, see P. J. C. Field, "Malory and the French Prose *Lancelot,*" *Malory: Texts and Sources,* pp. 199–223.
6. For the original postulation of this connection, see O[3], pp. 1472–1474. For an edition of *Sir Orfeo,* see MER, pp. 174–190 (esp. lines 237–330).
7. For further details, see Edward D. Kennedy, "Malory and his English Sources," in *Aspects of Malory,* ed. Toshiyuki Takamiya and Derek Brewer (Cambridge: Brewer, 1981), pp. 27–55; and P. J. C. Field, "Malory's Minor Sources," in *Malory: Texts and Sources,* pp. 27–31. For a consideration of the possibility of the influence of French verse, see Field's "Malory and Chrétien de Troyes" in the same volume, pp. 236–245.

pursuits of knights and gentry, on the vicissitudes of combat, and on the miseries of iniquity and imprisonment. To an extent these meditations must reflect shared experiences of the age, certainly in those cases where their manner of expression can be shown to be not entirely unique to Malory. They constitute a dimension of his work for which the selections printed in the "Responses to the Times" and "Tournament and Battle" sections are intended to offer some contextualization.

For direction to further investigation of Malory's sources and contemporary contexts—the latter an area of Malory studies undergoing considerable restoration and expansion—see the footnotes to the text and the selections printed in this section, see the essays by Batt, Cooper, McCarthy, Meale, and Riddy in the "Criticism" section, and research the Bibliography.

The selections printed in "Sources" are grouped in an order corresponding generally to that of the main divisions of the *Morte Darthur*. Unless otherwise noted, editorial procedures adopted for the Middle English selections are the same as those outlined on p. xliv for the text.

Sources

From the Prose Merlin

[Merlin's Conception and Birth]†

* * *

In this part the story says that the devil grew very angry after Our Lord had gone to Hell and freed Adam and Eve and as many others as He pleased, so that when the devils saw it they were very much afraid and they were greatly astounded by it.

So they met and said, "Who is this who so overwhelms us that no power we have can stop Him from doing whatever He pleases? We did not believe that any man born of woman could fail to belong to us, yet He overwhelms us! How can He have been born? * * * [H]ow can *we* have someone who might speak out and tell about our aims, our deeds, and our ways of life—who might have the power, like us, to know things done and said and past? If we had someone who had that power and who knew those things, and if he were on earth with other folk, then he could help us trick them. * * * And he could also foretell things that were to come about and be said soon and far in the future, so that he would be believed by everybody."

* * *

They undertook to engender a man who would teach the others. The devils were mad for thinking that Our Lord did not know this plan.

* * *

[Having killed the parents and siblings of a devout maiden, the devils eventually break the maiden's resolve.]

[One of the devils] reminded her of the time before the deaths of her father and mother and sister and brother. When she recalled all these things, she began to weep and to show her deep sorrow and great anger, and in this distress, she fell asleep. When the devil was sure that she had forgotten everything the good priest had told her, he said, "Now has this woman been led away from her teacher's watchful eye. Now we can put our man into her."

† This and the following selection copyright 1993, from *The Story of Merlin*, trans. Rupert T. Pickens, in *Lancelot-Grail: The Old French Arthurian Vulgate and Post-Vulgate in Translation*, 5 vols., Norris J. Lacy, Gen. Ed. (New York: Garland, 1993–96), I, pp. 167–172 and 196, respectively. Reproduced by permission of Routledge, Inc., part of the Taylor & Francis Group. The French prose *Merlin* is not a major source for Malory (as opposed to the *Suite de Merlin*), but the selections printed here represent the kind of information about the early days of Merlin's influence with which Malory seems to assume that his readership already has some familiarity.

This one devil had the power to lie with a woman and get her with child. Then he was all ready, and he lay with her carnally as she slept, and she conceived. After this had been done, the young woman awoke. As she was awakening, she remembered the [advice of her] wise priest, so she crossed herself and said, "Holy Lady Mary, what has happened to me? I feel so much worse than when I went to bed. Fair, glorious Mother of God, pray your dear Son to keep my soul and defend my body from torment and from the might of the devil." * * * [S]he left and made her way until she found her confessor.

When he saw her he said to her, "You are in trouble, for I see that you are very frightened."

"Sir," she told him, "something has happened to me that has never happened to any other woman. I come to you so that you'll tell me what to do." * * * And the worthy priest said to her, "If it is as you say, you will find out well enough. Yet you did a great sin when you broke the vow [against anger] I gave you to take. And because you transgressed, I will impose a penance on you today: that for as long as you live you will eat only once on Fridays. And for what you tell me about lustful behavior, although I do not believe you, I must impose another penance for all the days you will live henceforth, if you are willing to accept it just as I say." * * * "Do you mean," he went on, "to abide in the counsel of God and Holy Church and in the mercy of Jesus Christ, who redeemed us with the worthy ransom of His own precious blood and death? Is this a true confession and a sincere repentance, sworn to on your body and soul—everything you have told me by your own mouth? Do you hold it in your heart and body to be true in every way, in word and in deed?"

She answered, "I will very willingly hold to everything just as you have said it, God willing."

"As I believe in God," he said, "I believe that if what you have told me is true, you need not be afraid."

* * *

And she led a very good and simple life. When the devil saw that he had lost her—and he did not see that she was behaving otherwise than she always had—he became very angry.

* * *

[A]t last she had her child as it pleased God. And when he was born, he unavoidably had the power and the mind of a devil, and the cunning, because he was sired by one.

But the devil had behaved most unwisely, for Our Lord had bought true repentance with His death. The devil had ensnared the young woman through deceit and trickery while she was asleep. As soon as she felt that she had been beguiled, she confessed and cried out for mercy where she ought. And when she cried out, she put herself under the mercy and the commandments of the Lord God and Holy Church. This is why God did not want the child to lose, because of the devil, anything that belonged to him; rather He allowed the child to have what was his by right. Therefore, He bestowed on him the devils' art of knowing things that are done, said, and past—all this he knew. And Our Lord, who is all-knowing, knew, by the mother's repentance, by her good confession, by the cleansing of confession, and by the true repentance he knew to be in her heart, that she had not wanted or willed what had happened to her. By the power of the baptism with which the child was washed in the font, Our Lord willed that the sin of the mother should not harm him. And He also gave him the sense and the power to know the future.

This is the reason why he knew the things that were done, spoken, and past: he inherited this from the devil. Moreover, he knew things that were to come; Our Lord willed that he should know things contrary to those he knew from the other side. Now he could turn to whichever side he wanted, for if he wished, he could give the devils their due, or else His to God just as well.

Thus was he born. And when the women had received him, they were all deeply frightened, for they saw that he was hairier than they had ever seen any other child. After they had shown him to his mother she crossed herself and said, "This child frightens me very much."

And the other women said, "And we are so afraid of him that we can scarcely hold him."

She said to them, "Send him down and have him baptized."

They asked her, "What do you want him named?"

And she answered, "The same as my father's name."

Then they put him into a basket and sent him down with a rope, then they gave orders to have him baptized: "Let him bear the name of his grandfather on his mother's side; that good man was called Merlin by his father."

Thus the child was baptized and named Merlin after his grandfather. He was then given to his mother to be nursed, for no other woman dared do so. His mother nursed him until he was nine months old. The women who were with her told her many times that they were quite amazed that the child, who was so hairy, was only nine months old, yet he looked as if he were two years old or more.

* * *

[The Conception of the Round Table]

* * *

[Merlin said to Uther,] Our Lord ordered [Joseph of Arimathea] to make a table in the name of the table that was at the Last Supper and to put a cup he had on that table after he had covered it with a white cloth, and he was to cover the vessel fully as well. Sir, Jesus Christ gave that cup to him, and with this cup He divided the fellowship of the good from the wicked. And, sir, anyone who could sit at that table could fulfill his heart's desires in every way.

"Sir, at that table there was always an empty seat that stood for the place where Judas sat at the Last Supper when he understood what Our Lord was saying on his account and he left the fellowship of Jesus Christ. And his seat was left empty until Our Lord put another man there to take his place to bring the count to twelve. And the empty seat at the new table stands for that place. Thus these two tables are very much alike, and Our Lord perfects men's hearts at the second table. And they call the cup, from which they have that grace, the Grail.

"If you will believe me, you will set up the third table[1] in the name of the Trinity, and by these three tables will the Trinity be signified in its three Persons, the Father, the Son, and the Holy Ghost. I promise you that if you do this, great good will come to you from it and great honor to your soul and your body, and in your time will happen things that will utterly amaze you. If you will do this, I will help you, and I promise you that if you do, it will be one of the most talked about things ever. For Our Lord has indeed granted grace to those who will know how to speak well of it. And I tell you also that this cup and the people who keep it have drawn westward, by the will of Jesus Christ, to these parts. And even those who do not know where the cup is have come here, and Our Lord, who brings good things to pass, led them. If you believe me, you will do what I advise you to do about these things. If you do this, and if you will believe me, you will be very glad indeed."

Thus spoke Merlin to Uther Pendragon, and the king was very glad about it. And he answered, "I do not want Our Lord to lose, because of me, any part of the thing that must be done according to His will. Indeed, I want you to know that I love Him. I put it all onto you, and I will do anything you order me to do, if I can."

So King Uther Pendragon put the whole burden onto Merlin, who was very glad to bear it. And Merlin said, "Sir, now look to the place where you would like most to do what you must."

And the king answered, "I want it to be done where you would most like it done, where you know it can best be done according to the will of Jesus Christ."

Merlin replied, "We will do it at Carduel in Wales, so have your people gather there to meet you on Whitsunday, and you will be ready to give out great gifts and to be of good cheer. And I will go before you and have the table built, and you will give me silver and men who will do what I order them to do. And when you get there and your people are gathered, I will pick out the ones who are to stay there."

* * *

Merlin did just as he had said. It was Whitsunday, and Merlin chose fifty knights, and he bade them, and had others do likewise, to sit at the table and eat the food that was there, and they did so very willingly. And then Merlin, who was full of powerful craft, went among them and called to the king, when they had sat down, and showed him the empty seat. Many others saw it, but they did not know what it meant or why it was empty, except for the king and Merlin. * * * So they were for a whole week, and during the season of that feast the king gave away much wealth and many lovely jewels to ladies and unmarried gentlewomen.

And when it came time for leave-taking, the king went to his worthy companions and asked them how they were. And they answered him, "We have no wish ever to leave here, and we want always to be at this table at the hour of terce,[2] so we will have our wives and children come to this town. And so we will live here at our lord's pleasure, for this is what our hearts tell us to do."

---

1. It is not explicit until much later that the third table is the Round Table.
2. I.e., in the morning (around 9 A.M.) [Editor].

The king asked, "Do you all feel this way?"

And they all said, "Yes indeed! And yet we wonder at how this can be. For many of us have no bonds with any among us; others have not seen one other before, and few of us were friends before. And now we all love one other as much as a son should love his father, or more, and it does not seem to us that we will ever be parted unless it is by death."

When the king heard them speak in this way, he took it for a very great wonder, as did all those who heard it. And the king was most glad and ordered everyone in the town to love, believe, and honor them just as they would his own self. And so Uther Pendragon founded that table in his own time.

Then he came to Merlin and said to him, after the crowds had gone, "You told me the truth indeed, and now I really believe that Our Lord wills this table to be founded, but I wonder at the empty seat. I would like you please to tell me, if you know, who is the one that will sit there."

And Merlin answered, "I can tell you only that the place will not be taken in your time, and the one who will sit there has not yet been conceived. The one who will take that seat must fulfill the adventures of the Grail. This will not be in your time, but in the time of the king who will rule after you. And I bid you, hold all your gatherings and all your high courts in this town, and I ask you please to stay here and hold your court here three times every year."

And the king told him that he would gladly do this, and Merlin said to the king, "Sir, I will go away, and you will not see me again for a very long time."

* * *

From the Suite de Merlin†

[The Dolorous Stroke]¹

* * *

[Balin] looked and saw the open door of a third room, which was longer yet, and he headed that way to go inside, for he thought all the while to find some weapon there with which to defend himself against the man who pursued him so closely.

When he wanted to enter the room, he heard a voice, which cried to him, "Woe to you if you enter, for you are not worthy to enter such a noble place."

He heard the voice clearly but did not, for that, leave his path but dashed into the room and found that it was so beautiful and rich that he did not think the whole world held its equal for beauty. The room was square and marvelously large and sweet smelling, as if all the spices in the world had been brought there. In one part of the room was a silver table, broad and tall, supported on three silver legs. On the table, right in the middle, was a vessel of silver and gold, and standing in this vessel was a lance, the point up and the shaft down. And whoever looked long

---

† Copyright 1995, from The Post-Vulgate, Part 1: The Merlin Continuation, trans. Martha Asher, in Lancelot-Grail: The Old French Arthurian Vulgate and Post-Vulgate in Translation, 5 vols., Norris J. Lacy, Gen. Ed. (New York: Garland, 1993–1996), IV, pp. 212–214 and 246–248, respectively. Reproduced by permission of Routledge, Inc., part of the Taylor & Francis Group.
1. Cf. Morte Darthur p. 56, line 9–p. 57, line 8.

at the lance wondered how it stood upright, for it was not supported on any side.

The Knight with Two Swords looked at the lance, but he did not recognize it. He headed that way and heard another voice, which cried loudly to him, "Do not touch it! You will sin!"

In spite of this warning, he took the lance in both hands and struck King Pellehan, who was behind him, so hard that he pierced both his thighs. The king fell to the ground, severely wounded. The knight drew the lance back to himself and put it back in the vessel from which he had taken it. As soon as it was back there, it held itself as erect as it had before. When he had done this, he turned quickly toward the palace, for it seemed to him that he was well avenged, but before he got there the whole palace began to shake; all the rooms did the same, and all the walls shook as if they would instantly fall down and disintegrate. Everyone in the palace was so dumbfounded at this marvel that there was no one brave enough to remain standing, but they began to fall, one here, the other there, just as if they were all dead. They all had their eyes closed, so as not to see the hour they would all fall into the abyss. Because they saw that the palace shook and trembled as hard as if it would fall down at once, they thought that the end of the world had come and that they must now die.

Then came among them a voice as loud as a wild man's, which said clearly, "Now begin the adventures and marvels of the Kingdom of Adventures, which will not cease until a high price is paid for soiled, befouled hands having touched the Holy Lance and wounded the most honored of princes, and the High Master will avenge it on those who have not deserved it."

This voice was heard throughout the whole castle; all the people of the castle were terrified by it, so that they fainted everywhere. The true history says that they lay unconscious two nights and two days. And of this great fear more than one hundred died in the palace; of the others who were in the palace or outside, a great many died of fear. The others were wounded and crushed, for many of the houses of the village fell, and large sections of the walls collapsed with the castle's shaking, and many knights and peasants were wounded. There were some who received no harm, but there was no one so bold in all the village that he dared enter the palace during the first two days, and they would not have entered it even then, had it not been for Merlin, who came to the castle to see the great misery that had happened to poor and rich, for he well knew that the blow of the Lance of Vengeance could not be struck without great marvels happening.

* * *

Merlin went on all the while from room to room until he came near the room containing the Holy Lance and the Holy Vessel that men called the Grail.

He knelt at once and said to those who were near him, "Oh, God, how foolishly he acted, the wretched, unfortunate sinner who with his soiled, low-born hands, befouled by the base venom of sexual indulgence, touched such a noble, precious shaft as I see there and with it wounded such a noble man as King Pellehan. Oh, God! how dearly will this great outrage and forfeit be paid for, and how dearly will they pay for it who have not deserved it, and how much misery and torment the nobles and the good knights of the kingdom of Logres will suffer for it, and how many marvelous, perilous adventures will yet happen because of this Dolorous Stroke that has been struck."

* * *

Then Merlin * * * found a good, strong horse, and he brought it to the knight, for he found no man to stop him, and he gave it to the knight, who mounted.

Merlin asked him, "Do you know why I'm doing you this kindness? Know that it is not for you but for the love of King Arthur, whose knight you are; this I know."

The knight answered, "You have done me great kindness, and I would like, if you please, to know who you are."

"I shall tell you," said Merlin. "I am Merlin the magician, of whom so many people speak. I don't know if you ever heard of me."

Then the knight bowed deeply and said, "Merlin, I didn't know you, nor do those who are best acquainted with you. Perhaps I'll never see you again, and perhaps I will. But whether I see you or not, know that I am your knight, wherever I may be. And so I should be, for you have done more for me than any man ever did."

"I know well," said Merlin, "what you would do for me if I asked you. Go with God; may God guide you and keep you from misfortune wherever you go!"

With that they parted, and Merlin went into the castle. The knight, as he went along through the village, found his host beside the walls, dead from a crenel of the wall that had fallen on him. Then he was very sad, for at that he realized his misdeed better than he had done before. When he had looked for a long time, he started on his way again.

As he rode thus through the land, he found trees down and grain destroyed and all things laid waste, as if lightning had struck in each place, and unquestionably it had struck in many places, though not everywhere. He found half the people in the villages dead, both bourgeois and knights, and he found laborers dead in the fields. What can I tell you? He found the kingdom of Listinois so totally destroyed that it was later called by everyone the Kingdom of Waste Land and the Kingdom of Strange Land, because everywhere the land had become so strange and wasted.

* * *

[The Lake of Diana; Ninianne Increasingly Ensnares Merlin][2]

* * *

Merlin said to the maiden, "My lady, do you want to see the Lake of Diana[3] which you have so often heard about?"

"Yes, indeed," she said, "it would please me greatly to see it. Anything

---

2. Cf. *Morte Darthur* p. 79, lines 6–14.
3. This Diana is a vaguely recalled representation of the classical goddess of hunting and chastity [Editor].

of Diana's would please me, and I would gladly see it, for all her life she loved the pleasures of the forest as much as I do or more."

"Let us go, then," he said, "for I'll show it to you."

Then they went along the valley until they found a wide, deep lake.

"Here is the Lake of Diana," said Merlin.

They went on until they came to a block of stone. Beside the block was a marble tomb.

"My lady," said Merlin, "do you see this tomb?"

"Yes," she said, "I see it clearly."

"Know, then," he said, "that here lies Faunus, Diana's lover, who loved her to excess, and she was false to him and killed him by the greatest treachery in the world. Such was his reward for loving her faithfully."

"Indeed," said Ninianne, "Merlin, did Diana kill her lover?"

"Yes," he said, "unquestionably."

"Tell me how it was," she said, "for I want to know."

"Willingly," said Merlin, "I'll tell you.

"Diana, as you know, lived in the time of Virgil, a long time before Jesus Christ descended into the world to save sinners, and above all things she loved the pleasures of the forest. When she had roamed and hunted through all the forests of France and Britain, she found no wood that pleased her so much as this one did, and she stopped here and made her home on this lake, so that she went to hunt in the wood by day and at night returned to this lake. In this manner she stayed a long time in this country, which she served only by hunting and capturing beasts, until the son of a king who held all this country in his hands saw her and loved her for the beauty he saw in her and because she was so valiant and nimble that no man could endure the labor of the hunt as well as she. He was not yet a knight but a young man, handsome and open, and he begged her until she granted him her love on the condition that he would not return to his father or keep any company but hers. He promised and remained with her in this manner. For love of him and because the place pleased her, she made a rich, beautiful home on the lake. Thus Faunus was as if lost, for he left his father and his friends and all other company for the love of Diana. When he had stayed a good two years with her like this, she met another knight, whom she had encountered while hunting, as she had Faunus. She fell so deeply in love with this knight, who was called Felix, that it was nothing short of amazing. This Felix came of low lineage and poor people, but by his prowess he had become a knight; he knew well that Faunus was Diana's lover, and he knew that if Faunus found him, he would torture him or have him killed.

"Then he said to Diana, 'You love me, you tell me.'

" 'That's true,' said Diana, 'more than any other man I ever saw.'

" 'Of this,' he said, 'no good can come to me, for if I loved you well, I wouldn't have the courage to come to you, for I know that if Faunus knew it, he would have me and all my kin destroyed for it.'

" 'Have no fear of that,' she said; 'don't fail to come because of that.'

" 'By my faith,' he said; 'either free yourself completely, or I won't come near you.'

" 'I cannot free myself,' she said, 'as long as he is whole and healthy, for he loves me so deeply that he would never stand for it.'

" 'By my faith,' he said, 'in some way you have to free yourself.'

"Diana loved Felix so much that she wanted to die unless she had her will with him, and she thought she would make Faunus die in some way, either by poison or something else. This tomb you see was here then just as it is now, and it was usually full of water, and over the top was a tombstone. In this country there was then a devil, an enchanter they called Demophon, who had changed the water of the tomb so that all wounded who bathed here were healed, and this was by the devil's trickery and power.

"After this, it happened one day that Faunus came from the wood injured with a wound that a wild beast had given him. As soon as Diana, who thought of nothing but evil and suffering, heard that he was wounded, she had the water removed from the tomb so that he could not be healed.

"When he had come and found the water removed by which the wounded were healed, he was greatly frightened and said to Diana, 'What shall I do? I'm severely wounded.'

" 'Don't worry,' she said, 'for I'll heal you. Undress completely and get into the tomb and lie down, and we'll put the tombstone over you. When you are inside, we will throw herbs through the hole in the stone, and the herbs are of such efficacy that you will be healed as soon as you have endured the heat.'

"He had no suspicion that she wanted to betray him and said he would do whatever she told him. He went into the tomb stark naked, and the stone was put over him; it was so heavy that he could never get out unless someone lifted it.

"When he had put himself inside in this manner, Diana, who wanted to destroy him utterly, had boiling lead prepared and threw a great quantity of it inside the tomb, so that he was soon dead, for the lead burned his whole body at once.

"When she had killed him this way, she went to Felix and said to him, 'I've freed myself of the man you feared so much,' and told him how she had done it.

"When she had told him, he said, 'Certainly, all the world should hate you, and no one should love you, nor will I.' Then he drew his sword, took Diana by the hair, and cut off her head. Because Diana's body was thrown here and because she came here so gladly, this lake was called, and will be called as long as the world lasts, the Lake of Diana. Now I have shown you how Diana killed her lover and how this lake came to be called the Lake of Diana."

"Indeed, Merlin," said Ninianne, "you have truly told it well, but now tell me what became of the houses she had made here."

"Faunus's father destroyed them all," said Merlin, "as soon as he knew Faunus had been killed here, and he broke up all Diana's buildings."

"He did wrong," said the maiden, "for the house was built in a most lovely, pleasing spot. God help me, the place pleases and attracts me so much that I'll never leave it until I have made a home as beautiful and rich as once was made, if someone can make it here, where I'll stay all the rest of my life. I beg you, Merlin," she said, "for the love you have for me, to undertake it."

He said he would undertake it gladly, since she asked it of him.
So Merlin undertook to make a house beside the Lake of Diana.

* * *

So Merlin stayed with Ninianne and lived there night and day, and he loved her so passionately that he loved nothing else in the world so much. Because of the great love he had for her, he did not dare ask her to do anything for him, for he dared not anger her. He kept thinking that in some way it would happen that he could have his will with her completely.

He had already taught so much magic and necromancy to her that she alone knew more of it than anyone but Merlin, and no one could think of a good entertainment or game that she would not make by enchantment. But there was nobody in the world she hated so mortally as she did Merlin, because she knew well that he desired her maidenhead; and if she had dared to kill him, either by poison or in some other way, she would have undertaken it boldly, but she dared not, for she feared that he would know about it, since he was wiser than other men. Nevertheless, she had already so enchanted him by the very magic she had learned from him that she could say whatever she wanted before he knew a thing about it.

* * *

From the Alliterative Morte Arthure†

[Arthur's Dream of the Dragon and the Bear]¹

* * *

The Kynge was in a gret cogge° with knyghtez full many, *ship*
In a cabane enclosede, clenlyche° arayede; *splendidly*
Within on a ryche bedde rystys a littyll,
760 And with the swoghe° of the see in swefnynge° he *swell / dreaming*
    fell.
Hym dremyd of a dragon dredfull to beholde,
Come dryfande° over the depe to drenschen° hys *rushing / destroy*
    pople,
Ewen° walkande owte of the weste landez, *Directly*
Wanderande unworthyly overe the wale° ythez.° *surging / waves*
Bothe his hede and hys hals° ware halely° all over *neck / wholly*
765 Oundyde° of azure, enamelde full faire; *Colored in undulating patterns*

---

† Text of Lincoln Cathedral Library, MS 91 (the "Thornton MS"), printed with permission of the Dean and Chapter of Lincoln Cathedral. Ed. Stephen H. A. Shepherd from *The Thornton Manuscript*, a facsimile with introductions by D. S. Brewer and A. E. B. Owen (London: Scolar, 1977). Text in square brackets represents conjectural replacement of missing words and is informed by (but does not always follow) the record of scholarship in the standard edition by Mary Hamel (New York: Garland, 1984). Paragraphing follows that of the MS; paragraphing also represents the presence of three-line floriated lombardic capitals at lines 1870, 1892, 1912, and four-line capitals at lines 3840 and 3864. The MS is dated c. 1430, and the poem's date of composition is held to be c. 1400. The poem does not rhyme, but achieves a four-stress metrical regularity mainly through the use of alliteration. Nominally each line assumes a medial pause, or cæsura, and usually three of its four stresses fall on alliterating syllables, typically two in the first half-line and one in the second (thus, line 1874: "And felede them so feynte ~ they fall in the greves"; the pattern here can be represented in a shorthand form as *aa ~ ax*); often lines with the form *xa ~ ax* appear (i.e., having an initial nonalliterating stress), and other variations are found. Note that alliteration can also occur on vowels.
1. Cf. *Morte Darthur* p. 120, line 13–line 38.

His schoulders ware scalyde   all in clene sylvere;
Schreede over all the schrympe   with schrinkande poyntez[2]—
Hys wombe and hys wenges   of wondyrfull hewes—
In mervaylous maylys°   he mountede full hye: *armor, scales*
Whaym° that he towchede   he was tynt° for ever.   *Whomever / lost*
Hys feete ware floreschede   all in fyne sabyll;°   *heraldic black*
And syche a venymmous flayre   flawe fro his lyppez
That the flode of° the flawez°   all on fyre semyde.   *from / sparks*
   Thane come of the oryente   ewyn° hym agaynez   *directly*
A blake bustous° bere   abwen° in the clowdes,   *powerful / above*
With everyche a pawe as a poste   and paumes° full huge,   *palms*
With pykes° full perilous,   all plyande° tham   *claws / pliant*
      semyde;°   *seemed*
Lothen° and lothely   lokkes° and other,   *Shaggy / head-hair*
All with lutterde° legges,   lokerde° unfaire,°   *bent / curled / repulsively*
Filtyrde° unfrely,   wyth fomaunde° lyppez,   *Tangled / foaming*
The foulleste of fegure   that fourmede was ever.
He baltyrde, he bleryde,   he braundyschte[3] therafter,
To bataile he bounnez° hym   with bustous clowez;   *proceeds*
He romyede,° he rarede,°   that roggede° all the   *cried out / roared / shook*
      erthe,
So ruydly° he rappyd°   to ryot° hym selven.   *violently / hurried / indulge*
   Thane the dragon on dreghe   dressede hym agaynez,
And with hys dinttez hym drafe   one dreghe by the walkyn;[4]
He fares as a fawcon,   frekly° he strykez,   *fiercely*
Bothe with feete and with fyre   he feghttys° at ones.   *fights*
The bere in the bataile   the bygger hym semede,
And byttes hym boldlye   wyth balefull tuskez;
Syche buffetez he hym rechez   with hys brode klokes,°   *claws*
Hys brest and his brayell°   whas blodye all over.   *belly*
He rawmpyde° so ruydly   that all the erthe ryfez,°   *stormed / splits open*
Rynnande° on reede° blode   as rayne of the heven;   *Running / red*
He hade weryede° the worme°   by wyghtnesse°   *exhausted / dragon / force*
      of strenghte
Ne ware it fore the wylde fyre   that he hym wyth defendez.[5]
   Thane wandyrs the worme   awaye to hys heghttez,°   *heights*
Commes glydande fro the clowddez   and cowpez° full even,   *strikes*
Towchez hym wyth his talounez   and terez hys rigge°   *spine*
Betwyx the taile and the toppe   ten fote large:
Thus he brittenyde° the bere   and broghte hym o° lyfe,   *slew / from*
Lette hym fall in the flode,   fleete° whare hym lykes.   *float*
So they breen° the bolde Kyng   bynne° the schippe   *frighten / within*
      burde°   *board*
That nere he bristez for bale   on bede whare he lyggez.[6]
Than waknez the wyese Kynge,   wery° fore-travaillede°. . . .   *weary / worked over*

2. Jaggedly layered all over (was) the shriveled creature with sharply tapered points.
3. He wavered about, he bellowed, he swaggered.
4. The dragon at a distance readied himself against him, and with his strokes drove him away
   to the upper part of the sky.
5. If it were not for the fire with which he defended himself.
6. That he nearly bursts for grief in bed where he lies.

* * *

[*The End of the Battle of the Prisoner-Escort*][7]

* * *

1870	The Kynge of Surry the kene to Sir Cador es yolden,°	*yielded*
	The Synechall of Sotere to Segramoure hym selfen.	
	When the chevalrye saw theire cheftanes were nommen,°	*seized*
	To a cheefe forest they chesen° theire wayes,	*choose*
	And felede° them so feynte they fall in the greves°	*felt / groves*
1875	In the feryne° of the fyrthe,° fore ferde° of oure pople.	*ferned area / woods / fear*
	Thare myght men see the ryche° ryde in the schawes°	*noblemen* / *groves*
	To rype upe the Romaynez, ruydlyche° wondyde:°	*violently / wounded*
	Schowttes° aftyre [haythen]° men harageous° knyghttez—	*Shout / heathen / stern*
	Be° hunndrethez they hewede doun be the holte° eyvys.°	*By / woods* / *edges*
1880	Thus oure chevalrous men chasez the pople;	
	To a castell they eschewede,° a fewe that eschappede.	*withdrew*
	Thane relyez° the renkez° of the Rounde Table	*rally / warriors*
	For to ryotte° the wode ther the duke restez;	*search*
	Ransakes the ryndez all, raughte up theire feres[8]	
1885	That in the fightynge before fay° ware bylevyde.°	*mortally wounded / left*
	Sir Cador garte chare theym[9] and covere° them faire,	*caused*
	Kariede them to the Kynge with his beste knyghttez,	
	And passez unto Paresche° with presoners hym selfen;	*Paris*
	Betoke° theym the proveste,° pryncez and other,	*Entrusted / custodial officer*
1890	Tase° a sope° in the toure, and taryez no langere	*Takes / light meal*
	Bot tournes tytte° to the Kynge and hym wyth tunge telles:	*quickly*
	"Syr," sais Sir Cador "a caas° es° befallen:	*event / is*
	We hafe cownterede today in yone coste ryche	
	With kyngez and kayseres krouell° and noble	*fierce*
1895	And knyghtes and kene men clenlych° arayede.	*splendidly*
	Thay hade at yone forests forsette° us the wayes	*obstructed*
	At the furthe° in the fyrthe with ferse men of armes;	*path*
	Thare faughtte we in faythe and foynede° with sperys	*thrust*
	One felde° with thy foo-men° and fellyd them o° lyfe.	*field of battle / foes* / *from*
1900	The Kynge of Lebé es laide and in the felde levyde,	
	And manye of his legemen° that thare to hym langede;°	*vassals / belonged*
	Other lordez are laughte of uncouthe ledes—[1]	
	We hafe lede them at lenge° to lyf whilles the° lykez.	*length / thee*
	Sir Utolfe and Sir Ewaynedyre, theis honourable knyghttez,	
1905	Be an awntere° of armes Joneke has nommen,°	*fortuitous deed / taken*
	With erlez of the oryentte and austeren° knyghttez,	*stern*
	Of awncestrye the beste men that to the oste langede.	
	The Senatour Caruce es kaughte with a knyghtte,	

---

7. Cf. *Morte Arthur* p. 132, line 39–p. 133, line 34.
8. Search all the woods' edges, took up their comrades.
9. Had them placed in a cart.
1. Captured by men unknown (to me).

The Capitayne of Cornette, that crewell es halden,° *reputed*
10 The Syneschall of Sutere unsaughte° wyth thes other, *unreconciled*
The Kynge of Surry hym selfen and Sarazenes [ynowe].° *in plenty*
 "Bot fay of ours in the felde a fourtene knyghttez—
I will noghte feyne ne forbere, bot faythfully tellen:
Sir Berell es one, a banerette° noble, *leading knight*
15 Was killyde at the fyrste come with a kynge ryche;
Sir Alidoyke of Tyntajuel with his tende° knyghtez *afflicted*
Emange the Turkys was tynte° and in tym fonden;° *lost / found*
Gude Sir Mawrell of the Mannez and Mawren his brother,
Sir Meneduke of Mentoche with mervailous knyghttez.

* * *

[*The Death of Gawain; Mordred's Threnody*]²

* * *

40 Than he° moves to Sir Modrede amange all his *Then / Gawain*
   knyghttes
And mett hym in the myde-schelde and mallis° hym thorowe; *pierces*
Bot the schalke° for the scharpe,° he schownttes° *man / sharp point / hesitates*
   a littill.
He schare° hym one the schorte rybbys a schaft- *pierced*
   monde° large; *hand-breadth*
The schafte schoderede and schotte° in the schire° *penetrated / splendid*
   beryn,° *man*
45 That the schadande° blode over his schanke° rynnys *flowing / leg*
And schewede on his schynbawde° that was schire burneste.° *leg armor / flowing / leg*
And so they schyfte and schove; he° schotte to the erthe *Mordred*
With the lussche° of the launce: he lyghte° one hys *blow / landed*
   schuldyrs
Ane akere lenghe one a launde,³ full lothely wondide.
50 Than Gawayne gyrde° to the gome° and one the *rushes / man*
   groffe° fallis— *face*
Alls his grefe was graythede, his grace was no bettyre⁴—
He schokkes° owtte a schorte knyfe schethede with *quickly draws*
   silvere
And scholde have slottede hym in, bot no slytte° *opening in the armor*
   happenede:
His hand sleppid and slode o° slante one the mayles— *on (a)*
55 And the tother slely° slynges hym undire: *slyly*
With a trenchande knyfe the traytoure hym hyttes
Thorowe the helme and the hede, one heyghe one the
   brayne.
And thus Sir Gawayne es° gonn, the gude man of armes, *is*

---

2. This passage comes from the last quarter of the poem, which deals with Arthur's return
to England and his destruction in combating Mordred's rebellion. For his early tale of
Arthur and Lucius, Malory rejects that portion of *aMA* in favor of a conclusion that leaves
Arthur a triumphant imperial leader. There are possible echoes, however, of Mordred's
threnody in Malory's final tale, where Ector delivers his famous threnody for Launcelot,
p. 696, line 42–p. 697, line 7. Mordred's temporary regret over the effects of his rebellion
is not matched in earlier texts.
3. The distance of an acre on open land.
4. Since his grief was destined, his fortune was no better.

Withowttyn reschewe° of renke,° and rewthe° es the more;   *rescue / man / pity*

3860 Thus Sir Gawayne es gon, that gyede° many othire.   *led, commanded*

Fro Gowere to Gernesay all the gret lordys,

Of Glamour, of Galyslonde this galyarde° knyghtes,   *valiant*

For glent of gloppynyng⁵ glade be they never!

Kyng Froderike of Fres faythely° thareaftyre   *sincerely*

3865 Fraynes° at the false mane of° owre ferse° knyghte: *Inquires / about / fierce*

"Knew thow ever this knyghte in thi kithe° ryche,   *country*

Of whate kynde he was comen?° Beknowe now the sothe: *i.e., descended*

Qwat gome° was he, this with the gaye armes,°   *man / coat of arms*

With this gryffone° of golde, that es one growffe° fallyn?   *heraldic griffin / face*

3870 He has grettly greffede° us, sa me Gode helpe,   *grieved*

Gyrde° down oure gude men and grevede us sore;   *Struck*

He was the sterynneste in stoure° that ever stele° werryde,°   *battle / steel / wore*

Fore he has stonayede° oure stale° and stroyede° for ever!"   *stunned / company / destroyed*

Than Sir Mordrede with mouthe melis° full faire,   *speaks*

3875 "He was makles° one molde,° mane, be my trowthe.   *matchless / earth*

This was Sir Gawayne the gude, the gladdeste of othire°   *other people*

And the graciouseste gome that undire God lyffede;

Mane hardyeste of hande, happyeste° in armes,   *most fortunate*

And the hendeste° in hawle° undire heven riche,   *most gracious / hall*

3880 The lordelieste of ledynge° qwhylls° he lyffe myghte,   *leadership / while*

Fore he was [a] lyone allossede° in londes inewe.°   *made famous / in plenty*

Had thow knawen hym, sir kynge, in kythe thare he lengede,°   *belonged*

His konynge,° his knyghthode, his kyndly werkes,   *skill*

His doyng, his doughtynesse, his dedis of armes,

3885 Thow wolde hafe dole for his dede the° dayes of thy lyfe."   *i.e., all the*

Yit° that traytour alls tite° teris° lete he fall,   *Yet / immediately / tears*

Turnes hym furthe tite and talkes no more;

Went wepand awaye and weries the stowndys

That ever his werdes ware wroghte siche wandrethe to wyrke.⁶

3890 When he thoghte on this thynge, it thirllede° his herte;   *pierced*

For sake of his sybb° blode sygheande° he rydys.   *kindred / sighing*

When that renayede° renke remembirde hym selven   *renegade*

Of reverence and ryotes° of the Rownde Table,   *revels*

He remyd° and repent hym of all his rewthe° werkes;   *wept / grievous*

3895 Rode awaye with his rowte,° ristys° he no lengere,   *company / rests*

For rade° of oure riche Kynge,° ryve° that he scholde.   *fear / i.e., Arthur / arrive*

* * *

---

5. For a glimpse of the grief.
6. Went weeping away, and curses the occasions when his destinies were fashioned to work such misery.

From The Chronicle of John Hardyng†

[*The Coronation of Arthur at Rome*]¹

* * *

THE .LXXXII. CHAPTER.

⁋Howe the Senate and the citee of Roome mette hym in seven
processions, and crouned hym, and there wintred hym by all the
whole winter.

The senate sent unto the Kyng Arthure,
And prayed hym th'empire to admit,
Whiche became hym and semed° hym of nature,   *suited*
As Constantyne did in the honour sitte,
And al truage° forthward thei would remitte°   *tribute / return*
Of Greate Brytain, never to aske it more,
But make it free as it was ever before:

⁋To whiche prayer Kyng Arthure did consent,
And came to Roome in royall high astate,
Wher the citee, by good and whole assent,
Full richely hym mette, and the senate,
With greatest laude° that might been estimate,°   *praise / reckoned*
And every gate his triumphe and his glorie,
Full curyously was wrought in greate storie.²

⁋The seven orders in procession,
Full solemplye at Peters° churche hym mette;   *St Peter's*
The wifes wholé by good discrecion,
The wydowes after full devoutly sette,
In order came then nexte, as was there dette,°   *duty*
The virgyns then, of pure virgynitee,
And then th'ynnocentes of tender juventee.°   *youth*

⁋Th'orders all of good religion,
The preastes and clerkes seculer,

---

† Reprinted, with new glosses and explanatory notes, from *The Chronicle of Iohn Hardyng
. . . together with the Continuation of Richard Grafton* (London, 1812), pp. 144–145. The
version of Hardyng's popular verse *Chronicle* that Malory is likely to have known is the
last, the "shorter version," completed in 1460–1464 (when Hardyng had reached his late
eighties). Hardyng had spent much of his life writing and rewriting various documents,
including his *Chronicle,* with the intent, among others, of proving England's right to rule
Scotland. The *Chronicle* relates the history of Britain from its legendary founding up to
Hardyng's own time; and its account of Arthur, though based ultimately on the work of
Geoffrey of Monmouth, shows the influence of romances such as the French Vulgate
Queste del Saint Graal—a feature that may have attracted and inspired Malory in his early
reading for the *Morte Darthur.*
    Malory's most probable recourse to the *Chronicle* was to follow its otherwise unmatched
representation of the end of Arthur's Roman campaign as an extended triumph rather
than an abortive prelude to the final tragic war with Mordred. The relevant chapter from
Hardyng is printed here. For further study of Malory's other possible debts to Hardyng,
see Kennedy, "Malory and his English Sources," pp. 42–48. For further contextual study
of Hardyng, see Felicity Riddy, "John Hardyng's Chronicle and the Wars of the Roses,"
in *Arthurian Literature XII,* ed. James P. Carley and Felicity Riddy (Cambridge: Brewer,
1993), pp. 91–108.
1. Cf. *Morte Darthur* pp. 149, line 21–p. 150, line 5.
2. And on each gate were elaborately engraved stories attesting to his triumph and glory.

The byshop and cardinalles in unyon,
With the sacrement and lightes clere,
And belles ryngyng therewith in fere;°   *together*
Every order with laude and reverence,
5 Rejoysed greatly of his magnificence.

¶At the Capytole, in the sea° imperiall,   *(papal) see*
They crowned hym with crownes thre of golde
As emperoure moste principall,
And conquerour that daye moste worthy holde°   *held, esteemed*
10 Wher then he fested° the citee manyfolde,   *held feasts for*
Of Rome the byshop, and all his cardinals,
The senatours, with other estates als.

THE .LXXXIII. CHAPTER.

Howe that tydynges came to the Kynge at Roome that Mordred
had wedded his wyfe, and usurped the crowne of Englande; for
the whiche he came home agayne, and gave Mordred batayll at
Dover, where Arthure prevayled, and after again at Wynchester,
wher the Round Table began, and fell for ever.

*   *   *

From the Prose Lancelot†

[The First Meeting of Lancelot and Guinevere]

*   *   *

"Gawain," said the king, "have you heard? Our young man of
last evening already wants to be a knight!"

"Indeed," said Sir Gawain, "he's right. I think that knighthood
would be perfectly fitting in his case. He is very goodlooking and
seems to be of noble birth."

"Who," said the queen, "is this young man?"

"Who, my lady?" said Sir Yvain. "By far the handsomest young
man your eyes could ever see!"

Then he told her how the boy had been brought to the king the
day before and how striking his guardian was.

"Really!" said the queen. "He arrived at court last evening, and
he wants to be a knight tomorrow?"

"That's right, my lady," said Sir Yvain; "he is very eager."

"Oh, I would very gladly see him," said the queen.

The king said, "By God, you will! and in him surely the fairest
and most well-built youth you could ever see."

With that, he told Sir Yvain to go fetch him and "see that he is
dressed as splendidly as you know the occasion demands; I am
sure he has all the right clothes." Then the king himself told the
queen how the Lady of the Lake had required that he be knighted

† Copyright 1993, from *Lancelot, Part I*, trans. Samuel N. Rosenberg, in *Lancelot-Grail:
The Old French Arthurian Vulgate and Post-Vulgate in Translation*, 5 vols., Norris J. Lacy,
Gen. Ed. (New York: Garland, 1993–1996), II, pp. 64–65. Reproduced by permission of
Routledge, Inc., part of the Taylor & Francis Group. The passage is not matched in Malory.

in no arms or robes but his own, and that she was indeed called the Lady of the Lake.

The queen marveled greatly at it all and was impatient to see the boy.

Sir Yvain went to the young man and saw to it that he was dressed as elegantly as he could be, and when he found no more to improve, he led him to court on his own beautiful horse. Nor was there anything secret about their going, for the throng around them filled the whole street.

The news spread through the town that the beautiful young man who had come the evening before would be knighted the next day and that he was on his way to court in knightly dress. The townspeople, men and women, sprang to their windows, saying, as they saw him pass, that they had never seen so handsome a young man. He reached the palace courtyard and dismounted, and the news of him spread through the great hall and through all the rooms, and knights and ladies and maidens hurried forth, and even the king and queen came to the windows.

When the young man dismounted, Sir Yvain took him by the hand and led him up to the great hall. The king and queen came toward him, took him by the hands, and led him toward a couch, where they sat down. He sat down in front of them on the green rushes that covered the floor. The king gazed at him with pleasure; he had thought him handsome the day before, but it was nothing like the beauty that shone from him now; it seemed to him the boy had grown bigger and stronger. Meanwhile, the queen prayed that God make him a man of honor, for He had given him extraordinary beauty.

The queen looked at him tenderly, and he looked at her, too, every time he could do so without being noticed. He wondered where all the beauty could come from that he saw in her, and beside hers the beauty of the Lady of the Lake or of any other woman he had ever seen lost all its value for him. Nor was he wrong to admire no other woman as he did the queen, for she was the sovereign of all women and the very font of beauty. But if he had known all the great worthiness that was hers, he would have gazed at her even more gladly, for it surpassed that of every other woman, rich or poor.

She asked Sir Yvain the young man's name, and he answered that he did not know it.

"And do you know," she said, "whose son he is or where he was born?"

"No, my lady," he said, "only that he is from Gaul, since he speaks the language the right way."

Thereupon the queen took the boy's hand and asked him where he was from. At her touch, he started as if suddenly awakened, and he was so taken with the thought of her that he did not know what she was saying. She noticed how flustered he was, and asked him a second time, "Tell me," she said, "where you're from."

He looked at her helplessly and said with a sigh that he did not know. She then asked him what his name was, and he answered that he did not know that, either. The queen realized right away that he was flustered and troubled, but she dared not think that it was because of her; and yet she did somewhat suspect so, which made her stop her questioning. Not wanting to worsen the boy's confusion, she rose from her seat and, in order to keep anyone from having the wrong idea or noticing what she suspected, said that he did not strike her as being a very sensible young man and that, whether wise or foolish, he was in any case ill-bred.

* * *

[Mistaken Identity]‡[1]

* * *

He walked to the bed, but he found neither man nor woman on it, nor anyone in the tent. When he saw this, he went to his horse, removed its bridle and saddle, and led it to graze. Afterwards he took off his armor, put his sword at the head of the bed, removed his clothes and decided to lie down in it, since no one else was there. Then he put out the candles so the light would not disturb him, lay down, and fell right to sleep.

Not long afterwards, a knight arrived, to whom the tent belonged. When he saw the candles extinguished, he thought that his wife had fallen asleep and had put them out because of the brightness. He was not wearing his sword or armor, so he was quickly undressed and lying beside Lancelot; he snuggled up to him, hugged him, and began to kiss him; because he really thought it was his wife. As soon as Lancelot felt the knight kissing him, he leapt on him all confused, thinking it must be some lady or damsel, and grabbed him with both arms. The knight immediately realized it was a man, thought it was his wife's lover, loosed himself from Lancelot's grasp, and seized him with both arms; before Lancelot knew it, he had been thrown to the ground beneath him. The knight snarled, "Scoundrel! You'll be sorry that you've shamed me and slept with my wife in my own tent!" Then he landed a blow to Lancelot's teeth, almost knocking them out of his mouth, and blood spurted all over his chin.

When Lancelot felt himself so ill used, he seized the knight by the throat and threw him over his back onto a rock in the middle of the tent. The knight was badly hurt when he fell. Lancelot stood up, went to where he had left his sword, and drew it from its scabbard. The moon was shining so that one could see a little in the tent, and when the knight saw Lancelot coming with his sword drawn, he did not dare wait, but turned and fled naked toward the forest. But Lancelot was not about to let him go, so without stopping to dress he pursued him until he caught up with him and

---

‡ This and the following selection copyright 1995, from *Lancelot, Part V*, trans. William W. Kibler, in *Lancelot-Grail: The Old French Arthurian Vulgate and Post-Vulgate in Translation*, 5 vols. Norris J. Lacy, Gen. Ed. (New York: Garland, 1993–1996), III, pp. 158 and 215–216, respectively. Reproduced by permission of Routledge, Inc., part of the Taylor & Francis Group.

1. Cf. *Morte Darthur* p. 156, line 26–p. 157, line 5.

struck him a sword blow that split his head to the teeth, and the knight fell down dead. Lancelot then returned to the tent, lay down, and slept until morning; but he was very sore from the blow he had taken to the teeth.

* * *

[Lancelot Rescues a Maiden][2]

* * *

Now the story says that after Lancelot left the hill where he killed Tericam, he rode along terribly worn and weary, for he had suffered much pain and agony in the combat. But the maiden pushed relentlessly on, until she left the cobbled road and entered a narrow path. Then she said to Lancelot, "My lord, do you know where I am taking you?"

"I don't, my lady, unless you tell me."

"I am taking you," she said, "to do combat with a knight who lives nearby in this forest and performs an offensive office that everyone should condemn, for he turns aside all those who pass in front of him so that he can conquer them."

"And how do you know this?" asked Lancelot.

"I have had it happen to me," she said, "because yesterday as I was passing in front of him he seized my palfrey, the most handsome one you have seen in ages, and was about to dishonor me because I objected."

"Now I'll tell you what you must do," said Lancelot; "ride far ahead of me and I'll follow you at a distance, and when the knight sees you all alone I know he'll seize your palfrey if he's as villainous as you say."

"My lord," she replied, "you have spoken well, and I'll do just as you say."

Then she rode on ahead, with Lancelot following steadily at a distance; she rode until she reached a tall and strongly fortified tower situated in a marsh. The knight stood on his horse fully armed in front of the gate; as soon as he saw the maiden, he set out to steal her palfrey, first taking her in his arms and flinging her to the ground. She began to shout, "Help! Help!" She stood up again, seized her horse's reins, and said he would never get it. And Lancelot, who was not far behind, observed how he had struck her down; he was furious and spurred forward as fast as his horse could go, saying to the knight that he had met his death. Frightened, the knight was about to flee, but was unable to when Lancelot came and struck him so hard that neither shield nor hauberk could stop the point and shaft from piercing his body. He bore him backwards to the ground, and as Lancelot pulled out his spear the knight fainted in mortal anguish.

Lancelot dismounted, pulled the knight's helmet from his head, and said he would kill him if he refused to acknowledge defeat.

2. Cf. *Morte Darthur* p. 163, line 29–p. 165, line 4.

He was in such pain that he was unable to reply, and Lancelot, who had no mind to wait further, struck him a blow that knocked him to the ground dead.

He had the maiden remount her palfrey, and he remounted his horse and left that place. She urged him to come spend that night with her, "and you should," she added, "since it's late and time to seek lodging. And were you to leave here, I don't believe you'd find anywhere to stay this day, so I think it's better if you come with me."

He granted her wish and she was delighted. She led him through the forest a good league until they came to a shelter on the edge of the forest, and there they dismounted. That night Lancelot was well lodged, and his wounds were seen to by an old woman skilled in the matter. Lancelot remained there a week and more, until he was healed.

* * *

From Perlesvaus†

[*Lancelot at the Perilous Chapel*]¹

* * *

Launcelot . . . rode until he had come to the Chapel Perilous, which was set in a great valley of the forest, and it had a small cemetery around it which was well fenced on every side and had an ancient cross outside the entrance. The chapel and the cemetery were overshadowed by the great forest. Launcelot entered, fully armed; he crossed and blessed himself and commended himself to God. He saw in the cemetery many tombs here and there, and it seemed to him that he saw figures all around who spoke quietly to one another, but he could not hear what they said. He could not see them very clearly, but they seemed to be very big. He came close to the chapel and descended from his horse. He saw a shed outside the chapel which had fodder for horses. He went and put his horse there, and then placed his lance and his sword by the entrance to the chapel, and entered within—where it was very dark, for it had no light save for one lantern which gave out little light. He saw the tomb and the chapel where [Anurez the Bastard] lay.

When he had offered his prayers to an image of Our Lady, he went to the tomb. Then he opened it as quickly as he could, and saw the large and hideous knight who lay dead within. The shroud in which he was wrapped was all bloodied from his wounds. He

---

† Trans. by Stephen H. A. Shepherd from *Le Haut Livre du Graal: Perlesvaus*, 2 vols., ed. William A. Nitze and T. Atkinson Jenkins (Chicago: University of Chicago Press, 1932), I, pp. 343–345, lines 8312–8378. The selection begins with Lancelot arriving at the Perilous Chapel, where he hopes to retrieve the sword and a portion of the burial shroud from the tomb of Anurez the Bastard; a knight has told Lancelot that these things will heal Meliot of Logres, who had been wounded badly by Anurez.
1. Cf. *Morte Darthur* p. 171, line 18–p. 172, line 26.

took up the sword which lay beside him, and began to rip open the shroud; then he took the knight by the head to lift him upward, but he found him so heavy and so inert that only at great pains could he remove him. He cut away half of the shroud in which he was wrapped; and then the tomb began to crack so severely that it seemed that the chapel was collapsing. When he had taken the shroud and the sword, the tomb closed up completely. Thereafter he went to the door of the chapel and saw, mounted on horseback in the middle of the cemetery—he thought—large and horrible knights who were equipped ready for combat, and it seemed as if they were watching over and staring at him.

At that instant there came a damsel who went running through the cemetery at a great pace, and said to those who were there, "Make sure you do not move until I know who this knight is." She came to the chapel. "Sir knight," said she to Lancelot, "put down the sword and that which you have taken from the dead knight."

"Damsel, what harm is it to you that I have them?" said Lancelot. "Because," she said, "you have taken them without my consent, for I have them under my watch, and this place and the chapel— and I would like to know your name." "Damsel," said he, "what advantage is it to you to know my name?" "I do not know," said she, "if it will be a loss or an advantage to me, but there was a time when I would have been very unwilling to ask—for I have many times been deceived."

"Damsel," said he, "I am called Lancelot of the Lake." "You must indeed," said she, "have the sword and the shroud! But now you must come with me to my castle, for I have many times desired you, and Perceval and Sir Gawain—and you will see the three rich tombs which I have made for your use." "Damsel," said Lancelot, "I do not at all wish to see my sepulcher so soon!" "By my head," said she, "if you do not come, you will not be able to part from here without grief, because those who you see there are worldly devils who guard this cemetery and are under my command."

"Never, if it pleases God, damsel, will your devils have power to do harm to any Christian." "Ah, Lancelot," said she, "I require and beg of you that you come with me to my castle, and I will here save your life from those who are about to attack you; and if you do not want to do that, give back to me the sword which you have taken from the tomb, and go at once." "Damsel," said Lancelot, to you castle I cannot nor will not go—and do not ask me again, for I have another duty to perform—nor will I ever return the sword to you, no matter what happens to me; for a knight is to be healed with it, of whom it would be a great shame if he died."

"Ah Lancelot," said she, "how hard and cruel you are to me! And it grieves me greatly that you have the sword and that things must go so well for you. For if you did not have it with you, you would never part from here of your free will; and I would have taken all my pleasure of you and had you taken back to my castle; and, powerless, you would never escape. And I would be able to quit the watch of this chapel and having to come here in the manner that I do so often. But now I am thwarted, for no one can do you injury nor hold you while you have the sword."

This did not cause Lancelot much sorrow! He took leave of the damsel, who departed most unwillingly. He gathered his arms and then mounted his horse again and passed right through the cemetery, and looked at the evil figures, who were so ugly and large and hideous that they seemed as if they would entirely devour him. They made way for Lancelot, not having power to do him ill.

* * *

From the Prose Tristan†

[The Philtre Takes Effect]¹

* * *

They remained at sea for three days, happy and joyous at the fine weather which God had sent them. On the third day round about noon Tristan was playing chess with Iseut. It was extremely hot; Tristan was only wearing a light silken tunic, and Iseut was dressed in a green silk garment. Tristan, who was feeling the heat, asked Gorvenal and Brangain for a drink, and it so happened that they chanced upon the love potion, without however noticing what it was; there were so many other silver vessels standing around that they were deceived at that point. Gorvenal picked up the vessel without looking at it, and Brangain took the gold goblet and brought it to Tristan who was hot and thirsty drank it all up thinking it was good wine. And indeed so it was, but it contained much else besides wine of which he was quite unaware. When he had finished it, he asked them to give some to Iseut, which they did, and she drank it.

Ah! God, what a draught! What distress it caused them thereafter! Now they have drunk it; now they are in the grip of the suffering which will never leave them while their soul is in their body. Now they have embarked on the path on which they will have to endure anguish and torment all their life. God, what sorrow! They have drunk their destruction and their death. The draught was very enjoyable, but no joy was ever so dearly bought as this one. Their hearts changed and became completely transformed. As soon as they had drunk it, the one looked at the other and both of them were quite taken aback. Now their thoughts were very different from before. Tristan was thinking of Iseut, and Iseut of Tristan. King Mark was entirely forgotten. Tristan asked for nothing other than the love of Iseut.

* * *

When they had drunk the love potion as I have just described, Gorvenal looked at the vessel and recognized it, and became quite

---

† This, and the following selections, reprinted from *The Romance of Tristan*, trans. Renée L. Curtis (Oxford: Oxford University Press, 1994), pp. 86–89, 97, 177–178, 180, and 228–233, respectively. Reprinted with the permission of Oxford University Press.
1. Cf. *Morte Darthur* p. 256, line 37–p. 257, line 8.

alarmed. He drew back a little, looking at it a while longer, and then he knew for certain that it was the philtre. He was so upset that he wished he were dead, for now he realized that Tristan loved Iseut and Iseut loved Tristan. He and Brangain would be held responsible, and it was only right that they should bear the blame; it was not the fault of Tristan and Iseut who knew nothing of the drink.

* * *

[Gorvenal and Brangain] were upset, but those who had drunk the philtre had no misgivings; they were only intent on each other. Tristan looked at Iseut's noble bearing and it so roused and inflamed him that he desired nothing other than Iseut, and Iseut desired only Tristan. They were of one mind on this matter. It was all decided; there was no point in concealing it. Tristan revealed his thoughts to Iseut and said that he loved her with all his heart, and she told him openly:

'Tristan, I'm happy and delighted that you love me, for I also love no one else in the world but you, nor shall I as long as I live; and I tell you truly, I don't know how this has come about.'

What more shall I tell you? As soon as Tristan realized that Iseut shared his desires, there was nothing to hinder them, since they were all alone in the cabin, and did not have to worry about chance-comers nor to be afraid of anyone. He did with her what he wanted so that she lost her virginity.

This is how it happened that Tristan conceived such a passionate love for Iseut that never thereafter could he tear his heart away from her, nor did he love or sleep with any other woman. This passion which the philtre instilled in him caused him such great pain and anguish that no knight before or after was ever tormented by love as much as he was. He is to be greatly pitied because of this misadventure, it seems to me, for he was so valiant that in King Arthur's time there were few better knights in the world.

* * *

Brangain and the Serfs[2]

When Iseut had led this life for at least half a year without hearing her love mentioned or talked about, it seemed to her that she could go on living like this for ever and have her heart's desire whenever she wanted, if only she was not betrayed by Brangain who knew the whole truth. This made Iseut very apprehensive, even more so because she noticed that King Mark seemed to find greater pleasure in being with Brangain than with any other young girl, and she might well end up telling him everything. This possibility made her so frightened that she did not know what to say, except that Brangain must be put to death. If she were rid of her, then she

---

2. Cf. *Morte Darthur* p. 262, lines 6–14.

would be sure that no one would ever talk about the matter, for only Brangain and Gorvenal knew anything about it.

After she had thought for a long time, she called two of her serfs into a room and said to them:

'I want you to do something for me which I shall tell you, and it must be done so secretly that no one in the world will know anything about it except the two of you and myself.'

'My lady,' they replied, 'at your command. Tell us what it is, for we're prepared to do what you want.'

'Many thanks,' she said. 'You may be sure that I'll make it worth your while. Now I'll tell you what it is. You know well that I brought Brangain with me to this country and have always held her in high esteem. She paid no regard whatever to the honour I showed her, but has acted so wrongly as to sleep with my lord, King Mark, who now treats me with much less respect than he used to and greatly hates me. You must avenge me for this shame, and I'll tell you how. I shall send her with you to a forest on an errand; she herself will know well what it is. And when you've taken her right into the forest, kill her instantly with your own swords. Don't have pity on her whatever happens!'

* * *

Iseut of the White Hands[3]

* * *

Tristan for his part kept gazing at Iseut, for he found her very beautiful, and she pleased and attracted him greatly; and what was most instrumental in making him fall in love with her was the name Iseut, for it seemed to him that if he could have the company of this Iseut and his pleasure with her, he would never remember any other Iseut.

Such were Tristan's thoughts and that is how he planned to free himself of his love for Queen Iseut. He left one Iseut for the other, and believed he could forget his love for one by his love for the other. When he saw the bearing and countenance of this Iseut where one could find no flaw, it seemed to him there were many reasons why he ought to leave the other Iseut for this one, for his relationship with the other Iseut had been against God and against the law, since he should not rightfully have slept with his uncle's wife under any circumstances; moreover, there was no worthy man on earth who would not consider him treacherous and disloyal if he learnt the truth about what he had done. For that reason he decided it preferable, both with regard to his honour and his happiness, to leave Iseut of Cornwall and to take Iseut the daughter of King Hoel of Brittany. That is what he decided to do in the end; but he never gave any indication that the young girl meant anything to him.

3. Cf. *Morte Darthur* p. 271, line 37–p. 272, line 2.

Iseut, the noble maiden, who had no such thoughts, did her best day and night to make him recover. And when Tristan felt himself fit enough to wear armour, then he was happy and cheerful, then he was overjoyed and amused himself with everyone, then he was such that all who saw him said that if he was not a brave knight he really must hate his fine body. And in truth he was so handsome that Iseut herself, who was called Iseut of the White Hands, fell madly in love with him. She had never before thought of any man or fallen in love; now she loved so passionately that her heart and her thoughts were completely absorbed by Tristan, and she loved nobody else, nor was there anything she would not have done for him, even if she were sure that it would bring her great shame.

* * *

What shall I tell you? The wedding-day arrived. All the people of Brittany came there without exception, rich and poor alike, and there was much rejoicing and merriment. They spent the day in great jubilation. But the night was drawing near when Tristan had to sleep with Iseut. However, Queen Iseut of Cornwall forbade him to have intercourse with her. She did not forbid him such activities as embracing and kissing, but if the other act came into it, that would be the end of their love.[4]

What shall I tell you? When the night had come, Tristan lay down beside Iseut, who was so very beautiful that it is not surprising if he desired her. There was no one else in the room, and they lay in bed quite naked. The light in the bedroom was so bright that Tristan could see Iseut's beauty very clearly. She had white and tender breasts, lovely bright and laughing eyes, fine slender eyebrows and a clear, pure face. Tristan kissed and embraced her. But when he remembered Iseut of Cornwall, he could not bring himself to touch this one. Great was the battle of the two Iseuts. This Iseut was in front of him, the other was in Cornwall and knew absolutely nothing about the whole matter, and yet she forbade Tristan as he valued his life to go no further with this Iseut; since he was fit and well, let him come to Cornwall without delay, and on no account do anything which was blameworthy with this Iseut.

That is how Tristan remained with his wife: in the end he decided to go no further. Iseut, who did not know anything other than the joy of embracing, fell asleep in Tristan's arms, and Tristan did likewise.

[The Mortal Lay][5]

* * *

[Tristan spends more than eight days lamenting his rejection by Queen Iseut. Palamades' messenger-girl, who has been trying to console Tristan, comes to him at day break:]

4. * * * All this is just going on in Tristan's mind, since Queen Iseut was as yet quite unaware of his marriage.
5. Cf. *Morte Darthur* p. 301, lines 17–23.

As soon as she came up to him, she wished him good day and good fortune, and he returned her greeting.

'Maiden,' he said, 'now I'm quite prepared to fulfill the promise I made you yesterday evening.'

'Sir,' she replied, 'many thanks.'

And immediately he took up his harp and began to tune it to the best of his ability. And when he had tuned it correctly to harmonize with the song he wanted to sing, he said to the girl:

'Maiden, did you ever hear anyone mention the "Mortal Lay"?'

'No, sir,' she answered, 'I didn't, so help me God. I never heard anyone speak of it.'

'That's not surprising, maiden,' he said, 'since no one but myself has ever sung it. I only composed it last night; it's about my suffering and my death. And because I wrote it in anticipation of my end, I called it "Mortal Lay"; I derived the name from the event.'

After he had said this, he began to weep very tenderly, and in the midst of his tears he began to play the harp so melodiously that anyone who heard it would have declared that it would be impossible to hear a sweeter melody. And weeping like this he started his lay as follows:

> I've made many a song and lay
> But now abandon all I play.
> Here is my final legacy,
> This last lay, for Love's killing me.
>
> This is my very last lament,
> Clearly my flame of life is spent,
> My flesh bruised by grief's punishment
> As, singing, I voice my complaint.
>
> Joy has no place in this singing,
> Rather with sorrow beginning.
> Love treats me far too cruelly
> In taking harsh revenge on me.
>
> I rail against Iseut, oh she
> Whose service turns to slavery,
> Whose worship I regret, for I
> Now dying, don't deserve to die!
>
> Those knights who're on adventure bent,
> Don't suffer Love's predicament;
> In love they're far more fortunate
> Than Tristan, the disconsolate.
>
> Yet Love for me's too much to bear,
> Finishing life in black despair.
> Love's the beginning and end of me,
> Killed by my own heart's loyalty.
>
> While others' sing at ease, engrossed
> In love, I weep; trapped by the boast
> That now ensures my death: Tristan
> Loved more than any other man.

Death and Love have laid me low,
And transformed my joy to woe.
Before day dawns they'll cause my end,
And helplessly my head will bend.

Alas, who cares that I must die?
None will recall me with a sigh.
My knightly deeds are swept away
By Death who holds me in his sway.

Though often I've escaped and run
When to help me there was none,
With Death and Love my bitter foes,
Even King Porrus had lesser woes.[6]

Ah Lancelot, my dear sweet friend,
It is my wish someone will send
This lay to you. Love has killed me,
Its promise broken utterly.

I feel I suffer, for Love's sake,
Like one who let a poor cold snake
Take refuge on his breast; and thence
Was given death in recompense.

I've welcomed from the very start
The love I've honoured in my heart:
No arrow kills me of hard wood
But rather Love's ingratitude.

The noble Guinevere is not
My bane, nor fever makes me hot.
It is Iseut who causes this,
No reason but her wantonness.

How can I blame Love, how express
Reproach for causing my distress?—
When all too soon my lips are numb.
Love's deadly venom makes me dumb.

Against each leaf, however little,
Which lack of wind makes wet or brittle,
Love wields its power. Please God let
Love, on my death, feel deep regret.

What paltry chivalry Love shows
When it attacks a corpse! God knows
My strength is gone, and all my beauty.
I'm dead. What can Love get from me?

There's little profit Love will gain
Out of either my death or pain.

6. * * * This is probably a reference to the powerful Indian King Porrus (Porus) who lived in the fourth century BC and is mentioned in the twelfth-century *Roman d'Alexandre*. The "woes" alluded to no doubt refer to the Battle of Hydaspes in the summer of 327 BC where Alexander the Great totally defeated the army of Porus. The Indian losses were enormous and included two of Porus's sons and many of his high officers. Porus himself was taken prisoner.

Love knows that I do not pretend.
This last affliction is the end.

All of my strength has diminished,
Sorrow by sorrow replenished,
My grief and pain is now complete.
Tristan is sounding the retreat.

In Love's harsh prison I now lie.
Its cruel judgments make me die.
Can Love do more? It's been my end.
What's left of me may God defend.

Adieu, Iseut! And Love, adieu!
I'll make no more protests to you.
Because I loved so well, death's near.
But I have nothing else to fear.

Iseut, who once was my delight,
As I engage in this grim fight,
I beg you, my sweet enemy,
After my death, remember me!

I give Iseut my benison,
I, Tristan, give it, who is gone,
Who would have risked his life and limb
To gratify Iseut's least whim.

But since Iseut has been untrue,
All that is good now fails me too.
Death pounces on me suddenly—
I feel its final grip on me!

Once I was used to venery,
Now I'm the quarry. Death hunts me.
Death is mirrored in my face.
Its last assault is taking place.

No man on earth loved more than I.
I still love more, and that is why
Death appears like a dark doorway
Opened to me by this 'Mortal Lay'.

Feeling and reason, ears and eyes,
Even the soul which never dies
I gave to Love, and so I am
A lion slaughtered by a lamb.

And all of you who pass this way[7]
Come here: so that each one can say
If there were ever woes like those
Of Tristan in his final throes.

Song and tears in a single breath
Bring me right to the point of death.

---

7. *And all of you who pass this way:* an echo from the Bible; cf. the *Lamentation of Jeremiah*, 1:12: "all ye that pass by, behold, and see if there be any sorrow like unto my sorrow."

I sing and weep. To God the just
My soul and spirit I entrust.

When Tristan had finished singing his lay as I have described,
so beautiful and so sweet that no one could find fault with it, he
fell silent and said no more, and began to lament again as bitterly
as before, saying:

'God, what am I waiting for? Why don't I kill myself here and
now? Then my suffering would be finished at one go.'

And saying this, he stood up and looked all around him to see
if he could find a sword with which to kill himself. When he realized that it was impossible, his heart was filled with such great rage
and his head with such great madness that he lost his mind and
his memory so completely that he did not know what he was doing.
He no longer knew whether he was Tristan or not; he no longer
remembered my lady Iseut nor King Mark, nor indeed anything he
had ever done. He went running about through the Forest of Mor-
roiz, now here, now there, crying and shrieking like a mad animal.
And for that reason the maiden soon lost him, for she did not know
which way he had gone, and this upset and distressed her greatly.

* * *

From the Queste del Saint Graal†

[The Hermit Explains the Temptation of Perceval][1]

"The young woman you spoke to is the devil, the master of hell
who has power over everyone. It is true that she was formerly in
heaven,[2] in the company of angels, beautiful and luminous. But
the devil's great beauty made him proud and so eager to rival the
Trinity that he said, 'I will ascend to heaven and become equal to
the Good Lord.' As soon as he had said this, Our Lord, who did
not want His house to be defiled by the poison of pride, made him
fall from the high seat where He had placed him and sent him to
the dark house known as hell. When he found himself cast down
from the distinguished seat he had been occupying into everlasting
darkness, he decided to wage an all-out war against the one who
had put him there. But he did not know exactly how. Finally, he
became acquainted with Adam's wife, the first woman of the
human race. He watched her and trapped her into committing the
same mortal sin that had caused his expulsion from the glorious
heavens: the sin of covetousness. Encouraging her treasonous
impulses, he led her to pick the deadly fruit from the tree that
God's own voice had prohibited. When she had picked it, she ate
of the fruit and gave some to her husband Adam to eat, with the

† This and the following selections copyright 1995, from *The Quest for the Holy Grail*, trans.
E. Jane Burns, in *Lancelot-Grail: The Old French Arthurian Vulgate and Post-Vulgate in
Translation*, 5 vols., Norris J. Lacy, Gen. Ed. (New York: Garland, 1993–1996), IV, pp. 37,
44, and 68, respectively. Reproduced by permission of Routledge, Inc., part of the Taylor
& Francis Group.
1. Cf. *Morte Darthur* p. 531, lines 19–28.
2. I have maintained the ambiguity of pronouns here, which switch, interestingly, between
"she" and "he" since the devil was beautiful in his guise as a woman.

result that all their descendants have felt the mortal effect of this act. The devil, who advised Eve to do this, was the serpent that you saw the old woman riding the day before yesterday; it was also the young woman who paid you a visit last night. When she explained that she was fighting day and night, she spoke the truth, as you well know. She never ceases to stalk the knights of Jesus Christ, all worthy men and servants in whom the Holy Spirit resides.

"Once she had appeased you with her false words and cunning, she had the tent set up to protect you and said, 'Come and rest here, Perceval; sit here until nightfall. Move out of the sun; I have a feeling that you are getting too hot.' The words she spoke are not without great significance. She took them to mean something very different from what you understood. The tent, which was round like the circumference of the earth, clearly represents the world, which will never be without sin. It is because sin always resides therein that she did not want you to remain outside the tent; indeed, that is why she had it set up for you. When she called to you, she said, 'Perceval, come and rest here; sit here until night-fall.' By this she meant that you should be idle and nourish your body in gluttony with earthly foods. She did not encourage you to work in this world or sow seeds that wisemen could harvest on Judgment Day. She asked you to rest until nightfall, that is to say, until death overtook you. Indeed death is called night whenever it overtakes a man caught in mortal sin. She called to you because she thought the sun was heating you up too much. It is not sur-prising she would fear that. When the sun, by which we under-stand Jesus Christ, the true light, warms the sinner with the fire of the Holy Spirit, the cold and ice of the devil can do little to harm him, provided he has fixed his heart on the lofty sun. I have spoken about this lady long enough to let you know who she is and how her visit would have harmed rather than helped you."

* * *

[Lancelot's Genealogy][3]

"It is true [said the hermit,] that, forty-two years after Christ's passion, the wise man Joseph of Arimathea, a good and true knight, left Jerusalem at Our Lord's command to preach and spread the truth of the New Law and the commandments of the Gospel. When he came to the city of Sarras, he met a pagan king—named Evalach—who was waging war against his rich and powerful neigh-bor. Joseph gave Evalach such wise counsel that the king defeated his enemy in battle, thanks to the help of God. When Evalach returned to his city, he was baptized by Josephus, the son of Joseph. His brother-in-law, whose pagan name was Seraphe, took the baptismal name of Nascien. After his conversion, this knight's strong belief and intense love of God made him a pillar and foun-

3. Cf. *Morte Darthur* p. 534, line 38–p. 535, line 11.

dation stone of the faith. His goodness and loyalty were openly recognized when Our Lord allowed him to see the great secrets and mysteries of the Holy Grail. With the exception of Joseph, other knights of that time had hardly been able to glimpse them. And no knight has seen them fully since, except as you did, in a dream.

"At that time, Evalach had a vision of one of his nephews, Nascien's son. He saw a great lake pour forth from Nascien's belly, and from that lake nine rivers sprang. Eight of them were wide and deep, but the last one was even wider and deeper than the others. It was so swift and forceful that no one could have resisted it. At the source, this river was churned up and thick with mud. It was clear and clean in the middle, and different still at the end. For there it was a hundred times clearer and more beautiful than at the source, and so sweet to drink that no one would ever tire of it. Such was the ninth river. Then King Evalach saw a man come down from heaven who looked exactly like Our Lord. When he reached the lake, he washed his hands and feet in it, and in each of the rivers. But when he reached the ninth river, he washed his hands and feet and his entire body in it.

"This vision came to Mordrain in his sleep.[4] I will now tell you what it means. King Mordrain's nephew, from whom the lake issued, was Celidoine, Nascien's son, whom Our Lord sent to this land to confound and defeat the unbelievers. He was a true soldier of Christ and a true knight of God. He knew the paths of the stars and planets and the configuration of the firmament as well as or even better than the philosophers did. Because he was so learned in science, he appeared to you surrounded by stars. He was the first Christian king to hold the kingdom of Scotland. He was truly a source of science and knowledge from which one could derive all the principles and moving force of the divinity.

"From that lake, nine rivers flowed: they are his nine male descendants, but not his nine sons. Rather they issued one from the other in lineal descent. Of these nine, there were seven kings and two knights. The first king to descend from Celidoine was called Narpus, a virtuous man who loved the Holy Church. The second was called Nascien, in memory of his ancestor. He was so filled with the spirit of Our Lord that, in his time, no man was considered more virtuous. The third king was called Alan the Fat. He would have died rather than offend his Creator. The fourth was Isaiah, a good and loyal man who feared God above all else, and would never anger Him knowingly. The fifth was called Jonah, a good and loyal knight and braver than all others. He too never knowingly incited the anger of Our Lord. He left this land and went to Gaul, where he married the daughter of Maronel and inherited the kingdom. From him came your ancestor Lancelot, who left Gaul and came to this country where he wed the daughter of the King of Ireland. He was a virtuous man, as you heard when

---

4. Mordrain is the baptismal name of Evalach; the author uses it here without explanation.

you found the body of your ancestor at the fountain guarded by two lions. From this man there came King Ban, your father, who was a more noble and saintly man than people think. They believe that the grief over losing his land killed him. But it did not. He had asked Our Lord every day of his life to let him leave this world whenever he might request it. And Our Lord showed that he had heard that prayer. As soon as King Ban asked for bodily death, he received it and found the life of the soul.

"The seven people I have named, who are the source of your lineage, are the seven kings you saw in your dream, and they are seven of the rivers that flowed from the lake that King Mordrain saw in his sleep. Our Lord washed his hands and feet in all seven rivers.

* * *

[The Tree of Life]⁵

* * *

"Be assured [said Perceval's sister,] that virginity and maidenhood are not identical, but distinctly different. Maidenhood cannot be equated with virginity for the following reason: maidenhood is a virtue shared by all men and women who have not experienced carnal relations. But virginity is a loftier thing and more virtuous. It cannot be found in any man or woman who has even felt a desire for carnal coupling. Yet at the moment of her expulsion from paradise and the great delights it held, Eve possessed this kind of virginity. And when she planted the branch, she had not yet lost her virginity. Only later did God order Adam to know his wife, meaning that he should lie with her carnally, just as nature requires a man to lie with his wife and a woman with her lord. Thus did Eve lose her virginity, and from then on the couple were one flesh.

A long while after Adam knew his wife, as you have heard, it happened that the two were sitting beneath the tree. As Adam looked up at it, he began to lament his suffering and exile. Then they both began to weep bitterly for each other. And Eve said it was not surprising that the place reminded them of their pain and worry, since the tree contained those things within it. Indeed, no one, no matter how happy, could sit beneath it without feeling sad when he left. It was only right that they were unhappy, for this was the Tree of Death. No sooner had Eve uttered these words than a voice spoke to the couple, "Miserable wretches! Why do you predict and foretell death to each other? Do not prejudge things as hopeless, but comfort each other, for the tree has more life than death in it." Thus did the voice speak to the two unfortunate souls, and they were so comforted by it that from then on they called the tree the Tree of Life. And because of the great joy it gave them, they planted many more trees from this one. As soon as they broke

5. Cf. *Morte Darthur* p. 56, lines 5–22.

off a twig, they stuck it into the earth, where it came to life and readily took root, retaining the color of the original tree.

The original tree continued to grow and develop, and Adam and Eve sat beneath it more readily and more often than they had before, until one day, when they had been sitting together beneath it for a long while—the true story says it was a Friday—they heard a voice tell them that they should engage in carnal union. Both Adam and Eve were so overcome with shame that their eyes could not bear to watch each other do such a vile deed. The man felt as ashamed as the woman. Yet they did not know how they would defy the order of Our Lord, for they were still suffering the punishment of disobeying his first command. As they looked at each other with great shame, Our Lord saw their embarrassment and took pity on them. But since His command could not be breached, and because He wanted these two to establish the human race and restore the tenth legion of angels who had fallen from heaven because of their pride, He comforted them in their shame. He placed between them a darkness so thick that they could not see each other. The couple were amazed that this darkness had materialized between them so suddenly. They called to each other and touched each other without being able to see. Because everything must be accomplished according to the will of Our Lord, it was necessary that their bodies come together in carnal union, as the true Father had ordered. When they had lain together, they created a new seed in which their great sin was somewhat remedied. Adam had engendered and his wife had conceived Abel the Just, who first served his Creator by loyally rendering Him his tithes.

Thus was Abel the Just engendered beneath the Tree of Life, on a Friday, as you have heard. Then the darkness faded and the couple saw each other as before. They realized that Our Lord had done this to hide their shame, and they were delighted. Then an amazing thing happened. The Tree, which had been completely white, became as green as grass, and all the saplings that derived from it under this union had green trunks and leaves and bark.

Thus did the Tree change from white to green. But the saplings that had descended previously from it retained their original color. By contrast, the Tree of Life, having become thoroughly green, began from that day forward to flower and give fruit, though it had never done so before. The fact that the tree lost its white color and became green signifies that the woman who planted it had lost her virginity. The green color it took on and the flower and fruit represent the seed that had been sown beneath it, which would always be green in Our Lord; that is to say it would always have pious thoughts and feel love toward its Creator. The flower signifies that the creature engendered beneath this Tree would be chaste and clean and pure in body. The fruit signifies that he would work diligently and would exemplify the cause of religion and goodness in all his worldly deeds.

The Tree remained green for a long time, along with the saplings that derived from it after the couple's union. When Abel grew up, he was so devoted to his Creator and loved Him so much that he offered Him the tithes and the first fruits of the finest things he had. But his brother Cain offered the most vile and most despicable things he had. As a result, Our Lord gave a wonderful blessing to the one who had given the finest tithes, so that when Abel climbed the hill where he customarily burned his offerings, as Our Lord had commanded, the smoke rose straight up to heaven. But the smoke from Cain's offerings spread out through the fields, black and stinking, in contrast to the white and sweet-smelling smoke from Abel's sacrifice. When Cain realized that his brother Abel was more blessed for his sacrifice, which the Lord received more willingly than his own, he was very distraught and came to hate his brother beyond measure. Cain began to plot ways to take revenge and even considered murdering his brother, for he did not see how else he might be fully avenged."

* * *

[Galahad Dies][6]

One day, after a year had passed, Galahad complained to Our Lord, saying, "It seems to me, Sir, that I have lived in this world long enough. If You agree, please release me from it now." It happened that King Escorant lay ill on his death bed. He summoned the three companions and asked their forgiveness for having so mistreated them. They pardoned him readily, and he died.

When King Escorant was buried, the residents of the city were very concerned; they did not know who could be their king. They deliberated for a long time, and during their discussion, a voice said to them, "Choose the youngest of the three companions. He will protect you from harm and give sound advice while he is with you." They did as the voice had directed and chose Galahad to be their lord, despite his reluctance. When they placed the crown on his head, he was dismayed. But he realized he must accede to their wishes; otherwise they would kill him.

When Galahad had become lord of the land, he built an ark of gold and precious stones to cover the Holy Vessel, which sat on the silver table. Every morning, as soon as he awoke, he and his companions came before the Holy Vessel to say their prayers.

At the end of a year, on the very day that Galahad had been crowned, he and his companions rose early in the morning. When they came to the place that was called the heavenly palace, they looked in the direction of the Holy Vessel and saw a noble-looking man, dressed in a bishop's garb. He was kneeling in front of the table and saying confession. He was surrounded by as many angels as if he had been Jesus Christ himself. After kneeling for a long while, he rose and began to say the Mass of the glorious Mother of God. And when he came to the solemn part of the

6. Cf. *Morte Darthur* p. 585, line 37–p. 586, line 23.

Mass, he lifted the platen from the Holy Vessel and called to Galahad, saying, "Come forward, servant of Jesus Christ, and you will see what you have wanted to see for so long." Galahad drew near and looked into the Holy Vessel. As soon as he did, he began to tremble violently, for his mortal flesh had caught sight of spiritual mysteries.

Raising his hands toward heaven, Galahad said, "I worship You and give thanks that You have granted my desire. Now I see clearly what no tongue could describe and no heart could imagine. I see here the source of great deeds and the cause of all prowess. I see mysteries that surpass all other mysteries! And since, Dear Lord, You have allowed me to see what I have always hoped to see, I ask that You now permit me, in this state of bliss, to pass from earthly life into eternal life."

As soon as Galahad had made this request, the worthy man standing in front of the altar in priestly dress took the host from the table and offered it to Galahad. He received the body of Our Lord with humility and great devotion. And when he had partaken of it, the good man asked, "Do you know who I am?"

"No, indeed," replied Galahad, "not unless you tell me."

"Know that I am Josephus, son of Joseph of Arimathea, sent by Our Lord to be your companion. And do you know why He sent me rather than another? Because you are like me in two ways: you witnessed the mysteries of the Holy Grail, as I did, and you are a virgin, as I am. It is thus fitting that we be together."

Galahad went to Perceval and kissed him, and then he kissed Bors, and said to him, "Bors, give my greetings to Sir Lancelot, my father, when you see him." Then Galahad returned to the table and prostrated himself on hands and knees in front of it. He held that position only a short while before falling forward on the palace floor. His soul had already left his body and was being carried away by jubilant angels who blessed the name of the Lord.

At the moment of Galahad's death, an extraordinary thing took place. The two companions saw a hand reach down from heaven, though they could not see the body to which the hand belonged. The hand moved straight toward the Holy Vessel, seized it along with the Lance, and carried them both up to heaven. Since that time, no man has been bold enough to claim that he has seen the Holy Grail.

Galahad's death provoked an intense sadness in Perceval and Bors. If they had not been such valiant and virtuous men, they would have succumbed to despair over the loss of such a beloved friend. The people of the region mourned him deeply and were very distraught. They dug his grave there where he died, and as soon as he was buried, Perceval withdrew into a hermitage outside the city walls and began to wear the religious habit. Bors accompanied him but retained his secular clothing, for he intended to return to King Arthur's court. Perceval spent a year and three days at the hermitage before he died. He had Bors bury him with his sister and Galahad in the heavenly palace.

When Bors saw that he remained alone in the distant lands of the kingdom of Babylon, he left Sarras in full armor, went to the sea, and boarded a ship. After a short voyage, he arrived at the kingdom of Logres and rode as far as Camelot, where he found King Arthur. Never has there been such a joyous welcome as the one he received. Bors had been away from court so long that the others thought they had lost him forever.

After they had eaten, the king summoned the clerks who were putting into writing the adventures of the knights at court. When Bors had recounted the adventures of the Holy Grail, as he had seen them, they were recorded and kept in the archive at Salisbury. Master Walter Map withdrew them to write his book about the Holy Grail, for the love of his lord King Henry, who had the story translated from Latin into French.[7] But here the story stops, and tells no more about the adventures of the Holy Grail.

* * *

From the Stanzaic Morte Arthur†

[Launcelot in the Queen's Chambers][1]

* * *

1800 Whan he come to the lady shene,°	*splendid*
He kissid and clypped° that swete wyght°—	*embraced / creature*
Forsothe they nevyr wolde wene°	*expect*
That any treson was ther dyght.°	*planned*
So mykylle° love was hem bytwene	*much*
1805 That they noght° departe myght;	*not*
To bede he gothe with the Quene,	
And there he thoughte to dwelle alle nyght.	

He was not buskyd in hys bedde,[2]	
Launcelot in the Quenys boure,	
1810 Come Agrawayne and Syr Mordreit	
With twelve knyghtys stiffe° in stowre.°	*bold / fight*
Launcelot of tresson they begredde,°	*accused*
Callyd hym fals and kyngys treytoure;	
And he so strongly was bystedde°	*beset, constrained*
1815 Thereinne he hadde non armoure.	

"Welaway," than sayd the Quene,	
"Launcelot, what shall worthe° of us twoo?	*become*
The love that hathe bene us betwene,	
To suche endynge that it sholde goo.	

---

7. The historical Walter Map was a jurist and a man of letters at the court of King Henry II of England. But Map died before the *Quest* was composed and could not have been its actual author.

† Text of London, British Library, Harleian MS 2252, printed with permission of the British Library. The MS dates from the end of the 15th century, and the poem's date of composition is held to be c. 1400. The poem is written in eight-line stanzas of four-stress lines rhyming *ababab*. A number of the selections printed here are offered in parallel to those from Malory's concurrent source, the French *Mort le Roi Artu* (see p. 750 ff.).

1. Cf. *Morte Darthur* p. 649, line 1–p. 651, line 14.

2. He had barely got in bed.

<table>
<tr><td>20</td><td>Withe Agrawayne that is so kene,°</td><td>fierce</td></tr>
<tr><td></td><td>That nyght and day hathe bene oure foo,</td><td></td></tr>
<tr><td></td><td>Now I wote° withouten wene°</td><td>know / doubt</td></tr>
<tr><td></td><td>That alle oure wele° is tornyd to woo."</td><td>good fortune</td></tr>
</table>

<table>
<tr><td></td><td>"Lady," he sayd, "thow moste blynne,°</td><td>cease</td></tr>
<tr><td>25</td><td>Wyde I wote thes wordis bethe ryffe.³</td><td></td></tr>
<tr><td></td><td>Bot is here any armoure inne</td><td></td></tr>
<tr><td></td><td>That I may have to save my lyffe?"</td><td></td></tr>
<tr><td></td><td>"Certis, nay," she sayd thenne,</td><td></td></tr>
<tr><td></td><td>"Thys antoure is so wondyr stryffe,</td><td></td></tr>
<tr><td>30</td><td>That I ne may to none armoure wynne,⁴</td><td></td></tr>
<tr><td></td><td>Helme ne hauberke,° swerd ne knyffe."</td><td>coat of mail</td></tr>
<tr><td></td><td>Evyr Agrawayne and Syr Mordred</td><td></td></tr>
<tr><td></td><td>Callyd hym recreante° fals knyght,</td><td>recreant, craven</td></tr>
<tr><td></td><td>Bad hym ryse oute of hys bedde,</td><td></td></tr>
<tr><td>35</td><td>For he moste nedis° with them fyght.</td><td>necessarily</td></tr>
<tr><td></td><td>In hys robe than he hym cled,°</td><td>clad</td></tr>
<tr><td></td><td>Thoughe he none armoure gete myght,</td><td></td></tr>
<tr><td></td><td>Wrothely° oute hys swerd he bredde;°</td><td>Angrily / drew</td></tr>
<tr><td></td><td>The chamber dore he sette up ryght.⁵</td><td></td></tr>
</table>

<table>
<tr><td>40</td><td>An armyd knyght before in wente</td><td></td></tr>
<tr><td></td><td>And wende Launcelot wele to sloo;°</td><td>slay</td></tr>
<tr><td></td><td>Bot Launcelot gaffe hym soche a dynte</td><td></td></tr>
<tr><td></td><td>That to the grounde gonne he go.</td><td></td></tr>
<tr><td></td><td>The other all agayne than stente,°</td><td>stopped</td></tr>
<tr><td>45</td><td>Aftyr hym dorste° folowe no moo;°</td><td>durst / more</td></tr>
<tr><td></td><td>To the chambyr dore he sprente°</td><td>sprang</td></tr>
<tr><td></td><td>And claspid° it with barres twoo.</td><td>locked, barred</td></tr>
</table>

<table>
<tr><td></td><td>The knyght that Launcelot has slayne,</td><td></td></tr>
<tr><td></td><td>Hys armoure founde he fayre and bryght;</td><td></td></tr>
<tr><td>50</td><td>Hastely he hathe hem° of-drayne°</td><td>them / drawn off</td></tr>
<tr><td></td><td>And therin hymselfe dight.°</td><td>dressed</td></tr>
<tr><td></td><td>"Now know thou wele, Syr Agrawayne,</td><td></td></tr>
<tr><td></td><td>Thow presons° me no more tonyght!"</td><td>imprison</td></tr>
<tr><td></td><td>Oute than sprange he with mykell mayn,°</td><td>force</td></tr>
<tr><td>55</td><td>Hymselfe ayenste hem alle to fyght.</td><td></td></tr>
</table>

<table>
<tr><td></td><td>Launcelot than smote with herte goode;</td><td></td></tr>
<tr><td></td><td>Wete ye welle withouten lese,°</td><td>lie</td></tr>
<tr><td></td><td>Syr Agrawayne to dethe yode,</td><td>fell</td></tr>
<tr><td></td><td>And sythen° all the other presse—</td><td>then</td></tr>
<tr><td>60</td><td>Was non so stronge that hym withstode,</td><td></td></tr>
<tr><td></td><td>Be he had made a lytelle rese⁶—</td><td></td></tr>
<tr><td></td><td>Bot Mordreit fled as° he were wode:°</td><td>as if / mad</td></tr>
<tr><td></td><td>To save hys lyff full fayne° he was.</td><td>glad</td></tr>
</table>

3. I know that word of this will be widespread.
4. This mischance is so wondrously bad, that I can get to no armor.
5. I.e., he stood close to the door.
6. By the time Launcelot had made a small attack.

* * *

[Gawain's Objection to the Queen's Execution][7]

* * *

    The Kynge Arthure that ylke° tyde°   *same / time*
1935 Gawayne and Gaherys for sent;
    Here° answeres were noght for to hyde:°   *Their / be hidden*
    They ne wolde noght be of hys assente;
    Gawayne wolde nevyr be nere bysyde
    There any woman shuld be brente;°   *burned*
1940 Gaheriet and Gaheries, with lytell pryde,
    All unarmyd thedyr° they wente.   *thither*

* * *

[Launcelot Responds to His Besiegers][8]

* * *

2110 Aboute the Joyus Garde they° laye   *i.e., Arthur's forces*
    Seventene wokys° and well mare,   *weeks*
    Tille it felle uppon a day
    Launcelot home bad° hem fare:°   *bade / go*
    "Breke° youre sege, wendys° awaye!   *Break / go*
2115 You to slae° grete pyté it ware."°   *slay / were*
    He sayd, "Allas and weil-awaye,
    That evyr beganne thys sorewe sare."°   *sore*
    Evir the Kynge and Syr Gawayne
    Calde hym fals recreante knyght,
2120 And sayde he had hys bretherne slayne,
    And treytour was by day and nyght,
    Bad hym come and prove hys mayne°   *prowess*
    In the felde° with hem to fyghte.   *field of battle*
    Launcelot sighed, for sothe° o sayne,°   *truth / say*
    Grete duelle° it was to se with sight.   *dole, sorrow*

* * *

[Launcelot Hopes for Peace][9]

* * *

2580 Off Northe Gales were bretherne seven,
    Ferly° mekelle° of strenghe and pryde,   *Wondrously / great*
    Not full fele that men coude nevyne[1]
    Better° dorste° in bataile byde.°   *Who better / durst / stay*
    All they sayd with one steven,°   *voice*
2585 "Lordyngis, how longe wolle ye chyde?
    Launcelot, for Goddys love in heven,
    With Galehud forthe lette us ryde!"

    Than spake the lord that was so hende,°   *gracious*

---

7. Cf. *Morte Darthur* p. 655, line 9–p. 656, line 32.
8. Cf. *Morte Darthur* p. 660, line 2–p. 662, line 15.
9. Cf. *Morte Darthur* p. 673, lines 8–23.
1. There were not many who men could name.

Hymself, Syr Launcelot de Lake:
90 "Lordyngis, a whyle I rede° we lende,°   *advise / remain*
And oure worthy wallys wake.°   *watch*
A message wolle I to them sende,
A trews betwene us for to take;
My lord is so corteise° and hende   *courteous*
That yit° I hope a pees to make."   *yet, still*

*   *   *

[Arthur Finds Gawain Already Dead][2]

*   *   *

30 Arthur went to hys dyner thane°—   *then*
Hys frely folke hym folowed faste—
But whan he fand° Syr Gawayne   *found*
In a shyppe laye° dede by a maste,   *who lay*
Or evyr he coveryd myght or mayne,[3]
35 An hundreth tymes hys hert nyghe° braste.°   *nearly / burst*
Thay layd Syr Gawayne upon a bere,°   *bier*
And to the castell they hym bare.

And in a chapell, amydde the quere,°   *choir*
That bold baron they beryed thare.
40 Arthur than changyd all hys chere;°   *mood*
What wondyr thoghe° hys hert was sare?   *though*
Hys suster° sone that was hym° dere,   *sister's / to him*
Off hym shold he here° nevyr mare.   *hear*

*   *   *

[Arthur's Dream of the Wheel of Fortune][4]

*   *   *

At nyght whan Arthur was brought in bedd—
He shuld have batyle upon the morow—
70 In° stronge swevenys° he was bystedde°   *With / dreams / beset*
That many a man that day shuld have sorow.
Hym thowht° he satte in gold all gledde,°   *thought / clad*
As he was comely kynge with crowne,
Upon a whele° that full wyde spredd,   *wheel*
75 And all hys knyghtis to hym bowne.[5]

The whele was ferly ryche and rownd,
In world was nevyr none halfe so hye;
Thereon he satte rychely crownyd,
With many a besaunte,° broche, and be.°   *coin / ring*
80 He lokyd downe upon the grownd:
A blake water ther undyr hym see°   *saw*
With dragons fele° there lay unbownde,   *many*
That no man durst hem nyghe° nyee.°   *approach / near*

---

2. Cf. *Morte Darthur* p. 681, line 11–p. 682, line 37.
3. Before he could ever recover his strength or power.
4. Cf. *Morte Darthur* p. 683, lines 18–29.
5. And all his knights were gathered about him.

He was wondyr ferd° to falle   afraid
3185 Amonge the fendys° ther that faught.   fiends
The whele overtornyd° therwithall,   turned over
And everyche° by a lymme hym caught.   each one
The Kynge gan lowde crye and calle,
As marred man of wytte unsaught;[6]
3190 Hys chambyrlayns wakyd hym therwithall,
And woodely° oute of hys slepe he raught.°   madly / roused

* * *

[The Death of Arthur][7]

* * *

He° lede hys lord unto that stronde;°   Sir Bedwere / shore
3500 A ryche shyppe, with maste and ore,
Full of ladyes there they fonde.

The ladyes that were feyre and free
Curteysly the Kynge gan they fonge,°   take
And one that bryghtest was of blee°   complexion
3505 Wepyd° sore and handys wrange.   Wept
"Broder," she sayd, "wo ys me,
Fro lechyng hastow be to longe;[8]
I wote that gretely grevyth me,
For thy paynes ar full stronge."

3510 The knyght kest° a rewfull° rowne,°   cast, made / rueful / speech
There he stode, sore and unsownde,
And sayde, "Lord, whedyr° ar ye bowne?°   whither / bound
Allas, whedyr wyll ye fro me fownde?"°   set out
The Kynge spake with a sory sowne,
3515 "I wylle wende° a lytell stownde°   go / space of time
In5o the vale of Aveloune,
Awhyle to hele me of my wounde."

Whan the shyppe from the land was broght,
Syr Bedwere saw of hem no more.
3520 Throw the forest forthe he soughte
On hyllys and holtys° hore.°   woods / grey, old
Of hys lyffe rought° he ryght noght;   cared
All nyght he went wepynge sore.
Agaynste the day he fownde ther wrought
3525 A chapelle bytwene two holtes hore.

To the chapell he toke the way;
There myght he se a woundyr syght.
Than saw he where an ermyte° laye   hermit
Byfore a tombe that new was dyghte,°   fashioned
3530 And coveryd it was with marboll graye,
And with ryche lettres rayled° aryght,°   adorned / well

6. Like a disturbed and insane man.
7. Cf. *Morte Darthur* p. 687, line 45–p. 689, line 32.
8. You have been too long away from medical attention.

There on an herse° sothely to saye — *bier*
With an hundreth tappers° lyghte. — *tapers, candles*

35 Unto the ermyte wente he thare
And askyd who was beryed there.
The ermyte answeryd swythe yare,° — *very quickly*
"Thereof can I tell no more:
Abowte mydnyght were ladyes here,
In world ne wyste° I what° they were. — *knew / i.e., who*
40 Thys body they broght uppon a bere
And beryed it, with woundys sore.

Besauntis° offred they here bryght— — *Coins*
I hope° an hundreth pound and more— — *i.e., believe*
And bad me pray bothe day and nyght
45 For hym that is buryed in these moldys° hore — *earths*
Unto Ower Lady, bothe day and nyght,
That she hys sowle helpe sholde."
The knyght redde the lettres aryght;
For sorow he fell unto the folde.° — *ground*

50 "Ermyte," he sayd, withoute lesynge,
"Here lyeth my lord that I have lorne,
Bold Arthur, the beste kynge
That evyr was in Bretayne borne.
Yif° me som of thy clothynge, — *Give*
55 For° Hym that bare the Crowne of Thorne, — *i.e., For the sake of*
And leve° that I may with the° lenge° — *grant / thee / stay*
Whyle I may leve,° and pray hym forne.° — *live / for*

The holy ermyte wold not wounde;° — *delay*
60 Sometyme archebishop he was
That Mordred flemyd° oute of londe, — *put to flight*
And in the wode hys wonnyng° chase.° — *dwelling / chose*
He thankyd Jhesu all of hys sound
That Syr Bedwere was comyn in pease.
65 He resayved hym with herte and honde
Togedyr to dwelle, withouten lese.° — *lie*

Whan Quene Gaynor, the Kynges wyffe,
Wyste that all was gone to wrake,
Away she went with ladys fyve
To Aumysbery, a nonne hyr for to make.

*   *   *

[The Death of Launcelot]⁹

*   *   *

Hytte felle agayne an evyntyde,° — *evening*
35 That Launcelot sekenyd° sely° sare; — *grew sick / wondrously*
The bysshop he clepyd° to hys syde — *called*

9. Cf. *Morte Darthur* p. 695, line 25–p. 696, line 15.

And all hys felaws, lesse and mare:
He sayd, "Bretherne, I may no lenger abyde,
My baleffull blode of lyffe is bare.
3840 What bote° is it to hele° and hyde,   good / conceal
My fowle flesshe will to erthe fare.°   go

"But Bretherne, I pray yow tonyght,
Tomorow whan ye fynde me dede,
Upon a bere that ye wyll me dyght°   place
3845 And to Joyes Garde than me lede;
For the love of God Allmyght,
Bery my body in that stede.°   place
Sometyme my trowthe therto I plyght;[1]
Allas, me forthynketh° that I so dyd."   regret

3850 "Mercy, syr," they sayd all three,
"For Hys love that dyed on Rode,°   Cross
Yif any yvell° have grevyd the,°   evil, sickness / thee
Hyt ys bot hevynesse° of yower ° blode.   oppression / your
Tomorow ye shall better be,
3855 Whan were ye but of comforte gode."
Merely° spake all men but he,   Merrily
But streyght unto hys bed he yode,

And clepyd the bysshope hym untylle,
And shrove° hym of hys synnes clene,°   confessed / utterly
3860 Off all hys synnes loude and stylle—
And of hys synnes myche° dyd he mene.°   much / speak
Ther he resseyved° with good wylle   received the Sacrament
God, Maryis sonne, mayden clene.
(Than Bors of wepyng had nevyr hys fylle.)
3865 To bedde they yede than all bydene.°   together

A lytell whyle byfore the day,
As the bysshop lay in hys bed,
A laughter toke hym there he laye
That all they were ryght sore adred.°   afraid
3870 They wakenyd hym, for sothe to saye,
And askyd yif he were hard bysted.°   beset
He said, "Allas and wele-away!
Why ne had I lenger thus be ledd?[2]

Allas, why nyghed ye me nye
3875 To awake me in word or stevyn?°   voice
Here was Launcelot, bryght of blee,
With angellis thrytté thousand and sevyn;
Hym they bare upon hye;
Agaynste hym openyd the gatys of hevyn—

---

1. I once pledged my (word of) truth to that.
2. Why had I not been longer led in dreams?

380 Suche a syght ryght now I see
    Is none in erthe that myght it nevyn!"°   *tell*

    "Syr," thay sayd, "for Crosse on Rode,
    Dothe° suche wordys clene away.   *Put*
385 Syr Lancelot eylythe° nothynge but gode;   *suffers*
    He shall be hole by pryme° of day."   *first hour*
    Candell they lyght and to hym yode,
    And fownde hym dede, for sothe to saye,
    Rede° and fayer of flesshe and blode,   *Red*
    Ryght as he in slepynge laye.

                  *   *   *

[The Death of the Queen; Conclusion][3]

                  *   *   *

    Whan they came to Aumysbery,
955 Dede they faunde Gaynor the Quene
    With roddys° feyre and rede as chery;   *cheeks*
    And forthe they bare hyr theym bytwene,
    And beryed hyr with Masse full merry
    By Syr Arthur, as I yow mene.°   *relate*
960 Now hyght° there chapell Glassynbery,°   *is called / Glastonbury*
    An abbay full ryche of order° clene.   *religious order*

    Off Lancelot du Lake telle I no more,
    But thus byleve these ermytes sevyn.
965 And yit is Arthur beryed thore,°   *there*
    And Quene Gaynour, as I yow nevyn,
    With monkes that ar ryght of lore;
    They rede and synge with mylde stevyn,
    "Jhesu that suffred woundes sore
    Graunt us all the blysse of hevyn!"

    Amen.

    Explycit° *Le Morte Arthur*   *Here ends*

From the Mort le Roi Artu†

[The Maid of Escalot][1]

                  *   *   *

    The maiden stayed there with her brother until Lancelot was on his way to recovery, so that he could get around in the house. And

---

3. Cf. *Morte Darthur* p. 694, line 21–p. 697, line 38.
† This and the following selections copyright 1995, from *The Death of Arthur*, trans. Norris J. Lacy, in *Lancelot-Grail: The Old French Arthurian Vulgate and Post-Vulgate in Translation*, 5 vols., Norris J. Lacy, Gen. Ed. (New York: Garland, 1993–1996), IV, pp. 101–114, 121, 122, 148, 149–150, 155–156, 157, and 159, respectively. Reproduced by permission of Routledge, Inc., part of the Taylor & Francis Group. A number of these selections are offered in parallel to those from Malory's concurrent source, the *sMA* (p. 740 ff.).
1. Cf. *Morte Arthur* p. 614, line 7–p. 617, line 24.

when he was nearly healed and his handsome looks were restored, the maiden, who stayed with him night and day, loved him so much, both because others spoke so highly of him and because she found him so handsome, that she thought she could not go on living if she did not have his love.

She loved him with all her heart. And when she could no longer keep her thoughts to herself, she came to him one day, superbly adorned and wearing the most beautiful gown she could find, and without a doubt she was exceedingly beautiful. Thus she came to Lancelot and said to him, "Sir, wouldn't it be ignoble for a knight to refuse if I asked for his love?"

"Young lady," said Lancelot, "if his heart were at his disposal, so that he could do with it as he wished, he would be very ignoble to reject you; but if it happened that he didn't have sovereignty over himself and his heart, then if he rejected your offer of love, no one should blame him. And I'm speaking about myself, for, so help me God, if you were willing to give me your love, and if I were free to do as I would like, as many other knights are, I would consider myself generously rewarded to have your love; for, so help me God, it has been a long time since I've seen a woman more deserving of love than you."

"What, sir?" said the maiden. "Is your heart not yours to do with as you will?"

"Lady," he said, "I am doing with it as I will, because it's where I want it to be, and I have no desire for it to be anywhere else, since it could not be better placed than it is now. God forbid that it be removed from where I wish it to be, for then I couldn't live a single day as happy as I am now."

"Sir," said the maiden, "you have certainly told me enough that I have an idea of what's in your heart. It grieves me terribly that it's that way, for by what you have said and given me to understand in these few words, you'll soon cause my death. If you had told me this a little less directly, you would have let my heart languish in fond hope, and such hope might have let me live in all the joy and delight a love-stricken heart can know."

Then the maiden came to her brother and revealed everything to him; and she told him that she loved Lancelot so much that she would certainly die of it unless her brother could somehow arrange for her to have her will. He was saddened by that, and he said to her, "Fair sister, you must look elsewhere, for you can never succeed with him. I know for a fact that he has given his heart to someone so noble that he wouldn't deign to love a poor maiden like you, even though you're one of the most beautiful women in the world. If you wish to love someone, you should set your sights lower, for you can't pluck the fruit from such a high tree."

"That certainly distresses me, fair brother," said the maiden, "and I wish that, please God, I cared no more for him than I do for any other knight, and no more than before I met him. But now that can't be, for it's now my destiny to die for him, and you'll see me do so."

The maiden thus foresaw her death, and it happened just as she said it would, for she truly died for the love of Lancelot, as the story will tell later.[2]

*   *   *

[I]t happened that around noon a boat draped with rich silken cloths arrived beneath the tower at Camelot. The king had eaten with a large company of knights and was at the windows of the hall. He was looking down the river, very pensive and downcast because of the queen, for he knew she would have no aid from any knight there, since they had all seen clearly that she had given the knight the fruit that killed him. And because they all knew that beyond a doubt, none of them would dare to risk himself against those odds.

When the king, who was thinking about those things, saw the beautiful, rich boat arrive, he pointed it out to Sir Gawain and told him, "Dear nephew, there is the most beautiful boat I have ever seen. Let's go see what is in it."

"Let us go," said Sir Gawain. Then they went down from the palace, and when they reached the river, they saw the boat so beautifully decorated that they all marveled at it.

"My word," said Sir Gawain, "if this boat is as beautiful inside as out, it will be remarkable. I'm almost convinced that adventures are beginning anew."[3]

"I was going to say the same thing," said the king.

The boat was covered like a vault, and Sir Gawain lifted the edge of the cloth and said to the king, "Sir, let's go aboard and see what is there."

The king went aboard, and Sir Gawain after him, and there they found in the middle of the boat a very beautiful bed, adorned with every rich decoration imaginable, and in the bed lay a maiden who had not been dead for long and who, judging from her appearance, had been very beautiful.

Then Sir Gawain said to the king, "Oh, sir, don't you think death was evil and despicable to enter the body of a maiden as beautiful as this one was only recently?"

"To be sure," said the king, "I think she was a very beautiful creature, and it's a great pity that she died at such an age. And because of her great beauty, I'd like to know who she was and her identity and her lineage."

They looked at her for a long time, and when Sir Gawain looked more closely, he realized that this was the beautiful maiden whose love he had sought and who had told him she would never love anyone except Lancelot; and thereupon he said to the king, "Sir, I know who this maiden was."

2. The story resumes in the next selection printed here, after the "interlaced" relating of several other indirectly related episodes [Editor].

3. As the opening of the *Mort Artu* had suggested, the conclusion of the Grail Quest had put an end to the adventures that characterized the Arthurian world. See chapter 1, p. [3]: "the adventures of the kingdom of Logres had been brought to a close, so that scarcely anything more could occur."

"And who was she?" said the king. "Tell me."

"Willingly, sir," said Sir Gawain. "Do you remember the beautiful maiden I mentioned to you recently, the one I said Lancelot loved?"

"Yes, I remember it well," said the king. "You told me that you had asked for her love but that she had rejected you."

"Sir," said Sir Gawain, "this is the young woman we are talking about."

"I'm certainly sorry about that," said the king, "and I'd like to know the circumstances of her death, for I believe she died of grief."

As they were speaking of this matter, Sir Gawain looked intently at the maiden and saw a rich purse hanging from her belt, and it did not appear to be empty. He reached for it, opened it, and took out a letter. He gave it to the king, who began to read it and found that it contained the following words: "The Maiden of Escalot sends greetings to all the knights of the Round Table. I want you to hear my complaint, not because you can ever resolve it, but because I know you to be the most valiant and most congenial men in the world. I inform you that I met my death because of my faithful love. And if you ask for whose love I have suffered the pain of death, I answer that I died for the most valiant and yet the vilest man in the world: Lancelot of the Lake. He is the vilest man I know, for all my entreaties and laments and tears did not suffice to make him take pity on me; and my heart was so fixed on him that I died from loving faithfully."

That is what the letter said, and when the king had read it to Sir Gawain, he said, "To be sure, maiden, you can indeed say that he for whom you died is the most base man in the world and the most valiant; for the wicked thing he did to you is so terrible and so despicable that he should be condemned by all; and to be sure, I who am king and who should do no wrong would have given my finest castle to prevent your death."

* * *

[Lancelot in the Queen's Chambers][4]

* * *

Lancelot, who did not realize that he was being watched, came to the door that opened out from the room toward the garden; he opened it and entered and went from room to room until he came to the one in which the queen was waiting for him.

Once Lancelot was in the room, he closed the door behind him, as it was not his lot to be killed there. He undressed and went to bed with the queen. But he had not been there long before those who were lying in wait to capture him came to the door of the room; and when they found it closed, all of them were taken aback,

---

4. Cf. *Morte Arthur* p. 648, line 45–p. 652, line 19.

and they knew that their plan had been foiled. They asked Agravain how they could get in, and he advised them to break down the door, for otherwise they could not enter the room.

They knocked and beat on the door until the queen heard it; she said to Lancelot, "Dear friend, we're betrayed!"

"How, lady?" he said. "What is it?" Then he listened and heard a great noise outside, made by people trying in vain to break down the door.

"Oh, dear friend," said the queen, "now we're disgraced and doomed; now the king will know all about you and me. Agravain set this trap for us."

Lancelot said, "Lady, don't worry about that; he has arranged his own death, for he'll be the first to die." Then they both leapt out of bed and dressed as well as they could. "Oh, lady," said Lancelot, "do you have here a hauberk or some other armor with which I can protect my body?"

"None at all," said the queen. "Instead, our misfortune is so great that both of us are condemned to die here. And may God help me, that pains me more for your sake than for mine, for your death would be a much greater tragedy than mine. And yet, if God should grant that you escape from here safe and sound, I know that no man in the world would dare condemn me to death for this crime while he knew you were still alive."

When Lancelot heard that, he went fearlessly to the door and called to those who were beating on it, "Evil cowardly knights, wait for me; I'm going to open the door and see who will enter first!"

Then he drew his sword and opened the door and told them to come in. A knight named Tanaguin, who mortally hated Lancelot, stepped forward before the others. Lancelot raised his sword and, with all his power, struck him so hard that neither his helmet nor his iron coif could prevent him from being split down to his shoulders. Lancelot pulled out the sword and struck him dead. When the others saw what had happened to him, they all drew back so that the doorway was left empty.

When Lancelot saw that, he said to the queen, "Lady, this battle is finished; I'll leave when it pleases you, but I won't be kept here by any man."

The queen said that she wanted him to be safe, regardless of what might happen to her. Lancelot looked at the knight he had killed. The man had fallen inside the door; Lancelot pulled the body toward him and closed the door. Then he took his armor and armed himself as well as he could, and he said to the queen, "Lady, since I'm armed, I should be able to leave safely, may it please God."

She told him to go if he could. He went to the door, opened it, and said that they would not keep him there. Then he rushed into the middle of them, his sword drawn, and struck the first one he met so hard that he knocked him flat on the ground so that he was unable to rise. When the others saw that, they retreated, and even the boldest of them made way for him.

When he saw that they were leaving him alone, he went into the garden and set out for his lodging. There he found Bors, who greatly feared that Lancelot might not be able to return as he wished; for he had realized that the kinsmen of King Arthur had somehow spied on Lancelot in order to capture him. When Bors saw his lord approaching fully armed, whereas he had left unarmed, he understood that there had been a fight. He approached Lancelot and asked, "Sir, what made you arm yourself?"

Lancelot told him how Agravain and his two brothers had spied on him, wanting to catch him with the queen, and how they had brought a great many knights. "And they almost caught me, since I wasn't on my guard; but I defended myself vigorously, and I fought well enough, with God's help, that I escaped."

"Oh, sir," said Bors, "now matters are worse than before, for what we had hidden so long is now known! Now you'll see the war begin that will never end in our lifetime. For if the king has loved you more than any other man until now, he'll hate you all the more when he knows that you have offended him by shaming him with his wife. Now you must consider what we'll do, for I know that the king will henceforth be our mortal enemy. But, God help me, I'm most distressed about my lady the queen, who will be condemned to death on your account. And I would like for plans to be made, if possible, so that she might be rescued unharmed from her plight."

* * *

[Gawain's Objection to the Queen's Execution][5]

* * *

When Sir Gawain saw that deliberations had proceeded to the point that the queen's death was decided, he said that, if it pleased God, his sorrow would not allow him to see the one woman die who had accorded him the greatest honor. Then he came to the king and said to him, "Sir, I'm returning to you whatever I have received from you, and never again will I serve you if you permit this outrage." The king did not respond to what he had said, because his mind was on something else. Then Sir Gawain left the court and went directly to his lodging, grieving as much as if he saw everyone around him dead.

* * *

[The Death of Gawain][6]

* * *

One of the knights went to the king and said that Sir Gawain was asking for him. When the king came to him, he found Sir Gawain in such a grave state that no one could get a word from him. The king began to weep and lament bitterly; and when

5. Cf. *Morte Arthur* p. 655, line 9–p. 656, line 32.
6. Cf. *Morte Arthur* p. 681, line 14–p. 682, line 38.

Gawain heard his uncle grieving so for him, he opened his eyes and said with great effort, "Sir, I'm dying; in God's name, if you can avoid doing battle with Mordred, do so, because I tell you truly that if you die at the hand of any man, it will be his. And greet my lady the queen on my behalf; and you, lords, if any of you, God willing, should see Lancelot, tell him that I send more sincere greetings to him than to anyone I've ever known and that I ask his forgiveness. And I pray that God will keep him as I left him. And I ask that he not fail to come and see my tomb as soon as he knows that I'm dead; that way, he can't fail to take pity on me."

Then he said to the king, "Sir, I ask you to have me buried at Camelot with my brothers, and I want to be placed in the same tomb where Gaheriet was buried, because he was the man I loved most in the world. And have the tomb inscribed, "Here lie Gaheriet and Gawain, whom Lancelot killed through Gawain's folly." I want those words written there so that I will be blamed for my death, as I deserve to be."

When the king, who was grieving bitterly, heard Sir Gawain say that, he asked him, "What, dear nephew? Have you met your death through Lancelot?"

"Yes, sir, by the head wound he caused; and it would have healed, except that the Romans reopened it in the battle." After that, no one heard Gawain say anything else except, "Jesus Christ, Father, do not judge me by my faults." And then he left this world, his hands folded on his chest.

The king wept and lamented loudly and fainted repeatedly over the body, proclaiming himself miserable, distraught, and grief-stricken. He said, "Oh, hostile and perverse Fortune, the most perfidious thing in the world, why were you once so generous and kind to me, only to make me pay so dearly in the end? You once were my mother, but now you have become a cruel stepmother; and to make me die from grief, you've brought Death here with you, and you've dishonored me in two ways: with my friends and with my land. Oh, villainous Death, you should never have taken such a man as my nephew, who surpassed everyone in goodness!"

* * *

[*Arthur's Last Dreams*][7]

* * *

When he had retired and was asleep in his bed, he dreamed that Sir Gawain came to him, more handsome than he had ever seen him, and after him came a crowd of poor people, all saying, "King Arthur, we have won the house of God for Sir Gawain, your nephew, because of the great good he has done for us; do as he did and you'll be acting wisely."

The king answered that he would certainly do so. Then he ran to his nephew and embraced him; and Sir Gawain said to him,

7. Cf. *Morte Arthur* p. 683, line 18–p. 684, line 25.

weeping, "Sir, don't do battle with Mordred; if you do, you'll die or will be mortally wounded."

The king answered, "I most certainly will fight him, even if I must die as a result; for I'd be a coward not to defend my land against a traitor."

Then Sir Gawain left, grieving very bitterly and saying to his uncle the king, "Oh, sir, what a tragedy and a pity that you are rushing to your death!" Then he came back to the king and said to him, "Sir, send for Lancelot, for you can be sure that if you have him in your company, Mordred will never be able to hold out against you. But if you don't send for him in your need, you won't be able to escape death."

The king said that he would not summon him for this reason, because Lancelot had so wronged him that he did not think he would come if sent for. And Sir Gawain then turned away, weeping and saying, "Sir, you can be sure that this will be a pity for all good men." Such was the dream that King Arthur had.

In the morning, when he woke up, he crossed himself and said, "Oh, fair Lord God Jesus Christ, who have bestowed on me so many honors since I first became king and began to hold lands, fair dear Lord, by Your mercy, let me not lose honor in this battle, but instead give me victory over my enemies who have deceived and betrayed me."

When the king had said that, he rose and went to hear the Mass of the Holy Ghost, and after that, he had all his men eat a light breakfast, because he did not know when he might meet Mordred's men. When they had eaten, they set out and rode easily and in leisurely fashion all day, so that their horses would not be too tired whenever they had to do battle. That night they camped undisturbed on the plain of Lovedon. The king retired in his tent, all alone except for his chamberlains.

When he had fallen asleep, it seemed to him that the most beautiful lady in the world appeared before him and lifted him up from the earth and took him up onto the highest mountain he had ever seen; and there she set him upon a wheel. The wheel had seats, some of which rose as others sank. The lady asked him, "Arthur, where are you?"

"Lady," he said, "I'm on a large wheel, but I don't know what wheel it is."

She said, "It's the Wheel of Fortune." Then she asked him, "Arthur, what do you see?"

"Lady, it seems to me that I see the whole world."

"Indeed," she said, "you do see it, and in it there is little that you have not been lord of until now, and of all you see, you have been the most powerful king who ever was. But such are the effects of earthly pride that no one is so highly placed that he can avoid falling from worldly power." And then she took him and dashed him to earth so cruelly that it seemed to King Arthur that he was crushed and that he lost all the strength of his body and its members.

Thus did King Arthur see the misfortunes that were to befall him. In the morning, when he had risen, he heard Mass before taking up arms, and to an archbishop he confessed, to the best of his knowledge, all the sins he thought he had committed against his Creator. And when he had confessed and had asked for forgiveness, he revealed to the archbishop the two visions that had come to him during the two preceding nights. And when the wise man heard them, he said to the king, "Oh, sir, for the salvation of your soul and body and kingdom, turn back to Dover with all your army, and ask Lancelot to come to your aid, and he'll willingly come. For if you attack Mordred now, you'll be either mortally wounded or killed, and the tragedy that befalls us will last as long as the world. King Arthur, all this will happen if you do battle with Mordred."

* * *

[The Death of Arthur][8]

* * *

"In God's name," said the king, "I was right to think that my death was fast approaching." Then he became pensive, and tears came to his eyes; and when he had been lost in thought for a long time, he said to Girflet, "Now you must go from here and leave me, and you will never see me again."

"If that's the case, I'll never leave you," said Girflet.

"Yes, you will," replied the king, "or else I will have nothing but hatred for you."

"Sir," said Girflet, "how could I possibly leave you here all alone and go away, when you tell me that I'll never see you again?"

The king said, "You must do as I tell you. Leave here quickly, for you can't remain. And I ask this of you in the name of the love that you and I have had for each other."

When Girflet heard the king ask him so tenderly, he answered, "Sir, I'll do what you command, despite my terrible grief. But tell me, if you please, whether it's possible that I might see you again."

"No," said the king, "you may be assured of that."

"And where is it you are going, good sir?"

"I won't tell you that," answered the king.

When Girflet saw that he would learn nothing more, he mounted his horse and left the king. And as soon as he departed, a strong and wondrous rain began to fall, and it continued until he reached a hill half a league from the king. And when he came to the hill, he paused beneath a tree to wait for the rain to stop, and he began to look back toward the place where he had left the king. He saw coming across the water a ship with many ladies on board, and when the ship neared the shore where the king was, they gathered on that side of the ship. The first among them held Morgan, the sister of King Arthur, by the hand and began to

8. Cf. *Morte Arthur* p. 687, line 43–p. 688, line 48.

beckon to the king. And the king, as soon as he saw his sister Morgan, immediately rose from the ground where he was sitting and went aboard the ship, leading his horse after him and taking his arms and armor with him.

When Girflet, who was on the hill, had seen all this, he returned as fast as his horse could run. When he arrived at the shore, he saw King Arthur among the ladies, and he recognized Morgan the Fay, for he had seen her many times. In a very short time, the ship had gone farther from the shore than eight crossbow shots would have carried. When Girflet saw that the king was thus lost to him, he dismounted on the shore and mourned bitterly; and he stayed there all day and all night with neither food nor drink; nor had he had any the day before.

The next morning, after daybreak, when the sun had risen and the birds had begun to sing, Girflet was still suffering mightily from grief and pain. Sorrowful as he was, he mounted and left there and rode until he arrived at a nearby grove. In that grove lived a hermit whom he knew well. He went to him and remained with him two days, because he was ill from the grief he had suffered, and he told the holy man what he had seen happen to King Arthur.

On the third day, he left there and decided to go to the Black Chapel to see whether Lucan the Wine Steward had been buried. When he arrived there about noon, he dismounted at the entrance and tied his horse to a tree and went in. Before the altar he found two tombs, both of them very beautiful and rich, but one of them much more so than the other.

On the less beautiful was written the following: Here lies Lucan the Wine Steward, whom King Arthur crushed in his arms.[9] And on the tomb that was marvelous and rich were letters that said, Here lies King Arthur, who by his valor conquered twelve kingdoms. And when Girflet saw that, he fainted upon the tomb; and when he regained consciousness, he very gently kissed the tomb and began to grieve bitterly, and he remained there until evening, when the holy man came who was to serve at the altar. Upon his arrival, Girflet asked him immediately, "Sir, is it true that King Arthur lies here?"

"Yes, my friend, truly he does; some ladies whom I don't know brought him here."

Girflet understood that they were the ones who put Arthur on the ship. He said that since his lord had left this world, he would no longer remain in it, and he so entreated the hermit that he accepted him into his company. Thus Girflet became a hermit and served at the Black Chapel, but that was not to be for long, for after King Arthur's death he lived only eighteen days.

9. The dying Arthur, still in his armor, had inadvertently crushed the unarmed Lucan in an affectionate embrace [Editor].

* * *

[The Death of the Queen][1]

* * *

Lancelot and his company were approaching, and no one could have been more enraged and grief-stricken than he, for on the very day when the battle [with Mordred's sons] was to take place, he had received the news that his lady the queen had died and departed this world three days before. And it had happened just as he was told, for the queen had recently left the world. But never had a lady met a finer death or repented more nobly, nor had any lady more fittingly asked our Lord's mercy, than had she.

* * *

[The Death of Lancelot][2]

* * *

On the fifteenth day before May, Lancelot took to bed ill; and when he felt that he was going to die, he asked the archbishop and Blioberis to convey his body to Joyous Guard immediately after his death and to place it in the tomb containing the body of Galehaut, the lord of the Distant Isles. They promised him as his brothers that they would do so. Lancelot lived four days after that request and died on the fifth day. At the moment when his soul departed his body, the archbishop and Blioberis were not with him but were sleeping outside beneath a tree. It happened that Blioberis awoke first and saw the archbishop sleeping beside him. And in his sleep the archbishop saw a vision and rejoiced greatly and said, "Oh, God, blessed are You! For now I see what I wanted to see."

When Blioberis saw that he was laughing and talking in his sleep, he marveled greatly, and he feared that the enemy had entered him; for that reason he awoke him gently. When he opened his eyes and saw Blioberis, he said to him, "Oh, brother, why have you torn me away from the great joy I was experiencing?" Blioberis asked him what that joy was. He said, "I had such great joy and was in the company of so many angels that never have I seen so many people in one place, and they were taking the soul of our brother Lancelot up into heaven. Let's go then and see if he has really died."

"Yes, let's go," said Blioberis. They came to the place where Lancelot was and found that his soul had departed. "Oh, God!" said the archbishop. "Blessed are You. Now I know truly that the angels whom I saw rejoice so were celebrating for the soul of this man. Now I know well that penitence is more important than anything else, and never will I give it up as long as I live. Now we must take his body to Joyous Guard, for we promised him that before he died."

* * *

---

1. Cf. *Morte Arthur* p. 694, line 16–p. 695, line 24.
2. Cf. *Morte Arthur* p. 695, line 25–p. 696, line 20.

Backgrounds

Responses to the Times

FROM THE BERKELEY LETTERS

The letters printed here vignette the mid-fifteenth-century phase of what is sometimes called the "great Berkeley law suit" or the "Berkeley-Lisle dispute," which had begun in 1332 and was to last for nearly two hundred years: it is said to be "the longest family squabble in the whole course of English legal history."[1] The dispute centered on possession of the estates and inheritances of the Lords of Berkeley in Gloucestershire, including, at their heart, Berkeley Castle. In the fifteenth century, the dispute developed between two branches of the descendants of Thomas IV, Lord Berkeley, one branch represented by the Berkeleys of Berkeley Castle, the other by the famously militant Talbot Earls of Shrewsbury. This phase of the lawsuit, with its endemic threats of violence, often borne out by abductions, occupations, and localized battles is, like the Pastons' struggle with Lord Moleyns (see p. 763), regularly cited by historians as evidence of the high-minded and avaricious civil chaos—the "mischef," to use Malory's word (p. 680, line 25) that precipitated and attended the Wars of the Roses.

The letters are preserved in a Berkeley family history compiled from family documents in the early seventeenth century by the Berkeley steward John Smyth. Smyth's representation of the letters employs some modernization of spelling, but there is little reason to believe that their matter, word order, and vocabulary are not authentic.

---

1. J. R. Lander, "Family, 'Friends' and Politics in Fifteenth-Century England," in *Kings and Nobles in the Later Middle Ages*, ed. by Ralph A. Griffiths and James Sherborne (New York: St. Martin's Press, 1986), p. 29.

Isabel, Lady Berkeley, Warns Lord Berkeley of Plans to Seize His Lands†

To my right worshipfull and reverend lord and husband bee this lettre delivered.

Right worshipfull and reverend lord and husband, I commend mee to you with all my whole hart, desyring always to heare of your good welfare, the which God maintayne and increase ever to your worship. And it please you to heare how I fare * * *: Thomas Roger and Jacket have asked surety of peace[1] of mee, for their intent was to bringe mee into the Tower. But I trust in God tomorrow that I shall goe in bayle unto the next term,[2] and soe goe home, and then to come againe. And sir, I trust to God, and you will not treat with them, but keep your own in the most manlyest wise, yee shall have the land for ones and end.° Be well ware of Venables of Alderley, of Thom Mull,[3] and your false counsell; keep well your place. The Earle of Shroesbury lyeth right nye you, and shapeth all the wyles that hee can to distrusse you and yours, for he will not meddle with you openly noe manner of wise, but it bee with great falsdome that hee can bring about to beguile you, or els that hee caused that yee have so fewe peopull about you; then will hee set on you, for hee saith hee will never come to the King againe till hee have done you an ill turne. Sur, your matter speedeth and doth right well (save my daughter costeth° right good; at the reverence of God send money, or els I must lay my horse to pledge and come home on my feet). Keep well all about you till I come home, and trete° not without mee. And then all thinge shall bee well, with the grace of Almighty God, who have you in His keeping. Written at London the Wednesday next after Whitsunday.

for all

costs

negotiate

---

† Reprinted, with new glosses and explanatory notes, from John Smyth, *The Lives of the Berkeleys: Volume 2 of The Berkeley Manuscripts*, 3 vols., ed. Sir John Maclean (Glouces-ter: Bristol and Gloucestershire Archaeological Society, 1893–1895), pp. 62–63. The date of Lady Berkeley's letter to her husband, James IV, Lord Berkeley, is not certain, but is probably c. 1449–1451. Because her husband and sons had to stand guard, as it were, over the Berkeley estates in Gloucestershire, which were under constant threat of being taken over by agents of the Earl of Shrewsbury, Isabel operated as the family's legal rep-resentative in London. Her warnings about the insidious nature of the Shrewsbury threat would prove sadly prophetic for her, as she was later captured at the behest of Margaret, Countess of Shrewsbury, and imprisoned in Gloucester castle, where she died (the Ber-keleys insisted she was murdered). Cf. the responsibilities undertaken and the threats endured by Margaret Paston, according to her letter (p. 766).
1. *Surety of peace:* a payment as security for good behavior entered into with the Crown; nonpayment would result in imprisonment. *Thomas Roger and Jacket:* agents working on behalf of the Earl of Shrewsbury.
2. Go free on bail until the next period in which the court is in session.
3. Lawyers in the employ of the Earl of Shrewsbury.

Lord Berkeley Agrees to Trial by Combat with Viscount Lisle†

The Viscount's Challenge, March 19, 1469

William, called "Lord Berkeley," I marveill ye come not forth with all your carts of gunnes, bowes, with oder ordinance, that ye set forward to come to my manor of Wotton to bete it down upon my head. I let you wit, ye shall not nede to come so nye° for I trust to God to mete you nere home with English men of my own nation and neighbors—whereas ye by suttle craft have blowin° about in divers places of England that I should intend to bring in Welshmen for to destroy and hurt my one nation and cuntry; I lete the° wit, I was never soe disposed, nere° never will bee. And to the proof herof, I require thee of knighthood and of manhood to appoynt a day to meet me half way, there to try° between God and our two hands all our quarrell and title of right, for to eschew the shedding of Christian menns bloud—or els at the same day bring the uttermost of thy power[1]—and I shall mete thee. An answere of this by writinge, as ye will abide by, according to the honor and order of knighthood.

near

shouted, rumored

thee

nor

put to trial

Thomas Talbot, the Viscont Lisle.

[Lord Berkeley's Response, the Same Day]

Thomas Talbot, otherwise called "Viscont Lisle"—not longe continued in that name but a new-found thing brought out of strange contryes[2]—I marveill greatly of thy strange and lewd writinge,

---

† Reprinted, with new glosses and explanatory notes, from John Smyth, *The Lives of the Berkeleys*, Volume 2 of *The Berkeley Manuscripts*, 3 vols., ed. Sir John Maclean (Gloucester: Bristol and Gloucestershire Archaeological Society, 1893–95), pp. 109–111. These letters are written a generation later than the previous letter. Thomas Talbot is the son of the Earl of Shrewsbury. The exchange between Talbot and Berkeley has a strong Malorean flavor, concerned as it is with an appeal to deeds undertaken "of knighthood" against the inaction of respect for legal precedent; also, the sometimes verbatim repetition of Talbot's letter in Berkeley's response, though serving the legalistic and potentially public fuction of certifying a specific response to a specific charge, is reminiscent of what Terence McCarthy calls "a sense of verbal inevitability" in Malory's style (see McCarthy's essay [p. 860]; cf. also the note on John Paston's appeal to Parliament [n. †, p. 764]; for a comparable exchange between knights in Malory, see, for instance, pp. 660–62). The exchange between Berkeley and Talbot further realizes anxieties implicit throughout the *Morte Darthur* about the nature of knightly and masculine identity as dependent on authentication of word, name, title, landed heritage, and nationality.

   One might expect this exchange to have amounted to mere rhetorical bluster—a ventriloquizing of the values of popular chivalric fictions in an attempt to negotiate public opinion—but the battle was indeed joined at Nibley Green on the following day, reputedly the last battle to be fought in England by private armies. Talbot was killed. For further study of this and the similar case of *William, Lord Bonville v. Thomas Courtenay, Earl of Devon*, see Michael Hicks, "Idealism in Late Medieval English Politics," in *Richard III and His Rivals: Magnates and Their Motives in the War of the Roses* (London: Hambledon Press, 1991), pp. 48–51.

1. I.e., bring your armed supporters.
2. Berkeley mocks Talbot's rank of viscount as having no native English tradition; indicating a position between earl and baron, the title of viscount was derived from continental models, and its first use in England had been only as recent as 1440.

762 / Lord Berkeley Agrees to Trial by Combat

made I suppose by thy false untrue counsell that thou hast with thee, Hugh Mull[3] and Holt: as for Hugh Mull, it is not unknown to all the worshipfull men of this Relme, how hee is attaynt of falsenes and rasinge[4] of the Kings records; and as for the false mischevous Holt, what his rule hath be to the destruction of the Kings lege pepull in my lordship of Berkeley, as well to the hurt of their bodyes, as the losse of their goods, against Goddys lawe, consciens, and all reason, is openly known—so that every worshipfull man should refuse to have them in fellowship—and also of his own free will, undesired of mee, before worshipfull and sufficient witnes, was sworn on a Masse book, that hee never should bee against mee in noe matter that I had adoe, and especially in that untrue title that ye clayme, which ye hold my lyvelode with wronge.[5] And where thou requirest mee of knighthood that I should appoynt a day and mete thee in the myd way between my manor of Wotton and my castle of Berkeley, there to try betwyxt God and our two hands all our quarrell and title of right, for to eschewe the schedding of Christen mens bloud, or els the same day to bring the uttermost of my power, and thou would mete me: as for the determining of betwixt our two hands of thy untrue clayme, and my title and right of my land and inheritance, thou wottest right well there is noe such determinacion of land[6] in this relme used. And I ascertaine thee that my livelode, as well my manor of Wotton as my castle of Berkeley, be entayled to mee by fine of record[7] in the Kings courts by the advice of all the judges of this lond in that° dayes being. And if it were soe that this matter might bee determined by thy honds and myne, the King our soveraigne lord and his laws not offended, thou shouldst not so long desire but I would as soone answere thee in every poynt that belongeth to a knight: for thou art—God I take to record—in a false quarrell, and I in a true defence and title. And where thou desirest and requirest mee of knighthood and of manhood to appoynt a day, and that I should bee there with all the power that I could make, and that thou would mete mee half way, I will thou understand I will not bring the tenth part that I can make[8]—and I will appoint a short day to ease thy malitious hart and thy false counsell that is with thee: faile not tomorrow to be at Niblyes Green at eight

those

---

3. Hugh Mull, like his father Thomas (mentioned in Isabel Berkeley's letter, p. 760), was a Gloucestershire lawyer working in the service of the Talbot Earls of Shrewsbury. The family (*alias* Myll or Mill) were also avid Lancastrian supporters during the Wars of the Roses; after the throne fell into Yorkist hands in 1461, Hugh became for a time a notorious Lancastrian rebel and was eventually imprisoned in London for his involvement in a plot to circulate invasion plans for Henry VI's queen, Margaret of Anjou. P. J. C. Field has suggested that Malory was also involved in the plot: see *The Life and Times of Sir Thomas Malory* (Cambridge: Brewer, 1993), pp. 137–143; for contesting evidence, see Anne F. Sutton, "Malory in Newgate: A New Document," *The Library* 7th ser., 1 (2000), 243–262.
4. Convicted of deception and destruction.
5. With which you wrongly withhold my revenue-earning properties from me.
6. No such method of determining possession of land.
7. Bestowed to me as an untransferable possession by a final agreement of record.
8. I.e., the tenth part of an army I can assemble.

or nyne of the clock, and I will not faile, with Gods might and grace, to meete thee at the same place, the which standeth in the borders of the livelode that thou keepest untruly from me, redy to answere thee in all things, that I trust to God it shall be shewed° on thee and thine to thy great shame and disworshipp. And remember, thy self and thy false counsell have refused to abide the rule of the grete lordis of this lond, which by my will should have determyned this matter by thy evidences and mine; and therefore I vouch God to record, and all the company of heaven, that this fact and the scheddinge of Christen mens bloud which shall be atwixt us two and our fellowshipps, if any hap to bee, doth grow of thy quaryll, and not of mee (but in my defence, and in eschewing of reproche), and onely through thy malitious and mischevouse purpose, and of thy false counsell, and of thy own simple° discretion. And keepe thy day; and the truth shall be shewed by the marcy of God.

William, Lord of Berkeley

revealed

feeble

FROM THE PASTON LETTERS

Over the course of the fifteenth century, the Paston family of Norfolk rose from peasant to gentry status, along the way producing the largest body of private letters concerning a single family to survive from that century. The Pastons' rise was achieved through a combination of shrewd land acquisitions, marriages, and legal maneuvers. The rise was also sometimes attended by violence, usually in defense of attempts by noblemen to seize contested property, at a time—notably during the reign of Henry VI— when the administration of law and order was often at the discretion of local lords capable of raising their own private armies. Such virtual lawlessness as endured by the Pastons is often cited as one of the conditions that facilitated the Wars of the Roses (cf. the experiences recorded in the Berkeley letters on p. 760).

The selections printed here concern the family's struggle to regain possession of Gresham Manor, which was purchased by the family in 1427 but which had been forcibly occupied in 1448 by Robert Hungerford, Lord Moleyns, who claimed right of possession based on a vestigial family attachment to the property. The Pastons' legal efforts at reclaiming Gresham failed until 1451, when Moleyns's political misfortunes elsewhere caused him effectively to abandon his claim. For further discussion of the circumstances, see Colin Richmond, *The Paston Family in the Fifteenth Century: The First Phase* (Cambridge: Cambridge University Press, 1990), pp. 47–61. The standard scholarly edition of the Paston letters is by Norman Davis, *Paston Letters of the Fifteenth Century,* 2 vols. (Oxford: Clarendon Press, 1971–76).

Lord Moleyns Seizes Gresham Manor and Other Paston Holdings†

To the Kyng oure Soverayn Lord, and to the right wyse and discrete lordis assemblyd in this present Parlement.

Besechith mekly your homble liege man John Paston that, where he and oder° enfeffed° to his use have be pecybily poscessyd of the Maner of Gresham within the Counté of Norffolk 20 yere and more til the 17 day of Februarii the yere of your nobill regne 26°, that Robert Hungerford, knyght, the Lord Molyns, entred into the seyd Maner. And how be it that the seyd John Paston, after the seid entré, sued to the seid Lord Molyns and his councell, in the most louly° maner that he cowde, dayly fro tyme of the seid entré onto the fest of Mihelmes° than next folwyng, duryng which tyme divers° communicasyons were had betwix the councell° of the seid lord and the councell of your seid besechere;° and for as mych as in the seid communicasions no titill° of right at any tyme was shewed° for the seid lord but that was fully and clerly answeryd,° so that the seid lordes councell remitted your seid besechere to sewe° to the seid lord for his finall and rightfull answere; and after sute mad to the seid lord be your seid besechere—aswell at Salysbery as in oder places, to his gret coust—and non answere had but delays, which causyd your seid besechere the 6 day of Octobre last past to inhabite hym in a mansion within the seid town, kepyng stille there his poscession ontille the 28 day of Januarii last past; the seid lord sent to the seid mansion a riotous peple to the nombre of a thowsand persones * * * arrayd in maner of werre, with curesse, brigaunderes, jakkes, salettes, gleyfes, bowes, arows, pavyse, gonnes, pannys with fier and teynes brennyng therein,[1] long cromes° to draw doun howsis, ladderes, pikoys° with which thei myned down the walles, and long trees with which thei broke vp yates and dores; and so came into the seid mansion—the wiff° of your seid besechere at that tyme beyng therin, and 12 persones with here—the which persones thei dreve oute of the seid mansion and myned down the walle of the chambre wherein the wiff of your seid besechere was, and bare here oute at the yates,° and cutte asondre° the postes of the howses and lete them falle, and broke up all the chambres and coferes° within the seid mansion, and rifelyd and in maner of robery bare awey all the stuffe, aray,° and

others / enfeoffed

1448

lowly, humble
Michaelmas
various / counsel
Paston
title
demonstrated / refuted

sue

hooks / pickaxes

wife

gates
apart
coffers
decoration

---

† Text of London, British Library, Additional Charter 17,240, printed with permission of the British Library. Roman numerals have been converted to arabic numerals, and "li," when used to indicate currency in pounds, is represented by "£."

The letter, written by John Paston I, lawyer and head of the family, takes the form of a petition to the King and Parliament and was written sometime before July 16, 1449 (the last day of the Parliament), reporting events of the previous year. Even though it is a legal document characteristically replete with repetitive phrasing, the petition was probably written with the intention of being read aloud to the gathered Members of Parliament, and so presents a strong paratactic tendency: both are features of Malory's style (cf. the study by Terence McCarthy on p. 856 herein).

1. Equipped as if for war, with breast plates, body armor, military tunics, helmets, lances, bows, arrows, shields, guns, and fire-pans with tinder burning therein.

mony that your seyd besechere and his servauntes had there, onto
the valew of £200, and part thereof sold and part thereof yaffe,° —— *gave away*
and the remenaunt thei departed among them, to the grete and
outrageous hurt of your seid besechere—sayng opynly that if thei
myght have found there your seid besechere, and on° John Damme —— *one*
which is of councelle with hym, and divers oder of the servauntes
of your seid besechere, thei shuld haue died. And yet divers of the
seid mysdoeres and ryotous peple onknowyn, contrary to your
lawes, dayly kepe the seid maner with force and lyne° in wayte of —— *lie*
divers of the frendis, tenauntes, and servauntes of your seid
besecher, and grevously vexe and trobill° hem in divers wise, and —— *trouble*
seke hem in her howsis, ransakyng and serchyng her shevys and
strawe in her bernes and other places with bore speris, swerdes,
and gesernys,² as it semyth to sle hem if thei myght have found
hem, and summe have bete° and left for ded, so that thei, for —— *beaten*
doute° of here lyves, dare not go home to here houses ner° occupy —— *fear / nor*
here husbondry,° to the gret hurte, fere, and drede as wele of your —— *farm holdings*
seid besechere as of his seid frendis, tenauntes, and servauntes.
And also thei compelle pore tenauntes of the seid Maner, now
within ther daungere,° ageyn ther wille to take feyned pleyntes in —— *coercive power*
the courtes of the hundred³ there ageyn the seid frendis, tenaun-
tes, and servauntes of your seid besechere, whiche dare not apere
to answere for fere of bodily harme, ne can gete no copiis° of the —— *copies*
seid pleyntes to remedi them be the lawe, because he that kepyth
the seid courtis is of covyn° with the seid misdoeres and was on of —— *conspiracy*
the seid ryseres which, be coloure of the seid pleyntes grevously
amercy⁴ the seid frendes, tenauntes, and servauntes of your seid
besechere, to ther outrageous and importabille° hurt. —— *unbearable*

Please it your Hynesse, consideryng that if this gret insurrec-
cyon, ryottis, and wrongis, and dayly continuans therof, so heynosly° —— *heinously*
don° ageyn your crowne, dignité, and peas° shuld not, be your hye —— *act / peace*
myght, be duly punysshid, it shall gefe° grett boldnesse to them —— *give*
and alle oder mysdoeres to make congregacyouns and conventi-
cles° riottously, onabille to be seysed,⁵ to the subversyon and finall —— *gatherings*
distruccyon of your liege peple and lawes; and also how that your
seid besecher is not abille to sue the commune lawe in redressyng
of this heynos wrong for the gret myght and alyaunce° of the seid —— *alliance*
lord; and also that your seid besechere canne have non accyon° be —— *action*
your lawe ageyn the seid riotous peple for the godis° and catellis° —— *goods / chattels*
be hem so riottously and wrongfully take and bore awey, because
the seid peple be onknowe,° as welle here names as here persones, —— *unknown*
onto hym; to purvey° be the avyse° of the lordis spirituall and —— *provide / advice*
temporall assembled in this present Parlement that your seid
besechere may be restoryd to the seid godis and catellis thus
riotiously take awey, and that the seid Lord Molyns have suche

2. Searching their bundles of wheat and straw in their barns and other places with boar
spears, swords, and battle axes.
3. Against their will to take out fabricated complaints in the courts of the county subjuris-
diction.
4. One of the said rioters that, by pretext of the said complaints, grievously fine arbitrarily.
5. Unable to be ceased.

comaundment that your seid besechere be not thus, with force in maner of werre,° hold° oute of his seid Maner contrary to alle your statutes mad ageyn suych forcibille entrees and holdynges; and that the seid Lord Molyns and his servauntes be sette in suche a rewle° that your seid besechere, his frendis, tenauntes, and servauntes may be sure and saffe from hurt of here persones and pesibily ocupy here londes and tenementes vnder your lawes withoute oppressyoun or onrightfull vexasion of any of hem, and that the seid riseres and causeres therof may be punysshed that other may eschewe to make any suche rysyng in this your lond of peas in tyme comyng. And he shalle pray to God for yowe.

war / held

ruling

Moleyns's Men Threaten to Abduct Margaret Paston; Other Threats to Paston Holdings†

Ryt wurchypful hosbond,° I recommawnd me to you, desyryng hertyly to heryn of yowr welefare, beseching you that ye be not displesyd thow I be com fro that place that ye left me in; for be my trowth ther were browth° me seche tydyngys be dyverys personys,[1] qhiche° ben yowre wele-willerys and myn, that I durst no lengere abyd there, of qhyche personys I xall° late you have wetyng qhan° ye com hom. It was done me to wete° that dyverys of the Lord Moleynys men saydyn if thei myt gete me they xuld° stele° me and kepe me wythinne the kastell, and than they seyd thei wold that ye xuld feche me owth.° An thei seydyn it xuld ben "but a lytyll hert-brennyng"° to you. And after that I herd these tydyngys, I kowd° no rest have in myn hert tyl I was here,° nere° I durst nowt owt of the place that I was in tyll that I was redy to ryden; nere ther was non in the place wist° that I xul° com thens, save the godewyf,° notgh° an owre before that I kam thens. And I told here that I xuld com hedder° to don maken seche gere[2] as I wold have made for me and for the childer,° and seyd I sopposyd that I xuld be here a fowrtennythe° or 3 wekys. I pray you that the caws of my komyng away may ben kownsell° tyl I speke wyth you, for thei that lete me have warnyng therof wold not for no good that it were diskuryd.°

John Paston I

brought

which

shall

when / know

should / steal

out

heartburn

could / Norwich / nor

who knew / should

housemistress / not

hither

children

two weeks

secret

revealed

† Text of London, British Library, Additional MS 34,888, fol. 24, printed with permission of the British Library. Roman numerals have been converted to arabic numerals.
The letter is dated February 28, 1449. Since her husband spent most of his time as a lawyer in London, Margaret Paston was the one who assumed the leadership of the family back in Norfolk, and it was she who often had to deal firsthand with Moleyns's various assaults and attempts at demoralization. This and other letters of hers show her to be a shrewd defender of her own and her family's interests, with an acumen for discerning fine legal distinctions—as well as insincere diplays of friendship. Cf. Isabel Berkeley's letter to her husband, (p. 760). For further study of the lives of fifteenth-century gentlewomen, see ffiona [sic] Swabey, *Medieval Gentlewoman: Life in a Gentry Household in the Later Middle Ages* (Stroud: Sutton, 1999), with a helpful bibliography of secondary sources for further study.
1. Such news from various persons.
2. To have such necessary things gathered up.

I spac wyth yowr modyr as I kam hidderwardys, and sche profyrd me, if ye wold, that I xuld abydyn in this town. Sche wold wyth rytgh° *[right]* a good will that we xul abyde in here place, and delyveryn me seche° *[such]* gere° as sche myt forbere, to kepen wyth hwsold° tyl ye mytgh° ben *[provision / household / might]* purvayd of a place and stuff of yowr owyn to kepe wyth howsold. I pray you send me word be° the brynger of this how ye wil that I *[by]* be demenyd.° I wol ben rytgh sory to dwel so nere Gressam as I *[handling things]* dede tyl the mater were fully determynyd betwix the Lord Moleynis and you.

Barow° told me that ther ware no better evydens in Inglond than *[Moleyns' servant]* the Lord Moleynys hathe of the Maner of Gressam. I told hym I sopposyd that thei were seche evydens as Willyam Hasard seyd that yowr were: he seyd the sellys of hem were not yett kold.[3] I seyd I sopposyd his lordys evydens were seche. I seyd I wost° wele, *[knew]* as for yowr evydens, ther mytgh no man have non better than ye have, and I seyd the selys° of hem were to° hundred yere elder than *[seals / two]* he is. The seyd Barow sayd to me if he com to London qhil° ye *[while]* were there he wold drynk wyth you, for any angyr that was betwyx yow. He seyd he dede° but as a servawnt, and as he was com- *[did, acted]* mawndyd to don.° * * * I pray you hertyly, at the reverens of God, *[do]* be ware of the Lord Moleynys and his men, thow thei speke never so fayr to you, trost hem not, ne ete not nere drynk wyth hem, for thei ben so fals it is not for to trost in hem—and also I pray you beware qhat ye eten° ar° drynk wyth any othere felaschep, for the *[eat / or]* pepyll is ful ontrosty.° *[untrustworthy]*

I pray you hertylye that ye wil vowchesave° to send me word how *[promise]* ye don and how ye speden in yowr materis be the brynger of this.[4] I merveyl meche that ye send me no more tydyngys than ye have sent.

Rogere Foke of Sparham sent to me and seythe that he dare nott gon owt of his hows for bekawse of the sewte° that Heydon and *[lawsuit]* Wymdam[5] have agens hem, for he is thrett° that if he may be gette° *[threatened / taken]* he xal be ladde to preson. Heydon sent Spendlove and other to wayte° qhere he were, and to arest hym to the kastell; and the *[watch]* forseyd Roger is so aferd that his drede makyth hym so seke that but if he have sokowr° sone it is lyke to ben his dethe. Qherefor° *[help / Wherefore]* I pray you and he bothyn° that ye wil purvay a remedy for hym, *[both]* that he may gon at large, for it hurtit bothen yowr katel and hym: yowr closys° and yowr pastowr lythe all opyn bekawse he may not *[enclosures]* gon abrodde° to don hem amendyn,° and yowr schep ar not lokyd *[abroad / repair]* at as they xuld ben[6] for ther is no schepeherd but Hodgis sonys, for other schepherd dare non abyd ther ner com upon the comown° *[common land]* bekause that Wichyngham men thretyn hem to bete if thei comen

---

3. I.e., I believed that those evidences were of as high a quality as William Hasard (another servant of Moleyns's) said yours were: he said the wax seals attesting to their authenticity were not yet cold.
4. I.e., send me word how you are doing and how you get on in your affairs by way of a letter returned by the messenger who brings you this letter.
5. I.e., supporters of Moleyns.
6. Your enclosures and your pasture all lie open because he may not go about to repair them; and your sheep are not looked after as they should be.

on here komon. And but if yowr bestys° mown comown° ther it xall
ben gretto hurt to hem but if the° have more pasture than thei have
besyd thatt. * * * It is told me, as for Gressam, the Lord Moleynys
xuld not cleym it now nother be tayl nere be evydens, but be infef-
ment of on of his anseteris qhiche dyid sesynnyd, and in the same
wise it is seyd that Sweynysthorp xul be cleymyd.[7]

beasts / graze
they

* * *

The Holy Trynyté have you in His keping. Wretyn° at Norwyche
on the Fryday nexst after Puver° Weddenysday.

Written
Ash

Contemporary Accounts of
The Wars of The Roses[1]

From The Register of Abbot John Whetamstede†

[*The Duke of York Claims the Throne and Is Rejected*
(*c. October 10, 1460*)]

* * *

Arriving at [the Parliament chamber of Westminster Palace] at
last, [Richard, Duke of York] proceeded with forthright step until
he came to the throne of the King, and placing his hand over its
cushion, or bolster, in an act resembling that of a man taking possession of the law itself, he held his hand over it for a brief space
of time. Finally, withdrawing it from there, he turned his face to
the people, standing still under the cloth of the realm, and he
observed the gazing assembly.

While he stood there thus, his face turned to the people, awaiting their applause of him, Master Thomas Bourchier, Archbishop
of Canterbury, came upon him, and, having given a suitable greeting, asked if he wished to come and see the lord King. Somewhat
angered in his mind by this petition, he replied shortly, in this way:
"I know of no such person within this realm for whom it was not
fitting to sooner come to me and see my person, than that I should
go and visit him."

---

7. The Lord Moleyns would not claim it now either in tail (by freehold inheritance) nor by
   documentary evidence, but by the enfeoffment (holding of land from a feudal overlord)
   of one of his ancestors who died seisined (in lawful possession); and it is said that (our
   estate of) Swainsthorp will be claimed in the same fashion.
1. For a fuller sense of the context of the events described in the following selections, see
   the chronology on p. xix ff., and the Bibliography.
† Trans. Shelli Carnes Shepherd from *Registrum Abbatiae Johannis Whethamstede*, ed. H. T.
   Riley (London: Longman et al., 1872), pp. 377–78. John Whetamstede was Abbot of the
   Monastery of St. Albans and, as a member of the parliamentary House of Lords, was
   probably an eyewitness to the ill-fated Duke of York's extravagant failure to convince
   Parliament to grant him the throne—an event not dissimilar in import or scope to the
   failure of one of Malory's knights to pull a sword from a stone, achieve a quest, or indeed
   usurp a King. For a fuller sense of the context of the event, see the chronology on p. xxi.

The Archbishop, hearing this response, retreated in a hurry, and related the response to the King which he had heard from the mouth of the Duke. When the Archbishop retreated, [the Duke] too retreated—for the King lay in the lodgings of the Queen—to the most inner quarters of the entire Palace; and, breaking the bolts and opening the doors, in the manner of a king rather than of a duke, he resided for not a little time there. Naturally, when the haughty words of the lord Duke were put forth among the people, and in what manner, by his own unacceptable pretension to the throne, he thus entered—and not at all by some other perceptible deliberation—the people of every position and rank, age and sex, class and circumstance, began immediately to operate querulously against him, and to say it was through improper means.

* * *

From Gregory's Chronicle†

[*On the Battles of Mortimer's Cross and Second St. Albans, February 2–17, 1461*]

* * *

Edwarde Erle of Marche, the Duke of Yorke ys° sone and heyre, hadde a grete jornaye° at Mortymer ys Crosse in Walys the secunde day of Februar [1461], and there he put to flyght the Erle of Penbroke, the Erle of Wylteschyre. And there he toke and slowe of knyghtys and squyers * * * to the number of 3000.

Ande in that jornay was Owyn Tetyr° i-take° and brought unto Herfordeeste,° an he was beheddyde at the market place, and hys hedde sette apone the hygheyste gryce° of the market crosse; and a madde woman kembyd° hyss here and wysche away the blode of hys face, and she gate candellys and sette aboute hym brennynge° moo° then a 100. Thys Owyne Tytyr was fadyr unto the Erle of Penbroke, and hadde weddyd Quene Kateryn, Kyng Harry° the VI ys modyr, wenyng° and trustyng alleway that he shulde not be hedyd tylle he sawe the axe and the blocke; and whenn that he was in hys dobelet° he trustyd on pardon and grace—tylle the coler° of hys redde vellvet dobbelet was ryppyd of. Then he sayde, "That

his (or 's)
day's battle

Tudor / seized
Haverfordwest
shaft
combed
burning
more
Henry
believing

jacket / collar

---

† Reprinted, with new glosses and explanatory notes, from *Gregory's Chronicle*, in *The Historical Collections of a Citizen of London*, ed. James Gairdner, Camden Society, n.s. 17 (London: Royal Historical Society, 1876), pp. 211–215. Roman numerals have been converted to arabic numerals.

The *Chronicle* is named after William Gregory, a well-to-do member of the Skinner's Company, who had been Lord Mayor of London, 1451–52. Gregory wrote the entries of his *Chronicle* up to the period of his mayoralty, but another writer appears to have produced the entries for subsequent years. That writer was evidently a supporter of the Yorkist cause and may have been present with the foot soldiers at the events he describes. Stylistically, the selection is notable for its simple paratactic coordination of sentences—a feature of what P. J. C. Field has identified as a "Chronicle style," a style that Malory appears to emulate: see Field's *Romance and Chronicle: A Study of Malory's Prose Style* (London: Barrie and Jenkins, 1971), pp. 31–46. Of further note, and somewhat evocative of Malory, is the author's interest in public symbolism counterpoised with dramatic instances of personal conduct that are measured against an implied standard of honor and shame.

hede° shalle ly° on the stocke that was wonte to ly on Quene Kater- *head / lie*
yns lappe," and put hys herte and mynde holy unto God, and fulle
mekely toke hys dethe.

Alle soo the same day that the Erle of Marche shulde take hys
jornaye towarde Mortymer ys Crosse fro Herforde-este, he
mousterd° hys many° withowte the towne wallys in a mersche° *mustered/army/marsh*
that vs callyd Wygmersche. And ovyr hym men say° 3 sonnys *saw*
schynyng.[1]

Ande the 17 day nexte folowynge, Kyng Harry[2] roode to Synt
Albonys, and the Duke of Northefolke with hym, the Erle of Warwycke, the Erle of Arundelle, the Lorde Bouser,° the Lorde Bon- *Bourchier*
vyle, with many grete lordys, knyghtys, and squyers, and commyns
of an 100,000 men. And there they hadde a grete batayle° whythe *army*
the Quene, for she come ever on fro the jornaye of Wackefylde
tylle sche come to Synt Albonys, with alle the lordys aforesayde.
* * * I wene there were not 5000 men that fought in the Quenys *took to*
party, for the moste parte of Northeryn men fledde away, and sum
were take and spoylyd owte of hyr harnysse[3] by the way as they
fledde. And sum of them robbyd evyr as they yede°—a petyffulle° *went / pitiful*
thynge hit° ys to hyre hit. But the day before that batayle there was *it*
a jornay at Dunstapyl; but the Kyngys mayny lackyd good gydyng,° *leadership*
for sum were but newe men of warre, for the chevyste° captayne *highest*
was a boucher° of the same towne; and there were the Kyngys *butcher*
mayny ovyrthroughe° only by the Northeryn men. And sone aftyr *defeated*
the bocher, for schame of hys sympylle° gydynge and loste° of the *poor / loss*
men, the nombyr of 800, for very sorowe as hyt ys sayde, hynge° *hanged*
hymselfe; and sum men sayde that hyt was for loste of hys goode;° *property*
but dede he ys—God knowythe the trought.° *truth*

And in the myddys° of the batayle Kynge Harry wente unto hys *midst*
Quene and forsoke alle hys lordys, ande truste better to hyr party
thenne unto hys owne lordys. And thenn thoroughe grete labur the
Duke of Northefolke and the Erle of Warwycke aschapyd° awaye; *escaped*
the Byschoppe of Exceter, that tyme Chaunceler of Ingelond, and
brother unto the Erle of Warwycke, the Lorde Bouser, whythe
many othyr knyghtys, squyers, and comyns fledde, and many men
slayne in bothe partys. And the Lorde Bonevyle was beheddyd, the
comyn sayynge that hys longage causyd hym to dye.[4] The Prynce
was jugge ys owne sylfe.° Ande ther was slayne that manly knyght *self*
Syr Thomas Keryel. The number of ded men was 3500 an moo° *more*
that were slayne. The lordys in Kyng Harrys party pycchyd a fylde[5]
and fortefyd hyt fulle stronge—and lyke unwyse men brake hyr

---

1. The vision of the three suns—probably a natural phenomenon now known as a parhelion, caused by airborne ice crystals—was interpreted as a sign of Trinitarian favor for the Yorkist cause.
2. I.e., King Henry VI in the custody of the Yorkists; throughout this section the author somewhat confusingly identifies the Yorkist forces with the presence among them of the captured King. The Lancastrians are identified with the Queen, Margaret of Anjou.
3. Seized and robbed of their military equipment.
4. The commonfolk saying that it was the things he said which brought about his death.
5. Set up emplacements for the field of battle.

raye and fyld[6] and toke anothyr; and or that they were alle sette and buskyd° to batayle, the Quenys parte was at hond whythe hem in towne of Synt Albonys, and then alle thyng was to seke° and owte of ordyr, for hyr pryckyers° come not home to bryng no tydyng° howe ny° that the Quene was, save one come and sayd that she was 9 myle of. And ar the goners * * * couthe levylle hyr gonnys they were besely fyghtyng, and many a gynne of wer was ordaynyd that stode in lytylle avayle or nought.[7] * * * And as the substaunce of men of worschyppe that wylle not glose nor cory favyl for no parcyallyté, they cowthe not undyrstond that alle thys ordenaunce dyd any goode or harme but yf hit were among us in owre parte[8] * * *. There fore hyt ys moche lefte, and men take hem to mallys° of ledde, bowys, swyrdys, gleyvys,° and axys. As for speremen, they ben° good to ryde before the footemen and ete and drynke uppe hyr vetayle,° and many moo suche prety thyngys they doo; holde me excusyd—thoughe I say the beste—for in the fotemen ys alle the tryste.°

Ande at the nyght aftyr the batayle the Kynge blessyd hys sone the Prynce, and Doctor Morton[9] brought forthe a boke that was fulle of orysons,° and there the boke was oppenyd, and blessyd that yong chylde *cum pinguedine terre et cum rore celi,*[1] and made hym knyght. And the yong knyght weryd a payre of bregantyerys[2] i-coveryd with purpylle velvyt i-bete with goldesmythe ys worke. And the Prynce made many knyghtys. The fryste that he made was Androwe Trolloppe, for he was hurte and myght not goo for a calletrappe in hys fote;[3] and he sayde, "My lorde, I have not deservyd hit for I slowe but 15 men, for I stode stylle in oo° place and they come unto me, but they bode° stylle with me."* * *

Ande the Kynge and the Quene toke hyr jornay unto Yorke-wardys, for they demyde that the Northeryn men wolde have ben to creuelle in robbyng yf they hadde come to London. But by the avyse of Docter Morton they sende certayne knyghtys and men unto London and to Westemyster, but they myght not be sufferde° to entery into the towne. Ande sum of hyr mayny were slayne for hyr cursyd longege. Ande the Mayre ordaynyd bothe brede and vytayle to be sende unto the Quene, and a certayne sum of money with alle. But whenn men of London and comyns wyste that the cartysse° shulde goo to the Quene, they toke the cartys and depar-tyde the brede and vytayle amonge the comyns. And on° John

*readied
lost
scouts
news / near

maces
lances
are
victuals
trust, reliability

prayers

one
remained

permitted

carts
one*

6. Failed to keep their order and position on the field.
7. And before the gunners . . . could aim their weapons they were busily engaged in hand-to-hand fighting, and many a gadget of war was ordered into position that was of little or no use.
8. And, like most men of honor who will not critique others' actions or seek to ingratiate themselves with others, those in charge would not accept that all these devices were only effective against us ourselves.
9. Cardinal John Morton was chancellor to the seven-year-old Prince Edward.
1. "With the fatness of the earth, and the dew of heaven" (from Isaac's prayer on behalf of his son Esau, Genesis 27:28–29).
2. A set of body armor.
3. Wounded in the foot by a caltrop (a spiked ball designed to injure feet).

Byschoppe was a grete doer of thys mater, for he was chyffe coke°   *cook*
to the knyght Syr John Wenlocke.[4] But as for the mony, I wot not
howe hit was departyd; I trowe the pursse stale the money.[5]

Then come tydyngys of the comynge of the Erle of Marche unto
London; thenn alle the cytté were fayne,° and thonkyd God, and   *glad*
sayde that

> He° that had Londyn forsake   *Henry*
> Wolde no more to hem take,

and sayde, "Lette us walke in a newe wyne-yerde,° and lette us   *vineyard*
make us a gay gardon° in the monythe of March with thys fayre   *garden*
whyte ros and herbe, the Erle of Marche."[6]

GEORGE NEVILLE

Letter to Francesco Coppini
on the Battle of Towton†

*   *   *

I think it right to write and inform your lordship in a few words
about these events, as we have learned them by messengers and
letters, as well as by popular report.

*   *   *

[T]hey say that some 3,000 fell on one side and the other [at the
second battle of St. Albans]; but we,[1] being fortunate, amid so
many misfortunes, escaped [as] that puppet of a king[2] * * * turned
his face towards the North, pillaging in the country; and at length

---

4. John, Lord Wenlock was a supporter of the Yorkist cause, having changed sides after the
   first battle of St. Albans in 1455; he had been elected a Knight of the Garter on February
   8, 1461.
5. I.e., no one would admit to taking the money.
6. With this fair white rose and (medicinal) plant. An allusion to the emblem of the House
   of York, the white rose.
† Reprinted, with new explanatory notes, from *Calendar of State Papers and Manuscripts in
   the Archives and Collections of Milan:* Volume I, 1385–1618, ed. A. B. Hinds (London:
   His Majesty's Stationery Office, 1912) pp. 60–67. Roman numerals have been changed
   to arabic numerals. George Neville was at the time Bishop of Exeter and Chancellor of
   England, and a supporter of the Yorkist cause; the recipient of his letter, Francesco Coppini, was Bishop of Terni in Italy and former Apostolic Legate (i.e., an emissary of the
   Papacy) to England. The letter is dated April 7, 1461. It was the battle of Towton in
   Yorkshire that secured the throne for the recently proclaimed Edward IV; but it did so at
   a great cost, like the Battle of Antietam in the American Civil War producing the largest
   number of single-day casualties in the history of the nation. Neville's outcry against the
   "miserable and luckless" English is of a piece with Malory's complaint to "all Englysshemen" (p. 680, line 25.) about their self-destructive resistance to political stability. Certain
   distinctive features of the battle have led P. J. C. Field to propose that Malory had it in
   mind when describing the disastrous final battle of Arthur's reign: see "Malory and the
   Battle of Towton" in *The Social and Literary Contexts of Malory's "Morte Darthur,"* ed. D.
   Thomas Hanks Jr., pp. 68–74.
1. I.e., the Yorkist forces.
2. I.e., Henry VI.

the wife,[3] with her husband, arrived at York, glorying in their very bloody victory.

In the meantime our King Edward, then commonly known as the Earl of March, betook himself with an army of 30,000 men to London. With him went my brother the Earl of Warwick, as he had departed from the first battle and gone to join him. On the 25th [of February] they entered the city, and were joyfully received by all the people, and on the 4th of March [Edward] was nominated and practically by force created King by the nobles and people universally, near Westminster. They postponed the celebration of his coronation only for the most urgent reasons. Then on the 12th of March he set out towards the North with a large and magnificent army, having previously, on the 7th, sent on my brother to the West to collect troops.

The King, the valiant Duke of Norfolk, my brother aforesaid, and my uncle, Lord Fauconberg, travelling by different routes, finally united with all their companies and armies near the country round York. The armies having been re-formed and marchalled separately, they set forth against the enemy, and at length on Palm Sunday, near a town called Ferrybridge, about sixteen miles from the city, our enemies were routed and broken in pieces. Our adversaries had broken the bridge which was our way across, and were strongly posted on the other side, so that our men could only cross by a narrow way which they had made themselves after the bridge was broken. But our men forced a way by the sword, and many were slain on both sides.[4] Finally the enemy took to flight, and very many of them were slain as they fled.

That day there was a great conflict, which began with the rising of the sun, and lasted until the tenth hour of the night, so great was the pertinacity and boldness of the men, who never heeded the possibility of a miserable death. Of the enemy who fled, great numbers were drowned in the river near the town of Tadcaster, eight miles from York, because they themselves had broken the bridge to cut our passage that way, so that none could pass, and a great part of the rest who got away, who gathered in the said town and city, were slain; and so many dead bodies were seen as to cover an area six miles long by three broad and about four furlongs. In this battle eleven lords of the enemy fell, including the Earl of Devon, the Earl of Northumberland, Lord Clifford, and Nevill with some knights; and from what we hear from persons worthy of confidence, some 28,000 persons perished on one side and the other. O miserable and luckless race and powerful people, would you have no spark of pity for our own blood, of which we have lost so much of the fine quality by the civil war, even if you had no compassion for the French!

---

3. I.e., the Queen, Margaret of Anjou.
4. Here Neville alludes to the full-blown battle that developed near Towton after the encounter at Ferrybridge.

If it had been fought under some capable and experienced captain against the Turks, the enemies of the Christian name, it would have been a great stroke and blow. But to tell the truth, owing to these civil discords, our riches are beginning to give out, and we are shedding our own blood copiously among ourselves, while we were unwilling to give help in men and money to the army of his Holiness [the Pope] against the infidel Turks, despite all the instances of his Holiness and your Reverence.[5] But the limitations of writing do not permit me to state my mind on all these things.

* * *

From Edward IV's Act of Attainder,
December 16, 1461†

For as moche as Henry, late Kyng Henry the Sixt, ayenst the honoure and trouth that owe° to be established in every Christien prynce, dissimilyng° with the right noble and famous Prynce Richard, Duc of York, * * * procured, stered,° and excited, ayenst his promisse * * * the murdre of the same Duc: And where the seid Henry, usurpour, dissimilyng the destruction of other Lordes and persones of the same Reame,° * * * with Margarete, late called Quene of Englond, and hir son Edward, late called Prynce of Wales, entendyng° to the extreme destruction of the seid Reame, namely of the south parties therof, * * * to the spoile° by theym of Godds Chirch, of chalesses, crosses of sylver, boxes for the Sacrament, and other onourments longyng therunto, of defoulyng° and ravishing religious wymmen, wedowes and maydens, of unmanly and abhomynable entretyng of wymmen beyng in the naturall labour and bataille of travailyng of child—by the moyne° therof piteously disperaged, Heven sorowyng the lost therby of the soules that shuld have been of the felauship of Cristendom and of the blisse of Heven, not abhorryng of unmanly, unnaturall, and

ought
dissembling
stirred

Realm

intending
theft

defiling

means

5. On the Turkish threat, possibly alluded to by Malory, see n. 1, p. 689. In previous years, before having to flee England because of its political disruptions, Coppini had lobbied the throne on behalf of the Pope, at times threatening excommunication, to induce English participation in a crusade against the Turks.
† Reprinted, with new glosses and explanatory notes, from *Rotuli Parliamentorum*, 6 vols. (London, 1767), V, pp. 477–483. This was one of the first parliamentary acts enjoined after Edward IV's acquisition of the throne; attainder had first been employed through parliamentary act two years earlier, under the reign of Henry VI, and was used to punish, without recourse to judicial trial, those accused of treason in the dynastic wars: all property of those attainted, including those who had died in battle or were executed, was seized, and their rights to inherit and to bestow inheritance were taken away. The result was a condition known as "corruption of blood," tantamount to an erasure of public identity; this act of attainder takes the erasure even further by naming other quintessentially unchivalric crimes suborned by its targets (cf. the points of conduct upheld by the oath of the Order of the Bath, p. 781).
    Attainder's availing of property was a good source of revenue for the Crown and provided an immediate supply of landed rewards and other incentives for loyal followers—an important consideration in this period for usurper kings and their heirs, whose own claim to the throne (their own "public identity") was chronically contestable. The text of the act is many times longer than the selection printed here, but the selection retains one of several long lists of the names of those attainted. More than gloating catalogs of human "trophies," such lists operated as shorthand indexes of royal power; this might account in part for the gravity implicit in Malory's long lists of Arthurian knights, whose names are perhaps to be understood as ciphers of material dominion as well as chivalric reputation.

beestly cruelté to drawe wymmen beyng in childebedde from their bedds naked, and to spoile hem of all her° goods, a piteous deso- *their* lacion: The same Henry, actour, factour,° and provoker of the seid *agent* commocion, and assentyng of covyne° with the seid Margarete, *conspiracy* Henry Duc of Somerset, and Henry late Erle of Northumberlond, * * * in a feld° biside the Toune of Seint Albones, the 17 day of *field of battle* Feverer last past, not joynyng his persone and blode to the defence, tuition, and salvacion of the same Lordes persones commen° to *come* assist hym by his auctorité and commaundement, lyke a victorious and a noble captayne, but, lyke a disseyvable° coward, ayenst *deceptive* princely and knyghtly dueteé,° sodenly, privately, and shamefully *duty* refused theym, sufferyng and procuryng to, disseivably, th'effucion of their blode,[1] and horrible murdre and deth, not havyng therof sorowe, pitee or compassion, adheryng to the seid Margaret, and to the seid Duc of Somerset, and other Lordes and persones that comitted the seid orrible and cruell murdre of the seid Duc of York:

* * *

It be declared and adjuged, by th'assent and advis of the Lordes Spirituels and Temporels, and Commyns,[2] beyng in this present Parlement, and by auctorité of the same, that the seid Henry, late called Kyng Henry the Sixt, for the consideracions of the grete, haynouse, and detestable malice and offenses afore° specifyed, by *before* hym committed ayenst his feith and liegeaunce to oure seid Liege Lord, Kyng Edward the Fourth, his true, rightwisse,° and naturall *rightful* Liege Lord, offended and hurte unjustely and unlawfully the Roiall Magesté of oure seid Soverayne Lord, stand and be, by the seid advise and assent, convicted and atteinted of high treson: And that it be ordeyned and stablished,° by the seid advis, assent and auc- *established* torité, that the same Henry forfet° unto the same, oure Liege Lord *forfeit* Kyng Edward the Fourth, and to the seid Coroune° of Englond, all *Crown* castels, maners, lordships, tounes, touneships, honours, landes, tenantes, rentes, services, fee-fermes, knyghtes fees, advousons, hereditaments[3] and possessions, with their appurtenauncez, which he, or any other to his use, had the third day of Marche last past,[4] * * * And that the same Margarete, and also the seid Edward her son, be unabled, and taken, holden,° demed, and reputed unables *held* and unworthy to have, occupie, hold, enherit or joy,° any state, *enjoy use of* name of dignité, preemynence, or possessions within the Reame of Englond; * * * And also that the seid Henry Duc of Somerset, Thomas Courteney late Erle of Devonshire, Henry late Erle of Northumberlond, Thomas Lord Roos, John late Lord Clyfford, and John late Lord Nevill, be unabled for ever from hensforth to have,

1. Deceptively allowing and providing for the spilling of their blood.
2. I.e., the secular and ecclesiastical members of the parliamentary House of Lords, and the members of the House of Commons.
3. Estates held in absolute possession, lands of a value apportioned to knights for military service, rights to present clerics to benefices or livings in specific parishes, any property that can be inherited.
4. I.e., the day before Edward's proclamation as King at Westminster Abbey.

hold, enherit, or joy any name of dignité, estate or preemynence within the same Reame, in Irlond or Wales, or in Caleys,° or in the marches° therof, and that their heires be unable to cleyme° or have by theym any such name, estate, or preemynence: And that they—and also John Whelpdale clerk, Philip Lowys clerk, Bawdewyn Fulforth knyght, Alexander Hody knyght, Nicholas Latymer knyght, James Loterel knyght, Edmund Mountford knyght, Thomas Fyndern knyght, Henry Lowes knyght, John Heron of the Forde knyght, Richard Tustall knyght, Henry Belyngeham knyght, Robert Whityngham knyght, William Grymmesby late squier, Thomas Tunstall squier, Symonde Hammes knyght, Thomas Dalton gentilman, James Dalton gentilman, George Dalton, John Clapham, Andrewe Trollop, Antony Notehill knyght, John Botiller gentilman, Gawen Lamplewe gentilman, Edmund Fyssh, Thomas Fryzell, John Smothyng yoman, John Caterall, Thomas Barton late of Helmesley, William Fyppes, Henry Clyff, Robert Tomlynson, and Thomas Barton of York mason—for their traitors,° cruell, and horrible murdre of the seid right noble Prynce, Duc of York, afore declared, stand and be convycted and attainted of high treason, and forfett to the Kyng and his heires, all the castels, maners, lordships, landes, hereditaments, and possessions, with their appurtenauncez, which they or any of theym had, of estate° or enheritaunce, * * * or into which they, or any of theym aforeseid attaynted, or any other persone or persones, feoffees to the use or behofe° of any of the seid persones so attaynted, had * * * within Englond, Irlond or Wales, or the Marches therof.

Calais
borders / claim

traitorous

i.e., bestowal

advantage

* * *

And moreover it is ordeyned and established, by the seid advis, assent and auctorié, that every of the wyfes of every of the seid persone or persones nowe lyvyng, by this Acte attaynted, and every such woman as was the wyf of eny of the seid persones nowe dede, by this Acte atteynted—which wyfes or other wymmen were born under the obeysaunce° of the Coroune of Englond, in any place oute of the Reame of Fraunce, and of the Duchie of Normandie, or born oute of this Reame, and lawfully begoten by any Englishman—after the deth of their husbondes, frely enjoy, have, and possede° all their owne inheritaunces, to theym and to their heires other than been attaynted by this Acte.[5]

dominion

possess

* * *

5. This gracious measure strikes a chivalric contrast with the crimes against women with which Henry VI and his followers are above charged.

CHIVALRY IN PRINCIPLE

GILBERT HAY

From The Buke of Knychthede†

[*Properties of the Noble Order and Office of Knychthede*]¹

* * *

[F]irst and formast, knychthede was ordanyit to manetene and
defend haly° kirk,° and the faith, for the quhilk° God the fader of   *holy / church / which*
hevyn send his Sone in this warld to tak in him oure humanitee,
fleschly inumbrit,° and incarnate in the glorious Virgyne Mary, his   *unstained*
suete moder, be° the joyfull message brocht till hir be the angel   *by*
Gabriel * * * [R]ycht sa° the hye glorious God chesit° knychtis to   *so / chose*
be his campiouns, sa that the unworthy mystrowaris° and rebel-   *unbelievers*
louris agaynis his faith mycht be throu thame° chastisit, be force   *them*
of armes to vencus and ourecum² his inymyes, the quhilkis every
day fors thame at thair powar to put doun the fayth of haly kirk
* * * Bot the maist noble officeris and ordres in this erde° ar office   *earth*
and ordre of clerkis° and of knychtis, and the best lufe in this erde   *clerics*
is ay° betuix° thame; and tharfore rycht as clergy was nocht ordanyt   *always / between*
to be agayn° the ordre of knychthede, bot to honour it, and thame   *against*
that worthily beris° it, sa sulde° knychtis nocht be aganis the haly   *bear / should*
ordre and office of clergy.

* * *

The office alssua° of knychthede aw° to defend his naturale lord,   *also / ought*
and manetene him; for a king is bot a man allane° but° his men;   *alone / without*
and but tham thare may na king governe, na° deffend his peple na   *nor*
yit nane othir lord, for thai ar bot syngulere personis * * * But
commonly ane evill wikkit° knycht takis party° contrair with a kin-   *wicked / sides*
gis subditis° agayne himself, for he wald have his lord put doune,   *subjects*
that he mycht have sum part of the lordschip; bot than wirkis° he   *works*
agayne his awin° ordre and office that he is ordaynit for—that is   *own*
ane,° the faith of Jhesus Crist; ane othir, his naturale lord; the   *one*
thrid, the peple in thair richtis.°   *rights*

* * *

† Reprinted, with new glosses and explanatory notes, from Sir Gilbert Hay, *Gilbert of the
Haye's Prose Manuscript*, Volume 2; *The Buke of Knychthede and the Buke of the Governance of Princis*, ed. by J. H. Stevenson, Scottish Text Society 62 (Edinburgh: W. Black-
wood and Sons, 1914), pp. 18–33.
  Sir Gilbert Hay, a noted Scottish poet and translator, completed his *Buke* around 1456.
It is a translation and adaptation of Raymon Lull's 13th-century *Libre del ordre de cava-
leria*, arguably the classic chivalric manual of the Middle Ages and a work so popular in
Malory's day that it is hard to believe that he had not encountered it in some form; he
probably did not encounter it in Hay's translation, but Hay's text at least provides the
perspective of a contemporary British knight who, like Malory, read and produced chivalric
literature. For a study of Malory that makes extensive comparative use of the *Buke of
Knychthede*, see Beverly Kennedy, *Knighthood in the Morte Arthur* (Cambridge: Brewer,
1985). About thirteen years after Malory's death, William Caxton would produce his own
translation, *The Book of the Ordre of Chyvalry*.
1. The title is taken from Hay's Prologue (p. 2 of the edition cited in the title note).
2. Vanquish and overcome.

Knychtis suld be wele-ryddin,° and in youthede lere to be wele-   *adept at riding*
ryddin on destrellis and courseris,[3] till° haunte° justis and tour-   *to / attend*
naymentis, to hald table round, to hunt and hauk at hert and
hynde, daa and raa, bere and baare, loup and lyoun, and all sik
honourable plesauncis,[4] and sa mayntenand° the office and the   *maintaining*
ordre of knychthede worthily. And as all thir° properteis before said   *these*
pertenis till a knycht as to the habilnes° of his corps,° rycht sa is   *ableness / body*
thare othir proprieteis pertenand to the saule; as justice, force,°   *fortitude*
prudence, and temperaunce, charitee and veritee, lautee° and   *loyalty*
humilitee, faith, esperaunce,° subtilitee, agilitee, and with all othir   *hope*
vertues touchand° to wisedome, appertenis till him, as to the saule.   *pertaining*
And forthy,° when a knycht has all strenthis and habiliteis that   *therefore*
appertenis to the corps, and has nocht thame that appertenis to
the saule, he is nocht verray knycht, bot is contrarius to the ordre,
and inymy of knychthede.

* * *

Item,° office of knychtis is to manetene and governe landis and   *Also*
policy, and to defend thame; for the raddour° and the drede that   *fear*
the peple has of the knychtis, thai byde apon thair craftis and
labouragis, and grathis lyfing for the lordis,[5] for dout° to be undone,   *fear*
destroyit, and desertit; and thus ar the kingis dred° for the knychtis.   *feared*
And * * * a fals knycht that will nocht help to defend his king and
his lord naturale is lyke faith bot° gude charitable werkis, or kny-   *without*
chthede tume° and idill bot office, or heretike aganis the faith.   *empty*

* * *

Item, the order of knychthede standis in the corage, and nocht
in the corssage,° for ellis war° the ordre litill worth; for quhy?°   *body / were / why*
A lytill persone may quhilum throu habilitee of corps ourecum
a mekle,[6] and tak him, and enprisoun him. Bot a thousand
men, suppos° thai be never sa stark,° may nocht ourecum na ven°   *although / strong*
a gude knychtis curage. And thus is the ordre of knychte mare
worthily in the curage na in the corssage, for ellis war nocht that
the knychthede accordit° better to the body na to the saule. And   *accorded*
be that, the unworthy cowartis knychtis that fleis in bataillis fra
thair lordis ar nocht worthy to be callit knychtis * * * for thai drede
mare the distroublaunce° and malese° of thair corssage, na the   *disturbance / discomfort*
honoure and worschip of thair curage that appertenis to the ordre
of knychthede of rycht.

* * *

Item, office of knychthede is to mantene and defend wedowis,
maidenis, faderles and moderles barnis,° and pore miserable per-   *children*

---

3. War horses and chasing horses.
4. To attend feasts and contests in imitation of Arthurian institutions, to hunt and hawk in
   pursuit of hart and hind, doe and roe, bear and boar, wolf and lion, and all such honorable
   delights.
5. They attend to their crafts and labors and produce a living for the lords.
6. A little person may sometimes through physical ability overcome a large person.

sonis and piteable, and to help the wayke° agayne the stark, and
the pure° agayn the riche; for ofttymes sik folk ar, be mare stark
na thai, pelit and derobbit, and thair gudis tane,[7] and put to des-
tructioun and povertie, for fault° of power and defense. * * * For
rycht as the hewing ax is ordanyt to cutt doune treis that hynderis
labouragis° of landis, and cartis and chariotis and merchandices to
passe through the forestis, sa is the suerd of knychthede ordanyt
to kutt away and destroye the wickkit unworthy wedis and ronnis°
of thornis of evill men that lettis° labouraris, merchandis, and tra-
valouris to travale throu the warld, quhilk is as a forest and wild-
ernes quhen it is not wele redde;° off the quhilk evill men suld be
wedit° out be knychtis, keparis° of the lawe, that gude men mycht
lyve in lee;° and he that is a knycht, and dois° nocht this, bot dois
evyn the contrary, suld be tane be the prince, or be othir worthy,
faithfull, and honourable knychtis, and put till dede. For quhen a
knycht is a revare,° or a thef, or a traytour or a murtherar, or a
lollard,[8] scismatike or heretike, or in syk° crimys opinly knawin and
approvit,° than is he unworthy for to lyve, bot to be punyst in example of° otheris that defoulis° that maist noble and worthy ordre,
and abusit it aganis the poyntis° and the proprieteis of the order.

weak
poor

lack

ploughing

vines
hinders

tended
weeded / keepers
shelter / does

robber
such
proved
for / defile
principles

* * *

Item, ane othir poynt of the office of knychthede is, to halde his
armouris cleine and faire, and wele at poynt,° and to se° wele to the
governaunce of his hors, and nocht to play thame at playes° of
dice, and of tables, and othir licht° playis, quhilkis° ar nocht con-
tenyt° in the poyntis of the ordre.

condition / attend
games
frivolous / which
contained

* * *

Item, lordis na knychtis suld nocht brek the ath° of mariage
throw misordynate° lechery, for that is a poynt that discordis with
the poyntis of the ordre; for thare is thre gree° of chastitee, the
quhilkis all honourable personis ar behaldin till: that is, ane in
mariage, ane in widowhede, and ane in maidynhede that is callit
virginitee; of quhilk the haly writt biddis thame that may nocht
lyve chaste, mary thame, and syne° kepe thair mariage°—of quhilk
the haly writt biddis thame that may nocht lyve chaste, mary
thame, and syne kepe thair maryage. For gif thai do nocht, and
thai brek mariage, that brekis thair aithe° to God-wart,° the quhilk
is agayn the ordre and office of knychthede; for chastitee is vertu,
and misordanyt lechery is vice.

oath
aberrant
degrees

thereafter

oath / toward God

* * *

Item, justice and knychthede acordis togeder, and justice and
mariage: bresing° and othir disordinate lechery discordis with

embracing

7. Often such folk are, by more powerful people than they, beaten and rifled, and their goods
   taken.
8. Lollards were followers of the 14th-century theological reformer John Wyclif and were
   conventionally considered heretics.
9. 1 Corinthians 7:8–10.

justice; and thus knychthede and disordanyt lechery discordis, as
apperis be the lawis of haly kirk, quhilkis efferis° prelatis to correct. *suits*
And thus gif a prince, or a lord, or a knycht brekis mariage, he is mare
to blame na ony of lawar° degree; for the hyar degree the gretter *lower*
fault, and mare to be punyst in all excesse of vertu.

Item, ane othir poynt of knychthede is that a knycht suld be
meke and full of clemencé, and nocht prydy,° na presumptuous, *proud*
na orguillous;° for oft tymes of pryde and orguille and presump- *arrogant*
cione cummys injuré and discensioun; for orguille is contrary to
justice and inymy to concorde; and tharfore, thare sulde na knycht
be hautayn,° na feir,° na prydefull, na presumptuous, bot ever with *haughty / showy*
mekenes, and clemencé, and humilitee, be symple as a may° *maid*
amang peple, and in his inymyes presence be as lyoun rampand.° *rearing up*

❈   ❈   ❈

How Knyghtis of the Bath Shulde Be Made†

First the Kynge oure Sovereyne Lorde writith oute lettris unto certeyne squyers of this Rewme° and desirynge them for to make them *Realm*
redy for to receyve the hye and worshipfull ordir of knyghthode at
hye festis° of the yere, or at suche tyme as it likith° the Kynge for *feast days / pleases*
to desire them for to come.

The evyn° of the day of the feste, all the squyers that schall be *eve*
made knyghtis, they schall come all togedir unto the Kyngis palys;° *palace*
and then the statis° of the Kyngis hous schall mete with them and *dignitaries*
brynge hem up into the Kyngis presence. And then schall the Kyn-

---

† Reprinted, with new glosses and explanatory notes, from Harold Arthur, Viscount Dillon,
"On a MS. Collection of Ordinances of Chivalry of the fifteenth century, belonging to
Lord Hastings," *Archaeologia* 57, no. i (1900), 29–70. Dillon's transcription is from a MS
produced c. 1461 by Sir John Astley, a member of the Order of the Garter renowned in
his own time as a fighter in single combats (the MS is now New York, Pierpont Morgan
Library, 775). Roman numerals have been converted to arabic numerals. The Order of
the Bath was no doubt founded along similar lines to the Order of the Garter, a chivalric
institution established by Edward III in 1348, probably as a reflection of the institution
of Arthur's fellowship of the Round Table—and an oft-cited example of the interaction of
chivalric "life" and chivalric "art" in the later Middle Ages. The Order of the Bath had
been instituted by 1399, when it is mentioned in connection with the coronation of Henry
IV.

The language and tenets of the Order's oath are highly reminiscent of the "Pentecostal
Oath" of the Round Table which Malory introduces at the end of *The Weddyng of Kyng
Arthur* (p. 77); the language and tenets are also highly reminiscent of the implied definition of right chivalric conduct that appears at the beginning of Edward IV's first Act of
Attainder (see p. 774). Further, the ritual cleansing, fasting, waking in prayer, and hum-
bling changes of garb necessary for initiation into the order are reminiscent of the ascetic
prerogatives of the Grail Quest. All such points of correspondence can be traced to earlier
treatises on chivalry, such as the anonymous 13th-century *Ordene de chevalerie*, and to
practical custom: see Maurice Keen, *Chivalry* (New Haven: Yale University Press, 1984),
esp. pp. 6–8, and cf. the selections from Gilbert Hay's *Buke* (p. 777). For further consideration of Astley's MS and others like it in the context of the *Morte Darthur*, see Richard
Barber, "Malory's *Morte Darthur* and Court Culture under Edward IV," in *Arthurian Literature XII*, ed. James P. Carley and Felicity Riddy (Cambridge: Brewer, 1993), pp. 133–
155; and Karen Cherewatuk, "Sir Thomas Malory's 'Grete booke,'" in *The Social and
Literary Contexts of Malory's "Morte Darthur"* ed. by D. Thomas Hanks Jr. and Jessica G.
Brogdon (Cambridge: Brewer, 2000), pp. 42–67. See also the essay by Carol Meale on
p. 865 herein.

gis sewer° goo on to the kechyn for his mete° and all the squyers *officer / dinner*
with him that schall be made knyghtis, for eche on of them schall
bere a disshe, and they schall serve the Kynge out of the firste
course; * * * then they shall have ther service° into ther chambir *dinner service*
and dyne alle togedir; and when they have dynid, then schall the
gentilman usshere come into the seyde chambir and asyne every
squyer his plase for his bedde and for his bayne.° * * * Then schall *bath*
the Kyngis barboure come and shave all the squyers.

* * *

Then schall the seyde squyers goo unto ther bayne[1] * * * And
when they be in ther bayne, then schall the herawdis° of armys *heralds*
goo unto the Kynge and lete him have knowlege that the squyers
bene in ther bayne. * * * Then schall the stewards come with all
the lordis and knyghtis, the Kyngis mynstrellis and herawdis of
armys before them, unto the chambir dore; and then the lordis
entir into the chambir with the herawdis for to yeve° them ther *give*
charge as they been in the bayne, sayinge in this wise:° *manner*

Brothir, the Kynge oure Sovereyne Lorde woll° that ye take *wishes*
this hye and worshipfull ordir upon yow, the whiche I as a
knyght declare onto yow certeyne poyntis that longith° unto *pertain*
this hye and worshipfull ordir of kyghthode: ye shall love God
above all things and be stedfaste in the Feythe and sustene° *sustain*
the Chirche; and ye schall be trewe unto yowre Sovereyne
Lorde, and trewe of yowre worde and promys and sekirtee in
that oughte to be kepte;[2] also ye schall sustene wydowes in ther
right at every tyme they wol requere° yow, and maydenys in ther *require*
virginité, and helpe hem and socoure hem with yowre good° *goods, means*
that for lak of good they be not mysgovernyd° also ye schall *ill-treated*
sitte in noo plase where that eny jugement schulde be gevyn° *given*
wrongefully ayens enybody to yowre knowleche; also ye schall
not suffir noo murdreris nor extorcioners of the Kyngis pepill
within the contré there ye dwelle, but with yowre power ye
schall lete doo take them[3] and put them into the handis of
justice and that they be punysshid as the Kyngis lawe woll.

And then ye schall putte yowre hande into the bayne and take up
watir and make a crosse up on his lyfte schuldir before and
behynde, and kisse it and saye "*In nomine Patris [et Filius et Spir-
itus Sancti],*[4] God sende yow as moche worshipe as evyr had eny
of yowre kynne."° And thus muste doo all the lordis and knyghtis *family*
unto every squyer as he sittith in the bayne.

Then they schall goo oute of ther baynes into ther beddis.[5] And

1. The bath is understood as a baptism-like cleansing of sin and a return to childlike innocence.
2. True to assurances in agreements that ought to be kept.
3. Have them seized.
4. In the name of the Father, the Son, and the Holy Spirit.
5. The bed is understood as a reminder of the peace and rest of Heaven, that which knighthood should strive to establish.

then they schall arise and make them redy in hermytis aray of Colchestir russet.[6]

* * *

Than they schall goo alle togedir into the chapell and bee in ther preyeris° till in the mornyge unto 8 of the clokke. Than they schall have a Masse of the Holy Goste. * * * When Masse is done, then they schall goo unto ther chambris.

prayers

* * *

Than they schall chaunge them into anothr arayment. Firste they schall putte up on them dubletis with blak hosis chasemles, a reed° cote of reed tartaryn,° and a white ledir° girdill° aboute him, and the gyrdill may have noo bokill.[7] Then he muste have a white coyfe° upon his heed, and then a mantell of reed tarteryn purfild° aboute with ermyn, and that muste be putte above him and a white lase° muste be in the seyde mantell before at the breste, with a peyre of white glovys knyt° in the seyde lase.

red
silk / leather / belt
cap
furred
lace
tied

Then the servauntis and chambirleynes that bene asynid° to awayte upon them schall take ther swerdis—and the skabert schall be white ledir withoute any bokill—and a payre of gilte sporis° hangynge upon the hiltis of the same sworde, and the seyde servauntis and chambirleynes schall bere the seyde sworde with the sporis before them.[8]

assigned
spurs

* * *

Then they schall * * * come into the Kyngis presence with ther swordis borne before them, and makynge ther obeysaunce.° Then they schall come every° to the Kynge; then schall two knyghtis take the sporis of the sworde and doo° hem on ther helis;° then schall the Kynge gyrde his sworde aboute him. Then the squyer puttith bothe his thumbis within° the las of his mantell and lyftis up his armys ovyr his heed; then the Kynge puttith bothe his hondis within his armys, and takis him aboute the nekke with bothe his handis and kissis him, and plukkis° him be the nekke and sayes unto him "Sooyes bone chevalere."[9] Then he knelys downe and standis by till the Kynge hath made hem alle; than they schall be ladde unto the chapell with knyghtis.

submission
i.e., each
put / heels
under
tugs

When they come into the chapell, evyn before the hye auter,° then they shall ungirde him and leye his sworde upon the auter and then knele downe and ley his hande upon the auter; then the

altar

6. Dressed in the humble coarse cloth customary to hermits. The earthtones of the material are understood to represent burial or the earth itself and serve as a reminder of the transitory nature of worldly interests.
7. The red material is understood as a reminder of the knight's obligation to shed his blood when required, and the white belt is understood as a symbol of the restraints of virginity to which the knight should aspire.
8. The spurs are understood to represent the urge to follow God's commandments and to maintain loyalty. Beyond its obvious cruciform import, the sword is understood by its two edges to represent the just use of force.
9. Be a good knight. The tug at the neck serves as an immediate reminder of the power and authority of the lord bestowing the honor.

deen, or on for him that is asynid, for to say in this wise: "Be this holy auter that Oure Lordis Body is mynistrid° on, ye schall sus-teyne the Chirche and kepe this hye and worshipfull ordir that ye have takyn upon yow." * * * *

And when they be goynge oute of the chapell, then schall the Kyngis mayster cook[1] mete with hem at the dore, and he schall say unto them in this wise: "Sir, I as the Kyngis mayster cook come at this tyme to lete yow have knowlege what is myne office. Sire, myne office is, yf ye be untrewe to yowre sovereyne lorde or doo ayens this hye and worshipfull ordir that ye have takyn, myne office is that Y muste smyte of yowre hele be the small of yowre leggis;[2] and herefore I clayme yowre sporis, the whiche I pray yow remembir this in yowre mynde and yeve° yow grace to kepe this hye and worshipfull ordir, and yeve yow as moche worshipe as evyr had eny of yowre kynne."

Then they schall be brought into the halle; then the Kynge com-yth into the halle and wasshis and is sette. Then shall all the newe-made knyghtis wasshe and sitte at a side borde;° and when the Kynge is servid, then all the halle schalle be servid; but the newe-made knyghtis schalle ete noo mete. And when the Kyng is servid of the laste course * * * then they schall goo into ther chambris and doo of ther arayment. * * *

Then they shall doo upon them longe blewe gownis, and it muste be purfild aboute with ermyne, and a white lase of silke with golde in the toftis° muste be pynid° a° pyn upon his lyfte schuldir, and a hood of the same purfiled aboute (of the shappe as bacheleris of lawe hav) * * *. And then they schall goo alle togedir unto the Kyng; and when they come into his presence, on° shall say for them alle in this wise: "Most hye and excellent and most myghti prince, oure Sovereyne Lorde, we thanke yow of this hye and worshipfull ordir that ye have gyve unto us, and we as yowre liege men schall be redy at yowre comaundement." Then they schall bowe them downe alle at onys and arise and goo ther wey; then they schall goo into ther chambris and chaunge hem. * * * And then all the newe-made knyghtis may doo what them likis, for all is done and endid.

served

give

table

tufts / pinned / with

someone

[Oath of a Herald]†

In first ye shall swere that ye shall be trewe to oure high and excel-lent prince, oure Soverayn Lord that here is, and to hym that makys

1. I.e., a man adept at cutting meat.
2. Strike of your heel by the narrow part of your legs.
† Reprinted, with new glosses and explanatory notes, from Harold Arthur, Viscount Dillon, "On a MS. Collection of Ordinances of Chivalry of the fifteenth century, belonging to Lord Hastings," *Archaeologia* 57, no. i (1900), 29–70. About the MS and its original owner, see the title note, p. 780. By the 15th century in England heralds had assumed the status of official custodians and spokesmen of chivalric record. At tournaments and other notable occasions they would be responsible for announcing the entry of participant knights and nobles, identifying them by their coats of arms and often "heralding" their accomplishments and reputation. The same expertise at identification of arms made them

yow herold. And if ye have any knawlegyng° or here any ymagyn- *knowledge*
acion° or treson—the whiche God defend° that ye shuld—and in *plot / forbid*
cas° be that ye do, ye shall discovir° hit to his High Grace or to his *case / reveal*
noble counseill, and consaill° hit in no maner wyse, so helpe yow *conceal*
God and halydom.° *holiness*

Also ye shall promesse and swere that ye shall be connsamit° *accomplished*
and servyseable to all gentilmen to do their commaundementis to
their wurship° of knyghthod, and to excuse° their worship by youre *honor / defend*
good consaill that God sendys yow, and ever redy to offre youre
servyce unto them.

Also ye shall promesse and swere to be secrete and kepe thair
secretes, of knyghthes, squyers, ladyes, and gentylwomen, a con-
fessour of armes,¹ and not discover° them in no wyse except treson *reveal*
abovesaid.

Also ye shall promesse and swere if any fortune fall° yow in *befall*
dyvers° landes and contrayes that° ye goo or ryde, yf ye fynde any *various / such that*
gentilman of name and of armes that hath lost his goodes in wor-
ship of knyghthod, or in service of his lord, and fall° into poverté, *he fell*
and if he aske you of youre goodes to his sustynaunce ye shall geve° *give*
hym part of youre goodes to youre power and as ye may bere.²

Also ye shall promesse and swere, if ye be in any place that ye
here langage° betwene partie and partie that is not profitable ne *discourse*
vertuose, that ye kepe youre mouth closse and reporte it not forth
but° to their worship and the best. *except*

Also ye shall promisse and swere, if so be that ye be in any place
that ye here° debate or perill° betwene gentilman and gentilman *hear / threat*
the whyche ye be prevé° to, yf so be that ye be required by prynce, *privy*
juge, or ony other to bere wytnesse, ye shall not, withouten licence
of both parties; and whan ye have leve, ye shall for° any lust° or *despise / desire*
any good favour or awe but say the soth to youre knawynge.

Also ye shall promesse and swere to be trwe and secrete to gen-
tyllwomen, wydows, and maydyns. And in cas be that any man wold
doo theym wrong or forse them or disherite them of their lyfelo-
des,³ and they have no goodes° to pursue° for their ryght to the *means / sue*
princes or juges abovesayd, if thei require yow of youre supporta-
cion, ye shall supporte them with your good counseyll to prynces
and juges abovesaid.

---

authorities on the establishing of genealogy and pedigree; and on the field of battle it was
the heralds (themselves considered "neutral" noncombatants) who ascertained the identities of the armigerous dead—a procedure of great importance in the Wars of the Roses,
enabling in turn the disposition of the property of the deceased (cf. the title note, p. 774).

The oath printed here shares many of the chivalric principles enshrined by the investiture of Knights of the Bath (see the previous selection), but, through its greater emphasis
on discretion and probity, attempts to moderate that power over reputation that is germane
to the office of herald. It is perhaps worth thinking of Malory, in his writerly capacity as
a noncombatant recorder of chivalric endeavor and identity, as kind of herald (cf. n. 3,
p. 216). This model at least accomodates his text's resistance to being identified as categorically Yorkist or Lancastrian, despite its obvious allusions to the political troubles of
the day. And the directive to "kepe thair secretes, of knyghthes . . . and gentylwomen"
resonates well with Malory's famous demur concerning Launcelot and Guenevere (p. 649,
lines 1–5).

1. I.e., as a chivalric confidant.
2. To the best of your ability and as much as you can afford.
3. Disinherit them of their revenue-generating properties.

Also ye shall promesse and swere that ye shall forsake all places of dishonesté and hasardie° and of dishauntly[4] goyng to commyn tavernes and places of debates° and all maner vysys° and take you to vertous to your power.[5] This article and all other articles abovesaid ye shall trewly kepe, so helpe you God and halydome.

gambling
brawls / vices

TOURNAMENT AND BATTLE

CHRISTOPHER GRAVETT

Knights at Tournament: The 15th Century†

During this century the tournament perhaps reached its zenith as a colourful spectacle spiced with danger. Holinshed relates that the threat of regicide had not completely disappeared. In 1400 the Earl of Huntingdon arranged a joust with his followers and those of the Earl of Salisbury, but a plot against Henry IV was uncovered. However, kings and princes no longer felt threatened by the tournament. On the contrary, they vied with each other to put on memorable displays, which contained more and more elements of fantasy. During the 15th century it was at the courts of Aix and Burgundy that the tournament perhaps found most favour; here it was transformed almost to a science. In Burgundy the sovereign used these occasions to keep in touch with his knights and army leaders, and to provide entertainment for his subjects, who often had to pay towards his wars and pageants.

The lavish extravagances of the Burgundian court did not signify by any means that smaller gatherings were eclipsed. It should also be noted that bourgeois tournaments were popular, especially within Burgundian territory, hence the jousting societies in such places as Bruges, Tournai, and notably Lille, with its feast of the '*Espinette*'. Even Duke Philip the Good was prepared to joust with the bourgeois champions.

Italian tournaments were staged in every court which wanted to flaunt its wealth and social breeding, and formed useful vehicles for families like the Medici. In many cities such as Florence, Milan, Venice and even Rome, lavish spectacles were held in similar vein to those of the Burgundian court. In some versions towards the end of the 15th century the action was preceded by dramatic verse, as at Pesaro in 1475. Triumphal cars or 'pageants'

---

4. As an unattentive or unreliable person.
5. And give yourself over to virtues to the best of your ability.
† Reprinted from Christopher Gravett, *Knights at Tournament* (Oxford: Osprey, 1998), pp. 22–29. Reprinted with the permission of Osprey Publishing Ltd. For further reading, see the Bibliography.

were common; in 1466 the spectacle at Padua included a huge mounted figure of Jupiter, while in 1501 a ship was wheeled into one of the squares in Rome and assaulted.

In Germany the first half of the 15th century saw a remarkable lack of tourneying activity. Not until a meeting at Würzburg in 1479 did tournaments again become popular. Activities were largely in the hands of tournament societies such as those of Stein-bock, Rüden and Esel, which closely monitored the ceremonious gatherings. Latterly the *'grossen Turniergesellschaft'* [great Tour-nament Society] was formed from Swabia, Bavaria, Franconia and the Rhineland. The societies needed the backing of powerful nobles such as Graf Eberhard of Württemberg, who took part in a tourney at Stuttgart in 1484. The German nobility was not as wealthy as its Burgundian counterpart and so the spectacle was less fantastic. However, German princes took a keen interest in tournaments, often feeling it of great importance to be foremost in the contests. They kept horses especially for the occasion and made sure they were in fine fettle. Letters reveal that such animals were often requested for loan.

There was still a danger that in time of war tempers would boil over. In 1402 a contest *à outrance* [to the death] was held at Orleans between knights of the Duke of Orleans and some English opponents. The duke ignored calls to stop it because of ill-feeling. The French chronicle charges the English with conceiving the strategy of allowing two of their number to overpower one French-man, but the plan misfired. An Englishman died, and a bitter and bloody fight took place which the French finally won. Relations between English and French warriors became so bad that in 1409 the French king issued an ordinance forbidding all combats with sharp weapons. During a fight with axes in 1403 at Valencia a Spaniard grabbed a Frenchman by the leg and tried to knife him; the King of Aragon hastily threw down his baton to stop the fight.

Even in time of peace the sport remained hazardous. When the Dukes of Burgundy and Brabant wished to joust at a tournament at Brussels in 1428 they were dissuaded by the kings-of-arms, who feared an accident. Two years later two knights were badly wounded in separate incidents in the market place at Arras when their visors were pierced.

Tournaments were still held to celebrate great occasions. At the coronation of Henry IV's queen in 1403 Richard Beauchamp, Earl of Warwick, jousted for the queen. He challenged Sir Pandolf Mal-atesta to joust followed by foot combat with axes, then with arming swords, and lastly with sharp daggers. Sir Pandolf was wounded in the shoulder and saved from death when the fight was stopped. In 1467 a tournament was held to celebrate the coronation of Edward IV, in which Lord Scales won the ring and ruby. For the entry of Louis XII into Paris a lily, 30 feet high and bedecked with the shields of the challengers, was erected in Paris.

Formalities extended to the challenge beforehand. Some knights wore an *'emprise'* or token which must be touched to signify a challenge accepted. Thus in 1400 a squire from Aragon fixed on a piece of leg armour and refused to remove it until someone accepted his challenge. In 1445 the Castilian Galiot de Baltasin arrived to challenge Philippe de Ternant. With the assent of the Duke of Burgundy, de Ternant attached a lady's lawn sleeve to his shoulder with a jewelled knot. Galiot asked the custom of the country, saying that where he came from the act of tearing the token off roughly denoted a fight to the death, but touching it signified a wish to fight for honour. De Ternant that same day sent sealed 'chapitres' indicating the contests he desired.

The Treatise of King René of Anjou

Of special interest for the history of the tournament is the Traité de la forme et devis d'un tournoi [Treatise on the Form and Organization of a Tournament] of René, King of Anjou. In penning the events of a fictional meeting at Aix in about 1440 he left minute details of the formalities surrounding the tournament as it existed in France, Germany, Flanders and Brabant, though the customs of the varying areas are included together.

The lord who decides to give the tournament calls his king-of-arms (or in his absence a notable herald) and gives him a rebated tournament sword. On this occasion René relates how the Duke of Brittany sent the Duke of Bourbon a challenge to a 'Tournoy et Bouhordis d'armes' before ladies and girls. Four judges were to be appointed, two from the district of the defendant and two from elsewhere, all being worthy barons, knights or squires.

The destrier of the lord enters the town first, a small page in the saddle. The destriers of the other tourneying knights and squires follow in pairs. Behind come trumpeters and minstrels, then heralds, pursuivants and the tourneying knights and squires with their entourage. Four trumpeters lead the judges' procession; then come the king-of-arms, the four judges and the rest of the company.

Keeping their retinue together, the judges try to put up at a religious house, since the cloister was ideal for the display of crests the following day. The judges should have a canvas three feet by two in size, showing the banners and names of the two chief tourneyers (appellant and defendant) at the top, and at the foot the four banners with names, surnames, seigneuries, titles and offices of the four judges. On the day the banners of the princes are borne to the cloister by one of their chamberlain knights, and the pennons carried by the foremost valets or squires. The helms of princes are carried by the chief squire, those of other knights and squires by gentlemen or valets. The following day the contestants ride to the lists unarmed except for staves, with their banner bearers carrying furled banners. There, each raises his right hand and swears to obey the rules of the tournament.

Ordinances

Contestants often set out specific rules, such as types of weapon and number of blows, in 'Chapitres d' Armes' which might be formulated as much as a year before the actual event. A late 15th century example states that a contestant who withdraws beyond the 'barres' may not return that day.

In England a set of ordinances was drawn up in 1466 by John Lord Tiptoft, Earl of Worcester, at the command of Edward IV. They were to be kept in all manner of jousts of peace 'royall' in England; later ordinances tend to be very similar. Surviving copies show that the prize is awarded for the following feats, in order of preference:

> Unseating with the lance, or bearing horse and rider to earth.
> Striking the opponent's coronel twice.
> Striking the sight of the helm three times.
> Correctly breaking the most spears.
> Staying in the field longest and still helmed, and having run the fairest course and given the greatest strokes, best with the spear.

Prizes are lost for striking a horse, striking a man's back (turned or disarmed of his spear), hitting the tilt barrier three times, or unhelming oneself twice (unless the horse fails).

A spear is allowed for breaking a lance between saddle and the charnel (breast fixture) of the helm, or from the charnel upwards. Three spears are allowed for breaking a lance by unhorsing the opponent, or so disarming him that he cannot continue. A spear is disallowed, however, for breaking the lance on the saddle, whilst two spears are disallowed for striking the tilt and three if it happens twice. A lance which snaps within a foot of the coronel head is not considered as broken, simply a good 'attaint'.

Problems occurred which only the judges could solve. Lances and even horses must be of similar size. Jehan de Boniface was allowed a sharp lance, but not one furnished with four vicious points. Galiot de Baltasin appeared at Arras in 1446 on a horse whose chanfron and body armour were fitted with steel spikes, and was promptly told to remove them. His opponent, Philippe de Ternant, broke his sword belt in the combat so that his sword, turned in the scabbard, hung over the horse's crupper. Unable to reach it, he was forced to beat off Galiot with his hand until the sword fell out on to the sand. Only then was he considered disarmed so that his weapon could be restored to him in accordance with the 'chapitres'.

Some idea of the size of the lists may be gleaned from references to a meeting held at Smithfield in 1467. The area was 370 by 250 feet with a double palisade. Edward IV, acting as judge, sat in a stand reached by steps. Three other stands held knights, esquires and royal archers of the guard, whilst one on the opposite side housed the mayor and aldermen. Both the constable and the marshal of the lists were provided with chairs. The constable's guard of eight mounted men-at-arms took their place, together with a crowned king-of-arms and herald or pursuivant at each corner. Garter and other kings-of-arms were near Edward's right side in the stand. At St. Omer in 1446 a stone tribune had been built for the judges. At the Field of the Cloth of Gold in 1520 the arena measured 400 by 200 paces, encircled by a ditch and bank nine feet high; the lists measured 150 paces. Some references show them set east to west, perhaps to prevent the sun dazzling one of the contestants or the high lords present, since their stands seem to have been placed on the south side.

The most significant feature of the 15th century was the introduction of the tilt barrier to separate the contestants in a joust. Illustrations show that without a barrier jousters could meet their opponent on the left or right side. Not only did some deliberately 'ride down' their opponents, but collisions and close passes could cause injury to horses and severe bruising to the rider's knees. The tilt was designed to avoid this. First mentioned by Monstrelet in connection with a joust at Arras in 1429, the 'tilt' or 'toile' was initially a rope hung with cloth. The Count of St. Martin apparently preferred to ride from a corner of the lists, which proved to be his undoing: in a joust with Guillaume de Vaudray his oblique charge exposed his right arm because of a faulty piece of armour— Vaudray's lance struck this point, leaving the head embedded in the wound.

The tilt probably first appeared in Italy, since jousts using this innovation were referred to as the 'Italian Course'. It did not reach England until the 1430s, and was not popular in Germany until the end of the century. The tilt did not replace the older form of open jousting, which continued as an alternative form. It was never used in the mêlée. The rope was soon found to be inadequate, and was generally replaced by a wooden barrier up to six feet high. Sixteenth-century illustrations sometimes show the ends of the tilt bent out in such a way that at the end of the run the jouster must turn to his right; this would prevent him running on into the fences or tents beyond the tilt. Further, the other end was effectively blocked and so forced the rider to take the right hand path.

The Pas d'armes

Though terms such as 'tournois', 'joûtes' and 'pas d'armes' were sometimes used vaguely in the Middle Ages, it is possible to distinguish the 'pas' by certain characteristics. In concept it revolved around the idea that several challengers or 'tenans' would elect to hold a piece of ground (the 'pas') against all comers, knights or squires, called the 'venans'. As in other tournaments, this entertainment (especially popular in the 15th century) might comprise not only jousting but also foot combats and a mêlée involving all the contestants from both sides. From mid-century mounted contests with the 'baston' or club might be included.

The 'pas' mimicked the judicial duel before judges for honour, and was a re-enactment of the type of situation encountered in early epic literature. The influence of literature is especially seen in the frequent use of a 'perron' (artificial mound or pillar) often with a 'Tree of Chivalry' nearby. It was usual to hang on the perron shields which must be touched to signify a challenge. At the Pas of Perron Fée challengers blew a horn suspended from the tree. In 1443 one such was held at the 'Tree of Charlemagne' near Dijon. The challenge was thrown out to embrace most of Christian Europe, and it was held under the eye of Philip the Good, Duke of Burgundy. Thirteen of his nobles held the *'pas'* for 40 days (excluding Sundays and feast days).

Great ingenuity went into the settings for such events. At the Pas of La Bergière in 1449 Jeanne de Laval, mistress of René of Anjou, appeared dressed as a shepherdess in a corner of lists whose galleries were thatched. Two knights representing shepherds threw down the *gage* [challenge]. One bore a black shield to challenge those content in love, the other a white shield of happiness for dissatisfied amorists. That same year Jacques de Lalain held the Pas of Fontaine des Pleurs on an island in the River Saône. Before a pavilion stood models of a lady and unicorn, the latter with three tear-strewn shields about its neck. The colours of white, violet and black represented courses with axe, sword and lance respectively. Losers paid a forfeit; anyone brought to the ground by an axe must wear a gold bracelet for a year or find a lady with the key. Another unicorn made an appearance at a late 15th century *'pas'*: this time the shields (one on each leg) represented the opening jousts, the tourney of 12 sword strokes, foot combat with 12 sword strokes, and the defence and attack on a mock castle using shields, swords and pikes. This occurred each afternoon from 27 November to New Year's Day, and since combat went on until 7 p.m. the lists must have been illuminated by torches. At the Pas de la Pélerine at St. Omer in 1446 two shields represented Sir Lancelot and Tristan de Leonnois.

At the Smithfield *'pas'* of 1467 a knocking at the gate signalled the entry of 'Escallis' (Lord Scales), who was followed by about 12 richly caparisoned horses led by pages. In his joust with the Bastard of Burgundy, the latter's horse struck its head against the pommel of Scales' saddle and fell with its rider. Some chroniclers assert that a spike on the chanfron of Scales' *destrier* was thrust into the mouth of the other animal; the Bastard's comment was that he had fought a beast and tomorrow would fight a man. This was done on foot; the casting spears were considered too dangerous, and combat was agreed with axes and daggers. Olivier de la Marche, who was present, testifies to the great rents made in Scales' armour by the lower point of the Bastard's axe.

At the Pas à l'Arbre d'Or in 1468 a fir tree sheathed in gold was set up opposite the ladies' stand in the market place at Bruges. The festivities marked the marriage of Charles of Burgundy with the sister of Edward IV and were to last ten days. A pursuivant handed the duke a letter from a princess who would proffer favour to any knight who would deliver a giant from captivity, whom she had placed under protection of her dwarf. The latter entered in crimson and white satin, leading the giant. Together with the pursuivant of the Toison d'Or they were to take their place by three pillars on a stage set on a perron. Cleves Pursuivant knocked on one gate of the lists with a hammer, and on admittance his coat-of-arms was hung on the tree. Adolf of Cleves, Lord of Ravestein, was conducted into the lists disguised as a very old man (popular with organizers) and asked for permission to tilt. The Bastard of Burgundy entered within a rich portable pavilion. The dwarf turned a sand glass for half an hour's duration, and blew his horn. A banquet ended the first day's events. A *destrier* [war horse] was the prize, richly caparisoned and provided with panniers containing a jousting harness of the Bastard of Burgundy. Finally the tilt and stands were removed, and the mêlée took place with rebated swords. So ardent were the tourniers that they ignored all signals to cease until the duke, bare-headed and sword in hand, pushed his way into the press.

* * *

JOHN KEEGAN

Agincourt, 25 October 1415[†]

The Wounded

* * *

The heralds had watched the battle in a group together and, though the French army had left, the French heralds had not yet followed them. For the heralds belonged not to the armies but to the international corporation of experts who regulated civilized warfare. Henry was anxious to hear their verdict on the day's fighting and to fix a name for the battle, so that its outcome and the army's exploits could be readily identified when chroniclers came to record it. Montjoie, the principal French herald, confirmed that the English were the victors and provided Henry with the name of the nearest castle—Agincourt—to serve as eponym.

That decision ended the battle as a military and historical episode. The English drove their prisoners and carried their own wounded back to Maisoncelles for the night, where the twenty surgeons of the army set to work. English casualties had been few: the Duke of York, who was pulled from under a heap of corpses, dead either from suffocation or a heart-attack, and the Earl of Suffolk were the only notable fatalities. The wounded numbered only some hundreds. What were their prospects? In the main, probably quite good. The English had not undergone an arrow attack, so most of the wounds would have been lacerations rather than penetrations, clean even if deep cuts which, if bound up and

† "Agincourt, 25 October 1415," from *The Face of Battle* by John Keegan, copyright © 1976 by John Keegan. Used by permission of Viking Penguin, a division of Penguin Putnam Inc.

left, would heal quickly. There would also have been some fractures; depressed fractures of the skull could not be treated—the
secret of trepanning awaited rediscovery—but breaks of the arm
and lower leg could have been successfully set and splinted. The
French wounded enjoyed a much graver prognosis. Many would
have suffered penetrating wounds, either from arrows or from
thrusts through the weak spots of their armour. Those which had
pierced the intestines, emptying its contents into the abdomen,
were fatal: peritonitis was inevitable. Penetrations of the chest cav-
ity, which had probably carried in fragments of dirty clothing, were
almost as certain to lead to sepsis. Many of the French would have
suffered depressed fractures of the skull, and there would have
been broken backs caused by falls from horses in armour at speed.
Almost all of these injuries we may regard as fatal, the contemporary surgeons being unable to treat them. Many of the French,
of course, had not been collected from the battlefield and, if they
did not bleed to death, would have succumbed to the combined
effects of exposure and shock during the night, when temperatures
might have descended into the middle-30s Fahrenheit. It was,
therefore, not arbitrary brutality when, in crossing the battlefield
next morning, the English killed those whom they found alive.
They were almost certain to have died, in any case, when their
bodies would have gone to join those which the local peasants,
under the supervision of the Bishop of Arras, dug into pits on the
site. They are said to have buried about 6,000 altogether.

The Will to Combat

What sustained men in a combat like Agincourt, when the penalty
of defeat, or of one's own lack of skill or nimbleness, was so final
and unpleasant? Some factors, either general to battle—as will
appear—or more or less particular to this one are relatively easy
to isolate. Of the general factors, drink is the most obvious to mention. The English, who were on short rations, presumably had less
to drink than the French, but there was drinking in the ranks on
both sides during the period of waiting and it is quite probable that
many soldiers in both armies went into the mêlée less than sober,
if not indeed fighting drunk. For the English, the presence of the
King would also have provided what present-day soldiers call a
'moral factor' of great importance. The personal bond between
leader and follower lies at the root of all explanations of what does
and does not happen in battle: and that bond is always strongest
in martial societies, of which fifteenth-century England is one type
and the warrior states of India, which the British harnessed so
successfully to their imperial purpose, are another. The nature of
the bond is more complex, and certainly more materialistic than
modern ethologists would like to have us believe. But its importance must not be underestimated. And though the late-medieval
soldier's immediate loyalty lay towards his captain, the presence
on the field of his own and his captain's anointed king, visible to

all and ostentatiously risking his life in the heart of the mêlée, must have greatly strengthened his resolve.

Serving to strengthen it further was the endorsement of religion. The morality of killing is not something with which the professional soldier is usually thought to trouble himself, but the Christian knight, whether we mean by that the ideal type as seen by the chroniclers or some at least of the historical figures of whom we have knowledge, was nevertheless exercised by it. What constituted unlawful killing in time of war was well-defined, and carried penalties under civil, military and religious law. Lawful killing, on the other hand, was an act which religious precept specifically endorsed, within the circumscription of the just war; and however dimly or marginally religious doctrine impinged on the consciousness of the simple soldier or more unthinking knight, the religious preparations which all in the English army underwent before Agincourt must be counted among the most important factors affecting its mood. Henry himself heard Mass three times in succession before the battle, and took Communion, as presumably did most of his followers; there was a small army of priests in the expedition. The soldiers ritually entreated blessing before entering the ranks, going down on their knees, making the sign of the cross and taking earth into their mouths as a symbolic gesture of the death and burial they were thereby accepting.

Drink and prayer must be seen, however, as last-minute and short-term reinforcements of the medieval soldier's (though, as we shall see, not only his) will to combat. Far more important, and, given the disparity of their stations, more important still for the common soldier than the man-at-arms, was the prospect of enrichment. Medieval warfare, like all warfare, was about many things, but medieval battle, at the personal level, was about only three: victory first, of course, because the personal consequences of defeat could be so disagreeable; personal distinction in single combat—something of which the man-at-arms would think a great deal more than the bowman; but, ultimately and most important, ransom and loot. Agincourt was untypical of medieval battle in yielding and then snatching back from the victors the bonanza of wealth that it did; but it is the gold-strike and gold-fever character of medieval battle which we should keep foremost in mind when seeking to understand it.

We should balance it, at the same time, against two other factors. The first of these is the pressure of compulsion. The role which physical coercion or force of unavoidable circumstance plays in bringing men into, and often through, the ordeal of battle is one which almost all military historians consistently underplay, or ignore. Yet we can clearly see that the force of unavoidable circumstances was among the most powerful of the drives to combat at work on the field of Agincourt. The English had sought by every means to avoid battle throughout their long march from Harfleur and, though accepting it on 25 October as a necessary alternative to capitulation and perhaps lifelong captivity, were finally driven to attack by the pains of hunger and cold. The French had also hoped to avoid bringing their confrontation with the English to a fight; and we may convincingly surmise that many of those who went down under the swords or mallet-blows of the English had been drawn into the battle with all the free-will of a man who finds himself going the wrong way on a moving-staircase.

The second factor confounds the former just examined. It concerns the commonplace character of violence in medieval life. What went on at Agincourt appals and horrifies the modern imagination which, vicariously accustomed though it is to the idea of violence, rarely encounters it in actuality and is outraged when it does. The sense of outrage was no doubt as keenly felt by the individual victim of violence five hundred years ago. But the victim of assault, in a world where the rights of lordship were imposed and the quarrels of neighbours settled by sword or knife as a matter of course, was likely to have been a good deal less surprised by it when it occurred. As the language of English law, which we owe to the Middle Ages, reveals, through its references to 'putting in fear', 'making an affray', and 'keeping the Queen's peace', the medieval world was one in which the distinction between private, civil and foreign war, though recognized, could only be irregularly enforced. Thus battle, though an extreme on the spectrum of experience, was not something unimaginable, something wholly beyond the peace-loving individual's ken. It offered the soldier risk in a particularly concentrated form; but it was a treatment to which his upbringing and experience would already have partially inured him.

CRITICISM

CATHERINE BATT

Malory and Rape†

The evidence for Malory's historical identity has always prompted discussion about how to relate the physical man to the written word.[1] In *The Life and Times of Sir Thomas Malory* (1993), P.J.C. Field garners evidence to identify the author of the *Morte Darthur* with the criminal of Newbold Revel, but Field remains ambiguous about the fundamental question his research raises: how do lived experience and literary fiction inter-relate? The abstract of Field's argument on the book's back cover proclaims the description of Tristram's ghastly time in prison [p. 327, lines 28–37] as the elision of art and life—the observation that a prisoner without health is also without hope ('than hath he cause to wayle and wepe' [p. 327, line 34] carries, it says, 'the urgent note of personal experience.' This transference is not invoked in relation to the bodily integrity at issue in rape, which is also apparently a common element to the biography and the text. We shall see later that Field side-steps this question; and he concludes his study by reaffirming in general terms what he calls 'the gap between the book and the life,' for ultimately we have before us only the (apparently unmediated?) literary text.[2]

Responses to Field's research vary in their stress on the significance of biographical details. Helen Castor's review for *Arthuriana* agrees with Field's conclusion: the extant material offers 'no possibility of reconstructing Malory's emotional and intellectual life'[3] For Tom Shippey, however, in a piece for the *London Review of Books*, Field establishes Thomas Malory's identity beyond doubt and the closing of the interpretative 'gap' is thus a matter of some critical urgency. There are two strands to Shippey's argument: his own account draws text and life together by emphasizing a similarity in their expressions of violence.[4] To some degree he also seeks to maintain the binary opposition of lawless life versus idealizing narrative, and his argument is interesting for the way in

† Reprinted by permission from *Arthuriana* 7, no. 3 (1997), 78–99. The original "works cited" method of reference in this article has been converted to footnotes. For a summary of the criminal charges leveled at Malory, and references to studies of the known documentation, see the chronology on p. xxv.

1. An earlier version of this paper was presented at the 30th International Congress on Medieval Studies, Kalamazoo, 4–7 May, 1995. I wish to thank Ruth Evans and Jennifer Goodman for comments on the original paper, Jocelyn Wogan Browne for response to a subsequent draft, and Richard Ireland for information on the legal background to rape in the fifteenth and sixteenth centuries.
2. Field here raises, but does not directly address, an interesting question about the nature and function of literary biography.
3. Helen Castor, review of P.J.C. Field, *The Life and Times of Sir Thomas Malory*, *Arthuriana* 4.3 (1994): 273. Castor's review is also especially interesting for its astute observations on the complexity of fifteenth-century political culture, with which Field's reconstruction does not seem fully to engage.
4. Tom Shippey, 'Dark Knight.' Rev. of P.J.C. Field, *The Life and Times of Sir Thomas Malory*. *The London Review of Books*. 24 February 1994: 22–24. 'The chivalry [in the text] seems easily compatible with the settling of personal scores' (23). Compare Felicity Riddy's elegant observation, in her book-length study of Malory, that the book invites reading as 'the legitimization of a lawless man's fantasies' [*Sir Thomas Malory*. Leiden: Brill, 1987, p. 7].

which both here and in other studies of the *Morte,* rape is paradigmatic of the perceived hermeneutic difficulty (in this case, for
other scholars) of reconciling author and text. Shippey charts a
general discomfiture over the charges of rape against the historical
Malory, from earlier twentieth-century male critical embarrassment (from Kittredge to Hicks and C. S. Lewis), to the problems
that must now, he claims, surely arise for those whose study of
Malory incorporates contemporary critical approaches. Malory's
spectacular criminal career, says Shippey, must make him 'the
least politically correct author still commonly read. His potential
as a test-case for historicist, feminist, or anthropological
approaches has just been very much expanded.'

Shippey's own explanation, which he presents in such a way as
to suggest that it is free of troublesome ideological baggage, roots
itself in uncritical assumptions about class attitudes: in the *Morte*
the young Lancelot can express outrage at Sir Perys's abuse of
ladies—'(I)s he a theff and a knyght and a ravisher of women? He
doth shame unto the order of knyghthode, and contrary unto his
oth,' [p. 163, lines 33–35] but the historical Malory need see no
contradiction between this idealism and the rape of the non-
aristocratic Mrs Smith. As Shippey dissociates himself and his
explanation from rape as a critical problem, but intimates that it
continues to be a problem for others, the issue clearly emerges as
the site of other contentions. From (debatable) factual evidence
serving to focus the hermeneutic difficulties of relating a particular
author to a particular text, rape comes to be part of the self-
reflexive language of the activity of interpretation itself. Shippey's
writing posits, if only by semantic accident, a need for interpretative violence: in claiming that Field's research 'enforces . . . a
reconsideration' of the *Morte,* Shippey is using the same verb as
Malory's Pentecostal Oath employs for rape, where the knights
swear 'never to enforce' 'ladyes, damesels, and jantilwomen and
wydowes' [p. 77, lines 31–32]. (The verb 'to enforce' already has
more than one meaning in the *Morte* where, in a disturbing overlap
of terminology that echoes Old French literary practice, 'to
enforce' also features more commonly in its reflexive form, with
the sense of 'to exert oneself to feats of arms.'[5] But in Shippey's
review, assumptions about rape itself also appear more explicitly
as the site of aggressive challenges to and anxiety about the validity
and integrity of other critical approaches. Shippey's intimation that
his own stance somehow occupies ideologically and culturally neu-

5. For an example of this latter usage: ' . . . he paynyth hym and enforsyth hym to do grete
   dedys' [p. 217, lines 28–29]. For instances of 'esforcier' in Old French texts, see Kathryn
   Gravdal (*Ravishing Maidens: Writing Rape in Medieval French Literature and Law.* Philadelphia: University of Pennsylvania Press, 1991), who notes in her study of rape in these
   works that 'fame esforcier' can mean to exercise one's martial prowess as well as to violate,
   and suggests that 'rape is part of the feudal hegemony, built into the military culture in
   which force is applauded in most of its forms' (3–4), though I would want to add that
   rape's function and meaning within a discourse of violence need more careful examination
   than this generalization allows for. See also Philippa Maddern's thoughtful treatment of
   fifteenth-century institutionalizations of violence: *Violence and Social Order. East Anglia
   1422–1442.* Oxford Clarendon Press, 1992.

tral ground makes all the clearer the potential uses of rape as metaphor: there is no means of evading the personal in a discussion of
rape, even as one might claim to articulate the contrary.

I have mapped out some of the responses to Field's book, and
one in particular, because it seems to me significant that particular
anxieties about the function and interpretation of literature should
focus on the fact of rape and that they should also find expression
in language that uses rape figuratively. At the root of concern over
establishing who and what Malory was lies perhaps a humanist
anxiety about how to reconcile 'great writing' with a writer deemed
'unethical,' but the very terms of such discussions expose a subjective investment in the material which, left unexamined, produces its own critical impasse. The apparent split between Malory
as criminal and Malory as author of ethical prose constitutes just
such an investment, not so much an adequate representation of
either art or life, or a useful point of departure for literary investigation, as an artefact of the humanist approach, for the latter has
created both this problem-situation and its concomitant alarm over
the unlikelihood of being able to resolve it.[6]

If Malory's historical case rather neatly underlines an occluded
violence in the humanist project, this essay seeks to address the
issue of rape productively through acknowledging the inevitable
element of subjectivity inherent in its representation and investigation. Those critical perspectives that an outside point of view
might claim are embarrassed by rape can offer some of the most
rigorous, because self-aware, means of coming to terms with its
function in literary and cultural contexts. I thus own to the subjectivity of my own perspective in this inquiry.[7] And through an
awareness of what can be at stake in depictions of rape, I want to
look at the kinds of parameters the evidence suggests for the inter-
relations of art and life in this respect.

For, once one accepts the writer-rapist 'paradox' as a false
dichotomy, one can move beyond its limiting configuration of 'ethical' literature versus 'unethical' life and begin to understand something of the diversity of rape's manifestations as cultural and social
phenomenon, in particular what its inscription in Malory's work
reveals of that text. There emerges, from historical documentation
as well as literary writings and critical response, a complex of different attitudes as to what rape constitutes, what it means, and for
whom. Although I offer no new documentation for the historical
Malory's individual case, I would suggest that fifteenth-century life
and the late-medieval text of the *Morte* are not at odds in this

6. Stephanie Jed, in *Chaste Thinking*, offers an extended analysis of the relation between
humanist interpretation and violence (specifically in relation to the Lucretia legend) in
the not altogether different context of Italian Renaissance writings: *Chaste Thinking: The
Rape of Lucretia and the Birth of Humanism*. Bloomington: Indiana University Press, 1989.
7. Elaine Tuttle Hansen's concluding remarks, in her study of Chaucer, on the nature of
feminist approaches to medieval culture, are also relevant to responses to Malory. She
points out how the feminist medievalist 'cannot see her reflection in the texts of the Middle
Ages, and so her starting point and her ending point are different and her desire is different'
(*Chaucer and the Fictions of Gender*. Berkeley: University of California Press, 1992,
p. 290).

respect. The *Morte* too exhibits a range of cultural, legal and literary assumptions, anxieties, masculine concerns, glossings-over and confusion over physical violation and its consequences that would not be unfamiliar to a medieval (or even a modern) English subject. If we abandon the paradigm by which Malory in his private life betrays the idealism of his literary endeavors, we will be able to address more precisely the question of how and why Malory reflects and refracts contemporary legal and cultural concerns about rape in his writings.

English medieval law on rape, and the attitudes it encodes, are hardly uniform in either intention or concern, and the legal records, as we shall see, do not answer all the questions we might want to ask of them. In Malory's text, disparate though not unrelated issues similarly cluster around rape, and while Malory is not wholly systematic in his approach (that he should not be is part of my argument), the *Morte* incorporates some of his culture's legal assumptions and practice. I shall cite specific details and cases in discussion of aspects of Malory's text below. I want first, however, to look at some of the general issues that arise from a consideration of the charges of rape against Thomas Malory himself.

What do the legal documents reveal? The inquisition at Nuneaton of 23 August 1451 * * * shows the rapes as part of a series of violent crimes in which the Malory of Newbold Revel is alleged to have engaged in 1450, beginning with a plot to ambush the Duke of Buckingham on 4 January of that Year. On 23 May he is said to have broken into Hugh Smith's property at Monks Kirby, near Leicester, where he 'feloniously raped and carnally lay by' Joan Smith ('felonice rapuit & cum ea carnaliter concubit'). * * * On 6 August he is said to have again raped the same Joan Smith, in Coventry on this occasion, and stolen her husband's goods. * * * In Malory's case, as with that other famous apparent rapist Chaucer, the precise meaning of the details the extant documents offer, especially with regard to the actions and motives of those involved, is open to debate. The language of the law itself in large part creates this confusion, for it does not distinguish between rape as forced coition and rape as an abduction which does not necessarily involve forcible coition.[8] Argument over Chaucer's behavior towards Cecily Chaumpaigne who in May, 1380, released Chaucer from all actions 'such as they relate to my rape' (de raptu meo'), concentrates especially on this question of terminology, that is, whether *raptus* indicates abduction rather than penetration. Christopher Cannon's recent contextualization and analysis of a memorandum of the case in which the terms of accusation are carefully re-phrased suggests that *raptus* was indeed understood to involve sexual violation.[9] Some seventy years after the writing of this doc-

8. See Philippa Maddern's brief discussion of these terms (100–01), adapted from J.B. Post, 'Ravishment' [see n. 1, p. 801].
9. On the case of Chaucer and Cecily Chaumpaigne, and the modern academic debate surrounding it, see, in addition to Christopher Cannon's more detailed work, Carolyn Dinshaw, and Derek Pearsall: Christopher Cannon, '*Raptus* in the Chaumpaigne Release and a Newly Discovered Document Concerning the Life of Geoffrey Chaucer.' *Speculum*

ument, the record of the accusation against Malory in the *Coram Rege Roll* for Michaelmas term, 1451 * * * uses the same terminology, describing how Hugh Smith accuses Malory 'of the rape of Joan, wife of this same Hugh' (de raptu Johanne vxoris ipsius Hugonis').

If investigation of the documentation surrounding Chaucer's case strengthens the opinion that the charge against Malory is unequivocal, it by no means answers the difficulty of interpreting other aspects of the later case. Especially complicated is the task of determining the volition and intention of those involved, and especially of Joan Smith, in the light of the terms of Ricardian rape legislation, which served to consolidate interests rather different from those of a woman's personal safety and integrity. J. B. Post * * * has detailed with some precision how, from the twelfth century onwards, rape law evolves so as to serve less the needs of the woman concerned than a complex of other social interests.[1] The Statutes of Westminster (1275 and 1285) helped to blur the distinction between rape and abduction and whereas in earlier English law it was the woman who appealed her assailant,[2] the emphasis on abduction and elopement focused attention on the material interests of the woman's family rather than having regard to the woman herself. The details of Westminster II's provision that made 'ravishment' of woman a capital offence, 'although she consent afterwards' * * * seemed more designed to forestall attempts at frustrating family plans for an arranged marriage by absconding with the man of one's choice (and with some of the family fortune) than to offer women themselves protection under the law.

The Statute of Rapes of 1382, 6 Richard II, consolidates this shift in emphasis and accords the husband, the father, or next of kin, the right to make the accusation of rape even though the woman may have consented. Furthermore, the Statute's wording regarding the disinheritance of both 'ravishers . . . and ravished' shows that questions of material damage and compensation receive rather more attention than does the fact of sexual assault. * * * This Statute's primary concern with family and financial interests would be pertinent to any evidence (at present lacking) of a prior relationship between Malory and Joan Smith. But there are also, of course, medieval cases in which rape (as abduction, forced coition, or both) features (as in the later documentation of Malory's case) as elements in accounts of crimes against property,

68 (1993): 74–94; Carolyn Dinshaw, *Chaucer's Sexual Poetics*. Madison: University of Wisconsin Press, 1989, pp. 10–12; Derek Pearsall, *The Life of Geoffrey Chaucer: A Critical Biography*. Oxford: Clarendon Press, 1992, pp. 135–37.

1. See J.B. Post, 'Ravishment of Women and the Statutes of Westminster.' *Legal Records and the Historian*. Ed. J.H. Baker. London: Royal Historical Society, 1978, 150–64; and 'Sir Thomas West and the Statute of Rapes, 1382.' *Bulletin of the Institute of Historical Research* 53 (1980): 24–30.

2. See Patricia Orr, 'Men's Theory and Women's Reality: Rape Prosecutions in the English Royal Courts of Justice, 1194–1222.' *The Rusted Hauberk: Feudal Ideals of Order and Their Decline*. Eds. Liam O. Purdon and Cindy L. Vitto. Gainesville, Fla.: University Press of Florida, 1994, 121–59.

and the charge against Malory could conceivably pertain more closely to the issue of property crime than to a felony against Joan as an individual.[3]

Christine Carpenter, building on Post's researches, argues that the fact that Hugh Smith, and not Joan Smith, brings the charge of rape against Malory, exonerates the latter, because the husband brings the case under this 1382 statute, which suggests that for Joan Smith at least, Malory's behavior was not rape.[4] But the extant evidence also intimates that Joan Smith, as a married woman who had suffered a rape, would not have had any other remedy in law but to allow her husband to bring the case on her behalf. A literary analogue, in Caxton's The History of Reynard the Fox (1481), has Ysegrym the wolf, not the victim, complain to the Lion that Reynard has ravysshyd . . . and forcyed my wyf . . . knavisshly.'[5] This appears to reflect mid- and later-fifteenth century practice in that a rape case may be brought on behalf of a wife by a husband, whatever (and not necessarily 'in spite of') the woman's volition. On this question, Sir William Staunford, writing in 1557, asserts that although a single woman who is without a man's protection may bring a private prosecution, a married woman cannot appeal without her husband, and he cites case law from 1407 in support of this, together with the note that if a woman is raped, and afterwards 'consents' to her rapist/abductor ('ravishour'), her husband alone will have appeal, under the Richard II legislation. In the case to which Staunford refers, however, where a woman is raped in prison, her lack of consent seems beyond doubt, yet the court tells her she may not bring an appeal as an individual, because she has a husband * * * and this record cites the same Ricardian legislation in support of the need for the husband to act as his wife's proxy in the matter.[6]

It is not clear, then, that a full picture of the legal background would unequivocally reveal to us Joan Smith's personal view, especially as the case was never brought to trial.[7] The documents reveal

3. Barbara Hanawalt observes the difficulty, from earlier-fourteenth-century evidence, of distinguishing between rape as 'a personal crime against a woman' and rape as 'a property crime against her husband,' Crime and Conflict in English Communities 1300–1348. Cambridge, Mass.: Harvard University Press, 1978, p. 273. The charge of rape might thus serve to mask other concerns: Philippa Maddern cites cases from 1440 in which charges of housebreaking and rape seem to be a means of punishing a prostitute's customers (101–02).

4. Christine Carpenter, 'Sir Thomas Malory and Fifteenth-century Local Politics.' Bulletin of the Institute of Historical Research 53 (1980): 37–38, n. 54. Similarly, Field declares that in this instance 'the rape charges plainly involve rape in the modern sense rather than (as some have wanted to believe) abduction or assault' (106), but he cites this same statute, apparently in mitigation of Malory's alleged actions. As C.M. Adderley notes, 'Field's refusal to be drawn on this issue characterizes the book' [review of P.J.C. Field, The Life and Times of Sir Thomas Malory. Arthuriana 4.3 (1994): 278].

5. William Caxton, The History of Reynard the Fox. Ed. N.F. Blake. EETS, o.s. 263. London: Oxford University Press, 1970, p. 89.

6. See Sir William Staunford, Les Plees del Coron (1557). Facsimile rpt. Abingdon: Professional Books, 1971, Book II, 61; and Year Book Henry IV and Henry V. Les Reports dels cases en ley, que furent argues en le temps de tres Haut & Puissant Princes Les Roys Henry le IV. & Henry le V. Year Books 1307–1536, Vol. 6. London: George Sawbridge et al., 1679. Facsimile rpt. Abingdon: Professional Books, 1981, p. 21.

7. Emma Hawkes discusses historical evidence for the seriousness accorded women's testimony in medieval rape trials: for discussion of the complexity of Jane Boys's case (1452), from documentation about which Hawkes draws the title for her essay, see also Philippa

the difficulty (then as now) of establishing the woman's volition and show how considerations such as claims of family and concerns over property can make the issue of female volition irrelevant in law.[8] Meanwhile, modern critical discussion seems to interest itself in the case only in so far as it defines Malory: Joan Smith's consent or resistance makes Malory either a romantic gallant or a hooligan.

One of the most significant links between historical rape and rape in literature, from the reported circumstances of Malory's actions and the reactions of commentators, is then a male perspective, ratified in the legal system. Far from seeing the issue of woman's autonomy as central in rape, this view sees the crime as a mesh of other concerns, mediated through a specific male-defined construction of women as social and sexual beings. This ambiguity—rape as part of a masculine definition of social parameters, made real through the use of women's bodies, but not necessarily taking account of 'real' women, and rape as relating primarily to women's interests and the integrity of women as autonomous individuals—makes possible rather different interpretations of the same material. It also means that rape serves several functions within the text. For example, its incidence in the Pentecostal Oath illustrates a disfunction between description and practice, between the prescriptive regulation of society and its members the Oath encodes, and the somewhat different boundaries the pragmatics of chivalric experience reveal. In the episode of the Giant of St Michael's Mount in the *Arthur and Lucius* section of the narrative, meanwhile, rape has a different symbolic political resonance, and apparently figures a monstrous threat from outside the Arthurian community. Treatment of rape may also show the extent to which Malory accommodates Arthurian narrative to the exigencies of late-medieval legal and social practice, as the confusions surrounding the account of Torre's parentage, and the resolution of that episode, suggest [p. 64 ff.]. As the transgression of bodily integrity, rape also has a broad significance, throughout the *Morte,* as the violation of a moral order.

I want especially to examine how and why, although in the *Morte* rape does relate to female integrity, sexual violation is neither the only means of representing woman's wholeness, nor is it an experience unique to women. In general terms, as we shall see the instances mentioned above demonstrate, rape's significance may be 'displaced' from the female subject, to be subsumed into the issue of masculine chivalric identity and integrity (just as in law one might see women's desires subordinated to the demands of

Maddern (101). See Emma Hawkes, ' "She was ravished against her will, what so ever she say": Female Consent in Rape and Ravishment in late-medieval England.' *Limina* 1 (1995): 47–54.

8. On the issue of a woman's consent and the definition of rape in modern law, see Catharine MacKinnon, 'Feminism, Marxism, Method, and the State: Toward a Feminist Jurisprudence,' *Signs* 8 (1983): 635–58. Susan Edwards offers examples from the nineteenth and twentieth centuries of how law often serves to institutionalize prevalent ideological, often contradictory, perspectives on female sexuality: see *Female Sexuality and the Law*. Oxford: Martin Robertson, 1981.

male social control), on an individual as on a corporate level: but most important, Malory's narrative most tellingly investigates the consequences of rape—in terms of its effects on the physical person and its implications for the sense of a moral and social self—not in relation to a female character, but to the person of Lancelot, even though Lancelot's experiences of violation are partially on the planes of potentiality and fantasy.[9] In particular I shall look at how Malory appropriates for Lancelot the terms of the experience of rape, which is typically something men 'do' to women, as part of the definition of his narrative's hero, as a logical development of the uses of the physical in his discourse. For the fact of rape has particular significance in the *Morte* because of the intensity with which Malory invests the physical with a meaning beyond itself:[1] the body is the locus of honour and of shame, the site of strength and the means to the assertion of selfhood, yet simultaneously the locus of vulnerability. The language of the Pentecostal Oath apparently recognizes this and privileges respect for a woman's body and her autonomy at the same time as it guarantees her claim to legal rights:

> . . . than the Kynge stablysshed all the knyghtes and gaff them rychesse and londys—and charged them never to do outerage nothir mourthir . . . and allwayes to do ladyes, damesels, and jantilwomen and wydowes [socour], strengthe hem in hir ryghtes, and never to enforce them, upon payne of dethe.
>
> [p. 77, lines 27–33]

What one assumes is an eyeskip on the part of the Winchester manuscript scribe, produces, in the omission of the word 'socour,' an interesting dislocation of syntax which complements the ambiguity of the pronouncement here on woman's position in Arthurian society. The wording of the Oath, if it grants a woman legal rights, also places her in a social context in which her integrity might relate to concerns outside her self, specifically to the masculine definitions of the parameters of knighthood.[2] The Oath has echoes

9. Because I am specifically concerned with rape in this essay, I do not here discuss other extraordinary threats to Lancelot's physical person, which, though dramatic and significant, do not involve intentionality on the part of the agents. A typical example is the case of mistaken identity in Sir Belleus's pavilion, where the owner embraces Lancelot thinking him to be his female lover, which rewrites the situation in the French source, where the confusion is reciprocal and Lancelot, thinking Belleus to be a woman, takes him in his arms before each realizes his error, with rather more violent consequences than Malory's version records [see p. 722—Editor]. This change is part of the general objectification of Lancelot characteristic of his *Tale*, and which I am exploring at greater length in a separate study. Another (undignified) instance of Lancelot's accidental 'violation' is his wounding by a huntress in the latter part of the *Morte* [p. 619, line 3–p. 620, line 11]. For a scholarly, meticulous and thought-provoking account of this episode, which concentrates particularly on the constructions of gender and on the significance of unintentionality, see Catherine LaFarge, 'The Hand of the Huntress: Repetition and Malory's *Morte Darthur*.' *New Feminist Discourses. Critical Essays on Theories and Texts.* Ed. Isobel Armstrong. London: Routledge, 1992, 263–79.

1. The seminal work on Malory's articulation of meaning through the physical is Jill Mann's short piece 'Malory: Knightly Combat in *Le Morte D'Arthur*.' *The New Pelican Guide to English Literature.* Ed. Boris Ford. Vol. 1. Harmondsworth: Penguin, 1982: 331–39.

2. Caxton omits the prohibition of rape in his edition of the *Morte* (see the footnote to Field's revision of Vinaver's edition, [O³] 120), thus dismantling an important aspect of the *Morte*'s construction of violence and its ambivalence.

of the chivalric vows of Arthurian romance and of the regulations
pertaining to late medieval chivalric ritual, social as well as literary,
such as, Richard Barber has * * * pointed out, the investiture of
Knights of the Bath.³ But with respect to the treatment of women,
Malory's wording has closer parallels in documents relating to
other areas. It is reminiscent of earlier English jurisdiction on rape,
but also of fifteenth-century military provision for women's safety
in time of war, a provision we find expressed in other literary works
and in historical documents. The statute of Edward II, Westminster II (1285), Henry V's declaration at Mantes in 1419, and the
warning to Arthur's troops on campaign in the *Alliterative Morte
Arthure,* all share with Malory the threat of the death penalty for
rape and, in particular, the sovereign's interest in ensuring due
observance of the law.⁴

These echoes of legal provision, especially those for times of
heightened violence, stress the sovereign's judicial power, along
with his authority to prosecute rape as a crime primarily against
the king's peace. They also highlight the fact of woman's social
definition in the *Morte* as physically and sexually vulnerable, even
as they proclaim her 'rights.'⁵ But this cultural positioning of
woman, whereby the threat to and defence of her integrity potentially come from the same quarter, in addition emphasizes the
inherent tension in the operation of violence in the *Morte* as a

3. For an example of French 'Arthurian' regulations, see E. Sandoz, 'Tourneys in the Arthurian Tradition.' *Speculum* 19 (1944): 389–420. Richard Barber argues that the closest
parallel to the Pentecostal Oath is the text pertaining to the making of a Knight of the
Bath, but in relation to women the text for the ceremony asks only that 'ye schall sustene
wydowes in their right at every tyme they wol requere yow and maydenys in their virginite
and helpe hem and socoure hem with yowre good that for lak of good they be not mys-
governyd': See Richard Barber, 'Malory's *Le Morte Darthur* and Court Culture under
Edward IV.' *Arthurian Literature XII.* Ed. James P. Carley and Felicity Riddy. Cambridge:
D.S. Brewer, 1994, 133–55. [For the full text of the oath see p. 781, and cf. the other
texts printed under "Chivalry in Principle," p. 777—Editor.]
4. Thus Westminster II:
   'It is provided that if a man from henceforth do ravish a woman, married maid, or other,
where she did not consent, neither before or after, he shall have judgment of life and
member. And like-wise where a man ravisheth a woman, married lady, Damosel, or other,
with force, although she consent after he shall have such judgment as before is said, if he
attained at the king's suit, and there the king shall have the suit' (translated in John
Marshall Carter, *Rape in Medieval England: An Historical And Sociological Study.* New
York: University Press of America, 1985, pp. 36–37.
   Henry V's *Ordinances of War* declare that: 'no man be so hardy to sle ne enforte no
woman uppon (peyne of deth)'. *Ordinances of War Made by King Henry Vat Mawnt,* in
The Black Book of the Admiralty. Ed. Sir Travers Twiss. Rolls Series 55. London: Longman
and Company, 1871, I. 460. [For another example of regnal censure of rape, see Edward
IV's 1461 Act of Attainder, p. 774—Editor.] In the *Alliterative Morte Arthure,* the King
assures the Duchess of Lorraine, and other aristocratic ladies who plea for mercy (ll. 3049–
3053), that the inhabitants of their besieged city will not be violated: 'Shall no[n] myssedo
ȝow, ma dame, that to me lenges!' (l.3057), a promise Malory retains in his version of the
episode [p. 148, lines 1–4]. In the poem, after the fall of Como, Arthur stipulates the
death-penalty for rapists: * * *
   [In each division the king had proclaimed that no liegeman loyal to him should, on pain
of loss of life, limb, and property, lie with any woman, or with any faithful maidens, or
with any citizen's wife . . .]
   Again, Malory preserves this detail [p. 148, lines 37–41].
5. Malory is remarkably inclusive in his defence of women's rights. See Carter on the way
in which legal commentators view rape differently according to whether or not the victim
is a virgin, and Barber (149) for the different treatment of sexually-experienced women
and of maidens, recommended to the Knights of the Bath, cited in note 3 above: the
former have legal 'rights,' the latter have to be properly 'governed,' to ensure they are not
corrupted.

whole. The law acknowledges, and then seeks to contain and redirect, masculine aggression. The Oath assumes that it is women who are sexually violable, and whose identities relate to that sexual violability, while men are subject to more generalized forms of physical violence and may retaliate by exercising violence themselves. But in the context of the Oath, and in the rest of the narrative, the preservation of Woman's 'wholeness' can serve rather to figure an individual knight's integrity, and the consolidation of the rule of law, than to illuminate individual women's relation to their environment.

If rape in the Pentecostal Oath calls to our notice the internal tensions in the Arthurian social order, the *Morte* also develops a rhetoric for rape as signal of the anti-social, the threat from the margins, that against which the community defines itself.[6] The most horrifying details of male-female rape in the *Morte* are part of the description of the outrages committed by the Giant of Saint Michael's Mount. Here rape is unequivocally the mark of the monstrous. The Giant, the Old Woman tells a shocked Arthur, has abducted, raped and murdered the Duchess of Brittany: 'he forced hir by fylth of hymself, and so aftir slytte hir unto the navyll' [p. 122, lines 34–35]. It is his custom to kill women in the gratification of his appetite. The three women now preparing his food, says the Old Woman, 'shall be dede within foure oures or the fylth is fulfylled that his fleyshe askys' [p. 123, lines 12–13]. The account of the Duchess's death and of the fate that awaits the Giant's servants are from the *Alliterative Morte Arthure* (ll. 976–79, 1031–32, respectively). But Malory further invokes the violation of the feminine to emphasize the Giant's rapacity. In the source, the monster is anxious for Arthur's beard to add to a cloak already adorned with the hair of fifteen kings who are subject to him (ll. 998–1018). Here, however, although the cloak is mentioned, it is not the subject of a threat to Arthur's figurative and physical integrity, and the Giant's desire for Guinevere, whom the 'carefull wydow' twice expressly names as 'Arthurs wyff' [p. 122, line 40; p. 123, line 6], replaces this particular menace to Arthur's person. The gruesome physical details of the Giant's behaviour divert attention from what the Pentecostal Oath recognizes as the potential actuality of rape as a threat from within. In this adventure, rape (on the part of the Giant), and not raping (which Arthur's prohibition to his troops reinforces [p. 148, lines 37–41], are central to the definition of Arthur and his male Christian community. Guinevere, meanwhile, emblematizes the integrity of both ruler and Arthurian community in general. But if the stress on the Giant's sexual violence discourages us from considering too deeply to what extent Arthur and his opponent might have military ambitions and imperialist plans in common, the Duchess of Brittany's experience, abducted 'as she rode . . . with her ryche knyghtes' [p. 121,

---

6. For an argument that rape is in general to be characterized as such, see Roy Porter, 'Rape—Does it have a Historical Meaning?' *Rape: An Historical and Cultural Inquiry*. Eds Sylvana Tomaselli and Roy Porter. Oxford University Press, 1986, 216–36.

lines 23–25], in part foreshadows Guinevere's own abduction by Meleagaunt [p. 625, line 22–p. 626, line 37]. The implicit equation in the earlier narrative between the possible violation of Guinevere and the loss of the Arthurian kingdom's integrity will later work itself through in terms other than the figurative and speculative, with the threat of violence again coming from within the community.

Even when it seems most closely allied with a definition of the alien, rape is not simply definable in the text as the marker of an external threat to the social system. Anxiety about rape within the social order, and a consequent move to consolidate a propriety for that order, dominate Malory's revision of the story of Torre's parentage, which tells of Pellinor's rape of a beautiful young woman. In the source, the *Suite du Merlin,* this story is told twice, first by Merlin and later by the woman concerned. As in Malory's version, the truth comes to light when Tor appears before Arthur's wedding, anxious to be made a knight, to the bewilderment of his cowherd father. In the *Suite* there is no censure of Pellinor's rape of the young woman, though the narrative makes plain his violence and her distress and resistance and recounts his subsequent theft of her greyhound: indeed, the promise that Tor will make a 'bon chevalier' would seem to be enough to vindicate his behaviour. But this version also has the woman take upon herself the moral guilt attaching to the violence done to her: she speaks of her 'sin' which, she says, Merlin, unlike other devils who, as we know, always want individuals to hide and conceal their misdemeanours, forces her to 'reveal' to others. * * *

Malory's drastically abbreviated account of this episode substitutes a confusing testimony on the part of the woman involved which makes it impossible to establish either rape or consent: 'there mette with me a sterne knyght, and half be force he had my maydynhode' [p. 65, lines 5–6]. This has the effect of bypassing the moral issue, but an awareness of the legal context also suggests that, puzzling as this 'semi-rape' initially seems, Malory is trying to make sense of his source by correlating the facts of the case with late-medieval English law. Legal doctrine, drawing on medical knowledge as promulgated by Galen onwards, did not admit of the possibility of conception if the female did not consent to the act, and while there was later debate, both legal and medical, over the reliability of this long-lived opinion,[7] it certainly had some force in practice, as the records of an early-fourteenth-century case testify. A certain Joan sued an appeal of rape against 'E.', by whom she had borne a child, only to have the case dismissed because the existence of the child told against her: E. was deemed not guilty because 'it was said it was a wonder, for a child could not be conceived without the will of both.[8] * * * In Malory's

7. See Thomas Laquer, *Making Sex: Body and Gender from the Greeks to Freud.* Cambridge, Mass.: Harvard University Press, 1990, pp. 161–62.
8. See *Year Books of Edward II: The Eyre of Kent 6 & 7 Edward II. A.D. 1313–1314.* Eds F.W. Maitland, L.W.V. Harcourt and W.C. Bolland. Vol. 1. Selden Society 24. London: Bernard Quaritch, 1910, p. 111.

example, no one debates this biological assumption because the woman's own witness implicitly (and conveniently for the narrative focus on masculine chivalry) acknowledges what Torre's conception has itself 'proved.'

Malory compounds confusion over Torre's mother's social status by having her tell how this encounter took place while she was out milking, but following the *Suite* in having Pellinor steal the girl's greyhound, 'he . . . seyde he wolde kepe the grayhounde for my love' [p. 65, lines 8–9]. The *Suite* version reflects a brutal pastourelle-like world in which the claims of the masculine chivalric community override respect for fellow-beings,[9] but Malory, in the blurring of the woman's status, signals something of the otherness of the Arthurian world at the same time as he rationalizes it by confirming the familiar nature of its social structures. A concern with legal remedy emerges again when, in conversation with the son, Merlin speculates on the possibility of Pellinor's being of some material benefit to both mother and child: 'youre fadir . . . may ryght well avaunce you and youre modir both . . . ' [p. 65, lines 13–15]. This conforms to the fifteenth-century legal provision that absent fathers pay maintenance for their children.[1]

The report of 'half-rape' is not, however, aberrant in a narrative that does not accord any great prominence to woman's experience: it is telling that, for example, Torre's mother and the Duchess of Brittany remain anonymous, though we know the names of their husbands. In its tendency to obscure what constitutes 'full' assault on female physical integrity, the book, like the culture in which it is written, does not deploy a vocabulary of violation with any precision, nor does the language offer any sure guide to determining woman's sexual volition. From the very beginning, the *Morte* lacks a consistent terminology for rape. The Pentecostal Oath's technical term, 'enforce,' appears rarely: the imprecise 'to lie with' can signify casual brutality, as when it describes the Giant of St Michael's Mount's initial treatment of the Duchess of Brittany [p. 121, lines 24–25]. In *A Noble Tale of Sir Launcelot du Lake*, the damsel uses it in her terse report to the hero of the rapist-knight Perys's activities: 'at the leste he robbyth (ladyes) other lyeth by hem' [p. 163, lines 31–32]. Perys's crimes may be wholly sexual: 'to rob,' may suggest (by analogy with the Middle English idiom to rob one's virginity'[2]) the rape of a virgin, but this verb is not used consistently in the narrative to describe rape which is also defloration (as we have seen at [p. 148, lines 37–41]. But 'to lie with' can signal intercourse for which both partners are willing, as in,

9. See Kathryn Gravdal (104–21) for an examination of rape in the world of the pastourelle: Vitz offers a perspective on pastourelle as female fantasy diametrically opposed to Gravdal's stance and which suggests a greater scope for rape's literary function than Gravdal's reading allows, but this narrative stresses the sexual violence of the encounter, and the knight's control: See Evelyn Birge Vitz, 'Rereading Rape in Medieval Literature.' *Partisan Review* 63 (1996): 280–91.

1. See Richard Helmholz, *Marriage Litigation in Medieval England.* Cambridge: Cambridge University Press, 1974, pp. 108–09.

2. The *Middle English Dictionary*, under 'rob', 3a), cites examples of this idiom from Gower and the *Ayenbite of Inwit*.

for instance, Gawain's spring-time seduction of Ettarde [p. 104, lines 40–41].

Such vague terminology implicitly leads us to consider the relation between female volition and physical engagement in other sexual encounters. The fact of sexual deceit tends not to be cause for an in-depth analysis of feminine integrity: the women involved in the central conceptions in the *Morte,* of Arthur himself, and of Galahad, for example, resign themselves to greater forces, whether social or belonging to a higher destiny. At the beginning of the narrative Uther, with Merlin's help, tricks Ygerne, who has already resisted his advances, and who would certainly not have accepted him had she known his true identity. But the issue of near-rape and sexual betrayal is subsumed in Ygerne's articulation of sexual congress and the dangers of childbirth as elements of wifely loyalty and duty, in evidence when the pregnant queen tells Uther: 'ther came . . . a man lyke my lord . . . and soo I went unto bed with hym as I ought to do with my lord' [p. 6, lines 11–15], and when she later explains events to the assembled court [p. 33, lines 1–13]. Elaine too, in respect of the events necessary to ensure the conception of Galahad, while she suggests to Lancelot that he is under some obligation to her since she is not going to charge him with the irrevocable loss of her maidenhood, simultaneously declares her own acceptance of the workings of higher forces: 'I have obeyde me unto the prophesye that my fadir tolde me. And . . . I have gyvyn the the . . . fayryst floure that ever I had, and that is my maydenhode that I shall never have agayne. And therefore, jantyll knyght, owghe me youre good wyll' [p. 466, lines 9–14]. If female volition in sexual matters is glossed over, or briefly acknowledged and then overridden by other demands, whether social or narrative, the text does not so easily accommodate similar instances of Lancelot's loss of physical integrity and of his lack of volition in sexual matters.

Women's heroism then appears to relate to their consent to the use of their bodies in the service of particular institutions (often to the great convenience of the narrative): but while the Pentecostal Oath defines women's integrity and identity in terms of their rapeability and the defence of their bodies by others, such a definition by no means accounts for or delimits their function in the *Morte.* The narrative is particularly reticent on the subject of the consequences of violation for the individual. Often, those who suffer in this way die soon after their ordeal, and while we might ascribe to the author a range of impulses to account for these deaths, from a narratorial delicacy of feeling to simple lack of interest, the fact of death highlights the emblematic function the raped woman has in the story, as is the case with the Duchess of Brittany and the Giant's other victims in the *Arthur and Lucius* episode, or with the violated of the *Book of the Sankgreal.*

This latter set of adventures, which insists most markedly on the preservation of a sexually-defined bodily integrity (and for the Grail knights as for women), provides instances of women whose rapes

underline the heinousness of the evil against which the major characters are engaged: the duke's daughter raped by seven brothers at
the Castle of Maidens [p. 514, lines 14–37], and the lady raped
by her three brothers [p. 568, lines 38–45], are elements in episodes retrospectively glossed as exemplary of the continuing struggle against evil and the ultimate triumph of the good. These rape
stories may express compassion for, but do not dwell on, the
women's pain. Feminine integrity on an individuated level is
instead manifest in other ways. Perceval's Sister's blood sacrifice
on the Grail Quest, for example [p. 570, line 30–p. 572, line 34],
bespeaks her physical integrity and her spiritual wholeness
through other means than resistance to a threat to her virginity.
In Malory's narrative it is not then primarily in relation to rape that
women find heroic definition, though rape may serve to 'place'
some of the minor characters functionally. The narrative acknowledges the physical horrors of rape, but gives scant attention to
individual women's reactions to rape.

Catharine Coats has observed how in literary treatments of rape
'the response of the female to acts of violence may be far more
significant than the abuse of power by the male.'[3] As the above
examples demonstrate, feminine volition is not always at issue in
the *Morte*'s rape episodes. Instead, I have suggested, there is a
general tendency to accord a representational function to women
in rape situations, and the narrative displaces consideration of the
effects of rape and of the consequences of resistance to definition
in sexual terms, from the female subject to the person of Lancelot.
In the remainder of this essay I want to look at the importance of
this form of threat to Lancelot's integrity for the definition of the
hero, and for the *Morte*'s expression of anxiety about masculine
identity. For, through the hero, Malory problematizes the terms of
social sexual differentiation that the Pentecostal Oath establishes
for the narrative.

The Pentecostal Oath's demarcation of particular boundaries for
male and female behaviour does not admit of the possibility of
male on male rape. The only man in the *Morte* to suffer what one
assumes to be rape is one of the religious of the quest of the Sankgreal, who reports coyly to the Grail knights of his experience at
the hands of the criminal knights of the castle of Carteloyse ' . . .
such shame had never man as I had . . . with the three bretherne'
[p. 569, lines 5–6].[4] As with the other rapes in that section, as we
have seen, the physical horrors suffered by minor characters are
the measure of the evil of those dark forces against which the
chaste heroes contend and are successful. The indignities the man
suffers are passed over, but the most lurid account of attempted
sexual assault in the *Morte*, and of its potential aftermath, relates

---

3. Catharine Randall Coats, 'Rape as Narrative Strategy: En-texting Woman in "Her Place"—
   A Review Essay of Kathryn Gravdal, *Ravishing Maidens*.' *Romanic Review* 84 (1993): 215.
4. The French text is (a little) more explicit on this point: the priest's counterpart in the
   Queste del Saint Graal tells the grail knights that as soon as he arrived on the scene, the
   wicked knights 'wrought me such shame that I could not have suffered worse humiliation
   from the Saracens themselves, had they held me captive' * * *.

to another man, the young Lancelot. *A Noble Tale* initially presents us with what we might term normative examples of violence and assault and their relation to gender in this society: rape certainly figures generally as the marker of female integrity, and Lancelot does service to men and women alike in ridding the countryside first of an oppressor of knights and then of a rapist, who made it his business 'to destroy and dystresse ladyes, damesels, and jantyllwomen' [p. 164, lines 15–16]. But the *Morte*'s sexist (and of course unequal) terms of individual social integrity—women are rapeable, men risk defeat in battle—are remarkably fluid in relation to Lancelot, who is in his *Tale* especially the object of feminine interest, manipulation and desire in a largely female-controlled plot. Malory also changes some of the terms on which women relate to the hero in the source-text, omitting in his account several episodes in the French Prose *Lancelot* where women suffer violence from others because of some link with Lancelot, or where Lancelot himself is violent towards them.[5] In Malory's work, the more marked interest on the part of the female characters in Lancelot's sexuality and his sexual commitment is not, however, a comment on a woman's predatory nature as much as a projection of the reader's traditional apprehension of the Lancelot of romance (that is, one who is defined by his relationship with Guinevere). The ladies who throughout the *Tale* inquire about his sex life, such as the damsel who marvels that he is 'a knyght wyveles' [p. 164, line 24], simply echo the reader's prurient interest in what space the narrative is likely to afford the subject of adultery.

The Lancelot-Guinevere relationship is unspeakable, beyond the terms of the narrative's and the hero's language, but at the same time the narrative is predicated upon it, so it is fitting that desire for Lancelot, and for knowledge of what and who Lancelot is, should manifest itself as a transgressive desire for his body, one that also upsets the terms of the Pentecostal Oath. Lancelot's encounter with Hallewes the sorceress represents the culmination of the *Tale*'s general interest in his physical person and his commodification as hero. Lancelot experiences something of the dehumanizing effect of rape when Hallewes, foiled in her attempt to trap the hero, reveals how, had she succeeded, his body might have been simply the material witness of her ascendency over Guinevere:

' . . . and sytthen I myght nat rejoyse the nother thy body on lyve, I had kepte no more joy in this worlde but to have thy body dede:

¶ "Than wolde I have bawmed hit and sered hit, and so to have kepte hit my lyve dayes—and dayly I sholde have clypped

---

5. For comment on women's encounters with violence because of Lancelot in the French romance, see Albert Hartung, 'Narrative Technique, Characterization, and the Sources in Malory's "Tale of Sir Lancelot," ' *Studies in Philology* 70 (1973): 267. A striking incident Malory omits is the *Lancelot*'s report of the hero's behaviour in his madness, when 'he did not meet a woman nor a damsel to whom he did not do violence before he left her.' * * *

the and kyssed the, dispyte of Quene Gwenyvere [p. 172, lines 19–24].

Lancelot's adventure is of course very different from male-female rape, in the text or elsewhere, because Lancelot's assumed moral and social integrity together here guarantee his physical wholeness. Perhaps more specifically, his heroic and reflexive responses to adventure—such as his willingness to meet the threat of the thirty ghostly knights, and his refusal to give up the sword of the perilous chapel at the request of the lovely and imperious anonymous damsel [p. 171, line 18–p. 172, line 14]—seem to guard him from vulnerability to Hallewes's power, as though his chivalry functioned as some kind of protective grace. The threat to him is ultimately illusory: the frustrated Hallewes quickly pines away and dies 'within a fourtenyte' [p. 172, line 29], in her fate similar to the women who themselves suffer rape elsewhere in the *Morte*. But Hallewes's desire and the form it takes make a further comment on the nature of the reader's apprehension of Lancelot as literary hero. If one sees in Hallewes's covetousness of Lancelot's corpse (in default of his whole person) an impulse to possession as 'preservation' (albeit perverse) rather than as violation, that desire suitably figures a readerly impulse to 'fix' a 'consistent' Lancelot and his meaning in a definition that both grows out of the tradition of Lancelot as hero and yet can neither fully contain nor account for him, just as he is more than the sum of his admiring fellow-courtiers' reports of him at the end of the *Noble Tale*. At the same time, the repulsive fantasy of an obscene, 'out-of-bounds' physical possession of Lancelot also figures the transgressive nature of his heroic person, as lover and as knight. If Lancelot escapes this experience with virtue and body and apparently uncontaminated, the tensions surrounding that subjective definition of him do not disperse with Hallewes's death, but are to gather all the more worryingly later in the *Morte,* as part of Malory's anxiety-ridden configuration of the hero's masculine identity.

The anxiety evident in the possibilities of sexualizing and objectifying Lancelot's person extends also to the question of his volition in sexual matters. Lancelot's case is in marked contrast to both Ygrayne's and Elaine's response to their respective situations, and Lancelot is unique in the *Morte* for the attention he draws to the fact of his sexual betrayal: repeatedly he denies his consent to the fathering of Galahad: 'ye and Dame Brusen made me for to lye be you, magry myne hede' he tells Elaine [p. 485, lines 10–12][6]. Malory here registers Lancelot's distress, in equal measure with the redemptive aspect of his deception, the resultant 'good knight' Galahad. Lancelot seems here again to be resisting his traditional narrative definition, just as he has earlier resisted the move to make

6. Lancelot's lack of volition is made clear from the beginning: of the hero, Brusen promises Pelles that she will 'make hym to lye wyth youre doughter' [p. 464, line 33]. Later, Lancelot reports to Guinevere that 'he was made to lye by [Elaine]' [p. 470, line 15].

him into an object, which is similarly part of what we might call his narrative inheritance.

Like the fantasy of the rape of Lancelot's body, the hero's vigorous disavowal of responsibility for Galahad's conception presents us with another reversal of normative gender definitions, offering an unusual slant on masculine volition in the medieval formulation noted earlier, by which the consent of both parties is requisite for conception to take place. Indeed, Lancelot's position as unwilling father is even more traumatic for him in the light of what Vern Bullough observes is a 'widespread' medieval belief that female orgasm itself 'involved special efforts by the male.'[7] Arthur Brittan has suggested that central to hegemonic masculinity is the way in which 'men collectively appropriate women's reproductive labour in the family and in the public domain.'[8] The appropriation of Lancelot's reproductive power in the interests of the perpetuation and fulfilment of a chivalric ethos and of the Arthurian narrative leads to a crisis-point in the *Morte* Lancelot's sense of identity.

Ultimately, the community of readers, participating characters, the court and narrative pressures, all co-opt Lancelot into a heroic identity that does not fully account for him as an individual. And Lancelot's resistance to others control of him appears manifest in areas in which women's integrity is commonly defined; his body is recognizably vulnerable and violable. If the Pentecostal Oath defines women in these latter terms and men in terms of feats of arms and the regulation of their violent behaviour, Lancelot clearly belongs to both categories. But this perhaps presents us not so much with a 'feminized' Lancelot as with a critique of established classifying boundaries, pointing to a crisis in masculinity and its modes of control: Malory's modifications in his presentation of Lancelot are ultimately inconclusive gender reversals that draw on the fragmented and disjunctive nature of the hero's function already present in the source texts, but through them he registers a masculine identity in crisis straining against the narrative forms of heroic definition.

I would suggest then that to interpret rape as paradigmatic of the difficulties of resolving art and life, to view the *Morte* as exemplary of an ethical ideal, although its author appears unfortunately possessed of a shabby personal history, is to bypass the problems rape should make us confront, whether in literature or in reality, and to avoid difficult questions about how its treatment both implicates and reflects social, moral, literary and critical values in general. The issue of rape links the textual with the extratextual in that one cannot examine it in isolation from the politically and socially shaped narrative constructs in which it is embedded, whether those are literary, legal or historical documents. One might also observe that to appropriate rape's issues of integrity and volition

7. Vern Bullough, 'On Being a Male in the Middle Ages.' *Medieval Masculinities. Regarding Men in the Middle Ages.* Ed. Clare A. Lees, with Thelma Fenster and JoAnn McNamara. Minneapolis: University of Minnesota Press, 1994, 40.
8. Arthur Brittan, *Masculinity and Power.* Oxford: Basil Blackwell, 1989, p. 141.

for the purposes of illuminating a male literary character and, correlatively, to disregard or gloss over women's active and individual responses to rape, is not incompatible with the perspective of an apparent rapist.

At the same time, that very appropriation demonstrates an acute sensitivity to the issues at stake for the individual in cases of rape. Rape, particularly through the questions it raises about the interrelation of integrity and identity, writes large the tensions underlying the Arthurian world of the *Morte*. In the Pentecostal Oath, the law on rape serves to define the parameters of aggression and emblematizes the ambivalence of violence at the heart of the Arthuriad. But the narrative also makes clear, through the treatment of rape, through the diversity of roles women take up and through the person of Lancelot, that such definitions do not serve adequately either to describe or to prescribe social behaviour. In the story of Torre's parentage contemporary legal doctrine and provision disregard female volition in favour of what are perceived as 'broader' social claims. But in arguing that sexual assault on Lancelot's body can function as a logical conclusion to, and comment upon, traditional interpretative strategies of the hero, I would claim further that Malory appropriates the language of sex, power and coercion and deploys it across genders, not only in a manner that represents the inadequacy of regulation as a means of accounting for experience, but as part of an expression of anxiety, and perhaps disillusion, over the possible comforts for the masculine of the whole Arthurian project.

WILLIAM CAXTON

Prologue and Epilogue to the 1485 Edition†

[Prologue]

After that I had accomplysshed and fynysshed dyvers° hystoryes as wel of contemplacyon as of other hystoryal and worldly actes of grete conquerours and prynces, and also certeyn bookes of ensaumples° and doctryne,° many noble and dyvers gentylmen[1] of thys royame° of Englond camen and demaunded° me many and

diverse

morals / instruction

realm / asked of

---

† Ed. Stephen H. A. Shepherd from the text of the Pierpont Morgan copy of Caxton's 1485 edition, printed with permission of the Pierpont Morgan Library, New York. With the exception of references to book numbers in the edition, roman numerals have been converted to arabic numerals. Paragraphing is editorial. For an overview of the place of Caxton's edition in the history of Malory's work, see the chronology on p. xxvii. A good point of departure for further study of Caxton is Norman F. Blake, *William Caxton and English Literary Culture* (London: Hambledon Press, 1991).

1. There has been much informed speculation about the identity of the "noble gentlemen" who Caxton claims are the agents, if not patrons, of this edition, but no conclusive evidence has surfaced; their existence may even be a (marketable) fiction. For a discussion of the issue, see the essay by Carol Meale (reprinted in this volume, esp. p. 866).

oftymes, wherefore that I have not do° made and enprynte° the
noble hystorye of the Saynt Greal° and of the moost renomed°
Crysten kyng, fyrst and chyef of the thre best Crysten and Worthy,[2]
Kyng Arthur, whyche ought moost to be remembred emonge us
Englysshemen tofore° al other Crysten kynges; for it is notoyrly°
knowen thorough the unyversal world that there been 9 Worthy
and the best that ever were; that is to wete, thre paynyms,° thre
Jewes, and thre Crysten men. As for the paynyms, they were tofore°
the Incarnacyon of Cryst, whiche were named: the fyrst, Hector
of Troye, of whome th'ystorye is comen° bothe in balade and in
prose; the second, Alysaunder the Grete; and the thyrd, Julyus
Cezar, Emperour of Rome, of whome th'ystoryes ben wel kno° and
had. And as for the three Jewes whyche also were tofore
th'Yncarnacyon of our Lord, of whome the fyrst was Duc Josue,°
whyche brought the chyldren of Israhel into the Londe of Byheste,°
the second, Davyd, Kyng of Jherusalem, and the thyrd, Judas
Machabeus,° of these thre the Byble reherceth al theyr noble hystoryes and actes.

    And sythe° the sayd Incarnacyon have ben thre noble Crysten
men stalled° and admytted thorugh the unyversal world into the
nomber of the 9 Beste and Worthy, of whome was fyrst the noble
Arthur, whos noble actes I purpose to wryte in thys present book
here folowyng; the second was Charlemayn, or Charles the Grete,
of whome th'ystorye is had in many places bothe in Frensshe and
Englysshe; and the thyrd and last was Godefray of Boloyn,° of whos
actes and lyf I made a book unto th'excellent prynce and kyng of
noble memorye, Kyng Edward the Fourth.[3] The sayd noble jentylmen instantly° requyred me t'emprynte° th'ystorye of the sayd
noble kyng and conquerour Kyng Arthur and of his knyghtes, wyth
th'ystorye of the Saynt Greal, and of the deth and endyng of the
sayd Arthur, affermyng that I ought rather t'enprynte his actes and
noble feates than of Godefroye of Boloyne or ony° of the other
eyght, consyderyng that he was a man borne wythin this royame,
and kyng and emperour of the same, and that there ben in
Frensshe dyvers and many noble volumes of his actes and also of
his knyghtes.

    To whome I answerd that dyvers men holde oppynyon that there
was no suche Arthur, and that alle suche bookes as been maad of
hym ben but fayned° and fables, bycause that somme cronycles
make of hym no mencyon ne remembre hym noothynge, ne of his

had / printed
Holy Grail / renowned

ahead of / well

pagans

prior to

made available

known

Joshua
Promise

Maccabeus

since
honorably seated

Bouillon

insistently / to print

any

fictitious

<hr>

2. I.e., the three finest most worthy Christian kings. Caxton is about to summarize the theme
of the "Nine Worthies," a popular chivalric pantheon introduced by Jacques de Longuyon
in his *Voeux du Paon* ("Vows of the Peacock," 1312).
3. Godfrey of Bouillon was one of the leaders of the (for the West, remarkably successful)
First Crusade, and was elected King of Jerusalem in 1099. In 1481 (November 20) Caxton
had printed the *Siege of Jerusalem,* his own translation of a French source, and a somewhat
legendary account of Godfrey's exploits. The translation was dedicated to Edward IV, and
Caxton declared in its preface that one of his purposes in publishing it was to encourage
a renewed resistance to Muslim control of the East. To complete his representation of
the three Christian Worthies, Caxton would print, on December 1, 1485, just four months
after printing *Le Morte Darthur,* the prose romance of *Charles the Grete,* another of his
own translations from the French.

knyghtes. Wherto they answerd—and one in specyal[4] sayd—that in hym that shold say or thynke that there was never suche a kyng callyd Arthur myght wel be aretted° grete folye and blyndenesse; for he sayd that there were many evydences of the contrarye. Fyrst ye may see his sepulture° in the monasterye of Glastyngburye.° And also in *Polycronycon*,[5] in the 5° book, the syxte chappytre, and in the seventh book, the 23 chappytre, where his body was buryed and after founden and translated° into the sayd monasterye. Ye shal se also in th'ystory of Bochas, in his book *De Casu Principum*,[6] parte of his noble actes and also of his falle; also Galfrydus, in his *Brutysshe Book*,[7] recounteth his lyf. And in dyvers places of Englond many remembraunces ben yet of hym, and shall remayne perpetuelly, and also of his knyghtes. Fyrst in the Abbey of Westmestre° at Saynt Edwardes shryne remayneth the prynte° of his seal in reed° waxe closed in beryll, in which is wryton, *Patricius Arthurus Britannie, Gallie, Germanie, Dacie, Imperator.*[8] Item° in the Castel of Dover ye may see Gauwayns skulle[9] and Cradoks mantel;[1] at Wynchester, the Round Table;[2] in other places Launcelottes swerde and many other thynges.

    Thenne, al these thynges consydered, there can no man resonably gaynsaye° but there was a kyng of thys lande named Arthur. For in al places Crysten and hethen° he is reputed and taken for one of the 9 Worthy, and the fyrst of the thre Crysten men. And also he is more spoken of beyonde the see,° moo° bookes made of his noble actes, than there be in Englond; as wel in Duche, Ytalyen, Spaynysshe, and Grekysshe, as in Frensshe. And yet of record remayne in wytnesse of hym in Wales, in the toune of Camelot, the grete stones and mervayllous werkys° of yron° lyeng° under the grounde, and ryal vautes,° which dyvers now lyvyng hath seen. Wherfor it is a mervayl why he is nomore renomed in his owne contreye, sauf° onelye° it accordeth to the word of God, whyche sayth that no man is accept for a prophete in his owne contreye.

    Thenne, al these thynges forsayd aledged, I coude not wel denye but that there was suche a noble kynge named Arthur, and reputed one of the 9 Worthy, and fyrst and chyef° of the Cristen men. And

Marginal glosses: imputed · tomb / Glastonbury · fifth · moved · Westminster / impression · red · Also · retort · heathen · sea / more · works / iron / lying · regal vaults · except / only · chief

4. Again, the identity of this special (specious?) person—potentially the provider of the source copy of Malory, which Caxton refers to later—remains unknown; see n. 8, p. 866.
5. The *Polychronicon* was a universal history written in Latin in several versions from 1327 to 1360 by the English monk Ralph Higden. The work was immensely popular and was translated into English by John Trevisa in 1387 at the behest of Thomas IV, Lord Berkeley; Caxton printed his own edition of that translation on July 2, 1482.
6. The Italian writer Boccaccio produced *De Casibus Virorum Illustrium* ("Examples of Famous Men," completed 1360), a collection of monitory tales about the dissolution of great men.
7. The *History of the Kings of Britain* by Geoffrey of Monmouth, written c. 1136, was an extremely influential source of Arthurian lore (though we have no evidence that Malory was directly acquainted with it); for a very brief overview of the place of the work in Arthurian literature, see the chronology on p. xvii. See also the Bibliography.
8. Encased in beryl (transparent stone), in which is written, "The noble Arthur, Emperor of Britain, France, Germany, and Denmark."
9. Cf. n. 8, p. 682.
1. One stream of Arthurian legend held that only the wife of Sir Cradock (Caradoc) was able to wear a mantle (cloak) brought to Arthur's court which magically changed hue and fell apart on unchaste women.
2. See n. 5, p. 61.

many noble volumes be made of hym and of his noble knyghtes in Frensshe, which I have seen and redde beyonde the see, which been not had in our maternal tongue. But in Walsshe° ben many, and also in Frensshe (and somme in Englysshe, but nowher nygh° alle). Wherfore suche as have late ben drawen oute bryefly[3] into Englysshe, I have, after the symple connynge° that God hath sente to me, under the favour and correctyon of al noble lordes and gentylmen, enprysed° to enprynte° a book of the noble hystoryes of the sayd Kynge Arthur and of certeyn of his knyghtes, after° a copye unto me delyverd, whyche copye Syr Thomas Malorye dyd take oute of certeyn bookes of Frensshe and reduced it into Englysshe.

And I, accordyng to my copye, have doon sette it in enprynte, to the entente that noble men may see and lerne the noble actes of chyvalrye, the jentyl and vertuous dedes that somme knyghtes used° in tho dayes, by whyche they came to honour, and how they that were vycious° were punysshed and ofte put to shame and rebuke; humbly bysechyng° al noble lordes and ladyes, wyth al other estates° of what estate or degree they been of, that shal see and rede in this sayd book and werke, that they take the good and honest actes in their remembraunce and to folowe the same— wherin they shalle fynde many joyous and playsaunt hystoryes and noble and renomed actes of humanyté, gentylness, and chyvalryes. For herein may be seen noble chyvalrye, curtosye, humanyté, frendlynesse, hardynesse, love, frendshyp, cowardyse, murdre, hate, vertue, and synne. Doo after the good and leve the evyl, and it shal brynge you to good fame and renommee.° And for to passe the tyme, thys book shal be plesaunte to rede in; but for to gyve fayth and byleve° that al is trewe that is conteyned herin, ye be at your lyberté. But al is wryton° for our doctryne and for to beware° that we falle not to vyce ne synne, but t'excersyse and folowe vertu, by whyche we may come and atteyne to good fame and renomme in thys lyf, and after thys shorte and transytorye lyf to come unto everlastyng blysse in heven, the whyche He graunte us that reygneth in heven, the Blessyd Trynyté. Amen.

Thenne, to procede forth in thys sayd book—whyche I dyrecte unto alle noble prynces, lordes and ladyes, gentylmen or gen-tylwymmen, that desyre to rede or here° redde of the noble and joyous hystorye of the grete conquerour and excellent kyng, Kyng Arthur, somtyme kyng of thys noble royalme, thenne callyd Bry-taygne—I, Wyllyam Caxton, symple persone, present thys book folowyng, whyche I have enprysed t'enprynte, and treateth of the noble actes, feates of armes of chyvalrye, prowesse, hardynesse, humanyté, love, curtosye, and veray° gentylnesse, wyth many won-derful hystoryes and adventures. And for to understonde bryefly° the contente of thys volume, I have devyded it into 21 bookes, and every book chapytred as hereafter shal by Goddes grace folowe:

---

3. *drawen oute bryefly:* translated and abridged.

Welsh

near

ability

undertaken / print
according to

practiced
full of vice
asking
ranks of society

renown

belief
written / warn

hear

true
briefly

The fyrst book shal treate how Uther Pendragon gate° the noble   *begot*
    conquerour Kyng Arthur, and conteyneth 28 chappytres.

The second book treateth of Balyn, the noble knyght, and
    conteyneth 19 chapytres.

The thyrd book treateth of the maryage of Kyng Arthur to Quene
    Guenever, wyth other maters, and conteyneth fyftene
    chappytres.

The fourth book, how Merlyn was assotted,° and of warre maad°   *besotted / made*
    to Kyng Arthur, and conteyneth 29 chappytres.

The fyfthe book treateth of the conqueste of Lucius th'Emperour,
    and conteyneth 12 chappytres.

The syxthe book treateth of Syr Launcelot and Syr Lyonel and
    mervayllous adventures, and conteyneth 18 chapytres.

The seventh book treateth of a noble knyght called Syr Gareth
    and named by Syr Kaye "Beaumayns," and conteyneth 36
    chapytres.

The eyght book treateth of the byrthe of Syr Trystram, the noble
    knyght, and of hys actes, and conteyneth 41 chapytres.

The 9 book treateth of a knyght named by Syr Kaye "Le Cote Male
    Tayllé," and also of Syr Trystram, and conteyneth 44
    chapytres.

The 10 book treateth Syr Trystram and other mervayllous
    adventures, and conteyneth 88 chappytres.

The 11 book treateth of Syr Launcelot and Syr Galahad, and
    conteyneth 14 chappytres.

The 12 book treateth of Syr Launcelot and his madnesse, and
    conteyneth 14 chappytres.

The 13 book treateth how Galahad came fyrst to Kyng Arthurs
    courte, and the Quest, how the Sangreall° was begonne, and   *Grail Quest*
    conteyneth 20 chapytres.

The 14 book treateth of the Queste of the Sangreal, and
    conteyneth 10 chapytres.

The 15 book treateth of Syr Launcelot, and conteyneth 6
    chapytres.

The 16 book treateth of Syr Bors and Syr Lyonel, his brother, and
    conteyneth 17 chapytres.

The 17 book treateth of the Sangreal, and conteyneth 23
    chapytres.

The 18 book treateth of Syr Launcelot and the Quene, and
    conteyneth 25 chapytres.

The 19 book treateth of Quene Guenever and Launcelot, and
    conteyneth 13 chapytres.

The 20 book treateth of the pyteous deth of Arthur, and
    conteyneth 22 chapytres.

The 21 book treateth of his last departyng, and how Syr Launcelot
    came to revenge his dethe, and conteyneth 13 chapytres.

The somme° is 21 bookes, whyche conteyne the somme of 5 hon-   *sum, total*
dred and 7 chapytres, as more playnly shal folowe herafter.

            *   *   *

[Epilogue/Colophon]

❡Thus endeth thys noble and joyous book entytled *Le Morte Darthur*,[4] notwythstondyng it treateth of the byrth, lyf, and actes of the sayd Kyng Arthur, of his noble knyghtes of the Rounde Table, theyr mervayllous enquestes° and adventures, th'achyevyng of the Sangreal, and, in th'ende, the dolorous deth and departyng out of thys world of them al. Whiche book was reduced into Englysshe by Syr Thomas Malory, knyght, as afore° is sayd, and by me devyded into 21 bookes, chapytred and enprynted, and fynysshed in th'Abbey [of] Westmestre[5] the last day of Juyl,° the yere of Our Lord 1485.

❡*Caxton me fieri fecit*[6]

quests

beforehand

July

4. About this choice of title, see n. †, p. 1.
5. Caxton's press and bookshop were based near, if not on, the grounds of Westminster Abbey.
6. Caxton caused me (i.e., this book) to be made.

HELEN COOPER

Counter-Romance: Civil Strife and Father-Killing in the Prose Romances†

. . . down into the dyke, and thare he felle, and was all tofrusched; and than Alexander said unto hym one this wyse. 'Fals wreche,' quothe he, 'that presumes to tell thynges that ere to com, reghte als thou were a prophete, and knewe the prevatés of heven, now may thou see that thou lyes, and tharefore thou arte worthy to hafe swilke a dede.' And than Anectanabus ansuerd, and said: 'I wyste wele ynoghe,' quoth he, 'that I scholde die swylke a dede. Talde I noghte lange are to the, that myn awenn son schulde slae me?' 'Whi, ame I thi son?' than quoth Alexandire. 'Yaa, for sothe,' quoth Anectanabus, 'I gat the.' And with that word, he yalde the gaste.[1]

It is an accident of history, in the shape of a damaged manuscript, that the very first sentences to survive of what is probably the earliest English prose romance describe a son's killing of his father; but it is none the less a symbolic accident. The long-established tradition of metrical romances in English had occasionally allowed in ideas of family strife, but their general tenor was much more towards reunion, reconciliation, the due succession of father by heir—all the characteristics that are generally taken to be defining features of romance down through the Middle Ages to Shakespeare and beyond. The prose romance was

† From *The Long Fifteenth Century: Essays for Douglas Gray*, ed. Helen Cooper and Sally Mapstone (Oxford: Oxford University Press, 1997), pp. 141–162, reprinted by permission of Oxford University Press.
1. *The Prose Life of Alexander*, ed. J. S. Westlake, EETS OS 143 (1913), 7–8; from the Thornton MS, Lincoln Cathedral 91, fo. I[r].

the major contribution of the fifteenth century to the development of the whole genre in English, and its keynote is very different. Treachery and murder within the body politic or the kin group, the slaying of father by son, the failure to pass on good rule in a strong and righteous order of succession, and sometimes also incest, are repeated and urgent themes in these works. There are exceptions, of course, just as there are exceptions to the happy endings of metrical romances; but it is still true that the prose romances differ from the stanzaic ones not just in medium but in structure and content, to the point where they demand a rethinking of our conception of the genre.

The definition of genre as the conforming of a literary text to a certain horizon of expectation[2] has as its corollary that one has to bear in mind two sets of expectations: those contemporary with a work's composition and reception, and those of modern readers and scholars. There is an immediate problem with the prose romances, that the two sets may not be the same. Modern expectations have been shaped by the assumption that a prose romance is just a metrical romance in a different medium, and confirmed by their coexistence as an apparently authoritative single canon in such bibliographical compilations as the Romances volume of the *Manual of Writings in Middle English*.[3] But the modern plausibility of the volume's listings says nothing about whether the same categorization would have seemed plausible at the time the works were written. In the fifteenth century, there was more than just a change of medium involved in the writing of prose romance; a shift from verse into prose reflects a shift in association and literary context, a shift, therefore, of horizon. It seems that the very act of writing in prose, with its associations with genres such as chronicle history that made more direct claims to truth, brought with it different expectations for both authors and readers, and therefore also a shift in the centre of gravity of the romance genre. Furthermore, as Gabrielle Spiegel notes,

> The exact timing, location, and generic embodiment that give rise to prose composition are not necessarily the result of 'natural' linguistic process . . . The conditions under which prose narratives originate are as various as the cultures that produce them. In some cultures and at some times prose may represent a natural evolution of literary language, while in other places and periods it is socially generated by precise cultural needs and possesses ideological functions and meanings.[4]

2. Hans Robert Jauss, 'Theorie der Gattungen und Literatur des Mittelalters', in *Alterität und Modernität der mittelalterlichen Literatur: Gesammelte Aufsätze 1956–76* (Munich, 1977), 76–138 (p. 110).

3. *Manual*, vol. i: *Romances* (1967). Its listings for prose romances are supplemented by George R. Keiser, 'The Romances', in A. S. G. Edwards (ed.), *Middle English Prose: A Critical Guide to Major Authors and Genres* (New Brunswick, 1984), esp. 284–6. The earliest prose 'romance' listed by Keiser (p. 284), a version of King Arthur, is in fact an extract from the Middle English prose *Brut*, so is excluded from consideration here.

4. Gabrielle M. Spiegel, *Romancing the Past: The Rise of Vernacular Prose Historiography in Thirteenth-Century France* (Berkeley and Los Angeles, 1993), 2. The linguistic processes

The changes in content and ethos between English verse and prose romances suggest that there may be just such a cultural impetus behind the belated appearance of prose romance in England, over two centuries after the form had emerged in France.

Since the work of Johan Huizinga, the fifteenth century has often been accused of pursuing a fantasy of high chivalry that disguised the moribundity of its underlying ideology.[5] The abundance of copyings of metrical romances in this period, while war with France was briefly won and protractedly lost and England endured decades of intermittent civil war, could support just such an interpretation, though in the 1440s John Metham suggested rather that the increase in political unrest, 'encreasing of vexation', militated against new chivalric writing.[6] His own contribution to the genre, a rhyme-royal romance entitled *Amoryus and Cleopes,* is a version of the Pyramus and Thisbe story that incorporates a good deal of colorful chivalric action, and ends with a hermit resurrecting the dead lovers and baptizing them and their whole pagan society. The bulk of prose romances of the century, however, offer no such escape routes to a happy ending, not to any assertion of a providential ordering of human life. The testimony of these works indicates that their authors found a new literary form in which to express a more realistic and bleaker view of the world they lived in. The most famous of them, Sir Thomas Malory, makes the parallel explicit as he relates the civil war that makes the collapse of the Arthurian world to his own times, in his castigation of 'ye, all Englysshemen' who have not yet lost the old custom of being discontented with their king [p. 680]. The typical metrical romance ends with the succession of the true heir; the disrupted successions of the fifteenth century are much more accurately reflected in the prose romances.

I take as a working definition of prose romance those prose narratives with a primarily secular focus; aristocratic protagonists; a main concern generally with chivalry or love; and an exotic setting, far away or long ago, or both. The secularity distinguishes them from another genre moving more hesitantly into English prose in the fifteenth century, the saint's life, and it also excludes works such as the prose *Siege of Jerusalem.*[7] The exoticism of setting distinguishes them from histories such as the prose *Brut,* which may start long ago but which moves into the familiar present; and

at work in the shift to prose are discussed by John H. Fisher, 'Chancery and the Emergence of Standard Written English in the Fifteenth Century', *Speculum,* 52 (1977), 870–99.

5. Huizinga's *Waning of the Middle Ages* was first published in English in 1924, and continuing reprints testify to its continuing influence. Ironically, his faith in the rationalism of his own modern world and the unproblematic innocence of his references to male bonding make the book now appear itself the assertion of a dying ideology.

6. *The Works of John Metham,* ed. Hardin Craig, EETS OS 132 (1916), *Amoryus and Cleopes,* l. 2189. For an argument that verse romance was itself perceived in the fifteenth century as an active defence against threats to religious and political order, see Helen Cooper, 'Romance after 1400', in David Wallace (ed.), *The Cambridge History of Medieval English Literature* (Cambridge, 1999).

7. This is however included in the *Manual* (i. 163, #107); and see also Keiser, 'Romances', 276. There are two distinct fifteenth-century prose versions. Their content, which includes child cannibalism as well as the destruction of the city, would none the less fit well with my discussion here.

the distance of their subject-matter from the time or place they were written means that their contents are what we would broadly define as fiction, though much of the base material would have been taken in the fifteenth century as broadly historical. Six of the ten such works composed or translated before 1500 by authors other than Caxton, plus a seventh example from just after the turn of the century, illustrate this shift of generic centre, and form the focus of this essay. Of the other four pre-1500 romances, three are close translations of French originals that do not show the same tendency;[8] I largely exclude consideration of Caxton since his own generic assumptions were formed so extensively by the Burgundian literary milieu where he spent so many years, and because the systems of commercial publication by print, commission, and patronage within which he made his translations tended to generate a different set of 'cultural needs and ideological functions'. The first six of the seven romances with which I am concerned—the stories of Thebes, Troy, Alexander, Charlemagne, Arthur, and Melusine—fall into the category of legendary history, though the last two in particular edge over into the implausible and overtly fictional; the seventh and latest, *Valentine and Orson*, makes no claims at all to be other than fantasy, but is all the more interesting in showing the same resetting of generic expectation as the others.

Both the choice of prose over verse for stories of disaster, even when they also recount chivalric and amatory material, and the selection of such material for adaptation or translation into English prose, show that shift in the centre of gravity away from the comforting ideologies of the verse romances, with their calamities avoided or redeemed and political and familial order restored, to narratives that precisely deny those comforts. The outlines of the stories of many of the 'disaster romances' often pre-date the emergence of romance in the twelfth century; their immediate sources range over widely differing generic and linguistic backgrounds. Lydgate's English verse *Troy Book* and *Destruction of Thebes* provide the immediate source for two of the earliest, the prose epitomes the *Siege of Troy* and the *Siege of Thebes*;[9] Lydgate's own versions already downplay the elements in the stories associated in the Middle Ages with romance, such as high chivalry and love, to emphasize treason and destruction. Hector may elsewhere be treated as a chivalric hero on the romance model (as in the metrical *Laud Troy Book* of c.1400), Aeneas's descendants may go on to

8. These are *King Ponthus* and *Merlin* of the mid-century and *The Three Kings' Sons* of c.1500; the remaining work is the prose *Ipomedon* of c.1460, drawn from Hue de Rotelande's verse *Ipomedon*. A fifth prose work of before 1500, the Dublin *Alexander* fragments, is largely based on Caxton's *Dicts and Sayings of the Philosophers*.

9. They are edited by Friedrich Brie, 'Zwei mittelenglische Prosaromane: *The Sege of Thebes* und *The Sege of Troy*', *Anglia*, 130 (1913), 40–52, 269–85. The prose *Troy* draws on *Troilus and Criseyde* in addition to Lydgate's *Troy Book* (C. David Benson, 'Chaucer's Influence on the Prose "Sege of Troy"', *Notes and Queries* 261 (1971), 127–30). The epitomes were made between the completion of Lydgate's source poems in 1420/1422 and their mid-century copying; they are therefore likely to be closely contemporary with the *Life of Alexander*, which was copied into the Thornton manuscript around 1440.

found the nations of the West, but the story of Troy itself is one of catastrophe. The Oedipus story has notorious associations with the form that is almost the opposite of romance, tragedy, and no medieval narrative treatment altered its basic outline. The outlines of the story of Alexander were laid down by the facts of his own life as assimilated into Greek and Latin prose legendary biography. The very earliest, cryptic, reference to Arthur and Mordred is a bare note of their falling in battle; Malroy's own sources lie in French prose romance, English metrical and alliterative romance, and probably English verse chronicle as well, but he makes the threat of disaster more of a constant presence than in any of them. The anonymous English prose Charlemagne romance is a translation, made probably [c.1460] of the Latin *Pseudo-Turpin Chronicle,* which concludes with the death of Roland: the earliest version of the story is of course the *chanson de geste, Chanson de Roland.* Caxton's own romances include some with origins in chronicle (*Godfrey of Bouillon*) and, with prose intermediaries, *chanson de geste* (*The Four Sons of Aymon* and the end of *Charles the Great,* both on the Matter of France and both concerned with war or treachery within the polity). The English prose romance often therefore has more in common in terms of content and structure with the vernacular epic or the poems of the alliterative revival than with metrical romance. The bias towards disaster remains, however, even when the basic stories do belong to the age of romance, as in the instances of *Melusine* and, in particular, *Valentine and Orson.* The English versions of both are derived from French prose originals, but both stories also exist in metrical versions that show up just how uneasy is the generic relationship between prose and verse romance.

The episode quoted at the head of this essay, of Alexander's slaying of the magician Anectanabus—who had lain with his mother in the guise of a god, and who has just foreseen in the stars that his son will kill him—does not have any disastrous repercussions on Alexander's own triumphant career, though the number of figures he takes as in some sense fathers (Anectanabus, Philip, the god Amon) gains a retrospective irony with his own early death without a lineal heir to preserve his vast conquests. The pattern suggested by the unwitting act of parricide emerges more strongly when it is set beside the other two texts that compete with it for the possible earliest dating of prose romance texts, the *Siege of Troy* and the *Siege of Thebes.* The prominence of kin-killing and civil strife in the history of Thebes is too familiar to require exposition, but it is striking how closely Edippes' slaying of his father in the prose *Thebes* agrees with the narrative outline of the parallel episode in the *Alexander.* In both, the father knows by prophecy how he will die; each son learns without any advance preparation that the king he imagines to be his true father is not so; each kills his real father in a temper and without knowing his identity. The consequences of Edippes' action—his marriage to his mother; their incestuous sons' hatred for him, 'putting him onder fote so, that he died in grete myschef' (p. 49); the civil war between those sons; their destruction of each other along with the kingdom—make up the rest of the story.

> Fore hit preved well there of theym two, that weren so horribly gotten ayenst all nature and ordenaunce, for as clerkes seyn, blode to touche blode, bringeth forth corrupt frute. (p. 269)

Here, Edippes' initial parricide and incest initiates a cycle of kin-killing and political catastrophe that takes two generations to work itself out.

The history of the fall of Troy does not offer directly comparable models of incest and kin-slaying, but the prose *Siege of Troy* is none the less cast so as to emphasize the dark side of the war. The key word of the work, repeated in episode after episode, is 'treason'—destruction from within, from inside the family or the fellowship or the state. The epitome opens with an account of how Pelleus 'compassed tresoun' against his nephew Jason to prevent his succession to his father's crown, showing him 'hole love outeward, where there was ful dedely hate inward' (p. 273); it passes rapidly through Medea's betrayal of her homeland, abandonment by Jason, and her killing of her children; describes how Hecuba requites Achilles' 'fals treasoun' in mutilating Troilus' body with a further treacherous plot of her own to murder him (p. 284); finishes with the combined treachery of Calcas, Antenor, and Eneas in making the horse that brought the Greeks within the city; and signs off with the moral,

> And alwey the ende of every tresoun and falsenes to sorowe and myschef at the last. Amen. (p. 285)

By this reading, the whole history of Troy is driven by jealousy, hatred, and division within successive kin groups; and here, as in the *Siege of Thebes*, it ends not in happiness and restored order, as one expects of romances, but in personal and political disaster.

Betrayal from within is similarly the keynote of the fifteenth-century prose Charlemagne romances. Most of the verse romances concerned with the Matter of France tell of chivalric exploits, combats against pagan champions who are eventually baptized, Christian princesses who fall in love with them, Saracen princesses who fall in love with the peers, marvels, miracles, and relics. Only two of the ten surviving metrical romances (the English *Song of Roland* itself, and *Otuel and Roland*) recount Ganelon's treachery and the disaster at Roncesvalles. That, however, constitutes the narrative of the anonymous prose translation of the *Pseudo-Turpin Chronicle*;[1] and the two other fifteenth-century prose romances on Char-

---

1. See Stephen H.A. Shepherd, 'The Middle English *Pseudo-Turpin Chronicle*', *Medium Aevum* 65 (1996), 19–34; an [EETS] edition by Shepherd is [due in 2004]. [The introduction to the edition argues that the commissioner of the text was probably the ambitious lawyer and ardent Lancastrian, Thomas Mull (mentioned with distaste in one of the Berkeley Letters, printed above, p. 760; see also n. 3, p. 762, for further details and a possible Malorean connection)—Editor.] The work is not mentioned in the *Manual* [because its

lemagne, both translations by Caxton, similarly focus on disaster, *Charles the Great* again concluding with Roncesvalles, *The Four Sons of Aymon* recounting the long blood-feud waged by Charlemagne against Renaud of Montauban and his brothers—a feud that feeds on divided loyalties and amounts to a protracted civil war.

The most famous medieval example of the realm brought down by internal faction fostered by incest is Malory's Arthuriad; and the downfall and destruction of the Round Table is not a matter of historical or narrative interest alone. A drawing together of the legendary past and disordered present seems to lie behind much of his shaping of his Arthurian material. What happens in the *Morte Darthur*, and the fact that it is written in prose, may seem now to be inevitable: it is, after all, a translation from French prose originals that already included the story of Arthur's fall and his death at the hands of Mordred.[2] But to Malory in the 1460s, the choices facing him were not provided with any obvious answers. All but one of the earlier English translations of Arthurian prose romances had chosen verse as their medium, from the early fourteenth-century *Of Arthour and Merlin*, down through the stanzaic *Morte Arthur* (c. 1400) and the vast couplet versions of *Merlin* and the *History of the Holy Grail* produced by the Londoner Henry Lovelich in the 1420s; and writers after Malory were still making the same decision for verse, for instance the author of the Scottish *Lancelot of the Laik* (?1470s). The one exception to verse translation before Malory is the anonymous *Merlin* translated from the Vulgate cycle around the mid-century, which was apparently unknown to him (his own source for the equivalent material is the non-Vulgate *Suite du Merlin*). The English works he knew and used were all in verse of one kind or another: the stanzaic *Morte Arthur*, the alliterative *Morte Arthure*, even the substantial Arthurian section of John Hardying's mid-century rhyme-royal chronicle.[3] If P. J. C. Field is right, Malory himself may have tried his hand at composing Arthurian romance in verse too, as the prisoner author of *The Wedding of Sir Gawain and Dame Ragnell*.[4] So prose

existence was unknown at the time of publication]; for other Charlemagne romances, see [*Manual*] i. 80–100, ##45–61. *Huon of Burdeux* (c. 1534) is also a prose romance loosely attached to Charlemagne, but of a very different kind from the fifteenth-century examples.

2. It is widely accepted that the prose *remaniement* of Arthurian material in French was similarly a response to a cultural moment, and this has been taken as an argument against reading Malory's appropriation of them in analogous terms: see e.g. William Calin, *The French Tradition and the Literature of Medieval England* (Toronto, 1994), 506, 'The cultural crisis of the fifteenth century exemplified in *Le Morte Darthur* proves also to be a cultural crisis of the thirteenth century.' But this overlooks both Malory's reshaping of his sources, and the new significances that traditional material can assume in different circumstances (a notable modern example would be Sophocles' *Antigone*, banned by the Greek colonels). See also Elizabeth T. Pochoda, *Arthurian Propaganda: Le Morte Darthur as an Historical Ideal of Life* (Chapel Hill, NC, 1971).

3. See Edward D. Kennedy, 'Malory and his English Sources', in Toshiyuki Takamiya and Derek Brewer (eds.), *Aspects of Malory* (Cambridge and Totowa, NJ, 1981), 27–55 (pp. 42–8); and *The Chronicle of Iohn Hardyng*, ed. Henry Ellis (London, 1812), 118–49 (caps. lxxii–lxxxv).

4. P. J. C. Field, 'Malory's *The Wedding of Sir Gawain and Dame Ragnell*', *Archiv*, 219 (1982), 374–81. Field acknowledges the difference of ethos from the *Morte Darthur* as a problem; but this could be accommodated within the shift from verse romance to prose. [But see, n. 1, p. xxviii—Editor].

was not the natural medium that it seems with hindsight: it was deliberately chosen, and, it would seem, chosen to accommodate just such a generic shift away from romance, to civil war, treachery, and murder within the fellowship and the kin-group.

Malory's selection and treatment of topics from across the corpus of Arthurian romance was similarly deliberate: he did not just rework what was in front of him. The sources he was using offered him a range of different traditions, some of them incompatible or contradictory; he selects from those to present a single coherent vision of Arthurian history such as overrides the radical differences of story and interpretation between the *Suite du Merlin* and Hardyng, the alliterative *Morte Arthure* and the *Queste del Saint Graal*. In Malory, the greatest chivalric fellowship ever known is brought down, not so much by the moral and religious shortcomings revealed by the Grail Quest, as happens in the French Vulgate cycle, but by the splitting of the kingdom into viciously hostile magnate affinities in a manner analogous to his own age of the Wars of the Roses. The process is begun in his *Tristram*, when Gawain and his brothers, Arthur's nephews, avenge their father King Lot's death by murdering Sir Lamorak, son of Lot's killer Pellinore; it is continued in their jealous hatred of Lancelot and therefore also of his kin-group, and carried through to disaster in the blood-feud that follows Lancelot's accidental slaying of Gareth. The final battle pits Arthur against the nephew who is also his own incestuous son, Mordred.

The tradition that makes Mordred Arthur's son is first found in the Vulgate cycle; his mother is Arthur's half-sister (daughter of Ygerne by her first husband Gorlois), wife of King Lot of Lothian, and named by Malory as Morgause. This is far more subversive than the 'historical' tradition founded by Geoffrey of Monmouth that makes Mordred the legitimate son of Lot by Arthur's full sister, daughter to Uther and Ygerne, here named Anna.[5] Geoffrey's account was followed by the most widely known of the histories of England, the prose *Brut;* and Scottish historiographers from the late fourteenth through to the sixteenth century, keen to refute English claims over Scotland, go still further, making Mordred Lot's eldest son, and therefore, since they also argue that Arthur was begotten in adultery, Uther Pendragon's legitimate heir.[6] Hardyng also makes Mordred legitimate despite his familiarity with

5. Geoffrey of Monmouth in fact varies between identifying Anna as the daughter of Uther and Ygerne, therefore Arthur's full sister, or occasionally as his aunt, sister of Aurelius and Uther, and married to Lot in both identities (*Geoffrey of Monmouth: The History of the Kings of Britain*, trans. Lewis Thorpe (Harmondsworth, 1966), 208–9, 221, 223 n. (*Historia*, viii. 20–1, ix. II)). The *Brut* describes Anna as full sister and Mordred as nephew (*The Brut or the Chronicles of England*, Part I, ed. Friedrich W. D. Brie, EETS OS 131 (1906), 67, 83). See also Elizabeth Archibald, 'Arthur and Mordred: Variations on an Incest Theme', *Arthurian Literature*, 8 (1989), 1–27.

6. The tradition runs from John of Fordun (1385) to Hector Boece (1527) and his translators; for a summary, see Robert Huntington Fletcher, *The Arthurian Material in the Chronicles*, 2nd edn. expanded by Robert Sherman Loomis (New York, 1966), 241–9, modified by Flora Alexander, 'Late Medieval Scottish Attitudes to the Figure of King Arthur: A Reassessment', *Anglia*, 93 (1975), 17–34. Boece picks up the variant relationship of Arthur and Anna from Geoffrey to make Anna Aurelius' and Uther's elder sister (p. 247).

the Vulgate tradition (but not surprisingly given his concern to cleanse the whole Arthurian narrative of sexual irregularity: even his Lancelot and Elaine are married).[7] In the alliterative *Morte* too, more directly derived from Geoffrey than Hardyng's eclectic compilation, Mordred is Arthur's 'sister son', and if there is any hint of a closer relationship between them it is very muted indeed.[8] Even on this issue, then, Malory had the freedom to choose an alternative tradition if he had wished. The 'historical' Arthur has no direct heir to ensure a safe linear succession; but in the prose romance versions, any possibility of rightful succession is disastrously compromised by the existence of an incestuous son.

In no version do Arthur and his sister know each other's identity when Mordred is begotten, but the Vulgate *Merlin* does not even ascribe deliberate adultery to Lot's wife: she believes that the man in bed with her is her husband, when it is in fact the young squire Arthur who has crept in beside her from his lodging in a corner of the chamber. Despite having been smitten (more in the adolescent than the god-of-love sense) by the beauty of the queen, he at first dares do nothing more, until

> hit fill so that the lady awoke and turned hir toward hym, and toke hym in her armes as a woman slepynge, that wende verely it hadde ben her lorde. And that nyght was begete Mordred.[9]

Arthur tells her what he has done the next day while he kneels before her at table; but even when his true identity is discovered, she reacts with love (p. 181). Any sense of the enormity of the act is delayed until Merlin's later prophecy that 'the fader sholde sle the sone, and the sone sle the fader, and the londe of the grete breteigne abide withouten heir and lordles' (p. 579); and even that relates more to the broader context of civil war than to the specific act of incest.

In Malory and his immediate source,[1] Arthur and Morgause do not know they are related, but the act is one of deliberate adultery with none of the aura of adolescent innocence of the *Merlin* about it. Immediately afterwards, Arthur is given a dream in which he foresees the destruction of the country by griffins and serpents (Malory, [p. 30]) and Merlin relates the prophesied doom to the guilt incurred by the act:

---

7. *The Chronicle of Iohn Hardyng*, 120, 137 (l. 27 requires the variant reading 'mordred' to make sense), and 131 (caps. lxxii, lxxviii, lxxvii).
8. *Alliterative Morte Arthure*, l. 645, in *King Arthur's Death*, ed. Larry D. Benson (Exeter, 1986). The only indication that Mordred might be Arthur's son is Gawain's comment: on Mordred, 'Of such a engendure full little joy happens' (3743); but this could be no more than an analogue to the commonplace curse on the day an enemy was born.
9. This is from the anonymous mid-century prose translation of the *Estoire de Merlin: Merlin*, ed. Henry B. Wheatley, vol. i, part II, EETS OS 2I (rev. edn. 1877), 181.
1. This is the *Suite du Merlin* (also known as the 'Huth Merlin'; ed. Gaston Paris and Jacob Ulrich, *Merlin*, 2 vols., SATF (Paris, 1886)). For its relation to the Vulgate *Merlin*, see Alexandre Micha, 'The Vulgate *Merlin*', and Fanni Bogdanow, 'The *Suite du Merlin* and the Post-Vulgate *Roman du Graal*', in Roger Sherman Loomis (ed.), *Arthurian Literature in the Middle Ages* (corrected edn., Oxford, 1979), 319, 325–35.

Ye have done a thynge late that God ys displesed with you, for ye have lyene by youre syster and on hir ye have gotyn a childe that shall destroy you and all the knyghtes of youre realme. ([p. 32])

Malory's Arthur incurs further guilt in his next action. In the French, he orders all the children born in May to be sent to him, but the boat carrying Mordred to him is wrecked and he is the sole survivor. Arthur considers killing the children he has collected, but instead obeys a visionary instruction to set them adrift in a pilotless boat so that Christ may save or destroy whom He wishes; in the event, all of them come ashore safely, and are raised by Arthur's own care.² Malory conflates the two sea journeys into a single one: the boat carrying all the babies is wrecked, and Mordred is the only one to survive. All the innocent children therefore die as the direct result of Arthur's own action, in an episode that notoriously casts Arthur in the role of Herod. There is an additional irony in this, however, since it is the baby who will be most guilty who is the only one to survive. Malory is here rewriting, not just his Arthurian source, but the whole tradition of stories of setting adrift in which God preserves the innocent or the future hero: saints such as Mary Magdalene or the infant Gregorius, falsely accused women such as Constance, heroes such as Perseus of the Anglo-Norman Horn.³ The child of incest may elsewhere grow into a saint, as Gregorius does; but I know of only one survivor of casting adrift apart from Mordred who brings disaster on his community, and that is Judas, who himself grew up to commit the worse incest with his mother, and to make the ultimate betrayal.⁴ Malory's redrafting of his source rewrites it as if to make Judas the only survivor of the Massacre of the Innocents.

Malory's selection and rewriting of the various traditions of Mordred's parentage, birth, and upbringing extend to his account of Mordred's treachery and death. The historical tradition, exemplified among his known sources by the alliterative *Morte,* makes Guinevere a willing adulteress with Mordred: she betrays both her husband and her king as Mordred betrays his uncle and his king, in a relationship defined in the Christian world as itself prohibited (Mordred being her husband's nephew). This displacement of the incest motif further blackens Mordred, but it diverts the sense of retributive destiny from Arthur himself. In the stanzaic *Morte Arthur,* based on the Vulgate tradition, the fact that Mordred is Arthur's own son is mentioned only at the point when he is pursuing Guinevere, intensifying Mordred's incestuous intentions but

2. *Merlin,* ed. Paris and Ulrich, 203–12.
3. On the tradition, see J. R. Reinhard, 'Setting Adrift in Medieval Law and Literature', PMLA 56 (1941), 33–68, and Helen Cooper, 'Prospero's Boats: Magic, Providence, and Human Choice', in Sukanta Chaudhuri (ed.), *Renaissance Essays for Kitty Scoular Datta* (Oxford and Calcutta, 1995), 160–75.
4. The medieval legend of Judas has him cast away in the sea in a barrel at birth as the result of his mother's prophetic dream; he kills his foster-brother, then his own father, and unwittingly marries his mother (see e.g. *The South English Legendary,* ed. Charlotte d'Evelyn and Anna J. Mill, EETS OS 235–6 (1956), 692–7).

insulating Arthur himself from either blame or retribution.[5] The
Guinevere of the romance tradition, however, remains faithful to
Arthur even after Mordred spreads a false rumour of his death:
when he demands her in marriage, she escapes to the Tower of
London and faces a siege by him. This whole issue of feudal loyalty,
with its associated principle of the upholding of the common weal,
seems to matter far more to Malory in the apportioning or withholding of blame than the problematics of adultery, or indeed of
incest. Lancelot's adultery may worry the hermits on the Grail
quest, but Malory, in a passage without parallel in the Vulgate, has
God express His approval of Lancelot on his return to court by
allowing him his own personal miracle; the healing of Sir Urry.
The whole weight of blame can therefore be thrown, first on to the
jealousies and hatreds of Gawain and his brothers, then on to
the 'unhappy' Mordred—and the word is a strong one, carrying the
sense of being doomed to misfortune, almost accursed.[6] At the
moment when Arthur and Mordred meet in their final combat in
the French *Mort,* the primary syntactic and rhetorical emphasis
falls on God's anger (possibly, though not explicitly, for Arthur's
act of incest), and only secondarily on the killing of father by son
and son by father.[7] To Malory's Arthur—and there is no indication
of authorial dissent—Mordred is 'the traytoure that all thys woo
hath wrought' [p. 685]; and here it is emphasized that the greatest
treachery and sin is Mordred's deed of parricide, not the initial
sexual transgression that made it possible. Malory, moreover, gives
Mordred the most gruesome death of his entire work, and of all
versions of the final combat.

> And there Kyng Arthur smote Sir Mordred undir the shylde,
> with a foyne of hys speare, thorowoute the body more than a
> fadom. And whan Sir Mordred felte that he had hys dethys
> wounde, he threste hymselff with the myght that he had upp
> to the burre of Kyng Arthurs speare; and ryght so he smote
> hys fadir, Kynge Arthure, with hys swerde holdynge in both
> hys hondys, upon the syde of the hede, that the swerde per-
> ced the helmet and the tay of the brayne. And therewith Mor-
> dred daysshed downe starke dede to the erthe. [p. 686].

'Hys fadir, Kynge Arthure': it is the only time in the work that
Malory uses the dual formulation, and he holds it back until the
stroke that cuts down the whole Arthurian world.

The closing sections of Malory's work that recount the collapse
of the Round Table show a qualitative shift in the generic character
of the work, not only in their emphasis on civil war and destruction,

---

5. *Stanzaic Morte Arthur,* ll. 2954–61, in Benson (ed.), *King Arthur's Death.*
6. Malory uses it at two key moments, once to blame Mordred and Agravain together for
causing Arthur's fall through their hatred of Lancelot, once when Lucan tries to dissuade
the King from attacking him when Mordred alone of all his army is left alive at the end
of the final battle—'for he ys unhappy': Malory, [p. 646, line 11 and p. 685, line 32].
7. *La Morte le roi Artu,* ed. Jean Frappier, Textes littéraires français (2nd edn., Geneva,
1954), 245 (caps. 190–1), and the preceding prophecy, 211 (cap. 164); trans. James
Cable, *The Death of King Arthur* (Harmondsworth, 1971), 220, 192.

but in their avoidance or rejection of magic and the supernatural. Nothing intervenes to save Arthur: Excalibur's marvellous properties are never mentioned in the final battle, and the arm that draws the sword back into the lake withdraws whatever magic it may have had from the world. The possibility of Arthur's healing and return suggested by his departure in the barge to Avilion is frustrated by Bedivere's discovery of his tomb, and by Malory's refusal to endorse the idea that he may yet be *rex futurus*. Although romances frequently contain some kind of symbolic resurrection— lost children and wives restored after apparent death, Gawain returning home alive after his encounter with the death-dealing Green Knight—they seldom offer their protagonists perpetual life, though having a fairy mistress may, as in *Sir Launfal*, be a good way to set about it. That mortality might itself be an object of desire runs deeply counter both to the preference of romance for happy endings and to the escapism inherent in the supernatural.

* * *

P. J. C. FIELD

The Rhetoric of Dialogue†

* * *

If most readers finish the *Morte Darthur* with a memory of striking dignity of speech, this is because Malory's characters speak as they feel, and are often considerate, capable, and courageous. It is not because certain types of speech or action have been ruled out before the start. There is, as I have tried to show [earlier], a manner of speaking which is especially proper to knights at critical moments, as the natural expression of knightly character, but there is a great range of other styles and subjects open to them. Unlike Milton's angels, Malory's knights are not condemned to perpetual dignity. * * *

The range of the *Morte Darthur* is a little obscured to our eyes, because Malory does not individualize his characters by traits of speech to the extent to which the modern novel has accustomed us, and because his language is uniformly and inevitably distanced from us by five hundred years of linguistic change. But close reading shows us that all his characters can be strikingly colloquial, however heroic, good, aristocratic, or womanly they may be. Gentilesse is not yet the genteel, and for Malory there seem to be no prohibited subjects or phrases which are lower class or indelicate.[1] When Alexander the Orphan, who is the hero of his tale, discovers

---

† From *Romance and Chronicle: A Study of Malory's Style* (London: Barrie & Jenkins, 1971), pp. 123–129, reprinted with permission of Random House Publishers and P. J. C. Field.
1. For examples of the opposite extreme in translating Homer, see James Sutherland, *A Preface to Eighteenth Century Poetry* (Oxford, 1948), pp. 88–9.

from the damsel that Morgan le Fay wants him as her paramour, his response is:

> "I had levir kut away my hangers than I wolde do her ony suche pleasure!" [p. 385, line 36]

Alexander Pope did not feel that a hero's genitals should be the subject of polite conversation. The subject does come up in conversation once in his poetry; in his scurrilous little "Imitation of Chaucer". Pope allows himself this liberty in order to characterise what he sees as a distinctive side of medieval poetry. But his normal opinion can be seen when he lists The Prurient among the principal subdivisions of bad style, and describes it as "everywhere known by . . . Images of the Genital Parts of Men and Women. It consists wholly of Metaphors drawn from [these] two most fruitful Sources. . . ."[2] And he advises the bad poet with an ironic analogy:

> The Physician, by the Study and Inspection of Urine and Ordure, approves himself in the Science; and in like sort should our Author accustom and exercise his Imagination upon the Dregs of Nature.[3]

In Malory the matter is accepted, without the excitement which attaches itself to a prohibited subject.

A related freedom is seen when the most abusive language in the *Morte Darthur* is used by a lady in rank, Linette. "In the devyls name, thou bawdy kychyn knave!" is a chorus to her speeches to Gareth [e.g., pp. 183–86]. She later confesses that her abuse was "foule", and that Gareth showed a high degree of courtesy in enduring it; but the wrong lay in the falsity of her accusations, not in any abandonment of good manners [p. 204, line 13 ff.] There is no sign that, had Gareth really been a fraud, she or Malory would have felt it improper for a lady to abuse the impostor in violent terms.

In the speech of all Malory's characters, we find the recognisable accent of popular speech, in many particular phrases and in a general stress on forcefulness rather than precision. At one point Guenivere protests to Mellyagaunce: "I had levir kut myne owne throte in twayne rather than thou sholde dishonoure me!" Lancelot says (and to a lady): "The devyll made you a shoter!" And Arthur produces an obvious colloquial phrase to Gawain with: "What, nevew? . . . is the wynde in that dore?" [p. 627, line 6; p. 619, line 30; p. 224, line 44]. And these are the three most important characters in the story and the highest in rank. Phrases from common speech are found even in speeches of dignity. Before enlarging on Tor's future, Merlin says: "Nay, nay . . . thys ys but japis that he hath do. . . ." And Bors interrupts important speeches with

---

2. *Peri Bathous, or Martinus Scriblerus, his Treatise of the Art of Sinking in Poetry*, in [Swift-Pope] *Miscellanies, The Last Volume* (London, 1727), p. 67. His own "Imitation" is more clearly condemned by these words than anything Malory or Chaucer wrote.
3. Ibid., p. 29.

"howsomever the game goth" and the colloquial "by youre good will" [p. 73, line 20; p. 594, line 29; pp. 653, line 47] * * *.

We may also pause to notice three additional ways common to ordinary speech by which Malory chose frequently to intensify the effect of his dialogue: oaths, proverbs, and vocatives. Preachers in the middle ages complained that:

> No man now-a-daies unnethis [hardly] canne speke ony word but if an ooth be at the other eende.[4]

And with due allowance for overstatement, this is also true of Malory's dialogue at every social level. The oaths make the colloquial speeches the more forceful and the dignified ones the more elevated.

The extreme of the impersonal colloquial is found in the aphorisms, *sententiae*, catchphrases, and proverbs scattered throughout the dialogue of the *Morte Darthur*. All of them testify to a common experience shared by the narrator, characters, and the readers, who have formed the language in which these expressions have become accepted as authoritatively true.[5] The proverb proper, which has been defined as a generalisation not completely separated from a specific example, has a history of varied acceptability in literature. Most medieval and Renaissance writers found it a pleasing and persuasive way of expressing truth. One of the improvements in Speight's second edition of Chaucer (1602) was the marking out of Chaucer's proverbs by tiny pointing hands along the margin of the text. The Augustans began a reaction against the proverb, banishing it first from polite conversation and then from polite literature. As inhabitants of the Age of Reason, they preferred their generalisations pure rather than applied.

* * *

And after this time, proverbs came to have associations with the uneducated, which continue, though to a lesser degree, to our own day. The twentieth-century preference for the concrete rather than the abstract, or at least for the symbol rather than the unadorned concept, has allowed us a renewed sympathy with proverbs.

In late medieval and Renaissance high society, there was no aversion to proverbs, rather the reverse. In Malory's time, the king's brother-in-law, Earl Rivers, could translate a work based on proverbs, the *Dicts and Sayings of the Philosophers*. This was the first book which Caxton is known to have printed in England, and he

4. Quoted by Owst, *Literature and the Pulpit* (Oxford, 1961), pp. 420 ff.
5. See p. 7, line 15; p. 13, line 6; p. 42, line 26; p. 62, lines 22–23; p. 77, line 21; p. 83, line 1; p. 88, line 43–p. 89, line 1; p. 89, line 2; p. 96, line 13; p. 133, line 39; p. 137, line 15; p. 151, line 3; p. 179, lines 6 and 10–11; p. 187, line 7; p. 223, line 28; p. 224, line 44; p. 240, line 36; p. 245, lines 34, 39; p. 263, line 30; p. 264, line 7; p. 268, line 20; p. 277, line 14; p. 310, line 36; p. 314, lines 18–21; p. 331, line 10; p. 373, line 18; p. 408, line 42; p. 421, line 17; p. 440, line 17; p. 463, line 16; p. 466, line 12; p. 518, line 45; p. 522, line 4; p. 536, line 18; p. 537, line 38; p. 544, lines 33–34; p. 562, line 7; p. 571, line 29; p. 589, line 42; p. 610, line 36; p. 620, lines 8–9; p. 624, lines 18–20; p. 625, line 6; p. 629, line 34; p. 630, line 23; p. 631, lines 10–11; p. 634, lines 30–31; p. 652, line 1; p. 655, lines 22–24; p. 677, line 36; p. 679, line 35; p. 685, line 41; p. 691, line 23; p. 693, line 18.

twice reprinted it.[6] Other writers less exalted also used proverbs and proverbial sayings, some more, some less. In the Paston Letters, the family and their servants seem to use them equally: Margaret Paston is especially fond of bringing an argument to a climax with a proverb.[7] Richard Cely the Younger clinches a letter to his brother with:

> Be well ware how that ye do hyt ys better to pyttye than be pyttyd.[8]

Among the writers patronised by the court, the moral Gower found proverbs a useful source of *sententiae,* and Chaucer put them to varied uses in his different kinds of writing. He finds them telling, not only for instruction and for humorous effect, but also for characterisation, matching the kind of proverb with the character who uses it. Proverbs are particularly frequent in the speech of five of his characters: the Wife of Bath, John in the *Reve's Tale,* the falcon in the *Squire's Tale,* and Pandarus and Criseyde.[9] The last two are the most sophisticated and self-possessed aristocrats he ever drew. Both delight in resorting to the authority or consolation of proverbial wisdom.

With this in mind, we should be able to banish any lingering eighteenth-century suspicion that proverbs are the resort of stupid or uneducated minds, and we will not be surprised to find Malory, like most of his contemporaries, using them. A few stand out because they are explicitly called proverbs:

> Hit is an olde sawe, "Gyeff a chorle rule and thereby he woll nat be suffysed." [p. 421, line 17]
>
> Hyt ys an olde-seyde saw: "A good man ys never in daungere but whan he ys in the daungere of a cowhard." [p. 629, line 34]
>
> Hit ys an olde-seyde sawe, "there ys harde batayle thereas kynne and frendys doth batayle ayther ayenste other." [p. 610, line 36]

This formal setting-off makes them more conspicuous than the many others which occur unobtrusively throughout the book. It is consistent with the nature of the *Morte Darthur* that so high a proportion of the few explicit judgements on life which punctuate the action should be spoken by the characters rather than the narrator, and delivered in a traditional form. When Elaine says to Lancelot:

> "I have gyvyn the the grettyst ryches and the fayryst floure that ever I had, and that is my maydynhode. . . ." [p. 466, line 12]

---

6. 1477, 1479, 1489. Another and more accessible translation is ed. Curt F. Bühler, EETS (1941).
7. *Paston Letters,* ed. Davis (London, 1963), pp. 130, 173, 209, 219 (Margaret), and 232, 233, 260; ed. Gairdner (Westminster, 1900–01), I, 189, 195, 423, 444, II, 22, 23, 73(4), Supp., 68, 93, 124, 139; and Tilley *A Dictionary of the Proverbs in England in the Sixteenth and Seventeenth Centuries* (Ann Arbor, 1950), B740 (Margaret), C42, C868, C907, H638, M112, M371 S66, T496.
8. *Cely Papers,* ed. Malden (London, 1900), p. 14; cf. Tilley E177, P366.
9. V. B. J. Whiting, *Chaucer's Use of Proverbs* (Harvard, 1934), pp. 75, 152–4.

the phrase is striking not because it is original but because it is right. We may note at this point that with some few exceptions, the proverbs in Malory's book impress in conveying not an individual personality but a common humanity and shared attitudes. In loss or defeat, Malory's characters frequently find dignity and some resignation in those proverbs which, by their very existence as proverbs, testify that others have also faced the insuperable and have not been able to overcome it. Thus we find Merlin accepting his own inability to persuade Arthur at the beginning of the story:

> "But thereas mannes herte is sette he woll be loth to returne." [p. 62, lines 22–23]

And we see the same in Lancelot at the end:

> "That shall repente me whyle I lyve, but a ayenste deth may no man rebell."[p. 691, line 23]

One great authority has said that the use of this kind of proverb is characteristic of the late middle ages, and indeed, has gone on to say that proverbs never preach resistance.[1] Their accent, he tells us, is always of resignation. This is misleading if applied to Malory's characters. The proverbs and proverbial phrases they use help them towards the acceptance of a common idea, but the idea may be one which spurs them to action. Such phrases help to confirm Arthur's resolution to fight on in hopeless straits, to encourage Mellyagaunce to take on a formidable opponent, and to give Lancelot understanding to lift him out of despair [pp. 88–89, 634, 589]. One group which does try to instill resignation has an unusual individual quality, demonstrating that Dinadan's common sense is the sense of the common man:

> "Lo, sir Trystram, here may a man preve, be he never so good yet may he have a falle; and he was never so wyse but he myght be oversayne, and he rydyth well that never felle." [p. 314, lines 18–21]

But whether they urge the characters to action or passivity, the proverbs add a resonance to their lives. They become more rather than less frequent in the later books, and help to give an air of universality and impersonal authority to much of what is said in the final tragedy.

We are given an important but very different effect by Malory's use of the vocative. Vocatives serve to vary pace and emphasis, especially by doubling up the name and title together. Apart from any dignity in the title itself, and the emphasis put on it by its interruption of the plain-sense flow of the meaning, it divides the speech into significant portions, and often implies a deliberateness in the speaker which has a dignity of its own. The speaker is aware both of what he has to say, and to whom he is saying it. In this at least, Lord Chesterfield would have approved of Malory, as much as he would have disapproved of the casual practice of the twen-

---

1. J. Huizinga, *The Waning of the Middle Ages* (London, 1924), pp. 209–11.

tieth century.[2] The vocatives are part of the ineluctable courtesy of Malory's high moments. For instance:

> "My kynge, my lorde, and myne uncle," seyde Sir Gawayne, "wyte you well, now I shall make you a promyse whych I shall holde be my knyghthode. . . ." [p. 659, lines 14–16]

> "My moste redouted Kynge, ye shall undirstonde, by the Popis commaundemente and youres I have brought to you my lady the Quene, as ryght requyryth. And if there by ony knyght, of what degré that ever he be off, except your person, that woll sey or dare say but that she ys trew and clene to you, I here myselff, Sir Launcelot du Lake, woll make hit good uppon hys body that she ys a trew lady unto you. "But, sir lyars ye have lystened, and that hath caused grete debate betwyxte you and me. For tyme hath bene, my lorde Arthur, that ye were gretly pleased with me whan I ded batayle for my lady, youre Quene; and full well ye know, my moste noble Kynge, that she hathe be put to grete wronge or thys tyme. And sytthyn hyt pleased you at many tymys that I shulde feyght for her, therefore mese- myth, my good lorde, I had more cause to rescow her from the fyer whan she sholde have ben brente for my sake." [p. 666, lines 34–47]

The changes are rung: "my most redoubted King", "my lord Arthur", "my most noble King", "my good lord"; and each emphas- ises Arthur's dignity, Lancelot's self-control, and his awareness that he is not merely justifying himself *in vacuo,* but speaking to King Arthur. The vocatives also recall their past and irrecoverable relationship. A rather similar effect is achieved in Galahad's last brief speech, and it is the more impressive that so much of so short and crucial a speech should be taken up by it:

> "My fayre lorde, salew me unto my lorde Sir Launcelot, my fadir, and as sone as ye se hym, bydde hym remembir of this worlde unstable." [p. 586, lines 34–36]

The same effect is found everywhere in Malory, even in polite conversation like that of Pellinor and Meliot de Logres [p. 75]. And our casualness in everyday life probably makes it more effective for us than it was for our forebears.

* * *

GERALDINE HENG

Enchanted Ground: The Feminine Subtext in Malory†

Readings on women characters in Malory are by tradition tacitly inclined to concede to the feminine only a supporting place in the

2. V. Wyld, *A History of Modern Colloquial English* (Oxford, 1953) p. 21.
† From *Courtly Literature: Culture and Context,* edited by Keith Busby and Erik Kooper

Arthurian society of the text. The image of knightly culture on which that civilisation is posited must assume feminine presence and assistance for its completion, yet also constitute the feminine in essentially subsidiary relation to masculinity. Because the female is read as adjunctive (though necessary), a specifically feminine point of view in the work is never fully recovered, but remains only an inchoate potential, subsumed and dispersed within other discourses. A subtextual reading is needed to extricate and identify the outlines of that view, and restore thereby a certain equivalence. The disruptive gestures and energies, intrusions and interruptions that are lodged within surface textuality ultimately point to a sub-merged second narrative interplaying with and often prompting the first, and marked by a recognisably feminine voice.

To be conscious of the precise borders of a feminine hinterland, it is first necessary to be aware of the feminine origin of many of the enabling conditions for activity. The simplest form of this would be that tissue of gifts and material objects intruded into the narrative by women, which surrounds and underlies the textual drama. These timely insertions advance and mediate action, often by directly instigating it: such, for instance, is the purpose of the white hart and brachet which appear at Arthur's wedding feast to begin the cycles of quest for the Round Table. Indeed, this three-fold episode—a prologue of sorts to the later adventures—is exemplary in function, for it lays down the structures of appropriate behaviour toward the feminine in its explicit criticism of Gawain, even as it installs the right of the queen to arbitrate and judge knightly conduct.[1] Only after the action has been finalised and suitably glossed can the Round Table be formally inaugurated.[2] Women also possess devices that restore, such as Isode's brachet which reclaims Tristram to the world after an isolating madness.[3] Objects of protection, like Lyonesse's ring and Lyonet's magical ointment, both so effective in securing Gareth's good reputation, come from women, as do those of harm, such as Morgan le Fay's dangerous cloak, horn and shield. Devices of this nature suggest an extension of female presence in the narrative in the widest sense, since they encompass and symbolically fix the entire realm

(Amsterdam and Philadelphia: John Benjamins, 1990), pp. 283–300. Reprinted with kind permission from John Benjamins Publishing Co., Amsterdam/Philadelphia, www.benjamins.com/jbp.

1. Three models in the treatment of women are posed by the examples of Gawayn, Tor and Pellynor, constituting intertextual commentaries. See, [the equivalent of Caxton's] Book III.

2. Though the "Rounde Table" is mentioned in [Caxton equiv.] Book II [p. 41] it does not in fact formally exist till [Caxton equiv.] Book III [p. 77]. Significantly, the object designating the knightly order—the round table itself—has by this time come to be associated with Guenevere. When it first appears in Wace's Arthuriad, it is only associated with Arthur. In the chronicles, it is the king, of course, who exclusively "arranges the entire symbolic system, presides over its rites and orders its meaning" (Charles Méla, "Perceval," in Literature and Psychoanalysis: The Question of Reading: Otherwise, ed. Shoshanna Felman [Baltimore: Johns Hopkins Univ. Press, 1982], p. 258). That a shift has occurred to connect the queen with this symbolic object is appropriate to romance.

3. Originally given Tristram by a princess of France, King Faramon's daughter (Works, p. 378). We notice that Tristram's hound, Husdant, in earlier traditions (Béroul, Thomas) is not specifically a feminine gift, but merely appears as Tristram's hunter.

of human possibility—good and evil, success and failure, protection or destruction.

Perhaps the most enigmatic and dangerous items of this material trove are *swords*, the instruments on which all masculine accomplishment must turn, and therefore pivotal to conceptions of male identity and personal force.[4] These are so strongly associated with feminine sources and ownership as sometimes to be only temporarily accessible to men. The bestowal of Excaleber occasions the first of otherworldly feminine interventions in Arthur's life, when his own sword, an early motif of his royal authority through its free acquisition from stone and anvil, shatters, failing him. The meaning of this replacement is carefully elaborated in a deliberate pointing to the secret powers of the new weapon, contained not in blade, but in scabbard or sheath (Lat. *vagina*), a significance to which its royal custodian is at first insensitive. It takes Merlin, an authoritative reader of semiotic categories, to decipher the twin interlocking signs, and repeatedly tutor Arthur on the superior value of the scabbard. We notice that *women* never lose sight of these veiled significances, which they too are able to read: the king in tragic contrast never learns the language of emblems sufficiently, and between the theft of the weapon by Morgan, and its partial retrieval by Nyneve, has his fate irrevocably sealed. But if Arthur is blind to the sword's meaning, he is still able to perceive the borrowed character of its powers, a debt he symbolically acknowledges in the favour he agrees to give for their use, and in his unquestioning assumption that Excaleber is not his to keep or bequeath.[5] The negative image to Arthur's graceful submission is then Balyn, the self-willed knight who rejects such personal obligation. After being permitted by a maiden to establish his worth through the drawing of her mistress's word, he defiantly asserts his right to its ownership, illegitimately insisting on keeping what is not his. It is instructive that he goes on to destroy the brother who is an alter-ego of himself with the very sword he will not relinquish—a destiny, we are told by the prophetic female messenger, arising directly out of its misappropriation.[6] In the two men are thus offered polar models of conduct in

4. There is ritual acknowledgement of the importance of the sword, of course, in knighting ceremonies. Where these must be truncated of necessity, as for instance in the battlefield, they are abbreviated to the investment with the sword and the neck-blow, which may stand in for the other features. See Robert W. Ackerman, "The Knighting Ceremonies in the Middle English Romances," *Speculum*, 19 (1944), p. 294.

5. Arthur seems to know precisely what has to be done with Excaleber, and, in his chastisement of Bedyvere upon the latter's failure twice to carry out instructions, what nature of response to expect from the casting of the sword upon the waters. From Bedyvere's initial reluctance to comply, we might guess that it would be a very real temptation indeed to keep the weapon for its "precious stonys" and splendour, or to pass it on as a gift for loyal service. Arthur must be admired for doing neither. On the question of the sword's return to water, and its having come from a lady of the lake, we might note the interesting though arguable point that swords from the Anglo-Saxon and Medieval periods that have been recovered from rivers, lakes or boggy ground seem to have survived best. See H.R. Ellis Davidson, *The Sword in Anglo-Saxon England: Its Archaeology and Literature* (Oxford: Clarendon Press, 1962) and R. Ewart Oakeshott, *The Sword in the Age of Chivalry* (London: Arms and Armour, 1981).

6. I disagree with Jill Mann's contention that in keeping the sword, Balyn is merely "taking the adventure" assigned to him (see " 'Taking the Adventure': Malory and the *Suite du*

response to the feminine: one, acknowledging debt and steward-ship with the acceptance of a sword, and the other, repudiating these with the appropriation of a sword. Where Excaleber will pro-tect its masculine custodian, therefore, Balyn's weapon will destroy the very people who are closest in affection to its user, a legacy transmitted even after his death.[7]

It is possible to discover other swords, confirm a pattern of meaning. Galahad's has a girdle woven for it by Percivale's sister out of her own hair; and it is she who is appointed to draw the sword for him out of scriptural history and gird it upon him, a ceremonially significant act.[8] Lancelot's was "lapped . . . in [Guen-evere's] trayne" [p. 597] on the day he became a knight, a re-writing of the OF Vulgate Cycle episode where it is the queen, and not the king, who supplies the sword that ritually completes Lan-celot's entry into knighthood.[9]

The most suggestive trope for an analysis of feminine authority and presence in Malory, however, is that which is offered to us to describe two kinds of feminine play in the text—the tantalising, doubly-figurative trope of enchantment. In its most familiar con-formation, this refers to magic, and magical resources. While only one man, Merlin, is decisively associated with the practice of sor-cery, the reference of magic to women is almost casual, reflexive; even nameless figures who make the briefest appearances may pos-sess magical objects and spells, and work enchantment: it is a lan-guage depicted by the text as being ubiquitously familiar to women. There is, however, a second level of usefulness to the metaphor of enchantment in a courtly universe: that of the enchantment of love.[1] In a fictive discourse where love is valorised as a formidable motive power, and the female beloved identified with its source and regulation, even a territory of masculine endeavour is a ground

Merlin," in *Aspects of Malory*, eds. Toshiyuki Takamiya and Derek Brewer [D.S. Brewer, 1981], pp. 71–91). An adventure *might* have been assigned to him, one intended for him, had he returned the sword. His refusal signifies, rather, a flouting of the adventure-that-might-have-been, in favour of one of his own definition—a declaration of autonomy with unfortunate consequences for himself and all who encounter him. It is wilful self-assertion being recorded here, and not submission to chance, despite Balyn's—untrustworthy—claim to the contrary. The text goes on to depict him as notoriously inadequate in com-prehension.

7. Merlin predicts that Lancelot will slay Gawain with it, "the man in the worlde that he lovith beste" (*Works*, p. 91).

8. It is a brief knighting ceremony in itself, making Galahad her knight.

9. Guenevere's claims to Lancelot's loyalty are thus established over the king's, making *her*, and not Arthur, his symbolic overlord. See H. Oskar Sommer, ed., *The Vulgate Version of the Arthurian Romances* (Washington: Carnegie Institution, 1910–1912), Vol. III, pp. 131, 137.

1. I avoid applying the term "courtly love" here because of the instability of its status as a critical concept and its fluctuating meaning, which automatically render any application controversial and troublesome. See, e.g., the discussions in Richard Barber, *The Knight and Chivalry* (Ipswich: Boydell and Brewer, 1974); Roger Boase, *The Origins and Meaning of Courtly Love* (Manchester: Manchester Univ. Press, 1977); Julia Kristeva, *Desire in Language: A Semiotic Approach to Literature and Art*, ed. 'Leon S. Roudiez, trans. Thomas Gora, et al. (New York: Columbia Univ. Press, 1980); Jacques Lacan, "God and the *Jouiss-ance* of Woman," in *Feminine Sexuality: Jacques Lacan and the Ecole Freudienne*, eds. Juliet Mitchell and Jacqueline Rose, trans. Jacqueline Rose (New York: Norton, 1982); F.X. Newman, ed. *The Meaning of Courtly Love* (Albany: State Univ. of New York Press, 1968); Denis de Rougemont, *Love in the Western World*, trans. Montgomery Belgion (Princeton: Princeton Univ. Press, 1983); Irving Singer, *The Nature of Love Vol. II: Courtly and Romantic* (Chicago: Univ. of Chicago Press, 1984).

of feminine possibility. Each kind of enchantment traces a path by which the feminine may be active in the world, and constructs patterns of intelligibility specific to female interests and presences. Each must therefore be examined in turn.

The function of love, in the society of the narrative, is the displacement of a purely masculine and primarily martial discourse with another of greater civilising value: a sophisticated, feminine-presided discourse of emotion and relation. An ideology of war is only useful for the initial efforts of colonisation and consolidation which enable the establishment of Arthurian society, and for securing its preservation afterward from sporadic external threat. In textual terms this is to be found in the segments of narrative which manifest what we are used to identify as 'chronicle' behaviour,[2] where a fairly warlike Arthur[3] and the 'pre-romance' heroes of Kay, Lucan and Gryfflet, are the main actors.[4] For the distilling of an actual civilisation in the wake of victory, however, martial energies, always potentially disruptive and dangerous in peacetime, must be sublimated and re-assumed: and an ideology of war is therefore translated into an ideology of arms, or feats of prowess, for love. With this, a masculine orientation, turning upon allegiance to a king, warfare in the company of other men, massive group enterprises, and the goal of personal glory, is displaced and supplanted by a feminine-influenced one: involving instead allegiance to a lady, trial and effort out of the stimulus, inspiration or possibility of love, and in the essentially lonely conditions of the quest.[5] This substitution of orientation has been thought to create a motive logic of "greater moral potentiality" (Singer, p. 82) for the uses of violence,[6] and its dissemination seen to constitute "an

2. It is a mode apparently designed for the subsidiary role of framing actions to the main narrative interest—romance. The movements between what I call 'chronicle' and 'romance' modes are generally unobtrusive—mediated perhaps by the very nature of the model Professor Benson sees Malory's tales as comprising: the "brief prose cycle" (Larry D. Benson, *Malory's Morte Darthur* [Cambridge, MA: Harvard Univ. Press, 1976], p. 4). In a cycle, we would expect the beginning and end of a society to be very different from the treatment of its routine existence, and any sense of possible disjunction we might feel is accordingly minimised. To further ease the transitions, characters like Gawayn appear in both modes.

3. But even here the narrative makes him an Arthur who takes orders from Merlin, acting almost as a (royal) lieutenant. Malory's Arthur, even in the so-called 'chronicle' sections, never has the control and stature of Geoffrey's, Lazamon's or Wace's, or even that of the figure in the ME Alliterative *Morte Arthure* (Valerie Krishna, ed., *The Alliterative Morte Arthure: A Critical Edition*, [New York: B. Franklin, 1976]).

4. Once a society *has* emerged, the characterisation quickly turns against these 'chronicle' heroes, favouring instead the younger, women-serving knights of the Round Table, even as the figure of Arthur himself recedes and diminishes in stature. They are superseded in prowess, with Kay transmuting into a male shrew and a butt of jokes, and Arthur into a slightly buffoonish and ineffectual romance king. Not only is he typically powerless to affect the comings and goings of his knights, but he mutates into someone who takes falls in tournaments, and has to be re-horsed by Lancelot.

5. The knight may of course be accompanied by a maiden or a dwarf, or be temporarily in company. But the model is now *individual*, and not group activity—a paradigmatic "individualism" that arises largely out of a relation to the feminine. I owe the distinctions in this section to Peter Haidu's discussion of romance (Peter Haidu, "Romance: Idealistic Genre or Historical Text?," in *The Craft of Fiction: Essays in Medieval Poetics*, ed. Leigh A. Arrathoon [Rochester, MI: Solaris Press, 1984], p. 31).

6. Presumably because love of another, as opposed to love of self, is outward-directed, and implies a degree of altruism previously unthinkable. "Pagan love of fame was being brought under control".(Morton W. Bloomfield, "The Problem of the Hero in the Later Medieval

extension of the idea of conscience in the broad sense" (Bloom-field, p. 44).[7]

So fundamental to Arthurian society are the ideology of love and the claims of the feminine it inscribes, that those who are ignorant of or antagonistic to their spirit are shown to be necessarily outcast to society. In the fate of Balyn, a knight whose temperament attests a greater affiliation with the 'chronicle' than the 'romance' mode of assumptions, may be glimpsed the lineaments of such a suggestion. His career is a record of incomprehension and misplacement in a discourse intrinsically foreign to him. When first introduced, Balyn is a man already set apart from his civilisation by an earlier act of transgression against Arthur's family, and seeking reintegration into society through intended appeasement of the king [p. 41]. Before this can be attempted, however, his separation is further intensified through the addition of a second killing to the first, deepening his offence against Arthur. Whatever the moral stature of the lady of the lake he beheads,[8] Arthur is in her debt for the loan of Excaleber,[9] an obligation the king feels with sufficient force to cause him to expel Balyn from court [p. 44]. Indeed, it would appear to be out of his negative relations with the feminine, and his limited understanding of the feminine-pervaded discourse of romance society that Balyn's unfortunate fate is determined. We are told that his denial of the sword-bearing maiden's request for the weapon's return will produce his brother's death and his own; and Merlin categorically declares that Balyn will cause the Dolorous Stroke for his responsibility in the suicide of Columbe, whose life he renders unbearable:

> "Because of the dethe of that lady, thou shalt stryke a stroke moste dolerous that ever man stroke—excepte the stroke of Oure Lorde Jesu Cryste—for thou shalt hurte the trewyst knyght and the man of moste worship that now lyvith. And thorow that stroke three kyngdomys shall be brought into grete poverté, miseri, and wrecchednesse, twelve yere—and the knyght shall nat be hole of that wounde many yerys." [p. 48]

Period," in *Concepts of the Hero in the Middle Ages and the Renaissance,* eds. Norman T. Burns and Christopher J. Reagan [Albany: State Univ. of New York Press, 1975], p. 44).

7. "The great invention of the medieval romancers was to link love to glorious deeds so as to make love the direct cause and heroic personal identity and social position [only] the indirect consequences." (Césare Segre, "What Bakhtin Left Unsaid: The Case of the Medieval Romance," in *Romance: Generic Transformation from Chrétien de Troyes to Cervantes,* eds. Kevin Brownlee and Marina Scordilis Brownlee [Hanover: Univ. Press of New England, 1985] p. 35).

8. Whatever the ethical status of this lady of the lake, the enmity between Balyn and herself is oddly expressed in terms of a gender jurisdiction, with each of them being responsible for deaths in the other's family along sexually-divided lines, in a strangely elemental blood-struggle for dominion. Merlin is also singularly unconvincing here in his retrospective vindication of Balyn. Why did he not call the lady of the lake "the falsist damesell that lyveth" [p. 44] on the occasion of her presenting Excaleber to Arthur? We might notice instead that Merlin's later downfall, which he is able to foresee, but unable to prevent, is accomplished by *another* 'lady of the lake'. Perhaps a suggestion of competing spheres of influence and power exists here.

9. Balyn thus not only denies recognition of his debt to the sword-bearing maiden for her part in the drama at Arthur's court (which enables his moral worth to be proven), but with the slaughter of Excaleber's owner, he prevents Arthur from fulfilling *his* debt as well. Courtly society depends on the acknowledgement of just such relationships of duty and obligation, a basis of order.

That the assumptions of the courtly world to which he would belong are alien to him is partially indicated by the absence of any genuine relationship of intimacy with the feminine in Balyn's life. He is one of very few knights in the Arthurian constellation who has no lady, and never wins one, his closest human bond being, significantly, to another man, a brother who is in effect a double of himself. Balyn is therefore caught unawares by the intensity of Columbe's love for Lanceor, and in his wonder at the degree of commitment to the courtly ethos that would prompt so sacrificial an affirmation as hers, may be sensed his own remoteness and dislocation. Not being himself familiar to love, his presence is then inimical to the love-relation,[1] expressing an unintentional antipathy that has even posthumous consequences, for the world's two most famous lovers of women, Lancelot and Tristram, are inadvertently made to do battle later at the very site where Balyn has caused the deaths of Lanceor and Columbe.

Where Balyn's intentions and the outcome of his efforts correspond most closely is in the domain of warfare, an area in which he appears to be comfortable and effectual. Here, he is in his appropriate milieu, a 'chronicle' mode of action where his ungovernable and impulsive explosions of violence are useful.[2] It is only when the application of brute masculine force must be selectively tempered by obedience to social dictates[3] and the regulation of emotion—the peculiar specialities of a romance orientation—that his efforts are accordingly futile. His bewilderment then at his consistent failure to discharge that most basic of chivalric duties, the protection of those in his care, bespeaks the floundering confusion of a man stranded in a strange country with a map he cannot read: because the language, though familiar, has altered its codes of reference. The blank shield he finally accepts as replacement for his own arms is merely the outward mark of his capitulation to the unbreachable discontinuity between that world and himself, and acknowledgement of the subsequent loss of coordinates for identity. His original assertion of independent identity from the feminine, and separation from the matrix of courtly motivations, tragically concludes with the absence of all the saving attributes of such a connection. The aridity of Balyn's life, its squandered resources, and the sad absurdity of his death bear painful witness to that misplaced adaptation.

The love relation, which leaves few untouched in one or another of its forms, is a realm of special possibility for women, since it is indisputably their ground. Through its projection, not only may women condition an arena of masculine action by intervening in

---

1. His interventions are as disastrous for false lovers as for true ones—witness the case of Garnysh of the Mount and Duke Harmel's daughter.
2. Though in fact his best (and least morally ambiguous) accomplishments even in this realm are performed when he takes direction from Merlin. Interestingly, Balyn's story is literally sandwiched between 'chronicles' and 'romance' sections of the Arthuriad, between the close of wars and the start of the cycles of quest and adventure. Needless to say, his making off with Lyle of Avilion's sword does not itself constitute a genuine 'quest' as such.
3. His acts of destruction nearly always coincide with defiance of social law as well. For instance, he retains his sword in Pellam's hall in a rude breach of custom, and kills Garlon, his host's brother, under Pellam's roof, and without issuing prior warning or challenge.

the process of the 'adventure',[4] but even the most sedentary may manifest a presence in knightly acts. By receiving a knight's dedication and being ascribed his motivations, resources and accomplishments, a woman is at once immanent in his deeds, her place and influence permanently inscribed in the record of his gestures. Conversely, knightly obedience to and cooperation with the feminine supply effective means for actualisations of feminine will, creating an agency by which women may be active in the world. Knightly actions, where they are an extension of feminine will are, in this sense, transparent, and have been described as "*Gesta dominarum per milites*, the exploits of ladies through the medium of knights."[5]

Nowhere are the implications of the love-ideology more thoroughly celebrated than in the life and career of that legendary servitor of women, the great Lancelot himself. By his own profession, the meaning of his acts is to be sought only in a strict context of relation with his beloved, and valued only to the degree that they install the advocacy of his lady:

> "And all my grete dedis of armys that I have done, for the moste party was for the Quenys sake, and for hir sake wolde I do batayle were hit ryght other wronge; and never dud I batayle all only for Goddis sake, but for to wynne worship and to cause me the bettir to be beloved—and litill or nought I thanked never God of hit."[p. 519]

In expressly assigning the queen the purpose and uses of his life, Lancelot subsumes his identity within her own,[6] his volition existing separately only insofar as it is a force for instituting her authority and spatial presence within the world. To this end, it is to *Guenevere* and not Arthur that he sends defeated knights for their fealty and homage, an act of empowerment underwriting her supremacy in the courtly universe.[7] Indeed, his submission to his lady's will is so perfect[8]—taking precedence even over allegiance

4. In a courtly society not at war or under foreign threat, the identity-forging requirements of 'adventure' (see Mann) are most often to be met in service to the feminine, whose causes prompt and invite a wide field of knightly activity. Since female interests are thus quintessential to the formation of masculine personality, the agents of chance—like Fortune herself—typically tend to be feminine.
5. Hermann J. Weigand, *Three Chapters on Courtly Love in Arthurian France and Germany* (Chapel Hill: Univ. of North Carolina Press, 1956), p. 33.
6. See Whitehead's sensitive reading of the final, moving events in the Lancelot-Guenevere relationship, where even Lancelot's "resolution to retire from the world . . . is an act of self-identification with his lady" (F. Whitehead, "Lancelot's Penance," in *Essays on Malory*, ed. J. A. W. Bennett [Oxford: Clarendon Press, 1963], pp. 110–13).
7. While also simultaneously "bring[ing] his relation to Guenevere to the center of action" (Benson, p. 90). Where the OF Vulgate Cycle has a number of knights send their captives to surrender to the queen, Malory re-works the features of the story to emphasise Lancelot's unique subservience to Guenevere. See Benson, pp. 82–88, for an account.
8. Even the act of fathering Galahad, so necessary to the Grail Quest element, is depicted as involuntary, the result of wily manipulations by Elayne and Dame Brusen. Maureen Fries is of course correct in positing a suspect Tristram as the foil to Lancelot's unswervingly loyal character ("The Tragic Pattern in Malory's *Morte Darthur*: Medieval Narrative as Literary Myth," in *The Early Renaissance* (Acta 5), ed. Aldo S. Bernado [Binghamton: State Univ. of New York Press, 1979], pp. 81–99). The sordid affair with Segwarydes' wife, and his marrying of the second Isode testify to a corrupt fidelity. Ironically, it is Tristram's love that should be perfect, since unlike Lancelot he is constrained to love by

to God and concern for his soul—that it is awarded the supreme accolade of being suspected to be founded in supernatural causes. The occasional voicing of female speculation that Guenevere exercises the enchantment of sorcery as much as that of love over Lancelot is perhaps supreme testimony to the power and efficacy of feminine domination through the 'spell' of emotion [p. 171]. Indeed, the characterisation of Lancelot answers the requirements of masculine dedication to feminine will so satisfyingly that it has often been felt to contain the lineaments of an ideal women's fantasy. Lancelot is "an example . . . of what the modern analytical psychologist terms the 'animus archetype', the dream image of manliness that inhabits the woman's psyche,"[9] largely because he enacts the willing and symbolic capture of the best attributes of masculinity by feminine elements. That he is the premier knight[1] in a theatre of pure masculine ability and the finest specimen of secular civilisation is necessary to establish the pleasure of his voluntary self-subordination. For not only is the obedience and devotion of chivalry's best knight immensely desirable, but it sets in place a paradigm of idealism of special advantage to the feminine,[2] through its assuming the absolute priority of female interests. Lancelot is the most effective agent in the text for the transliteration of female will and desire because the emotional logic of serving a particular lady translates polysemously for him into dedication to a feminine principle, affirmed in the enormous variety of requests successfully made of him by women.[3] Ultimately it is in this that the meaning of his characterisation is to be found, located within a world of feminine purpose without which a Lancelot as we know him would be unimaginable: seen thus, Lancelot's desire, then, is the desire not *for* the feminine, but *of* the feminine.

Yet however fascinating its operations or useful for individual female causes, the enchantment of love defines clear limits in the end for feminine play. By its nature it allows only an indirect presence and vicarious participation for women, since it is dependent

---

a magic potion. It speaks much for the power of freely-given love that it is Lancelot who is the superior lover.

9. Heinrich Zimmer, *The King and the Corpse: Tales of the Soul's Conquest of Evil* (New York: Pantheon Press, 1956), p. 133.

1. See Benson (pp. 224, 231) on the resuscitation of Lancelot's supremacy after the Grail Quest section with the healing of Sir Urré, and Malory's careful placing of the Quest within "the context of worldly chivalry." To Jessie Weston, Galahad is merely "his father's representative" in a spiritual context, "vicarious achiever of the quest" for Lancelot (*The Legend of Sir Lancelot du Lac* [London: David Nutt, 1901], p. 142). We might note that Lancelot's first name *is* 'Galahad' [p. 79], and see Galahad as a Lancelot stripped of the adulterous relationship with Guenevere that is anathema to the clerical mind.

2. The more attractive younger knights in particular are linked to Lancelot in surreptitious ways by the text and their lives similarly manifest a brand of idealism that is inextricable from a pervasive feminine presence. See especially the characterisations of Gareth, La Cote Male Taylé, and Alysaundir le Orphelyne.

3. That is, all but requests of a sexual nature are effective. Obviously, obedience to Guenevere would preclude compliance to others in this area, though Lancelot is lamentably attractive to women (see, e.g., the importuning of him by the two Elaynes, Hellawes, Morgan and the three queens, the maiden who frees him from Mellygaunce's captivity, etc.). From the earliest traditions, and even in the so-called parallel tradition of the MHG *Lanzelet* (Ulrich von Zatzikhoven, trans. Kenneth G.T. Webster [New York: Columbia Univ. Press, 1951]), Lancelot's characterisation has been of a man to whom women are irresistably drawn, and whose adventures invariably involve the feminine. In Malory's text, women recognise him even when he is disguised.

on knighthood to work its design. For a *direct* mode of feminine play, we must look to a different emphasis in the image of enchantment —the actual practice of magic itself. Love is a spell optimistic in attitude, possible only in a collaborative discourse of shared, mutual, emotional interrelation. Magic, on the other hand, is an independent force, and requires little concession from the human counters with which it transacts. Its dispositions therefore lodge formidable sources of power in the text, to far exceed the mechanism of arms. And, because its operations are secret or indecipherable, and may press even the unwilling into service, it is a thing to be feared, particularly by a warrior ethic, for its mysterious compulsion.[4]

An early demonstration of the control available with magical resources occurs at the very beginning of the text where it is Merlin's supervision of war that enables the victories on which Arthurian society rests. His instigation, management and termination of conflicts is almost arbitrary—a measure of the freedom available to a manipulator of magic. Interestingly, the outward sign of such control and freedom is indicated through the metaphor of *writing:* with the completion of the wars, Merlin narrates and glosses them for record by his predecessor magician, so that they erect a permanent testament to the authori(ci)ty of magic [p. 27].[5] The suggestion that enchantment gives access to textual control hardly surprises, for the place of its practitioners *is* a privileged one in the text, analogous to an author's. It is particularly significant, then, that the one masculine practitioner, Merlin, is excised very early from the narrative, and the mantle of authority and authorship quickly passes from him to female users of magic. Where Merlin once shepherded Uther to a night of illicit love with a duped Ygrayne by means of a clever blurring of identities, Dame Brusen later shepherds Elayne to a similar night with an equally-deceived Lancelot by a parallel trick.[6] Where the enchanter once importuned a damosel of the lake for her love, enchantresses of various persuasions—Hallewes, Annowre, Morgan, the queens of North Galys, Estlonde, and the Oute Iles—now importune men for

4. That enchantment is feared by warriors is axiomatic in all literatures, including the oral. Underlying that response are the competitive structures of two divergent forms of power with a similar goal—domination. Warrior culture, so visible in its trapping, is naturally fearful of a force whose operations are mysterious and invisible, and which it suspects of being more efficacious than (merely) human physical strength.
5. There is, moreover, a manifestly literary quality to many of Merlin's displays of power, several of his forecasts turning upon a trick of writing: since he is able to bring about what he 'foresees' through manipulation of those around him, who co-operate with his arrangements, his assertions, like any author's notes-in-progress, are intrinsically self-fulfilling. The implication of this handling is detectable in Merlin's love of dramatic disguise, hoax and deception, each instance of which playfully puts his audience in doubt of the relationship between the appearance of a thing, and its referent—to fracture the signifying process so that he remains the most accurate reader of signs in the sections he inhabits.
6. The basis of Merlin's trick is merely the creating of a slide between signifier (here, a person's appearance) and signified (that person's identity), switching 'meanings' between Uther and the Duke of Cornwall for a night. Dame Brusen does precisely the same thing, confusing the codes of identity (Elayne's with Guenevere's) through the substituted sign of the queen's ring. From Merlin's manipulation, Arthur, king in the secular realm, is born, while from Brusen's comes Galahad, a spiritual king of a spiritual country.

theirs. Indeed, Merlin's own position as advisor and rescuer of Arthur is filled by the very woman who authors his defeat.

The two principal enchantresses who construct different dispositions of power after Merlin's removal—Nyneve, the principal Lady of the Lake, and Morgan le Fay—are incomprehensible merely by the standards of chivalry. Despite their intermittent conflict with each other, the distinction between them is slight, and far less than their mutual distinction from the realm of commonplace mortals that is their occasional tramping-ground. It is only by a clearly partial standard of reference that Nyneve is identified as beneficent and Morgan as malign—estimated, that is, only by the relative usefulness or threat of their presence for knightly society. Both are women possessed of such powers as confer an extraordinary autonomy upon them, an untrammelled freedom to act that is denied others. Released from the normal codes circumscribing mortal relations, they unleash actions which may playfully mimic the gestures of the courtly-chivalric ethos, but without self-conscription. An ironic tension prevails even as they invoke the formalities of contact—positive or negative by Arthurian standards—with knightly culture, suggesting always their distance.

Nyneve's capture and disposal of Merlin is accomplished through a delicately ironic interrogation of the familiar courtly role of the beloved mistress. Only here, the lady is a maiden, who through sexual withholding keeps perfect her control over her professed lover, and intact her personal powers.[7] The discrepancy between the sage maiden, virginal but canny, and the old magician, powerful but besotted, holds considerable potential for humour or pathos, and is perhaps finally elemental in its configuration. It may be inevitable that she supplants him, as spring replaces winter,[8] but the textual attention is to her clever application of the courtly metaphor at hand. Merlin as would-be lover is eager and compliant, revealing secrets and doing her will in his own version of a knight's performance of deeds for his lady's pleasure. She enacts the elusive beloved, whose extraction of his promise not to enforce her, here through sorcery, should conventionally yield to an eventual submission and acceptance of his love. But Nyneve stages instead an alternative outcome, interpolating a scene in which the anticipated sexual surrender is substituted by her ascension to greater power. To approve and confirm her freedom for such extemporising—a freedom once exercised exclusively by Merlin—the text underwrites her intervention by placing responsibility for

7. An inner fragmentation would seem to attend the loss of virginity, dramatised in folklore and myth by the motif of sudden loss of magical powers with the onset of sexual experience. Brünhilde, in the *Nibelungenlied*, is a notable literary example. Power passes on with the surrender of one's sexual being to another. Something of this may possibly glimmer in the idea of sexual withholding that is one strain in the original configuration of courtly love in lyric poetry. By retaining intact her physical and psychic self, Nyneve continues to hold a palpable form of power over him who loves her.

8. In Merlin's complete resignation to his projected end may be sensed a faint shadow of mythic inexorability, and the structure of cyclical replacement. " 'A', sayde the Kyng, 'syn ye knowe of youre evil adventure, purvey for hit, and putt hit away by youre crauftes, that mysseadventure.' 'Nay', seyde Merlion, 'hit woll not be.' " [p. 78].

his demise with Merlin himself, marking him as a victim of his own lust and folly.[9] This is a displacement that perhaps corresponds to textual shifts in orientation. Merlin's presence is largely useful for the setting-up of Arthurian society, and the accurate deployments required for its early success. With the transposition to romance imperatives, however, his presence is superannuated, and a shift of authority to feminine disseminators of enchantment is timely and appropriate.[1] The text dramatises this transition by juxtaposing an ascent with a decline, and insists that it is by the efficacy of the new powers that the old are subjugated: "So by hir subtyle worchyng she made Merlyon to go undir that stone to latte hir wete of the mervayles there; *but she wrought so there for hym* that he come never oute *for all the craufte he coude do*" [p. 79] emphasis mine). With the supplanting of her predecessor is bequeathed some obligation to the Arthurian world, and Nyneve works with sporadic attention on its behalf. We are given to feel, however, that it is far less central to her interests than it was to Merlin, whose preoccupation with its concerns was obsessive. Our impression, instead, is of her moving in a separate and wholly other reality, her own centres of interest, from which she may be recalled only when more-than-human intervention is exigent.[2] She interrupts when the odds are overwhelmingly weighted by magic against merely human abilities, employing her superior perspective to even the advantage, but does not, unlike Merlin, interfere in the purely human struggle of social destiny.

Having refused to be constructed as a beloved object in the frame of relations proposed by Merlin, Nyneve eventually improvises a construction of her own, with the acquisition of the knight Pelleas for a husband. She does this in a display of her own form of prowess, in playful imitation of the typical chivalric pattern of rescue.[3] Her winning her knight through the defeat of the initial contender for his love is as much a manifestation of feminine desire acting for itself as an independent force in the world, as it is a dispensation of exact justice to two mortals deadlocked by their emotions. To deliver Pelleas from the excesses of Ettarde's cruelty and pride, she enchants him, turning his love away from Ettarde and toward herself, thereby fully transacting Merlin's role by completing the very spell she made Merlin promise never to cast on her, and gaining what she had been unwilling to surrender before.[4]

9. "And allwayes he lay aboute to have hir maydynhode, and she was ever passynge wery of hym and wolde have bene delyverde of hym, for she was aferde of hym for cause he was a devyls son, and she cowde not be skyfte of him by no meane" [p. 79]. The text justifies Nyneve's response by making Merlin too pressing and importunate, and her "wery" resistance only natural. The bringing back of the old slur on Merlin's origins weighs against him conclusively.
1. In the chronicle versions of Geoffrey, Wace and Lazamon, Merlin is of course not even associated with the Arthuriad at all, but only the 'Utheriad,' so to speak.
2. What this 'other reality' might be like is far plainer in the OF Vulgate Cycle or the Middle High German *Lanzelet*, where she is clearly an otherworldly fay, ruling a feminine domain.
3. Through magic, a woman's equivalent of a knight's skill at arms, and a means of accomplishing a purpose by her own efforts. Pelleas' assigned role in the episode is that of the besieged 'lady' who requires succour from a distress he is unable to alleviate on his own.
4. Nyneve is also now a representative of divine authority, as Merlin once was. Where Merlin used to discourse on the will of God, chastising Arthur for squandering his military

Pelleas is thus a twice-enchanted subject, bound by a spell of magic, and one of emotion. We are told that his lady, true to the familiar pattern of other women practising enchantment, thereafter extends protection to her chosen knight in the form of safeguarding his reputation, by ensuring he is never upstaged by Launcelot in tournament.[5]

If Morgan and Nyneve may be said to differ—and some have argued that they are both merely divided aspects of a single magical being[6]—it is a difference of *intensity*, rather than of kind. Nyneve, in spite of her occasional compassion for Arthur, is more impersonal in her relations with the Arthurian world, less interested in its quotidian operations. Morgan, on the other hand, is intensely interested in the Arthurian ethos as a stage for her powers, and the disruptions she manufactures for the king and his knights point to a pleasure in their competitive display. Yet underlying the details of their surface gestures is an abiding similarity of nature. Both have a capacity for force that is not containable by knightly society alone, and therefore a level of independence which establishes them as unique. Each selects whom she will love, rather than being herself selected, and is not above a degree of coercion in the exercise of choice. Both are superb readers of the language of signs, whether it is to secretly encode, or to publicly decipher meaning, in the form of such symbolic objects as shield, horn, cloak or sword; and both are represented, finally, in the feminine escort that will deliver Arthur beyond the regions of his geographical authority.

These similarities shared by Nyneve and Morgan are themselves an expression of their *dissimilarity* from the rest of ordinary humankind. That is to say, they are factors for identifying their otherness within the context of narrative values—constructions to acknowledge the persistence of alternative voices and levels within the text. The presence of enchantresses and enchantment is thus a recognition of alterity in the Arthurian worldview, and of the active pressure of submerged discourses. Distinctions in moral judgement as applied to Morgan and Nyneve therefore tend to be founded less in any genuine opposition of their natures than on a difference in the *perception* and *interpretation* of their otherness. Because Nyneve is more detached from Arthurian society, functioning less visibly, the sense of her alienness is, ironically,

---

resources and for sexual incest [pp. 26, 32], Nyneve now delivers God's judgement to Ettarde for excesses of cruelty and pride [pp. 105–6].

5. We note that Lyonesse similarly guarantees Gareth's reputation with a magical ring of invulnerability [p. 214]. Like a number of other knights, Pelleas virtually disappears from the narrative after the formalisation of his relations with his lady. There are occasions when he accompanies Nyneve to court as her consort, described in much the same way as when wives or mistresses accompany male personages on celebratory occasions ("So agayne the feste of Pentecoste cam the Damesell of the Laake, and brought with hir Sir Pelleas . . ." [p. 111]).

6. For L.A. Paton, this is the "fairy mistress" who is healer and protectress, seductive *amie* and vengeful antagonist, schemer and shape-shifter—an elemental goddess who exists outside the realm of human morality, and for whom its categories are inapplicable, perhaps impertinent (Lucy Allen Paton, *Studies in the Fairy Mythology of Arthurian Romance* [Boston: Athenaeum, 1903]).

reduced. By contrast, Morgan's febrile dynamism and repeated appearances on the Arthurian stage are highly visible, and the tension and suspense generated by her acts draw almost continuous attention to her as a foreign presence. Of the two, Morgan is then the enchantress far more recognisable as different, and other, from the human—a condition that is essential, Fredric Jameson shows us, to a definition of someone as evil:

> Evil . . . continues to characterize whatever is radically different from me, whatever by virtue of precisely that difference seems to constitute a real and urgent threat to my own existence. So from the earliest times, the stranger from another tribe, the "barbarian" who speaks an incomprehensible language and follows "outlandish" customs, but also the woman, whose biological difference stimulates fantasies of castration and devoration . . . behind whose apparently human features a malignant and preternatural intelligence is thought to lurk: these are some of the archetypal figures of the Other, about whom the essential point to be made is not so much that [s]he is feared because [s]he is evil; [but] rather, [that] [s]he is evil *because* [s]he is Other, alien, different, strange, unclean, and unfamiliar.[7]

To compound the palpable impression of her difference, Morgan is also openly defiant of Arthurian values. Where Nyneve has quietly defeated and replaced Merlin—surely an act as destructive as any of Morgan's[8]—Morgan must hurl gloating challenges at Arthur when she out-manoeuvres him, or boastfully delight in her abilities: " ' . . . and tell hym I feare hym nat whyle I can make me and myne in lyknesse of stonys—and lette hym wete I can do much more whan I se my tyme' " [p. 95]. Furthermore, her energies are unruly, her instincts unabashedly competitive. She desires not one, but several lovers [pp. 154–55, 333–34, 385–86, *passim*] and not only magical power, but the temporal authority of the king. The episode of the False Excaleber is set up so that she and Accolon may enact a replacement of Arthur and Uryens, for expressly ambitious reasons [p. 90]; and the hostility she bears Guenevere, revealed in the episodes of the magical horn and insinuating shield she directs toward Arthur's court, arises from merely

7. Fredric Jameson, *The Political Unconscious: Narrative as a Socially Symbolic Act* (Ithaca: Cornell Univ. Press, 1981), p. 115. Jameson observes that romance is a medium for women ("the most characteristic protagonists of romance") because of the room it makes for *guile* as an operating force, over the "sheer physical power" that distinguishes a masculine medium (p. 113). In this light, Morton Bloomfield's lament for the absence of "a hero of any sort worthy of note in the English tradition between Beowulf and Spenser"—by which he means an *epic* hero of supremely and unambiguously masculine proportions— is significant. He finds instead a proliferation of protagonists in the later Middle Ages (Bloomfield, pp. 33–37). This 'de-heroicisation' of literature and proliferation of characters testifies of course to a widening and varying of an original concept of heroism narrowly male, and which makes possible, and is itself the effect of, an entrance of the feminine and feminine kinds of heroism into textual life, that were previously (by definition) excluded.

8. Nyneve has in fact removed from Arthurian society a significant source of benevolent patronage, but escapes censure for having accomplished this discreetly, away from general observation. Her habitual understatement, and Morgan's customary overstatement, leads to their respective vindication and vilification by society.

acquisitive hopes. Like Nyneve, she too is linked to Merlin by the text—he is "a devlys son" [p. 79], she "an erthely fende" [p. 92], a suitable description perhaps for one who is ultimately an over-reacher, and whose form of enchanted play testifies to an intense interest in the demonstration and extension of her powers.

In the final analysis, however, Morgan's impact is not as destructive as it might superficially seem. The trials she provides Arthur's knights serve to increase their abilities and reputations with successful endurance; and the potentially subversive instruments she sends to Arthur are deflected from their purpose when Nyneve publicly discloses their concealed meanings. Indeed, her last appearance in the text with her sister-enchantress, in the barge to Avilion, offers us a curiously suggestive image for a retrospective re-vision of her acts. Here she addresses Arthur not agonistically, but as a fellow player in a drama that has now concluded all its scenes, with their former identities irrelevant and discarded. Arthur's last actions have been enigmatic, seeming to indicate his anticipation of the barge and its women,[9] and eager to entrust his final destiny to them. Morgan's greeting to her brother—the only speaking voice among the women—is accordingly affectionate, concerned: " 'A, my dere brothir! Why [ha]ve ye taryed so longe frome me? Alas, thys wounde on youre hede hath caught over-much coulde!' " [p. 688]. The tones are the gentle, chiding ones of a protectress and healer, not those of a mortal enemy, and in them may be discerned a suggestion of the final instability and impermanence of all constructed identity. An affinity between them is at once suggested: the bond perhaps of two actors finally away from the pageant, who need no longer play their temporarily assigned roles.

In Malory's text, I have attempted to show, is a subtext of feminine presences—direct and indirect manifestations which together inscribe a range of play that perhaps yields, in the fullest sense, what has been called "the recovery of a possible operation of the feminine in language."[1]

MARK LAMBERT

Shame and Guilt†

* * *

The usefulness of the shame-guilt distinction for an understanding of how Lancelot and other characters behave in Le Morte Darthur

---

9. "Though Arthur returns Excalibur to the Lady of the Lake to signal his mortal distress, it seems a signal arranged with Morgan, for she immediately appears with the greeting 'A, my dere brothir!' (III, 1240) and bears Arthur away" (Myra Olstead, "Morgan le Fay in Malory's Morte Darthur," BBIAS, 19 [1967], p. 138).
1. Luce Irigaray, Ce Sexe qui n'en est pas Un (Paris: Minuit, 1977), p. 74.
† From Malory: Style and Vision in "Le Morte Darthur," (New Haven and London: Yale University Press, 1975), pp. 179–194. Reprinted with permission of Yale University Press.

was first pointed out by D. S. Brewer in his edition of Malory's final tales,[1] and his insight is of fundamental importance. It seems to me, in fact, that the distinction is even more basic than Professor Brewer considers it to be. It is Malory himself, not just his characters, for whom honor and shame are more real than innocence and guilt. *Le Morte Darthur* is *of* rather than *about* a shame ethos. When Malory describes Lancelot's [morally outrageous] speech [p. 666, line 33 ff.] as "full knightly" he is not being ironic.

For the author as for the character the *fact* of the lie does not really exist; or we might say it exists only in the ghostly way the mountain and valley of Perceval's island exist: it has no imaginative weight. The narrative style of *Le Morte Darthur*, as I have been describing it in this book, obviously works well with an emphasis on public recognition rather than private knowledge. Guilt may matter in Lancelot's world; in the imagined world of Sir Lancelot, where one's official, social identity is one's real identity, shame is more significant. Malory's style presents values and states as objectively demonstrable and palpable, existing on the same plane of reality as physical objects. It is what might be called the stylistic converse of this demonstrability of states and values that the state which is not demonstrated does not fully exist: shame matters, not guilt. The important thing is not one's own knowledge of what one has done (the inner life is not very significant in Malory), but public recognition of one's actions. Lancelot really is indignant. His observable behavior is what it always was, and he has passed the tests: what right do people have to make trouble? "Liars," for him, means almost "those who say what they cannot make good" rather than "those who say what is false." Strange as it may seem, he believes what he says here about the might of God. In the entrapment itself he exclaims, just before opening the door to fight his accusers, ". . . God deffende me frome such a shame! But, Jesu Cryste, be Thou my shylde and myne armoure" [p. 650].[2] He does not think at all about the morality of his presence in the queen's chamber; what matters is the attempt of Aggravain and the others to cause trouble about that presence: God would side with Lancelot rather than Aggravain, the stirrer up of strife.

When we think of Malory as a writer to whose imagination shame and honor were more vivid than guilt and innocence a good many things in *Le Morte Darthur* make more sense than they did before: things ranging from Malory's attitude toward the adultery of Lancelot and Guinevere to the paragraph to paragraph emphases of the narration. Inconsistencies remain, of course; here as

---

1. *The Morte Darthur: Parts Seven and Eight* "Introduction," part vi, pp. 23–35. See also the discussion of shame, appearance and reality in S. J. Miko's extremely interesting "Malory and the Chivalric Order," *Medium Aevum* 25 (1966): 211–230. My idea of the nature of shame in *Le Morte Darthur* is closer to Brewer's than to Miko's, but I am more nearly in agreement with Miko than with Brewer on the relation of the author's attitudes to the characters'.

2. This passage is original with Malory, though I suspect there is a memory of Ephesians VI in it [cf. n. 4, p. 569—Editor.]. Lancelot and the Red Crosse knight are protected by the same armor.

elsewhere Malory's imagination recasts but does not reblend. Yet the reader will find that a shame-reading solves more puzzles than it creates. In this section I want to look at some of the ways in which Malory's shame-orientation manifests itself; but I should take a moment first to say a few things about the context of this shame/guilt contrast and its appropriateness for the study of a late medieval writer.

In literary criticism the shame/guilt distinction occurs most commonly when Homeric and post-Homeric values are being compared.[3] We have learned to see Homer as the poet of a shame-culture, and Aeschylus, his contemporaries, and successors as the poets (perhaps even the creators) of a guilt-culture, Generally speaking, there is a value judgment explicit or implicit in these contrasts: shame cultures are "primitive," guilt-cultures "more sophisticated";[4] the discovery of guilt, responsiveness to internal sanctions, is an advance in civilization. Is it not improbable then that Malory, living in a society well acquainted with the values of innocence and guilt, would respond more deeply to the primitive values of honor and shame? Not as improbable as it may seem, I think.

First, the shame-culture/guilt-culture distinction is not really like a quill/fountain pen distinction. It is obvious enough from a glance at any day's newspaper that "shame" and "honor" never become obsolete concepts. Classicists such as Snell and Dodds tell us not that shame and honor do not matter in post-Homeric writings but that new and sometimes competing values have been introduced. For any anthropologist, I believe, a guilt-culture is one in which internal sanctions matter more than external sanctions, rather than one in which shame and honor are entirely replaced by guilt and innocence.[5] Second, it is unnecessary to assume that because Christian thought stressed guilt and innocence all of medieval Christendom was a single guilt-culture. Honor can be more important than innocence even for those who have been "exposed" to the more advanced value and might know better; it is quite possible for ideas of guilt and innocence to exist, but not lodge as deeply or as widely in a society's imagination as its ideas of shame and honor. Even now a good many parts of Christendom are better described as shame-cultures than as guilt-cultures. Our fifteenth-century Englishman may seem rather out of place among samurai, Homeric, and Navaho warriors; but a twentieth-century village in Andalusia might also be called a shame-culture,[6] and in

---

3. See the first two chapters of E. R. Dodds, *The Greeks and the Irrational* (Berkeley and Los Angeles, 1951) and the first chapter of Bruno Snell, *Scenes from Greek Drama* (Berkeley and Los Angeles, 1964).
4. Snell, *Scenes from Greek Drama*, p. 11.
5. I think most contemporary anthropologists would also maintain that there are guilt elements in all shame-cultures. See, e.g., Philip K. Bock, *Modern Cultural Anthropology: An Introduction* (New York, 1969), p. 69.
6. For a study of honor in such a village, see Julian Pitt-Rivers, "Honour and Social Status," in *Honour and Shame: The Values of Mediterranean Society*, ed. J. G. Peristiany (London, 1966), pp. 19–77. Professor Brewer uses this volume, and particularly the Pitt-Rivers essay, as points of reference for his discussion of honor in Malory. The title of this book is of course quite relevant to what I am saying here. I might also point out,

this setting Malory looks somewhat more at home. Perhaps the most important point to be made here, however, is that the terms "shame" and "guilt" are meaningful for psychological as well as anthropological description and classification.[7] All men—like all or most cultures—have both a sense of shame and a sense of guilt, and the relative strengths of the two will vary from individual to individual. Now assuming that (however much the psychologist may want to refine the anthropologist's understanding of the origins, dynamics and interrelationships of shame and guilt) both psychologist and anthropologist are referring to the same or closely related things when they use these terms, we may stress the variety of attitudes possible not only from culture to culture but also within a given culture. Saying that shame was more real, that it loomed larger in Malory's imagination than guilt, and that Malory was likely far less sensitive to guilt and innocence than, say, Chaucer, does not mean we see *Le Morte Darthur* as an inexplicable throwback to the Homeric age.[8]

* * *

[L]et me turn to some slight but illuminating changes in wording Malory makes in adapting an important scene from *La Queste del Saint Graal*: the interview in which Lancelot confesses to a hermit that he has "loved a quene unmesurably and oute of mesure longe" [p. 519, line 38].

Just before the interview, Malory's Lancelot speaks bitterly of the failure in the quest his sinfulness has brought him. This speech is explicitly concerned with shame and honor in a way its source is not:

> And then he begins a great and marvellous lament, and calls himself a miserable wretch and says: "Ah, God, now my sin and my wicked life appear! Now well I see that more than any other thing my wretchedness has undone me. For when I ought to have amended myself, then the fiend destroyed me, who so blinded me that I could see nothing that was of God. And it is no marvel that I cannot see clearly: for since I was first a knight, there has been no hour in which I was not covered by the shadows of deadly sin, for more than anyone else I have dwelled altogether in lust and in this world's vileness."

---

while on the subject of shame-orientation in a Christian society, that Eugene Vance has described *The Song of Roland* as the expression of a shame-culture. (*Reading the song of Roland*, p. 36.) Despite the Christian context of the *Roland*, "respect for public opinion" is "the strongest moral force its characters know." In the terms I used before, there has been exposure to "higher" values, but those higher values have not really taken. We might also recall that the last word in *Beowulf* is *lofgeornost*, "most eager for praise."

7. Gerhart Piers, in Part I of the influential *Shame and Guilt: A Psychoanalytic and a Cultural Study* by Gerhart Piers and Milton B. Singer (New York, 1971 [originally published 1953]) offers a post-Freudian description: "Whereas guilt is generated whenever a boundary (set by the superego) is touched or transgressed, shame occurs when a goal (presented by the ego ideal) is not being reached. It thus indicates a real 'shortcoming.' Guilt anxiety accompanies transgression; shame, failure" (p. 24). I am certainly not competent to evaluate this description (or Singer's critique of earlier anthropological work) but it does seem to me that for both Malory and his hero failure is indeed more real than transgression.

8. It would be useful to consider the relation between Malory's shame-orientation and his taste for English heroic poems.

And then he called hymselff a verry wrecch, and moste unhappy of all knyghtes; and there he seyde, "My synne and my wyckednes *hath brought me unto grete dishonoure.* For whan I sought worldly adventures for worldely desyres, I ever encheved them and had the bettir in every place—and never was I discomfite in no quarell, were hit ryght, were hit wronge. And now I take uppon me the adventures to seke of holy thynges, now I se and undirstonde that myne olde synne hyndryth *and shamyth me,* that I had no power to stirre nother speke whan the holy bloode appered before me." [p. 518]

* * *

Later in their conversation Lancelot tells the *Queste* hermit that he will live chastely, but cannot give up the life of chivalric adventure. The hermit rejoices to hear him say so, and tells him, "if you would leave the sin of the queen, I tell you truly that Our Lord would love you again and send you succour and look upon you with pity and give you power to achieve many things your sin now keeps you from." Malory changes the power to accomplish things to the reward for accomplishment—worship:

"Sir, loke that your harte and your mowth accorde," seyde the good man, "and I shall ensure you ye shall have the more worship than ever ye had." [p. 520, lines 5–7]

The shift in emphasis is subtle but it is there; and there not just in the attitude of Malory's hero, but of Malory's work as a whole.

Another thing worth considering here is what might be called the argument from loose ends: a consideration * * * of what kind of thing Malory is careless about when he is careless. The loose end I want to consider here * * * is found in the story of Meliagaunt, the most contemptible of Malory's villains. On coming into the queen's chamber, Meliagaunt discovers that her bed had been bloodied. He then accuses Guinevere of treason in the form of adultery with one of the wounded knights who lay in her chamber during the night. Technically, the queen is not guilty of the charge. But only technically: it was Lancelot, not one of those wounded knights who shared her bed, and the blood came from a deep cut in Lancelot's hand. After reprimanding him for opening the queen's bed without permission, Lancelot agrees to act as Guinevere's champion against Meliagaunt, and eventually fights and kills him. This section, "The Knight of the Cart," then closes with the words "And than the kynge and the quene made more of sir Lancelot, and more was he cherysshed than ever he was aforehande" [p. 638, lines 32–34].

The problem is that bloodied bed. Don't the characters wonder whose blood it is and how it got there?

* * *

It seems to me that Malory's silence about the blood and stress on Arthur's gratitude make sense if we understand Malory, Arthur, and Lancelot to be concerned with the queen's shame rather than her guilt: we focus not on whether adultery was committed, but on whether the charge of treason can be made good. I do not think the non-resolution of the blood question is a literary strategy: it is simply a loose end. * * * The question "what did Arthur think about the bloody bed?" has much the same answer as the question "what happens to the fool in *King Lear*?": nothing; the question may matter to us, but it did not matter to the author.[9]

Malory's shame-orientation is important for our understanding of the love of Lancelot and Guinevere and the kind of responsibility those lovers have for the ruin in the eighth book. If we assume the author must want us not to look at questions of shame but to look through them to the real issues of guilt, we will see "and that caused sir Agravain" as Malory being banal in interpreting his own work, and most of the other causes I have discussed will seem fake columns in the tragic edifice. If we see the tragedy primarily in terms of a shame-ethos, Aggravain does really cause it: we view Lancelot and Guinevere as victims rather than culprits, their love as the occasion and not the root of the anger and unhap. For Malory, I believe, Lancelot's tragedy is not so much the tragedy of having caused as of having failed to prevent disaster.

* * * Here I want to conclude by looking at a structural pattern whose full importance we don't feel until we realize the centrality of shame in *Le Morte Darthur*. The pattern is the recurrent motif of noise.

Just before Lancelot dies, he summons his last companions, the hermit and his remaining fellows, and speaking "wyth drery steven" asks to be given the last rites. They tell him this is not necessary; he will be "wel mended" in the morning. Lancelot replies, "My fayr lordes . . . wyt you wel my careful body wyll into th'erthe—I have warnyng more than now I wyl say; therefore gyve me my ryghtes"

9. See also Miko's discussion of this loose end, "Malory and the Chivalric Order," p. 215. Let me suggest two other points in the story of Meliagaunt's accusation where a shame interpretation is useful. Lancelot's first reaction to the story of Meliagaunt's discovery and accusation is fury at Meliagaunt's breach of etiquette in touching the queen's bed [p. 634, lines 14–20]; Meliagaunt has done "unworshypfully and shamefully." The accuser then answers "Sir, I wote nat what ye meane . . . but well I am sure there hath one of the hurte knyghtes layne with her thys nyght" [p. 634, lines 21–23]. Now here, as with Lancelot's speech when he returns Guinevere to Arthur, we see Malory's hero as either a peculiarly brazen hypocrite, very stupid, or shame-oriented. Surely the third possibility is the most attractive. If Meliagaunt does not understand what Lancelot means it is because he is a churl as well as a coward.

The wounded knights are "sore ashamed" when they see the blood discovered by Meliagaunt [p. 634, line 6]. What is likely to be our first assumption here—that they are "ashamed" because they think the queen had committed adultery—may well be right. But perhaps not. These knights are all willing to champion the queen's cause after seeing the evidence as well as before seeing it, and Malory doesn't suggest either that they have to struggle with their consciences or that they continue to be willing to champion the queen *in spite of* the evidence they have seen. When Malory says these knights are "ashamed," his emphasis, I suspect, is on their embarrassment that the hated Meliagaunt has the queen "at suche avauntage," rather than on the guilt that evidence points toward; their reaction may be like that of a defense attorney when the prosecution introduces unexpected new evidence. Perhaps the most curious manifestation of the shame ethos here is the obliviousness of both Malory and his characters to the nature of the ancient motif at the center of this episode. No one seems very interested in the fact that the queen is innocent only through a technicality, that it is merely the letter of the law which puts her "in the right." Lancelot could not be more single-willed defending Una's chastity than he is defending Guinevere's innocence.

[p. 695]. That "I have warnyning more than now I wyl say" is not in the sources, and it is somehow very moving; if Lancelot dies as a Christian man, he also dies as a Malorian knight, anxious to do rather than talk about. "But he seyth but lytil, but he doth much more," Arthur's praise of Torre in the first book [p. 83 lines 1–2] might apply to any of the Round Table knights; most recently to the dying Lucan [p. 686, lines 25–43], and here to the greatest of those heroes even when all that is left to do is to prepare for his own death and burial. This laconism is the mark of Arthurian knighthood, and the thing which destroys that knighthood is its opposite: an insistent noise, a saying which cannot be ignored.

We are told, at the beginning of the seventh tale, that when Lancelot and Guinevere resumed their love "many in the courte spake of hit—and in especiall Sir Aggravayne, Sir Gawaynes brothir, for he was ever opynne-mowthed" [p. 588, lines 18–20].[1] Thus, although Aggravain can in fact use the laconic style on occasion (" 'Lat us deale,' seyde Sir Aggravayne and Sir Mordred" [p. 648, line 14]), Malory makes us associate his destructive quality with an unchivalric garrulousness. We find this same emphasis on unbearable noise and open speech in the first of the calamities of the eighth tale:

> So hyt myssefortuned Sir Gawayne and all hys brethirne were in Kynge Arthurs chambir; and than Sir Aggravayne *seyde thus opynly, and nat in no counceyle, that manye knyghtes myghte here.* . . .[2] [p. 646, lines 16–18]
>
> But thus as they were togydir, there cam Sir Aggravayne and Sir Mordred wyth twelve knyghtes with them of the Rounde Table; and they seyde *with grete cryying and scaryng voyce,*
>
> "Thou traytoure, Sir Launcelot, now ar thou takyn!"
>
> *And thus they cryed with a lowde voyce, that all the courte myght hyre hit.* [p. 649, lines 5–9]
>
> But ever Sir Aggravayne and Sir Mordred cryed, "Traytour knyght! come oute of the Quenys chambir, for wyte thou well thou arte besette so that thou shalt nat ascape!"
>
> "A, Jesu mercy!" seyde Sir Launcelot, "*thys shamefull cry and*

---

1. In his note to this passage Vinaver suggests that "open-mouthed" came from a misreading of the French. This seems to me possible, but the epithet is powerful and right, however it got there.

2. This passage, and especially the words "opynly, and nat in no counceyle," are particularly striking if we know the French *Mort*. There, on an earlier occasion, Aggravain had spoken to Arthur of the adultery in this way: * * * "Sire, I would tell you a thing *in counsel,* if I did not think it would grieve you. And know that I tell you it to avenge your shame." "My shame?" said the king. "Is it then so high a thing that my shame lies there?" "Sire, yes," said Aggravain. "And I shall tell you how." [*Then he drew him to one side and said to him in counsel.* . . .] In the French scene which corresponds to Malory's, Aggravain and his brothers are [speaking of this matter very privately]. The king draws near, Gawain tells Aggravain to keep quiet, and Aggravain says he will not. The king overhears this, and wants to know what Aggravain was speaking about so loudly. Arthur insists on knowing: Aggravain will not tell him, nor will the others; Arthur only extracts the information from Aggravain by taking up a sword and threatening to cut off his head if he doesn't speak. The French Aggravain, obviously, is far less open-mouthed than the Malorian one. The Aggravain of the *Stanzaic Morte* occupies a more-or-less intermediate position between the discreet French accuser and the reckless Malorian one. See 11.1672 ff.

noyse I may nat suffer, for better were deth at onys than thus
to endure *thys payne.*" [p. 649, lines 30–32]

* * *

That high volume of sound—sound which not only marks but
brings about the ruin of Arthur's kingdom—probably has a good
deal to do with the mysterious poignancy of one bit of detail late
in the work. After Lancelot's final interview with Guinevere, all
day and night he rides weeping through a forest; then he comes to
the place where he will remain for the rest of his life: "And atte
last he was warre of an ermytage and a chappel stode betwyxte two
cliffes, and than he herde a lytel belle rynge to masse. And thyder
he rode and alyght, and teyed his hors to the gate, and herd Masse"
[p. 693, lines 10–13]. Less than a page later, Bors too comes upon
this chapel: "And so Syr Bors herde a lytel belle knylle that range
to Masse . . ." [p. 693, lines 32–33]. Malory is working from the
stanzaic poem here, but one of his additions to the story is that
little describing the bell. Not an astonishing epithet, but exactly
right: after all the noise and shouting, the audibility of a *little* bell
suggests the quiet of the life Lancelot and his fellows now take up.

* * *

TERENCE McCARTHY

On Malory's Style†

* * *

'Who the deuce would begin talking about the style,' asked C. S.
Lewis, 'till all else was given up?' He was referring in particular to
the novel, but many people would be ready to express more general
agreement. With Malory, however, it is impossible to consider style
as a merely secondary topic—one taken up to ensure an exhaustive
survey—for the simple reason that Malory's style has been almost
universally admired, whereas there is little agreement about anything else in the *Morte Darthur.* It is a powerful and intensely
moving style and yet, apparently so simple; indeed, almost artless,
unexpected. And just as the realism and characterisation of the
Morte Darthur are not as 'modern' as some would have us believe—
Malory does not really lead forward to the novel; its assumptions
and interests are not his—so his style seems to look back rather
than ahead. It is plain, formal, stately, and more akin to older,
oral modes of narration; it is never learned, sophisticated or
refined. Malory's turn of mind, as D. S. Brewer points out, is
'archaic', and the bases of his style are also those of the traditional
writer; they have their roots in oral tradition.

† From *An Introduction to Malory* (Cambridge: Brewer, 1988), pp. 124–134. Reprinted with
permission of Boydell & Brewer Ltd.

Oral Tradition

Much emphasis has been placed in recent years on the impact of writing on culture and thought. Writing does not merely provide thought with a new mode of expression, it has totally transformed it. Literate and oral (preliterate) cultures do not merely express themselves differently, their perception is not the same. The thought processes of literate cultures are those we take for granted, they are the assumptions we work with every day; but oral cultures function in other ways.

A useful definition of oral cultures can be found in W. J. Ong's *Orality and Literacy,* and although he has nothing to say about Malory, the relevance of his remarks to the style of the *Morte Darthur* is, I think, immediately evident.

The cultures of orality and literacy have an entirely different attitude to memory. We write something down in case we forget. If the spoken word is forgotten, it is lost. Writing replaces memory; oral cultures must, unless they are ready to accept oblivion, defend memory at all costs. They therefore devise all sorts of mnemonic aids: charms, lists, alliterations, formulae, devices which will stimulate recall. In this respect there are times when Malory writes as though he were not *writing* at all, writes not as though he were *recording* great deeds, but trying to anchor them in our minds.

Oral cultures are additive rather than subordinate; they rely on accumulation not a hierarchy of ideas. They prefer to organise items into appropriate groups rather than separate identity, and their expression tends to be repetitive, never too dense for the attention or the memory. What is presented often enough rather than what is presented persuasively carries weight. They prefer to concentrate on situation rather than on abstraction, and their point of view is not distanced, objective, or ironic, but participatory and committed. They see from within not from without.

This is a useful context in which to consider Malory's style. Malory is very much a traditional writer with his roots in an oral tradition. Indeed, it is more than likely that his first literary inspiration was the writings of the alliterative tradition, which look back to oral cultures, and there are still signs within his book that occasionally Malory is thinking in terms of a listening audience. His famous apostrophe on the state of the realm in his day—'Lo, ye, all Englysshemen' [p. 680]—is a collective address not a private aside to the reader. Malory's style has been analysed at length and very well by a number of eminent specialists; I merely wish to draw attention to certain (isolated) features of style which, like Malory's use of realism and characterisation, are indicative of his outlook. Style is not the icing on a cake, but an essential ingredient. To this extent, critics who fall back on Malory's style for want of something else to praise, have, in fact, singled out a vital aspect of his art.

Coordination

One thing which distinguishes Malory from the French prose romances he was working with is his attitude to subordination. It has been suggested that the structures of Malory's prose are based on French models, but this is probably wrong. French prose uses a highly developed system of subordination; Malory's sentences are almost exclusively coordinated: he rarely strays beyond 'and' and 'but'. The use of parataxis was a common feature of fifteenth century translation and was, perhaps, one aspect of its low level of competence, and yet in Malory it gives a deceptively simple appearance totally in keeping with the author's outlook and presentation.

Malory's prose is accumulative not causal; emphasis is clearly placed on events not the relationship between events. The important question is 'What happened?' not 'What happened next?' Malory's eye is on the act not on the interpretation, and he provides a kind of objectivity by letting everything speak for itself. He presents what happened, and then what, and then, without organising things into a pattern or analysis. He reports the news, as it were, without commentary and without organising the details in such a way that a point of view comes across. Subordination inevitably reveals the analytic mind of the narrator, who fits events into a hierarchy of importance and cause. Malory merely provides us with the facts; we are free to assess them as we read. His parataxis is not mere artlessness, it implies an outlook. It gives an appearance of objectivity, of historicity. Malory is a historian recording great deeds; he is not a journalist writing an editorial.

Malory's prose is not totally without subordination, but he tends to say what he has to say by piling one detail on top of another rather than with the aid of complex organisations of the thought. Cumulative weight not logical force is the basis of his prose, and even when explanations are being offered, Malory still uses a paratactic presentation. At times he appears to use subordinating conjunctions, but they turn out to be 'ands' in disguise. The words suggesting logical analysis are mere sand in our eyes: information is being added not sifted. Consider the sentences:

> wyte thou well I am sette in suche a plyght to gete my soule hele. And *yet* I truste, thorow Goddis grace and thorow Hys Passion of Hys woundis wyde, that aftir my deth I may have a syght of the blyssed face of Cryste Jesu . . .
>
> [p. 692, lines 3–7]

and:

> And if that I had nat had my prevy thoughtis to returne to youre love agayne as I do, I had sene as grete mysteryes as ever saw my sonne Sir Galahad, Percivale, other Sir Bors. And *therefore*, madam, I was but late in that Queste . . .
>
> [p. 589, lines 1–5]

The italicised 'yet' and 'therefore' are present under false pretences.

The use of parataxis gives a semblance of objectivity; it is also responsible for there being little or no simultaneity of action in Malory. We have no sense of things going on at the same time: when Malory describes a mêlée there is little to distinguish it from a series of individual encounters. It is as though knights stand by inactive until the narrator can turn his attention to them. As Malory's sentences are sequential in structure, so are the events he describes in time.

Repetition

Malory does not rely on the logical force of reasoned structures but the emotional force of insistence. The accumulation and repetition of loaded words arouse a massive response and achieve an effect logical structures would miss. There are several kinds of repetition. First of all, at moments of intensity, Malory repeats key words frequently in a very short space. One eloquent example is from the Grail book, in a passage which is, uncharacteristically, a very free rendering of the French:

> 'Now,' seyde the Kynge, 'I am sure at this Quest of the San-kegreall shall all ye of the Rownde Table departe, and nevyr shall I se you agayne holé togydirs. Therefore ones shall I se you togydir in the medow, all holé togydirs— therefore I woll se you all holé togydir in the medow of Camelot, to juste and to turney, that aftir youre dethe men may speke of hit that such good knyghtes were here, such a day, holé togydirs.'
> [p. 501, line 46–p. 502, line 5]

It is Malory who chooses to load the force of this passage by repeating the key word. The effectiveness is perhaps a matter of opinion, and the editor of the version of the *Morte Darthur* published by Caxton clearly considered the passage to be a scribal error, and reduced it. But it is a feature of style Malory uses regularly and although it can appear artless, this is precisely how emotional speech works. In the heat of a moment of intense feeling we do repeat ourselves; it is only later that we are cool enough to vary our discourse.

I would not always want to defend Malory's use of repetition. At times the repeated words are too banal to suggest intended effects and he would have done well to revise. A good example of this poverty of expression is the very first page of the *Morte Darthur*: it is as though the challenge of actually getting started took the words from his mouth. When key words are concerned, however, their repetition is essential to the emotional impact. There are even passages where the power of the language resides entirely in the verbal repetition, for the syntax, less important, disintegrates. The famous

May passage is a good example of this: it is worth examining its structure logically and then considering the impact of the words. Most obviously, in the dialogue of scenes of dramatic interest verbal repetition plays an important part. Consider the passage where Lancelot arrives at Meliagaunt's castle, for example [p. 630, line 40–p. 632, line 11]. Repetition is still a forceful linguistic device, of course. It is one of the tricks of the advertiser's trade to repeat the name of the product as often as possible.

Not only does Malory repeat words over a brief passage, the descriptions he gives throughout the book rely heavily on the same limited set of adjectives and stock phrases time and again. To modern eyes this inevitably looks like poverty of expression; in fact it reveals a different outlook. A modern writer would look for variation; Malory relies entirely on conventional vocabulary. His knights are forever noble, his ladies all passing fair. Just as he never attempts to individualise his characters through any analysis of their personalities, so he never distinguishes them in description. They all belong to the appropriate category; they all conform to the pattern. The adjectives he singles out with which to describe them are, in a way, the ones which make them least singular, least worth the attribution of an adjective at all. Even when Malory seems to give an exceptional detail of information or an unusual comparison, we can be fairly sure it will crop up later. When knights come rushing together like two wild boars, we feel that the image is vivid and unusual, until it turns out to be a part of the standard vocabulary of combat. The image does not single out one battle from many, it links it to all the others. And so too with the vocabulary of warfare in general. Malory employs the same range of stock vocabulary each time he takes up the same kind of context. To some extent perhaps the repeated vocabulary reflects the repetitions of life—the number of actions in battle and the number of outcomes is limited—but it is also a way of relating each incident to its proper context. What some will see as a sign of Malory's lack of imagination is, for others, a legitimate aspect of his art. There are appropriate terms for each event. It is Malory's version of the proper word in the proper place. The right words are more important than mere embellishment. Malory's repetitions do not betray a pedestrian lack of verbal imagination; his traditional, normative language accords to everything its proper category or role. It is part of the decorum both of his style and his outlook.

There are repetitions within Malory's narrative and within the speech of his characters; at times they and their author share the same vocabulary, and in this way Malory introduces a sense of verbal inevitability. As the author confirms the choice of words of the characters, or as they speak as he does, so the words seem doubly appropriate to the situation. What we have is not merely one point of view (the author's or a character's), but the right words for the occasion. By disappearing behind his characters, the author gives weight to what they say. He is not analysing or suspecting their speech, he is—in a literal sense—taking their word for it.

Consider the following extract, where the repetitions underline the
support the author is giving his characters:

> '. . . . But I se well,' seyde Sir Bors, 'by her *dyligence* aboute
> you that she lovith you intyerly.'
>   ¶'That me repentis,' seyde Sir Launcelot. 'Well,' seyde Sir
> Bors, 'she ys nat the firste that hath loste hir payne uppon you,
> and that ys the more pyté.' And so they talked of many mo
> thynges. And so within three or foure dayes Sir Launcelot
> wexed *bygge and* lyght. (*stronge,* Caxton) . . .
>   ' . . . I fele myself resonabely *bygge and stronge.*'
>   ¶'Blessed be God,' seyde Sir Bors. Than they were there
> nyghe a moneth togydirs, and ever thys maydyn Elayne ded
> ever hir *dyligence* and labour both nyght and day unto Sir
> Launcelot . . .
>   [p. 611, lines 13–28]

Repetition always runs the risk of appearing artless, but the simple,
emphatic style of Malory's prose owes a lot to it. What we are told
three times is not necessarily true, but at least it sticks.

The Sliding Scale of Values

The coordinating structures, which present without analysis, help
to give Malory's prose a veneer of objectivity, as does his readiness
to insert detailed lists. What should also be noticed is the way in
which Malory's extremely subjective glance parades as objectivity
too. As we have seen, for him the moral and the physical exist on
a single plane of perception, and he is constantly passing from one
to the other. Where we would expect a physical description Malory
gives a moral one, constantly offering value judgments and assuming our agreement. He takes the truth of a moral statement for
granted and repeats it so regularly that our acquiescence is readily
achieved. For Malory, to describe is to evaluate; a knight's moral
worth is part of the only description Malory is interested in giving.
And strangely enough, as we read, we begin to suspend our moral
disbelief rather than scream out our indignation. It is as though in
a prose narrative which appears so plain and in which no attempt
is made to manipulate or embellish, the subjectivity goes unnoticed. Malory rigs out his prose with the trappings of an objectivity
which disguises his total commitment. He is not consciously
deluding us; the implication is that the nobility of a Lancelot is as
patent for all to see as the colour of his eyes or hair, which, being
so much less important, are not even mentioned.

All those lists which seem so drearily objective for our tastes,
which link Malory to older, oral traditions and give a semblance
of history, exist side by side with a subjective gaze of the most
unashamed kind. Nor is this the only way in which Malory's objectivity is suspect. His use of the superlative mode is another. When
a knight is the best of a category it suggests that an objective scale

of evaluation exists and that an attempt at reasonable judgment is being made. In fact the assessments implicit in the use of superlatives are just a front. Since all the knights are the best in the world, all the ladies the fairest in the land, the scale of evaluation is without value, except in that it gives the impression that unbiased assessment itself is something which counts. But it is an impression only, for Malory is not the distant narrator scrutinising with cold irony the world he creates. Indeed, the word 'narrator' is itself inappropriate, with all that it suggests of detachment and criticism. Malory is part of the world he describes, the traditional writer who participates, and his moral judgments are inevitable because he is clearly on the side of the community he describes. Arthur's knights, we have seen, are our noble men of merry England.

Dialogue

Malory's use of dialogue also reveals his commitment to the Arthurian world. His voice is frequently confused with those of his characters: he slips in and out of dialogue in a way which is disconcerting for a modern reader and something of a headache for editors of the *Morte Darthur*, who have to take special care with the punctuation. When Malory seems to be describing events he suddenly withdraws to let the actors in those events speak for themselves: their voice is heard through his, or his through theirs. It is an important feature of his prose, and one which becomes more obvious towards the end of the *Morte Darthur* as the sheer mass of dialogue there makes clear. In the final tales, of course, speech and deeds go together: what certain characters say leads to further events. When Gareth refuses to be a party to Agravain and Mordred's plottings he says he 'woll nat be knowyn of your dedis' [p. 646, lines 26–27], but the deed he will not 'be knowyn of' is the speech his brothers are about to make to Arthur.

Malory lets his characters speak, but makes no attempt to individualise them by their speech. Lancelot at one point is said to have a distinctive voice [p. 157, lines 16–17], but the detail, once mentioned, is at once forgotten. No one in Malory can be recognised by the way they speak. This does not mean that Malory's dialogue does not ring true, for it often does, and superbly so. Quite simply, speech never identifies a character. For us it is one aspect of a man's individuality; for Malory, on the contrary, it is a way for a man to reveal his allegiance to a group. In the *Morte Darthur* speech is normative not particular, appropriate to a knight's role, never to his character. Malory shows us proper, fitting speech, not idiosyncratic discourse. 'That is knyghtly spokyn' is a compliment they all deserve.

The clearest example of normative discourse is one which is totally unbelievable for twentieth century readers, but an example of the extremely formal, public, non-naturalistic attitude of Malory: his knights speak together with a collective voice, chorus-like, referring to themselves in the plural. In modern fiction the only equivalent is always expressed through indirect speech. No one could hope to make us believe that several characters said exactly the same words, at the same time and speaking of themselves in the plural as a group—except fans in a theatre chanting 'We want . . .' whoever it is.

Malory's collective discourse shows the abandonment of the individual for the group, and this, in the *Morte Darthur* is a healthy state of mind. For Malory, virtue and prowess involve living up to a standard, behaving in a fitting and characteristic manner, and in this Malory's style expresses his outlook well. He does not hesitate to make his knights speak with one voice because, ideally, this is how they should speak.

* * *

Plain History

* * *

There is none of the *romancier*'s desire to organise and embellish, rather the sobriety of the chronicle style proper to the historian.

This, of course, is seen in Malory's readiness to add lists and identify names; the historian must record evidence, and evidence is not presented in vague generalities. It is also seen in his respect for the past. Malory does not try to recreate the atmosphere of the past in terms of the present. If we do not understand its assumptions and conventions, Malory is not going to bring them up to date. Rather he states plainly 'custom was those days'. There is nothing more to say.

Moreover, like the historian, Malory writes sparely, with little decoration or description. This, in part, is due to his desire to reduce his source material and write a single manageable history instead of a bulky collection of tales. Description is always easy to remove. But the absence of description is also essential to his outlook. Malory is not presenting an elegant, decorative fiction, but a record of deeds. If information is not essential, it can be taken for granted and overlooked. Consequently, there is little or none of the ordinary business of life in the *Morte Darthur*. Knights appear not to eat unless a meal is an important social occasion and they seek repose when it is convenient in the plot to do so; otherwise they are tireless. The *Morte Darthur* contains none of the mundane affairs of fiction and real life—the French romances are far more aware of the realities of physical surroundings—and Malory rarely takes time to offer any sort of description to set the scene.

Moreover, as we have seen, Malory's use of description tends to be normative not individualising. We may occasionally be struck by an added detail—instead of riding in on a horse, a knight will arrive on a white horse—but the extra information is usually gratuitous, for other knights arrive on white (or black) horses for no apparent reason. We begin to discard the information and no longer pay attention. When, rarely, someone arrives on a dun horse we scarcely even notice, and rightly so, for 'white horse', 'black horse' or 'dun horse' add little more than 'horse'. Descriptive details of the kind seem arbitrary and, remembering Malory's moral bias, far less telling than an appreciative assessment. Had Malory said 'noble horse' we really would have sat up. Malory's concern for group not individual identity, and for moral not physical description is part of his outlook as a traditional writer. He writes not so much to make us visualise, but to help us recognise.

Alliteration

One final detail of Malory's style should be mentioned; it is also linked to his outlook as a traditional writer: alliteration. It is more than likely that the works of the alliterative poets were Malory's initial source of inspiration, and throughout the *Morte Darthur* he is always ready to use alliteration himself, not regularly or structurally, but in particular at moments of high intensity.

Some of Malory's alliteration, perhaps the least important, is the result of direct borrowing from his sources. All of Book II is like this, and there are numerous examples in Book VIII. Some alliteration is not Malory's choice but the nature of the English language. When the king kisses the queen, he cannot help alliterating as he does so. But Malory regularly uses alliteration (or fails to resist its influence) and in this way gives force to what he writes. There is no need to give examples, alliteration can be found throughout the *Morte Darthur*, especially in passages where the emotional impact is strong.

For us, alliteration can be a dangerous literary feature. It adds a falsely popular ring to our writing and can result in bathos. In Malory there is a long tradition behind it and it adds stateliness and force, the weight perhaps of a popular tradition of proverbial wisdom. It also adds to the deceptively simple appearance of Malory's prose. He does not strike us as a *littérateur*. He has been criticised for being a careless writer, gauche and artless, but his prose at its best is extraordinarily moving. For all his apparent lack of manipulation he has a way of controlling our responses that no modern author could hope to get away with, but he does so less as a man of letters organising and anticipating our reactions, than as a soldier wholly committed to an ethic which commands respect and which, with the force of his own persuasion, he calls on us to admire. He relies less on any literary devices he might have at his disposal, than on the power of a traditional outlook and his own natural good taste. Derek Brewer has described Malory's style as 'the style of a gentleman'. Malory was a knight and, appropriately, his book is, to adapt his own words, 'knyghtly written'.

CAROL MEALE

Manuscripts, Readers, and Patrons in Fifteenth-Century England: Sir Thomas Malory and Arthurian Romance[†]

On 31 August 1422 the victor of Agincourt, Henry V, died in his newly-acquired French territories. His untimely death was followed in October of the same year by that of his father-in-law, Charles VI of France. The demise of these two monarchs meant that, under the terms of the Treaty of Troyes,[1] the ten-month-old son of Henry and his queen, Catherine of Valois, became Henry VI, titular ruler of both countries. The man to whom fell the not altogether enviable task of governing France in the new king's stead was John Duke of Bedford, the eldest surviving son of Henry IV of England.[2] Apparently one of Bedford's earliest acts as regent was to instigate enquiries as to the contents and value of the French royal library, a magnificent collection of over eight hundred volumes assembled with care by Charles V during the fourteenth century.[3] The task of cataloguing the books took from 11–15 April, 1423, but Bedford himself did not visit the library, housed in a tower of the Louvre, until 1425; in June of that year he became its legal owner, the sum of money which was eventually handed over to Charles VI's executors being even less than the modest evaluation of the collection's worth arrived at by the team of assessors.[4]

Amongst the MSS which Bedford acquired, according to the inventory which he had commissioned, were thirteen volumes of Arthurian texts, including two *Lancelots*, three *Grails*, a *Tristan*, and two *Merlins*, plus other books described as 'du Saint Graal et du Tristan', 'Tristan et Lancelot et des ses faiz de la Table rond', and 'un romant de la Table ronde'; all of these were in prose, and in addition there were two copies of 'Perceval le Galois' in verse.[5] It has recently been suggested, by Professor Richard Griffith, that within the next forty years this library passed, almost complete, into the hands of Anthony Wydville, Lord Scales and (from 1469) 2nd Earl Rivers, and that he undertook the patronage of Sir

† From *Arthurian Literature IV*, ed. Richard Barber (Cambridge, D.S. Brewer, 1985), pp. 93–126. Reprinted with permission of Boydell & Brewer Ltd.
1. E. F. Jacob, *The Fifteenth Century* (Oxford, 1961) pp. 184–6.
2. See E. Carleton Williams, *My Lord of Bedford* (London, 1963).
3. On the royal library see especially Léopold Delisle, *Recherches sur la librairie de Charles V*, 2 vols (Paris, 1907); and on Bedford's interest in the library, Alfred Franklin, *Histoire Générale de Paris. Les Anciennes Bibliothèques de Paris* (Paris, 1867–73) 3 vols, vol. 2, pp. 129ff, and L. Douët d'Arcq, ed., *Inventaire de la bibliothèque du Roi Charles VI, fait au Louvre en 1423, par ordre du régent duc de Bedford* (Paris, 1867). See also, M. J. Barber, 'The Book and Patronage of Learning of a Fifteenth Century Prince,' *The Book Collector*, 12 (1963) 308–15.
4. Delisle, *Recherches*, 1, p. 138; Franklin, *Anciennes Bibliothèques*, pp. 129–30.
5. Delisle, *Recherches*, 2, nos. 1132, 1133, 1113, 1115, 1116, 1190, 1142, 1143, 1117, 1198, 1189, 1151, 1153. * * *

Thomas Malory's *Morte d'Arthur,* probably in the middle and latter part of the decade 1460–70; the line of descent of the books, it is proposed, would have been through Anthony's mother, Jacquetta of Luxembourg, whose first marriage, of only two years duration, was to Bedford.[6] This is an intriguing hypothesis and one which, at first glance, appears to solve as many questions as it raises, for a constant preoccupation amongst Malorian scholars has been the issue of where, exactly, Malory could have obtained the large number of French romances needed for his translation and reworking of the Arthurian story.

An early theory, and one dependent upon the identification of the author with the Sir Thomas Malory of Newbold Revel in Warwickshire, was that whilst officially in prison in Newgate, Malory could have had access to the library of Greyfriars Abbey (in which institution he was later buried), founded by Sir Richard Whittington, who had himself donated £400 towards the cost of buying books; however, no convincing argument, or proof, was ever brought forward to support such an idea.[7] More recent, though, has been Professor Griffith's advancement of the claims of Anthony Wydville to be considered, not only as the person responsible for the transference of the work from manuscript into the medium of the printed book (an idea which has received wide acclaim since it was first mooted some years since),[8] but also as the provider of source materials for the author, and as the patron active in the creation of the work, fifteen to twenty years earlier. Professor Griffith is, of course, the most eloquent proponent of the theory that the author of the *Morte* can be identified as the Cambridgeshire Thomas Malory, of Papworth St Agnes, and he adduces evidence from many different sources in support of his contention that this man and Anthony Wydville knew one another. But advocates of the claims of the Warwickshire Sir Thomas have

6. See Richard R. Griffith, 'The Authorship Question Reconsidered', in *Aspects of Malory,* ed. Toshiyuki Takamiya and Derek Brewer (Woodbridge, 1981) pp. 159–77; also 'Arthur's Author: The Mystery of Sir Thomas Malory', *Ventures in Research,* I (1972) 7–43. * * *

7. See Edward Hicks, *Sir Thomas Malory: His Turbulent Career* (Cambridge, Mass., 1928) pp. 65–70, on Malory's time in Newgate, and pp. 74–6, on his burial; on the latter see also C. L. Kingsford, ed., *Stow's Survey of London* (Oxford, 1908, repr. 1971) I, p. 321, and cf. P. J. C. Field, 'The Last Years of Sir Thomas Malory', *Bulletin of the John Rylands Library,* 64 (1982) 433–56, p. 440. On the library at Greyfriars see *Stow's Survey,* I, p. 318, and Caroline M. Barron, 'Richard Whittington: the Man behind the Myth' in *Studies in London History presented to P. E. Jones,* ed. A. E. J. Hollaender and William Kellaway (London, 1969) p. 232.

8. The idea that political considerations led to the concealment of the patron's name in Caxton's edition of the *Morte* was first put forward by N. F. Blake, 'Investigations into the Prologues and Epilogues by William Caxton', *Bulletin of the John Rylands Library,* 49 (1966) 23–44, pp. 39, 40, and cf. Blake, *Caxton and His World* (London, 1969) pp. 94–5; see also George D: Painter, *William Caxton: A Quincentenary Biography of England's First Printer* (London, 1976) p. 147, and Lotte Hellinga, *Caxton in Focus,* The British Library (London, 1982) pp. 89–94. Professor Blake has more recently argued, however, that the events recounted by Caxton in the prologue to the *Morte* were entirely fictitious, and that the story was devised as an advertisement, in which apparent recommendation by 'courtly' readers would increase the likelihood of sales; see 'Caxton Prepares His Edition of the *Morte Darthur', Journal of Librarianship,* 8 (1976) 272–85, esp. pp. 282–4; and, more generally, 'William Caxton: the Man and His Work', *Journal of the Printing Historical Society,* 11 (1975/6) 64–80, pp. 73–5; 'Continuity and Change in Caxton's Prologues and Epilogues: the Bruges Period' and 'Continuity and Change in Caxton's Prologues and Epilogues: Westminster', *Gutenberg Jahrbuch* (1979) pp. 72–7, (1980) pp. 38–43.

also enthusiastically embraced the idea of a connection between their man and Wydville. Hilton Kelliher, for instance, in his essay 'The Early History of the Malory Manuscript', on equally plausible grounds transposes the supposed relationship from East Anglia to the Midlands.[9]

Nevertheless, whilst scholars from both camps have expended considerable energy and ingenuity in establishing that Malory and Wydville lands virtually adjoined each other in both parts of the country (and both parties agree that the two men could have met one another at the siege of Alnwick in 1462),[1] it would seem desirable to step back in order to address some fairly basic questions. For instance, what justification is there for assuming, first, that the French library did remain intact after Bedford's death, and that it did pass to Anthony Wydville? Secondly, can we be sure that there was no comparable collection of potential source materials in England at the time? Thirdly, is it reasonable to assume that, in the context of fifteenth-century England, Malory would have had to rely on either the motivation and/or the resources offered by a patron in order to compose his work? The latter issue, it should be said, is one which reaches beyond the bound of Arthurian literary history. I cannot pretend to offer conclusive answers to any of these questions, but the hope behind this paper is to reopen the field of enquiry, to suggest ways of approaching the subject, and indicate areas which appear to need a more thorough investigation if we are ever to achieve a fuller understanding of the circumstances under which Malory wrote.

The first step is to consider the evidence concerning the existence and extent of English libraries and collections of books in the fifteenth century; and it is from within this context that it is appropriate to look in greater detail at the possibility that the French royal library was either taken, or sent, to England. The theory, as outlined above, runs that on Bedford's death his books were inherited directly by his young widow, Jacquetta, and hence, it is said, they passed to Jacquetta's eldest son by her second marriage, Anthony Wydville. Leaving aside the fact that both the Cambridgeshire and the Warwickshire Malorys predeceased Jacquetta,[2] scholars on both sides of the channel have long been

9. *Aspects of Malory*, ed. Takamiya and Brewer, pp. 153–6. This essay is a revised version of the article by Kelliher and Lotte Hellinga, 'The Malory Manuscript', *British Library Journal*, 3 (1977) 91–113, pp. 101ff. Cf. Field, 'The Last Years', pp. 455–6.

1. Professor Griffith's case rests in large part upon the assumption that Malory and Wydville met one another at Alnwick during the northern campaign; see 'The Authorship Question', p. 172. Kelliher attaches less importance to this possibility; see 'The Early History', p. 155. For an analysis of the record which indicates that Malory was at the siege see P. J. C. Field, 'Thomas Malory: the Hutton Documents', *Medium Aevum*, 48 (1979) 213–39, pp. 225–9, 235–9 (on p. 238 Field makes the point that there may have been 'more than one Thomas Malory' at the siege).

2. Jacquetta died on 30 May 1472; Sir Thomas Malory of Newbold Revel died on either 12 or 14 March 1471 (see Field, 'The Hutton Documents', p. 231 and n.80); and the Thomas Malory of Papworth St Agnes was dead by 1 September 1469 (see Griffith, 'The Authorship Question', p. 174 and n.62). Jacquetta's husband, Richard Wydville, 1st Earl Rivers, was executed on 12 August 1469. Given these facts, the theory that Anthony was in a position to supply the author with books from his mother's collection during the 1460s would seem to need further elaboration.

unanimous in their agreement that the library was broken up either before Bedford's death in September 1435, or immediately afterwards. Although ideas as to the destination of the bulk of the books have varied, the fact that only just over one hundred of the volumes have been traced (the majority of these being now in France)[3] argues for a fairly thorough dispersal. M. J. Barber, for example, in an authoritative survey of Bedford's interest in books and learning in general, makes the point that 'no large body of his official or private papers or possessions' survived in either England or France in the confusion of the years following his death, as the English were driven steadily from their French territories.[4] * * *

There is in fact only one manuscript known to have been in the possession of Anthony Wydville which was owned originally by a member of the French royal family, and this is BL Harley 4431, a volume of Christine de Pisan's works collected together before 1415 for presentation to Charles VI's queen, Isabeau of Bavaria.[5] On a flyleaf are the signatures of Jacquetta, Anthony himself, and Louis de Bruges, seigneur de Gruthuyse, the Burgundian nobleman with whom Anthony and his brother-in-law, Edward IV, stayed whilst in exile from the readeption Lancastrian government in England in 1470/71.[6] The volume is not listed, however, in Bedford's 1423 inventory, and it is unlikely that it formed part of the royal library in the Louvre.[7]

The issue is complicated by the possibility that although Bedford is known to have been active as a buyer and commissioner of MSS, his motives in procuring the collection may not have been solely those of a book lover, as has on occasion been assumed.[8] There is an undoubted chronological coincidence between the acquisition and disappearance from contemporary record of the library, and the acquisition and loss of the French crown by the English and, as Dr Jonathan Alexander has recently pointed out, Bedford's purchase may well have been directed by a propagandist desire to

3. See *La Librairie de Charles V*, catalogue of an exhibition held at the Bibliothèque Nationale, Paris, 1968; also Delisle, *Recherches*, 1, pp. 142ff.

4. Barber, 'Books and Patronage', p. 313; the view favored by Barber is that the books were removed from Paris in 1429 to Rouen, where repairs to the library were carried out at the Duke's orders in 1433; it is suggested further that Bedford may have 'thought to use Charles V's books as a foundation library for the projected university at Caen' (cf. p. 311). E. Carleton Williams, *My Lord of Bedford*, p. 198, is also of the opinion that the books went to Rouen when they were removed from the Louvre, in 1429.

5. For an analysis of the MS, and an account of the process by which it was assembled, see Sandra Hindman, 'The Composition of the MS of Christine de Pisan's Collected Works in the British Library: A Reassessment', *British Library Journal*, 9 (1983) 93–123.

6. This page of the MS is reproduced as pl.43 in Hellinga, *Caxton in Focus*. Since Jacquetta died in May 1472 (see n.11 above) it is possible that Louis de Gruthuyse was given the volume by Anthony during the former's visit to England in the autumn of that year; see F. Madden, 'Narratives of the arrival of Louis de Bruges, Seigneur de la Gruthuyse, in England, and of his Creation as Earl of Winchester in 1472', *Archaeologia*, 26 (1836) 265–86. However, it may be that Anthony used this MS for his translation of Christine's *Moral Proverbs* which were not printed by Caxton until 1477/78, in which case the transfer is not likely to have taken place as early as this. Anthony's translations are discussed further, below.

7. Delisle discusses Isabeau of Bavaria's book, *Researches*, 1, pp. 132–5, and see also Valet de Viriville, 'La Bibliothèque d'Isabeau de Bavière', *Bulletin du Bibliophile*, 14 (1858) 663–87.

8. E.g. by Franklin, *Anciennes Bibliothèques*, p. 121; Delisle, *Recherches*, 1, pp. 139–40; McFarlane, *op. cit.*, p. 205.

acquire 'a prestige possession of the French monarchy'; and he speculates further that 'As the union collapsed the library was allowed to be dispersed.[9] A similar understanding of the potential significance of patronage and book-ownership as a political tool could also, perhaps, have lain behind Bedford's commissioning of fine service books and translations from Parisian workshops;[1] it almost certainly dictated the action of his first duchess, Anne of Burgundy who, in a move of undeniable diplomatic flair, presented the magnificent Book of Hours acquired by the couple at the time of their marriage, to Henry VI, when he spent Christmas with them at Rouen in 1430.[2] The issue of the public face of patronage has obvious implications for any study of the inception and subsequent dissemination of Malory's work, and it is one to which I shall return in due course.

If the lack of specific evidence should incline us to discount the French royal library as the source of Malory's various texts, this conclusion is reinforced when we examine the rider to it, that there was in effect no alternative available to him. It was Professor William Matthews who, in his book *The Ill-Framed Knight*, came to the conclusion that there was no library in England which could have provided the Arthurian writer with all his materials.[3] Following the line of enquiry prompted by his conviction that the author came from the Yorkshire family of Malory's, he commented upon the 'pitifully few' bequests of Arthurian books in the north, and went on to remark: 'Nor indeed is there any evidence that anyone in England ever owned such a collection. The most that can be proved is that various people owned a copy of this romance or that . . . ' On the basis of these observations he concluded that Malory wrote his work abroad, most probably under the auspices of Jacques d'Armagnac, duc de Nemours, whose tastes in the way of Arthurian literature are well documented.[4] This dismissal of the potential of the resources likely to have been held by English book

9. J. J. G. Alexander, 'Painting and Manuscript Illumination for Royal Patrons in the Later Middle Ages' in *English Court Culture in the Later Middle Ages*, ed. V. J. Scattergood and J. W. Sherborne (London, 1983) p. 161.
1. The books which Bedford ordered from Parisian workshops included: a Breviary of the use of Sarum (BN Latin 17294, begun in 1426, went after Bedford's death to Philippe de Morvilliers, 1st president of the Parlement de Paris); a Missal completed after Bedford's death for Jacques Juvenal des Ursins, Bishop of Poitiers, (lost in a fire at the Hôtel de Ville, 1871); two Latin translations of the *Pèlerinage de l'Âme* (Lambeth 326, BN fr. 602—the miniatures in the latter are unfinished); *Le Vif Table de Confession* (no longer extant, but copied by the same scribe as Lambeth 326); *La Somme du Roi Philippe, ou somme des vices et des vertus* (Reims 570); *Scientia de numerq et virtute numerii*, written by Roland Lisbon, a master in the medical faculty of Paris (Columbia University, Plimpton 173); Jean Tourtier, *Traduction du commentaire de Galien sur les aphorismes d'Hippocrate* (BN fr. 24246, finished 1429); *Le Livre du jugement des étoiles*, a French translation by Guillaume Harnoys of an Arabian work, commissioned 1430 (BN fr. 1352). On these MSS see Barber, 'Books and Patronage'; Eric G. Millar, *Les principaux manuscrits à peintures du Lambeth Palace à Londres* (Paris, 1924) pp. 74–7 and pl.XLII, repr. from the *Bulletin de la Société française pour reproductions de manuscrits à peintures*, 8ᵉ année (1924) and 9ᵉ année (1925); M. R. James and Claude Jenkins, *A Descriptive Catalogue of the Manuscripts in the Library of Lambeth Palace* (Cambridge, 1932) pp. 427–31; E. Carleton Williams, *My Lord of Bedford*, pp. 249–52. * * *
2. Henry VI's physician made a note on f.256r of the MS recording the gift. * * *
3. William, Matthews, *Ill-Framed Knight* (Berkeley and Los Angeles, 1966) pp. 141–2.
4. Matthews, *Ill-Framed Knight*, pp. 145–9. * * * For a refutation of Matthews' view on historical grounds see Field, 'The Hutton Documents', pp. 224–5.

collectors, whilst somewhat abrupt, does serve to highlight the problems which are to be encountered in any study of book ownership in England.

The first of these is the inadvisability of placing too great a reliance upon wills as evidence of ownership. These documents are, in fact, notoriously unreliable as guides either to general interest in literature or to the actual subjects of the books which people possessed. It is by no means uncommon, for example, for known book-owners either not to list a single MS in their bequests, or to omit mention of volumes which, because they are still extant, and bear contemporary *ex libris* inscriptions or other identifying marks, can be confidently assigned to them.[5] It is similarly no rarity to find books described collectively, and this applies to other kinds of record, as well as to wills. Thus in 1395, Lady Alice West of Hynton Marcel in Hampshire left all her 'bokes . . . of latyn, englisch, and frensch' to her daughter-in-law, and over a century later, in the inventory of the goods of John de Vere, Earl of Oxford, which was made after his death, although his service books were described in some detail, the contents of 'A chest full of frenshe and englisshe bokes', together valued at £3 6s. 8d., are not specified.[6] Again, books may be described by their appearance rather than their content; in 1415 Michael de la Pole, Earl of Suffolk, bequeathed to his wife, Katherine, 'a little book with tablets of silver and gold', and five years later, Dame Matilda Bowes left 'ye boke with ye knotts'.[7] Another of Dame Matilda's bequests, of 'unum romance boke', is scarcely any more informative, except perhaps about the language of the text contained within it.[8] The reasoning behind the adoption of the latter types of description was, no doubt, pragmatic, in that it would have facilitated identification of volumes for the executors,[9] and the same criterion may have led testators to refer to books by only one of several component texts. * * *

Usually we have no means of checking on particular bequests to see how accurately books have been described by their owners. But there is one case where we do, and it is one which is most appropriate in the context of the present discussion. Sir Richard Roos, in his will made in March 1481/2, left his 'grete booke called

5. See K. B. McFarlane, *The Nobility of Later Medieval England* (Oxford, 1973) pp. 236–7; A. I. Doyle, Appendix B to *Stephen Scrope: The Epistle of Othea*, ed. Curt F. Bühler, EETS OS 264 (1970) p. 127 * * *

6. See F. J. Furnivall, *The Fifty Earliest English Wills*, etc., EETS OS 78 (1882) p. 5; Sir William H. St John Hope, 'The Last Testament and Inventory of John de Vere, 13th Earl of Oxford', *Archaeologia*, 66 (1914/15) 275–348, pp. 341, 342; (the latter example is quoted by McFarlane, *Nobility*, p. 237).

7. Nicolas, ed., *Testamenta Vetusta*, pp. 189–90; *Testamenta Eboracensia*, I, Surtees Society, 2 (1835) pp. 63–5.

8. Another of the books left by Dame Matilda was 'j romance boke is called ye gospelles'; 'romance', therefore, in the context of this will, seems to mean that the text was in French; cf. R. M. Wilson, *The Lost Literature of Medieval England* (London, 1952) p. 120.

9. In other cases elaborate descriptions of the coverings of books can be taken as an indication of the owner's pride in their value, whether this is seen in monetary, or social, terms; see, e.g. the will of Thomas Burgeys, citizen and cissor of London, 1468, H. R. Plomer, 'Books Mentioned in Wills', *Transactions of the Bibliographical Society*, 7 (1902–4) 99–121, p. 117.

saint Grall bounde in boordes coerde with rede leder and plated with plates of laten' to his niece, 'Alianore hawte'. This volume, complete with the signatures of Roos, Alianore, and that of the next owner, Elizabeth Wydville, Edward IV's wife and first cousin to Alianore's husband, survives; it is now BL MS Royal 14.E.III, and in addition to the *Queste* it contains an *Estoire* and a *Mort*.[1] The number of texts within this one book should act as a cautionary reminder, in any assessment of the size of an individual's library, of the possibility that there may well be a marked discrepancy between the actual contents of a given book collection and our immediate perception of it.

It should be stressed that the existence of composite volumes is not an argument that Malory would not have had to consult several books. His major French sources, for example, are generally agreed to have been the *Suite du Merlin*, the *Lancelot*, *Tristan*, the *Queste* and the *Mort*; and the *Lancelot* in particular was a bulky compilation. Still, there is no reason to suppose that he need have found them in so many separate volumes as has usually been thought. It is of note in this respect that Eugène Vinaver indicated the likelihood that Malory had access to such multiple-text volumes in his editorial reference to the authorial comment at the end of the book of *Sir Tristrem*, which reads: 'here ys no rehearsall of the thirde booke'; Professor Vinaver observes that in the two MSS of the French text which are closest to Malory's redaction (BN fr. 99 and Chantilly 316) there is a similar textual division and comment at this stage in the narrative, and that in both these books, as in Malory's compendium, the work which follows is the *Queste*.[2]

Problems similar to those encountered when dealing with references to books in wills must be recognised in considering the use which it is possible to make of other kinds of contemporary records, ranging from inventories which might list books to household and other accounts which could be expected to detail expenditure upon them. Again, knowledge of book collections drawn from sources such as these is dependent largely upon the accidents of survival, and we should be wary of drawing too firm conclusions from the evidence which they offer.[3] It has often been assumed, for instance, that an interest in literature is more pronounced amongst the French and Burgundian nobility than amongst the English, but it is not generally acknowledged that a contributory factor to this apparent state of affairs is the paucity of relevant documentation which is extant from this period in England. As Richard Green has remarked:

1. See the transcription of this will in Ethel Seaton, *Sir Richard Roos* (London, 1961) pp. 547–50. * * * For a description of the MS see G. F. Warner and J. P. Gilson, *Catalogue of Western MSS in the Old Royal and King's Collections* (London, 1921), II, p. 140, and IV; pl.85. Matthews mentions this MS (*Ill-Framed Knight*, p. 141) but he does not follow up the implications, which affect his own argument, of the structure and contents of the volume.
2. Eugène Vinaver, ed., *The Works of Sir Thomas Malory* (Oxford, 1967) III, p. 1519.
3. Cf. McFarlane's comments on the survival of inventories of books belonging to men convicted of treason, for example, Sir Simon Burley, Thomas of Woodstock and Henry Lord Scrope of Masham, which 'are likely to suggest a very unlikely correlation between crime, in particular treason, and literacy'; he adds, 'By comparison, few inventories of the possessions of the law-abiding' have been preserved; (*Nobility*, p. 237).

Not only royal household records and library inventories, but also the records of a number of seigneural establishments . . . are sparser in England than are their counterparts on the continent. If we possessed a fraction of the information about the day-to-day activities of men like John Montagu, earl of Salisbury, William de la Pole, duke of Suffolk, Humphrey of Gloucester, John Tiptoft, and Anthony Wydville, that we have for the dukes of Burgundy and Orléans, or Jean duc de Berri, or René of Anjou, our knowledge of the literature of the English court and of its social background would be increased enormously.[4]

An illustration of the amount and probable nature of the material which has been lost is provided by the fact that wardrobe accounts for Edward IV are available only for a short period from the latter part of his reign, from 1480–81, and yet these papers give valuable information regarding the rebinding of various of the King's books, and the arrangements which were made for them to accompany him on his travels.[5] * * *

However, in spite of these constraints, piece by piece an understanding of patronage and book production in England is being built up; that this is so is due partly to the work which is being carried out on cataloguing the medieval contents of modern libraries; partly to the systematic research being devoted to documenting the lives of individuals, from whatever class of society; and partly to discoveries as felicitous as that of the Winchester Malory MS itself in 1934.[6] Thus our knowledge is far from being full and, whilst it may never be possible to build up a definitive picture, it is only reasonable to anticipate further developments which will cause a realignment of present views. I would suggest, therefore, that the assertion that there was no library in England in the mid-fifteenth century from which Malory could have drawn his source texts is unwarranted.

Although it is almost certain that Malory did have recourse to a library, or collection of sorts, for the French books he used, it should not be forgotten that he could well have owned one or more volumes himself. Instances in the fifteenth century of members of the gentry or lesser knightly classes possessing Arthurian romances in French include Dame Matilda Bowes, who bequeathed 'unum librum yat is called Trystram'; and the Mauleverers of Ribston in Yorkshire, who have been associated with Cambridge, UL Addi-

---

4. Richard Firth Green, *Poets and Princepleasers: Literature and the English Court in the Later Middle Ages* (Toronto, Buffalo and London, 1980) pp. 7–8.
5. See Nicholas Harris Nicolas, ed., *Privy Purse Expenses of Elizabeth of York: Wardrobe Accounts of Edward IV* (London, 1830, repr. 1972) pp. 117, 125–6, 152. * * *
6. The work which is currently being carried out on the *Index of Middle English Prose* may be cited as the kind of research which will uncover much new information; see the discussion of the aims of the project in *Middle English Prose: Essays in Bibliographical Problems*, ed. A. S. G. Edwards and D. A. Pearsall (New York and London, 1981). Where the literary interests of individuals are concerned, the extent and nature of Edward III's tastes have been reassessed by Juliet Vale, in the light of her work on documentary material from the period; see her *Edward III and Chivalry: Chivalric Society and Its Context 1270–1350* (Woodbridge, 1982) Chapter 3.

tional MS 7071, which contains an *Estoire* and a *Merlin*.[7] Allowing
for the fact that owing to their cost, and his relatively low income,
Malory is unlikely to have been in possession of more than a few
volumes, it still does not follow that a bookowner acting in the
capacity of a patron supplied him with the rest of the texts he
required.[8] There is ample evidence of books being loaned amongst
groups of people who lived within the same social or geographical
sphere. BL Royal 17. D. VI, for instance, containing works by Hoc-
cleve (including his *Regiment of Princes*) appears to have been
owned by William Fitzalan, Earl of Arundel, and his wife Joan
Neville, Countess of Salisbury, who died in 1487 and 1462 respectively; but a number of signatures and mottoes at the beginning of
the volume, most of which can be attributed to people who were
connected with the Arundels by ties of marriage or friendship,
seems to indicate that its use may have been communal.[9] Lower
down the social scale, the Lambeth Palace copy of the *Awntyrs off
Arthure* (MS 491) contains the names of several individuals who
seem to have formed a kind of informal literary circle amongst the
Essex gentry in the early sixteenth century; (one of the owners has
written on f.273r, albeit in jest, the popular ownership rhyme 'he
that styleth thys boke shall be hangyd on hoke').[1] This form of
dissemination of literary texts must have been common in the Middle Ages, particularly before the introduction of printing.[2]

With regard to the English works which Malory apparently
knew, even if he did not have them in front of him when he wrote,[3]
access to most of these would have been straightforward. The
English translation of the Vulgate *Merlin*, the stanzaic *Morte
Arthur*, the *Awntyrs off Arthure*, and the treatise on hunting

7. For details of Dame Matilda's will see [n. 7, p. 870] above; on the Mauleverers see Vinaver, ed., *Works of Sir Thomas Malory*, III, pp. 1277–80; also Matthews, *Ill-Framed Knight*, pp. 108–13. The speculations in the latter work should be treated with caution.
8. Malory's income has been assessed at something over £20, which was fairly low for some-one of his social standing; see P.J.C. Field, 'Sir Thomas Malory, M. P.', *Bulletin of the Institute of Historical Research*, 46 (1973) 24–35, p. 27. It would be helpful in this con-nection to know what prices Arthurian texts commanded on the second-hand market; half a century before, the inventory of Thomas of Woodstock's books records a *Merlin*, price 3s. 4d., a *Lancelot*, price 13s. 4d., and a 'Tretiz de Roy Arthur', price 4s. 4d.; see Viscount Dillon and W. H. St John Hope, 'Inventory of Goods . . . belonging to Thomas, duke of Gloucester', *Archaeological Journal*, 54 (1897) 275–308, pp. 300–3. Even allowing for the inflation of prices during the fifteenth century, it is not impossible that a knight might own several such books, which could have been cheaper than new ones of comparable length. The cost of producing the MS of Malory's work is estimated below, pp. [879–880].
9. See Warner and Gilson, *Catalogue of Royal MSS*, II, pp. 251–2 and IV, pl.101.
1. I hope to discuss the ownership of this MS in more detail elsewhere. Cf. [n. 4, p. 881].
2. On this subject cf. the introduction to *John Benet's Chronicle for the years 1400 to 1462*, ed. G. L. Harriss and M. A. Harriss, Camden Miscellany Vol. 24, Camden Society, 4th ser. 9 (1972) pp. 172–3. * * *
3. On the English Arthurian texts which Malory knew, and for suggestions as to other minor sources, see: Robert H. Wilson, 'Malory's Naming of Minor Characters', *Journal of English and Germanic Philology*, 43 (1943) 364–85, 'Malory's Early Knowledge of Arthurian Romance', *University of Texas Studies in English*, 29 (1950) 33–50, 'Notes on Malory's Minor Sources', *Modern Language Notes*, 66 (1951) 22–6; E. D. Kennedy, 'Malory's Use of Hardyng's *Chronicle*', *Notes and Queries*, 114 (1969) 100–3; Wilson, 'More Borrowings by Malory from Hardyng's *Chronicle*', *Notes and Queries*, 115 (1970) 208–10; Diane Born-stein, 'Military Strategy in Malory and Vegetius' *De Re Militari*', *Comparative Literature Studies*, 9 (1972) 123–9; E. M. Bradstock, 'The Source for Book XVIII of Malory's *Morte Darthur*', *Notes and Queries*, 124 (1979) 105–7; P. J. C. Field, 'Malory's Minor Sources', *Notes and Queries*, 124 (1979) 107–10; Kennedy, 'Malory and His English Sources' in *Aspects of Malory*, ed. Takamiya and Brewer.

ascribed to Sir Tristrem (to which Malory seems to be referring at the beginning of his tale of *Tristrem*), were all available in relatively inexpensive booklets, and all were in circulation in London, as well as farther north. Furthermore, the text on hunting and the *Awntyrs* were combined by two stationers or purchasers within the same volume.[4] Amongst the romances, only the alliterative *Morte Arthure* and the *Avowinge of Arthur,* to judge from the evidence of extant MSS (in itself not an infallible guide) seem to have had a more restricted geographical distribution.[5] The extent to which copies of Chaucer's *Canterbury Tales* multiplied throughout the fifteenth century is well documented.[6] Even works like Hardyng's *Chronicle* and the English translation of Vegetius' treatise *De re militari* could have been obtained without too much difficulty, and the audience for both texts seems to have been drawn from a broad social spectrum. Whilst it may be open to doubt whether Henry VI or Edward IV ever read the copies of Hardyng's *Chronicle* presented to them by the author, Hunterian MS V. 2.20 is a modestly-produced volume on paper, which would have been well within the reach of someone of limited means, and the same is true of Douce 378.[7] Vegetius' treatise, on the other hand, was owned and presumably read by members of the gentry in Norfolk, Warwickshire and Devon, as well as by Richard III, members of the Hastings family, and the Berkeleys of Gloucestershire for whom Walton made the translation.[8] In short, none of the texts which have been proposed as sources for Malory in his work would have been out-of-the-way for someone of his social standing to acquire, or borrow, without the aid of a patron.

At this point it is appropriate to look more closely at the surviving copies of Malory's work, to see whether they offer any more defi-

4. On the *Merlin* MSS see below, pp. [878–79]. The stanzaic *Morte Arthur* is extant in Harley 2252; the *Awntyrs* in Lincoln Cathedral 91, Lambeth 491, Douce 324, and the Ireland-Blackburn MS (now Mr. R. H. Taylor's MS, Princeton University Library). The *Book on Hunting* appears together with the *Awntyrs* in Lambeth 491, and in the composite volume of which Douce 324 once formed a part; (see K. L. Smith, 'A Fifteenth Century Vernacular Manuscript Reconstructed', *Bodleian Library Record,* 7 (1962–67) pp. 234–41). On the hunting text itself see Rachel Hands, 'Sir Tristrem's "Boke of Huntyng": the case for the Rawlinson manuscript', *Archiv für neuere Sprachen,* 21 (1973) 58–74. *Torrent of Portyngale,* which Kennedy suggested as a source for Malory ('Malory and his English Sources') survives in only one copy, in Chetham A.6.31 (8009), which dates from 1480–1500, but this is, again, in inexpensive booklet format; see Meale, 'The Middle English Romance of *Ipomedon:* A Late Medieval 'Mirror' for Princes and Merchants', *Reading Medieval Studies,* forthcoming.
5. The romances survive uniquely in Lincoln Cathedral 91 and the Ireland Blackburn MS, respectively.
6. See Field, 'Malory's Minor Sources', p. 109 for a comparison of lines in Malory with lines from the *Franklin's Tale;* and for descriptions of MSS of the *Canterbury Tales,* and information on their provenance and ownership, see J. M. Manly and Edith Rickert, *The Text of the Canterbury Tales,* I (Chicago, 1940).
7. On Hardyng's life, and his presentation of his work to the two monarchs, see C. L. Kingsford, *English Historical Literature in the Fifteenth Century* (Oxford, 1913) pp. 140–4; on Hunterian V.2.20 (400) see John Young and P. Henderson Aitken, *A Catalogue of the MSS in the Hunterian Museum in the University of Glasgow* (Glasgow, 1904) pp. 319–20; and on Douce 378 (SC 21953) see F. Madan *et al., Summary Catalogue of Western MSS in the Bodleian Library* (Oxford, 1895–1953) IV, p. 613.
8. See, respectively, BL MSS Lansdowne 285 (Pastons of Norfolk); Sloane 2027 (Brandons of Warwickshire); Douce 291 (Chalons of Devon); Royal 18.A.XII (Richard III); Digby 233 (Hastings). A limited amount of information on these MSS may be found in Charles R. Shrader, 'A Handlist of Extant Manuscripts Containing the *De Re Militari* of Flavius Vegetius Renatus', *Scriptorium,* 33 (1979) 280–305, pp. 302–5.

nite clues as to the circumstances of its composition. With reference to the unique MS of the *Morte*, BL Additional 59678, the first gathering is lost and, as Professor Griffith rightly remarks, calculating on the basis that this would have comprised the same number of leaves as the majority of the other gatherings, there could well have been room for the inclusion of a dedicatory preface, addressed to a patron.[9] But two principal arguments may be brought against this theory. The first of these arises from consideration of the MS version. On those occasions when Malory the author breaks into his translation at the end of certain of the tales, the information which he gives is limited to his name, his social status, and a brief indication of his personal misfortunes.[1] It is true that the last few leaves of the MS are also lost, and that Caxton may have simplified the author's conclusion to a greater extent than we suspect, just as elsewhere he omitted to make any mention of the 'knyght presoner' at all, but it still seems unlikely that a writer, dependent upon the goodwill and the financial recompense presumably in the gift of a patron, should have neglected to record the relationship, or debt, in any of the other, well-marked, breaks in the narrative.[2] It could be countered, of course, that since the MS appears to have been copied at an unspecified number of removes from the author's holograph, all references which were deemed irrelevant to the purposes for which the present copy was being made, were excised. However, this explanation would not account for the retention in the colophons, as they stand in the MS, of highly personal details which could scarcely be said to lend the work any prestige by association, whereas information about a patron who, by definition, has to be in a position of some superiority to the author, would have supplied it for the literary market with a pedigree guaranteeing respectability and, perhaps, even fashionableness.[3]

This social aspect of the appeal of literature to a potential audience should not be underestimated. Indeed, it is a factor which Caxton understood and exploited in his marketing techniques, and the absence from the printer's preface to his edition of the *Morte*

9. Griffith, 'Arthur's Author', p. 23; cf. Field, 'The Last Years', p. 455 and n. 2. All the quires save one consisted of eight bifolia; the exception is the present quire 5, which was a six; see the introduction to the facsimile of the MS by N. R. Ker, EETS SS 4 (1976) pp. x–xi.

1. Vinaver, ed., *Works*, books 1, 4, 5, 6, 7, 8; and see the facsimile, ff. 70v, 148r, 346v, 409r, 449r.

2. On Caxton's excision of personal detail see Blake, 'Caxton Prepares His Edition of the *Morte Darthur*', pp. 277–8. On the relationship of patron to writer generally see, e.g., Green, *Poets and Princepleasers, passim*; and the important article by Peter J. Lucas, 'The Growth and Development of English Literary Patronage in the Later Middle Ages and Early Renaissance', *The Library*, 6th ser., 4 (1982) 219–48.

3. The fact that Lydgate's *Troy Book* was written at the command of Henry, Prince of Wales, later Henry V, seems to have accounted in part for its status as a 'fashionable' text; on the MSS see Lesley Lawton, 'The Illustration of Late Medieval Secular Texts, with Special Reference to Lydgate's *Troy Book*' in *Manuscripts and Readers in Fifteenth Century England*, ed. Derek Pearsall (Woodbridge, 1983) pp. 41–69. See also the retention of the colophon explaining the circumstances which prompted the translation of Vegetius' treatise in, e.g., the Pastons' copy, Lansdowne 285; this is transcribed in *A Catalogue of the Lansdowne MSS in the British Museum* (London, 1819) p. 101. Cf. the retention of details of literary 'pedigree' in a late copy of John Russell's 'boke of kervyng and nortur,' Meale, 'The Middle English romance of *Ipomedon*', n. 64.

of any reference to a patron as being involved in the creation of the work suggests that he had nothing to impart on the subject. It may perhaps be that the one gentleman 'in specyal' who, Caxton tells us, requested publication of the *Morte* was (whether before or after death) in sufficient political disfavor to have made it unwise for the printer to give his name, but Caxton had a habit, wherever he had relevant information to hand, of discussing the genesis of the work he was issuing.[4] In this case he is conspicuously silent on the history of the text before it arrived in his shop, and this implies that the copy from which he printed contained no details as to how the work came to be written other than those with which we are familiar.[5] To sum up, the textual evidence, fragmentary though it undoubtedly is, allows for the possibility that Caxton enjoyed the offices of a patron but suggests, rather more strongly, that Malory did not.

The discussion so far has tended to concentrate on the function of patronage in relation to the writer and/or distributor of literary texts; but it is also important to consider the subject from the point of view of the patron. It is reasonable to assume that the activity of patronage implies an expectation on the part of the patron, whether male or female, an individual or a corporate body, that he, she or they would derive reciprocal benefits of some kind, whether in the area of politics, learning, or religion.[6] The essentially public nature of much of the patronage which the Duke of Bedford embarked upon has already been alluded to, and he was not unusual amongst his contemporaries. Thus, when Bedford commissioned Laurence Calot to write a pedigree of Henry VI, which was posted on the walls of the major churches of northern France as part of the English propaganda campaign, Richard Beauchamp, Earl of Warwick, who was a military administrator in France under Bedford, and tutor to the young Henry VI from 1428–1436, commissioned Lydgate, who was also in Paris at the time, to write an English translation of the poem; this can be seen as a politic move in the light of the divisions between the war and anti-war parties which developed in England once the euphoria at Henry V's victories had died with the King.[7] A more obvious desire to enhance personal reputation lay behind other patrons' encouragement of Lydgate and other writers and artists. For example, Beauchamp's daughter, Margaret, later Lady Talbot and Countess of Shrewsbury, commissioned Lydgate to write the story of *Guy of Warwick*, in celebration of her father's legendary ancestor and his

4. On the question of whether or not Caxton's one gentleman 'in specyal' actually did exist, see the articles by Blake cited in [n. 8, p. 866] above. The printer's prologues and other writings are edited by N.F. Blake, *Caxton's Own Prose* (London, 1973).
5. For a presentation of the evidence that BL Additional MS 59678 was in Caxton's shop, as well as the copy from which the printer and compositors worked principally, see Lotte Hellinga, 'The Malory Manuscript' in *Aspects of Malory*, ed. Takamiya and Brewer, pp. 127–42 and cf. Hellinga, *Caxton in Focus*, pp. 90–4.
6. Cf. Lucas, 'English Literary Patronage'. * * *
7. See B. J. H. Rowe, 'King Henry VI's Claim to France in Picture and Poem', *The Library*, 4th ser., 13 (1932–33) 77–88, also J.W. McKenna, 'Henry VI of England and the Dual Monarchy: Aspects of Royal Political Propaganda, 1422–1432', *Journal of the Warburg and Courtauld Institutes*, 28 (1965) 145–63; cf. Derek Pearsall, *John Lydgate* (London, 1970) pp. 166–7.

chivalric exploits.[8] A desire to recover political standing, as well as her estates, probably lay behind the production of the beautiful series of drawings with accompanying texts known as the *Beauchamp Pageants*, executed, it has been suggested, at the request of another of Beauchamp's daughters, Anne Neville, widow of Richard Neville, Earl of Warwick, in the mid-1480s.[9] Patrons of Lydgate's religious writings, inspired, no doubt, in part by thoughts of a spiritual reward for their devotion,[1] included Thomas Montacute, Earl of Salisbury (*The Pilgrimage of the Life of Man*), his wife, Alice Chaucer, later Duchess of Suffolk (*The Virtues of the Masse*), and John Whethamstede, Abbot of St Albans (*The Lives of St Albon and St Amphabell*).[2]

Returning to the question of a possible connection between Malory and Anthony Wydville, it is clear that the latter, too, was conscious of how reputation could be enhanced by certain judicious acts of patronage. In November 1473 Wydville was appointed tutor to the young Prince of Wales, his nephew, and the books which he translated himself, and had issued through Caxton's press (the *Dicts and Sayings of the Philosophers*, published 18 November 1477, the *Moral Proverbs* of Christine de Pisan, published 20 February 1477/78, and the *Cordyale*, published 24 March 1478/79) were of a kind to impress with their sober, thoughtful, and didactic intent. In the realm of chivalric activity, too, Wydville seems to have been well aware, in an age of conspicuous consumption, of the propagandist potential of ordered, but ostentatious, display. This is suggested, for instance, by his involvement in the Anglo-Burgundian jousts held at Smithfield in 1467, which accompanied the negotiations for the marriage of Edward IV's sister, Margaret, to Charles the Bold; and by his participation in the wedding celebrations in Bruges the following year.[3] Given the evident care with which Wydville promoted his interests both in general[4] and in respect of his role as patron, if he

8. Pearsall, *Lydgate*, pp. 167–8.
9. See Kathleen L. Scott, *The Caxton Master and His Patrons*, Cambridge Bibliographical Society Monograph, no. 8 (Cambridge, 1976) pp. 55–66, and for a discussion of the patronage of the volume, pp. 61–3. There are two complete facsimiles of the MS: William, Earl of Carysfoot, *The Pageants of Richard Beauchamp, Earl of Warwick* (Oxford, for the Roxburghe Club, 1908); and Viscount Dillon and W. H. St John Hope, *Pageant of the birth, life and death of Richard Beauchamp, Earl of Warwick, K. G., 1389–1439* (London, 1914).
1. Cf. Lucas, 'English Literary Patronage', p. 230.
2. On these patrons and the texts they commissioned, see Pearsall, *Lydgate*, pp. 172–3 and plate facing p. 166; 162; 280; 283–5. For the debate as to whether the translation of Deguileville is actually by Lydgate, see K. Walls, 'Did Lydgate Translate the *Pèlerinage de la Vie Humaine?*', *Notes and Queries*, 222 (1977) 103–5, and R.F. Green, 'Lydgate and Deguileville Once More', *Notes and Queries*, 223 (1978) 105–6. On the cost of producing this copy of the saints' lives see n. 75 below.
3. See Sydney Anglo, 'Anglo-Burgundian Feats of Arms: Smithfield, June 1467', *Guildhall Miscellany*, 2 (1965) 271–83. A measure of Wydville's success as a self-publicist is the preservation in contemporary MSS of accounts of his deeds, e.g. in the Pastons' MS, Lansdowne 285, ff.18–22, 29v–42; see *Catalogue of Lansdowne MSS*, nos. 12–15, 20–37; (on the changing relations between Wydville and the Pastons see Davis, *Paston Letters*, Part 1 (Oxford, 1971) p. xviii). It is also of some note that ten years after the Smithfield jousts Edward IV proposed Wydville as husband for Mary of Burgundy, his sister's stepdaughter.
4. See Hicks, 'Changing Role of the Wydvilles', and on Wydville's management of his affairs, E. W. Ives, 'Andrew Dymmock and the Papers of Antony, Earl Rivers, 1482–83', *Bulletin of the Institute of Historical Research*, 41 (1968) 216–29.

had been instrumental in the composition of the *Morte,* it is almost inconceivable, even making due allowance for his family's downfall, that no record of such an involvement should be traceable in either manuscript or printed copies of the text. This contention receives support from the argument outlined above, that the only apparent deliberate omissions of material in either version relate to Malory himself.

The evidence would thus seem to leave Malory with the status of 'gentleman amateur' rather than that of professional writer, a role for which there were ample precedents from the fourteenth century onwards.[5] * * * In order to set Malory as an author more firmly within the context of his age it would be worthwhile to compare his position to that of other translators.[6] Whilst such a task calls for a closer study than is practicable here, a few observations concerning a near-contemporary Arthurian translation may be of use to emphasise the fact that patronage did not provide the sole means by which writers could work in the fifteenth century. The only other Arthurian romance in Middle English to approach Malory's in terms of physical magnitude is the prose *Merlin;* even so, this work is only just over half the length of the *Morte,* covering in its most complete copy (some leaves are missing at the end) 245 as opposed to the original 500 leaves of the Additional MS.[7] I should add that I do not equate the *Merlin* qualitatively with the *Morte,* since it is a relatively straightforward translation from the French, but quantitatively the comparison does have validity.

The romance survives in two copies. One, almost complete, is Cambridge UL Ff.3.11, and the other, of which only a leaf remains, is in a Rawlinson miscellany in the Bodleian (D.913, f.43). The latter is in the hand of a scribe with a prolific output, who worked in London during the reign of Edward IV. * * * This fragment of the *Merlin* is of paper, and though the scribe is competent, there is little of note about the quality of the copy. It seems justifiable to conclude that the buying public for this MS would not have needed to be particularly wealthy. The history of the Cambridge MS, on the other hand, appears to have been rather different. Ff.3.11 is a vellum book with some, though not a great deal of, illumination; the opening page of text is framed by a demi-vinet border, and smaller painted initials are scattered through the copy thereafter.[8] * * * The characteristics of the copyist's hand and the style of the decoration indicates a date of sometime after 1450 for its manufacture and it is, therefore, almost contemporaneous with the Rawlinson copy. The conclusion to which all this evidence tends is that at much the same time copies of the *Merlin* were

---

5. See, e.g., McFarlane, *Nobility,* pp. 241–2.
6. Malory's style has been compared with that of other prose writers in the fifteenth century by P. J. C. Field, *Romance and Chronicle* (London, 1971), but a study of the development of prose in relation to audience and/or patronage would be of some interest.
7. The *Merlin* is edited by H. B. Wheatley, EETS OS 10, 21, 36, 112 (1865, 1866, 1869, 1899, repr. in 1 vol., 1973).
8. For examples of contemporary usage of the term 'demi-vinet' see Margaret Rickert's chapter on 'Illumination' in Manly and Rickert, *Canterbury Tales,* pp. 562–3.

being executed for different kinds of market, though whether they were made for the retail or the bespoke trade is not clear.[9] This pattern of production in turn throws doubt upon the idea that the translation was made at the behest of a patron. It may be, of course, that a slightly earlier MS, now lost, contained some dedicatory material, but the chances of this do not appear to be strong; the Cambridge MS is complete at the beginning, but there is no reference to the circumstances of composition. Perhaps, as happened in the case of some of the prose redactions of romances issued by Caxton and the printers who came after him, the translation of the *Merlin* was undertaken on a speculative, commercial basis.[1]

Mention of the commercial considerations involved in the production of books leads to a last point concerning the physical make-up of the unique MS of the *Morte d'Arthur*, namely that it can in no way be described as a *de luxe* volume; this fact has considerable implications for an understanding of the kind of ownership for which it was intended. The names of characters and of some places are, it is true, highlighted by being written in red ink, but this sign of careful and thoughtful presentation (the switch between pens would have been a time-consuming process) is not matched by other aspects of its production, in particular the lack of uniformity of lay-out adopted by the two scribes, the overall lack of supervision, and the fact that the volume is composed of paper, and that it contains no illustrations or painted decoration.[2] This is not to say that it would have been a cheap book to buy, as can be demonstrated by an approximate valuation based on contemporary rates of copying. For example, at around the time that Malory was completing his compilation, the scribe John Ebesham was submitting a bill to John Paston II for the numerous pieces of work he had carried out for him, and the charges he made were 1d. for a leaf of verse, and 2d. for one of prose.[3] One of the books which Ebesham copied for Paston is still extant, that is, Lansdowne 285, the 'Grete Booke'. The number of lines to a page and the size of the writing space are roughly equal in this MS and Additional 59678 and so, assuming that rates were fairly standard in different

9. See, for general discussion of this problem, A.I. Doyle and M. B. Parkes, 'The production of copies of the *Canterbury Tales* and the *Confessio Amantis* in the early fifteenth century' in *Medieval Scribes, Manuscripts and Libraries: Essays presented to N. R. Ker*, ed. M. B. Parkes and Andrew G. Watson (London, 1978) pp. 163–210.

1. On the rationale behind the translation and publication of romances by de Worde and his associates, see N. F. Blake, 'Wynkyn de Worde: The Early Years' and 'Wynkyn de Worde: The Later Years', *Gutenberg Jahrbuch* (1971) pp. 62–9, (1972) pp. 128–38. Commercial considerations may have governed the composition of romances in the fourteenth century as well; see the introduction to the facsimile of the Auchinleck MS by Derek Pearsall and I. C. Cunningham (London, 1977), and cf. Nicolas Jacobs, '*Sir Degarré, Lay le Freine, Beves of Hamtoun* and the "Auchinleck Bookshop" ', *Notes and Queries*, 29 (1982) 294–301.

2. On the scribes' use of red ink see Ker, introd. to the facsimile, pp. xiv–xv: it seems that, rather than the names being filled in after the rest of the text was copied, a different pen was picked up each time red ink was required. Other features of the manuscript's production are analysed in this same introduction.

3. See *Paston Letters*, Pt 2, pp. 391–2 and also 386–7; and A. I. Doyle, 'The Work of a Late Fifteenth Century English Scribe, William Ebesham' *Bulletin of the John Rylands Library*, 39 (1956–57) 298–325, pp. 299–307.

parts of the country,[4] this would suggest that the basic cost of this copy of the *Morte* was £4 3s. 8d., although it is not certain whether this sum would include the cost of the scribal insertions in red ink. On top of this there would have been a charge for rubrication, in this case the addition of around 120 large initials at divisions within the text (only 111 remain, owing to the loss of two quires); this could have been carried out by a separate craftsman. Only two of the initials are at all elaborate; these, on ff.71r and 409v, occupy five lines and have a pen and ink infilling of a formalised, but rather clumsy, leaf design. Apart from these there is one three line initial on f.349r, of blue with red pen-work decoration, and the remainder are all plain red lombards either of three, but more usually of two, lines; the execution of all of these is rather crude. John Ebesham charged John Paston 3s. 4d. for 'the Rubrissheyng of Alle the booke', which implies that he did it himself; allowing for the relative lengths of the Additional and Lansdowne MSS, an estimate of 8s. for the rubrication of the former may not be too wide of the mark. A final cost would be that of binding. Charges for this work varied with the size of the book to be covered and with the type of materials chosen. Assuming the covering in this case to have been fairly basic—wooden boards with an outer layer of leather— 2s. to 3s. would be an adequate sum to allow, perhaps. * * * An estimated total cost of around £4. 15s. for the book therefore seems reasonable.

Whoever bought the Additional MS must have had at least a moderate income, but its quality suggests that the purchaser is unlikely to have come from the nobility because, even leaving out of consideration the sumptuous painted books which Edward IV and his close associates obtained from Flemish workshops,[5] the quality of the books commissioned and owned by the nobility at this time is very different from that of the Malory MS. Since the suggestion has been made that the latter may have been commissioned by Anthony Wydville,[6] a particularly apt comparison may be drawn between it and Lambeth 265, the presentation copy of Wydville's translation of *The Dicts and Sayings of the Philosophers*, which was completed on 24 December 1477, and perhaps given to Edward by his brother-in-law as a Christmas gift. In terms of luxuriousness this volume scarcely rivals others which the King owned, but it reveals nevertheless several expensive features of production. There is only one illustration (the famous scene in which Wydville presents the book to Edward, who is surrounded by his family and members of the court)[7] but aside from this, large

4. It is not clear where the MS of Malory's work was written, although Professor Angus McIntosh has tentatively localised the dialect of the two scribes in West Northamptonshire; see his review of Matthews, *The Ill-Framed Knight*, in *Medium Aevum*, 37 (1968) 346–8.
5. See Margaret Kekewich, 'Edward IV, William Caxton and Literary Patronage in Yorkist England', *Modern Languages Review*, 66 (1971) 481–7; Alexander, 'Painting and Illumination for Royal Patrons', pp. 152–3 and additional references cited there; see pl.14 in the latter work for an illustration of a MS typical of those owned by Edward.
6. Hilton Kelliher, 'The Early History of the Malory Manuscript', pp. 155–6.
7. This has often been reproduced; see, e.g., R. Strong, *Tudor and Jacobean Portraits*, 2 vols,

illuminated initials of an unusual design abound and the beginning
of each sentence is picked out alternately with a blue mark decorated with red penwork, or a gold mark with blue penwork.[8] The
material of the book, which is used lavishly, is vellum, and the
pages are attractively prepared with ruling in an ink which is now
a light-purplish colour.[9] The text is written in a clear and fluent
secretary script.[1] Compared with this MS the Additional volume
gives the impression of competent, but routine, production. More
telling correspondences with regard to execution can be noted
between the *Morte* MS and other late fifteenth-century paper copies of English romances, for example: the MS of *Partenay,* now
Trinity College Cambridge R.3.17; the version of *Partonope of
Blois* now Additional 35288; and the fragmentary remains of the
story of *Ponthus* preserved as ff.1–2 of Douce 384.[2] Moreover, the
analogy may be extended to the probable ownership of the various
volumes. On the basis of scribbled names which appear in the MS
of Malory's work, Hilton Kelliher has presented a convincing
case for the ownership in the later sixteenth century to be attributed to a relatively well-to-do family of Northamptonshire gentry.
The evidence which he has gathered, together with the conclusions prompted by the physical characteristics of the volume,
suggests that the original owners are likely to have come from
a similar background.[3] Such a history would be in accord with
what is known about the other romance MSS which have been
mentioned.[4]

The discussion so far has emphasised the desirability, in our
present state of knowledge, of keeping open as many avenues of
enquiry as possible in the approach to an understanding of how
Malory was able to write his Arthurian work, despite the problems

---

National Portrait Gallery (London, 1969) pl.162, and the enlarged detail of the portrait
of Anthony Wydville, pl. V in Hellinga, *Caxton in Focus.*

8. See Hellinga, *Caxton in Focus,* pl.III for a colour illustration of f.17v, and cf. the description of the MS by James and Jenkins, *Catalogue of MSS at Lambeth Palace,* pp. 412–14.
9. There are generous borders around the text: the page measurement is 278mm × 198mm,
and the writing space is 176mm × 97mm.
1. The scribe signs his work on f.105r: 'Apud sanctum Jacobum/in campis per *haywarde*';
Doyle, 'English Books In and Out of Court', p. 181 n. 54, describes his work as 'accomplished', and suggests that he may have been a cleric at the hospital of St. James in the
Fields at Westminster.
2. See, respectively: M. R. James, *Catalogue of the Western MSS in the Library of Trinity
College Cambridge* (Cambridge, 1901) II, pp. 66–7, and Julia Boffey, *The Manuscript
Context of English Courtly Love Lyrics, c.1450–1530,* D. Phil., University of York, 1983,
pp. 203–5; Gisela Guddat-Figge, *A Catalogue of Manuscripts Containing Middle English
Romances* (Munich, 1976), pp. 164–5 (ff.2–19 of this MS are of vellum, ff.1, 20–154 of
paper) and pp. 268–9.
3. 'The Early History of the Malory Manuscript'. The MS contains the signature (repeated
several times) of one 'Richard Followell', who can probably be identified as a member of
the Followell family of Litchborough. Kelliher has proved a connection, during the sixteenth century, between this family and the lords of the manor of Litchborough, the
Malorys, who were distantly related to the Malorys of Newbold Revel, though whether
this series of associations has any bearings on the origins of the MS is, as yet, a matter
for speculation only.
4. Trinity College Cambridge R.3.19 is connected with inhabitants of York and two nearby
villages, Elvington and Sutton-on-Derwent, in the late fifteenth century; see James, *Catalogue of Trinity MSS,* and Boffey, *Manuscript Context.* BL Additional MS 35288 contains
various names, including: Thomas Altherton, 'frauncissi babisonis' and 'melady babsin',
'Dorythe Couper', and 'Robarte Gascoygne'; none of these individuals has been identified,
though inscriptions in Altherton's hand imply that the MS was loaned amongst a group of
friends; see Guddat-Figge, *MSS Containing Romances,* p. 165.

of interpretation inherent in the nature of the evidence with which we have to deal. Thus, it has been argued, it is not necessary to assume that Malory had a patron in order to account for his access to a number of source texts, since there were several different ways in which he could have obtained them. One of the possibilities raised was that he borrowed, or had access to, books owned by someone with a larger collection than he, in all probability, possessed, and investigation into the contents of the libraries of individuals and families who may have been known to Malory does seem to hold out the offer of potentially rich rewards.

* * *

FELICITY RIDDY

Divisions†

* * *

History, courtesy, right conduct and the claims of the next world: I have been suggesting so far that it is possible to see the *Morte Darthur* as composed of a series of tales which are pulled in different directions by the connected yet divergent concerns—which Malory shares—of fifteenth-century readers of romances. Because of their diverse origins the tales provide for the constant redirection of focus which has been my concern up till now. The separate books of the *Morte Darthur* are ordered in a roughly chronological sequence, bounded by Arthur's birth and death, but are not unified. Their continuity derives as much as anything from their juxtaposition in a single volume; it is spatial as well as temporal, as several of the colophons acknowledge. The colophon to Book Two, for example, promises: 'and here folowyth afftir many noble talys of Sir Launcelot de Lake' [p. 151], while the colophon to Book Three, *Sir Lancelot*, looks forward in turn to Book Four, *Sir Gareth*, in a sentence that has unfortunately been omitted in Vinaver's edition: 'Here folowyth Sir Gareth is tale of Orkeney that was callyd Bewmaynes By Sir Kay' [p. 177]. Nevertheless the connectives offered by the colophons are no more consistent or complete than the temporal or casual links made within the tales: the *explicit* to Book One, for example, raises the possibility of a continuation but points in no particular direction:

> Here endyth this tale, as the Freynshe booke seyth, . . . And this booke endyth whereas Sir Launcelot and Sir Trystrams com to courte. Who that woll make ony more, lette hym seke other bookis of Kynge Arthure or of Sir Launcelot or Sir Trystrams. [p. 112]

† From *Sir Thomas Malory* (Leiden: Brill, 1987), pp. 139–153. Reprinted with permission of E.J. Brill publishers.

This peculiarly open-ended closure, and the self-contained *explicit* to the *Sankgreal* which simply brings it to an end and does not link it with Book Seven, point to the likelihood that these tales existed more or less independently before the final compilation of the *Morte Darthur*. Many manuscripts—and this is particularly true of miscellanies containing romances—are made up of separate booklets consisting of one or more gatherings, which were not necessarily copied at the same time or by the same person and which had had an independent existence before being assembled and bound in the order in which they have survived.[1] Richard Heege's manuscript, Advocates 19.3.1, and C.U.L. Ff.II.38, * * * are made up in this way. Caxton's redivision of the *Morte Darthur* into twenty-one books, each one carefully linked to the next—even if by no more than *Explicit Liber Quartus. Incipit Liber Quintus,* for example—reveals the printer's more fixed understanding of what a 'hoole booke' is. Moreover Caxton had the Winchester manuscript to hand as a model: bound, complete, and manifestly a single volume. Malory's own sense of the wholeness of the 'hoole booke' must have been very different, and was presumably cumulative; by the time he wrote the final *explicit* he had obeyed his own injunction at the end of Book One to 'seke other bookis of Kynge Arthure or of Sir Launcelot or Sir Trystrams' and had assembled the stories—which were probably in a series of different booklets (though not necessarily one to each booklet)—and placed them one after another so that they could be bound together in a single volume. It may have been only at this stage that he went back over the various stories and introduced those passages, especially at the beginnings and endings of the tales, which seem designed to create connections between them. In the end, the wholeness of the 'hoole booke' in its manuscript form rests on the tales' contiguity; the book itself contains them and holds them together, physically, between its two covers.

The last two books—and particularly the final one—are about fracture, separation, and the dissolution of wholeness. That is, they take as their subject the fissile tendencies of the book, both as a compilation of originally separate booklets and as a collection of tales drawn from various sources which respond differently to different strains in fifteenth-century culture. Malory's sources for these books are the Vulgate *La Mort Artu* and it's derivative the English stanzaic *Le Morte Arthur,* both of which interlace the stories of the Fair Maid of Astolat and the Poisoned Apple in a continuous sequence which leads into the story of the discovery of Lancelot's and Guinevere's adultery and the destruction of the Round Table that ensues from that discovery. Malory has not only divided the unified matter of the *Mort Artu* into two books, but he has broken up the first of those books into separate tales as well. Book Eight, however, is constructed on different principles from

---

1. See P.R. Robinson, 'The "Booklet": a Self-Contained Unit in Composite Manuscripts', *Codicologica*, 3 (1980), 46–69.

those of Book Seven. Vinaver's division of it into five sections is—
as elsewhere—his own; there is little authority for such a structure
in the Winchester manuscript and Caxton treated it quite differently. It could just as well be printed as one continuous unit, since
it has a narrative coherence that is new to the *Morte Darthur,* in
which events are linked in a chain of cause and effect and are not
simply juxtaposed. It is striking that this kind of coherence should
emerge precisely—and only—at the final point of collapse, as if
the new form provides Malory with a means whereby the narrative
itself can hold disintegration at bay.[2]

These last books, one fragmented and the other coherent,
embody the ideas of separation and affinity in their very form and
are held together in ways which simultaneously assert and deny
the possibility of continuity. 'The Tale of Sir Urry', the last tale in
Book Seven, ends with an ominous foreboding of what is to come
in the next book: 'But every nyght and day Sir Aggravayne, Sir
Gawaynes brother, awayted Quene Gwenyver and Sir Launcelot
to put hem bothe to a rebuke and a shame' [p. 644]. But before
this note can be picked up and developed in Book Eight (as it will
be), the narrator interrupts himself and moves out of the narrative
altogether:

> And so I leve here of this tale, and overlepe grete bookis of sir
> Launcelot, what grete adventures he ded when he was called
> le Shyvalere de Charyot. For, as the Freynshe booke sayth . . .
> [p. 644]

And he goes on, with grand irrelevance, to describe what the
French book in fact does not say. The narrator's intervention at
this point has the effect of reminding the reader that the conti-
nuities of fiction are themselves fictional, while the statement at
the end of this digression, that 'here on the othir syde folowyth the
moste pyteuous tale of the *Morte Arthure Saunz Gwerdon*' affirms
this even more explicitly: it is on the pages of books that tales
connect.

Nevertheless, contiguity has its own tantalizing and minimal way
of suggesting coherence, just as the paratactic chronicle style * * *
implies without asserting the possibility of some kind of casual
relationship between events. The meaning that contiguity offers
lies in the disjunctive structure itself, which seems to long for a
design and a completeness which it cannot quite assert. The fragmentation of the self and the world underlies Malory's presentation of the end of Arthur's reign, but the longing to transcend this
fragmentation is there also. It is not only discernible in the form
itself but is also more directly expressed. The meditation on love
in Book Seven which serves as a bridge between the episodes of
the Great Tournament and the Knight of the Cart expresses both

---

2. I disagree with the persuasive argument of Stephen Knight, *The Structure of Sir Thomas
Malory's Arthuriad* (Sydney, 1969), that Malory's narrative method is episodic up to the
end of *Sir Tristram* but that the 'book is a unity from that point; its qualities are those of
a unified work of art and its failings are where it turns away from its strong unified theme'
(p. 60). I do not regard the disunity of the *Morte Darthur* as a failing.

this longing and the impossibility of achieving it [pp. 624–25].[3] The passage, too long to quote in full, is poetic, exploratory and reflective. Equally apparent are the impulses to renewal and the impulses to destructiveness; it rests on a shifting pattern of contrasts—between summer and winter, heat and cold, remembering and forgetting, true love and negligence, the present and the old days—and its development proceeds in a similarly ambivalent and contrastive way, with assertions which are then qualified or denied. The whole passage carries in its structure that shiftingness which it seeks to confront, and which derives from the divisions of experience. The way in which it ends is characteristic:

> Wherefore I lykken love nowadayes unto sommer and wynter: for, lyke as the tone ys colde and the othir ys hote, so faryth love nowadayes. And therefore all ye that be lovers, calle unto youre remembraunce the monethe of May, lyke as ded Quene Gwenyver, for whom I make here a lytyll mencion, that whyle she lyved she was a trew lover, and therefor she had a good ende. [p. 625]

The words 'calle unto youre remembraunce the monethe of May' turn back to the opening of the whole passage: 'And thus hit passed on frome Candylmas untyll after Ester, that the moneth of May was com, whan every lusty harte begynnyth to blossome and to burgyne' [p. 624]. Calling May 'unto youre remembraunce' seems to provide a way of taking it out of the passage of time in which Easter succeeds Candlemas and summer gives way to winter: memory recalls the month of May as a permanent present, suggests that there is a time when the heart may flower and not be defaced or laid apart by 'a lytyll blaste of wyntres rasure' [p. 624]. But once that moment has been created in the text, Guinevere enters it— summoned there, it seems, by the association of 'lovers,' 'remembraunce' and 'May'—and then destroys it, as it must be destroyed for there is no such season, by bringing with her her own mortality. Guinevere is 'a trew lover, and therefor she had a good ende' [p. 625]: Malory's 'therefor' does not conceal the disjunction between the desire for permanence and the fact of impermanence. The contrast between the seasons as they change, now hot, now cold, is an emblem not only of love's alteration but of the restless and desiring modern sensibility which Malory deplores but out of which his own book issues. The narrator returns to this subject again in 'The Day of Destiny' when the people of England desert Arthur for the usurper Mordred: 'Alas, thys ys a great defaughte of us Englysshemen, for there may no thynge please us no terme' [p. 680]. The *Morte Darthur* confronts those contemporary instabilities but is unable to transcend them.

3. * * * Professor Norton-Smith points out that Malory may have drawn here on Lydgate's 'That Now is Hay Some-tyme was Grase', of which two texts survive, one in Boldl. Lib., MS Rawlinson C. 86 where it is bound with *Sir Launfal* and *The Weddyng of Sir Gawen and Dame Ragnell*. See *The Minor Poems of John Lydgate*, ed. H.N. MacCracken, II, EETS, OS 192 (London, 1934; repr. 1961), pp. 809–13.

The last two books seem to be peculiarly the products of that late-medieval dividedness about the validity of the things of this world which * * * is an aspect of the *Morte Darthur*'s own instability. The previous book, the *Sankgreal*, turned the whole narrative inward, but introspection is not to be the final perspective. From the beginning of Book Seven the settings of the stories are translated into familiar and identifiable locations: 'the good ermyte here besyde Wyndesore' [p. 589] the 'pryvy dynere in London' [p. 590]. In the episode of the Fair Maid, Camelot is 'otherwyse callyd Wynchester' and Astolat 'ys in Englysh Gylforde' [p. 599], while in 'The Knight of the Cart' Lancelot 'toke the watir at Westmynster Brydge and made hys horse swymme over the Temmys unto Lambyth' [p. 629]. As in *King Arthur and the Emperor Lucius*, the narrative assumes that there is an external world and thus that the *locus* of action is not within. The struggles of the moral life in Book Seven are not the Platonic and Pauline battles with the self with which the *Sankgreal* was concerned, but arise out of the pressing and contradictory demands that are created in relationships with other people. Percival in the *Sankgreal* is confronted by a naked woman who is a fiend summoned up by his own desire, and his encounter with her takes place in a pavilion that vanishes in a puff of smoke when he rejects her. In Book Seven, however, Malory moves back into the historian's or the novelist's domain: Lancelot is confronted by a Guinevere whose otherness is guaranteed by those real locations and who makes the complicated demands that other people make, unsatisfiable precisely because they are other. In this book London cannot vanish into thin air nor Guinevere simply retreat 'with the wynde, rorynge and yellynge' [p. 530]. She has to be endured, placated, and fought for, and the long struggle is called love. In this book Lancelot's and Arthur's dilemmas are not presented as crossroads with signposts helpfully explaining that 'if thou go on the lyffte honde thou shall nat there lyghtly wynne prouesse' [p. 510]. Since the paths the characters take are not within themselves they are crossed by other people's paths; the opaque realism of this book derives from its presentation of the competing and conflicting intentions out of which the action is created. The plots of 'The Poisoned Apple' and 'The Knight of the Cart' both make use of misunderstanding, deception and intrigue, while in 'The Great Tournament' an arrow meant for a hind wounds Lancelot ignominiously in the buttock. But nothing presents more poignantly the inscrutable otherness of other people than the baffled death of the Fair Maid of Astolat, who understands her own predicament even less than the other characters do theirs[4]. Moreover in the final 'Tale of Sir Urry' we as readers share that limitation of vision, when Lancelot is granted a power to unspell sir Urry that he does not seem to deserve, and after which he weeps like a beaten child for reasons which we can only partly comprehend.

---

4. See my 'Structure and Meaning in Malory's "The Fair Maid of Astolat" ', *Forum for Modern Language Studies*, 12 (1976), 354–66.

After the *Sankgreal,* then, Book Seven re-establishes the ground of action as being the place where other people are, where their intentions collide as they love, quarrel, defend or betray one another, and the realistic mode both assumes and asserts its validity. In Book Eight, however, there is a loss of confidence in that place and a retreat from it into various kinds of isolation. This isolation is not the same as the introspective solitariness of the *Sankgreal* since there is now no coherent sense of self towards which to turn. Nothing seems able to hold together: not the fellowship, nor the characters, nor even language itself. Malory's version of the end of the Round Table is the product of his own and his generation's insecurities.

The end of the fellowship of the Round Table is expressed in metaphors of dispersal, fracture and the division of that wholeness of which it is an emblem. At the beginning of 'Slander and Strife' Gawain foresees that ' "the noble felyship of the Rounde Table shall be disparbeled" ' [p. 647], meaning 'scattered' or 'dispersed'. Arthur echoes him a little later, saying: ' "me sore repentith that ever Sir Launcelot sholde be ayenste me, for now I am sure the noble felyshyp of the Rounde Table ys brokyn for ever" ' [p. 654], and when Lancelot is finally banished to France his knights use Arthur's words: ' "in thys realme woll be no quyett, but ever debate and stryff, now the felyshyp of the Rounde Table ys brokyn" ' [p. 671]. After the chaotic melée of Guenevere's rescue, Arthur says: ' "Alas, my good knyghtes be slayne and gone away fro me . . . for now I may never more holde hem togydirs with my worshyp" ' [p. 657]. Neither in the stanzaic *Le Morte Arthur* nor in the *Mort Artu* does Gawain or Arthur express what is to ensue in these terms. In the English poem, which Malory seems to have been following closely at this point, Gawain foresees 'werre and wrake'[5]. After Lancelot's rescue of the queen, Arthur weeps for the loss of his knights: ' "Suche knyghtys as there ar slayne, / In all thys worlde there is no mo" ' (1975–6), while at the equivalent moment in the *Mort Artu,* Arthur curses Lancelot ' "car il a destruit moi et mon lingnage" '[6]. There are loss and destruction here, but not the sense contained in Malory's metaphors, that something which has been held together is finally falling apart. This is the leading theme of the final book and is expressed in a number of ways, of which one is the reiteration of departure.

'To depart' in Middle English means to leave, to separate, to divide, and to come to an end[7]. In this book lovers, friends, enemies, lands, love itself: all are departed. There are many leave-takings, the most expansive of which is Lancelot's banishment to his own lands in France after he has returned Guinevere to Arthur. It is both a separation of the lovers and a sundering of the Round

---

5. Line 1183. Quotations are from *Le Morte Arthur,* ed. J.D. Bruce, EETS, ES 87 (London, 1903, repr. 1959).
6. P. 129. (' . . . for he has destroyed me and my lineage.') Quotations are from *La Mort Le Roi Artu,* ed. Jean Frappier (Paris and Geneva, 1964).
7. See *Middle English Dictionary,* departen, 1, 2, 3, 4.

Table, as Lancelot acknowledges: ' "Madame, now I muste departe from you and thys noble felyshyp for ever" ' [p. 670]. And as he goes, 'there was nother kynge, duke, erle, barowne, nor knyght, lady nor jantyllwoman, but they all wepte as people oute of mynde . . . ' [p. 670]. In that brief hierarchy is a last glimpse of the order and unity which Lancelot's going will destroy for ever, and the simile 'as people oute of mynde' reaches out to other areas of the book: in its obvious sense 'oute of mynde' is another version of the separation from oneself which the vengeful Gawain, 'nygh oute of hys mynde' [p. 657] after Gareth's death, adumbrates in the larger narrative. At the same time the other sense of 'oute of mynde'—as in 'time out of mind'—suddenly locates that social order, and its grief for itself, as beyond recall. The separation of past from present is, as I shall show, another of the partings of this last book.

When Lancelot goes into exile the long-standing alliance between England and France, which began in Book One when King Bors and King Ban came to Arthur's aid, is severed. It is difficult to avoid finding a contemporary implication in Malory's choice of the romance version of the downfall of Arthur's kingdom, which inevitably entails, as the chronicle version does not, an English king's loss of French allegiance and the internal devastation that follows on that loss. But the exile of Lancelot and his followers also introduces another of the senses of 'depart': that of division. No longer maintained by Arthur as knights of the Round Table, Lancelot's supporters turn to him for the good lordship that he promises them as he divides his lands among them:

> 'And ye shall undirstonde, suche lyvelode as I am borne unto I shall departe with you in thys maner of wyse: that ys for to say, I shall departe all my lyvelode and all my londis frely amonge you; . . . and I truste to God to maynteyne you on my londys as well as ever ye were maynteyned.' [p. 671]

Out of this division of his lands Lancelot creates a different and separate social order from that one which had wept its own passing at his departure, as he makes his followers kings, dukes and earls in some of those very territories of France which England had lost in Malory's lifetime.[8]

Depart also means 'come to an end', and this is the sense in which Lancelot uses it early in the book when, trapped in Guinevere's bedroom, he tells her: ' "syth hit ys so that the day ys com that oure love muste departe, wyte you well I shall selle my lyff as dere as I may" ' [p. 650]; here he is picking up what Guinevere has already said: ' "I dred me sore oure longe love ys com to a myscheyvus ende" ' [p. 649]. But Lancelot is wrong; this is not the day on which their love is to depart. That departure will take place much later, in a convent in Amesbury, when he asks Guinevere to kiss him and she refuses:

8. See Vinaver, *Works,* III, pp. 1640–1.

'Nay', sayd the Quene, 'that shal I never do, but absteyne you from such werkes.' And they departed; but there was never so harde an herted man but he wold have wepte to see the dolour that they made . . . [p. 693]

Now 'they departed' brings together a number of the meanings that have been established in the interval between that encounter in the bedroom and this one. The obvious meaning—that they separate and take their leave of each other—also includes the others: they are divided by their different vocations, she a nun and he still a knight, and they have also come to the end.

The disintegration of unity takes other forms in the book as well. Arthur's dream of falling from fortune's wheel on the eve of the last battle is a nightmarish image of dismembering which is developed from the stanzaic *Le Morte Arthur*. In the *Morte Artu* the dream has a direct moral explicitness: Arthur is raised up on the highest part of a wheel, which he is told is the wheel of fortune, and from where he can see the whole world. ' "Mes" ', says Fortune, ' "tel sont li orgueil terrien qu'il n'i a nul si haut assiz qu'il ne le coviegne cheoir de la poesté del monde" ', and with that she pushes him to the ground so that it seems as if he 'perdoit tout le pooir del cors et des membres'[9]. It is a dream of pride, power and their opposites, and its implications are public and political. In the stanzaic *Le Morte Arthur* the dream is less explicit but nevertheless its public significance is still unmistakable. Arthur on the wheel is associated with the opulent trappings of proud authority [see p. 743, lines 3172–79]: Malory's version begins with a moment of self-detachment, in which the dreaming Arthur sees himself momentarily from the outside, wearing the cloth of gold that signifies his kingship:

> Kynge Arthure dremed a wondirfull dreme, and in hys dreme hym semed that he saw uppon a chafflet a chayre, and the chayre was faste to a whele, and thereuppon sate Kynge Arthure in the rychest cloth of golde that myght be made. [p. 683]

Then the dreamer's perspective becomes that of the king on the chair, looking down. From here he does not see 'tout le monde' [all the world]: his vision is, as in the stanzaic *Le Morte Arthur*, more private, more terrifying and more vertiginous:

> And the Kynge thought there was undir hym, farre from hym, an hydeous depe blak watir, and therein was all maner of serpentis and wormes and wylde bestis, fowle and and orryble. [p. 683]

With the shift from outside to inside comes the possibility that the ugly forms that Arthur sees are within. They are 'undir hym'—that is, not only beneath him physically but subordinated to him as

---

9. p. 227. ('But such is earthly pride that there is no-one seated so high that he can avoid falling from worldly power.') (' . . . he lost all the strength from his body and limbs')

well—and also 'farre from hym', distanced and seemingly unrelated to that hieratic figure in his Byzantine dress. But the poise and self-possession of this perspective are illusory; suddenly the wheel turns and 'he felle amonge the serpentes, and every beste toke hym by a lymme.' This fall does not seem to be merely an emblem of reversal; Arthur's dream at this point is not just of himself as another Hector or Alexander, to whom Lancelot likens himself at his banishment: ' "whan they were moste in her royalte, they alyght passyng lowe" ' [p. 669]. The 'hydeous depe blak watir' ('A blake watir' in the stanzaic Le Morte Arthur) is a zone where kingliness is obliterated. It is inhabited by creatures who are not human, but whose dismembering of the king begins with gestures ('and every beste toke hym by a lymme') that seem almost to be those of greeting. The dream has a public meaning, of course: it alludes to the events to come, and to the region of savage nightmare into which Arthur will be plunged in the final battle. It has a private signification as well, however. It suggests the disintegration of the self, presented first as a king in apparent control of his powers, using the metaphor of the moral drama, as in Rex Vivus in the *Pride of Life* or King Humanity in the later *Satyre of the Thrie Estaites*. Then the king-self is torn apart, no longer able to 'holde togydirs' in unity, but preyed upon by monstrous forms that it knows of old.

This symbolic dismembering of the king is enacted in a different way in the final battle which follows, when Arthur and Mordred finally confront and kill each other. Traditionally, Mordred has two identities, as Arthur's nephew and Arthur's son. In the *Historia Regum Britanniae* he is a nephew, the son of Arthur's sister by her husband, King Lot of Lothian (in the *Morte Darthur*, of Lothian and Orkney), and this relationship is preserved in the alliterative *Morte Arthure*. The Mordred who is Arthur's son, begotten in an act of unwitting incest on his sister, derives from the French romance tradition. This Mordred was invented, according to Frappier, by the 'architect' of the *Lancelot-Queste-Mort Artu* trilogy, from where an elaborated version of the birth story entered the Vulgate *Merlin* and post-Vulgate *Suite du Merlin* [1]. Malory used the *Suite* for Book One and tells the story there of Mordred's incestuous conception and Arthur's vain attempt to kill his son in order to forestall Merlin's prophecy that Mordred will destroy him. Nevertheless when Mordred reappears in Books Three and Five (he is not mentioned in Books Two, Four or Six) he is never identified as Arthur's son, but instead as Gawain's brother. In Book Five, *Sir Tristram,* it is his identity as his mother's son, not his father's, that is required: he is one of the clannish and treacherous Orkney brethren who kill their mother and her lover, Sir Lamorak, in accordance with the violent imperatives of that book. In Book Seven, and early in Book Eight, he is still presented as a member of a fraternal solidarity, and is con-

1. Frappier, ed. cit., pp. xxiii–iv.

stantly coupled with his dangerous brother Agravaine until the latter is killed in the fight with Lancelot which the pair of them have instigated. After the deaths of Gareth and Gaheris only two of the Orkney brothers are left. From 'The Vengeance of Sir Gawain' until Arthur's death, the impetus for the action is provided by the differing relationships of Gawain and Mordred with Arthur, rather than with each other, as one drives Arthur to war in France and the other brings him back. That is, now that the Orkney clan does not exist except as a motive for Gawain's mad hatred, Mordred—no longer needed as a brother—can reassume at the beginning of 'The Siege of Benwick' the identity of the incestuously-begotten son that he has not had since Book One: 'bycause sir Mordred was kynge Arthurs son, he gaff hym the rule off hys londe and off hys wyff' [p. 672]. The plot alone does not require this homecoming. In the alliterative *Morte Arthure*, as I have already said, the usurper is a sister's son; at the end of the poem it is the powerful ironies of Mordred's kinship with Gawain— whom he kills and whose death he laments—which are exploited, rather than his relationship with Arthur. The presence of the son in the last part of the last book of the *Morte Darthur* has to do with that fragmentation of the world and the self to which Malory continually returns.

The fact that Arthur is Mordred's father is reiterated in 'The Day of Destiny' when Mordred proposes to marry Guinevere ('which was hys unclys wyff and hys fadirs wyff', as the narrator reminds us), in an extended speech by the Bishop of Canterbury which derives from the stanzaic *Le Morte Arthur*:

❡"For ys nat Kynge Arthur youre uncle, and no farther but youre modirs brothir, and uppon her he hymselffe begate you, uppon hys owne syster? Therefore how may ye wed youre owne fadirs wyff?' [p. 679]

It is alluded to again by the narrator when Mordred prepares to meet Arthur's army at Dover: 'and so he thought to beate hys owne fadir fro hys owne londys' [p. 680], and a few lines later: 'there was Sir Mordred redy awaytyng uppon hys londynge—to lette hys owne fadir to londe uppon the londe that he was kynge over' [pp. 680–81]. In the final preparations for the truce made at Salisbury Plain, both leaders draw up their armies and warn them to expect treachery from the other side. Arthur's mistrust of Mordred is justified in the light of what has happened, but the mistrust of Arthur which Mordred voices at this point is less explicable and does not have its source in Arthur's public self. Mordred's speech indicates the origin of his mistrust: ' "in no wyse I woll nat truste for thys tretyse . . . for I know well my fadir woll be avenged uppon me" ' [p. 684]. In these, the last words that are heard from him, Mordred acknowledges for the first time that Arthur is his father. Arthur never refers to Mordred as his son; he is always 'that traytoure, sir Mordred' [pp. 684 and 685], 'the traytoure that all thys woo hath wrought' [p. 685] ' "Traytoure, now ys thy dethe-day com!" ' [p. 686] is

Arthur's last cry to Mordred before he kills him. When Arthur calls Mordred a traitor there is a private implication alongside the public one: Arthur has been betrayed by Mordred's very being. Mordred's ' "I know well my fadir woll be avenged uppon me" ' is a voice which reaches down into the 'hydeous depe blak watir' of the destructive family, in which the father rejects the son, and where the grudging adult speaks like a frightened child. It is the same voice which is heard at the end of *Athelston*, when the traitor Wymound is asked the reason for his treachery to his sworn brother, and replies: ' "He lovyd hym to mekyl and me to lyte; / Ther-ffore envye I hadde" '2. * * *

I do not intend to suggest that Mordred is what he is because Arthur tried to have him killed as an infant. The characters in the *Morte Darthur* do not have that kind of psychological depth or that kind of historical consistency. It is rather the other way round: because Mordred is what he is—the product of an act of incest—he must be rejected. And when Merlin prophesies to Arthur in Book One that ' "ye have gotyn a childe that shall destroy you and all the knyghtes of youre realme" ' [p. 32], he is defining Mordred through the prophecy, adding another proposition about him, but this time one which accounts for his function in the plot of the final book. The Mordred who is brought back into the *Morte Darthur* in Book Eight is thus both that-which-must-be-rejected and that-which-will-destroy; more than this, it is because he is these things that he is there at all. That is, the plot requires that-which-will-destroy, who is also, as it happens, that-which-must-be-rejected. These two aspects of Mordred create his identity as the usurping son of Book Eight; they correspondingly divide Arthur into king and father. Moreover, these inseparable dualities make the final battle between Arthur and Mordred inevitable: the son must kill the father and destroy his realm, while the father must kill the usurper whom he himself has begotten in incest.

Malory's presentation of the last battle on Salisbury Plain is much shorter and less varied than in the *Mort Artu* and is even more abbreviated than in the stanzaic *Le Morte Arthur*. Its purpose is to focus on the final confrontation between father and son, for which the battle provides a context as well as an occasion. In the *Mort Artu* there are three hundred left on both sides, including four knights of the Round Table, at the beginning of the last attack in which Mordred and Arthur are killed. Malory has turned to the terse account in the stanzaic *Le Morte Arthur*, where by nightfall only Arthur, Lucan, Bedivere and Mordred are still living, for his eerie depiction of Arthur and Mordred as kings of the dead. At the end of the day there are 'an hondred thousand leyde dede uppon the erthe. Then was Kynge Arthure wode wroth oute of mesure, whan he saw hys people so slayne frome hym' [p. 685] and he can see no-one left alive but Lucan and Bedivere.

2. *Athelston*, in *Medieval English Romances*, ed. A.V.C. Schmidt and Nicholas Jacobs, 2 vols (London, 1980), I, p. 150.

"Jesu mercy!" seyde the Kynge, "where ar all my noble knyghtes becom? Alas, that ever I shulde se thys doleful day! For now", seyde Kynge Arthur, "I am com to myne ende. But wolde to God," seyde he, "that I wyste now where were that traytoure Sir Mordred that hath caused all thys myschyff." Than Kynge Arthur loked aboute and was ware where stood Sir Mordred leanyng uppon hys swerde amonge a grete hepe of dede men. [p. 685]

The answer to the literal sense of Arthur's question, ' "where ar all my noble knyghtes become?" ', is obvious: they lie 'ded uppon the erthe' all around him, and at Mordred's feet. * * * Arthur at this point is man *in extremis,* a king without a kingdom, and the figure of Mordred in that final sentence mirrors him, an image of desolate and desolating power. Then the two kings of nowhere, father and son, who have come to an end that is both a conclusion and a goal, run towards one another as if to some fearful embrace, seeking their own and each other's deaths. Mordred's action—'he threste hymselff with the myght that he had upp to the burre of kyng Arthurs speare' [p. 686]—is the interloper's final piece of aggressive self-assertion. At the same time it is also in some terrible way the action of the child who will not be fended off, who impales himself on the parent's hatred, reaching out to destroy what does not love him. The inseparable dualities remain: 'and ryght so he smote hys fadir, Kynge Arthure, with hys swerde holdynge in both hys hondys . . . ' [p. 686]. In the paragraph describing their final encounter from which this quotation comes, the two men are held together, their names intertwined—Mordred, Arthur, Arthur, Mordred, Arthur, Arthur, Mordred—and then they fall apart.

The end of Arthur's rule over himself and his kingdom is confirmed when he is twice unable to assert his will over Bedivere, in a scene which takes place in an extension of the nightmare landscape of the battlefield. Arthur is carried to a little chapel 'nat farre from the see', about which one editor comments sharply: 'Malory's geography is in error: the sea nowhere comes to the edge of Salisbury Plain'[3]. Quite so; this is no longer an England that can be clearly mapped. Other boundaries have dissolved also: 'pyllours and robbers' invade the field to murder the wounded and rob the dead; the Bishop of Canterbury has already fled to a hermitage; the forest encroaches. The ladies who take Arthur away may or may not have buried him in the grave which bears his name; it is not even certain that Arthur is dead. Almost his last words to Bedivere are: ' "Comforte thyselff . . . and do as well as thou mayste, for in me ys no truste for to truste in" ' [p. 688]. The noun 'truste' is unusual in Malory's vocabulary and there is no other occurrence in the *Morte Darthur* quite like this. It means something like 'source of assurance'; Arthur, unkinged, participates in

---

3. *Le Morte Darthur. The Seventh and Eighth Tales,* ed. P.J.C. Field (London, 1978), p. 277.

the instability of his world. The barge on which he is taken away by the queens is 'rowed fromward the londe' [p. 688], a movement into insolidity. The dispersal of the Round Table has left nothing at the centre, and Arthur's mysterious departing is a departing from himself.

* * *

PAUL STROHM

Mellyagant's Primal Scene†

A recent diatribe * * * accuses theoretical practitioners of disingenuousness in using early texts as vehicles for their own more contemporary interests: "It seems to me wrong to seek to advance your career by professing to be concerned with Shakespeare, while actually writing about what happens to interest you more, forcing a limited set of new interests onto the old topic, using that topic as an excuse to write about these more fashionable concerns."[1] A different essay might pause to refute the sour assumption that only career-mongers and fashion victims pursue theory. I wish, however, to address the more substantial accusation that theory encourages effacement of the text. This is obviously a possible consequence of theory ill applied, yet theory holds out the equal and opposite promise that it might foster valued (and otherwise unobtainable) interpretative understandings.

One would be disingenuous to deny theory's possible problems; paramount among them is the power to enforce a reading, to discover in any text exactly what the theory was programmed to find. Against this possible pitfall I would, however, adduce a major benefit, which is the capacity of theory to reveal new and important aspects of a text that might otherwise have escaped notice. My intention in this essay is to weigh these two poles of possibility, by reading a passage in the light of a "strong" theory—strong in such senses as its capacity to discover its own preconditions in the widest variety of texts and its temporal and conceptual distance from the possible intentions of any medieval author, but also strong in its capacity to illuminate unnoticed aspects of a text, allowing us to see them in a new way. I mean, in short, to attempt a kind of "cost-benefit" analysis, between theory that, on the one hand, threatens to interpose itself between reader and text, and theory that, on the other, earns its way by sheer suggestiveness about the text. The occasion will be a scene at once familiar and disturbing

† From *Theory and the Premodern Text,* (Minneapolis and London, University of Minnesota Press, 2000), pp. 201–214. Reprinted with permission of University of Minnesota Press.
1. Frank Kermode, "Writing about Shakespeare," *London Review of Books,* 9 December 1999, 3.

to readers of medieval literature: a bloodied bed, in this case, that of Malory's Guinevere. The theory will be drawn from Freud's several discussions of what he came to call the "primal scene."

Guinevere's Bloody Bed

Bloody beds are rife in late medieval literature. The Wife of Bath claims to dream of one.[2] Julian of Norwich imagines herself in a bed bloodied by the wounds of Christ.[3] The Tristan of Béroul opens a wound leaping across a barrier to land, and bleed, in Yseut's bed.[4] Chrétien's Lancelot gets into an analogous scrape, injuring his fingers entering Guinevere's chamber and then notoriously bloodying her bed—even as her ten wounded knights simultaneously bloody theirs.[5] This story reaches Malory via a lost intermediate *Shyvalere le Charyote,* and to his "Knight of the Cart" I turn for the incident that provokes this essay. I choose this instance as a case in which meaning is both ostentatiously exhibited and arrantly withheld, in which a debate about meaning is foregrounded and fully thematized in the text, even as all the most promising interpretative avenues are blocked, rerouted, and systematically disavowed.

Guinevere is semiprisoner in Mellyagant's castle, tending over her wounded knights. Lancelot has arrived in his *charyott,* or cart, and boisterously spent the night with Guinevere, after ripping the bars off her window and wounded his own hands in the process. After "wacching" the night away, he withdraws. The wretched Mellyagant then arrives and opens the bed-curtain:

> And therewithall he opened the curtayn for to beholde her; and than was he ware where she lay, and all the hede-sheete, pylow, and over-shyte was all be-bled of the bloode of Sir Launcelot and of hys hurte honde.
>
> ¶Whan Sir Mellyagaunt aspyed that blood, than he demed in her that she was false to the Kynge and that som of the wounded knyghtes had lyene by her all that nyght. [p. 633, lines 29–35]

In typically craven fashion, he resolves to accuse her of treason before King Arthur.

2. "The Wife of Bath's Prologue," III.577–79.
3. *A Book of Showings to the Anchoress Julian of Norwich,* ed. E. Colledge and J. Walsh (Toronto: Pontifical Institute, 1978), long version, chap. 12, 343.
4. Béroul, *The Romance of Tristan,* ed. Alfred Ewert, vol. I (Oxford: Blackwell, 1977), lines 693–826. See also his valuable commentary on these lines and their analogues, vol. 2 (Oxford: Blackwell, 1970), 125–27. As noted by Ewert, Gottfried von Strassburg and others repeat versions of this episode. The prose Tristan, followed by Malory, shifts the bloodied bed to the wife of Segurades, who confesses that the blood was Tristan's; see Malory for his spectacularly bloody effusion in the bed of Segwarydes' wife: "and so Sir Trystrames bledde bothe the over-shete and the neyther-sheete, and the pylowes and the hede-shete." [p. 244] * * *
5. In Malory and elsewhere, Tristan and Iseult are repeatedly likened to Lancelot and Guinevere, and the four regularly indulge in congratulatory recognition of their own similitude. Thus, it is no surprise to find a scene highly similar to that of the Béroul Tristan in Chrétien's *Lancelot,* where (as in Malory) Lancelot injures his fingers forcing entry to Guinevere's chamber, and her obtrusive admirer Meleaganz reaches the reasonable but erroneous conclusion that she has slept with Kay, a bedtime bleeder in his own right. See *Lancelot,* ed. and trans. W. Kibler, vol. I (New York: Garland, 1981), lines 4633–986.

Both captor and petitioner, Mellyagant finds himself obliged to spy upon the woman whom he would possess, demoted to the role of standby and witness of a situation he had thought to control. We here encounter him as an interpreter of other people's activities, and not even a very good one at that. For this scene hinges on a point of interpretation, becomes a virtual allegory of the necessity and fallibility of the interpretative process. Mellyagant's "deeming" that she has slept with one of the wounded knights represents a misperception of the situation; but, since her wounded knights did in fact spend the night in her chamber and since Lancelot is nowhere to be seen, it is an entirely reasonable misperception. Such, in fact, seems always to have been this sorry character's role. In the same situation in Chrétien's *Lancelot,* his attempts at reasoned assessment are even more labored, and no less wrong:

> I have found
> Blood on your sheets, clear proof ["que le tesmoingne"],
> Since you must be told.
> This is how I know ["par ce le sai"], and this my proof,
> For on your sheets and his I have found
> Blood that dripped from his wounds.
> This evidence ["ansaignes"] is irrefutable![6]

For all the proof he is able to adduce, the secure knowledge he believes he has achieved, the evidence he brings to bear, he is off the mark; Guinevere's companion is neither innocent Kex (in Chrétien) nor any of the equally innocent knights (in Malory) but Mellyagant's actual nemesis Lancelot.

For all his hapless folly, Mellyagant is, in a sense, *our*—that is, the reader's—representative in this scene. He is condemned to an act of interpretation, and carries it forward in the most reasonable and empirical way, only to fall short of anything approaching an account of what has actually transpired. Adding insult to injury, Mellyagant is further chastised for his role in this sorry interpretative scene. For one thing, as Lancelot then makes clear to him, his viewing of the bed constituted an impermissible breach. As befits a man of action, Lancelot offers us an action-oriented interpretation. In the bedchamber, "looking" (as opposed to "doing") is a doubly contemptible pursuit:

> ❡"Now truly," seyde Sir Lancelot, "ye ded nat youre parte, nor knyghtly, to touche a Quenys bed whyle hit was drawyn, and she lyyng therein—and I dare say . . . my lorde Kynge Arthur hymselff wolde nat have displayed hir curtaynes, she beyng within her bed, onles that hit had pleased hym to have layne hym downe by her; and therefore, Sir Mellyagaunce, ye have done unworshypfully and shamefully to youreself."
> [p. 634, lines 14–20]

---

6. *Lancelot,* ed. Kibler, lines 4768–74.

Note, of course, that this wretched bedstead snooper is able only to do things "to himself" and not to Guinevere at all. He is, in this sense, a Peeping Tom, a scopophile, a would-be beholder of events from which he is otherwise excluded. Even the cuckolded Arthur would have known enough to enter Guinevere's bed ready for action, or not to enter it at all, but never just to snoop around. Here, as in every other episode in which we encounter him, Mellyagant displays his incapacity for chivalric norms of behavior, his inability to be properly "knightly." And, to the extent that he is our fellow interpreter, and thus our representative within the world of this tale, we must accept a share in his shame. But the full dimensionality of Mellyagant's shame remains unexpressed. He has, indeed, improperly entered Guinevere's bed, just as he improperly assaulted her knights, detained her, will trick Lancelot, and the like. Yet he is, in spite of all, not *wrong;* something untoward *did* happen in Guinevere's bed that night, and for all Lancelot's success in seizing the offensive, Mellyagant should hardly have to bear the entire burden of shame for its disclosure. Something more, in other words, remains to be said about the character and intensity—and ultimately the source—of Mellyagant's shame.

Mellyagant's "Primal Scene"

One might—and here I choose to take a theoretical step—elicit additional aspects of this situation that have the effect of guaranteeing Mellyagant's shame by recourse to Freud's discussions of the "primal scene." This is Freud's evocation of the young child's real or imagined witness of parental intercourse, with its accompanying confusion about the event witnessed,[7] uneasy surmise that violence is somehow involved,[8] inevitable feelings of rivalry, and guilty fear of punishment springing from those feelings and from a sense of impermissible viewing.[9] Excluded by the curtained bed, forced boisterously to intrude by thrusting the curtains aside,[1] then required to engage in an after-the-fact reconstruction of an imperfectly understood event, Mellyagant is discovered in a situation similar to that of Freud's young Wolf Man. This is the patient who,

7. As with the issue of the seduction fantasy, Freud takes different positions at different times on the question of whether the primal scene is real, a product of fantasy, or—for that matter—even phylogenetic. Speaking of primal, among other severe childhood experiences, Freud observed in 1916–17, "If they have occurred in reality, so much to the good; but if they have been withheld by reality, they are put together from hints and supplemented by phantasy"; *Introductory Lectures on Psycho-Analysis, Standard Edition* (London: Hogarth Press, 1957), 16:370 (hereafter, *Standard Edition*). See also *From the History of an Infantile Neurosis, Standard Edition,* 17:48–60.
8. "If [the child] finds traces of blood on his mother's bed . . . he takes it as a sign that she has been injured by his father"; *Introductory Lectures on Psycho-Analysis, Standard Edition,* 1:318–19. See also *From the History of an Infantile Neurosis, Standard Edition,* 17:45.
9. "What was essentially new for him in his observation of his parents' intercourse was the conviction of the reality of castration"; *Standard Edition,* 17:45. Within Freud's system the castration fear may be explained in part by the introjection of a sense of deserved punishment, owing to feelings of hostility and rivalry toward the father. See, for a pertinent analytical moment, the case of little Hans, *Analysis of a Phobia in a Five-Year-Old Boy, Standard Edition,* 10:42.
1. On the child's propensity for interruption, see Freud, *Infantile Neurosis, Standard Edition,* 17:80.

tormented by his sense of being veiled from reality,[2] is aided in his own reconstruction of what occurred during the parental siesta one early childhood afternoon.

I must address a frequent misconception by asserting that I do not introduce Freud in order to psychoanalyze the character Mellyagant—or, for that matter, Béroul, Chrétien, Malory, medieval culture, or the original readers of this scene. Mellyagant is, after all, only marks on a page, without depth or specific personal history of the sort that would justify such an analytical enterprise. The conceptual gain in relating this moment to Freud's "primal scene" lies elsewhere; lies, in this case like so many others, with Freud's astounding analytical capacity to identify and describe particular meaning-making structures and effects. In this case, Freud recognizes a particular typology—that of the "primal scene"—that enables him to stipulate particular roles for the various participants. Freud's typology allows us, in other words, certain expectations about which participants are inside the bed and which destined to remain outside; who actually performs the purported deed and who watches or imagines the performance; who is or is not entitled to lay claim to emotions such as anger, fear, or embarrassment; and so on.

Lancelot and Guinevere, after all, enjoy a provisional entitlement to share her bed. I say "provisional" because they are not, in fact, a marital or parental couple, but an adulterous one. Nonetheless, Lancelot occupies the place of the king, and even, when lecturing Mellyagant, presumes to speak on his behalf concerning matters of bedroom decorum, and Guinevere is indeed the Queen. They are, in this sense, a satisfactory metonym for the parental couple, with its full rights of private enjoyment—enjoyment from which, needless to say, Mellyagant is structurally excluded. The role of the child observer of the parental scene is, of course, an abject role, in the sense that it is founded on nonparticipation, disempowerment, necessary exclusion. Occupying the structural role of the child observer of parental enjoyment, Mellyagant must accept the bitter truth that the scene in question is engineered for its immediate participants' enjoyment, that it is not "about" or "for" Mellyagant at all. Confronted in the primal scene is the child's sense of having no rights in the matter; that any participation engineered by the child will probably be unwelcome and cannot occur without demonstrating feelings of rivalry and inviting possible punishment.

To be sure, the narrative already has a good deal to tell us about the impropriety of Mellyagant's behavior and the fecklessness of his attempt to know what transpired there in the curtained bed; we have already seen the passage in which Lancelot fully informs him of the chivalric shortcomings of his curiosity. Here as elsewhere in the narrative, we might conclude that Mellyagant's abjec-

2. Ibid., 17:74–75. However, Freud later (99–100) draws an utterly nonliteral conclusion from this preoccupation.

tion is already fully commented upon and sufficiently explained. Yet Mellyagant's impropriety is also so flagrant as to be susceptible to more than one kind of explanation, at more than one textual level. Indeed the overly curious Mellyagant is a boorish and coercive and unchivalric lover, and it is no wonder that Guinevere resists his unwelcome importunings; and he is no less deficient in a number of other categories of analysis, some of which are highlighted via a consideration of his role in "primal" and psychological terms. In the first place, Mellyagant's desire to know more about potential rivals in Guinevere's bed is only peripherally related to the progress of his own menacing courtship—may, in a sense, be seen as a distraction from his stated aims—yet his curiosity becomes a principal motive of the narrative. Also prominent within Freud's analysis is a humiliating (but necessary—the Wolf Man was only eighteen months old!) preference for looking over doing. Like the child observer, Mellyagant is perforce a kind of scopophile, with the additional increment of shame attending that role. Like the child observer, Mellyagant is troubled and puzzled by a confusion about the nature of the event that bloodied the bed in the first place. The child of Freud's primal scene surmises the presence of some violent misbehavior, and the violent origins of this blood as a product of struggle and injury are not far to be sought. In the case both of Mellyagant's mistaken theory (in which the blood belongs to one or more of the knights injured in his treacherous ambuscade) and of the true event (in which the blood is the product of Lancelot's forced entry through the barred window), the hypothesis of violence is sustained. Although the latter's violent exploit did not occur in the bed itself, we may see it as only slightly displaced from the bed, since it is motivated by love and the desire to enjoy love's pleasures:

¶ "Than shall I prove my myght," seyde Sir Launcelot, "for youre love." And than he sette hys hondis uppon the barrys of iron and pulled at them with suche a myght that he braste hem clene oute of the stone wallys—and therewithall one of the barres of iron kutte the brawne of hys hondys thorowoute, to the bone—and than he lepe into the chambir to the Quene [p. 633, lines 8–13].

Mellyagant's confused deeming about the nature of the event in Guinevere's bed is, in a sense, the reaction of a child—who is guaranteed a full measure of ignorance and agitation about an event not supposed to have been seen in the first place. Something other than simple sexual jealousy—some childish sense of broader impropriety—attaches itself to his response.

Freud's formulation of the primal scene also speaks to the oddly lopsided assignment of guilt within the narrative. Although an adulterous couple, Lancelot and Guinevere feel no guilt at all. Their imperviousness is undoubtedly associated with qualities of blindness and arrogance implicated in the ultimate fall of Arthur's court, but it may also be associated with the symbolic prestige owed to the parental couple—the couple in authorized possession of the nuptial bed—within the primal narrative. Similarly, the frustrated Mellyagant, who really is onto something but is unable to make anyone see it, is dogged by that imputation of guilt which will always fall upon the unsanctioned or illicit beholder. Lancelot's behavior throughout suggests that no guilt is to be assigned to himself, as Arthur's worthy stand-in, but that all guilt rests with the craven on-looker, the supposition-ridden interpreter—*our* representative in the narrative, the hapless Mellyagant.

Furthermore, this typology helps me to understand the assurance and even serenity with which this text is able to protect its own central event—the commerce between Lancelot and Guinevere in her bed—from our, as well as Mellyagant's, gaze. For no sooner has Lancelot left Guinevere's soiled bed than the text propels itself into a strenuous and extended program of disavowal. Denied is the possibility that the soiled sheets testify to much of anything. Certainly to be rejected is Mellyagant's attempt to place blame on the wounded knights. But the text goes on more ambitiously to reject any suggestion of untoward behavior of any kind. For the taint of treason against Arthur, which would ordinarily attach itself to Lancelot's adulterous invasion of his bed, is promptly and decisively withdrawn from the adulterous act and rebounds upon Mellyagant the accuser. Mellyagant first introduces the subject of treason, accusing Guinevere of being "a traytouras unto my lorde Arthur" [p. 633], yet Mellyagant's "treson" against Lancelot soon overshadows any other possible offense [p. 637]: once "the kynge and queen and all the lordis knew off the treson of sir Mellyagante, they were all ashamed on hys behalffe" [p. 637]. Thus, the burden of shame lies entirely upon Lancelot's accuser, even as Lancelot ends up "more . . . cherysshed than ever he was aforehande" [p. 638].

A part of the work of this text is to protect its own most ambitious fantasy of proscribed/authorized indulgence between Lancelot and the queen. Mellyagant is a pleasure-seeker, too, yet his desire is degraded by a variety of means, not excluding his infantilization and exclusion from rightful participation via the typology of the primal scene. By this and other means, the text moves treason out from its center to its periphery, away from Lancelot's bloody tumble with his queen and toward Mellyagant's impermissible viewings and base (though not, except technically, erroneous) imputations. I should say that I am not surprised by this textual operation: texts routinely—one might even say inevitably—engage in such self-protective stratagems, whereby their origins, and constitutive exclusions and, especially, central preoccupations are shielded from (rather than exposed to) view.

This text talks constantly about treason and is always assigning blame for treason, but the accusations tend to cluster about Mellyagant rather than to fall where they are most deserved, upon Lancelot's impermissible relation with the queen. Mellyagant's much discussed treasonous behavior is significant as an instance of "overdetermination"—by which Freud describes the effect whereby a dream's preoccupations will be multiply restated (sometimes even in random or incidental ways) within the dream. In this sense Mellyagant functions as a kind of litmus or beacon, attracting to himself multiple evidences of the treason that saturates the entire narrative, at once concealing and broadcasting the ultimate importance of treason *somewhere* within the total narrative scene. This use of Mellyagant's character requires that he be placed at a certain distance from the central action of the seduction scene, a state of acute curiosity unrelieved by any possibility of actual participation. In other words, the typology of the primal scene, and Mellyagant's role in it, well serves the mingled motives of secrecy and disclosure that mark the handling of treason in this tale.

I have thus far made a kind of "soft" or selective use of Freud, in the sense of emphasizing those potentially Freudian insights which rest most easily with the more literal motives and purposes of the narrative. Naturally, a truly "Freudian" reading will also work back against the grain of the text, emphasizing those insights to be gained which are at some level disguised or negated by the text or even actively contest its more literal sense. By way of example, I might return to the case of the young Wolf Man, to elicit another aspect of the primal experience as Freud describes it. For, by way of simplifying a highly complicated exposition, I might simply mention that Freud characterizes his infantile observer as highly uncertain about his particular attachment to the scene he has witnessed—a scene that had the effect of "splintering" his sexual life for years to come. If the obvious point of entry to the scene was identification with the father and desire to enjoy the mother, a strong countertheme as identified by Freud is adoption of a passive attitude toward the father and "to be given sexual satisfaction in the same way as his mother."[3] Yet this satisfaction had its potential cost, for this is a satisfaction "whose attainment seemed to involve the renunciation of [the male] organ." Thus, along with his confusion about object choice, the infant observer also reaped an emphatically unwelcome consequence: "What was essentially new for him in his observation of his parents' intercourse was the conviction of the reality of castration."

Returning to the situation of Mellyagant, whose own sexuality is of a stunted and only partially participatory form, we must notice that the event for which he has paid the greatest price in lost prestige and for which he will ultimately forfeit his life—that is, the rape of Guinevere—has not and never does occur in this narrative. Instead he turns to connivance, the dubious penal pleasures of incarceration, and endless curiosity about the whereabouts and doings of Lancelot. The plot to detain Guinevere, in fact, soon gives way to a plot to detain Lancelot in a kind of thinly disguised "love cave" reminiscent of other favored resorts in medieval romance. Guinevere is permitted simply to return to

3. *Standard Edition*, 17:45–48.

Westminster—albeit under accusation—as the momentum of the story shifts to the final struggle between Mellyagant and Lancelot.

Here rests an interpretative avenue that I will not fully pursue but that I believe lies open to intelligent investigation, which is the homoerotics of chivalry and the sense in which Guinevere here as elsewhere serves as a chivalric pretext, enabling a relation of greater intensity between men. I do, however, wish to return to the matter of castration anxiety, which resurfaces in an extraordinary way at the end of the narrative. Here Mellyagant, after characteristic chicanery and evasion, finds himself in combat with Lancelot only to avoid its consequences by yielding in a most craven way. Certainly, in the literal terms of the story, we have here yet one more illustration of Mellyagant's utter incapacity to inhabit exterior chivalric norms. Yet a complementary point can be made at the psychoanalytical level, involving the terms of Mellyagant's identification with Lancelot and the former's faltering ability to recognize himself in the latter—and thus to constitute himself as his proper opponent. It is only when Lancelot offers to accept an impairment—literally to expose one side of his body and tie one arm behind his back—that the combat can resume: "I shall unarme my hede and my lyffte quarter of my body . . . and I woll lette bynde my lyfft honde behynde me there hit shall nat helpe me, and ryght so I shall do batayle with you" [p. 638]. This narrative has already been supersaturated with images of castration, including Lancelot's own mangled fingers (a severed finger in Chretien [lines 4642–43]), and here Lancelot offers to place himself on Mellyagant's plane by accepting an impairment. Literally, he appeals to his opponent's cowardice and opportunism. Psychoanalytically, he accepts the symbolic wound Mellyagant has already received as a result of his infantile demotion within the framework of the primal scene, rendering himself recognizable to Mellyagant, an object of identification and hence an appropriate opponent in the final struggle between the two knights.

Costs and Benefits

Has looking at Guinevere's bloody bed through the lens of the primal scene done any harm so far? The reader who might think so has probably long since closed this book. I suppose one might argue that, tarrying with Freud, I have failed or neglected to do something else more worthwhile, such as performing a historicist analysis of this scene—in terms, perhaps, of various detained, maligned, and abused fifteenth-century English queens, or fears of ungallantry associated with the rise of the commercial system, or some other presenting topic. But the critic's choice of subject presumably falls within the zone of taste and tactics, rather than some more absolute criterion. No, the *real* issue here is whether Freud is actually necessary to any of the points I have made. I have had the pleasure of debating Freudian criticism with Lee Patterson on several occasions, at a University of Oklahoma forum and elsewhere, and he has more than once observed, with characteristic penetration, "Sure, but did you need Freud for that?"

In this essay, I have made several "Freudian" observations about my text, and each might have been made at some level without reference to Freud at all. I have noted an emphasis on situations of impermissible looking—of eavesdropping or spying. Yet, from Pandarus to Frocin (in Béroul's *Tristan*) to Agravain (in the *Morte*), medieval texts afford us numerous condemnations of onlookers, snoops, and spies. I have noted that Mellyagant's demeaning role as unsanctioned onlooker repeats the confusion and consternation of the excluded child in the primal triangle. Yet excluded claimants, from Absolon (in the "Miller's Tale") to the Pardoner (in the Prologue to the *Tale of Beryn*), are *always* inherently ridiculous, and liable not only to victimization but to infantilization as well. I have noted that this scene is permeated by guilt and that issues pertaining to guilt's final assignment are illuminated with reference to the guilty anxieties of the child observer in the primal scene. Yet medieval analysts have their own proven strengths in the attestation and assignment of guilt; the fine-tuning of guilt in the closing lines of *Sir Gawain and the Green Knight* overcomes any suggestion that the medievals need Freud's help in that area. Besides, Malory is clearly aware of his own central ironies—that Guinevere really is guilty of treason against Arthur (though not the variety of treason that Mellyagant has claimed) and that Lancelot really is the most guilty party, even though the temporary effect of this episode is to enhance his position and increase his esteem.

Nevertheless, I would resist the suggestion that Freud has nothing at all to add here. Each imaginative text is, to be sure, wholly a product of its own times, articulated at its own moment and within available discursive and explanatory systems. Whatever its debts to the past and hopes for the future, its meanings are refocused around the Now of its composing process. Yet each imaginative text simultaneously records more general strivings and desires, for which contemporary terms of reference provide a grounding and occasion and partial object, but which speak more broadly to matters of persistence and recurrence. I would never go so far as to argue—as Freud at least considered arguing, in the case of the primal scene—that some propensities and desires altogether escape time, to become the birthright of persons in all times and places.[4] Yet I would argue that texts work on both levels: accommodating full renderings of their immediate cultural circumstances and other less intelligible impulses. Thus, to say that Mellyagant is "infantile" in his headstrong desires and readiness to defy chivalric codes and to say that he is "infantile" as a result of his regressive reduction to confusion and passive spectatorship within the presuppositions of the primal scenario is to say two slightly different things—the one dependent on the text's overt instructions and the other more analytically derived. My

4. See note 7 [p. 897] on phylogenetic properties.

contention is that both things are worth saying, and that the reading that acknowledges both of them strengthens itself. Always to be preferred is that reading which illuminates the text in several of its dimensions. In this respect, the final obligation of theory is not to permanence or even to truth; the best theory is the most *suggestive* one, the one most completely suggestive of added riches in the text.

Premature Knowledge

The enemy of good criticism is what might be called "premature knowledge," which I would define as knowledge achieved the easy way, by acceptance of the text's own self-descriptions. In my view Freud's wise caution is to be respected; temporarily adrift in his analysis of little Hans, he observes, "I can only advise those of my readers who have not yet conducted an analysis not to try to understand everything at once, but to give a kind of unbiased attention to every point that arises and to await further developments."[5] Also to be resisted is the subsequent error, which is to become so arrogant about the capacities of one's critical tools that one indiscriminately overrides or reverses what the text seems to be trying to tell us about itself. Returning for a moment to Mellyagant's splintered desires: although the text leaves some leeway for a relation between Mellyagant and Lancelot as object of affective identification, I am reluctant to go so far against its grain as to claim that Mellyagant wishes to be enjoyed by Lancelot, or (thinking of little Hans's long afternoon of spectatorship) that he wishes Lancelot to take him violently or from behind.

Preferable either to accepting everything a text says about itself or to negating its self-descriptions is a middle way that accepts theory as a partner in inquiry without signing away all our rights in the matter. One aspect of this middle way, 'as I have said, is not to be hasty about conclusions. Another is to invest particular confidence in those moments at which the text's different levels of statement are found to be mutually reinforcing. Yet another is not to imagine that everything about a text can be known. Some aspects of the "truth" about what happened in Guinevere's bed can never be known to us. We know that Lancelot "toke hys pleasaunce and hys lykynge untyll hit was the dawning of the day," and we are in an excellent position for surmise, but in the end we do not know or experience a good deal more than the balked and baffled Mellyagant. At the center of every text lies a blind spot—Freud's *omphalos* or dream navel—that resists full disclosure.[6] This evokes Lacan's vacuole, the empty place at the center of every signifier, best epitomized in Lacan's view by the enigmas of desire, the occlusion of the love object, and the detours and obstacles that constitute the gift of love: "Where, in effect, is the vacuole created

5. Freud, *Analysis of a Phobia, Standard Edition*, 10:65.
6. Freud, *Interpretation of Dreams*, Standard Edition, 5:525.

for us? It is at the center of the signifiers—insofar as that final demand to be deprived of something real is essentially linked to the primary symbolization that is wholly contained in the signification of the gift of love."[7] We have a certain explanatory choice here. The text's blind spot may be unreadable because, in the Freudian system, it is overfull, overimplicated in too many different kinds of inextricable meanings. Or it may be unreadable because, in the Lacanian system, it is an "empty place," hollowed out, awaiting colonization only by our own inferences and desires. Either way, we are not finally to know everything about Guinevere's bloody bed and what happened there.

Whether because of its inherent richness or the inexhaustible creativity of our own object-seeking desires, this bed must remain a hot spot of alternative interpretation. For example, the blood in Guinevere's bed may be read as another kind of symptom altogether: as a symptom of woman's secrets, the obscurity and terror of her gynecological functions, the inviolable and unknowable character of her private space. It may, in other words, be read as an occasion and symptom of male bafflement—in which not only the hapless Mellyagant, but also the ten knights and Lancelot himself must be supposed to share.

The right use of theory is not to "settle things." Quite the contrary: its use is to *un*settle things, first by evading the text's own self-serving simplifications, and second by displaying the multiplicity (or silence) at the text's core. In this I would recommend to the critic some of the inscrutability maintained by Arthur himself about the precise character of relations between his best knight and his queen. At the opening of the *Morte,* when the literal minded Agravain thinks he knows the one and only true thing about Lancelot and Guinevere, Malory comments,

> For, as the Freynshe booke seyth, the Kynge was full lothe that such a noyse shulde be uppon Sir Launcelot and his Quene; for the Kynge had a demyng of hit, but he wold nat here thereoff, for Sir Launcelot had done so much for hym and for the Quene so many tymes that, wyte you well, the kynge loved hym passyngly well. [p. 647, lines 40–45]

A certain "deeming"—partly knowing without claiming fully to know—certainly turns out to be the best thing for the maintenance of Arthurian society. Only when Arthur lets himself be drawn into the camp of those literalists who claim emphatically to know do the real troubles begin. I propose Arthur's posture as a chastening model for the critic, who forms certain inferences and suppositions about the concealed act at the text's center . . . but should not claim overrapid or overcomplete knowledge of all that has happened there.

7. Lacan, *The Seminar,* book 7, 150.

Glossary

The following entries address words and phrases in Malory likely to be unfamiliar in spelling or meaning to modern readers. In instances where Malory's use of a particular form includes both modern and premodern senses, for the most part only the premodern sense is glossed (for example, *and* is glossed as *if, he* glossed as *it* or *she,* and *quest(e)* is glossed as *inquest,* even though the narrower modern senses of these words are also prevalent in Malory).

Except in special circumstances, verbs are listed in the infinitive and nouns in the singular. For a summary of the usual inflexions for different parts of speech, see "Reading Malory's English," p. xxxv.

A semicolon distinguishes subsenses of a particular word. Wholly different senses having the same spelling are distinguished by numbers in parentheses. *Y/y is given the alphabetic status of I/i when used as a vowel.*

The following abbreviations are used:

1 first person	*adv.* adverb	*ppl.a.* participial adjective
2 second person	*art.* article	*prep.* preposition
3 third person	*cj.* conjunction	*prep.* present
(1) sense one	*interj.* interjection	*pron.* pronoun
(2) sense two	*pa.t.* past tense	*sg.* singular
(3) sense three	*pl.* plural	*v.*verb
a. adjective	*pp.* past participle	

A

a, *v.* have

a, *pron.* he

a, *prep.* at, in, of, on

a, *interj.* ah

a, *indefinite art.* indicating a collective entity when used with numerals—e.g., *a ten,* a quantity of ten

abacke, abak(ke), *prep.* to the rear, backwards; *gaff . . . abak,* gave way

aba(y)sshed, *ppl.a.* brought down, ashamed; taken aback, astonished

abaysshe, abeyse, *v.* beat down, lower; astonish

abbas, *n.* (*possessive sg.*) abbess's

abate, *v.* (1) cast down, reduce; (2) bait or chase prey

abeyse, see *abaysshe, v.*

abyde, *v.* wait (for), stay, withstand; *abyde by,* perform; **abithe,** 3 *sg. pres.*; **abyd(d)yn,** *pp.*; **abode,** *pa.t.*; **abydith,** *imperative*

abyte, see *(h)abyte,* sb.

abithe, see *abyde, v.*

able, *a.* sufficient, "do-able"

ablemente, *n.* (military) equipment

abode, see *abyde, v.*

abought, *v. pa.t.* paid for

aboute, *prep.* near; *adv.* in all directions; *lay aboute,* was seeking about, scheming; *be aboute to,* be scheming to

aboven, abovyn, *adv.* above

abovynseyde, *ppl. a.* mentioned above

abrayded, *v. pa.t.* sprang

abrode, *adv.* abroad, far and about

absteyne, *v.* abstain

accompany, *v.* join in company with, associate oneself

ac(c)ompte, *v.* reckon, count

ac(c)orde, *v.* bring to accord, reconcile

accordemente, *n.* accord, reconciliation

accounseyle, *a.* complicit

achyeve, *v.* conclude successfully

acombird, *pp.* encumbered

acquyte, *v.* repay

actuall, *a.* active, vigorous

actually, *adv.* actively, vigorously

addir, *n.* adder, snake

adew, *interj.* adieu, farewell

admyrall, *n.* Saracen emir, prince

ado, *n.* business; cause, reason; sexual intercourse; *have ado,* fight, be occupied

adoyng, *pres. participle* going on, happening

adouted, *pp.* afraid

adrad(de), *pp.* afraid, in dread

adretched, *pp.* troubled, disturbed

advaunte-garde, *n.* advance guard

a(d)venture, *n.* chance event, fortune; risk, danger; hazardous task; *in adventure, at risk, in doubt*

a(d)venture, *v.* risk

a(d)ventures, *a.* adventurous; seeking adventure; perilous

a(d)vyce, a(d)vyse, *n.* advice, reckoning; consent

a(d)vyse, *v.* advise; study; ponder, reflect to oneself

a(d)vysed, *ppl. a.* informed, deliberative

a(d)vysement(e), *n.* deliberation, reflection

advyssyon, *n.* vision, dream

advoutrer, *n.* adulterer

afarre, *adv.* from afar, at a distance

aferde, *ppl. a.* afraid

affray, *n.* disturbance

affyaunce, *n.* trust

affye, *v.* trust

affinité, *n.* relationship; the support network of a powerful lord

afonned, *a.* doting

afo(o)te, *adv.* on foot

afore, *prep.* ahead of, in front of; before, in the presence of; beforehand

aforehande, aforehonde, *adv.* beforehand, previously

aforetyme, *adv.* beforehand

aforne, *adv.* previously

af(f)ter, aftir, *prep.* according to; *adv.* later, thereafter

agayne, ageyne, *prep.* against; in preparation for; *adv.* in return, in reply; in retaliation

agayne-commynge, *n.* return

agaynesay, agaynesey, *v.* gainsay, speak against

agaynewarde, *adv.* in return, back

agaynste, see *ayenst(e),* prep.

agone, *a.* ago

agré, *v.* agree

agreved, *pp.* aggrieved, offended

ayge, *n.* age

ayle, *v.* ail, suffer

ayre, *n.* heir

ayther, aythir, eythir, eyther, *pron. a.* each; either; *ayther . . . other,* each . . . the other

aknowyn, *ppl. a.* acknowledging; *be aknowyn,* acknowledge

alayed, *pp.* alleviated

Al Halowmas, All Halowmasse, *n.* November 1, Feast of All Saints

alyauntes, alyauntis, *n. pl.* aliens, foreigners

alyed, *pp.* allied

alyes, *n. pl.* allies

alyegemente, *n.* alleviation

alygeaunce, *n.* alleviation

alyght(e), alight, *v. pp. pa.t.* dismounted

all, *a.* every; *adv.* completely, throughout

alledged, *pp.* lessened

al(l)ther, althers, *a. gen. pl.* of all; *oure al(l)ther,* of all of us

al(l)thernexte, althirnexte, *adv.* nearest of all, next most

allway, allwey, *adv.* always

almeryes, *n. pl.* repositories

almesdede, *n.* deed of charity (alms)

alow, *v.* praise, acknowledge

alowde, *adv.* aloud

als, *adv.* also

also, allso, *cj. adv.* (just) as, thus; when, as soon as

amased, *ppl. a.* bewildered

amated, *pp.* confused

ambular, *n.* ambling horse

amende, *v.* cure, repair

amerall, see *admyrall* n.

amonyshment, *n.* exhortation

amoved, *pp.* angry

an, see *a, indefinite art.*

an: see *a, prep.;* **an-hontynge,** engaged in hunting

an(d), *cj.* if; *and if,* if

angirfull, *a.* wrathful

angirly, *adv.* angrily

angred, *v. pa.t.* became angered

angurly, see *angirly, adv.*

angwyshlye, *adv.* full of anguish

anone, *adv.* anon, forthwith

anvylde, *n.* anvil

aparte, *adv.* partially

apeche, appeyche, *v.* impeach, accuse

apoynted, *pp.* resolved; directed

appayre, *v.* impair

apparayled, *pp.* dressed; furnished; equipped

appeyche, see *apeche, v.*

appele, *v.* accuse

appertenaunce, apportenaunce, *n.* due rights and privileges belonging to an estate

ap(p)oyntemente, *n.* agreement

ar, *prep., cj., adv.* before

arace, *v.* raze, erase

araged, *ppl. a.* enraged; frenzied

aray, *n.* garb, outfit; preparation; condition

aray, *v.* clothe; situate

araymente, *n.* clothing

arayse, areyse, *v.* raise; waken

araunte, *a.* errant, roving, seeking adventure

aredy, *a.* ready

areyse, see *arayse v.*

arere, *v.* raise a force, call to arms; raise up

areste, *v.* commandeer

aryght, *adv.* rightly

aryve, *v.* land on shore

armes, armys, *n. pl.* coat of arms, heraldic bearings; deeds of arms

armytayge, see *ermytayge, n.*

armyte, *n.* hermit
aroos, *v. pa.t.* rose up
arraunte, see *araunte, a.*
array, aray, *n.*
arred, *pp.* erred
ars, *n.* "arse;" hind quarters
arson, *n.* saddle-bow
arst(e), *adv.* beforehand; sooner, earlier
as, *cj.* as if; where; when; also; *but as,* except; *lyke as,* as if; *as for, as in,* with regard to
asay, see *assay, v.*
asawte, *n.* military assault
ascawnce, *adv.* hypocritically
asoted, *ppl. a.* besotted
aspye *v.* notice; spy; become familiar with, learn about
assay, *v.* try, test; challenge; endure
assemble, *n.* encounters
assente, *n.* agreement
assigne, *v.* agree; arrange; appoint
assoyle, *v.* absolve
assomon, assumpne, *v.* summon; **assomned, assumned** *pp.*
assomons, *n.* summoned military retinue
assot(t)ed, see *asoted, ppl. a.*
asspye, see *aspye, v.*
assumned, assumpne, see *assomon, v.*
assure, *n.* azure, heraldic blue
astate, *n.* condition; ceremony; rank, people of the gentry and nobility
asto(o)ned, *pp.* astonished; stunned
asure, see *assure, n.*
aswaged, *pp.* assuaged, subdued
at, *prep.* to, into, against; with, by; from
ataynte, *ppl. a.* exhausted
a-to(o), *adv.* in two
attayne, *v.* succeed
attame, *v.* pierce
attempt, *v.* tempt
attyre, *v.* equip
attende, *v.* lie in wait
attyre, *v.* equip, set in order
auctorysed, *ppl. a.* authorized, having authority
audiens, *n.* hearing
auter, aulter *n.* altar
auncetrye, *n.* ancestry; **auncet(t)ryes,** ancestors
auncyen, *a.* elder, distinguished
availle, avayle, *n.* benefit, advantage
avayded, see *avoyde, v.*
avaylyd, *v. pa.t.* dismounted
ava(u)nta(y)ge, *n.* advantage
avaunce, *v.* advance, ennoble
avaunte, *n.* boast; **avauntynge,** boasting
aventryd, *v. pa.t.* readied, set (a lance)
aventure, see *adventure, n.* and *adventure, v.*
aventures, see *adventures, a.*
avyce, avys(e), avysed, see *a(d)vyce, n., a(d)vyse, v., a(d)vysed, ppl. a.*
avysement, see *a(d)vysement(e), n.*
avision, see *advysyon, n.*
avoydaunce, *n.* emptying

avoyde, *v.* vacate, leave; dismount; dismiss
avow(e), *n.* vow, promise
avow, *v.* swear to; admit
away, *v.* go away, turn away
awayte, *n.* watchfulness
awayte, *v.* attend; watch shrewdly; lay in wait upon
awarde, *n.* ward, guard; care
awepte, *v. pa.t.* wept
awghe, see *ow(gh)e, v.*
a-wyte, *v.* find out
awke, *a.* backhanded
awkewarde, *a.* with a backward stroke
awnciente, *a.* ancient
awne, *a.* own; *my nowne, my nawne,* my own
awntis, *n. (possessive)* aunt's
a-worke, *adv.* at work
awroke, *pp.* avenged
awter, see *au(l)ter, n.*
axe, *v.* ask (for); demand
ayen, *adv.* again; back
ayenst(e), *prep.* against, next to, opposite; toward; in advance of

B

bad(de), see *bede, v.*
baptyme, *n.* baptism
bacheler, *n.* young knight
backer, *adv.* further back
bay, *a.* reddish brown
bayne, *n.* bath
bayte, *v.* (1) feed (**baytande,** feeding); (2) tempt with bait
bak, rear; *on bak,* in retreat
baladis, *n.* poems
bakyn, *pp.* baked
balefull, *a.* wretched
baly, see *bealy, n.*
bandis, see *bondys, n.*
barayne, *a.* barren, infertile
barbycan, *n.* fortification at the entrance to a castle or town
bare, see *bere, v.*
barget, *n.* small boat
baronnery, *n.* barony, baronial estate
baronny, *n.* constituency of barons
barown, *n.* baron
basyn, *n.* hollow vessel
basnet, *n.* helmet
batayle, *n.* battle, fight; battalion, army
bate, *n.* (1) debate, dispute; (2) baited pursuit
batyd, *pp.* abated
bavoure, *n.* lower face-guard
bawdy, *a.* filthy
bawme, *v.* embalm, annoint
be, *prep.* by; by way of, through: see also *by,* prep.
be, *v.,* see *be(ne), pp.*
beadis, *n.* rosary
b(e)aly, *n.* belly

beamys, *n.pl.* bugles

be(a)nded, *ppl. a.* having (diagonal) heraldic stripes

beate, *v.* drive

beaulté, *n.* beauty

be-bled(de), *ppl. a.* covered in blood, bled upon

becalled, *pp.* accused

becam, see *becom*

beclosed, *pp.* enclosed

becom, becam, *v. pp.* gone; *pa.t.* went

bedaysshed, *pp.* bedecked

bede, *v.* bid, command; **bodyn,** *pp.*, **bad(de),** *pa.t.*

bedrad, *ppl. a.* dreaded; revered

beeke, *v.* bake, warm

bee, bye, *n.* torque or neck ring

beere, *n.* (funeral) bier

before, *adv.* in front of, ahead of; *prep.* beyond, above

beforne, *adv.* beforehand

befurred, *pp.* wrapped in fur

begone, *ppl. a.* become; beset

begrype, *v.* grip

behanged, *pp.* hung

behated, *pp.* hated

behyght, see *behote, v.*

behylde, see *beholde, v.*

behynde, *adv.* still to come, delayed; left behind

beholde, *v.* behold, see; **beholde,** *pp.*; **behylde,** *pa.t.*

beholde, *ppl.a.* beholden, indebted, bound (a. **beholdyng(e)**)

behote, *v.* promise; **behyght,** *pa.t.*

behove, *v.* behoove, be necessary

beynge, *n.* presence

beystys, *n.pl.* beasts

belaffte, belef(f)te, *v. pa.t.* remained

beleve, see *bel(y)eve, n.*

belye, *v.* belie, slander

bel(y)eve, belyve, *n.* belief

bemoone, *v.* bemoan, grieve over

bended, see *be(a)nded, ppl. a.*

bendis, bondis, *n. pl.* heraldic stripes

ben(e), *v. 3 pl. pres.* are

be(ne), *pp.* been, existed

beneth *prep.* below

benyghtyd *pp.* overtaken by night

benomme, *pp.* taken from; deprived

bente, *n.* grassy area

beraffte, berauf(f)te: see *bereve, v.*

beré, byry, *n.* (black)berry

bere, *n.* momentum

bere, *v.* bear, carry; uphold, advance; display; **boren, born(e),** *pp.*; **bare, bere,** *pa.t.*; **be(e)rynge,** bearing

berenne, covered; *blody berenne,* covered in blood

bereve, beryve, *v.* deprive of; seize from; **bera(u)ffte, bereved,** *pp.*; **beraufte,** *pa.t.*

berye, *v.* bury

beryellys, buryellys, *n.* burial

beryve, see *bereve, v.*

besayne, see *bese(y)ne, ppl. a.*

besaunt, *n.* bezant, gold coin

bese(y)ne, besayne, bisene, *ppl.a.* equipped, dressed, appointed; *well besene,* good-looking

beseke, *v.* seek; beseech (**besought,** *pp.*)

beseme, *v.* seem, appear; be appropriate for, suit

besette, *v.* place, bestow; suit; **besett(e),** *pp.*

besy, bysy, *a.* busy; anxious; interfering

besparcled, *pp.* spattered

besprente, *v. pa.t.* sprinkled

bestad(de), *pp.* beset, situated; *harde bestad(de), straytely bestad,* hard pressed, attacked

beste, *n.* beast

bestrade, bestrode, *v. pa.t.* straddled

beswette, *ppl. a.* covered in sweat

betaught(e), betoke, *v. pa.t.* commended; entrusted

bet(t)he, *v. 2 pl. pres.* are

betyde, *v.* befall, happen to

betyme(s), *adv.* at once, early, in good time

betyn, *pp.* beaten

betoke, see *betaught(e), v.*

betoken, *v.* symbolize

betrappe, *v.* entrap

bettir, *a.* better

betwene, *adv.* between; *ever betwene,* meanwhile

betwyxte, *prep.* between

bewared, *ppl. a.* bestowed

by, *prep.* by way of, through, not later than, concerning, (I swear) by; *cj.* by the time that; *adv.* nearby; *by that,* when

bycause, see *because, cj.*

bycompast *ppl. a.* surrounded

byd, *v.* request

byde, *v.* remain; **byddyn,** *pp.*

bye, see *bee, n.*

bygge, *a.* strong, powerful (rarely indicates large size); **bygger,** stronger

byghe, *v.* buy

byghte, *v.* bite; **bo(o)te,** *pa.t.*

bygly, *adv.* strongly, powerfully

byry, see *beré, n.*

bisene, see *bese(y)ne, ppl. a.*

bysy, see *besy, a.*

bysshopryche, *n.* diocese or jurisdiction of a bishop

bitake, *v.* entrust to; **bitaken,** *pp.*; **bytoke,** *pa.t.*

byver, *v.* tremble

ble, *n.* complexion

bledde, *v. ppl.a.* bled upon; *pa.t.* stained with blood

blesse, see *blysse, v.*

blyeth, *a.* happy, blithe

blyndefelde, *a.* blindfolded

blysse, blesse, *v.* bless; cross oneself

blyssed, *a.* blessed

blissyng, *n.* blessing

blyve, *adv.* quickly

bloode, *n.* bloodline, kin

blow(e), *v.* summon (with trumpet); speak out

bobbaunce, *n.* boasting, boastful conduct

bodyn, see *bede, v.*

boyes, *n. pl.* boys, delinquents

boysh, boyshemente, see *buys(s)h, n., hu(y)shemente, n.*

boysteous, boystouse, *a.* rude; violent, strong; immense

bonde(n), *ppl. a.* bound

bondis, bondys, bandes *n.pl.* (1) bands of people; (2) bonds; (3) bounds, constraint bondis: see *bendis, n. pl.*

bone, *n.* boon, request

boole, *n.* bole, trunk

bo(o)ne, *n.* bone, tusk

boorde, see *b(o)urde, n.*

bo(o)re, *n.* boar

booster, *n.* boaster

boote, *n.* remedy, good

boote, *n.* boat (**botis** *pl.*)

boote, see *byghte, v.*

boren, borne, see *bere, v.*

bore, see *bere, v., bo(o)re, n.*

borow, *n.* (1) billet, claimed lodging; (2) pledge

borow, *v.* ransom

bote, see *byghte, v.*

boteneth, *v.* 3 *sg.* avails

botis, see *boote, n.*

bought, see *byghe, v.*

bounde, *a.* starting

bounden, *pp.* bound, encircled

bounden, *ppl. a.* indebted

bounté, bownté, *n.* goodness; generosity; excellence; gifts

b(o)urde, boorde, *n.* table; floorboard; gunwale of a ship

bourde, *v.* jest, joke

bourder, *n.* joker

bourely, bowerly, *a.* large and strong, burly

bowe, see *bow(gh)e, v.*

bowe-draught, bowe-drawght, *n.* (distance of a) bowshot

bowerly, see *bourely, a.*

bowghe, *n.* archer's bow

bow(gh)e, *v.* bend, bow (in submission)

bowys, *n.pl.* tree boughs

bownti, see *bounti, n.*

bowske, see *buske, v.*

boxe, *n.* blow

brace, *v.* embrace, set

brachet, brachett(e), *n.* female hound

bray, *n.* skirmish

brayde, *n.* sudden movement, quick action

brayde, *v.* remove quickly

brayle, *n.* belly

brayne-panne, *n.* skull

brake, see *breke, v.*

braste, breste, *v. pa.t.* burst, broke

brawne, *n.* flesh, meat

breche, see *breke, n.*

brede, *n.* (1) bread; (2) roasted meat; (3) breadth

breeth, see *brethe, v.*

breff, *v.* keep brief; shorten

breke, *n.* breeches

breke, *v.* break out, rush out; reveal; disturb; *brake . . . fast*, take breakfast; **brokyn**, *pp.*; **brake**, *pa.t.*

brekelys, *a.* without breeches

bren(ne), *v.* burn; to be burnt, to be burnt with strong emotion; **brente, brenned**, *pa.t. and pp.*

brese, see *bruse, v.*

brest, see *braste, v. pa.t.*

brethe, breeth, *v.* rest, catch one's breath

brethid, *ppl. a.* in phrase *bettir brethid,* more aerobically fit

brethirn(e), see *broder, n.*

brewte, *n.* fame

brym, *a.* fierce

brymme, *n.* bank

bryse, see *bruse, v.*

broche, *n.* spit, skewer

broche, *v.* skewer, open holes in

brochys, *n.pl.* brooches

brode, *a.* broad; *n.* broad part

broder, *n.* brother; *pl.* **brethirn(e)**

brokyn, see *breke, v.*

bronde, *n.* sword

broute, *v. pa.t.* brought, took

browes, *n.* broth

bruntis, *n.pl.* sharp blows

bruse, bryse, brese, *v.* bruise; crush; break

brutyll, *a.* brittle

buff, *a.* blow-receiving (usually assuming the left-hand side)

buys(s)h, boysh, *n.* bush, body of vegetation

b(y)shemente, bu(y)sshement, boyshemente, *n.* ambush

burbely, *a.* burbling

burde, see *b(o)urde, n.*

burge(y)s(s)e, *n.* burgess, townsman

burgyne, *v.* burgeon

buryellys, see *beryellys, n.*

burre, *n.* hand-protecting ring

bushement, see *bu(y)shemente, n.*

buske, bowske, *v.* hasten; ready oneself

but, *n.* (1) butt, blunt end; (2) target

but *prep. cj.* except, only, unless, than; *but as,* but; *but if,* unless

C

caban, *n.* cabin

cayser, *n.* emperor

caytyff, *a.* miserable

calle, *v.* accuse; deem

cam(e), see *com(e), v.*

can, *v.* be able; know

Candilmasse, February 2, Feast of the

Purification of the Blessed Virgin (see n. 9, p. 10)

canellbone, *n.* neck-bone

cankyrde, *ppl. a.* malignant

cantel(l), *n.* piece, slice, splinter

care, *v.* worry

care *n.* sorrow, trouble

carefull *a.* troubled, sorrowful

carff, *v. pa.t.* carved, cut

caryage, *n.* collection of equipment, baggage, transport

cary(c)k, *n.* large (merchant) ship

carle, *n.* churl

carpe, *v.* speak

case, *n.* (1) situation, the case; (2) cover

caste, *n.* batches

caste, keste, kyst, *v., pp. pa.t.*, cast, throw; intend, devise; be inclined; anticipate; *caste on*, put on, don

caughte, *v. pa.t.* seized

cause, cawse, *n.* matter; *pl.* motives, causes; *by cause, cause why*, because; *for cause*, because, so that

cerche, see *serch(e)*, *v.*

cerclet, *n.* circlet, band

cered, *ppl. a.* waxed

cese, sece, se(a)se, *v.* cease, desist; stop

cetyl, *v.* settle, calm

cewe, see *sew(e)*, *v.*

chace, *n.* pursuit, hunt

chase, *v.* pursue

chacer, *n.* hunter

chaffed, see *cha(u)ffe*, *v.*

chafflet, *n.* platform, riser

chayre, *n.* chair

chambirlayne, *n.* chief steward

champayne, champion, *n.* open country, clear ground

charbuckkle, *n.* carbuncle, rubious gemstone

charge, *n.* command; responsibility, duty; task, burden; care, custody

charge, *v.* order, request; entrust

charyot(t)e, *n.* cart

chartyrs, *n.pl.* pardons

chastisement, *n.* mortification

cha(u)ffe, *v.* heat; stir to anger

chauffynge, *n.* chafing, abrasion

chaunceler, *n.* official secretary of a great lord

chaundeler, *n.* candlestick

checked, *v. pa.t.* ascertained

cheff, *n.* upper section of a heraldic blazon on a shield

cheff, chy(e)ff, *a.* chief, foremost; main, central

chek(ke), *n.* band of warriors

chere, chire, chyre, *n.* expression, display, disposition; courteous welcome; amusement; *what chere?* how are you doing?

chere, *v.* cheer, encourage

chese, *v.* choose

chest, *n.* coffin

chevalry, see *chyvalry*, *n.*

cheve, *v.* achieve

chydde, *v. pa.t.* chided

chy(e)ke, *n.* cheek

chyff, see *cheff*, *a.*

chyfften, *n.* chieftain

chykyns, *n.pl.* chicks

chyld(e), *n.* youth of noble birth; **chyldir(ne)**, *pl.* children

chylde, see *shylde*, *n.*

chyre, see *chere*, *n.*

chyvalry, chevalry, shevalry, *n.* knights; reputation; martial prowess

chyvetayn, see *chyfften*, *n.*

chonge, *v.* change; exchange

chongyng, *n.* change; decomposition

chorle, *n.* churl

claffe, clave, *v. pa.t.* cleaved, split

clarke, see *clerke*, *n.*

clatir, *v.* chatter

clave, see *claffe*, *v. pa.t.*

clegged, see *cleyght(e)*

cleyght(e), clegged, clyched, *v. pp. and pa.t.* clutched, seized

clene, *a.* excellent; pure; complete

clene, *adv.* utterly, completely; **clennyst**, most utterly

clenly, *adv.* completely, fully

clennes, *n.* cleanness, purity

clennyst, see *clene, adv.*

clennyst-myghted, *a.* utterly strongest

clepe, *v.* call, name

clere, *a.* splendid, beautiful

clerenesse, *n.* brightness, splendor

clerke, clarke, *n.* scholar, cleric

clevid, *v. pa.t.* clung, stuck

clyched, see *cleyght(e)*.

clyere *a.* clear; unblemished

clyernes, see *clerenesse n.*

clyerly, *adv.* clearly; without complications

clyppe, *v.* embrace

cloce, *a.* in phrase *in cloce*, secret

clokys, *n. pl.* cloaks

close, *v.* enclose

clothe, *n.* cloth; *clothe of Raynes,* fine linen

clowys, *n.pl.* steep valleys

cnokke, *v.* knock

cofyr, coffir, *n.* coffer, strongbox

cog, *n.* broad transport ship

co(g)nyssaunce, cognysshauns, *n.* knowledge; heraldic sign

coyff(e), *n.* under-cap, skullcap

coystron, *n.* scullion, kitchen-knave

colys, *n. pl.* coals; cinders

comberaunce, *n.* encumbrance

com(e) *v.* come; descend; become; *com off,* proceed

comfortable, *a.* comforting; **com(myn), cam**, *pp.*; **com(e), cam(e), cum**, *pa.t.*

comyn, *a.* common

comynalté, *n.* common people

comyns, *n.pl* common people

comly, *a.* handsome; *adv.* becomingly

commaunde, *v.* command; commend, recommend

commaundemente, *n.* command, authority

commyn, see *com(e)*, *v.*

compace, *n.* confines, compass

compare, *v.* contend

compaste, *v. pa.t.* realized

complayne, *v.* lament, grieve

complevysshed, *pp.* accomplished, achieved

complysshed, *pp.* filled

conceyte, *n.* judgment

conde(s)cende(d), condiscended, *v. pa.t. ppl.a.*, agreed

condis(s)ion, condusion, *n.* character, disposition; condition

conduyte, *n.* safe conduct; responsibility of escort

conduyte, *v.* conduct, escort

condusion, see *cond(s)ion*, *n.*

con(e)stable, *n.* chief military officer, chief representative of a king

conyes, *n.pl.* rabbits

conyssaunce, see *co(g)nyssaunce*, *n.*

conj(e)oure, *v.* constrain

constable, see *con(e)stable*, *n.*

contray(e)s, see *co(u)ntrey*, *n.*

contrary, *v.* contradict

contrey, see *co(u)ntrey*, *n.*

convenyent, *a.* suitable

co(n)versaunte, *a.* dwelling, living

cooper, *n.* copper

coorse, see *corse*, *n.*

coote, *n.* coat

corage, see *corrayge*, *v.*

coryous, *a.* skillful

corne, *n.* wheat

corne-boote, *n.* proper payment

coronal(l), *n.* coronet; circlet on a helmet

corownemente, *n.* coronation

corpus. *n.* corpse

corrage, cor(r)ayge, courage, curra(y)ge, *n.* motivation, desire; spirit, zeal

corrayge, corage, *v.* encourage

corroure, curroure, *n.* courier

corse, coorse, *n.* corpse

corseynte, *n.* reliquary body of a saint

cosyn(e), *n.* kinsman, cousin

coste, *n.* side, flank

coste, *v.* (out)flank

costis, *n. pl.* expense(s)

costys, *n.pl.* regions; coasts

couche, *n.* bed

couche, *v.* go to bed; ready a lance (in its brace) for attack

coulde, *n.* cold

counceyle, counsayle, counseyle, *n.* counsel, body of advisors; advice; secret

counceyle, *v.* advise

counsayle, counseyle, see *counceyle*, *n.*

countenaunce, *n.* appearance; pretense

countes, *n.* countess

countir, *v.* encounter

co(u)ntrey, *n.* district, region; **contray(e)s**, *pl.*

couper, *n.* copper

coupyl, *n.* couple, pair of

courage, see *corrage*, *n.*

coure, see *cowre*, *v.*

cours(e), *n.* charge

courser, *n.* war horse

court(e)la(y)ge, *n.* house with courtyard, enclosed yard

couthe, cowth(e), cow(u)de, *v. pa.t.* could; knew; had learned: see *can*

covenaunte, *n.* agreement, contract; condition; promise

covente, *n.* religious community

cover, *v.* relieve, cure

coversaunte: see *co(n)versaunte*, *a.*

coverte, *n.* cover, protection

covetyse, *n.* covetousness

coward, see *cowherde*, *n.*

cowde, see *couthe*, *v. pa.t.*

cowherde, *n.* (1) coward (*a.* cowardly); (2) (*also spelled* **coward**) cow-herd

cowre, *v.* hide, cower

cowth(e), cowude, see *couthe*, *v. pa.t.*

craffte, see *cra(u)ffle*, *n.*

crake, *v.* proclaim boastfully

cra(u)ffte, *n.* magical power; enchantment, deceit; skill

creature, *n.* creator; God

credence, *n.* message

creyme, *n.* chrism, consecrated oil

cryature, *n.* creature

cry(e), *n.* proclamation; outcry

cry(e), *v.* proclaim, announce; beg

cryyng, *ppl a.* loud

crysemed, *pp.* anointed with consecrated oil

Crysten, *a.* Christian

crystynde, *ppl. a.* christened; converted to Christianity

croked, *ppl. a.* crooked, bent over (with age)

crosse, *n.* crossroads

croufte, *n.* undercroft, crypt

croupe, croupen, croupyn, crowpen, *n.* hindquarters

crowper, *n.* strap that prevents a saddle from lurching forward

crucchis, *n. pl* crutches

cum, see *com(e)*, *v.*

cunnyngyst, *a.* most cunning, most learned

curra(y)ge, see *coryage*, *n.*

curroure, see *corroure*, *n.*

cursednesse, *n.* wickedness

cursynge, *n.* (rite of) excommunication

curte(y)st, *a.* most courteous

curtyll, *n.* tunic, coat

customme, *n.* manner, disposition

D

daffysshe, *a.* foolish

day, *n.* daylight; lifetime

dayssh(e), *n.*, blow

daysshe, *v.* dash, rush down

dalys, *n.pl.* dales, valleys

dalt(e), see *de(a)le, v.*

dame, *n.* noble woman, lady

damesel(l), see *damoysel(le), n.*

dam(m)age, *n.* (matter for) regret; injury; loss

dampned, *pp.* condemned; damned

dare, *v.* remain motionless

darste, *v.* 2. *sg.* dare

darf, *v.* need

daunger(e), *n.* power; captivity; risk, jeopardy

daungerous, *a.* powerful; arrogant

dawe, *v.* dawn; revive

de(a)le, *v.* do what is necessary; deal out; deled, dalt(e), *pp. and pa.t.*

de(a)re, *v.* harm

debate, *n.* conflict; fight

debonayre, *a.* gracious

ded(e); see *do, v.*

dede, *n.* deed, effort

dede, deed, *a.* dead

ded(e)ly, *a.* deadly; deathly

dedes, dedis, *n. pl.* deeds, accomplishments

deed, see *dede, a.*

defaded, *ppl. a.* pale

defame, *v.* speak ill of; speak well of

defau(gh)te, *n.* default, lack; absence; failing

defendaunte, *n.* self defense

def(f)ame, see *defame, v.*

def(f)ende, *v.* forbid; prevent; warn

defyghe, *v.* defy

defoyle, defowle, *v.* defile; put to shame; deflower; trample

degré, degri, *n.* rank; generation; prize; situation

dey(e), *v.* die

deyntés, deyntees, *n.pl.* delicacies

deyse, *n.* dais, raised platform for dining

dele, *n.* part; (significant) quantity; *every dele*, completely

dele, see *de(a)le, v.*

delyver, *v.* release; entrust; dispose of

delyveraunce, *n.* handing over

delyverly, *adv.* quickly, adroitly

demaynes, demenys, *n. pl.* landed estates

deme, *v.* deem, judge; declare; suspect, think, guess

demeanys, *n. pl.* demeanor

dente, see *dynte, n.*

deore, *n. pl.* deer

departe, *v.* separate; divide; distribute

departicion, *n.* separation; departure

depe, *a.* deeply mired

depnes, *n.* depth

deppyst, *a.* deepest

deprave, *v.* accuse; defame

dere, *a.* dear; costly; noble; **derar, derrer,** *adv.* more expensively

dere, *v.*, see *de(a)re, v.*

deserve, *v.* reward; earn

desesed, see *disease, n.*

desyre. *v.* request; invite

desyrous, *a.* eager

desmaye, *v. reflexive* be afraid

despite, dispite, *n.* act of contempt

desportys, *n.pl.* games, amusements

destresse, see *distresse, v.*

deuches, *n.* duchess

deuke, dewke, *n.* duke

dever, devoure, *n.* duty

devyse, *n.* appointment, arrangement

devyse, *v.* plan; conjecture

devoyde, *v.* get clear from; put aside

devoure, *v.* destroy

devoure, see *dever, n.*

devowrer, *n.* destroyer

dewke, see *deuke, n.*

dyche, *n.* ditch, moat

dyched, *ppl.a.* defended with a ditch or moat

dyght, *v. pp. pa.t.* prepare; furnish; cut up

dygnyté, *n.*, in phrase *dygnyté of his hondys,* his martial excellence

dyked, see *dyched, ppl.a.*

dyndled, *v. pa.t.* trembled

dynte, dente, *n.* blow

dyryge, *n.* dirge, Office of the Dead

disadventure, *n.* misadventure

dyscevir, *v.* separate

discever, *v.* distinguish

discomfite(d), *pp.* defeated

discover, *v.* reveal; inform on; search out

discrece, *v.* decrease

discryve, discreve, *v.* describe, explain

disease, *n.* tribulation; sorrow; discomfort; diseased, desesed, *ppl.a.*

disherytaunce, *n.* disinheriting

dis(h)eryte, *v.* disinherit, dispossess

disparbeled, *pp.* dispersed

dispercle, *v.* disperse

disperysshed, *v. pa.t.* perished utterly

dispite, see *despite, n.*

displase, *v.* displease

dispoyle, *v.* strip; *reflexive* undress

disporte, *n.* amusement

disporte, *v.* amuse

dissayved, *pp.* deceived

dysseyvable, *a.* deceptive

distayned, *ppl.a.* disdained, rejected

distracke, *a.* distracted

distresse, destresse, *v.* defeat

dysworship, *n.* disgrace

dyvers, *a.* diverse, several

do, *v.* put; hold; cause, perform; *have done,* cease, stop; **doon, do,** *pp.;* **ded(e), dud,** *pa.t.*

doctour, *n.* learned man

dole, *n.* (1) distribution of gifts; (2) sorrow, grief

dolefull, *a.* dreadful; grievous (**dolefully,** *adv.*)

dolerous(e), *a.* grievous, sorrowful

dombe, see *dom(m)e, a.*

dome, see *do(o)me, n., dom(m)e, a.*

dommage, see *dam(m)age, n.*

dom(m)e, doome, dombe, *a.* dumb, without speech

domyneth, *v. 3. sg.* holds dominion

done, *n.* donation, gift

doole, see *dole, n.* (2)

do(o)me, *n.* judgment; decision

doome, *a.*, see *dom(m)e, a.*

dore, *n.* door; direction; **dorys, durres**, *pl.*

dotage, *n.* infatuation

doted, *ppl.a.* foolish

doth, see *do, v.*

doubte, see *dout(e), n.*

d(o)uches, see *deuches, n.*

dought(e), see *dout(e), n.* and, *v.*

dou(gh)ty, *a.* valiant; as, *n.*, valiant man

doughted, *pp.* feared

doughtly, *adv.* valiantly

dout(e), dought, doubte, *n.* fear; fearsome thing; doubt

doute, doughte, dowt, *v.* fear; doubt

douteful, *a.* fearsome

douty, see *dou(gh)ty, a.*

downeryght, *adv.* thoroughly

downys, *n.pl.* downs, rolling hills

dowré, *n.* dowry, endowment

dowse, *a.* (*French*) sweet

dowte, see *doute, v.*

dowve, *n.* dove

doynge, *n. gerund,* doing, work; achievement; happening

do(y)st(e), see *do, v.*

dra(d)d(e), see *drede, v.*

draught, drawght, *n.* current; coming and going

draw(e), *v.* withdraw; incline; approach; tear; translate; **drew(e)**, *pa.t.*

dred(e), *n.* fear

drede, *v.* fear, be afraid; **dred(de), drad(de)**, *pa.t.*

dreme-reder, *n.* interpreter of dreams

drenche, *v.* drown

dresse, *v.* prepare (military equipment); direct, lead; advance; *reflexive* raise or prepare (oneself)

dretched, *ppl.a.* afflicted, troubled; **dretchyng**, *n.* affliction, disturbance

drevyn, dryvyn, see *dryve, v.*

drew(e), see *draw(e), v.*

dryve, *v.* drive forward, hasten; **drevyn, dryvyn**, *pp.*; **droff(e)**, *pa.t.*; **dryvande** *pres. participle*

droupe, *v.* droop

dubled, dublette, *n.* doublet, jacket

duches, see *deuches, n*

dud, see *do, v.*

durable, *a.* inexhaustible

duras, *n.* duress, affliction; corruption

dure, *v.* endure, last; exist; **durynge**, enduring

durke, *a.* dark; **durked**, *ppl.a.*, darkened, gone dark

durres, durrys: see *dore, n.*

durst, *pa.t.* dared

dwelle, *v.* linger

dwere, *n.* doubt, quandary

dwyne, *v.* dwindle, waste

E

earthely, *adv.*, see n. 6, p. 507

ease, *n.* (1) health; (2) see *evyse*

ease, *v.* refresh; cure

ec(c)hone, *pron.* each one

effte, *adv.* again, after

egg, *v.* incite

egir, *a.* angry, eager

egirly, egerly, *adv.* angrily; quickly

egirnesse, *n.* fierceness; anxiety

eyen, see *y(gh)e, n.*

eyle, *v.* ail, suffer

eythir, see *aythir, a.* and *pron.*

elder, *n.* ancestor; man of high rank

elffe, *n.* diminutive creature

elis, ell(i)s, els, *adv.* else, otherwise

elle, *n.* measure of forty-five inches

elther, *a.* elder

eme, *n.* uncle

emerawde, *n.* emerald

emonge, *prep.* among

empeyre, *v.* become impaired, weaken

empyreship, *n.* office of emperor

emprise, *v.* undertake

en, *prep.* in

enamyled, *ppl.a.* enameled, painted

enbrayde, *v.* upbraid, admonish

enbrowdred, *ppl.a.* embroidered

encense, *v.* imbue with incense

enchace, *v.* chase, expel

enchaff, *v.* exercise; arouse, inflame

encheve, enchy(e)ve, *v.* achieve, acquire; complete successfully

enchevynge, *n.* achieving

encres(e), encrece, *v.* increase; grow stronger

end(e)longe, enlonge, endlynge, *prep. adv.*, head on; along the length of

endented, *ppl.a.* set with a scalloped (heraldic) pattern

endewe, *v.* endow

endite, *v.* compose; dictate

enewed, *ppl.a.* colored

enforce, enforse, *v.* force, exert (oneself); overpower, rape

enfourme, *v.* inform

engendirde, *ppl.a.* begotten, conceived

engyn(n)e, *n.* contrivance, scheme; ingenuity; siege weapon

enlonge, see *end(e)longe*

enoynted, *ppl.a.* anointed

enpoysen, enpoyson, *v.* poison

enquere, *v.* inquire

ensa(u)mple, insample, *n.* example; warning
enstraunged, *pa.t.* estranged
ensure, *v.* assure
entent(e), *n.* intent, desire; reason; intention
entere, entyre, *v.* inter, bury
enterement, *n.* burial
entermete, *v.* be occupied
entirdytynge, *n. gerund* interdiction
entirmete, *v.* interfere
entyre, see *entere, v.*
entré, *n.* entrance
entreté, *n.* negotiation
entrete, *v.* entreat, appeal to; negotiate; deal with
entromedled, *pp.* intermixed
envyro(w)ne, *adv.* around, about
erbys, *n.pl.* herbs, plants
ere, *prep.* before
eregned, *ppl.a.* heretical
erewhyle, *adv.* earlier
erys, *n.pl.* ears
ermyne, *n.* ermine (see n. 2, p. 206)
ermyta(y)ge, armytayge, *n.* hermitage, hermit's retreat
er(e)myte, *n.* hermit
erste, *adv.* before
erthely, *a.*, see n. 6, p. 507
espye, *n.* spy
estate, see *astate, n.*
esturys, *n.pl.* rooms
ete, *v.pa.t.* ate
etynge, *n.* eating
even, see *evyn,* adv.
ever, *adv.* for ever; continuously
every, everych(e), *a. pron.* each
evyl(l), yevell, yevil, *a. adv.* bad; badly, poorly; ill; evil
evyn, *n.* evening before
evyn, even, *adv.* right, directly, straight; close; evenly
evynlongis, *prep.* along
evynner, *adv.* more evenly
evynsonge, *n.* evening prayer
evyse, ease, *n.* edge, margin
exemple, *n.* (moral) illustration

F

fa(a)re, *n.* behavior, conduct; method
fade, *v.* lose strength
fadir, *n.* father
fadom, fadum, *n.* fathom, measure of six feet
fayle, *v.* miss, lack
fayne, *v. reflexive* feign
fayne, *a.* glad, eager; *adv.* gladly; faynyst, most gladly
faynte, *n.* faintness
faynte, *v.* weaken, grow tired, falter
fayre, fair *a.* fair, welcoming; beautiful; fayrar, more fair; fayryst, most fair; *adv.* courteously, graciously; deferentially; gently

fayrenes(se), *n.* civility, gentility
faytoure, *n.* impostor
fall(e), *v.* befall, happen; be appropriate; fall; fallyn, *pp.;* fyll(e), fyl, felle, *pa.t.*
fals(e)hed(e), *n.* falsehood, lies; treachery
falselyar, *a.* more false
falsyst, *a.* most false
famuste, *a.* most famous
fantasy, *n.* fancy, love
fare, *v.* behave, carry on; happen; faryn, *pp.* treated
fare, see *fa(a)re, n.*
farme, *n.* rent, tax
farther, *v.* advance, further
faste, *adv.* securely; close; quickly
fastenys, *v. imperative* fasten
faucon, *n.* falcon
faught, see *feyght, v.*
fau(gh)te, *n.* fault
faught(e), *v.* go without, lack
fauntekyn, *n.* tiny infant
favour(e), *n.* bias
fe(a)re, *v.* frighten; be afraid
feaute, see *fewte, n.*
feauté, see *feawté, n.*
feauter, fewter, *v.* ready (a lance) in its rest for combat
feautyr, feawter, *n.* dedicated rest for a lance on armor
feaw, *a.* few
feawté *n.* fealty (see n. 6, p. 9)
feawter, see *feautyr, n.*
fecche, fette, *v.* fetch; reach; fet(te), *pp. and pa.t.*
fee, *n.* reward
fe(e)rys, *n. pl.* companions
feffed, *v. pa.t.* populated
feyght, *v.* fight; faught, *pa.t*
feyste, see *feste, n.*
felaushyp, *v.,* see *felyship, v.*
feld(e), *n.* field of battle
felde, *v. pp. pa.t.* felled, brought down
feldys, *n.pl.* fields
fele, *v.* feel, sense; realize; experience; felt, *pp.,* felte, *pa.t.*
fele, *pron.* many
felyshep, felyshyp, felysship, *n.* companions; band, military forces
felyship, felaushyp, *v.* enjoy company, associate
felle, *n.* wild, open country
fel(l)on, *a.* wicked
felonne, *n.* villain
felon(ou)s, felownse, *a.* wicked; violent
felonsly, *adv.* recklessly, violently
felt(e), see *fele, v.*
fende, *n.* fiend, devil
fendly, *adv.* like a fiend
fenyshe, *v.* finish
ferde, *n.* fear
fere, *n.* companionship; *in fere,* together
fere, *adv.* far; *on fere* afar

fere, see *fe(a)re*, *v.*

ferys, see *fe(e)rys*, *n. pl.*

fer(re), see *farre*, *a.*

fers(e), *a.* fierce, determined

fersely, *adv.* fiercely; **ferselyer**, more fiercely

ferther, *adv.* further

feste, feyste, *n.* feast

fested, *ppl.a.* sitting at the feast

fet(te), see *fecche*, *v.*

fetys, *n.pl.* feats

fewte, feaute, *n.* trace, trail

fewter, see *feauter*, *v.*

fyaunce, *n.* promise

fyeble, *v.* weaken

fyete, see *foote*, *n.*

fyll(e), see *fall(e)*, *v.*

filde, fylde, see *feld(e)*, *n.*

fyll(e), see *fall(e)*, *v.*

fylth, *n.* lust; foul internal matter

fynde, see *fende*, *n.*

fynde, *v.* find; notice; **founde**, *pp.*, **fond(e)**, *pa.t.*

fyndely, see *fendly*, *adv.*

fyndynge, *n.* provision

fine, fyne, *a.* superior

fyrys, *n.pl.* fires

fyrse, see *fers(e)*, *a.*

fyse, *n.* (*French*) son

fysshers, *n.pl.* fishermen

fittlockys, fyttlokkes, *n.pl.* projections above (horses') hoofs

flayne, *pp.* flayed, skinned

flaket(te), *n.* flask

flamand, see *fla(w)me*, *v.*

flange, see *flynge*, *v.*

flappys, *v.* 3.sg. cuts

flatlynge, *adv.* at full length; with the flat side (of a sword)

fla(w)me, *v.* flame; **flamand**, *pres. participle*, flaming

fle, flye, *v.* fly, flee; **flye, flow(e), flowghe**, *pa.t*

fleamed, fleymed, flemyd, *v. pp. pa.t.* forced to flee; banished

fle(e)te, *v.* float

fleymed, flemyd, see *fleamed*, *v.*

fleyng, flyynge, *pres. participle* fleeing

fleyshly, *adv.* physically; carnally

flye, see *fle*, *v.*

flynge, *v.* hasten; fling; **flange**, *pa.t.*

flytte, *v.* move

floode, *n.* river; flood tide

florys(s)h, *v.* bloom; make thrive

florys(s)hed, *ppl.a.* decorated

floter, *v.* flutter

floure, *n.* (1) floor; (2) flower; best part

flow(e), flowghe, see *fle*, *v.*

foyne, *n.* thrust

foyne, *v.* thrust

fole, *n.* fool

foo, *n.* foe; **foomen**, *n.pl.* enemies

fond(e), see *fynde*, *v.*

fo(o)ys, *n.pl.* enemies

foote, *n.*, **fyete**, *pl.* foot

footehote, *adv.* immediately, without pause

footemen, *n.pl.* foot-soldiers

for, *cj.* and; because

for(e), *prep.* because of, out of; concerning; *for to*, in order to

forbe(a)re, *v.* be patient with, tolerate; leave alone; desist; resist; **forborne**, *pp.*; **forbare**, *pa.t.*

forbled(de), *ppl.a.* drained of blood, so weakened

forbode, *n.* forbidding

forborne, see *forbe(a)re*, *v.*

force, forse, *n.* power, strength, exertion; *no force*, that does not matter; *take no force*, do not care

force, forse, *v.* exert; rape

fordo, *v.* **fordyd**, *pa.t.* defeat; do away with

forecaste, *n.* design, scheme

forecaste, *ppl.a.* premeditated

foreryder, *n.* scout

forestage, *n.* forecastle

forewarde, *a.* ready to go

forfare, *v.* destroy

forfende, *v. infinitive and pp.* forbid

forfete, *a.* lost, forfeit

forfette, *n.* offense

forfoughtyn, *ppl.a.* fought to exhaustion

forgyff, *v.* forgive; renounce

forhewyn, *ppl.a.* cut to pieces

forjusted, *pa.t.* defeated at jousting

forlonde, *n.* promontory

formyst(e), *a.* foremost, first

forrey, *v.* forage in

forsake, *v.* refuse (contact with)

forse, see *force*, *n.* and *v.*

forsoth(e), *adv.* truly

forstall, *v.* cut off, block

fo(r)ster, *n.* forester

fo(r)stred, *pp.* raised; cared for

forsworne, *pp.* made a liar

forthynke, *v.* regret; grieve

forthwithal, furth(e)withal(l), *adv.* forthwith

fortune, *v.* happen, befall

foryaf, *v.pa.t.* forgave

foryevenes, *n.* forgiveness

foster, see *fo(r)ster*, *n.*

fostred, see *fo(r)stred*, *pp.*

foule, fowle, *adv.* with evil

founde(n), see *fynde*, *v.*

foundred, *pa.t.* collapsed

fountayne, fowntayne, *n.* spring; font

fourde, *n.* stream crossing

fourme, *n.* (1) condition; (2) bench

fourme, *v.* make

fowle, see *foule*, *adv.*

fowler, *a.* more foul

fowlys, *n.pl.* birds

fownder, *n.* finder

frankensens, *n.* incense, frankincense

frayke, freyke, *n.* man, warrior; creature

fraysted, *ppl.a.* proven
fraunchyse, *n.* district
fre, *a.* generous; noble; unrestrained
freyke, see *frayke, n.*
freynship, *n.* friendship
freys(s)h(e), *a.* fresh, vigorous
freys(s)hly, *adv.* freshly, with new strength; happily; severely
freysshid, *v. pa.t.* eased
frely, *adv.* nobly; generously
frende, *v.* befriend
frendly, *adv.* in a friendly fashion
frycke, *a.* strong, vigorous
frynde, *n.* friend; **fryndely,** *a.*
fryth, *n.* wood(s)
fro, frome, *prep.* from; away from; *cj.* from the time when
fro(m)ward(e), *prep.* from, away from
fruys(s)he, *v.* knock, dash
fruyte, *n.* fruit
frunte, *n.* front line of battle
fulfyle, *v.* complete, realize; fill to, replace to
ful(l), fulle, *adv.* fully, wholly; very; severely
full-but, *adv.* directly, head-on
furlonge, *n.* one eighth of a mile
furnysshe, *v.* provision, prepare for
furth(e), *adv.* forth
furthewith, *adv.* forthwith
furth(e)withal(l), see *forthwithall, adv.*
fy, *interj.* expression of disgust

G

gabbe, *v.* lie
gadde, *n.* bar
gadir, *v.* gather; **gadird(e), gadred,** *pa.t.*
gadlynges, *n.pl.* worthless fellows
gaf(f), see *gyff(e), v.*
gayne-commynge, *n.* return
gayneste, *a.* quickest; *at the gaynyste,* by the shortest way
gal(e)y, *n.* galley
galyard, *a.* spirited
galyottys, *n.pl.* fast galleys with sails and oars
gan, *v. pa.t.* began
gaper, *n.* joker
gar, *v.* cause; **garte,** *p.a.t.*
garneson, *n.* reward
garnyson, *n.* defending force
garnysshe, garnysh, *v.* equip for defence; provision
garte, see *gar, v.*
gastfull, *a.* ghastly, frightening
gate, *n.* pathway, road
gate, see *ge(e)te, v.*
geaunte, *n.* giant
ge(e)te, gett, *v.* get, obtain; seize, take control over; gather up; beget, conceive; compel to move; go; **goten,** *pp.;* **gate,** *pa.t.*
geff, geffyn, see *gyff(e), v.* and *gyff, cj.*
genytrottys, *n.pl.* genitals

gerde, see *gurde, v.(2)*
gere, *n.* battle-gear
germayne, jarmayne, jermayne, *a.* closely related by blood; *cosyne germayne,* first cousin
gesseraunte, jesseraunte, *n.* coat of armor
geste, *n.* guest; stranger
gete, gett, see *ge(e)te, v.*
getynge, *n.* getting, acquisition
gettles, *a.* empty-handed
geve, gevyn, see *gyff(e), v.*
ghost, *n.* soul, spirit
gyaunt, *n.* giant
gyde, *v.* guide (oneself)
gyeff, see *gyff(e), v.*
gyese, *n.pl.* geese
gyff, geff, *cj.* if
gyff(e), geve, gyeff, gyve, yeff, yeve, *v.* give; emit; appoint; incline; **geffyn, gyffyn, gevyn, yeffyn,** *pp.;* **gaf(f),** *pa.t.*
gylden, *a.* golden
gyle, *n.* guile
gyrde, see *gurde, v.* (1) and (2)
gyse, *n.* fashion; habit, custom
gysarne, gyserne, *n.* battle-axe
gyve, see *gyff(e), v,*
glad, *v.* please, gladden
glayve, *n.* lance, spear
glatys(s)aunte, glatissynge, *a.* yelping (see n. 9, p. 31)
glemerynge, *n.* glimpse
glystrand, *ppl.a.* glittering
gloore, *v.* glare
gloove, *n.* glove
gloton, *n.* glutton
gnaste, *v.* gnash
go, *v.* walk; suffice
gobbettis, *n.pl.* pieces
godelye, see *godly, a.*
good, *n.* **go(o)dis, gooddys,** *pl.* goods; spoils; wealth
goodly, godelye, *a.* beautiful; courteous; *adv.* courteously
gooldys, gouldes, *n.* heraldic red, gules
gorge, *n.* throat
gost(e)ly, *a.* spiritual; *gostly fadir,* priest, confessor
goten, gotyn, see *ge(e)te, v.*
gouldes, see *gooldys, n.*
governaunce, *n.* authority, leadership
grace, *n.* mercy; permission; (heavenly) privilege
grame, *n.* harm, grief
gramercy, see *graunt(e)mercy*
graunte, *n.* promise
graunte, *v.* (and *pa.t.*) consent; agree, allow
graunt(e)mercy, gramercy, many thanks
grauntesyre, *n.* grandfather
gravyn, *pp.* interred, buried
gré, *n.* prize; first place; reward
grece, *n.* fatness
grecis, *n.pl.* stairs
greff, *n.* grief

grekynge, *n.* dawn

grene, gryne, *a.* green, fresh

grenne, *v.* grin

gres(e)ly, *a.* grisly, horrific; *adv.* terribly

gresylde, *a.* grizzled, gray

grete, *v.* greet

grete, *a.* large; boastful; powerful; **gretter,** greater; **grettest,** greatest

grevaunces, *n.pl.* sufferings

greve, *n.* thicket, grove

greve, gryff, *v.* grieve

gry(e)ff, *n.* grief

gryff, see *greve, v.*

gryffen, *n.* gryphon, beast with the head and wings of an eagle and the body of a lion

grymly, *a.* grim; severe

grymme, *a.* grim; severe

gryne, see *grene, a.*

grype, *v.* grasp, hold; lift

grounden, *ppl. a.* sharply ground

grovelyng(e), *adv.* facedown, headlong

growunde, *n.* ground

grucche, *v.* grumble; begrudge, resist

grucchynge, *n.* reluctance

gummys, *n.pl.* gums, resins

gurde, gyrde, *v.* (1) gyrde, gurde, gurte, *pp. and pa.t,* girded; (2) gerde, gyrde, gurde, *pa.t.,* struck out; rushed; drew out

gurdyll, *n.* belt; waist

gwardonles, *a.* without reward

gwerdon, *n.* reward

H

(h)abyte, *n.* garment

had, see *have, v.*

haylese, *v.* greet

haynxman, *n.* henchman, page

hayre, see *heyre, n.*

hakeney, *n.* horse-drawn carriage

hale, *v.* pull

halfendele, *n.* half (of)

halff, *n.* side

halow, *v.* (1) consecrate; (2) shout

Halowma(se), see *Al Halowmas*

halpe, *v.* stumble

halpe, see *helpe, v.*

halse, *n.* neck

halse, *v.* embrace

hampred, *ppl. a.*

hand(e), see *honde, n.*

hande-brede, *n.* handsbreadth

handels, hondils, *n.pl.* hilt

handyll, *v.* grasp, clutch; touch; capture; hand(e)led, *pp. pa.t.*

hangers, *n.pl.* testicles

hansell, *n.* gift

hap(pe), *n.* luck, chance

hap(pe), *v.* happen, chance; **happed,** *pa.t.* chanced, happened; benefited

happely, *adv.* by a lucky chance

happy, *a.* lucky, fortunate

harberow, harborow, see *herborow, v.*

harde, *a.* difficult; frugal

hardé, *a.* brave, bold

harde, *adv.* with difficulty; severely

harde, *v. pa.t.* heard

hardé-herted, *ppl a.* brave-hearted

hardely, *adv.* indeed

hardy, *a.* bold

hardynes(se), hardines, *n.* boldness; callousness

harys, *n.pl.* hares

harlot, *n.* rascal

harmys, *n.pl.* harms, injuries

harneys(e), harneysse, harnoys, *n.* equipment, armor

harneyst(e), *ppl.a.* equipped; decorated

harson: see *arson, n.*

harte: see *hert(e), n.* (1) and (2)

hartely, *a.* heartfelt, grievous

hartely, see *hertely, adv.*

hast(e), *v.* hasten

hastely, *adv.* quickly

hasty, *a.* pressing, urgent

hastynes, *n.* haste

hauffte, *n.* haft, handle

haunche, *n.* shoulder

haunte, *v.* attend, frequent

hauté, hawté, *a.* haughty, proud

hauthorne, *n.* hawthorn tree

have, *v.* bring, take; *have done,* stop, that is enough; **had,** *pp.*

haven, *n.* harbor

hawbirke, hawbarke, *n.* coat of mail

hawté, see *hauté, a.*

he, *pron.* it; she

he(a)le, *n.* health; advantage

hede, heed, *n.* (1) head; chief; *magré . . . hede,* against . . . will; (2) care, heed; *uppon hede,* with malice aforethought

hede-shete, *n.* sheet at the head of a bed

hedyous, hedeous, *a.* hideous

heed, see *hede, n.* (1) and (2)

heyre, hayre, here, *n.* hair shirt (see n. 9, p. 532); hair

helde, see *holde, v.*

hele, *v.* (1) heal, restore; (2) cover

hele, see *he(a)le, n.*

helys, *n. pl.* heels

helme, *n.* helmet; armed man

helpe, *v.* help, assist; **holpyn,** *pp;* **halpe, holpe,** *pa.t.*

hem, *pron.* them

hemynge, *n.* clearing the throat

hemselff, *pron.* themselves

hende, *a.* courteous

hens, *adv.* hence, from there

hensforewarde, *adv.* henceforth

hente, *v.* (pa.t.) take, seize

hepe, *n.* band, group

her, see *hir,* possessive *a.* (1) and (2)

herberow, see *herborow, n.* and *v.*

herbygeour, *n.* official procurer and preparer of lodgings

herbys, *n.pl.* plants, herbs

herborgage, herbo(u)rage, *n.* lodging

herborow, herberow, *n.* lodging

herborow, herberow, harberow, harborow, *v.* procure lodging; take lodging, lodge; **herbourde,** *pp.*

herborowles, *a.* without lodging

herbourage, see *herborgage, n.*

herde, see *hyre, v.*

here, see *heyre, n.*

hereby, *adv.* nearby

heretoforne, *adv.* from before, previously

heryed, *v. pa.t.,* harried

heryng, hyryng, *n. pres. participle,* hearing

herken, *v.* listen

her(r)od, herowd, *n.* herald

hert(e), harte, *n.* (1) heart, spirit; (2) hart, male deer

hertely, hartely, *adv.* heartily, profoundly, thoroughly

hertys, *n.pl.* hurts, injuries

hete, *n.* (1) anger; (2) rebuke

heth(e), *n.* heath, open ground

hethyn, *n.* heathen

hethynde, *a.* heathen

heve, *v.* heave, raise; **heve, hove,** *pa.t.*

hevy, *v.* grieve

hevy, *a.* sad; **hevyar,** more sad

hevyly, *adv.* sadly

hevyn, *n.* heaven

hevynesse, *n.* sadness

hew, *n.* hue

hew, *v.* cut up; **hewed** *pa.t.;* **hewen, hewyn** *pp.* hewn

hyd(d)ir, hyd(d)er, *adv.* hither, to here

hyde, *n.* (1) skin; (2) heed

hye, see *hy(gh)e, v.*

hy(g)he, *n. a.* high; noble; loud; *an/on hyghe,* loudly, above, in height

hy(gh)e, *v.* hasten (oneself)

hyght, *n.* height; *on hyght* loudly

hyght(e), *v. pres. pa.t.* be called, be named

hyhe, see *hy(g)he, n. a.*

hylde, *v.* fill

hyide; see *holde, v.*

hyltis, *n.pl.* hilt

hym, *pron.* himself

hynge, honged, *v. pa.t.* hung

hir, her, hyr(e), *a. possessive* (1) her; (2) their

hyre, *v.* hear; understand, acknowledge; **harde, herde,** *pp.* and *pa.t.*

hyre, *adv.* here

hyryng, see *heryng, n.* and *pres. participle*

his, hys, *a. possessive,* used as genitive extension after proper names: e.g., *Galeron hys spear:* Galeron's spear

hit(te), *pron.* it

holde, *n.* stronghold

holde, *v.* hold, grasp; preserve, keep, possess

(sexually); hold in opinion; owe allegiance; **holde(n),** *pp.;* **helde, hylde,** *pa.t.*

hole, hool, *a.* whole, entire; healthy, healed; **holer,** in better health

hole, *adv.* fully

holy, holé, *adv.* wholly

holpe, holpyn, see *helpe, v.*

holsom, *a.* beneficial, healthy

holt, *n.* wood(s)

honde, hand(e), *n.* hand; side; *hande-for-hande,* hand-to-hand; *better/higher honde,* victory; *on honde,* in hand, to do; *evyn honde,* stalemate; *stronge honde,* military force; *at ... honde,* near

honde-faste, *a.* betrothed

hondils, see *handels, n.*

hondredsom, *n.* group of a hundred

honesté, *n.* credit

honeste, *a.* decent

honestely, *adv.* decently

honged, see *hynge, v. pa.t.*

honoure, *n.* renown, repute

hool, see *hole, a.*

hooly, *n.* holly

ho(o)st(e), *n.* army

hoote, see *hote, a.*

hore, *a.* hoary, gray; old

horle, see *hurle, v.*

horse, *n.* horseman; and *sg. genitive,* horse's

horse, *v.* provide with a horse; set on horseback

horse-bere, *n.* horse-drawn bier

horse-lettir, -litter, -lyttar, *n.* horse-drawn stretcher

hote, hoote, *a.* hot, passionate

houseld, howseled, *pp.* administered the Eucharist

hove, *v.* wait; float

hove, see *heve, v.*

howbehit, *adv.* nevertheless; *cj.* even though, although

howge, *a.* huge

howghe-boone, *n.* rear thigh bone

howre, *n.* hour

hows, *n.* (religious) house

howseled, see *houseld, pp.*

howund, *n.* hound

hunderthes, hundrethis, *n. pl.* hundreds

hunteres, hunteras, *n.* huntress

hurle, horle, *v.* rush; be thrown violently

hurlynge, *n.* commotion

hurtel, *v.* rush; throw

I, *Vowel-Form Y*

i-, y-, *prefix of pp.*

Y, *pron.* I

i-bake, *pp.* baked

i-cleyght, *pp.* clutched

i-dyght, *pp.* prepared

i-drawyn, *pp.* drawn

ye(e), ien, yen, see y(gh)e, n.
yf, if, cj. if; but if, unless
y-fared, pp. treated
i-founde, pp. found
y(gh)e, yee, n. eye; y(gh)en, ien, yen, iyen, eyen, pl. eyes
yghesyght, n. surveillance, watch
i-gyffyn, pp. given
i-horsed, pp. horsed
iyen, see y(gh)e, n.
yle, ile, n. island
ylle, n. evil; ill-will, evil intent
ylle, adv. ill, poorly; evil
ilonde, n. island
imboced, inboced, ppl.a. fled into a wood
in, prep. on; concerning; in the power of; at, near
inboced, see imboced, ppl.a.
inbusshemente, n. ambush
inchaffed, ppl.a. heated, excited
incoronacion, n. coronation
inde, n. indigo, deep blue dye of India
infelyshyp, v. join (oneself) in company
infortunate, a. unfortunate
inly(c)ke, inlyche, adv. alike, equally
inne, n. lodging
inow(ghe), a. adv. enough, (in) plenty
insample, see ensa(u)mple, n.
instaunce, n. insistence, entreaty
intyerly, adv. entirely
into, prep. used as cj. until
invenymed, pp. poisoned
inward(e)ly, adv. thoroughly, fully
ipocresye, n. hypocrisy
i-purveyed, pp. provided
ys, a. his
i-sente, pp. sent
i-sette, pp. set, appointed
i-sowdred, pp. adhered, reunited
issew, v. issue, go
yssue, n. gate; issuing out, sortie
i-taught, ppl.a. instructed
i-tyed, pp. tied
ivery, n. ivory
iwys, adv. indeed

J

jantely, adv. nobly
jantil(l), a. noble, gentle
jantillwoman, n. woman of gentle birth
jantilman, n. man of gentle birth
jantilnes(se), n. nobility, courtesy
japyng, n. jesting
jape, n., japys, pl. jest, trifle
jarfaucon, jarfawcoun, n. gyrfalcon, large falcon
jarmayne, see germayne, a.
jelosy, jolesy, n. concern, anxiety; jealousy
jermayne, see germayne, a.
jesseraunte, see gesseraunte, n.

jocounde, a. jocund, cheerful
joye, v. rejoice
joyne, v. (1) join (battle), begin, direct; (2) enjoin, assign
jolesy, see jelosy, n.
jolowse, a. jealous
jolyar, a. more high-spirited
j(o)uge, jowge, v. judge, sentence
j(o)ugement, n. decision; punishment
jouparté, jouperdé, joupardye, jupardé, n. jeopardy, danger
jouparté, jouparté, v. risk, place in jeopardy
j(o)urnay, j(o)urney(e), n. day's fighting, day's work; journey, campaign
joustys, see justes, n.
jowge, see j(o) uge, v.
jowke, v. knock
jubett, n. gibbet, gallows
juell, n. jewell
juge, jugement, see j(o)uge, v., j(o)ugement, n.
jupardé, see jouparté, n.
jurnay, jurney: see j(o)urnay, n.
juste, v. joust
justenynge, n. jousting, tournament followed by a feast
justes, justis, j(o)ustys, justus, justyse, n. (1) jousting
justyse, n. (2) punishment

K

kay, n. key
keele, v. cool
ke(e)ne, a. brave
keep, see lepe, v.
kempys, n. pl. champions
ken, v. make known
kene, see ke(e)ne, a.
kepe, n. care, interest; take kepe take care, pay attention
kepe, keep, v. watch, guard; maintain; await; hinder, conceal
keper, n. warden
kepyng(e), n. guarding
kerve, v. carve, cut
kerver, n. carver
keste, see caste, v.
keverchoff, n. kerchief
kybbet, n. cubit, length of a forearm
kyd(de), ppl.a. well known; notorious
kynde, n. nature; right of birth
kynde, a. natural; appropriate, lawful; kynde elders, ancestors
kyndely, a. natural
kyndenes, n. affection
kyne, n. pl. cows
kynne, n. kin, family, bloodline
kynred(e), n. kindred, family
kyrke, n. church
kyrtyl, kurdyll, n. gown
kyst(e), see caste, v. pa.t.

knave, *n.* boy; servant; wretch
knyghtly, *adv.* befitting a knight, chivalrously
knylle, *v.* knell, ring
knytte, *pp.* knit, clasped
kneled, *v. pa.t.* kneeled
knowe, *v.* know; recognize; **knowe,** *pp.*
knowlecchynge, *n.* knowledge; heraldic blazon
knowleche, *n.* knowledge
knowleche, *v.* acknowledge
knowyn, *ppl.a.* knowing, cognizant; made known, recognized
knowynge, *a.* knowledgeable, cunning
kurdyll, see *kyrtyl, n.*
kut(te), *v. pa.t.* cut

L

lacke, *v.* miss
lad(de), see *lede, v.*
laddys, *n.pl.* lads, servants
lade, lode, *pp.* laden, loaded
ladyles, *a.* lady-less, single
ladyll, *n.* ladle
lay, *n.* song
lay(ne), see *ly(ghe), v.*
layne, *v.* conceal
layrge, see *large, n., a., adv.*
laysshe, *v.* strike, lash out
lake, *n.* lack, want
Lammas, *n.* Lammas Day, August 1, a harvest festival day, also celebrating St. Peter's deliverance from prison
langa(y)ge, *n.* language, talk; verbal abuse
langeryng, *pres. participle* lingering
langoure, *n.* lamentation
lappe, *v.* wrap
large, layrge, *n., a., adv.* liberty, freedom; will; good; ful(ly); generous(ly); boastful(ly); *at . . . large,* at liberty
largely, *adv.* generously; freely; boastfully; **largelyer,** more fully
largenesse, *n.* generosity
laste, *v.* extend, reach
laste, *cj.* lest
late, *adv.* lately, recently
latyne, laton, *n.* latten, brass-like alloy
lat(t)e, see *let(e), v.*
laughte, *v. pa.t.* seized
launde, lawnde, *n.* glade, clearing, plain
lawde, *n.* praise
lawghe, *v.* laugh; **lough, lowghe,** *pa.t.*
lawnde, see *launde, n.*
lawles, *a.* lawless
lazar-cote, *n.* house for lepers
leade, see *lede, n.*
leagis, *n.pl.* leagues, twenty-mile distances
leane, see *lene, v.*
learys, *n.pl.* cheeks
leche, *n.* physician
lechecra(u)ffte, *n.* skill of physicians, surgical skill

lechourere, *n.* lecher
lede, leade, leed, *n.* lead metal; lead seal; lead coffin
lede, *v.* **lad(de),** *pp.;* **lad(de),** *pa.t.;* (1) lead, direct; (2) carry
leder, *n.* leader
leeff, see *leve, a.*
leepe, see *lepe, v.*
leete, see *let(e) v.*
lefft(e), see *leve, v.*
legeaunce, *n.* allegiance
ley, *v.* lay
ley, see *ly(ghe), v.*
leyde, *ppl. a.* set, positioned
leyne, see *ly(ghe), v.*
leyser, *n.* leisure, opportunity
lemman, *n.* lover
lende, *v.* remain
lendys, *n. pl.* loins, buttocks
lene, leane, *v.* (1) lend; (2) lean; **lente,** *pa.t.*
lenger, lengist, lengyst, see *longe, adv.*
lente, see *lene, v.*
lepe, *v.* leap; **lopyn,** *pp.;* **le(e)pe, lope,** *pa.t.*
lerne, *v.* teach
lese, see *loose, v.*
leste, *a.* least; fewest
let, *n.* hindrance
let(e), lette, lat(e), latte, *v.* (1) cause; allow; release; (2) hinder; stop; deprive; **lette, latte, lette(d),** *pp.;* **let(t)e, late,** *pa.t.*
letter, lettir, *n.* litter, stretcher; cot, bed
lettirs, *n.pl.* writings
leve, *n.* leave, permission
leve, *v.* (1) leave off, desist, yield; remain; (2) (*also* **lyve**) believe (3) (*also* **lyff**) *imperative,* live, remain alive; *on lyve,* alive; **lefft(e),** **leved,** *pp.;* **lefte,** *pa.t.;*
leve, leeff, lyff, *a.* beloved, dear; **lever,** dearer; **levyste,** dearest
leved, *ppl.a.* leafy
lever, see *leve, a.; lyff, adv.*
levir, see *lyff, adv.*
levynge, *n.* condition of life
levyste, see *leve, a.*
lewde, *a.* rude, ill-mannered
ley(ne), ly, see *ly(ghe), v.*
lybard(e), *n.* leopard
lyck(e)ly, lycly, see *lyk, a.*
lycence, *n.* permission
lycoure, *n.* greed
lycoures, *a.* lecherous
lyeff, *n.* leaf
ly(e)ff, lyve, *n.* life, lifetime; *on lyve,* alive
lyeff, *adv.,* see *lyff, adv.*
lyeffloode, see *lyvelod(e), n.*
lyefftenaunte, *n.* lieutenant
lyege, *a.* liege, feudally bound to give or receive allegiance
lyen(e), see *ly(ghe), v.*
lyer, *n.* liar
lyff, lyeff, *adv.* preferably, sooner, willingly; **lever, levir,** more willingly

lyff, see *ly(e)ff, n.; leve, a.; leve, v.* (3)
lyfft(e), *v. pa.t.* lifted
lyf(f)te, *a.* left
lyggyng(e), *ppl.a.* lying
lygge, ly(ghe), ley, lay, *v.* lie; rest, remain; set at risk; **lyggys,** 3 *sg. pres.;* **ley(ne), layne, lyen(e),** *pp.;* **lay,** *pa.t.*
lyght, *a.* active; wanton
lyght(e), *v.* (1) mount; settle; (2) grow cheerful
lyghtene, *v.* flash with lightning
lyghtly, *adv.* quickly; summarily
lygnage, see *lynage n.*
lyke, *v.* please
lyke, *a.* alike, likely; *adv.* equally; according to; *lyke to,* as if; *like as,* just as
lykynge, *n.* pleasure; rejoicing
lykynge, *a.* pleasant
lykly, lyck(e)ly, lycly, *a.* likeable; good-looking
lyklyhode, *n.* likelihood
lyknes(se), *n.* likeness, appearance
lymme, *n.* limb
lym-meale, *adv.* limb-for-limb
lynage *n.* lineage, ancestry
lyne, *n.* line of descent
lysence, see *lycence, n.*
lyst(e), *n.* desire
lyst(e), *v.* desire, wish; please; **lyst(e),** *pa.t.*
lystened, *pp.* listened to
lystis, lystys, *n.pl.* lists, tournament arena
lytyll, *a.* few
littur, lytter, see *letter, n.*
lyve, see *leve, v.*(2) and (3); *ly(e)ff, n.*
lyvis, see *ly(e)ff, n.*
lyvelod(e), lyeffloode, *n.* livelihood, endowment, income; estates
lo, *v., interj.* behold
lode, see *lade, pp.*
loffte, *n.* sky; *(upp)on loffte,* aloft, on high
logge, *n.* lodge, house
logged, *pp.* lodged
loke, looke *v.* look; take care; **loked,** *pp.* **loke,** *pa.t.; imperative,* see that, make sure that
lokys, *n. pl.* (1) signs; (2) looks, stares; (3) locks of hair
lond, *n.* land
longe, *v.* belong, be appropriate
longe, *a.* due
longe, *adv.* for a long time; **lenger,** longer; **lengist,** longest
longys, *n.pl.* lungs
longyng, *ppl.a.* belonging
loo, see *lo, v.*
looke, see *loke, v.*
loos(e), *n.* fame, renown
loose, lese, *v.* lose; destroy; **loste,** *pp.*
lope, lopyn, see *lepe, v. pa.t.*
lorde, *n.* feudal superior and protector
lordely, *adv.* in a fashion befitting a lord
lorne, *pp.* lost
lose, see *lowse, v.*
loste, see *loose, v.*

loth(e), *a.* loath, unwilling; hateful
lotles, *a.* without harm
lough, see *lawghe, v.*
louse, see *lawse, v.*
love, luff, *n.* love, beloved; great concern
lovear, *n.* lover
lovely, *a.* loving
lovynge, *n.* praise
lowde, *a.* loud; *on lowde,* aloud, on high
lowe, *n.* hill
lowghe, see *lawghe, v.*
lowly, *adv.* with humility
lowse, louse, *v.* loose, set free
lowse, *adv.* loose
luff, see *love, n.*
lugerande, *ppl.a.* lowering, hanging
lunes, *n. pl.* jesses, short leg-straps to which a leash may be fastened
luske, *n.* slacker, lazy person
lust(e), *n.* desire; wish
lusty, *a.* vigorous; delightful

M

maade, see *make, v.*
macche, *n.* equal, match
macche, matche, *v.* fight with; equal in combat; unite in marriage
macchecolde, *pp.* machiolated, having projecting galleries at the tops of the walls
mad(e), see *make, v.*
madde, *a.* passionate
madyn, see *mayden, n.*
magré, *n.* ill-will
magré, magry, malgré, *prep.* in spite of; *magré . . . hede,* against . . . will
mayden, ma(y)dyn, *n.* virgin; girl
mayynge, mayinge, *n.* gathering of spring flowers
mayles, *n.pl.* chain mail armor, coats of mail
maymes, *n.pl.* injuries
mayné, meyny, *n.* household, group of (feudal) retainers
mayneall, *a.* domestic
maynelondis, *n.pl.* (continental) mainland
maynteyne, *v.* support, maintain
maysterlesse, *a.* masterless, powerless
maystership, *n.* mastery
maystir, mayster, *n.* master, conqueror
maystir-man, *n.* master-man, ruler
ma(y)stry, *n.* power; deed of superiority; game, contest
make, *v.* versify, write, translate; cause to happen, assemble; do; **mad(e), maade,** *pa.t.*
makeles, *a.* matchless
maker, *n.* author, poet
male *a.* evil, ill
malefortune, *n.* misfortune
malgré see *magré, prep.*
malyncoly, *n.* anger

maner, *n.* (1) manor, estate; (2) kind, nature, fashion; *in . . . maner,* in some way

manhode, *n.* valor, manliness

manly, *adv.* manfully

mannehandeled, *pp.* handled roughly

man-sleer, *n.* manslayer, murderer

mantel(l), *n.* cloak

marchall, *n.* marshal

marche, *n.;* **marchis, marchys,** *pl.* region; borderland

marche, *v.* border upon

marys, *n. genitive sg.* mare's

marys(e), *n.;* **mares,** *pl.* marsh

marke, *v.* (1) notice, target; (2) set out a boundary

marquesse, *n.* marquis, nobleman ranking below a duke but above an earl or count

marter, *n.* martyr

mased, *ppl. a.* crazed

masse-peny, *n.* a sum of money given to a priest for celebration of a requiem Mass

mastry see *ma(y)stry, n.*

matche see *macche, v.*

mater, *n.* matter; task; cause

matyns, *n.* morning prayer

meane, *n.,* **meanys,** *pl.,* means, power; strategy, efforts; mediation, intermediary

meane, mene, *v.* (1) tell, say (**mente,** *pa.t.*); (2) pity (as **meaned,** *pa.t.*)

meane, *a.* ordinary, average

meanewhyle, *n.* intervening time; same time

med(d)yll, med(d)el, *v.* mix in; join in combat; have sex; interfere

mede, *n.* reward

medlé, medly, *n.* hand-to-hand fighting

meedys, *n.pl.* meadows

megir, *a.* meager, weak; emaciated

meyny, see *mayné, n.*

meke, *v.* humble (oneself)

meke, *a.* humble, submissive; **mekar,** more submissive

mekly, *a.* humbly

membir, *n.* limb

mene, see *meane, v.* (1)

menyvere, *n.* fur trimming

mensyon, *n.* mention, record; epitaph

mente, see *meane, v.* (1)

mery, merthe, see *myr(r)y, myrthe.*

mervayle, *v.* astonish

mervayl(l)e, merveyl, *n.* wondrous thing or event; wonderment

mervayl(l)ous, mervalous, mervayles, *a. adv.* marvelous(ly), wondrous(ly); bewlidering(ly); **mervayloust, mervaylyste,** most marvelous

mervaylously, *adv.* wonderingly

mesemes, mesemythe, *v.* it seems to me

messa(y)ge, *n.* messenger; errand, business

messe, *n.* dish, meal

messynge, *n.* messenger

mesure, *n.* music; *oute of mesure,* immeasurably, unrestrainedly

mete, *n.* food

mete, *a.* (close) fitting, appropriate

mete, see *mette, v. pa.t.*

metewhyle, *n.* mealtime

methynke, *v.* it seems to me

met(t)e, *v. pa.t.* (1) dreamed; (2) met

meve, *v.* move, bring; inspire; propose

mevear, *n.* mover

mevynge, *n.* arrangement

Mychael(l)masse, *n.* festival of the archangel Michael, September 29

myckyll, mykyll, mykel, *a.* much, great; *adv.* greatly

myddys, *n.* middle

myghted, *a.* endowed with strength

mylde, *a. n.* gentle (person)

myle, *n.pl.* miles

myne, *v.* undermine

mynster, *n.* monastery church

myre, *n.* mud

myr(r)y, mery, *a.* merry; pleasant

myrroure, *n.* mirror; example

myrthe, merthe, *n.* mirth, merriment

myschevous, *a.* wicked, shameful; **myschevuste,** most wicked

myschyff, myscheffe, *n.* trouble; wickedness

myschyff, *v.* harm, bring to ruin; **myscheved,** *pp.*

myscomfort, *v.* distress (oneself)

myscreaunte, *n.* unbeliever, infidel

myssadventure, *n.* bad luck

myssaye, see *mys(se)say(e), v.*

mysse, *n.* wrong, that which is amiss

myssecreature, *n.* person of inferior belief

mys(s)ededys, *n.pl.* misdeeds; sins, trespasses

myssedo, *v.* mistreat, offend; **mysseded,** *pa.t.*

myssease, mysse-ease, *n.* ill health, disease; distress

myssefortune, *n.* ill fortune

myssefortune, *v.* subject to ill fortune

myssehappe, mysshape, *n.* mishap, unlucky incident

myssehappe, *v.* happen unfortunately

mysselyvyng, *n.* sinful life

mys(se)say(e), *v.* speak ill of, insult; **mysseseyde,** *pa.t.*

mysshape, see *myssehappe, n.*

myst(e), *v. pp. pa.t.* missed

myster, mystir, *n.* need

mo, see *mo(o), a.*

moche, see *much(e), a. adv.*

moder, modir, *n.* mother

mokkis, *n.pl.* mockery

molde, *n.* earth

mollehyllys, *n.pl.* molehills

mon, *v.* must

mone, see *mo(o)ne, n.*

monester, see *mynster, n.*

moneth-day, *n.* period until this day next month

monkys, *n.pl.* monks

mo(o), *a.* more

mo(o)ne, *n.* moan, complaint

more, *a.* larger; *adv.* again

mores, *n.pl.* moors, exposed grassland
morne-tyde, *n.* morning time
morow, *n.* morning
mourthir, mourthur, *n.* murder
moste, *a.* greatest
motis, *n.pl.* horn blasts
mountenaunce, mowntenaunce, *n.* amount; extent; duration
mourtheryng, *n.* murdering
mow(e), *v. pa.t.* may
mowyn, *pp.* mown
much(e), moche, *a.* big; many; *n.* much; *adv.* fast
muffeled, *ppl.* veiled
murtherer, *n.* murderer
murthir, *n.* murder
mutte, *v.* must

N

nayed, *v. pa.t.* drew nearer
naked, *a.* poorly dressed; unarmed; unsheathed
named, *ppl. a.* reputed
namely, *adv.* especially
nat(e), *adv.* not
natforthan, notforthan, *cj.* although; *adv.* nevertheless
naught, *adv.* not; never
navyll, *n.* navel
nawne, see *awne, a.*
ne, *cj.* nor; **ne . . . but,** nothing but; *adv.* not
nede, *v.* be necessary
nedely, *adv.* out of need
nedys, nedis, *adv.* necessarily
neyssh, *a.* soft
neyther, *a.* nether, lower; **neyther-sheete,** under-sheet
neyther, *pron.* in phrase *neyther nother,* neither one nor the other; *cj.* nor
nere, *a.,* closely related; *comparative* nearer
nere, *adv.* (1) nearly; (2) never
nerehonde, nerehande, *adv.* near at hand, soon; nearly
neve(a)w, *n.* nephew
newe, *adv.*
Newerys, *n.* New Year's
new-fangill, *a.* fickle
next(e), *a.* nearest, closest
nyce, *n.* niece
ny(e), nygh(e), *a.* near; *adv.* nearly
nyghe, *v.* (1) draw near, approach; (2) neigh (**nayed,** *pa.t.*)
nyghehonde, nyhonde, *adv.* near at hand; nearly
nyghted, *ppl. a.* benighted, concealed by night
nygromancye, *n.* necromancy, magic
nylle, *v.* will not
nymell, *a.* nimble
nys, *v.* is not
nob(e)ley, *n.* pomp, high celebration
nob(e)les, *n.* nobility

noy, *v.* annoy, aggravate; harm
noyous, *a.* annoying; harmful
noyse, *n.* rumor, scandal; opinion (of the crowd)
noyse, *v.* spread rumors about; defame; say loudly
nombir, numbir, *v.* count
none, *n.* noon
none, *pron.* neither; *a.* no; *adv.* not
northir, *a.* northern
noselynge, *adv.* headlong
notforthan see *natforthan, adv.*
nother, *pron.* neither (cf. *neyther, pron.*)
nought, *adv.* not at all
nourisshe, *v. pp.* nurse; foster
nourisshyng, *n.* upbringing, nursing
nouryture, nurture, *n.* upbringing; disipline (or arms)
nowhyle, *adv.* for no length of time
nowne, see *awne, a.*
numbir, see *nombir, v.*
nunry(e), *n.* nunnery
nurture, see *nouryture, n.*

O

o, oo, *a.* one; *prep.,* see *of, prep.*
obeysaunce, obeissaunce, *n.* rule; obedience, gesture of respect
obley, *n.* wafer
odir, see *other, a.* and *pron.*
of, *adv.* off
of(f), o, *prep.* for; about, as to, pertaining to; with; by; from; during
offenser, *n.* offender
offerynge, *n.* offertory
oftymes, *adv.* often
oynemente, *n.* healing balm
oke, *n.* oak tree
oldenes, *n.* age
olde-seyde, *ppl. a.* said of old, ancient
olyff, *n.* olive
olyvaunte, *n.* elephant
oma(y)ge, *n.* homage (see n. 6, p. 9)
onarme, *v.* unarm
on(e) *prep.* on; in; to; for; concerning; *adv.* on
on(e), *pron.* someone
oncrystynde, *ppl.a.* unchristened
ony, *a. pron.* any
onys, *adv.* once
onythynge, *n., adv.* anything; to any extent
onles(se), *cj.* unless
on-lofte, *adv.* aloft, on high
ons, see *onys, adv.*
oo, see *o, a.*
opynyon, *n.* judgment
opynly, *adv.* publicly
opynne-mowthed, *a.* talkative
or, *cj. prep.* before
ordayne, ordeyne, *v.* arrange; command

ordynaunce, *n.* ordnance, marshalling of weaponry; military gathering

ore, *n.* oar

orgule, *n.* arrogance

orgulyté, *n.* pride

orgul(o)us, *a.* arrogant, zealous; orguluste, most zealous

oryson, *n.* oration, prayer

orryble, *a.* horrible

os, see *as, cj.*

oste, *n.* host, army

ostré, ostry, *n.* lodging

other, othir, odir, *a.* other; *pron.* the other(s), each other; *cj.* either; or; *other . . . (n)other,* either . . . (n)or

othyrwayes, *adv.* otherwise

othirwhyle, *adv.* at other times

otis, *n.pl.* oats

oufte, *adv.* often

ouftyn, *adv.* often

ought, *n.* anything

ought(e), see *oute, adv., ow(gh)e, v.*

oure, owre, *n.* hour, time

oure, owre, *pron. pl. possessive* our, of us

oute, *a.* outlying

oute, ought, *adv.* out; publicly

outebrynge, *v.* bring forth

outecepte, *v.* except

outerage, *n.* excessive rage

out(e)rage, *v.* commit excesses

outerageousnes, *n.* reckless aggression

outetake, *v.* except

outetake, *prep.* except for

outewarde, *adv.* outwardly

overall, *adv.* very

overcast, *v. pa.t.* tangled about

overcharged, *v.pa.t.* overbore

over-evenynge *n.* yesterday evening

overfallen, *pp.* overcome

overgete, *v.* overtake

overgovernyd, *pp.* ruled

overheled, *ppl. a.* covered

overlad, *pp.* oppressed

over-largely, *adv.* overgenerously

overleder, *n.* overlord

overlepe, *v.* skip over; digress

overlonge, *prep.* along

overmacche, *v.* overwhelm

overpasse, *v.* pass

overren(ne), *v.* overrun

overryde, *v.* overrun; harry; overredyn, *pp.*

oversayne, *ppl.a.* proved wrong

oversé, *v.* read over; make sure

over-shyte,-shete *n.* upper sheet

overslyppe, *v.* pass

overt(h)wart(e), ovirtwarte, *a.* crosswise; contrary, backhanded; *prep.* across; *adv.* crosswise

overthwartely, *adv.* askew

overtwart(e), see *overt(h)wart(e)*

ovirbledde, *ppl. a.* covered with blood

owchys, *n.pl.* decorative clasps

ow(gh)e, awghe, *v.* own; owe; ought(e), *pa.t.*

owre, see *oure, n.*

o(w)ther, owthyr, othir, see *other, cj.*

P

paale, *a.* pale

pace, paas(e), *n.* (1) pace; *a . . . pace,* at high speed; (2) pass, passage

pageaunte, *n.* role, scene

pagis, *n.pl.* pageboys

paye, *v.* satisfy; pay

paylet, *n.* mattress; paylattes, *pl.*

payn(e), *n.* penalty; effort

payne, *v.* trouble (oneself)

paynym, *n.* pagan

paytrels, *n.pl.* breastplates for horses

palferey, *n.* saddle horse

palyse, *n.* palace

palle, *n.* fine cloth

paltokkys, *n.pl.* short coats

pappis, *n.pl.* breasts, nipples

parage, *n.* peerage, rank

paramour(e), *n.* lover

paramour(s), *adv.* as a lover

pardé, perde(us), *interj.* by God, indeed

parelous, see *perelous, adv.*

parfyte, perfite, *a.* (morally) perfect

parler, *n.* parlor

parte, *n.* share, portion; duty

parte, *v.* go, depart

parté, party, *n.* region, side; group; circumstance

parter, *n.* marshal

passe, *v.* surpass, go beyond; escape, go away; pass judgment; paste, *pa.t.*

passyng(e), passyngly, *adv.* surpassingly, exceedingly

patryarkys, *n.* patriarchs

pauper, paupir, *n.* paper

paveloun, pavelyon, pavilon, pavylon, *n.* pavilion, grand tent, military tent

pavilys, *n.* tent

pe(a)ce, pyce, *n.* piece; *at all pecis,* fully armed

peas, see *pees, n.*

pease, *v.* pacify

peasab(e)ly, pesiblé, *adv.* in peace

pece, see *pe(a)ce, n.*

peere, pere, p(y)ere, *n.* peer, equal

pees, peas, py(e)se, *n.* (1) peace, silence (*so as interj.*); (2) vessel

penowne, *n.* battle flag

pensell, *n.* narrow banner borne on a lance

pensiff, pensyff, *a.* thoughtful

Pentecoste, *n.,* see n. 1, p. 10

pera(d)venture, *adv.* perhaps

perclose, *n.* enclosure

perde(us), see *pardé, interj.*

pere, see *peere, n.*

pereles, *a.* peerless, without equal

perelest, see *perelous, a.*

perelys, perelles, *n.pl.* pearls

perell(e), *n.* peril, danger; risk of losing salvation

perelous, parelous, perelles, perellus, perleous(e), *a.* perilous, dangerous, intimidating; **perelest**, most dangerous

perfay, *interj.* by my faith

perfite, see *parfyte, a.*

perische, perish, peryssh, *v.* destroy

perleous(e), see *perelous, a.*

perowne, perron, *n.* signal block of stone

pesiblé, see *peasab(e)ly, adv.*

pesyble, *a.* peaceable

peté, see *pité, n.*

peteuous, *a.* pitiful

philozopher, phylozopher, *n.* learned man

pyce, see *pe(a)ce, n.*

pycch, *v.* pitch

py(c)ke, *v.* take (oneself)

piereles, p(y)ereles, pyerles, see *pereles, a.*

p(y)ere, see *peere, n.*

pyese, see *pees, n.*

pyesemealys, *n.pl.* pieces

pyght(e), *v. pa.t.* pitched, erected; thrust

pyke, see *pycke, v.*

pykyll, *n.* sauce

pylde, *v. pa.t.* pulled

pylle, *v.* plunder

pyllour(e), *n.* pillager

pyloure, *n.* pillar

pynche, *v.* bite

pirvey, see *purvey, v.*

pyse, see *pees, n.*

pité, peté, *n.* pity

piteuously, pyteuously, *adv.* pitiably

play, *n.*(1) wound (2) pastime, play

play(e), *v.* pass the time; join in

playne, *a. adv.* open(ly), honest(ly), regular(ly)

playne, *v.* complain, protest

plesaunce, *n.* pleasure

plenoure, *adv.* with the full number

plyght(e), *v.* pledge

plyte, *n.* plight

plumpe, *n.* block, clump

poynte, *n.* part; *at all poyntis,* in every respect

poynte, *v.* care for

poyntelynge, *adv.* point first

poyntemente, *n.* arrangement; appointment

poysen, *v.* poison

ponyshemente, *n.* punishment

porely, *a.* of poor manufacture

porte, *n.* gate

portecoly(e)s, portcolyse, *n.* sliding grille of a gateway

porter, *n.* gatekeeper

postels, *n.pl.* apostles

posterne, postren, *n.* gate

potestate, *n.* potentate, independent ruler

pouder, *n.* powder, ashes

poure, *a.* poor

pousté, *n.* power

power, *n.* army; ability

powse, *n.* pulse

pray, *n.* prize

prece, pre(e)s, prease, *n.* press of battle, congregation (in combat)

prece, prese, *v.* press; compel

precessour, *n.* predecessor

pre(e)st(e), *n.* priest; *preste-ermyte,* hermit priest

preff, see *preve, v.*

prefyxte, *ppl.a.* prearranged

preson, *v.* imprison

presonment, *n.* imprisonment

prestly, *adv.* eagerly

pretende, *v.* extend

prevayle, *v.* avail, help

preva(y)y, prevely, pryvaly, pryvely, *adv.* privately, secretly; with constraint

preve, preff, prove, *v.* prove, put to the test; establish (the genuineness of), determine; attempt; demonstrate; learn by experience

preved, proved, *ppl.a.* proven, established; well-tried

prevely, see *preva(y)ly, adv.*

prevy, pryvy, pryvé, *a.* secret, confidential; **pryvyst**, most secret

prevydence, *n.* advance vision

prevys, *n.pl.* proof

prevyté, *n.* privacy, secret contents

pryce, pryse, *n.* prize, first place; honor

pryce, *a.* excellent

prycke, *v.* spur, ride on

prycker, *n.* horseman

pryme, *n.* first hour of the day (see n. 4, p. 86)

pryory, *n.* priory, monastery or convent governed by a prior or prioress

pryse, see *pryce, n.*

pryste, *n.* priest

pryvaly, pryvely, see *preva(y)ly, adv.*

pryvy, pryvé, see *prevy, a.*

proces, *n.* due course

procurour, *n.* procurator, manager

proferre, *v.* prefer, promote

prof(f)yr, profer, *v.* offer, proffer

profir, profyr, *n.* offer

pronosticacion, *n.* prognostication, prediction

proues(se), *n.* prowess, valor; deed of arms

prove, proved, see *preve, v.; preved, ppl.a.*

provydence, *n.* providing

provisions, *n.* provision

puyssaunce, *n.* power, might; ability

purfyl, *v.* trim; **purfilde**, *pp.*

purphile, *n.* trimming

purpose, *v.* intend (oneself)

pursyvauntis, *n.pl.* heralds

purvey, pirvey, *v.* arrange, prepare (oneself); ordain, assign

purveyde, *ppl.a.* prepared; provided

purv(e)yaunce, purveyans, *n.* arrangements; provisions

pusell, pusyll, *n.* virgin

put, *v.* knock; push; entrust; **putt,** *pp.*; **put(te),** *pa.t.*

Q

quarel(l), *n.* (1) dispute; cause; (2) short arrow
quarters, *n.pl.* hips
quene, quy(e)ne, *n.* queen
quere, quyre, *n.* choir of a chapel, chancel
queste, *n.* inquest
queste, *v.* yelp, bark
questyng, *n.* barking (see n. 9, p. 31)
quycke, quyk, *a.* alive
quy(e)ne, see *quene, n.*
quyre, see *quere, n.*
quyte, *v.,* **quytte,** *pp.* repay, take vengeance on; acquit oneself
quyte, *adv.* quite, completely
quyt(t)e, *a.* free, unhindered; acquitted

R

race, rasse, *v.* (1) strip (off), snatch (off); (2) rush
rack, rake, *n.* feeding rack
rad, *v. pa.t.* read
rafe, *v. pa.t.* tore
raffte, *v. pa.t.* bereft, deprived
rag(e)ynge, *n.* raging, passion
rayed, *ppl.a.* dressed
rayge, *n.* rage, passion
rayke, *v.* go
rayle, *v.* (1) rail, speak mockingly; (2) gush down, flow
rayne, *n.* rein
rayne, *v.* reign, rule
raynke, see *ren(c)k, n.*
rak(e), see *rack, n.*
random, see *ra(u)ndom, n.*
range, *v. pa.t.* rang, resounded
ranke, *a.* strong
ransake, see *rensake, v.*
rase, *v.* slash, raze, obliterate
rasse, see *race, v.*
rasure, *n.* obliteration
rate, *v.* berate
rathly, *adv.* quickly
raught(e), *v. pp. pa.t.* reached, caught, struck
raumpe, *v.* trample ragefully
ra(u)ndom, rawndom, *n.* violence
raunge, *n.* tournament ground
raunsom, *v.* hold for ransom
ravyshe, *v.* fetch
rea(u)me, *n.* realm
rebounde, *v.* echo
rebuke, *n.* shame
rebuke, *v.* defeat, hurt; put to shame, insult
rebukyng, *n.* repulse
rechace, *n.* (horn-call signaling) the driving back of the deer into the forest

reche, *v.* reach, extend to
recke, rek, *v.* care, be concerned with; **rought,** *pa.t.*
recommaunde, *v.* commend
recountir, recounter, *n.* (military) encounter
recountir, *v.* meet
recover, recovir, *n.* recovery (from hardship); escape, way out
recover, recovir, *v.* gain, regain; restore, correct; retreat
recr(e)ayed, recr(e)ayde, *ppl.a.* recreant, craven; having the condition of an abject coward
recreaunte, *a.* recreant, craven
rede, *n.* advice
rede, *a.* red
rede, *v.* advise
redy, rydy, *a.* fast; ready
redyly, *adv.* suddenly; readily
redouted, *ppl.a.* dreaded
redresse, *v.* improve; relieve; stand (oneself) up
reed, *adv.* in red
reest, reyste, *n.* rest (for a lance or spear, on the saddle)
refygowred, *ppl. a.* restored to vigor
refreysshe, *v.* assist; brace
refresshynge, *n.* refreshment
regeaunte, *ppl.a.* regent, ruling
regne, *v.* reign
rehersall, *n.* retelling
rehers(e), reherce, *v.* relate, retell
reygne, *n.* rein
reyse, *v.* raise, lift up; gladden
reyste, see *reest, n.*
rejoyse, *v.* enjoy; possess
rek, see *recke, v.*
rekeyst(e), *n.* request; disposition
rekles, *n.* recluse
rele, *v.* reel (back)
rele(a)ce, rele(a)s, *v.* release; exonerate
releve, *v.* relieve; rally; revive
remanaunte, remenaunte, remanent, *n.* remainder, (the) rest
remedy(e), *v.* restore, cure
remeve, *v.* remove, retreat, leave
renayne, *v.* disown
ren(c)ke, raynke, *n.* man, warrior, knight
rencountre, *n.*
renke, see *ren(c)ke, n.*
ren(ne), *v.* run; **renne,** *pp.*; **ronne,** *pa.t.*; **rennynge,** running
reno(w)med, *ppl.a.* renowned
rensake, ransake, *v.* search; examine the wounds of
rente, *v.* tear apart
rentes, *n.pl.* revenues
repayre, repeyre, *v.* dwell; resort, return
repeyre, *n.* resort
repente, *v.* regret; repent
replenysshed, *ppl.a.* filled
reporte, *v.* appeal for confirmation
repreff, *n.* shame

repreve, *v.* blame, reprove
rere, *v.* rear, raise
rere-brace, *n.* upper-arm armor
reremayne, *n.* backhand blow
rerewarde, *n.* rearguard
resceyve, ressayve, resseyve, *v.* receive; accept
rescowe, *n.* rescuer
rescowe, reskow, *v.* rescue
rescows, *n.* (opportunity for) rescue
resyne, *v.* hand over
reskow, see *rescowe, v.*
reson, *n.* reason; reasonable conduct
resortis, *n. pl.* visits
ressayve, see *resceyve, v.*
resseite, resseyte, *n.* lodging; reinforcements
rether, *adv.* rather
retynew, *n.* retinue
retorne, see *returne, v.*
retray, *v.* retreat
returne, retorne, *v.* turn; turn away; return
reule, *v.* rule, govern
rever, *n.* river
revers, *adv.* backwards
rew, rowe, *n.* row, order, succession
rewarde, *v.* award
rewe, *v.* have pity, take pity on; grieve; **ruys, r(e)wyth,** 3 *sg.*
ryall, *a.* royal; magnificent; **ryally,** *adv.*
ryalté, see *r(o)yalty, n.*
rychelyar, *adv.* more richly
rychesse, *n.* riches, treasure
rydge, *n.* backbone
rydy, see *redy, a.*
ryghtes, *n. pl.* (1) in phrase *at all . . . ryghtes,* in every respect; (2) last rights
ryght, *v.* correct, set right
ryght, *adv.* very; correctly
ryght(e)uouse, *a.* righteous, just
righteuously, *adv.* correctly, rightfully
rightwys, ryghtwos, *a.* rightful
ryme, *n.* poem
rynde, *n.* bark
ryvage, *n.* shore
ryve, *v.* stab; split; tear; **roofe, rooff(e), rove, roff,** *pa.t.*
roche, *n.* rock
r(o)yalté, *n.* magnificence
royam(m)e, *n.* realm
rolled, *ppl.a.* enrolled
rollys, *n.pl.* rolls, lists of soldiers
rome, *n.* confines; room
rome, *v.* (1) roar (**romyng(e),** roaring); (2) go
ronne, see *ren(ne), v.*
Roode, *n.* Cross
roofe, rooff(e), see *ryve, v.*
rosshe, see *russhe, v.*
rosteled, *v. pa.t.* fell
rotyn, *a.* rotten
rought, see *recke, v.*
route, rought(e), *n.* band (of warriors)
r(o)uthe, *n.* pity

rove, see *ryve, v.*
rowe, see *rew, n.*
rowgh, *a.* rough, boisterous; **rowghly,** *adv.*
rowysshe, see *russhe, v.*
rude, *a.* violent
rudely, *adv.* roughly; loudly
ruffler, *a.* more sorrowful
ruys, see *rewe, v.*
rule, *n.* control; authority
rule, *v.* direct, control, conduct (oneself)
russhe, rowysshe, rosshe, *v.* rush (down); pull; knock down
ruthe, see *r(o)uthe, n.*
rwyth, see *rewe, v.*

S

sable, *n.* expensive fur
sable, sabyl(l) *a.* heraldic black
sad(de), *a.* valiant; heavy, grievous
sadly, *adv.* soundly; fully
saff, see *sauff, prep.*
say, *v.* try, test; prove
say(e)(nge), see *sey, v.*
sakarynge, sakerynge, *n.* consecration (of the bread and wine of the Eucharist)
sale, *n.* hall
salew, *v.* welcome, salute
salve, salff, *n.* remedy; salve, healing balm
salve, *v.* anoint
same, *adv.* in same, together
samyte, *n.* rich silk
sarezen, saresyn, sarysen, saryson, *n.* saracen (see n. 6, p. 27)
sarpis, *n.pl.* chains
sauff, save, *v.* save, keep
sauf(f), *adv.* safely
sauff, saff, *prep.* except for, save
sauffconduyghte, *n.* guarantee of safe conduct
sauffgarde, *n.* custody
saufté, *n.* safety
saulter, *n.* psalter
saunz, *prep.* without
savely, *adv.* safely
savyté, *n.* safety
Saveoure, *n.* Savior, Christ
savour(e), *n.* aroma, scent
savoure, *v.* give off a foul smell
saw, see *se, v.*
sawdon, see *sowdon, n.*
sawe, *n.* saying; word; message
sawte, *n.* assault
scape, *v.* escape
scaryng, *ppl.a.* terrifying
scarlet, *n.* scarlet cloth
scathe, *n.* injury
scawberd, scawberte, scawbard, *n.* scabbard, sheath
scholde, see *shold(e), v. pa.t.*
sclaundir, sclawndir, *n.* slander
scole, *n.* school

scomfyte, *v.* defeat

score, *n.* twenty

scowte-wacche, *n.* sentinel

scripture, *n.* inscription

se, *v.* see; look; *lat se,* let us see; **seyth,** 3 *sg. pres.;* **seyne,** *pp.;* **se(y), sy(e), sygh(e),** saw, *pret.*

sease, see *cese, v.*

se(a)son, *n.* opportunity; right time

sece, see *cese, v.*

secrete, *adv.* confidentially

sedull, *n.* short letter

se(e), *n.* sea

se(e)ge, see *syege, n.*

seek, see *seke, a.*

se(e)kene, *v.* sicken, become ill

sey, say, *v.* say; tell: **saynge, seyynge,** *pres. participle;* **seth, seyth,** 3 *sg. pres.;* **seyde,** *pp.* and *pa.t.*

seyght, *n.* scene, sight

seyne, *ppl.a.* seen, manifest

sey(ne), see *se, v.*

seynge, *n. take seynge* take seisin, take legal possession

seynte, *n.* saint

seynte, *a.* holy

seyth, see *se, v.*

segynge, *n.* besieging

sege, *n.* seat

seke, syke, *v.* seek; search out; advance against; make way **sought,** *pp.;* **sought(e),** *pa.t.*

seke, seek, syke, *a.* sick, ill

sekene, see *se(e)kene, v.*

selff, *a.* same

semb(e)launte, *n.* appearance; pretense

semble, *a.* dissembling, fraudulent

seme, *v.* seem, appear; think

semely, *a.* seemly, good-looking

semyng(e), *n.* appearance; thinking

senatoure, *n.* senator, senior Roman official

send, *v. pa.t.* sent

sendele, sendell, *n.* rich silk

senceall, sencial, senesciall, *n.* seneschal, steward, head administrative official

sengly, *adv.* singly, unaccompanied

sensar, senser, *n.* censer, incense vessel

senshyp, see *shendeshyp, n.*

septure, *n.* scepter

serch(e), cerche, *v.* search (for); find out; examine medically

sere, *v.* wrap in waxed cloth

sere, *a.* dry; withered

sertayne, *n.* certainty; certain number; *adv.* certainly

sertaynté, *n.* certainty

sertes, serteyse, *adv.* certainly, indeed

servayge, *n.* servitude

serve, *v.* serve; treat; allow

servyse, *n.* service; serving staff; church service; homage

servyture, *n.* servitor, attendant

sese, see *cese, v.*

seson, see *se(a)son, n.*

seteled, *pp.* seated

seth, see *sey, v.*

sette, *v.* bestow, send; assign; care; be disposed; **sette,** *pp.;* **set(te),** *pa.t.*

setthen, see *sytthen, adv.*

sevennyght, *n.* week

severally, *adv.* one after the other

sew(e), cewe, *v.* follow, pursue; sue; **swith,** imperative

sewear-cheyff, *n.* chief server

sewte, *n.* attendance at court; matching appearance; manner of dress

shafftemonde, *n.* hand span (six to eight inches)

shake, *n.* pace

shapyn, *ppl.a.* shaped, formed

shappe, *n.* shape, form

shap(p)e, *v.* shape, form; aim a blow; **shope,** *pa.t.*

sharpe, *a.* bitter, harsh

shawe, *n.* edge

she(a)rte, shurte, *n.* (under)shirt

shende. *v.* destroy, ruin; **shente,** *pp.*

shendeshyp, senshyp, *n.* disgrace

shene, *a.* bright; well-formed

sherys, *n.pl.* shears

sherpe, *a.* sharp

shete, *n.* sheet

shet(t), *v. pa.t.* shut

shevalry, see *chyvalry, n.*

shewed, *v.* show, reveal

shewyng, *n.* appearance

shylde, chylde, *n.* shield

shipbourde, *n.* in phrase *on the shipbourde,* on board ship

shyperdis, *n.pl.* shepherds

shirly, *adv.* shrilly

shyvalere, *n.* knight

shyver, *n.* splinter

shold(e), scholde, *v. pa.t.* would; could; should

sholdir, see *shulder, n.*

shooke, *v. pa.t.* departed

shope, see *shap(p)e, v.*

shorne, *pp.* cut through

shorte, *a. adv.* curtly

shortecomyng, *n.* deficient welcome

short(e)ly, *adv.* promptly

shoter, *n.* shooter

shotynge, *pres. participle* shooting

shotte, *v. pa.t.* launched

shovyn, *pp.* shoved, launched

showre, *n.* shower; conflict

shrede, *v.* cut

shrewde, shrewed. *a.* dangerous; mischievous

shrew(e), *n.* dangerous one; villain

shryche, *n.* shriek

shryke, *v.* shriek

shryve, *v.* confess

shulder, sholdir, *n.* shoulder

shunte, *v.* dodge

shurte: see *she(a)rte, n.*

sybbe, *n*. kin, blood relative
syde-bourd, *n*. side table
sydelynge, *adv*. sideways
sy(e), sie, see *se, v*.
sy(e)ge, se(e)ge, *n*. seat; siege
sygh(e), see *se, v*.
syeth, *v*. 3 *sg. pres.* sighs
sygamoure, *n*. sycamore
sygne, *n*. sign, token; coat of arms
sygnyfycacion, *n*. sign; symbol
signyfye, *v*. compare symbolically
syke, see *seke, a.* and *v*.
syker, *a*. sure, certain; trusty
sykerly, *adv*. surely, thoroughly
sykernesse, *n*. surety, agreement
sykynge, *n*. search, seeking
sylden, *adv*. seldom
syler, *n*. canopy
symple, *a*. poor; feeble; trivial; **symplyst**, lowest-ranking
syn(e), *prep. cj. adv.* since, afterwards
synles, *adv*. guiltless
syns, *adv*. since
syrrys, *n.pl.* sirs
syses, *n.pl.* musical pitches
sytte, *v*. withstand; sit; **syttande**, sitting
syt(t)h(e), sith, *adv*. since; afterwards
sytthen, sytthyn, setthen, *adv. cj.* since then; then
skyffte, *n*. effort; dealing
skyffte, *v*. settle; divide
skyfte, *a*. rid
skymme, *v*. skim, survey quickly
slad(e), *n*. valley; glade
slake, *v*. slacken
sle(e), *v*. slay, kill; **sleyth**, 3 *sg. pres.*; **slow(ghe), slew**, *pa.t.*
sleynge, *n*. slaying, killing
slente, *v*. slant
slepe, *n*. sleep
slepe, *v. pa.t.* slept
sleve, see *sl(y)eve, n*.
slew, see *sle(e), v*.
sl(y)eve, slyve, *n*. sleeve
slyght, *n*. sleight of hand
slyly, *adv*. skillfully; secretly
slypped, *ppl.a.* directed
slyve, see *sl(y)eve, n*.
slo(o)de, *v. pa.t.* slid
slow(ghe), see *sle(e), v*.
sloughis, *n.pl.* swampy lowlands
small, smale, *a*. fine; small
smyte, *v*. strike; impress; **smyte, smytten, smeten**, *pp.*; **smote**, *pret.*
so(o), *cj. adv.* so long as; then; now; as
soc(c)our, *n*. help
sodde, *pp.* boiled
soddeyn, *a*. sudden
soffte, see *so(u)ffte, a*.
soyle, *n*. wallowing place; soil, land
solempnité, *n*. solemnity, ceremony
som, *a*. some

som, *n*., see *som(me), n*.
somen, *v*. summon
somer, *n*. summer
somever, see *whatsomever, pron.* and *a*.
som(me), *n*. sum, number
somo(u)ns, *n*. summons
somtyme, *adv*. sometimes; once
sondys, *n.pl.* sands, shores
sondis, *n.pl.* messengers
sondismen, *n.pl.* messengers
sondry, *a*. different, separate
sone, *adv*. soon, quickly
sonnebeame, *n*. sunbeam
sonne, sunne, *n*. son
sonner, sunner, *adv*. sooner; **sonneste**, soonest
soo, see *so, cj. adv*.
soppe, *n*. dipped bread
sore, *adv*. deeply, violently
sorou, sorow, *n*. sorrow
sorseres, sorseras, *n*. sorceress
sorte, *n*. band, group
soth(e), *n*. truth
soth(e), *a*. true
sotte, *n*. sot, fool
so(u)ffte, *a*. soft, easy; steady
sought(e), see *seke, v*.
soupe, sowpe, *v*. sup, dine
souper, *n*. supper
sowde, *v*. adhere, reunite
sowdyar, *n*. (paid) soldier
sowdon, sowdan, sawdon, *n*. sultan
sowghe, *n*. rushing sound
sowghe, see *swow(gh)e, n*.
sowne, *n*. (1) sound; (2) swoon
sowne, *v*. swoon
sownynge, *ppl.a.* swooning
sowpe, see *soupe, v*.
sowsed, *pa.t.* soused, drenched
space, *n*. space of time
sparde, *v. pa.t.* barred
Spaynardis, *n.pl.* Spaniards
spaynell, *n*. spaniel
spare, see *spirre, v*.
spare, *v*. desist
sparhawke, *n*. sparrowhawk
speache, *n*. speech
spede, *n*. help
spede, spyede, *v*. succeed; fare; help; dispatch, consume; **spedde**, *pp.*
spedfull, *a*. fast-moving
spend, *v*. make use of
spendynge, *n*. provision for expenses
spere, see *spirre, v*.
speretes, *n.pl.* spirits
spette, *v. pa.t.* spat
spycery, *n*. spices
spyede, see *spede, v*.
spyyng, *n*. spying, observation
spyndyll, spyndel, *n*. spindle
spynnesse, *n.pl.* pinnaces, small escort boats
spiritualités, *n. pl.* consecrated ground

spirre, spyrre, spurre, spare, spere, *v.* inquire, ask; find out

spite, *n.* injury, wrong

spyteuous, *a.* contemptuous

spiteuously, *adv.* angrily; without pity

spore, *n.* spur

spore, *v.* spur

sporte, *v.* enjoy oneself

sprynge, *v.* spring; reveal; **spronge,** *pp.*

spurre, see *spirre, v.*

square, *a.* of square cross-section

squyar, *n.* squire, apprentice knight

sqwatte, *v. pa.t.* squashed

stabely, *adv.* firmly

stablisshe, stab(e)lysshe, *v.* establish; stabilize; set in office

stack, see *stake, v. pa.t.*

stadde, *ppl.a.* beset

stayre-foote, *n.* foot of the stairs

stake, stack, *v. pa.t.* stuck; joined

stakir, *v.* stagger

stale, *n.* body of warriors

stale, *v. pa.t.* stole

stalke, *n.* stalking of game

standarde, (heraldic) flag

stange, *v. pa.t* stung.; **stonge,** *pp.*

starke, sterke, *a.* thorough; *adv.* thoroughly, plainly

starte: see *sterte, v.*

staunche, *v.* stanch

stavys, *n.pl.* staves, clubs

ste(a)vyn, *n.* assignation; occasion

stede, *n.* (1) stead, place; (2) (also **styede**) steed, warhorse

steyrred, see *stir(r)e, v.*

stelyd, *ppl. a.* steeled, made of steel

steppynge, *v. pres. participle* advancing

stere, see *stir(r)e, v.*

sterke, see *starke*

sterne, *a.* stern, strong; grim

sterris, *n.pl.* stars

sterte, *v.* start, rush, jump, advance ; **sterte, starte,** *pret.*

steven, *n.* voice

stevyn, see *ste(a)vyn, n.*

styede, see *stede, n.* (2)

styew, *n.* heated bathhouse

styff, *a.* strong

styke, *v.* slaughter

stylle, *adv.* still, quiet; always, continuously

stylly, *adv.* quietly

stynte, *n.* value

stynte, *v.* stop, cease; **stynte,** *pret.*

stir(r)e, steyrre, stere, *v.* stir, move, urge; steer

stirre, *n.* star

stonde, *v.* withstand (from); stand; remain; **stonde,** *pp.;* **stoode,** *pa.t.*

stone, see *sto(o)ne, v.*

stonge, see *stange, v. pa.t.*

stoode, see *stonde, v.*

stoolyn, *pp.* stolen, snuck

sto(o)ne, *v.* stun; crush

stoupe, stowpe, *v.* stoop, bend

stoure, stowre, *n.* battle, conflict

stoute, *a.* stern

stoutly, *adv.* vigorously

stowpe, see *stoupe, v.*

stowre, see *stoure, n.*

straike, see *stryke, v.*

strayne, *v.* exert

strayte, strete, streyt(e), streyghte, *a.*, narrow; severe, hard; *adv.* straight; directly; strictly; severely

strayt(e)ly, *adv.* strictly, severely

strake, *n.* hunting-horn signal of success or failure; *v.* to produce such a signal

strake, see *stryke, v.*

straunge, *a.* unknown, foreign, exotic

straunger, *n.* stranger

stredys, see *stryddys, n.pl.*

streyghte, streyt(e), see *strayte, a. adv.*

streke, strekyn, see *stryke, v.*

stre(y)me, *n.* stream, current, sea

strendus, *n.pl.* streams

strene, *n.* strain, family

strenge, *n.* leash

strenger, strengyst, see *stronge, a.*

strength, *n.* stronghold

strengthe, *v.* enforce; support

strete, *n.* street

strete, see *strayte, a. adv.*

stryddys, stredys, *n. pl.* strides

stryff, *n.* strife

stryke, *v.* strike; fight; **strykyn, strekyn,** *pp.;* **stra(i)ke, stroke, streke, strekyn,** *pa.t*

stroke, see *stryke, v.*

stronde, *n.* strand, shore

stronge, *a.* (1) strong; arduous, heavy; **strenger,** stronger; **strengyst,** strongest; (2) strange

strongely, *adv.* violently

strooff, *v. pa.t.* strove, fought

study, *n.* condition of thought

stuff(e), *n.* forces; (military) provisions

stuff(e), *v.* furnish for defense with men and provisions

subjette, sudgette, *n.* subject

subtylé, see *suttelly, adv.*

subtyle, see *suttyle, a.*

sudgette, see *subjette, n.*

suerd, see *swerd, n.*

suffer, suffir, suffyr, *v.* allow, permit; be patient with, endure

sufferaunce, *n.* forbearance

sufferynge, *ppl.a.* patient

suffyse, *v.* provide for

suffrygan, *n.* bishop

suggeourne, *v.* sojourn, remain

sundir, *n.* in phrase *in sundir,* asunder, apart, at a distance

sundry, see *sondry, a.*

sunne, see *sonne, n.*

sunner, see *sonner, adv.*

suppyngis, *n.pl.* food to sip, broth

suppose, *v.* believe; think
suraunce, *n.* assurance
sure, *a.* secure, safe; reliable; *adv.* certainly; safely
surely, *adv.* securely; well
sureté, *n.* assurance of safety or reparations; assurance of getting
surmyse, *v.* surplice, loose-fitting white gown
sursynglys, *n.pl.* saddle-girths
sustayne, *v.* support
suttelyté, *n.* subtle ability
suttelly, subtylé, *adv.* skillfully
suttyle, subtyle, *a.* skillful, subtle
swall, *v. pa.t.* swelled
swalowe, *n.* whirlpool
swamme, *v. pa.t.* floated
swange, *v. pa.t.* pulled
swappe, *v.* strike
sware, *v. pa.t* swore
swarffe, *n.* ground
swarve, *v.* swerve
swerd, suerd, *n.* sword
swettest, *a.* sweetest
swettnes, *n.* sensation of rapture
swevyn, *n.* dream
swith, see *sew(e), v.*
swoghe, see *swow(gh)e, n.*
swone, *n.* swoon
sworne, *pp.* made to swear an oath
swow(gh)e, swoghe, swoughe, sowghe, *n.* swoon

T

tabours, *n.pl.* tabors, drums
tacchis, tacchys, *n.pl.* qualities, traits, habits
tay, *n.* outer membrane
tay, tey, *v.* tie
take, *v.* take; strike; receive; understand; betake oneself; imprison; **takyn, tane,** *pp.;* **toke, took,** *pa.t.*
takyn, *ppl.a.* set
tale, *n.* tally, count; false story
talente, *n.* desire
talis, *n.pl.* tales
tame, *v.* pierce, injure; damage
tane, see *take, v.*
tapir, *n.* taper, slender candle
tar(r)y, tarye, *v.* dwell; wait, stay; delay; **tarrynge,** *pres. participle*
tatyrs, *n.pl.* tatters
teche, *v.* direct; teach; **taughte,** *pp.*
tey, see *tay, v.*
te(i)the, *n.pl.* teeth
tempte, *v.* test
tene, *n.* suffering
terme, *n.* duration; appointment; term, time-span
than, *a. cj.* then; when; *be than,* by the time, by that time

that, *pron. a.* that which, that, what; who, whom
that, *cj.* so that, such that; because; unless
the, *pron.* thee, thyself
theffis, *n.pl.* thieves
thens, thence, from there
theras, see *ther(e)as, adv. cj.*
there, *a. possessive* their
ther(e), *adv.* there; where
thereaf(f)tir, *adv.* afterwards; in accord
thereagaynste, *adv.* in return
ther(e)as, *adv. cj.* there; where; whereas
therefor(e), *adv.* for that reason; thereto
theretyll, *adv.* to that; concerning that
therewithall, *adv.* thereupon
therto, *adv.* concerning that; moreover
thycke, *a.* powerful
thycke, *adv.* powerfully; intensely
thyder, *adv.* thither, (to) there
thyes, *n.pl.* thighs
thynge, *n. pl.* things
thynke, *v.* seem; imagine, think of; discover; **thought,** *pa.t. pp.*
thirle, thryle, *v.* pierce; flow
thirstelew, *a.* thirsty
this, thys, *a. pron.* these
tho, *adv.* then
tho(o), *a. pron.* those
thorne, *n.* hawthorne tree
thorowborne, *pp.* run through, pierced
thorow(e), thorugh, *prep. adv.* through; by way of; because of
thorowoute, *prep. adv.* through; because of
thorugh, see *thorow(e), prep. and adv.*
thought, *n.* worry, anxiety
thought, see *thynke, v.*
thralle, *n.* bondage
thrange, *n.* throng (of fighting knights)
thrange, *v. pa.t.* pressed, forced
thredys, *n.pl.* threads
threst(e), *v. pa.t.* thrust (into); **thriste,** *pp.*
thretyng(e), *n.* threatening
thryle, see *thirle, v.*
throoff, *v. pa.t.* throve, prospered
throtis, *n.pl.* throats
throwe, *pp.* thrown
throwys, *n.pl.* throes, violent attacks of pain
thrumbelyng, *adv.* compressing
tyde, *n.* time
tyde, *v.* betide, befall
tyll, *v.* tell
tyll(e), *prep.* to; unto
tyme, *n.*
tyraunte, see *tirraunte, n.*
tyred, *ppl.a.* armed, equipped
tirraunte, tyr(r)aunte, *n.* tyrant
tyssew, *n.* tissue
tytil, *n.* title, claim
to, *adv.* too, also
to, *prep.* at; against; until; for; of; in order to; according to; comparable to
to, see *to(o), a.*

to-bete, *v. pa.t.* beaten
to-braste, *v. pa.t. pp.* burst apart, shattered
to-cracched, *ppl.a.* deeply scratched
todir, see *tother, a. pron.*
to-dryve, *v.* break apart
tofore, toforne, *prep., cj., adv.* before, in front of; beforehand; previously; until
toforetyme, *adv.* previously
toforne, *adv,* see *tofore*
tofornehande, toforehonde, *adv.* beforehand
togedyrs, togidirs, togydyr, *adv.* together
to-hew, *v. pa.t.* cut to pieces
toke, see *take, v.*
tokenynge, *n.* sign
tokyn, *n.* token; symbolism
tombe, see *to(u)mbe, n.*
tomorne, *adv.* tomorrow
tone, *a. pron.* one (of two)
to(o), *a.* two
took, see *take, v.*
toolys, *n.pl.* weapons
to-rongeled, *ppl.a.* wrinkled
toryn, *pp.* torn apart
to-rove, *v. pa.t.;* **to-ryven,** *pp.* riven, split apart
to-shevir, *v.* shatter
to-tatered, *ppl.a.* thoroughly tattered
tother, todir, *a. pron.* other (of two or more)
to(u)mbe, towmbe, tumbe, *n.* tombe
tourcheis, *n.pl.* torches
tour(e), *n.* (fortified) tower
tourneye, *v.* participate in a tournament
to(u)rnoye, *n.* tournament
toward(e), *prep. adv.* supporting
towche, *v.* touch; reach; be concerned with
towmbe, see *to(u)mbe, n.*
trace, *n.* track
traced, *v. pa.t.* tracked
trade, *v. pa.t.* trod
tray, *n.* pain
trayle, *v.* trickle
trayne, *n.* (1) train of a dress; (2) enticement
tra(y)toures, traytouras, *n.* female traitor
traytourly, *adv.* treacherously
trappe, *n.* trapdoor
trapped, *ppl.a.* dressed, fitted with trappings, adorned
trappour(e), trap(o)ur, trapper, *n.* trapping, horse's harness
trase, *v.* track, pursue; tread
tratoures, see *tra(y)toures, n.*
travayle, *n.* labor
travayle, traveille, *v.* labor; belabor, trouble; travel; **traveilling,** traveling
travayled, *ppl.a.* troubled; tired
travaillyng, *n.* labor
traveille, see *travayle, v.*
travers, *n.* crossing
traverse, *adv.* crosswise
tre, *n.* tree; wood; **treys,** *pl.*
trencheaunte, *a.* sharp; cutting
treson, *n.* treachery; treason
tresoure, *n.* treasure

trespasce, *v.* offend
treste, *n.* trap, point of ambush
tretable, *a.* cooperative
trete, *v.* negotiate
tretyse, *n.* negotiation; treaty
trew, *a.* trustworthy; faithful
tr(e)wage, tr(e)wayge, truage, *n.* (extraction of) tribute
trybet, *n.* tribute
troncheon, see *trouncheoun, n.*
trouble, *v.*
trouncheoun, truncheoune, truncheon, troncheon, *n.* broken-off portion
trouth(e), trowthe, *n.* truth; word; honor; pledge of homage
trouthe-plyght, *v. pa.t.* pledged truth (in love)
trow(e), *v.* think, trust, believe
trowthe, see *trouth(e), n.*
truage, see *tr(e)wage, n.*
truncheon, truncheoune, see *trouncheoun, n.*
trusse, *v.* equip; pack up
trussynge, *n.* packing
truste, *n.* faith, confidence
trwa(y)ge, see *tr(e)wage, n.*
trwe, see *trew, a.*
tumbe, see *to(u)mbe, n.*
tunge, *n.* tongue
turmentis, *n.pl.* torments
turne, *v.* change, transform; return
turret(te), *n.* small tower
turvis, *n.pl.* clumps of turf
twayne, tweyne, *a.* two
twelvemonth, *n.* year

U

umbecaste, *v. pa.t.* cast about
umbelyclose, *v.* surround
umbir, *n.* shade
umbrell, *n.* visor
umbrere, *n.* visor
unarm, *v.* disarm
unavysed, *adv.* uncautiously; thoughtlessly
unbethought, *v. pa.t.* recalled (to oneself); concluded
unbegotyn, *ppl.a.* unconceived
uncoupelynge, *n.* releasing of hounds
uncouth, *a.* unkown, strange
uncklys, *n.pl.* uncles
uncrystened, *ppl.a.* unchristened
uncurteyse, *a.* dishonorable
under, undir, *prep.* beneath; on condition of
underne, undirn, undyrn, *n.* about 9 a.m.
undirstonde, *v.* perceive; believe; **undirstonde,** *pp.*
undirtake, *v.* take upon oneself, accept responsibility; seize; **undirtake,** *pp.*
undo, *v.* unfasten
ungerde, *v. pa.t.* took off
ungoodly, *adv.* discourteously
unhappe, *n.* bad luck, (event of) ill fortune

unhappely, see *unhappyly, adv.*

unhappy, *a.* unlucky; disastrous; dire, objectionable

unhappyly, unhappely, *adv.* by unlucky chance

unhappynes, *n.* misfortune, mischance

unhylle, *v.* uncover

unkyndely, *a.* unnatural

unkyndenesse, *n.* ill-feeling

unlyckly, *a.* unlikeable

unmesurabely, *adv.* excessively

unnailled, *v. pa.t.* disintegrated

unneth(e), *adv.* with difficulty; hardly, scarcely

unresonablé, *adv.*

unsyker, *a.* uncertain, unstable

unsounde, *a.* unwell

untyl(l), *prep.* unto, toward

unto, *prep. cj.* until; to; as far as; in; for; at; with regard to; in accordance with; compared with

untrouthe, *n.* wickedness

untrwyste, *a.* most untrue

unwarely, *adv.* by surprise

unwares, *a.* unawares

unwrayste, *v. pa.t.* wrenched free

upborne, *ppl.a.* supported

upholdyn, *pp.* upheld

up(p)on, *prep.* over; against; concerning; from; for; *adv.* on

upryght, *adv.* flat on one's back

up-so-downe, *adv.* upside down

upwarde, *adv.* flat on one's back

usage, *n.* practice

usurppe, *v.* encroach aggressively

utas, *n.* eighth day after a festival

utteraunce, *n.* end, utmost

utteryst(e), *n.* utmost

uttermuste, uttirmust, uttermoste, uttermest, *n.* end, utmost

uttir, *a.* deadly; *adv.* further away

uttirde, *v. pa.t.* uttered, declared

V

vayne, *n.* vein

valyaunte, *a.* brave

valure, *n.* valor

varyaunte, *a.* variable

varlet, verlatte, *n.* servant

vawarde, voward, *n.* forward, vanguard

vawm-brace, *n.* forearm armor

veary, see *ver(r)y, a.*

velony, see *vilony, n.*

venery, *n.* beasts of the chase, game

vengeabely, *adv.* strictly

vengeable, *a.* inclined to vengeance

venquyshe, vynquysshe, *v.* vanquish

ventayles, *n.pl.* air-vent holes

vergyne, *n.* virgin

very, see *ver(r)y, a.*

veryly, *adv.* truly

verlatte, see *varlet, n.*

vermaynes, *n.pl.* vermin, noxious animals (especially reptiles)

Vernacle, see n. 7, p. 116

ver(r)y, verrey, veary, *a.* true; undoubted; authentic

vertue, *n.* power; virtue, worth

vyall, *n.* vial, container

vyande, *n.* food

vycounte, see *vy(s)counte, n.*

vygyle, *n.* eve

vigoure, *n.* figure

vylayne, *n.* man of low birth

vylaunce, vylans *a.* villainous, wicked, harsh

vylaunsly, *adv.* wickedly, disrespectfully

vilony, velony, *n.* wickedness

vynys, *n.pl.* vines

vynquysshe, *v.*, see *venquyshe, v.*

vysage *v.* stare at

vysaged, see *well vysaged, a.*

vysa(y)ge, *n.* face

vy(s)counte, *n.* viscount

vysour, *n.* visor

vitayle, *n.* victuals, food; provisions

vytayle, vytaille, *v.* provision; provide food

voyde, *v.* leave; dismount; remove

voyde, *a.* empty; unmanned

voyse, *n.* voice

voward, see *vawarde, n.*

W

wacche, *v.* keep watch; lie awake; lie in wait

wage, *v.* pay; fight

wagge, *v.* nod; shake

waycche, *n.* watch

wayes, weyes, *n. (pl.)* way

wayke, wayk(e)ly, see *weyke, a.*

wayshen, *ppl.a.* washed

waysher, *n.* washer

wayte, *n.* waiting, watch; watchman

wayte, *v.* (1) watch; look; stand guard; lie in wait for; beset; take care that; (2) treat

wake, *v.* stay awake; awaken

walop, *v.* gallop

walow, *v.* tumble about

walterynge, *n.* tossing or rolling about

waltyrde, waltred, *v. pa.t.* tossed or rolled about

wan, see *w(h)an*

wanhope, *n.* despair

wanne, *v.* grow dark

wan(ne), see *wynne, v.*

wante, *v.* lack

wantis, *n.pl.* wants, needs

wap, *v.* lap, splash

waraunte, see *war(r)aunte, n. v.*

warde, *n.* guard

ward(e), see *toward(e), prep.*

wardeyn, *n.* governor

wardrop(e), *n*. dressing room; king's private quarters

ware, *v. pa.t.* were

ware, *a*. aware (of)

waryson, *n*. reward

warke, see *worke, n*.

warly, *a*. warlike

warlow, werlow, *n*. monster

warne, *v*. refuse; forbid; inform

war(r)aunte, *n*. protector, champion

war(r)aunte, *v*. guarantee; protect

warre, werre, *n*. war

warre, wars, wers, *a*. (*used as n.*) worse, inferior; *put . . . to the warre*, defeated

warste, *a*. worst

warwolff, *n*. werewolf

waste, *n*. waist; *in waste*, in vain

wastys, *n.pl.* wastelands

wasted, *ppl.a.* ruined

watir, watyr, *n*. body of water; river

wawis, *n.pl.* waves

waxe, wexe, *v*. grow, become; **waxen, wexen, woxen**, *pp.;* **waxed, waxte, wexed, woxe**, *pa.t.*

we(a)le, weall, welle, *n*. good, welfare; good fortune, prosperity

webbe, *n*. wrapping

wed(d)ir, *n*. weather

wede, *n*. vestment, habit, garment; **wedys**, *pl.*

weete, see *wyte, v*.

wey, *n*. way

weyke, wayke, *a*. weak; **wayker**, weaker; **waykest**, weakest

weyk(e)ly, wayk(e)ly, *adv*. weakly; with difficulty

weyte, see *wyte, v*.

weke, wyke, *n*. week

welde, *v*. wield, rule; carry

wele, see *we(a)le, n*.

well-besyene, *ppl.a.* good-looking

well-brethed, *ppl.a.* aerobically fit, of high stamina

well-condyssyonde, *ppl.a.* full of good qualities

welle, *n*. spring

welle, see *we(a)le, n*.

welle-stremys, *n.pl.* streams flowing from a well

well-farynge, *ppl.a.* impressive

well-ny(gh)e, *adv*. very nearly

well-ruled, *ppl.a.* well-behaved

well-visaged, *ppl.a.* handsome

well-wyllar, well-wyller, *n*. well-wisher

well-wylled, well-wyllynge, *ppl.a.* well-disposed

well-wynded, *ppl.a.* aerobically fit

weltryng, *ppl.a.* tossing or rolling

wende, *v*. go

wene, wyne, *v*. believe, think; expect, intend; **wenys**, 3 *sg. pres.;* **went(e), wende**, *pa.t.*

wepyn, *n*. weapon; **wepynles**, *adv*. without weapon

wepyngly, *adv*. with weeping, tearfully

were, *v*. wear; **wered**, *pa.t.*

wery, *a*. weary; **weryar**, more weary

werynesse, *n*. weariness, fatigue

werke, see *worke, n*.

werlow, see *warlow, n*.

werre, *v*. make war

werre, see *warre, n*.

wers, see *warre, a*.

westirly, *adv*. westward

wete, see *wyte, v*.

wetynge, see *wyt(t)ynge, n*.

wexe, *n*. wax

wexe(d), wexen, see *waxe, v*.

w(h)an, *cj*. when

what, *pron. a. adv*. whatever, whichever; who

whatsomever, whatsumever, *pron. a.* whatever, whatsoever

whele, whyle, *n*. wheel

whelpe, *n*. baby

whens, *adv*. whence, from where

wher(e), *adv*. wherever

where, see *whethir, pron. and cj*.

whereas, *adv*. wherever

whereby, *adv*. why

whereof, *adv*. concerning that, of that

wheresomever, *adv*. wherever

wherethorow, *conj. prep*. whereby

whethir, whother, *adv*. whither, to where

whethir, where, *pron. cj*. which (of two); whichever; whereas

whethirsomever, *pron*. whichever

which, *pron*. who

why, whyghe, *adv*. why; *for why*, for, because

whycht, wyghte, *n*. creature

whyghe, see *why, adv*.

whyght(e), *a*. white

whyghtsauff, *v*. vouchsafe, guarantee

whyle, *n*. (1) length of time; (2) wheel

whyle, whylys, *cj*. until; for the time that

whylom, *adv*. a while ago

whyrle, whorle, *v*. whirl, rush; jump

Whytsonday, Pentecost, (see n. 1, p. 10); **Whytsontide**, *n*. the week beginning with Pentecost

who, *pron*. whoever

who(o), *interj*. whoa, stop

whorle, see *whyrle, v*.

whoso, *pron*. whoever

whosomever, *pron*. whoever

whother, see *whethir, adv*.

Whotherward(e), whothirward(e), *adv*. which way

wyght, *a*. strong, valiant; **wyghteste**, most valiant

wyght(e), see *whycht, n.;* *wyte, v*. (1) and (2); and *wyte, n*.

wyghty, *a*. strong

wyghtly, *adv*. quickly

wyghtnesse, *n*. prowess

wyke, see *weke, n*.

wylde, *a*. mad; **wyldar**, more reckless

wyld(e) woode, *a.* insane, utterly mad
wylde-fyre, *n.* highly flammable compound used in warfare
wylfulnesse, *n.* stubbornness
wylys, *n.pl.* wiles
wyll(e), *n.* intention, will; *in wyll,* willing
wyllfull, *a.* deliberate
wyllynge, *n.* intention
wylsom, *a.* lonely
wympled, *ppl.a.* veiled
wynde, *n.* breath, air
wynde, *v.* (1) exhaust the breath of; (2) go, turn
wyne, *n.* wine
wyne, *v.,* see *wene, v.*
wynne, *v.* defeat; win, capture; gain way, escape; profit; wonne, *pp.*; won, wan(ne), *pa.t.*
wyntir, *n.pl.* years
wyse, *n.* manner, fashion, way
wyse, *a.* shrewd
wysshe, *v. pa.t.* washed
wyst(e), see *wyte, v.* (1)
wyte, wyght, *n.* blame
wyte, wytte, wyght(e), we(e)te, weyte, a-wyte, *v.* (1) know, find out; wote, *pres. indicative;* wyste, *pa.t.*; (2) blame (on)
with, wyt(h), *prep.* by; *with that/this,* provided that
withal(l), *prep. adv.* with; by
wythdraughtes, *n.pl.* recesses
withholde, *v.* retain in feudal service; withholdyn, witholde, *pp.*; withhylde, *pa.t.*
withinfurthe, withinforthe, *adv.* inside
withoute, *adv., prep., cj.* outside; unless
withoutefurth, wythouteforthe, *adv.* outside
withsey, *v.* refuse
wythstonde, *v.* withstand, oppose; withstonde, *pp.*
withturne, *v.* turn
wytynge, see *wyt(t)ynge, n.*
wytte, witte, *n.* mind, wits, reason
wytte, see *wyte, v.* (1)
wytty, *a.* wise
wyttyly, *adv.* wisely
wyt(t)ynge, wetynge, *n.* knowledge
wyttyngly, *adv.* knowingly
wyveles, *a.* without wife
wo, *n.* woe
wode, see *wood(e), a. adv.*
woddys, *n.pl.* woods
wofull, *a.* woeful, sad
woll, wyll, *v.* 1 sg. wish, intend; be about to do, have, or go ; wold(e), *pp.* and *pa.t.* should, would
wombe, *n.* belly
won, see *wynne, v.*
wondir, *a. adv.* wondrous, wonderful
wondirfully, *adv.* with wonder
wondirly, *adv.* wondrously
wonne, see *wynne, v.*
woode, *n.* wood, trees; woodys, *pl.*

wood(e), wode, *a. adv.* mad(ly), insane(ly), fierce(ly)
woodly, *adv.* madly, fiercely
woodnes, woodenesse, *n.* madness, rage
woodshaw, *n.* edge of the wood
worche, *v.* work, bring about; ache, hurt; wrought, *pp. pa.t.*
worchyng, *n.* contriving
worke, warke, werke, *n.* work, matter, doing; behavior
worme, *n.* dragon
worse, see *warre, a.*
worship, worshyp, *n.* worth, honor; good name; honorable deed; worship
worship, worshyp, *v.* honor
worshipfull, *a.* honorable
worshypfully, *adv.* honorably
worth(e), *a.* worthy
worthe, *v.* befall
wortis, *n.* edible plants
wote, see *wyte, v.* (1)
wowe, *v.* woo
woxe(n), see *waxe, v.*
wrake, *n.* ruin; strife
wrakke, *v.* (ship)wreck
wrange, see *wrynge, v.*
wraste, *v. pa.t.* wrested, wrung
wrath, see *wroth(e), v. pa.t.*
wratth, wretth, *v.* make angry
wretyn, see *wryte, v.*
wretthe, *n.* wrath
wretth, see *wraith, v.*
wryght, see *wryte, v.*
wrynge, *v.* wring; wrange, wronge, *pa.t.*; wryngande, wringing
wryte, wryght, *v.* write; wryt(t)en, wretyn, *pp.* written
wrytte, *n.* writ, summons; letter
wrokyn, *pp.* wreaked, inflicted
wronge, see *wrynge, v.*
wroth(e), wrath, *v. pa.t.* writhed
wroth(e), *a.* angry; wrotther, more angry
wrought, see *worche, v.*

Y[1]

yalow, yalew, yealow *a.* yellow, blond
yarde, yerde, *n.* rod; branch, tribe
yate, *n.* gate
ye, *pron.* you
yede, see *yode, v. pa.t.*
ye(e), *adv.* yes
yeete, *v. pa.t.* ate
yeff(yn), see *gyff(e), v.*
yef(f)te, *n.* gift
yelde, *v.* yield, surrender; pay; yoldyn, yolden, yelden, *pp.*; yelde(d), *pa.t.*
yeode, see *yode, v. pa.t.*

1. For words beginning with vowel-form Y, see entries under I.

yerde, see *yarde, n.*
yere, *n.pl.* years
yerely, *adv.* yearly
yette, *adv.* yet; since
yeve, see *gyff(e), v.*
yevell, yevil, see *evyl(l), a. adv.*

yode, yoode, ye(o)de, *v. pa.t.* went
yolden, yoldy–yoldyn, see *yelde, v.*
yoman, *n.* yeoman, servant
yon, *a.* yonder, those
yonge, *a.* young
yoode, see *yode, v. pa.t.*

Selected Guide to Proper Names

The following guide is intended mainly to assist readers (1) in clarifying familial or other defining relationships bewteen characters; (2) in identifying variant spellings of the same name; (3) in distinguishing two or more characters or places sharing the same name; (4) in identifying single characters or places which go by more than one name; and (5) when they can be identified, in identifying place names in terms accessible by reference to modern maps. For the names of holy/feast days, see the Glossary. As with the Glossary, *Y/y is given the alphabetic status of I/i when used as a vowel.*

Adrawns, uncle of King Arthur

Ag(g)lova(y)le, son of Pellynore and brother of Percyvale

Ag(g)ravayne, son of King Lot

Almayn(e), Germany

Albons, Saynt, town of St. Albans in Hertfordshire

Alymsbury(e)/Amysbyry/Amysbery, Amesbury in Wiltshire

Alyne, (1) daughter of Pellynore and the Lady of the Rule; (2) brother of Tryan

Alys/Alis, le Beall Pylgryme/la Bealle Pellaron, "the beautiful Pilgrim," la Beale Alys, wife of Alysaundir le Orphelyne

Alysaundir le Orpheline, nephew of King Mark and son of Prince Bodwyne

Alysa(u)ndir, (1) Alexander the Great; (2) the city in Egypt named after him, Alexandria

Andret/Andred, cousin of Trystram

Angeoy, region of Anjou in France

Angwys(s)h(e)/Angwyss(c)haunce, King of Ireland and father of La Beal Isode

Anwyk, (castle of) Alnwick in Northumberland

Aramathy, Arimathea

Argayle, Argyllshire in Scotland

Aryes, cowherd and foster father to Tor(re)

Armynake, region of Armagnac in France

Arnolde; Raynold(e), brother of Gylmere and Gauter

Arnolde le Bruse/Brewse, brother of Garrarde le Bruse

Arrabé, Arabia

Arrage, Arcadia

Arthur(e), King of Britain, son of Uther Pendragon and Igrayne

Arundell, castle in Sussex (identified with Magouns)

Asclabor, father of Palomydes

Ascolat(e)/Ascolot(t), Fayre Maydyn of, Elayne le Blanke, daughter of Barnarde

Assy, Asia

Aufryke, Africa

Aunserus, father of Alys le Beall Pylgryme

Avylion/Avilion/Avyl(y)on, (1) valley to which the dying Arthur is carried; (2) island home of Gryngamour; (3) home of the Lady Lyle

Avoutres, see **Uwayne le(s) Avoutres**

Babilonye, Babylon

Bagdemagus, King of Gore and cousin of King Urience

Balan, brother of Balyn

Balyn(e)/Balen, le Savea(i)ge, also known as **the Knight with the Two Swerdis**: brother of Balan

Bamborow, (castle of) Bamburgh in Northumberland

Ban(ne)/Bayan, King of Benwick and father of Launcelot

Baram/Bareon Downe, Barham Down in Kent

Barflete, port of Barfleur in France

Barnarde/Bernarde, of Ascolat, father of Elayne le Blanke and Tirry

Barraunte/Berraunt(e), le Apres, see **Hundred Knyghtes, King with the**

Bartelot, brother of Breunys Sanze Pyté

Baudewen/Bawdewyn, of Bretayn(e)/Brytaygne, a hermit

Bayan, Bayonne in France

Beawme, Beaune in France

Be(a)wmaynes, see **Gareth**

Bedyvere/Bedwer(e), the Bolde, brother of Lucan

Bedyvere, of the Streyte Marchys/Strayte Marche, knight defeated by Bors

Bellyas/Bellyaunce, le Orgulous, brother of Froll of the Oute Ilys

Ector, (1) foster father to Arthur; (2) Hector of Troy

Ector, de Marys/Mares/Maris, brother of Launcelot

Edwarde, son of Roulonde

Edward(e), of Orkeney, brother of Sadok(e)

Edwarde, of Carnarvan, brother of Priamus and Hectimer

Elayne, (1) wife of King Nauntres; (2) wife of King Ban; (3) daughter of King Pelles and mother of Launcelot

Elayne, le Blanke, see Ascolat(e)

Elayne/Elyan/Hel(a)yne, le Blank(e), son of Bors

Eliazar/Elyazar, son of Pelles

Eliodyn, see Galy(h)odyn

Elyne, mother of the Emperor Constantine

Elyzabeth, mother of Trystram and wife of Melyodas

Epynogrys, son of the King of Northumberland

Ermynde, see Hermynde

Ermony, Armenia

Esax, Essex

Escans(e), Duke of Candebenet, opponent of Arthur

Estrake, Astarac in France

Ethyope, Ethiopia

Ettarde, sought in love by Pelleas

Eufrate, the River Euphrates in the Near East

Evelake, pagan king renamed Mordrains upon baptism

Ewayn(e), see Uwayne/Ewayne

Excaliber/Excalibir/Excalibur/Excaleber/ Excalebir, Arthur's sword

Farmagos, Famagusta in Spain

Fayre Maydyn of Ascolat, see Ascolat(e)

Fyleloly, sister of Urry

Fyze de Vaysshoure, "Son of the Cowherd," name given to Tor(re), foster son of Aryes the cowherd

Flaundirs/Flaunders/Flaundyrs, region of Flanders in Belgium

Florence/Florens, son of Gawain

Foyse, region of Foix in France

Gaheris/Gaherys, son of Lot and brother of Gawayne

Galahad, Launcelot's name at baptism

Gala(h)ad, son of Launcelot

Galahalt(e), the Haute/Hawte/Noble Prince, of the Longe Iles, ruler of Surluse

Galantyne, Gawain's sword

Galely, Galilee in Palestine

Galy(h)odyn/Galyhuddyn/Eliodyn, sub-king of Surluse

Galyhud, Arthurian knight, *distinct from* Galahad

Galys, Wales

Galowey/Gal(o)way/Galeway, district of Galloway in Scotland

Garaunte, cousin of Gwenyvere

Gareth(e), son of King Lot and nephew of Arthur; named Beawmaynes by Kay

Gar(r)arde le Breuse/Brewse, brother of Arnolde le Bruse and *distinct from the Welsh knight* Garrarde

Gaulle/Gawle, Gaul (France)

Gauter/Gawter(e), brother of Arnolde and Gylmere

Gavernayle, see Governayle

Gawayn(e)/Gaweyn, son of King Lot and nephew to Arthur

Ge(e)ne, Genoa in Italy

Gyan, Guienne in France

Gylforde, Guildford in Surrey

Gylmere, Gyllymer(e), brother of Gauter and Arnolde

Gyngalyn(e), son of Gawain

Glassyngbyry/Glastynburye, Glastonbury in Wiltshire

God of Cardal, see Du

Godarde/Godarte, Pass of St. Gotthard in Switzerland

Governayle/Govirnayle/Gavernayle, manservant and confidant to Trystram

Graale see Sank(e)greal(l)

Grekis, Greeks

Grene Knyght, the, Pertolype

Gryfflet(te), le/la Fyz(e) de D(e)u, son of God of Cardal

Gryngamour(e), brother of Lady Lyones

Gromore Somer Joure, associate of Mordred and Agravayne; also named Grummor Grummorson

Gwenbaus, brother of kings Ban and Bors

Gwenyver(e)/Gwenyvir/Gwenivere/ Guenyver(e)/Guenever(e), daughter of Lodegreance and wife of Arthur

Harde Roche, castle, identical with Roche Deure, "[of the] Hard Rock"

Hardy Harte, Ozanna wyth the, Ozanna le Cure Hardy

Harleus(e), le Berbeus/Berbuse, see n. 6, p. 387

Harmaunce/Hermaunce, King of the Red City

Haute Prince, the, see Galahalte

Hebes le Renowné(s),"the Renowned," Ebes le Renownys

Hectimer/Hectymere, brother of Edwarde of Carnarvan and Priamus

Helayne le Blanke, see Elayne le Blanke

Hellyas le Grose, ancestor of Launcelot: son of Nacien, grandson of Nappus

Hermynde/Ermynde, brother of Harmaunce

Howell, King of Brittany and father of Isode le Blaunche Maynes (? identical with Howell the Hende, relative of Arthur)

Humbir, the River Humber in northeastern England

Hungré, Hungary

Ider/Idres/Idrus, the yonge, son of Uwayne, grandson of Uriens

Idres, King of Cornwall

Igrayne, mother of Arthur

Inde, Ynde, India

Ing(e)londe, England

Yrland, Ireland

Ironsyde, the Rede Knyght of the Rede Laundis

Isod(e), La Beale/Beall, "the beautiful," wife of King Mark and daughter of King Angwysh

Isod(e)/Isolde, le Blaunche Maynes/Maynys, "of the White Hands," daughter of King Howell

Jesu, Jesus

Jonas, ancestor of Launcelot: son of Lysays

Joseph(e), off Aramathy, see n. 7, p. 464

Joseph, son of Joseph of Arimathea

Josué, Joshua

Joyo(u)s Gard(e), castle renamed Dolerouse Garde by Launcelot, identified with Anwyk or Bamborow: see n. 2, p. 670

Kayhidius/Kayhydyus/Keyhidyus/Keyhydius/ Keyhydyus, son of King Howell

Kay(nus)/Kay(y)us, the Senesciall/Senceall, the Sty(e)warde, son of Ector and foster brother to Arthur: distinct from Kay(nes) le Straunge/d'Estraunges

King with the Hundred Knyghtes, the, Barraunte/Berraunt(e) le Apres

Knight with the Two Swerdis, the, Balyn

La Beale Alys, see Alys

La Beale/Beall Isod(e), see Isod(e)

La Beall Pellaron/Pelleryn, see Alys

La Cote/Kote Male Taylé, "the Badly-Tailored Coat," nickname given to Brunor by Kay

Lady of the Lake, the, woman beheaded by Balyn, distinct from the Chief Lady of the Lake, Nynyve

Lambyth, Lambeth (now a central London suburb)

Lamerok(e)/Lamerake/Lamorak(e), de Galys/Galis/of Walis, son of Pellynor

Landok/Langeduke, region of Languedoc in France

Launcelo(t)(e), du/de La(a)ke, son of King Ban

Launceor, son of the King of Ireland

Lavayn(e), son of Barnarde of Ascolat

Le Beall Pylgryme, see Alys

Lybye, Libya

Lymosyn, region of Limousin in France

Lyonel(l), cousin of Launcelot

Lyones(se), (1) land of Trystram; (2) Lady of the Castell Perelus

Lyonet(t)/Lynet, also named the Damesell Savea(i)ge, sister of Lyones

Lyonors, mother of Boarte (by Arthur)

Lysays, ancestor of Launcelot: son of Hellyas le Grose

Lytyll Brytayne, see Bretayne

Lodegr(e)aunce/Lodegreauns/Lodegrean,
King of Camelarde and father of Gwenyvere

Logrys/Logris/Logres/Logrus/Logurs/ Logyrs, England

Longeus, Longinus, soldier who pierced Christ's side with a lance

Lorayne, region of Lorraine in France

Lot(t)/Lotte, King of Lothian and Orkney (now parts of Scotland)

Lovell, son of Gawain

Lowe Contrey, land around the estuary of the River Seine in France

Lowthean see Lot(t)

Lucan(e)/Lucas/Lucanere, de/the Butler(e)/ Butler, son of Corneus

Lucius/Lucyus, Emperor of Rome

Lumbardy, region of Lombardy in Italy

Lusarne, Lucerne in Switzerland

Lushburne, Luxembourg

Macabeus, Judas, Judas Maccabeus, legendary Jewish warrior

Macidony, Macedonia

Magouns/Magowns, castle identified with Arundell

Maledysaunte, (ill-speaking), the Damesell, aided by, and then married to, La Cote Male Taylé: also named Byeaue Vyvante and Byeau Pansaunte

Mal(l)eorré/Maleoré/Malorye, (Sir) Thomas, author of the Morte Darthur

Marhalte, King of Ireland

Marhalt(e)/Marhau(l)t(e)/Marhaus, brother of the Queen of Ireland

Mark(e), King of Cornwall and uncle of Trystram

Maymed Kynge, see Pellam (and cf. Pelles)

Mausank, Marsan in France

Melayne/Myllayne, Milan in Italy

Melias/Mel(l)yas/Melyaus de Lyle/de le Ile, son of the King of Denmark

Meliot/Mel(l)yot de Logris/Logrys/Logyrs/ Logurs, cousin of Nyneve

Mellyagaunce/Mellyagauns/Mellyagaunt/ Mellyagaunte, son of King Bagdemagus

Melyodas, King of Lyones and father of Trystram

Myllayne, see Melayne

Moyses, Moses

Mordrains/Mordrayns, see Evelake

Mordrede, son of Arthur and Morgawse

Morgan le Fay/Fey, sister of Arthur and wife of Uriens

Morgawse/Morgause/Margawse, Queen of Orkney (and wife of King Lot)

Nacien/Nacyen, (1) Grandfather of Nappus, and great grandfather of (2) Nacien, ancestor of Launcelot

Nacien the Er(e)myte, "the Hermit," descendant of Joseph of Aramathy

Nappus, grandson of Nacien (1)

Nauntres/Nayntres/Nentres, King of Garlot

Nenyve, see Nynyve

Nero, brother of King Royns

Nynyve/Nenyve, Lady/Damsel/Chief Lady of the Lake

Northefolke, county of Norfolk

Orkenay/Orkeney, island realm of Lot (now part of Scotland)

Out(e)lake/Oughtlake, brother of Damas, *distinct from* Outelake of Wentelonde

Overn, region of Auvergne in France

Ozanna le Cure Hardy, see Hardy Harte

Payters, region of Poitiers in France

Palomydes/Palamydes, the Saresyn, son of Asclabor and brother of Segwarydes and Saffyre

Pampoyle, Pamphilia in Asia Minor (Turkey)

Pardyak, Pardiac in France

Parsaunte/Persaunte, of Inde, the Blue Knight

Part(h)olype, see Pertolype

Parys(e), Paris in France

Pavye, Pavia in Italy

Pavynes Londis, the heathen lands

Pecchere, Pescheor, the Fisher King

Pelaundris, brother of Plenoryus

Pellam of Lystenoyse, the Maymed Kynge, son of Labor and father of Pelles

Pelleas, lover of Ettarde

Pelles/Pelleaus, father of Elayne, the mother of Launcelot: mistakenly called the Maymed Kynge (who is actually King Pellam)

Pellogres, brother of Plenoryus

Pellynor(e)/Pellinore/Pellenor(e), of Lystenoyse, Kynge of the Ilis, father of Tor, Aglovale, Darnarde, Percyvale, Lamorak, and Alyne (1)

Pellynore, knight who seeks Trystram's identity

Pellownes, father of Persydes de Bloyse

Perarde, the Blak Knyght of the Blak Laundis

Percivale/Percivall/Percyva(y)le/Percyvall/Percyvele/Persyvale, de Galys, son of Pellynore

Perygot, Périgord region in France

Perymones/Perimones, the Red Knyght

Perysie see Parys(e)

Persaunte, see Parsaunte

Persydes/Persides, de Bloyse, son of Pellownes

Pertolyp(e)/Pertolope/Pertholepe/Part(h)olype, the Grene Knyght

Pescheor, see Pecchere

Pyllownes, brother of Plenoryus

Pyn(n)el(l)/Pyonell, le Saveaige/Saveayge, relative of Lamerok

Playne de Amoris, "Full of Love," brother of Plenoryus

Playne de Fors, "Full of Strength," brother of Plenoryus

Plenoryus, brother of Pelaundris, Pellogres, Playne de Amoris, Playne de Fors, and Pyllownes

Plesaunce, Piacenza in Italy

Poynte Tremble/Porte Trembyll, Pontremoli in Italy

Portyngale, Portugal

Pounce, region of Pontus in Asia Minor (Turkey)

Pounte de Corbyn, see Carbone(c)k(e)

Preter Johan, Prester John: see n. 9, p. 118

Priamus/Pryamus, brother of Hectimer and Edwarde of Carnarvan

Provynce, region of Provence in France

Questyng(e) Beste, see Beste Glatys(s)aunte

Raynes, Rennes in France

Raynold(e), see Arnolde

Rede Knyght of the Rede Laundis/Laundys, Ironsyde

Red Knyght, Perimones

Roche Deure, see Harde Roche

Rodis, the, Rhodes

Roerge, Rouergue in France

Royens/Royns/Ryens/Ryons, King of North Wales/Galys

Romaynes, Roman people

Roome, Rome in Italy

Roone, Rouen in France

Roulonde, father of Edwarde and Raynolde

Rule, Lady of the, mother of Alyne

Sado(c)k(e)/Saduk, associate of Alexander and Trystram

Sadoke, cousin of Gawayn and brother of Edward(e) of Orkeney

Saf(f)yr(e)/Saf(f)ir/Safer(e)/Saphyr(e)/Saphir/Sapher, brother of Palomydes

Sayne, the River Seine in France

Salamon, King Solomon

Salysbiry/Salysbury/Salusbyry, Salisbury in Wiltshire

Sand(e)wych(e), port of Sandwich in Kent

Sank(e)greal(l)/Sancgreal(l)/Sangreall, (1) the Holy Grail; (2) Malory's *Noble Tale of the Sankgreal*

Sautre/Sawtre, Roman senator

Segwarydes, brother of Palomydes

Seynte Mychael's Mount, Mont St. Michel in France

Selyses, of the Dolerous Towre, nephew of the King with the Hundred Knyghtes

Selyvaunte, brother of Blyaunte

Sentonge, region of Saintonge in France

Sessoyne, (1) Soissons in France; (2) Saxony (also spelled Syssoyne)

Sessoynes, Saxons

Sevarne, the River Severn

Sherewood, Sherwood Forest in Nottinghamshire

Shevalere/Shyvalere de/le Charyot(e)/Charyotte, the, "the Knight of the Cart," name given to Launcelot

Shyvalere (Ill) Mafe(e)te, the, "the Knight who Has Trespassed," name Launcelot gives to himself

Symyan, associate of Joseph of Aramathy and distant relative of Galahad

Southsex, county of Sussex in England

Spaynardis, Spaniards

Spolute, Spoleto in Italy

Surré, Syria

Tarquyn(e)/Terquyn(e) Turquyn, enemy to Arthur

Tars, Tarsus in Asia Minor (Turkey)

Taulas/Tauleas, giant, brother of Taulurd

Taulurd, giant, brother of Taulas

Temmys, the River Thames

Tholomé, la Feyntis, cousin of Evelake

Tyntagyl(l)/Tyntagil/Tyntigail(l)/Tyntygaill, castle in Cornwall

Tirry/Tyrré/Tyrry/Tyrré, son of Barnarde

Tor(re), le Fyze Aryes/le Fyze de Vaysshoure, "the Son of Aryes/the son of the Cowherd," foster son of Aryes the cowherd

Tramtryst, transpositional name Trystram gives himself as a disguise

Tryan, brother of Alyne

Trystram(s)/Trystrames/Trystramys/Tristram(s)/Tristrames/Trystran, de Lyones(se), nephew of King Mark and son of Melyodas, King of Lyones

Troyes, city of Troyes in France

Turké, Turkey

Turquyn, see Tarquyn(e)

Tursanke, region of Tursan in France

Tuskayne, region of Tuscany in Italy

Urbyne, Urbino in Italy

Uriens, Uryen(s), Uryence, of Go(o)re, King of Gore and father of Uwayne

Uther Pendragon, father of Arthur

Uwayne/Ewayne, le Blaunche Maynes/Maynys, "of the White Hands," le Fyze de Roy Uryens, "the Son of King Uryens," *distinct from* **Uwayne le(s) Avoutres/Avowtres/Adventurys**, "child of adultery"

Vyterbe, Viterbo in Italy

Waalis/Walis/Walys, Wales

Watlynge Strete, old Roman road extending from Kent to North Wales

Wes(e)mynster, Westminster (now a central London suburb)

Westwallie, region of Westphalia in Wales

Wynchester/Wynchestir, Winchester in Hampshire (identified with Camelot: see n. 5, p. 61)

Wyndesore, Windsor in Berkshire

Selected Bibliography

Editions

Listed in reverse chronological order:

Complete Text

Malory, Sir Thomas. *The Works of Sir Thomas Malory*. Ed. Eugene Vinaver. 3rd ed. Rev. P. J. C. Field. 3 vols. Oxford, 1990. [The standard scholarly edition of Malory, based on the Winchester MS.]

———. *Caxton's Malory*. Ed. James W. Spisak. 2 vols. Berkeley and Los Angeles, 1983. [Scholarly edition, with limited commentary, based on Caxton's print of 1485.]

———. *Sir Thomas Malory: Le Morte D'Arthur*. Ed. Janet Cowen. Introduction by John Lawlor. 2 vols. London, 1969 [Based on Caxton.]

———. *Le Morte Darthur by Sir Thomas Malory*. Ed. H. Oskar Sommer. 3 vols. London, 1889–91. [A diplomatic edition of Caxton, with a still-useful guide to some of Malory's sources.]

Abridged

Malory, Sir Thomas. *Le Morte Darthur: The Winchester Manuscript*. Ed. Helen Cooper. Oxford, 1998.

———. *Le Morte Darthur, The Seventh and Eighth Tales*. Ed. P. J. C. Field. London, 1978.

———. *King Arthur and his Knights: Selected Tales by Sir Thomas Malory*. Ed. Eugène Vinaver. London, 1978.

———. *The Morte Darthur, Parts Seven and Eight*. Ed. Derek Brewer. London, 1968.

Facsimiles

Malory, Sir Thomas. *The Winchester Malory: A Facsimile*. Introduced by N. R. Ker. Early English Text Society. London, 1976.

———. *Sir Thomas Malory, Le Morte d'Arthur, printed by William Caxton, 1485*. Ed. and introduced by Paul Needham. London, 1976.

Bibliographies and Other Useful Resources

Aarne, Antii. *The Types of the Folk-Tale*. Trans. and enlarged by Stith Thompson. Folklore Fellows Communications, no. 184. Helsinki, 1961.

Ackerman, Robert W. *An Index of the Arthurian Names in Middle English*. Stanford, 1952.

Alford, John A. *'Piers Plowman': A Glossary of Legal Diction*. Cambridge, 1988.

Annual Bibliography of English Language and Literature. Published annually for the Modern Humanities Research Association. Cambridge.

Arthuriana. Published quarterly. [Frequently administered by guest editors producing topic-based numbers. Formerly *Quondam et Futurus: A Journal of Arthurian Interpretations;* formerly *Quondam et Futurus* and *Arthurian Interpretations.*]

Bibliographical Bulletin of the International Arthurian Society. Published annually.

Bordman, Gerald. *Motif-index of the English Metrical Romances.* Folklore Fellows Communications, no. 190. Helsinki, 1963.

Bruce, Christopher W. *The Arthurian Name Dictionary.* New York, 1999.

Coghlan, Ronan. *The Encyclopaedia of Arthurian Legends.* London, 1991.

Gaines, Barry. *Sir Thomas Malory: An Anecdotal Bibliography of Editions 1485–1985.* New York, 1990.

International Medieval Bibliography. Published twice a year under the auspices of the University of Leeds.

Kato, Tomomi, *A Concordance to the Works of Sir Thomas Malory.* Tokyo, 1974. [Keyed to O^2/O^3.]

Lacy, Norris J. ed. *The New Arthurian Encyclopedia.* Rev. ed., New York and London, 1996.

———. ed. *Medieval Arthurian Literature: A Guide to Recent Research.* New York, 1996.

———, and Geoffrey Ashe. *The Arthurian Handbook.* 2nd ed. New York, 1997.

Life, Page West. *Sir Thomas Malory and the "Morte Darthur:" A Survey of Scholarship and Annotated Bibliography.* Charlottesville, Va. 1980.

A Manual of the Writings in Middle English 1050–1500. 10 vols. Gen. ed. J. Burke Severs (vols. 1–2), and Alber E. Hartung (vols. 3–10). New Haven, 1967–98.

The Middle English Dictionary. Ann Arbor, 1952–

MLA International Bibliography of Books and Articles on the Modern Languages and Literatures. Published annually by the Modern Language Association of America, New York.

Moorman, Charles and Ruth. *An Arthurian Dictionary.* Chicago, 1990.

The Oxford English Dictionary. 2nd ed. 20 vols. Oxford, 1989.

Parry, John J. *A Bibliography of Critical Arthurian Literature for the Years 1922–1929.* New York, 1931.

———, and Margaret Schlauch. *A Bibliography of Critical Arthurian Literature for the Years 1930–1935.* New York, 1936.

Pickford, C. E., R. W. Last, C. R. Barker, Caroline Palmer, and Elaine Barber., eds. *The Arthurian Bibliography.* 4 vols. to date: *Arthurian Studies* 3, 6, 31, and 49. Cambridge, 1981–2002.

Reiss, Edmund, Louise Horner Reiss, and Beverly Taylor. *Arthurian Legend and Literature: An Annotated Bibliography, I: The Middle Ages.* New York, 1984.

Rice, Joanne A. *Middle English Romance: An Annotated Bibliography, 1955–1985.* New York, 1987.

Wallace, David, ed. *The Cambridge History of Medieval English Literature.* Cambridge, 1999.

Whiting, B. J. *Proverbs, Sentences and Proverbial Phrases from English Writings Mainly before 1500.* Cambridge, Mass., 1968.

The Year's Work in English Studies. Published for the English Association, London.

Web Site

This volume has a dedicated Web site with supporting resources similar to those offered for *Middle English Romances: A Norton Critical Edition,* including links to the leading Arthurian sites. Given the notorious instability of Internet addresses, this site is most reliably reached by following links from the publisher's Web site (www.wwnorton.com) to the Norton Critical Editions page (www.wwnorton.com/college/english/nce).

Surveys of Extra-Literary Representations

See also Arthurian titles in the previous section. For a select survey of early treatments, see the chronology on p. xxvii and notes thereto.

Harty, Kevin J., ed. *Cinema Arthuriana, Essays on Arthurian Film.* New York, 1991.

———. *The Reel Middle Ages: American, Western and Eastern European, Middle Eastern and Asian Films about Medieval Europe.* Jefferson, N.C. 1998.

Loomis, Roger Sherman. *Arthurian Legend in Medieval Art.* Oxford, 1938.

Lupack, A., and B. T. Lupack. *King Arthur in America.* Cambridge, 1999.

Mancoff, D. N. *The Arthurian Revival in Victorian Art.* New York, 1990.

———. *The Return of King Arthur: The Legend through Victorian Eyes.* New York, 1995.

———, ed. *The Arthurian Revival: Essays on Form, Tradition, and Transformation.* New York, 1992.

Michelsson, Elisabeth. *Appropriating King Arthur: The Arthurian Legend in English Drama and Entertainment 1485–1625.* Uppsala, 1999.

Poulson, Christine. "Arthurian Legend in Fine and Applied Art of the Nineteenth and Early Twentieth Centuries: A Catalogue of Artists." *Arthurian Literature* 9 (1989), 81–142. [Subject Index in *Arthurian Literature* 10 (1990), 111–134; Update by Roger Simpson in *Arthurian Literature* 11 (1992), 81–96.]

Torregrossa, Michael A. "Camelot 3000 and Beyond: An Annotated Listing of Arthurian Comic Books Published in the United States c. 1980–1998." *Arthuriana* 9, no. 1 (1999), 67–109.

Umland, Rebecca A., and Samuel J. Umland. *The Use of Arthurian Legend in Hollywood Film from Connecticut Yankees to Fisher Kings.* Westport, Conn., 1996.

Ward, B. J. "King Arthur in Traditional Music." *Keystone Folklore* 2 (1984); 23–33.

Whitaker, Muriel. *The Legends of King Arthur in Art.* Cambridge, 1990.

Studies of Malory's Era, Contextual Studies, Sources

Arthurian Origins

See also Arthurian titles under "Bibliographies and Other Useful Resources," above.

Aneirin. *The 'Gododdin' of Aneirin: Text and Context from Dark-Age North Britain.* Ed. and trans. J. T. Koch. Cardiff, 1997.

Ashe, Geoffrey. "The Origins of the Arthurian Legend." *Arthuriana* 5, no. 3 (1995), 1–24.

Barber, Richard. *King Arthur: Hero and Legend.* Woodbridge, 1986.

Barron, W. R. J., ed. *The Arthur of the English: The Arthurian Legend in Medieval English Life and Literature.* Cardiff, 1999.

Beroul. *The Romance of Tristan.* Ed. and trans. Norris J. Lacy. New York, 1989.

de Boron, Robert. *Merlin and the Grail.* "Joseph of Arimathea," "Merlin," "Perceval:" The Trilogy of Arthurian Prose Romances attributed to Robert de Boron. Trans. Nigel Bryant. Cambridge, 2001.

Bromwich, Rachel A., O. H. Jarman, and Brynley F. Roberts, eds. *The Arthur of the Welsh: The Arthurian Legend in Medieval Welsh Literature.* Cardiff, 1991.

Castleden, Rodney. *King Arthur: The Truth behind the Legend.* London and New York, 2000.

Chrétien de Troyes. *Arthurian Romances.* Trans. D. D. R. Owen. London, 1987.

Coe, J. B. and Young, S. *The Celtic Sources for the Arthurian Legend.* Llanerch, 1995. [Texts with English translations.]

Cohen, Jeffrey Jerome. *Of Giants: Sex, Monsters, and the Middle Ages.* Minneapolis, Minnesota, 1999.

Culhwch and Olwen: An Edition and Study of the Oldest Arthurian Tale. Ed. R. Bromwich and D. S. Evans. Cardiff, 1992.

Darrah, John. *Paganism in Arthurian Romance.* Woodbridge, 1994.

Echard, Siân. *Arthurian Narrative in the Latin Tradition.* Cambridge, 1998.

Ellis, Peter Beresford. *A Dictionary of Irish Mythology.* London, 1987.

de France, Marie. *The Lais of Marie de France.* Ed. and trans. G. Burgess and K. Busby. London, 1986.

Geoffrey of Monmouth. *The History of the Kings of Britain.* Trans. L. Thorpe. London, 1966.

Green, Miranda. *The Gods of the Celts.* Stroud, 1986.

Lacy, Norris J. *Text and Intertext in Medieval Arthurian Literature.* New York, 1996.

Littleton, Scott, and Linda Malcor. *From Scythia to Camelot: A Radical Reassessment of the Legends of King Arthur, the Knights of the Round Table, and the Holy Grail.* New York, 1994.

Loomis, Roger Sherman, ed. *Arthurian Literature in the Middle Ages: A Collaborative History.* Oxford, 1961.

John Morris. *Arthurian Sources.* 9 vols. Chichester, 1995.

Nennius. *Historia Brittonum.* In *British History and the Welsh Annals.* Ed. and trans. J. Morris. London, 1980.

Snyder, Christopher, and Samuel Valentino. *The World of King Arthur.* London and New York, 2000. [Excellent guide to further introductory reading and Internet resources.]

Wace and Layamon. *The Life of King Arthur.* Trans. Judith Weiss and R. Allen. London, 1997.

Warren, Michelle R. *History on the Edge: Excalibur and the Borders of Britain, 1100–1300*. Minneapolis, Minnesota, 2000.

Wilhelm, James J., ed. *The Romance of Arthur: New, Expanded Edition. An Anthology of Medieval Texts in Translation*. New York, 1994.

Malory's Major Sources

For guides to Malory's suspected "minor" sources, see the references in the headnote on p. 701.

The Death of King Arthur. Trans. James Cable. London, 1971 [Translation of the *Mort le Roi Artu*.]

Hardyng, John. *The Chronicle of Iohn Hardyng . . . together with the Continuation of Richard Grafton*. London, 1812.

King Arthur's Death. Ed. Larry D. Benson. Exeter, 1986. [Normalized editions of the alliterative *Morte Arthure* and stanzaic *Morte Arthure*.]

Lancelot. Ed. Alexandre Micha. Textes littéraires français. 9 vols. Geneva, 1978–83.

Lancelot-Grail: The Old French Arthurian Vulgate and Post-Vulgate in Translation. 5 vols. Gen. Ed. Norris J. Lacy. New York, 1993–1996. [An invaluable resource for Malory studies. Includes complete English translations of the *Suite de Merlin, Lancelot, Queste del Saint Graal*, and *Mort le Roi Artu*.]

Le Haut Livre du Graal: Perlesvaus. 2 vols. Ed. William A. Nitze and T. Atkinson Jenkins. Chicago, 1932.

Merlin. Ed. Gaston Paris and Jacob Ulrich. Société des anciens textes français. Paris, 1886. [*Suite du Merlin*: this version also known as "The Huth Merlin."]

Morte Arthur [stanzaic]. Ed. J. Douglas Bruce. Early English Text Society. Extra Series 88. Oxford, 1903.

Morte Arthur [stanzaic]. Ed. P. F. Hissiger. The Hague, 1975.

Morte Arthure [alliterative]. Ed. John Finlayson. London, 1967. [Selections, with summaries. of omitted material.]

Morte Arthure [alliterative]. Ed. Mary Hamel. New York, 1984.

La Morte le roi Artu. Ed. Jean Frappier. Geneva, 1964.

Tristan 1489. Facsimile with introduction by C. E. Pickford. London, 1976. [Version closer in places to Malory's source than those represented in the editions cited in the next two entries.]

La Queste del Saint Graal. Ed. Albert Pauphilet. Paris, 1921.

The Quest of the Holy Grail. Trans. P. Matarasso. London, 1969.

Le Roman de Tristan en Prose. 3 vols. Ed. Renée Curtis. Munich, 1963; Leiden, 1976; Cambridge, 1985.

Le Roman de Tristan en Prose. 9 vols. Gen. ed. Phillipe Ménardé. Geneva, 1987–97.

The Romance of Tristan. Trans. Renée Curtis. Oxford, 1994. [Selections.]

The Vulgate Version of the Arthurian Romances. 8 vols. Ed. H. Oskar Sommer. Washington, D.C., 1908–16.

English Writing and Literary Patronage in and around Malory's Time

See also the subsections above and below.

Beckwith, Sarah. *Christ's Body: Identity, Culture and Society in Late Medieval Writings*. London, 1993.

Cherewatuk, Karen. "Sir Thomas Malory's 'Grete booke.'" In *The Social and Literary Contexts of Malory's "Morte Darthur."* Ed. D. Thomas Hanks, Jr., and Jessica G. Brogdon. Cambridge, 2000, pp. 42–67.

Coleman, Joyce. *Public Reading and the Reading Public in Late Medieval England and France*. Cambridge, 1996.

Connolly, Margaret. *John Shirley: Book Production and the Noble Household in Fifteenth-Century England*. Aldershot, 1998.

Crane, Susan. *Insular Romance: Politics, Faith and Culture in Anglo-Norman and Middle-English Literature*. Berkeley, 1986.

Davis, Norman, ed. *Paston Letters of the Fifteenth Century*. 2 vols. Oxford, 1971–76.

Dobson, R. B., ed. *The Church, Politics and Patronage in the Fifteenth Century*. Gloucester, 1984.

Doyle, A. I. "English books In and Out of Court from Edward III to Henry VII." In *English Court Culture in the Later Middle Ages*. Ed. V. J. Scattergood and J. W. Sherborne. New York, 1983, pp. 163–181.

Edwards, A. S. G., ed. *Middle English Prose: A Critical Guide to Major Authors and Genres.* New Brunswick, 1984.

Gray, Douglas, ed. *The Oxford Book of Late Medieval Verse and Prose.* Oxford, 1985. [The most comprehensive single-volume survey available of the wide variety of English texts produced in and around Malory's time.]

Green, Richard Firth. *Poets and Princepleasers: Literature and the English Court in the Later Middle Ages.* Toronto, 1980.

Hanna, Ralph. "Sir Thomas Berkeley and His Patronage." *Speculum* 64 (1989), 878–916.

———. *Pursuing History: Middle English Manuscripts and Their Texts.* Stanford, 1996.

Kekewich, Margaret. "Edward IV, William Caxton, and Literary Patronage in Yorkist England." *Modern Language Review* 66 (1971), 481–487.

Krochalis, Jeanne. "The Books and Reading of Henry V and His Circle." *Chaucer Review* 23, no. 1 (1988), 50–77.

Lester, G. A. *Sir John Paston's 'Grete Boke.'* Cambridge, 1984.

———. "The Books of a Fifteenth-Century English Gentleman, Sir John Paston." *Neuphilologische Mitteilungen* 88 (1987), 200–217.

Lucas, Peter J. "The Growth and Development of English Literary Patronage in the Later Middle Ages and Early Renaissance." *The Library* 6th ser., 4, no. 3 (1982), 219–248.

Meale, Carol M. "Manuscripts, Readers, and Patrons in Fifteenth-Century England: Sir Thomas Malory and Arthurian Romance." In *Arthurian Literature IV.* ed. Richard Barber. Cambridge, 1985, pp. 93–126.

———. " '. . . all the bokes that I haue of latyn, englisch, and frensche:' Laywomen and Their Books in Late Medieval England." In *Women and Literature in Britain 1100–1500.* Ed. Carol M. Meale. Cambridge, 1993, pp. 128–158.

Pearsall, Derek. "The English Romance in the Fifteenth Century." *Essays and Studies* 29 (1976), 56–83.

Powell, Sue. "Lady Margaret Beaufort and Her Books." *The Library* 6th ser. 20 (1998), 197–240.

Shepherd, Stephen H. A. *Turpines Story: A Middle English Translation of the Pseudo-Turpin Chronicle.* Early English Text Society. Oxford, 2004. [See n. 1, p. 824.]

Spiegel, Gabrielle M. *The Past as Text: The Theory and Practice of Medieval Historiography.* Baltimore, 1997.

Sutton, Anne F., and Livia Visser-Fuchs. *Richard III's Books: Ideals and Reality in the Life and Library of a Medieval Prince.* Stroud, 1997.

Politics, War, Chivalric Theory, and Empirical Knighthood

Barber, Richard. *The Knight and Chivalry.* London, 1970.

———, and Juliet Barker. *Tournaments: Jousts, Chivalry and Pageants in the Middle Ages.* Woodbridge, 1989.

———. "Malory's *Morte Darthur* and Court Culture under Edward IV." In *Arthurian Literature XII.* Ed. James P. Carley and Felicity Riddy. Cambridge, 1993, pp. 133–155.

Bennett, H. S. *The Pastons and Their England.* Cambridge, 1991.

Boardman, A. W. *The Battle of Towton.* Stroud, 1994.

Calendar of State Papers and Manuscripts in the Archives and Collections of Milan. Volume I, 1385–1618. Ed. A. B. Hinds. London, 1912. [Includes letters from England on the Wars of the Roses.]

Carpenter, Christine. *The Wars of the Roses: Politics and Constitution in England 1437–1509.* Cambridge, 1997.

Caxton, William. *The Book of the Ordre of Chyualry.* Ed. Alfred T. P. Byles. Early English Text Society 168. Oxford, 1926.

Cline, Ruth. "The Influence of Romance on the Tournaments of the Middle Ages." *Speculum* 20 (1945), 204–211.

Daniel, Christopher. *Death and Burial in Medieval England 1066–1550.* London, 1997.

Dillon, Viscount (Harold Arthur). "On a MS. Collection of Ordinances of Chivalry of the Fifteenth Century, Belonging to Lord Hastings." *Archaeologia* 57, no. 1 (1900), 29–70.

Duggan, Anne J., ed. *Queens and Queenship in Medieval Europe.* Woodbridge, 1997.

Gillingham, John. *Wars of the Roses: Peace and Conflict in the 15th Century.* London, 2001.

Goodman, Anthony. *The Wars of the Roses: Military Activity & English Society, 1452–97.* London, 1981.

Gravett, Christopher. *Knights at Tournament.* Oxford, 1998.

Gregory's Chronicle. In *The Historical Collections of a Citizen of London.* Ed. James Gairdner, Camden Society, new ser., 17. London, 1876.

Griffiths, Ralph A. *The Reign of Henry VI: The Exercise of Royal Authority, 1422–1461*. Berkeley and Los Angeles, 1981.

Hay, Sir Gilbert. *Gilbert of the Haye's Prose Manuscript*. Volume 2, *The Buke of Knychthede and the Buke of the Governance of Princis*. Ed. J. H. Stevenson, Scottish Text Society, 62. Edinburgh, 1914.

Hicks, Michael. *Richard III and His Rivals: Magnates and Their Motives in the War of the Roses*. London, 1991.

———. *Warwick the Kingmaker*. Oxford, 1998.

Jefferson, Lisa. "Tournaments, Heraldry and the Knights of the Round Table: A Fifteenth-Century Armorial with Two Accompanying Texts." *Arthurian Literature* 14. Ed. James P. Carley and Felicity Riddy. Cambridge, 1996, pp. 69–157.

Keegan, John. *The Face of Battle*. New York and London, 1976.

Keen, Maurice. *Chivalry*. New Haven and London, 1984.

Kim, Hyonjin. *The Knight without the Sword: A Social Landscape of Malorian Chivalry*. Cambridge, 2000.

Knight, Stephen. "From Jerusalem to Camelot: King Arthur and the Crusades." In *Medieval Codicology, Iconography, Literature, and Translation: Studies for Keith Val Sinclair*. Ed. Peter Rolfe Monks and D. D. R. Owen. Leiden, 1994, pp. 223–232.

Lander, J. R. *Crown and Nobility 1450–1509*. Montreal, 1976.

———. "Family, 'Friends' and Politics in Fifteenth-century England." In *Kings and Nobles in the Later Middle Ages*. Ed. Ralph A. Griffiths and James Sherborne. New York, 1986, pp. 27–40.

———. *The Wars of the Roses*. New York, 1990.

McFarlane, K. B. *The Nobility of Later Medieval England*. Oxford, 1973.

Richmond, Colin. *The Paston Family in The Fifteenth Century: The First Phase*. Cambridge, 1990.

Riddy, Felicity. "Contextualizing *Le Morte Darthur*: Empire and Civil War." In *A Companion to Malory*. Ed. Elizabeth Archibald and A. S. G. Edwards. Cambridge, 1996, pp. 55–73.

Rotuli Parliamentorum, 6 vols. London, 1767. [Acts of Parliament, mostly in English.]

Seward, Desmond. *The Wars of the Roses through the Lives of Five Men and Women of the Fifteenth Century*. New York, 1995.

Smyth, John. *The Lives of the Berkeleys*. Vol. 2 of *The Berkeley Manuscripts*. 3 vols. Ed. Sir John Maclean. Gloucester, 1893–95.

Storey, R. L. *The End of the House of Lancaster*. Stroud, 1999.

Strohm, Paul. "Counterfeiters, Lollards, and Lancastrian Unease." *New Medieval Literatures* 1 (1997), 31–58.

Swabey, ffiona [sic]. *Medieval Gentlewoman: Life in a Gentry Household in the Later Middle Ages*. Stroud, 1999.

Tyerman, Christopher. *England and the Crusades 1095–1588*. Chicago, 1988.

Warm, Robert. "Arthur and the Giant of Mont St. Michel: The Politics of Empire Building in the Later Middle Ages." *Nottingham Medieval Studies* 41 (1997); 57–71.

Watts, John. *Henry VI and The Politics of Kingship*. Cambridge, 1996.

Wolffe, Bertram. *Henry VI*. London, 1981.

Caxton

Adams, Tracy. "Printing and the Transformation of the Middle English Romance." *Neophilologus* 82 (1998), 291–310.

Blake, Norman F. *Caxton's Own Prose*. London, 1973.

———. "Caxton Prepares His Edition of the *Morte Darthur.*" *Journal of Librarianship* 8, no. 4 (1976): 272–285.

———. "William Caxton." In *Middle English Prose: A Critical Guide to Major Authors and Genres*. A. S. G. Edwards. Ed. New Brunswick, 1984, pp. 389–412.

———. *William Caxton and English Literary Culture*. London, 1991.

Coleman, Joyce. "The Audible Caxton: Reading and Hearing the Writings of England's First Publisher." *Fifteenth-Century Studies* 16 (1990), 83–109.

Fichte, Joerg. "Caxton's Concept of 'Historical Romance' within the Context of the Crusades: Conviction, Rhetoric and Sales Strategy." In *Tradition and Transformation in Medieval Romance*. Ed. Rosalind Field. Cambridge, 1999, pp. 101–113.

Field, P. J. C. "Caxton's Roman War." In *Malory: Texts and Sources*. Ed. P. J. C. Field. Cambridge 1998, pp. 126–161. [Counters the proposition that Caxton's edition represents later revisions by Malory.]

Goodman, Jennifer R. "Malory and Caxton's Chivalric Series, 1481–85." In *Studies in Malory*. Ed. James W. Spisak. Kalamazoo, 1985, pp. 257–274.

Hellinga, Lotte. "The Malory Manuscript and Caxton." *Aspects of Malory*. Ed. D. S. Brewer. Woodbridge and Totowa, 1986. pp. 127–114.

Housman, John E. "Higden, Trevisa, Caxton and the Beginnings of Arthurian Criticism." *Review of English Studies* 23 (1947), 209–217.

Kato, Takako. *Caxton's "Morte Darthur": The Printing Process and the Authenticity of the Text*. Medium Ævum Monograph. Oxford, forthcoming.

Kirk, Elizabeth. " 'Clerkes, Poetes and Historiographs': The *Morte Darthur* and Caxton's 'Poetics' of Fiction." In *Studies in Malory*. Ed. James W. Spisak. Kalamazoo, 1985, pp. 275–295.

Kuskin, William. "Caxton's Worthies Series: The Production of Literary Culture." *ELH* 66 (1999), 511–551.

Matthews, William. *William Matthews on Caxton and Malory*. Ed. Robert L. Kindrick with the assistance of Michele R. Crepeau. *Arthuriana* [Special issue] 7, no. 1 (1997), 3–133.

Meale, Carol M. "Caxton, de Worde, and the Publication of Romance in Late Medieval England." *The Library* 6th ser., 14 (1992), 283–298.

Moorman, Charles. "Caxton's *Morte Darthur*: Malory's Second Edition?" *Fifteenth-Century Studies* 12 (1987), 99–113.

Mukai, Tsuyoshi. "De Worde's 1498 *Morte Darthur* and Caxton's Copy-Text." *Review of English Studies* 51 (2000), 24–40.

Nakao, Yuji. "Does Malory really Revise His Vocabulary?—Some Negative Evidence." *Poetica* 25–6 (1987), 93–109. [Counters the proposition that Caxton's edition represents later revisions by Malory.]

Noguchi, Shunichi. "Caxton's Malory." *Poetica* 8 (1977): 72–84.

———. "Caxton's Malory Again." *Poetica* 20 (1984): 33–38.

Rutter, Russell. "William Caxton and Literary Patronage." *Studies in Philology* 84 (1987): 440–470.

Sandved, Arthur O. *Studies in the Language of Caxton's Malory and That of the Winchester Manuscript*. Oslo, 1968.

Šimko, Ján. *Word-Order in the Winchester Manuscript and in William Caxton's Edition of Thomas Malory's "Morte Darthur" (1485)—A Comparison*. Halle, 1957.

Shaw, Sally. "Caxton and Malory." *Essays on Malory*. Ed. J. A. W. Bennett. Oxford, 1963, pp. 114–145.

Smith, Jeremy. "Some Spellings in Caxton's Malory." *Poetica* 24 (1986): 58–63.

Criticism and Textual Studies, Mainly Since 1934

For a selected survey of earlier treatments, see the chronology on p. xxvii and notes thereto. For a statement on principles of selection, see the note to "Individual Essays," below.

Book-Length Studies

Batt, Catherine. *Malory's Morte Darthur: Remaking Arthurian Tradition*. New York, 2002.

Benson, Larry D. *Malory's Morte Darthur*. Cambridge, Mass., 1976.

Dillon, Bert. *A Malory Handbook*. Boston, 1978.

Edwards, Elizabeth. *The Genesis of Narrative in Malory's "Morte Darthur."* Cambridge, 2001.

Field, P. J. C. *Romance and Chronicle: A Study of Malory's Prose Style*. London, 1971.

———. *The Life and Times of Sir Thomas Malory*. Cambridge, 1993. [The standard source of (necessarily speculative) biographical information about Malory.]

Kennedy, Beverly. *Knighthood in the Morte Darthur*. Cambridge, 1992.

Kraemer, Alfred Robert. *Malory's Grail Seekers and Fifteenth-Century English Hagiography*. New York, 1999.

Lambert, Mark. *Malory: Style and Vision in Le Morte Darthur*. New Haven, 1975.

Lumiansky, R. M. *Malory's Originality*. Baltimore, 1963.

Lynch, Andrew. *Malory's Book of Arms: The Narrative of Combat in "Le Morte Darthur."* Cambridge, 1997.

Matthews, William. *The Ill-Framed Knight: A Skeptical Inquiry into the Identity of Sir Thomas Malory*. Berkeley, 1966.

McCarthy, Terence. *An Introduction to Malory*. Cambridge, 1991.

Moorman, Charles. *The Book of Kyng Arthur: The Unity of Malory's "Morte Darthur."* Lexington, 1965.

Pochoda, Elizabeth. *Arthurian Propaganda: Le Morte Darthur as an Historical Ideal of Life*. Chapel Hill, 1971.
Reiss, Edmund. *Sir Thomas Malory*. New York, 1966.
Riddy, Felicity. *Sir Thomas Malory*. Leiden, 1987.
Schofield, William H. *Chivalry in English Literature: Chaucer, Malory, Spenser, and Shakespeare*. Boston, 1912.
Scudder, Vida D. *"Le Morte Darthur" of Sir Thomas Malory and Its Sources*. New York, 1921.
Taylor, Beverly, and Elisabeth Brewer. *The Return of King Arthur*. Cambridge, 1983. [On nineteenth- and early twentieth-century receptions of Arthurian legend in English.]
Vinaver, Eugène. *Malory*. Oxford, 1929.
———. *The Rise of Romance*. Oxford, 1971.
Wilson, Robert H. *Characterization in Malory: A Comparison with His Sources*. Chicago, 1934.

Collections of (Reprinted) Essays

Archibald, Elizabeth, and A. S. G. Edwards, eds. *A Companion to Malory*. Cambridge, 1996.
Bennett, J. A. W., ed. *Essays on Malory*. Oxford, 1963.
Field, P. J. C. *Malory: Texts and Sources*. Cambridge 1998. [Convenient collection of important reprinted essays by Field, with some new material.]
Hanks, D. Thomas Jr., and Jessica G. Brogdon, eds. *The Social and Literary Contexts of Malory's "Morte Darthur."* Cambridge, 2000.
Lumiansky, R. M., ed. *Malory's Originality: A Critical Study of "Le Morte Darthur."* Baltimore, 1964.
Lupack, Alan, ed. *New Directions in Arthurian Studies*. Cambridge, 2002.
Mahoney, Dhira B., ed. *The Grail: A Casebook*. New York, 2000.
Parins, Marylyn Jackson. *Malory: The Critical Heritage*. London and New York, 1995.
Shichtman, Martin B., and James P. Carley, eds. *Culture and the King: The Social Implications of the Arthurian Legend*. Albany, 1994.
Spisak, James W., ed. *Studies in Malory*. Kalamazoo, 1985.
Suzuki, Takashi, and Tsuyoshi Mukai, eds. *Arthurian and Other Studies presented to Shunichi Noguchi*. Cambridge, 1993.
Takamiya, Toshiyuki, and Derek Brewer, eds. *Aspects of Malory*. Woodbridge and Totowa, 1986.
Wheeler, Bonnie, Robert L. Kindrick, and Michael N. Salda, eds. *The Malory Debate: Essays on the Texts of "Le Morte Darthur."* Cambridge, 2000. [Reprinted matter from *Arthuriana*, with some new essays.]

Individual Essays

No selected bibliography of Malory studies can do justice to the prolific body of excellent work available. The titles listed here tend to relate to all of Malory's Arthuriad rather than its parts, and are offered as stimulating and various—sometimes conflicting—points of departure for further study. Shortened titles refer to listings under "Collections of Essays," above; not every essay from those collections is listed below, but newcomers to Malory are strongly encouraged to explore those collections (and the book-length studies) in their entirety, not least for preliminary coverage of the constituent books or smaller subsections of the *Morte Darthur*. • indicates items included or exerpted in this Norton Critical Edition.

Allen, Judson Boyce. "The Medieval Unity of Malory's Morte Darthur." *Mediaevalia* 6 (1980), 279–309.
Archibald, Elizabeth. "Malory's Ideal of Fellowship." *Review of English Studies*, new ser., 43 (1992), 311–328.
Batt, Catherine. "Malory's Questing Beast and the Implications of Author as Translator." In *The Medieval Translator: The Theory and Practice of Translation in the Middle Ages*. Ed. Roger Ellis. Cambridge, 1989, pp. 143–166.
———. " 'Hand for Hand' and 'Body for Body': Aspects of Malory's Vocabulary of Identity and Integrity with Regard to Gareth and Lancelot." *Modern Philology* 91 (1994), 269–287.
• ———. "Malory and Rape." *Arthuriana* 7, no. 3 (Fall 1997), 78–99.
Benson, C. David. "The Ending of the Morte Darthur." In *A Companion to Malory*, pp. 221–238.
Brewer, Derek. "The Hoole Book." In *Essays on Malory*, pp. 41–63.

———. "Malory: The Traditional Writer and the Archaic Mind." In *Arthurian Literature 1*. Ed. Richard Barber. Cambridge, 1981, pp. 94–120.

Clough, Andrea. "Malory's *Morte Darthur*: The 'Hoole Book.'" *Medievalia et Humanistica*, new ser., 14 (1986), 139–56.

Cole, Harry E. "Forgiveness as Structure: 'The Book of Sir Lancelot and Queen Guinevere.'" *Chaucer Review* 31, no. 1 (1996), 36–44.

• Cooper, Helen. "Counter-Romance: Civil Strife and Father-Killing in the Prose Romances." In *The Long Fifteenth Century*. Ed. Helen Cooper and Sally Mapstone. Oxford, 1997, pp. 141–162.

———. "M. for Merlin: The Case of the Winchester Manuscript." In *Medieval Heritage: Essays in Honour of Tadahiro Ikegami*. Ed. Masahiko Kanno et al. Tokyo, 1997, pp. 93–107.

———. "Opening Up the Malory Manuscript." In *The Malory Debate*, pp. 255–284.

Davis, Rebecca A. "More Evidence for Intertextuality and Humorous Intent in *The Weddynge of Syr Gawen and Dame Ragnell*." *The Chaucer Review* 35, no. 4 (2001), 430–439. [Supports the view of the poem as a reception of Malory rather than as a work by Malory.]

Donavin, Georgiana. "Locating a Public Forum for the Personal Letter in Malory's *Morte Darthur*." *Disputation* 1 (1996), 19–36.

Edwards, A. S. G. "The Reception of Malory's Morte Darthur." In *A Companion to Malory*, pp. 241–252.

Evans, Murray J. "The Explicits and Narrative Division in the Winchester MS: A Critique of Vinaver's Malory." *Philological Quarterly* 58 (1979), 263–228.

———. "*Ordinatio* and Narrative Links: The Impact of Malory's Tales as a 'hoole book.'" In *Studies in Malory*, pp. 29–52.

Field, P. J. C. "The Malory Life-Records." In *A Companion to Malory*, pp. 115–130.

———. "Malory's Minor Sources." In *Malory: Texts and Sources*, pp. 27–31.

———. "Fifteenth-Century History in Malory's *Morte Darthur*." In *Malory: Texts and Sources*, pp. 47–71.

———. "Author, Scribe and Reader in Malory: The Case of Harleuse and Peryne." In *Malory: Texts and Sources*, pp. 72–88.

———. "Malory and the French Prose *Lancelot*." In *Malory: Texts and Sources*, pp. 199–223.

———. "Malory and Chrétien de Troyes." In *Malory: Texts and Sources*, pp. 236–245.

———. "The Source of Malory's Tale of Gareth.'" In *Malory: Texts and Sources*, pp. 246–260.

———. "Malory and *The Wedding of Sir Gawain and Dame Ragnell*." In *Malory: Texts and Sources*, pp. 284–294.

———. "Malory and the Battle of Towton." In *The Social and Literary Contexts of Malory's "Morte Darthur*," pp. 68–74.

———. "Malory's Own Marginalia." *Medium Ævum* 70 (2001), 226–239.

Fletcher, Alan J. "King Arthur's Passing in the *Morte D'Arthur*." *English Language Notes* 31, no. 4 (1994), 19–24.

Hanks, D. Thomas, and Jennifer Fish, "Beside the Point: Medieval Meanings vs. Modern Impositions in Editing Malory's *Morte Darthur*." *Neuphilologische Mitteilungen*, 3rd ser., 98 (1997), 273–289.

• Heng, Geraldine. "Enchanted Ground: The Feminine Subtext in Malory." In *Courtly Literature: Culture and Context*. Ed. Keith Busby and Erik Kooper. Amsterdam and Philadelphia, 1990, pp. 283–300.

Kelly, Robert L. "Penitence as a Remedy for War in Malory's *Tale of the Death of Arthur*." *Studies in Philology* 91, no. 2 (1994), 11–25.

Kennedy, Beverly. "Adultery in Malory's *Le Morte d'Arthur*." *Arthuriana* 7, no. 4 (1997), 63–91.

Kennedy, Edward D. "Malory and His English Sources." In *Aspects of Malory*, pp. 27–55

Knight, Stephen. *The Structure of Sir Thomas Malory's Arthuriad*. Sydney, 1969.

Lynch, Andrew. "Gesture and Gender in Malory's *Le Morte Darthur*." In *Arthurian Romance and Gender: Masculin/Feminin dans le roman arthurien médiéval*. Ed. Friedrich Wolfzettel. Amsterdam, 1995, pp. 295–295.

MacBain, Danielle Morgan. "The Tristramization of Malory's Lancelot." *English Studies*. 74, no. 1 (1993), 57–65.

Mann, Jill. "Taking the Adventure:' Malory and the *Suite du Merlin*." In *Aspects of Malory*, pp. 71–91.

———. *The Narrative of Distance, The Distance of Narrative in Malory's "Morte Darthur*." The William Matthews Lectures. London, 1991.

McCarthy, Terence. "*Le Morte Darthur* and Romance." In *Studies in Medieval English Romances*. Ed. Derek Brewer. Cambridge, 1988, pp. 148–75.

———. "Malory and His Sources." In *A Companion to Malory*, pp. 75–95.

• Meale, Carol M. "The Hoole Book': Editing and the Creation of Meaning in Malory's Text." In *A Companion to Malory*, pp. 3–17.

Moorman, Charles. "Malory's Treatment of the Sankgreal," *PMLA*, 71 (1956), 496–509.

Olefsky, Ellyn. "Chronology, Factual Consistency, and the Problem of Unity in Malory." *Journal of English and Germanic Philology* 68 (1969), 57–73.

Parry, Joseph D. "Following Malory Out of Arthur's World." *Modern Philology* 95, no. 2 (1997), 147–69.

Tsuyoshi Mukai. "De Worde's 1498 Morte Darthur and Caxton's Copy-Text." *Review of English Studies* 51 (2000), 24–40.

Ricciardi, Marc. " 'Se What I Shall Do as for My Trew Parte': Fellowship and Fortitude in Malory's 'Noble Tale of King Arthur and the Emperor Lucius.' " *Arthuriana* 11, no. 2 (2001), 20–31.

Riddy, Felicity. "John Hardyng's Chronicle and the Wars of the Roses." In *Arthurian Literature XIII*. Ed. James P. Carley and Felicity Riddy. Cambridge, 1993, pp. 91–108.

Saunders, Corinne J. "Malory's *Booke of Huntynge*: The *Tristram* section of the *Morte Darthur*." *Medium Ævum* 62 (1993), 270–284.

Shepherd, Stephen H. A. "No poet has his travesty alone: *The Weddynge of Sir Gawen and Dame Ragnell*." In *Romance Reading on the Book: Essays on Medieval Narrative Presented to Maldwyn Mills*. Ed. J. Fellows et al. Cardiff, 1996, pp. 112–127. [Advances the view of the poem as a reception of Malory rather than a work by Malory.]

Shunichi Noguchi. "Reading Malory's Text Aloud." In *The Malory Debate*, pp. 117–125.

———. "The Winchester Malory." In *The Malory Debate*, pp. 301–314.

Sklar, Elizabeth S. "The Undoing of Romance in Malory's *Morte Darthur*." *Fifteenth-Century Studies*. 20 (1993), 309–327.

Stewart, George R. "English Geography in Malory's *Morte Darthur*." *Modern Language Review* 30 (1935): 204–209.

• Strohm, Paul. "Mellyagant's Primal Scene." In *Theory and the Premodern Text*. Minneapolis and London, 2000, pp. 201–214.

Sutton, Anne F. "Malory in Newgate: A New Document." *The Library* 7th ser. 1 (2000), 243–62.

Taylor, Paul Beekman. "Myths and Etymologies behind Malory's Gareth." *English Studies* 78 (1997), 506–512.

Vinaver, Eugène. "Malory's *Morte Darthur* in the Light of a Recent Discovery." *John Rylands Library Bulletin* 19 (1935), 438–457.

Weiss, Victoria L. "Grail Knight or Boon Companion? The Inconsistent Sir Bors of Malory's *Morte Darthur*." *Studies in Philology* 94 (1997), 417–427.

White, Hayden. "The Historical Text as Literary Artifact." In *The Writing of History: Literary Form and Historical Understanding*. Ed. R. H. Canary and H. Kozicki. Madison, 1978, pp. 41–62.

Wilson, R. H. "Malory's French Book Again." *Comparative Literature* 2 (Spring, 1950), 172–181.

———. "Malory's Early Knowledge of Arthurian Romance." *University of Texas Studies in English* 29 (1950), 33–50.

———. "How Many Books Did Malory Write?" *University of Texas Studies in English* 30 (1951), 1–23.

Withrington, John. "The Arthurian Epitaph in Malory's *Morte Darthur*." *Arthurian Literature VII*, Ed. Richard Barber. Cambridge, 1987, pp. 103–144.